Piaggio/Vespa Scooters
Service and Repair Manual

by Matthew Coombs & Phil Mather

(3492-416-12AE3)

Models covered

Piaggio Sfera 50	50 cc	1991 to 1998
Piaggio Sfera 80	80 cc	1993 to 1998
Piaggio Sfera 125	125 cc	1996 to 1998
Piaggio Typhoon 50	50 cc	1993 to 2005
Piaggio Typhoon 80	80 cc	1994 to 1998
Piaggio Typhoon 125	125 cc	1995 to 2004
Piaggio Zip	50 cc	1993 to 1999
Piaggio Zip SP	50 cc	1997 to 2005
Piaggio Zip 50	50 cc	2000 to 2005
Piaggio Zip 4T	50 cc	2001 to 2006
Piaggio Zip 125	125 cc	2001 to 2004
Piaggio Fly 50	50 cc	2005 to 2006
Piaggio Fly 50 4T	50 cc	2006
Piaggio Fly 125	125 cc	2005 to 2006
Piaggio Skipper	125 cc	1993 to 2000
Piaggio Skipper ST	125 cc	2001 to 2004
Piaggio Hexagon	125 cc	1994 to 2000
Piaggio Super Hexagon	125 cc	2001 to 2003
Piaggio Liberty 50	50 cc	1997 to 2006
Piaggio Liberty 50 4T	50 cc	2001 to 2006
Piaggio Liberty 125	125 cc	2000 to 2006
Piaggio NRG MC²	50 cc	1997 to 2000
Piaggio NRG MC³ DT	50 cc	2001 to 2004
Piaggio NRG MC³ DD	50 cc	2001 to 2004
Piaggio NRG Power DT	50 cc	2005 to 2006
Piaggio NRG Power DD	50 cc	2005 to 2006
Piaggio B125/Beverly	125 cc	2002 to 2006
Piaggio X9 125	125 cc	2001 to 2006
Piaggio X8 125	125 cc	2005 to 2006
Vespa ET2	50 cc	1997 to 2004
Vespa ET4 50	50 cc	2001 to 2004
Vespa ET4 125	125 cc	1996 to 2004
Vespa LX2 50	50 cc	2005 to 2006
Vespa LX4 50	50 cc	2005 to 2006
Vespa LX4 125	125 cc	2005 to 2006
Vespa GT125	125 cc	2003 to 2006
Vespa GT200	200 cc	2003 to 2006

© Haynes Publishing 2006

ABCDE
FGHIJ
K

A book in the Haynes Service and Repair Manual Series

All rights reserved. No part of this book may be reproduced or transmitted in any form or by any means, electronic or mechanical, including photocopying, recording or by any information storage or retrieval system, without permission in writing from the copyright holder.

ISBN 1 84425 299 X

British Library Cataloguing in Publication Data
A catalogue record for this book is available from the British Library

Printed in the USA

Haynes Publishing
Sparkford, Yeovil, Somerset BA22 7JJ, England

Haynes North America, Inc
861 Lawrence Drive, Newbury Park, California 91320, USA

Editions Haynes
4, Rue de l'Abreuvoir
92415 COURBEVOIE CEDEX, France

Haynes Publishing Nordiska AB
Box 1504, 751 45 UPPSALA, Sweden

Contents

LIVING WITH YOUR SCOOTER

Introduction
The Piaggio Story	Page	0•4
Acknowledgements	Page	0•7
About this manual	Page	0•7
Identification numbers	Page	0•8
Buying spare parts	Page	0•8
Safety first!	Page	0•9

Daily (pre-ride checks)
Engine oil level check – four-stroke models	Page	0•10
Fuel and two-stroke engine oil checks	Page	0•10
Coolant level check – liquid-cooled models	Page	0•11
Brake fluid level check – disc brake models	Page	0•12
Tyre checks	Page	0•13
Suspension and steering checks	Page	0•13
Legal and safety checks	Page	0•13

MAINTENANCE

Routine maintenance and servicing
Model specifications and service schedules	Page	1•2
Routine maintenance and servicing procedures	Page	1•68

Contents

REPAIRS AND OVERHAUL

Engine, transmission and associated systems

Air-cooled two-stroke engines (Sfera 50/80, all Typhoons, Liberty 50, Zip and Zip 50, NRG MC3 DT, NRG Power DT, ET2, Skipper, Fly 50, LX2 50) — Page 2A•1

Liquid-cooled two-stroke engines (NRG MC2, NRG MC3 DD, NRG Power DD, Zip SP, Hexagon) — Page 2B•1

Four-stroke engines (Sfera 125, Liberty 125, ET4) — Page 2C•1

Four-stroke engines (ET4 50, Liberty 50 4T, Zip 50 4T, Fly 50 4T, LX4 50) — Page 2D•1

LEADER air-cooled four-stroke engines (Zip 125, Skipper ST, Liberty 125, ET4, Fly 125, LX4 125) — Page 2E•1

LEADER liquid-cooled four-stroke engines (Super Hexagon, B125, X9 125, X8 125, GT125, GT200) — Page 2F•1

Transmission — Page 2G•1

Cooling system (liquid-cooled engines) — Page 3•1

Fuel and exhaust systems — Page 4•1

Ignition system — Page 5•1

Chassis components

Steering and suspension — Page 6•1

Frame and bodywork — Page 7•1

Brakes, wheels and tyres — Page 8•1

Electrical system — Page 9•1

Wiring diagrams — Page 9•27

REFERENCE

Conversion factors — Page REF•1

Fault Finding — Page REF•2

Index — Page REF•10

Introduction

The Piaggio Story

by Julian Ryder

Outside of its native Italy, Piaggio is in a strange position. Everyone has heard of one of its products while comparatively few know the name of the parent company itself. That products is, of course, the Vespa, the first mass-produced scooter and the vehicle that got Italy mobile after World War II before becoming a style icon for generations all over the world.

The first Vespa was completed in April 1946, after just three months design work by the gifted aeronautical engineer Corradino d'Ascanio. Piaggio itself was founded as long ago as 1884 by Rinaldo Piaggio, then only 20 years of age, to manufacture components for naval and railway applications. At the outbreak of World War I, Piaggio branched out into aeronautical parts and by 1923 had built a monoplane fighter with cantilever wing. He also started Italy's first airline and became a member of the Italian Senate. In 1924 the company took over the Pontadera factory near Pisa to build seaplanes and bombers. Today, it is the Piaggio group's biggest manufacturing facility.

After Rinaldo Piaggio died in 1938, his sons Armando and Enrico took over the company, and it was Enrico who, with d'Ascanio, developed the first Vespa. He was responsible for redeveloping the Pontedera plant, which had been blown up by the retreating Germans and bombed by the advancing allies. He realised that the country was crying out for mobility, and it would have to be mobility at the lowest possible price and with the toughness and ease of use that could cope with the prevailing conditions. Enrico had already started thinking about this problem before the end of the War, he stared with a small motorcycle built for parachute troops which was modified with unsatisfactory results. This prototype, the MP5 or Paperino – Italian for Donald Duck – was then handed over to d'Ascanio, a man who did not like motorcycles because of their bulk, the difficulty involved in changing wheels and the fact that exposed drive chains made them dirty.

In an astonishingly short period of time (around three months) d'Ascanio had refined his ideas and laid out a totally new and original vehicle that is still recognisable today. He attached the motor to a load-bearing single-sided swinging arm with direct gearing to the rear wheel, he put the gearchange on the handlebar, he used an aircraft-undercarriage strut design for the stub-axle front suspension thus allowing instant wheel changing both front and rear, and he clothed the whole thing in lightweight bodywork that protected the rider from the elements.

It was christened when Piaggio himself saw the first prototype, the MP6, and he remarked that with its wide engine housing and narrow central 'waist' it looked like a wasp.

The Italian word for wasp is *vespa*.

The first 98 cc Vespa was an instant success. In the first year 2484 were sold, 10,535 in the following year, and in 1948 just under 20,000 were built. Piaggio did his first deal for licensed-production in 1950 with Germany. Already, the Vespa was becoming a cult object. By 1953 there were 10,000 Piaggio dealers all over the World, and that same year production passed the half-million mark. The millionth Vespa left the production line in June 1956, the two-millionth in 1960, the four-millionth in 1970, the ten-millionth in 1980, and production is now past 15,000,000 in eighty-nine different models. Worldwide, the Vespa is still Piaggio's top-selling two-wheeler.

But it would be wrong to think that Piaggio is nothing but Vespa. In 1967 the company started making mopeds and in '69 took over one of the Italian motorcycle industry's greatest names – Gilera. In 1980 it absorbed Bianchi one of the greatest names in the Italian bicycle industry (as well as an occasional motorcycle manufacturer) and seven years later took-over the Austrian company Steyr-Daimler-Puch. And that's just the two-wheeled business: there are also Piaggio companies involved in chemicals, textiles, mechanical engineering (which supplied machinery to Toyota's new plant in Derby, England), powder technology, automation, and industrial plant, to name but a few.

The Vespa 150 Sportique of 1964

Introduction

The main Piaggio company, Piaggio Veicoli Europei SpA, is the biggest manufacturer of two and three-wheeled vehicles in Europe and the third biggest in the World, marketing vehicles under the Piaggio, Gilera and Puch banners. It runs Motovespa SA in Spain which manufactures as well as markets mopeds and scooters, and national distributors Vespa GmbH in Germany, Vespa Diffusion SA in France, and Piaggio Ltd in the UK. Piaggio VE SpA also controls 25% of LML Ltd of Kampur, India's second largest scooter manufacturer and owns 51% of P&D SpA, a joint venture with Daihatsu of Japan to co-ordinate the manufacture and marketing of lightweight three- and four-wheeled light commercial vehicles worldwide. In some countries they're sold as Daihatsus, in others as Piaggios.

Piaggio is a big company, a major player on the world scene, but you can trace it all back to that revolutionary little scooter – the Vespa.

Of course the original 98 cc Vespa has developed over the years. It grew to 125 cc as early as 1948 and the 150 cc model of 1955 was the first of the really modern scooters. A few years ago, scooters were thought of, in the UK at least, as only of interest to born-again mods. Nothing of course is further from the truth. Great chunks of Europe, mainly the southern half, gained mobility thanks to the Vespa. In more remote areas, a scooter can still be the mainstay of a family's transport. Now, the northern half of Europe is starting to cotton on.

Much of the thanks for that must go to the Italian industry in general and Piaggio in particular. In the UK, the big four Japanese manufacturers had effectively given up on what used to be called the 'soft bike' market. Can you remember any publicity for any Japan's soft bikes since the days of the Honda Express as demonstrated by Twiggy and the line "You meet the nicest people on a Honda". Thought not.

At the start of the '90s, Piaggio UK gave the rest of the industry a lesson in marketing. The accepted wisdom was that the British wouldn't buy scooters because of the country's less than two-wheeler friendly weather. Piaggio were already selling vast numbers of scooters in Germany and didn't really see any difference between the climate of Manchester and Dusseldorf, so with a minimal budget and cleverly targeted marketing they started pointing out to people that modern scooters were the most convenient form of inner-city transport yet invented. More to the point they were very affordable, reliable and clean.

Piaggio UK got the non-motorcycling press to ride these press-and-go scooters and the word started to spread. Scooter tests appeared in the motoring pages of the daily press, fashionable young things from the fashion and music world were pictured on their new transport. The message got across. When I moved out of central London in 1990 there was hardly a scooter of any description to be seen. Now, when I find myself back in the great wen I can't help noticing the serried ranks of scooters, not just Piaggios but Italjets, Malaguttis, Peugeots, plus a few of Japan's attempts to cash-in on the boom, packing two-wheeler parking bays in the city centre or formed up outside expensive town houses in fashionable areas. The UK scooter market has been expanding at over 30% year on year since 1995 and shows no signs of slowing down.

Scooters are a familiar sight in European cities

The traditional styled semi-automatic scooters in the PX range

Introduction

Increasing concern over congestion and pollution in cities isn't confined to the UK. Back in Italy, there are many medieval city centres that are particularly unsuited to or suffer badly from modern traffic. Vehicles powered by internal combustion engines are banned from many of them, so Piaggio came up with what may be the first compound-engined vehicle offered for sale. The 'Zip & Zip' looks like any other 50 cc scooter but as well as Piaggio's conventional two-stroke motor it also has an electric motor. The rider selects which engine he or she wants to use by a conventional switch on the handlebar. When you reach the perimeter of the old town where petrol-burning motors are prohibited, you stop and switch to the electric motor.

On Vespa's 50th anniversary in 1996, Piaggio unveiled the Vespa ET2 Injection, an attempt to make two-stroke motors cleaner by using fuel injection. So far the Injection has only been launched in a few European markets but shows graphically how you don't have to be building 150 hp rocketships to be at the forefront of two-wheel technology.

Scooters aren't the type of vehicles that you associate with sport, but there is a healthy scooter racing series in Italy and other countries. Scooter racing came to the UK for the first time in 1997 and the championship was won by Leon Haslam, son of ex-GP hero Ron. On the world stage, Piaggio's biggest successes have been in the Paris-Dakar Rally in the late '80s and early '90s with single-cylinder Gileras. The legendary marque's return to the Grand Prix circuits in the ultra-competitive 250 cc class wasn't so happy and only lasted a couple of seasons.

But these are side issues, Piaggio's core business is scooters, and they make them in a seemingly bewildering variety of specifications. The good old Vespa still lives on of course in 50, 80, 125 and 200 cc forms plus a special classic edition for the Japanese home market where it is the most successful European two-wheeler. Modern Vespas look very like their ancestors but nowadays have such refinements as electric starters and electronic ignition. All PX Vespas still use steel bodywork whereas all the new designs from the Sfera onwards are based on a tubular and sheet steel frame and plastic bodywork. The original left-handlebar mounted gearshifter is still available on the 200 and some 125 models, but every scooter covered by this manual uses the modern constantly variable automatic transmission that makes them such easy bikes to ride, especially in city traffic.

The Sfera 50 of 1991 was the first of the new generation of these modern scooters, and although it wasn't a radical design it won the Compasso d'Oro, a top design prize. The Zip and Free models that followed in 1993 were budget models, the Zip was a good deal lighter and aimed at female riders. The Typhoon 50 was launched the same year as the top-of-the-range 50 cc scooter. This was the first of the really radical looking, innovative scooters with racy lines, chunky tyres – a real trend setter and the scooter that became the paddock bike of choice in car and motorcycle GPs. 80 cc versions of the Sfera and Typhoon appeared in 1993 and '94, respectively, but the next major breakthrough was the Skipper 125, the first 125 cc two-stroke scooter to use automatic transmission. All these bikes used air-cooled two-stroke motors.

The Quartz 50 that appeared in 1993 was the first Piaggio scooter with liquid-cooling, and was followed in '94 by a new top-of-the range model, the Hexagon 125 with a liquid-cooled two-stroke motor. This scooter was more luxurious and aimed at the older customer than some of the flashier 50 cc models that were intended primarily for Italy's fickle teenage market. The Hexagon had a longer wheelbase, more laid-back riding position, sculpted seat with flip-up backrest for the solo rider, and enough luggage space to take two crash helmets. This 'boot' was even carpeted.

The Sfera 125 was Piaggio's first four-stroke engined scooter

Introduction 0•7

The next technical breakthrough was in the use of four-stroke engines from 1996 on in the new Sfera 125 and the Vespa ET4 – yes, a four-stroke Vespa! While Piaggio carries on its ground-breaking research into fuel-injecting two-strokes to clean them up, the company is also moving to cleaner, quieter four-strokes. Sporting rides needn't worry though, if you want to go racing there's the Zip 50 SP (as in Sport Production), a very different animal from the standard Zip. Add the Malossi race kit and you have a seriously cheap route into seriously fast racing.

Four-stroke development went a stage further in 1999 with the launch of the 125 cc LEADER engine, its name being an acronym for Low Emission ADvanced Engine Range. This engine is produced in 2-valve air-cooled and 4-valve liquid-cooled forms and is fitted in the Skipper ST, Super Hexagon, B125, X9 125, X8 125, Zip 125, Liberty 125, Fly 125, LX4 125, later ET4 125, and the GT125/200 models.

The 50 cc two-stroke engine is now fitted in only a small number of models, and is equipped with a catalytic converter and secondary air system to ensure it meets low emission requirements. It has already given way to a 2-valve 50 cc four-stroke engine and will eventually be superseded by Piaggio's new 'Purejet' fuel injected two-stroke engine.

The budget price Zip scooter

Acknowledgements

Our thanks are due to Fowlers Motorcycles of Bristol, South West Scooters of Yeovil and Bridge Motorcycles of Exeter who supplied the scooters featured in the photographs throughout this manual. We would also like to thank NGK Spark Plugs (UK) Ltd for supplying the colour spark plug condition photos.

Special thanks are due to Piaggio UK Ltd for supplying service literature, technical support and model photographs, and to Piaggio VE SpA, Italy, for permission to reproduce artwork from their publications.

The introduction, "The Piaggio Story" was written by Julian Ryder.

About this Manual

The aim of this manual is to help you get the best value from your scooter. It can do so in several ways. It can help you decide what work must be done, even if you choose to have it done by a dealer; it provides information and procedures for routine maintenance and servicing; and it offers diagnostic and repair procedures to follow when trouble occurs.

We hope you use the manual to tackle the work yourself. For many simpler jobs, doing it yourself may be quicker than arranging an appointment to get the scooter into a dealer and making the trips to leave it and pick it up. More importantly, a lot of money can be saved by avoiding the expense the shop must pass on to you to cover its labour and overhead costs. An added benefit is the sense of satisfaction and accomplishment that you feel after doing the job yourself.

References to the left or right side of the scooter assume you are sitting on the seat, facing forward.

We take great pride in the accuracy of information given in this manual, but motorcycle manufacturers make alterations and design changes during the production run of a particular motorcycle of which they do not inform us. No liability can be accepted by the authors or publishers for loss, damage or injury caused by any errors in, or omissions from, the information given.

Illegal copying

It is the policy of Haynes Publishing to actively protect its Copyrights and Trade Marks. Legal action will be taken against anyone who unlawfully copies the cover or contents of this Manual. This includes all forms of unauthorised copying including digital, mechanical, and electronic in any form. Authorisation from Haynes Publishing will only be provided expressly and in writing. Illegal copying will also be reported to the appropriate statutory authorities.

0•8 Identification numbers

Frame and engine numbers

The frame serial number (or VIN (Vehicle Identification Number) as it is often known) is stamped into the frame, and also appears on an identification plate; your owner's manual will give exact details of its location. The engine number is stamped into the rear of the transmission casing at the back of the engine. Both of these numbers should be recorded and kept in a safe place so they can be furnished to law enforcement officials in the event of a theft.

The frame and engine numbers should also be kept in a handy place (such as with your driving licence) so they are always available when purchasing or ordering parts for your scooter.

Each model type can be identified by its engine and frame number prefix – refer to *Model specifications and service schedules* in Chapter 1.

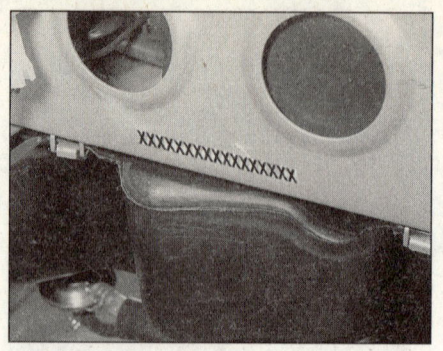

The frame number is stamped into the frame . . .

. . . which is sometimes behind a removable panel

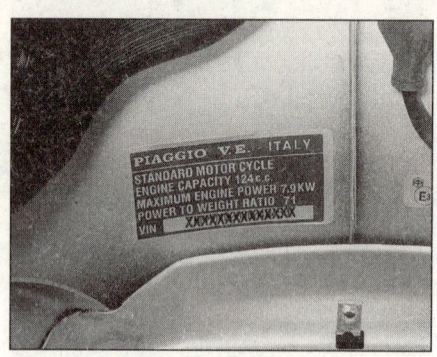

The frame number also appears on the identification plate

The engine number is stamped into the transmission casing at the back of the rear hub

Buying spare parts

When ordering new parts, it is essential to identify exactly the machine for which the parts are required. While in some cases it is sufficient to identify the machine by its title, eg, 'Typhoon 50', any modifications made to components mean that it is usually essential to identify the scooter by its year of production, or better still by its frame or engine number prefix.

To identify your own scooter, refer to the engine and frame number prefix information in *Model specifications and service schedules* in Chapter 1. Note that Piaggio have used the term RST for some later models (meaning Restyle), and this description has been used in the manual.

To be absolutely certain of receiving the correct part, not only is it essential to have the scooter engine or frame number prefix to hand, but it is also useful to take the old part for comparison (where possible). Note that where a modified component has superseded the original, a careful check must be made that there are no related parts which have also been modified and must be used to enable the new part to be correctly fitted; where such a situation is found, purchase all the necessary parts and fit them, even if this means renewing apparently unworn items.

Purchase new parts from an authorised Piaggio dealer or someone who specialises in scooter parts; they are more likely to have the parts in stock or can order them quickly from the importer. Pattern parts are available for certain components; if used, ensure these are of recognised quality brands which will perform as well as the original.

Expendable items such as lubricants, spark plugs, some electrical components, bearings, bulbs and tyres can usually be obtained at lower prices from accessory shops, motor factors or from specialists advertising in the national motorcycle press.

Safety first!

Professional mechanics are trained in safe working procedures. However enthusiastic you may be about getting on with the job at hand, take the time to ensure that your safety is not put at risk. A moment's lack of attention can result in an accident, as can failure to observe simple precautions.

There will always be new ways of having accidents, and the following is not a comprehensive list of all dangers; it is intended rather to make you aware of the risks and to encourage a safe approach to all work you carry out on your bike.

Asbestos

● Certain friction, insulating, sealing and other products - such as brake pads, clutch linings, gaskets, etc. - contain asbestos. Extreme care must be taken to avoid inhalation of dust from such products since it is hazardous to health. If in doubt, assume that they do contain asbestos.

Fire

● Remember at all times that petrol is highly flammable. Never smoke or have any kind of naked flame around, when working on the vehicle. But the risk does not end there - a spark caused by an electrical short-circuit, by two metal surfaces contacting each other, by careless use of tools, or even by static electricity built up in your body under certain conditions, can ignite petrol vapour, which in a confined space is highly explosive. Never use petrol as a cleaning solvent. Use an approved safety solvent.

● Always disconnect the battery earth terminal before working on any part of the fuel or electrical system, and never risk spilling fuel on to a hot engine or exhaust.
● It is recommended that a fire extinguisher of a type suitable for fuel and electrical fires is kept handy in the garage or workplace at all times. Never try to extinguish a fuel or electrical fire with water.

Fumes

● Certain fumes are highly toxic and can quickly cause unconsciousness and even death if inhaled to any extent. Petrol vapour comes into this category, as do the vapours from certain solvents such as trichloro-ethylene. Any draining or pouring of such volatile fluids should be done in a well ventilated area.
● When using cleaning fluids and solvents, read the instructions carefully. Never use materials from unmarked containers - they may give off poisonous vapours.
● Never run the engine of a motor vehicle in an enclosed space such as a garage. Exhaust fumes contain carbon monoxide which is extremely poisonous; if you need to run the engine, always do so in the open air or at least have the rear of the vehicle outside the workplace.

The battery

● Never cause a spark, or allow a naked light near the vehicle's battery. It will normally be giving off a certain amount of hydrogen gas, which is highly explosive.

● Always disconnect the battery ground (earth) terminal before working on the fuel or electrical systems (except where noted).
● If possible, loosen the filler plugs or cover when charging the battery from an external source. Do not charge at an excessive rate or the battery may burst.
● Take care when topping up, cleaning or carrying the battery. The acid electrolyte, even when diluted, is very corrosive and should not be allowed to contact the eyes or skin. Always wear rubber gloves and goggles or a face shield. If you ever need to prepare electrolyte yourself, always add the acid slowly to the water; never add the water to the acid.

Electricity

● When using an electric power tool, inspection light etc., always ensure that the appliance is correctly connected to its plug and that, where necessary, it is properly grounded (earthed). Do not use such appliances in damp conditions and, again, beware of creating a spark or applying excessive heat in the vicinity of fuel or fuel vapour. Also ensure that the appliances meet national safety standards.
● A severe electric shock can result from touching certain parts of the electrical system, such as the spark plug wires (HT leads), when the engine is running or being cranked, particularly if components are damp or the insulation is defective. Where an electronic ignition system is used, the secondary (HT) voltage is much higher and could prove fatal.

Remember...

✗ Don't suddenly remove the pressure cap from a hot cooling system - cover it with a cloth and release the pressure gradually first, or you may get scalded by escaping coolant.
✗ Don't attempt to drain oil until you are sure it has cooled sufficiently to avoid scalding you.
✗ Don't grasp any part of the engine or exhaust system without first ascertaining that it is cool enough not to burn you.
✗ Don't allow brake fluid or antifreeze to contact the machine's paintwork or plastic components.
✗ Don't siphon toxic liquids such as fuel, hydraulic fluid or antifreeze by mouth, or allow them to remain on your skin.
✗ Don't inhale dust - it may be injurious to health (see Asbestos heading).
✗ Don't allow any spilled oil or grease to remain on the floor - wipe it up right away, before someone slips on it.
✗ Don't use ill-fitting spanners or other tools which may slip and cause injury.
✗ Don't lift a heavy component which may be beyond your capability - get assistance.
✗ Don't rush to finish a job or take unverified short cuts.

✗ Don't allow children or animals in or around an unattended vehicle.
✗ Don't inflate a tyre above the recommended pressure. Apart from overstressing the carcass, in extreme cases the tyre may blow off forcibly.

✓ Do ensure that the machine is supported securely at all times. This is especially important when the machine is blocked up to aid wheel or fork removal.
✓ Do take care when attempting to loosen a stubborn nut or bolt. It is generally better to pull on a spanner, rather than push, so that if you slip, you fall away from the machine rather than onto it.
✓ Do wear eye protection when using power tools such as drill, sander, bench grinder etc.
✓ Do use a barrier cream on your hands prior to undertaking dirty jobs - it will protect your skin from infection as well as making the dirt easier to remove afterwards; but make sure your hands aren't left slippery. Note that long-term contact with used engine oil can be a health hazard.
✓ Do keep loose clothing (cuffs, ties etc. and long hair) well out of the way of moving mechanical parts.

✓ Do remove rings, wristwatch etc., before working on the vehicle - especially the electrical system.
✓ Do keep your work area tidy - it is only too easy to fall over articles left lying around.
✓ Do exercise caution when compressing springs for removal or installation. Ensure that the tension is applied and released in a controlled manner, using suitable tools which preclude the possibility of the spring escaping violently.
✓ Do ensure that any lifting tackle used has a safe working load rating adequate for the job.
✓ Do get someone to check periodically that all is well, when working alone on the vehicle.
✓ Do carry out work in a logical sequence and check that everything is correctly assembled and tightened afterwards.
✓ Do remember that your vehicle's safety affects that of yourself and others. If in doubt on any point, get professional advice.

● **If** in spite of following these precautions, you are unfortunate enough to injure yourself, seek medical attention as soon as possible.

0•10 Daily (pre-ride) checks

Note: *The daily (pre-ride) checks outlined in your owner's manual covers those items which should be inspected on a daily basis.*

Engine oil level check – four-stroke models

Before you start:
✔ Support the machine in an upright position on its centre stand. Make sure it is on level ground.
✔ Make sure you have a supply of the correct oil available.

✔ Check the oil level when the engine is cold. Wait at least 5 minutes after the engine has been run.

Bike care:
● If you have to add oil frequently, you should check whether you have any oil leaks. If there is no sign of oil leakage from the joints and gaskets the engine could be burning oil due to worn piston rings or failed valve stem seals.

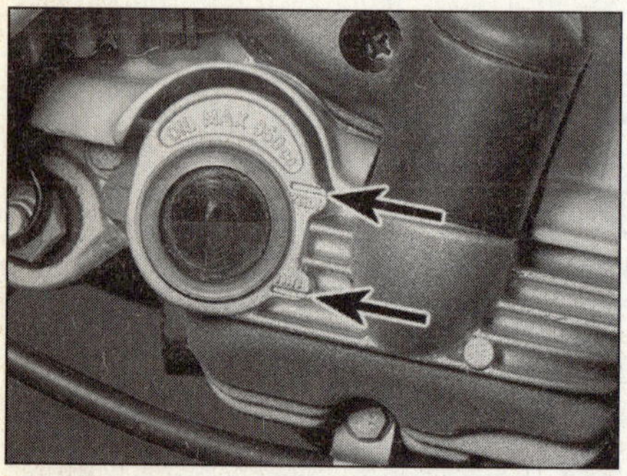

1 Some engines have a sightglass in the left-hand side of the crankcase. Wipe the window clean if necessary. The oil level should lie between the MAX and MIN level lines (arrowed).

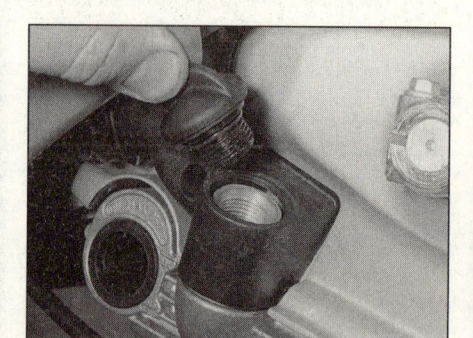

2 If the level is below the MIN line, unscrew the oil filler cap.

3 Top the engine up with the recommended grade and type of oil, to bring the level up to the MAX line on the sightglass. Do not overfill.

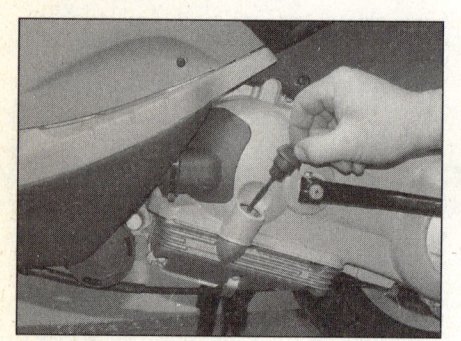

4 Some engines have a dipstick on the oil filler cap. Unscrew the cap and wipe the dipstick on some clean rag, then insert the clean dipstick back into the engine and screw the cap fully in.

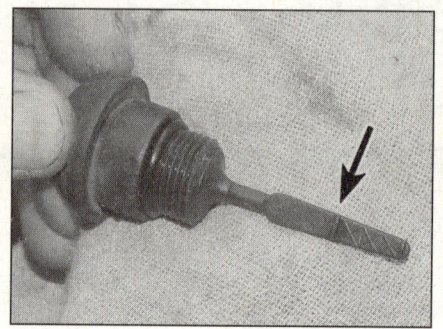

5 Unscrew the cap - the oil level should be up to the MAX line (arrowed).

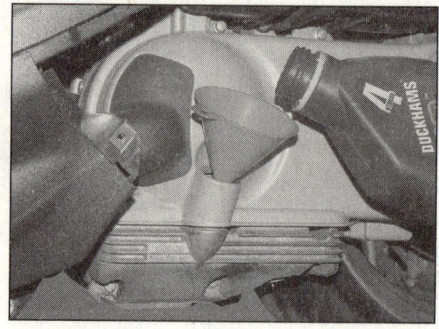

6 If necessary, top the engine up with the recommended grade and type of oil, to bring the level up to the MAX line. Do not overfill.

Fuel and two-stroke engine oil checks

Fuel
● This may seem obvious, but check that you have enough fuel to complete your journey. If you notice signs of leakage – rectify the cause immediately.
● Ensure you use the correct grade of unleaded fuel, minimum 95 octane.

Two-stroke oil
● On all two-stroke models check that the oil level warning light extinguishes immediately after the engine is started. If the light stays on or if it comes on whilst the scooter is being ridden, the oil tank requires topping-up.
● Do not rely on the oil warning light to tell you that the oil tank needs topping-up. Get into the habit of checking the level of oil in the oil tank at the same time as you fill up with fuel.
● If the engine is run without oil, even for a short time, engine damage and very soon engine seizure will occur. It is advised that a bottle of two-stroke oil is carried in the storage compartment for such emergencies.

Top-up the oil tank with a good quality two-stroke oil designed for motorcycle oil injection systems.

Daily (pre-ride) checks 0•11

Coolant level check – liquid-cooled models

⚠️ *Warning: DO NOT leave open containers of coolant about, as it is poisonous.*

Before you start:
✔ Make sure you have a supply of coolant available (a mixture of 50% distilled water and 50% corrosion inhibited ethylene glycol anti-freeze is needed).
✔ Always check the coolant level when the engine is cold.
Caution: Do not run the engine in an enclosed space such as a garage or workshop.
✔ Support the scooter in an upright position whilst checking the level; make sure it is on level ground.

Bike care:
● Use only the specified coolant mixture. It is important that anti-freeze is used in the system all year round, and not just in the winter. Do not top the system up using only water, as the system will become too diluted.
● Do not overfill the reservoir tank, which is located behind the fairing on all models. If the coolant is significantly above the UPPER or MAX line at any time, the surplus should be syphoned or drained off to prevent the possibility of it being expelled under pressure.

● If the coolant level falls steadily, check the system for leaks (see Chapter 1). If no leaks are found and the level continues to fall, it is recommended that the machine is taken to a Piaggio dealer for a pressure test.

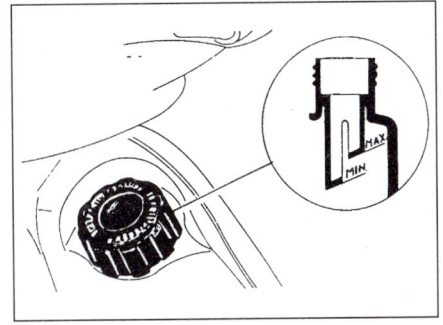

1 On all Hexagon, B125, X8 and X9 models, the coolant MAX and MIN level lines are visible by looking down the filler neck...

2 ...top-up if necessary with the specified coolant mixture.

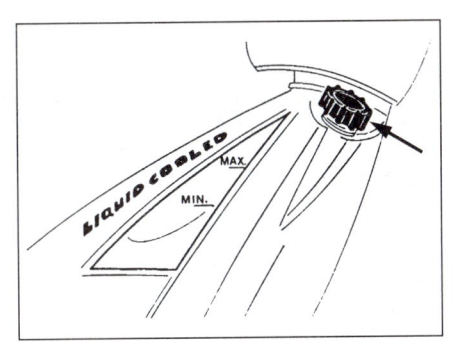

3 On the NRG MC2 and MC3 models, the level can be viewed through the cutout in the front panel left-hand side and topped up by removing the filler cap (arrowed).

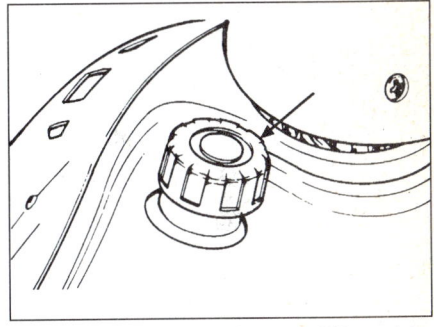

4 On Zip SP and NRG Power DD models, remove the filler cap (arrowed) from the kick panel...

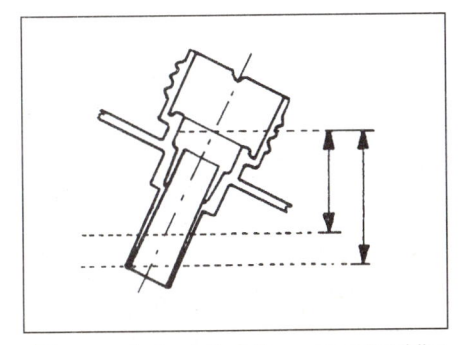

5 ...and check that the coolant level lies just above the base of the filler neck.

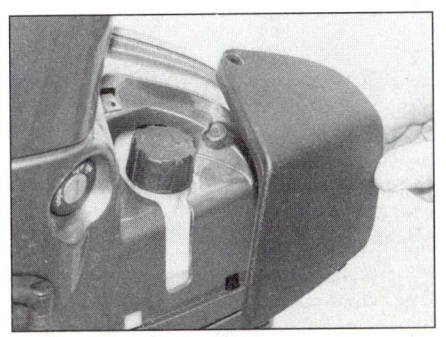

6 On Vespa GT models, remove the access panel...

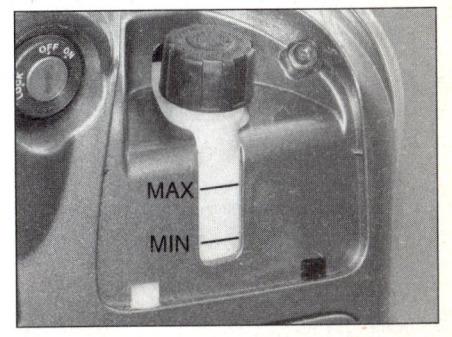

7 ...and check that the coolant level lies between the MAX and MIN level lines.

Daily (pre-ride) checks

Brake fluid level check – disc brake models

⚠️ **Warning:** Brake hydraulic fluid can harm your eyes and damage painted surfaces, so use extreme caution when handling and pouring it and cover surrounding surfaces with rag. Do not use fluid that has been standing open for some time, as it absorbs moisture from the air which can cause a dangerous loss of braking effectiveness.

Before you start:
✔ Support the scooter in an upright position.

✔ Make sure you have a supply of DOT 4 hydraulic fluid.

✔ Wrap a rag around the reservoir to ensure that any spillage does not come into contact with painted or plastic surfaces.

Bike care:
● The fluid in the front brake master cylinder reservoir will drop slightly as the brake pads wear down.

● If the fluid reservoir requires repeated topping-up this is an indication of an hydraulic leak somewhere in the system, which should be investigated immediately.

● Check for signs of fluid leakage from the hydraulic hoses and components – if found, rectify immediately.

● Check the operation of the brake before riding the scooter; if there is evidence of air in the system (spongy feel to lever), it must be bled as described in Chapter 8.

1 On models with a handlebar-mounted master cylinder, the brake fluid level is visible through the window in the reservoir body (arrowed). If necessary, remove the reservoir cover or the handlebar cover (see Chapter 7) to check the level. The level must be above the MIN level line.

2 If the level is below the MIN level line, remove the two reservoir cap screws and remove the cover, the diaphragm plate and the diaphragm.

3 Top-up with new clean hydraulic fluid of the recommended type, until the level is above the MIN mark. Take care to avoid spills (see **Warning** above).

4 Ensure that the diaphragm is correctly seated before installing the plate and cover.

5 On models with a cable-operated master cylinder and separate reservoir, the brake fluid level is visible through the reservoir body via the aperture in the kick panel – it must be above the MIN level line.

6 If the level is below the MIN level line, unscrew the reservoir cap and remove the diaphragm plate and diaphragm.

7 Top-up with new clean hydraulic fluid of the recommended type, until the level is above the MIN mark. Take care to avoid spills (see **Warning** above).

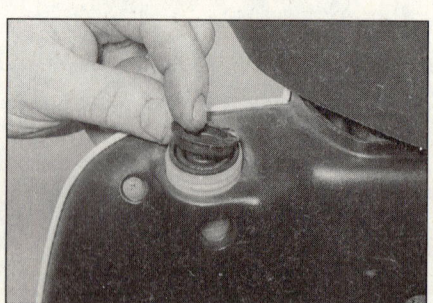

8 Ensure that the diaphragm is correctly seated before installing the plate and cover. Tighten the cap securely.

9 The NRG MC² brake fluid reservoir is located behind the front panel on the right-hand side. The fluid level can be viewed through the panel cutout and the panel must be removed if topping-up is required.

Daily (pre-ride) checks   0•13

Tyre checks

The correct pressures:
● The tyres must be checked when **cold**, not immediately after riding. Note that low tyre pressures may cause the tyre to slip on the rim or come off. High tyre pressures will cause abnormal tread wear and unsafe handling.
● Use an accurate pressure gauge.
● Proper air pressure will increase tyre life and provide maximum stability and ride comfort.
● Refer to *Model specifications* in Chapter 1 for the correct tyre pressures for your model.

Tyre care:
● Check the tyres carefully for cuts, tears, embedded nails or other sharp objects and excessive wear. Operation of the scooter with excessively worn tyres is extremely hazardous, as traction and handling are directly affected.
● Check the condition of the tyre valve and ensure the dust cap is in place.
● Pick out any stones or nails which may have become embedded in the tyre tread. If left, they will eventually penetrate through the casing and cause a puncture.
● If tyre damage is apparent, or unexplained loss of pressure is experienced, seek the advice of a tyre fitting specialist without delay.

Tyre tread depth:
● At the time of writing UK law requires that tread depth on machines over 50 cc must be at least 1 mm over 3/4 of the tread breadth all the way around the tyre, with no bald patches. Many riders, however, consider 2 mm tread depth minimum to be a safer limit.
● For machines with an engine size not greater than 50 cc, UK law states that tread depth may be less than 1 mm if the tread pattern is clearly visible across the whole of the tread breadth all the way around the tyre. Many riders, however, consider 2 mm tread depth minimum to be a safer limit.
● Many tyres now incorporate wear indicators in the tread. Identify the triangular pointer on the tyre sidewall to locate the indicator bar and replace the tyre if the tread has worn down to the bar.

1 Check the tyre pressures when the tyres are **cold** and keep them properly inflated.

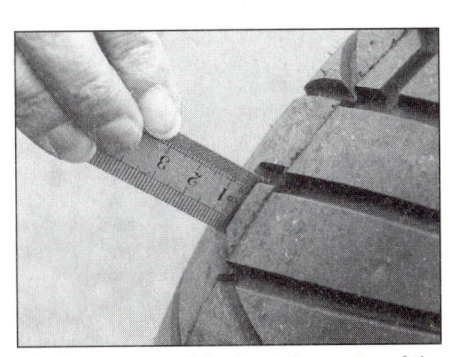

2 Measure tread depth at the centre of the tyre using a tread depth gauge or ruler.

3 Tyre tread wear indicator bar and its location marking (usually either an arrow, a triangle or the letters TWI) on the sidewall (arrowed).

Suspension and steering checks

● Check that the front and rear suspension operates smoothly without binding.
● Check that the rear suspension is adjusted as required.
● Check that the steering moves smoothly from lock-to-lock.

Legal and safety checks

Lighting and signalling
● Take a minute to check that the headlight, tail light, brake light, instrument lights and turn signals all work correctly.
● Check that the horn sounds when the switch is operated.
● A working speedometer graduated in mph is a statutory requirement in the UK.

Safety
● Check that the throttle grip rotates smoothly and snaps shut when released in all steering positions.
● Check that the stand return spring holds the stand securely up when retracted.
● Check that both brakes work correctly when applied and free off when released.

Notes

Chapter 1
Routine maintenance and servicing

Contents

Air filter and transmission filter – cleaning	1
Battery – check	2
Brake cables – check, adjustment and lubrication	5
Brake fluid (disc brake) – change	4
Brake hose (disc brake) – renewal	6
Brake lever pivots – lubrication	7
Brake shoes/pads – wear check	8
Brake system – check	3
Cooling system – check	9
Cooling system – draining, flushing and refilling	10
Cylinder head – decarbonisation (two-stroke engines)	11
Drivebelt – inspection and renewal	12
Engine oil and filter – change (four-stroke engines)	13
Fuel system – check	14
Gearbox oil – change	16
Gearbox oil – level check	15
Headlight aim – check and adjustment	17
Idle (tickover) speed – check and adjustment	18
Nuts and bolts – tightness check	19
Oil pump drivebelt – renewal (two-stroke engines)	20
Secondary air system – clean	21
Spark plug – renewal	23
Spark plug gap – check and adjustment	22
Speedometer cable and drive gear – lubrication	24
Stands – check and lubrication	25
Steering head bearings – freeplay check and adjustment	26
Suspension – check	27
Throttle cable and oil pump – check and adjustment	28
Valve clearances – check and adjustment (four-stroke engines)	29
Variator and clutch – check	30
Wheel bearings – check	32
Wheels and tyres – general check	31

Degrees of difficulty

Easy, suitable for novice with little experience	**Fairly easy,** suitable for beginner with some experience	**Fairly difficult,** suitable for competent DIY mechanic	**Difficult,** suitable for experienced DIY mechanic	**Very difficult,** suitable for expert DIY or professional

Introduction

This Chapter is designed to help the home mechanic maintain his/her scooter for safety, economy, long life and peak performance.

Deciding where to start or plug into the service schedule depends on several factors. If the warranty period on your scooter has just expired, and if it has been maintained according to the warranty standards, you may want to pick up routine maintenance as it coincides with the next mileage or calendar interval. If you have owned the machine for some time but have never performed any maintenance on it, then you may want to start at the nearest interval and include some additional procedures to ensure that nothing important is overlooked. If you have just had a major engine overhaul, then you may want to start the maintenance routine from the beginning. If you have a used machine and have no knowledge of its history or maintenance record, you may desire to combine all the checks into one large service initially and then settle into the maintenance schedule prescribed.

Before beginning any maintenance or repair, the machine should be cleaned thoroughly, especially around the engine and transmission covers. Cleaning will help ensure that dirt does not contaminate the engine and will allow you to detect wear and damage that could otherwise easily go unnoticed.

Certain maintenance information is sometimes printed on decals attached to the scooter. If the information on the decals differs from that included here, use the information on the decal.

Note 1: *The Daily (pre-ride) checks detailed at the beginning of this Manual cover those items which should be inspected on a daily basis. Always perform the pre-ride inspection at every maintenance interval (in addition to the procedures listed).*

Note 2: *An initial (one-off) service will be performed by a Piaggio dealer after the first 600 miles (1000 km) from new. Thereafter, the scooter should be serviced according to the intervals specified in the service schedules which follow. The intervals listed below are the intervals recommended by the manufacturer for each particular operation during the model years covered in this manual. Your owner's manual may have different intervals for your model.*

Note 3: *The 2500 mile (4000 km) tasks should be included with the 5000 mile (8000 km) service, etc.*

Note 4: *The service intervals were increased from every 2500, 5000 and 10,000 miles (4000, 8000, and 16,000 km) to every 3125, 6250 and 12,500 miles (5000, 10,000 and 20,000 km) in January 1996. Refer to the Scheduled Maintenance Program in the Three Year Warranty booklet supplied with the scooter for the correct intervals for your machine.*

1•2 Model specifications and service schedules

Piaggio Sfera 50/80

Model identification

Engine ....50 cc or 80 cc single cylinder air-cooled two-stroke
Transmission ....Variable speed automatic, belt-driven
Ignition ....Electronic
Suspension
   Front ....Trailing link and monoshock
   Rear ....Swingarm and monoshock
Brakes ....Drum (front and rear)
Engine no. prefix ....NSL 1M (50 cc), NS8 1M (80 cc)
Frame no. prefix ....NSL 1T (50 cc), NS8 1T (80 cc)
Wheelbase ....1200 mm
Overall length ....1705 mm
Overall width ....700 mm
Overall height (excl. mirrors) ....1070 mm
Weight (dry) ....81 kg
Fuel tank capacity
   Total ....5.2 litres
   Reserve ....1.4 litres
Introduced ....Jul '91 (50 cc), Feb '93 (80 cc)
Modifications
   November 1994 (MAQ2 model) ....Rear carrier, new seat

Servicing specifications and lubricants

Spark plug type ....Champion N2C or NGK B9ES
Spark plug electrode gap ....0.5 to 0.6 mm
Idle speed ....1800 to 2000 rpm
Tyre size 90/90-10
Front tyre pressure ....16 to 17.5 psi (1.1 to 1.2 Bar)
Rear tyre pressure
   Rider only ....23 to 24.5 psi (1.6 to 1.7 Bar)
   Rider and passenger ....36.5 psi (2.5 Bar)
Fuel type ....Petrol (unleaded) min 95 octane
Engine oil type ....Good quality two-stroke injector oil
Engine oil tank capacity
   Total ....1.42 litres
   Reserve ....0.38 litre
Gearbox oil type ....80W90 or 85W90 gear oil
Gearbox oil quantity ....approx. 85 cc
Air filter oil ....Synthetic oil (eg Selenia HI 2T)
Variator ....Lithium soap grease (NLGI 3)
Speedometer drive gear ....Lithium soap grease (NLGI 3)
Brake levers ....Calcium soap grease (NLGI 1-2)
Control cables ....Synthetic oil (eg Selenia HI 2T)

Model specifications and service schedules

Service intervals – Piaggio Sfera 50/80

Note: *Always perform the Daily (pre-ride) checks before every service interval – see the beginning of this Manual*

	Text section in this Chapter	Every 2500 miles (4000 km) or 12 months	Every 5000 miles (8000 km) or 2 years	Every 10,000 miles (16,000 km) or 3 years
Air filter – clean	1	✔		
Battery – check	2	✔		
Brake cables – check and lubrication	5	✔		
Brake levers – lubrication	7	✔		
Brake shoes – wear check	8	✔		
Brake system – check	3	✔		
Cylinder head – decarbonise	11			✔
Drivebelt – check	12	✔		
Fuel system – check	14	✔		
Gearbox oil level – check	15	✔		
Gearbox oil – change	16		✔	
Headlight aim – check and adjustment	17		✔	
Idle speed – check and adjustment	18	✔		
Nuts and bolts – tightness check	19		✔	
Oil pump drivebelt – renew	20			✔
Spark plug – gap check and adjustment	22	✔		
Spark plug – renew	23		✔	
Speedometer cable and drive gear – lubrication	24		✔	
Stand – check and lubrication	25		✔	
Steering head bearings – check and adjustment	26		✔	
Suspension – check	27		✔	
Throttle cable/oil pump – check and adjustment	28	✔		
Variator and clutch – check	30	✔ variator		✔ clutch
Wheels and tyres – general check	31	✔		
Wheel bearings – check	32		✔	

1•4 Model specifications and service schedules

Piaggio Sfera 50/80 (RST – restyle)

Model identification
Engine . . . . . . .50 cc or 80 cc single cylinder air-cooled two-stroke
Transmission . . . . .Variable speed automatic, belt-driven
Ignition . . . . .Electronic
Suspension
 Front . . . . .Trailing link and monoshock
 Rear . . . . .Swingarm and monoshock
Brakes . . . . .Single disc (front), drum (rear)
Engine no. prefix . . . . .CO 11M (50 cc)
Frame no. prefix . . . . . .ZAP CO 1000 (50 cc), ZAP MO 3000 (80 cc)
Wheelbase . . . . .1230 mm
Overall length . . . . .1760 mm
Overall width . . . . .700 mm
Overall height (excl. mirrors) . . . . .1080 mm
Weight (dry) . . . . .90 kg
Fuel tank capacity
 Total . . . . .8.0 litres
 Reserve . . . . .1.8 litres
Introduced . . . . .August 1995

Servicing specifications and lubricants
Spark plug type .Champion N2C or NGK B9ES
Spark plug electrode gap . . . . .0.5 to 0.6 mm
Idle speed . . . . .1600 to 1800 rpm
Front tyre size 100/80-10
Rear tyre size 110/80-10
Front tyre pressure . . . . .22 psi (1.5 Bar)
Rear tyre pressure
 Rider only . . . . .26 psi (1.8 Bar)
 Rider and passenger . . . . .32 to 33.5 psi (2.2 to 2.3 Bar)
Fuel type . . . . .Petrol (unleaded) min 95 octane
Engine oil type . . . . .Good quality two-stroke injector oil
Engine oil tank capacity
 Total . . . . .1.42 litres
 Reserve . . . . .0.38 litres
Gearbox oil type .80W90 or 85W90 gear oil
Gearbox oil quantity . . . . .approx. 75 cc
Brake fluid . . . . .DOT 4
Air filter oil . . . . .Synthetic oil (eg Selenia HI 2T)
Variator . . . . .Lithium soap grease (NLGI 3)
Speedometer drive gear . . . . .Lithium soap grease (NLGI 3)
Brake levers .Calcium soap grease (NLGI 1-2)
Control cables . . . . .Synthetic oil (eg Selenia HI 2T)

Model specifications and service schedules 1•5

Service intervals – Piaggio Sfera 50/80 (RST – restyle)

Note: *Always perform the Daily (pre-ride) checks before every service interval – see the beginning of this Manual*

	Text section in this Chapter	Every 2500 miles (4000 km) or 12 months	Every 5000 miles (8000 km) or 2 years	Every 10,000 miles (16,000 km) or 3 years
Air filter – clean	1	✔		
Battery – check	2	✔		
Brake cable – check and lubrication	5	✔		
Brake fluid – change	4		✔*	
Brake hose – renew	6			✔*
Brake levers – lubrication	7	✔		
Brake pads/shoes – wear check	8	✔		
Brake system – check	3	✔		
Cylinder head – decarbonise	11			✔
Drivebelt – check	12	✔		
Fuel system – check	14	✔		
Gearbox oil level – check	15	✔		
Gearbox oil – change	16		✔	
Headlight aim – check and adjustment	17		✔	
Idle speed – check and adjustment	18	✔		
Nuts and bolts – tightness check	19		✔	
Oil pump drivebelt – renew	20			✔
Spark plug – gap check and adjustment	22	✔		
Spark plug – renew	23		✔	
Speedometer cable and drive gear – lubrication	24		✔	
Stand – check and lubrication	25		✔	
Steering head bearings – check and adjustment	26		✔	
Suspension – check	27		✔	
Throttle cable/oil pump – check and adjustment	28	✔		
Variator and clutch – check	30	✔ variator		✔ clutch
Wheels and tyres – general check	31	✔		
Wheel bearings – check	32		✔	

*The brake fluid must be changed every 2 years and the brake hose renewed every 3 years, irrespective of mileage.

1•6 Model specifications and service schedules

Piaggio Sfera 125

Model identification

Engine	125 cc single cylinder air-cooled four-stroke
Transmission	Variable speed automatic, belt-driven
Ignition	Electronic
Suspension	
Front	Trailing link and monoshock
Rear	Swingarm and monoshock
Brakes	Single disc (front), drum (rear)
Engine no. prefix	MO 11M
Frame no. prefix	ZAP MO 1000
Wheelbase	1230 mm
Overall length	1760 mm
Overall width	700 mm
Overall height (excl. mirrors)	1080 mm
Weight (dry)	104 kg
Fuel tank capacity	
Total	7.5 litres
Reserve	1.5 litres
Introduced	January 1996

Servicing specifications and lubricants

Spark plug type	Champion RG4 HC or NGK CR8E
Spark plug electrode gap	0.5 to 0.6 mm
Idle speed	1500 to 1700 rpm
Valve clearances (COLD engine)	0.12 to 0.15 mm
Front tyre size	100/80-10
Rear tyre size	130/70-10
Front tyre pressure	22 psi (1.5 Bar)
Rear tyre pressure	
Rider only	26 psi (1.8 Bar)
Rider and passenger	29 psi (2.0 Bar)
Fuel type	Petrol (unleaded) min 95 octane
Engine oil type	20W50 multigrade engine oil
Engine oil quantity	850 cc (dry fill)
Gearbox oil type	80W90 or 85W90 gear oil
Gearbox oil quantity	approx. 90 cc
Brake fluid	DOT 4
Air filter oil	Air filter oil
Variator	Lithium soap grease (NLGI 3)
Speedometer drive gear	Lithium soap grease (NLGI 3)
Brake levers	Calcium soap grease (NLGI 1-2)
Control cables	Synthetic oil (eg Selenia HI 2T)

Model specifications and service schedules 1•7

Service intervals – Piaggio Sfera 125

Note: *Always perform the Daily (pre-ride) checks before every service interval – see the beginning of this Manual*

	Text section in this Chapter	Every 2500 miles (4000 km) or 12 months	Every 5000 miles (8000 km) or 2 years	Every 10,000 miles (16,000 km) or 3 years
Air filter – clean	1	✔		
Battery – check	2	✔		
Brake cable – check and lubrication	5	✔		
Brake fluid – change	4		✔*	
Brake hose – renew	6			✔*
Brake levers – lubrication	7	✔		
Brake pads/shoes – wear check	8	✔		
Brake system – check	3	✔		
Drivebelt – check	12	✔		
Engine oil change and strainer clean	13	✔		
Engine oil filter – change	13		✔	
Fuel system – check	14	✔		
Gearbox oil level – check	15	✔		
Gearbox oil – change	16		✔	
Headlight aim – check and adjustment	17		✔	
Idle speed – check and adjustment	18	✔		
Nuts and bolts – tightness check	19		✔	
Spark plug – gap check and adjustment	22	✔		
Spark plug – renew	23		✔	
Speedometer cable and drive gear – lubrication	24		✔	
Stand – check and lubrication	25		✔	
Steering head bearings – check and adjustment	26		✔	
Suspension – check	27		✔	
Throttle cable – check and adjustment	28	✔		
Valve clearances – check and adjustment	29		✔	
Variator – check	30	✔		
Wheels and tyres – general check	31	✔		
Wheel bearings – check	32		✔	

* The brake fluid must be changed every 2 years and the brake hose renewed every 3 years, irrespective of mileage.

1•8 Model specifications and service schedules

Piaggio Typhoon 50/80

Model identification
Engine . . . . . . .50 cc or 80 cc single cylinder air-cooled two-stroke
Transmission . . . . .Variable speed automatic, belt-driven
Ignition . . . . .Electronic
Suspension
   Front . . . . .Upside-down telescopic forks
   Rear . . . . .Swingarm and monoshock
Brakes . . . . .Single disc (front), drum (rear)
Engine no. prefix . . . . .TEC 1M (50 cc), TE8 1M (80 cc)
Frame no. prefix . . . . .TEC 1T (50 cc), TE8 1T (80 cc)
Wheelbase . . . . .1280 mm
Overall length . . . . .1800 mm
Overall width . . . . .700 mm
Overall height (excl. mirrors) . . . . .1085 mm
Weight (dry) . . . . .83 kg (50 cc), 94 kg (80 cc)
Fuel tank capacity
   Total . . . . .5.5 litres (50 cc), 8.0 litres (80 cc)
   Reserve . . . . .1.5 litres (50 cc), 2.0 litres (80 cc)
Introduced . . . . .Feb '93 (50 cc), Jul '94 (80 cc)
Modifications
   August 1995 . . . . .Starter jet in carburettor (50 cc only)

Servicing specifications and lubricants
Spark plug type . . . . .Champion N2C or NGK B9ES
Spark plug electrode gap . . . . .0.5 to 0.6 mm
Idle speed . . . . .1800 to 2000 rpm
Tyre size 120/90-10
Front tyre pressure . . . . .17.5 to 19 psi (1.2 to 1.3 Bar)
Rear tyre pressure
   Rider only . . . . .24.5 to 26 psi (1.7 to 1.8 Bar)
   Rider and passenger . . . . .32 to 33.5 psi (2.2 to 2.3 Bar)
Fuel type . . . . .Petrol (unleaded) min 95 octane
Engine oil type . . . . .Good quality two-stroke injector oil
Engine oil tank capacity
   Total . . . . .1.5 litres
   Reserve . . . . .0.5 litre
Gearbox oil type . . . . .80W90 or 85W90 gear oil
Gearbox oil quantity . . . . .approx. 85 cc
Brake fluid . . . . .DOT 4
Air filter oil . . . . .Synthetic oil (eg Selenia HI 2T)
Variator . . . . .Lithium soap grease (NLGI 3)
Speedometer drive gear . . . . .Lithium soap grease (NLGI 3)
Brake levers . . . . .Calcium soap grease (NLGI 1-2)
Control cables . . . . .Synthetic oil (eg Selenia HI 2T)

Model specifications and service schedules 1•9

Service intervals – Piaggio Typhoon 50/80

Note: *Always perform the Daily (pre-ride) checks before every service interval – see the beginning of this Manual*

	Text section in this Chapter	Every 2500 miles (4000 km) or 12 months	Every 5000 miles (8000 km) or 2 years	Every 10,000 miles (16,000 km) or 3 years
Air filter – clean	1	✔		
Battery – check	2	✔		
Brake cable – check and lubrication	5	✔		
Brake fluid – change	4		✔*	
Brake hose – renew	6			✔*
Brake levers – lubrication	7	✔		
Brake pads/shoes – wear check	8	✔		
Brake system – check	3	✔		
Cylinder head – decarbonise	11			✔
Drivebelt – check	12	✔		
Fuel system – check	14	✔		
Gearbox oil level – check	15	✔		
Gearbox oil – change	16		✔	
Headlight aim – check and adjustment	17		✔	
Idle speed – check and adjustment	18	✔		
Nuts and bolts – tightness check	19		✔	
Oil pump drivebelt – renew	20			✔
Secondary air system (cat models) – clean	21			✔
Spark plug – gap check and adjustment	22	✔		
Spark plug – renew	23		✔	
Speedometer cable and drive gear – lubrication	24		✔	
Stand – check and lubrication	25		✔	
Steering head bearings – check and adjustment	26		✔	
Suspension – check	27		✔	
Throttle cable/oil pump – check and adjustment	28	✔		
Variator and clutch – check	30	✔ variator		✔ clutch
Wheels and tyres – general check	31	✔		
Wheel bearings – check	32		✔	

*The brake fluid must be changed every 2 years and the brake hose renewed every 3 years, irrespective of mileage.

Model specifications and service schedules

Piaggio Typhoon 125

Model identification

Engine ....125 cc single cylinder air-cooled two-stroke
Transmission ....Variable speed automatic, belt-driven
Suspension
   Front ....Upside-down telescopic forks
   Rear ....Swingarm and monoshock
Brakes ....Single disc (front), drum (rear)
Engine no. prefix ....CO 21M, RST model MO 21M
Frame no. prefix ....ZAP CO 2000, RST model ZAP MO 2000
Wheelbase ....1280 mm
Overall length ....1800 mm
Overall width ....700 mm
Overall height (excl. mirrors) ....1085 mm
Weight (dry) ....106 kg
Fuel tank capacity
   Total ....8.0 litres, RST model 5.2 litres
   Reserve ....1.5 litres, RST model 1.4 litres
Introduced ....Jun '95, RST (restyle) model Aug '87

Servicing specifications and lubricants

Spark plug type ....Champion N2C or NGK B9ES
Spark plug electrode gap ....0.5 to 0.6 mm
Idle speed ....1600 to 1800 rpm
Tyre size 120/90-10
Front tyre pressure ....19 psi (1.3 Bar)
Rear tyre pressure
   Rider only ....26 psi (1.8 Bar)
   Rider and passenger ....36.5 psi (2.5 Bar)
Fuel type ....Petrol (unleaded) min 95 octane
Engine oil type ....Good quality two-stroke injector oil
Engine oil tank capacity
   Total ....1.5 litres
   Reserve ....0.5 litre
Gearbox oil type ....80W90 or 85W90 gear oil
Gearbox oil quantity ....approx. 85 cc
Brake fluid ....DOT 4
Air filter oil ....Synthetic oil (eg Selenia HI 2T)
Variator ....Lithium soap grease (NLGI 3)
Speedometer drive gear ....Lithium soap grease (NLGI 3)
Brake levers ....Calcium soap grease (NLGI 1-2)
Control cables ....Synthetic oil (eg Selenia HI 2T)

Model specifications and service schedules

Service intervals – Piaggio Typhoon 125

Note: *Always perform the Daily (pre-ride) checks before every service interval – see the beginning of this Manual*

	Text section in this Chapter	Every 2500 miles (4000 km) or 12 months	Every 5000 miles (8000 km) or 2 years	Every 10,000 miles (16,000 km) or 3 years
Air filter – clean	1	✔		
Battery – check	2	✔		
Brake cable – check and lubrication	5	✔		
Brake fluid – fluid change	4		✔*	
Brake hose – renew	6			✔*
Brake levers – lubrication	7	✔		
Brake pads/shoes – wear check	8	✔		
Brake system – check	3	✔		
Cylinder head – decarbonise	11			✔
Drivebelt and clutch – check	12	✔		
Fuel system – check	14	✔		
Gearbox oil level – check	15	✔		
Gearbox oil – change	16		✔	
Headlight aim – check and adjustment	17		✔	
Idle speed – check and adjustment	18	✔		
Nuts and bolts – tightness check	19		✔	
Oil pump drivebelt – renew	20			✔
Spark plug – gap check and adjustment	22	✔		
Spark plug – renew	23		✔	
Speedometer cable and drive gear – lubrication	24		✔	
Stand – check and lubrication	25		✔	
Steering head bearings – check and adjustment	26		✔	
Suspension – check	27		✔	
Throttle cable/oil pump – check and adjustment	28	✔		
Variator and clutch – check	30	✔ variator		✔ clutch
Wheels and tyres – general check	31	✔		
Wheel bearings – check	32		✔	

* The brake fluid must be changed every 2 years and the brake hose renewed every 3 years, irrespective of mileage.

1•12 Model specifications and service schedules

Piaggio Zip/Zip 50

Model identification
Engine ....50 cc single cylinder air-cooled two-stroke
Transmission ....Variable speed automatic, belt-driven
Ignition ....Electronic
Suspension
  Front ....Telescopic forks
  Rear ....Swingarm and monoshock
Brakes
  Front ....Drum (Zip), single disc (Zip 50)
  Rear ....Drum
Engine no. prefix
  Zip ....NSL 1M
  Zip 50 ....C25 1M
Frame no. prefix
  Zip ....SSL 1T, RST model ZAP CO 6000
  Zip 50 ....ZAP C25
Wheelbase
  Zip ....1160 mm
  Zip 50 ....1180 mm
Overall length
  Zip ....1630 mm
  Zip 50 ....1690 mm
Overall width
  Zip ....640 mm
  Zip 50 ....630 mm
Overall height (excl. mirrors)
  Zip ....1050 mm
  Zip 50 ....1070 mm
Weight (dry)
  Zip ....71 kg
  Zip 50 ....84 kg
Fuel tank capacity   Total   Reserve
  Zip ....4.0 litres   0.9 litre
  Zip 50 ....6.0 litres   1.5 litres
Introduced ....1993, RST (restyle) model 1997, Zip 50 2000

Servicing specifications and lubricants
Spark plug type
  Zip ....Champion N2C or NGK B9ES
  Zip 50 ....Champion RN2C
Spark plug electrode gap
  Zip ....0.5 to 0.6 mm
  Zip 50 ....0.6 to 0.7 mm
Idle speed
  Zip ....1800 to 2000 rpm
  Zip 50 ....1700 to 1900 rpm
Tyre size
  Zip 90/90-10
  Zip 50 ....100/80-10 (Front); 120/70-10 (Rear)
Front tyre pressure
  Zip ....16 to 17.5 psi (1.1 to 1.2 Bar)
  Zip 50 ....19 psi (1.3 Bar)
Rear tyre pressure
  Zip ....23 to 24.5 psi (1.6 to 1.7 Bar)
  Zip 50 ....26 to 29 psi (1.8 to 2.0 Bar)
Fuel type ....Petrol (unleaded) min 95 octane
Engine oil type ....Good quality two-stroke injector oil
Engine oil tank capacity
  Total ....1.15 litres
  Reserve ....0.5 litre
Gearbox oil type ....80W90 or 85W90 gear oil
Gearbox oil quantity ....approx. 85 cc
Brake fluid ....DOT 4
Front fork oil type ....20W fork oil
Front fork oil quantity ....30 cc
Air filter oil ....Synthetic oil (eg Selenia HI 2T)
Variator
  Zip 50 ....Lithium soap grease (NLGI 3)
Speedometer drive gear ....Lithium soap grease (NLGI 3)
Brake levers ....Calcium soap grease (NLGI 1-2)
Control cables ....Synthetic oil (eg Selenia HI 2T)

Model specifications and service schedules

Service intervals – Piaggio Zip/Zip 50

Note: Always perform the Daily (pre-ride) checks before every service interval – see the beginning of this Manual

	Text section in this Chapter	Every 2500 miles (4000 km) or 12 months	Every 5000 miles (8000 km) or 2 years	Every 10,000 miles (16,000 km) or 3 years
Air filter – clean	1	✔ (Zip)	✔ (Zip 50)	
Battery – check	2	✔		
Brake cables – check and lubrication	5	✔		
Brake fluid (Zip 50) – change	4		✔	
Brake hose (Zip 50) – renew	6			✔
Brake levers – lubrication	7	✔		
Brake pads/shoes – wear check	8	✔		
Brake system – check	3	✔		
Cylinder head – decarbonise	11			✔
Drivebelt – check	12	✔ (Zip)		✔ (Zip 50)
Fuel system – check	14	✔		
Gearbox oil level – check	15	✔		
Gearbox oil – change	16		✔	
Headlight aim – check and adjustment	17		✔	
Idle speed – check and adjustment	18	✔ (Zip)	✔ (Zip 50)	
Nuts and bolts – tightness check	19		✔	
Oil pump drivebelt – renew	20			✔
Secondary Air System (Zip 50) - clean	21			✔
Spark plug – gap check and adjustment	22	✔		
Spark plug – renew	23	✔ (Zip 50)	✔ (Zip)	
Speedometer cable and drive gear – lubrication	24		✔	
Stand – check and lubrication	25		✔	
Steering head bearings – check and adjustment	26		✔	
Suspension – check	27		✔	
Throttle cable/oil pump – check and adjustment	28	✔		
Variator and clutch (Zip) – check	30	✔ variator		✔ clutch
Variator and clutch (Zip 50) – check	30			✔
Wheels and tyres – general check	31	✔		
Wheel bearings – check	32		✔	

* The brake fluid must be changed every 2 years and the brake hose renewed every 3 years, irrespective of mileage.

1•14 Model specifications and service schedules

Piaggio Zip SP

Model identification
Engine ....50 cc single cylinder liquid-cooled two-stroke
Transmission ....Variable speed automatic, belt-driven
Ignition ....Electronic
Suspension
   Front ....Trailing link and monoshock
   Rear ....Swingarm and monoshock
Brakes ....Single disc (front), drum (rear)
Engine no. prefix ....C 111M
Frame no. prefix ....ZAPC 11000
Wheelbase ....1160 mm
Overall length ....1630 mm
Overall width ....640 mm
Overall height (excl. mirrors) ....1050 mm
Weight (dry) ....77 kg
Fuel tank capacity
   Total ....4.0 litres
   Reserve ....0.9 litre
Introduced ....Apr '97

Servicing specifications and lubricants
Spark plug type ....Champion N2C or NGK B9ES
Spark plug electrode gap ....0.5 to 0.6 mm
Idle speed ....1800 to 2000 rpm
Tyre size 100/80-10
Front tyre pressure ....20.5 psi (1.4 Bar)
Rear tyre pressure
   Rider only ....26 psi (1.8 Bar)
   Rider and passenger ....38 psi (2.6 Bar)
Fuel type ....Petrol (unleaded) min 95 octane
Engine oil type ....Good quality two-stroke injector oil
Engine oil tank capacity
   Total ....1.15 litres
   Reserve ....0.5 litre
Coolant type ....50% distilled water and 50% ethylene glycol anti-freeze
Cooling system quantity ....approx. 1 litre
Gearbox oil type ....80W90 gear oil
Gearbox oil quantity ....approx. 80 cc
Brake fluid ....DOT 4
Air filter oil ....Synthetic oil (eg Selenia HI 2T)
Variator ....Lithium soap grease (NLGI 3)
Speedometer drive gear ....Lithium soap grease (NLGI 3)
Brake levers ....Calcium soap grease (NLGI 1-2)
Control cables ....Synthetic oil (eg Selenia HI 2T)

Model specifications and service schedules 1•15

Service intervals – Piaggio Zip SP

Note: *Always perform the Daily (pre-ride) checks before every service interval – see the beginning of this Manual*

	Text section in this Chapter	Every 3000 miles (5000 km) or 12 months	Every 6000 miles (10,000 km) or 2 years	Every 12,000 miles (20,000 km) or 3 years
Air filter – clean	1	✔		
Battery – check	2	✔		
Brake cable – check and lubrication	5	✔		
Brake fluid – change	4		✔*	
Brake hose – renew	6			✔*
Brake levers – lubrication	7	✔		
Brake pads/shoes – wear check	8	✔		
Brake system – check	3	✔		
Cooling system – check	9	✔		
Cooling system – draining, flushing and refilling	10			✔**
Cylinder head – decarbonise	11			✔
Drivebelt – check	12	✔		
Fuel system – check	14	✔		
Gearbox oil level – check	15	✔		
Gearbox oil – change	16		✔	
Headlight aim – check and adjustment	17		✔	
Idle speed – check and adjustment	18	✔		
Nuts and bolts – tightness check	19		✔	
Oil pump drivebelt – renew	20			✔
Spark plug – gap check and adjustment	22	✔		
Spark plug – renew	23		✔	
Speedometer cable and drive gear – lubrication	24		✔	
Stand – check and lubrication	25		✔	
Steering head bearings – check and adjustment	26		✔	
Suspension – check	27		✔	
Throttle cable/oil pump – check and adjustment	28	✔		
Variator and clutch – check	30	✔variator		✔clutch
Wheels and tyres – general check	31	✔		
Wheel bearings – check	32		✔	

*The brake fluid must be changed every 2 years and the brake hose renewed every 3 years, irrespective of mileage.
**The coolant must be changed every 3 years, irrespective of mileage.

1•16 Model specifications and service schedules

Piaggio Zip 50 4T

Model identification

Engine	50 cc single cylinder air-cooled four-stroke
Transmission	Variable speed automatic, belt driven
Ignition	Electronic
Suspension	
Front	Telescopic forks
Rear	Swingarm and monoshock
Brakes	Single disc (front), drum (rear)
Engine no. prefix	C 252M
Frame no. prefix	ZAPC250
Wheelbase	1250 mm
Overall length	1690 mm
Overall width	680 mm
Overall height (excl. mirrors)	1070 mm
Weight	84 kg
Fuel tank capacity	
Total	7.5 litres
Reserve	1.5 litres
Introduced	2001

Servicing specifications and lubricants

Spark plug type	Champion RG4 PHP or Champion RG4 HC
Spark plug electrode gap	0.7 to 0.8 mm
Idle speed	1900 to 2000 rpm
Valve clearances (COLD engine)	
Intake	0.10 mm
Exhaust	0.15 mm
Front tyre size	100/80-10
Rear tyre size	120/70-10
Front tyre pressure	19 psi (1.3 Bar)
Rear tyre pressure	
Rider only	23 psi (1.6 Bar)
Rider and passenger	26 psi (1.8 Bar)
Fuel type	Petrol (unleaded) min 95 octane
Engine oil type	5W40 API SJ synthetic oil
Engine oil quantity	850 cc
Gearbox oil type	80W90 API GL3 gear oil
Gearbox oil quantity	approx. 80 cc
Brake fluid	DOT 4
Air filter oil	Air filter oil
Speedometer drive gear	Lithium soap grease (NLGI 3)
Brake levers	Calcium soap grease (NLGI 1-2)
Control cables	Synthetic oil (eg Selenia HI 2T)

Model specifications and service schedules

Service intervals – Piaggio Zip 50 4T

Note: *Always perform the Daily (pre-ride) checks before every service interval – see the beginning of this Manual*

	Text section in this Chapter	Every 3750 miles (6000 km) or 12 months	Every 7500 miles (12,000 km) or 2 years	Every 11,000 miles (18,000 km) or 3 years
Air filter – clean	1	✔		
Battery – check	2	✔		
Brake cable – check and lubrication	5	✔		
Brake fluid – change	4		✔*	
Brake hose – renew	6			✔*
Brake levers – lubrication	7	✔		
Brake pads/shoes – wear check	8	✔		
Brake system – check	3	✔		
Drive belt – change	12		✔	
Engine oil change and strainer clean	13	✔		
Fuel system – check	14	✔		
Gearbox oil level – check	15	✔		
Gearbox oil – change	16			15,000 miles/ 24,000 km
Headlight aim – check and adjustment	17		✔	
Idle speed – check and adjustment	18		✔	
Nuts and bolts – tightness check	19		✔	
Spark plug – check	22		✔	
Speedometer cable and drive gear – lubrication	24		✔	
Stand – check and lubrication	25		✔	
Steering head bearings – check and adjustment	26		✔	
Suspension – check	27		✔	
Throttle cable – check and adjustment	28		✔	
Valve clearances – check and adjustment	29			15,000 miles/ 24,000 km
Variator – check	30	✔		
Wheels and tyres – general check	31	✔		
Wheel bearings – check	32		✔	

* The brake fluid must be changed every 2 years and the brake hose renewed every 3 years, irrespective of mileage.

Model specifications and service schedules

Piaggio Zip 125

Model identification
Engine ......125 cc single cylinder air-cooled four-stroke LEADER
Transmission ....Variable speed automatic, belt-driven
Ignition ....Electronic
Suspension
   Front
      2001 models ....Trailing link and monoshock
      2002-on models ....Telescopic forks
   Rear ....Swingarm and monoshock
Brakes ....Single disc (front), drum (rear)
Engine no. prefix M251M
Frame no. prefix ....ZAP M25
Wheelbase ....1220 mm
Overall length ....1695 mm
Overall width ....680 mm
Overall height (excl. mirrors) ....1115 mm
Weight ....95 kg
Fuel tank capacity
   Total ....7.5 litres
   Reserve ....1.2 litres
Introduced 2001

Servicing specifications and lubricants
Spark plug type ....Champion RG 6YC or NGK CR7EB
Spark plug electrode gap ....0.7 to 0.8 mm
Idle speed ....1600 to 1700 rpm
Valve clearances (COLD engine)
   Intake ....0.10 mm
   Exhaust ....0.15 mm
Front tyre size 100/80-10
Rear tyre size 120/70-10
Front tyre pressure ....19.0 psi (1.3 Bar)
Rear tyre pressure
   Rider only ....23 to 26 psi (1.6 to 1.8 Bar)
   Rider and passenger ....29 psi (2.0 Bar)
Fuel type ....Petrol (unleaded) min 95 octane
Engine oil type ....5W40 API SJ synthetic oil
Engine oil quantity ....approx. 1 litre
Gearbox oil type ....80W90 API GL3 gear oil
Gearbox oil quantity ....approx. 150 cc
Brake fluid ....DOT 4
Foam air filter oil ....Air filter oil
Speedometer drive gear ....Lithium soap grease (NLGI 3)
Brake levers ....Calcium soap grease (NLGI 1-2)
Control cables ....Synthetic oil (eg Selenia HI 2T)

Model specifications and service schedules 1•19

Service intervals – Piaggio Zip 125

Note: *Always perform the Daily (pre-ride) checks before every service interval – see the beginning of this Manual*

	Text section in this Chapter	Every 2500 miles (4000 km) or 12 months	Every 5000 miles (8000 km) or 2 years	Every 10,000 miles (16,000 km) or 3 years
Air filter – clean	1		✓	
Battery – check	2	✓		
Brake cable – check and lubrication	5	✓		
Brake fluid – change	4		✓*	
Brake hose – renew	6			✓*
Brake levers – lubrication	7	✓		
Brake pads/shoes – wear check	8	✓		
Brake system – check	3	✓		
Drivebelt – renew	12		✓	
Engine oil and filter change	13	✓		
Fuel system – check	14	✓		
Gearbox oil level – check	15	✓		
Gearbox oil – change	16			✓
Headlight aim – check and adjustment	17		✓	
Idle speed – check and adjustment	18		✓	
Nuts and bolts – tightness check	19		✓	
Spark plug – gap check and adjustment	22	✓		
Spark plug – renew	23		✓	
Speedometer drive gear – lubrication	24		✓	
Stand – check and lubrication	25		✓	
Steering head bearings – check and adjustment	26		✓	
Suspension – check	27		✓	
Throttle cable – check and adjustment	28		✓	
Valve clearances – check and adjustment	29			✓
Variator – check	30	✓		
Wheels and tyres – general check	31	✓		
Wheel bearings – check	32		✓	

* The brake fluid must be changed every 2 years and the brake hose renewed every 3 years, irrespective of mileage.

1•20 Model specifications and service schedules

Piaggio Skipper

Model identification

Engine ....125 cc single cylinder air-cooled two-stroke
Transmission ....Variable speed automatic, belt-driven
Ignition ....Electronic
Suspension
    Front ....Trailing link and monoshock
    Rear ....Swingarm and monoshock
Brakes ....Single disc (front), drum (rear)
Engine no. prefix ....CSM 1M
Frame no. prefix ....CSM 1T
Wheelbase ....1250 mm
Overall length ....1750 mm
Overall width ....710 mm
Overall height (excl. mirrors) ....1120 mm
Weight (dry) ....95 kg
Fuel tank capacity
    Total ....8.0 litres
    Reserve ....1.5 litres
Introduced ....Nov '93

Servicing specifications and lubricants

Spark plug type ....Champion N2C or NGK B9ES
Spark plug electrode gap ....0.5 to 0.6 mm
Idle speed ....1600 to 1800 rpm
Front tyre size 100/80-10
Rear tyre size 110/80-10
Front tyre pressure ....17.5 to 19 psi (1.2 to 1.3 Bar)
Rear tyre pressure
    Rider only ....24.5 to 26 psi (1.7 to 1.8 Bar)
    Rider and passenger ......32 to 33.5 psi (2.2 to 2.3 Bar)
Fuel type ....Petrol (unleaded) min 95 octane
Engine oil type ....Good quality two-stroke injector oil
Engine oil tank capacity
    Total ....1.5 litres
    Reserve ....0.5 litre
Gearbox oil type ....85W90 gear oil
Gearbox oil quantity ....approx. 100 cc
Brake fluid ....DOT 4
Foam air filter oil ....Synthetic oil (eg Selenia HI 2T)
Speed governor ....Lithium soap grease (NLGI 3)
Speedometer drive gear ....Lithium soap grease (NLGI 3)
Brake levers ....Calcium soap grease (NLGI 1-2)
Control cables ....Synthetic oil (eg Selenia HI 2T)

Model specifications and service schedules

Service intervals – Piaggio Skipper

Note: *Always perform the Daily (pre-ride) checks before every service interval – see the beginning of this Manual*

	Text section in this Chapter	Every 2500 miles (4000 km) or 12 months	Every 5000 miles (8000 km) or 2 years	Every 10,000 miles (16,000 km) or 3 years
Air filter and transmission filter – cleaning	1	✔		
Battery – check	2	✔		
Brake cable – check and lubrication	5	✔		
Brake fluid – change	4		✔*	
Brake hose – renew	6			✔*
Brake levers – lubrication	7	✔		
Brake pads/shoes – wear check	8	✔		
Brake system – check	3	✔		
Cylinder head – decarbonise	11			✔
Drivebelt – check	12	✔		
Fuel system – check	14	✔		
Gearbox oil level – check	15	✔		
Gearbox oil – change	16		✔	
Headlight aim – check and adjustment	17		✔	
Idle speed – check and adjustment	18	✔		
Nuts and bolts – tightness check	19		✔	
Oil pump drivebelt – renew	20			✔
Spark plug – gap check and adjustment	22	✔		
Spark plug – renew	23		✔	
Speedometer cable and drive gear – lubrication	24		✔	
Stand – check and lubrication	25		✔	
Steering head bearings – check and adjustment	26		✔	
Suspension – check	27		✔	
Throttle cable/oil pump – check and adjustment	28	✔		
Variator and clutch – check	30	✔variator		✔clutch
Wheels and tyres – general check	31	✔		
Wheel bearings – check	32		✔	

*The brake fluid must be changed every 2 years and the brake hose renewed every 3 years, irrespective of mileage.

1•22 Model specifications and service schedules

Piaggio Skipper ST125

Model identification
Engine ......125 cc single cylinder air-cooled four-stroke LEADER
Transmission ....Variable speed automatic, belt-driven
Ignition ....Electronic
Suspension
   Front ....Upside-down telescopic forks
   Rear ....Swingarm and monoshock
Brakes ....Single disc (front), drum (rear)
Engine no. prefix M121M
Frame no. prefix ....ZAP M
Wheelbase ....1291 mm
Overall length ....1855 mm
Overall width ....680 mm
Seat height ....815 mm
Weight ....108 kg
Fuel tank capacity
   Total ....9.5 litres
   Reserve ....1.5 litres
Introduced 2001

Servicing specifications and lubricants
Spark plug type ....Champion RG 4HC
Spark plug electrode gap ....0.7 to 0.8 mm
Idle speed ....1600 to 1700 rpm
Valve clearances (COLD engine)
   Intake ....0.10 mm
   Exhaust ....0.15 mm
Front tyre size 120/70-12
Rear tyre size 130/70-12
Front tyre pressure ....20.5 to 22 psi (1.4 to 1.5 Bar)
Rear tyre pressure
   Rider only ....23 to 24.5 psi (1.6 to 1.7 Bar)
   Rider and passenger ....26 psi (1.8 Bar)
Fuel type ....Petrol (unleaded) min 95 octane
Engine oil type ....5W/40 API SJ synthetic oil
Engine oil quantity ....approx. 1 litre
Gearbox oil type ....80W90 API GL3 gear oil
Gearbox oil quantity ....approx. 150 cc
Brake fluid ....DOT 4
Foam air filter oil ....Air filter oil
Speedometer drive gear ....Lithium soap grease (NLGI 3)
Brake levers ....Calcium soap grease (NLGI 1-2)
Control cables ....Synthetic oil (eg Selenia HI 2T)

Model specifications and service schedules

Service intervals – Piaggio Skipper ST125

Note: *Always perform the Daily (pre-ride) checks before every service interval – see the beginning of this Manual*

	Text section in this Chapter	Every 2500 miles (4000 km) or 12 months	Every 5000 miles (8000 km) or 2 years	Every 10,000 miles (16,000 km) or 3 years
Air filter – clean	1	✔		
Battery – check	2	✔		
Brake cable – check and lubrication	5	✔		
Brake fluid – change	4		✔*	
Brake hose – renew	6			✔*
Brake levers – lubrication	7	✔		
Brake pads/shoes – wear check	8	✔		
Brake system – check	3	✔		
Drivebelt – renew	12		✔	
Engine oil and filter change	13	✔		
Fuel system – check	14	✔		
Gearbox oil level – check	15	✔		
Gearbox oil – change	16		✔	
Headlight aim – check and adjustment	17		✔	
Idle speed – check and adjustment	18	✔		
Nuts and bolts – tightness check	19		✔	
Spark plug – gap check and adjustment	22	✔		
Spark plug – renew	23		✔	
Stand – check and lubrication	25		✔	
Steering head bearings – check and adjustment	26		✔	
Suspension – check	27		✔	
Throttle cable – check and adjustment	28	✔		
Valve clearances – check and adjustment	29		✔	
Variator – check	30	✔		
Wheels and tyres – general check	31	✔		
Wheel bearings – check	32		✔	

* The brake fluid must be changed every 2 years and the brake hose renewed every 3 years, irrespective of mileage.

1•24 Model specifications and service schedules

Piaggio Hexagon

Model identification

Engine . . . . .125 cc single cylinder liquid-cooled two-stroke
Transmission . . . . .Variable speed automatic, belt-driven
Ignition . . . . .Electronic
Suspension
   Front . . . . .Trailing link and monoshock
   Rear . . . . .Swingarm and monoshock
Brakes . . . . .Single disc (front), drum (rear)
Engine no. prefix . . . . .EXS 1M
Frame no. prefix . . . . .EXS 1T
Wheelbase . . . . .1400 mm
Overall length . . . . .1960 mm
Overall width . . . . .725 mm
Overall height . . . . .1170 mm
Weight (dry) . . . . .138 kg
Fuel tank capacity
   Total . . . . .10.0 litres
   Reserve . . . . .2.0 litres
Introduced . . . . .Jul '94

Servicing specifications and lubricants

Spark plug type . . . . .Champion N2C or NGK B9ES
Spark plug electrode gap . . . . .0.5 to 0.6 mm
Idle speed . . . . .1600 to 1800 rpm
Front tyre size 100/80-10
Rear tyre size 130/70-10
Front tyre pressure . . . . .26 psi (1.8 Bar)
Rear tyre pressure
   Rider only . . . . .33.5 psi (2.3 Bar)
   Rider and passenger . . . . .36.5 psi (2.5 Bar)
Fuel type . . . . .Petrol (unleaded) min 95 octane
Engine oil type . . . . .Good quality two-stroke injector oil
Engine oil tank capacity
   Total . . . . .1.5 litres
   Reserve . . . . .0.5 litre
Coolant type . . . . .50% distilled water and 50% ethylene
                                                                                     glycol anti-freeze
Cooling system capacity . . . . .approx. 1 litre
Gearbox oil type . . . . .85W90 gear oil
Gearbox oil quantity . . . . .approx. 85 cc
Brake fluid . . . . .DOT 4
Grey air filter element oil . . . . .Synthetic oil (eg Selenia HI 2T)
Variator . . . . .Lithium soap grease (NLGI 3)
Speedometer drive gear . . . . .Lithium soap grease (NLGI 3)
Brake levers .Calcium soap grease (NLGI 1-2)
Control cables . . . . .Synthetic oil (eg Selenia HI 2T)

Model specifications and service schedules 1•25

Service intervals – Piaggio Hexagon

Note: *Always perform the Daily (pre-ride) checks before every service interval – see the beginning of this Manual*

	Text section in this Chapter	Every 2500 miles (4000 km) or 12 months	Every 5000 miles (8000 km) or 2 years	Every 10,000 miles (16,000 km) or 3 years
Air filter and transmission filter – cleaning	1	✔		
Battery – check	2	✔		
Brake cable – check and lubrication	5	✔		
Brake fluid (disc) – change	4		✔*	
Brake hose (disc) – renew	6			✔*
Brake levers – lubrication	7	✔		
Brake pads/shoes – wear check	8	✔		
Brake system – check	3	✔		
Cooling system – check	9	✔		
Cooling system – draining, flushing and refilling	10			✔**
Cylinder head – decarbonise	11			✔
Drivebelt – check	12	✔		
Fuel system – check	14	✔		
Gearbox oil level – check	15	✔		
Gearbox oil – change	16		✔	
Headlight aim – check and adjustment	17		✔	
Idle speed – check and adjustment	18	✔		
Nuts and bolts – tightness check	19		✔	
Oil pump drivebelt – renew	20			✔
Spark plug – gap check and adjustment	22	✔		
Spark plug – renew	23		✔	
Speedometer cable and drive gear – lubrication	24		✔	
Stand – check and lubrication	25		✔	
Steering head bearings – check and adjustment	26		✔	
Suspension – check	27		✔	
Throttle cable/oil pump – check and adjustment	28	✔		
Variator and clutch – check	30	✔ variator		✔ clutch
Wheels and tyres – general check	31	✔		
Wheel bearings – check	32		✔	

* The brake fluid must be changed every 2 years and the brake hose renewed every 3 years, irrespective of mileage.
** The coolant must be changed every 3 years, irrespective of mileage.

Model specifications and service schedules

Piaggio Super Hexagon

Model identification
Engine ....124 cc single cylinder liquid-cooled four-stroke LEADER
Transmission ....Variable speed automatic, belt-driven
Ignition ....Electronic
Suspension
   Front ....Trailing link and monoshock
   Rear ....Swingarm and twin shock
Brakes ....Single disc (front and rear)
Engine no. prefix M201M
Frame no. prefix ....ZAP M20
Wheelbase ....1450 mm
Overall length ....2012 mm
Overall width ....730 mm
Overall height ....1462 mm
Weight (dry) .... 139 kg
Fuel tank capacity
   Total ....11.4 litres
   Reserve ....2.0 litres
Introduced 2001

Servicing specifications and lubricants
Spark plug type ....Champion RG4HC or NGK CR 9EB
Spark plug electrode gap ....0.7 to 0.8 mm
Idle speed ....1570 to 1630 rpm
Valve clearances (COLD engine)
   Intake ....0.10 mm
   Exhaust ....0.15 mm
Front tyre size 120/70-11
Rear tyre size 130/70-11
Front tyre pressure ....26 psi (1.8 Bar)
Rear tyre pressure
   Rider only ....32 psi (2.2 Bar)
   Rider and passenger ....36.5 psi (2.5 Bar)
Fuel type ....Petrol (unleaded) min 95 octane
Engine oil type ....SAE 5W40 synthetic oil
Engine oil quantity ....approx. 1 litre
Coolant type ....50% distilled water and 50% ethylene glycol anti-freeze
Cooling system capacity ....approx. 1 litre
Gearbox oil type ....80W90 API GL3 gear oil
Gearbox oil quantity ....approx. 150 cc
Brake fluid ....DOT 4
Foam air filter oil ....Air filter oil
Speedometer drive gear ....Lithium soap grease (NLGI 3)
Brake levers ....Calcium soap grease (NLGI 1-2)
Control cables ....Synthetic oil (eg Selenia HI 2T)

Model specifications and service schedules

Service intervals – Piaggio Super Hexagon

Note: *Always perform the Daily (pre-ride) checks before every service interval – see the beginning of this Manual*

	Text section in this Chapter	Every 2500 miles (4000 km) or 12 months	Every 5000 miles (8000 km) or 2 years	Every 10,000 miles (16,000 km) or 3 years
Air filter – clean	1		✓	
Battery – check	2	✓		
Brake cable – check and lubrication	5	✓		
Brake fluid – change	4		✓*	
Brake hose – renew	6			✓*
Brake levers – lubrication	7	✓		
Brake pads/shoes – check	8	✓		
Brake system – check	3	✓		
Cooling system – check	9	✓		
Cooling system – draining, flushing and refilling	10		✓**	
Drivebelt – check	12	✓		
Drivebelt – renew	12		✓	
Engine oil and filter – change	13	✓		
Fuel system – check	14	✓		
Gearbox oil level – check	15	✓		
Gearbox oil – change	16		✓	
Headlight aim – check and adjustment	17		✓	
Idle speed – check and adjustment	18	✓		
Nuts and bolts – tightness check	19		✓	
Spark plug – gap check and adjustment	22	✓		
Spark plug – renew	23		✓	
Stand – check and lubrication	25		✓	
Steering head bearings – check and adjustment	26		✓	
Suspension – check	27		✓	
Throttle cable – check and adjustment	28	✓		
Valve clearances – check and adjustment				✓
Variator – check	30	✓		
Wheels and tyres – general check	31	✓		
Wheel bearings – check	32		✓	

* The brake fluid must be changed every 2 years and the brake hose renewed every 3 years, irrespective of mileage.
** The coolant must be changed every 3 years, irrespective of mileage.

1•28 Model specifications and service schedules

Liberty 50

Model identification

Engine	.50 cc single cylinder air-cooled two-stroke
Transmission	Variable speed automatic, belt-driven
Ignition	Electronic
Suspension	
Front	Telescopic forks
Rear	Swingarm and monoshock
Brakes	Single disc (front), drum (rear)
Engine no. prefix	C151M
Frame no. prefix	ZAPC 15
Wheelbase	1285 mm
Overall length	1885 mm
Overall width	670 mm
Overall height (excl. mirrors)	1100 mm
Weight	88 kg
Fuel tank capacity	
Total	5.5 litres
Reserve	1.2 litres
Introduced	1997

Servicing specifications and lubricants

Spark plug type	Champion N2C
Spark plug electrode gap	0.5 to 0.6 mm
Idle speed	1700 to 1900 rpm
Tyre size	
Front	70/90-16
Rear	90/80-16
Front tyre pressure	26 psi (1.8 Bar)
Rear tyre pressure	29 psi (2.0 Bar)
Fuel type	Petrol (unleaded) min 95 octane
Engine oil type	Good quality two-stroke injector oil
Engine oil tank capacity	
Total	1.7 litres
Reserve	0.4 litre
Gearbox oil type	80W90 or 85W90 gear oil
Gearbox oil quantity	approx. 100 cc
Brake fluid	DOT 4
Air filter oil	Synthetic oil (eg Selenia HI 2T)
Variator	Lithium soap grease (NLGI 3)
Speedometer drive gear	Lithium soap grease (NLGI 3)
Brake levers	Calcium soap grease (NLGI 1-2)
Control cables	Synthetic oil (eg Selenia HI 2T)

Model specifications and service schedules 1•29

Service intervals – Liberty 50

Note: *Always perform the Daily (pre-ride) checks before every service interval – see the beginning of this Manual*

	Text section in this Chapter	Every 2500 miles (4000 km) or 12 months	Every 5000 miles (8000 km) or 2 years	Every 10,000 miles (16,000 km) or 3 years
Air filter – clean	1	✔		
Battery – check	2	✔		
Brake cable – check and lubrication	5	✔		
Brake fluid – change	4		✔*	
Brake hose – renew	6			✔*
Brake levers – lubrication	7	✔		
Brake pads/shoes – wear check	8	✔		
Brake system – check	3	✔		
Cylinder head – decarbonise	11			✔
Drivebelt – check	12			✔
Fuel system – check	14	✔		
Gearbox oil level – check	15	✔		
Gearbox oil – change	16		✔	
Headlight aim – check and adjustment	17		✔	
Idle speed – check and adjustment	18		✔	
Nuts and bolts – tightness check	19		✔	
Oil pump drivebelt – renew	20			✔
Spark plug – gap check and adjustment	22	✔		
Speedometer cable and drive gear – lubrication	24		✔	
Stand – check and lubrication	25		✔	
Steering head bearings – check and adjustment	26		✔	
Suspension – check	27		✔	
Throttle cable/oil pump – check and adjustment	28	✔		
Variator and clutch – check	30			✔
Wheels and tyres – general check	31	✔		
Wheel bearings – check	32		✔	

* The brake fluid must be changed every 2 years and the brake hose renewed every 3 years, irrespective of mileage.

1•30 Model specifications and service schedules

Liberty 50 4T

Model identification
Engine . . . . .50 cc single cylinder air-cooled four-stroke
Transmission . . . . .Variable speed automatic, belt-driven
Ignition . . . . .Electronic
Suspension
　Front . . . . .Telescopic forks
　Rear . . . . .Swingarm and monoshock
Brakes . . . . .Single disc (front), drum (rear)
Engine no. prefix C282M
Frame no. prefix . . . . .ZAPC 28 / ZAPC282
Wheelbase . . . . .1285 mm
Overall length . . . . .1885 mm
Overall width . . . . .670 mm
Overall height (excl. mirrors) . . . . .1100 mm
Weight . . . . .94 kg
Fuel tank capacity
　Total . . . . .7.0 litres
　Reserve . . . . .1.5 litres
Introduced 2001

Servicing specifications and lubricants
Spark plug type . . . . .Champion RG4 PHP or Champion RG4 HC
Spark plug electrode gap . . . . .0.7 to 0.8 mm
Idle speed . . . . .1900 to 2000 rpm
Valve clearances (COLD engine)
　Intake . . . . .0.10 mm
　Exhause . . . . .0.15 mm
Front tyre size 70/90-16
Rear tyre size 90/80-16
Front tyre pressure . . . . .26 psi (1.8 Bar)
Rear tyre pressure . . . . .29 psi (2.0 Bar)
Fuel type . . . . .Petrol (unleaded) min 95 octane
Engine oil type . . . . .5W40 API SJ synthetic oil
Engine oil quantity . . . . .850 cc
Gearbox oil type . . . . .80W90 API GL3 gear oil
Gearbox oil quantity . . . . .approx. 80 cc
Brake fluid . . . . .DOT 4
Air filter oil . . . . .Air filter oil
Speedometer drive gear . . . . .Lithium soap grease (NLGI 3)
Brake levers . . . . .Calcium soap grease (NLGI 1-2)
Control cables . . . . .Synthetic oil (eg Selenia HI 2T)

Model specifications and service schedules 1•31

Service intervals – Liberty 50 4T

Note: *Always perform the Daily (pre-ride) checks before every service interval – see the beginning of this Manual*

	Text section in this Chapter	Every 2500 miles (4000 km) or 12 months	Every 5000 miles (8000 km) or 2 years	Every 10,000 miles (16,000 km) or 3 years
Air filter – clean	1		✔	
Battery – check	2	✔		
Brake cable – check and lubrication	5	✔		
Brake fluid – change	4		✔*	
Brake hose – renew	6			✔*
Brake levers – lubrication	7	✔		
Brake pads/shoes – wear check	8	✔		
Brake system – check	3	✔		
Drivebelt – change	12		✔	
Engine oil change and strainer clean	13	✔		
Fuel system – check	14	✔		
Gearbox oil level – check	15	✔		
Gearbox oil – change	16			✔
Headlight aim – check and adjustment	17		✔	
Idle speed – check and adjustment	18		✔	
Nuts and bolts – tightness check	19		✔	
Spark plug – renew	22		✔	
Speedometer cable and drive gear – lubrication	24		✔	
Stand – check and lubrication	25		✔	
Steering head bearings – check and adjustment	26		✔	
Suspension – check	27		✔	
Throttle cable – check and adjustment	28		✔	
Valve clearances – check and adjustment	29			✔
Variator – check	30	✔		
Wheels and tyres – general check	31	✔		
Wheel bearings – check	32		✔	

*The brake fluid must be changed every 2 years and the brake hose renewed every 3 years, irrespective of mileage.

1•32 Model specifications and service schedules

Liberty 125

Model identification
Engine	124 cc single cylinder air-cooled four-stroke
Transmission	Variable speed automatic, belt-driven
Ignition	Electronic
Suspension	
Front	Telescopic forks
Rear	Swingarm and monoshock
Brakes	Single disc (front), drum (rear)
Engine no. prefix	
Pre-LEADER engine	M111 M000
LEADER engine	M222 M000
Frame no. prefix	
Pre-LEADER engine	ZAPM 11
LEADER engine	ZAPM 22
Wheelbase	1285 mm
Overall length	1885 mm
Overall width	670 mm
Overall height (excl. mirrors)	1100 mm
Weight	97 kg
Fuel tank capacity	
Total	7.0 litres
Reserve	1.5 litres
Introduced	2000

Servicing specifications and lubricants
Spark plug type	
Pre-LEADER engine	Champion RG4 HC or NGK CR8E
LEADER engine	Champion RG4 6YC or NGK CR7EB
Spark plug electrode gap	
Pre-LEADER engine	0.5 to 0.6 mm
LEADER engine	0.7 to 0.8 mm
Idle speed	
Pre-LEADER engine	1500 to 1700 rpm
LEADER engine	1600 to 1700 rpm
Valve clearances (COLD engine)	
Pre-LEADER engine	0.12 to 0.15 mm
LEADER engine	
Intake	0.10 mm
Exhaust	0.15 mm
Tyre size	
Front	80/80-16
Rear	110/80-14
Front tyre pressure	26 psi (1.8 Bar)
Rear tyre pressure	
Rider only	29 psi (2.0 Bar)
Rider and passenger	32 to 36.5 psi (2.2 to 2.5 Bar)
Fuel type	Petrol (unleaded) min 95 octane
Engine oil type	
Pre-LEADER engine	20W50 multigrade engine oil
LEADER engine	5W40 API SJ synthetic oil
Engine oil quantity	
Pre-LEADER engine	850 cc
LEADER engine	approx. 1 litre
Gearbox oil type	80W90 API GL3 gear oil
Gearbox oil quantity	
Pre-LEADER engine	80 to 90 cc
LEADER engine	approx. 150 cc
Brake fluid	DOT 4
Air filter oil	Air filter oil
Speedometer drive gear	Lithium soap grease (NLGI 3)
Brake levers	Calcium soap grease (NLGI 1-2)
Control cables	Synthetic oil (eg Selenia HI 2T)

Model specifications and service schedules 1•33

Service intervals – Liberty 125

Note: *Always perform the Daily (pre-ride) checks before every service interval – see the beginning of this Manual*

	Text section in this Chapter	Every 2500 miles (4000 km) or 12 months	Every 5000 miles (8000 km) or 2 years	Every 10,000 miles (16,000 km) or 3 years
Air filter (pre-LEADER engine) – clean	1	✔		
Air filter (LEADER engine) – clean	1		✔	
Battery – check	2	✔		
Brake cable – check and lubrication	5	✔		
Brake fluid – change	4		✔*	
Brake hose – renew	6			✔*
Brake levers – lubrication	7	✔		
Brake pads/shoes – wear check	8	✔		
Brake system – check	3	✔		
Drivebelt (pre-LEADER engine) – check	12	✔		
Drivebelt (LEADER engine) – change	12		✔	
Engine oil change and strainer clean (pre-LEADER engine)	13	✔		
Engine oil filter (pre-LEADER engine) – change	13		✔	
Engine oil and filter (LEADER engine) – change	13	✔		
Fuel system – check	14	✔		
Gearbox oil level – check	15	✔		
Gearbox oil (pre-LEADER engine) – change	16		✔	
Gearbox oil (LEADER engine) – change	16			✔
Headlight aim – check and adjustment	17		✔	
Idle speed – check and adjustment	18	✔		
Nuts and bolts – tightness check	19		✔	
Spark plug – gap check and adjustment	22	✔		
Spark plug – renew	23		✔	
Speedometer cable and drive gear – lubrication	24		✔	
Stand – check and lubrication	25		✔	
Steering head bearings – check and adjustment	26		✔	
Suspension – check	27		✔	
Throttle cable – check and adjustment	28		✔	
Valve clearances (pre-LEADER engine) – check and adjustment	29		✔	
Valve clearances (LEADER engine) – check and adjustment	29			✔
Variator – check	30	✔		
Wheels and tyres – general check	31	✔		
Wheel bearings – check	32		✔	

* The brake fluid must be changed every 2 years and the brake hose renewed every 3 years, irrespective of mileage.

1•34 Model specifications and service schedules

Piaggio Fly 50

Model identification
Engine . . . . .50 cc single cylinder air-cooled two-stroke
Transmission . . . . .Variable speed automatic, belt driven
Ignition . . . . .Electronic
Suspension
   Front . . . . .Telescopic forks
   Rear . . . . .Swingarm and monoshock
Brakes . . . . .Single disc (front), drum (rear)
Engine no. prefix C44 1M
Frame no. prefix . . . . .ZAPM 44100
Wheelbase . . . . .1340 mm
Overall length . . . . .1880 mm
Overall width . . . . .735 mm
Overall height (excl. mirrors) . . . . .1150 mm
Weight (dry) . . . . .97 kg
Fuel tank capacity
   Total . . . . .7.2 litres
   Reserve . . . . .1.5 litres
Introduced 2005

Servicing specifications and lubricants
Spark plug type . . . . .Champion RGN2C
Spark plug electrode gap . . . . .0.6 to 0.7 mm
Idle speed . . . . .1800 to 2000 rpm
Tyre size 120/70-12
Front tyre pressure . . . . .26 psi (1.8 Bar)
Rear tyre pressure
   Rider only . . . . .29 psi (2.0 Bar)
   Rider and passenger . . . . .33.5 psi (2.3 Bar)
Fuel type . . . . .Petrol (leaded or unleaded) min 95 octane
Engine oil type . . . . .Selenia HI 2T two-stroke injector oil
Engine oil tank capacity . . . . .1.2 litres
Gearbox oil type . . . . .75W85 API GL4 gear oil
Gearbox oil quantity . . . . .approx. 85 cc
Brake fluid . . . . .DOT 4
Air filter oil . . . . .Synthetic oil (e.g. Selenia HI 2T)
Speedometer drive gear . . . . .Lithium soap grease (NLGI 3)
Brake levers . . . . .Calcium soap grease (NLGI 1-2)
Control cables . . . . .Synthetic oil (e.g. Selenia HI 2T)
Driven pulley shaft grease . . . . .Molybdenum bisulphide grease

Model specifications and service schedules 1•35

Service intervals – Piaggio Fly 50

Note: *Always perform the Daily (pre-ride) checks before every service interval – see the beginning of this Manual*

	Text section in this Chapter	Every 2500 miles (4000 km) or 12 months	Every 5000 miles (8000 km) or 2 years	Every 10,000 miles (16,000 km) or 3 years
Air filter – clean	1	✔		
Battery – check	2	✔		
Brake cable – check and lubrication	5		✔	
Brake fluid – change	4		✔*	
Brake hose – renew	6			✔*
Brake levers – lubrication	7	✔		
Brake pads/shoes – wear check	8	✔		
Brake system – check	3	✔		
Cooling system – check	9			✔
Drive belt – check	12		✔	Renew belt
Gearbox oil level – check	15	✔		
Gearbox oil – change	16		✔	
Headlight aim – check and adjustment	17		✔	
Idle speed – check and adjustment	18		✔	
Nuts and bolts – tightness check	19		✔	
Oil pump drive belt – renew	20			Every 12,000 miles (20,000 km)
Secondary air system - clean	21			✔
Spark plug – gap check and adjustment	22	✔		
Spark plug – renew	23		✔	
Speedometer cable and drive gear – lubrication	24		✔	
Steering head bearings – check and adjustment	26		✔	
Suspension – check	27		✔	
Throttle cable/oil pump – check and adjustment	28	✔		
Variator	30		Renew rollers	
Wheels and tyres – general check	31	✔		

* The brake fluid must be changed every 2 years and the brake hose renewed every 3 years, irrespective of mileage.

Model specifications and service schedules

Piaggio Fly 50 4T

Model identification

Engine ....50 cc single cylinder air-cooled four-stroke
Transmission ....Variable speed automatic, belt driven
Ignition ....Electronic
Suspension
   Front ....Telescopic forks
   Rear ....Swingarm and monoshock
Brakes ....Single disc (front), drum (rear)
Engine no. prefix ....C 442M
Frame no. prefix ZAPM44200
Wheelbase ....1340 mm
Overall length ....1880 mm
Overall width ....735 mm
Overall height (excl. mirrors) ....1150 mm
Weight ....102 kg
Fuel tank capacity
   Total ....7.2 litres
   Reserve ....1.5 litres
Introduced 2006

Servicing specifications and lubricants

Spark plug type ....NGK CR 8EB
Spark plug electrode gap ....0.7 to 0.8 mm
Idle speed ....1900 to 2000 rpm
Valve clearances (COLD engine)
   Intake ....0.10 mm
   Exhaust ....0.15 mm
Tyre size 120/70-12
Front tyre pressure ....26 psi (1.8 Bar)
Rear tyre pressure
   Rider only ....29 psi (2.0 Bar)
   Rider and passenger ....33.5 psi (2.3 Bar)
Fuel type ....Petrol (unleaded) min 95 octane
Engine oil type ....5W40 API SJ synthetic oil
Engine oil quantity ....850 cc
Gearbox oil type ....80W90 API GL3 gear oil
Gearbox oil quantity ....approx. 85 cc
Brake fluid ....DOT 4
Air filter oil ....Air filter oil
Speedometer drive gear ....Lithium soap grease (NLGI 3)
Brake levers ....Calcium soap grease (NLGI 1-2)
Control cables ....Synthetic oil (e.g. Selenia HI 2T)

Model specifications and service schedules

Service intervals – Piaggio Fly 50 4T

Note: *Always perform the Daily (pre-ride) checks before every service interval – see the beginning of this Manual*

	Text section in this Chapter	Every 3750 miles (6000 km) or 12 months	Every 7500 miles (12,000 km) or 2 years	Every 15,000 miles (24,000 km) or 3 years
Air filter – clean	1		✔	
Battery – check	2	✔		
Brake cable – check and lubrication	5		✔	
Brake fluid – change	4		✔*	
Brake hose – renew	6			✔*
Brake levers – lubrication	7		✔	
Brake pads/shoes – wear check	8	✔		
Brake system – check	3	✔		
Cooling system – check	9			✔
Drive belt – change	12		✔	
Engine oil change and strainer clean	13	✔		
Gearbox oil – check	15		✔	
Gearbox oil – change	16			✔
Headlight aim – check and adjustment	17		✔	
Idle speed – check and adjustment	18		✔	
Secondary air system - clean	21		✔	
Spark plug – check	22	✔		
Speedometer cable and drive gear – lubrication	24		✔	
Steering head bearings – check and adjustment	26	✔		
Suspension – check	27		✔	
Throttle cable – check and adjustment	28	✔		
Valve clearances – check and adjustment	29			✔
Variator – check	30	✔		
Wheels and tyres – general check	31	✔		

* The brake fluid must be changed every 2 years and the brake hose renewed every 3 years, irrespective of mileage.

1•38 Model specifications and service schedules

Piaggio Fly 125

Model identification
Engine	125 cc single cylinder air-cooled four-stroke LEADER
Transmission	Variable speed automatic, belt driven
Ignition	Electronic
Suspension	
Front	Telescopic forks
Rear	Swingarm and monoshock
Brakes	Single disc (front), drum (rear)
Engine no. prefix	M421M
Frame no. prefix	ZAPM 42100
Wheelbase	1330 mm
Overall length	1870 mm
Overall width	735 mm
Seat height	785 mm
Weight	112 kg
Fuel tank capacity	
Total	7.2 litres
Reserve	1.5 litres
Introduced	2005

Servicing specifications and lubricants
Spark plug type	Champion RG 6YC or NGK CR7EB
Spark plug electrode gap	0.7 to 0.8 mm
Idle speed	1600 to 1800 rpm
Valve clearances (COLD engine)	
Intake	0.10 mm
Exhaust	0.15 mm
Tyre size	120/70-12
Front tyre pressure	26 psi (1.8 Bar)
Rear tyre pressure	
Rider only	29 psi (2.0 Bar)
Rider and passenger	33.5 psi (2.3 Bar)
Fuel type	Petrol (leaded or unleaded) min 95 octane
Engine oil type	5W/40 API SG synthetic oil
Engine oil quantity	approx. 1 litre
Gearbox oil type	80W90 API GL3 gear oil
Gearbox oil quantity	approx. 200 cc
Brake fluid	DOT 4
Foam air filter oil	Air filter oil
Speedometer drive gear	Lithium soap grease (NLGI 3)
Brake levers	Calcium soap grease (NLGI 1-2)
Control cables	Engine oil

Model specifications and service schedules 1•39

Service intervals – Piaggio Fly 125

Note: *Always perform the Daily (pre-ride) checks before every service interval – see the beginning of this Manual*

	Text section in this Chapter	Every 3750 miles (6000 km) or 12 months	Every 7500 miles (12,000 km) or 2 years	Every 15,000 miles (24,000 km) or 3 years
Air filter – clean	1	✔		
Battery – check	2	✔		
Brake cable – check and lubrication	5	✔		
Brake fluid – change	4		✔*	
Brake hose – renew	6			✔*
Brake levers – lubrication	7	✔		
Brake pads/shoes – wear check	8	✔		
Brake system – check	3	✔		
Cooling system – check	9			✔
Drive belt – check	12	✔	Renew belt	
Engine oil and filter change	13	✔		
Gearbox oil level – check	15	✔		
Gearbox oil – change	16			✔
Headlight aim – check and adjustment	17		✔	
Idle speed – check and adjustment	18	✔		
Nuts and bolts – tightness check	19		✔	
Secondary air system – clean	21		✔	
Spark plug – gap check and adjustment	22	✔		
Spark plug – renew	23		✔	
Speedometer cable and drive gear – lubrication	24		✔	
Stand – check and lubrication	25	✔		
Steering head bearings – check and adjustment	26		✔	
Suspension – check	27		✔	
Throttle cable – check and adjustment	28		✔	
Valve clearances – check and adjustment	29	✔		
Variator – check	30	✔	Renew rollers	
Wheels and tyres – general check	31	✔		
* The brake fluid must be changed every 2 years and the brake hose renewed every 3 years, irrespective of mileage.			

1•40 Model specifications and service schedules

Piaggio NRG MC² / MC³ DD

Model identification
Engine ....50 cc single cylinder liquid-cooled two-stroke
Transmission ....Variable speed automatic, belt-driven
Ignition ....Electronic
Suspension
  Front ....Upside-down telescopic forks
  Rear ....Swingarm and monoshock
Brakes
  MC² ....Single disc (front), drum (rear)
  MC³ DD ....Single disc (front and rear)
Engine no. prefix ....CO 41M
Frame no. prefix
  MC² ....ZAP CO 4000
  MC³ DD ....ZAP C1800
Wheelbase
  MC² ....1260 mm
  MC³ DD ....1280 mm
Overall length
  MC² ....1830 mm
  MC³ DD ....1870 mm
Overall width
  MC² ....700 mm
  MC³ DD ....720 mm
Overall height (excl. mirrors)
  MC² ....1080 mm
  MC³ DD ....1140 mm
Weight (dry) ....94 kg
Fuel tank capacity
  Total
    MC² ....5.5 litres
    MC³ DD ....7.5 litres
  Reserve ....2.0 litres
Introduced
  MC² ....March 1997
  MC³ DD 2001

Servicing specifications and lubricants
Spark plug type
  MC² ....Champion N84 or Bosch W2CC
  MC³ DD ....Champion RN2C or NGK BR9 ES
Spark plug electrode gap ....0.5 to 0.6 mm
Idle speed
  MC² ....1800 to 2000 rpm
  MC³ DD ....1700 to 1900 rpm
Tyre size 130/60-13
Front tyre pressure ....17.5 to 19 psi (1.2 to 1.3 Bar)
Rear tyre pressure ....23 to 24.5 psi (1.6 to 1.7 Bar)
Fuel type ....Petrol (unleaded) min 95 octane
Engine oil type ....Good quality synthetic two-stroke injector oil
Engine oil tank capacity
  Total ....1.3 litres
  Reserve ....0.5 litre
Coolant type ....50% distilled water and 50% ethylene glycol anti-freeze
Cooling system capacity ....approx. 1 litre
Gearbox oil type ....80W90 gear oil
Gearbox oil quantity ....approx. 80 cc
Brake fluid ....DOT 4
Air filter oil ....Synthetic oil (eg Selenia HI 2T)
Variator
  MC² ....Lithium soap grease (NLGI 3)
Speedometer drive gear ....Lithium soap grease (NLGI 3)
Brake levers ....Calcium soap grease (NLGI 1-2)
Control cables ....Synthetic oil (eg Selenia HI 2T)

Model specifications and service schedules 1•41

Service intervals – Piaggio NRG MC2/MC3 DD

Note: *Always perform the Daily (pre-ride) checks before every service interval – see the beginning of this Manual*

	Text section in this Chapter	Every 3000 miles (5000 km) or 12 months	Every 6000 miles (10,000 km) or 2 years	Every 12,000 miles (20,000 km) or 3 years
Air filter – clean	1	✔		
Battery – check	2	✔		
Brake cable (NRG MC2) – check and lubrication	5	✔		
Brake fluid – change	4		✔*	
Brake hose – renew	6			✔*
Brake levers – lubrication	7	✔		
Brake pads/shoes – wear check	8	✔		
Brake system – check	3	✔		
Cooling system – check	9	✔		
Cooling system – draining, flushing and refilling	10			✔**
Cylinder head – decarbonise	11			✔
Drivebelt (NRG MC2) – check	12	✔		
Drivebelt (NRG MC3) – renew	12			Renew every 9000 miles (15,000 km)
Fuel system – check	14	✔		
Gearbox oil level – check	15	✔		
Gearbox oil – change	16		✔	
Headlight aim – check and adjustment	17		✔	
Idle speed – check and adjustment	18	✔		
Nuts and bolts – tightness check	19		✔	
Oil pump drivebelt – renew	20			✔
Secondary air system (cat models) - clean	21			✔
Spark plug – gap check and adjustment	22	✔		
Spark plug – renew	23		✔	
Speedometer cable and drive gear – lubrication	24		✔	
Stand – check and lubrication	25		✔	
Steering head bearings – check and adjustment	26		✔	
Suspension – check	27		✔	
Throttle cable/oil pump – check and adjustment	28	✔		
Variator and clutch (NRG MC2) – check	30	✔variator		✔clutch
Variator and clutch (NRG MC3) – check	30		✔variator	✔clutch
Wheels and tyres – general check	31	✔		
Wheel bearings – check	32		✔	

* The brake fluid must be changed every 2 years and the brake hose renewed every 3 years, irrespective of mileage.
** The coolant must be changed every 3 years, irrespective of mileage.

1•42 Model specifications and service schedules

Piaggio NRG MC³ DT

Model identification

Engine	.50 cc single cylinder air-cooled two-stroke
Transmission	Variable speed automatic, belt-driven
Ignition	Electronic
Suspension	
Front	Upside-down telescopic forks
Rear	Swingarm and monoshock
Brakes	Single disc (front), drum (rear)
Engine no. prefix	C215M
Frame no. prefix	ZAP C2100
Wheelbase	1280 mm
Overall length	1870 mm
Overall width	720 mm
Overall height (excl. mirrors)	1180 mm
Weight	96 kg
Fuel tank capacity	
Total	7.5 litres
Reserve	2.0 litres
Introduced	2001

Servicing specifications and lubricants

Spark plug type	Champion RN2C or NGK BR9 ES
Spark plug electrode gap	0.5 to 0.6 mm
Idle speed	1700 to 1900 rpm
Tyre size	130/60-13
Front tyre pressure	19 psi (1.3 Bar)
Rear tyre pressure	26 to 29 psi (1.8 to 2.0 Bar)
Fuel type	Petrol (unleaded) min 95 octane
Engine oil type	Good quality synthetic two-stroke injector oil
Engine oil tank capacity	
Total	1.3 litres
Reserve	0.5 litre
Gearbox oil type	80W90 API GL3 gear oil
Gearbox oil quantity	approx. 85 cc
Brake fluid	DOT 4
Air filter oil	Synthetic oil (eg Selenia HI 2T)
Speedometer drive gear	Lithium soap grease (NLGI 3)
Brake levers	Calcium soap grease (NLGI 1-2)
Control cables	Synthetic oil (eg Selenia HI 2T)

Model specifications and service schedules

Service intervals – Piaggio NRG MC³ DT

Note: *Always perform the Daily (pre-ride) checks before every service interval – see the beginning of this Manual*

	Text section in this Chapter	Every 3000 miles (5000 km) or 12 months	Every 6000 miles (10,000 km) or 2 years	Every 12,000 miles (20,000 km) or 3 years
Air filter – clean	1		✔	
Battery – check	2	✔		
Brake cable – check and lubrication	5	✔		
Brake fluid – change	4		✔*	
Brake hose – renew	6			✔*
Brake levers – lubrication	7	✔		
Brake pads/shoes – wear check	8	✔		
Brake system – check	3	✔		
Cylinder head – decarbonise	11			✔
Drivebelt – renew	12			Renew every 9000 miles (15,000 km)
Fuel system – check	14	✔		
Gearbox oil level – check	15	✔		
Gearbox oil – change	16		✔	
Headlight aim – check and adjustment	17		✔	
Idle speed – check and adjustment	18	✔		
Nuts and bolts – tightness check	19		✔	
Oil pump drivebelt – renew	20			✔
Secondary Air System (cat models) - clean	21			✔
Spark plug – gap check and adjustment	22	✔		
Spark plug – renew	23		✔	
Speedometer cable and drive gear – lubrication	24		✔	
Stand – check and lubrication	25		✔	
Steering head bearings – check and adjustment	26		✔	
Suspension – check	27		✔	
Throttle cable/oil pump – check and adjustment	28	✔		
Variator and clutch – check	30		✔variator	✔clutch
Wheels and tyres – general check	31	✔		
Wheel bearings – check	32		✔	

*The brake fluid must be changed every 2 years and the brake hose renewed every 3 years, irrespective of mileage.

Model specifications and service schedules

Piaggio NRG Power DD

Model identification

Engine . . . . .49 cc single cylinder liquid-cooled two-stroke
Transmission . . . . .Variable speed automatic, belt driven
Ignition . . . . .Electronic
Suspension
  Front . . . . .Upside-down telescopic forks
  Rear . . . . .Swingarm and monoshock
Brakes . . . . .Single disc (front and rear)
Engine no. prefix C451M
Frame no. prefix . . . . .ZAP C45100
Wheelbase . . . . .1270 mm
Overall length . . . . .1790 mm
Overall width . . . . .850 mm
Overall height . . . . .1170 mm
Weight . . . . .99 kg
Fuel tank capacity
  Total . . . . .6.5 litres
  Reserve . . . . .1.5 litres
Introduced 2005

Servicing specifications and lubricants

Spark plug type . . . . .Champion RN1C
Spark plug electrode gap . . . . .0.6 to 0.7 mm
Idle speed . . . . .1800 to 2000 rpm
Front tyre size 120/70-13
Rear tyre size 140/60-13
Front tyre pressure . . . . .17.5 psi (1.2 Bar)
Rear tyre pressure
  Rider only . . . . .24.5 psi (1.7 Bar)
  Rider and passenger . . . . .27.5 psi (1.9 Bar)
Fuel type . . . . .Petrol (leaded or unleaded) min 95 octane
Engine oil type . . . . .API TC synthetic two-stroke injector oil
Engine oil tank capacity
  Total . . . . .1.3 litres
  Reserve . . . . .0.5 litres
Gearbox oil type . . . . .75W85 API GL4 gear oil
Gearbox oil quantity . . . . .approx. 85 cc
Brake fluid . . . . .DOT 4
Air filter oil . . . . .Synthetic oil (e.g. Selenia HI 2T)
Speedometer drive gear . . . . .Lithium soap grease (NLGI 3)
Brake levers . . . . .Calcium soap grease (NLGI 1-2)
Control cables . . . . .Synthetic oil (e.g. Selenia HI 2T)

Model specifications and service schedules

Service intervals – Piaggio NRG Power DD

Note: *Always perform the Daily (pre-ride) checks before every service interval – see the beginning of this Manual*

	Text section in this Chapter	Every 3000 miles (5000 km) or 12 months	Every 6000 miles (10,000 km) or 2 years	Every 9000 miles (15,000 km) or 3 years
Air filter – clean	1	✔		
Battery – check	2	✔		
Brake fluid – change	4		✔*	
Brake levers – lubrication	7	✔		
Brake pads – wear check	8	✔		
Brake system – check	3	✔		
Cooling system – check	9	✔		
Cooling system – draining, flushing and refilling	10		✔**	
Drive belt – check	12		✔	Renew belt
Gearbox oil level – check	15	✔		
Gearbox oil – change	16		✔	
Headlight aim – check and adjustment	17		✔	
Idle speed – check and adjustment	18		✔	
Nuts and bolts – tightness check	19		✔	
Oil pump drive belt – renew	20			12,000 miles (20,000 km)
Secondary Air System - clean	21			✔
Spark plug – gap check and adjustment	22	✔		
Spark plug – renew	23		✔	
Speedometer cable and drive gear – lubrication	24		✔	
Steering head bearings – check and adjustment	26		✔	
Suspension – check	27		✔	
Throttle cable/oil pump – check and adjustment	28	✔		
Variator	30		Renew rollers	
Wheels and tyres – general check	31	✔		

*The brake fluid must be changed every 2 years and the brake hose renewed every 3 years, irrespective of mileage.
**The coolant must be changed every 2 years, irrespective of mileage.

Model specifications and service schedules

Piaggio NRG Power DT

Model identification

Engine	.49 cc single cylinder air-cooled two-stroke
Transmission	Variable speed automatic, belt driven
Ignition	Electronic
Suspension	
Front	Upside-down telescopic forks
Rear	Swingarm and monoshock
Brakes	Single disc (front), drum (rear)
Engine no. prefix	C453M
Frame no. prefix	ZAP C45300
Wheelbase	1270 mm
Overall length	1790 mm
Overall width	850 mm
Seat height	795 mm
Weight	95 kg
Fuel tank capacity	
Total	6.5 litres
Reserve	1.5 litres
Introduced	2005

Servicing specifications and lubricants

Spark plug type	Champion RN2C
Spark plug electrode gap	0.6 to 0.7 mm
Idle speed	1800 to 2000 rpm
Front tyre size	120/70-13
Rear tyre size	140/60-13
Front tyre pressure	17.5 psi (1.2 Bar)
Rear tyre pressure	
Rider only	24.5 psi (1.7 Bar)
Rider and passenger	27.5 psi (1.9 Bar)
Fuel type	Petrol (leaded or unleaded) min 95 octane
Engine oil type	Good quality synthetic two-stroke injector oil
Engine oil tank capacity	
Total	1.2 litres
Reserve	0.5 litres
Gearbox oil type	75W85 API GL4 gear oil
Gearbox oil quantity	approx. 85 cc
Brake fluid	DOT 4
Air filter oil	Synthetic oil (e.g. Selenia HI 2T)
Speedometer drive gear	Lithium soap grease (NLGI 3)
Brake levers	Calcium soap grease (NLGI 1-2)
Control cables	Synthetic oil (e.g. Selenia HI 2T)

Model specifications and service schedules

Service intervals – Piaggio NRG Power DT

Note: *Always perform the Daily (pre-ride) checks before every service interval – see the beginning of this Manual*

	Text section in this Chapter	Every 3000 miles (5000 km) or 12 months	Every 6000 miles (10,000 km) or 2 years	Every 9000 miles (15,000 km) or 3 years
Air filter – clean	1		✔	
Battery – check	2	✔		
Brake cable – check and lubrication	5		✔	
Brake fluid – change	4		✔*	
Brake levers – lubrication	7	✔		
Brake pads/shoes – wear check	8	✔		
Brake system – check	3	✔		
Cooling system – check	9			12,000 miles (20,000 km)
Drive belt – check	12		✔	✔renew
Gearbox oil level – check	15	✔		
Gearbox oil – change	16		✔	
Headlight aim – check and adjustment	17		✔	
Idle speed – check and adjustment	18		✔	
Nuts and bolts – tightness check	19		✔	
Oil pump drive belt – renew	20			12,000 miles (20,000 km)
Secondary Air System – clean	21			✔
Spark plug – gap check and adjustment	22	✔		
Spark plug – renew	23		✔	
Speedometer cable and drive gear – lubrication	24		✔	
Steering head bearings – check and adjustment	26		✔	
Suspension – check	27		✔	
Throttle cable/oil pump – check and adjustment	28	✔		
Variator	30		change rollers	
Wheels and tyres – general check	31	✔		
Wheel bearings – check	32		✔	

* The brake fluid must be changed every 2 years and the brake hose renewed every 3 years, irrespective of mileage.

1•48 Model specifications and service schedules

Piaggio B125 Beverly

Model identification
Engine . . .124 cc single cylinder liquid-cooled four-stroke LEADER
Transmission . . . . .Variable speed automatic, belt-driven
Ignition . . . . .Electronic
Suspension
   Front . . . . .Telescopic forks
   Rear . . . . .Swingarm and twin shock
Brakes . . . . .Single disc (front and rear)
Engine no. prefix M281M
Frame no. prefix . . . . .ZAP M281
Wheelbase . . . . .1470 mm
Overall length . . . . .2120 mm
Overall width . . . . .760 mm
Seat height . . . . 975 mm
Weight (dry) . . . . .149 kg
Fuel tank capacity
   Total . . . . .10.0 litres
   Reserve . . . . .2.5 litres
Introduced 2002

Servicing specifications and lubricants
Spark plug type . . . . .NGK CR 8EB
Spark plug electrode gap .0.7 to 0.8 mm
Idle speed . . . . .1600 to 1700 rpm
Valve clearances (COLD engine)
   Intake . . . . .0.10 mm
   Exhaust . . . . .0.15 mm
Front tyre size 110/70-16
Rear tyre size 140/70-16
Front tyre pressure . . . . .29 psi (2.0 Bar)
Rear tyre pressure
   Rider only . . . . .32 psi (2.2 Bar)
   Rider and passenger . . . . .36.5 psi (2.5 Bar)
Fuel type . . . . .Petrol (unleaded) min 95 octane
Engine oil type . . . . .SAE 5W40 synthetic oil
Engine oil quantity . . . . .approx. 1 litre
Coolant type . . . . .50% distilled water and 50% ethylene
                                                                                               glycol anti-freeze
Cooling system capacity . . . . .approx. 1 litre
Gearbox oil type .80W90 API GL3 gear oil
Gearbox oil quantity . . . . .approx. 150 cc
Brake fluid . . . . .DOT 4
Foam air filter oil . . . . .Air filter oil
Brake levers .Calcium soap grease (NLGI 1-2)
Control cables . . . . .Synthetic oil (eg Selenia HI 2T)

Model specifications and service schedules 1•49

Service intervals – Piaggio B125 Beverly

Note: *Always perform the Daily (pre-ride) checks before every service interval – see the beginning of this Manual*

	Text section in this Chapter	Every 2500 miles (4000 km) or 12 months	Every 5000 miles (8000 km) or 2 years	Every 10,000 miles (16,000 km) or 3 years
Air filter – clean	1		✔	
Battery – check	2	✔		
Brake fluid – change	4		✔*	
Brake hose – renew	6			✔*
Brake levers – lubrication	7	✔		
Brake pads/shoes – wear check	8	✔		
Brake system – check	3	✔		
Cooling system – check	9			
Cooling system – draining, flushing and refilling	10		✔**	
Drivebelt – check	12	✔		
Drivebelt – renew	12		✔	
Engine oil and filter change	13	✔		
Fuel system – check	14	✔		
Gearbox oil level – check	15	✔		
Gearbox oil – change	16			✔
Headlight aim – check and adjustment	17		✔	
Idle speed – check and adjustment	18		✔	
Nuts and bolts – tightness check	19		✔	
Spark plug – gap check and adjustment	22	✔		
Spark plug – renew	23		✔	
Stand – check and lubrication	25		✔	
Steering head bearings – check and adjustment	26		✔	
Suspension – check	27		✔	
Throttle cable – check and adjustment	28	✔		
Valve clearances – check and adjustment	29			✔
Variator – check	30	✔		
Wheels and tyres – general check	31	✔		
Wheel bearings – check	32		✔	

* The brake fluid must be changed every 2 years and the brake hose renewed every 3 years, irrespective of mileage.
** The coolant must be changed every 3 years, irrespective of mileage.

1•50 Model specifications and service schedules

Piaggio X8 125

Model identification
Engine . . .124 cc single cylinder liquid-cooled four-stroke LEADER
Transmission . . . . .Variable speed automatic, belt driven
Ignition . . . . .Electronic
Suspension
    Front . . . . .Telescopic forks
    Rear . . . . .Swingarm and twin shock
Brakes . . . . .Single disc (front and rear)
Engine no. prefix M363M
Frame no. prefix ZAPM36300
Wheelbase . . . . .1490 mm
Overall length . . . . .2050 mm
Overall width . . . . .760 mm
Overall height . . . . .1370 mm
Weight (dry) . . . . .157 kg
Fuel tank capacity
    Total . . . . .9.5 litres
    Reserve . . . . .2 litres
Introduced 2005

Servicing specifications and lubricants
Spark plug type . . . . .Champion RG4HC
Spark plug electrode gap .0.7 to 0.8 mm
Idle speed . . . . .1600 to 1700 rpm
Valve clearances (COLD engine)
    Intake . . . . .0.10 mm
    Exhaust . . . . .0.15 mm
Front tyre size 120/70-14
Rear tyre size 130/70-12
Front tyre pressure . . . . .29 psi (2.0 Bar)
Rear tyre pressure
    Rider only . . . . .32 psi (2.2 Bar)
    Rider and passenger . . . . .37 psi (2.6 Bar)
Fuel type . . . . .Petrol (leaded or unleaded) min 95 octane
Engine oil type . . . . .SAE 5W40 API SG synthetic oil
Engine oil quantity . . . . .approx. 1 litre
Coolant type 50% distilled water and 50% ethylene glycol anti-freeze
Cooling system capacity . . . . .approx. 2 litre
Gearbox oil type .80W90 API GL3 gear oil
Gearbox oil quantity . . . . .approx. 150 cc
Brake fluid . . . . .DOT 4
Foam air filter oil . . . . .Air filter oil
Speedometer drive gear . . . . .Lithium soap grease (NLGI 3)
Brake levers . . . . .Calcium soap grease (NLGI 1-2)
Control cables . . . . .Engine oil

Model specifications and service schedules

Service intervals – Piaggio X8 125

Note: *Always perform the Daily (pre-ride) checks before every service interval – see the beginning of this Manual*

	Text section in this Chapter	Every 3750 miles (6000 km) or 12 months	Every 7500 miles (12,000 km) or 2 years	Every 15,000 miles (24,000 km)
Air filter – clean	1	✔		
Battery – check	2	✔		
Brake fluid – change	4		✔*	
Brake levers – lubrication	7		✔	
Brake pads/shoes – wear check	8	✔		
Brake system – check	3	✔		
Cooling system – check	9	✔		
Cooling system – draining, flushing and refilling	10		✔**	
Drive belt – check	12	✔		
Drive belt – renew	12		✔	
Engine oil and filter change	13	✔		
Gearbox oil level – check	15	✔		
Gearbox oil – change	16			✔
Headlight aim – check and adjustment	17		✔	
Idle speed – check and adjustment	18		✔	
Nuts and bolts – tightness check	19		✔	
Secondary air system – clean	21		✔***	
Spark plug – gap check and adjustment	22	✔		
Spark plug – renew	23		✔	
Steering head bearings – check and adjustment	26		✔	
Suspension – check	27		✔	
Throttle cable – check and adjustment	28		✔	
Valve clearances – check and adjustment	29	First 3750 miles		Thereafter every 15,000 miles
Variator – check	30	✔		
Wheels and tyres – general check	31	✔		

* The brake fluid must be changed every 2 years and the brake hose renewed every 3 years, irrespective of mileage.
** The coolant must be changed every 2 years, irrespective of mileage.
*** The secondary air system filter must be cleaned every 2 years, irrespective of mileage.

Model specifications and service schedules

Piaggio X9 125

Model identification
Engine . . .124 cc single cylinder liquid-cooled four-stroke LEADER
Transmission . . . . .Variable speed automatic, belt-driven
Ignition . . . . .Electronic
Suspension
   Front . . . . .Telescopic forks
   Rear . . . . .Swingarm and twin shock
Brakes . . . . .Double disc (front), single disc (rear)
Engine no. prefix M223M
Frame no. prefix ZAPM23
Wheelbase . . . . .1495 mm
Overall length . . . . .2100 mm
Overall width . . . . .865 mm
Overall height . . . . .1350 mm
Weight (dry) . . . . .159 kg
Fuel tank capacity
   Total . . . . .14.5 litres
   Reserve . . . . .2.5 litres
Introduced 2001

Servicing specifications and lubricants
Spark plug type . . . . .NGK CR 8EB
Spark plug electrode gap . . . . .0.7 to 0.8 mm
Idle speed . . . . .1600 to 1700 rpm
Valve clearances (COLD engine)
   Intake . . . . .0.10 mm
   Exhaust . . . . .0.15 mm
Front tyre size 120/70-14
Rear tyre size 140/60-14
Front tyre pressure . . . . .30.5 psi (2.1 Bar)
Rear tyre pressure
   Rider only . . . . .33.5 psi (2.3 Bar)
   Rider and passenger . . . . .36.5 psi (2.5 Bar)
Fuel type .Petrol (unleaded) min 95 octane
Engine oil type . . . . .SAE 5W40 synthetic oil
Engine oil quantity . . . . .approx. 1 litre
Coolant type . . . . .50% distilled water and 50% ethylene
                                                      glycol anti-freeze
Cooling system capacity . . . . .approx. 1 litre
Gearbox oil type . . . . .80W90 API GL3 gear oil
Gearbox oil quantity . . . . .approx. 150 cc
Brake fluid . . . . .DOT 4
Foam air filter oil . . . . .Air filter oil
Speedometer drive gear . . . . .Lithium soap grease (NLGI 3)
Brake levers . . . . .Calcium soap grease (NLGI 1-2)
Control cables . . . . .Synthetic oil (eg Selenia HI 2T)

Model specifications and service schedules 1•53

Service intervals – Piaggio X9 125

Note: *Always perform the Daily (pre-ride) checks before every service interval – see the beginning of this Manual*

	Text section in this Chapter	Every 3750 miles (6000 km) or 12 months	Every 7500 miles (12,000 km) or 2 years	Every 15,000 miles (24,000 km) or 3 years
Air filter – clean	1	✔		
Battery – check	2	✔		
Brake fluid – change	4		✔*	
Brake hose – renew	6			✔*
Brake levers – lubrication	7		✔	
Brake pads/shoes – wear check	8	✔		
Brake system – check	3	✔		
Cooling system – check	9	✔		
Cooling system – draining, flushing and refilling	10		✔**	
Drivebelt – check	12	✔		
Drivebelt – renew	12		✔	
Engine oil and filter change	13	✔		
Fuel system – check	14	✔		
Gearbox oil level – check	15	✔		
Gearbox oil – change	16			✔
Headlight aim – check and adjustment	17		✔	
Idle speed – check and adjustment	18		✔	
Nuts and bolts – tightness check	19		✔	
Spark plug – gap check and adjustment	22	✔		
Spark plug – renew	23		✔	
Stand – check and lubrication	25		✔	
Steering head bearings – check and adjustment	26		✔	
Suspension – check	27		✔	
Throttle cable – check and adjustment	28		✔	
Valve clearances – check and adjustment	29	First 3750 miles		Thereafter every 15,000 miles
Variator – check	30	✔		
Wheels and tyres – general check	31	✔		
Wheel bearings – check	32		✔	

* The brake fluid must be changed every 2 years and the brake hose renewed every 3 years, irrespective of mileage.
** The coolant must be changed every 3 years, irrespective of mileage.

Model specifications and service schedules

Vespa ET2

Model identification

Engine	50 cc single cylinder air-cooled two-stroke
Transmission	Variable speed automatic, belt-driven
Ignition	Electronic
Suspension	
Front	Trailing link and monoshock
Rear	Swingarm and monoshock
Brakes	Single disc (front), drum (rear)
Engine no. prefix	C161M000
Frame no. prefix	ZAPC160000000
Wheelbase	1260 mm
Overall length	1780 mm
Overall width	710 mm
Overall height (excl. mirrors)	1100 mm
Weight (dry)	98 kg
Fuel tank capacity	
Total	8.6 litres
Reserve	1.5 litres
Introduced	Jul '97

Servicing specifications and lubricants

Spark plug type	Champion N2C or NGK B9ES
Spark plug electrode gap	0.5 to 0.6 mm
Idle speed	1600 to 1800 rpm
Front tyre size	100/80-10
Rear tyre size	120/70-10
Front tyre pressure	19 psi (1.3 Bar)
Rear tyre pressure	
Rider only	26 psi (1.8 Bar)
Rider and passenger	29 psi (2.0 Bar)
Fuel type	Petrol (unleaded) min 95 octane
Engine oil type	Good quality two-stroke injector oil
Engine oil tank capacity	
Total	1.35 litres
Reserve	0.4 litre
Gearbox oil type	80W90 gear oil
Gearbox oil quantity	approx. 75 cc
Brake fluid	DOT 4
Air filter oil	Synthetic oil (eg Selenia HI 2T)
Variator	Lithium soap grease (NLGI 3)
Speedometer drive gear	Lithium soap grease (NLGI 3)
Brake levers	Calcium soap grease (NLGI 1-2)
Control cables	Synthetic oil (eg Selenia HI 2T)

Model specifications and service schedules 1•55

Service intervals – Vespa ET2

Note: *Always perform the Daily (pre-ride) checks before every service interval – see the beginning of this Manual*

	Text section in this Chapter	Every 3000 miles (5000 km) or 12 months	Every 6000 miles (10,000 km) or 2 years	Every 12,000 miles (20,000 km) or 3 years
Air filter – cleaning	1	✔		
Battery – check	2	✔		
Brake cable – check and lubrication	5	✔		
Brake fluid – change	4		✔*	
Brake hose – renew	6			✔*
Brake levers – lubrication	7	✔		
Brake pads/shoes – wear check	8	✔		
Brake system – check	3	✔		
Cylinder head – decarbonise	11			✔
Drivebelt – check	12	✔		
Fuel system – check	14	✔		
Gearbox oil level – check	15	✔		
Gearbox oil – change	16		✔	
Headlight aim – check and adjustment	17		✔	
Idle speed – check and adjustment	18	✔		
Nuts and bolts – tightness check	19		✔	
Oil pump drivebelt – renew	20			✔
Spark plug – gap check and adjustment	22	✔		
Spark plug – renew	23		✔	
Speedometer cable and drive gear – lubrication	24		✔	
Stand – check and lubrication	25		✔	
Steering head bearings – check and adjustment	26		✔	
Suspension – check	27		✔	
Throttle cable/oil pump – check and adjustment	28	✔		
Variator and clutch – check	30	✔ variator		✔ clutch
Wheels and tyres – general check	31	✔		
Wheel bearings – check	32		✔	

* The brake fluid must be changed every 2 years and the brake hose renewed every 3 years, irrespective of mileage.

1•56 Model specifications and service schedules

Vespa ET4 50

Model identification

Engine	50 cc single cylinder air-cooled four-stroke
Transmission	Variable speed automatic, belt-driven
Ignition	Electronic
Suspension	
Front	Trailing link and monoshock
Rear	Swingarm and monoshock
Brakes	Single disc (front), drum (rear)
Engine no. prefix	C382M
Frame no. prefix	ZAPC382
Wheelbase	1275 mm
Overall length	1780 mm
Overall width	710 mm
Overall height (excl. mirrors)	1090 mm
Weight	105 kg
Fuel tank capacity	
Total	9.0 litres
Reserve	2.3 litres
Introduced	2001

Servicing specifications and lubricants

Spark plug type	Champion RG4 PHP or Champion RG4 HC
Spark plug electrode gap	0.7 to 0.8 mm
Idle speed	1900 to 2000 rpm
Valve clearances (COLD engine)	
Intake	0.10 mm
Exhaust	0.15 mm
Front tyre size	100/80-10
Rear tyre size	120/70-10 or 130/70-10
Front tyre pressure	19 psi (1.3 Bar)
Rear tyre pressure	
Rider only	26 psi (1.8 Bar)
Rider and passenger	29 psi (2.0 Bar)
Fuel type	Petrol (unleaded) min 95 octane
Engine oil type	5W40 API SJ synthetic oil
Engine oil quantity	850 cc
Gearbox oil type	80W90 API GL3 gear oil
Gearbox oil quantity	approx. 80 cc
Brake fluid	DOT 4
Air filter oil	Air filter oil
Speedometer drive gear	Lithium soap grease (NLGI 3)
Brake levers	Calcium soap grease (NLGI 1-2)
Control cables	Synthetic oil (eg Selenia HI 2T)

Model specifications and service schedules

Service intervals – Vespa ET4 50

Note: *Always perform the Daily (pre-ride) checks before every service interval – see the beginning of this Manual*

	Text section in this Chapter	Every 2500 miles (4000 km) or 12 months	Every 5000 miles (8000 km) or 2 years	Every 10,000 miles (16,000 km) or 3 years
Air filter – clean	1		✔	
Battery – check	2	✔		
Brake cable – check and lubrication	5	✔		
Brake fluid – change	4		✔*	
Brake hose – renew	6			✔*
Brake levers – lubrication	7	✔		
Brake pads/shoes – wear check	8	✔		
Brake system – check	3	✔		
Drivebelt – change	12		✔	
Engine oil change and strainer clean	13	✔		
Fuel system – check	14	✔		
Gearbox oil level – check	15	✔		
Gearbox oil – change	16			✔
Headlight aim – check and adjustment	17		✔	
Idle speed – check and adjustment	18		✔	
Nuts and bolts – tightness check	19		✔	
Spark plug – renew	22		✔	
Speedometer cable and drive gear – lubrication	24		✔	
Stand – check and lubrication	25		✔	
Steering head bearings – check and adjustment	26		✔	
Suspension – check	27		✔	
Throttle cable – check and adjustment	28		✔	
Valve clearances – check and adjustment	29			✔
Variator – check	30	✔		
Wheels and tyres – general check	31	✔		
Wheel bearings – check	32		✔	

*The brake fluid must be changed every 2 years and the brake hose renewed every 3 years, irrespective of mileage.

Model specifications and service schedules

Vespa ET4 125

Model identification
Engine ....125 cc single cylinder air-cooled four-stroke
(LEADER engine on later models)
Transmission ....Variable speed automatic, belt-driven
Ignition ....Electronic
Suspension
  Front ....Trailing link and monoshock
  Rear ....Swingarm and monoshock
Brakes ....Single disc (front), drum (rear)
Engine no. prefix ....MO 41M
Frame no. prefix
  1996 to 1998 models ....ZAP MO 4000
  LEADER engine ....ZAP M19
Wheelbase ....1275 mm
Overall length ....1780 mm
Overall width ....710 mm
Overall height (excl. mirrors) ....1090 mm
Weight (dry) ....109 kg
Fuel tank capacity
  Total ....9.0 litres
  Reserve ....2.3 litres
Introduced ....Sept '96

Servicing specifications and lubricants
Spark plug type ....Champion RG4 HC or NGK CR8E
Spark plug electrode gap ....0.7 to 0.8 mm
Idle speed
  1996 to 1998 models ....1570 to 1630 rpm
  LEADER engine ....1600 to 1800 rpm
Valve clearances (COLD engine)
  1996 to 1998 models (both valves) ....0.15 mm
  LEADER engine
    Intake ....0.10 mm
    Exhaust ....0.15 mm
Front tyre size 100/80-10
Rear tyre size ....120/70-10 or 130/70-10
Front tyre pressure ....19 psi (1.3 Bar)
Rear tyre pressure
  Rider only ....26 psi (1.8 Bar)
  Rider and passenger ....29 psi (2.0 Bar)
Fuel type ....Petrol (unleaded) min 95 octane
Engine oil type
  1996 to 1998 models ....20W synthetic engine oil
  LEADER engine ....5W40 API SJ synthetic oil
Engine oil quantity
  1996 to 1998 models ....850 cc (dry fill)
  LEADER engine ....1 litre
Gearbox oil type ....80W90 API GL3 gear oil
Gearbox oil quantity ....90 to 100 cc
Brake fluid ....DOT 4
Air filter oil ....Air filter oil
Variator (1996 to 1998 models) ....Lithium soap grease (NLGI 3)
Speedometer drive gear ....Lithium soap grease (NLGI 3)
Brake levers ....Calcium soap grease (NLGI 1-2)
Control cables ....Synthetic oil (eg Selenia HI 2T)

Model specifications and service schedules 1•59

Service intervals – Vespa ET4 125

Note: *Always perform the Daily (pre-ride) checks before every service interval – see the beginning of this Manual*

	Text section in this Chapter	Every 3000 miles (5000 km) or 12 months	Every 6000 miles (10,000 km) or 2 years	Every 12,000 miles (20,000 km) or 3 years
Air filter – clean	1	✔		
Battery – check	2	✔		
Brake cable – check and lubrication	5	✔		
Brake fluid – change	4		✔*	
Brake hose – renew	6			✔*
Brake levers – lubrication	7		✔	
Brake pads/shoes – wear check	8	✔		
Brake system – check	3	✔		
Drivebelt – check (1996 to 1998 models)	12	✔		
Drivebelt – change (LEADER engine)	12		✔	
Engine oil change and strainer clean (1996 to 1998 models)	13	✔		
Engine oil filter – change (1996 to 1998 models)	13		✔	
Engine oil and filter – change (LEADER engine)	13	✔		
Fuel system – check	14	✔		
Gearbox oil level – check	15	✔		
Gearbox oil (1996 to 1998 models) – change	16		✔	
Gearbox oil (LEADER engine) – change	16			✔
Headlight aim – check and adjustment	17		✔	
Idle speed – check and adjustment	18	✔		
Nuts and bolts – tightness check	19		✔	
Spark plug – gap check and adjustment	22	✔		
Spark plug – renew	23		✔	
Speedometer cable and drive gear – lubrication	24		✔	
Stand – check and lubrication	25		✔	
Steering head bearings – check and adjustment	26		✔	
Suspension – check	27		✔	
Throttle cable – check and adjustment	28	✔		
Valve clearances – check and adjustment	29			✔
Variator – check	30	✔		
Wheels and tyres – general check	31	✔		
Wheel bearings – check	32		✔	

* The brake fluid must be changed every 2 years and the brake hose renewed every 3 years, irrespective of mileage.

1•60 Model specifications and service schedules

Vespa LX2 50

Model identification

Engine	50 cc single cylinder air-cooled two-stroke
Transmission	Variable speed automatic, belt driven
Ignition	Electronic
Suspension	
Front	Trailing link and monoshock
Rear	Swingarm and monoshock
Brakes	Single disc (front), drum (rear)
Engine no. prefix	C38 1M
Frame no. prefix	ZAPC 38101
Wheelbase	1280 mm
Overall length	1755 mm
Overall width	740 mm
Overall height (excl. mirrors)	1140 mm
Weight (dry)	96 kg
Fuel tank capacity	
Total	8.6 litres
Reserve	2.0 litres
Introduced	2005

Servicing specifications and lubricants

Spark plug type	Champion RGN2C
Spark plug electrode gap	0.6 to 0.7 mm
Idle speed	1800 to 2000 rpm
Tyre size	
Front	110/70-11
Rear	120/70-10
Front tyre pressure	23 psi (1.6 Bar)
Rear tyre pressure	29 psi (2.0 Bar)
Fuel type	Petrol (leaded or unleaded) min 95 octane
Engine oil type	Selenia HI 2T two-stroke injector oil
Engine oil tank capacity	1.2 litres
Gearbox oil type	75W85 API GL4 gear oil
Gearbox oil quantity	approx. 85 cc
Brake fluid	DOT 4
Air filter oil	Synthetic oil (e.g. Selenia HI 2T)
Speedometer drive gear	Lithium soap grease (NLGI 3)
Brake levers	Calcium soap grease (NLGI 1-2)
Control cables	Synthetic oil (e.g. Selenia HI 2T)
Driven pulley shaft grease	Molybdenum bisulphide grease

Model specifications and service schedules 1•61

Service intervals – Vespa LX2 50

Note: *Always perform the Daily (pre-ride) checks before every service interval – see the beginning of this Manual*

	Text section in this Chapter	Every 3000 miles (5000 km) or 12 months	Every 6000 miles (10,000 km) or 2 years	Every 9000 miles (15,000 km) or 3 years
Air filter – clean	1	✔		
Battery – check	2	✔		
Brake cable – check and lubrication	5		✔	
Brake fluid – change	4		✔*	
Brake hose – renew	6			✔*
Brake levers – lubrication	7	✔		
Brake pads/shoes – wear check	8	✔		
Brake system – check	3	✔		
Cooling system – check	9			✔
Drive belt – check	12		✔	Renew belt
Gearbox oil level – check	15	✔		
Gearbox oil – change	16		✔	
Headlight aim – check and adjustment	17		✔	
Idle speed – check and adjustment	18		✔	
Nuts and bolts – tightness check	19		✔	
Oil pump drive belt – renew	20			Every 12,000 miles (20,000 km)
Secondary air system – clean	21			✔
Spark plug – renew	23	✔		
Speedometer cable and drive gear – lubrication	24		✔	
Steering head bearings – check and adjustment	26		✔	
Suspension – check	27		✔	
Throttle cable/oil pump – check and adjustment	28	✔		
Variator	30		Renew rollers	
Wheels and tyres – general check	31	✔		

*The brake fluid must be changed every 2 years and the brake hose renewed every 3 years, irrespective of mileage.

1•62 Model specifications and service schedules

Vespa LX4 50

Model identification
Engine ....50 cc single cylinder air-cooled four-stroke
Transmission ....Variable speed automatic, belt driven
Ignition ....Electronic
Suspension
   Front ....Trailing link and monoshock
   Rear ....Swingarm and monoshock
Brakes ....Single disc (front), drum (rear)
Engine no. prefix ....C 383M
Frame no. prefix ZAPC38300
Wheelbase ....1290 mm
Overall length ....1755 mm
Overall width ....740 mm
Overall height (excl. mirrors) ....1140 mm
Weight ....102 kg
Fuel tank capacity
   Total ....8.5 litres
   Reserve ....2.0 litres
Introduced 2006

Servicing specifications and lubricants
Spark plug type ....NGK CR 8EB
Spark plug electrode gap ....0.7 to 0.8 mm
Idle speed ....1900 to 2000 rpm
Valve clearances (COLD engine)
   Intake ....0.10 mm
   Exhaust ....0.15 mm
Tyre size
   Front 110/70-11
   Rear 120/70-10
Front tyre pressure ....23 psi (1.6 Bar)
Rear tyre pressure ....29 psi (2.0 Bar)
Fuel type ....Petrol (unleaded) min 95 octane
Engine oil type ....5W40 API SG synthetic oil
Engine oil quantity ....850 cc
Gearbox oil type ....75W85 API GL4 gear oil
Gearbox oil quantity ....approx. 85 cc
Brake fluid ....DOT 4
Air filter oil ....Air filter oil
Speedometer drive gear ....Lithium soap grease (NLGI 3)
Brake levers ....Calcium soap grease (NLGI 1-2)
Control cables ....Synthetic oil (e.g. Selenia HI 2T)
Driven pulley shaft grease ....Molybdenum bisulphide grease

Model specifications and service schedules 1•63

Service intervals – Vespa LX4 50

Note: *Always perform the Daily (pre-ride) checks before every service interval – see the beginning of this Manual*

	Text section in this Chapter	Every 3750 miles (6000 km) or 12 months	Every 7500 miles (12,000 km) or 2 years	Every 15,000 miles (24,000 km) or 3 years
Air filter – clean	1		✔	
Battery – check	2	✔		
Brake cable – check and lubrication	5		✔	
Brake fluid – change	4		✔*	
Brake hose – renew	6			✔*
Brake levers – lubrication	7		✔	
Brake pads/shoes – wear check	8	✔		
Brake system – check	3	✔		
Cooling system – check	9			✔
Drive belt – change	12		✔	
Engine oil change and strainer clean	13	✔		
Gearbox oil – check	15	✔		
Gearbox oil – change	16			✔
Headlight aim – check and adjustment	17		✔	
Idle speed – check and adjustment	18		✔	
Secondary air system - clean	21		✔	
Spark plug – check	22	✔		
Speedometer cable and drive gear – lubrication	24		✔	
Steering head bearings – check and adjustment	26		✔	
Suspension – check	27		✔	
Throttle cable – check and adjustment	28	✔		
Valve clearances – check and adjustment	29			✔
Variator – check	30	✔		
Wheels and tyres – general check	31	✔		

*The brake fluid must be changed every 2 years and the brake hose renewed every 3 years, irrespective of mileage.

1•64 Model specifications and service schedules

Vespa LX4 125

Model identification
Engine ......125 cc single cylinder air-cooled four-stroke LEADER
Transmission ....Variable speed automatic, belt driven
Ignition ....Electronic
Suspension
  Front ....Trailing link and monoshock
  Rear ....Swingarm and monoshock
Brakes ....Single disc (front), drum (rear)
Engine no. prefix MXXXM1001
Frame no. prefix ....ZAPM 44100
Wheelbase ....1280 mm
Overall length ....1800 mm
Overall width ....740 mm
Seat height ....785 mm
Weight ....110 kg
Fuel tank capacity
  Total ....8.6 litres
  Reserve ....2.0 litres
Introduced 2005

Servicing specifications and lubricants
Spark plug type ....Champion RG 6YC or NGK CR7EB
Spark plug electrode gap ....0.7 to 0.8 mm
Idle speed ....1600 to 1800 rpm
Valve clearances (COLD engine)
  Intake ....0.10 mm
  Exhaust ....0.15 mm
Tyre size 120/70-12
Front tyre pressure ....23 psi (1.6 Bar)
Rear tyre pressure
  Rider only ....29 psi (2.0 Bar)
  Rider and passenger ....33.5 psi (2.3 Bar)
Fuel type ....Petrol (leaded or unleaded) min 95 octane
Engine oil type ....5W/40 API SG synthetic oil
Engine oil quantity ....approx. 1 litre
Gearbox oil type ....80W90 API GL3 gear oil
Gearbox oil quantity ....approx. 100 cc
Brake fluid ....DOT 4
Foam air filter oil ....Air filter oil
Speedometer drive gear ....Lithium soap grease (NLGI 3)
Brake levers ....Calcium soap grease (NLGI 1-2)
Control cables ....Engine oil

Model specifications and service schedules 1•65

Service intervals – Vespa LX4 125

Note: *Always perform the Daily (pre-ride) checks before every service interval – see the beginning of this Manual*

	Text section in this Chapter	Every 3750 miles (6000 km) or 12 months	Every 7500 miles (12,000 km) or 2 years	Every 15,000 miles (24,000 km) or 3 years
Air filter – clean	1	✔		
Battery – check	2	✔		
Brake cable – check and lubrication	5	✔		
Brake fluid – change	4		✔*	
Brake hose – renew	6			✔*
Brake levers – lubrication	7		✔	
Brake pads/shoes – wear check	8	✔		
Brake system – check	3	✔		
Cooling system – check	9			✔
Drive belt – check	12	✔	Renew belt	
Engine oil and filter change	13	✔		
Gearbox oil level – check	15	✔		
Gearbox oil – change	16			✔
Headlight aim – check and adjustment	17		✔	
Idle speed – check and adjustment	18		✔	
Nuts and bolts – tightness check	19		✔	
Secondary air system – clean	21		✔	
Spark plug – gap check and adjustment	22	✔		
Spark plug – renew	23		✔	
Speedometer cable and drive gear – lubrication	24		✔	
Stand – check and lubrication	25		✔	
Steering head bearings – check and adjustment	26		✔	
Suspension – check	27		✔	
Throttle cable – check and adjustment	28		✔	
Valve clearances – check and adjustment	29	First 3750 miles		Thereafter every 22,000 miles
Variator – check	30	✔	Renew rollers	
Wheels and tyres – general check	31	✔		

*The brake fluid must be changed every 2 years and the brake hose renewed every 3 years, irrespective of mileage.

1•66 Model specifications and service schedules

Vespa GT125/200

Model identification
Engine
  GT125 ...124 cc single cylinder liquid-cooled four-stroke LEADER
  GT200 ...198 cc single cylinder liquid-cooled four-stroke LEADER
Transmission ....Variable speed automatic, belt driven
Ignition ....Electronic
Suspension
  Front ....Trailing link and monoshock
  Rear ....Swingarm and twin shock
Brakes ....Single disc (front and rear)
Engine no. prefix
  GT125 .... M311M1001
  GT200 .... M312M1001
Frame no. prefix
  GT125 ....ZAPM311000000
  GT200 ....ZAPM312000000
Wheelbase ....1395 mm
Overall length ....1940 mm
Overall width ....755 mm
Seat height ....800 mm
Weight (dry) ....138 kg
Fuel tank capacity
  Total ....10 litres
  Reserve ....2 litres
Introduced 2003

Servicing specifications and lubricants
Spark plug type
  GT125 ....NGK CR 8EB
  GT200 ....Champion RG6YC
Spark plug electrode gap ....0.7 to 0.8 mm
Idle speed ....1600 to 1700 rpm
Valve clearances (COLD engine)
  Intake ....0.10 mm
  Exhaust ....0.15 mm
Front tyre size 120/70-12
Rear tyre size 130/70-12
Front tyre pressure ....26 psi (1.8 Bar)
Rear tyre pressure
  Rider only ....29 psi (2.0 Bar)
  Rider and passenger ....32 psi (2.2 Bar)
Fuel type ....Petrol (leaded or unleaded) min 95 octane
Engine oil type ....SAE 5W40 synthetic oil
Engine oil quantity ....approx. 1 litre
Coolant type 50% distilled water and 50% ethylene glycol anti-freeze
Cooling system capacity ....approx. 2 litre
Gearbox oil type ....80W90 API GL3 gear oil
Gearbox oil quantity ....approx. 150 cc
Brake fluid ....DOT 4
Foam air filter oil ....Air filter oil
Speedometer drive gear ....Lithium soap grease (NLGI 3)
Brake levers ....Calcium soap grease (NLGI 1-2)
Control cables ....Engine oil

Model specifications and service schedules

Service intervals – Vespa GT125/200

Note: *Always perform the Daily (pre-ride) checks before every service interval – see the beginning of this Manual*

	Text section in this Chapter	Every 3750 miles (6000 km) or 12 months	Every 7500 miles (12,000 km) or 2 years	Every 11,250 miles (18,000 km) or 3 years
Air filter – clean	1	✔		
Battery – check	2	✔		
Brake fluid – change	4		✔*	
Brake hose – renew	6			✔*
Brake levers – lubrication	7		✔	
Brake pads – wear check	8	✔		
Brake system – check	3	✔		
Cooling system – check	9	✔		
Cooling system – draining, flushing and refilling	10		✔**	
Drive belt – check	12	✔		
Engine oil and filter change	13	✔		
Gearbox oil level – check	15	✔		
Gearbox oil – change	16			✔
Headlight aim – check and adjustment	17		✔	
Idle speed – check and adjustment	18		✔	
Nuts and bolts – tightness check	19		✔	
Secondary air system – clean	21		✔***	
Spark plug – gap check and adjustment	22	✔		
Steering head bearings – check and adjustment	26		✔	
Suspension – check	27		✔	
Throttle cable – check and adjustment	28		✔	
Valve clearances – check and adjustment (125)	29	First 3750 miles		Thereafter every 15,000 miles
Valve clearances – check and adjustment (200)	29	First 3750 miles		Thereafter every 22,000 miles
Variator – check	30	✔		
Wheels and tyres – general check	31	✔		

* The brake fluid must be changed every 2 years and the brake hose renewed every 3 years, irrespective of mileage.
** The coolant must be changed every 3 years, irrespective of mileage.
*** The secondary air system filter must be cleaned every 2 years, irrespective of mileage.

1•68 Routine maintenance and servicing procedures

1.2a Remove the screws securing the filter cover and detach the cover . . .

1.2b . . . then remove the filter – Typhoon 50/80, NRG models

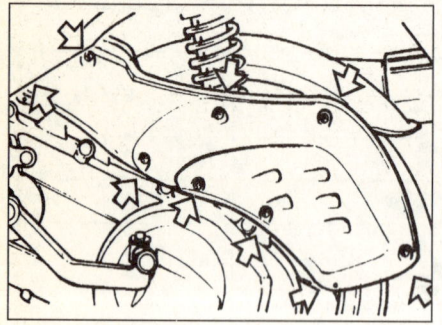

1 Air filter and transmission filter – cleaning

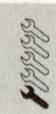

Caution: If the machine is often ridden in wet or dusty conditions, the filter should be cleaned more frequently.

1 Remove the body panels as required on your model to access the air filter housing, located above the transmission casing on the left-hand side of the engine (see Chapter 7).

2 Remove the screws securing the air filter cover and detach the cover **(see illustrations)**.

3 On models fitted with a paper filter element, undo the screw securing the filter, then lift it out of the housing. Lay the filter face down on a clean surface and tap it gently to dislodge any dust. If available, clean the filter with compressed air. If the filter is damaged or excessively dirty, renew it. Installation is the reverse of removal.

4 On models fitted with a foam filter element, remove the filter and wash it in hot soapy water **(see illustrations)**. Blow the filter dry using compressed air – never wring the filter dry as it may tear.

5 Most models incorporate a filter element in the drivebelt cover air intake or breather cap – remove the intake and lift the element out

1.2c Air filter cover – Zip SP and later Zip

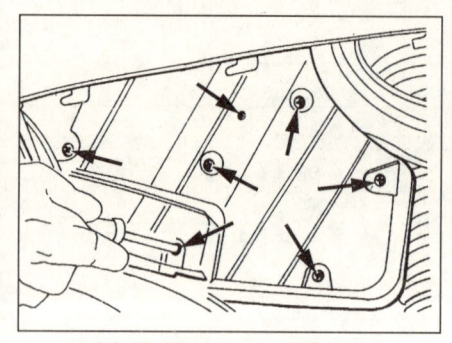

1.2d Air filter cover – Hexagon

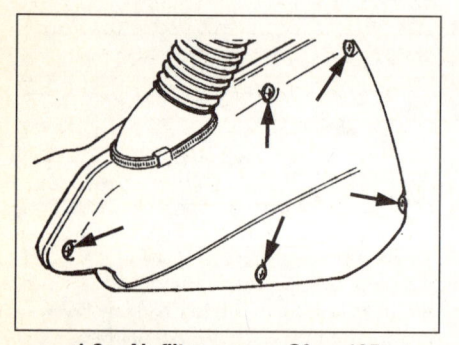

1.2e Air filter cover – Sfera 125

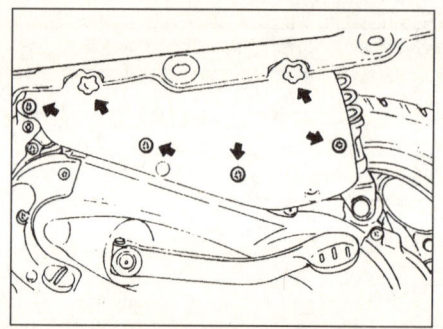

1.2f Air filter cover – ET2, ET4

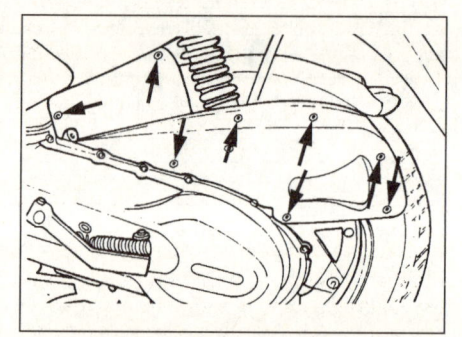

1.2g Air filter cover – Skipper and Typhoon 125

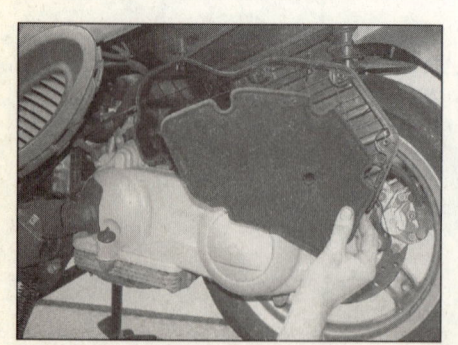

1.2h Air filter – X9

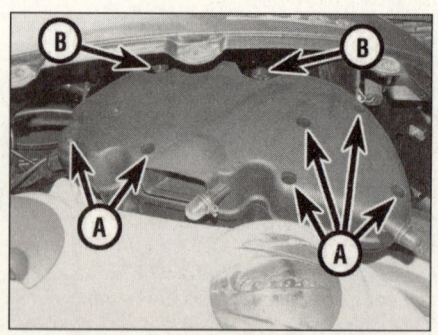

1.2i Air filter cover screws (A) and knurled knobs (B) – Vespa GT models

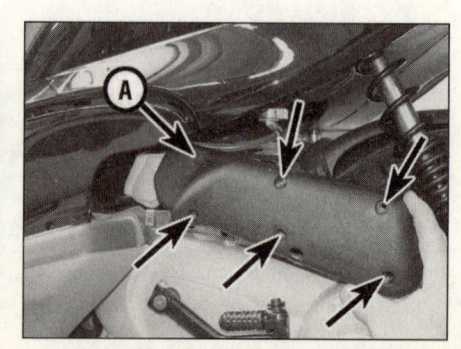

1.2j On Fly 50 models use a cranked screwdriver to access screw (A)

Routine maintenance and servicing procedures 1•69

1.4a Lift the foam element out of the cover . . .

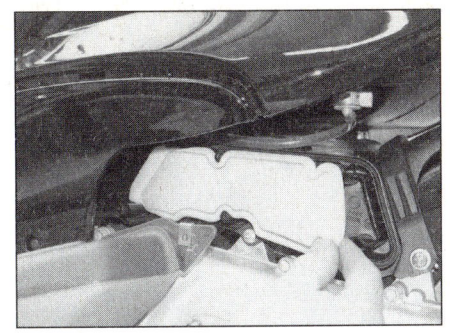

1.4b . . . or the filter housing

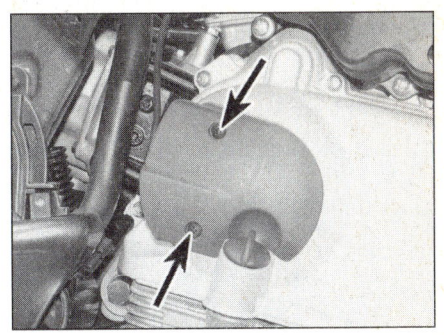

1.5a Where fitted, undo the screws . . .

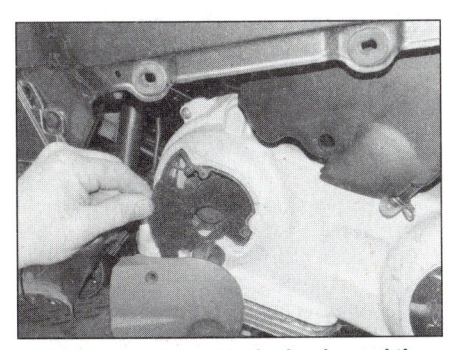

1.5b . . . then remove the intake and the filter element

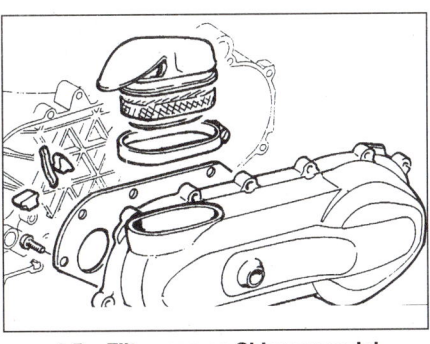

1.5c Filter cap on Skipper model

1.7 If required, remove the caps (arrowed) to drain off excess oil

carefully **(see illustrations)**. Note that on the NRG Power DT scooter we photographed for this manual, no filter element was fitted in the drivebelt cover cap and the air intake was blanked off. On the two-stroke Skipper model, remove the filter from the top of the drivebelt cover, having first removed the filter cap **(see illustration)**. Clean the filter as described above but do not oil the drivebelt cover filter before installation.

6 When it is dry, soak the foam air filter element either in special air filter oil, or a 50/50 mixture of petrol and two-stroke oil, then gently squeeze out the excess liquid, making sure you do not damage the filter by twisting it. On the two-stroke Hexagon model, only oil the smaller (grey) element.

2.1 Battery electrolyte level must be between level marks

7 Allow the filter to dry for a while, then fit it back into the housing and install the cover, making sure that the cover seal is in good condition. If fitted, drain caps in the cover can be removed to drain off excess oil **(see illustration)**.

8 If the filter is excessively dirty and cannot be cleaned properly, or is torn or damaged in any way, fit a new one.

2 Battery – check

Caution: Be extremely careful when handling or working around the battery. The electrolyte is very caustic and an explosive gas (hydrogen) is given off when the battery is charging.

Conventional battery

1 Remove the battery cover and partially lift the battery out of its holder (see Chapter 9). Check the electrolyte level which is visible through the translucent battery case – it should be between the UPPER and LOWER level marks **(see illustration)**.
2 If the electrolyte is low, disconnect the battery terminals (see Chapter 9) and move the battery to the work bench. Remove the cell caps and fill each cell to the upper level mark with distilled water. Do not use tap water (except in an emergency), and do not overfill. The cell holes are quite small, so it may help to use a clean plastic squeeze bottle with a small spout to add the water. Install the battery cell caps, tightening them securely, then install the battery (see Chapter 9).

Maintenance-free battery

3 On models fitted with a sealed battery, no maintenance is required. **Note:** Do not attempt to remove the battery caps to check the electrolyte level or battery specific gravity. Removal will damage the caps, resulting in electrolyte leakage and battery damage. All that should be done is to check that its terminals are clean and tight and that the casing is not damaged or leaking. See Chapter 9 for further details.

3 Brake system – check

1 A routine general check of the brake system will ensure that any problems are discovered and remedied before the rider's safety is jeopardised. Refer to Sections 4 to 8.
2 Check the brake cables and levers for looseness, improper or rough action, excessive play, bends, and other damage. Renew any damaged parts (see Chapter 8).
3 Make sure all brake fasteners are tight. Check the brake shoes (drum brake) and pads (disc brake) for wear (see Section 8) and on disc brake models make sure the fluid level in

1•70 Routine maintenance and servicing procedures

5.1a Front brake cable adjuster (arrowed)

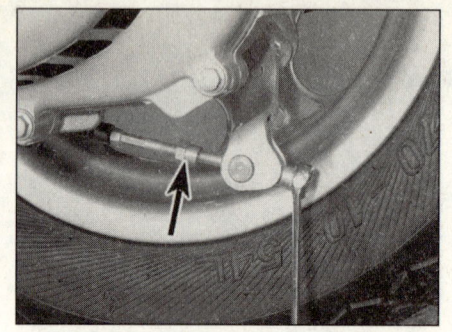

5.1b Slacken the locknut (arrowed) and adjust the rear brake cable as required

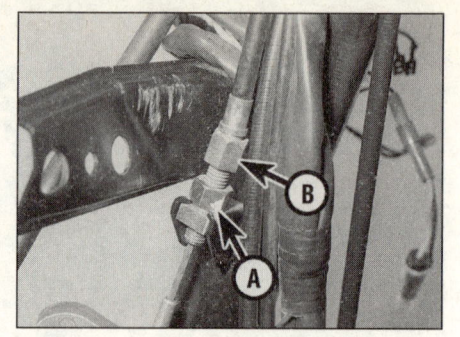

5.2 Slacken the locknut (A) and turn the adjuster (B) as required

the reservoirs is correct (see *Daily (pre-ride) checks*). Look for leaks at the hose connections and check for cracks in the hoses. If the lever is spongy, bleed the brakes (see Chapter 8).

4 Make sure the brake light operates when each brake lever is pulled in. The brake light switches are not adjustable. If they fail to operate properly, check them (see Chapter 9).

4 Brake fluid (disc brake) – change

1 Brake fluid will degrade over a period of time. It should be changed at the prescribed interval or whenever a master cylinder or caliper overhaul is carried out. Follow the procedure described in the brake bleeding section in Chapter 8.

5 Brake cables – check, adjustment and lubrication

Drum brake

1 On drum brakes, check that there is not an excessive amount of freeplay in the brake lever before the brake takes effect. The wheel should spin freely when the brake is not activated, but the brake should come on when the lever is just pulled in. The actual amount of freeplay is not specified and is a matter of personal taste. To take up freeplay in the lever, slacken the locknut (where fitted) and tighten the adjuster nut on the end of the cable until the excess is taken out **(see illustrations)**. If the brakes are binding without the lever being pulled, slacken the adjuster nut to provide some freeplay.

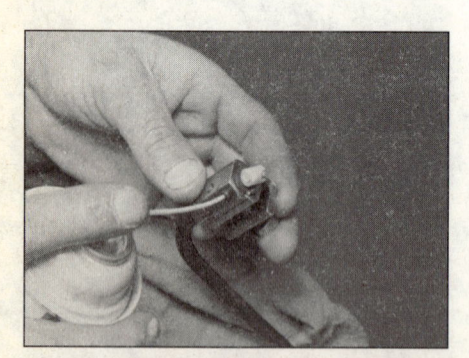

Disc brake

2 Where the hydraulic master cylinder is activated by a cable from the handlebar lever, remove the fairing (see Chapter 7) and check that there is no slack in the cable. If there is, loosen the cable adjuster locknut and turn the adjuster anti-clockwise until all the slack is taken up, but make sure the lever arm is not activated and pressurising the system **(see illustration)**. If the brakes are binding without the lever being pulled, turn the adjuster clockwise until the lever arm is at rest but make sure that no slack is created in the cable. Tighten the locknut securely on completion.

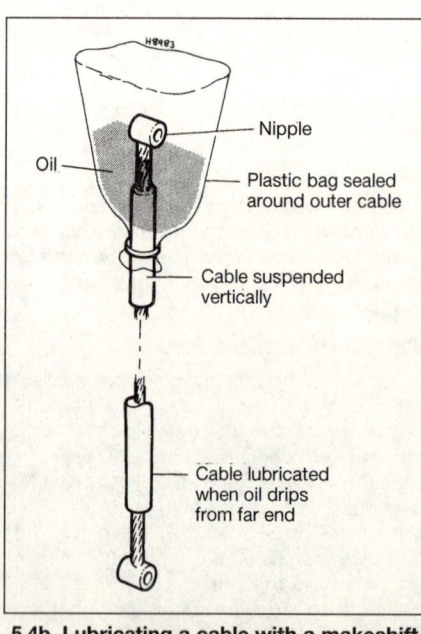

5.4a Lubricating a cable with a pressure lubricator. Make sure the tool seals around the inner cable

5.4b Lubricating a cable with a makeshift funnel and motor oil

Cable check and lubrication

3 Since the cables are exposed to the elements, they should be lubricated periodically to ensure safe and trouble-free operation.

4 To lubricate the cables, disconnect the relevant cable at its upper end, then lubricate the cable with a pressure adapter or, if one is not available, using the set-up shown **(see illustrations)**.

5 Check along the length of the outer cable for splits and kinks, and at the ends of the inner cable for frays. Check that the inner cable slides smoothly and freely in the outer cable. Renew the cable if necessary (see Chapter 8).

6 Brake hose (disc brake) – renewal

1 The flexible hydraulic hose will deteriorate with age and should be renewed at the specified interval, regardless of its apparent condition.

2 Refer to Chapter 8 and disconnect the brake hose from the master cylinder and caliper. Always renew the banjo union sealing washers.

7 Brake lever pivots – lubrication

1 Since the lever pivots are exposed to the elements, they should be lubricated periodically to ensure safe and trouble-free operation.

2 In order for the lubricant to be applied where it will do the most good, the lever should be removed (see Chapter 6). However, if chain and cable lubricant is being used, it can be applied to the pivot joint gaps and will usually work its way into the areas where friction occurs. If motor oil or light grease is being used, apply it sparingly as it may attract dirt (which could cause the controls to bind or wear at an accelerated rate). **Note:** *One of the best lubricants for the control lever pivots is a dry-film lubricant.*

Routine maintenance and servicing procedures 1•71

8 Brake shoes/pads – wear check

1 The brake shoes and pads are not marked with wear indicators, meaning that the only sure way of knowing the extent of wear is to remove them and check them visually (see Chapter 8). If the amount of friction material remaining on either the shoes or the pads is below 1.5 mm they must be renewed (see illustration).

2 The front drum brake fitted to Zip and Sfera 50/80 models may be equipped with a wear indicator arrow on the inner end of the brake arm and a corresponding index mark on the brake plate (see illustration). As the shoes wear and the cable is adjusted to compensate, the arm moves round and the marks will become closer together. When they align the shoes are worn to their limit.

3 On LEADER engined models fitted with a rear drum brake there is an indicator arrow on the brake arm and two index marks on the gearbox casing (see illustration). The shoes are worn to their limit when the arrow aligns with the lower mark. Have an assistant apply the brake firmly and check the position of the arrow. Remove the rear wheel to check the condition of the brake shoes if necessary (see Chapter 8).

9 Cooling system – check

Air-cooled engines

1 On air-cooled models, a fan mounted on the alternator rotor forces air into the engine cowling to cool the cylinder and cylinder head.

2 Check that the air intake in the fan cowling is unobstructed and that the sections of the engine cowling are fitted together correctly and secured with their mounting screws (see illustration). Note: *If any sections of the engine cowling are missing the engine will not be properly cooled.*

3 Remove the fan cowling and inspect the fan (see illustration). If any of the vanes are broken renew the fan. Check that the fan mounting screws are tight; if the screws are loose or if the screw holes are worn oversize, the fan will run out of true and cause engine vibration.

Liquid-cooled engines

Warning: *The engine must be cool before beginning this procedure.*

4 Check the coolant level (see *Daily (pre-ride) checks*).

5 The entire cooling system should be checked for evidence of leaks. Examine each coolant hose and pipe along its entire length, noting that you will need to remove much of the bodywork to access the hoses. Look for cracks, abrasions and other damage. Squeeze each flexible hose at various points. They should feel firm, yet pliable, and return to their original shape when released. If they have become hardened, replace them with new ones.

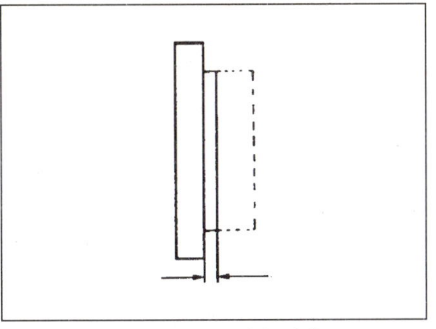

6 Check for evidence of leaks at each cooling system joint. Tighten the hose clips carefully to prevent future leaks. On early models, check the crankcase drain hole in the left-hand crankcase half for signs of leakage (see Chapter 3). On LEADER engines check below the water pump for signs of leakage. If the internal seal in the water pump fails, coolant will leak out from the bottom of the alternator cover.

7 Check the radiator for leaks and other damage. Leaks in the radiator leave tell-tale scale deposits or coolant stains on the outside of the core below the leak. If leaks are noted, remove the radiator (see Chapter 3) and have it repaired or fit a new one.

Caution: *Do not use a liquid leak stopping compound to try to repair leaks.*

8 Check the radiator fins for mud, dirt and insects, which may impede the flow of air through the radiator. If the fins are dirty, remove the radiator (see Chapter 3) and clean it using water or low pressure compressed air directed through the fins from the back. If the fins are bent or distorted, straighten them carefully with a screwdriver. If the air flow is restricted by bent or damaged fins over more than 30% of the radiator's surface area, replace the radiator.

9 Check the condition of the coolant in the reservoir. If it is rust-coloured or if accumulations of scale are visible, drain, flush and refill the system with new coolant (see Section 10).

10 Check the antifreeze content of the coolant with an antifreeze hydrometer (see illustration). Sometimes coolant looks like it's in good condition, but might be too weak to

8.1 Brake friction material minimum wear limit

8.2 Front drum brake wear indicator

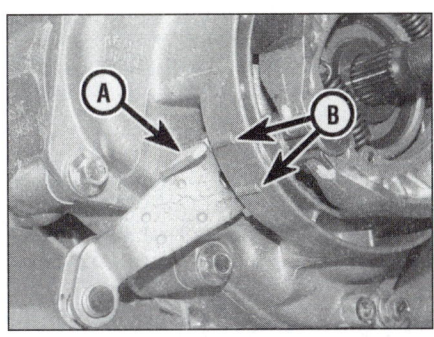

8.3 Indicator arrow (A) and index marks (B)

9.2 Fan cowling (A) and engine cowling sections (B) and (C)

9.3 Check the fan for broken vanes and ensure the screws (arrowed) are tight

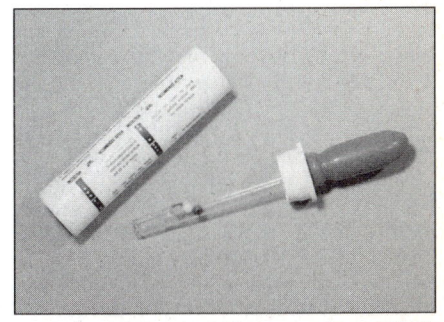

9.10 An antifreeze hydrometer is required to check coolant strength

1•72 Routine maintenance and servicing procedures

10.1 Remove the cap from the coolant reservoir

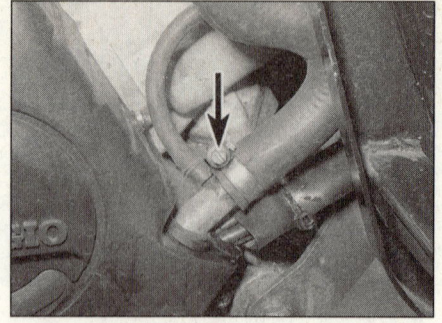

10.2a Slacken the clamp (arrowed) and detach the coolant hose

10.2b Detach the lower coolant hose on LEADER engined models

offer adequate protection. If the hydrometer indicates a weak mixture, drain, flush and refill the system (see Section 10).

11 Start the engine and let it reach normal operating temperature, then check for leaks again.

12 If the coolant level is consistently low, and no evidence of leaks can be found, have the entire system pressure checked by a Piaggio dealer.

10 Cooling system – draining, flushing and refilling

⚠ *Warning: Allow the engine to cool completely before performing this maintenance operation. Also, don't allow antifreeze to come into contact with your skin or the painted or plastic surfaces of the scooter. Rinse off spills immediately with plenty of water. Antifreeze is highly toxic if ingested. Never leave antifreeze lying around in an open container or in puddles on the floor; children and pets are attracted by its sweet smell and may drink it. Check with local authorities (councils) about disposing of antifreeze. Many communities have collection centres which will see that antifreeze is disposed of safely. Antifreeze is also combustible, so don't store it near open flames.*

Draining

1 Remove the cap from the coolant reservoir **(see illustration)**. If you hear a hissing sound as you unscrew it (indicating there is still pressure in the system), wait until it stops.

2 Position a suitable container beneath the engine on the right-hand side at the front. On two-stroke models, loosen the clip securing the coolant hose to the pipe on the side of the engine, then detach the hose and allow the coolant to completely drain from the system **(see illustration)**. On LEADER engined models, loosen the clip on the lower hose on the water pump and detach the hose and allow the coolant to drain **(see illustration)**. **Note:** *Do not dispose of the old coolant by pouring it down the drain. Instead pour it into* a heavy plastic container, cap it tightly and take it into an authorised disposal site or garage – see **Warning** at the beginning of this Section.

Flushing

3 Flush the system with clean tap water by inserting a garden hose in the reservoir filler neck. Allow water to run through the system until it is clear and flows cleanly out of the detached hose. If there is a large amount of rust or sediment in the water, remove the radiator and flush it out separately (see Chapter 3).

4 Reconnect the coolant hose to the pipe or water pump and secure it with its clip (see Step 2).

5 Fill the cooling system via the reservoir filler with clean water mixed with a flushing compound. Make sure the flushing compound is compatible with aluminium components, and follow the manufacturer's instructions carefully. Fit the reservoir cap.

6 Start the engine and allow it to reach normal operating temperature. Let it run for about five minutes.

7 Stop the engine. Let it cool for a while, then remove the reservoir cap.

8 Drain the system once again.

9 Fill the system with clean water and repeat the procedure in Steps 6 to 8.

Refilling

LEADER engined models

10 Attach the coolant hose to the water pump and secure it with its clip.

10.16 Cooling system bleed screw – Hexagon

11 Fill the system all the way up to the MAX level mark in the reservoir filler neck with the proper coolant mixture (see this Chapter's Specifications). Install the reservoir cap. **Note:** *Pour the coolant into the reservoir slowly to minimise the amount of air entering the system.*

12 Start the engine and allow it to idle for 2 to 3 minutes. Flick the throttle twistgrip part open 3 or 4 times, so that the engine speed rises, then stop the engine.

⚠ *Warning: Make sure that the scooter is on its centre stand and that the rear wheel is off the ground before starting the engine. If necessary, place a support under the engine to prevent the rear wheel contacting the ground.*

13 Let the engine cool then remove the reservoir cap. Check that the coolant level is still up to MAX level mark. Top-up the reservoir if necessary, then refit the cap.

14 Check the system for leaks.

Two-stroke models

15 Attach the coolant hose to the pipe and secure it with its clip.

16 Remove the engine cover (see Chapter 7). Locate the bleed screw, either on the top edge of the cylinder head, or secured to the bodywork adjacent to the engine **(see illustration)**. Fully loosen the bleed screw and attach one end of a suitable length of clear flexible tube to it. Place the other end into the coolant reservoir.

17 Fill the system all the way up to the MAX level line on the reservoir with the proper coolant mixture (see this Chapter's Specifications). **Note:** *Pour the coolant into the reservoir slowly to minimise the amount of air entering the system.* As you fill the reservoir, air will bubble up from the tube attached to the bleed screw.

18 When the system is full and no more air is coming out of the tube, tighten the bleed screw and install the reservoir cap.

19 Start the engine and allow it to idle for 2 to 3 minutes. Flick the throttle twistgrip part open 3 or 4 times, so that the engine speed rises, then stop the engine. Loosen the bleed screw to allow any air trapped in the system to come out, then tighten the screw.

Routine maintenance and servicing procedures 1•73

⚠️ **Warning:** *Make sure that the scooter is on its centre stand and that the rear wheel is off the ground before starting the engine. If necessary, place a support under the engine to prevent the rear wheel contacting the ground.*

20 Let the engine cool then remove the reservoir cap. Check that the coolant level is still up to MAX level line. Top-up the reservoir if necessary, then refit the cap.
21 Check the system for leaks.

11 Cylinder head – decarbonisation (two-stroke engines)

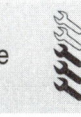

Caution: If the machine is continually ridden on short journeys which do not allow the engine to reach and maintain its normal operating temperature, the cylinder head should be decarbonised more frequently.

1 Remove the cylinder head (see Chapter 2A or 2B).
2 Remove all accumulated carbon from the cylinder head using a blunt scraper.
Caution: The cylinder head and piston are made of aluminium which is relatively soft. Take great care not to gouge or score the surface when scraping.
3 Turn the engine over until the piston is at the very top of its stroke. Smear grease all around the edge of the piston to trap any particles of carbon, then scrape the piston crown clean, again taking care not to score or gouge it or the cylinder bore.
4 Clean out the carbon, then lower the piston and wipe away the grease and any remaining particles. Also scrape or wipe clean the intake and exhaust ports in the cylinder. If the exhaust port is heavily coked, the exhaust system will probably also require cleaning (see Chapter 4).

HAYNES HiNT *Finish the piston head and combustion chamber off using a metal polish. A shiny surface is more resistant to the build-up of deposits.*

5 Install the cylinder head (see Chapter 2A and 2B).

12 Drivebelt – inspection and renewal

1 Referring to Chapter 2G, remove the drivebelt cover, then inspect the belt as described and renew it if necessary.

13 Engine oil and filter – change (four-stroke engines)

Note: On earlier, pre-LEADER engines, the engine oil is changed and the oil strainer cleaned at every service interval; the oil filter is changed at every other service interval. If only performing an oil change and strainer clean, ignore the procedure for the oil filter. On LEADER engines, a new oil filter should be fitted whenever the oil is changed.

⚠️ **Warning:** *Be careful when draining the oil, as the exhaust pipe, the engine, and the oil itself can cause severe burns.*

1 Consistent routine oil and filter changes are the single most important maintenance procedure you can perform on a four-stroke engine. The oil not only lubricates the internal parts of the engine, but it also acts as a coolant, a cleaner, a sealant, and a protector. Because of these demands, the oil takes a terrific amount of abuse and should be renewed often with oil of the recommended grade and type.
2 Before changing the oil, warm up the engine so the oil will drain easily. Stop the engine and turn the ignition OFF. Put the scooter on its centre stand, and position a clean drain tray below the engine.
3 Unscrew the oil filler plug from the left-hand side of the engine to vent the crankcase and to act as a reminder that there is no oil in the engine **(see illustration)**.

Pre-LEADER engines

4 Unscrew the oil drain plug from the bottom of the engine, and allow the oil to flow into the drain tray **(see illustration)**. Discard the sealing washer on the drain plug as a new one must be used on reassembly.
5 Remove the exhaust heat shield **(see illustration)**. Unscrew the oil strainer plug below the alternator cover on the right-hand side of the engine **(see illustration)**. Withdraw the gauze strainer and clean it in solvent and remove any debris caught in the mesh **(see illustration)**. Check the gauze for splits or holes and renew it if necessary. Install the strainer, fit a new sealing washer or O-ring to the plug if necessary, then install the plug and tighten it securely.
6 When the oil has completely drained, fit the drain plug using a new sealing washer, and tighten it to 26 Nm. Avoid overtightening, as damage to the threads will result.

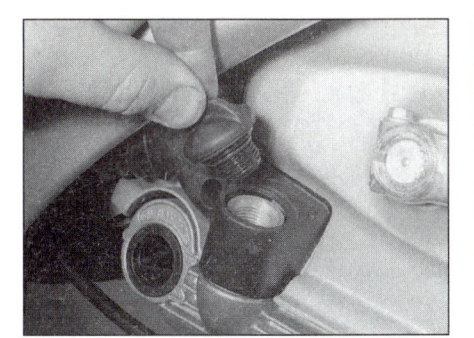

13.3 Remove the oil filler plug

13.4 Remove the drain plug (arrowed)

13.5a Remove the screws (arrowed) and detach the shield

13.5b Unscrew the plug (arrowed) . . .

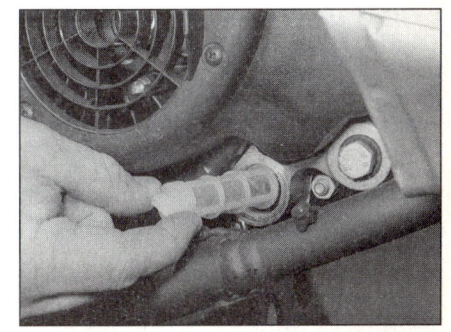

13.5c . . . and withdraw the strainer

Routine maintenance and servicing procedures

13.7a Unscrew the bolts (arrowed) . . .

13.7b . . . and remove the cover, spring and filter

13.7c Remove the O-rings and discard them

7 Now place the drain tray below the oil filter. Unscrew the two bolts securing the oil filter cover, then remove the cover, the spring and the filter **(see illustrations)**. Tip any residual oil into the drain tray. Discard the O-rings on the cover and in the filter housing as new ones should be used **(see illustration)**.

8 Fit the new housing O-ring, then install the new filter and fit the spring and the cover, again using a new O-ring **(see illustration 13.7b)**. Tighten the cover bolts to 12 Nm.

9 Refill the engine to the proper level using the recommended type and amount of oil (see *Daily (pre-ride) checks)*; you may find that due to a certain amount of oil remaining in the engine, only 600 to 650 cc will be required. Install the filler plug and tighten it by hand. Start the engine and let it run for two or three minutes. Shut it off, wait five minutes, then check the oil level. If necessary, add more oil to bring the level up to between the level marks on the sightglass. Check around the drain plug and the oil filter/strainer for leaks.

LEADER engines

10 Unscrew the oil drain plug below the alternator cover on the right-hand side of the engine and allow the oil to flow into the drain tray **(see illustration)**. Withdraw the gauze strainer and clean it in solvent and remove any debris caught in the mesh **(see illustration)**. Check the gauze for splits or holes and renew it if necessary.

11 Unscrew the oil filter and tip any residual oil into the drain tray **(see illustration)**. Smear clean engine oil onto the seal of the new filter, then install the filter and tighten it securely by hand **(see illustration)**.

12 Install the strainer, fit a new sealing washer or O-ring to the drain plug if necessary, then install the plug and tighten it to 24 to 30 Nm.

13 Refill the engine to the proper level using the recommended type and amount of oil (see *Daily (pre-ride) checks)*; you may find that due to a certain amount of oil remaining in the engine, only 600 to 650 cc will be required. Install the filler plug and tightening it by hand. Start the engine and let it run for two or three minutes. Shut it off, wait five minutes, then check the oil level. If necessary, add more oil to bring the level up to between the level marks on the dipstick. Check around the drain plug and the oil filter for leaks.

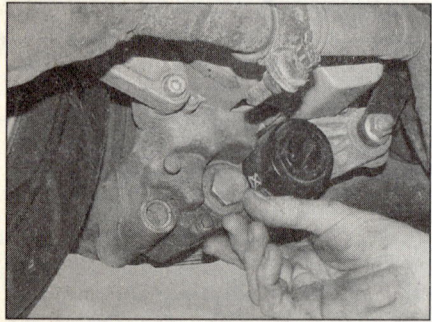

All engines

14 The old oil drained from the engine cannot be re-used and should be disposed of properly. Check with your local refuse disposal company, disposal facility or environmental agency to see whether they will accept the used oil for recycling. Don't pour used oil into drains or onto the ground.

13.10a Unscrew the oil drain plug . . .

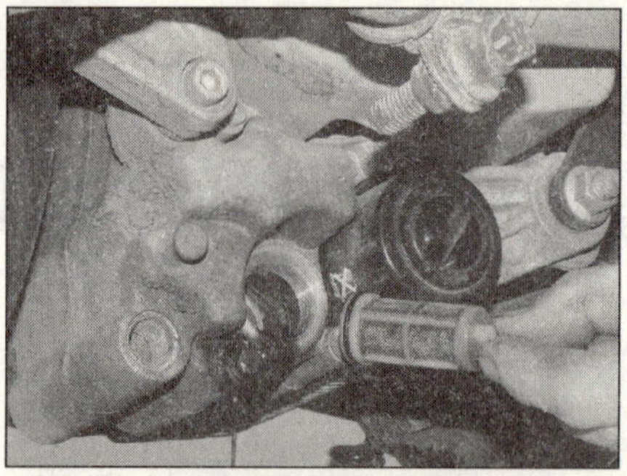

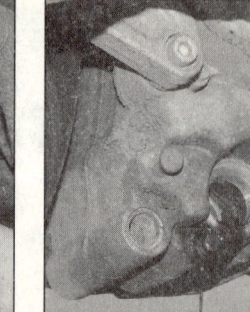

13.10b . . . then withdraw the gauze strainer

13.11a Unscrew the oil filter

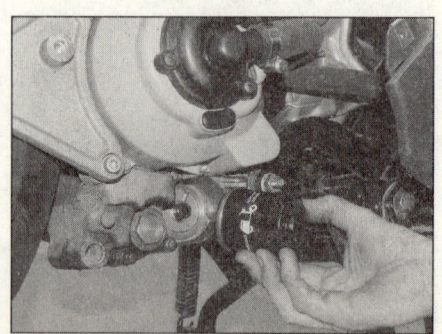

13.11b Lubricate the seal on the new filter and tighten it securely

> **HAYNES HiNT** Check the old oil carefully – if it is very metallic coloured, then the engine is experiencing wear from break-in (new engine) or from insufficient lubrication. If there are flakes or chips of metal in the oil, then something is drastically wrong internally and the engine will have to be disassembled for inspection and repair.

14 Fuel system – check

Warning: Petrol is extremely flammable, so take extra precautions when you work on any part of the fuel system. Don't smoke or allow open flames or bare light bulbs near the work area, and don't work in a garage where a natural gas-type appliance is present. If you spill any fuel on your skin, rinse it off immediately with soap and water. When you perform any kind of work on the fuel system, wear safety

Routine maintenance and servicing procedures 1•75

glasses and have a fire extinguisher suitable for a Class B type fire (flammable liquids) on hand.

Check

1 Remove the body panels as necessary to access the fuel tank, tap, fuel pump (where fitted) and carburettor. Check the tank, tap, pump and the fuel and vacuum hoses for signs of leakage, deterioration or damage; in particular check that there is no leakage from the fuel hoses. Renew any hoses which are cracked or deteriorated.
2 If the fuel tap or pump is leaking it must be renewed – individual parts are not available for the tap or pump.
3 If the carburettor gaskets are leaking, the carburettor should be disassembled and rebuilt using new gaskets and seals (see Chapter 4).

Filter cleaning

4 Cleaning or renewal of the fuel filter is advised after a particularly high mileage has been covered. It is also necessary if fuel starvation is suspected.
5 Hexagon and some LEADER engined models are fitted with an in-line fuel filter. Refer to Chapter 4 for renewal details.
6 On all other models, the fuel filter is mounted in the tank and is integral with the fuel tap. Remove the tap (see Chapter 4). Clean the gauze filter to remove all traces of dirt and fuel sediment. Check the gauze for holes. If any are found, a new tap must be fitted. Check the condition of the O-ring and renew it if it is in any way damaged or deteriorated.

15 Gearbox oil – level check

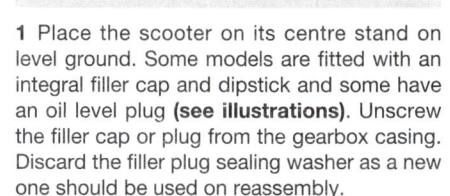

1 Place the scooter on its centre stand on level ground. Some models are fitted with an integral filler cap and dipstick and some have an oil level plug **(see illustrations)**. Unscrew the filler cap or plug from the gearbox casing. Discard the filler plug sealing washer as a new one should be used on reassembly.
2 On models with a dipstick, use a clean rag

15.1a Gearbox oil filler cap and dipstick

or paper towel to wipe off the oil. Several different dipstick level markings are used on Piaggio scooters and it is important to have the right information for checking the oil level on your specific machine. Either consult your *Owner's Manual* or Piaggio dealer for details. Also check whether the dipstick should be screwed back into the casing or not when the level reading is being taken.

> **Warning: Do not risk under-filling or over-filling the gearbox as a transmission seizure or dangerous oil leakage may result.**

3 On models with a level plug, remove the plug – the oil level should come up to the lower threads so that it is just visible on the threads **(see illustration 15.1b)**.
4 If the oil level is below the appropriate line on the dipstick, or below the level of the plug threads, top the gearbox up with the recommended grade and type of oil (see Specifications at the beginning of the Chapter). Use a pump-type oil can to top up gearboxes with a level plug **(see illustrations)**. Do not overfill.
5 Install the filler cap and tighten it securely by hand, or fit a new sealing washer to the level plug and tighten it securely.

16 Gearbox oil – change

1 Remove the exhaust system (see Chapter 4).

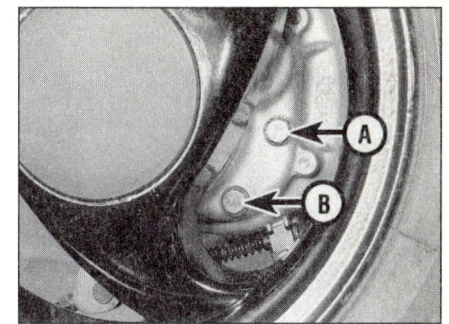

15.1b Gearbox oil filler plug (A) and drain plug (B)

2 Remove the rear wheel (see Chapter 8). On models with a rear disc brake, care must be taken to avoid spilling oil on the disc – remove the disc if necessary.
3 Position a clean drain tray below the gearbox. Unscrew the filler cap or level plug (as applicable) to vent the case and to act as a reminder that there is no oil in it.
4 Unscrew the oil drain plug from the gearbox casing **(see illustration)**. On scooters fitted with a filler plug and a drain plug, the drain plug is the lower one **(see illustration 15.1b)**, and allow the oil to flow into the drain tray. Discard the sealing washers on the drain and level plugs as new ones should be used.
5 When the oil has completely drained, fit the drain plug using a new sealing washer, and tighten it securely. Avoid overtightening, as damage to the casing will result. On LEADER engined models, tighten the drain plug to 15 to 17 Nm.
6 Refill the gearbox to the proper level using the recommended type and amount of oil (see Section 15). Install the filler cap and tighten it securely by hand, or fit a new sealing washer to the level plug and tighten it securely.
7 Check the oil level again after riding for a few minutes and, if necessary, add more oil. Check around the drain plug for leaks.
8 The old oil drained from the gearbox cannot be re-used and should be disposed of properly. Check with your local refuse disposal company, disposal facility or environmental agency to see whether they will accept the used oil for recycling. Don't pour used oil into drains or onto the ground.

15.4a Top up the oil . . .

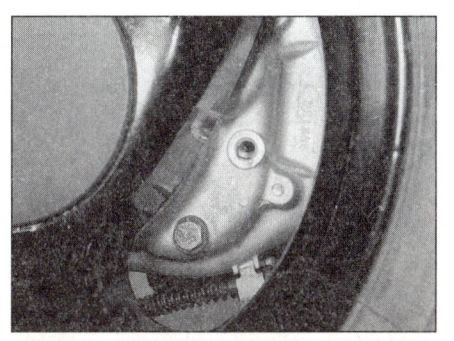

15.4b . . . until it is level with the threads

16.4 Unscrew the gearbox oil drain plug (arrowed)

1•76 Routine maintenance and servicing procedures

17.2a Headlight adjuster screw – models with handlebar-mounted headlight

17.2b Remove the badge . . .

17.2c . . . to access the adjuster screw (arrowed) – X8 shown

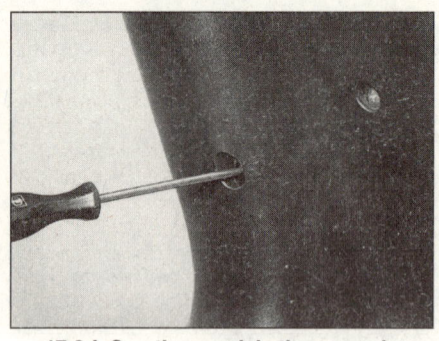

17.2d On other models the screw is accessed through the kick panel

17 Headlight aim – check and adjustment

Note: *An improperly adjusted headlight may cause problems for oncoming traffic or provide poor, unsafe illumination of the road ahead. Before adjusting the headlight aim, be sure to consult with local traffic laws and regulations.*

1 The headlight beam can adjusted vertically. Before making any adjustment, check that the tyre pressures are correct and the suspension is adjusted as required. Make any adjustments to the headlight aim with the machine on level ground, with the fuel tank half full and with an assistant sitting on the seat. If the bike is usually ridden with a passenger on the back, have a second assistant to do this.

2 Adjustment is made by turning the adjuster screw, located below the headlight unit on models with a handlebar mounted headlight, between the headlights on dual headlight models or via the hole in the back of the kick panel **(see illustrations)**. Turn the adjuster clockwise to move the beam up, and anti-clockwise to move it down.

18 Idle (tickover) speed – check and adjustment

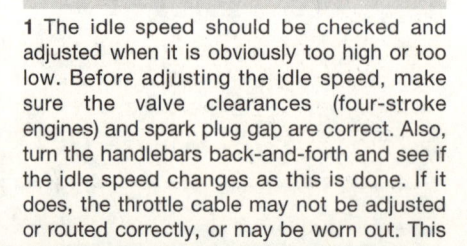

1 The idle speed should be checked and adjusted when it is obviously too high or too low. Before adjusting the idle speed, make sure the valve clearances (four-stroke engines) and spark plug gap are correct. Also, turn the handlebars back-and-forth and see if the idle speed changes as this is done. If it does, the throttle cable may not be adjusted or routed correctly, or may be worn out. This is a dangerous condition that can cause loss of control of the scooter. Be sure to correct this problem before proceeding.

2 The engine should be at normal operating temperature, which is usually reached after 10 to 15 minutes of stop-and-go riding. Place the scooter on its centre stand and make sure that the rear wheel is clear of the ground. No tachometer is fitted to enable the idle speed to be compared with that specified, but ensure that at idle (twistgrip closed) the engine speed is steady and does not falter, also that it is not too high otherwise the automatic transmission will engage.

3 The idle speed adjuster screw is located either on the carburettor, or is clipped into the front of the air filter housing **(see illustrations)**. With the engine idling, turn the screw clockwise to increase idle speed, and anti-clockwise to decrease it.

4 Snap the throttle open and shut a few times, then recheck the idle speed. If necessary, repeat the adjustment procedure.

5 If a smooth, steady idle can't be achieved, the fuel/air mixture may be incorrect or the carburettor may need overhauling (see Chapter 4).

6 With the idle speed correctly adjusted, recheck the throttle cable freeplay (see Section 28).

19 Nuts and bolts – tightness check

1 Since vibration of the machine tends to loosen fasteners, all nuts, bolts, screws, etc, should be periodically checked for proper tightness.

2 Pay particular attention to the following:
Spark plug.
Carburettor clamps.
Engine oil drain plug (four-stroke engines).
Stand bolts.
Engine mounting bolts.
Suspension and swingarm bolts.
Handlebar lever clamp bolts.
Wheel bolts.
Brake caliper and disc mounting bolts (disc brakes).
Brake hose banjo bolts (disc brakes).
Exhaust system bolts/nuts.

18.3a The idle speed adjuster is on the side of the carburettor (arrowed) . . .

18.3b . . . or on the top (arrowed) . . .

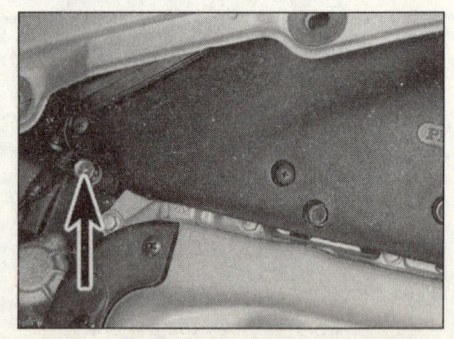

18.3c . . . or is clipped onto the air filter housing (arrowed)

Routine maintenance and servicing procedures 1•77

21.3a Release the hose clip . . .

21.3b . . . then undo the screws . . .

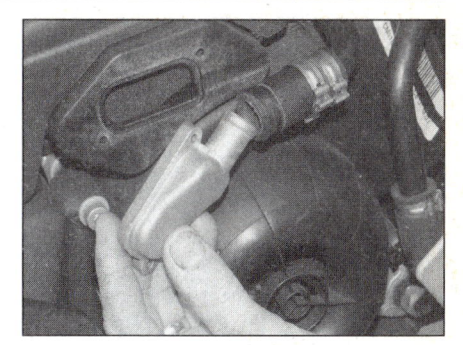

21.3c . . . and detach the reed valve housing

21.4a Lift off the cover . . .

21.4b . . . and the filter element

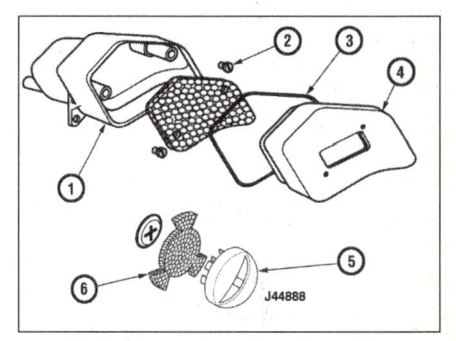

21.4c Secondary air system filter components

1 Housing
2 Filter
3 O-ring
4 Cover
5 Breather cap
6 Drive belt filter

3 If a torque wrench is available, use it along with the torque specifications given in this manual.

20 Oil pump drivebelt – renewal (two-stroke engines)

1 Refer to Chapter 2A or 2B, remove the oil pump and renew the drivebelt.

21 Secondary air system – clean

1 The secondary air system (SAS) is fitted to all two-stroke and four-stroke models with Hi-Per2 and Hi-Per4 engines, and to later LEADER-engines models. All these models have a catalytic converter exhaust system (see Chapter 4, Section 12).
2 The system components are located on the alternator cover on the right-hand side of the machine. Remove the right-hand body panel as necessary to access the system components (see Chapter 7).

Hi-Per2 engines

3 Release the clip securing the hose to the reed valve housing, then undo the screws securing the housing and detach it (see illustrations). Note the location of the reed valve inside the housing.
4 Lift off the plastic cover and the filter element (see illustrations). Note the position of the cover O-ring, if fitted. If the O-ring is damaged, discard it and fit a new one on reassembly.
5 Lever the breather cap out of the drivebelt cover with a small screwdriver and carefully pull the filter element out of the cap (see illustrations). Note that on the NRG Power DT photographed, no filter element was fitted in the drivebelt cover cap and the air intake was blanked off (see illustration). The air outlet at the rear end of the drivebelt cover was partially blanked off – if your machine has

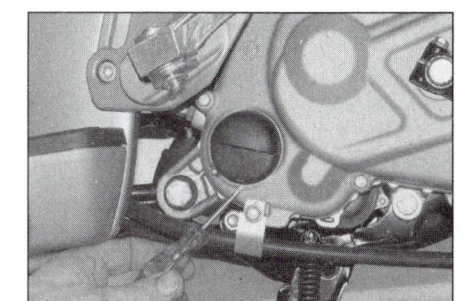

21.5a Lever off the breather cap . . .

21.5b . . . and remove the filter element carefully

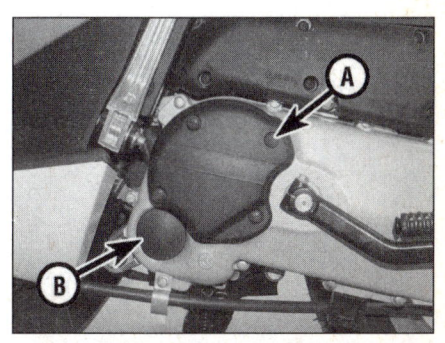

21.5c Drivebelt air intake (A) and cover cap (B) are blanked off – NRG Power DT shown

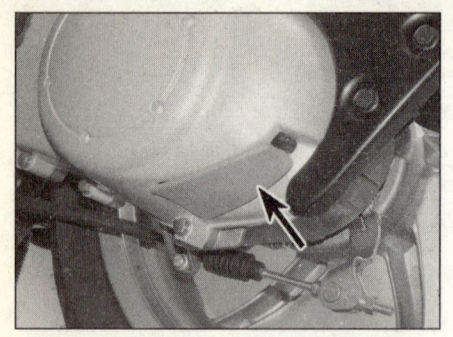

1•78 Routine maintenance and servicing procedures

21.5d If applicable, ensure the blanking piece (arrowed) is a firm fit

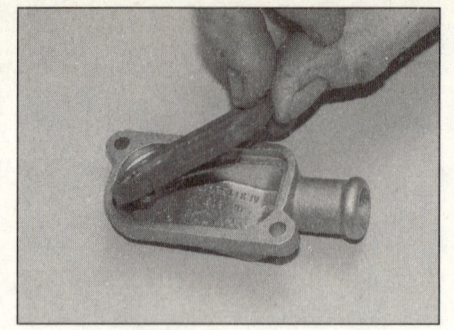

21.7a Lift out the reed valve

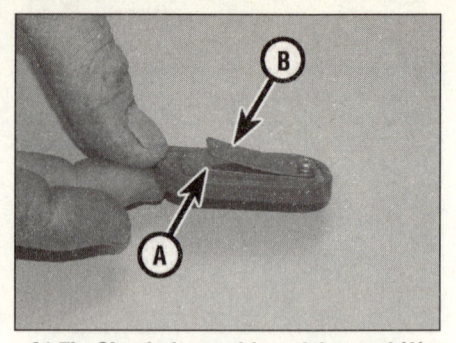

21.7b Check the position of the reed (A) and note the position of the stopper plate (B)

this system, ensure the blanking piece is a firm fit – water and road dirt will enter the housing if it is missing **(see illustration)**.
6 Wash the filters in hot soapy water then blow them dry using compressed air. Never wring the filters dry as they may tear. If the filters are excessively dirty and cannot be cleaned properly, or are torn or damaged in any way, fit new ones.
7 Lift the reed valve out of the housing, noting which way round it fits **(see illustration)**. To check the condition of the reed valve, hold it up to the light. The valve should be closed. If light can be seen around the edge of the reed a new valve should be fitted **(see illustration)**. Clean the reed and stopper plate carefully with a suitable solvent to remove any gum.
8 Install the components in the reverse order of disassembly. If necessary, fit a new O-ring to the filter housing cover. The hose clip should be secured with pliers **(see illustration)**.

Hi-Per4 engines

9 Release the clip securing the hose to the reed valve cover, then undo the screws securing the cover and detach it. Note the location of the cover gasket. If the gasket is damaged, discard it and fit a new one on reassembly.
10 Remove the filter element from the housing and wash it in hot soapy water, then blow it dry using compressed air. Never wring the filter dry as it may tear. If the filter is excessively dirty and cannot be cleaned properly, or is torn or damaged in any way, fit a new one.
11 Lift the reed valve out of the housing, noting which way round it fits. Follow the procedure in Step 7 to check and clean the reed valve.
12 Install the components in the reverse

order of disassembly. If necessary, fit a new gasket to the filter housing cover. The hose clip should be secured with pliers **(see illustration 21.7)**.

LEADER engines

13 Remove the silencer (see Chapter 4). If necessary, displace the fuel pump and filter assembly to allow access to the reed valve housing **(see illustration)**.
14 On liquid-cooled models, follow the procedure in Section 10 to drain the cooling system, then undo the screws securing the water pump body to the alternator cover and displace the pump body. Discard the body O-ring as a new one must be used (see Chapter 3).
15 Remove the luggage compartment to gain access to the top of the reed valve housing (see Chapter 7).
16 Release the clip securing the vacuum hose to the SAS diaphragm and disconnect the hose **(see illustration)**.
17 Undo the bolts securing the lower end of the SAS pipe to the cylinder head and disconnect the pipe; discard the gasket as a new one must be used. Either remove the screws securing the reed valve cover on the upper end of the SAS pipe to the reed valve housing, or release the clip securing the pipe, then lift off the pipe **(see illustrations)**. If the reed valve cover had been removed, note the cover O-ring.
18 On liquid-cooled models, undo the screws securing the reed valve housing and

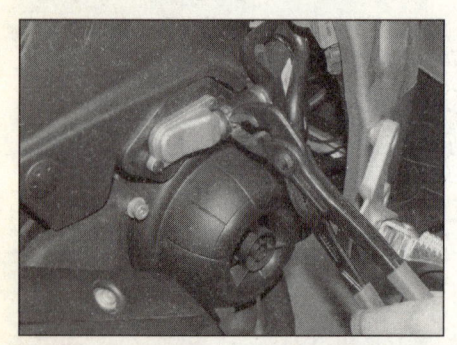

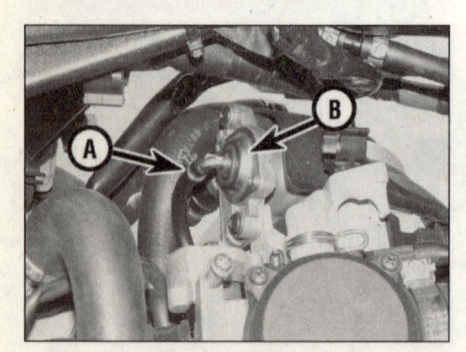

21.8 Secure the hose clip with pliers

21.13 Fuel pump (arrowed) is secured to the underside of the fuel tank – Vespa GT model shown

21.16 Disconnect the hose (A) from the SAS diaphragm (B)

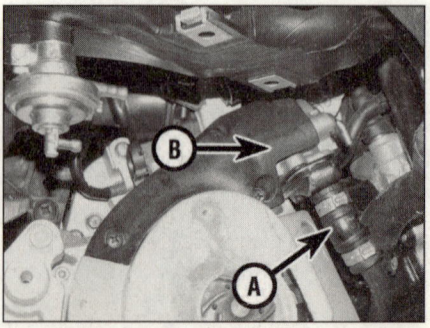

21.17a Disconnect the upper end of the SAS pipe (A) from the reed valve housing (B) . . .

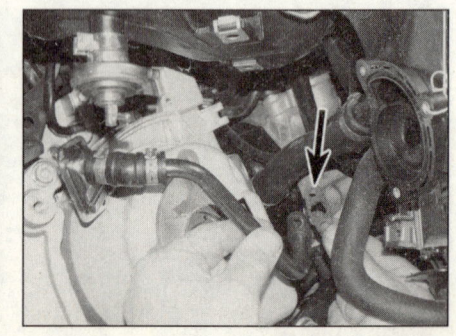

21.17b . . . and lift off the pipe. Note the gasket (arrowed)

Routine maintenance and servicing procedures 1•79

21.18a Undo the three screws on the right-hand side . . .

21.18b . . . and the screw on the front . . .

21.18c . . . and remove the reed valve housing

lift it off **(see illustrations)**. Note the location of the cover gasket.

19 On air-cooled models, undo the screws securing the outer alternator cover and lift it off.

20 Remove the filter element from the alternator cover **(see illustration)**. Wash the filter in hot soapy water, then blow it dry using compressed air. Never wring the filter dry as it may tear. If the filter is excessively dirty and cannot be cleaned properly, or is torn or damaged in any way, fit a new one.

21 On liquid-cooled models, a second filter element is fitted inside the alternator cover. Remove the alternator cover (see Chapter 2F). Prise out the filter cover and remove the filter element, noting how it fits **(see illustration)**. Follow the procedure in Step 20 to clean the filter. When it is dry, install the filter in the cover, ensuring it is fitted the correct way round, then align the filter and cover with the recess in the alternator cover and press them into position **(see illustrations)**. Install the alternator cover (see Chapter 2F).

22 On air-cooled models, undo the screws securing the reed valve housing in the inner alternator cover and pull it out. On all models, if not already done, undo the screws securing the reed valve cover and lift it off. Lift the reed valve out of the housing, noting which way round it fits **(see illustration)**. Follow the procedure in Step 7 to check and clean the reed valve. Note that on LEADER engined models the reed valve is not listed as a separate item; if the valve is faulty, a new valve housing assembly must be fitted.

23 Install the components in the reverse order of disassembly. If necessary, fit a new O-ring to the reed valve cover and the filter housing cover. The hose clip on the SAS pipe should be secured with pliers **(see illustration 21.8)**. Ensure the vacuum hose is pushed fully onto its union and secured with the clip. Fit a new gasket on the union between the lower end of the SAS pipe and the cylinder head.

24 On liquid-cooled models, follow the procedure in Chapter 3 and install the alternator cover and water pump body, then refill the cooling system (see Section 10).

22 Spark plug gap – check and adjustment

⚠️ *Warning: Access to the spark plug is extremely restricted on some models. Ensure the engine and exhaust system are cool*

21.20 Lift out the filter element

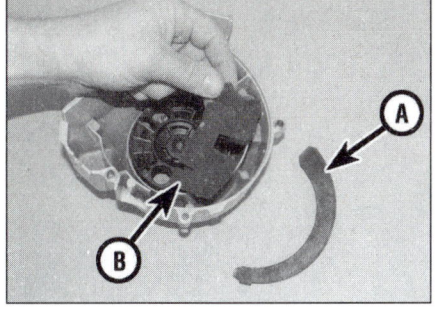

21.21a Remove the cover (A) then lift out the inner filter element (B)

21.21b Ensure that the filter is correctly installed its cover . . .

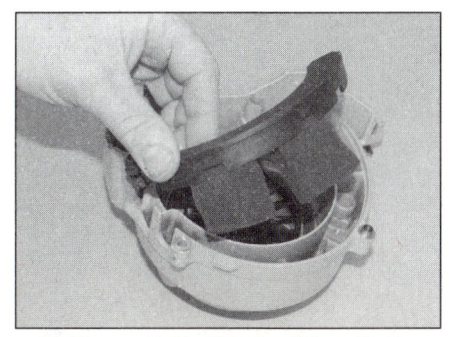

21.21c . . . then align the filter with the recess in the alternator cover . . .

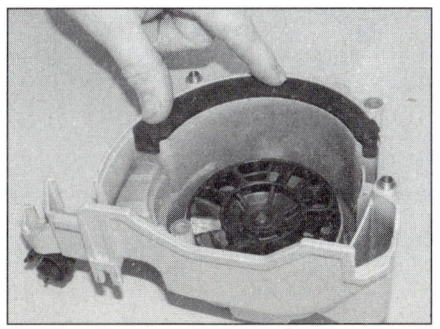

21.21d . . . and press filter cover into place

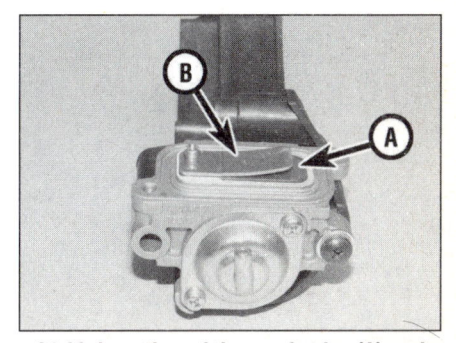

21.22 Location of the reed valve (A) and stopper plate (B) – liquid-cooled LEADER shown

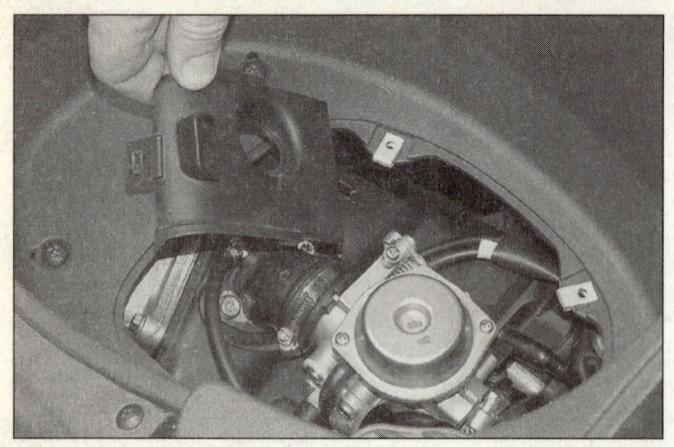

1•80 Routine maintenance and servicing procedures

22.1 Remove the spark plug access panel on air-cooled LEADER models

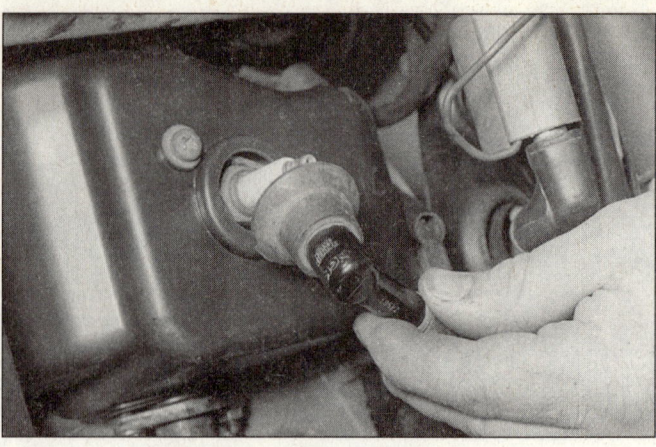

22.2a Remove the spark plug cap . . .

before attempting to remove the spark plug.

1 Make sure your spark plug socket is the correct size before attempting to remove the plug – a suitable plug socket is supplied in the scooter's toolkit. Where appropriate, remove the engine access panel or side cover (see Chapter 7). On air-cooled LEADER engined models, first undo the screw then unclip the access panel in the engine cowling and slide it out **(see illustration)**.

2 Pull the spark plug cap off the spark plug, then unscrew the plug from the cylinder head **(see illustrations)**.

3 Inspect the electrodes for wear. Both the centre and side electrode should have square edges and the side electrode should be of uniform thickness. Look for excessive carbon deposits and evidence of a cracked or chipped insulator around the centre electrode. Compare your spark plug to the colour spark plug reading chart at the end of this manual. Check the threads, the washer and the ceramic insulator body for cracks and other damage.

4 If the electrodes are not excessively worn, and if the deposits can be easily removed with a wire brush, the plug can be regapped and re-used. If in doubt concerning the condition of the plug, renew it, as the expense is minimal.

5 Cleaning a spark plug by sandblasting is permitted, provided you clean it with a high flash-point solvent afterwards.

6 Before installing the plug, make sure it is the correct type (see Specifications at the beginning of the Chapter). Check the gap between the electrodes **(see illustrations)**. Compare the gap to that specified and adjust as necessary. If the gap must be adjusted, bend the side electrode only and be very careful not to chip or crack the insulator nose **(see illustration)**. Make sure the washer is in place before installing the plug.

7 Since the cylinder head is made of aluminium, which is soft and easily damaged, thread the plug into the head by hand. Once the plug is finger-tight, the job can be finished with the plug socket **(see illustration)**. Take care not to over-tighten the plug.

8 Reconnect the spark plug cap.

HAYNES HiNT *A stripped plug thread in the cylinder head can be repaired with a thread insert.*

23 Spark plug – renewal

1 Ensure the new plug is the correct type (see Specifications at the beginning of the

22.2b . . . then unscrew the spark plug

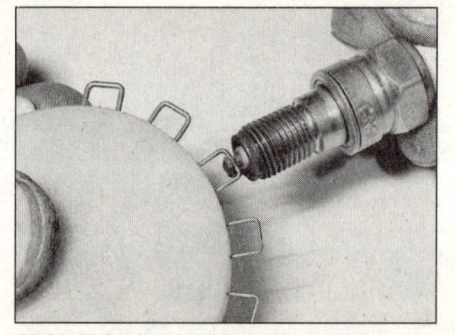

22.6a Using a wire type gauge to measure the spark plug electrode gap

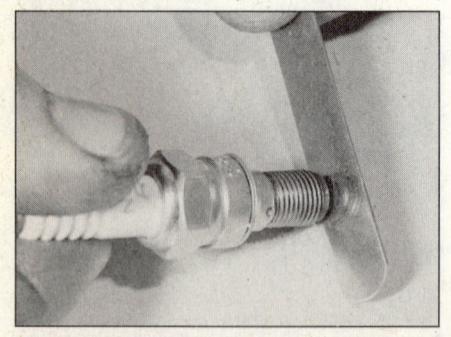

22.6b Using a feeler gauge to measure the spark plug electrode gap

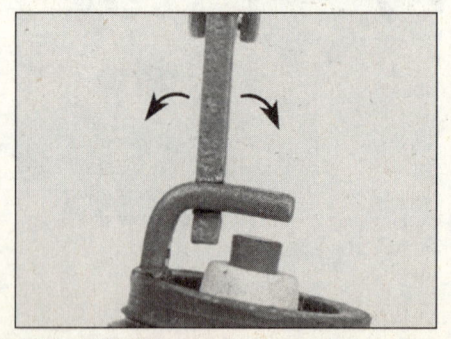

22.6c Adjust the electrode gap by bending the side electrode only

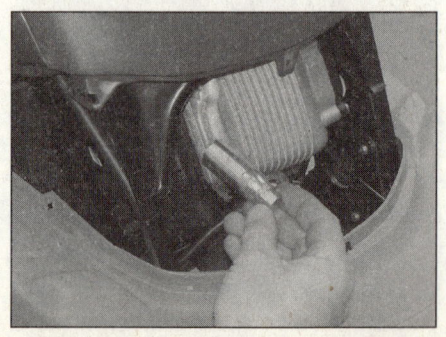

22.7 Use the correct socket to tighten the plug

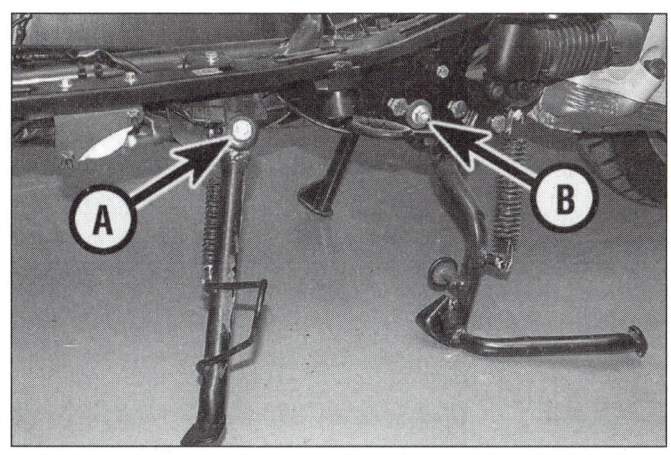

Routine maintenance and servicing procedures 1•81

25.1 Lubricate the side stand (A) and centre stand (B) pivots

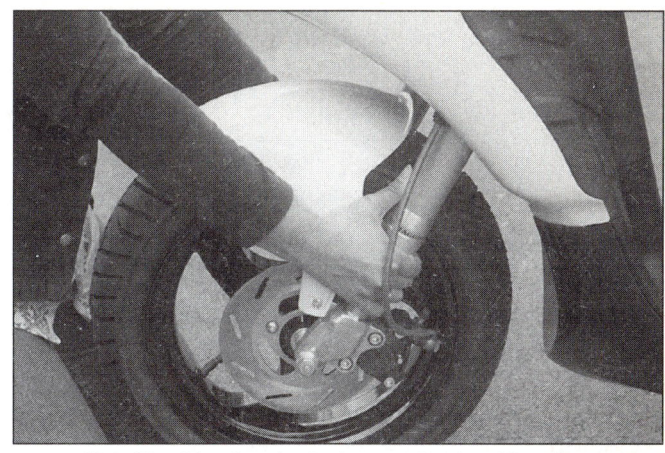

26.4 Checking for play in the steering head bearings

Chapter). Check the gap between the electrodes and adjust it if necessary. Remove the old spark plug as described in Section 22 and install the new one.

24 Speedometer cable and drive gear – lubrication

Note: *Some later models are fitted with electronic speedometers. Do not attempt to disconnect the cable from the drive housing.*

1 Remove the speedometer cable (see Chapter 9).
2 Withdraw the inner cable from the outer cable and lubricate it with motor oil or cable lubricant. Do not lubricate the upper few inches of the cable as the lubricant may travel up into the instrument head.
3 On models with monoshock front suspension, remove the drive gear (see Chapter 9). On models with telescopic front suspension, remove the front wheel and remove the drive housing (see Chapter 8). Clean all the old grease from the speedometer drive gear/drive housing, then lubricate the components with clean grease and reassemble them as descried in the relevant chapters.

25 Stands – check and lubrication

1 Since the stand pivots are exposed to the elements, they should be lubricated periodically to ensure safe and trouble-free operation **(see illustration)**.
2 In order for the lubricant to be applied where it will do the most good, the component should be disassembled. However, if chain or cable lubricant is being used, it can be applied to the pivot joint gaps and will usually work its way into the areas where friction occurs. If motor oil or light grease is being used, apply it sparingly as it may attract dirt (which could cause the pivots to bind or wear at an accelerated rate).
3 The return springs must be capable of retracting the stand fully and holding the stand retracted when the scooter is in use. If any spring has sagged or broken it must be renewed (see Chapter 7).

26 Steering head bearings – freeplay check and adjustment

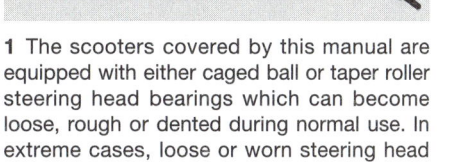

1 The scooters covered by this manual are equipped with either caged ball or taper roller steering head bearings which can become loose, rough or dented during normal use. In extreme cases, loose or worn steering head bearings can cause steering wobble – a condition that is potentially dangerous.

Check

2 Place the scooter on the centre stand. Raise the front wheel off the ground either by having an assistant push down on the rear or by placing a support under the frame. **Note:** *Do not rest the weight of the machine on the bodywork; if necessary, remove the belly panel to expose the frame (see Chapter 7).*
3 Point the front wheel straight-ahead and slowly move the handlebars from side-to-side. Any dents or roughness in the bearing races will be felt and the bars will not move smoothly and freely. If the bearings are damaged they must be renewed (see Chapter 6).
4 Next, grasp the front suspension and try to move it forward and backward **(see illustration)**. Any freeplay in the steering head bearings will be felt as front-to-rear movement of the steering stem. If play is felt in the bearings, adjust them as follows.

Adjustment

5 Remove the handlebar covers (see Chapter 7).

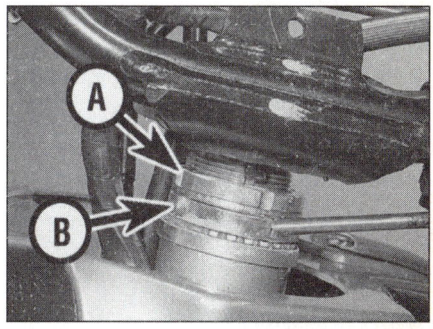

26.6 Slacken the locknut (A), then turn the adjuster (B) using a C-spanner or drift

6 Slacken the adjuster locknut using either a C-spanner or a suitable drift located in one of the notches **(see illustration)**.
7 Using either the C-spanner or drift, slacken the bearing adjuster nut slightly to release pressure on the bearings, then tighten the nut until all freeplay (front-to-rear movement) is removed. Check that the steering still moves freely from side-to-side. The object is to set the adjuster nut so that the bearings are under a very light loading, just enough to remove any freeplay.

Caution: Take great care not to apply excessive pressure because this will cause premature failure of the bearings.

8 With the bearings correctly adjusted, hold the adjuster nut to prevent it from moving, then tighten the locknut securely. Piaggio specify a torque setting of 33 Nm for the locknut on the X9 and 40 Nm for the locknut on all other models. However to apply this a Piaggio service tool (Part No. 020055Y), or a suitable old socket fabricated into a peg spanner is required and the handlebars must be removed (see Chapter 6).
9 Check the bearing adjustment as described above and re-adjust if necessary.
10 Over a period of time the grease in the bearings will harden or may be washed out. Disassemble the steering head for regreasing of the bearings. Refer to Chapter 6 for details.

Routine maintenance and servicing procedures

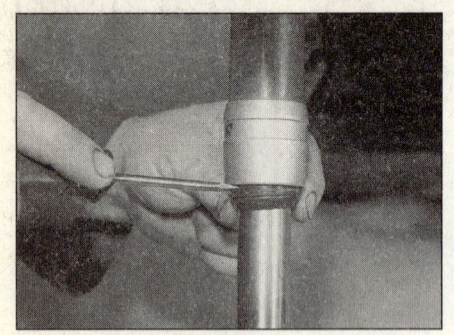

27.4a Lever off the seal . . .

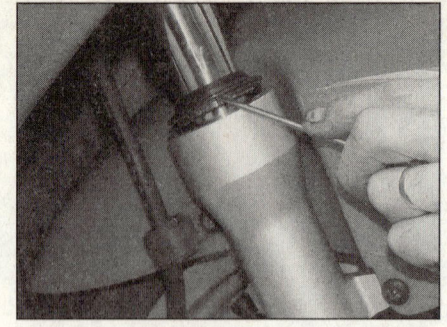

27.4b . . . and check for corrosion on the fork tube

27.4c Corrosion such as this wrecks seals

27 Suspension – check

1 The suspension components must be maintained in top operating condition to ensure rider safety. Loose, worn or damaged suspension parts decrease the scooter's stability and control.

Front suspension

2 While standing alongside the scooter, apply the front brake and push on the handlebars to compress the suspension several times. See if it moves up-and-down smoothly without binding. If binding is felt, the suspension should be disassembled and inspected (see Chapter 6).
3 On models with a monoshock, inspect the shock for fluid leaks and tightness of its mountings. If leaks are found, the shock should be renewed (see Chapter 6).
4 On models with telescopic forks, inspect the area around the dust seal for signs of grease or oil leaks, then carefully lever off the dust seal using a flat-bladed screwdriver and inspect the area behind it **(see illustrations)**. If corrosion due to the ingress of water is evident, the seals must be renewed (see Chapter 6). The chromed finish on the forks is prone to corrosion and pitting, so it is advisable to keep them as clean as possible and to spray them regularly with a rust inhibitor, otherwise the seals will not last long **(see illustration)**. If corrosion and pitting is evident, tackle it as early as possible to prevent it getting worse.
5 Check the tightness of all suspension nuts and bolts to ensure none have worked loose.

Rear suspension

Note: *For models fitted with twin rear shocks, both shocks must be in good condition. If either is found to be faulty, renew the shocks as a pair.*

6 Inspect the rear shock for fluid leaks and tightness of its mountings. If a leak is found, the shock should be renewed (see Chapter 6).
7 With the aid of an assistant to support the bike, compress the rear suspension several times. It should move up-and-down freely without binding. If any binding is felt, the worn or faulty component must be identified and renewed. The problem could be due to either the shock absorber or the pivoting silentblock assembly between the engine unit and the frame.
8 Support the scooter so that the rear wheel is off the ground. Grab the engine at the rear and attempt to rock it from side-to-side – there should be no discernible freeplay between the engine and frame. If there is movement, inspect the tightness of the silentblock assembly and engine mounting bolts, referring to the torque settings specified at the beginning of Chapters 2 and 6, then recheck for movement. If freeplay is still felt, disconnect the rear shock(s) at its lower mounting and check again – any freeplay should be more evident. If there is freeplay, inspect the silentblock assembly for wear (see Chapter 6).
9 Next, grasp the top of the rear wheel and pull it upwards – there should be no discernible freeplay before the shock absorber begins to compress **(see illustration)**. Any freeplay indicates worn shock absorber mountings. The worn components must be renewed (see Chapter 6).

28 Throttle cable and oil pump – check and adjustment

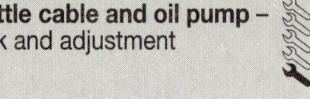

Two-stroke engines

1 With the engine stopped, make sure the throttle grip rotates easily from fully closed to fully open with the front wheel turned at various angles. The grip should return automatically from fully open to fully closed when released.
2 If the throttle sticks, this is probably due to a cable fault. Remove the cables (see Chapter 4) and check and lubricate them using the same method as for the brake cables (see Section 5). Install the cables, making sure they are correctly routed. If this fails to improve the operation of the throttle, the cable(s) must be renewed. Note that in very rare cases the fault could lie in the carburettor or oil pump rather than the cable (see Chapters 4 or 2 respectively).
3 With the throttle operating smoothly, check for a small amount of freeplay in the twistgrip before the throttle opens **(see illustration)**. If there is insufficient or excessive freeplay, loosen the locknut on the cable adjuster and turn the adjuster until freeplay is just evident, then retighten the locknut **(see illustration)**.

27.9 Checking for freeplay in the suspension mountings

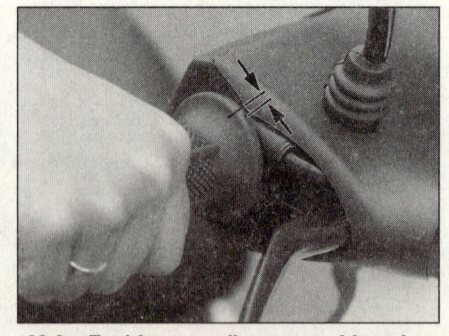

28.3a Feel for a small amount of freeplay in the throttle twistgrip

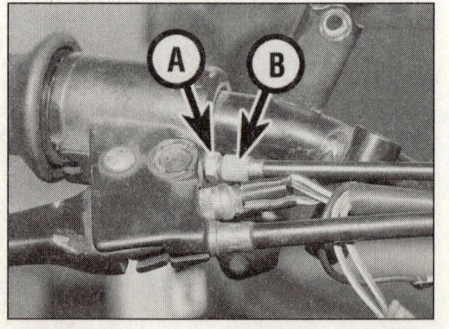

28.3b Slacken the locknut (A) and turn the adjuster (B) until the desired amount of freeplay is obtained

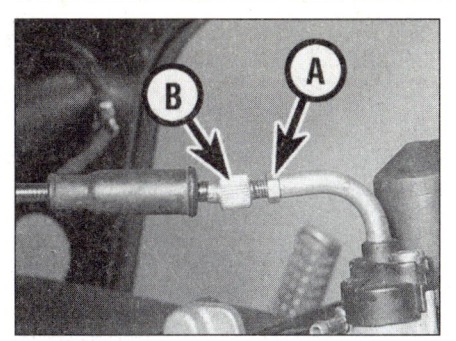

Routine maintenance and servicing procedures 1•83

28.4 Slacken the locknut (A) and turn the adjuster (B) as required

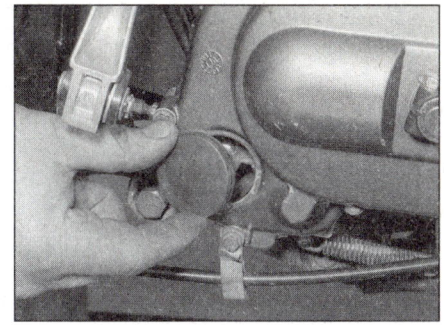

28.5a Remove the plug from the transmission cover

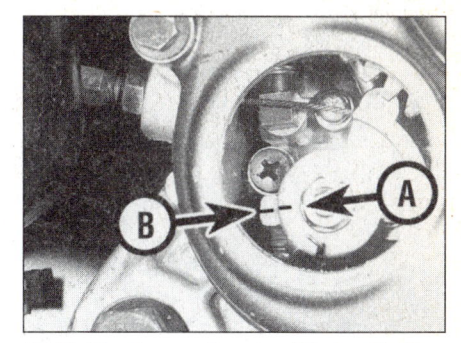

28.5b The line on the cam (A) should align with the index line (B) on the body

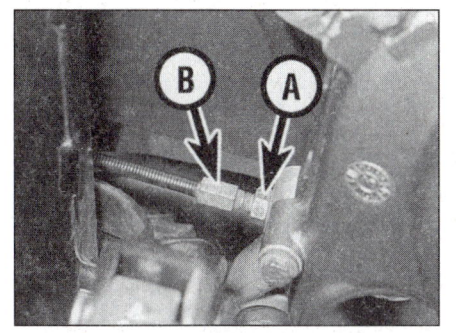

28.5c Slacken the locknut (A) and turn the adjuster (B) as required

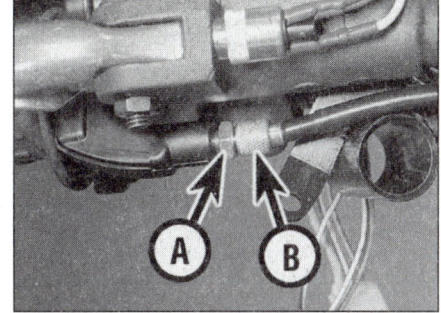

28.9a Slacken the locknut (A) and turn the adjuster (B) until the desired amount of freeplay is obtained

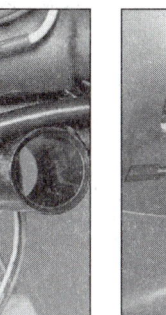

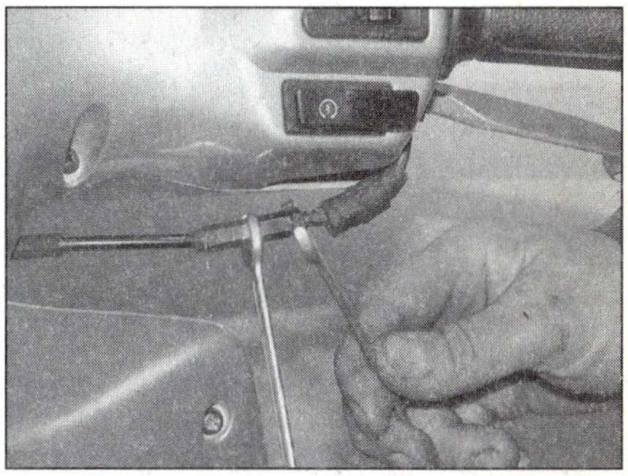

28.9b Adjusting an exposed throttle cable

Note: *It may be necessary to remove the handlebar covers to access the cable adjuster (see Chapter 7). If the adjuster has reached its limit of adjustment, renew the cable (see Chapter 4). If the idle speed cannot be set properly, this could be due to incorrect adjustment of the cable. Turn the adjuster in – if the idle speed falls as you do, this is the case. Set the adjuster so that a small amount of freeplay is evident.*

4 There should be no freeplay in the cable from the splitter to the carburettor. If any is evident, pull back the rubber boot at the carburettor end, then slacken the locknut on the adjuster, and turn the adjuster out until all freeplay has just been removed, but not so far as to start to lift the throttle valve in the carburettor **(see illustration)**. To check the exact position, slacken the locknut and turn the adjuster in until freeplay just becomes evident, then turn it out until it is taken up again, but again not too far.

5 Remove the rubber plug from the transmission cover **(see illustration)**. With the throttle closed, check that the cable from the splitter to the oil pump is correctly adjusted so that the scribe mark on the pump cam aligns with the mark on the pump body **(see illustration)**. If they are not aligned, slacken the cable adjuster locknut on the transmission housing, turn the adjuster in or out as required until the marks align, then retighten the locknut **(see illustration)**.

6 Start the engine and check that the idle speed does not rise as the handlebars are turned. If it does, a cable is routed incorrectly. Correct the problem before riding the scooter.

Four-stroke engines

7 With the engine stopped, make sure the throttle grip rotates easily from fully closed to fully open with the front wheel turned at various angles. The grip should return automatically from fully open to fully closed when released.

8 If the throttle sticks, this is probably due to a cable fault. Remove the cable (see Chapter 4) and lubricate it using the same method as for the brake cables (see Section 5). Install the cable, making sure it is correctly routed. If this fails to improve the operation of the throttle, the cable must be renewed. Note that in very rare cases the fault could lie in the carburettor rather than the cable, necessitating the removal of the carburettor (see Chapter 4).

9 With the throttle operating smoothly, check for a small amount of freeplay in the twistgrip before the throttle opens **(see illustration 28.3a)**. If there is insufficient or excessive freeplay, loosen the locknut on the cable adjuster and turn the adjuster until freeplay is just evident, then retighten the locknut **(see illustrations)**. **Note:** *It may be necessary to remove the handlebar covers to access the cable adjuster (see Chapter 7). If the adjuster has reached its limit of adjustment, renew the cable (see Chapter 4). If the idle speed cannot be set properly, this could be due to incorrect adjustment of the cable. Turn the adjuster in – if the idle speed falls as you do, this is the case. Set the adjuster so that a small amount of freeplay is evident.*

10 Start the engine and check that the idle speed does not rise as the handlebars are turned. If it does, a cable is routed incorrectly. Correct the problem before riding the scooter.

29 Valve clearances – check and adjustment (four-stroke engines)

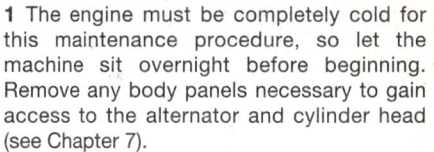

1 The engine must be completely cold for this maintenance procedure, so let the machine sit overnight before beginning. Remove any body panels necessary to gain access to the alternator and cylinder head (see Chapter 7).

2 Remove the spark plug (see Section 22).

3 Remove the valve cover (see Chapter 2). Discard the cover gasket or O-ring as a new one must be fitted on reassembly.

4 Turn the engine in a clockwise direction until the timing mark on the camshaft sprocket aligns with the timing mark on the camshaft holder **(see illustration)**; you can do this by removing the alternator cover and rotating the crankshaft via the rotor retaining

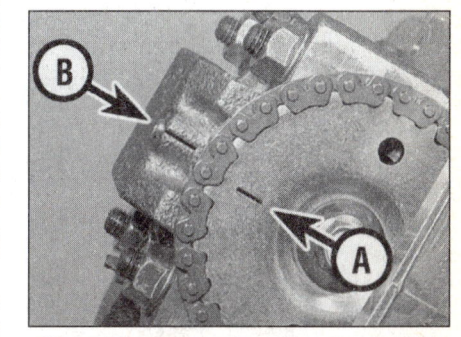

29.4a Align the mark on the sprocket (A) with that on the camshaft holder (B)

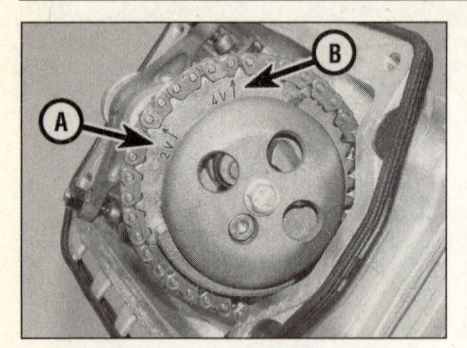

1•84 Routine maintenance and servicing procedures

29.4b Timing mark (A) for two valve and (B) for four valve LEADER engines

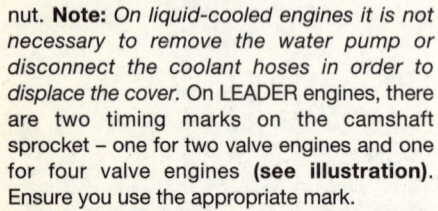

29.6 Check each valve clearance using a feeler gauge

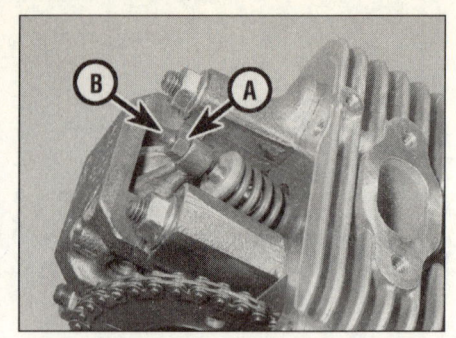

29.7a Slacken the locknut (A) and turn the adjuster (B) . . .

nut. **Note:** *On liquid-cooled engines it is not necessary to remove the water pump or disconnect the coolant hoses in order to displace the cover.* On LEADER engines, there are two timing marks on the camshaft sprocket – one for two valve engines and one for four valve engines **(see illustration)**. Ensure you use the appropriate mark.

5 The valve clearances are checked with the engine at top dead centre (TDC) on its compression stroke; i.e., the valves are closed and a small clearance can be felt at each rocker arm. If the engine is not on its compression stroke, rotate the crankshaft clockwise one full turn (360°) so that the camshaft sprocket mark once again aligns with that on the camshaft holder.

6 Insert a feeler gauge of the same thickness as the correct valve clearance (see Specifications) between the rocker arm and stem of each valve and check that it is a firm sliding fit – you should feel a slight drag when the you pull the gauge out **(see illustration)**.

7 If the clearance is either too small or too large, slacken the locknut and turn the adjuster until a firm sliding fit is obtained, then tighten the locknut securely, making sure the adjuster does not turn as you do so **(see illustrations)**. Recheck the clearances.

8 Apply some engine oil to the valve assemblies, rockers and camshaft before installing the valve cover and fit a new cover gasket or O-ring. Install the remaining components in the reverse order of removal.

30 Variator and clutch – check

Variator

1 Remove the drive pulley and the variator (see Chapter 2G). Disassemble the variator and check all components for wear as described. If applicable, grease the rollers and the roller tracks in the housing.

Clutch

2 On two-stroke models, remove the clutch and driven pulley assembly (see Chapter 2G). Disassemble the pulley assembly and check all the components as described, paying particular attention to the bearing surfaces of the inner and outer pulley halves, and the condition of the needle roller bearing.

31 Wheels and tyres – general check

Wheels

1 Cast wheels are virtually maintenance-free, but they should be kept clean and checked periodically for cracks and other damage. Also check the wheel runout and alignment (see Chapter 8). Never attempt to repair damaged cast wheels; they must be renewed.

2 Check the valve rubber for signs of damage or deterioration and have it renewed if necessary. Also, make sure the valve cap is in place and tight. If fitted, check that the wheel weights are firmly attached to the rim **(see illustration)**.

Tyres

3 Check the tyre condition and tread depth thoroughly – see *Daily (pre-ride) checks*.

32 Wheel bearings – check

1 Wheel bearings will wear over a period of time and cause handling problems.

2 Support the scooter upright on its centre stand. Check for any play in the bearings by pushing and pulling the wheel against the hub **(see illustration)**. Also rotate the wheel and check that it revolves smoothly.

3 If any play is detected in the hub, or if the wheel does not rotate smoothly (and this is not due to brake or transmission drag), the wheels must be removed and the bearings inspected for wear or damage. Check first that any freeplay is not due to loose wheel mountings.

4 The front wheel bearings are housed in the wheel hub on telescopic fork models and in the separate hub assembly on monoshock models (see Chapter 8). There are no rear wheel bearings as such; the driveshaft bearings are housed in the gearbox (see Chapter 2G).

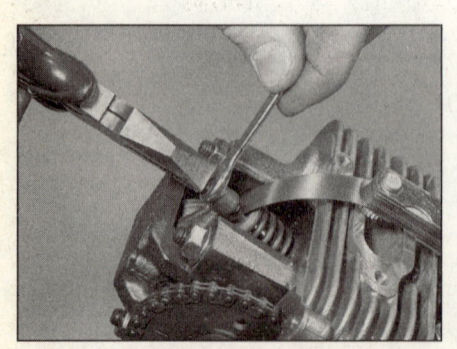

29.7b . . . until the clearance is correct

31.2 Check that the wheel weights are firmly attached

32.2 Checking for play in the wheel bearings

Chapter 2 Part A:
Air-cooled two-stroke engines
(Sfera 50/80, all Typhoons, Zip and Zip 50, ET2, NRG MC³ DT, Liberty 50, NRG Power DT, Fly 50, LX2 50, Skipper)

Refer to the beginning of Chapter 1 for model identification details

Contents

Alternator rotor and stator – removal and installation 12	Major engine repair – general note 4
Cooling fan – removal and installation 11	Operations possible with the engine in the frame 2
Crankcase halves, crankshaft and connecting rod and bearings ... 15	Operations requiring engine removal 3
Cylinder – removal, inspection and installation 8	Oil pump and belt – removal, inspection, installation and bleeding . 14
Cylinder head – decarbonisation .... see Chapter 1	Piston – removal, inspection and installation 9
Cylinder head – removal, inspection and installation 7	Piston rings – inspection and installation 10
Disassembly and reassembly – general information 6	Recommended running-in procedure 17
Engine/transmission unit – removal and installation 5	Spark plug gap – check and adjustment .... see Chapter 1
General information 1	Starter motor – removal and installation .... see Chapter 9
Idle speed – check and adjustment .... see Chapter 1	Starter pinion assembly – removal, inspection and installation 13
Initial start-up after overhaul 16	

Degrees of difficulty

Easy, suitable for novice with little experience	Fairly easy, suitable for beginner with some experience	Fairly difficult, suitable for competent DIY mechanic	Difficult, suitable for experienced DIY mechanic	Very difficult, suitable for expert DIY or professional

Specifications

Sfera 50, Typhoon 50, Zip, ET2, NRG MC³ DT 50, Liberty 50

General

Type	Single cylinder two-stroke
Capacity	49.4 cc
Bore	40.0 mm
Stroke	39.3 mm
Compression ratio	10.9 to 1

2A•2 Air-cooled two-stroke engines

Cylinder bore
Standard
    Size-code A .... 39.995 mm
    Size-code B .... 40.000 mm
    Size-code C .... 40.005 mm
    Size-code D .... 40.010 mm
    Size-code E .... 40.015 mm
1st oversize .... 40.195 to 40.215 mm
2nd oversize .... 40.395 to 40.415 mm

Connecting rod
Small-end internal diameter
    Size I .... 17.007 to 17.011 mm
    Size II .... 17.003 to 17.007 mm
    Size III .... 17.001 to 17.003 mm

Piston
Piston diameter (measured 25 mm down from lower ring groove, at 90° to piston pin axis)
  Standard
    Size-code A .... 39.940 mm
    Size-code B .... 39.945 mm
    Size-code C .... 39.050 mm
    Size-code D .... 39.955 mm
    Size-code E .... 39.960 mm
1st oversize .... 40.140 to 40.160 mm
2nd oversize .... 40.340 to 40.360 mm
Piston-to-bore clearance .... 0.050 to 0.060 mm
Piston pin diameter .... 11.999 to 12.005 mm

Piston rings
Ring end gap (installed) .... 0.10 to 0.25 mm

Crankshaft
Runout (max)
    At middle and left-hand end .... 0.03 mm
    At right-hand end .... 0.02 mm
Endfloat .... 0.03 to 0.09 mm

Torque settings
Engine front mounting bolt .... 33 to 41 Nm
Rear shock absorber lower mounting .... 33 to 41 Nm
Cylinder head nuts .... 10 to 11 Nm
Crankcase bolts .... 12 to 13 Nm
Alternator rotor nut .... 40 to 44 Nm

Hi-Per2 engine: Zip 50, Fly 50, Liberty 50 from frame prefix no. ZAPC 37200, NRG Power DT, ET2 from frame prefix no. ZAPC 38100, LX2 50

General
Type .... Single cylinder two-stroke
Capacity .... 49.4 cc
Bore .... 40.0 mm
Stroke .... 39.3 mm
Compression ratio .... 10.3 to 1

Cylinder bore
Standard
    Size code M .... 40.005 to 40.012 mm
    Size code N .... 40.012 to 40.019 mm
    Size code O .... 40.019 to 40.026 mm
    Size code P .... 40.026 to 40.033 mm
1st oversize .... 40.205 to 40.233 mm
2nd oversize .... 40.405 to 40.433 mm

Connecting rod
Small-end internal diameter
    Standard .... 17.001 to 17.011 mm
    Service limit .... 17.060 mm

Piston

Piston diameter (measured 25 mm down from lower ring groove, at 90° to piston pin axis)
   Standard
      Size code M .... 39.943 to 39.950 mm
      Size code N .... 39.950 to 39.957 mm
      Size code O .... 39.957 to 39.964 mm
      Size code P .... 39.964 to 39.971 mm
   1st oversize .... 40.143 to 40.171 mm
   2nd oversize .... 40.343 to 40.371 mm
Piston-to-bore clearance .... 0.055 to 0.069 mm
Piston pin diameter .... 12.001 to 12.005 mm
Piston pin bore diameter in piston .... 12.007 to 12.012 mm

Piston rings

Ring end gap (installed) .... 0.10 to 0.25 mm

Crankshaft

Runout (max)
   At middle and left-hand end .... 0.03 mm
   At right-hand end .... 0.02 mm
Endfloat .... 0.03 to 0.09 mm

Torque settings

Engine front mounting bolt .... 33 to 41 Nm
Rear shock absorber lower mounting .... 33 to 41 Nm
Cylinder head nuts .... 10 to 11 Nm
Crankcase bolts .... 12 to 13 Nm
Alternator rotor nut .... 40 to 44 Nm

Sfera 80, Typhoon 80

General

Type .... Single cylinder two-stroke
Capacity .... 74.7 cc
Bore .... 46.5 mm
Stroke .... 44.0 mm
Compression ratio .... 10.4 to 1

Cylinder

Bore .... 46.495 to 46.525 mm

Connecting rod

Small-end internal diameter
   Size I .... 17.007 to 17.011 mm
   Size II .... 17.003 to 17.007 mm
   Size III .... 17.001 to 17.003 mm

Piston

Piston diameter (measured 25 mm down from lower ring groove, at 90° to piston pin axis)
   Standard .... 46.465 to 46.495 mm
Piston-to-bore clearance .... 0.025 to 0.035 mm
Piston pin diameter .... 11.999 to 12.005 mm

Piston rings

Ring end gap (installed) .... 0.10 to 0.25 mm

Crankshaft

Runout (max)
   At middle and left-hand end .... 0.03 mm
   At right-hand end .... 0.02 mm
Endfloat .... 0.03 to 0.09 mm

Torque settings

Engine front mounting bolt .... 33 to 41 Nm
Rear shock absorber lower mounting .... 33 to 41 Nm
Cylinder head nuts .... 10 to 11 Nm
Crankcase bolts .... 12 to 13 Nm
Alternator rotor nut .... 40 to 44 Nm

Typhoon 125, Skipper

General
Type	Single cylinder two-stroke
Capacity	124 cc
Bore	55.0 mm
Stroke	52.0 mm
Compression ratio	10.2 to 1

Cylinder bore
Standard
Size-code A	54.990 to 54.995 mm
Size-code B	54.995 to 55.000 mm
Size-code C	55.000 to 55.005 mm
Size-code D	55.005 to 55.010 mm
Size-code E	55.010 to 55.015 mm
Size-code F	55.015 to 55.020 mm
Size-code G	55.020 to 55.025 mm
Size-code H	55.025 to 55.030 mm
Size-code I	55.030 to 55.035 mm

Connecting rod
Small-end internal diameter
Size I	20.009 to 20.013 mm
Size II	20.005 to 20.010 mm
Size III	19.999 to 20.006 mm
Size IIII	19.997 to 20.002 mm

Piston
Piston diameter (measured 35 mm down from lower ring groove, at 90° to piston pin axis)
Standard
Size-code A	54.945 to 54.950 mm
Size-code B	54.950 to 54.955 mm
Size-code C	54.955 to 54.960 mm
Size-code D	54.960 to 54.965 mm
Size-code E	54.965 to 54.970 mm
Size-code F	54.970 to 54.975 mm
Size-code G	54.975 to 54.980 mm
Size-code H	54.980 to 54.985 mm
Size-code I	54.985 to 54.990 mm
Piston-to-bore clearance	0.040 to 0.050 mm
Piston pin diameter	15.999 to 16.006 mm

Piston rings
Ring end gap (installed)	0.20 to 0.35 mm

Crankshaft
Runout (max)	0.03 mm
Endfloat	0.03 to 0.09 mm

Torque settings
Engine front mounting bolt	33 to 41 Nm
Rear shock absorber lower mounting	33 to 41 Nm
Cylinder head nuts	22 to 23 Nm
Crankcase bolts	13 Nm
Alternator rotor nut	52 to 56 Nm

Air-cooled two-stroke engines 2A•5

1 General information

The engine unit is a single cylinder two-stroke, with fan-assisted air cooling. The fan is mounted on the alternator rotor, which is on the right-hand end of the crankshaft. The crankshaft assembly is pressed, incorporating the connecting rod, with the big-end running on the crankpin on a needle roller bearing. The piston also runs on a needle roller bearing fitted in the small-end of the connecting rod. The crankshaft runs in caged ball main bearings. The crankcase divides vertically.

2 Operations possible with the engine in the frame

All components and assemblies, with the exception of the crankshaft/connecting rod and its bearings, can be worked on without having to remove the engine/transmission assembly from the frame. If, however, a number of areas require attention at the same time, removal of the engine is recommended, as it is easy to do so.

3 Operations requiring engine removal

To access the crankshaft and connecting rod and its bearings, the engine must be removed from the frame and the crankcase halves must be separated.

4 Major engine repair – general note

1 It is not always easy to determine when or if an engine should be completely overhauled, as a number of factors must be considered.
2 High mileage is not necessarily an indication that an overhaul is needed, while low mileage, on the other hand, does not preclude the need for an overhaul. Frequency of servicing is probably the single most important consideration. An engine that has regular and frequent maintenance will most likely give many miles of reliable service. Conversely, a neglected engine, or one which has not been run-in properly, may require an overhaul very early in its life.
3 If the engine is making obvious knocking or rumbling noises, the connecting rod and/or main bearings are probably at fault.
4 Loss of power, rough running, excessive noise and high fuel consumption rates may also point to the need for an overhaul, especially if they are all present at the same time. If a complete tune-up does not remedy the situation, major mechanical work is the only solution.
5 An engine overhaul generally involves restoring the internal parts to the specifications of a new engine. The piston rings and main and connecting rod bearings are usually renewed and, if necessary, the cylinder is rebored (50cc engine only). The end result should be a like-new engine that will give as many trouble-free miles as the original.
6 Before beginning the engine overhaul, read through the related procedures to familiarise yourself with the scope and requirements of the job. Overhauling an engine is not all that difficult, but it is time consuming. Check on the availability of parts and make sure that any necessary special tools, equipment and supplies are obtained in advance.
7 Most work can be done with typical workshop hand tools, although a number of precision measuring tools are required for inspecting parts to determine if they must be renewed. Often a dealer will handle the inspection of parts and offer advice concerning reconditioning and renewal. As a general rule, time is the primary cost of an overhaul so it does not pay to install worn or substandard parts.
8 As a final note, to ensure maximum life and minimum trouble from a rebuilt engine, everything must be assembled with care in a spotlessly-clean environment.

5 Engine/transmission unit – removal and installation

Caution: The engine is not heavy, although engine removal and installation should be carried out with the aid of an assistant; personal injury or damage could occur if the engine falls or is dropped.

Removal

1 Support the scooter securely in an upright position. Work can be made easier by raising the machine to a suitable working height on a hydraulic ramp or a suitable platform. Make sure the scooter is secure and will not topple over.
2 Remove the bodywork as required according to model (see Chapter 7).
3 If the engine is dirty, particularly around its mountings, wash it thoroughly before starting any major dismantling work. This will make work much easier and rule out the possibility of dirt falling inside.
4 Disconnect the battery negative terminal (see Chapter 9). Trace the wiring from the alternator/pulse generator coil on the right-hand side of the engine and disconnect it at the connector(s). Free the wiring from any clips on the engine. Pull the spark plug cap off the plug.
5 Either remove the carburettor, leaving the throttle cable attached if required, or just disconnect the fuel hose and vacuum hose from their unions on the carburettor and inlet manifold respectively, and disconnect the throttle cable (see Chapter 4). Where fitted, disconnect the automatic choke wiring connector. Also disconnect the oil hose from the oil tank and the pump cable from the pump (see Chapter 4). On Typhoon 80 and 125 models, disconnect the fuel pump vacuum hose from the engine.
6 Either remove the starter motor if required, or disconnect the starter motor leads (see Chapter 9).
7 Remove the air filter housing (see Chapter 4). Where fitted, detach the drivebelt air duct from the front of the cover. On some models, there is a spring attached to the engine mounting below the front of the drivebelt cover – detach the spring.
8 Remove the exhaust system (see Chapter 4).
9 If required, remove the rear wheel (see Chapter 8). **Note:** *The rear wheel and centre stand provide a convenient support for the engine unit once it is removed from the scooter. However, it is useful to loosen the rear wheel nut at this point before disconnecting the rear brake.*
10 Disconnect the rear brake cable from the brake (see Chapter 8).
11 Remove the bolt securing the rear shock absorber to the transmission casing and lower the engine unit carefully **(see illustration)**. If the rear wheel has been removed, support the engine unit on a wood block to prevent damage to the casing. Undo the nut securing the upper end of the shock to the frame and remove the shock.
12 Check that all wiring, cables and hoses are well clear, then remove the front engine mounting bolt and manoeuvre

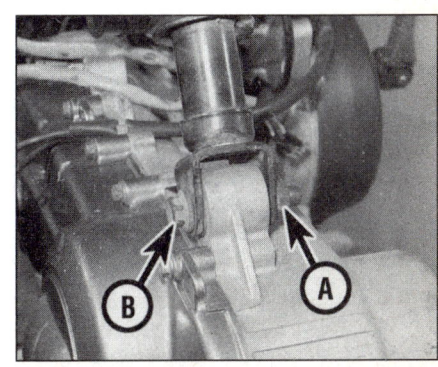

5.11 Remove the nut (A) and withdraw the shock absorber bolt (B)

2A•6 Air-cooled two-stroke engines

5.12a Remove the nut (arrowed) . . .

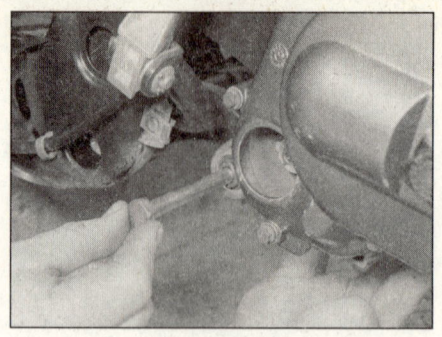

5.12b . . . and withdraw the bolt

the engine back and out of the frame **(see illustrations)**.

Installation

13 Installation is the reverse of removal, noting the following points:
a) Make sure no wires, cables or hoses become trapped between the engine and the frame when installing the engine.
b) Tighten the engine mounting bolt and shock absorber bolt to the torque settings specified at the beginning of the Chapter.
c) Use new gaskets on the exhaust pipe connections, and tighten the exhaust mounting nuts securely, having applied a smear of copper-based grease to their threads to aid future removal.
d) Make sure all wires, cables and hoses are correctly routed and connected, and secured by any clips or ties.
e) Adjust the throttle and oil pump cable, and the rear brake cable (see Chapter 1).

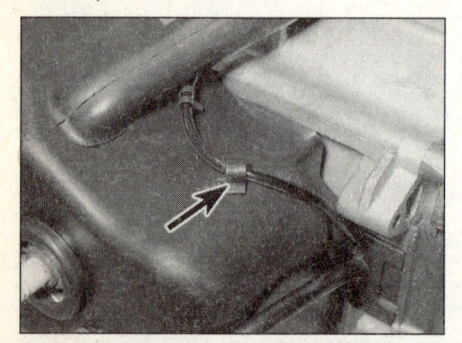

7.2a Free the oil pipe clip (arrowed) . . .

7.3a Unscrew the nuts . . .

6 Disassembly and reassembly – general information

Disassembly

1 Before disassembling the engine, the external surfaces of the unit should be thoroughly cleaned and degreased. This will prevent contamination of the engine internals, and will also make working a lot easier and cleaner. A high flash-point solvent, such as paraffin can be used, or better still, a proprietary engine degreaser such as Gunk. Use old paintbrushes and toothbrushes to work the solvent into the various recesses of the engine casings. Take care to exclude solvent or water from the electrical components and inlet and exhaust ports.

⚠️ **Warning: The use of petrol (gasoline) as a cleaning agent should be avoided because of the risk of fire.**

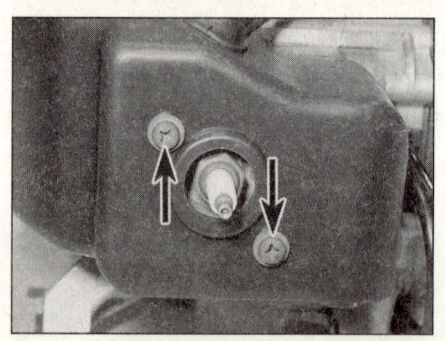

7.2b . . . then remove the screws and lift off the cover

7.3b . . . and draw the head off the cylinder

2 When clean and dry, arrange the unit on the workbench, leaving a suitable clear area for working. Gather a selection of small containers and plastic bags so that parts can be grouped together in an easily identifiable manner. Some paper and a pen should be on hand to permit notes to be made and labels attached where necessary. A supply of clean rag is also required.

3 Before commencing work, read through the appropriate section so that some idea of the necessary procedure can be gained. When removing components it should be noted that great force is seldom required, unless specified. In many cases, a component's reluctance to be removed is indicative of an incorrect approach or removal method – if in any doubt, recheck with the text.

4 When disassembling the engine, keep 'mated' parts that have been in contact with each other during engine operation together. These 'mated' parts must be re-used or renewed as an assembly.

5 Complete engine disassembly should be done in the following general order with reference to the appropriate Sections. Refer to Chapter 2G for details of transmission components disassembly.
Remove the cylinder head.
Remove the cylinder.
Remove the piston.
Remove the alternator.
Remove the variator (see Chapter 2G).
Remove the starter motor (see Chapter 9).
Remove the oil pump and drivebelt.
Remove the reed valve (see Chapter 4).
Separate the crankcase halves.
Remove the crankshaft.

Reassembly

6 Reassembly is accomplished by reversing the general disassembly sequence.

7 Cylinder head – removal, inspection and installation

Note: *The cylinder head can be removed with the engine in the frame. If the engine has been removed, ignore the steps which don't apply.*

Caution: *The engine must be completely cool before beginning this procedure or the cylinder head may become warped.*

Removal

1 Remove the engine cover and, if required, the side panels (see Chapter 7).

2 Pull out the clip securing the oil hose to the cylinder head cover **(see illustration)**. Remove the two screws securing the cylinder head cover and remove the cover, noting how it fits **(see illustration)**. Where fitted, detach the air cooling duct from the fan housing.

3 Unscrew the four cylinder head nuts evenly and a little at a time in a criss-cross sequence until they are all loose, then draw the head off the cylinder studs **(see illustrations)**. If it is

Air-cooled two-stroke engines 2A•7

7.12a Fit the nuts . . .

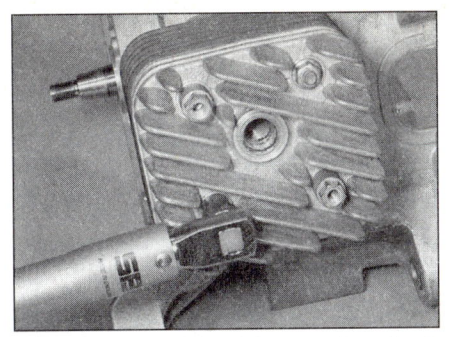

7.12b . . . then tighten them as described to the specified torque

stuck, tap around the joint faces of the cylinder head with a soft-faced mallet to free the head. Do not attempt to free the head by inserting a screwdriver between the head and cylinder – you'll damage the sealing surfaces. Note the relative positions of the different type of cylinder head nuts – two of them are threaded in the top to house the cover screws.

4 There is no cylinder head gasket fitted as standard, the machined face of the cylinder head fitting directly against the machined face of the cylinder. It may found, however, that a gasket is fitted on aftermarket top-end kits.

Inspection

5 Refer to Chapter 1 and decarbonise the cylinder head.
6 Inspect the head very carefully for cracks and other damage. If cracks are found, a new head will be required.
7 Check the mating surfaces on the cylinder head and cylinder for signs of leakage, which could indicate warpage.
8 Using a precision straight-edge, check the head mating surface for warpage. Check vertically, horizontally and diagonally across the head, making four checks in all.

Installation

9 Lubricate the cylinder bore with the recommended two-stroke oil.
10 Ensure both cylinder head and cylinder mating surfaces are clean.
11 Carefully fit the cylinder head onto the cylinder **(see illustration 7.3b)**.
12 Install the four nuts, making sure the special nuts are positioned to accept the cover screws, and tighten them all finger-tight **(see illustration)**. Now tighten them evenly and a little at a time in a criss-cross pattern to the torque setting specified at the beginning of the Chapter **(see illustration)**.
13 Install the cylinder head cover, making sure it locates correctly against the alternator cover, and clip the oil hose to it **(see illustrations 7.2b and 7.2a)**, then install the engine cover and, if removed, the side panels (see Chapter 7).

8 Cylinder – removal, inspection and installation

Note: *The cylinder can be removed with the engine in the frame.*

Removal

1 Remove the exhaust system (see Chapter 4) and the cylinder head (see Section 7).
2 Lift the cylinder up off the studs, supporting the piston as it becomes accessible to prevent it hitting the crankcase **(see illustration)**. If the cylinder is stuck, tap around the joint faces with a soft-faced mallet to free it from the crankcase. Don't attempt to free the cylinder by inserting a screwdriver between it and the crankcase – you'll damage the sealing surfaces. When the cylinder is removed, stuff a clean rag around the piston to prevent anything falling into the crankcase.
3 Remove the gasket and discard it, as a new one must be used **(see illustration)**.

Inspection – 50 cc engines

4 Inspect the cylinder bore carefully for scratches and score marks. A rebore will be necessary to remove any deep scores (see Step 7).
5 Using telescoping gauges and a micrometer, check the dimensions of the cylinder to assess the amount of wear, taper and ovality. Measure near the top (but below the level of the top piston ring at TDC), centre and bottom (but above the level of the bottom ring at BDC) of the bore both parallel to and across the crankshaft axis **(see illustration)**. Calculate any differences between the measurements to determine any taper or ovality in the bore. Compare the results to the cylinder bore specifications at the beginning of this Chapter.
6 Calculate the piston-to-bore clearance by subtracting the piston diameter (see Section 9) from the bore diameter. If the cylinder is in good condition and the piston-to-bore clearance is within specifications, the cylinder can be re-used.
7 If the cylinder is tapered, oval, or worn, badly scratched, scuffed or scored, have it rebored by a Piaggio dealer or motorcycle engineer. If the cylinder is rebored, it will require an oversize piston and rings. If the cylinder has already been rebored to the maximum oversize and is worn or damaged, the cylinder must be renewed. **Note:** *Cylinders and pistons are size-coded during manufacture and it is important that they are of the same size-code. Piaggio list five size-codes (A to E) for the original 50 cc air-cooled two-stroke engine and four (M to P) for the Hi-Per2 engine; see the specifications at the beginning of this Chapter. The size-code is stamped in the gasket surface at the top or base of the cylinder, and in the piston crown. When purchasing a new cylinder or piston, always supply the size-code letter.*
8 Check that all the cylinder head studs are tight in the crankcase halves. If any are loose, remove them and clean their threads. Apply a suitable permanent thread locking compound and tighten them securely.

Inspection – 80 cc and 125 cc models

9 On these engines the cylinder bore is coated with Nicasil, which has a high

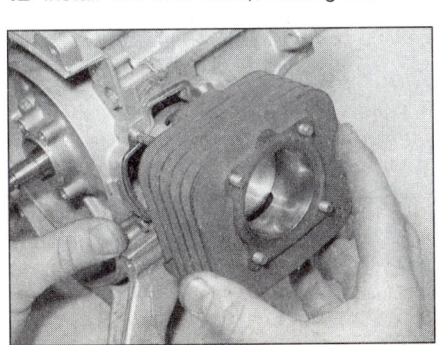

8.2 Draw the cylinder up off the studs

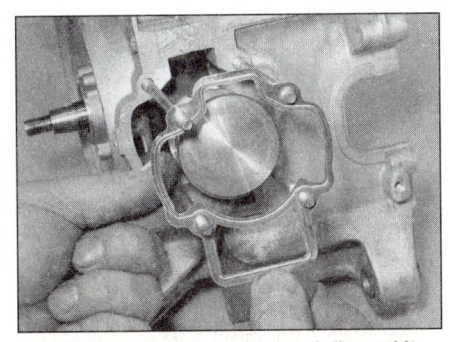

8.3 Remove the gasket and discard it

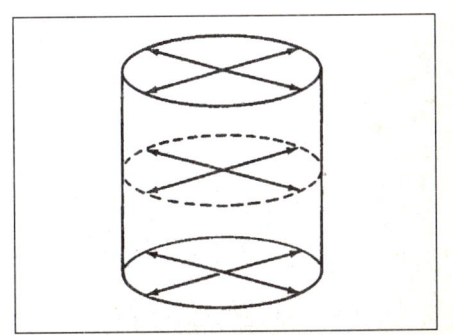

8.5 Measure the cylinder bore in the directions shown

2A•8 Air-cooled two-stroke engines

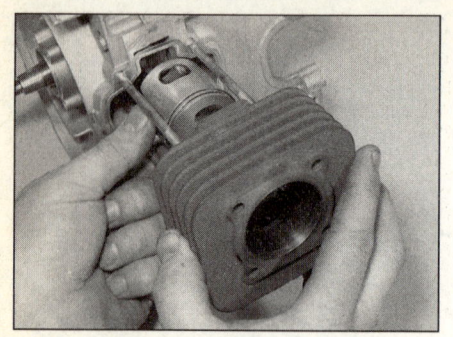

8.14 Fit the cylinder onto the studs

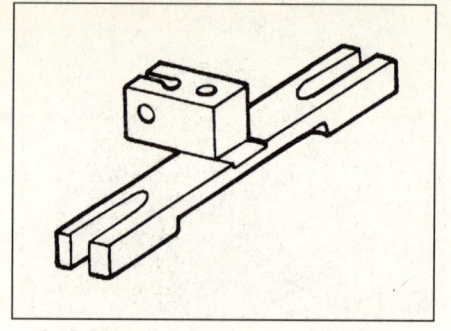

8.18 Mounting bracket for dial gauge

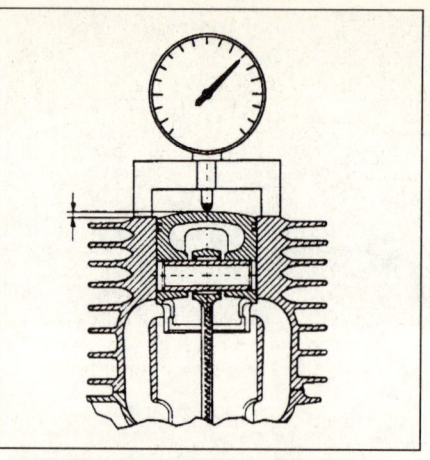

8.21 Checking the cylinder surface-to-piston crown relationship

resistance to wear. The Nicasil coating should last the life of the engine unless serious engine damage, such as seizure, has occurred.

10 Check the cylinder walls carefully for scratches and score marks. If damage is noted, yet the bore is still within the size specification (measure as described above in Step 5), seek the advice of a Piaggio dealer or motorcycle engineer as to its suitability for continued use. If the bore is too badly damaged, a new cylinder must be fitted.
Note: *Cylinders and pistons are size-coded during manufacture and it is important that they are of the same size-code. Piaggio list nine size-codes (A to I) for the original 125 cc air-cooled two-stroke engine; see the specifications at the beginning of this Chapter. The size-code is stamped in the gasket surface at the top or base of the cylinder, and in the piston crown. When purchasing a new cylinder or piston, always supply the size-code letter. Details of size-codes for later 125cc and all 80 cc air-cooled two-stroke engines are not available, but the identification letters on the cylinder and piston should always match.*

11 Calculate the piston-to-bore clearance by subtracting the piston diameter (see Section 9) from the bore diameter. If the cylinder is in good condition and the piston-to-bore clearance is within specifications, the cylinder can be re-used.

12 Check that all the cylinder head studs are tight in the crankcase halves. If any are loose, remove them and clean their threads. Apply a suitable permanent thread locking compound and tighten them securely.

Installation

Note: *On Typhoon 125 and Skipper models, different thickness cylinder base gaskets are available to allow the cylinder top gasket surface to be set at the specified distance of 2.99 ± 0.05 mm below the top of the piston crown (see illustration 8.21). Assemble the cylinder as described below but without a base gasket, and measure the distance with a dial gauge and suitable mounting as described in Steps 18 to 22.*

13 Remove any rag from the crankcase mouth. Lay the new base gasket in place on the crankcase making sure it is the correct way round **(see illustration 8.3)**. Never re-use the old gasket – it will have become compressed.

14 Check that the piston rings are correctly positioned so that the ring locating pin in the piston grooves is between the ring gaps **(see illustration 10.6)**. Lubricate the cylinder bore, piston and piston rings, and the connecting rod big- and small-ends, with two-stroke oil, then fit the cylinder down over the studs until the piston crown fits into the bore **(see illustration)**.

15 Gently push down on the cylinder, making sure the piston enters the bore squarely and does not get cocked sideways. Carefully compress and feed each ring into the bore as the block is lowered. If necessary, use a soft mallet to gently tap the cylinder down, but do not use force if the cylinder appears to be stuck as the piston and/or rings will be damaged.

16 When the piston is correctly installed in the cylinder, press the cylinder down onto the base gasket.

17 On 50 cc and 80 cc models, install the cylinder head (see Section 7).

18 On Typhoon 125 and Skipper models, Piaggio advises that the distance between the cylinder top gasket surface and the piston crown is checked at this stage **(see Note above)**. For this purpose you will require a dial gauge and a mounting plate; Piaggio provide a mounting plate (Pt. No. 020268Y) **(see illustration)**.

19 Set the dial gauge in the mounting plate, and with the mounting plate feet and gauge tip resting against the cylinder top gasket surface, zero the gauge. Rotate the engine so that the piston is part way down the bore.

20 Clamp the mounting plate diagonally across two of the cylinder studs and tighten the stud nuts to 20 to 22 Nm to ensure that the cylinder is held firmly against the crankcase.

21 Rotate the crankshaft via the alternator rotor nut so the piston rises to the top of its stroke (TDC). At this point read off the dial gauge **(see illustration)**. The reading represents the distance between the cylinder top gasket surface and the top of the piston crown. Subtract the specified distance of 2.99 ± 0.05 mm from the reading and the result is the thickness of the base gasket required. Base gaskets are available in 0.2, 0.3, 0.4, 0.5, 0.6, 0.7 and 0.8 mm sizes.

22 Install the cylinder head (see Section 7).

9 Piston – removal, inspection and installation

Note: *The piston can be removed with the engine in the frame.*

Removal

1 Remove the cylinder (see Section 8).

2 Before removing the piston from the connecting rod, stuff a clean rag into the hole around the rod to prevent the circlips or anything else from falling into the crankcase. The piston should have an arrow marked on its crown which should face down towards the exhaust port. If this is not visible, mark the piston accordingly so that it can be installed the correct way round. Note that the arrow may not be visible until the carbon deposits have been scraped off and the piston cleaned.

3 Carefully prise out the circlip on one side of the piston using a pointed instrument or a small flat-bladed screwdriver inserted into the notch **(see illustration)**. Push the piston pin out from the other side to free the piston from

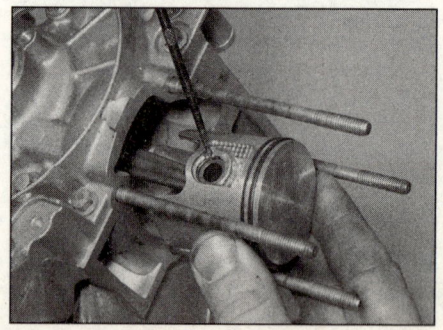

9.3a Remove the circlip . . .

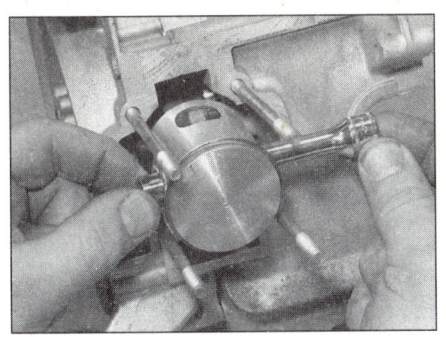

9.3b . . . and push out the piston pin, using a socket extension if required

9.5a Remove the piston rings carefully using your thumbs . . .

9.5b . . . or a thin blade

the connecting rod **(see illustration)**. Remove the other circlip and discard them, as new ones must be used. Use a socket extension to push the piston pin out if required.

> **HAYNES HiNT** To prevent the circlip from pinging away or from dropping into the crankcase, pass a rod or screwdriver with a greater diameter than the gap between the circlip ends, through the piston pin. This will trap the circlip if it springs out.

> **HAYNES HiNT** If a piston pin is a tight fit in the piston bosses, heat the piston gently with a hot air gun – this will expand the alloy piston sufficiently to release its grip on the pin.

Inspection

4 Before the inspection process can be carried out, the piston must be cleaned and the old piston rings removed. Note that if the cylinder is being rebored, piston inspection can be overlooked as a new one will be fitted.

5 Using your thumbs or an old feeler gauge blade, carefully remove the rings from the piston **(see illustrations)**. Do not nick or gouge the piston in the process. Note which way up each ring fits and in which groove, as they must be installed in their original positions if being re-used. The upper surface of each ring should be marked at one end.

6 Scrape all traces of carbon from the top of the piston. A hand-held wire brush or a piece of fine emery cloth can be used once most of the deposits have been scraped away. Do not, under any circumstances, use a wire brush mounted in a drill motor to remove deposits from the piston; the piston material is soft and will be eroded away by the wire brush.

7 Use a piston ring groove cleaning tool to remove any carbon deposits from the ring grooves. If a tool is not available, a piece broken off an old ring will do the job. Be very careful to remove only the carbon deposits. Do not remove any metal and do not nick or gouge the sides of the ring grooves.

8 Once the deposits have been removed, clean the piston with solvent and dry it thoroughly.

9 Carefully inspect the piston for cracks around the skirt, at the pin bosses and at the ring lands. Also check that the circlip grooves are not damaged.

10 Normal piston wear appears as even, vertical wear on the thrust surfaces of the piston and slight looseness of the top ring in its groove. If the skirt is scored or scuffed, the engine may have been suffering from overheating and/or abnormal combustion, which caused excessively high operating temperatures.

11 A hole in the piston crown is an extreme indication that abnormal combustion (pre-ignition) has occurred. Burned areas at the edge of the piston crown are usually evidence of spark knock (detonation). If any of the above problems exist, the causes must be corrected or the damage will occur again.

12 Check the piston-to-bore clearance by measuring the bore (see Section 8) and the piston diameter. Measure the piston 25 mm down from the bottom of the lower piston ring groove and at 90° to the piston pin axis **(see illustration)**. Subtract the piston diameter from the bore diameter to obtain the clearance. If it is greater than the specified figure, the piston must be renewed (assuming the bore itself is within limits, otherwise a rebore is necessary).

13 Apply clean two-stroke oil to the piston pin, insert it into the piston and check for any freeplay between the two **(see illustration)**. Measure the pin external diameter and compare the measurement to the specifications at the beginning of the Chapter **(see illustration)**. Renew the pin if it is worn beyond the specified limits.

14 Check the condition of the needle roller bearing in the connecting rod small-end (see

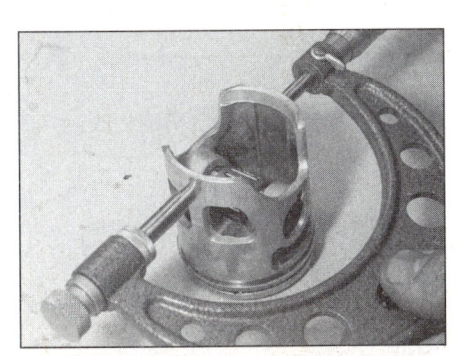

9.12 Measure the piston diameter with a micrometer at the specified distance from the bottom of the lower ring groove

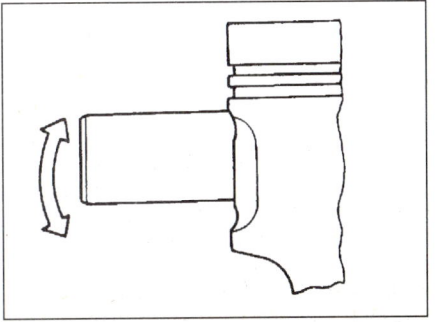

9.13a Slip the pin into the piston and try to rock it back-and-forth. If it's loose, renew the piston and pin

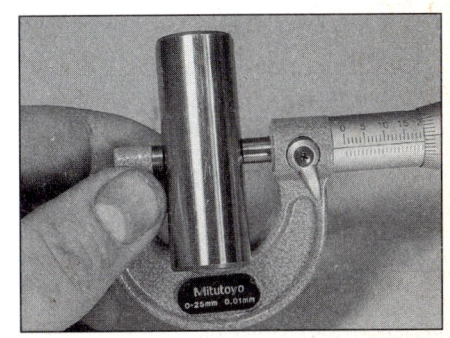

9.13b Measure the external diameter of the pin

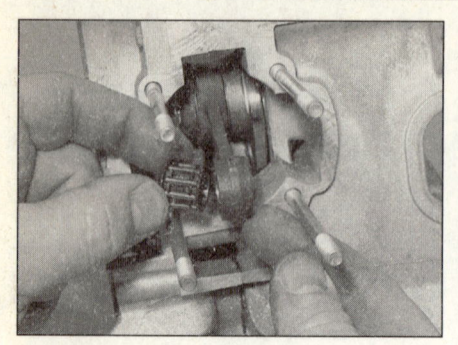

2A•10 Air-cooled two-stroke engines

9.14 Remove the needle roller bearing and check its condition

9.18a Make sure the arrow on the piston faces the exhaust port

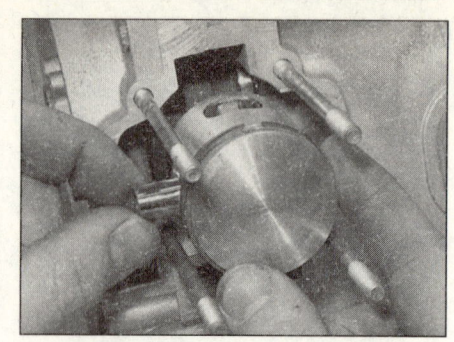

9.18b Line up the piston and insert the pin . . .

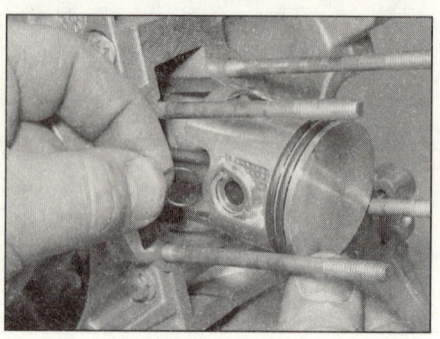

9.18c . . . and secure it with the circlip

illustration). A worn small-end bearing will produce a metallic rattle, most audible when the engine is under load, and increasing as engine speed rises. This should not be confused with big-end bearing wear, which produces a pronounced knocking noise. Assemble the bearing and the piston pin on the connecting rod; there should be no discernible freeplay between the piston pin, the bearing and the connecting rod. If the piston pin is good (see Step 13), measure the internal diameter of the small-end bore and compare it to the Specifications. If the small-end has worn, the connecting rod and crankshaft assembly must be renewed (see Section 15). If the small-end is good, fit a new bearing.

15 Ensure that the correct bearing is fitted. A mark on the connecting rod, either a I, II, III or IIII indicates the small-end size, and this mark must be matched with a similar mark on the new bearing, or by a colour code.

Connecting rod marked I –
bearing colour copper or gold.
Connecting rod marked II –
bearing colour blue.
Connecting rod marked III –
bearing colour white or silver.
Connecting rod marked IIII –
bearing colour green.

16 If a new piston is to be fitted, ensure the correct size of piston is ordered. Compare the piston size with the specifications at the beginning of this Chapter to determine if the piston is standard, or oversize, indicating a rebored cylinder. Note the piston size-code. The size-code is stamped in the piston crown, and the same size-code is stamped in the gasket surface at the top or base of the cylinder. When purchasing a new piston, always supply the size-code letter.

Installation

17 Inspect and install the piston rings (see Section 10).
18 Lubricate the piston pin, the piston pin bore and the connecting rod small-end bore with two-stroke oil. Install a new circlip in one side of the piston (do not re-use old circlips). Line up the piston on the connecting rod, making sure the arrow on the piston crown faces down towards the exhaust, and insert the piston pin from the other side **(see illustrations).** Secure the pin with the other new circlip **(see illustration).** When installing the circlips, compress them only just enough to fit them in the piston, and make sure they are properly seated in their grooves with the open end away from the removal notch.
19 Install the cylinder (see Section 8).

10 Piston rings –
inspection and installation

1 New piston rings should be fitted whenever an engine is being overhauled. Before installing the new piston rings, the ring end gaps must be checked.
2 Insert the top ring into the bottom of the cylinder and square it up with the cylinder walls by pushing it in with the top of the piston. The ring should be about 20 mm from the bottom edge of the cylinder. To measure the end gap, slip a feeler gauge between the ends of the ring and compare the measurement to the specifications at the beginning of the Chapter **(see illustration).**
3 If the gap is larger or smaller than specified, double check to make sure that you have the correct rings before proceeding.
4 Excess end gap is not critical unless it is greater than 0.7 mm. Again, double-check to make sure you have the correct rings for your engine and check that the bore is not worn.

10.2 Measuring piston ring installed end gap

5 Repeat the procedure for the other ring.
6 Once the ring end gaps have been checked/corrected, the rings can be installed on the piston. First identify the ring locating pin in each piston ring groove – the rings must be positioned so that the pin is in between the open ends of the ring **(see illustration).**
7 The upper surface of each ring should be marked at one end. Install the lower ring first. Make sure that the identification letter near the end gap is facing up. Fit the ring into the lower groove in the piston. Do not expand the ring any more than is necessary to slide it into place **(see illustrations 9.5a and 9.5b).**
8 Now install the top ring into the top groove in the piston. Make sure the identification letter near the end gap is facing up.
9 Once the rings are correctly installed check that their gaps are positioned each side of the pin.

10.6 Make sure the pin in each groove is between the ends of the ring (arrow)

Air-cooled two-stroke engines 2A•11

11.3 Remove the alternator cover

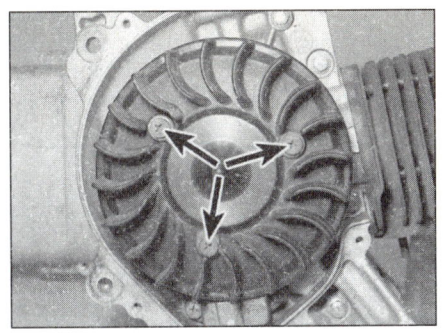

11.4 The fan is secured by three screws (arrowed)

11 Cooling fan – removal and installation

Note: *The cooling fan can be removed with the engine in the frame.*

Removal

1 Remove the bodywork (see Chapter 7).
2 Pull out the clip securing the oil hose to the cylinder head cover (see illustration 7.2a). Remove the two screws securing the cylinder head cover and remove the cover, noting how it fits **(see illustration 7.2b)**. Where fitted, detach the air cooling duct from the fan housing. Where fitted, unclip the secondary air system from the alternator cover (see Chapter 1, Section 21).
3 Remove the three screws securing the alternator cover to the crankcase and remove the cover **(see illustration)**.

4 Remove the three screws securing the cooling fan to the alternator rotor and remove the fan **(see illustration)**.

Installation

5 Installation is the reverse of removal.

12 Alternator rotor and stator – removal and installation

Note: *The alternator can be removed with the engine in the frame.*

Removal

1 Remove the cooling fan (see Section 11).
2 Trace the wiring back from the alternator and pulse generator coil and disconnect it at the connectors. Free the wiring from any clips or guides and feed it through to the alternator.
3 To remove the rotor nut it is necessary to stop the rotor from turning. A strap wrench can be used around the rotor periphery, although be careful not to damage the ignition pulse generator coil, or you can make up a tool which engages the slots in the rotor face (see *Tool Tip*) **(see illustration)**. With the rotor securely held, unscrew the nut.

> **TOOL TIP** *A rotor holding tool can easily be made using two strips of steel bolted together in the middle, with a bolt through each end which locates into the slots in the rotor. Do not allow the bolts to extend too far through the rotor slots otherwise the coils could be damaged.*

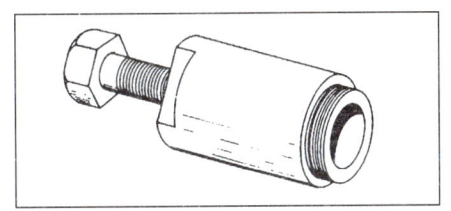

4 To remove the rotor from the shaft it is necessary to use the Piaggio service tool (Part No. 020162Y) **(see illustration)** or a two-legged puller. If using the service tool, screw the body of the tool into the threads provided in the rotor, then tighten the centre bolt down so that the rotor is drawn off the end of the crankshaft; hold the body of the tool using a spanner on its flats. If using a two-legged puller, assemble the puller legs through the rotor slots and tighten the centre bolt down onto the crankshaft end until the rotor is drawn off **(see illustration)**. If it is loose, remove the Woodruff key from the shaft, noting how it fits **(see illustration)**.
5 To remove the stator from the crankcase, it is also necessary to remove the pulse generator coil, as they come as a linked assembly. Unscrew the three screws securing the stator and the two screws securing the coil and remove them together **(see illustration)**. Draw the rubber wiring boot out of the crankcase and carefully pull the wiring through the hole, taking care not to snag it **(see illustration)**.

12.3 With the rotor securely held, unscrew the rotor nut (arrowed)

12.4a The Piaggio rotor removal tool

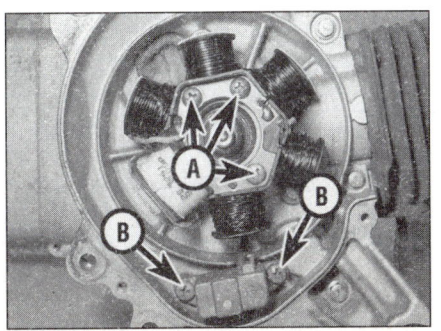

12.4b Using a two-legged puller to remove the rotor

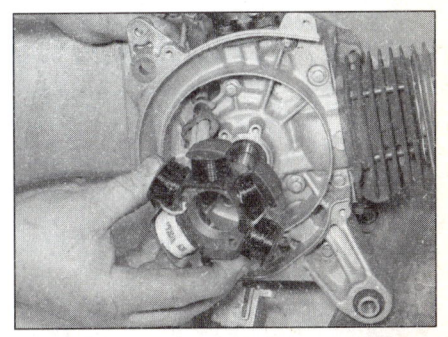

12.4c Remove the Woodruff key for safekeeping

12.5a Remove the stator screws (A) and the pulse generator coil screws (B) . . .

12.5b . . . and remove the assembly, feeding the wiring through the casing

2A•12 Air-cooled two-stroke engines

12.6a Feed the wiring through the hole ...

12.6b ... then install the stator and coil

12.7a Fit the Woodruff key (arrowed) ...

12.7b ... then align the slot in the rotor (arrowed) with the key and install the rotor

12.8a Fit the nut ...

12.8b ... and tighten it to the specified torque, using the tool to hold the rotor

Installation

6 Feed the wiring through the hole in the crankcase and press the rubber boot into the hole, then install the stator and pulse generator coil onto the crankcase (see illustration). Apply a suitable non-permanent thread locking compound to the stator screw threads, then install the screws and tighten them securely (see illustration).
7 Clean the tapered end of the crankshaft and the corresponding mating surface on the inside of the rotor with a suitable solvent. Make sure that no metal objects have attached themselves to the magnets on the inside of the rotor. If removed, fit the Woodruff key into its slot in the shaft, then install the rotor onto the shaft, aligning the slot in the rotor with the key (see illustrations).
8 Install the rotor nut and its washer, and tighten it to the torque setting specified at the beginning of the Chapter, using the method employed on removal to prevent the rotor from turning (see illustrations).
9 Reconnect the wiring at the connectors and secure it with any clips or ties.
10 Install the cooling fan (see Section 11).

13 Starter pinion assembly – removal, inspection and installation

Note: *The starter pinion assembly can be removed with the engine in the frame.*

Removal

1 Remove the drivebelt cover (see Chapter 2G).
2 Remove the starter pinion assembly, noting how it fits (see illustration).

Inspection

3 Check the starter pinion assembly for any signs of damage or wear, particularly for chipped or broken teeth on either of the pinions.
4 Rotate the outer pinion and check that it moves smoothly up-and-down the shaft, and that it returns easily to its rest position (see illustration).
5 The starter pinion assembly is supplied as a complete unit; if any of the component parts is worn or damaged, the unit will have to be renewed.
6 The starter pinion mechanism should not be lubricated; apply a smear of grease to both ends of the pinion shaft before reassembly.

Installation

7 Installation is the reverse of removal. Ensure the inner pinion engages with the starter motor shaft

14 Oil pump and belt – removal, inspection, installation and bleeding

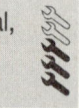

Note: *The oil pump and drivebelt can be removed with the engine in the frame.*

Removal

1 Remove the drivebelt cover; to access the pump drivebelt, also remove the variator (see Chapter 2G). Remove the starter pinion assembly (see Section 13). If the pump is being removed rather than just being

13.2 Remove the pinion assembly, noting how it fits

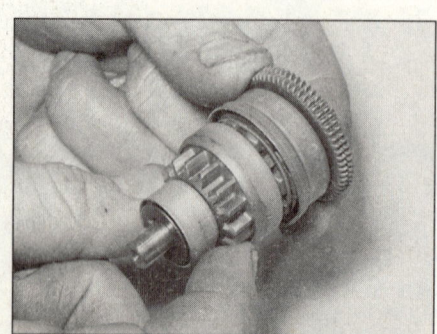

13.4 Check the pinion as described

Air-cooled two-stroke engines 2A•13

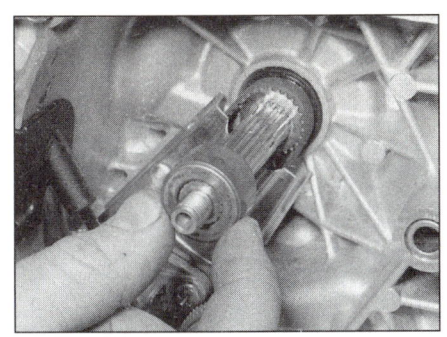

14.2 Slide the spacer off the shaft

14.3a Inlet hose (A), outlet hose (B). Remove the two screws (C) . . .

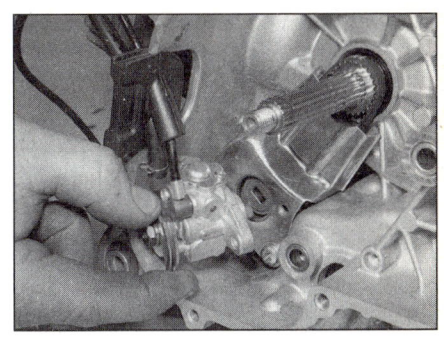

14.3b . . . and remove the pump, along with the hoses, if still attached

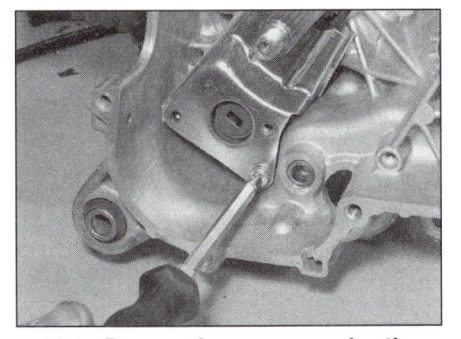

14.4a Remove the screw securing the guard plate . . .

14.4b . . . and remove the inner plate (arrowed)

14.4c Remove the belt, the driven pulley (A) and its washer, and the drive pulley (B)

displaced for belt renewal, detach the oil inlet and outlet hoses from either the pump itself **(see illustration 14.3a)**, noting which fits where, or from the oil tank and carburettor respectively. Seal the end of the inlet hose or plug the outlet from the oil tank to prevent the tank from draining. Also disconnect the cable from the pump cam (see Chapter 4).

2 Draw the spacer off the shaft (not necessary if only removing the pump, leaving the belt in place) **(see illustration)**.

3 Remove the two screws securing the oil pump, then remove the pump, sliding the rubber grommet securing the hoses out of its cutout in the crankcase in the process (if the hoses are still attached) **(see illustrations)**.

Note how the drive tab on the back of the pump locates in the slot in the driven pulley.

4 Remove the remaining screw securing the guard plate and remove the plate and the inner plate behind it **(see illustrations)**. Slip the drivebelt off the pulleys, then remove the driven pulley and the thrustwasher behind it, and slide the drive pulley off the shaft **(see illustration)**.

Inspection

5 Check the pump for obvious signs of damage. Turn the drive tab by hand and check that the pump rotates smoothly and freely **(see illustration)**. Also check that the cable cam turns smoothly and returns to rest

under pressure of the return spring **(see illustration)**.

6 If the operation of the pump is suspect, or for internal cleaning, remove the screws securing both cover plates and remove the plates. Clean the pump using a solvent, and inspect the internal components for wear and damage. No individual components are available, so if the pump is faulty it must be renewed as a unit.

7 Check along the length of the drivebelt for splits, cracks or broken teeth and renew the belt if necessary. The belt should be renewed regardless of its condition at the service interval specified in Chapter 1, or during the course of dismantling.

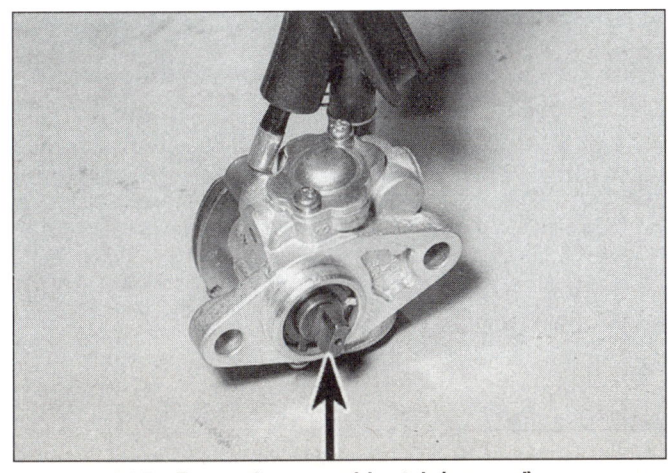

14.5a Rotate the pump drive tab (arrowed) . . .

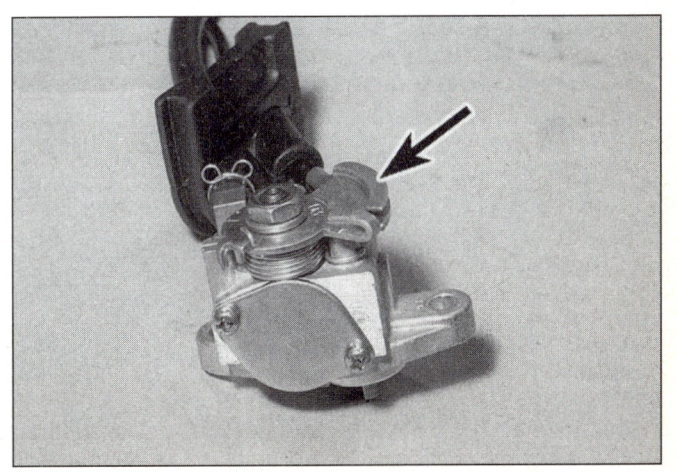

14.5b . . . and the cable cam (arrowed) by hand

2A•14 Air-cooled two-stroke engines

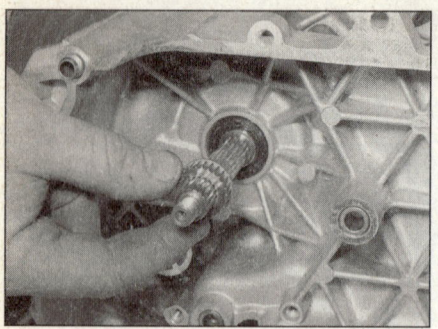

14.8a Fit the drive pulley . . .

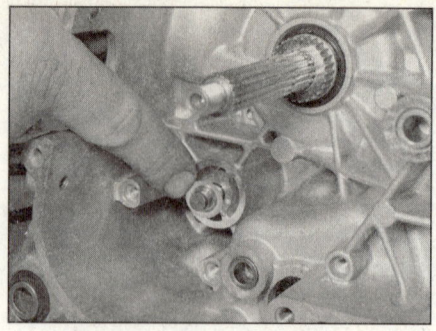

14.8b . . . the thrustwasher . . .

14.8c . . . the driven pulley . . .

14.8d . . . and the new drivebelt

14.9a Fit the inner plate . . .

14.9b . . . and the guide plate

Installation

8 Slide the drive pulley, with its shouldered side innermost, onto the crankshaft, then fit the thrustwasher and the driven pulley, with its slot for the pump drive tab outermost **(see illustrations)**. Fit the belt onto the pulleys, making sure the teeth mesh correctly **(see illustration)**.

9 Fit the inner plate, locating the raised sections on the inside in the recesses in the screw holes **(see illustration)**. Fit the guard plate and secure it with the single screw **(see illustration)**.

10 Install the pump, locating the drive tab in the slot in the driven pulley and the hose grommet in its cutout (if removed) **(see illustration 14.3b)**, and secure it with its screws **(see illustration)**.

11 If detached, connect the oil inlet and outlet hoses to the pump, oil tank or carburettor, according to how they were removed, making sure they are secured by their clamps, where fitted. Also connect the cable to the pump cam (see Chapter 4). Bleed the pump as described below, then adjust the cable (see Chapter 1).

Caution: Note that cable adjustment is important to ensure that the oil pump delivers the correct amount of oil to the engine and is correctly synchronised with the throttle.

12 Slide the spacer onto the crankshaft **(see illustration 14.2)**, then install the variator (see Chapter 2G) and the starter pinion assembly (see Section 13).

Bleeding

13 Bleeding the pump is the process of removing the air from it and allowing it to be filled with oil. Simply remove the bleed screw, and wait until oil, without any air mixed with it, starts to flow out of the hole, then refit the screw **(see illustration)**.

14 It is important that the oil lines are bled of air as well as the pump. Ensure the ignition switch is OFF. Disconnect the oil outlet hose from the carburettor and crank the engine with the kickstarter until oil, without any air mixed with it, flows out the hose, then reconnect the hose and secure it with the clip.

15 Crankcase halves, crankshaft and connecting rod and bearings

Note: To separate the crankcase halves, the engine must be removed from the frame.

Separation

1 To access the crankshaft and its bearings, the crankcase must be split into two parts.

2 To enable the crankcases to be separated, the engine must be removed from the frame (see Section 5). Before the crankcases can be separated the following components must be removed:
a) *Cylinder head (Section 7)*
b) *Cylinder (Section 8)*
c) *Alternator rotor and stator (Section 12)*
d) *Reed valve (Chapter 4)*
e) *Starter motor (Chapter 9)*
f) *Oil pump and drivebelt (see Section 14)*

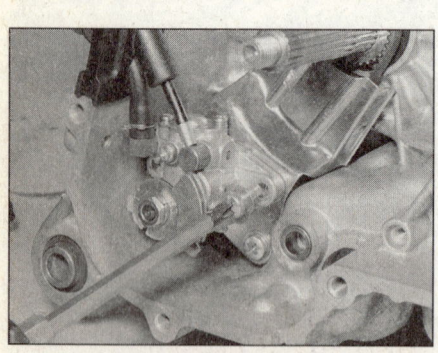

14.10 Install the pump and secure it with its screws

14.13 Remove the bleed screw (arrowed) and allow the air to bleed out

Air-cooled two-stroke engines 2A•15

15.3 The crankcase halves are secured by eight bolts (arrowed)

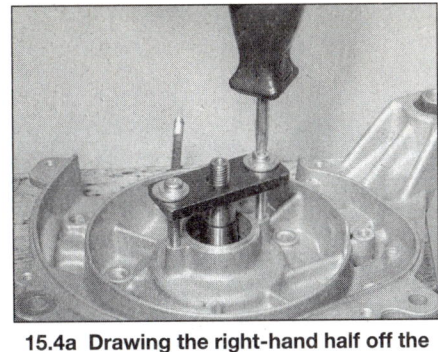

15.4a Drawing the right-hand half off the crankshaft

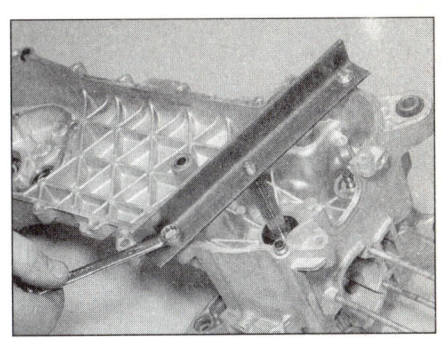

15.4b Pressing the crankshaft out of the left-hand half

3 Unscrew the eight crankcase bolts evenly, a little at a time and in a criss-cross sequence until they are all finger-tight, then remove them **(see illustration)**.
4 Carefully remove the right-hand crankcase half from the left-hand half. If necessary, Piaggio produce a service tool (Part No. 020163Y) to aid separation of the crankcase halves. Alternatively, heat the crankcase around the outside of the bearing housing, and/or use the set-ups shown **(see illustrations)**. The first will draw the right-hand half off the crankshaft, leaving the shaft in the left-hand half. The second will press the crankshaft out of the left-hand half. The end of the crankshaft can be tapped using a soft-faced mallet to help free it, but take great care not to use too much force and make sure the crankshaft is supported by an assistant to prevent it from dropping if it suddenly comes free. The crankshaft is a pressed-together unit, so any undue shock or force could upset the relative positions of the two sections. **Note:** *If the halves do not separate easily, make sure all fasteners have been removed. Do not try and separate the halves by levering against the crankcase mating surfaces as they are easily scored and will not seal correctly afterwards.*
5 Before removing the oil seals, measure their set depth in each crankcase half, as the new ones must be correctly positioned. Drive the oil seal out of each crankcase half using a punch inserted from the inside **(see illustration)**.
6 Remove the main bearings from either the crankcase halves or from the crankshaft itself. To remove them from the crankcases, heat the bearing housings using a hot air gun, then use an internal bearing puller to draw the bearings out **(see illustration)**. Alternatively they can be driven out from the outside of the crankcase. To remove them from the crankshaft, use an external bearing puller. Check the condition of the bearings – they should spin freely and smoothly without any rough spots or excessive noise. Renew them if there is any doubt as to their condition.

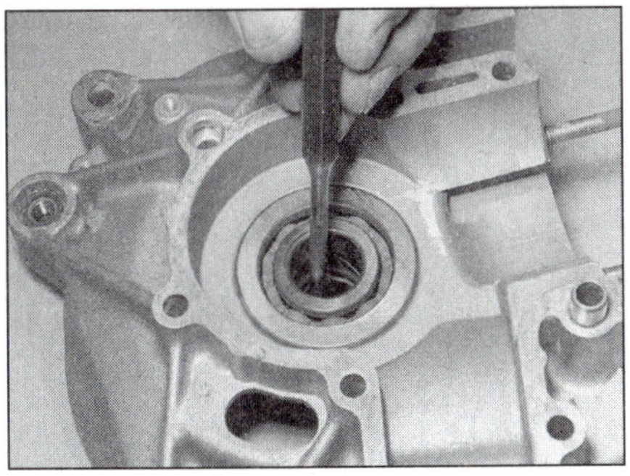

Inspection

7 The crankcases should be cleaned thoroughly with new solvent and dried with compressed air.
8 All traces of old gasket sealant should be removed from the mating surfaces. Minor damage to the surfaces can be cleaned up with a fine file.
Caution: *Be very careful not to nick or gouge the crankcase mating surfaces or oil leaks will result. Check both crankcase halves very carefully for cracks and other damage.*
9 Small cracks or holes in aluminium castings may be repaired with an epoxy resin adhesive as a temporary measure. Permanent repairs can only be effected by argon-arc welding, and only a specialist in this process is in a position to advise on the economy or practical aspect of such a repair. If any damage is found that can't be repaired, renew both crankcase halves as a set.
10 Damaged threads can be economically reclaimed by using a diamond section wire insert, of the Heli-Coil type, which is easily fitted after drilling and retapping the affected thread.
11 Sheared studs or screws can usually be removed with screw extractors, which consist of a tapered, left-thread screw of very hard steel. These are inserted into a predrilled hole in the stud, and usually succeed in dislodging the most stubborn stud or screw **(see illustrations)**.
12 The crankshaft should not give any problems under normal use. The most likely problems will be worn main bearings or a worn big-end bearing, due most likely to a lubrication failure. If the main bearings have failed, excessive rumbling and vibration will be felt when the engine is running. Sometimes

15.5 Driving out the oil seals

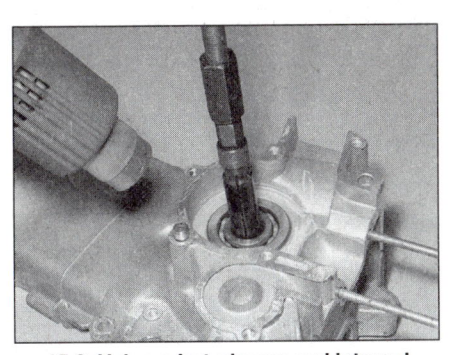

15.6 Using a hot-air gun and internal bearing puller to remove the bearing

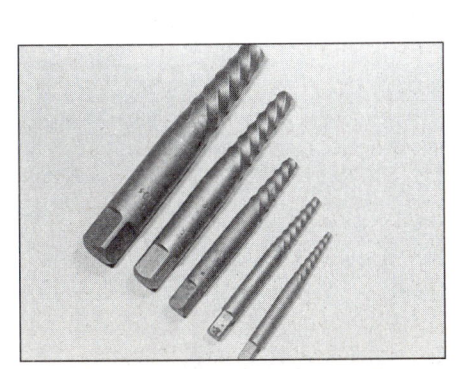

15.11a A set of screw extractors is a useful addition to the workshop

15.11b This type of screw extractor is screwed anti-clockwise into the broken off fastener

2A•16 Air-cooled two-stroke engines

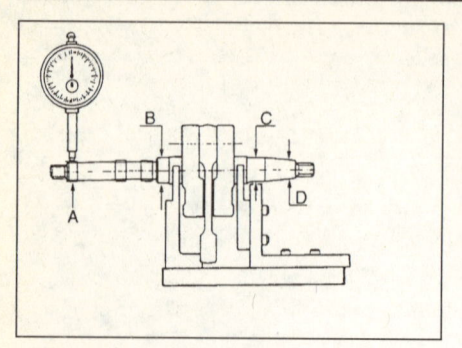

15.14 Check crankshaft runout at points A, B, C and D

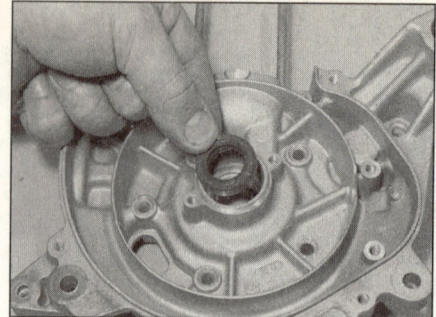

15.15a Fit the new oil seals . . .

15.15b . . . and drive them in to the correct depth

this may cause the oil seals to fail, resulting in a loss of compression and poor running.

13 A worn big-end bearing will produce a pronounced knocking noise, most audible when the engine is under load, and increasing as engine speed rises. This should not be confused with small-end bearing wear, which produces a lighter, metallic rattle. To assess the condition of the big-end bearing, grasp the small-end of the connecting rod and alternately pull it away from and push it into the crankshaft, checking for any freeplay between the two. If any freeplay is noted, the bearing is worn and the crankshaft assembly must be renewed. Take care not confuse the small amount of side-to-side play between the rod and the crankshaft webs with play in the bearing itself. Refer to Section 9 for small-end bearing checks.

14 Place the crankshaft on V-blocks and check the runout at the main bearing journals using a dial gauge **(see illustration)**. Compare the reading to the maximum specified at the beginning of the Chapter. If the runout exceeds the limit, the crankshaft must be renewed, although it may be possible to have the crankshaft trued by an engineer.

Reassembly

15 Fit the new crankshaft oil seals into the crankcase halves and drive them to the previously measured set-depth using a seal driver or socket, making sure they enter squarely **(see illustrations)**.

16 Fit the bearings onto the crankshaft. It will be necessary to first heat the bearings in an oil bath to around 100°C, then to tap them onto the shaft using a suitable length of tube that just fits over the shaft and bears onto the inner race only of the bearing - do not drive the bearings on using the outer race as they will be damaged **(see illustration)**. If the bearings do not fit easily they are not hot enough.

⚠ *Warning: This must be done very carefully to avoid the risk of personal injury.*

17 If not already done, remove all traces of sealant from the crankcase mating surfaces. Generously lubricate the crankshaft, particularly around the bearings, with the recommended two-stroke oil, then use a rag soaked in high flash-point solvent to wipe over the mating surfaces of both crankcase halves to remove all traces of oil.

18 Now heat the right-hand crankcase half around the main bearing housing, then fit the crankshaft into the case, making sure the bearing is pushed fully into its housing **(see illustrations)**. If required, a freeze spray can be used on the bearing itself to aid installation. Allow the case to cool, then apply a small amount of suitable sealant to the mating surface of the case **(see illustrations)**. Heat the left-hand crankcase half around the bearing housing and fit the halves together, again using the freeze spray on the bearing if required, and making sure the main bearing is fully pushed home.

Caution: Do not apply an excessive amount of sealant as it will ooze out when the case halves are assembled.

19 Check that the crankcase halves are correctly seated. **Note:** *If they have been sufficiently heated, they should fit together without force.* If the casings are not correctly

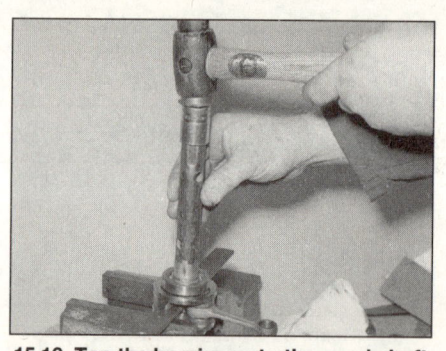

15.16 Tap the bearing onto the crankshaft – do not use excessive force

15.18a Heat the crankcase . . .

15.18b . . . and install the crankshaft

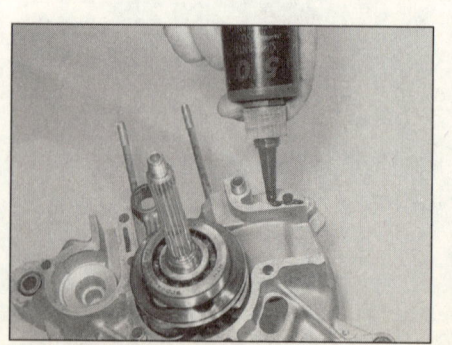

15.18c Apply the sealant and join the halves

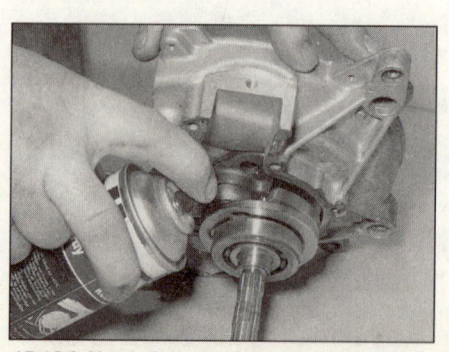

15.18d Use a freeze spray on the bearings to ease installation if required

15.20 Tighten the crankcase bolts to the specified torque

15.21 Tap the end of the crankshaft until the endfloat is correct and the shaft turns freely

seated, remove the right-hand crankcase half and investigate the problem. Do not attempt to pull them together using the crankcase bolts as the casing will crack and be ruined.
20 Clean the threads of the crankcase bolts and secure them finger-tight at first, then tighten them evenly a little at a time in a criss-cross sequence to the torque setting specified at the beginning of the Chapter **(see illustration)**. Do not worry at this stage if the crankshaft appears stiff or tight when turned – this should be rectified when the endfloat is set.
21 Check the amount of crankshaft endfloat using a dial gauge and compare the result to the amount specified at the beginning of the Chapter. The dial gauge should be supported so that its tip rests against the end of the crankshaft – push and pull the crankshaft to obtain a reading on the gauge. If the amount recorded is less than the amount specified, lightly tap the end of the crankshaft with a soft-faced mallet until the specified amount is achieved **(see illustration)**. Rotate the crankshaft by hand – if there are any signs of undue stiffness, tight or rough spots, or of any other problem, the fault must be rectified before proceeding further.
22 Install all other removed assemblies in the reverse of the sequence given in Step 2.

16 Initial start-up after overhaul

1 Make sure the oil tank is at least partly full and the pump is correctly adjusted (see Chapter 1) and bled of air (see Section 14).
2 Make sure there is fuel in the tank.
3 With the ignition OFF, operate the kickstart a couple of times to check that the engine turns over easily.
4 Turn the ignition ON, start the engine and allow it to run at a slow idle until it reaches operating temperature. Do not be alarmed if there is a little smoke from the exhaust – this will be due to the oil used to lubricate the piston and bore during assembly and should subside after a while.
5 If the engine proves reluctant to start, remove the spark plug and check that it has not become wet and oily. If it has, clean it and try again. If the engine refuses to start, go through the fault finding charts at the end of this manual to identify the problem.

17 Recommended running-in procedure

1 Treat the engine gently for the first few miles to allow any new parts to bed-in.
2 Even greater care is necessary if the engine has been rebored or a new crankshaft has been installed. In the case of a rebore, the engine will have to be run-in as when new. This means a restraining hand on the throttle until at least 600 miles (1000 km) have been covered. There's no point in keeping to any set speed limit – the main idea is to keep from labouring the engine and to gradually increase performance up to the 600 mile (1000 km) mark. Make sure that the throttle position is varied to vary engine speed, and use full throttle for only short bursts, but do not allow the machine to attain more than 80% full speed (70% on Skipper and Typhoon 125) or to maintain any one speed for too long. Experience is the best guide, since it's easy to tell when an engine is running freely.

Chapter 2 Part B:
Liquid-cooled two-stroke engines (NRG MC², NRG MC³ DD, NRG Power DD, Zip SP, Hexagon)

Refer to the beginning of Chapter 1 for model identification details

Contents

Alternator rotor and stator – removal and installation	11
Crankcase halves, crankshaft and connecting rod and bearings	14
Cylinder – removal, inspection and installation	8
Cylinder head – decarbonisation	see Chapter 1
Cylinder head – removal, inspection and installation	7
Disassembly and reassembly – general information	6
Engine/transmission unit – removal and installation	5
General information	1
Idle speed – check and adjustment	see Chapter 1
Initial start-up after overhaul	15
Major engine repair – general note	4
Operations possible with the engine in the frame	2
Operations requiring engine removal	3
Oil pump and drivebelt – removal, inspection, installation and bleeding	13
Piston – removal, inspection and installation	9
Piston rings – inspection and installation	10
Recommended running-in procedure	16
Spark plug gap – check and adjustment	see Chapter 1
Starter motor – removal and installation	see Chapter 9
Starter pinion assembly – removal, inspection and installation	12
Water pump – check, removal and installation	see Chapter 3

Degrees of difficulty

Easy, suitable for novice with little experience	Fairly easy, suitable for beginner with some experience	Fairly difficult, suitable for competent DIY mechanic	Difficult, suitable for experienced DIY mechanic	Very difficult, suitable for expert DIY or professional

Specifications

NRG MC², NRG MC³ DD, Zip SP

General

Type	Single cylinder two-stroke
Capacity	49.4 cc
Bore	40.0 mm
Stroke	39.3 mm
Compression ratio	10.9 to 1

Cylinder

Bore
Standard	39.99 to 40.01 mm
1st oversize	40.19 to 40.21 mm
2nd oversize	40.39 to 40.41 mm

Connecting rod

Small-end internal diameter
Size I	17.007 to 17.011 mm
Size II	17.003 to 17.007 mm
Size III	17.001 to 17.003 mm

Piston

Piston diameter (measured 25 mm down from lower ring groove, at 90° to piston pin axis)
Standard	39.94 to 39.96 mm
1st oversize	40.14 to 40.16 mm
2nd oversize	40.34 to 40.36 mm
Piston-to-bore clearance	0.045 to 0.055 mm
Piston pin diameter	11.999 to 12.005 mm

Piston rings
Ring end gap (installed) .... 0.10 to 0.25 mm

Crankshaft
Runout (max)
   At middle and right-hand end .... 0.03 mm
   At left-hand end .... 0.02 mm
Endfloat .... 0.03 to 0.09 mm

Cylinder base gasket selection
Cylinder top gasket surface-to-piston crown measurement   **Gasket thickness**
   3.26 mm to 3.45 mm .... 0.75 mm
   3.10 mm to 3.25 mm .... 0.5 mm
   2.85 mm to 3.09 mm .... 0.4 mm

Torque settings
Engine front mounting bolt .... 33 to 41 Nm
Shock absorber lower mounting bolt .... 33 to 41 Nm
Cylinder head nuts .... 10 to 11 Nm
Crankcase bolts .... 12 to 13 Nm
Alternator rotor nut .... 40 to 44 Nm

NRG Power DD

General
Type .... Single cylinder two-stroke
Capacity .... 49.4 cc
Bore .... 40.0 mm
Stroke .... 39.3 mm
Compression ratio .... 11.3 to 1

Cylinder bore
Standard
   Size code M .... 39.997 to 40.004 mm
   Size code N .... 40.004 to 40.011 mm
   Size code O .... 40.011 to 40.018 mm
   Size code P .... 40.018 to 40.025 mm
1st oversize .... 40.197 to 40.225 mm
2nd oversize .... 40.397 to 40.425 mm

Connecting rod
Small-end internal diameter
   Standard .... 17.001 to 17.011 mm
   Service limit .... 17.060 mm

Piston
Piston diameter (measured 25 mm down from lower ring groove, at 90° to piston pin axis)
Standard
   Size code M .... 39.943 to 39.950 mm
   Size code N .... 39.950 to 39.957 mm
   Size code O .... 39.957 to 39.964 mm
   Size code P .... 39.964 to 39.971 mm
1st oversize .... 40.143 to 40.171 mm
2nd oversize .... 40.343 to 40.371 mm
Piston-to-bore clearance .... 0.047 to 0.061 mm
Piston pin diameter .... 12.001 to 12.005 mm
Piston pin bore diameter in piston .... 12.007 to 12.012 mm

Piston rings
Ring end gap (installed) .... 0.10 to 0.25 mm

Crankshaft
Runout (max)
   At middle and left-hand end .... 0.03 mm
   At right-hand end .... 0.02 mm
Endfloat .... 0.03 to 0.09 mm

Cylinder base gasket selection
Cylinder top gasket surface-to-piston crown measurement   **Gasket thickness**
   3.24 mm to 3.48 mm .... 0.8 mm
   3.04 mm to 3.24 mm .... 0.6 mm
   2.80 mm to 3.04 mm .... 0.4 mm

Torque settings
Engine front mounting bolt	33 to 41 Nm
Shock absorber lower mounting bolt	33 to 41 Nm
Cylinder head nuts	10 to 11 Nm
Crankcase bolts	12 to 13 Nm
Alternator rotor nut	40 to 44 Nm

Hexagon

General
Type	Single cylinder two-stroke
Capacity	124 cc
Bore	55.0 mm
Stroke	52.0 mm
Compression ratio	10.2 to 1

Cylinder bore
Standard
Size-code A	54.990 to 54.995 mm
Size-code B	54.995 to 55.000 mm
Size-code C	55.000 to 55.005 mm
Size-code D	55.005 to 55.010 mm
Size-code E	55.010 to 55.015 mm
Size-code F	55.015 to 55.020 mm
Size-code G	55.020 to 55.025 mm
Size-code H	55.025 to 55.030 mm
Size-code I	55.030 to 55.035 mm
1st oversize	55.190 to 55.235 mm
2nd oversize	55.390 to 55.435 mm
3rd oversize	55.590 to 55.610 mm

Connecting rod
Small-end internal diameter
Size I	20.009 to 20.013 mm
Size II	20.005 to 20.010 mm
Size III	19.999 to 20.006 mm
Size IIII	19.997 to 20.002 mm

Piston
Piston diameter (measured 35 mm down from lower ring groove, at 90° to piston pin axis)
Standard
Size-code A	54.935 to 54.940 mm
Size-code B	54.940 to 54.945 mm
Size-code C	54.945 to 54.950 mm
Size-code D	54.950 to 54.955 mm
Size-code E	54.955 to 54.960 mm
Size-code F	54.960 to 54.965 mm
Size-code G	54.965 to 55.970 mm
Size-code H	54.970 to 54.975 mm
Size-code I	54.975 to 54.980 mm
1st oversize	55.135 to 55.180 mm
2nd oversize	55.335 to 55.380 mm
3rd oversize	55.535 to 55.555 mm
Piston-to-bore clearance	0.050 to 0.060 mm
Piston pin diameter	15.999 to 16.006 mm

Piston rings
Ring end gap (installed)	0.20 to 0.35 mm

Crankshaft
Runout (max)	0.03 mm
Endfloat	0.03 to 0.09 mm

Torque settings
Engine front mounting bolt	33 to 41 Nm
Rear shock absorber lower mounting	33 to 41 Nm
Cylinder head nuts	20 to 22 Nm
Crankcase bolts	13 Nm
Alternator rotor nut	52 to 56 Nm

2B•4 Liquid-cooled two-stroke engines

1 General information

The engine unit is a single cylinder two-stroke, with liquid-cooling. The alternator rotor is on the right-hand end of the crankshaft. The crankshaft assembly is pressed, incorporating the connecting rod, with the big-end running on the crankpin on a needle roller bearing. The piston also runs on a needle roller bearing fitted in the small-end of the connecting rod. The crankshaft runs in caged ball main bearings. The crankcase divides vertically.

2 Operations possible with the engine in the frame

All components and assemblies, with the exception of the crankshaft/connecting rod assembly and its bearings, and the water pump impeller, can be worked on without having to remove the engine/transmission assembly from the frame. If however, a number of areas require attention at the same time, removal of the engine is recommended, as it is easy to do so.

3 Operations requiring engine removal

To access the crankshaft and connecting rod assembly and its bearings, and the water pump impeller, the engine must be removed from the frame and the crankcase halves must be separated.

4 Major engine repair – general note

1 It is not always easy to determine when or if an engine should be completely overhauled, as a number of factors must be considered.
2 High mileage is not necessarily an indication that an overhaul is needed, while low mileage, on the other hand, does not preclude the need for an overhaul. Frequency of servicing is probably the single most important consideration. An engine that has regular and frequent maintenance will most likely give many miles of reliable service. Conversely, a neglected engine, or one which has not been run-in properly, may require an overhaul very early in its life.
3 If the engine is making obvious knocking or rumbling noises, the connecting rod and/or main bearings are probably at fault.
4 Loss of power, rough running, excessive noise and high fuel consumption rates may also point to the need for an overhaul, especially if they are all present at the same time. If a complete tune-up does not remedy the situation, major mechanical work is the only solution.
5 An engine overhaul generally involves restoring the internal parts to the specifications of a new engine. The piston rings and main and connecting rod bearings are usually renewed and, if necessary, the cylinder is rebored. The end result should be a like-new engine that will give as many trouble-free miles as the original.
6 Before beginning the engine overhaul, read through the related procedures to familiarise yourself with the scope and requirements of the job. Overhauling an engine is not all that difficult, but it is time consuming. Check on the availability of parts and make sure that any necessary special tools, equipment and supplies are obtained in advance.
7 Most work can be done with typical workshop hand tools, although a number of precision measuring tools are required for inspecting parts to determine if they must be renewed. Often a dealer will handle the inspection of parts and offer advice concerning reconditioning and renewal. As a general rule, time is the primary cost of an overhaul so it does not pay to install worn or substandard parts.
8 As a final note, to ensure maximum life and minimum trouble from a rebuilt engine, everything must be assembled with care in a spotlessly-clean environment.

5 Engine/transmission unit – removal and installation

Caution: *The engine is not heavy, although engine removal and installation should be carried out with the aid of an assistant; personal injury or damage could occur if the engine falls or is dropped.*

Removal

1 The procedure for removing the engine is the same as for air-cooled models, with the following addition: drain the cooling system (see Chapter 1). Release the clamps securing the cooling system hoses to the cylinder head and to the water pipe just ahead and below the alternator on the right-hand side of the engine, and detach the hoses from their unions, noting which fits where **(see illustrations)**. Also pull back the rubber cover on the coolant temperature sensor wiring terminal and pull off the connector.
2 Refer to Chapter 2A, Section 5, for the rest of the procedure.

Installation

3 Installation is the reverse of the procedure in Chapter 2A, noting the additional points:
a) *Make sure the cooling system hoses are properly connected and secured by their clamps* **(see illustrations 5.1a and 5.1b)**. *Do not forget to connect the temperature sensor wiring cover.*
b) *Fill the cooling system (see Chapter 1).*

6 Disassembly and reassembly – general information

Disassembly

1 Before disassembling the engine, the external surfaces of the unit should be thoroughly cleaned and degreased. This will prevent contamination of the engine internals, and will also make working a lot easier and cleaner. A high flash-point solvent, such as paraffin can be used, or better still, a proprietary engine degreaser such as Gunk. Use old paintbrushes and toothbrushes to work the solvent into the various recesses of the engine casings. Take care to exclude solvent or water from the electrical components and inlet and exhaust ports.

Warning: *The use of petrol (gasoline) as a cleaning agent should be avoided because of the risk of fire.*

2 When clean and dry, arrange the unit on the workbench, leaving a suitable clear area for working. Gather a selection of small containers and plastic bags so that parts can be grouped together in an easily identifiable manner. Some paper and a pen should be on hand to permit notes to be made and labels attached where necessary. A supply of clean rag is also required.

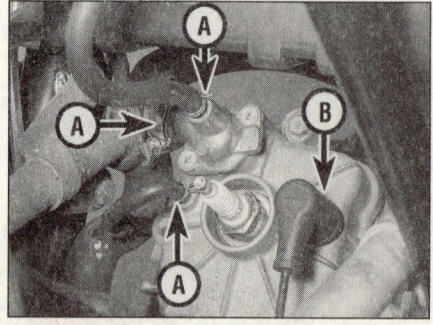

5.1a Detach the hoses (A) from their unions and disconnect the wiring connector (B)

5.1b Detach the hose (arrowed) from its union

Liquid-cooled two-stroke engines 2B•5

3 Before commencing work, read through the appropriate section so that some idea of the necessary procedure can be gained. When removing components it should be noted that great force is seldom required, unless specified. In many cases, a component's reluctance to be removed is indicative of an incorrect approach or removal method – if in any doubt, recheck with the text.

4 When disassembling the engine, keep 'mated' parts that have been in contact with each other during engine operation together. These 'mated' parts must be reused or renewed as an assembly.

5 A complete engine disassembly should be done in the following general order with reference to the appropriate Sections and Chapters.
Remove the cylinder head.
Remove the cylinder.
Remove the piston.
Remove the alternator.
Remove the variator (see Chapter 2G).
Remove the starter motor (see Chapter 9).
Remove the oil pump and drivebelt.
Remove the reed valve (see Chapter 4).
Remove the water pump (see Chapter 3).
Separate the crankcase halves.
Remove the crankshaft.

Reassembly

6 Reassembly is accomplished by reversing the general disassembly sequence.

7 Cylinder head – removal, inspection and installation

Note: *The cylinder head can be removed with the engine in the frame. If the engine has been removed, ignore the steps which don't apply.*
Caution: The engine must be completely cool before beginning this procedure or the cylinder head may become warped.

Removal

1 Remove the bodywork as required by your model (see Chapter 7).

2 Drain the cooling system (see Chapter 1). Release the clamps securing the cooling system hoses to the cylinder head, and detach the hoses from their unions, noting which fits where **(see illustration 5.1a)**. Also pull back the rubber cover on the coolant temperature sensor wiring terminal and pull off the connector. If required, remove the thermostat and housing (see Chapter 3).

3 On Hexagon models, remove the four bolts securing the cylinder head cover and remove the cover **(see illustration)**. Remove the O-ring from the plug housing and discard it, as a new one must be used **(see illustration)**.

4 Unscrew the four cylinder head nuts evenly and a little at a time in a criss-cross sequence until they are all loose, then draw the head off the cylinder and the studs **(see illustrations)**.

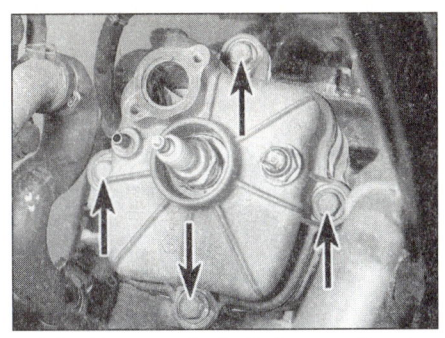

7.3a Unscrew the bolts (arrowed) and remove the cover

7.3b Remove the O-ring and discard it

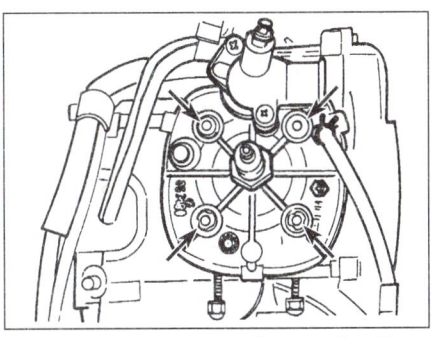

7.4a Cylinder head nuts (arrowed) – 50 cc engine

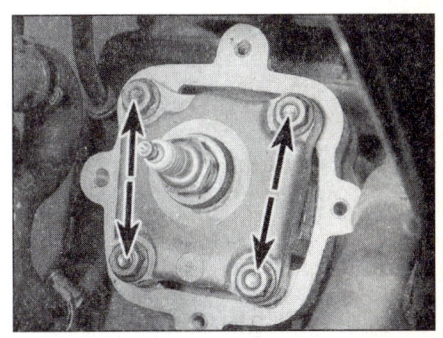

7.4b Cylinder head nuts (arrowed) – 125 cc engine

If it is stuck, tap around the joint faces of the cylinder head with a soft-faced mallet to free the head. Do not attempt to free the head by inserting a screwdriver between the head and cylinder – you'll damage the sealing surfaces. Discard the cylinder head O-ring and gasket (where fitted), as new ones must be used.

Inspection

5 Refer to Chapter 1 and decarbonise the cylinder head.

6 Inspect the head very carefully for cracks and other damage. If cracks are found, a new head will be required.

7 Check the mating surfaces on the cylinder head and cylinder for signs of leakage, which could indicate warpage.

8 Using a precision straight-edge, check the head mating surface for warpage. Check vertically, horizontally and diagonally across the head, making four checks in all.

Installation

9 Lubricate the cylinder bore with two-stroke oil.

10 Ensure both cylinder head and cylinder mating surfaces are clean.

11 Carefully fit the cylinder head onto the cylinder using a new gasket (where fitted) and O-ring **(see illustrations)**.

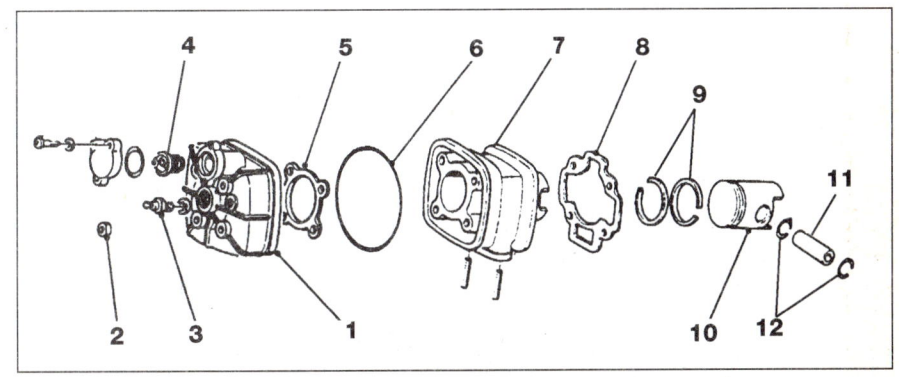

7.11a Cylinder head and cylinder components – 50 cc engine

1 Cylinder head
2 Cylinder head nut – 4 off
3 Temperature sender
4 Thermostat
5 Cylinder head gasket
6 O-ring
7 Cylinder
8 Base gasket
9 Piston rings
10 Piston
11 Piston pin
12 Circlips

2B•6 Liquid-cooled two-stroke engines

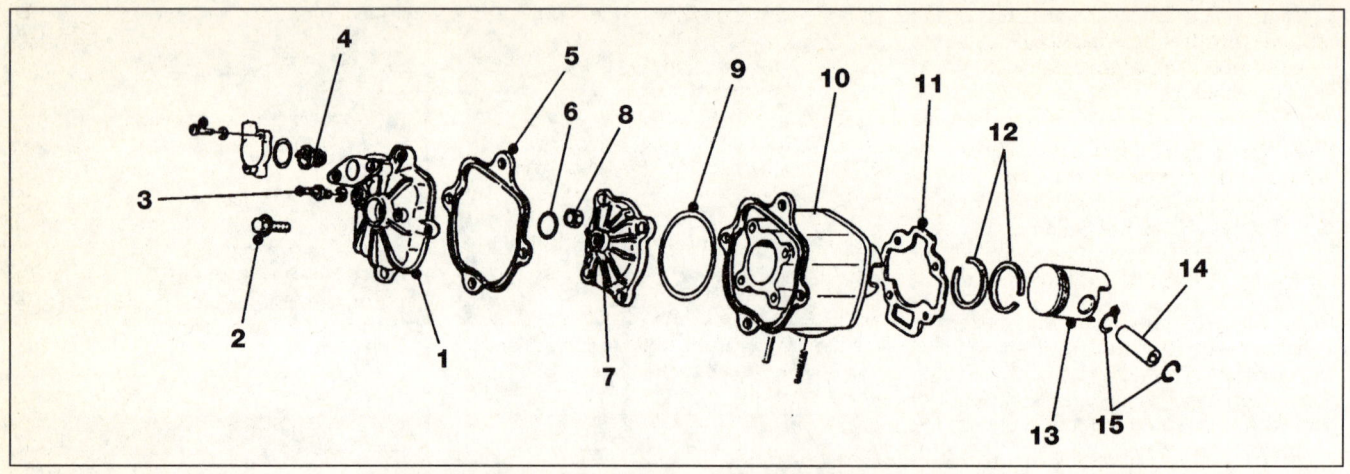

7.11b Cylinder head and cylinder components – 125 cc engine

1 Cylinder head cover
2 Cover bolt – 4 off
3 Temperature sender
4 Thermostat
5 Cover seal
6 O-ring
7 Cylinder head
8 Cylinder head nut – 4 off
9 O-ring
10 Cylinder
11 Base gasket
12 Piston rings
13 Piston
14 Piston pin
15 Circlips

12 Install the four nuts and tighten them all finger-tight **(see illustration 7.4a or 7.4b)**. Now tighten them evenly and a little at a time in a criss-cross pattern to the torque setting specified at the beginning of the Chapter.

13 On the Hexagon, check the condition of the head cover gasket and fit a new one if necessary **(see illustration)**. Also fit a new O-ring around the plug housing **(see illustration 7.3b)**.

14 Install the remaining components in a reverse of their removal sequence, referring to the relevant Sections or Chapters.

15 Refill the cooling system (see Chapter 1).

8 Cylinder – removal, inspection and installation

Note: *The cylinder can be removed with the engine in the frame.*

1 Remove the exhaust system (see Chapter 4) and the cylinder head (see Section 7).

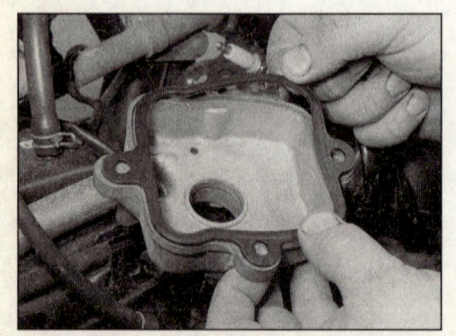

7.13 Check the cover gasket and renew if necessary

The procedure for removal, inspection and installation of the cylinder is basically the same as for air-cooled models. Refer to Chapter 2A, Section 8, for details.

2 Note that the cylinder base gasket thickness on 50 cc liquid-cooled two-stroke engines has to be calculated in the same way as on 125 cc engines (see Step 4). All cylinders and pistons are size-coded as on air-cooled engines.

3 Note that some 125 cc liquid-cooled two-stroke engines are fitted with iron cylinders which can be rebored, and some are fitted with Nicasil coated aluminium cylinders which cannot. Specifications for oversize cylinders and pistons are listed at the beginning of this Chapter. To assess the amount of wear in a Nicasil coated cylinder, compare the measurements taken with the standard cylinder bore specifications. Likewise, the appropriate piston sizes in the specifications are those for standard pistons.

4 When installing the cylinder, note that different thickness base gaskets are available. For the Zip SP and NRG models, gaskets are available in 0.4, 0.5 and 0.75 mm thicknesses, and for the Hexagon they are available in 0.2, 0.3, 0.4, 0.5, 0.6, 0.7 and 0.8 mm thicknesses. To determine which thickness of gasket to use, assemble the cylinder on the crankcase and piston without any base gasket fitted. Mount the dial gauge as described in Chapter 2A and measure the distance between the cylinder top gasket surface and the top of the piston crown. On Zip SP and NRG models, use the specifications at the beginning of this Chapter to determine the gasket thickness. On Hexagon models, subtract 2.79 mm from the reading to obtain the gasket thickness.

9 Piston – removal, inspection and installation

1 The procedure for removal, inspection and installation of the piston is the same as for air-cooled engines. Refer to Chapter 2A, Section 9, for the procedure.

10 Piston rings – inspection and installation

1 The procedure for inspection and installation of the piston rings is the same as for air-cooled models. Refer to Chapter 2A, Section 10, for the procedure.

11 Alternator rotor and stator – removal and installation

Note: *The alternator can be removed with the engine in the frame.*

1 Where fitted, unclip the secondary air system from the alternator cover (see Chapter 1, Section 21). Remove the screws securing the alternator cover and remove the cover, noting how it fits.

2 The remainder of the procedure for removal, inspection and installation of the alternator rotor and stator is the same as for air-cooled models, though liquid-cooled models have no cooling fan attached to the rotor. Refer to Chapter 2A, Section 12, for the procedure.

12 Starter pinion assembly – removal, inspection and installation

Note: *The starter pinion assembly can be removed with the engine in the frame.*

1 The procedure for removal, inspection and installation of the starter pinion assembly is the same as for air-cooled models. Refer to Chapter 2A, Section 13, for the procedure.

13 Oil pump and drivebelt – removal, inspection, installation and bleeding

1 The procedure for removal, inspection, installation and bleeding of the oil pump and drivebelt is the same as for air-cooled models. Refer to Chapter 2A, Section 14, for the procedure.

14 Crankcase halves, crankshaft and connecting rod and bearings

Note: *To separate the crankcase halves, the engine must be removed from the frame.*

Separation

1 To access the crankshaft and its bearings, the crankcase must be split into two parts.
2 To enable the crankcases to be separated, the engine must be removed from the frame (see Section 5). Before the crankcases can be separated the following components must be removed:

a) Cylinder head (Section 7).
b) Cylinder (Section 8).
c) Alternator rotor and stator (Section 11).
d) Reed valve (Chapter 4).
e) Starter motor (Chapter 9).
f) Oil pump and drivebelt (Section 13).

3 The remainder of the procedure for separation and joining of the crankcase halves and for removal, inspection and installation of the crankshaft/connecting rod and bearings is the same as for air-cooled models, though liquid-cooled models have the water pump assembly housed within the left-hand side of the crankcase. Refer to Chapter 2A, Section 15, for the procedure. Remove the water pump from the crankcase after the halves have been separated, noting how it fits.

Reassembly

4 Do not forget to install the water pump before joining the crankcase halves (see Chapter 3).

15 Initial start-up after overhaul

1 Make sure the oil tank is at least partly full and the pump is correctly adjusted (see Chapter 1) and bled of air (see Section 13).
2 Fill the coolant reservoir with fresh coolant (see Chapter 1).
3 Make sure there is fuel in the tank.
4 With the ignition OFF, operate the kickstart a couple of times to check that the engine turns over easily.
5 Turn the ignition ON, start the engine and allow it to run at a slow idle until it reaches operating temperature. Do not be alarmed if there is a little smoke from the exhaust – this will be due to the oil used to lubricate the piston and bore during assembly and should subside after a while.
6 If the engine proves reluctant to start, remove the spark plug and check that it has not become wet and oily. If it has, clean it and try again. If the engine refuses to start, go through the fault finding charts at the end of this manual to identify the problem.
7 Check the coolant level after the engine has cooled down and bleed the cooling system of air as described in Chapter 1.

16 Recommended running-in procedure

1 Treat the engine gently for the first few miles to allow any new parts to bed-in.
2 Even greater care is necessary if the engine has been rebored or a new crankshaft has been installed. In the case of a rebore, the bike will have to be run-in as when new. This means a restraining hand on the throttle until at least 600 miles (1000 km) have been covered. There's no point in keeping to any set speed limit – the main idea is to keep from labouring the engine and to gradually increase performance up to the 600 mile (1000 km) mark. Make sure that the throttle position is varied to vary engine speed, and use full throttle for only short bursts, but do not allow the machine to attain more than 80% full speed (70% on Hexagon) or to maintain any one speed for too long. Experience is the best guide, since it's easy to tell when an engine is running freely.

Chapter 2 Part C: Four-stroke engines (Sfera 125, Liberty 125, ET4 125)

Refer to the beginning of Chapter 1 for model identification details

Contents

Alternator rotor and stator – removal and installation	19
Cam chain tensioner – removal, inspection and installation	9
Camshaft holder, camshaft and rockers – removal, inspection and installation	11
Cam chain, blades and sprockets – removal, inspection and installation	10
Cooling fan – removal and installation	18
Crankcase halves, crankshaft and connecting rod	22
Cylinder – removal, inspection and installation	15
Cylinder head – removal and installation	12
Cylinder head and valves – disassembly, inspection and reassembly	14
Disassembly and reassembly – general information	6
Engine/transmission unit – removal and installation	5
General information	1
Idle speed – check and adjustment	see Chapter 1
Initial start-up after overhaul	23
Major engine repair – general note	4
Oil and filter – change	see Chapter 1
Oil cooler and pipes – removal and installation	8
Oil level – check	see *Daily (pre-ride) checks*
Oil pump and relief valve – removal, inspection and installation	21
Operations possible with the engine in the frame	2
Operations requiring engine removal	3
Piston – removal, inspection and installation	16
Piston rings – inspection and installation	17
Recommended running-in procedure	24
Spark plug gap – check and adjustment	see Chapter 1
Starter motor – removal and installation	see Chapter 9
Starter pinion assembly – removal, inspection and installation	20
Valve clearances – check and adjustment	see Chapter 1
Valve cover – removal and installation	7
Valves/valve seats/valve guides – overhaul	13

Degrees of difficulty

Easy, suitable for novice with little experience	Fairly easy, suitable for beginner with some experience	Fairly difficult, suitable for competent DIY mechanic	Difficult, suitable for experienced DIY mechanic	Very difficult, suitable for expert DIY or professional

Specifications

General
Type	Single cylinder four-stroke
Capacity	124 cc
Bore	57.0 mm
Stroke	48.6 mm
Compression ratio	10.6 to 1

Valves, guides and springs
Valve clearances	See Chapter 1
Intake valve	
Stem diameter	
Standard	4.987 to 4.972 mm
Service limit (min)	4.96 mm
Guide bore diameter	
Standard	5.000 to 5.012 mm
Service limit (max)	5.022 mm
Seat width	1.8 mm
Exhaust valve	
Stem diameter	
Standard	4.975 to 4.960 mm
Service limit (min)	4.96 mm
Guide bore diameter	
Standard	5.000 to 5.012 mm
Service limit (max)	5.022 mm
Seat width	1.8 mm
Valve springs free length (intake and exhaust)	
Standard	29.9 mm
Service limit (min)	29.5 mm

Cylinder head
Warpage (max) .... 0.05 mm

Cylinder bore
Standard
    Size-code A .... 56.990 to 56.995 mm
    Size-code B .... 56.995 to 57.000 mm
    Size-code C .... 57.000 to 57.005 mm
    Size-code D .... 57.005 to 57.010 mm
    Size-code E .... 57.010 to 57.015 mm
1st oversize .... 56.190 to 57.215 mm
2nd oversize .... 57.390 to 57.415 mm
3rd oversize .... 57.590 to 57.615 mm
Service limit (all sizes) .... 0.030 mm more than nominal diameter

Piston
Piston diameter (measured 25 mm down from piston oil ring groove, at 90° to piston pin axis)
Standard
    Size-code A .... 56.935 to 56.939 mm
    Size-code B .... 56.940 to 56.944 mm
    Size-code C .... 56.945 to 56.949 mm
    Size-code D .... 56.950 to 56.954 mm
    Size-code E .... 56.955 to 56.959 mm
1st oversize .... 57.135 to 57.159 mm
2nd oversize .... 57.335 to 57.359 mm
3rd oversize .... 57.535 to 57.559 mm
Piston-to-bore clearance (when new) .... 0.0505 to 0.0606 mm
Piston pin diameter
    Size A .... 14.000 to 14.002 mm
    Size B .... 13.998 to 14.000 mm
    Service limit (min) .... 13.995 mm
Piston pin bore diameter in piston (max) .... 14.015 mm
Piston pin-to-piston clearance (max) .... 0.02 mm

Piston rings
Ring end gap (installed)
  Top ring
    Standard .... 0.15 to 0.30 mm
    Service limit (max) .... 0.50 mm
  2nd ring
    Standard .... 0.10 to 0.25 mm
    Service limit (max) .... 0.40 mm
  Oil control ring
    Standard .... 0.15 to 0.30 mm
    Service limit (max) .... 0.50 mm
Ring-to-groove clearance (max) .... 0.08 mm

Lubrication system
Oil pump
  Inner rotor tip-to-outer rotor clearance (max) .... 0.12 mm
  Outer rotor-to-body clearance (max) .... 0.20 mm
  Rotor endfloat (max) .... 0.09 mm
Relief valve spring free length (min) .... 14.0 mm

Connecting rod
Small-end internal diameter
  Size I .... 14.0085 to 14.0120 mm
  Size II .... 14.0050 to 14.0085 mm
  Service limit (max) .... 14.020 mm
Big-end side clearance
  Standard .... 0.14 to 0.41 mm
  Service limit (max) .... 0.50 mm
Big-end radial freeplay
  Standard .... 0.015 to 0.025 mm
  Service limit (max) .... 0.35 mm

Crankshaft and bearings
Runout (max) .... 0.06 mm

Torque settings

Valve cover bolts	12 Nm
Camshaft holder/cylinder head nuts	29 Nm
Cylinder head-to-block bolt	13 Nm
Oil cooler mounting bolts	8 Nm
Oil cooler pipe banjo bolts	13 Nm
Cam chain tensioner spring cap bolt	10 Nm
Cam chain tensioner blade bolt	9 Nm
Camshaft sprocket bolt	13 Nm
Rocker shaft stopper bolt	6 Nm
Oil pump mounting screws	5.5 Nm
Oil pump driven sprocket bolt	13 Nm
Sump cover bolts	12 Nm
Alternator rotor nut	40 to 44 Nm
Crankcase bolts	11 to 13 Nm

1 General information

The engine unit is a single cylinder, overhead-camshaft four-stroke, with fan-assisted air cooling. The fan is mounted on the alternator rotor, which is on the right-hand end of the crankshaft. The camshaft is chain-driven off the left-hand end of the crankshaft, and operates two valves via rocker arms.

The crankshaft assembly is pressed together, incorporating the connecting rod. The crankcase divides vertically.

2 Operations possible with the engine in the frame

All components and assemblies, with the exception of the crankshaft assembly and its bearings, can be worked on without having to remove the engine/transmission unit from the frame. If, however, a number of areas require attention at the same time, removal of the engine is recommended, as it is easy to do so.

3 Operations requiring engine removal

To access the crankshaft and connecting rod asssembly and its bearings, the engine must be removed from the frame and the crankcase halves must be separated.

4 Major engine repair – general note

1 It is not always easy to determine when or if an engine should be completely overhauled, as a number of factors must be considered.
2 High mileage is not necessarily an indication that an overhaul is needed, while low mileage, on the other hand, does not preclude the need for an overhaul. Frequency of servicing is probably the single most important consideration. An engine that has regular and frequent oil and filter changes, as well as other required maintenance, will most likely give many miles of reliable service. Conversely, a neglected engine, or one which has not been run-in properly, may require an overhaul very early in its life.
3 Exhaust smoke and excessive oil consumption are both indications that piston rings and/or valve guide oil seals are in need of attention, although make sure that the fault is not due to oil leakage.
4 If the engine is making obvious knocking or rumbling noises, the connecting rod and/or main bearings are probably at fault.
5 Loss of power, rough running, excessive valve train noise and high fuel consumption rates may also point to the need for an overhaul, especially if they are all present at the same time. If a complete service does not remedy the situation, major mechanical work is the only solution.
6 An engine overhaul generally involves restoring the internal parts to the specifications of a new engine. The piston and piston rings are renewed and the cylinder is rebored. The valve seats are reground and new valve springs are fitted. The main bearings in the crankcase are renewed and, if the connecting rod bearings are worn, a new crankshaft assembly is fitted. The end result should be a like-new engine that will give as many trouble-free miles as the original.
7 Before beginning the engine overhaul, read through the related procedures to familiarise yourself with the scope and requirements of the job. Overhauling an engine is not all that difficult, but it is time-consuming. Plan on the scooter being tied up for a minimum of two weeks. Check on the availability of parts and make sure that any necessary special tools, equipment and supplies are obtained in advance.
8 Most work can be done with typical workshop hand tools, although a number of precision measuring tools are required for inspecting parts to determine if they must be renewed. Often a dealer will handle the inspection of parts and offer advice concerning reconditioning and renewal. As a general rule, time is the primary cost of an overhaul, so it does not pay to install worn or substandard parts.
9 As a final note, to ensure maximum life and minimum trouble from a rebuilt engine, everything must be assembled with care in a spotlessly-clean environment.

5 Engine/transmission unit – removal and installation

Caution: The engine is not heavy, although engine removal and installation should be carried out with the aid of an assistant; personal injury or damage could occur if the engine falls or is dropped.

Removal

1 The procedure for removing the engine is the same as for air-cooled two-stroke models. If required, drain the engine oil (see Chapter 1).
Note: *There is no external oil feed or external oil pump on the four-stroke engine.*
2 Refer to Chapter 2A, Section 5, for the rest of the procedure.

Installation

3 Installation is the reverse of the procedure in Chapter 2A. Note that if the engine oil was drained, or if any oil has been lost during overhaul, the engine must be filled with the specified quantity of oil (see Chapter 1 Specifications) and the oil level checked as described in *Daily (pre-ride) checks*.

6 Disassembly and reassembly – general information

Disassembly

1 Before disassembling the engine, the external surfaces of the unit should be thoroughly cleaned and degreased. This will prevent contamination of the engine internals, and will also make working a lot easier and cleaner. A high flash-point solvent, such as paraffin can be used, or better still, a proprietary engine degreaser such as Gunk. Use old paintbrushes and toothbrushes to work the solvent into the various recesses of the engine casings. Take care to exclude solvent or water from the electrical components and intake and exhaust ports.

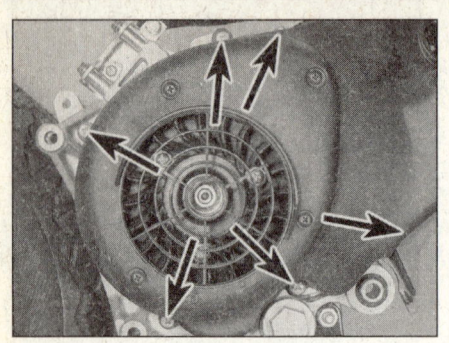

2C•4 Four-stroke engines (Sfera 125, Liberty 125, ET4 125)

7.2 Remove the screws (arrowed) securing the alternator cover . . .

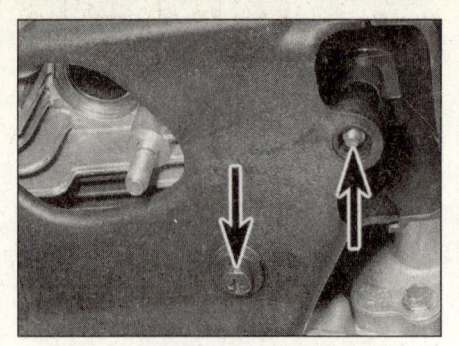

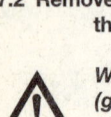

7.3 . . . and the engine lower cover (arrows)

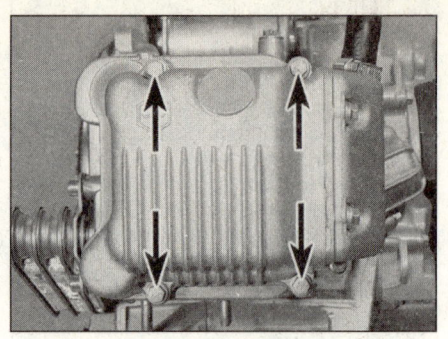

7.4 The valve cover is secured by four bolts (arrowed)

⚠ *Warning: The use of petrol (gasoline) as a cleaning agent should be avoided because of the risk of fire.*

2 When clean and dry, arrange the unit on the workbench, leaving a suitable clear area for working. Gather a selection of small containers and plastic bags so that parts can be grouped together in an easily identifiable manner. Some paper and a pen should be on hand to permit notes to be made and labels attached where necessary. A supply of clean rag is also required.

3 Before commencing work, read through the appropriate section so that some idea of the necessary procedure can be gained. When removing components it should be noted that great force is seldom required, unless specified. In many cases, a component's reluctance to be removed is indicative of an incorrect approach or removal method – if in any doubt, recheck with the text.

4 When disassembling the engine, keep 'mated' parts that have been in contact with each other during engine operation together. These 'mated' parts must be re-used or renewed as an assembly.

5 Complete engine disassembly should be done in the following general order with reference to the appropriate Sections. Refer to Chapter 2G for details of transmission components disassembly.
Remove the valve cover.
Remove the camshaft and rockers.
Remove the cylinder head.
Remove the cylinder.
Remove the piston.
Remove the alternator.
Remove the variator (see Chapter 2G).
Remove the starter motor (see Chapter 9).
Remove the sump cover.
Remove the oil pump.
Separate the crankcase halves.
Remove the crankshaft.

Reassembly

6 Reassembly is accomplished by reversing the general disassembly sequence.

7 Valve cover – removal and installation

Note: *The valve cover can be removed with the engine in the frame. If the engine has been removed, ignore the steps which do not apply.*

Removal

1 Remove the bodywork as required by your model to access the engine (see Chapter 7).
2 Pull the cap off the spark plug, then remove the screws securing the alternator cover and remove the cover **(see illustration)**.
3 Remove the screws securing the lower engine cover and remove the cover **(see illustration)**.
4 Unscrew the four bolts securing the valve cover, then lift the cover off the cylinder head **(see illustration)**. If it is stuck, do not try to lever it off with a screwdriver. Tap it gently around the sides with a rubber hammer or block of wood to dislodge it. Remove the gasket and discard it, as a new one must be used.

Installation

5 Clean the mating surfaces of the cylinder head and the valve cover with lacquer thinner, acetone or brake system cleaner.
6 Lay the new gasket onto the valve cover, making sure it fits correctly into the groove **(see illustration)**.
7 Position the valve cover on the cylinder head, making sure the gasket stays in place **(see illustration)**. Install the cover bolts with their washers. Tighten the bolts evenly and in a criss-cross sequence to the torque setting specified at the beginning of the Chapter.
8 Install the remaining components in the reverse order of removal.

8 Oil cooler and pipes – removal and installation

Note: *The oil cooler can be removed with the engine in the frame. If the engine has been removed, ignore the steps which do not apply.*

Removal

1 Remove the bodywork as required by your model to access the engine (see Chapter 7).
2 Drain the engine oil (see Chapter 1).
3 Remove the screws securing the alternator cover and remove the cover **(see illustration 7.2)**.
4 Unscrew the banjo bolt securing each pipe union to the crankcase **(see illustration)**. Now

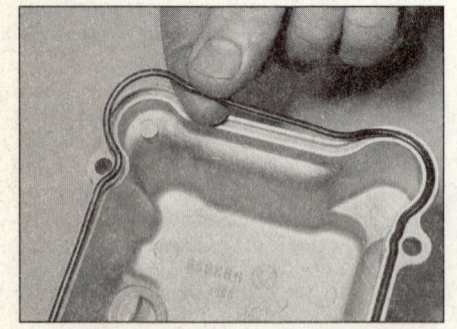

7.6 Fit a new gasket into the groove . . .

7.7 . . . then install the cover

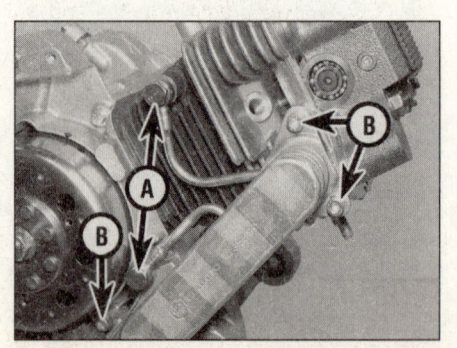

8.4 Oil pipe banjo bolts (A) and cooler mounting bolts (B)

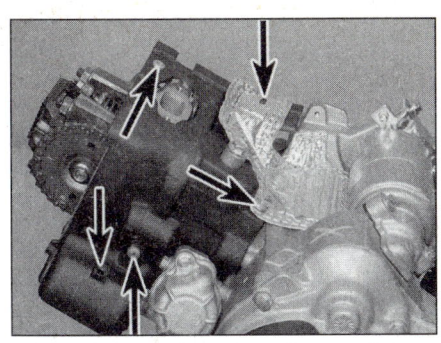

Four-stroke engines (Sfera 125, Liberty 125, ET4 125) 2C•5

9.3a Remove the screws (arrowed) . . .

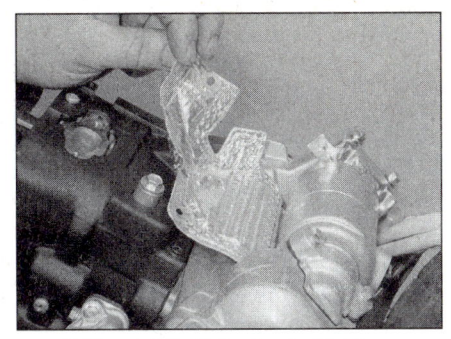

9.3b . . . lift off the heat shield . . .

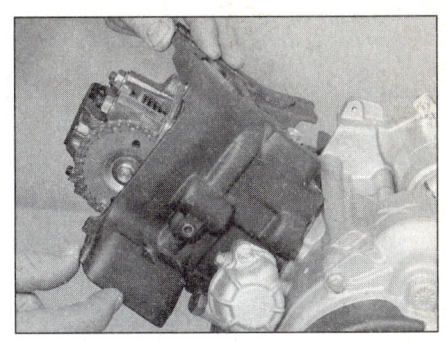

9.3c . . . and remove the cover

unscrew the three cooler mounting bolts, noting the fitting of the washers, and remove the cooler and pipes. If required, unscrew the banjo bolt securing each pipe to the cooler and detach the pipes. Discard the pipe sealing washers, as new ones must be used.

Installation

5 Installation is the reverse of removal, noting the following:
a) Check the condition of the cooler mounting washers and renew them if they are damaged or deteriorated.
b) Always use new sealing washers on the pipe unions.
c) Tighten the cooler bolts and the banjo bolts to the torque settings specified at the beginning of the Chapter.
d) Fill the engine with oil (see Chapter 1) and check the oil level (see Daily (pre-ride) checks).

9 Cam chain tensioner – removal, inspection and installation

Note: The cam chain tensioner can be removed with the engine in the frame.

Removal

1 Remove the bodywork as required by your model to access the engine (see Chapter 7).
2 Remove the carburettor and the intake manifold (see Chapter 4).
3 Remove the screws securing the engine lower cover to the upper engine cover (see illustration 7.3), followed by the screws securing the engine upper cover to the engine and alternator cover, then lift off the heat shield and remove the upper cover (see illustrations).
4 Unscrew the two tensioner mounting bolts and withdraw the tensioner from the cylinder (see illustration).
5 Remove the gasket from the base of the tensioner or from the cylinder and discard it, as a new one must be used.

Inspection

6 Unscrew the tensioner spring cap bolt and withdraw the spring from the tensioner body (see illustration 9.4).
7 Examine the tensioner components for signs of wear or damage.
8 Release the ratchet mechanism from the tensioner plunger and check that the plunger moves freely in and out of the tensioner body (see illustration 9.11).
9 If the tensioner or any of its components are worn or damaged, or if the plunger is seized in the body, they must be renewed. Individual components are available.

Installation

10 Remove the cooling fan (see Section 18). Turn the engine in a clockwise direction using the alternator rotor nut. This removes all the slack between the crankshaft and the camshaft in the front run of the chain and transfers it to the back run where it will be taken up by the tensioner.
11 Release the ratchet mechanism and press the tensioner plunger all the way into the tensioner body (see illustration).
12 Place a new gasket on the tensioner body, then install it in the engine and tighten the bolts (see illustration).
13 Install a new sealing washer on the spring cap bolt. Install the spring and cap bolt and tighten the bolt to the torque setting specified at the beginning of the Chapter (see illustrations).

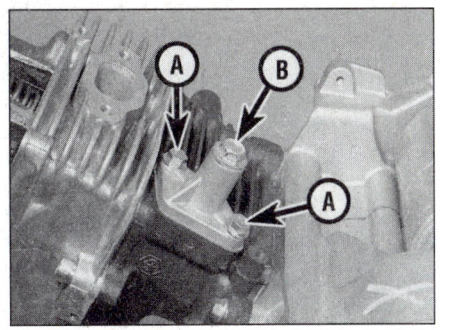

9.4 Tensioner mounting bolts (A) and spring cap bolt (B)

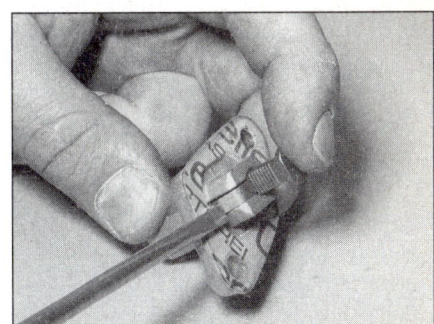

9.11 Release the ratchet and press the plunger fully in

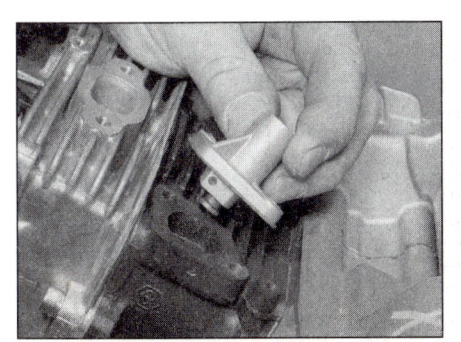

9.12 Install the tensioner . . .

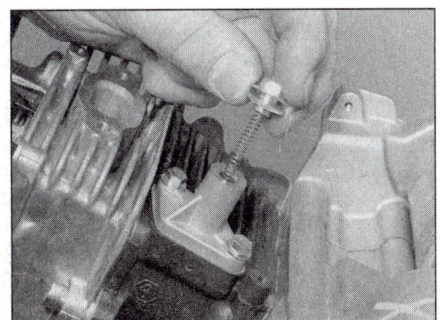

9.13a . . . then fit the spring and cap bolt . . .

9.13b . . . and tighten the bolt to the specified torque

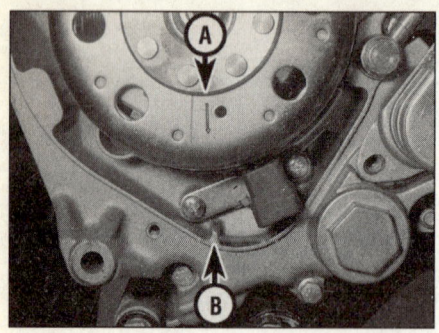

2C•6 Four-stroke engines (Sfera 125, Liberty 125, ET4 125)

10.3a Turn the engine until the arrow (A) aligns with the index mark (B) . . .

10.3b . . . and the mark on the sprocket (C) aligns with that on the camshaft holder (D)

10.5a Unscrew the bolt (arrowed), using a tool to hold the sprocket . . .

14 It is advisable to remove the valve cover (see Section 7) and check that the cam chain is tensioned. If it is slack, the tensioner plunger did not release when the bolt was tightened.

15 Install the cooling fan (see Section 18), the engine covers, and the carburettor and intake manifold (see Chapter 4).

10 Cam chain, blades and sprockets – removal, inspection and installation

Note: *The cam chain and sprockets can be removed with the engine in the frame.*

Removal

1 Remove the valve cover (see Section 7).

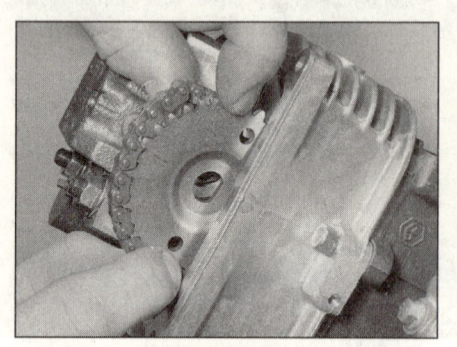

10.5b . . . and slip the sprocket off the shaft and out of the chain

2 If the cam chain or tensioner blade is being removed, remove the oil pump driven sprocket, drive chain and drive sprocket (see Section 21).

10.6a Remove the thrustwasher . . .

10.6b . . . then lower the chain and draw it out of the engine

10.6c Note how the sprocket locates over the pin (arrowed)

10.7a The tensioner blade is secured by a pivot bolt (arrowed)

10.5c Remove the spacer for safekeeping if required

3 Remove the cooling fan (see Section 18). Turn the engine in a clockwise direction using the alternator rotor nut, until the timing mark on the rotor aligns with the index mark on the crankcase, and the timing mark on the sprocket aligns with the index mark on the camshaft holder **(see illustrations)**. At this point the engine is at TDC (top dead centre) on the compression stroke (both valves closed).

4 Remove the cam chain tensioner (see Section 9).

5 Unscrew the bolt securing the sprocket to the camshaft **(see illustration)**. To prevent the sprocket from turning, use the Piaggio service tool (Part No. 020565Y) or a suitable holding tool fitted into the hole(s) in the sprocket. Discard the bolt and its washer, as new ones must be used. Draw the sprocket off the end of the camshaft and disengage it from the camchain **(see illustration)**. Remove the sprocket spacer for safekeeping if required **(see illustration)**.

6 Remove the thrustwasher from the end of the crankshaft, then lower the cam chain down its tunnel and slip it off the sprocket on the crankshaft, and draw the chain out of the engine **(see illustrations)**. If required, remove the sprocket from the crankshaft, noting how it locates over the pin **(see illustration)**.

7 If required. remove the bolt securing the cam chain tensioner blade to the crankcase and withdraw the blade, noting which way round it fits **(see illustration)**. Also remove the

Four-stroke engines (Sfera 125, Liberty 125, ET4 125) 2C•7

10.7b Lift the guide blade out

10.10 Make sure the guide blade is properly fitted

10.12a Use a new bolt and washer...

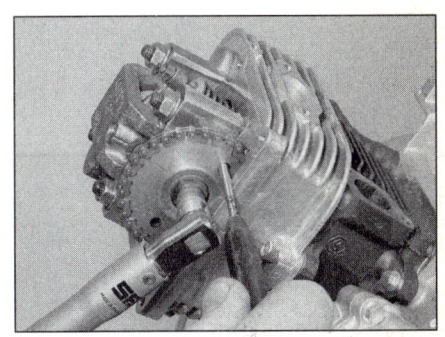

10.12b ... and tighten the bolt to the specified torque

guide blade, noting how it fits **(see illustration)**.

Inspection

8 Check the sprockets for wear, cracks and other damage, renewing them if necessary. If the sprocket teeth are worn, the chain is also worn. If wear this severe is apparent, the entire engine should be disassembled for inspection.

9 Check the chain tensioner blade and guide blade for wear or damage and renew them if necessary. If they are worn or damaged, the chain may be worn out or improperly tensioned. Check the operation of the cam chain tensioner (see Section 9).

Installation

10 If removed, install the tensioner blade and guide blade, making sure they are the correct way round **(see illustration)**. Tighten the tensioner blade bolt to the torque setting specified at the beginning of the Chapter.

11 If removed, install the sprocket onto the crankshaft, aligning the cutout in the sprocket with the pin on the crankshaft **(see illustration 10.6c)**. Also fit the camshaft sprocket spacer, if removed **(see illustration 10.5c)**.

12 Slip the cam chain down through the tunnel and engage it with the crankshaft sprocket **(see illustration 10.6b)**. Slip the camshaft sprocket into the top of the chain, then fit the sprocket onto the camshaft, aligning the squared edges between the sprocket and the shaft end, and making sure any slack in the chain is at the back of the engine so that it is later taken up by the tensioner, and that all the timing marks align as described in Step 3 **(see illustration 10.5b)**. Secure the sprocket with a new bolt and washer, then, using the method employed on removal to prevent the sprocket turning, tighten the bolt to the torque setting specified at the beginning of the Chapter **(see illustrations)**. Fit the thrustwasher onto the end of the crankshaft **(see illustration 10.6a)**, then install the oil pump drive sprocket, chain and driven sprocket (see Section 21).

Caution: If the marks are not aligned exactly as described, the valve timing will be incorrect and the valves may strike the piston, causing extensive damage to the engine.

13 Install the cam chain tensioner (see Section 9). After installation, rotate the engine and check again that all the timing marks align as described in Step 3. If not, remove the sprocket and align the marks correctly.

14 Install the remaining components in the reverse order of removal.

11 Camshaft holder, camshaft and rockers – removal, inspection and installation

Note: *The camshaft and rockers can be removed with the engine in the frame. Place rags over the cam chain tunnel to prevent any component from dropping into the engine.*

Removal

1 Remove the valve cover (see Section 7). Remove the rubber insulating pad from the top of the camshaft holder for safekeeping, noting how it fits **(see illustration)**.

2 Remove the cooling fan (see Section 18). Turn the engine in a clockwise direction using the alternator rotor nut, until the timing mark on the rotor aligns with the index mark on the crankcase, and the timing mark on the sprocket aligns with the index mark on the camshaft holder **(see illustration 10.3a and 10.3b)**. At this point the engine is at TDC (top dead centre) on the compression stroke (both valves closed).

3 Remove the cam chain tensioner (see Section 9).

4 Unscrew the bolt securing the sprocket to the camshaft **(see illustration 10.5a)**. To prevent the sprocket from turning, use the Piaggio service tool (Part No. 020565Y) or a suitable holding tool fitted into the hole in the sprocket. Discard the bolt and its washer, as new ones must be used. Draw the sprocket off the end of the shaft and disengage the camchain **(see illustration 10.5b)**. Secure the top of the chain to the cylinder head using a tie to prevent it dropping into the engine.

5 Slacken the bolt securing the cylinder head to the cylinder **(see illustration)**. Now unscrew the camshaft holder nuts, which also secure the cylinder head, evenly and a little at a time in a criss-cross pattern, until they are all loose **(see illustration)**. Remove the nuts

11.1 Remove the rubber pad

11.5a Slacken the bolt (arrowed)...

11.5b ...then unscrew the nuts (arrowed)...

2C•8 Four-stroke engines (Sfera 125, Liberty 125, ET4 125)

11.5c . . . and remove the holder

11.6a Remove the spacer . . .

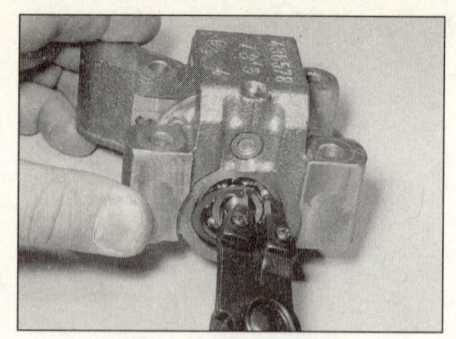

11.6b . . . and the circlip . . .

11.6c . . . and draw out the camshaft

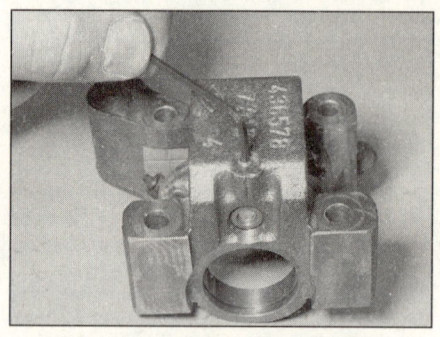

11.7a Unscrew the stopper bolt . . .

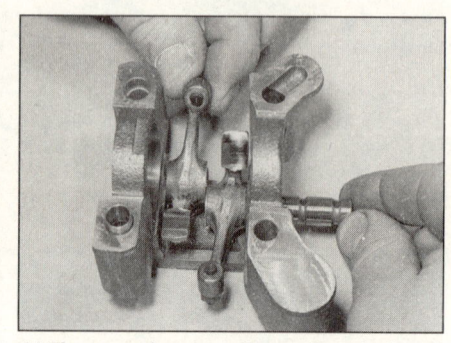

11.7b . . . and remove the rocker shaft and arms

then lift off the camshaft holder **(see illustration)**.

6 To separate the camshaft from the holder, remove the camshaft sprocket spacer, then remove the circlip securing the bearing in the holder **(see illustrations)**. Grasp the end of the camshaft and draw it out of the holder along with the bearing **(see illustration)**. The bearing on the right-hand end of the shaft will stay in the holder.

7 To remove the rocker arms and shaft, remove the shaft stopper bolt from the camshaft holder **(see illustration)**. Draw the shaft out of the holder and remove the rockers and the washer that fits between them, noting carefully which fits where, as they must be installed in their original positions **(see illustration)**.

Inspection

8 Clean all of the components with solvent and dry them off. Check the camshaft lobes for heat discoloration (blue appearance), score marks, chipped areas, flat spots and spalling **(see illustration)**. If damage is noted or wear is excessive, the camshaft must be renewed.

9 Check the condition of the camshaft bearings. If they are in any way worn, damaged, run noisily or roughly, or have excessive play, they must be renewed. Draw the bearing off the camshaft using a suitable puller, and drive the bearing out of the holder using a suitable piece of tubing or a socket that bears on the outer race only. Take care not to damage the holder. When installing the bearing onto the camshaft, heat the bearing to aid installation and use a drift which bears on the inner race only. When installing the bearing into the holder, use a drift that bears on the outer race only; apply heat to the holder to aid bearing installation.

⚠️ *Warning: When heating components, take great care not to burn your hands.*

10 Blow through the oil passages in the rocker arms with compressed air, if available. Inspect the rocker arm faces for pits, spalling, score marks and rough spots **(see illustration)**. If the faces of the rocker arms are damaged, the rocker arms and the camshafts should be renewed as a set. Check the rocker arm-to-shaft contact areas. Look for cracks in each rocker arm. Check the contact areas between the adjusting screws and the valve stems. If they are worn, rounded or damaged in any other way, they should be renewed as a set.

Installation

11 Lubricate the rocker shaft with engine oil. Slide the shaft into the holder, making sure the groove for the stopper bolt is correctly positioned, and fit each rocker arm and the washer that fits between them **(see illustration)**. Make sure each rocker is installed in its original position **(see**

11.8 Check the camshaft for wear and damage

11.10 Check the rocker arms for wear and damage

11.11a Do not forget the washer between the rocker arms

Four-stroke engines (Sfera 125, Liberty 125, ET4 125) 2C•9

11.11b Fit the stopper bolt and tighten it to the specified torque

11.13 Lubricate all components with clean engine oil

illustration 11.7b). Fit the stopper bolt and tighten it to the torque setting specified at the beginning of the Chapter (see illustration).
12 Slide the camshaft into the holder, making sure the bearing enters its housing squarely and is pressed fully home (see illustration 11.6c). Fit the bearing circlip, making sure it locates correctly into its groove, then fit the sprocket spacer (see illustrations 11.6b and 11.6a).
13 Locate the camshaft holder onto the cylinder head, with the sprocket end on the left-hand side of the engine (see illustration 11.5c). Fit the holder nuts and tighten them evenly and a little at a time in a criss-cross sequence to the torque setting specified at the beginning of the Chapter (see illustration 11.5b). Now tighten the bolt securing the cylinder head to the cylinder to the specified torque (see illustration 11.5a). Lubricate all the camshaft holder components with clean engine oil (see illustration).
14 Slip the camshaft sprocket into the top of the chain (see illustration 10.5b), then fit the sprocket onto the camshaft, aligning the squared edges between the sprocket and the shaft end. Ensure any slack in the chain is at the back of the engine so that it is later taken up by the tensioner, and that all the timing marks align as described in Step 2 (see illustration 10.3b). Secure the sprocket with a new bolt and washer, then, using the method employed on removal to prevent the sprocket turning, tighten the bolt to the torque setting

specified at the beginning of the Chapter (see illustration 10.12a and 10.12b).
Caution: If the marks are not aligned exactly as described, the valve timing will be incorrect and the valves may strike the piston, causing extensive damage to the engine.
15 Install the cam chain tensioner (see Section 9). After installation, rotate the engine and check again that all the timing marks align as described in Step 2. If not, remove the sprocket and align the marks correctly.
16 Check the valve clearances and adjust them if necessary (see Chapter 1).
17 Install the remaining components in the reverse order of removal.

12 Cylinder head – removal and installation

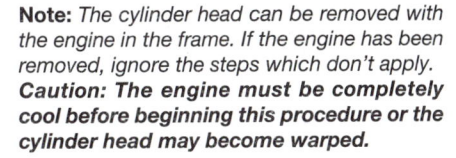

Note: *The cylinder head can be removed with the engine in the frame. If the engine has been removed, ignore the steps which don't apply.*
Caution: The engine must be completely cool before beginning this procedure or the cylinder head may become warped.

Removal

1 Remove the oil cooler (see Section 8).
2 Remove the exhaust system (see Chapter 4).
3 Remove the camshaft holder (see Section 11).

4 Remove the previously-slackened bolt securing the cylinder head to the cylinder (see illustration 11.5a), then pull the cylinder head up off the cylinder (see illustration). If it is stuck, tap around the joint faces of the cylinder head with a soft-faced mallet to free the head. Do not attempt to free the head by inserting a screwdriver between the head and cylinder – you'll damage the sealing surfaces. Remove the old cylinder head gasket and discard it, as a new one must be used (see illustration).
5 Check the cylinder head gasket and the mating surfaces on the cylinder head and cylinder for signs of leakage, which could indicate warpage. Refer to Section 14 and check the flatness of the cylinder head.
6 Clean all traces of old gasket material from the cylinder head and cylinder. If a scraper is used, take care not to scratch or gouge the soft aluminium. Be careful not to let any of the gasket material fall into the crankcase, the cylinder bore or the oil passages.

Installation

7 Lubricate the cylinder bore with engine oil.
8 Ensure both cylinder head and block mating surfaces are clean, then lay the new head gasket in place on the cylinder block, making sure all the holes are correctly aligned (see illustration 12.4b). Never re-use the old gasket.
9 Carefully fit the cylinder head onto the block (see illustration 12.4a).
10 Install the camshaft holder (see Section 11).
11 Install the remaining components in a reverse of their removal sequence, referring to the relevant Sections or Chapters.

13 Valves/valve seats/valve guides – overhaul

1 If a valve spring compressor is available, the home mechanic can remove the valves from the cylinder head, grind in the valves and renew the valve stem seal. If the necessary measuring tools are available, you can assess the amount of wear on the valves and guides and measure the valve-to-seat contact areas.

12.4a Lift the head off the cylinder . . .

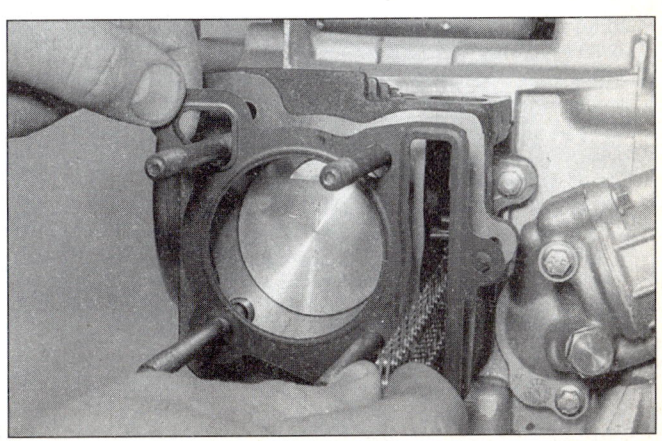

12.4b . . . and remove the gasket

2C•10 Four-stroke engines (Sfera 125, Liberty 125, ET4 125)

2 If the valve guides or the valve seats in the cylinder head are worn beyond their service limits a new head will have to be fitted.

3 After any servicing or repair work, be sure to clean the head very thoroughly before installation on the engine to remove any metal particles or abrasive grit that may still be present. Use compressed air, if available, to blow out all the holes and passages.

14 Cylinder head and valves – disassembly, inspection and reassembly

1 Disassembly, cleaning and inspection of the valves and related components can be done by the home mechanic if the necessary special tools are available. If there is any doubt about the condition of any components, have them checked by a Piaggio dealer.

2 To disassemble the valve components without the risk of damaging them, a valve spring compressor suitable for motorcycle engines is absolutely necessary.

Disassembly

3 Before proceeding, arrange to label and store the valves and their related components so that they can be returned to their original location without getting mixed up (see illustration).

4 If not already done, clean all traces of old gasket material from the cylinder head. If a scraper is used, take care not to scratch or gouge the soft aluminium.

5 Compress the valve spring on the intake valve with a spring compressor, making sure it is correctly located onto each end of the valve assembly. Do not compress the spring any more than is absolutely necessary. Remove the collets, using either needle-nose pliers, tweezers, a magnet or a screwdriver with a dab of grease on it (see illustration). Carefully release the valve spring compressor and remove the spring retainer, noting which way up it fits, the spring, the spring seat, and the valve from the head. If the valve binds in the guide (won't pull through), push it back into the head and deburr the area around the collet groove with a very fine file or whetstone (see illustration). Once the valve has been removed, pull the valve stem oil seal off the top of the valve guide with pliers and discard it (the old seal should never be re-used).

6 Repeat the procedure for the exhaust valve, noting that it has an oil cup in place of the spring seat and stem oil seal. Remember to keep the parts for each valve together and in order so they can be reinstalled in the same location.

7 Next, clean the cylinder head with solvent and dry it thoroughly. Compressed air will speed the drying process and ensure that all holes and recessed areas are clean.

8 Clean the valve springs, collets, retainers, spring seat or oil cup with solvent and dry

1 Gasket
2 Valves
3 Cylinder head
4 Collets
5 Retainer
6 Spring
7 Oil seal
8 Spring seat
9 Oil cup

14.3 Cylinder head components

14.5a Remove the collets with needle-nose pliers, tweezers, a magnet or a screwdriver with a dab of grease on it

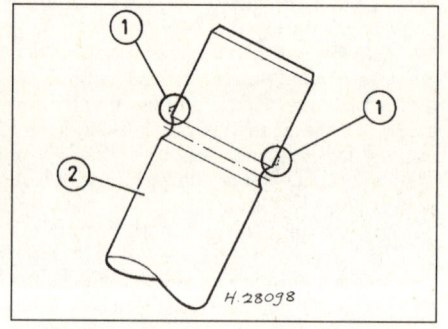

14.5b If the valve stem (2) won't pull through the guide, deburr the area (1) above the collet groove

them thoroughly. Work on the parts from one valve at a time so as not to mix them up.

9 Scrape off any deposits that may have formed on the valve, then use a motorised wire brush to remove deposits from the valve heads and stems. Again, make sure the valves do not get mixed up.

Inspection

10 Inspect the head very carefully for cracks and other damage. If cracks are found, a new head will be required.

11 Using a precision straight-edge and a feeler gauge set to the warpage limit listed in the specifications at the beginning of the Chapter, check the head gasket mating surface for warpage. Lay the straight-edge lengthways, across the head and diagonally, intersecting the stud holes, and try to slip the feeler gauge under it on either side of the combustion chamber. If the feeler gauge can be inserted between the straight-edge and the cylinder head, the head is warped and must be either machined or, if warpage is excessive, renewed.

12 Examine the valve seats in the combustion chamber. If they are deeply pitted, cracked or burned, it may be possible to have them repaired by a specialist engineer, otherwise a new head will be required. Measure the valve seat width and compare it to this Chapter's Specifications (see illustration).

13 Measure the valve stem diameter (see illustration). If the valve is worn beyond its service limit a new one must be fitted. Clean the valve guides to remove any carbon build-up, then measure the inside diameter of each guide with a small hole gauge. Insert the

14.12 Measuring the valve seat width (for greater precision use a vernier caliper)

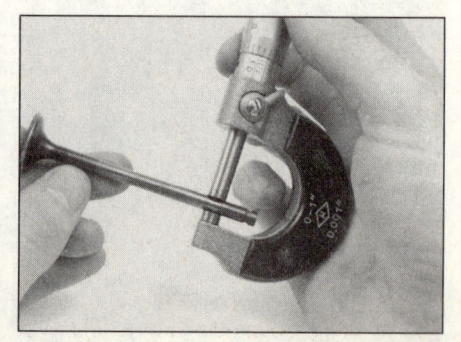

14.13a Measure the valve stem diameter with a micrometer

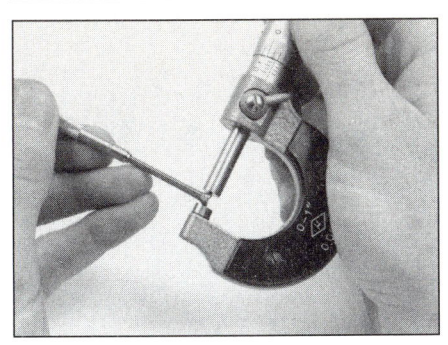

Four-stroke engines (Sfera 125, Liberty 125, ET4 125) 2C•11

14.13b Measuring the small hole gauge with a micrometer

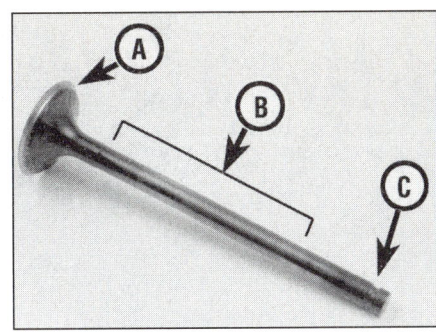

14.14 Check the valve face (A), stem (B) and collet groove (C) for signs of wear and damage

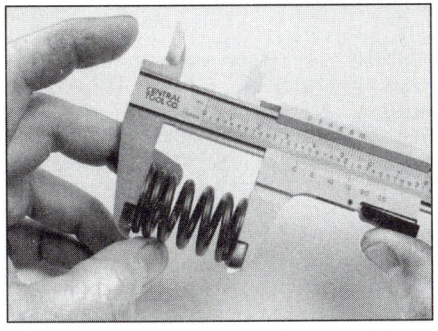

14.15a Measure the free length of the valve springs

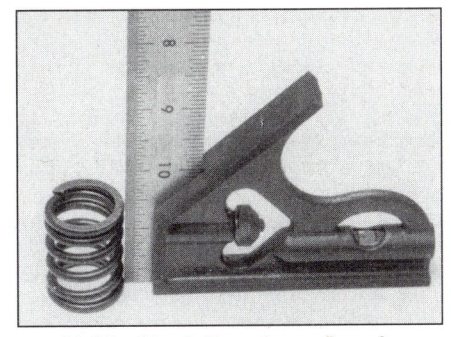

14.15b Check the valve springs for squareness

gauge into the guide and expand it so there's a slight drag when it's pulled out. Measure the gauge with a micrometer **(see illustration)**. Take measurements at both ends and at the centre of the guide to determine if it is worn unevenly. Piaggio do not list new valve guides, so if the guide is worn beyond its limit, have the head checked by a specialist engineer who may be able to bore out the guide and fit a sleeve in it. Otherwise a new cylinder head will have to be fitted.

14 Carefully inspect each valve face for cracks, pits and burned spots. Check the valve stem and the collet groove area for cracks **(see illustration)**. Rotate the valve and check for any obvious indication that it is bent. Check the end of the stem for pitting and excessive wear. The presence of any of the above conditions indicates the need for valve overhaul. If the stem end is pitted or worn, also check the contact area of the valve clearance adjuster in the rocker arm.

15 Check the end of each valve spring for wear and pitting. Measure the spring free length and compare it to that listed in the specifications **(see illustration)**. If either spring is shorter than specified it has sagged and must be renewed. Also place the spring upright on a flat surface and check it for bend by placing a square against it **(see illustration)**. If the bend in the spring is excessive, it must be renewed.

16 Check the spring retainers and collets for obvious wear and cracks. Any questionable parts should not be re-used, as extensive damage will occur in the event of failure during engine operation.

17 If the inspection indicates that no overhaul work is required, the valve components can be reinstalled in the head.

Reassembly

18 Unless a valve overhaul has been performed, before installing the valves in the head they should be ground in (lapped) to ensure a positive seal between the valves and seats. This procedure requires coarse and fine valve grinding compound and a valve grinding tool. If a grinding tool is not available, a piece of rubber or plastic hose can be slipped over the valve stem (after the valve has been installed in the guide) and used to turn the valve.

19 Apply a small amount of coarse grinding compound to the valve face, then slip the valve into the guide **(see illustration)**. **Note:** *Make sure each valve is installed in its correct guide and be careful not to get any grinding compound on the valve stem.*

20 Attach the grinding tool (or hose) to the valve and rotate the tool between the palms of your hands. Use a back-and-forth motion (as though rubbing your hands together) rather than a circular motion (ie, so that the valve rotates alternately clockwise and anti-clockwise rather than in one direction only) **(see illustration)**. Lift the valve off the seat and turn it at regular intervals to distribute the grinding compound properly. Continue the grinding procedure until the valve face and seat contact area is of uniform width and unbroken around the entire circumference of the valve face and seat **(see illustration)**.

21 Carefully remove the valve from the guide and wipe off all traces of grinding compound. Use solvent to clean the valve and wipe the seat area thoroughly with a solvent-soaked cloth.

22 Repeat the procedure with fine valve grinding compound, then repeat the entire procedure for the other valve.

23 Lay the spring seat for the intake valve in place in the cylinder head, then install a new valve stem seal onto the guide. Use an appropriate size deep socket to push the seal over the end of the valve guide until it is felt to clip into place. Don't twist or cock it, or it will not seal properly against the valve stem. Also, don't remove it again or it will be damaged.

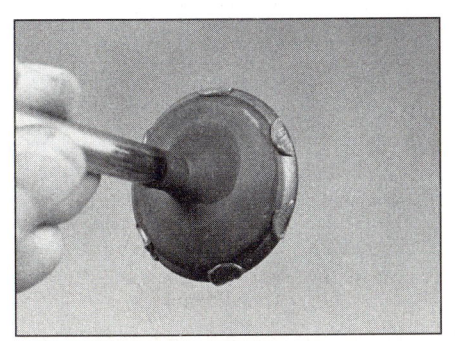

14.19 Apply the grinding compound very sparingly, in small dabs, to the valve face only

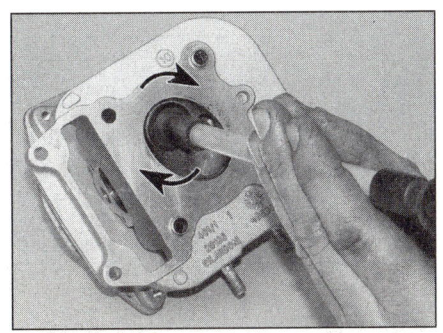

14.20a Rotate the tool back-and-forth between the palms of your hands

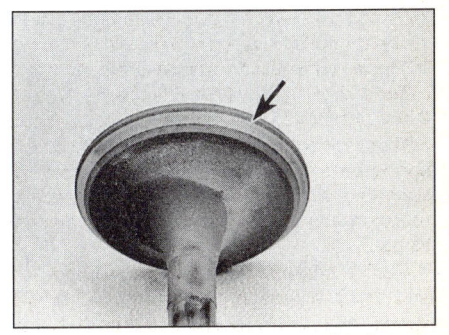

14.20b Valve contact area should show a uniform unbroken ring

2C•12 Four-stroke engines (Sfera 125, Liberty 125, ET4 125)

24 Lubricate the intake valve stem with molybdenum disulphide grease, then install it into its guide, rotating it slowly to avoid damaging the seal. Check that the valve moves up and down freely in the guide. Next, install the spring, with its closer-wound coils facing down into the cylinder head, followed by the spring retainer, with its shouldered side facing down so that it fits into the top of the spring.

25 Apply a small amount of grease to the collets to help hold them in place as the pressure is released from the spring (see illustration). Compress the spring with the valve spring compressor and install the collets (see illustration 14.5a). When compressing the spring, depress it only as far as is absolutely necessary to slip the collets into place. Make certain that the collets are securely locked in their retaining grooves.

26 Fit the oil cup for the exhaust valve onto the guide, then repeat the procedure in Steps 24 and 25 for that valve (see illustration).

27 Support the cylinder head on blocks so the valves can't contact the workbench top, then very gently tap each of the valve stems with a soft-faced hammer. This will help seat the collets in their grooves.

HAYNES HINT: *Check for proper sealing of the valves by pouring a small amount of solvent into each of the valve ports. If the solvent leaks past any valve into the combustion chamber area the valve grinding operation on that valve should be repeated.*

14.25 A small dab of grease will help to keep the collets in place on the valve while the spring is released

14.26 Make sure the oil cup is correctly installed

15 Cylinder – removal, inspection and installation

Note: *The cylinder can be removed with the engine in the frame.*

Removal

1 Remove the cylinder head (see Section 12).
2 Undo the bolt securing the cylinder to the crankcase (see illustration).
3 Lift the cylinder up off the studs, supporting the piston as it becomes accessible to prevent it hitting the crankcase. If the cylinder is stuck, tap around its joint faces with a soft-faced mallet to free it from the crankcase. Don't attempt to free the cylinder by inserting a screwdriver between it and the crankcase – you'll damage the sealing surfaces. When the cylinder is removed, stuff a clean rag around the piston to prevent anything falling into the crankcase.
4 Remove the gasket and discard it; a new one should be used on reassembly.

Inspection

5 Inspect the cylinder bore carefully for scratches and score marks. A rebore will be necessary to remove any deep scores (see Step 7).

6 Using telescoping gauges and a micrometer, check the dimensions of the cylinder to assess the amount of wear, taper and ovality. Measure near the top (but below the level of the top piston ring at TDC), centre and bottom (but above the level of the bottom ring at BDC) of the bore both parallel to and across the crankshaft axis (see illustration). Calculate any differences between the measurements to determine any taper or ovality in the bore. Compare the results to the cylinder bore specifications at the beginning of this Chapter. **Note:** *Cylinders and pistons are size-coded during manufacture and it is important that they are of the same size-code. Piaggio list five size-codes (A to E) for this engine. The size-code is stamped in the gasket surface at the top or base of the cylinder, and in the piston crown. When purchasing a new cylinder or piston, always supply the size-code letter.*

7 Calculate the piston-to-bore clearance by subtracting the piston diameter (see Section 16) from the bore diameter. If the cylinder is in good condition and the piston-to-bore clearance is within specifications, the cylinder can be re-used.

8 If the cylinder is tapered, oval, or worn beyond the service limit, badly scratched, scuffed or scored, have it rebored by a Piaggio dealer or motorcycle engineer. If the cylinder is rebored, it will require an oversize piston and rings. If the cylinder has already been rebored to the maximum oversize and is worn or damaged, the cylinder must be renewed.

9 Check that all the cylinder head studs are tight in the crankcase halves. If any are loose, remove them and clean their threads. Apply a suitable permanent thread locking compound and tighten them securely.

Installation

10 Check that the mating surfaces of the cylinder and crankcase are clean. Three different thicknesses of cylinder base gasket are available from Piaggio. To establish which size is required, the cylinder must be assembled on the crankcase and piston without a base gasket, and a dial gauge mounted against the crown of the piston. Set the dial gauge in the mounting plate, and with the mounting plate feet and gauge tip resting against the cylinder sealing face, zero the gauge dial (see illustration 8.18 in Chapter 2A). Rotate the engine so that the piston is part way down the bore, then clamp the mounting plate diagonally across two of the cylinder studs and tighten the stud nuts to 28 to 30 Nm to ensure that the cylinder is held firmly against the crankcase.

11 Rotate the crankshaft via the alternator rotor nut so the piston rises to the top of its stroke (TDC). At this point read off the dial gauge (see illustration 8.21 in Chapter 2A). If the reading is between –0.1 and +0.2 mm a 0.7 mm gasket is required, between +0.1 and +0.3 mm a 0.6 mm gasket is required, and between +0.3 and +0.5 mm a 0.4 mm gasket is required – refer to your Piaggio dealer for

15.2 Remove the bolt (arrowed) securing the cylinder to the crankcase

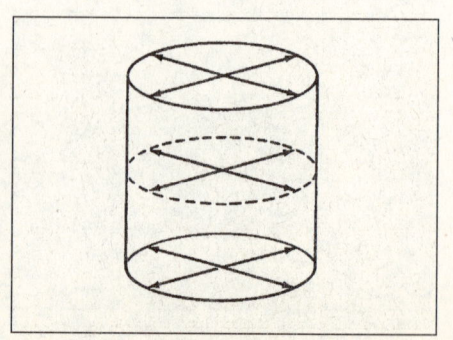

15.6 Measure the cylinder bore in the directions shown

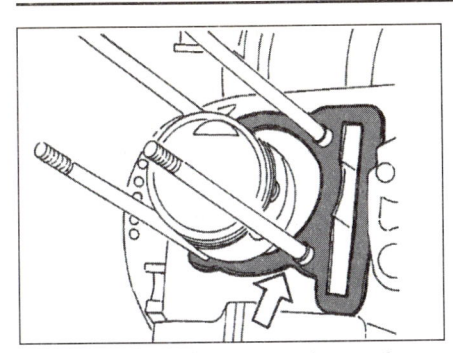

Four-stroke engines (Sfera 125, Liberty 125, ET4 125)   2C•13

15.11 Lay a new base gasket on the crankcase

details. Having established the correct gasket thickness, fit it to the crankcase **(see illustration)**. Never re-use the old gasket.

12 If required, install a piston ring clamp onto the piston to ease its entry into the bore as the cylinder is lowered. This is not essential as the cylinder has a good lead-in enabling the piston rings to be hand-fed into the bore. If possible, have an assistant to support the cylinder while this is done. Check that the piston ring end gaps are positioned as described in Section 17.

13 Lubricate the cylinder bore, piston and piston rings, and the connecting rod big- and small-ends, with the clean engine oil, then fit the cylinder down over the studs until the piston crown fits into the bore.

14 Gently push down on the cylinder, making sure the piston enters the bore squarely and does not get cocked sideways. If a piston ring clamp is not being used, carefully compress and feed each ring into the bore as the cylinder is lowered. If necessary, use a soft mallet to gently tap the cylinder down, but do not use force if it appears to be stuck as the piston and/or rings will be damaged. If a clamp is used, remove it once the piston is in the bore.

15 When the piston is correctly installed in the cylinder, press the cylinder down onto the base gasket.

16 Install the cylinder bolt and tighten it finger-tight only at this stage **(see illustration 15.2)**.

17 Install the cylinder head (see Section 12), then tighten the cylinder block bolt.

16 Piston – removal, inspection and installation

Note: *The piston can be removed with the engine in the frame.*

Removal

1 Remove the cylinder (see Section 15). Before removing the piston from the connecting rod, stuff a clean rag into the hole around the rod to prevent the circlips or anything else from falling into the crankcase. The piston should have an arrow marked on its crown which should face towards the exhaust valve. If this is not visible, mark the piston accordingly so that it can be installed the correct way round **(see illustration)**. Note that the arrow may not be visible until the carbon deposits have been scraped off and the piston cleaned.

2 Carefully prise out the circlip on one side of the piston using a pointed instrument or a small flat-bladed screwdriver inserted into the notch **(see illustration)**. Push the piston pin out from the other side to free the piston from the connecting rod. Remove the other circlip and discard them both, as new ones must be used. Use a socket extension to push the piston pin out if required.

> **HAYNES HiNT** *To prevent the circlip from flying away or from dropping into the crankcase, pass a rod or screwdriver with a greater diameter than the gap between the circlip ends through the piston pin. This will trap the circlip if it springs out.*

> **HAYNES HiNT** *If a piston pin is a tight fit in the piston bosses, heat the piston gently with a hot air gun – this will expand the alloy piston sufficiently to release its grip on the pin.*

Inspection

3 Before the inspection process can be carried out, the piston rings must be removed and the piston must be cleaned. Note that if the cylinder is being rebored, piston inspection can be overlooked as a new one will be fitted. All three piston rings can be removed by hand; a ring removal and installation tool can be used on the two compression rings, but do not use it on the oil control ring **(see illustration)**. Carefully note which way up each ring fits and in which groove, as they must be installed in their original positions if being re-used. The upper surface of each ring should be marked at one end. Do not nick or gouge the piston in the process.

4 Scrape all traces of carbon from the top of the piston. A hand-held wire brush or a piece of fine emery cloth can be used once most of the deposits have been scraped away. Do not, under any circumstances, use a wire brush mounted in a drill motor to remove deposits from the piston; the piston material is soft and will be eroded away by the wire brush.

5 Use a piston ring groove cleaning tool to remove any carbon deposits from the ring grooves. If a tool is not available, a piece broken off an old ring will do the job. Be very careful to remove only the carbon deposits. Do not remove any metal and do not nick or gouge the sides of the ring grooves. Once the deposits have been removed, clean the piston with solvent and dry it thoroughly.

6 Inspect the piston for cracks around the skirt, at the pin bosses and at the ring lands. Normal piston wear appears as even, vertical wear on the thrust surfaces of the piston and slight looseness of the top ring in its groove. If the skirt is scored or scuffed, the engine may have been suffering from overheating and/or abnormal combustion, which caused excessively high operating temperatures. Also check that the circlip grooves are not damaged.

7 A hole in the piston crown is an extreme example that abnormal combustion (pre-ignition) was occurring. Burned areas at the edge of the piston crown are usually evidence of spark knock (detonation). If any of the above problems exist, the causes must be corrected or the damage will occur again.

8 Check the piston-to-bore clearance by measuring the bore (see Section 15) and the

16.1 Mark the piston before removing it

16.2 Prise the circlip out carefully

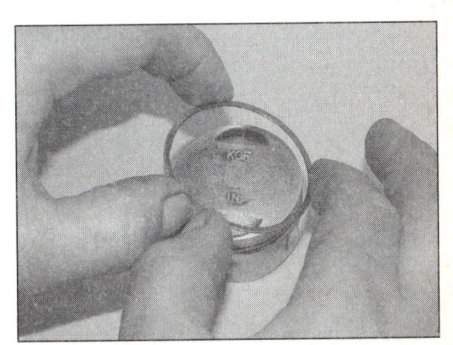

16.3 Removing the piston rings

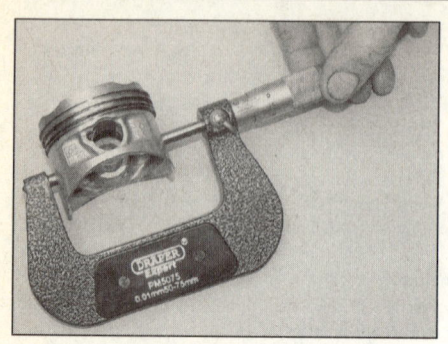

2C•14 Four-stroke engines (Sfera 125, Liberty 125, ET4 125)

16.8 Measuring the piston diameter

16.9a Measure the piston pin diameter at each end . . .

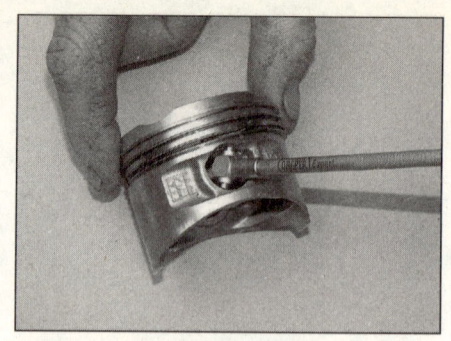

16.9b . . . and the boss diameter on each side of the piston

piston diameter. Measure the piston 25 mm down from the bottom of the lower piston ring groove and at 90° to the piston pin axis **(see illustration)**. Subtract the piston diameter from the bore diameter to obtain the clearance. If it is greater than the specified figure, the piston must be renewed (assuming the bore itself is within limits, otherwise a rebore is necessary).

9 Use a micrometer and a small hole gauge to determine whether there is wear between the piston pin and piston. Measure the piston pin diameter at the ends and the diameter of each pin boss in the piston and compare the results with the Specifications **(see illustrations)**.

10 To check for wear between the piston pin and connecting rod small-end, measure the piston pin diameter at its centre and the internal diameter of the rod small-end **(see illustrations)**. There are two size groups for the piston pin (A or B) and connecting rod small-end (I or II). Look for identification marks on the components and supply these to the dealer when ordering new parts.

11 Piston ring-to-groove clearance can be measured to determine whether the ring grooves in the piston are worn. Install the rings on the piston (see Section 17), then use a feeler gauge to measure the clearance between the ring and groove and compare the result with the specifications **(see illustration)**. If the clearance is greater than the limit, repeat the check using new rings, if the clearance is still too great, the piston should be renewed.

Installation

12 Inspect and install the piston rings (see Section 17).

13 Lubricate the piston pin, the piston pin bore and the connecting rod small-end bore with clean engine oil. Install a new circlip in one side of the piston (do not re-use old circlips). Line up the piston on the connecting rod, making sure the arrow on the piston crown faces towards the exhaust, and insert the piston pin **(see illustration)**. Secure the pin with the other new circlip **(see illustration)**. When installing the circlips, compress them only just enough to fit them in the piston, and make sure they are properly seated in their grooves with the open end away from the removal notch **(see illustration)**.

14 Install the cylinder (see Section 15).

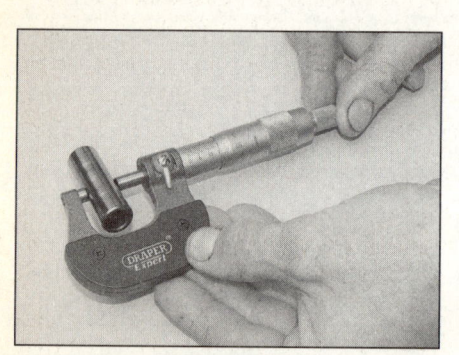

16.10a Measure the piston pin diameter in the middle . . .

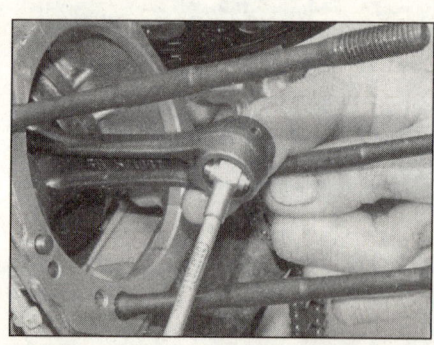

16.10b . . . and the rod small-end diameter

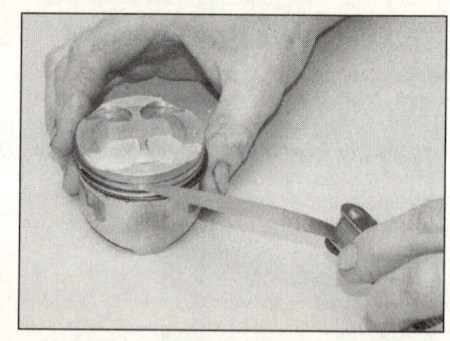

16.11 Measuring piston ring-to-groove clearance

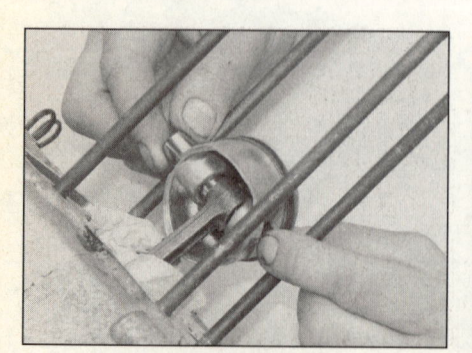

16.13a Insert the piston pin . . .

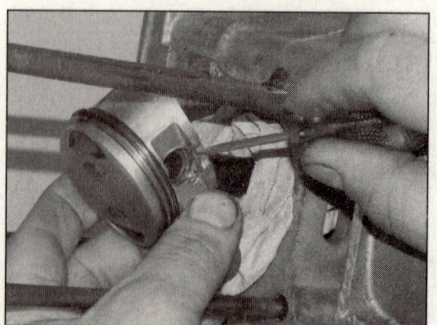

16.13b . . . and secure it with a new circlip

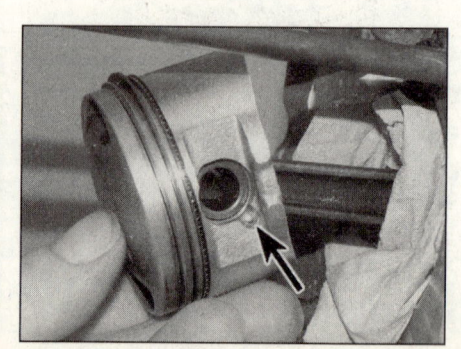

16.13c Ensure the ends of the circlip are clear of the notch (arrowed)

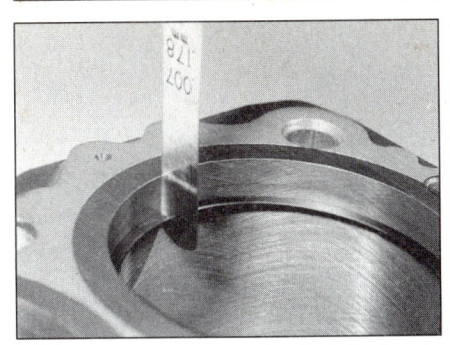

Four-stroke engines (Sfera 125, Liberty 125, ET4 125) 2C•15

17.2 Measuring piston ring installed end gap

17 Piston rings – inspection and installation

1 New piston rings should be fitted whenever an engine is being overhauled. Before installing the new piston rings, the ring end gaps must be checked with the rings installed in the bore.
2 To measure the installed ring end gap, insert the top ring into the bottom of the bore and square it up with the bore walls by pushing it in with the top of the piston. The ring should be about 20 mm from the bottom edge of the bore. To measure the end gap, slip a feeler gauge between the ends of the ring and compare the measurement to the specifications at the beginning of the Chapter (see illustration).
3 If the gap is larger or smaller than specified, double check to make sure that you have the correct rings before proceeding. If the gap is too small the ends may come in contact with each other during engine operation, which can cause serious damage. Check the piston and bore diameters with the specifications to confirm whether they are standard or oversize.
4 Excess end gap is not critical unless it exceeds the service limit. Again, double-check to make sure you have the correct rings for your engine and check that the bore is not worn.
5 Repeat the procedure for the other two rings.
6 Once the ring end gaps have been checked, the rings can be installed on the piston.
7 The oil control ring (lowest on the piston) is installed first. Always install this ring by hand and do not expand the ring any more than is necessary to slide it into place. Next install the 2nd compression ring, noting that there is usually a marking or letter near the gap to denote the upper surface of the ring. Finally install the top ring into its groove. A ring installation tool can be used on the two compression rings if desired.
8 Once the rings are correctly installed, check they move freely without snagging and stagger their end gaps as shown (see illustration).

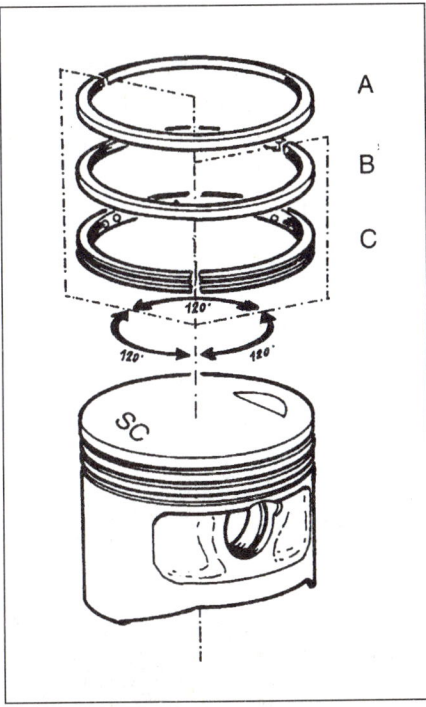

17.8 Ensure that the ring end gaps are positioned at 120° intervals
A First (top) compression ring
B Second (middle) compression ring
C Oil control ring

18 Cooling fan – removal and installation

Note: *The cooling fan can be removed with the engine in the frame.*

Removal
1 Remove the bodywork as required by your model to access the alternator cover on the right-hand side of the engine (see Chapter 7).
2 Remove the screws securing the alternator cover and remove the cover (see illustration 7.2).
3 Remove the three screws securing the cooling fan to the alternator rotor and remove the fan (see illustration 11.4 in Chapter 2A).

Installation
4 Installation is the reverse of removal.

19 Alternator rotor and stator – removal and installation

Note: *The alternator can be removed with the engine in the frame*
1 Remove the cooling fan (see Section 18).
2 The remainder of the procedure for removal, inspection and installation of the alternator rotor and stator is the same as for two-stroke models. Refer to Chapter 2A, Section 12, for the procedure.

20 Starter pinion assembly – removal, inspection and installation

Note: *The starter pinion assembly can be removed with the engine in the frame.*
1 The procedure for removal, inspection and installation of the starter pinion assembly is the same as for two-stroke models, except that it is located in the top of the transmission housing rather than the bottom (see illustration). Refer to Chapter 2A, Section 13, for the procedure.

21 Oil pump and relief valve – removal, inspection and installation

Note: *The oil pump and pressure relief valve can be removed with the engine in the frame.*

Oil pump
Removal
1 Remove the air filter housing (see Chapter 4).
2 Remove the drive pulley and variator (see Chapter 2G).
3 Remove the screws securing the pump drive chain cover and remove the cover (see illustration). Discard the cover O-ring as a new one should be used.

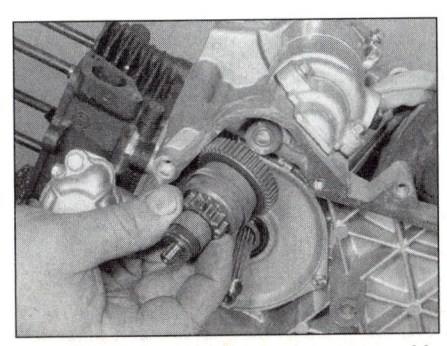

20.1 Removing the starter pinion assembly

21.3 The cover is secured by three screws (arrowed)

2C•16 Four-stroke engines (Sfera 125, Liberty 125, ET4 125)

4 Remove the bolts securing the sump cover and remove the cover (see illustration).

5 Remove the screws securing the driven sprocket plate and remove the plate, noting how it fits (see illustration).

6 Insert a pin punch or screwdriver through one of the holes in the driven sprocket and locate it against part of the casing to prevent the sprocket turning, then unscrew the sprocket bolt (see illustration).

7 Draw the sprocket off the pump and slip it out of the chain (see illustration). If required, draw the chain up into the transmission housing and remove it from the drive sprocket (see illustration). Slide the drive sprocket off the end of the crankshaft (see illustration).

8 Remove the two screws securing the oil pump and remove the pump (see illustration). Also remove the gasket from behind the pump and discard it as a new one must be used.

Inspection

9 Remove the two screws securing the cover to the pump body, then remove cover (see illustrations).

10 Clean the pump in solvent. Inspect the pump body and rotors for scoring and wear. If any damage, scoring or uneven or excessive wear is evident, renew the pump (individual components are not available). Dry the pump with compressed air.

11 Measure the clearance between the inner rotor tip and the tip of one of the crescents on the outer rotor with a feeler gauge and compare it to the maximum clearance listed in the specifications at the beginning of the Chapter (see illustration). If the clearance measured is greater than the maximum listed, renew the pump.

12 Measure the clearance between the outer rotor and the pump body with a feeler gauge and compare it to the maximum clearance listed in the specifications at the beginning of

21.4 The sump cover is secured by six bolts (arrowed)

21.5 The driven sprocket plate is secured by two screws (arrowed)

21.6 Unscrew the sprocket bolt (arrowed) using a tool in one of the holes to prevent it turning

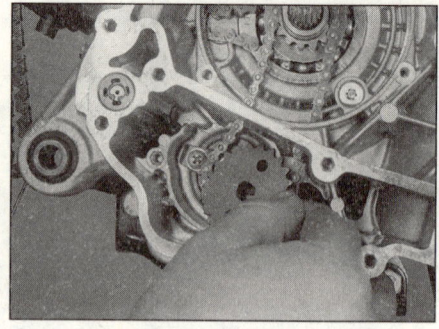

21.7a Remove the driven sprocket . . .

21.7b . . . the chain . . .

21.7c . . . and the drive sprocket

21.8 The pump is secured by two screws (arrowed)

21.9a Remove the screws . . .

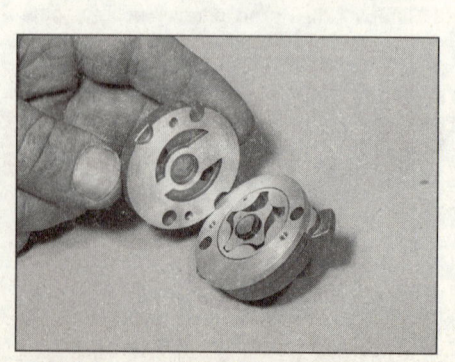

21.9b . . . and lift off the pump cover

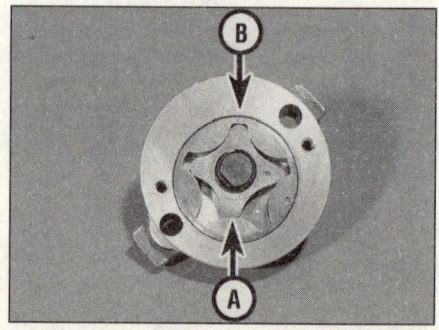

21.11 Measure inner-to-outer rotor clearance (A) and outer rotor-to-body clearance (B)

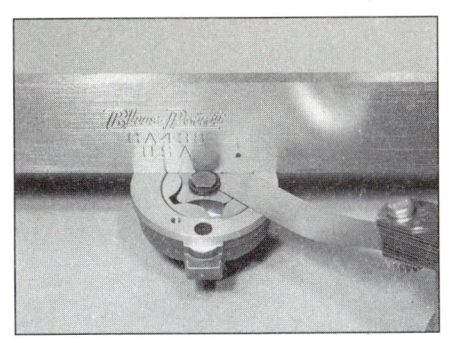

Four-stroke engines (Sfera 125, Liberty 125, ET4 125) 2C•17

21.13 Measuring rotor endfloat

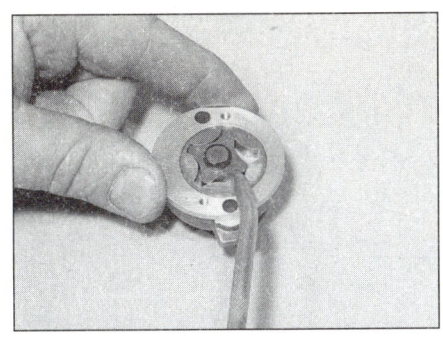

21.15 Lubricate the pump with clean oil

21.18 Fit a new gasket (arrowed)

21.19a Install the pump . . .

21.19b . . . and tighten its screws to the specified torque

21.21a Fit the sprocket then install the bolt . . .

the Chapter **(see illustration 21.11)**. If the clearance measured is greater than the maximum listed, renew the pump.

13 Lay a straight-edge across the rotors and the pump body and, using a feeler gauge, measure the rotor endfloat (the gap between the rotors and the straight-edge) **(see illustration)**. If the clearance measured is greater than the maximum listed, renew the pump.

14 Check the pump drive chain and sprockets for wear or damage, and renew them as a set if necessary.

15 If the pump is good, make sure all the components are clean, then lubricate them with new engine oil **(see illustration)**.

16 Fit the cover, noting that it can only be fitted one way, and tighten the screws securely **(see illustrations 21.9b and 21.9a)**.

17 Rotate the pump shaft by hand and check that the rotors turn smoothly and freely.

Installation

18 Lay a new pump gasket onto the crankcase, making sure the holes in the gasket align correctly with the oil holes **(see illustration)**.

19 Install the pump, noting that it can only be fitted one way, and tighten the screws to the torque setting specified at the beginning of the Chapter **(see illustrations)**. Piaggio specify that this torque setting is crucial.

20 Slide the drive sprocket, with its shouldered end facing out, onto the crankshaft **(see illustration 21.7c)**. Fit the drive chain around the sprocket and slip it down into the sump **(see illustration 21.7b)**.

21 Fit the driven sprocket into the chain **(see illustration 21.7a)**, then fit the sprocket onto the pump, aligning the flat with that on the pump shaft **(see illustration)**. Install the bolt, and using the method employed on removal to prevent the sprocket turning, tighten the sprocket bolt to the specified torque **(see illustration)**.

22 Install the driven sprocket plate and tighten its screws securely **(see illustration)**.

23 Remove any traces of old sealant from the

21.21b . . . and tighten it to the specified torque

21.22 Install the sprocket plate

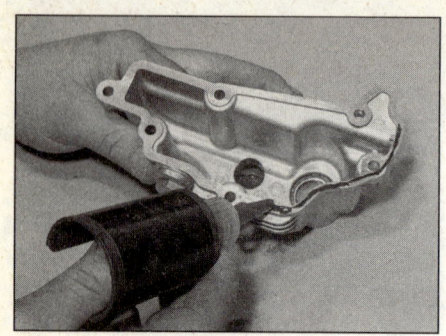

2C•18 Four-stroke engines (Sfera 125, Liberty 125, ET4 125)

21.24a Apply a sealant...

21.24b ...then install the cover...

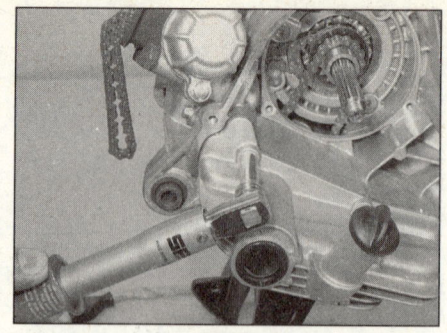

21.24c ...and tighten the bolts to the specified torque

sump cover and crankcase mating surfaces and make sure they are clean. If a scraper is used, take care not to scratch or gouge the soft aluminium.

24 Apply a suitable sealant (such as Loctite 501) to the sump cover, then fit the cover and tighten the bolts to the specified torque **(see illustrations)**.

25 Check the condition of the oil seal and the chain guide in the drive chain cover and renew them if there are any signs of oil leakage on the cover or crankshaft or wear on the guide **(see illustration)**. Fit a new O-ring onto the cover, then install the cover with its flat edge at the bottom, making sure the chain fits correctly around the guide shoe, and tighten its screws securely **(see illustration)**.

26 Install the drive pulley and variator (see Chapter 2G).

27 Install the air filter housing (see Chapter 4).

28 Fill the engine with the correct type and quantity of oil as described in Chapter 1. Start the engine and check that there are no leaks around the sump.

Oil pressure relief valve

Removal

29 Remove the air filter housing (see Chapter 4).

30 Remove the transmission cover (see Chapter 2G).

31 Remove the bolts securing the sump cover and remove the cover **(see illustration 21.4)**.

32 The valve is a push-fit in the crankcase **(see illustration)**. Draw it out and discard the O-ring, as a new one must be used.

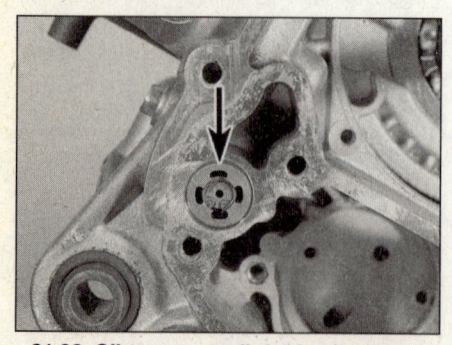

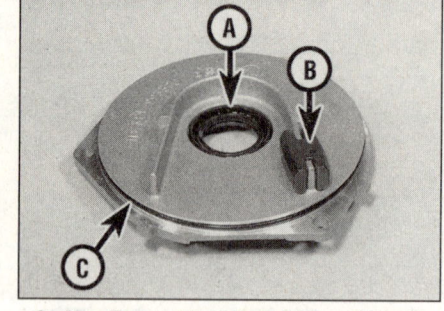

21.25a Renew the oil seal (A) and chain guide (B) if necessary, and fit a new O-ring (C)

Inspection

33 Push the valve ball and plunger on the inner end of the valve into the valve body and check that it moves smoothly and freely against the spring pressure. If not, renew the relief valve – individual components are not available.

34 Carefully remove the circlip from the outer end of the valve, noting that it is under spring pressure, and withdraw the washer, spring, plunger and ball from the valve **(see illustration)**. Inspect all components for wear or damage and renew the valve if any is found.

35 Measure the free length of the spring. If it is less than the minimum specified at the beginning of the Chapter, renew the valve.

Installation

36 Fit the ball, plunger, spring and washer into the valve body and secure them with the circlip.

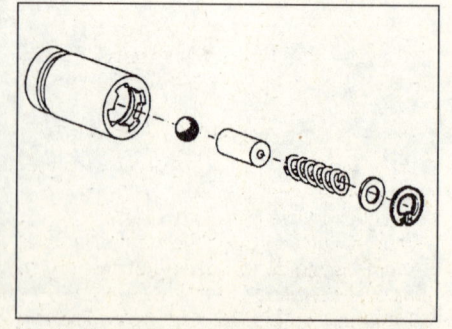

21.25b Install the cover with its flat edge at the bottom

37 Smear the new valve body O-ring with clean engine oil, then fit it onto the body. Press the valve into its bore in the crankcase **(see illustration 21.32)**.

38 Apply a suitable sealant (such as Loctite 501) to the sump cover, then fit the cover and tighten the bolts to the specified torque **(see illustrations 21.24a, 21.24b and 21.24c)**.

39 Fit the transmission cover (see Chapter 2G), then install the air filter housing (see Chapter 4).

22 Crankcase halves, crankshaft and connecting rod

Note: *To separate the crankcase halves, the engine must be removed from the frame.*

Separation

1 To access the crankshaft and its bearings, the crankcase must be split into two parts.

2 To enable the crankcases to be separated, the engine must be removed from the frame (see Section 5). Before the crankcases can be separated the following components must be removed:

a) Camchain, blades and sprockets (see Section 10).
b) Cylinder head (see Section 12).
c) Cylinder (see Section 15).
d) Alternator rotor and stator (see Section 19).
e) Variator (see Chapter 2G).
f) Starter motor (see Chapter 9).
g) Oil pump (see Section 21).

21.32 Oil pressure relief valve (arrowed)

21.34 Oil pressure relief valve components

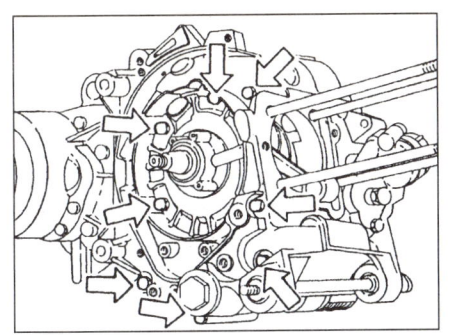

22.3 Crankcase bolt locations (arrowed)

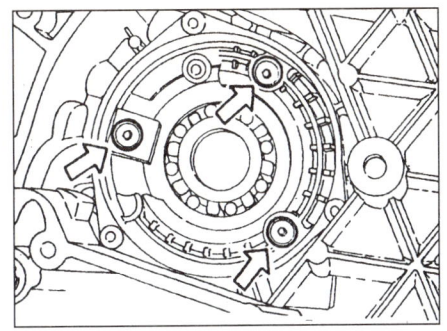

22.5 Left-hand main bearing retaining plate screws (arrowed)

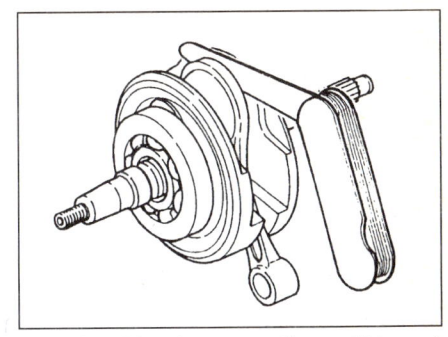

22.7 Checking the connecting rod big-end bearing side clearance

3 Unscrew the eight crankcase bolts evenly, a little at a time and in a criss-cross sequence until they are all finger-tight, then remove them **(see illustration)**. Carefully lift the right-hand crankcase half off the left-hand half. Lift the crankshaft out of the left-hand (transmission side) crankcase.

4 Remove the oil seals from each crankcase half, having taken careful note of their fitted positions.

Inspection

5 Check the condition of the crankshaft main bearings. The crankshaft right-hand bearing will remain on the crankshaft and the left-hand bearing will be held in the left-hand crankcase half. The bearings should spin freely and smoothly without any rough spots or excessive noise. Renew them if there is any doubt about their condition. The right-hand bearing should be removed from the crankshaft using an external bearing puller – make sure that the puller clamp or legs fit securely behind the bearing and are in no danger of slipping out. Before removing the left-hand bearing, remove the three screws which secure the bearing retaining plate to the crankcase **(see illustration)**. Use a suitable diameter tube to drive the bearing out of the crankcase; if necessary heat the bearing housing using a hot air gun to aid bearing removal.

6 Refer to Chapter 2A, Section 15, for inspection procedures, referring also to the Specifications section of this Chapter.

7 Check the connecting rod big-end side clearance using feeler gauges **(see illustration)**.

Reassembly

8 Install new crankshaft oil seals in the crankcase halves in the same position as noted on removal. Use a bearing driver or a suitably-sized socket which contacts only the outer face of the seal to drive it into position.

9 To fit the right-hand main bearing onto the crankshaft, the manufacturer advises that the bearing is first heated in an oil bath to around 120°C, then driven onto the crankshaft using a tubular drift which contacts the inner race of the bearing only – not the balls or outer race **(see illustration 15.16 in Chapter 2A)**. To aid the fitting of the left-hand bearing in the left-hand crankcase half it is recommended that the bearing housing in the crankcase is first heated using a hot air gun. Use a tubular drift which contacts only the outer race of the bearing to drive it into its housing. Fit the bearing retaining plate (it can only be fitted one way due to its offset screw holes), apply thread locking compound to the threads of the three retaining plate bolts and tighten them securely.

10 If not already done, remove all traces of old gasket sealant from both crankcase halves. Use a rag moistened with high flash-point solvent to degrease the mating surfaces.

11 Lubricate the crankshaft big-end and main bearings with engine oil and insert the crankshaft into the left-hand half, positioning the connecting rod in line with the crankcase mouth. Apply a suitable gasket sealant to the crankcase mating surfaces. Guide the crankcase right-hand half over the crankshaft end, pressing it over the right-hand main bearing. Use a soft-faced mallet to help the casing seat, but don't apply too much pressure. **Note:** *If the crankcases do not meet, remove the right-hand half and investigate the problem – do not be tempted to pull the crankcases together using the bolts.*

12 Clean the threads of the crankcase bolts and install them finger-tight. Tighten the bolts evenly, in a criss-cross sequence, to the torque setting specified at the beginning of this Chapter. Rotate the crankshaft to check that it is moves freely.

13 Install all other components in a reverse of the order given in Step 2.

23 Initial start-up after overhaul

1 Make sure the engine oil level is correct (see *Daily (pre-ride) checks*).

2 Make sure there is fuel in the tank.

3 With the ignition OFF, operate the kickstart a couple of times to check that the engine turns over easily.

4 Turn the ignition ON, start the engine and allow it to run at a slow idle until it reaches operating temperature. Do not be alarmed if there is a little smoke from the exhaust – this will be due to the oil used to lubricate the piston and bore during assembly and should subside after a while.

5 If the engine proves reluctant to start, remove the spark plug and check that it has not become wet and oily. If it has, clean it and try again. If the engine refuses to start, go through the fault finding charts at the end of this manual to identify the problem.

6 Check carefully for oil leaks and make sure the transmission and controls, especially the brakes, function properly before road testing the machine. Refer to Section 24 for the recommended running-in procedure.

7 Upon completion of the road test, and after the engine has cooled down completely, recheck the valve clearances (see Chapter 1) and check the engine oil level (see *Daily (pre-ride) checks*).

24 Recommended running-in procedure

1 Treat the machine gently for the first few miles to make sure oil has circulated throughout the engine and any new parts installed have started to seat.

2 Even greater care is necessary if the engine has been rebored or a new crankshaft has been installed. In the case of a rebore, the bike will have to be run-in as when new. This means a restraining hand on the throttle until at least 600 miles (1000 km) have been covered. There's no point in keeping to any set speed limit – the main idea is to keep from labouring the engine and to gradually increase performance up to the 600 mile (1000 km) mark. Make sure that the throttle position is varied to vary engine speed, and use full throttle for only short bursts, but do not allow the machine to attain more than 80% full speed, or to maintain any one speed for too long. Experience is the best guide, since it's easy to tell when an engine is running freely.

3 If a lubrication failure is suspected, stop the engine immediately and try to find the cause. If an engine is run without oil, even for a short period of time, severe damage will occur.

Chapter 2 Part D:
Four-stroke engines
(ET4 50, Liberty 50 4T, Zip 50 4T, Fly 50 4T, LX4 50)

Refer to the beginning of Chapter 1 for model identification details

Contents

Alternator rotor and stator – removal and installation	18
Cam chain tensioner – removal, inspection and installation	8
Camshaft and rockers – removal, inspection and installation	10
Cam chain, blades and sprockets – removal, inspection and installation	9
Cooling fan – removal and installation	17
Crankcase halves, crankshaft and connecting rod	21
Cylinder – removal, inspection and installation	14
Cylinder head – removal and installation	11
Cylinder head and valves – disassembly, inspection and reassembly	13
Disassembly and reassembly – general information	6
Engine/transmission unit – removal and installation	5
General information	1
Idle speed – check and adjustment	see Chapter 1
Initial start-up after overhaul	22
Major engine repair – general note	4
Oil and filter – change	see Chapter 1
Oil level – check	see *Daily (pre-ride) checks*
Oil pump – removal, inspection and installation	20
Operations possible with the engine in the frame	2
Operations requiring engine removal	3
Piston – removal, inspection and installation	15
Piston rings – inspection and installation	16
Recommended running-in procedure	23
Spark plug gap – check and adjustment	see Chapter 1
Starter motor – removal and installation	see Chapter 9
Starter pinion assembly – removal, inspection and installation	19
Valve clearances – check and adjustment	see Chapter 1
Valve cover – removal and installation	7
Valves/valve seats/valve guides – overhaul	12

Degrees of difficulty

Easy, suitable for novice with little experience	**Fairly easy,** suitable for beginner with some experience	**Fairly difficult,** suitable for competent DIY mechanic	**Difficult,** suitable for experienced DIY mechanic	**Very difficult,** suitable for expert DIY or professional

Specifications

General
Type	Single cylinder four-stroke
Capacity	49.9 cc
Bore	39.0 mm
Stroke	41.8 mm
Compression ratio	11.5 to 12.0 : 1

Camshaft
Intake and exhaust lobe height	25.935 mm
Left-hand journal diameter	
Standard	12.002 to 12.010 mm
Service limit (min)	11.98 mm
Right-hand journal diameter	
Standard	15.977 to 15.985 mm
Service limit (min)	15.96 mm
Camshaft endfloat (max)	0.50 mm

Cylinder head
Warpage (max)	0.05 mm
Left-hand camshaft bearing housing diameter	32.015 to 32.025 mm
Right-hand camshaft journal housing diameter	16.000 to 16.018 mm
Rocker arm shaft housing	11.000 to 11.018 mm
Rocker arm shaft diameter (min)	10.970 mm
Rocker arm internal diameter (max)	11.030 mm

Valves, guides and springs

Valve clearances	See Chapter 1
Intake valve	
Overall standard length	70.1 mm
Stem diameter	
Standard	4.985 mm
Service limit (min)	4.970 mm
Guide bore diameter	
Standard	5.000 to 5.012 mm
Service limit (max)	5.022 mm
Face width	1.5 mm
Seat width	1.6 mm
Exhaust valve	
Overall standard length	69.2 mm
Stem diameter	
Standard	4.975 mm
Service limit (min)	4.960 mm
Guide bore diameter	
Standard	5.000 to 5.012 mm
Service limit (max)	5.022 mm
Face width	1.6 mm
Seat width	1.6 mm
Valve spring free length (inlet and exhaust)	n/a

Cylinder bore – ET4 50, Liberty 50 4T, Zip 50 4T

Note: *The following specifications are for parts supplied for ET4 50, Liberty 50 4T and Zip 50 4T models when first introduced. Specifications for parts supplied at a later date may differ (see **Cylinder bore** – Fly 50 4T, LX4 50).*

Standard	
Size-code A	38.986 to 38.993 mm
Size-code B	38.993 to 39.000 mm
Size-code C	39.000 to 39.007 mm
Size-code D	39.007 to 39.014 mm
1st oversize	39.186 to 39.214 mm
2nd oversize	39.386 to 39.414 mm
3rd oversize	39.586 to 39.614 mm

Piston – ET4 50, Liberty 50 4T, Zip 50 4T

Note: *The following specifications are for parts supplied for ET4 50, Liberty 50 4T and Zip 50 4T models when first introduced. Specifications for parts supplied at a later date may differ (see **Piston** – Fly 50 4T, LX4 50).*

Piston diameter (measured 27 mm down from top edge of the piston, at 90° to piston pin axis)	
Standard	
Size-code A	38.954 to 38.961 mm
Size-code B	38.961 to 38.968 mm
Size-code C	38.968 to 38.975 mm
Size-code D	38.975 to 38.982 mm
1st oversize	39.154 to 39.182 mm
2nd oversize	39.354 to 39.382 mm
3rd oversize	39.554 to 39.582 mm
Piston-to-bore clearance (when new)	0.025 to 0.039 mm
Piston pin diameter	
Standard	12.996 to 13.000 mm
Service limit (min)	12.990 mm
Piston pin bore diameter in piston	13.005 to 13.010 mm

Cylinder bore – Fly 50 4T, LX4 50

Note: *The following specifications are for parts supplied originally for Fly 50 4T and LX4 50 models.*

Standard	
Size-code A	38.993 to 39.000 mm
Size-code B	39.000 to 39.007 mm
Size-code C	39.007 to 39.014 mm
Size-code D	39.014 to 39.021 mm
1st oversize	39.193 to 39.221 mm
2nd oversize	39.393 to 39.421 mm
3rd oversize	39.593 to 39.621 mm

Four-stroke engines (ET4 50, Liberty 50 4T, Zip 50 4T, Fly 50 4T, LX4 50) 2D•3

Piston – Fly 50 4T, LX4 50
Note: The following specifications are for parts supplied originally for Fly 50 4T and LX4 50 models.
Piston diameter (measured 27 mm down from top edge of the piston, at 90° to piston pin axis)
  Asso piston – standard
    Size-code A .... 38.954 to 38.961 mm
    Size-code B .... 38.961 to 38.968 mm
    Size-code C (with Asso cylinder) .... 38.968 to 38.975 mm
    Piston-to-bore clearance (when new) .... 0.032 to 0.046 mm
  Asso piston – standard
    Size-code C (with Shiram cylinder) .... 38.963 to 38.970 mm
    Piston-to-bore clearance (when new) .... 0.037 to 0.051 mm
    Size-code D .... not available
  Shiram piston – standard
    Size-code A .... 38.949 to 38.956 mm
    Size-code B .... 38.956 to 38.966 mm
    Size-code C .... not available
    Size-code D (with Shiram cylinder) .... 38.970 to 38.977 mm
    Piston-to-bore clearance (when new) .... 0.037 to 0.051 mm
  Shiram piston – standard
    Size-code D (with Asso cylinder) .... 38.975 to 38.982 mm
    Piston-to-bore clearance (when new) .... 0.032 to 0.046 mm
  1st oversize .... 39.154 to 39.182 mm
  2nd oversize .... 39.354 to 39.382 mm
  3rd oversize .... 39.554 to 39.582 mm
  Piston-to-bore clearance (when new) .... 0.032 to 0.046 mm
Piston pin diameter (all)
  Standard .... 12.996 to 13.000 mm
  Service limit (min) .... 12.990 mm
Piston pin bore diameter in piston (all) .... 13.005 to 13.010 mm

Piston rings
Ring end gap (installed)
  Top ring
    Standard .... 0.08 to 0.20 mm
    Service limit (max) .... 0.35 mm
  2nd ring
    Standard .... 0.05 to 0.20 mm
    Service limit (max) .... 0.30 mm
  Oil control ring
    Standard .... 0.20 to 0.70 mm
    Service limit (max) .... 0.80 mm
Ring-to-groove clearance
  Top ring
    Standard .... 0.030 to 0.065 mm
    Service limit (max) .... 0.080 mm
  2nd ring
    Standard .... 0.020 to 0.055 mm
    Service limit (max) .... 0.070 mm
  Oil control ring
    Standard .... 0.040 to 0.160 mm
    Service limit (max) .... 0.200 mm

Lubrication system
Oil pump
  Inner rotor tip-to-outer rotor clearance (max) .... 0.15 mm
  Outer rotor-to-body clearance (max) .... 0.20 mm
  Rotor endfloat (max) .... 0.09 mm

Connecting rod
Small-end internal diameter
  Standard .... 13.015 to 13.025 mm
  Service limit (max) .... 13.030 mm
Big-end side clearance
  Standard .... 0.15 to 0.30 mm
  Service limit (max) .... 0.50 mm
Big-end radial freeplay
  Standard .... 0.006 to 0.018 mm
  Service limit (max) .... 0.25 mm

2D•4 Four-stroke engines (ET4 50, Liberty 50 4T, Zip 50 4T, Fly 50 4T, LX4 50)

Crankshaft

Combined width of flywheels and big end	45 mm
Runout A (max)	0.15 mm
Runout B (max)	0.02 mm
Runout C (max)	0.10 mm

Torque settings

Valve cover bolts	8 to 10 Nm
Cam chain tensioner spring cap bolt	5 to 6 Nm
Cam chain tensioner blade bolt	5 to 7 Nm
Cam chain tensioner bolts	8 to 10 Nm
Camshaft sprocket bolt	12 to 14 Nm
Rocker shaft stopper bolt	3 to 4 Nm
Cylinder head nuts	
Initial setting	6 to 7 Nm
Final setting	+ 90°+ 90°
Cylinder head-to-block bolts	8 to 10 Nm
Oil pump driven sprocket bolt	12 to 14 Nm
Oil pump mounting screws	5 to 6 Nm
Oil pump cover screws	0.7 to 0.9 Nm
Alternator rotor nut	40 to 44 Nm
Crankcase bolts	8 to 10 Nm
Engine front mounting bolt	33 to 41 Nm
Rear shock absorber lower mounting bolt	33 to 41 Nm

1 General information

The engine unit is a single cylinder four-stroke, with fan-assisted air cooling. The fan is mounted on the alternator rotor, which is on the right-hand end of the crankshaft. The crankshaft assembly is pressed, incorporating the connecting rod, with the big-end running on the crankpin on a needle roller bearing. The crankshaft runs in caged ball main bearings. The crankcase divides vertically.

The camshaft is chain-driven off the left-hand end of the crankshaft, and operates two valves via rocker arms.

2 Operations possible with the engine in the frame

All components and assemblies, with the exception of the crankshaft/connecting rod assembly and its bearings, can be worked on without having to remove the engine/transmission assembly from the frame. If, however, a number of areas require attention at the same time, removal of the engine is recommended, as it is easy to do so.

3 Operations requiring engine removal

To access the crankshaft and connecting rod assembly and its bearings, the engine must be removed from the frame and the crankcase halves must be separated.

4 Major engine repair – general note

1 It is not always easy to determine when or if an engine should be completely overhauled, as a number of factors must be considered.
2 High mileage is not necessarily an indication that an overhaul is needed, while low mileage, on the other hand, does not preclude the need for an overhaul. Frequency of servicing is probably the single most important consideration. An engine that has regular and frequent oil and filter changes, as well as other required maintenance, will most likely give many miles of reliable service. Conversely, a neglected engine, or one which has not been run-in properly, may require an overhaul very early in its life.
3 Exhaust smoke and excessive oil consumption are both indications that piston rings and/or valve guides are in need of attention, although make sure that the fault is not due to oil leakage.
4 If the engine is making obvious knocking or rumbling noises, the connecting rod and/or main bearings are probably at fault.
5 Loss of power, rough running, excessive valve train noise and high fuel consumption rates may also point to the need for an overhaul, especially if they are all present at the same time. If a complete tune-up does not remedy the situation, major mechanical work is the only solution.
6 An engine overhaul generally involves restoring the internal parts to the specifications of a new engine. The piston rings and main and connecting rod bearings are usually renewed and, if necessary, the cylinder is rebored. Generally the valve seats are reground, since they are usually in less than perfect condition at this point. The end result should be a like-new engine that will give as many trouble-free miles as the original.
7 Before beginning the engine overhaul, read through the related procedures to familiarise yourself with the scope and requirements of the job. Overhauling an engine is not all that difficult, but it is time-consuming. Plan on the scooter being tied up for a minimum of two weeks. Check on the availability of parts and make sure that any necessary special tools, equipment and supplies are obtained in advance.
8 Most work can be done with typical workshop hand tools, although a number of precision measuring tools are required for inspecting parts to determine if they must be renewed. Often a dealer will handle the inspection of parts and offer advice concerning reconditioning and renewal. As a general rule, time is the primary cost of an overhaul, so it does not pay to install worn or substandard parts.
9 As a final note, to ensure maximum life and minimum trouble from a rebuilt engine, everything must be assembled with care in a spotlessly-clean environment.

5 Engine/transmission unit – removal and installation

Caution: The engine is not heavy, although engine removal and installation should be carried out with the aid of an assistant; personal injury or damage could occur if the engine falls or is dropped.

Removal

1 The procedure for removing the engine is the same as for air-cooled LEADER models (see Chapter 2E, Section 5), with the following additions.
2 Undo the three screws that secure the drivebelt air duct to the front of the belt cover,

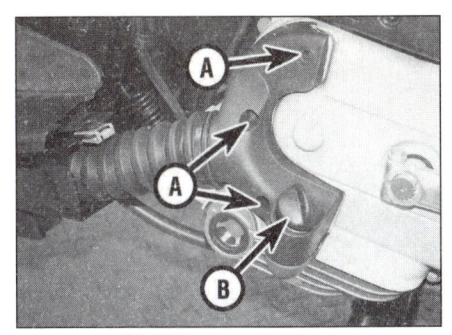

Four-stroke engines (ET4 50, Liberty 50 4T, Zip 50 4T, Fly 50 4T, LX4 50) 2D•5

5.2a Undo the screws (A) and the cap (B) . . .

5.2b . . . then displace the duct

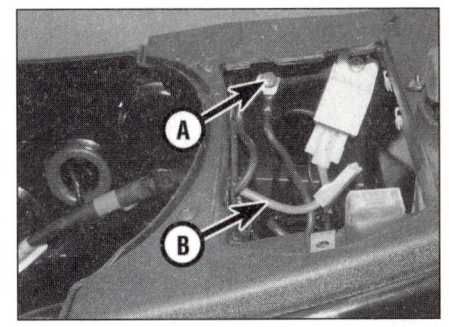

5.3 Engine earth (A) and starter motor wire (B)

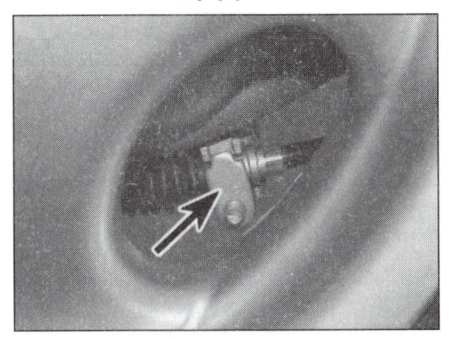

5.5 Location of rear brake cable clamp (arrowed)

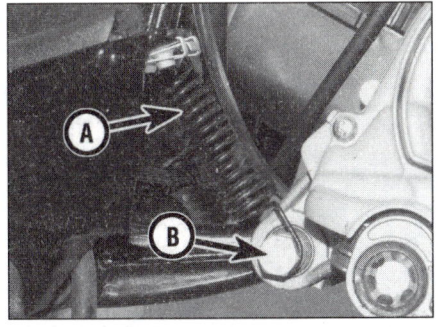

5.6 Disconnect the spring (A) from the engine bolt (B)

5.8a Undo the nut (arrowed) on the front mounting bolt . . .

then unscrew the oil filler cap and displace the duct **(see illustrations)**.

3 Remove the battery (see Chapter 9). Trace the red wire from the starter motor to the solenoid mounted on the right-hand side of the battery location and disconnect it, then undo the screw securing the engine earth wire **(see illustration)**. Cut the cable ties securing the starter motor and earth wire to the frame and secure the wires to the engine unit.

4 No carburettor heater is fitted.

5 The rear brake cable is clamped at the back of the drivebelt cover **(see illustration)**.

6 Place a suitable temporary support under the metal section of frame forward of the engine mounting bracket, then disconnect the lower end of the spring from the head of the front engine mounting bolt, noting how it fits **(see illustration)**.

7 Remove the rear shock absorber and rest the weight of the scooter on the temporary support.

8 Remove the front engine mounting bolt and manoeuvre the engine unit out of the frame **(see illustrations)**. Note the spacer on the left-hand side of the mounting bolt.

Installation

9 Installation is the reverse of the removal procedure. If required, fill the engine with the specified quantity of oil (see Chapter 1 Specifications) and check the oil level as described in *Daily (pre-ride) checks*.

6 Disassembly and reassembly – general information

Disassembly

1 Before disassembling the engine, the external surfaces of the unit should be thoroughly cleaned and degreased. This will prevent contamination of the engine internals, and will also make working a lot easier and cleaner. A high flash-point solvent, such as paraffin can be used, or better still, a proprietary engine degreaser such as Gunk. Use old paintbrushes and toothbrushes to work the solvent into the various recesses of the engine casings. Take care to exclude solvent or water from the electrical components and inlet and exhaust ports.

⚠ **Warning: The use of petrol (gasoline) as a cleaning agent should be avoided because of the risk of fire.**

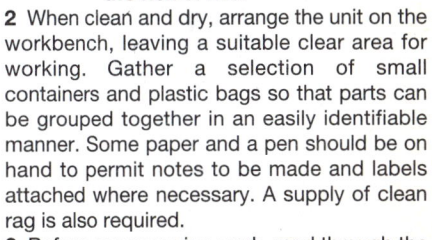

2 When clean and dry, arrange the unit on the workbench, leaving a suitable clear area for working. Gather a selection of small containers and plastic bags so that parts can be grouped together in an easily identifiable manner. Some paper and a pen should be on hand to permit notes to be made and labels attached where necessary. A supply of clean rag is also required.

3 Before commencing work, read through the appropriate section so that some idea of the necessary procedure can be gained. When removing components it should be noted that great force is seldom required, unless specified. In many cases, a component's reluctance to be removed is indicative of an incorrect approach or removal method – if in any doubt, recheck with the text.

4 When disassembling the engine, keep 'mated' parts that have been in contact with each other during engine operation together. These 'mated' parts must be re-used or renewed as an assembly.

5.8b . . . then withdraw the bolt, noting the position of the spacer (arrowed) . . .

5.8c . . . and manoeuvre the engine out

2D•6 Four-stroke engines (ET4 50, Liberty 50 4T, Zip 50 4T, Fly 50 4T, LX4 50)

7.4 Remove the valve cover; note the breather hose union (arrowed)

8.4a Location of alternator cover fixings

8.4b Upper end of cover is secured by knurled knob (arrowed)

5 Complete engine disassembly should be done in the following general order with reference to the appropriate Sections. Refer to Chapter 2G for details of transmission components disassembly.
  Remove the valve cover.
  Remove the camshaft and rockers.
  Remove the cylinder head.
  Remove the cylinder.
  Remove the piston.
  Remove the alternator.
  Remove the starter motor (see Chapter 9).
  Remove the sump cover.
  Remove the oil pump.
  Separate the crankcase halves.
  Remove the crankshaft.

Reassembly

6 Reassembly is accomplished by reversing the general disassembly sequence.

7 Valve cover – removal and installation

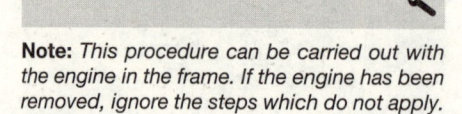

Note: *This procedure can be carried out with the engine in the frame. If the engine has been removed, ignore the steps which do not apply.*

Removal

1 Remove the bodywork as required by your model to access the engine (see Chapter 7).
2 Release the clip securing the breather hose to the union on the valve cover and pull off the hose **(see illustration 7.4)**.
3 Undo the cam chain tensioner cap bolt and withdraw the spring from the tensioner body (see Section 8). **Note:** *A lug inside the valve cover pretensions the (lower) cam chain guide blade. The tensioner cap bolt and spring must be removed before the valve cover is removed, and installed after the valve cover is fitted to avoid over-tightening the cam chain.*
4 Undo the bolts securing the valve cover, then lift the cover off the cylinder head **(see illustration)**. If it is stuck, do not try to lever it off with a screwdriver. Tap it gently around the sides with a rubber hammer or block of wood to dislodge it. Remove the gasket and discard it, as a new one must be used.

Installation

5 Clean the mating surfaces of the cylinder head and the valve cover with a suitable solvent.
6 Lay the new gasket onto the groove in the valve cover, making sure it fits correctly.

7 Position the valve cover on the cylinder head, making sure the gasket stays in place, then install the cover bolts. Tighten the bolts evenly and in a criss-cross sequence to the torque setting specified at the beginning of the Chapter.
8 Install the cam chain tensioner spring and cap bolt, then install the remaining components in the reverse order of removal.

8 Cam chain tensioner – removal, inspection and installation

Note: *This procedure can be carried out with the engine in the frame. If the engine has been removed, ignore the steps which do not apply.*

Removal

1 Remove the bodywork as required by your model to access the engine (see Chapter 7).
2 Remove the carburettor and the inlet manifold (see Chapter 4).
3 On machines fitted with a secondary air system, release the clip securing the hose to the reed valve cover and disconnect the hose. Release the clip securing the hose to the back of the cover and disconnect the hose.
4 Undo the screws securing the alternator cover and lift off the cover **(see illustration)**. Note the upper cover fixing is a knurled knob **(see illustration)**. Remove the cooling fan (see Section 17).
5 Undo the screws securing the rear half of the engine cowling to the front half of the cowling and to the crankcase **(see illustrations)**. Note

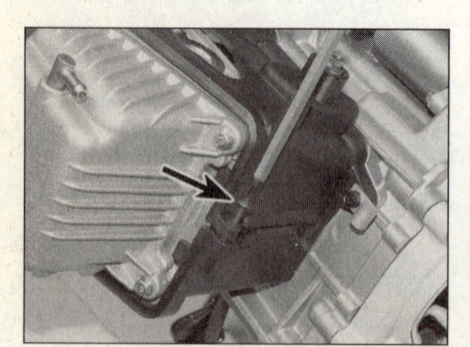

8.5a Cowling halves are joined by screws on the right-hand side . . .

8.5b . . . and the left-hand side

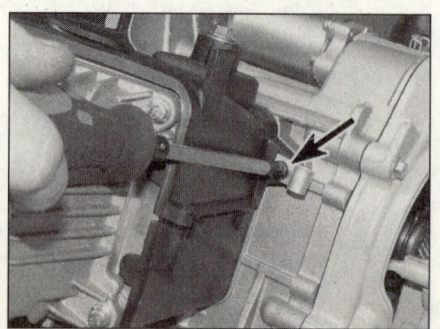

8.5c Rear cowling half is secured to crankcase. Note the clip (arrowed)

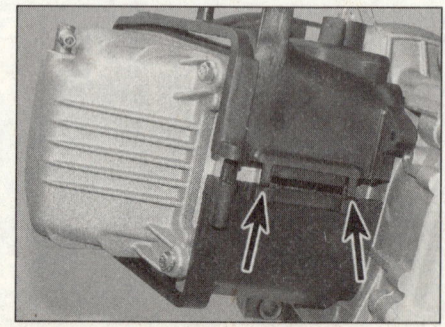

8.5d Release the clips (arrowed) . . .

Four-stroke engines (ET4 50, Liberty 50 4T, Zip 50 4T, Fly 50 4T, LX4 50) 2D•7

8.5e . . . then ease the cowling apart carefully

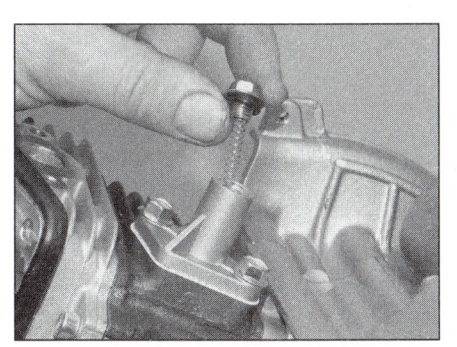

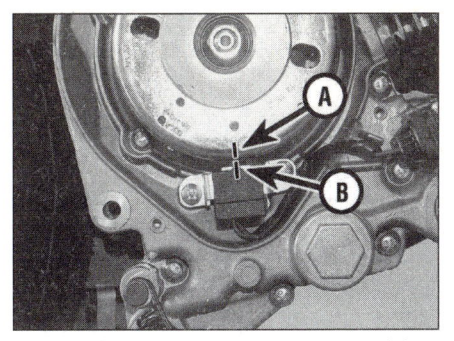

8.7a Second timing mark on rotor (A) should align with pulse generator pick-up (B)

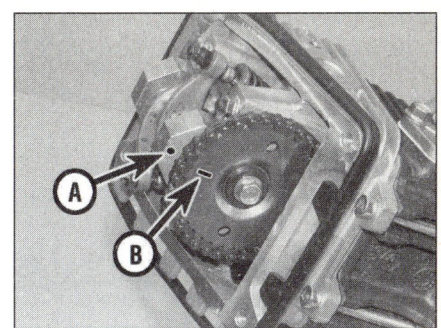

8.7b Index mark (A) should align with timing mark (B)

8.8 Remove the cap bolt and spring

the clip for the carburettor breather hose secured by the crankcase screw **(see illustration)**. The two halves of the cowling are clipped together on the left-hand side – carefully ease them apart and lift the rear half off **(see illustrations)**.
6 Remove the valve cover (see Section 7).
7 Turn the engine in a clockwise direction using the alternator rotor, until the second timing mark on the rotor aligns with the pulse generator coil pick-up, and the timing mark on the camshaft sprocket aligns with the index mark on the camshaft holder **(see illustrations)**. At this point the engine is at TDC (top dead centre) on the compression stroke (both valves closed).
8 Unscrew the chain tensioner cap bolt and withdraw the spring from the tensioner body **(see illustration)**.

9 Unscrew the two tensioner mounting bolts and withdraw the tensioner from the cylinder **(see illustration)**.
10 Remove the gasket from the base of the tensioner or from the cylinder and discard it, as a new one must be used.

Inspection
11 Examine the tensioner components for signs of wear or damage.
12 Release the ratchet mechanism from the tensioner plunger and check that the plunger moves freely in and out of the tensioner body **(see illustration)**.
13 If the tensioner or any of its components are worn or damaged, or if the plunger is seized in the body, they must be renewed. Individual components are available.

Installation
14 Turn the engine in a clockwise direction using the alternator rotor. This removes all the slack between the crankshaft and the camshaft in the front run of the chain and transfers it to the back run where it will be taken up by the tensioner.
15 Release the ratchet mechanism and press the tensioner plunger all the way into the tensioner body **(see illustration 8.12)**.
16 Place a new gasket on the tensioner body, then install it in the engine and tighten the bolts to the torque specified at the beginning of the Chapter **(see illustration 8.9)**.
17 Install the valve cover (see Section 7).
Note: *A lug inside the valve cover pretensions the (lower) cam chain guide blade. The tensioner cap bolt and spring must be installed after the valve cover is fitted to avoid over-tightening the cam chain.*
18 If necessary, install a new O-ring on the cap bolt. Install the spring and cap bolt and tighten the bolt to the specified torque **(see illustration 8.8)**.
19 Install the remaining components in the reverse order of removal.

9 Cam chain, blades and sprockets – removal, inspection and installation

Note: *This procedure can be carried out with the engine in the frame. If the engine has been removed, ignore the steps which do not apply.*

Removal
1 Remove the cam chain tensioner (see Section 8).
2 If the cam chain and crankshaft sprocket are being removed, remove the oil pump driven sprocket, drive chain and drive sprocket (see Section 20).
3 Undo the camshaft sprocket centre bolt **(see illustration)**. To prevent the sprocket from turning, use the Piaggio service tool (Part No. 020565Y) or a suitable holding tool fitted into the hole(s) in the sprocket. If necessary, protect the gasket surface of the cylinder head with a piece of wood.
4 Remove the centre bolt and Belleville

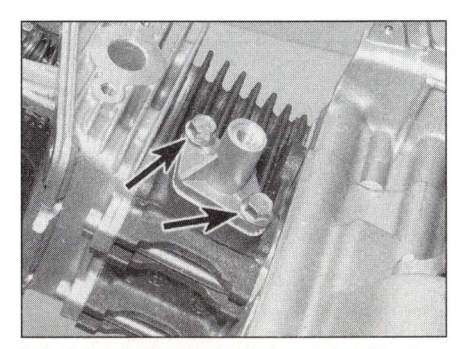

8.9 Cam chain tensioner is retained by two bolts (arrowed)

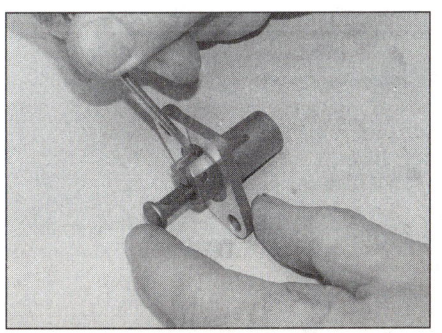

8.12 Check the operation of the ratchet and plunger

9.3 Lock the sprocket and undo the centre bolt

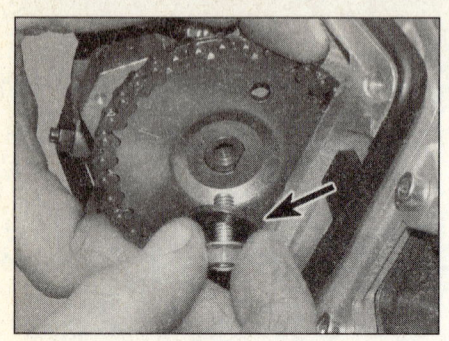

2D•8 Four-stroke engines (ET4 50, Liberty 50 4T, Zip 50 4T, Fly 50 4T, LX4 50)

9.4 Remove the bolt and Belleville washer (arrowed)

9.5a Note how the centre hole aligns with the end of the camshaft . . .

9.5b . . . then lift off the sprocket . . .

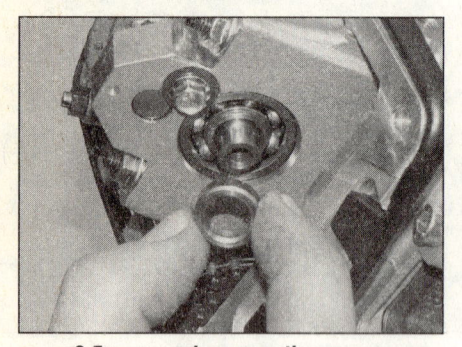

9.5c . . . and remove the spacer

9.6a Remove the thrustwasher . . .

washer, noting which way round the washer fits **(see illustration)**.
5 Note how the straight-edge on the end of the camshaft aligns with the centre hole in the sprocket, then lift off the sprocket and disengage it from the camchain **(see illustrations)**. Remove the sprocket spacer for safekeeping **(see illustration)**.
6 If required, secure the chain with a cable tie to prevent it falling into the engine. If the chain is to be removed, mark it with paint so that if it is re-used it can be fitted the same way round. Remove the thrustwasher from the end of the crankshaft, then lower the chain down its tunnel and slip it off the sprocket on the crankshaft **(see illustrations)**. Draw the sprocket off the crankshaft, noting how it locates over the pin on the shaft **(see illustration)**.
7 If required remove the bolt securing the cam chain tensioner blade to the crankcase

and withdraw the blade, noting which way round it fits, and the spacer **(see illustration)**.
8 The cam chain guide blade is secured by the cylinder head. To remove the blade, first remove the head (see Section 11), then lift out the blade. Note how the lower end of the blade locates in the U-shaped lug in the crankcase **(see illustration 9.7)**.

Inspection
9 Check the sprockets for wear, cracks and other damage, renewing them if necessary. If the sprocket teeth are worn, the chain is also worn. If wear this severe is apparent, the entire engine should be disassembled for inspection.
10 Check the chain tensioner blade and guide blade for wear or damage and renew them if necessary. If they are worn or damaged, the chain may be worn out or improperly tensioned. Check the operation of the cam chain tensioner (see Section 8).

Installation
11 If removed, install the guide blade and the tensioner blade, making sure they are the correct way round. Tighten the tensioner blade bolt to the torque setting specified at the beginning of the Chapter.
12 If removed, install the sprocket onto the crankshaft, aligning the cutout in the sprocket with the pin on the crankshaft **(see illustration 9.6c)**. Also fit the camshaft sprocket spacer **(see illustration 9.5c)**.
13 Lower the cam chain down through the tunnel and fit it onto the sprocket. If the chain is being re-used, ensure it is fitted the right way round (see Step 6).
14 Check that the timing mark on the alternator rotor still aligns with the pulse generator pick-up **(see illustration 8.7a)**. Slip the camshaft sprocket into the top of the chain, then fit the sprocket onto the camshaft, aligning the straight-edges between the sprocket and the shaft end **(see illustration 9.5a)**. Ensure that any slack in the chain is at the back of the engine so that it is later taken up by the tensioner, and that the timing mark on the camshaft sprocket aligns with the index mark on the camshaft holder **(see illustration 8.7b)**. Secure the sprocket with the centre bolt and Belleville washer. **Note:** *The outer edge of the Belleville washer should be positioned against the sprocket on installation.* Insert a length of dowel or a similar tool through the hole in the cylinder for the cam chain tensioner, then press it against the tensioner blade and ensure that the timing marks are still aligned.

9.6b . . . then lift out the cam chain

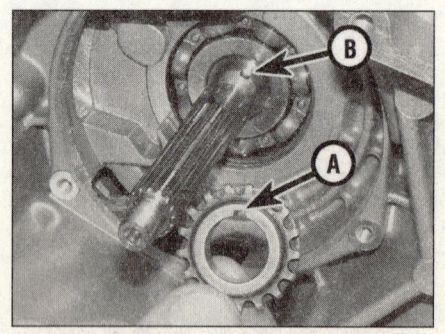

9.6c Notch in sprocket (A) locates on pin (B)

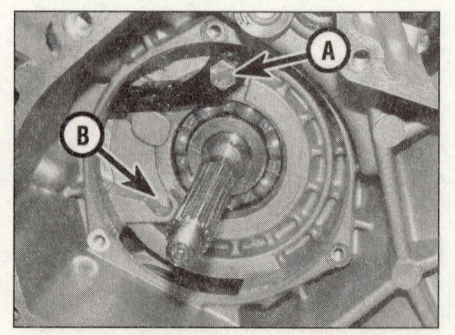

9.7 Tensioner blade is secured by bolt (A). Guide blade locates in lug (B)

Four-stroke engines (ET4 50, Liberty 50 4T, Zip 50 4T, Fly 50 4T, LX4 50) 2D•9

Caution: *If the marks are not aligned exactly as described, the valve timing will be incorrect and the valves may strike the piston, causing extensive damage to the engine.*

15 Using the method employed on removal to prevent the camshaft sprocket turning, tighten the bolt to the torque setting specified at the beginning of the Chapter **(see illustration 9.3)**.
16 If removed, fit the thrustwasher onto the end of the crankshaft **(see illustration 9.6a)**, then install the oil pump drive sprocket, chain and driven sprocket (see Section 20).
17 Install the remaining components in the reverse order of removal.

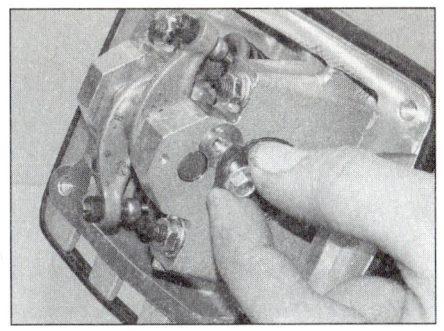

10 Camshaft and rockers – removal, inspection and installation

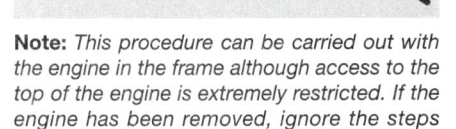

Note: *This procedure can be carried out with the engine in the frame although access to the top of the engine is extremely restricted. If the engine has been removed, ignore the steps which do not apply.*

Removal

1 Remove the valve cover (see Section 7).
2 Remove the camshaft sprocket (see Section 9). Secure the chain with a cable tie to prevent it dropping into the engine. Stuff a clean rag into the cam chain tunnel to prevent anything falling into the engine.
3 Undo the stopper bolt and remove the bolt and washer **(see illustration)**.
4 Mark the rocker arms so that they can be installed in their original positions, then insert a screwdriver into the right-hand end of the camshaft holder and press out the rocker shaft **(see illustration)**. Support the exhaust valve (right-hand) rocker arm as the shaft is withdrawn and remove it once it is free **(see illustration)**. Withdraw the shaft completely and remove the intake valve rocker arm, then assemble the rockers in their original positions on the shaft **(see illustration)**.
5 Before removing the camshaft, temporarily install the stopper bolt and washer and check that the camshaft rotates freely with no discernible up-and-down movement. If available, measure the camshaft endfloat with a dial gauge and compare the result to the specification at the beginning of the Chapter. If the endfloat is excessive, remove the camshaft and inspect the shaft journal, bearings and bearing housings for wear.
6 Remove the stopper bolt and washer. The camshaft and bearing must be drawn out of the camshaft holder – Piaggio provide a service tool (Part No. 020450Y) to do this. Alternatively, use the set-up shown **(see illustration)**. Thread the centre bolt all the way into the end of the camshaft, then gradually turn the outside bolts exerting even pressure against the face of the camshaft holder to pull out the camshaft **(see illustration)**.

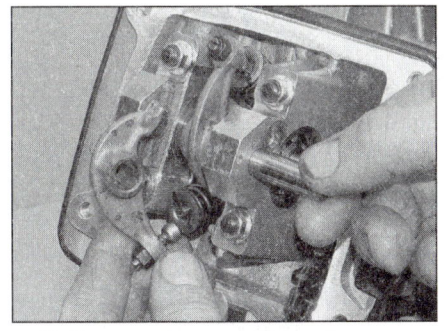

Inspection

7 Clean all of the components with solvent and dry them. Inspect the camshaft lobes for heat discoloration (blue appearance), score marks, chipped areas, flat spots and spalling **(see illustration)**. Measure the height of both lobes with a micrometer and compare the results to the specifications at the beginning of the Chapter **(see illustration 10.7b in Chapter 2E)**. If damage is noted or wear is excessive, the camshaft must be renewed.
8 Check the condition of the camshaft bearing **(see illustration 10.7)**. If it is in any way worn, runs noisily or roughly, or has excessive play, it must be renewed. If necessary, draw the bearing off the camshaft using a suitable puller. When installing the new bearing, heat it to aid installation and press it onto the shaft, pressing on the inner race only.
9 Measure the camshaft journal with a micrometer and, if available, measure the internal diameter of the housing journal with a telescoping gauge and micrometer **(see**

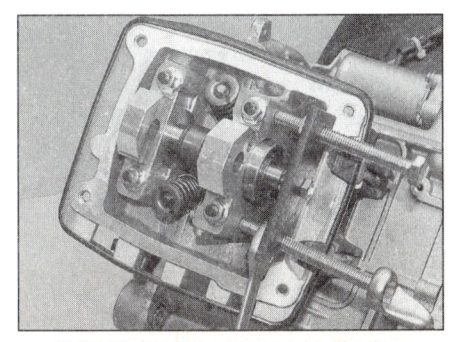

10.3 Remove the stopper bolt and washer

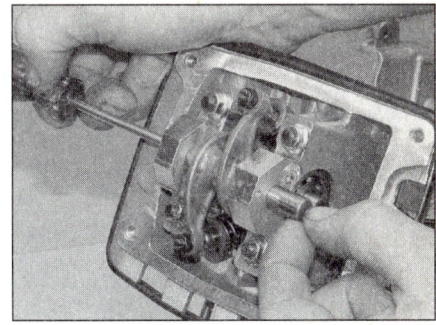

10.4a Press out the rocker shaft . . .

10.4b . . . and remove the rocker arms

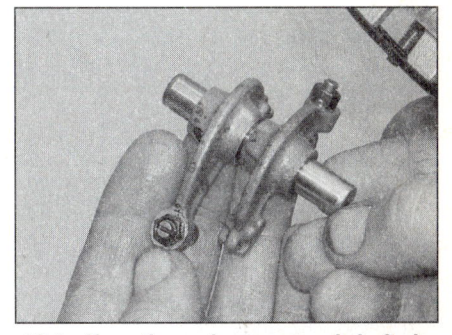

10.4c Keep the rocker arms and shafts in their original positions

10.6a Using the set-up described . . .

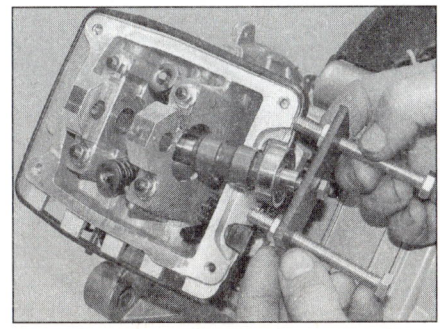

10.6b . . . to remove the camshaft and bearing

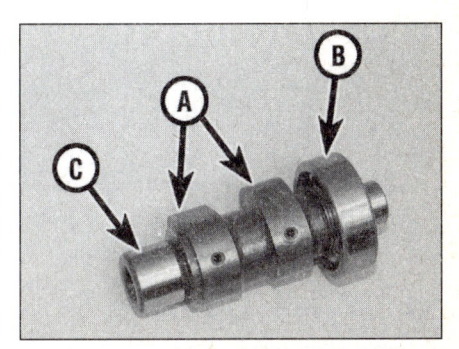

10.7 Inspect the camshaft lobes (A), bearing (B) and bearing journal (C)

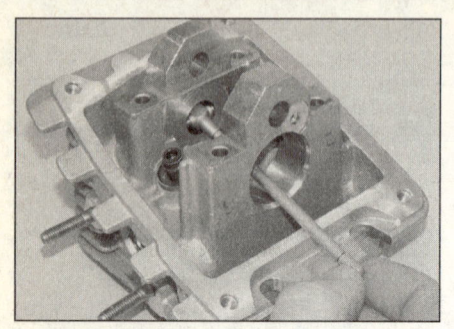

2D•10 Four-stroke engines (ET4 50, Liberty 50 4T, Zip 50 4T, Fly 50 4T, LX4 50)

10.9 Measuring the internal diameter of the camshaft housing journal

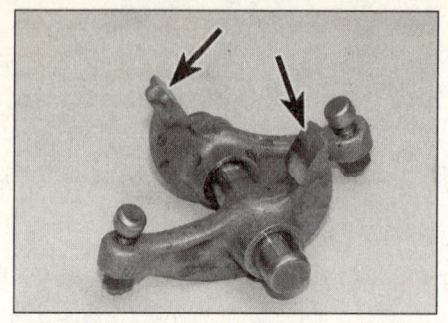

10.10a Inspect the rocker arm faces . . .

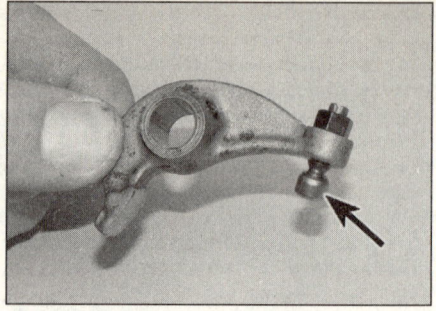

10.10b . . . and the articulated tip of the adjusting screw (arrowed)

10.11a Ensure the camshaft is pressed all the way into its holder

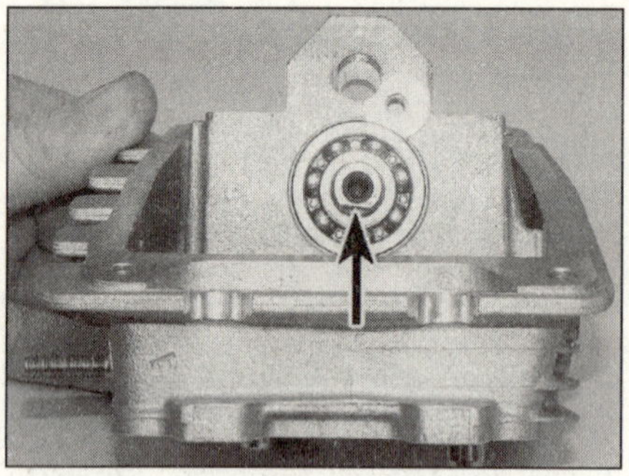

10.11b Straight-edge should face downwards

illustration). Compare the results to the specifications at the beginning of the Chapter and, if damage is noted or wear is excessive, renew the faulty component.

10 Blow through the oil passages in the rocker arms with compressed air, if available. Inspect the rocker arm faces for pits and spalling **(see illustration)**. Check the articulated tip of the adjusting screw for wear **(see illustration)**. The tip should move freely but not be loose. Measure the internal diameter of each rocker arm, the internal diameters of the rocker shaft housings and the diameter of the rocker shaft and compare the results to the specifications at the beginning of the Chapter. If damage is noted or wear is excessive, renew the faulty component.

Installation

11 Lubricate the camshaft bearing and journal with clean engine oil, then install the camshaft. The camshaft should be pressed all the way into its holder; if necessary, use a suitably-sized socket that bears on the inner race of the camshaft bearing only, to tap the shaft into place **(see illustration)**. Ensure the camshaft is positioned with the straight-edge on the end of the shaft facing downwards **(see illustration)**.

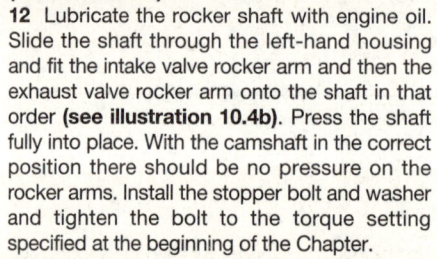

12 Lubricate the rocker shaft with engine oil. Slide the shaft through the left-hand housing and fit the intake valve rocker arm and then the exhaust valve rocker arm onto the shaft in that order **(see illustration 10.4b)**. Press the shaft fully into place. With the camshaft in the correct position there should be no pressure on the rocker arms. Install the stopper bolt and washer and tighten the bolt to the torque setting specified at the beginning of the Chapter.

13 Follow the procedure in Section 9 to install the camshaft sprocket, then check the valve timing.

Caution: If the marks are not aligned exactly as described, the valve timing will be incorrect and the valves may strike the piston, causing extensive damage to the engine.

14 Check the valve clearances and adjust them if necessary (see Chapter 1).

15 Install the remaining components in the reverse order of removal.

11 Cylinder head – removal and installation

Note: *This procedure can be carried out with the engine in the frame although access to the top of the engine is extremely restricted. If the engine has been removed, ignore the steps which do not apply.*

Caution: The engine must be completely cool before beginning this procedure or the cylinder head may become warped.

Removal

1 Remove the exhaust system (see Chapter 4). Pull the spark plug cap off the plug.

2 Follow the procedure in Section 8 to remove the cam chain tensioner, then follow the procedure in Section 9 to remove the camshaft sprocket. Secure the cam chain with a cable tie to prevent it falling into the engine.

3 Lift off the engine cowling seal, noting how it fits **(see illustration)**.

4 Undo the two cylinder head bolts on the left-hand side of the engine **(see illustration)**. Undo the four cylinder head nuts evenly, a little at a time, in a criss-cross pattern and remove them **(see illustration)**.

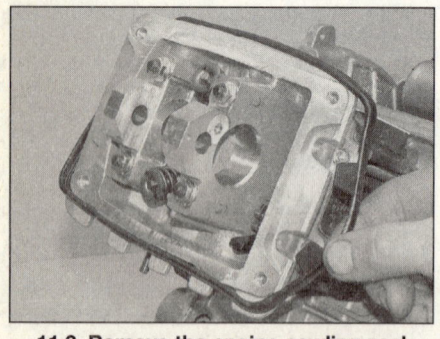

11.3 Remove the engine cowling seal

11.4a Undo the external cylinder head bolts (arrowed) . . .

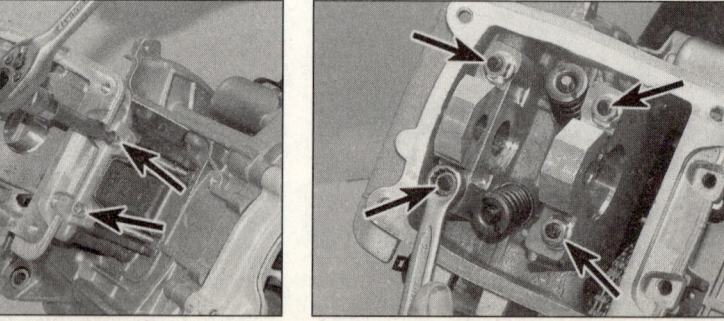

11.4b . . . then the internal cylinder head nuts (arrowed)

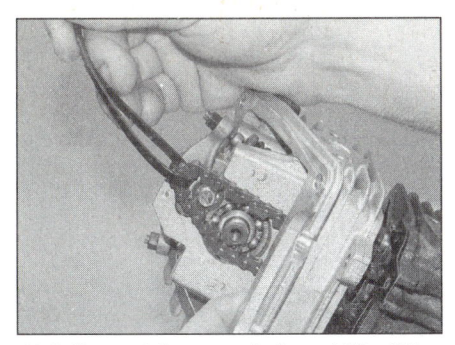

Four-stroke engines (ET4 50, Liberty 50 4T, Zip 50 4T, Fly 50 4T, LX4 50) 2D•11

11.5 Support the cam chain and lift off the cylinder head

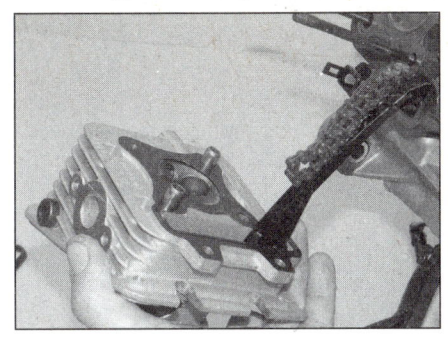

11.6a Note how the guide blade fits . . .

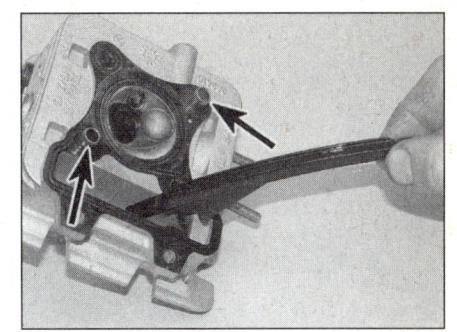

11.6b . . . then remove it from the head. Note the dowels (arrowed)

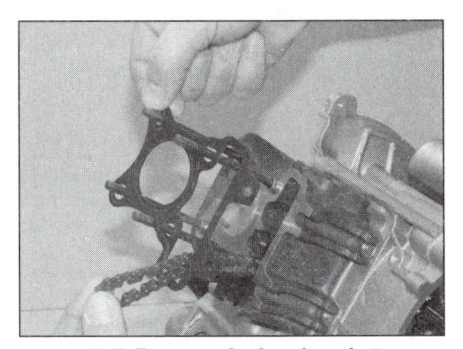

11.7 Remove the head gasket

11.10 Install the dowels in the top of the cylinder

11.12 Using a torque angle gauge to tighten the cylinder head nuts

5 Lift the cylinder head off carefully, feeding the cam chain down through the tunnel in the head **(see illustration)**. If the head is stuck, tap around the joint face with a soft-faced mallet to free it. Do not attempt to free the head by inserting a screwdriver between the head and cylinder – you'll damage the sealing surfaces. **Note:** *Avoid lifting the cylinder off the crankcase when the head is removed, otherwise a new cylinder base gasket will have to be fitted (see Section 14).*

6 The cam chain guide blade is clipped to the lower edge of the chain tunnel in the head and will lift out with it – detach the blade, noting how it fits **(see illustrations)**. Note the location of the two dowels either in the head or the cylinder, and remove them for safekeeping if they are loose.

7 Remove the old cylinder head gasket **(see illustration)**. Two types of gasket are fitted – a steel gasket (approximately 0.3 mm thick when new) or a fibre gasket (approximately 0.95 mm thick when new). Always fit a new gasket of the same type when installing the cylinder head.

8 Inspect the cylinder head gasket and the mating surfaces on the head and cylinder for signs of leakage, which could indicate that the head is warped. Refer to Section 13 and check the head gasket mating surface for warpage.

9 Clean all traces of old gasket material from the cylinder head and cylinder with a suitable solvent. Take care not to scratch or gouge the soft aluminium. Be careful not to let any dirt fall into the crankcase, the cylinder bore or the oil passage.

Installation

10 Ensure both cylinder head and cylinder mating surfaces are clean. Slide the dowels down the cylinder studs and install them in the top of the cylinder **(see illustration)**. Lay the new gasket in place on the cylinder, making sure the oil passage holes are correctly aligned. Never re-use the old gasket.

11 Carefully lower the head onto the cylinder, feeding the cam chain up through the tunnel **(see illustration 11.5)**. Make sure the dowels are correctly aligned with the head and the gasket.

12 Install the cylinder head nuts finger tight. Tighten the nuts evenly, in a criss-cross pattern, to the initial torque setting specified at the beginning of the Chapter. Now tighten

HAYNES HiNT *If a degree disc is not available, the angle for the torque setting can be determined by using the points on the cylinder head nut. Select one point on the nut as a reference and mark it with paint or a marker. Now select the second point clockwise 90° from it and mark its position on the head. Tighten the nut – when the mark on the first point aligns with the mark made on the head, it will have turned through the requisite number of degrees. Repeat the procedure to achieve the final torque setting.*

them one at a time and in the same sequence, through 90° in one continuous movement, using a torque angle gauge **(see illustration)**. Now tighten them through a further 90°. **Note:** *If a torque angle gauge is not available see Haynes Hint.*

13 Install the two cylinder head bolts on the left-hand side of the engine and tighten them to the specified torque setting **(see illustration 11.4a)**.

14 Install the camshaft sprocket and the remaining components in the reverse order of removal, referring to the relevant Sections or Chapters.

12 Valves/valve seats/valve guides – overhaul

1 If a valve spring compressor is available, the home mechanic can remove the valves from the cylinder head, grind in the valves and renew the valve stem seals. If the necessary measuring tools are available, you can assess the amount of wear on the valves and guides and measure the valve-to-seat contact areas.

2 If the valve guides or the valve seats in the cylinder head are worn beyond their service limits a new head will have to be fitted.

3 After any servicing or repair work, be sure to clean the head thoroughly to remove any metal particles or abrasive grit that may still be present. Use compressed air, if available, to blow out all the holes and passages.

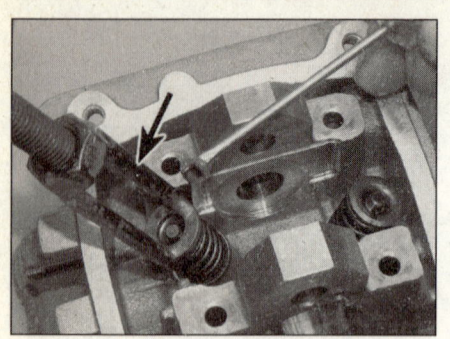

2D•12 Four-stroke engines (ET4 50, Liberty 50 4T, Zip 50 4T, Fly 50 4T, LX4 50)

13.5 Using an adapter (arrowed) on the valve spring compressor

13.6 Measuring the valve seat width with a vernier caliper

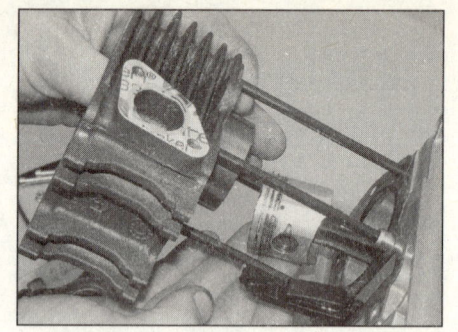

14.2 Support the piston as the cylinder is raised

13 Cylinder head and valves – disassembly, inspection and reassembly

1 Disassembly, cleaning and inspection of the valves and related components can be done by the home mechanic if the necessary special tools are available. If there is any doubt about the condition of any components, have them checked by a Piaggio dealer.
2 To disassemble the valve components without the risk of damaging them, a valve spring compressor suitable for motorcycle engines is absolutely necessary.
3 Before proceeding, arrange to label and store the valves and their related components so that they can be returned to their original location without getting mixed up **(see illustration 13.3 in Chapter 2E)**.
4 The procedure for disassembly, inspection and reassembly of the cylinder head and valves is the same as for air-cooled LEADER models (see Chapter 2E, Section 13), with the following additions.
5 When compressing the valve springs, it may be necessary to place a suitable spacer against the valve head to prevent the compressor pressing on the inside of the cylinder head. It may also be necessary to use an adapter to locate the compressor onto the spring retainer **(see illustration)**.
6 For greater accuracy, measure the valve seat width with a vernier caliper **(see illustration)**.

14 Cylinder – removal, inspection and installation

Note: *This procedure can be carried out with the engine in the frame although access to the top of the engine is extremely restricted. If the engine has been removed, ignore the steps which do not apply.*

Removal

1 Remove the cylinder head (see Section 11).
2 Lift the cylinder up off the studs, carefully feeding the cam chain down through the tunnel. Support the piston as it becomes accessible to prevent it hitting the crankcase **(see illustration)**. If the cylinder is stuck, tap around its joint faces with a soft-faced mallet to free it from the crankcase. Don't attempt to free the cylinder by inserting a screwdriver between it and the crankcase – you'll damage the sealing surfaces. When the cylinder is removed, stuff a clean rag around the piston to prevent anything falling into the crankcase.
3 Note the two dowels in the crankcase and remove them for safekeeping if they are loose.
4 Remove the gasket carefully **(see illustration)**. If the gasket is marked with a thickness (0.4 or 0.5) make a note of the thickness. If the original cylinder and piston are used on reassembly, a new gasket of the same thickness should be used. If the gasket is not marked, the piston height will have to be measured on reassembly (see Steps 9 to 11). Discard the old gasket.

Inspection

5 The procedure for inspection of the cylinder is the same as for air-cooled LEADER models (see Chapter 2E, Section 14), with the following additions.
6 Piaggio recommend the bore is measured at 10 mm, 30 mm and 50 mm down from the top edge, both parallel to and across the crankshaft axis.
7 The cylinder size-code is stamped into the outside of the cylinder adjacent to the cam chain tensioner location **(see illustration)**.

Installation

8 The procedure for installation of the cylinder is the same as for air-cooled LEADER models (see Chapter 2E, Section 14), with the following additions.
9 Two different size cylinder base gaskets are available from Piaggio. If the original cylinder and piston are being re-used, fit a gasket the same thickness as the original (see Step 4). If the original gasket was not marked, or if new components are being used, the cylinder must be assembled on the crankcase and piston without a base gasket, and a dial gauge mounted against the crown of the piston to establish which thickness is required.
10 Use suitable spacers and the cylinder head nuts to tighten the cylinder down against the crankcase. Set the dial gauge in the mounting plate, and with the gauge tip resting against the cylinder top gasket face, zero the gauge dial **(see illustration)**. Rotate the crankshaft so that the piston is a small distance down the bore.

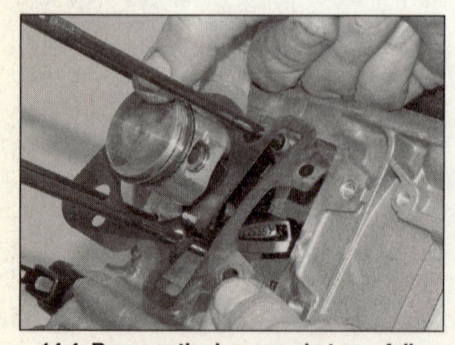

14.4 Remove the base gasket carefully

14.7 Piston and cylinder are stamped with a size-code as shown

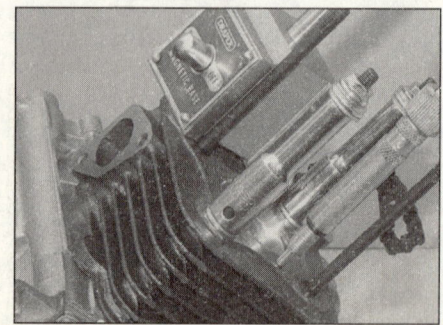

14.10 Zero the dial gauge on the cylinder top gasket face

Four-stroke engines (ET4 50, Liberty 50 4T, Zip 50 4T, Fly 50 4T, LX4 50)   2D•13

14.11 Take the reading off the piston crown at TDC

11 Now rest the tip of the gauge on the centre of the piston crown and rotate the crankshaft via the alternator rotor so the piston rises to the top of its stroke (TDC). At this point read off the dial gauge **(see illustration)**. The further the piston crown is above the top of the cylinder bore, the thicker the base gasket should be. If the engine is fitted with a steel head gasket and the reading is between 0.15 and 0.25 mm a 0.4 mm gasket is required, between 0.25 and 0.35 mm a 0.5 mm gasket is required. If the engine is fitted with a fibre head gasket and the reading is between 0.85 and 0.95 mm a 0.4 mm gasket is required, between 0.95 and 1.05 mm a 0.5 mm gasket is required.

15 Piston – removal, inspection and installation

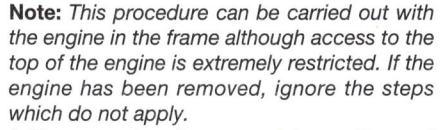

Note: *This procedure can be carried out with the engine in the frame although access to the top of the engine is extremely restricted. If the engine has been removed, ignore the steps which do not apply.*

1 The procedure for removal, inspection and installation of the piston is the same as for four-stroke engines described in Chapter 2C, Section 16, with the following additions.

2 To avoid breaking the rings, use an old feeler gauge blade to ease them off the piston **(see illustration)**. Note which way up each ring fits and in which groove as they must be installed in their original positions if being re-used. The upper surface of each ring should be marked at one end **(see illustration)**.

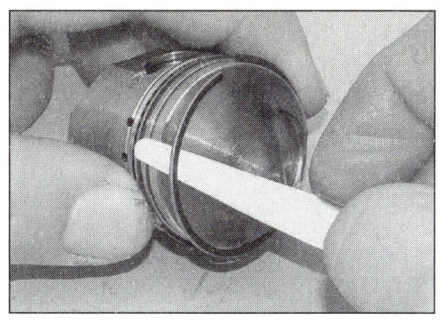

15.2a Using a thin blade to remove the piston rings

3 When checking the piston-to-bore clearance, measure the piston 27 mm down from the top edge of the piston and at 90° to the piston pin axis.

16 Piston rings – inspection and installation

1 The procedure for inspection and installation of the piston rings is described in Chapter 2C, Section 17.

17 Cooling fan – removal and installation

Note: *This procedure can be carried out with the engine in the frame. If the engine has been removed, ignore the steps which do not apply.*

Removal

1 Remove the bodywork as required by your model to access the alternator cover on the right-hand side of the engine (see Chapter 7).
2 Remove the screws securing the alternator cover and remove the cover **(see illustrations 8.3a and 8.3b)**.
3 Remove the three screws securing the cooling fan to the alternator rotor and remove the fan **(see illustration)**.

Installation

4 Installation is the reverse of removal. Note that the screw holes are offset so that the fan can only be fitted in one position on the rotor.

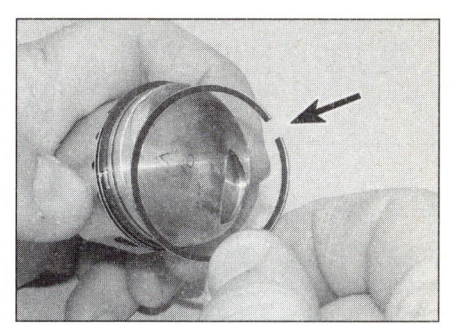

15.2b Check for a mark at one end of the piston ring

18 Alternator rotor and stator – removal and installation

Note: *This procedure can be carried out with the engine in the frame. If the engine has been removed, ignore the steps which do not apply.*

Removal

1 Remove the cooling fan (see Section 17).
2 To remove the rotor nut it is necessary to stop the rotor from turning. Piaggio produce a service tool (Part No. 020656Y) which locates in the holes in the rotor. A similar tool can be made **(see illustration)**. With the rotor held securely, unscrew the nut.

> **HAYNES HiNT** A rotor holding tool can easily be made using two strips of steel bolted together in the middle, with a bolt through each end which locates into the holes in the rotor. Do not allow the bolts to extend too far through the rotor holes otherwise the coils could be damaged.

3 To remove the rotor from the crankshaft it is necessary to use the Piaggio service tool (Part No. 020162Y) or a two-legged puller. If using the service tool, ensure that the centre bolt is backed-out sufficiently to allow the body of the tool to be screwed all the way into the threads provided in the rotor **(see illustration)**. With the tool in place, hold the body of the tool using a spanner on its flats while tightening the

17.3 Cooling fan is secured by three screws (arrowed)

18.2 Hold the alternator rotor and undo the centre nut

18.3a Service tool screws into threads provided

2D•14 Four-stroke engines (ET4 50, Liberty 50 4T, Zip 50 4T, Fly 50 4T, LX4 50)

18.3b Using the service tool to remove the alternator rotor

18.3c Using a two-legged puller to remove the alternator rotor

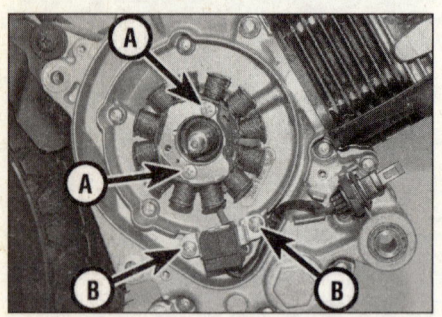

18.4a Alternator stator is secured by screws (A), pulse generator coil is secured by screws (B)

18.4b Lift off the stator/generator coil assembly

centre bolt (turn it clockwise) to draw the rotor off the end of the shaft **(see illustration)**. If using a two-legged puller, assemble the puller legs through the holes in the rotor and tighten the centre bolt down onto the crankshaft end until the rotor is drawn off **(see illustration)**. If it is loose, remove the Woodruff key from the shaft, noting how it fits.

4 To remove the stator, it is also necessary to remove the pulse generator coil as they come as a linked assembly. Disconnect the alternator wiring multi-pin connector, noting how it locates in the crankcase, then undo the screws that secure the stator and the pulse generator coil **(see illustration)**. Lift off the stator/pulse generator coil assembly **(see illustration)**.

Installation

5 Install the stator and pulse generator coil onto the crankcase; ensure the multi-pin connector positioned. Install the stator and generator coil screws and tighten them securely.

6 Clean the tapered end of the crankshaft and the corresponding mating surface on the inside of the rotor with a suitable solvent. Make sure that no metal objects have attached themselves to the magnets on the inside of the rotor. If removed, fit the Woodruff key into its slot in the shaft, then install the rotor onto the shaft, aligning the slot in the rotor with the key.

7 Install the rotor nut and tighten it to the torque setting specified at the beginning of the Chapter, using the method employed on removal to prevent the rotor from turning.

8 Install the remaining components in the reverse order of removal.

19 Starter pinion assembly – removal, inspection and installation

Note: *This procedure can be carried out with the engine in the frame.*

1 Follow the procedure in Chapter 2G to remove the drivebelt cover and the starter driven gear.

2 Hold the variator in position on the crankshaft and lift out the starter pinion assembly, noting how it fits **(see illustration)**.

3 The procedure for inspection of the starter pinion assembly is the same as for air-cooled LEADER models (see Chapter 2E, Section 19).

4 Installation is the reverse of removal. Ensure the inner pinion engages with the starter motor shaft.

19.2 Lift out the starter pinion assembly

20.3 Undo the sump cover bolts

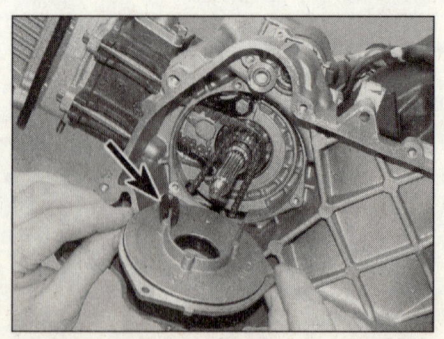

20 Oil pump – removal, inspection and installation

Note: *This procedure can be carried out with the engine in the frame.*

Removal

1 Drain the engine oil (see Chapter 1).

2 Remove the drive pulley and variator (see Chapter 2G).

3 Undo the bolts securing the sump cover, noting the position of the clip for the rear brake cable, and remove the cover **(see illustration)**. Be prepared to catch any residual oil when the cover is removed. Discard the gasket, as a new one must be used on reassembly.

4 Undo the bolts securing the pump drive chain cover, then carefully lever the cover out **(see illustration)**. Discard the cover O-ring, as a new one should be used. Note the chain guide on the back of the cover **(see illustration)**.

5 Undo the bolts securing the pump sprocket

20.4a Undo the cover bolts (arrowed) and lever out the cover

20.4b Note the location of the chain guide (arrowed)

Four-stroke engines (ET4 50, Liberty 50 4T, Zip 50 4T, Fly 50 4T, LX4 50) 2D•15

20.5 Remove the pump sprocket plate

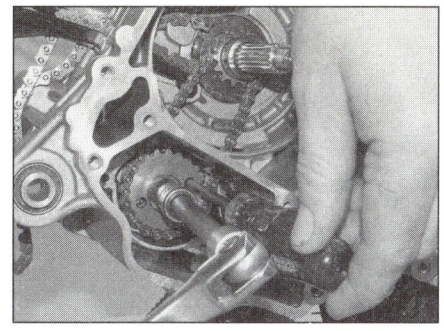

20.6a Undo the pump sprocket bolt

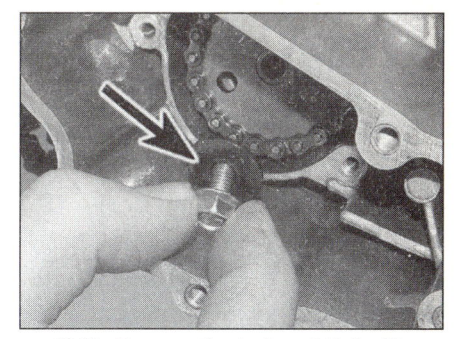

20.6b Remove the bolt and Belleville washer (arrowed)

20.6c Pull the sprocket off the pump

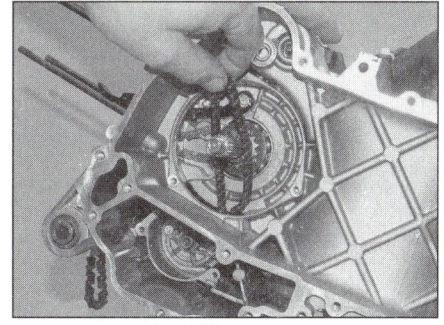

20.7a Remove the chain . . .

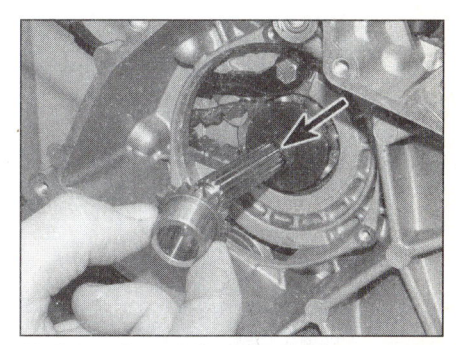

20.7b . . . then slide off the sprocket noting the O-ring (arrowed)

20.7c Remove the O-ring from the crankshaft

plate and remove the plate, noting how it fits **(see illustration)**.

6 Insert a pin punch or screwdriver through one of the holes in the driven sprocket and locate it against the pump body to stop the sprocket turning, then unscrew the sprocket bolt **(see illustration)**. Remove the bolt and Belleville washer, noting which way round the washer fits **(see illustration)**. Pull the sprocket off the pump and slip it out of the chain **(see illustration)**.

7 If required, draw the chain up into the transmission housing and remove it from the drive sprocket **(see illustration)**. **Note:** *Before the chain is removed, mark it so that it can be fitted the same way round.* Slide the drive sprocket off the end of the crankshaft, noting which way round it fits. Note the position of the O-ring on the shaft **(see illustration)**. Slide the O-ring off the shaft and discard it, as a new one must be fitted **(see illustration)**.

8 Undo the two screws securing the oil pump and remove the pump. Also remove the gasket from behind the pump and discard it, as a new one must be used.

Inspection

Note: *No relief valve is fitted to this lubrication system.*

9 The procedure for disassembly and inspection of the oil pump is the same as for air-cooled LEADER models (see Chapter 2E, Section 20), with the following addition.

10 Check the condition of the oil seal in the drive chain cover and renew it if it is damaged or if oil is leaking into the drivebelt casing.

Check the chain guide and renew it if it is worn **(see illustration 20.4b)**.

Installation

11 Installation is the reverse of removal, noting the following:
a) Make sure the holes in the pump gasket align with the oil holes.
b) Tighten the pump mounting screws to the torque setting specified at the beginning of the Chapter.
c) Lubricate the new crankshaft O-ring with clean engine oil and fit it onto the crankshaft carefully to avoid damage.
d) Install the drive sprocket with its shouldered end facing out.
e) Fit the Belleville washer on the pump sprocket bolt with the outer edge of the washer against the sprocket.
f) Tighten the sprocket bolt to the specified torque setting.
g) Fit a new O-ring to the drive chain cover.
h) Fit a new gasket to the sump cover.
i) Fill the engine with the correct type and quantity of oil (see Chapter 1). Start the engine and check for oil leaks around the sump.

21 Crankcase halves, crankshaft and connecting rod

Note: *To separate the crankcase halves, the engine must be removed from the frame.*

Separation

1 To access the crankshaft and its bearings, the crankcase must be split into two parts.
2 To enable the crankcases to be separated, the engine must be removed from the frame (see Section 5). Before the crankcases can be separated the following components must be removed:
a) Camchain, blades and sprockets (see Section 9).
b) Cylinder head (see Section 11).
c) Cylinder (see Section 14).
d) Alternator rotor and stator (see Section 18).
e) Variator (see Chapter 2G).
f) Starter motor (see Chapter 9).
g) Oil pump (see Section 20).
h) Centre stand (see Chapter 7).

3 Unscrew the ten crankcase bolts evenly, a little at a time and in a criss-cross sequence until they are all finger-tight, then remove them

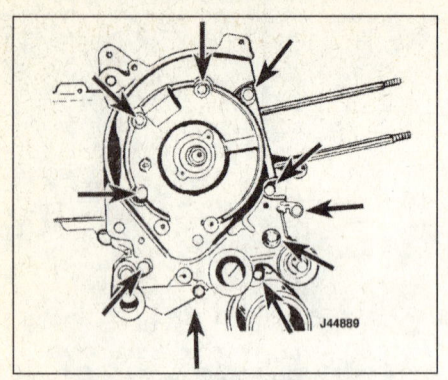

2D•16 Four-stroke engines (ET4 50, Liberty 50 4T, Zip 50 4T, Fly 50 4T, LX4 50)

21.3 Crankcase bolt locations (arrowed)

(see illustration). Carefully lift the right-hand crankcase half off the left-hand half. Lift the crankshaft out of the left-hand (transmission side) crankcase. Note the two dowels and remove them for safekeeping if they are loose.

4 Remove the oil seal from the right-hand crankcase half, having taken careful note of its fitted position. Clean all traces of old gasket sealant from both crankcase halves with a suitable solvent. Take care not to scratch or gouge the soft aluminium.

Inspection

5 Refer to Chapter 2E, Section 21 for general crankcase inspection procedures.

6 Check the condition of the main bearings. The right-hand bearing will remain on the crankshaft and the left-hand bearing will be held in the crankcase half. The bearings should spin freely and smoothly without any rough spots or excessive noise. Renew them if there is any doubt about their condition.

7 The right-hand bearing should be removed from the crankshaft using an external bearing puller. Make sure that the puller clamp or legs fit securely behind the bearing and are in no danger of slipping out, and thread the alternator rotor nut onto the crankshaft to protect the end of the shaft **(see illustration)**. Note which way round the bearing is fitted. To fit the new bearing the crankshaft must be supported securely with the right-hand end uppermost. Heat the new bearing in an oil bath to 120°C then install it on the shaft and press it into position with a suitable length of tube that bears on the inner race only.

8 Before removing the left-hand bearing, heat the bearing housing using a hot air gun to aid removal, then drive the bearing out with a bearing driver or suitably-sized socket. Note which way round the bearing is fitted. Reheat the bearing housing then press the new bearing into position with a suitably-sized socket that bears on the outer race only.

9 Measure the connecting rod big end side clearance with a feeler gauge and compare it with the specifications at the beginning of the Chapter **(see illustration)**. Measure the up-and-down (radial) play on the rod with a dial gauge and measure the width of the flywheels at several points to ensure they are not out of alignment **(see illustrations 21.17b and 21.17c in Chapter 2E)**. Compare the results with the specifications at the beginning of this Chapter.

10 Place the crankshaft assembly on V-blocks and check the runout at the main bearing journals and at the ends of the shafts **(see illustration 21.18 in Chapter 2E)**. **Note:** *The right-hand main bearing must be removed from the shaft for this check.* If the runout exceeds the specified limit, or if either of the connecting rod measurements exceed the limit, the crankshaft assembly must be renewed.

Reassembly

11 Lubricate the new crankcase oil seal with clean engine oil and install it in the right-hand crankcase half in the same position as noted on removal. Use a bearing driver or a suitably-sized socket which contacts only the outer face of the seal to drive it into position.

12 Lubricate the big-end and main bearings with engine oil and insert the crankshaft into the left-hand crankcase half, positioning the connecting rod in line with the crankcase mouth. Apply a suitable gasket sealant to the crankcase mating surface. Guide the right-hand crankcase half over the crankshaft end, pressing it over the right-hand main bearing. If necessary, heat the bearing housing with a hot air gun and use a soft-faced mallet to help the casing seat, but don't apply too much pressure. **Note:** *If the crankcases do not meet, remove the right-hand half and investigate the problem – do not be tempted to pull the crankcases together using the bolts.*

13 Clean the threads of the crankcase bolts and install them finger-tight. Tighten the bolts evenly, in a criss-cross sequence, to the torque setting specified at the beginning of this Chapter. Support the connecting rod and rotate the crankshaft to check that it is moves freely.

14 Install the remaining components in the reverse order of removal.

22 Initial start-up after overhaul

1 Make sure the engine oil level is correct (see *Daily (pre-ride) checks*).

2 Make sure there is fuel in the tank.

3 With the ignition OFF, operate the kickstart a couple of times to check that the engine turns over easily.

4 Turn the ignition ON, start the engine and allow it to run at a slow idle until it reaches operating temperature. Do not be alarmed if there is a little smoke from the exhaust – this will be due to the oil used to lubricate the piston and bore during assembly and should subside after a while.

5 If the engine proves reluctant to start, remove the spark plug and check that it has not become wet and oily. If it has, clean it and try again. If the engine refuses to start, go through the fault finding charts at the end of this manual to identify the problem.

6 Check carefully for oil leaks and make sure the transmission and controls, especially the brakes, function properly before road testing the machine. Refer to Section 23 for the recommended running-in procedure.

7 Upon completion of the road test, and after the engine has cooled down completely, recheck the valve clearances (see Chapter 1) and check the engine oil level (see *Daily (pre-ride) checks*).

23 Recommended running-in procedure

1 Treat the machine gently for the first few miles to make sure oil has circulated throughout the engine and any new parts installed have started to seat.

2 Even greater care is necessary if the engine has been rebored or a new crankshaft has been installed. In the case of a rebore, the bike will have to be run-in as when new. This means a restraining hand on the throttle until at least 600 miles (1000 km) have been covered. There's no point in keeping to any set speed limit – the main idea is to keep from labouring the engine and not to maintain any one speed for too long. Experience is the best guide, since it's easy to tell when an engine is running freely. Once past the 600 mile (1000 km) mark, gradually increase performance, using full throttle for short bursts to begin with.

3 If a lubrication failure is suspected, stop the engine immediately and try to find the cause. If an engine is run without oil, even for a short period of time, severe damage will occur.

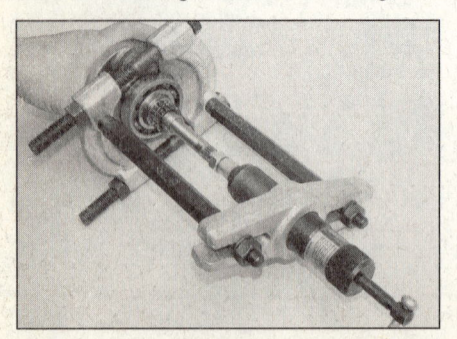

21.7 Removing the main bearing from the crankshaft

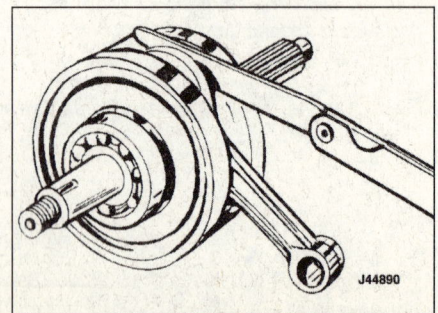

21.9 Checking the connecting rod big-end bearing side clearance

Chapter 2 Part E:
LEADER air-cooled four-stroke engines (Zip 125, Skipper ST, Liberty 125, ET4 125, Fly 125, LX4 125)

Refer to the beginning of Chapter 1 for model identification details

Contents

Alternator rotor and stator – removal and installation	18
Cam chain tensioner – removal, inspection and installation	8
Cam chain, blades and sprockets – removal, inspection and installation	9
Camshaft and rockers – removal, inspection and installation	10
Cooling fan – removal and installation	17
Crankcase halves, crankshaft and connecting rod	21
Cylinder – removal, inspection and installation	14
Cylinder head – removal and installation	11
Cylinder head and valves – disassembly, inspection and reassembly	13
Disassembly and reassembly – general information	6
Engine/transmission unit – removal and installation	5
General information	1
Idle speed – check and adjustment	see Chapter 1
Initial start-up after overhaul	22

Major engine repair – general note	4
Oil and filter – change	see Chapter 1
Oil level – check	see *Daily (pre-ride) checks*
Oil pump and relief valve – pressure check, pump removal, inspection and installation	20
Operations possible with the engine in the frame	2
Operations requiring engine removal	3
Piston – removal, inspection and installation	15
Piston rings – inspection and installation	16
Recommended running-in procedure	23
Spark plug gap – check and adjustment	see Chapter 1
Starter motor – removal and installation	see Chapter 9
Starter pinion assembly – removal, inspection and installation	19
Valve clearances – check and adjustment	see Chapter 1
Valve cover – removal and installation	7
Valves/valve seats/valve guides – overhaul	12

Degrees of difficulty

Easy, suitable for novice with little experience	Fairly easy, suitable for beginner with some experience	Fairly difficult, suitable for competent DIY mechanic	Difficult, suitable for experienced DIY mechanic	Very difficult, suitable for expert DIY or professional

Specifications

General
Type	Single cylinder four-stroke
Capacity	124.01 cc
Bore	57.0 mm
Stroke	48.6 mm
Compression ratio	10.1 to 11.1 : 1

Camshaft
Intake and exhaust lobe height	
Zip 125, Skipper ST, Liberty 125, ET4	27.8 mm
Fly 125, LX 125	
Intake	27.5 mm
Exhaust	27.2 mm
Left-hand journal diameter	
Standard	32.50 mm
Service limit (min)	32.44 mm
Right-hand journal diameter	
Standard	20.00 mm
Service limit (min)	19.95 mm
Camshaft endfloat	
Standard	0.11 to 0.41 mm
Service limit	0.42 mm

Cylinder head

Warpage (max)	0.05 mm
Left-hand camshaft bearing housing diameter	32.500 to 32.525 mm
Right-hand camshaft journal housing diameter	20.000 to 20.021 mm
Rocker arm shaft housing	12.000 to 12.018 mm
Rocker arm shaft diameter	11.977 to 11.985 mm
Rocker arm internal diameter	12.000 to 12.011 mm
Valve seat width (max)	1.6 mm

Valves, guides and springs

Valve clearances	See Chapter 1
Intake valve	
Overall standard length	80.6 mm
Stem diameter	
Service limit (min)	4.960 mm
Guide bore diameter	
Standard	5.022 mm
Stem/valve guide clearance	
Standard	0.013 to 0.040 mm
Service limit	0.062 mm
Face width	3.1 mm
Exhaust valve	
Overall standard length	79.6 mm
Stem diameter	
Service limit (min)	4.950 mm
Guide bore diameter	
Standard	5.022 mm
Stem/valve guide clearance	
Standard	0.025 to 0.052 mm
Service limit	0.072 mm
Face width	3.0 mm
Valve spring free length (intake and exhaust)	n/a

Cylinder bore – aluminium cylinder

Bore diameter (measured 38.5 mm down from top edge of the cylinder, at 90° to piston pin axis)

Standard	
Size-code A	56.980 to 56.987 mm
Size-code B	56.987 to 56.994 mm
Size-code C	56.994 to 57.001 mm
Size-code D	57.001 to 57.008 mm
1st oversize	57.180 to 57.208 mm
2nd oversize	57.380 to 57.408 mm
3rd oversize	57.580 to 57.608 mm

Piston – aluminium cylinder

Piston diameter (measured 36.5 mm down from top edge of the piston, at 90° to piston pin axis)

Standard	
Size-code A	56.933 to 56.940 mm
Size-code B	56.940 to 56.947 mm
Size-code C	56.947 to 56.954 mm
Size-code D	56.954 to 56.961 mm
1st oversize	57.133 to 57.161 mm
2nd oversize	57.333 to 57.361 mm
3rd oversize	57.533 to 57.561 mm
Piston-to-bore clearance (when new)	0.040 to 0.054 mm
Piston pin diameter	14.996 to 15.000 mm
Piston pin bore diameter in piston	15.001 to 15.006 mm

Cylinder bore – cast iron cylinder

Bore diameter (measured 38.5 mm down from top edge of the cylinder, at 90° to piston pin axis)

Standard	
Size-code M	56.997 to 57.004 mm
Size-code N	57.004 to 57.011 mm
Size-code O	57.011 to 57.018 mm
Size-code P	57.018 to 57.025 mm
1st oversize	57.197 to 57.225 mm
2nd oversize	57.397 to 57.425 mm
3rd oversize	57.597 to 57.625 mm

Piston – cast iron cylinder
Piston diameter (measured 36.5 mm down from top edge of the piston, at 90° to piston pin axis)
    Standard
        Size-code M .... 56.944 to 56.951 mm
        Size-code N .... 56.951 to 56.958 mm
        Size-code O .... 56.958 to 56.965 mm
        Size-code P .... 56.965 to 56.972 mm
    1st oversize .... 57.144 to 57.172 mm
    2nd oversize .... 57.344 to 57.372 mm
    3rd oversize .... 57.544 to 57.572 mm
Piston-to-bore clearance (when new) .... 0.046 to 0.060 mm
Piston pin diameter .... 14.996 to 15.000 mm
Piston pin bore diameter in piston .... 15.001 to 15.006 mm

Piston rings
Ring end gap (installed) – Zip 125, Skipper ST, Liberty 125, ET4
    Top ring
        Standard .... 0.15 to 0.30 mm
        Service limit (max) .... 0.40 mm
    2nd ring
        Standard .... 0.20 to 0.40 mm
        Service limit (max) .... 0.50 mm
    Oil control ring
        Standard .... 0.20 to 0.40 mm
        Service limit (max) .... 0.50 mm
Ring end gap (installed) – Fly 125, LX 125
    Top ring
        Standard .... 0.15 to 0.30 mm
        Service limit (max) .... 1.0 mm
    2nd ring
        Standard .... 0.10 to 0.30 mm
        Service limit (max) .... 1.0 mm
    Oil control ring
        Standard .... 0.15 to 0.30 mm
        Service limit (max) .... 1.0 mm
Ring-to-groove clearance – all models
    Top ring
        Standard .... 0.025 to 0.070 mm
        Service limit (max) .... 0.080 mm
    2nd ring
        Standard .... 0.015 to 0.060 mm
        Service limit (max) .... 0.070 mm
    Oil control ring
        Standard .... 0.015 to 0.060 mm
        Service limit (max) .... 0.070 mm

Lubrication system
Engine oil pressure (at 90°C) .... 0.5 to 1.2 Bars @ 1650 rpm / 3.2 to 4.2 Bars @ 6000 rpm
Oil pump
    Inner rotor tip-to-outer rotor clearance (max) .... 0.12 mm
    Outer rotor-to-body clearance (max) .... 0.20 mm
    Rotor endfloat (max) .... 0.09 mm
Relief valve spring free length .... 54.2 mm

Connecting rod
Small-end internal diameter
    Standard .... 15.015 to 15.025 mm
    Service limit (max) .... 15.030 mm
Big-end side clearance
    Standard .... 0.20 to 0.50 mm
Big-end radial freeplay
    Standard .... 0.006 to 0.018 mm
    Service limit (max) .... 0.25 mm

Crankshaft

Combined width of flywheels and big-end	51.4 mm
Runout A (max)*	0.15 mm
Runout B (max)*	0.01 mm
Runout C (max)*	0.10 mm
Endfloat	0.15 to 0.40 mm

See illustration 21.18 for runout measurement points

Torque settings

Valve cover bolts	11 to 13 Nm
Cam chain tensioner spring cap bolt	5 to 6 Nm
Cam chain tensioner blade bolt	10 to 14 Nm
Cam chain tensioner bolts	11 to 13 Nm
Camshaft sprocket bolt	11 to 15 Nm
Camshaft retaining plate bolts	4 to 6 Nm
Cam timing mechanism bolt	7 to 8.5 Nm
Cylinder head nuts	
Initial setting	7 Nm
Final setting	+ 90°+ 90°
Cylinder head bolts (outside)	11 to 13 Nm
Oil pressure switch	12 to 14 Nm
Oil pump cover screws	0.7 to 0.9 Nm
Oil pump mounting screws	5 to 6 Nm
Oil pump sprocket bolt	10 to 14 Nm
Oil pump drive chain cover screws	3.5 to 4.5 Nm
Sump cover bolts	10 to 14 Nm
Alternator rotor nut	52 to 58 Nm
Alternator stator screws/pulse generator coil screws	3 to 4 Nm
Engine front mounting bolt	33 to 41 Nm
Crankcase bolts	11 to 13 Nm

1 General information

The engine unit is a single cylinder four-stroke, with fan-assisted air cooling. The fan is mounted on the alternator rotor, which is on the right-hand end of the crankshaft. The crankshaft assembly is pressed together, incorporating the connecting rod, with the big-end running on the crankpin on a bronze bearing. The crankshaft runs in plain main bearings. The crankcase divides vertically.

The camshaft is chain-driven off the left-hand end of the crankshaft, and operates two valves via rocker arms.

2 Operations possible with the engine in the frame

All components and assemblies, with the exception of the crankshaft/connecting rod assembly, can be worked on without having to remove the engine/transmission unit from the frame. However, access is extremely limited and if a number of areas require attention at the same time, removal of the engine is recommended.

3 Operations requiring engine removal

To access the crankshaft and connecting rod assembly and its bearings, the engine must be removed from the frame and the crankcase halves must be separated.

4 Major engine repair – general note

1 It is not always easy to determine when or if an engine should be completely overhauled, as a number of factors must be considered.
2 High mileage is not necessarily an indication that an overhaul is needed, while low mileage, on the other hand, does not preclude the need for an overhaul. Frequency of servicing is probably the single most important consideration. An engine that has regular and frequent oil and filter changes, as well as other required maintenance, will most likely give many miles of reliable service. Conversely, a neglected engine, or one which has not been run-in properly, may require an overhaul very early in its life.
3 Exhaust smoke and excessive oil consumption are both indications that piston rings and/or valve guides are in need of attention, although make sure that the fault is not due to oil leakage.
4 If the engine is making obvious knocking or rumbling noises, the connecting rod and/or main bearings are probably at fault.
5 Loss of power, rough running, excessive valve train noise and high fuel consumption rates may also point to the need for an overhaul, especially if they are all present at the same time. If a complete tune-up does not remedy the situation, major mechanical work is the only solution.
6 A full engine overhaul generally involves restoring the internal parts to the specifications of a new engine. The piston and piston rings are renewed and the cylinder is rebored. The valve seats are re-ground and new valve springs are fitted. If the connecting rod bearings are worn a new crankshaft assembly is fitted. The end result should be a like-new engine that will give as many trouble-free miles as the original.
7 Before beginning the engine overhaul, read through the related procedures to familiarise yourself with the scope and requirements of the job. Overhauling an engine is not all that difficult, but it is time-consuming. Plan on the scooter being tied up for a minimum of two weeks. Check on the availability of parts and

LEADER air-cooled four-stroke engines (Zip 125, Skipper ST, Liberty 125, ET4 125, Fly 125, LX4 125)

make sure that any necessary special tools, equipment and supplies are obtained in advance.

8 Most work can be done with typical workshop hand tools, although a number of precision measuring tools are required for inspecting parts to determine if they must be renewed. Often a dealer will handle the inspection of parts and offer advice concerning reconditioning and renewal. As a general rule, time is the primary cost of an overhaul so it does not pay to install worn or substandard parts.

9 As a final note, to ensure maximum life and minimum trouble from a rebuilt engine, everything must be assembled with care in a spotlessly-clean environment.

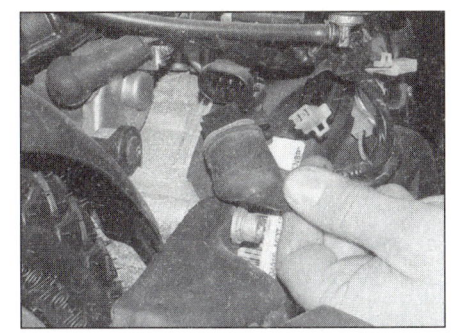

5 Engine/transmission unit – removal and installation

Caution: *The engine is not heavy, although engine removal and installation should be carried out with the aid of an assistant; personal injury or damage could occur if the engine falls or is dropped.*

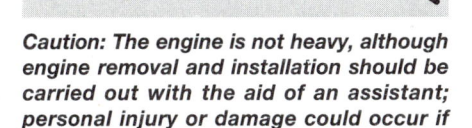

Removal

1 Support the scooter securely in an upright position. Note that the centre stand is bolted to the engine – if required, remove the belly panel (see Chapter 7) and support the frame on wooden blocks forward of the front engine mounting. Work can be made easier by raising the machine to a suitable working height on a hydraulic ramp or a suitable platform. Make sure the scooter is secure and will not topple over. If the sump is going to be removed, or the crankcases separated, drain the engine oil (see Chapter 1).

2 Remove the bodywork as required according to model (see Chapter 7). Remove the exhaust silencer (see Chapter 4).

3 If the engine is dirty, particularly around its mountings, wash it thoroughly before starting any major dismantling work. This will make work much easier and rule out the possibility of dirt falling inside.

4 Disconnect the battery negative terminal (see Chapter 9). Trace the wiring from the alternator/pulse generator coil on the right-hand side of the engine and disconnect it at the multi-pin connector **(see illustration)**. Free the wiring from any clips and secure it clear of the engine. Pull the spark plug cap off the plug. Undo the nut securing the starter motor lead to the starter motor terminal **(see illustration)**.

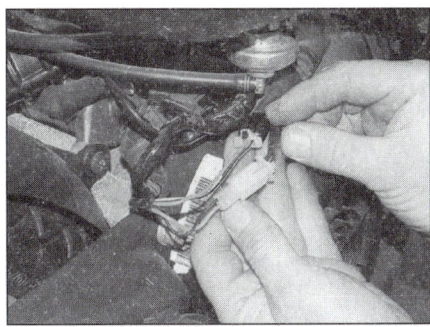

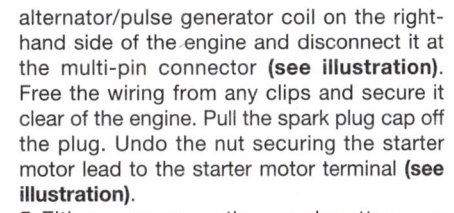

5 Either remove the carburettor, or disconnect the fuel hose and vacuum hose from their unions on the fuel tap, and disconnect the throttle cable (see Chapter 4). If the carburettor is left in place, disconnect the automatic choke and carburettor heater wiring connectors **(see illustration)**.

6 If not already done, temporarily undo the bolt on the drivebelt cover that secures the throttle cable clip and free the clip and cable **(see illustration)**.

7 Cut the cable tie that secures the drivebelt air duct to the front of the belt cover and detach the duct, then undo the bolt that secures the engine unit earth wire to the drivebelt cover **(see illustration)**.

8 If required, remove the rear wheel (see Chapter 8). **Note:** *The rear wheel and centre stand provide a convenient support for the engine unit once it is removed from the scooter. However, it is useful to loosen the rear wheel nut at this point before disconnecting the rear brake.*

9 Disconnect the rear brake cable from the brake and detach the cable from the clamp and clips on the underside of the drivebelt cover **(see illustration)**.

10 Remove the bolt securing the lower end of the rear shock absorber to the transmission casing and lower the engine unit carefully **(see illustration)**. If the rear wheel has been removed, support the engine unit on a wood block to prevent damage to the casing. Undo the nut securing the upper end of the shock to

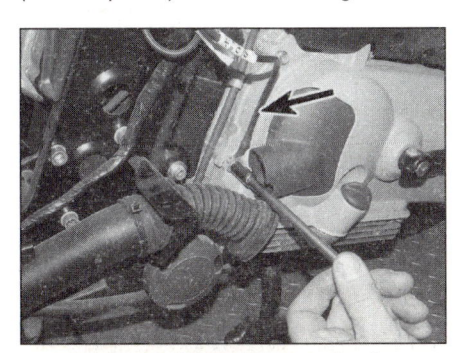

5.4a Disconnect the multi-pin wiring connector

5.4b Disconnect the lead from the starter motor terminal (arrowed)

5.5 Disconnect the choke and carburettor heater wiring connectors

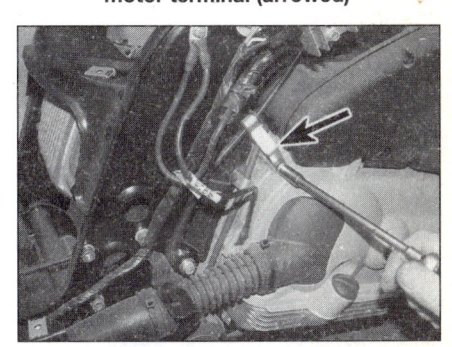

5.6 Free the throttle cable clip (arrowed) . . .

5.7 . . . and the engine earth wire (arrowed)

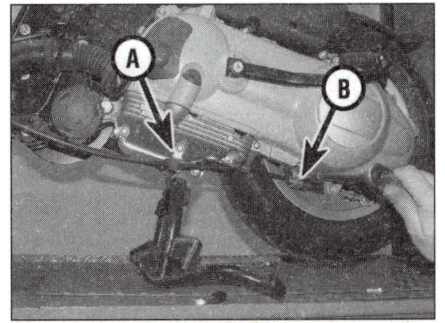

5.9 Free the brake cable from the clip (A) and clamp (B)

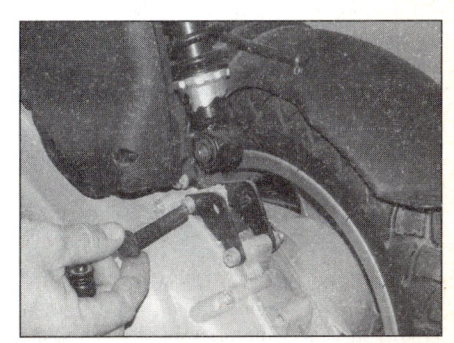

5.10a Undo the lower shock mounting bolt

2E•6 LEADER air-cooled four-stroke engines (Zip 125, Skipper ST, Liberty 125, ET4 125, Fly 125, LX4 125)

5.10b Undo the upper shock mounting . . .

5.10c . . . and remove the shock

5.11a Undo the nut on the front mounting bolt . . .

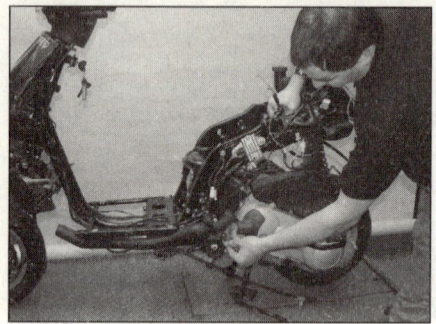

5.11b . . . then support the frame and withdraw the bolt

the frame and remove the shock **(see illustrations)**.

11 Check that all wiring, cables and hoses are well clear, then remove the front engine mounting bolt and lift the frame off the engine unit **(see illustrations)**.

Installation

12 Installation is the reverse of removal, noting the following:
a) Make sure no wires, cables or hoses become trapped between the engine and the frame when installing the engine.
b) Tighten the engine mounting bolt and shock absorber bolt to the torque settings specified at the beginning of this Chapter and Chapter 6.
c) Make sure all wires, cables and hoses are correctly routed and connected, and secured by any clips or ties.

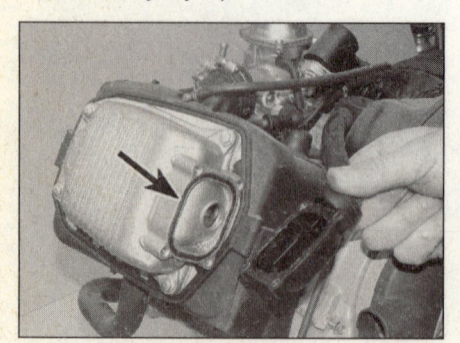

7.2 Remove the breather unit; note the O-ring (arrowed)

7.3 Lift off the valve cover

d) Adjust the throttle and the rear brake cable (see Chapter 1).
e) If required, fill the engine with the specified quantity of oil (see Chapter 1 Specifications) and check the oil level as described in Daily (pre-ride) checks.

6 Disassembly and reassembly – general information

Disassembly

1 Before disassembling the engine, the external surfaces of the unit should be thoroughly cleaned and degreased to rule out the possibility of dirt falling inside. A high flash-point solvent, such as paraffin can be used, or better still, a proprietary engine degreaser. Use old paintbrushes and toothbrushes to work the solvent into the various recesses of the engine casings. Take care to exclude solvent or water from the electrical components and intake and exhaust ports.

⚠ **Warning:** *The use of petrol (gasoline) as a cleaning agent should be avoided because of the risk of fire.*

2 When clean and dry, arrange the unit on the workbench, leaving suitable clear area for working. Gather a selection of small containers and plastic bags so that parts can be grouped together in an easily identifiable manner. Some paper and a pen should be on hand to permit notes to be made and labels attached where necessary. A supply of clean rag is also required.

3 Before commencing work, read through the appropriate section so that some idea of the necessary procedure can be gained. When removing components it should be noted that great force is seldom required, unless specified. In many cases, a component's reluctance to be removed is indicative of an incorrect approach or removal method – if in any doubt, recheck with the text.

4 When disassembling the engine, keep 'mated' parts that have been in contact with each other during engine operation together. These 'mated' parts must be re-used or renewed as an assembly.

5 Complete engine disassembly should be done in the following general order with reference to the appropriate Sections. Refer to Chapter 2G for details of transmission components disassembly.
Remove the valve cover.
Remove the camshaft and rockers.
Remove the cylinder head.
Remove the cylinder.
Remove the piston.
Remove the alternator.
Remove the starter motor (see Chapter 9).
Remove the sump cover.
Remove the oil pump.
Separate the crankcase halves.
Remove the crankshaft.

Reassembly

6 Reassembly is the reverse of the general disassembly sequence.

7 Valve cover – removal and installation

Note: *This procedure can be carried out with the engine in the frame. If the engine has been removed, ignore the steps which do not apply.*

Removal

1 Remove the bodywork as required by your model to access the engine (see Chapter 7).
2 Undo the bolts securing the breather unit to the valve cover and lift it off **(see illustration)**. Discard the O-ring, as a new one must be fitted.
3 Unscrew the bolts securing the valve cover, then lift the cover off the cylinder head **(see illustration)**. If it is stuck, do not try to lever it

LEADER air-cooled four-stroke engines (Zip 125, Skipper ST, Liberty 125, ET4 125, Fly 125, LX4 125) 2E•7

8.3 Undo the screws (arrowed)

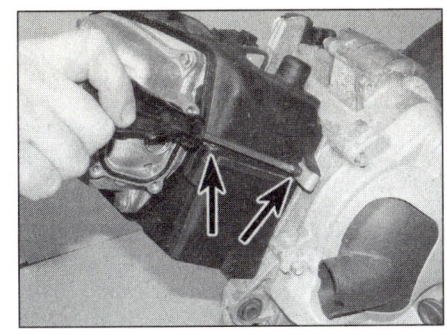

8.4 Undo the screws (arrowed)

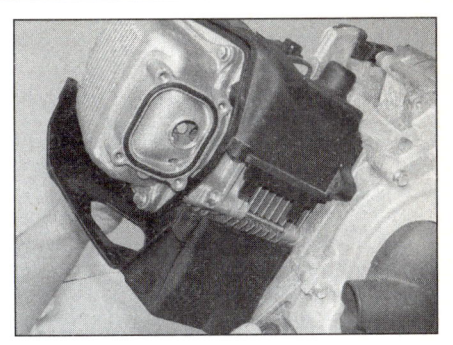

8.5 Ease the cowling apart carefully

off with a screwdriver. Tap it gently with a rubber hammer or block of wood to dislodge it. Remove the gasket and discard it, as a new one must be used.

4 If required, release the clip that secures the breather unit to the hose and disconnect the hose. Discard the clip, as a new one must be fitted on reassembly.

Installation

5 Clean the mating surfaces of the cylinder head and the valve cover with a suitable solvent.

6 Lay the new gasket into the groove in the valve cover, making sure it fits correctly.

7 Position the valve cover on the cylinder head, making sure the gasket stays in place, then install the cover bolts. Tighten the bolts evenly and in a criss-cross sequence to the torque setting specified at the beginning of the Chapter.

8 Install the remaining components in the reverse order of removal.

8 Cam chain tensioner – removal, inspection and installation

Note: *This procedure can be carried out with the engine in the frame. If the engine has been removed, ignore the steps which do not apply.*

Removal

1 Remove the bodywork as required by your model to access the engine (see Chapter 7).

2 Remove the carburettor and the intake manifold (see Chapter 4).

3 On the right-hand side of the engine, remove the screws securing the rear half of the engine cowling to the front half of the cowling and to the alternator cover **(see illustration)**.

4 On the left-hand side of the engine, remove the screws securing the rear half of the engine cowling to the front half of the cowling and to the crankcase **(see illustration)**. Note the clip for the carburettor breather hose secured by the crankcase screw.

5 The two halves of the cowling are clipped together on the left-hand side – carefully ease them apart and lift the rear half off **(see illustration)**.

6 Remove the valve cover (see Section 7).

7 Remove the cooling fan (see Section 17). Turn the engine in a clockwise direction using the alternator rotor nut, until the timing mark on the rotor aligns with the index mark on the crankcase, and the timing mark (2V) on the camshaft sprocket aligns with the index mark on the camshaft holder **(see illustrations 9.3a and 9.3b)**. At this point the engine is at TDC (top dead centre) on the compression stroke (both valves closed).

8 Unscrew the chain tensioner spring cap bolt and withdraw the spring from the tensioner body **(see illustration)**. Discard the sealing washer, as a new one must be fitted on reassembly

9 Unscrew the two tensioner mounting bolts and withdraw the tensioner from the back of the cylinder **(see illustration)**.

10 Remove the gasket from the base of the tensioner or from the cylinder and discard it, as a new one must be used.

Inspection

11 Examine the tensioner components for signs of wear or damage.

12 Use a small screwdriver to release the ratchet mechanism on the tensioner plunger and check that the plunger moves freely in and out of the tensioner body **(see illustration)**.

13 If the tensioner mechanism or the spring are worn or damaged, or if the plunger is seized in the body, the tensioner must be renewed as an assembly. Individual components are not available.

Installation

14 Turn the engine in a clockwise direction using the alternator rotor nut. This removes all the slack in the front run of the cam chain between the crankshaft and the camshaft and transfers it to the back run where it will be taken up by the tensioner.

15 Release the ratchet mechanism and press the tensioner plunger all the way into the tensioner body **(see illustration 8.12)**.

16 Place a new gasket on the tensioner body, then install it in the cylinder and tighten the bolts to the torque specified at the beginning of the Chapter **(see illustration 8.9)**.

17 Install a new sealing washer on the spring cap bolt. Install the spring and cap bolt and

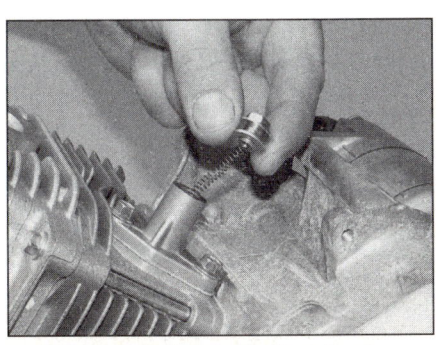

8.8 Remove the cap bolt and spring

8.9 Remove the cam chain tensioner

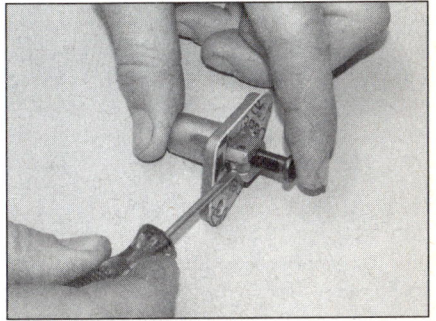

8.12 Check the operation of the ratchet and plunger

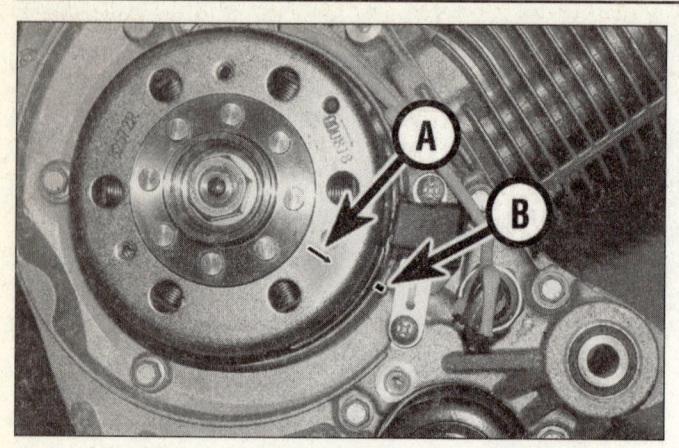

2E•8 LEADER air-cooled four-stroke engines (Zip 125, Skipper ST, Liberty 125, ET4 125, Fly 125, LX4 125)

9.3a Align rotor timing mark (A) with index mark (B)

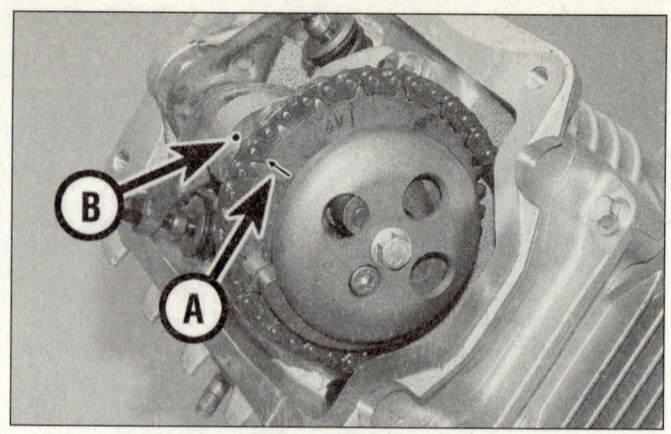

9.3b Align 2V timing mark (A) with index mark (B)

tighten the bolt to the specified torque **(see illustration 8.8)**.

18 Check that the cam chain is tensioned as it passes over the camshaft sprocket. If it is slack, the tensioner plunger did not release when the cap bolt was tightened. Remove the tensioner and check the operation of the plunger again.

19 Install the cooling fan (see Section 17) and the valve cover (see Section 7). Install the remaining components in the reverse order of removal.

9 Cam chain, blades and sprockets – removal, inspection and installation

Note 1: *This procedure can be carried out with the engine in the frame although access to the top of the engine is extremely restricted. If the engine has been removed, ignore the steps which do not apply.*

Note 2: *The engine used to illustrate this Section was fitted with an automatic decompressor mechanism. This feature was discontinued during the production run of the LEADER engine. For details of the LEADER engine without this feature refer to Chapter 2F, Section 9).*

Removal

1 Remove the valve cover (see Section 7).
2 If the cam chain and crankshaft sprocket are to be removed, remove the oil pump driven sprocket, drive chain and drive sprocket (see Section 20).
3 Remove the cooling fan (see Section 17). Turn the engine in a clockwise direction using the alternator rotor nut, until the timing mark on the rotor aligns with the index mark on the crankcase, and the timing mark (2V) on the camshaft sprocket aligns with the index mark on the camshaft holder **(see illustrations)**. At this point the engine is at TDC (top dead centre) on the compression stroke (both valves closed).

4 Undo the camshaft sprocket centre bolt and lift off the decompressor mechanism cover **(see illustrations)**. Hold the alternator to prevent the sprocket from turning.
5 Undo the decompressor mechanism bolt, then hold the bob weight return spring and withdraw the bolt and static weight **(see illustrations)**.
6 Lift off the bob weight – note the nylon bush on the back of the weight and how it locates in the slot in the cam chain sprocket **(see illustration)**. Remove the bush for safekeeping.
7 Remove the cam chain tensioner (see Section 8).
8 Lift the sprocket and its backing plate off

9.4a Undo the centre bolt . . .

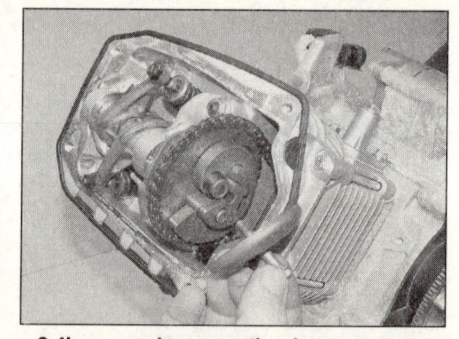

9.4b . . . and remove the decompressor mechanism cover

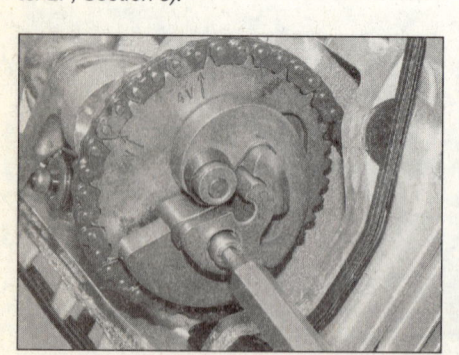

9.5a Undo the decompressor mechanism bolt . . .

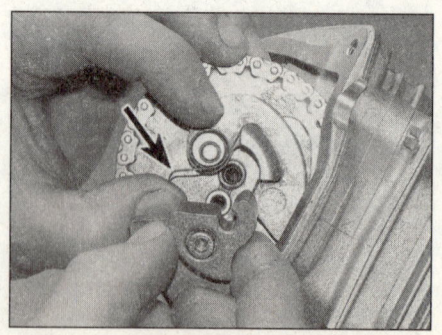

9.5b . . . and remove the static weight. Note the return spring (arrowed)

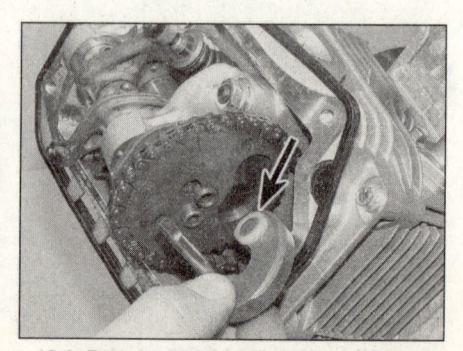

9.6 Remove the bob weight. Note the position of the bush (arrowed)

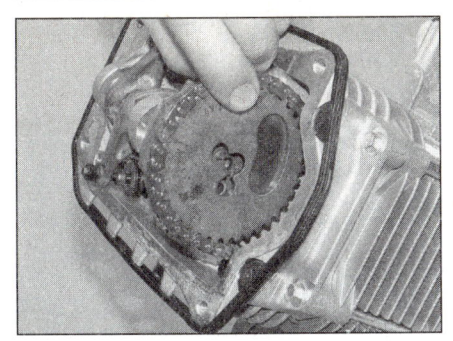

LEADER air-cooled four-stroke engines (Zip 125, Skipper ST, Liberty 125, ET4 125, Fly 125, LX4 125) 2E•9

9.8a Lift off the sprocket and backing plate . . .

9.8b . . . and disengage it from the chain

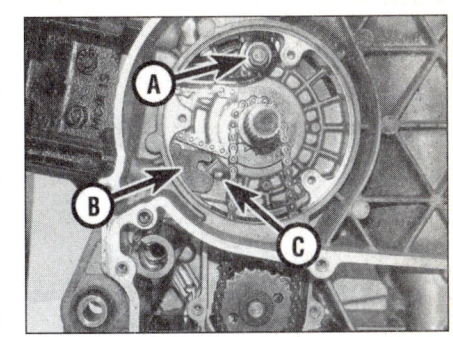

9.10 Cam chain tensioner blade is secured by bolt (A). Lower blade (B) locates on peg (C)

the end of the camshaft, then disengage it from the camchain (see illustrations).

9 If required, secure the chain with a cable tie to prevent it falling into the engine. If the chain is to be removed, mark it with paint so that if it is re-used it can be fitted the same way round. Remove the thrustwasher from the end of the crankshaft, then lower the chain down its tunnel and slip it off the sprocket on the crankshaft (see illustrations 9.6a and 9.6b in Chapter 2D). Draw the sprocket off the crankshaft, noting how it locates on the pin on the shaft (see illustration 9.6c in Chapter 2D).

10 If required, remove the bolt securing the cam chain tensioner blade to the crankcase and withdraw the blade, noting which way round it fits, and the spacer. The lower cam chain blade locates in a groove in the front edge of the cam chain tunnel in the cylinder. To remove the blade, first remove the cylinder head (see Section 11), then lift out the blade, noting how the lower end locates on the peg in the crankcase (see illustration).

Inspection

11 Check the sprockets for wear and damaged teeth, renewing them if necessary. If the sprocket teeth are worn, the chain will also be worn and should be renewed.

12 Check the chain tensioner blade and guide blade for wear or damage and renew them if necessary. Damaged or severely worn blades are an indication of a worn or improperly tensioned chain. Check the operation of the cam chain tensioner (see Section 8).

13 Inspect the components of the decompressor mechanism. Check the nylon bush for wear and flat spots and renew it if necessary. Temporarily assemble the mechanism on the camshaft (see below) and check its operation – check the spring tension and ensure the bob weight does not bind on the cover.

Installation

14 If removed, install the lower cam chain blade (see Step 10). If removed, install the tensioner blade and spacer, then tighten the retaining bolt to the torque setting specified at the beginning of the Chapter. Ensure both blades are fitted the correct way round.

15 Install the sprocket on the crankshaft, aligning the notch in the sprocket with the pin on the shaft. Lower the cam chain down through the tunnel and fit it onto the sprocket. If the chain is being re-used, ensure it is fitted the right way round (see Step 9).

16 Check that the timing mark on the alternator rotor still aligns with the index mark on the crankcase and that the engine is at TDC on the compression stroke (see Step 3). Install the camshaft sprocket backing plate on the end of the camshaft (see illustration). Slip the camshaft sprocket into the top of the chain, then take up the slack in the lower run of the chain and fit the sprocket onto the camshaft, aligning the timing mark on the sprocket with the index mark on the camshaft holder (see illustration). Note: *To prevent the backing plate falling off the end of the camshaft while the sprocket is being installed, pass the blade of a small screwdriver through the centre of the sprocket, the backing plate and the camshaft.*

Caution: *If the marks are not aligned exactly as described, the valve timing will be incorrect and the valves may strike the piston, causing extensive damage to the engine.*

17 Apply some grease to the nylon bush and fit it onto the back of the cam timing bob weight, then install the bob weight – ensure the bush locates in the slot in the cam chain sprocket (see illustration).

18 Lift the bob weight return spring and install the static weight, ensuring that the spring is located over the top of the static weight (see illustration 9.5b). Tighten the decompressor mechanism bolt finger tight. Check the operation of the decompressor mechanism – the bob weight should move freely on its spindle and return to the rest position under the tension of the spring.

19 Install the decompressor mechanism cover, aligning the small hole in the cover with the head of the decompressor mechanism

9.16a Install the backing plate . . .

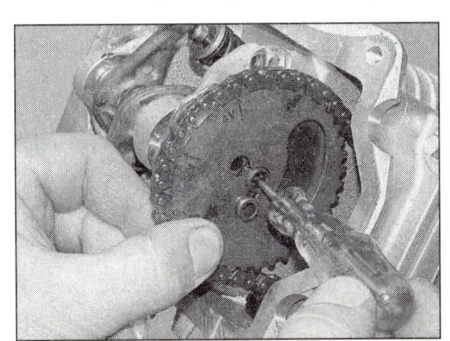

9.16b . . . and the camshaft sprocket

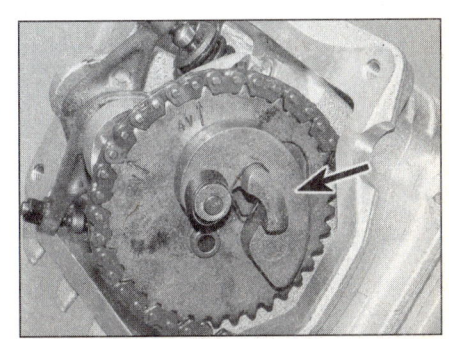

9.17 Install the bob weight (arrowed)

2E•10 LEADER air-cooled four-stroke engines (Zip 125, Skipper ST, Liberty 125, ET4 125, Fly 125, LX4 125)

9.19 Install the cover and centre bolt

bolt. Fit the camshaft sprocket centre bolt and tighten it finger tight **(see illustration)**.
20 Install the cam chain tensioner (see Section 8).
21 Tighten the camshaft sprocket bolt and the decompressor mechanism bolt. Hold the alternator to prevent the sprocket from turning.
22 Fit the thrustwasher onto the end of the crankshaft, then install the oil pump drive sprocket, chain and driven sprocket (see Section 20).
23 Install the remaining components in the reverse order of removal.

10 Camshaft and rockers –
removal, inspection and installation

Note: *This procedure can be carried out with the engine in the frame although access to the top of the engine is extremely restricted. If the engine has been removed, ignore the steps which do not apply.*

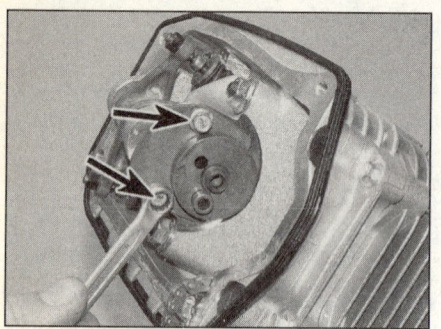

10.5a Undo the bolts (arrowed) . . .

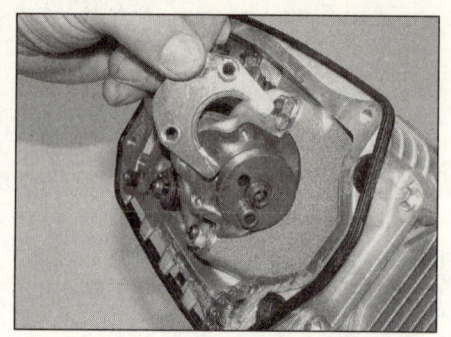

10.5b . . . and lift out the plate

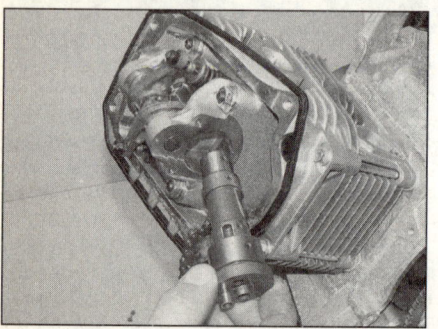

10.5c Withdraw the camshaft

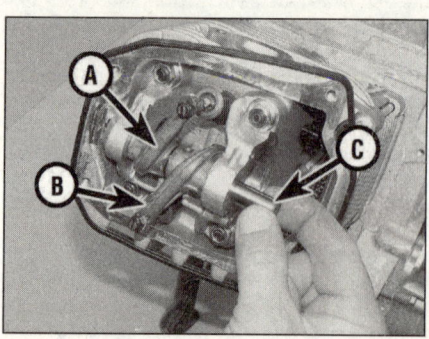

10.6a Intake rocker arm (A), exhaust rocker arm (B) and shaft (C)

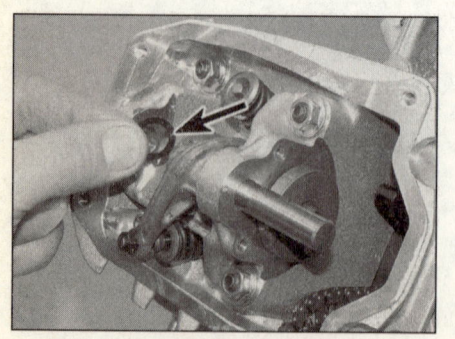

10.6b Thrustwasher (arrowed) is fitted between the rocker arms

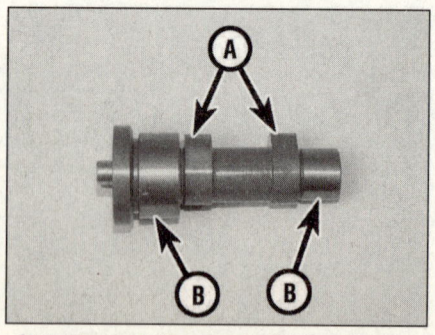

10.7a Inspect the camshaft lobes (A) and bearing journals (B)

10.7b Measuring the camshaft lobe height

Removal

1 Remove the valve cover (see Section 7).
2 Remove the cooling fan (see Section 17). Turn the engine in a clockwise direction using the alternator rotor nut, until the timing mark on the rotor aligns with the index mark on the crankcase, and the timing mark (2V) on the camshaft sprocket aligns with the index mark on the camshaft holder **(see illustration 9.3a and 9.3b)**. At this point the engine is at TDC (top dead centre) on the compression stroke (both valves closed).
3 If applicable, remove the decompressor mechanism (see Section 9).
4 Remove the camshaft sprocket (see Section 9), then secure the cam chain with a cable tie or length of wire to prevent it dropping into the engine. Stuff a clean rag into the cam chain tunnel to prevent anything falling into the engine.
5 Undo the two bolts securing the camshaft retaining plate and lift out the plate **(see illustrations)**. Mark the end of the camshaft so that it can be refitted in the same position (TDC, both valves closed), then withdraw the camshaft from its housing **(see illustration)**.
6 Mark the rocker arms so they can be installed in their original positions. Support the intake valve (right-hand) rocker arm and slowly withdraw the rocker shaft until the arm is free and can be removed **(see illustration)**. Remove the thrustwasher located on the shaft between the rocker arms, then withdraw the shaft completely and remove the exhaust valve rocker arm **(see illustration)**.

Inspection

7 Clean all the components with a suitable solvent and dry them. Inspect the camshaft lobes for heat discoloration (blue appearance), score marks, chipped areas, flat spots and spalling **(see illustration)**. Measure the height of both lobes with a micrometer and compare the results to the Specifications at the beginning of the Chapter **(see illustration)**. If damage is noted or wear is excessive, the camshaft must be renewed.
8 Check the condition of the camshaft bearing journals and the housing journals in the cylinder head **(see illustration 10.7a)**. Measure the camshaft journals with a

LEADER air-cooled four-stroke engines (Zip 125, Skipper ST, Liberty 125, ET4 125, Fly 125, LX4 125) 2E•11

10.8 Measuring the internal diameter of the camshaft housing journals

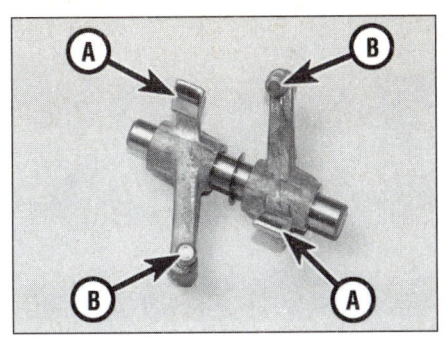

10.10 Inspect the rocker arm faces (A) and adjuster screw tips (B)

11.3 Remove the engine cowling seal

micrometer and, if available, measure the internal diameter of the housing journals with a telescoping gauge and micrometer **(see illustration)**. Compare the results to the Specifications at the beginning of the Chapter and, if damage is noted or wear is excessive, renew the faulty component.

9 Lubricate the camshaft journals with clean engine oil, install the camshaft in the cylinder head and secure it with the retaining plate. The camshaft should rotate freely with no discernible up-and-down movement. If available, measure the camshaft endfloat with a dial gauge and compare the result to the Specifications at the beginning of the Chapter. If the endfloat is excessive, inspect the retaining plate and the slot in the camshaft for wear and renew the worn component.

10 Blow through the oil passages in the rocker arms with compressed air, if available. Inspect the rocker arm faces for pits and spalling **(see illustration)**. Check the articulated tip of the adjusting screw for wear. The tip should move freely but not be loose. Measure the internal diameter of each rocker arm, the internal diameters of the rocker shaft housings and the diameter of the rocker shaft and compare the results to the Specifications at the beginning of the Chapter. If damage is noted or wear is excessive, renew the faulty component.

Installation

11 Lubricate the camshaft journals with clean engine oil, then install the camshaft in the cylinder head. Ensure the cam lobes are facing the same way as on disassembly (see Step 5).

12 Lubricate the rocker shaft with engine oil. Slide the shaft through the left-hand housing and fit the exhaust valve rocker arm, the thrustwasher and the intake valve rocker arm onto the shaft in that order. Press the shaft fully into place. With the camshaft in the correct position there should be no pressure on the rocker arms. Align the camshaft retaining plate with the slot in the camshaft, slide the plate into position and secure it with the bolts. Tighten the bolts to the specified torque setting.

13 Follow the procedure in Section 9 to install the camshaft sprocket, decompressor mechanism and cam chain tensioner as applicable, then check the valve timing.

Caution: If the marks are not aligned exactly as described, the valve timing will be incorrect and the valves may strike the piston, causing extensive damage to the engine.

14 Check the valve clearances and adjust them if necessary (see Chapter 1).

15 Install the remaining components in the reverse order of removal.

11 Cylinder head – removal and installation

Note: *This procedure can be carried out with the engine in the frame although access to the top of the engine is extremely restricted. If the* engine has been removed, ignore the steps which do not apply.

Caution: The engine must be completely cool before beginning this procedure or the cylinder head may become warped.

Removal

1 Remove the exhaust system (see Chapter 4) and the cooling fan (see Section 17). Pull the spark plug cap off the plug.

2 Follow the procedure in Section 8 to remove the engine cowling.

3 Remove the valve cover (see Section 7). Lift off the engine cowling seal **(see illustration)**.

4 If applicable, remove the decompressor mechanism (see Section 9).

5 Remove the camshaft sprocket, then secure the cam chain with a cable tie or length of wire to prevent it dropping into the engine (see Section 9).

6 Undo the two cylinder head bolts on the left-hand side of the engine **(see illustration)**. Undo the four cylinder head nuts evenly, a little at a time, in a criss-cross pattern and remove them **(see illustration)**.

7 Lift the cylinder head off carefully, feeding the cam chain down through the tunnel in the head **(see illustration)**. If the head is stuck, tap around the joint face with a soft-faced mallet to free it. Do not attempt to free the head by inserting a screwdriver between the head and cylinder – you'll damage the sealing surfaces. **Note:** *Avoid lifting the cylinder off the crankcase when the head is removed, otherwise a new cylinder base gasket will have to be fitted (see Section 14).*

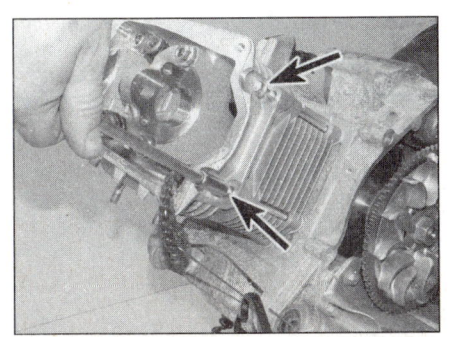

11.6a Undo the external cylinder head bolts (arrowed) . . .

11.6b . . . then the internal cylinder head nuts (arrowed)

11.7 Secure the cam chain and lift off the cylinder head

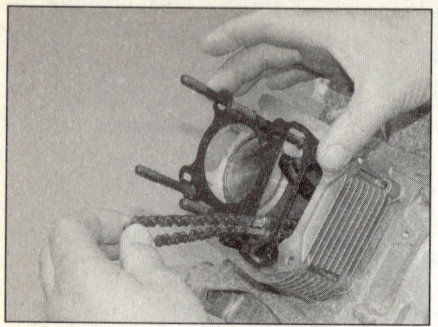

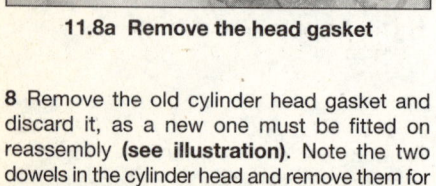

2E•12 LEADER air-cooled four-stroke engines (Zip 125, Skipper ST, Liberty 125, ET4 125, Fly 125, LX4 125)

11.8a Remove the head gasket

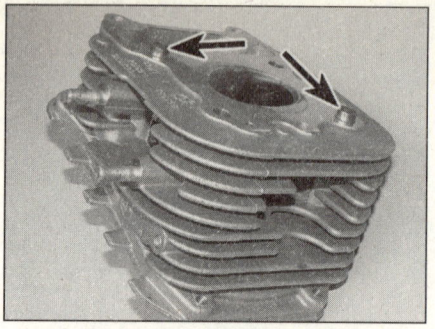

11.8b Note the dowels (arrowed) in the underside of the cylinder head

11.13 Using a torque angle gauge to tighten the cylinder head nuts

8 Remove the old cylinder head gasket and discard it, as a new one must be fitted on reassembly **(see illustration)**. Note the two dowels in the cylinder head and remove them for safekeeping if they are loose **(see illustration)**.
9 Inspect the cylinder head gasket and the mating surfaces on the head and cylinder for signs of leakage, which could indicate that the head is warped. Refer to Section 13 and check the head gasket mating surface for warpage.
10 Clean all traces of old gasket material from the cylinder head and cylinder with a suitable solvent. Take care not to scratch or gouge the soft aluminium. Be careful not to let any dirt fall into the crankcase, the cylinder bore or the oil passage.

Installation

11 Ensure both cylinder head and cylinder mating surfaces are clean, then lay the new gasket in place on the cylinder, making sure the oil passage holes are correctly aligned. Never re-use the old gasket.
12 Ensure both the dowels are in place in the head, then carefully lower the head onto the cylinder, feeding the cam chain up through the tunnel **(see illustration 11.8b)**. Make sure the dowels are correctly aligned with the gasket and the cylinder.
13 Lubricate the seating surfaces of the cylinder head nuts with clean engine oil, then install the nuts finger tight. Tighten the nuts evenly, in a criss-cross pattern, to the initial torque setting specified at the beginning of the Chapter. Now tighten them one at a time and in the same sequence, through 90° in one continuous movement, using a torque angle gauge **(see illustration)**. Now tighten them through a further 90°. **Note:** *If a torque angle gauge is not available see **Haynes Hint**.*

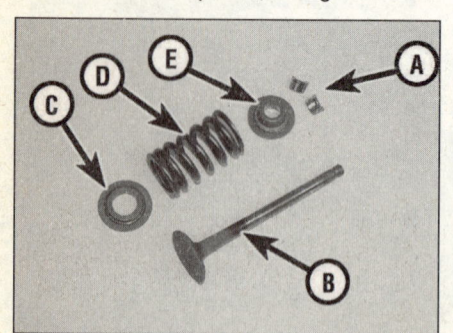

HAYNES HiNT *If a degree disc is not available, the angle for the torque setting can be determined by using the points on the cylinder head nut. Select one point on the nut as a reference and mark it with paint or a marker. Now select the second point clockwise 90° from it and mark its position on the head. Tighten the nut – when the mark on the first point aligns with the mark made on the head, it will have turned through the requisite number of degrees. Repeat the procedure to achieve the final torque setting.*

14 Install the two cylinder head bolts on the left-hand side of the engine and tighten them to the specified torque setting **(see illustration 11.6a)**.
15 Install the camshaft sprocket and the remaining components in the reverse order of removal, referring to the relevant Sections or Chapters.

12 Valves/valve seats/valve guides – overhaul

1 If a valve spring compressor is available, the home mechanic can remove the valves from the cylinder head, grind in the valves and renew the valve stem seal. If the necessary measuring tools are available, you can assess the amount of wear on the valves and guides and measure the valve-to-seat contact areas.
2 If the valve guides or the valve seats in the cylinder head are worn beyond their service limits a new head will have to be fitted.
3 After any servicing or repair work, be sure to clean the head thoroughly to remove any metal particles or abrasive grit that may still be present. Use compressed air, if available, to blow out all the holes and passages.

13 Cylinder head and valves – disassembly, inspection and reassembly

1 Disassembly, cleaning and inspection of the valves and related components can be done by the home mechanic if the necessary special tools are available. If there is any doubt about the condition of any components, have them checked by a Piaggio dealer.
2 To disassemble the valve components without the risk of damaging them, a valve spring compressor suitable for motorcycle engines is absolutely necessary.

Disassembly

3 Before proceeding, arrange to label and store the valves and their related components so that they can be returned to their original location without getting mixed up **(see illustration)**.
4 If not already done, remove the camshaft and rockers (see Section 10), then clean all traces of old gasket material from the cylinder head with a suitable solvent. Take care not to scratch or gouge the soft aluminium.
5 Compress the valve spring on the intake valve with a spring compressor, making sure it is correctly located onto each end of the valve assembly. Do not compress the spring any more than is absolutely necessary to release the collets. Remove the collets, using either needle-nose pliers, tweezers, a magnet or a screwdriver with a dab of grease on it **(see illustration)**. Carefully release the valve spring compressor and remove the spring retainer,

13.3 Valve components – collets (A), valve (B), spring seat (C), spring (D) and spring retainer (E)

13.5a Compress the valve spring and remove the collets

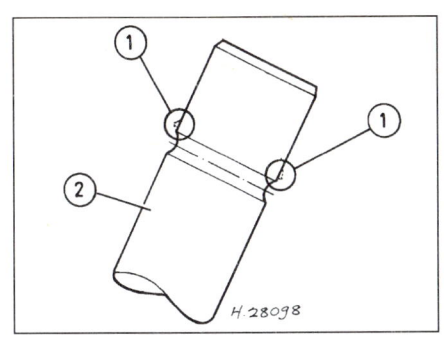

LEADER air-cooled four-stroke engines (Zip 125, Skipper ST, Liberty 125, ET4 125, Fly 125, LX4 125) 2E•13

13.5b If the valve stem (2) won't pull through the guide, deburr the area (1) above the collet groove

13.5c Pull the stem seal off with pliers

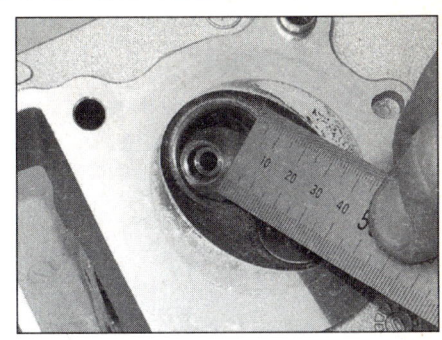

13.12 Measuring the valve seat width (for greater precision use a vernier caliper)

noting which way up it fits, the spring, and the valve from the head. If the valve binds in the guide (won't pull through), push it back into the head and deburr the area around the collet groove with a very fine file **(see illustration)**. Once the valve has been removed, pull the valve stem oil seal off the top of the valve guide with pliers and discard it (the old seal should never be re-used) and remove the spring seat **(see illustration)**.

6 Repeat the procedure for the exhaust valve. Remember to keep the parts for each valve together and labelled so they can be reinstalled in the correct location.

7 Next, clean the cylinder head with solvent and dry it thoroughly. Compressed air will speed the drying process and ensure that all holes and recessed areas are clean.

8 Clean the valve springs, collets, retainers, and spring seats with solvent and dry them thoroughly. Work on the parts from one valve at a time so as not to mix them up.

9 Scrape off any deposits that may have formed on the valve, then use a motorised wire brush to remove deposits from the valve heads and stems. Again, make sure the valves do not get mixed up.

Inspection

10 Inspect the head very carefully for cracks and other damage. If cracks are found, a new head will be required.

11 Using a precision straight-edge and a feeler gauge, check the head gasket mating surface for warpage. Lay the straight-edge across the head lengthways and diagonally, intersecting the stud holes, and try to slip the feeler gauge under it on either side of the combustion chamber. If the feeler gauge can be inserted between the straight-edge and the cylinder head, the head is warped and should be machined. Consult a Piaggio dealer or specialist engineer. If warpage has reached the limit listed in the Specifications at the beginning of the Chapter, a new head will have to be fitted.

12 Examine the valve seats in the combustion chamber. If they are deeply pitted, cracked or burned, it may be possible to have them repaired by a specialist engineer, otherwise a new head will be required. Measure the valve seat width and compare it to this Chapter's Specifications **(see illustration)**.

13 Measure the valve stem diameter **(see illustration)**. If the stem is worn beyond its service limit a new valve must be fitted. Clean the valve guides to remove any carbon build-up, then measure the inside diameters of the guides (at both ends and the centre of the guide) with a small hole gauge and micrometer. The guides are measured at the ends and at the centre to determine if they are worn unevenly. Piaggio do not list new valve guides, so if any guide is worn unevenly, or if the valve stem/guide clearance is more than the service limit, have the head checked by a specialist engineer. It may be possible to bore out the guide and fit a sleeve in it, otherwise a new cylinder head will have to be fitted.

14 Inspect each valve face for cracks, pits and burned spots; measure the valve face and compare the result with the Specifications. Check the valve stem and the collet groove area for cracks **(see illustration)**. Rotate the valve and check for any obvious indication that it is bent. Check the end of the stem for pitting and excessive wear. Worn valve faces, or the presence of any of the above conditions indicates the need for new valves. If the stem end is pitted or worn, also check the contact area of the valve clearance adjuster in the rocker arm

15 Inspect the end of each valve spring for wear and pitting. Stand the spring upright on a flat surface and check it for bend by placing a square against it **(see illustration)**. If the bend in a spring is excessive, it must be renewed. Piaggio do not specify a service limit for the valve springs, but it is good practice to fit new springs when the head has been disassembled for valve servicing.

16 Check the spring retainers and collets for obvious wear and cracks. Any questionable parts should not be re-used, as extensive damage will occur in the event of failure during engine operation.

17 If the inspection indicates that no overhaul work is required, the valve components can be reinstalled in the head.

Reassembly

18 Unless a valve overhaul has been performed, before installing the valves in the head they should be ground in (lapped) to

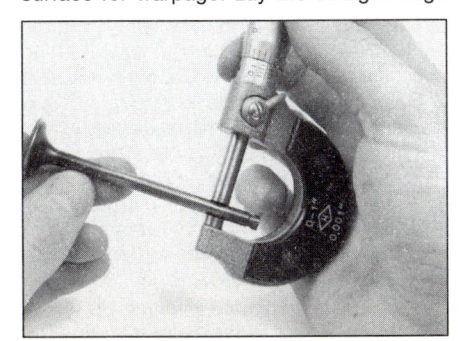

13.13 Measuring the valve stem diameter with a micrometer

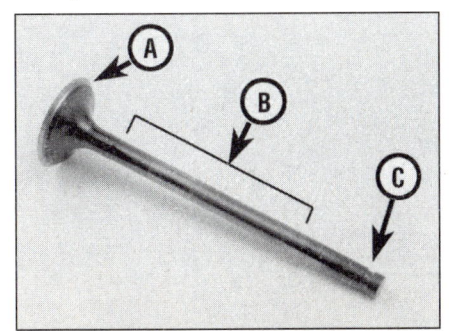

13.14 Check the valve face (A), stem (B) and collet groove (C) for signs of wear and damage

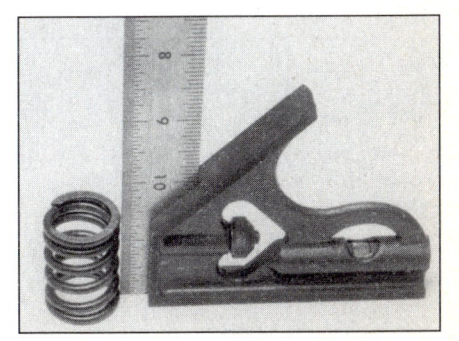

13.15 Check the valve springs for squareness

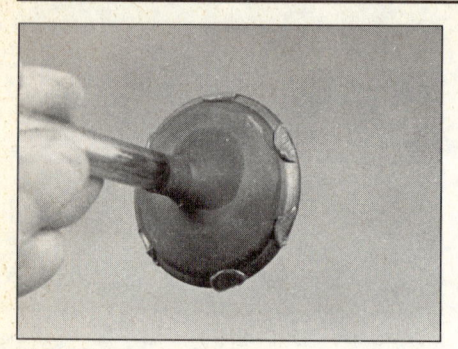

13.19 Apply the grinding compound very sparingly, in small dabs, to the valve face only

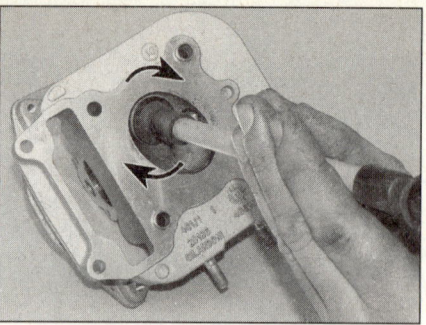

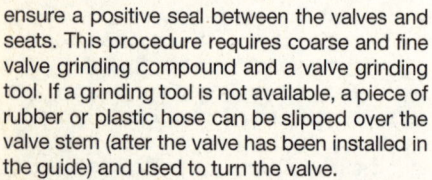

13.20a Rotate the tool back-and-forth between the palms of your hands

13.20b Valve contact area should show a uniform unbroken ring

ensure a positive seal between the valves and seats. This procedure requires coarse and fine valve grinding compound and a valve grinding tool. If a grinding tool is not available, a piece of rubber or plastic hose can be slipped over the valve stem (after the valve has been installed in the guide) and used to turn the valve.

19 Apply a small amount of coarse grinding compound to the valve face, then slip the valve into the guide **(see illustration)**. **Note:** *Make sure each valve is installed in its correct guide and be careful not to get any grinding compound on the valve stem.*

20 Attach the grinding tool (or hose) to the valve and rotate the tool between the palms of your hands. Use a back-and-forth motion (as though rubbing your hands together) rather than a circular motion (ie, so that the valve rotates alternately clockwise and anti-clockwise rather than in one direction only) **(see illustration)**. Lift the valve off the seat and turn it at regular intervals to distribute the grinding compound properly. Continue the grinding procedure until the valve face and seat contact areas are of uniform width and unbroken around the circumference **(see illustration)**.

21 Carefully remove the valve from the guide and wipe off all traces of grinding compound. Use solvent to clean the valve and wipe the seat area thoroughly with a solvent-soaked cloth.

22 Repeat the procedure with fine valve grinding compound, then repeat the entire procedure for the other valve.

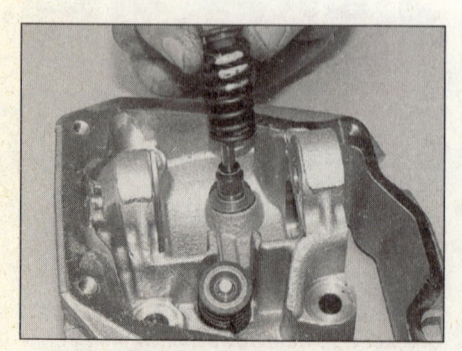

HAYNES HiNT *Check for proper sealing of each valve by pouring a small amount of solvent into the valve port while holding the valve shut. If the solvent leaks past the valve into the combustion chamber the valve grinding operation should be repeated.*

23 Lay the spring seat for the intake valve in place in the cylinder head, then install a new valve stem seal onto the guide. Use an appropriate size deep socket to push the seal over the end of the valve guide until it is felt to clip into place. Don't twist or cock it, or it will not seal properly against the valve stem. Also, don't remove it again or it will be damaged.

24 Lubricate the intake valve stem with molybdenum disulphide grease, then install it into its guide, rotating it slowly to avoid damaging the seal. Check that the valve moves up and down freely in the guide. Next, install the spring, with its closer-wound coils facing down into the cylinder head, followed by the spring retainer, with its shouldered side facing down so that it fits into the top of the spring **(see illustration)**.

25 Apply a small amount of grease to the collets to help hold them in place as the pressure is released from the spring. Compress the spring with the valve spring compressor and install the collets **(see illustration 13.5a)**. When compressing the spring, depress it only as far as is necessary to slip the collets into place. Make certain that the collets are securely locked in their retaining grooves.

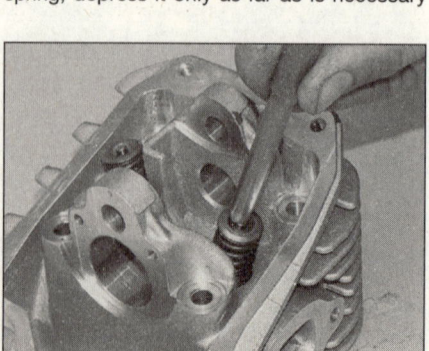

26 Repeat the procedure for the exhaust valve.

27 Support the cylinder head on blocks so the valves can't contact the workbench top, then very gently tap each of the valve stems with a soft-faced hammer **(see illustration)**. This will help seat the collets in their grooves.

14 Cylinder – removal, inspection and installation

Note: *This procedure can be carried out with the engine in the frame although access to the top of the engine is extremely restricted. If the engine has been removed, ignore the steps which do not apply.*

Removal

1 Remove the cylinder head (see Section 11).
2 Note how the lower cam chain blade locates in a groove in the front edge of the cam chain tunnel in the cylinder, then lift out the blade, noting which way round it fits.
3 Lift the cylinder up off the studs, carefully feeding the cam chain down through the tunnel. Support the piston as it becomes accessible to prevent it hitting the crankcase. If the cylinder is stuck, tap around its joint face with a soft-faced mallet to free it from the crankcase. Don't attempt to free the cylinder by inserting a screwdriver between it and the crankcase – you'll damage the sealing surfaces. When the cylinder is removed, stuff a clean rag around the piston to prevent anything falling into the crankcase.
4 Note the two dowels in the cylinder and remove them for safekeeping if they are loose.
5 Remove the gasket carefully and make a note of the thickness (0.4, 0.6 or 0.8) stamped into the material. If the original cylinder and piston are used on reassembly, a new gasket of the same thickness should be used. Discard the old gasket.

Inspection

6 Inspect the cylinder bore carefully for

13.24 Install the spring with the closer wound coils facing the head

13.27 Tap the valve stems to seat the collets

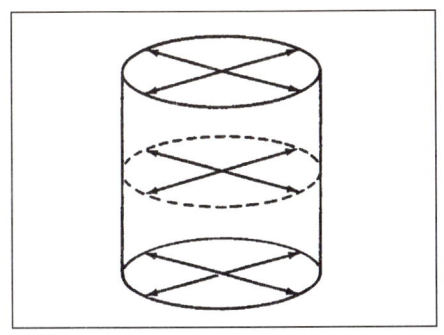

LEADER air-cooled four-stroke engines (Zip 125, Skipper ST, Liberty 125, ET4 125, Fly 125, LX4 125) 2E•15

14.7 Measure the cylinder bore in the directions shown

14.13 Zero the dial gauge on the cylinder top gasket face

scratches and score marks. A rebore will be necessary to remove any deep scores (see Step 7).

7 Using telescoping gauges and a micrometer, check the dimensions of the cylinder to assess the amount of wear, taper and ovality. Piaggio recommend the bore is measured at 10 mm, 38.5 mm and 75 mm down from the top edge, both parallel to and across the crankshaft axis **(see illustration)**. Compare the results to the cylinder bore Specifications at the beginning of this Chapter. **Note:** *Cylinders and pistons are size-coded during manufacture and it is important that they are of the same size-code. Piaggio list four size-codes (A to D) for this engine, in standard size and first, second and third oversizes (rebored cylinders). The size-code is stamped in the gasket surface at the top or base of the cylinder, and in the piston crown. When purchasing a new cylinder or piston, always supply the size-code letter.*

8 Calculate any differences between the measurements to determine any taper or ovality in the bore. Piaggio specify a wear limit of 0.05 mm between any of the measurements. If the cylinder is worn beyond this service limit, badly scratched, scuffed or scored, have it rebored by a Piaggio dealer or motorcycle engineer. If the cylinder is rebored, it will require an oversize piston and rings. If the cylinder has already been rebored to the maximum oversize and is worn or damaged, the cylinder must be renewed.

9 Measure the cylinder bore diameter 38.5 mm down from the top edge, then calculate the piston-to-bore clearance by subtracting the piston diameter (see Section 15) from the bore diameter. If the cylinder is in good condition and the piston-to-bore clearance is within specifications, the cylinder can be re-used.

10 Check that all the cylinder head studs are tight in the crankcase halves. If any are loose, remove them and clean their threads. Apply a suitable permanent thread locking compound and tighten them securely.

Installation

11 Check that the mating surfaces of the cylinder and crankcase are clean.

12 Three different thicknesses of cylinder base gasket are available from Piaggio. If the original cylinder and piston are being re-used, fit a gasket the same thickness as the original (see Step 5). If new components are being used, the cylinder must be assembled on the crankcase and piston (see Steps 17 to 19) without a base gasket, and a dial gauge mounted against the crown of the piston to establish which thickness is required.

13 Set the dial gauge in the mounting plate, and with the gauge tip resting against the cylinder top gasket face, zero the gauge dial **(see illustration)**. Rotate the crankshaft so that the piston is part way down the bore.

14 Clamp the mounting plate diagonally across two of the cylinder studs, and secure it by tightening the stud nuts to 28 to 30 Nm.

15 Rotate the crankshaft via the alternator rotor nut so the piston rises to the top of its stroke (TDC) and the gauge tip rests on the centre of the piston crown. At this point read off the dial gauge **(see illustration)**. The further the piston crown is below the top of the cylinder bore, the thinner the base gasket should be. If the reading is between 0 and 0.1 mm a 0.8 mm gasket is required, between 0.1 and 0.3 mm a 0.6 mm gasket is required, and between 0.3 and 0.4 mm a 0.4 mm gasket is required – refer to your Piaggio dealer for details.

16 Having established the correct gasket thickness, fit it to the crankcase **(see illustration)**. Never re-use the old gasket.

17 If required, install a piston ring clamp onto the piston to ease its entry into the bore as the cylinder is lowered. This is not essential as the cylinder has a good lead-in enabling the piston rings to be hand-fed into the bore. If possible, have an assistant to support the cylinder while this is done. Check that the piston ring end gaps are positioned as described in Section 16.

18 Lubricate the cylinder bore, piston and piston rings, and the connecting rod big- and small-ends, with the clean engine oil, then fit the cylinder down over the studs until the piston crown fits into the bore.

19 Gently push down on the cylinder, making sure the piston enters the bore squarely and does not get cocked sideways. If a piston ring clamp is not being used, carefully compress and feed each ring into the bore as the cylinder is lowered. If necessary, use a soft mallet to gently tap the cylinder down, but do not use force if it appears to be stuck as the piston and/or rings will be damaged. If a clamp is used, remove it once the piston is in the bore.

20 When the piston is correctly installed in the cylinder, press the cylinder down onto the base gasket.

21 Fit the lower cam chain guide into the cam chain tunnel (see Step 2), then install the cylinder head (see Section 11).

15 Piston – removal, inspection and installation

Note: *This procedure can be carried out with the engine in the frame although access to the top of the engine is extremely restricted. If the engine has been removed, ignore the steps which do not apply.*

Removal

1 Remove the cylinder (see Section 14). Before removing the piston from the connecting rod, stuff a clean rag into the hole around the rod to prevent the circlips or anything else from falling into the crankcase. The piston should have an arrow marked on its crown which should face towards the exhaust valve. If this is not visible, mark the piston accordingly so that it can be installed the correct way round **(see illustration 16.1 in Chapter 2C)**. Note that the arrow may not be visible until the carbon deposits have been scraped off and the piston cleaned. There

14.15 Take the reading off the piston crown at TDC

14.16 Fit a new cylinder base gasket onto the crankcase

should also be a valve head recess on the intake valve side of the piston crown.

2 Carefully prise out the circlip on one side of the piston using a pointed instrument or a small flat-bladed screwdriver inserted into the notch **(see illustration 16.2 in Chapter 2C)**. Push the piston pin out from the other side to free the piston from the connecting rod. Remove the other circlip and discard them both, as new ones must be used. Use a socket extension to push the piston pin out if required.

> **HAYNES HINT**: *To prevent the circlip from flying away or from dropping into the crankcase, pass a rod or screwdriver with a greater diameter than the gap between the circlip ends, through the piston pin. This will trap the circlip if it springs out.*

> **HAYNES HINT**: *If a piston pin is a tight fit in the piston bosses, heat the piston gently with a hot air gun – this will expand the alloy piston sufficiently to release its grip on the pin.*

Inspection

3 Before the inspection process can be carried out, the piston rings must be removed and the piston must be cleaned. Note that if the cylinder is being rebored, piston inspection can be overlooked, as a new one will be fitted. All three piston rings can be removed by hand; a ring removal and installation tool can be used on the two compression rings, but do not use it on the oil control ring **(see illustration 16.3 in Chapter 2C)**. Carefully note which way up each ring fits and in which groove as they must be installed in their original positions if being re-used. The upper surface of each ring should be marked at one end. Do not nick or gouge the piston in the process.

4 Scrape all traces of carbon from the top of the piston. A hand-held wire brush or a piece of fine emery cloth can be used once most of the deposits have been scraped away. Do not, under any circumstances, use a wire brush mounted in a drill motor to remove deposits from the piston; the piston material is soft and will be eroded away by the wire brush.

5 Use a piston ring groove cleaning tool to remove any carbon deposits from the ring grooves. If a tool is not available, a piece broken off an old ring will do the job. Be very careful to remove only the carbon deposits. Do not remove any metal and do not nick or gouge the sides of the ring grooves. Once the deposits have been removed, clean the piston with solvent and dry it thoroughly.

6 Inspect the piston for cracks around the skirt, at the pin bosses and at the ring lands. Normal piston wear appears as even, vertical wear on the thrust surfaces of the piston and slight looseness of the top ring in its groove. If the skirt is scored or scuffed, the engine may have been suffering from overheating and/or abnormal combustion, which caused excessively high operating temperatures. Also check that the circlip grooves are not damaged.

7 A hole in the piston crown is an extreme example that abnormal combustion (pre-ignition) was occurring. Burned areas at the edge of the piston crown are usually evidence of spark knock (detonation). If any of the above problems exist, the causes must be corrected or the damage will occur again.

8 Check the piston-to-bore clearance by measuring the bore (see Section 14) and the piston diameter. Measure the piston 36.5 mm down from the top edge of the piston and at 90° to the piston pin axis **(see illustration 16.8 in Chapter 2C)**. Subtract the piston diameter from the bore diameter to obtain the clearance. If it is greater than the specified figure, the piston must be renewed (assuming the bore itself is within limits, otherwise a rebore is necessary). Remember that the pistons and cylinders are size-coded – make sure you have matched components.

9 Use a micrometer and a telescoping gauge to determine whether there is wear between the piston pin and piston. Measure the piston pin diameter at both ends and the internal diameter of each pin boss in the piston and compare the results with the Specifications **(see illustrations 16.9a and 16.9b in Chapter 2C)**.

10 To check for wear between the piston pin and connecting rod small-end, measure the piston pin diameter at its centre and the internal diameter of the rod small-end **(see illustrations 16.10a and 16.10b in Chapter 2C)**. The piston pin should not be worn below its specified diameter and the small-end measurement should not be greater then the specified service limit. Renew any worn components; if the small-end is worn, a new connecting rod and crankshaft assembly will have to be fitted (see Section 21).

11 Piston ring-to-groove clearance can be measured to determine whether the ring grooves in the piston are worn. Install the rings on the piston (see Section 16), then use a feeler gauge to measure the clearance between the ring and groove and compare the result with the Specifications **(see illustration 16.11 in Chapter 2C)**. If the clearance is greater than the service limit, repeat the check using new rings, if the clearance is still too great, the piston should be renewed.

Installation

12 Inspect and install the piston rings (see Section 16).

13 Lubricate the piston pin, the piston pin bore and the connecting rod small-end bore with clean engine oil. Install a new circlip in one side of the piston (do not re-use old circlips). Line up the piston on the connecting rod, making sure the arrow on the piston crown faces down towards the exhaust, and insert the piston pin **(see illustration 16.13a in Chapter 2C)**. Secure the pin with the other new circlip **(see illustration 16.13b in Chapter 2C)**. When installing the circlips, compress them only just enough to fit them in the piston, and make sure they are properly seated in their grooves with the open end away from the removal notch **(see illustration 16.13c in Chapter 2C)**.

14 Install the cylinder (see Section 14).

16 Piston rings – inspection and installation

1 New piston rings should be fitted whenever an engine is being overhauled. Before fitting the new rings, the end gaps must be checked with the rings installed in an unworn part of the bore.

2 To measure the installed ring end gap, insert the top ring into the bottom of the bore and square it up with the bore walls by pushing it in with the top of the piston. The ring should be about 15 mm from the bottom of the bore. To measure the end gap, slip a feeler gauge between the ends of the ring and compare the measurement to the Specifications at the beginning of the Chapter **(see illustration 17.2 in Chapter 2C)**.

3 If the gap is larger or smaller than specified, double-check to make sure that you have the correct rings before proceeding. If the gap is too small the ends may come in contact with each other during engine operation, which can cause serious damage. Check the piston and bore diameters with the Specifications to confirm whether they are standard or oversize.

4 Excess end gap is not critical unless it exceeds the service limit. Again, double-check to make sure you have the correct rings for your engine and check that the bore is not worn.

5 Repeat the procedure for the other two rings.

6 Once the ring end gaps have been checked, the rings can be installed on the piston.

7 The oil control ring (lowest on the piston) is installed first. Always install this ring by hand and do not expand the ring any more than is necessary to slide it into place. Next install the 2nd compression ring, noting that there is usually a marking or letter near one end to denote the upper surface of the ring. Finally install the top ring into its groove. A ring installation tool can be used on the two compression rings if desired.

8 Once the rings are correctly installed, check they move freely without snagging and stagger their end gaps as shown **(see illustration 17.8 in Chapter 2C)**.

LEADER air-cooled four-stroke engines (Zip 125, Skipper ST, Liberty 125, ET4 125, Fly 125, LX4 125) 2E•17

17.4 Unclip the connector (arrowed) from the cover

17.5 Lift off the alternator cover

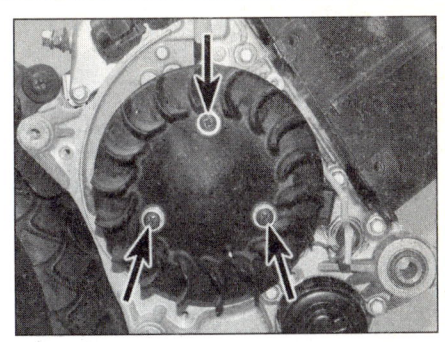

17.6 Cooling fan is secured by three screws (arrowed)

17 Cooling fan – removal and installation

Note: *This procedure can be carried out with the engine in the frame. If the engine has been removed, ignore the steps which do not apply.*

Removal

1 Remove the bodywork as required by your model to access the alternator cover on the right-hand side of the engine (see Chapter 7).
2 If required, remove the exhaust system or silencer to gain clearance to draw the cover off the alternator rotor (see Chapter 4). If required, displace the fuel pump and filter assembly (see Chapter 4).
3 On machines fitted with a secondary air system, disconnect the SAS vacuum hose and the SAS pipe from the reed valve housing (see Chapter 1, Section 21).
4 Undo the clip that secures the wiring harness to the top of the alternator cover, then detach the alternator multi-pin connector from the cover **(see illustration)**.
5 Remove the screws securing the alternator cover and remove the cover **(see illustration)**.
6 Remove the three screws securing the cooling fan to the alternator rotor and remove the fan **(see illustration)**.

Installation

7 Installation is the reverse of removal.

18 Alternator rotor and stator – removal and installation

Note: *This procedure can be carried out with the engine in the frame. If the engine has been removed, ignore the steps which do not apply.*

Removal

1 Remove the cooling fan (see Section 17).
2 To remove the rotor nut it is necessary to stop the rotor from turning **(see illustration)**. Piaggio produce a service tool (Part No. 020656Y) which locates in the holes in the rotor. A similar tool can be made **(see illustration 12.3 in Chapter 2A)**. A strap wrench can be used around the rotor

HAYNES HiNT *A rotor holding tool can easily be made using two strips of steel bolted together in the middle, with a bolt through each end which locates into the holes in the rotor. Do not allow the bolts to extend too far through the rotor holes otherwise the coils could be damaged.*

periphery, although be careful not to damage the ignition pulse generator coil. With the rotor held securely, unscrew the nut.
3 To remove the rotor from the crankshaft it is necessary to use the Piaggio service tool (Part No. 020162Y) **(see illustration 12.4a in Chapter 2A)** or a two-legged puller. If using the service tool, ensure that the centre bolt is backed-out sufficiently to allow the body of the tool to be screwed all the way into the threads provided in the rotor. With the tool in place, hold the body of the tool using a spanner on its flats while tightening the centre bolt (turn it clockwise) to draw the rotor off the end of the shaft. If using a two-legged puller, assemble the puller legs through the holes in the rotor and tighten the centre bolt down onto the crankshaft end until the rotor is drawn off **(see illustration 12.4b in Chapter 2A)**. If it is loose, remove the Woodruff key from the shaft, noting how it fits **(see illustration 12.4c in Chapter 2A)**.
4 To remove the stator, it is also necessary to remove the pulse generator coil as they come as a linked assembly. Disconnect the alternator wiring multi-pin connector. Undo

the screw that secures the alternator wiring guide to free the wiring from the crankcase. Disconnect the oil pressure switch wiring connector **(see illustration)**.
5 Undo the screws that secure the pulse generator coil **(see illustration 18.2)**, then undo the screws that secure the stator and remove the two units together.

Installation

6 Install the stator and pulse generator coil onto the crankcase; ensure that the wiring for the generator coil and the oil pressure switch is correctly positioned. Install the stator and generator coil screws and tighten them to the specified torque.
7 Connect the oil pressure switch wiring connector, the alternator wiring multi-pin connector, and install the alternator wiring guide.
8 Clean the tapered end of the crankshaft and the corresponding mating surface on the inside of the rotor with a suitable solvent. Make sure that no metal objects have attached themselves to the magnets on the inside of the rotor. If removed, fit the Woodruff key into its slot in the shaft, then install the rotor onto the shaft, aligning the slot in the rotor with the key **(see illustrations 12.7a and 12.7b in Chapter 2A)**.
9 Install the rotor nut and tighten it to the torque setting specified at the beginning of the Chapter, using the method employed on removal to prevent the rotor from turning.
10 Position the rotor so that the raised section aligns with the pulse generator coil, then measure the air gap between the rotor

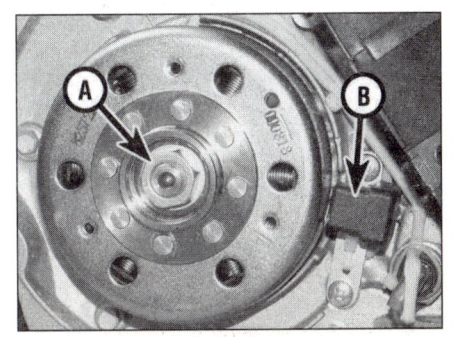

18.2 Alternator rotor nut (A). Note the pulse generator coil (B)

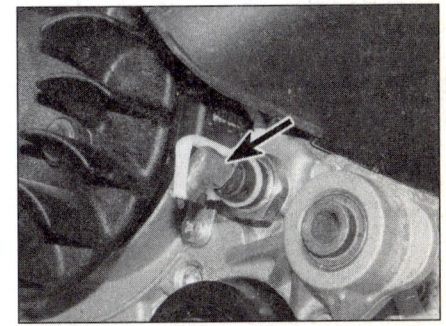

18.4 Oil pressure switch wiring connector (arrowed)

2E•18 LEADER air-cooled four-stroke engines (Zip 125, Skipper ST, Liberty 125, ET4 125, Fly 125, LX4 125)

and the coil with a feeler gauge. The air gap should be between 0.34 to 0.76 mm. If the gap is outside the specified limits inspect the coil mounting for distortion. If the gap is too small the rotor may strike to coil and damage it; if the gap is too large the performance of the ignition system will be reduced.

11 Install the cooling fan (see Section 17).

19 Starter pinion assembly – removal, inspection and installation

Note: *This procedure can be carried out with the engine in the frame.*

Removal
1 Remove the drivebelt cover (see Chapter 2G).
2 Lift out the starter pinion assembly, noting how it fits **(see illustration)**.

Inspection
3 Check the starter pinion assembly for any signs of damage or wear, particularly for chipped or broken teeth on either of the pinions. Check the corresponding teeth on the starter motor pinion and the starter driven gear.
4 Rotate the outer pinion and check that it moves smoothly up and down the shaft, and that it returns easily to its rest position **(see illustration)**.
5 The starter pinion assembly is supplied as a complete unit; if any of the component parts are worn or damaged, the unit will have to be renewed.

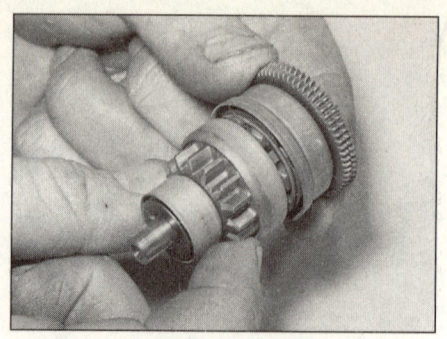

Installation
6 Installation is the reverse of removal. Ensure the inner pinion engages with the starter motor shaft.

20 Oil pump and relief valve – pressure check, pump removal, inspection and installation

Note: *This procedure can be carried out with the engine in the frame.*

Pressure check
1 This engine is fitted with an oil pressure switch and warning light. The function of the circuit is described in Chapter 9.

19.2 Location of the starter pinion assembly

2 If there is any doubt about the performance of the engine lubrication system, the oil pressure should be checked. The check provides useful information about the condition of the lubrication system. If you do not have the facilities to check the oil pressure yourself, have it done by a Piaggio dealer.
3 To check the oil pressure, a suitable pressure gauge (which screws into the crankcase) will be needed. Piaggio produce a gauge (Part No. 020193Y) and gauge adapter (Part. No. 020434Y) for this purpose.
4 Check the engine oil level (see *Daily (pre-ride) checks*), then warm the engine up to normal operating temperature and stop it. Support the scooter so that the rear wheel is clear of the ground.
5 Remove the alternator cover (see Section 17). Disconnect the oil pressure switch wiring connector **(see illustration 18.4)**, then unscrew the oil pressure switch from the crankcase and screw in the gauge adapter. Connect the pressure gauge to the adapter. Discard the pressure switch sealing washer, as a new one must be fitted on reassembly. If necessary, temporarily reconnect the exhaust system.

⚠️ **Warning:** *Take great care not to burn your hands on the hot engine unit, exhaust pipe or with engine oil when connecting the gauge adapter to the crankcase. Do not allow exhaust gases to build-up in the work area; either perform the check outside or use an exhaust gas extraction system.*

6 Start the engine and increase the engine speed to 6000 rpm whilst watching the pressure gauge reading. The oil pressure

19.4 Check the pinion as described

should be similar to that given in the Specifications at the beginning of the Chapter.
7 If the pressure is significantly lower than the standard, either the oil strainer or filter is blocked, the pressure relief valve is stuck open, the oil pump is faulty, the piston oil jet in the crankcases has become dislodged, or there is considerable engine main bearing wear. Begin diagnosis by checking the oil filter and strainer (see Chapter 1), then the relief valve and oil pump (see Steps 11 to 38). If those items check out okay, the crankcases will have to be split to check the oil jet and the main bearings (see Section 21).
8 If the pressure is too high, either an oil passage is clogged, the relief valve is stuck closed or the wrong grade of oil is being used.
9 Stop the engine and unscrew the gauge and adapter from the crankcase.
10 Fit a new sealing washer to the oil pressure switch and install the switch. Tighten the switch, then check the oil level (see *Daily (pre-ride) checks*). **Note:** *Rectify any problems before running the engine again.*

Oil pump and relief valve
Removal
11 Drain the engine oil (see Chapter 1).
12 Remove the drive pulley and variator (see Chapter 2G).
13 Remove the screws and washers securing the pump drive chain cover and remove the cover **(see illustrations)**. **Note:** *The cover is a tight fit in the casing; pull it out carefully by the cast projections. Discard the cover O-ring, as a new one must be fitted on reassembly. Note the chain guide on the back of the cover* **(see illustration)**

20.13a Undo the cover screws (arrowed) ...

20.13b ... and pull out the cover ...

20.13c ... noting the location of the chain guide (arrowed)

LEADER air-cooled four-stroke engines (Zip 125, Skipper ST, Liberty 125, ET4 125, Fly 125, LX4 125)

20.14a Undo the sump cover bolts . . .

20.14b . . . and remove the cover

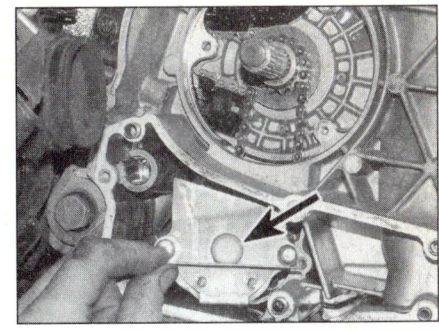

20.15 Remove the pump sprocket plate (arrowed)

14 Undo the bolts securing the sump cover and remove the cover **(see illustrations)**. Note the position of the guide for the rear brake cable. Discard the gasket, as a new one must be used. Note how the relief valve spring locates on the lug on the inside of the cover and remove it carefully. If necessary, withdraw the relief valve from its location in the sump. Note the location of the cover dowels and remove them for safekeeping if they are loose.

15 Remove the screws securing the pump sprocket plate and remove the plate, noting how it fits **(see illustration)**.

16 Insert a pin punch or screwdriver through one of the holes in the pump sprocket and locate it against the pump body to stop the sprocket turning, then unscrew the sprocket bolt **(see illustration)**. Note the Belleville washer on the bolt.

17 Draw the sprocket off the pump and slip it out of the chain **(see illustration 21.7a in Chapter 2C)**. If required, draw the chain up into the transmission housing and remove it from the drive sprocket. **Note:** *Before the chain is removed, mark it so that it can be fitted the same way round.* Slide the drive sprocket off the end of the crankshaft **(see illustration 21.7c in Chapter 2C)**.

18 Remove the pump drive pinion and discard the O-ring, as a new one must be fitted. Undo the two screws securing the oil pump and remove the pump, noting how it fits **(see illustration 21.8 in Chapter 2C)**. Also remove the gasket from behind the pump and discard it, as a new one must be fitted.

Inspection

19 Clean the relief valve and spring in solvent. Inspect the surface of the valve for wear and scoring. Measure the free length of the spring and compare the result with the Specifications at the beginning of the Chapter. If the valve is worn or the spring has shortened, renew them. Inspect the valve housing in the casing; any dirt lodged in the housing will prevent the valve from seating properly and must be cleaned out carefully to avoid scratching the surface of the housing.

20 Remove the two screws securing the cover to the pump body, then remove cover **(see illustration)**.

21 Note the position of the reference marks on the pump rotors. It is not be necessary to disassemble the pump (individual components are not available) but, if required, remove the central circlip with circlip pliers, then lift out the rotors. Clean the pump body and rotors in solvent and dry them with compressed air, if available. Inspect the body and rotors for scoring and wear. If any damage, scoring, uneven or excessive wear is evident, renew the pump. If the pump has been disassembled, fit the rotors back into the body, ensuring that the reference marks are visible, and install the circlip.

22 Measure the clearance between the inner rotor tip and the outer rotor with a feeler gauge as shown, and compare the result to the Specifications at the beginning of the Chapter **(see illustration)**.

23 Measure the clearance between the outer rotor and the pump body and compare the result to the Specifications at the beginning of the Chapter **(see illustration 20.22)**. If either clearance measured is greater than the maximum listed, fit a new pump.

24 Lay a straight-edge across the rotors and the pump body and, using a feeler gauge, measure the rotor endfloat (the gap between the rotors and the straight-edge. If the clearance measured is greater than the maximum listed, fit a new pump.

25 Check the pump drive chain and sprockets for wear or damage, and renew them as a set if necessary.

26 If the pump is good, make sure all the components are clean, then lubricate them with clean engine oil.

27 Fit the cover, noting that it can only be fitted one way, and tighten the screws securely.

28 Rotate the pump shaft by hand and check that the rotors turn smoothly.

Installation

29 Lay a new pump gasket onto the crankcase, making sure the holes in the gasket align correctly with the oil holes.

30 Install the pump, noting that it can only be fitted one way, and tighten the screws to the torque setting specified at the beginning of the Chapter. Fit a new O-ring to the drive pinion and install the pinion.

31 Slide the drive sprocket, with its shouldered end facing out, onto the crankshaft, then fit the drive chain around the sprocket and slip it down into the sump (see Step 17).

20.16 Undo the pump sprocket bolt (arrowed)

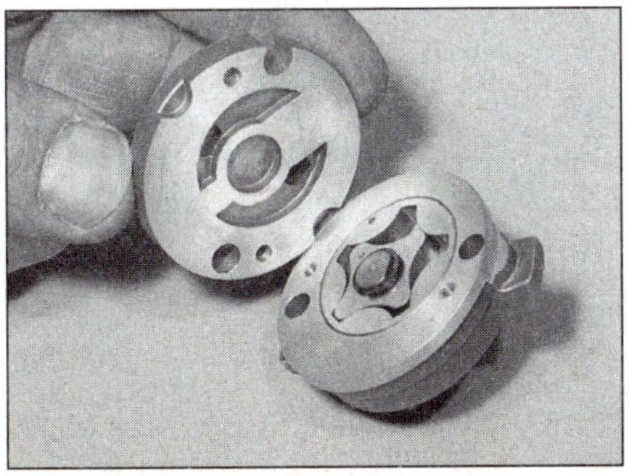

20.20 Remove the pump cover

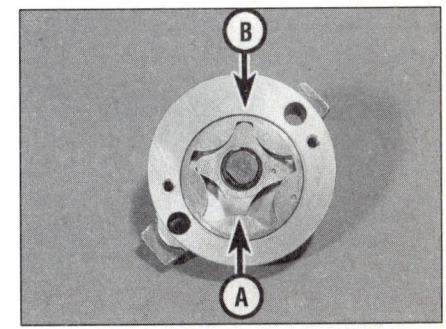

20.22 Measure inner-to-outer rotor clearance (A) and outer rotor-to-body clearance (B)

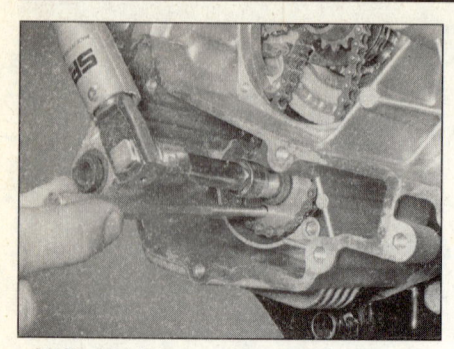

20.32 Hold the sprocket and tighten the bolt to the specified torque

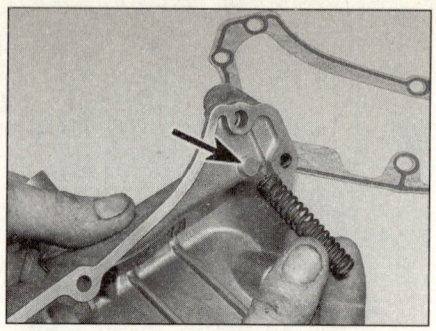

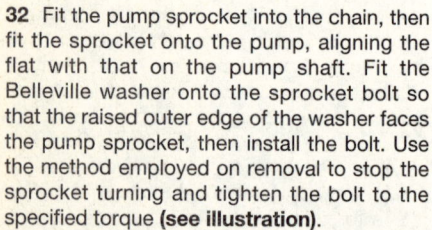

20.35 Relief valve spring locates on lug (arrowed) inside cover

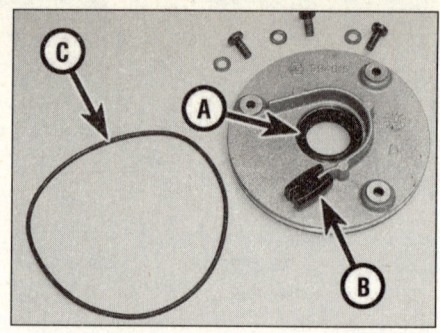

20.36 Pump drive chain cover oil seal (A), chain guide (B) and O-ring (C)

32 Fit the pump sprocket into the chain, then fit the sprocket onto the pump, aligning the flat with that on the pump shaft. Fit the Belleville washer onto the sprocket bolt so that the raised outer edge of the washer faces the pump sprocket, then install the bolt. Use the method employed on removal to stop the sprocket turning and tighten the bolt to the specified torque **(see illustration)**.
33 Install the pump sprocket plate and tighten its screws securely.
34 Remove any traces of old gasket from the sump cover and crankcase mating surfaces with solvent. Take care not to scratch or gouge the soft aluminium.
35 Lubricate the relief valve with clean engine oil, then install the valve into the casing. Fit the spring onto the lug on the inside of the sump cover **(see illustration)**. Ensure the dowels for the sump cover are in place and install the cover using a new gasket. Install the cover bolts and the clip for the rear brake cable, then tighten the cover bolts to the specified torque.
36 Check the condition of the centre oil seal in the pump drive chain cover **(see illustration)**. If there are any signs of oil leakage inside the drivebelt casing, renew the seal. If the chain guide is worn, unclip it and fit it the other way round, or fit a new guide. Fit a new O-ring onto the cover and smear it with grease. Slide the cover carefully over the crankshaft to avoid damaging the centre seal, align the holes for the fixing screws and install

the screws and washers finger tight. Tighten the screws a little at a time, in turn, to draw the cover into the casing, then ensure the screws are tightened to the specified torque.
37 Install the drive pulley and variator (see Chapter 2G).
38 Fill the engine with the correct type and quantity of oil (see Chapter 1). Start the engine and check that there are no leaks around the sump.

21 Crankcase halves, crankshaft and connecting rod

Note: To separate the crankcase halves, the engine must be removed from the frame.

Separation

1 To access the crankshaft and its bearings, the crankcase must be split into two parts.
2 To enable the crankcases to be separated, the engine must be removed from the frame (see Section 5). Before the crankcases can be separated the following components must be removed:
a) Camchain, blades and sprockets (see Section 9).
b) Cylinder head (see Section 11).
c) Cylinder (see Section 14).
d) Alternator rotor and stator (see Section 18).
e) Variator (see Chapter 2G).
f) Starter motor (see Chapter 9).
g) Oil pump (see Section 20).
h) Centre stand (see Chapter 7).
3 Before separating the crankcases, measure the crankshaft endfloat with a dial gauge and compare the result with the Specifications at the beginning of the Chapter. Excessive endfloat is an indication of wear on the crankshaft or the crankcases and should be investigated when the cases have been separated.
4 Unscrew the eleven crankcase bolts evenly, a little at a time and in a criss-cross sequence until they are all finger-tight, then remove them **(see illustration)**. Support the engine unit on the work surface left-hand (transmission) side down. Carefully lift the right-hand crankcase half off the left-hand half, taking care not to score the surface of

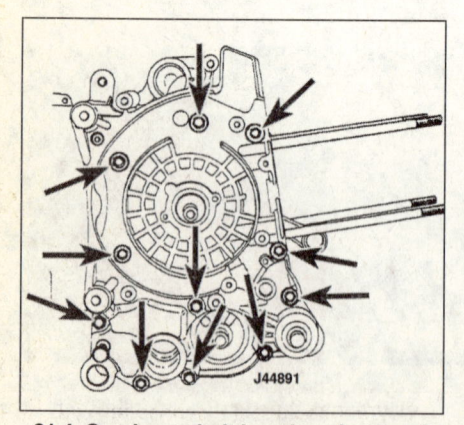

21.4 Crankcase bolt locations (arrowed)

the right-hand main bearing on the crankshaft. If the halves do not separate easily, tap around the joint with a soft-faced mallet. *Note: Do not try and separate the halves by levering against the crankcase mating surfaces as they are easily scored and will not seal correctly afterwards.* Note the position of the two crankcase dowels and remove them for safekeeping if they are loose.
5 Lift the crankshaft assembly out of the left-hand crankcase, again taking care not to mark the bearing surface. Discard the gasket, as a new one must be fitted on reassembly.
6 Clean the crankcases thoroughly with solvent and dry them with compressed air. Clean the crankshaft assembly with solvent. *Note: Piaggio warn against blowing compressed air through the connecting rod oil passage to avoid the danger of compacting dirt and blocking the passage to the big-end bearing.*
7 Remove all traces of old gasket from the mating surfaces with solvent. Take care not to scratch or gouge the soft aluminium.
Caution: Be very careful not to nick or gouge the crankcase mating surfaces, or oil leaks will result. Check both crankcase halves very carefully for cracks and other damage.
8 Note the position of the crankshaft oil seal in the right-hand crankcase half, then drive the seal out with a bearing driver or suitably-sized socket. Take care not to damage the surface of the main bearing.

Inspection

Crankcases

9 Small cracks or holes in aluminium castings can be repaired with an epoxy resin adhesive as a temporary measure. Permanent repairs can only be effected by argon-arc welding, and only a specialist in this process is in a position to advise on the economy or practical aspect of such a repair. If any damage is found that can't be repaired, renew the crankcase halves as a set.
10 Damaged threads can be economically reclaimed by using a diamond section wire insert, of the Heli-Coil type, which is easily fitted after drilling and retapping the affected thread. Sheared studs or screws can usually

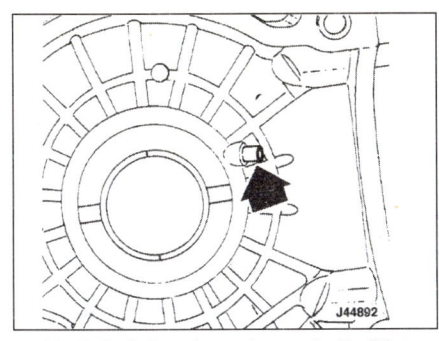

LEADER air-cooled four-stroke engines (Zip 125, Skipper ST, Liberty 125, ET4 125, Fly 125, LX4 125) 2E•21

21.13 Left-hand crankcase half oil jet (arrowed)

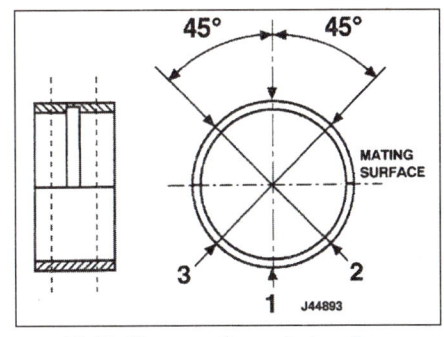

21.15 Measure the main bearings

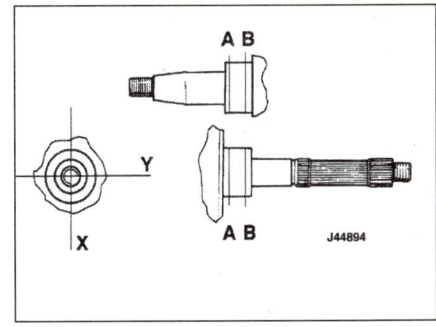

21.16 Measure the crankshaft journals

be removed with stud or screw extractors; if you are in any doubt consult a Piaggio dealer or specialist motorcycle engineer.

11 Always wash the crankcases thoroughly after any repair work to ensure no dirt or metal swarf is trapped inside when the engine is rebuilt.

12 Inspect the engine mounting bushes. If they show signs of deterioration, renew them both at the same time. To remove a bush, first note its position in the casing. Heat the casing with a hot air gun, then support the casing and drive the bush out with a hammer and a suitably-sized socket. Clean the bush housing with steel wool to remove any corrosion, then reheat the casing and fit the new bush. **Note:** *Always support the casing when removing or fitting bushes to avoid breaking the casing.*

13 Blow out the oil passages for the oil pump, relief valve, main bearing and piston oil jet in the left-hand crankcase half with compressed air **(see illustration)**. Blow out the oil passages for the main bearing, the cylinder head oil supply and the oil seal drain in the right-hand crankcase half.

14 Check the condition of the main bearings in each crankcase half. Each bearing comprises two halves – the surface of the lower half is plain and the upper half has an oilway in it. The surface of each bearing should be smooth with no scoring or scuff marks. The condition of the bearings and the corresponding crankshaft journals is vital to the performance of the engine lubrication system. If the bearings are damaged or worn, oil pressure will drop and the oil feed to the connecting rod big end and the cylinder head will be insufficient to prevent rapid wear and possible seizure.

15 Use a telescoping gauge and a micrometer to measure the internal diameter of each bearing in three directions as shown **(see illustration)**. Ensure that the measurements are taken in the centre of the bearing surface, either side of the oilway. The bearings are colour coded – on Zip 125, Skipper ST, Liberty 125 and ET4 models they are coded red, blue or yellow and on Fly 125 and LX4 125 models they are coded yellow, green and blue. Ensure all three measurements for each bearing are within the specifications in the tables below. Piaggio do not supply new bearings; if any of the bearings are worn beyond the specifications new crankcase halves will have to be fitted. If there is any doubt about the condition of the bearings consult a Piaggio dealer.

Crankshaft

16 Check the condition of the crankshaft journals. The surface of each journal should be smooth with no scoring, pitting or scuff marks. Use a micrometer to measure the diameter of each journal in two positions (A and B) and in two directions as shown **(see illustration)**. There are two size categories for the crankshaft journals, Class 1 and Class 2, which should match the colour-coding of the crankcase bearings. Compare the results with the appropriate table and ensure that the journal size is within the specifications for the appropriate bearing. If the crankshaft journals are damaged or worn beyond the specifications a new crankshaft will have to be fitted.

17 Measure the connecting rod big-end side clearance with a feeler gauge and compare it with the Specifications at the beginning of the Chapter **(see illustration)**. Measure the up-and-down (radial) play on the rod with a dial gauge and measure the width of the flywheels at several points to ensure they are not out of

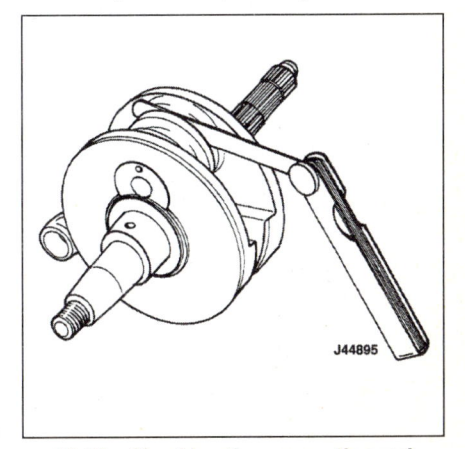

Table 1: Crankshaft/main bearing fit – Zip 125, Skipper ST, Liberty 125, ET4

Crankcase main bearing		Crankshaft journal diameter	
Code	Internal diameter	Class	External diameter
Blue	29.019 to 29.034 mm	1	28.994 to 29.000 mm
Red	29.025 to 29.040 mm		
Yellow	29.022 to 29.037 mm	2	29.000 to 29.006 mm
Blue	29.028 to 29.043 mm		

Table 2: Crankshaft/main bearing fit – Fly 125, LX4 125

Crankcase main bearing		Crankshaft journal diameter	
Code	Internal diameter	Class	External diameter
Yellow	28.999 to 29.005 mm	1	28.998 to 29.004 mm
Green	28.999 to 29.005 mm		
Blue	29.005 to 29.011 mm	2	29.004 to 29.010 mm
Yellow	29.005 to 29.011 mm		

21.17a Checking the connecting rod big-end bearing side clearance

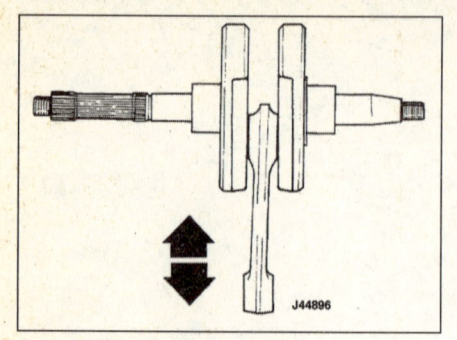

21.17b Measure the radial play on the connecting rod

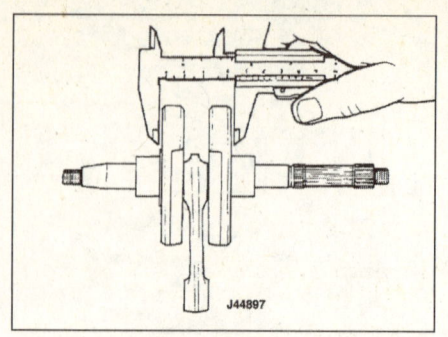

21.17c Measure the width of the flywheels as described

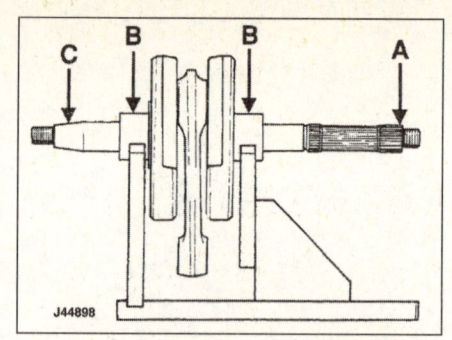

21.18 Check the crankshaft runout

alignment **(see illustrations)**. Compare the results with the Specifications at the beginning of the Chapter.

18 Place the crankshaft assembly on V-blocks and check the runout at the main bearing journals and at the ends of the shafts **(see illustration)**. If the runout exceeds the specified limit, or if either of the connecting rod measurements exceed the limit, the crankshaft assembly must be renewed.

Reassembly

19 Support the engine unit on the work surface left-hand (transmission) side down. Ensure that the crankcase mating surfaces are clean and that the crankcase dowels are in place, then install a new gasket.

20 Lubricate the main bearings and crankshaft journals with clean engine oil, then insert the crankshaft all the way into the left-hand half, positioning the connecting rod in line with the crankcase mouth. Guide the crankcase right-hand half over the crankshaft end and press it down until the two halves meet. Use a soft-faced mallet to help the casing seat, but don't apply too much pressure. **Note:** *If the crankcases do not meet, remove the right-hand half and investigate the problem – do not be tempted to pull the crankcases together using the bolts.*

21 Clean the threads of the crankcase bolts and install them finger-tight. Tighten the bolts evenly, in a criss-cross sequence, to the specified torque setting. Hold the connecting rod to prevent it hitting the crankcase mouth, then rotate the crankshaft to check that it is moves freely. If necessary, trim any excess crankcase gasket off the cylinder mating surface with a sharp knife.

22 Lubricate the new crankshaft oil seal with clean engine oil, then install it in the right-hand crankcase half in the same position as noted on removal. Use a bearing driver or a suitably-sized socket which contacts only the outer face of the seal to drive it into position. **Note:** *Do not press the oil seal too far into the casing.*

23 Install the remaining components in the reverse order of removal.

22 Initial start-up after overhaul

1 Make sure the engine oil level is correct (see *Daily (pre-ride) checks*).

2 Make sure there is fuel in the tank.

3 With the ignition OFF, operate the kickstart a couple of times to check that the engine turns over easily.

4 Turn the ignition ON, start the engine and allow it to run at a slow idle until it reaches operating temperature. Do not be alarmed if there is a little smoke from the exhaust – this will be due to the oil used to lubricate the piston and bore during assembly and should subside after a while.

5 If the engine proves reluctant to start, remove the spark plug and check that it has not become wet and oily. If it has, clean it and try again. If the engine refuses to start, go through the fault finding charts at the end of this manual to identify the problem.

6 Check carefully for oil leaks and make sure the transmission and controls, especially the brakes, function properly before road testing the machine. Refer to Section 23 for the recommended running-in procedure.

7 Upon completion of the road test, and after the engine has cooled down completely, recheck the valve clearances (see Chapter 1) and check the engine oil level (see *Daily (pre-ride) checks*).

23 Recommended running-in procedure

1 Treat the machine gently for the first few miles to make sure oil has circulated throughout the engine and any new parts installed have started to seat.

2 Even greater care is necessary if the engine has been rebored or a new crankshaft has been installed. In the case of a rebore, the machine will have to be run-in as when new. This means a restraining hand on the throttle until at least 600 miles (1000 km) have been covered. There's no point in keeping to any set speed limit – the main idea is to keep from labouring the engine and not to maintain any one speed for too long. Experience is the best guide, since it's easy to tell when an engine is running freely. Once past the 600 mile (1000 km) mark, gradually increase performance, using full throttle for short bursts to begin with.

3 If a lubrication failure is suspected, stop the engine immediately and try to find the cause. If an engine is run without oil, even for a short period of time, severe damage will occur.

Chapter 2 Part F:
LEADER liquid-cooled four-stroke engines (Super Hexagon, B125, X9 125, X8 125, GT125, GT200)

Refer to the beginning of Chapter 1 for model identification details

Contents

Alternator rotor and stator – removal and installation	17
Cam chain tensioner – removal, inspection and installation	8
Cam chain, blades and sprockets – removal, inspection and installation	9
Camshaft and rockers – removal, inspection and installation	10
Crankcase halves, crankshaft and connecting rod	20
Cylinder – removal, inspection and installation	14
Cylinder head – removal and installation	11
Cylinder head and valves – disassembly, inspection and reassembly	13
Disassembly and reassembly – general information	6
Engine/transmission unit – removal and installation	5
General information	1
Idle speed – check and adjustment	see Chapter 1
Initial start-up after overhaul	21
Major engine repair – general note	4
Oil and filter – change	see Chapter 1
Oil level – check	see *Daily (pre-ride) checks*
Oil pump and relief valve – pressure check, pump removal, inspection and installation	19
Operations possible with the engine in the frame	2
Operations requiring engine removal	3
Piston – removal, inspection and installation	15
Piston rings – inspection and installation	16
Recommended running-in procedure	22
Spark plug gap – check and adjustment	see Chapter 1
Starter motor – removal and installation	see Chapter 9
Starter pinion assembly – removal, inspection and installation	18
Valve clearances – check and adjustment	see Chapter 1
Valve cover – removal and installation	7
Valves/valve seats/valve guides – overhaul	12
Water pump – check, removal and installation	see Chapter 3

Degrees of difficulty

Easy, suitable for novice with little experience	**Fairly easy,** suitable for beginner with some experience	**Fairly difficult,** suitable for competent DIY mechanic	**Difficult,** suitable for experienced DIY mechanic	**Very difficult,** suitable for expert DIY or professional

Specifications

General
Note: GT200 specifications, where different, in brackets

Type	Single cylinder four-stroke
Capacity	124. cc (198 cc)
Bore	57.0 mm (72.0 mm)
Stroke	48.6 mm
Compression ratio	11.5 to 13.0 : 1

Cylinder head

Warpage (max)	0.05 mm
Left-hand camshaft bearing housing diameter	37.000 to 37.025 mm
Right-hand camshaft journal housing diameter	20.000 to 20.021 mm
Rocker arm shaft housing	12.000 to 12.018 mm
Rocker arm shaft diameter	11.977 to 11.985 mm
Rocker arm internal diameter	12.000 to 12.011 mm
Valve seat width (max)	1.6 mm

2F•2 LEADER liquid-cooled four-stroke engines (Super Hexagon, B125, X9 125, X8 125, GT125, GT200)

Camshaft
Intake lobe height	30.285 mm
Exhaust lobe height	29.209 mm
Left-hand journal diameter	
Standard	36.950 to 36.975 mm
Service limit (min)	36.940 mm
Right-hand journal diameter	
Standard	19.959 to 19.980 mm
Service limit (min)	19.950 mm
Camshaft endfloat	
Standard	0.11 to 0.41 mm
Service limit	0.42 mm

Valves, guides and springs
Valve clearances	See Chapter 1
Intake valve	
Overall standard length	94.6 mm
Stem diameter	
Standard	4.972 to 4.987 mm
Service limit (min)	4.960 mm
Guide bore diameter	
Standard	5.000 to 5.012 mm
Service limit (max)	5.022 mm
Stem/valve guide clearance	
Standard	0.013 to 0.040 mm
Service limit	0.062 mm
Face width	
Standard	0.99 to 1.27 mm
Service limit (max)	1.6 mm
Exhaust valve	
Overall standard length	94.4 mm
Stem diameter	
Standard	4.960 to 4.975 mm
Service limit (min)	4.950 mm
Guide bore diameter	
Standard	5.000 to 5.012 mm
Service limit (max)	5.022 mm
Stem/valve guide clearance	
Standard	0.025 to 0.052 mm
Service limit	0.072 mm
Face width	0.99 to 1.27 mm
Valve spring free length (inlet and exhaust)	n/a

Cylinder bore – 125 cc engine
Bore diameter (measured 41.0 mm down from top edge of the cylinder, at 90° to piston pin axis)

Standard	
Size-code A	56.997 to 57.004 mm
Size-code B	57.004 to 57.011 mm
Size-code C	57.011 to 57.018 mm
Size-code D	57.018 to 57.025 mm
1st oversize	57.197 to 57.225 mm
2nd oversize	57.397 to 57.425 mm
3rd oversize	57.597 to 57.625 mm

Piston – 125 cc engine
Piston diameter (measured 41.1 mm down from top edge of the piston, at 90° to piston pin axis)

Standard	
Size-code A	56.945 to 56.952 mm
Size-code B	56.952 to 56.959 mm
Size-code C	56.959 to 56.966 mm
Size-code D	56.966 to 56.973 mm
1st oversize	57.145 to 57.173 mm
2nd oversize	57.345 to 57.373 mm
3rd oversize	57.545 to 57.573 mm
Piston-to-bore clearance (when new)	0.045 to 0.059 mm
Piston pin diameter	14.996 to 15.000 mm
Piston pin bore diameter in piston	15.001 to 15.006 mm

Cylinder bore – 200 cc engine
Bore diameter (measured 33.0 mm down from top edge of the cylinder, at 90° to piston pin axis)
  Standard
    Size-code A .... 71.990 to 71.997 mm
    Size-code B .... 71.997 to 72.004 mm
    Size-code C .... 72.004 to 72.011 mm
    Size-code D .... 72.011 to 72.018 mm

Piston – 200 cc engine
Piston diameter (measured 33.0 mm down from top edge of the piston, at 90° to piston pin axis)
  Standard
    Size-code A .... 71.953 to 71.960 mm
    Size-code B .... 71.960 to 71.967 mm
    Size-code C .... 71.967 to 71.974 mm
    Size-code D .... 71.974 to 71.981 mm
Piston-to-bore clearance (when new) .... 0.030 to 0.044 mm
Piston pin diameter .... 14.996 to 15.000 mm
Piston pin bore diameter in piston .... 15.001 to 15.006 mm

Piston rings
Ring end gap (installed) – 125 cc engine
  Top ring
    Standard .... 0.15 to 0.30 mm
    Service limit (max) .... 1.0 mm
  2nd ring
    Standard .... 0.10 to 0.30 mm
    Service limit (max) .... 1.0 mm
  Oil control ring
    Standard .... 0.15 to 0.35 mm
    Service limit (max) .... 1.0 mm
Ring end gap (installed) – 200 cc engine
  Top ring
    Standard .... 0.15 to 0.30 mm
    Service limit (max) .... 1.0 mm
  2nd ring
    Standard .... 0.20 to 0.40 mm
    Service limit (max) .... 1.0 mm
  Oil control ring
    Standard .... 0.20 to 0.40 mm
    Service limit (max) .... 1.0 mm
Ring-to-groove clearance
  Top ring
    Standard .... 0.025 to 0.070 mm
    Service limit (max) .... 0.080 mm
  2nd ring
    Standard .... 0.015 to 0.060 mm
    Service limit (max) .... 0.070 mm
  Oil control ring
    Standard .... 0.015 to 0.060 mm
    Service limit (max) .... 0.070 mm

Lubrication system
Oil pump
  Inner rotor tip-to-outer rotor clearance (max) .... 0.12 mm
  Outer rotor-to-body clearance (max) .... 0.20 mm
  Rotor endfloat (max) .... 0.09 mm
Relief valve spring free length .... 54.2 mm

Connecting rod
Small-end internal diameter
  Standard .... 15.015 to 15.025 mm
  Service limit (max) .... 15.030 mm
Big-end side clearance .... 0.20 to 0.50 mm
Big-end radial play .... 0.036 to 0.054 mm

Crankshaft

Combined width of flywheels and big-end	55.75 to 55.90 mm
Runout A (max)*	0.15 mm
Runout B (max)*	0.01 mm
Runout C (max)*	0.10 mm
Endfloat	0.15 to 0.40 mm

See illustration 21.18 in Chapter 2E for runout measurement points

Torque settings

Valve cover bolts	11 to 13 Nm
Cam chain tensioner spring cap bolt	5 to 6 Nm
Cam chain tensioner blade bolt	10 to 14 Nm
Cam chain tensioner bolts	11 to 13 Nm
Camshaft sprocket bolt	11 to 15 Nm
Camshaft retaining plate bolts	4 to 6 Nm
Cylinder head nuts	28 to 30 Nm
Cylinder head bolts (outside)	11 to 13 Nm
Sump cover bolts	10 to 14 Nm
Oil pressure switch	12 to 14 Nm
Oil pump drive chain cover screws	3.5 to 4.5 Nm
Oil pump driven sprocket bolt	10 to 14 Nm
Oil pump mounting screws	5 to 6 Nm
Oil pump cover screws	0.7 to 0.9 Nm
Alternator rotor nut	54 to 60 Nm
Alternator stator screws/pulse generator coil screws	3 to 4 Nm
Engine front mounting bolt	33 to 41 Nm
Crankcase bolts	11 to 13 Nm

1 General information

The engine unit is a liquid-cooled, single cylinder four-stroke. The water pump is mounted on the alternator rotor, which is on the right-hand end of the crankshaft. The crankshaft assembly is pressed together, incorporating the connecting rod, with the big-end running on the crankpin on a bronze bearing. The crankshaft runs in plain main bearings. The crankcase divides vertically.

The camshaft is chain-driven off the left-hand end of the crankshaft, and operates four valves via rocker arms.

2 Operations possible with the engine in the frame

All components and assemblies, with the exception of the crankshaft/connecting rod assembly, can be worked on without having to remove the engine/transmission unit from the frame. However, access is extremely limited and if a number of areas require attention at the same time, removal of the engine is recommended, as it is easy to do so.

3 Operations requiring engine removal

To access the crankshaft and connecting rod assembly and its bearings, the engine must be removed from the frame and the crankcase halves must be separated.

4 Major engine repair – general note

1 It is not always easy to determine when or if an engine should be completely overhauled, as a number of factors must be considered.
2 High mileage is not necessarily an indication that an overhaul is needed, while low mileage, on the other hand, does not preclude the need for an overhaul. Frequency of servicing is probably the single most important consideration. An engine that has regular and frequent oil and filter changes, as well as other required maintenance, will most likely give many miles of reliable service. Conversely, a neglected engine, or one which has not been run-in properly, may require an overhaul very early in its life.
3 Exhaust smoke and excessive oil consumption are both indications that piston rings and/or valve guides are in need of attention, although make sure that the fault is not due to oil leakage.
4 If the engine is making obvious knocking or rumbling noises, the connecting rod and/or main bearings are probably at fault.
5 Loss of power, rough running, excessive valve train noise and high fuel consumption rates may also point to the need for an overhaul, especially if they are all present at the same time. If a complete tune-up does not remedy the situation, major mechanical work is the only solution.
6 A full engine overhaul generally involves restoring the internal parts to the specifications of a new engine. The piston and piston rings are renewed and the cylinder is rebored. The valve seats are reground and new valve springs are fitted. If the connecting rod bearings are worn a new crankshaft assembly is fitted. The end result should be a like-new engine that will give as many trouble-free miles as the original.
7 Before beginning the engine overhaul, read through the related procedures to familiarise yourself with the scope and requirements of the job. Overhauling an engine is not all that difficult, but it is time-consuming. Plan on the scooter being tied up for a minimum of two weeks. Check on the availability of parts and make sure that any necessary special tools, equipment and supplies are obtained in advance.
8 Most work can be done with typical workshop hand tools, although a number of precision measuring tools are required for inspecting parts to determine if they must be renewed. Often a dealer will handle the inspection of parts and offer advice concerning reconditioning and renewal. As a general rule, time is the primary cost of an overhaul so it does not pay to install worn or substandard parts.
9 As a final note, to ensure maximum life and minimum trouble from a rebuilt engine, everything must be assembled with care in a spotlessly-clean environment.

5 Engine/transmission unit – removal and installation

Caution: *The engine is not heavy, although engine removal and installation should be carried out with the aid of an assistant; personal injury or damage could occur if the engine falls or is dropped.*

LEADER liquid-cooled four-stroke engines (Super Hexagon, B125, X9 125, X8 125, GT125, GT200) 2F•5

5.7a Undo the nut on the front mounting bolt . . .

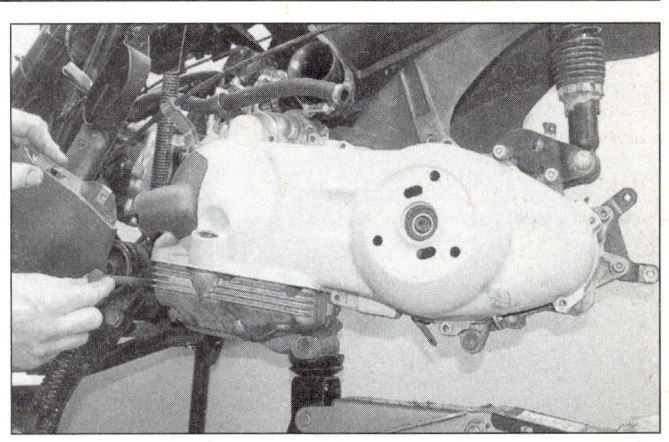

5.7b . . . then support the engine unit and withdraw the bolt

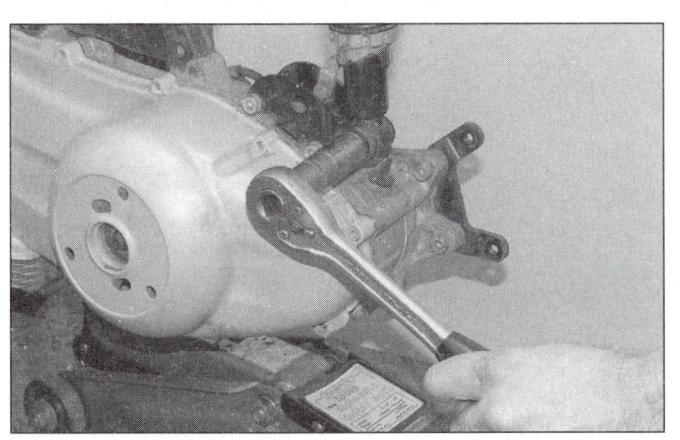

5.8a Undo the lower shock mounting bolt . . .

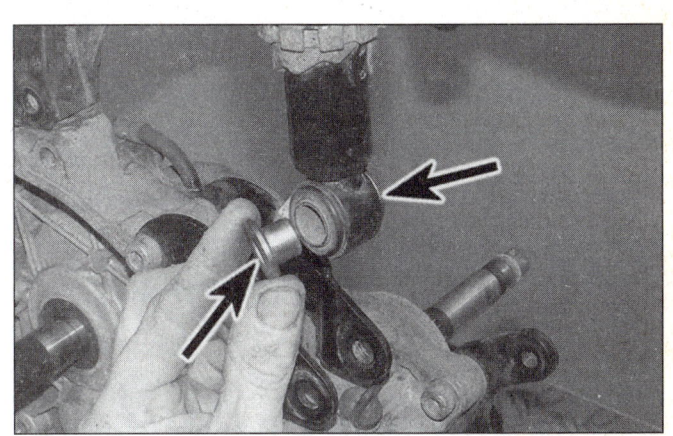

5.8b . . . noting the position of the spacers (arrowed)

Removal

1 The procedure for removing the engine is the same as for air-cooled LEADER models (see Chapter 2E, Section 5), with the following additions.

2 The centre stand is bolted to the frame – provision, such as a trolley jack, should be made to support the engine unit once the front engine mounting bolt is removed (see Step 7).

3 After removing the bodywork as required, drain the cooling system (see Chapter 1), then disconnect the coolant hoses from the water pump and the thermostat housing (see Chapter 3). Disconnect the coolant temperature sensor wiring connector.

4 Disconnect the fuel hose from the carburettor and the vacuum hose from the union on the intake manifold.

5 Displace the rear disc brake caliper and secure the caliper clear of the engine unit (see Chapter 8). Pull the disc and hub off the driveshaft.

6 Remove the right-hand rear shock to facilitate engine removal (see Chapter 6).

7 Undo the nut securing the front engine mounting bolt **(see illustration)**. Place a suitable support under the engine unit and remove the front engine mounting bolt **(see illustration)**.

8 Have an assistant steady the engine unit, then remove the bolt securing the lower end of the left-hand shock absorber to the transmission casing **(see illustration)**. Manoeuvre the engine unit out of the frame. Note the spacers in the lower shock mounting and remove them for safekeeping **(see illustration)**.

Installation

9 Installation is the reverse of the removal procedure, noting that the cooling system must be filled with the specified coolant mixture (see Chapter 1). If required, fill the engine with the specified quantity of oil (see Chapter 1 Specifications) and check the oil level as described in *Daily (pre-ride) checks*.

6 Disassembly and reassembly – general information

Disassembly

1 Before disassembling the engine, the external surfaces of the unit should be thoroughly cleaned and degreased to rule out the possibility of dirt falling inside. A high flash-point solvent, such as paraffin can be used, or better still, a proprietary engine degreaser. Use old paintbrushes and toothbrushes to work the solvent into the various recesses of the engine casings. Take care to exclude solvent or water from the electrical components and inlet and exhaust ports.

⚠ **Warning:** *The use of petrol (gasoline) as a cleaning agent should be avoided because of the risk of fire.*

2 When clean and dry, arrange the unit on the workbench, leaving suitable clear area for working. Gather a selection of small containers and plastic bags so that parts can be grouped together in an easily identifiable manner. Some paper and a pen should be on hand to permit notes to be made and labels attached where necessary. A supply of clean rag is also required.

3 Before commencing work, read through the appropriate section so that some idea of the necessary procedure can be gained. When removing components it should be noted that great force is seldom required, unless specified. In many cases, a component's reluctance to be removed is indicative of an incorrect approach or removal method – if in any doubt, recheck with the text.

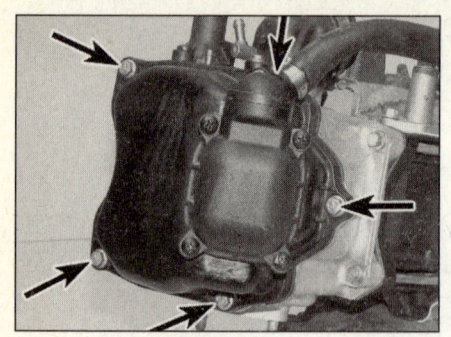

2F•6 LEADER liquid-cooled four-stroke engines (Super Hexagon, B125, X9 125, X8 125, GT125, GT200)

7.1a Location of valve cover bolts (arrowed)

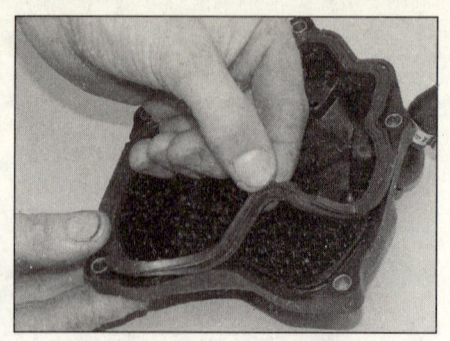

7.1b Ensure the gasket is fitted correctly into the groove in the cover

4 When disassembling the engine, keep 'mated' parts that have been in contact with each other during engine operation together. These 'mated' parts must be re-used or renewed as an assembly.

5 Complete engine disassembly should be done in the following general order with reference to the appropriate Sections. Refer to Chapter 2G for details of transmission components disassembly.
  Remove the valve cover.
  Remove the camshaft and rockers.
  Remove the cylinder head.
  Remove the cylinder.
  Remove the piston.
  Remove the alternator.
  Remove the starter motor (see Chapter 9).
  Remove the sump cover.
  Remove the oil pump.
  Separate the crankcase halves.
  Remove the crankshaft.

Reassembly

6 Reassembly is the reverse of the general disassembly sequence.

7 Valve cover – removal and installation

Note: *This procedure can be carried out with the engine in the frame. If the engine has been removed, ignore the steps which do not apply.*

1 The procedure for removal and installation of the valve cover is the same as for air-cooled LEADER models (see Chapter 2E, Section 7). Note that on liquid-cooled models, the valve cover is secured by five bolts **(see illustration)**. Ensure the gasket is fitted correctly into its groove before installing the cover **(see illustration)**.

8 Cam chain tensioner – removal, inspection and installation

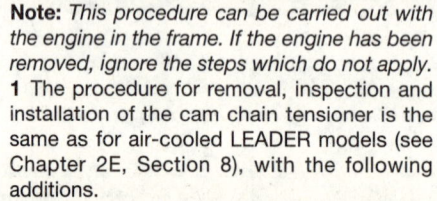

Note: *This procedure can be carried out with the engine in the frame. If the engine has been removed, ignore the steps which do not apply.*

1 The procedure for removal, inspection and installation of the cam chain tensioner is the same as for air-cooled LEADER models (see Chapter 2E, Section 8), with the following additions.

2 No cowling is fitted to the liquid-cooled engines, so it is not necessary to remove the carburettor and intake manifold.

3 To turn the engine using the alternator rotor nut, first displace or remove the alternator cover as required (see Section 17).

4 On the engine used to illustrate this section there was no timing mark on the alternator rotor.

5 The appropriate timing mark on the camshaft sprocket for the liquid-cooled engine is 4V **(see illustration)**. Align the 4V mark with the index mark on the camshaft holder to position the engine at TDC (top dead centre) on the compression stroke. **Note:** *All the valves should be closed at TDC on the compression stroke.*

9 Cam chain, blades and sprockets – removal, inspection and installation

Note 1: *This procedure can be carried out with the engine in the frame although access to the top of the engine is extremely restricted. If the engine has been removed, ignore the steps which do not apply.*

Note 2: *The engine used to illustrate this Section was not fitted with an automatic decompressor mechanism. This feature was discontinued during the production run of the LEADER engine. For details of the LEADER engine with this feature refer to Chapter 2E, Section 9).*

Removal

1 Remove the valve cover (see Section 7).

2 If the cam chain and crankshaft sprocket are to be removed, remove the oil pump driven sprocket, drive chain and drive sprocket (see Section 19).

3 Displace or remove the alternator cover as required (see Section 17). Turn the engine in a clockwise direction using the alternator rotor nut, until the timing mark on the rotor aligns with the index mark on the crankcase **(see illustration 9.3a in Chapter 2E)**. **Note:** *On the engine used to illustrate this section there was no timing mark on the alternator rotor. To ensure correct reassembly a mark was painted on the rotor aligned with the edge of the crankcase* **(see illustration)**. Ensure the timing mark (4V) on the camshaft sprocket aligns with the index mark on the camshaft holder **(see illustration 8.5)**. At this point the engine is at TDC (top dead centre) on the compression stroke (all valves closed).

4 Loosen the camshaft sprocket centre bolt and the offset bolt **(see illustration 9.7a)**. Hold the alternator to prevent the sprocket from turning.

5 Remove the cam chain tensioner (see Section 8).

6 Lift the chain off the camshaft sprocket **(see illustration)**. If required, secure the chain with a cable tie to prevent it falling into the engine. If the chain is to be removed, mark it with paint so that if it is re-used it can be fitted the same way round. Remove the

8.5 4V (four valve) timing mark on the camshaft sprocket

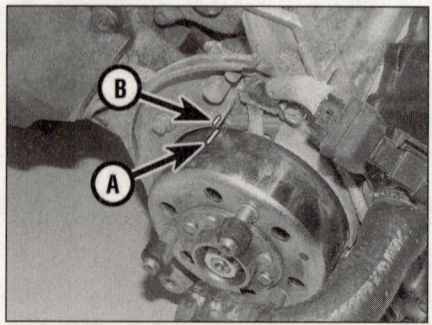

9.3 Painted mark on rotor (A) aligns with edge of casing (B)

9.6 Lift the cam chain off the sprocket

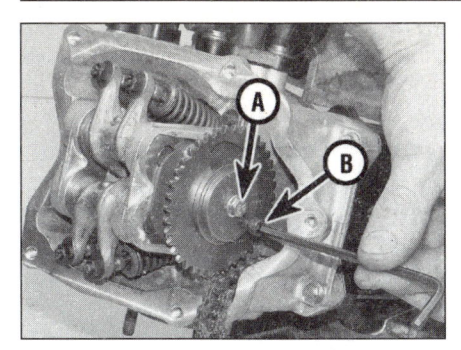

LEADER liquid-cooled four-stroke engines (Super Hexagon, B125, X9 125, X8 125, GT125, GT200) 2F•7

9.7a Undo the centre bolt (A) and the offset bolt (B) . . .

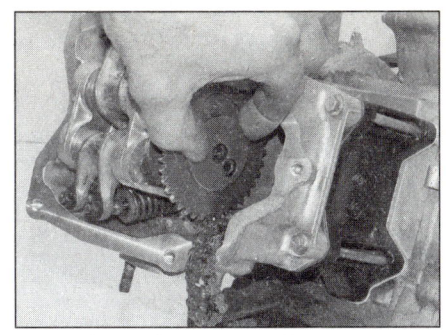

9.7b . . . then remove the spacers

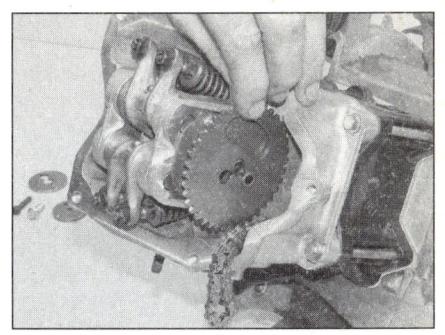

9.8a Lift off the camshaft sprocket . . .

thrustwasher from the end of the crankshaft, then lower the chain down its tunnel and slip it off the sprocket on the crankshaft **(see illustrations 9.6a and 9.6b in Chapter 2D)**. Draw the sprocket off the crankshaft, noting how it locates on the pin on the shaft **(see illustration 9.6c in Chapter 2D)**.

7 Undo the camshaft sprocket centre bolt and the offset bolt, then lift off the two spacers, noting how they fit **(see illustrations)**.

8 Lift the sprocket and its backing plate off the end of the camshaft, noting how they fit **(see illustrations)**.

9 If required, remove the bolt securing the cam chain tensioner blade to the crankcase and withdraw the blade, noting which way round it fits, and the spacer. The lower cam chain blade locates in a groove in the front edge of the cam chain tunnel in the cylinder. To remove the blade, first remove the cylinder head (see Section 11), then lift out the blade, noting how the lower end locates on the peg in the crankcase **(see illustration 9.10 in Chapter 2E)**.

Inspection

10 Check the sprockets for wear and damaged teeth, renewing them if necessary. If the sprocket teeth are worn, the chain will also be worn and should be renewed **(see illustration)**.

11 Check the chain tensioner blade and guide blade for wear or damage and renew them if necessary. Damaged or severely worn blades are an indication of a worn or improperly tensioned chain. Check the operation of the cam chain tensioner (see Section 8).

Installation

12 If removed, install the lower cam chain blade (see Step 9). If removed, install the tensioner blade and spacer, then tighten the retaining bolt to the torque setting specified at the beginning of the Chapter. Ensure both blades are fitted the correct way round.

13 Install the sprocket on the crankshaft, aligning the notch in the sprocket with the pin on the shaft. Lower the cam chain down through the tunnel and fit it onto the sprocket. If the chain is being re-used, ensure it is fitted the right way round (see Step 6).

14 Check that the timing mark on the alternator rotor still aligns with the index mark on the crankcase and that the engine is at TDC on the compression stroke (see Step 3). Install the camshaft sprocket backing plate on the end of the camshaft, then install the sprocket **(see illustrations 9.8b and 9.8a)**. Ensure the timing mark (4V) on the sprocket is aligned with the index mark on the camshaft holder.

15 Fit the two spacers onto the sprocket, then install the centre bolt and the offset bolt finger tight **(see illustration 9.7a)**.

16 Take up the slack in the lower run of the cam chain and slip it onto the camshaft sprocket. Ensure the timing mark (4V) on the sprocket is still aligned with the index mark on the camshaft holder, then install the cam chain tensioner (see Section 8). After installation, rotate the engine and check again that all the timing marks align (see Step 3). If not, remove the tensioner and chain and align the marks correctly.

Caution: If the marks are not aligned exactly as described, the valve timing will be incorrect and the valves may strike the piston, causing extensive damage to the engine.

17 Hold the alternator to prevent the camshaft sprocket from turning and tighten

9.8b . . . and the backing plate

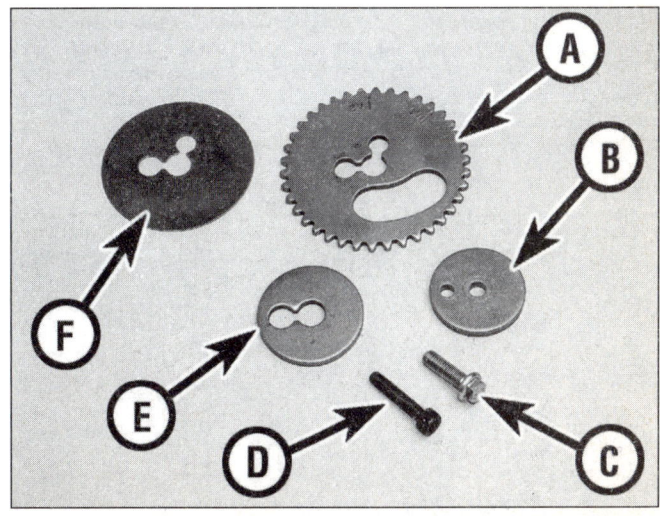

9.10 Camshaft sprocket components – sprocket (A), outer spacer (B), centre bolt (C), offset bolt (D), inner spacer (E) and backing plate (F)

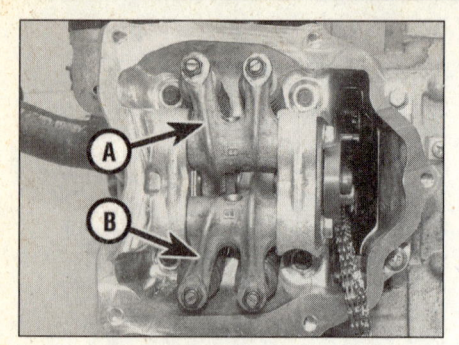

2F•8 LEADER liquid-cooled four-stroke engines (Super Hexagon, B125, X9 125, X8 125, GT125, GT200)

10.3 Layout of the intake (A) and exhaust (B) rocker arms

10.4 Remove the camshaft retaining plate

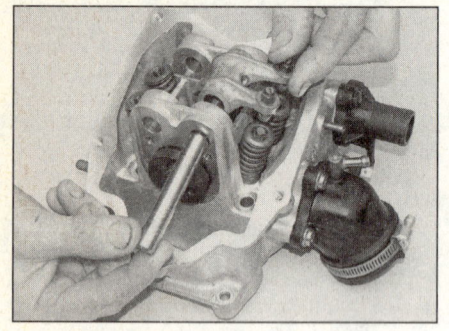

10.5a Withdraw the rocker shafts

10.5b Keep each rocker arm and its shaft together

the centre bolt to the specified torque setting. Tighten the offset bolt securely.
18 Fit the thrustwasher onto the end of the crankshaft, then install the oil pump drive sprocket, chain and driven sprocket (see Section 19).
19 Install the remaining components in the reverse order of removal.

10 Camshaft and rockers –
removal, inspection and installation

Note: *This procedure can be carried out with the engine in the frame although access to the top of the engine is extremely restricted. If the engine has been removed, ignore the steps which do not apply.*

1 The procedure for removal, inspection and installation of the camshaft and rockers is the same as for air-cooled LEADER models (see Chapter 2E, Section 10), with the following additions.
2 After removing the valve cover, refer to Section 9 for details of the alternator rotor and camshaft sprocket timing marks.
3 The rocker arms are fitted on two separate shafts (see illustration). The intake rocker arm is on the intake (carburettor) side of the cylinder head, and the exhaust arm is on the exhaust side of the head. Mark the rocker arms so that they can be installed in their original positions.
4 Remove the camshaft retaining plate, then mark the ends of the shafts so that they can be refitted in the same position (see illustration).
5 Support each rocker arm in turn and withdraw its shaft (see illustration). Do not mix the rocker arms and shafts up – they must be installed in their original positions (see illustration).

11 Cylinder head –
removal and installation

Note: *This procedure can be carried out with the engine in the frame although access to the top of the engine is extremely restricted. If the engine has been removed, ignore the steps which do not apply.*
Caution: *The engine must be completely cool before beginning this procedure or the cylinder head may become warped.*

Removal

1 Remove the carburettor and exhaust system (see Chapter 4)
2 Drain the cooling system (see Chapter 1).
3 Release the clips securing the cooling system hoses to the cylinder head and detach the hoses form their unions, noting where they fit.
4 Disconnect the coolant temperature sensor wiring connector. Pull the spark plug cap off the plug.
5 Remove the valve cover (see Section 7).
6 Follow Steps 4 to 10 in Chapter 2E, Section 11, to remove the camshaft sprocket and the cylinder head. On 125 cc liquid-cooled engines, note that two types of cylinder head gasket are fitted – a steel gasket (approximately 0.3 mm thick when new) or a fibre gasket (approximately 1.1 mm thick when new). Always fit a new gasket of the same type when installing the cylinder head.

Installation

7 Ensure both cylinder head and cylinder mating surfaces are clean. Ensure both the dowels are in place either in the cylinder or the head (see illustration). Lay the new gasket in place on the cylinder, making sure the oil and coolant passage holes are correctly aligned (see illustration). Never re-use the old gasket.
8 Carefully lower the head onto the cylinder, feeding the cam chain up through the tunnel (see illustration). Make sure the dowels are correctly aligned with the gasket and the cylinder head or cylinder.

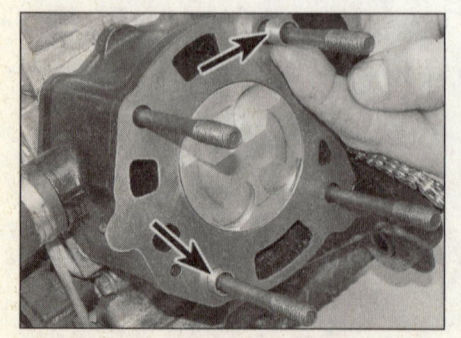

11.7a Ensure the dowels (arrowed) are in place

11.7b Ensure the gasket is fitted correctly

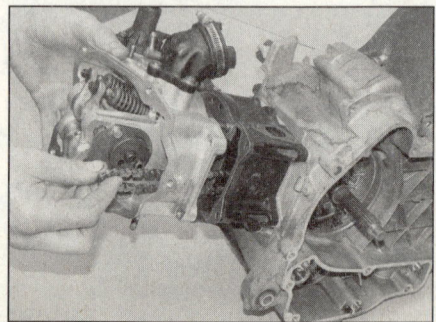

11.8 Install the cylinder head carefully

LEADER liquid-cooled four-stroke engines (Super Hexagon, B125, X9 125, X8 125, GT125, GT200) 2F•9

11.9 Tighten the cylinder head nuts in stages

9 Install the cylinder head nuts finger tight, then tighten them in a criss-cross pattern, in two or three stages to the torque setting specified at the beginning of the Chapter **(see illustration)**.
10 Install the two cylinder head bolts on the left-hand side of the engine and tighten them to the specified torque setting.
11 Install the camshaft sprocket and the remaining components in the reverse order of removal, referring to the relevant Sections or Chapters.

12 Valves/valve seats/valve guides – overhaul

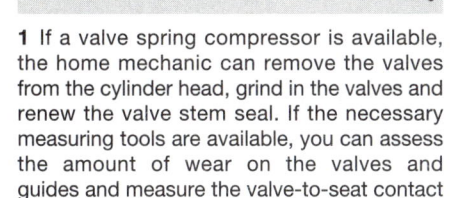

1 If a valve spring compressor is available, the home mechanic can remove the valves from the cylinder head, grind in the valves and renew the valve stem seal. If the necessary measuring tools are available, you can assess the amount of wear on the valves and guides and measure the valve-to-seat contact areas.
2 If the valve guides or the valve seats in the cylinder head are worn beyond their service limits a new head will have to be fitted.
3 After any servicing or repair work, be sure to clean the head very thoroughly to remove any metal particles or abrasive grit that may still be present. Use compressed air, if available, to blow out all the holes and passages.

13 Cylinder head and valves – disassembly, inspection and reassembly

1 Disassembly, cleaning and inspection of the valves and related components can be done by the home mechanic if the necessary special tools are available. If there is any doubt about the condition of any components, have them checked by a Piaggio dealer.
2 To disassemble the valve components without the risk of damaging them, a valve spring compressor suitable for motorcycle engines is absolutely necessary.

Disassembly

3 Before proceeding, arrange to label and store the valves and their related components so that they can be returned to their original location without getting mixed up **(see illustration 13.3 in Chapter 2E)**.
4 If not already done, remove the camshaft and rockers (see Section 10), then undo the bolts securing the thermostat housing to the head and remove the housing and thermostat (see Chapter 3). Clean the sealing surfaces of the cylinder head and thermostat housing with a suitable solvent. Take care not to scratch or gouge the soft aluminium.
5 Compress the valve spring on the first valve with a spring compressor, making sure it is correctly located onto each end of the valve assembly. On the underside of the head, make sure the plate on the compressor only contacts the valve and not the soft aluminium of the head – if the plate is too big for the valve, use a spacer between them. Do not compress the spring any more than is absolutely necessary to release the collets. Remove the collets, using either needle-nose pliers, tweezers, a magnet or a screwdriver with a dab of grease on it **(see illustration)**. Carefully release the valve spring compressor and remove the spring retainer, noting which way up it fits, and the spring, and lift the valve from the head **(see illustrations)**. If the valve binds in the guide (won't pull through), push it back into the head and deburr the area around the collet groove with a very fine file **(see illustration 13.5b in Chapter 2E)**. Once the valve has been removed, pull the valve stem oil seal off the top of the valve guide with pliers and discard it (the old seal should never be re-used) and remove the spring seat **(see illustration)**.
6 Repeat the procedure for the remaining valves. Remember to keep the parts for each valve together and labelled so they can be reinstalled in the correct location.
7 Next, clean the cylinder head with solvent and dry it thoroughly. Compressed air will speed the drying process and ensure that all holes and recessed areas are clean.
8 Clean the valve springs, collets, retainers, and spring seats with solvent and dry them thoroughly. Work on the parts from one valve at a time so as not to mix them up.
9 Scrape off any deposits that may have formed on the valve, then use a motorised wire brush to remove deposits from the valve heads and stems. Again, make sure the valves do not get mixed up.

Inspection and reassembly

10 The procedure for inspection and reassembly of the cylinder head and valves is the same as for air-cooled LEADER models (see Chapter 2E, Section 13), with the following addition.
11 Install the thermostat housing (see Chapter 3).

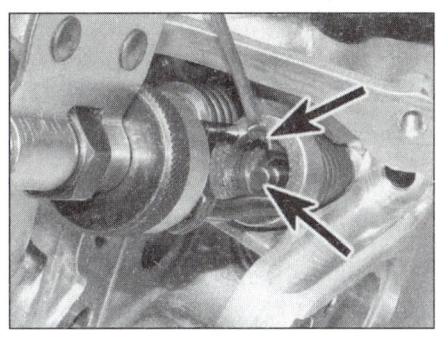

13.5a Compress the valve spring and remove the collets (arrowed)

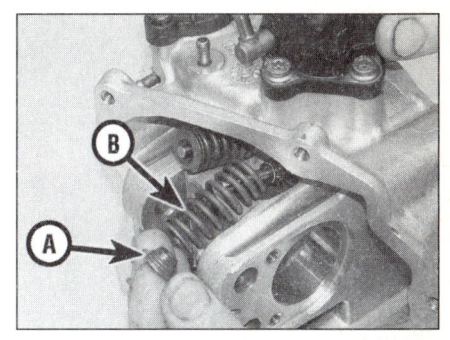

13.5b Remove the spring retainer (A) and spring (B) . . .

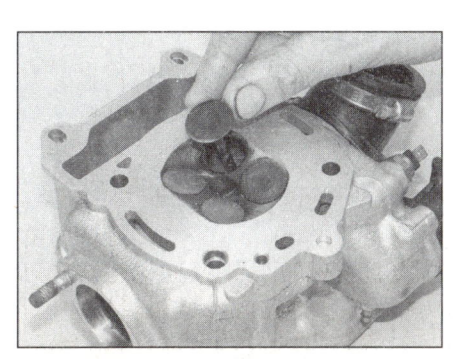

13.5c . . . then lift out the valve

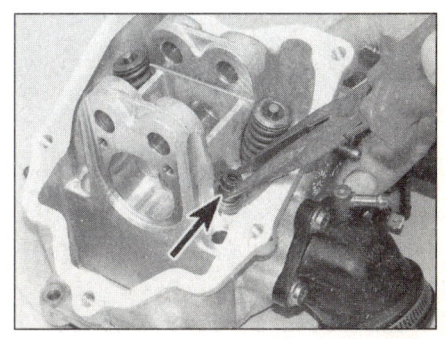

13.5d Pull the stem seal (arrowed) off with pliers

2F•10 LEADER liquid-cooled four-stroke engines (Super Hexagon, B125, X9 125, X8 125, GT125, GT200)

14.2 Lift out the lower cam chain blade

14.4a Lower the cam chain (arrowed) through the cylinder ...

14.4b ... then support the piston to prevent damage

14 Cylinder – removal, inspection and installation

Note: *This procedure can be carried out with the engine in the frame although access to the top of the engine is extremely restricted. If the engine has been removed, ignore the steps which do not apply.*

Removal

1 Remove the cylinder head (see Section 11).
2 Note how the lower cam chain blade locates in a groove in the front edge of the cam chain tunnel in the cylinder, then lift out the blade, noting which way round it fits **(see illustration)**.
3 If required, release the clip securing the cooling system hose to the cylinder and detach the hose from its union.
4 Lift the cylinder up off the studs, carefully feeding the cam chain down through the tunnel; support the piston as it becomes accessible to prevent it hitting the crankcase **(see illustrations)**. If the cylinder is stuck, tap around its joint face with a soft-faced mallet to free it from the crankcase. Don't attempt to free the cylinder by inserting a screwdriver between it and the crankcase – you'll damage the sealing surfaces. When the cylinder is removed, stuff a clean rag around the piston to prevent anything falling into the crankcase.
5 Note the two dowels in the cylinder and remove them for safekeeping if they are loose.

6 Remove the gasket carefully and make a note of the thickness (0.4, 0.6 or 0.8) stamped into the material. If the original cylinder and piston are used on reassembly, a new gasket of the same thickness should be used. Discard the old gasket.

Inspection

7 The procedure for inspecting the cylinder is the same as for air-cooled LEADER models (see Chapter 2E, Section 14), with the following additions.
8 To check the amount of cylinder wear, taper and ovality, Piaggio recommend the bore is measured at 6 mm, 41 mm and 78 mm down from the top edge, both parallel to and across the crankshaft axis **(see illustration)**. Calculate any differences between the measurements to determine any taper or ovality in the bore – the maximum allowable difference is 0.05 mm. The size-code for the cylinder is stamped into the lower edge, the size-code for the piston is stamped into the crown **(see illustrations)**.
9 Measure the cylinder bore diameter 41 mm down from the top edge on 125 cc engines and 33 mm on 200 cc engines, then calculate the piston-to-bore clearance.

Installation

10 Check that the mating surfaces of the cylinder and crankcase are clean. The procedure for measuring the piston height and installing the cylinder is the same as for air-cooled LEADER models (see Chapter 2E, Section 14), with the following additions.

11 On 125 cc engines, with the piston at TDC, the dial gauge reading will be the distance the centre of the piston crown is above the top of the cylinder bore. The further the piston crown is above the top of the bore, the thicker the base gasket should be. On Super Hexagon, B125 and X9 125 models, if the dial gauge reading is between 2.25 and 2.35 mm a 0.4 mm gasket is required, between 2.35 and 2.55 mm a 0.6 mm gasket is required, and between 2.55 and 2.65 mm a 0.8 mm gasket is required. On X8 125 and GT125 models fitted with a steel head gasket, if the dial gauge reading is between 1.40 and 1.65 mm a 0.4 mm gasket is required, between 1.65 and 1.90 mm a 0.6 mm gasket is required. On X8 125 and GT125 models fitted with a fibre head gasket, if the dial gauge reading is between 2.20 and 2.45 mm a 0.4 mm gasket is required, between 2.45 and 2.70 mm a 0.6 mm gasket is required.
12 On 200 cc engines, with the piston at TDC, the dial gauge reading will be the distance the centre of the piston crown is below the top of the cylinder bore. The further the piston crown is below the top of the bore, the thinner the base gasket should be. If the dial gauge reading is between 1.3 and 1.4 mm a 0.8 mm gasket is required, between 1.4 and 1.6 mm a 0.6 mm gasket is required, and between 1.6 and 1.7 mm a 0.4 mm gasket is required.
13 If removed, fit the coolant hose to the cylinder and secure it with the clip after the cylinder head has been installed to avoid damaging the seating of the cylinder base gasket.

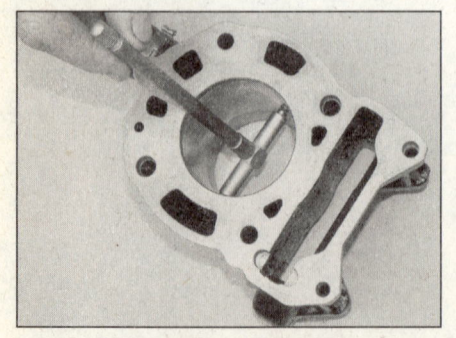

14.8a Measure the cylinder bore with a telescoping gauge

14.8b Cylinder size-code (arrowed) stamped into the lower edge

14.8c Piston size-code (arrowed) stamped into the crown

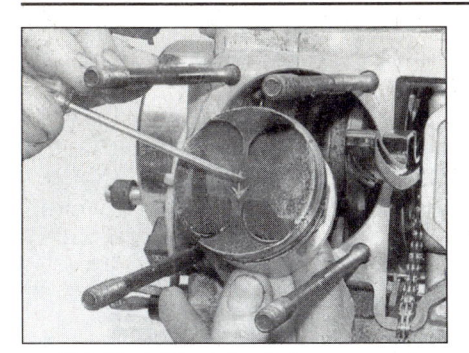

LEADER liquid-cooled four-stroke engines (Super Hexagon, B125, X9 125, X8 125, GT125, GT200) 2F•11

15.2 Mark the piston before removal

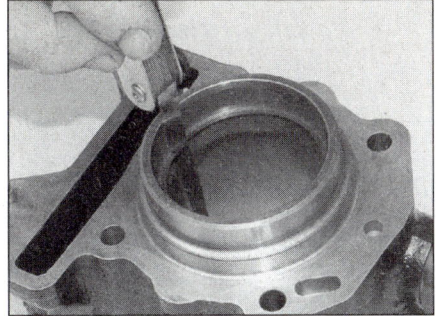

16.1a Measuring piston ring installed end gap

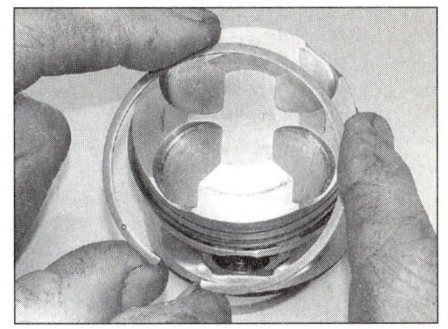

16.1b Fitting new piston rings by hand

15 Piston – removal, inspection and installation

Note: *This procedure can be carried out with the engine in the frame although access to the top of the engine is extremely restricted. If the engine has been removed, ignore the steps which do not apply.*

1 Remove the cylinder (see Section 14). The procedure for removal, inspection and installation of the piston is the same as for air-cooled LEADER models (see Chapter 2E, Section 15), with the following additions.
2 Mark the piston crown so that it can be installed the correct way round – there should be recesses for all four valves in the piston crown **(see illustration)**.
3 Measure the piston diameter 41.1 mm down (125 cc engines) or 33 mm down (200 cc engines) from the top edge of the piston and at 90° to the piston pin axis when calculating the piston-to-bore clearance.

16 Piston rings – inspection and installation

1 New piston rings should be fitted whenever an engine is being overhauled **(see illustrations)**. The procedure for inspection and installation of the piston rings is the same as for air-cooled LEADER models (see Chapter 2E, Section 16).

17 Alternator rotor and stator – removal and installation

Note: *This procedure can be carried out with the engine in the frame. If the engine has been removed, ignore the steps which do not apply.*

1 Remove the bodywork as required by your model to access the alternator cover and water pump on the right-hand side of the engine (see Chapter 7).
2 If required, remove the exhaust system or silencer to gain clearance to draw the cover off the alternator rotor (see Chapter 4). If required, displace the fuel pump and filter assembly (see Chapter 4).
3 Drain the cooling system and disconnect the coolant hoses from the water pump (see Chapter 1).
4 On machines fitted with a secondary air system, disconnect the SAS vacuum hose and the SAS pipe from the reed valve housing (see Chapter 1, Section 21).
5 Undo the clip that secures the wiring harness to the top of the alternator cover.
6 Undo the bolts securing the alternator cover and draw the cover off, then detach the alternator multi-pin connector and remove the cover **(see illustrations)**. Note how the dampers on the alternator rotor locate in the water pump drive.
7 The remainder of the procedure for removal, inspection and installation of the alternator rotor and stator is the same as for air-cooled LEADER models (see Chapter 2E, Section 18) with the following additions.
8 When fitting the alternator cover, ensure the dampers on the alternator rotor align with the water pump drive.
9 Connect the SAS vacuum hose and the SAS pipe to the reed valve housing (see Chapter 1, Section 21).
10 Connect the coolant hoses to the unions on the water pump and refill the cooling system (see Chapter 1, Section 10).

18 Starter pinion assembly – removal, inspection and installation

Note: *The starter pinion assembly can be removed with the engine in the frame.*

1 The procedure for removal, inspection and installation of the starter pinion assembly is the same as for air-cooled LEADER models (see Chapter 2E, Section 19).

19 Oil pump and relief valve – pressure check, pump removal, inspection and installation

Note: *The oil pump and pressure relief valve can be removed with the engine in the frame.*

1 The procedure for checking the oil pressure is the same as for air-cooled LEADER models (see Chapter 2E, Section 20). **Note:** *The alternator cover must be displaced in order to connect the oil pressure gauge and the cover*

17.6a Undo the alternator cover bolts (arrowed)

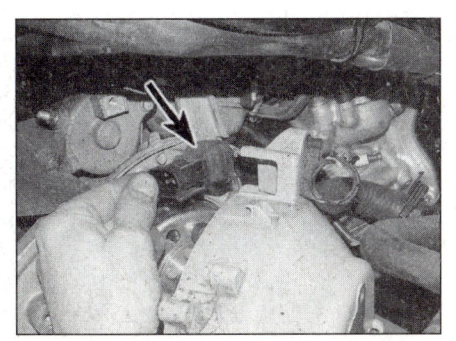

17.6b Detach the wiring connector (arrowed) from the cover . . .

17.6c . . . and remove the cover noting how the dampers locate in the water pump drive

cannot be installed with the gauge in place. The water pump drive is therefore disconnected during the test and care should be taken so as not to overheat the engine. Also ensure that the pump drive dampers on the alternator rotor do not foul the alternator cover when the engine is running.

2 To install the oil pressure gauge adapter, first displace the alternator cover (see Section 17).

3 The procedure for removal, inspection and installation of the oil pump is the same as for air-cooled LEADER models (see Chapter 2E, Section 20). Note that on liquid-cooled models there is no guide for the rear brake cable attached to the sump bolts.

20 Crankcase halves, crankshaft and connecting rod

Note: *To separate the crankcase halves, the engine must be removed from the frame.*

1 The procedure for separating and joining the crankcase halves, and for removal, inspection and installation of the crankshaft assembly is the same as for air-cooled LEADER models (see Chapter 2E, Section 21).

21 Initial start-up after overhaul

1 Make sure the engine oil and coolant levels are correct (see *Daily (pre-ride) checks*).
2 Make sure there is fuel in the tank.
3 Turn the ignition ON, start the engine and allow it to run at a slow idle until it reaches operating temperature. Do not be alarmed if there is a little smoke from the exhaust – this will be due to the oil used to lubricate the piston and bore during assembly and should subside after a while.
4 If the engine proves reluctant to start, remove the spark plug and check that it has not become wet and oily. If it has, clean it and try again. If the engine refuses to start, go through the fault finding charts at the end of this manual to identify the problem.
5 Check carefully for oil leaks and make sure the transmission and controls, especially the brakes, function properly before road testing the machine. Refer to Section 22 for the recommended running-in procedure.
6 Upon completion of the road test, and after the engine has cooled down completely, recheck the valve clearances (see Chapter 1) and check the engine oil and coolant level (see *Daily (pre-ride) checks*).

22 Recommended running-in procedure

1 Treat the machine gently for the first few miles to make sure oil has circulated throughout the engine and any new parts installed have started to seat.
2 Even greater care is necessary if the engine has been rebored or a new crankshaft has been installed. In the case of a rebore, the machine will have to be run-in as when new. This means a restraining hand on the throttle until at least 600 miles (1000 km) have been covered. There's no point in keeping to any set speed limit – the main idea is to keep from labouring the engine and not to maintain any one speed for too long. Experience is the best guide, since it's easy to tell when an engine is running freely. Once past the 600 mile (1000 km) mark, gradually increase performance, using full throttle for short bursts to begin with.
3 If a lubrication failure is suspected, stop the engine immediately and try to find the cause. If an engine is run without oil, even for a short period of time, severe damage will occur.

Chapter 2 Part G:
Transmission

Refer to the beginning of Chapter 1 for model identification details

Contents

Clutch and driven pulley – removal, inspection and installation 4	General information 1
Drive pulley and variator – removal, inspection and installation 3	Drivebelt and support roller – inspection and renewal 5
Gearbox – removal, inspection and installation 6	Drivebelt cover and kickstart – removal, inspection and installation . 2

Degrees of difficulty

Easy, suitable for novice with little experience	**Fairly easy,** suitable for beginner with some experience	**Fairly difficult,** suitable for competent DIY mechanic	**Difficult,** suitable for experienced DIY mechanic	**Very difficult,** suitable for expert DIY or professional

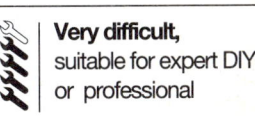

Specifications

Variator
Roller diameter (min)
   50 cc, 80 cc and 125 cc models .... 18.5 mm
   200 cc models .... 20.0 mm
Collar diameter (min)
   50/80 cc two-stroke engines .... 19.95 mm
   ET4 50, Liberty 50 4T, Zip 50 4T, Fly 50 4T, LX4 50 .... 19.95 mm
   ET4 125, Sfera 125, Liberty 125 .... 21.90 mm
   Typhoon 125, Skipper, Hexagon .... 25.93 mm
   LEADER models .... 25.95 mm
Bush diameter (max)
   50/80 cc two-stroke engines .... 26.10 mm
   ET4 50, Liberty 50 4T, Zip 50 4T, Fly 50 4T, LX4 50 .... 20.12 mm
   ET4 125, Sfera 125, Liberty 125 .... 22.035 mm
   Typhoon 125, Skipper, Hexagon .... 26.10 mm
   LEADER models .... 26.12 mm

Clutch and driven pulley
Clutch drum diameter (max)
   50/80 cc two-stroke engines .... 107.5 mm
   ET4 50, Liberty 50 4T, Zip 50 4T, Fly 50 4T, LX4 50 .... 107.5 mm
   ET4 125, Sfera 125, Liberty 125 .... 120.6 mm
   Typhoon 125, Skipper, Hexagon, LEADER models .... 134.5 mm
Clutch drum out-of-round (max)
   LEADER models .... 0.15 mm
   all other models .... 0.20 mm
Inner pulley shaft diameter (min)
   50/80 cc two-stroke engines .... 33.96 mm
   ET4 50, Liberty 50 4T, Zip 50 4T, Fly 50 4T, LX4 50 .... 33.96 mm
   ET4 125, Sfera 125, Liberty 125 .... 40.955 mm
   Typhoon 125, Skipper, Hexagon, LEADER models .... 40.96 mm
Outer pulley bore diameter (max)
   50/80 cc two-stroke engines .... 34.08 mm
   ET4 50, Liberty 50 4T, Zip 50 4T, Fly 50 4T, LX4 50 .... 34.08 mm
   ET4 125, Sfera 125, Liberty 125 .... 41.035 mm
   Typhoon 125, Skipper, Hexagon, LEADER models .... 41.08 mm
Spring free length (min)
   50/80 cc two-stroke engines .... 110 mm
   ET4 50, Liberty 50 4T, Zip 50 4T, Fly 50 4T, LX4 50 .... 110 mm
   ET4 125, Liberty 125 .... 127 mm
   Sfera 125 .... 121 mm
   Typhoon 125, Skipper, Hexagon .... 136 mm
   LEADER models .... 106 mm
Clutch lining material thickness (min) - all models .... 1 mm

2G•2 Transmission

Drivebelt

Minimum width of outer run
- All 50/80 cc two-stroke engines .... 17.5 mm
- ET4 50, Liberty 50 4T, Zip 50 4T, Fly 50 4T, LX4 50 .... 17.5 mm
- ET4 125, Sfera 125, Liberty 125 .... 17.2 mm
- Typhoon 125, Skiper, Hexagon .... 21.0 mm
- LEADER models .... 21.5 mm

Torque settings

- Kickstart lever pinch-bolt .... 12 to 13 Nm
- Drivebelt cover screws .... 11 to 13 Nm
- Drivebelt support roller centre bolt .... 11 to 13 Nm
- Drive pulley nut
  - 50/80 cc two-stroke models .... 40 to 44 Nm
  - ET4 50, Liberty 50 4T, Zip 50 4T, Fly 50 4T, LX4 50 .... 20 Nm + 90°
  - ET4 125, Sfera 125, Liberty 125 .... 40 to 44 Nm
  - Skipper, Hexagon, Typhoon 125, LEADER .... 75 to 80 Nm
- Clutch assembly nut
  - 50/80 cc models .... 40 to 44 Nm
  - 125 cc models .... 55 to 60 Nm
  - LEADER models .... 55 to 60 Nm
- Clutch drum nut
  - 50/80 cc two and four-stroke models .... 40 to 44 Nm
  - 125 cc two-stroke models .... 50 to 56 Nm
  - ET4 125, Sfera 125, Liberty 125 .... 40 to 44 Nm
- Gearbox input shaft nut
  - LEADER models .... 54 to 60 Nm
- Gearbox cover bolts
  - All 50/80 cc two-stroke models .... 12 to 13 Nm
  - All 125 cc two-stroke model .... 13 to 15 Nm
  - ET4 50, Liberty 50 4T, Zip 50 4T, Fly 50 4T, LX4 50 .... 11 to 13 Nm
  - ET4 125, Sfera 125, Liberty 125 .... 11 to 13 Nm
  - LEADER models .... 24 to 27 Nm

1 General information

The transmission on all models is fully automatic in operation. Power is transmitted from the engine to the rear wheel by belt, via a variator on the drive pulley, which automatically varies the gearing with engine speed, an automatic clutch on the driven pulley, and a reduction gearbox. Both the variator and the automatic clutch work on the principal of centrifugal force.

Note: *On some models the internal components of the transmission may differ slightly to those components described or shown. When dismantling, always note the fitted position, order and way round of each component as it is removed.*

2 Drivebelt cover and kickstart – removal and installation

Removal

1 If the engine is still in the frame, remove any bodywork as required to access the drivebelt cover on the left-hand side of the engine (see Chapter 7).

2 Remove the air filter housing (see Chapter 4).

3 Release the rear brake cable and, where appropriate, the throttle cable from its clips on the drivebelt cover. Where fitted, detach the air cooling duct from the front of the cover **(see illustration)**.

4 On Hexagon models fitted with a plastic trim over the drivebelt cover, remove the kickstart lever pinch-bolt and draw the lever off the shaft, then remove the bolts securing the plastic **(see illustrations)**. Refit the kickstart lever to the shaft – this is to prevent the shaft being accidentally knocked through the cover and dislodging the mechanism return spring.

5 On later models and LEADER engined models, the gearbox input shaft passes through the drivebelt cover and is supported

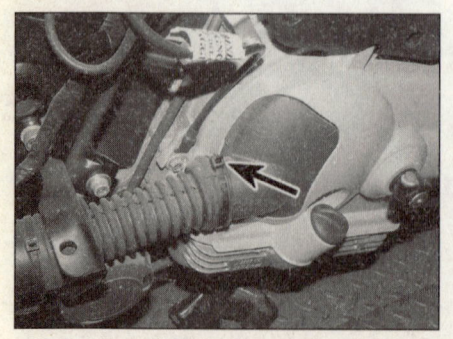

2.3 Cut the cable tie (arrowed) and detach the air duct

2.4a Remove the pinch-bolt (arrowed) and slide off the kickstart lever

2.4b Unscrew the bolts and remove the trim cover

Transmission 2G•3

2.5a Remove the plastic cap

2.5b Lock the clutch drum as described . . .

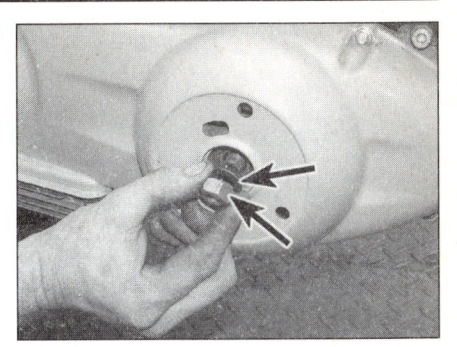

2.5c . . . and remove the nut and washer (arrowed)

by a bearing in the cover. To undo the nut on the outer end of the shaft, first unclip the plastic cap on the clutch bearing housing **(see illustration)**. The clutch drum must be locked against the belt cover to prevent the shaft turning while the nut is undone; Piaggio produce a service tool (Part No. 020423Y) to do this. Alternatively, insert two large screwdrivers through the holes in the belt cover to engage the holes in the clutch drum and have an assistant hold the screwdrivers while the nut is undone, then remove the nut and washer **(see illustrations)**. On LEADER engined models, remove the oil filler cap **(see illustration)**.

6 Unscrew the bolts securing the drivebelt over, noting the position of the clips on the bolts, then remove the cover, noting how it fits **(see illustration)**. On models where the gearbox input shaft passes through the belt cover, note the spacer on the shaft **(see illustration)**.

7 On 50 cc four-stroke models, a spring clip secures the end of the gearbox shaft in the cover bearing **(see illustration)**. Note the position of the clip but do not remove it unless it is damaged and needs to be renewed.

Inspection

Note: *It is not advisable to disassemble the kickstart mechanism unless a component needs to be renewed – the return spring can be very difficult to fit.*

8 Where fitted, remove the kickstart mechanism cover on the inside of the belt cover **(see illustration)**. Remove any old and hardened grease. Manually operate the lever and check that the mechanism operates smoothly and returns to its rest position under pressure of the spring. Check for any signs of wear or damage on the pinion teeth, and check for rounded dogs on the engaging pinion and its corresponding plate on the drive pulley **(see illustration)**.

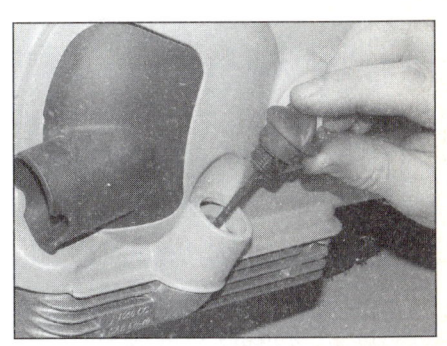

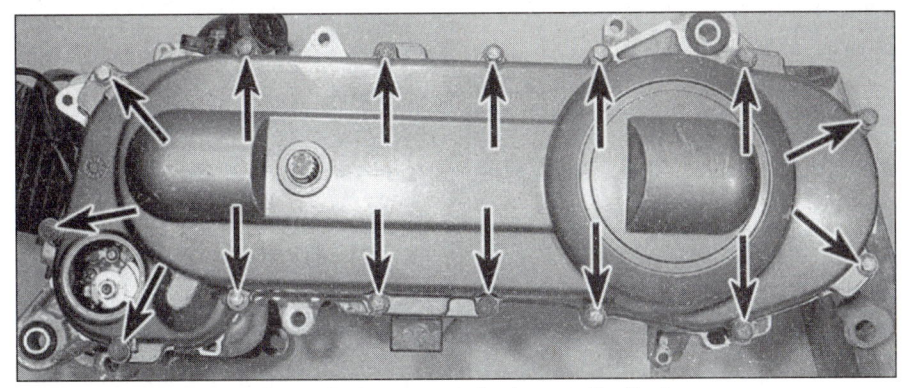

2.5d Remove the oil filler cap

2.6a Transmission cover bolts (arrowed) – Typhoon

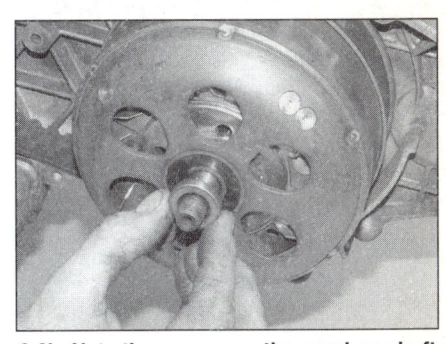

2.6b Note the spacer on the gearbox shaft

2.7 Note the spring clip (arrowed) on the gearbox shaft

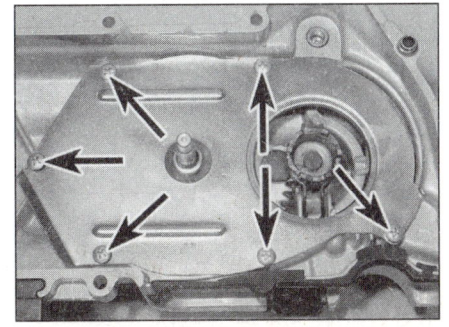

2.8a Where fitted, remove the screws securing the kickstart mechanism cover (arrowed)

2.8b Check the engaging pinion dogs and their mating plate for wear and damage

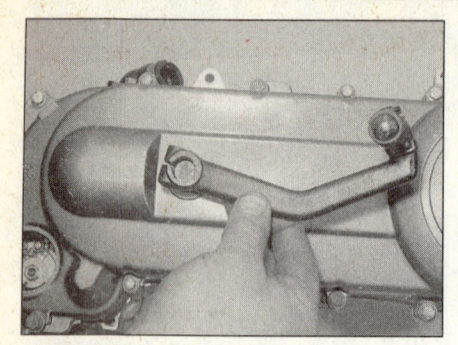

2G•4 Transcription

2.9a Unscrew the bolt and remove the kickstart lever

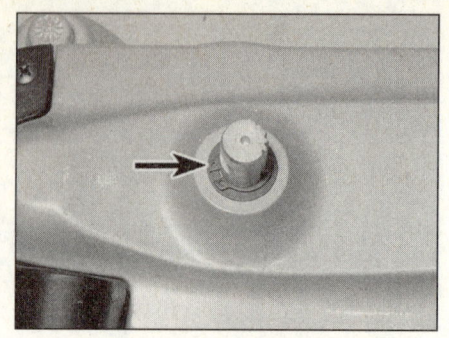

2.9b Remove the circlip (arrowed) securing the shaft

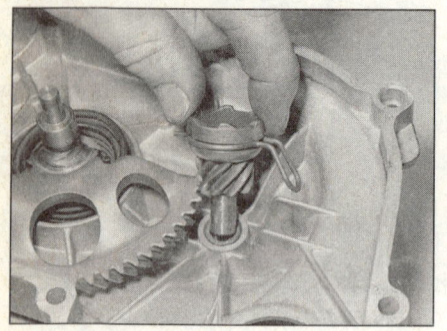

2.9c Remove the engaging pinion, noting how it fits

2.9d Note how the spring ends (A) locate, and how the pinion butts against the rubber pad (B)

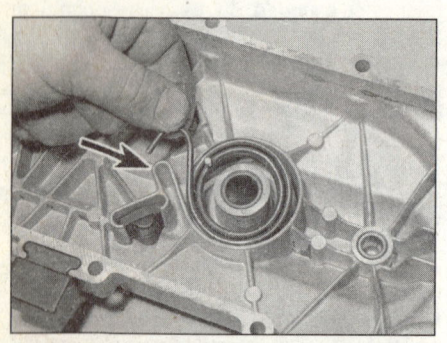

2.11a Fit the return spring, locating its hooked end against the raised section (arrowed)

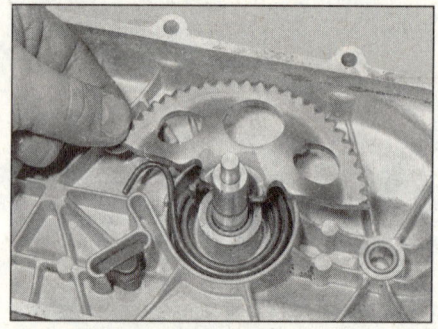

2.11b Install the pinion as shown . . .

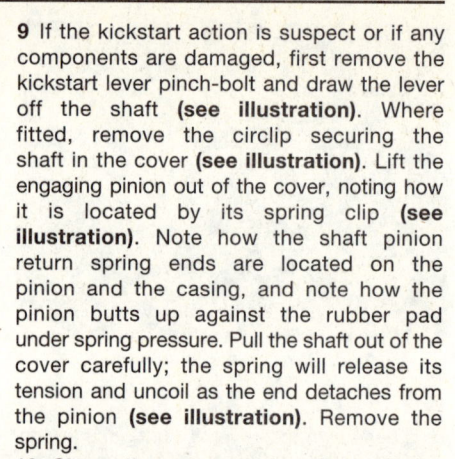

2.11c . . . then locate the steel rod onto the spring end and against the pinion . . .

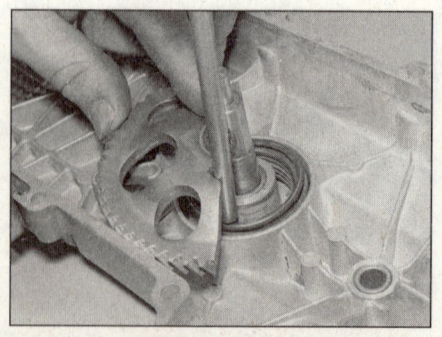

2.11d . . . and move the pinion around, bringing the spring with it . . .

2.11e . . . until the pinion end clears the rubber pad and can be tapped down against it

9 If the kickstart action is suspect or if any components are damaged, first remove the kickstart lever pinch-bolt and draw the lever off the shaft **(see illustration)**. Where fitted, remove the circlip securing the shaft in the cover **(see illustration)**. Lift the engaging pinion out of the cover, noting how it is located by its spring clip **(see illustration)**. Note how the shaft pinion return spring ends are located on the pinion and the casing, and note how the pinion butts up against the rubber pad under spring pressure. Pull the shaft out of the cover carefully; the spring will release its tension and uncoil as the end detaches from the pinion **(see illustration)**. Remove the spring.

10 Clean all components in solvent. Check the spring for cracks and distortion and the shafts and their bushes in the cover for wear. Check the condition of the rubber pad. Renew any components that are worn or damaged.

11 To reassemble the mechanism, first install the pinion return spring, locating its hooked end against the raised section in the cover **(see illustration)**. Apply some grease to the kickstart shaft and its bore. Fitting the shaft pinion and tensioning the return spring can be difficult. Piaggio produce a service tool (Part No. 020261Y) for this purpose. Alternatively, obtain a length of steel rod and drill a hole up one end deep enough to accommodate the upturned end of the return spring. Locate the pinion in its bore, with the cutout in the pinion adjacent to the end of the spring, then fit the drilled rod over the end of the spring **(see illustrations)**. Hold the rod against the pinion and use the rod to turn the pinion anti-clockwise so that the spring is tensioned. When the pinion clears the rubber pad, press or tap it down into its installed position, so that it butts against the pad **(see illustrations)**. Pull the rod off the spring end, which will automatically locate itself in the cutout in the pinion.

12 Apply some grease to the engaging pinion shaft and fit it into its bore **(see illustration 2.9c)**, locating the spring clip end as

Transmission 2G•5

2.12 The installed assembly should be as shown, though on some models the engaging spring end locating section is positioned differently

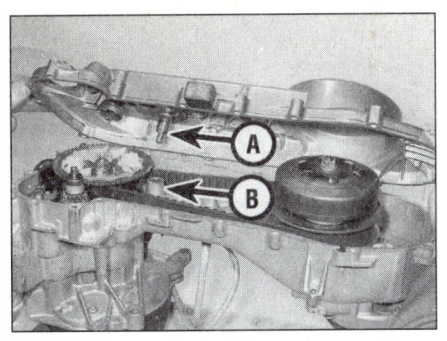

2.14 Where applicable, make sure the shaft (A) locates in its bore (B)

shown (see illustration). Secure the kickstart shaft with the circlip, where fitted (see illustration 2.9b). Fit the kickstart lever and tighten the bolt to the specified torque (see illustration 2.9a). Check the operation of the mechanism. Where fitted, install the mechanism cover (see illustration 2.8b).

13 Where fitted, check the condition of the bearing in the cover. The bearing should turn smoothly and freely without excessive play between the inner and outer races. If there is any doubt about the condition of the bearing, replace it with a new one. On models where the gearbox shaft passes through the cover, remove the retaining circlip on the inside of the cover, then press the bearing out from the outside with a driver or suitably sized socket. If necessary, heat the cover on the inside around the bearing housing with a hot air gun to aid removal. Note which way round the bearing is fitted. Drive the new bearing in with a socket that contacts the outer race only, then fit the circlip. On some two-stroke models, the bearing locates in a blind hole in the cover and must be removed with a bearing puller and slide hammer. Alternatively, heat the cover around the bearing housing, then tap it face down on the work surface to dislodge the bearing. Take care to avoid damaging the surface of the cover's edge.

Installation

14 Installation is the reverse of removal. Ensure the kickstart shaft end locates correctly in its bore next to the drive pulley where applicable (see illustration). On models where the gearbox input shaft passes through the belt cover, ensure the spacer is in place on the shaft before fitting the cover (see illustration 2.6b). Employ the method used on removal to prevent the shaft turning, then fit the washer and tighten the input shaft nut to the specified torque.

3 Drive pulley and variator – removal, inspection and installation

Removal

1 Remove the drivebelt cover (see Section 2).
2 To remove the drive pulley nut, the pulley must be locked to prevent it turning. Piaggio produce a service tool (Part No. 020165Y or 020451Y depending on model) which bolts onto the engine case and has a toothed section which locates into the drive pulley (see illustration). A similar home-made tool can be made. Alternatively, locate a large flat-bladed screwdriver between the teeth of the starter driven gear and hold it firmly against the engine casing (see illustration). With the pulley locked, unscrew the nut and remove the kickstart engaging pinion mating plate, the plastic finned plate (where fitted) and the starter driven gear (see illustrations). Piaggio

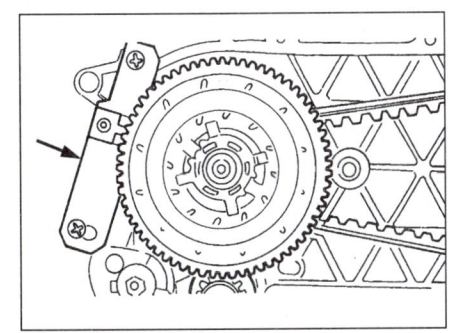

3.2a Piaggio tool (arrowed) used to lock drive pulley

3.2b Lock the starter driven gear with a screwdriver (arrowed)

3.2c Remove the nut . . .

3.2d . . . the mating plate . . .

3.2e . . . the finned plate . . .

3.2f and the starter driven gear

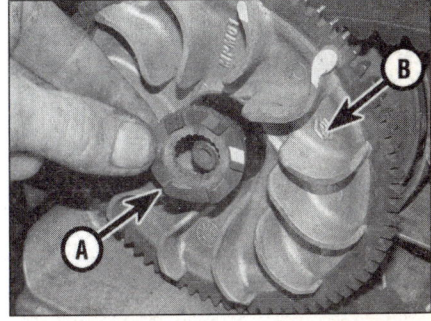

3.2g Starter mating plate (A) and driven gear (B) on X9 LEADER engine

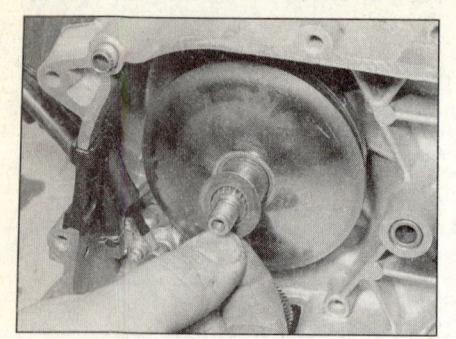

2G•6 Transmission

3.3a Remove the washer . . .

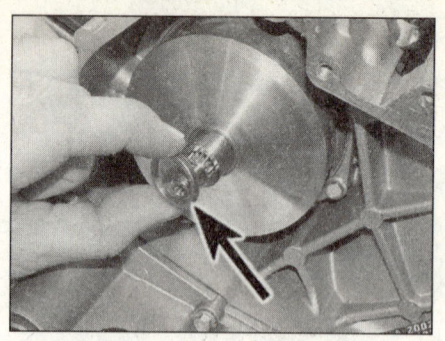

3.3b . . . or spacer (arrowed)

3.3c Draw out the collar . . .

3.3d . . . and slide the variator off the shaft

recommend that a new nut is used on assembly.

3 Move the drivebelt aside, and remove the washer from the end of the shaft or the spacer from off the collar, then draw out the collar and slide the variator off the shaft **(see illustrations)**.

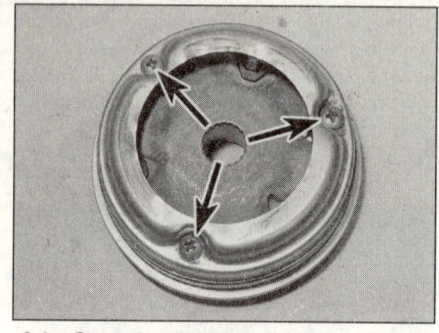

3.4a On early models remove the screws (arrowed) . . .

Note: *Two types of variator are fitted; on early models the variator rollers are greased and the variator has a cover, on later models the rollers are not greased and no cover is fitted.*

4 To disassemble the early-type variator, first remove the three screws and lift off the cover, then remove the O-ring and discard it, as a new one must be used **(see illustrations)**. On all models, lift out the ramp plate, then remove the rollers, noting which fits where as, unless new ones are used, they should be installed in their original locations **(see illustrations)**. Clean and, where applicable, degrease all the components.

Inspection

5 Check the rollers and the corresponding ramps in the variator housing and ramp plate for damage, wear and flat spots, and renew the rollers, the housing and the plate if necessary **(see illustration)**. Measure the diameter of the rollers and compare the result to the Specifications at the beginning of the Chapter. Renew the rollers as a set if any are worn below the minimum diameter **(see illustration)**. **Note:** *Always specify the model and year of your scooter when buying new variator rollers. If supplied, later non-greased rollers can be fitted in the earlier type variator,*

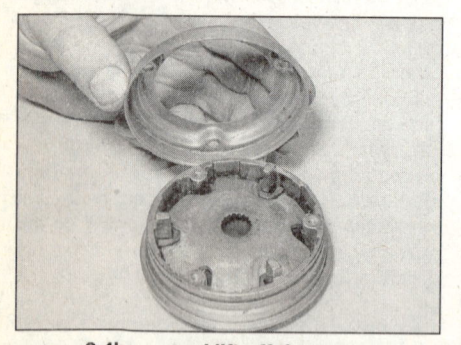

3.4b . . . and lift off the cover

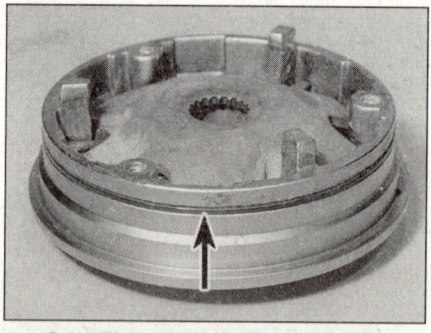

3.4c Discard the O-ring (arrowed)

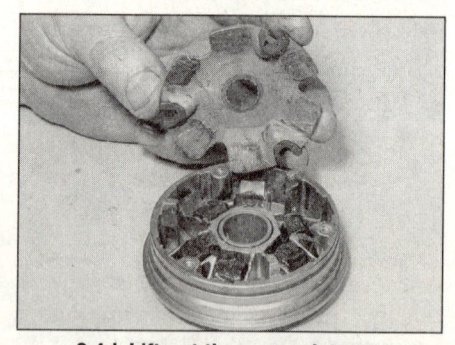

3.4d Lift out the ramp plate . . .

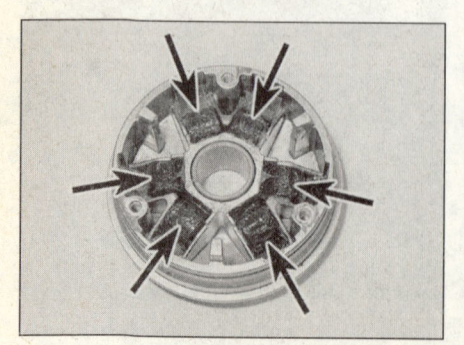

3.4e . . . and remove the rollers (arrowed)

3.5a Check the ramps for wear

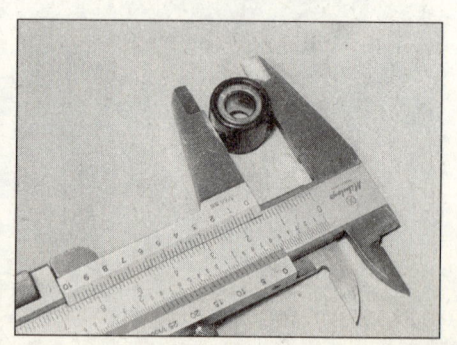

3.5b Measure the diameter of the rollers

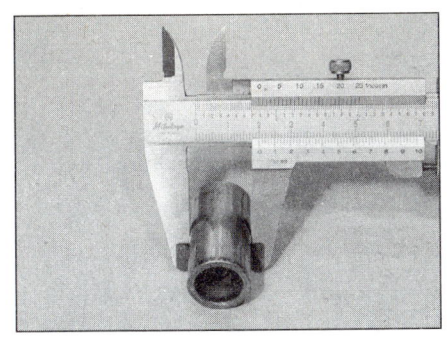

Transmission 2G•7

3.6a Measure the collar external diameter . . .

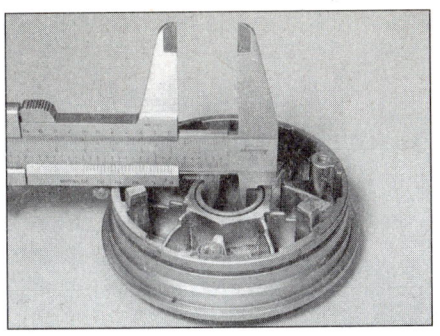

3.6b . . . and the bush internal diameter

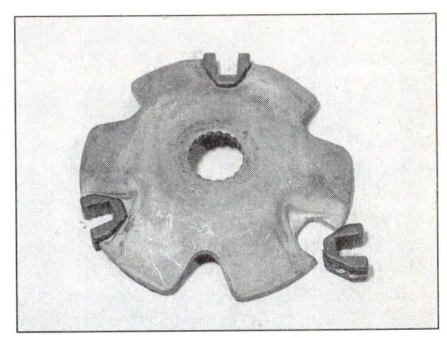

3.7 Check the guide shoes and replace them if necessary

but the variator should be cleaned thoroughly and the rollers should not be greased.

6 Check the collar and its bush in the housing for wear and damage and renew them if necessary. Measure the external diameter of the collar and the internal diameter of the bush and compare the results to the Specifications at the beginning of the Chapter. Renew either or both if they are worn beyond their limit **(see illustrations)**.

7 Check the condition of the guide shoes on the ramp plate and renew them if they are worn or damaged **(see illustration)**. Also check the splines on the plate and renew the plate if they are worn.

Installation

8 On early models fitted with the original rollers, grease the rollers and the ramps with lithium soap-based grease (NLGI 3). On all models, fit the rollers into the housing, making sure they are fitted in their original positions (unless new ones are used) **(see illustration)**. Check that the guide shoes are correctly fitted on the ramp plate, then install the plate **(see illustration)**. On early models, if the original greased rollers are fitted, fit a new O-ring around the housing, then install the cover and tighten its screws securely **(see illustrations 3.4c, 3.4b and 3.4a)**.

9 Grip the variator so that the ramp plate is held into the housing and slide the variator onto the crankshaft **(see illustration)**. Install the collar, then fit the washer or spacer **(see illustrations 3.3c and 3.3a or 3.3b)**. Note: *If the ramp plate moves and the rollers are dislodged, disassemble the variator and reposition the rollers correctly.*

10 Position the drivebelt around the shaft **(see illustration)**, then fit the starter driven gear, the finned plate (where fitted) and the mating plate **(see illustrations 3.2g, 3.2f, 3.2e, and 3.2d)**, making sure the mating plate is correctly located **(see illustration)**. Fit a new nut and apply a suitable non-permanent thread locking compound to its threads. Use the method employed on removal to prevent the pulley turning and tighten the nut to the torque setting specified at the beginning of the Chapter **(see illustrations 3.2a or 3.2b)**. If required, tighten the nut with a torque angle gauge **(see illustration)**. Note: *If a torque angle gauge is not available see* **Haynes Hint** *overleaf.* Note: *It is important the nut tightens against the mating plate, and does not bottom on the shouldered end of the crankshaft.*

11 Install the drivebelt cover (see Section 2).

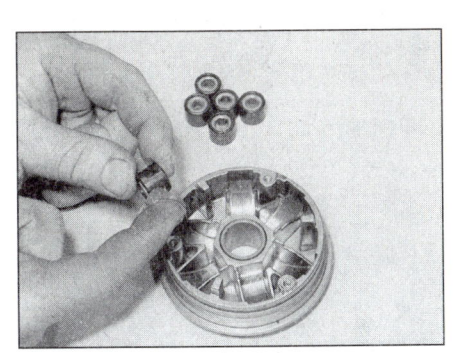

3.8a On early models, grease the rollers and fit them into the housing . . .

3.8b Fit the inner plate, locating the guide shoes as shown

3.9 Hold the variator assembly together to keep the rollers in place

3.10a Locate the belt over the shaft

3.10b Make sure the tabs (arrowed) are correctly located

3.10c Tightening the nut with a torque angle gauge

HAYNES HINT: *If a degree disc is not available, the angle for the torque setting can be determined by using the points on the nut. Select one point on the nut as a reference and mark it with paint or a marker. Now select the second point clockwise 90° from it and mark its position on the driven gear. Tighten the nut – when the mark on the nut aligns with the mark made on the gear, it will have turned through the requisite number of degrees.*

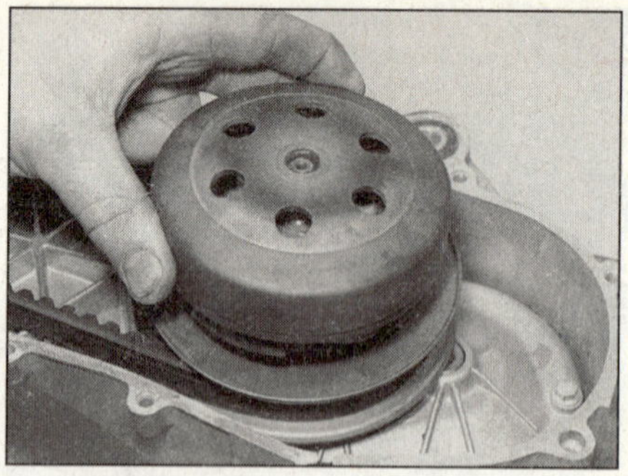

4.3a Remove the clutch drum . . .

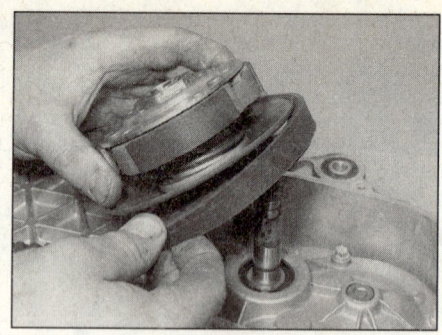

4.3b . . . then draw the assembly off the shaft and disengage the belt

4 Clutch and driven pulley – removal, inspection and installation

TOOL TIP: *A holding tool can easily be made using two strips of steel bolted together in the middle, and with a bolt through each end which locate into the slots in the rotor.*

Removal

1 Remove the drivebelt cover (see Section 2). On models where the gearbox input shaft passes through the belt cover, remove the spacer on the end of the shaft **(see illustration 2.6b)**.

2 On early models, to remove the clutch drum nut it is necessary to hold the clutch and stop it from turning. Piaggio produce a service tool (Part No. 020565Y) for this purpose, or alternatively a home-made equivalent can be made (see **Tool Tip**). With the drum securely held, unscrew the nut **(see illustration 4.12b)**. Piaggio recommend that a new nut is used on assembly.

3 Remove the clutch drum, then draw the clutch/driven pulley assembly off the shaft and disengage the drivebelt from it **(see illustrations)**.

4 To disassemble the clutch and driven pulley assembly, it is necessary to clamp the assembly against the pressure of the spring so that it does not fly apart when the clutch nut is unscrewed – the tool set-up described in Step 10 can be used. Alternatively, if an assistant is available, position the assembly on a bench and have the assistant press down hard on the top of the clutch. With the assembly clamped or securely held, unscrew the nut **(see illustration)**. Slowly release the clutch and allow the spring to expand, then remove the clutch, the upper spring seat, where fitted, and the spring. Remove the lower spring seat, then draw out the guide pins and separate the pulley halves **(see illustrations)**. Remove the seal and the O-rings from the pulley outer half and discard them as new ones must be used **(see illustration)**. Degrease and clean all components.

Inspection

5 Check the inner surface of the clutch drum for damage and scoring; renew it if necessary. Measure the internal diameter of the drum at several points to determine if it is worn or out-of-round **(see illustration)**. If it is worn or out-of-round beyond the limits, renew it.

4.4a Press down hard on the clutch and unscrew the nut (arrowed)

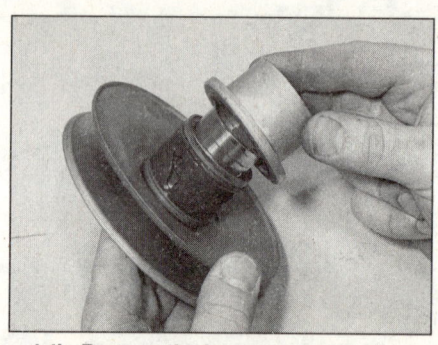

4.4b Remove the lower spring seat . . .

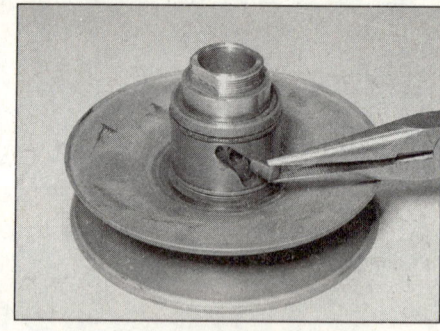

4.4c . . . then withdraw the pins . . .

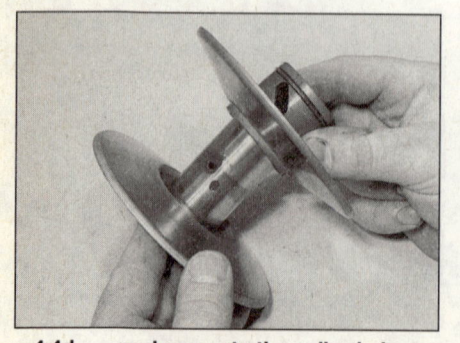

4.4d . . . and separate the pulley halves

4.4e Lever out the seal (A) and remove the O-rings (B)

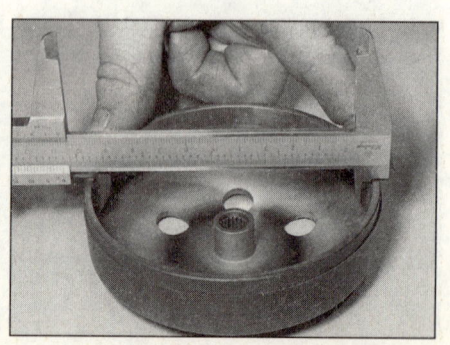

4.5 Measure the drum diameter

Transmission 2G•9

4.6a Check the friction material on the shoes . . .

4.6b . . . and check the springs and pivots

6 Check the amount of friction material remaining on the clutch shoes and renew the clutch if any shoe is worn to its limit **(see illustration)**. Do not try to disassemble the clutch and renew any of the shoes individually because the clutch is balanced during manufacture, and will cause severe vibration if it becomes out of balance. Check the condition of the shoe springs and renew the clutch if any are weakened or broken, and check that the shoes are securely held on their pivots by the circlips **(see illustration)**. Check that the shoes are not seized on their pivots by pressing them out with your hands or a screwdriver.

7 Check the pulley halves for any signs of damage and wear and renew them if necessary. Measure the external diameter of the inner pulley shaft and the internal diameter of the outer pulley bore and compare the results to the Specifications at the beginning of the Chapter. Renew either or both if they are worn beyond their limits **(see illustrations)**. Also check the condition of the needle roller bearing in the inner pulley and renew it if necessary **(see illustration)**. Drive out the old bearing using a suitable piece of tubing or a drift.

8 Check the condition of the spring. If it is bent or appears weak, renew it. Measure the free length of the spring and compare it with the figure in the Specifications **(see illustration)**. Renew the spring if it has sagged to less than the limit.

Installation

9 Fit a new seal and O-rings onto the outer pulley **(see illustration 4.4e)**. Apply grease to the inner pulley shaft **(see illustration)**. Fit the inner pulley shaft into the outer pulley bore, then fit the guide pins into their holes **(see illustrations 4.4d and 4.4c)**. Apply some grease to the guide pin slots and around the O-rings **(see illustration)**, then fit the lower spring seat **(see illustration 4.4b)**.

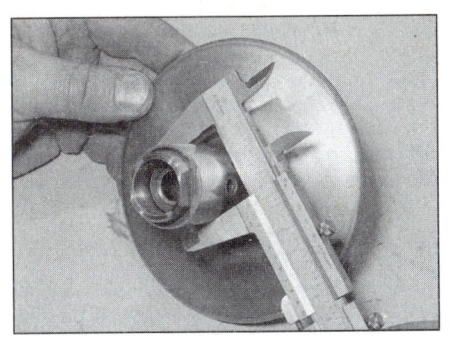

4.7a Measure the diameter of the inner pulley shaft . . .

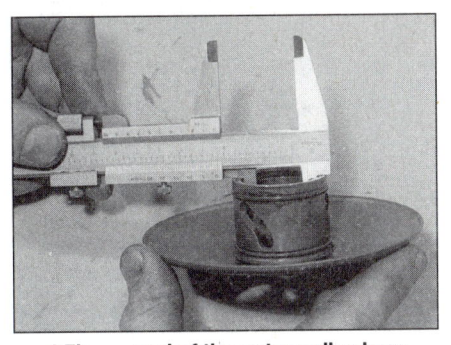

4.7b . . . and of the outer pulley bore

4.7c Check the needle bearing (arrowed) in the inner pulley

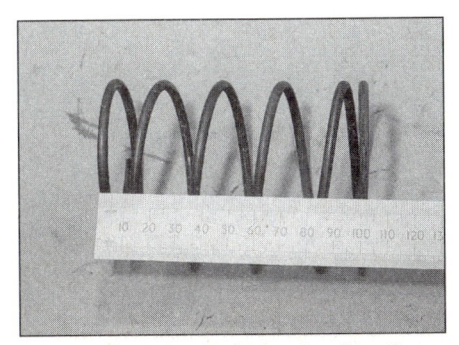

4.8 Measure the spring free length

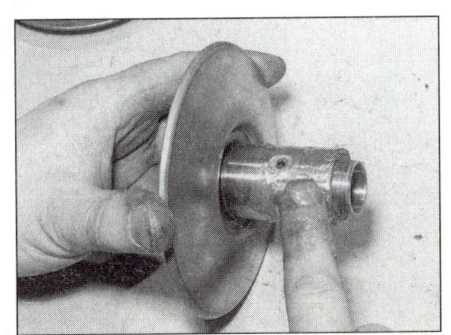

4.9a Apply grease to the inner pulley shaft

4.9b Apply grease to the slots and around the O-rings

2G•10 Transmission

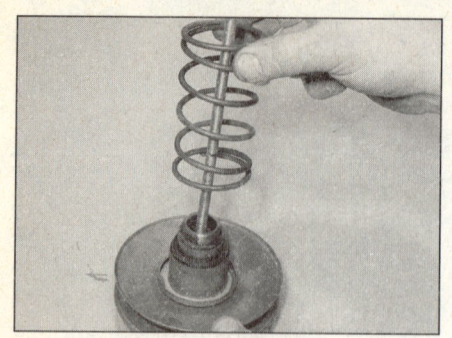

4.10a Fit the spring ...

4.10b ... the upper spring seat (where fitted) ...

4.10c ... the clutch ...

4.10d ... and the nut

4.10e Position the oil filter tool ...

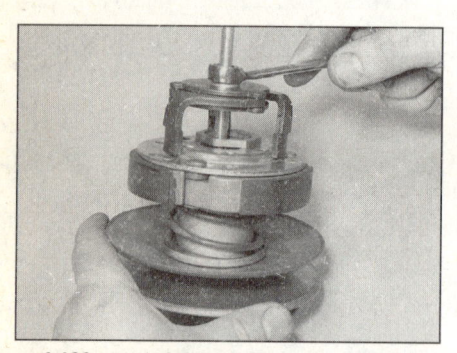

4.10f ... and tighten the nut onto it to compress the spring

4.10g Hold the clutch as shown and tighten the nut to the specified torque

10 To assemble the clutch and driven pulley it is necessary to compress the spring and keep it compressed while the clutch nut is tightened. If an assistant is available, have them press down on the clutch to compress the spring while you tighten the nut. Otherwise, a clamping tool can be made up using a piece of threaded rod and an oil filter removing tool as follows: fit a washer and two nuts onto one end of the rod and tighten the nuts together. Pass the other end of the rod up through the pulley and locate the washer against the back of the inner pulley. Fit the spring, the upper spring seat (where fitted) and the clutch onto the pulley, then apply a suitable non-permanent thread locking compound to the clutch nut and rest the nut on top of the clutch (see illustrations). Fit the oil filter removing tool with its legs down on the clutch, then thread a nut down the rod and onto the tool (see illustration). Tighten the nut, thereby compressing the spring, until the clutch nut threads are fully exposed and tighten the clutch nut as tight as possible by hand (see illustration). Remove the tool and the threaded rod, then hold the clutch with the tool used on removal and tighten the nut to the torque setting specified at the beginning of the Chapter (see illustration).

11 Apply some grease to the needle bearing in the inner pulley half and to the gearbox input shaft (see illustration). Engage the driven pulley with the drivebelt, then, if the drive pulley has not been removed, squeeze the belt to force the pulley halves apart, thereby providing some slack in the belt, and slide the assembly onto the shaft (see illustrations).

12 Fit the drum onto the clutch. On early models, apply a suitable non-permanent thread locking compound to the drum nut. Using the method employed on removal to prevent the clutch turning, tighten the nut to the specified torque setting (see

4.11a Grease the bearing and shaft ...

4.11b ... then squeeze the belt to part the pulleys if slack is needed ...

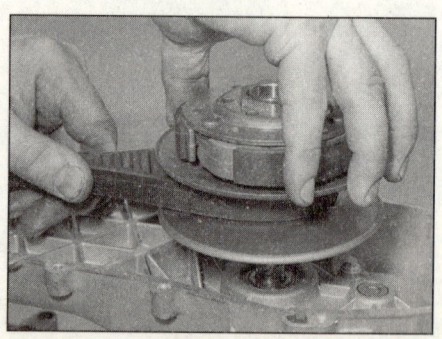

4.11c ... and fit the assembly onto the shaft

4.12a Fit the clutch drum and its nut . . .

4.12b . . . and tighten it to the specified torque

illustrations). On models where the gearbox input shaft passes through the belt cover, install the spacer on the end of the shaft (see illustration 2.6b).
13 Install the drivebelt cover (see Section 2).

5 Drivebelt and support roller – inspection and renewal

Inspection

1 Remove the drivebelt cover (see Section 2). Check along the entire length of the belt for cracks, splits, frays and damaged teeth and renew the belt if any damage is found.
2 Measure the width of the outside of the belt and compare the measurement to the minimum width specified (see illustration). If the belt has worn below the limit, renew it.
3 The belt should be inspected regularly, according the service interval (see Chapter 1).
Note: *Oil or grease inside the casing will contaminate the belt and prevent it gripping the pulleys. Any evidence of oil inside the casing suggests a worn seal on either the crankshaft or the gearbox input shaft; evidence of grease suggests worn seals in the clutch centre.*

4 On GT200 models, a belt support roller is fitted midway between the variator and the clutch pulley (see illustration). Check that the roller turns smoothly and freely. If the roller centre bearing is worn or damaged, undo the centre bolt and remove the roller (see illustration). Remove the retaining circlip and press the bearing out from the back of the roller with a driver or suitably sized socket. Note which way round the bearing is fitted. Press the new bearing in with a socket that contacts the outer race only and secure it with the circlip.

Renewal

5 Follow the procedure in Section 3 and remove the starter driven gear. **Note:** *Hold the variator in position on the crankshaft when the gear is removed to avoid dislodging the rollers. If the ramp plate moves and the rollers are dislodged, disassemble the variator and reposition the rollers correctly.*
6 Lift the belt off the crankshaft and ease it out of the clutch pulley. If necessary, pull the outer clutch pulley half back against the spring tension and manoeuvre the belt out (see illustration).
7 Fit the new belt, making sure any directional arrows point in the direction of normal rotation (see illustration). Ensure there is sufficient slack in the belt to avoid it

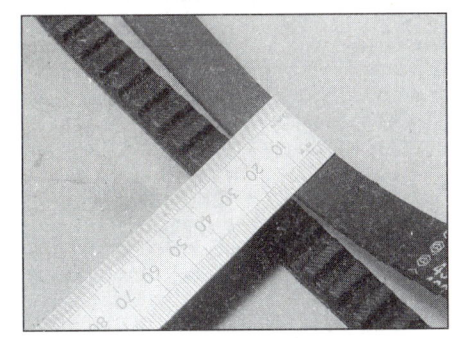

5.2 Measure the width of the belt to determine wear

5.4a Location of the belt support roller (arrowed)

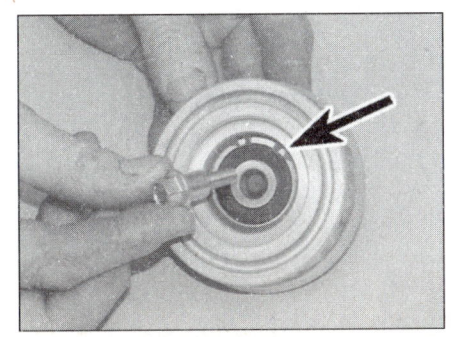

5.4b Roller is retained by centre bolt. Note the circlip (arrowed)

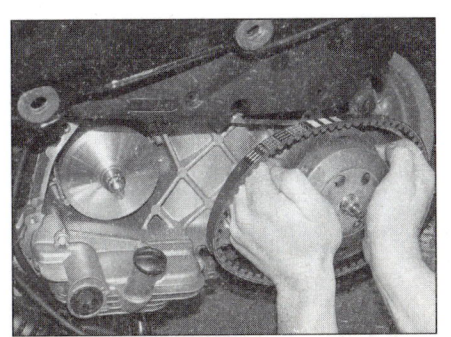

5.6 Compress the clutch to release the drivebelt

5.7 Arrows should point in the normal direction of rotation

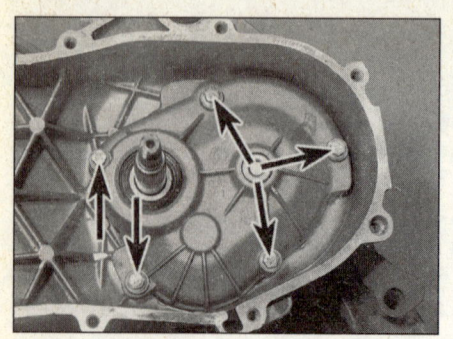

2G•12 Transcription

(figures)

6.3a Undo the bolts (arrowed) . . .

6.3b . . . and remove the gearbox cover with the input shaft

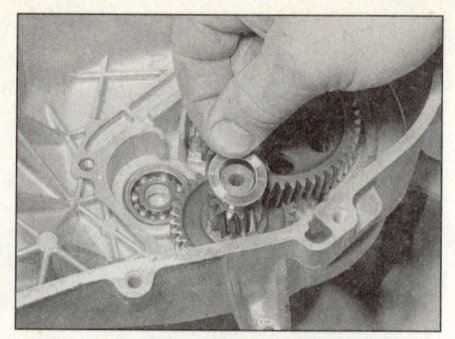

6.4a Remove the outer thrustwasher . . .

6.4b . . . the output shaft . . .

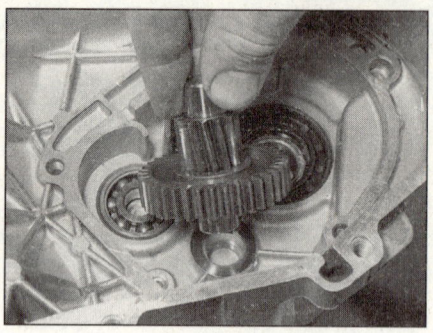

6.4c . . . the reduction gear . . .

being trapped when the starter driven gear is installed.

8 Install the starter driven gear (see Section 3) and the belt cover.

6 Gearbox – removal, inspection and installation

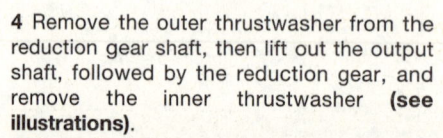

Removal

1 Remove the clutch and driven pulley (see Section 4) and the rear wheel (see Chapter 8).
2 Drain the gearbox oil (see Chapter 1).

Gearbox cover behind clutch

3 Unscrew the bolts securing the gearbox cover and remove the cover – the input shaft will come away with it **(see illustrations)**.

4 Remove the outer thrustwasher from the reduction gear shaft, then lift out the output shaft, followed by the reduction gear, and remove the inner thrustwasher **(see illustrations)**.
5 If required, drive the input shaft from the gearbox cover using a soft hammer on the shaft end, but note that the bearing and oil seal will have to be renewed if you do so. If there are no signs of oil leakage on the outside of the cover (behind the clutch), and if the shaft turns smoothly and freely with no signs of freeplay in the bearing or between the shaft and the bearing, it is better not to remove it, unless it is worn or damaged.

Gearbox cover behind rear wheel

6 Displace the disc brake caliper and remove the rear hub (see Chapter 8).

7 Unscrew the bolts securing the gearbox cover and remove the cover **(see illustration)**. Note the location of the bolts – the three bolts on the right-hand side of the cover are shorter than the others. Note the location of the guides for the gearbox breather hose. Discard the gasket, as a new one must be fitted on reassembly.
8 Lift out the output shaft and the reduction gear. If required, press the input shaft out of its bearing in the transmission casing, but note that the shaft oil seal will have to be renewed if you do so (see Step 5).

Inspection

9 Remove all traces of old sealant or gasket from the gearbox and cover mating surfaces, taking care not to nick or gouge the soft aluminium if a scraper is used. Wash all of the components in clean solvent and dry them off.
10 Check the gear teeth for cracking, chipping, pitting and other obvious wear or damage. Any pinion that is damaged must be renewed. Check the splines on the shafts for wear and damage.
11 Check for signs of scoring or bluing on the pinions and shaft. This could be caused by overheating due to inadequate lubrication. Renew any damaged pinions. On early models, remove the circlip securing the pinion on the output shaft and check the splines on both the shaft and the pinion for wear and damage **(see illustration)**.
12 Check the thrustwashers where fitted and

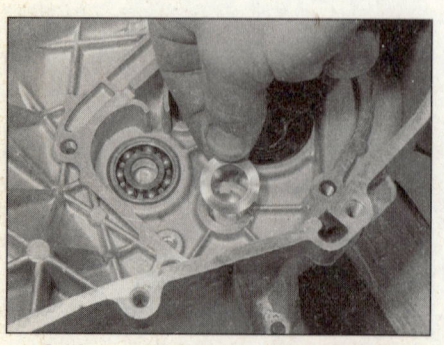

6.4d . . . and the inner thrustwasher

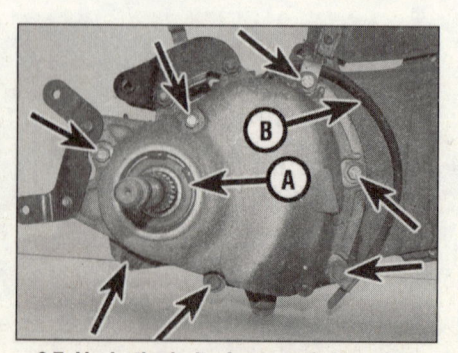

6.7 Undo the bolts (arrowed). Note the breather (B) and bearing circlip (A)

6.11 Remove the circlip (arrowed) and slide the pinion off the output shaft

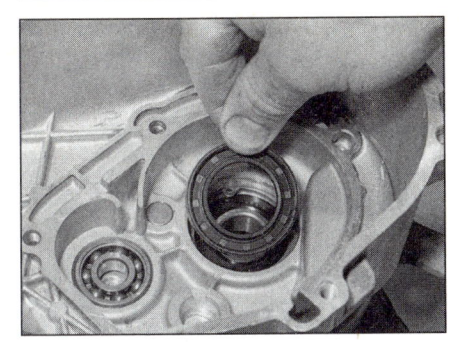

6.13a Lever out the seal . . .

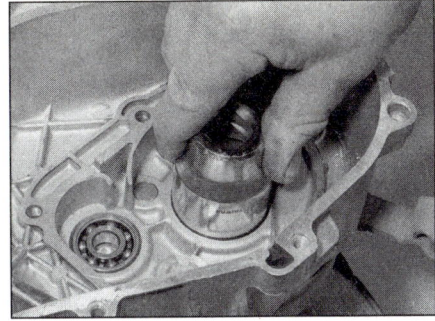

6.13b . . . and drive a new one in using a socket

6.15 The output shaft bearing is secured by a circlip (arrowed)

renew them if they are bent or appear weakened or worn. Use new ones if in any doubt.

13 Note which way round the output shaft oil seal is fitted, then lever it out and discard it, as a new one must be used **(see illustration)**. After checking the bearing (Step 14), fit the new seal and drive it in using a seal driver or suitable socket, making sure it enters squarely **(see illustration)**.

14 Check that all the bearings turn smoothly and freely without excessive play between the inner and outer races. The bearings should be a tight fit in the casing; if a bearing is loose, and the casing is not damaged, use a suitable bearing locking compound to hold it in place. On some models the inner end of the output shaft runs in a needle bearing. Inspect the surface of the rollers for wear and pitting. Renew any bearing that is worn.

15 To renew a bearing, first lever out the oil seal where fitted **(see illustration 6.13a)**. If the bearing is secured by a circlip, remove the circlip **(see illustration)**. Note the position of the bearing, then heat the cover using a hot air gun and drive the bearing out with a bearing driver or suitably-sized socket. Install the new bearing with a bearing driver or socket large enough to contact the outer race of the bearing. Install the circlip and new oil seal as required.

16 Bearings fitted in blind holes require an internal bearing puller to extract them without damaging the case; consult a Piaggio dealer or specialist motorcycle engineer if they need removing.

Installation

Gearbox cover behind clutch

17 Fit the inner thrustwasher, followed by the reduction gear, then the output shaft, and fit the outer thrustwasher onto the reduction gear **(see illustrations 6.4d, 6.4c, 6.4b and 6.4a)**. If removed, fit the input shaft into the cover.

18 Apply a suitable sealant, such as Loctite 501, to the cover mating surface, then fit the cover, making sure the dowels locate correctly **(see illustration)**. Tighten the cover bolts evenly and in a criss-cross pattern to the torque setting Specified at the beginning of

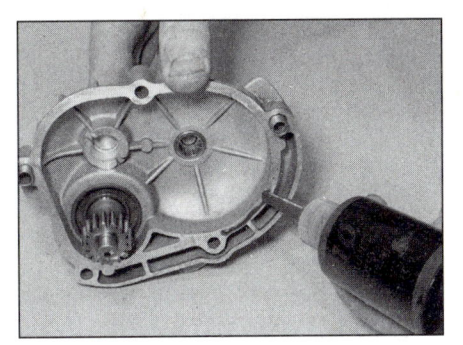

6.18a Apply a suitable sealant . . .

the Chapter **(see illustration)**. Ensure that the input and output shafts turn freely.

19 Install the clutch and driven pulley (see Section 4) and the rear wheel (see Chapter 8).

20 Fill the gearbox with the specified amount and type of oil (see Chapter 1).

Gearbox cover behind rear wheel

21 If removed, press the input shaft into its bearing, then install the reduction gear and the output shaft.

22 Fit a new gasket over the dowels on the transmission casing, then fit the cover. Install the cover bolts with the guides for the breather hose (see Step 7). Tighten the cover bolts evenly and in a criss-cross pattern to the torque setting specified at the beginning of the Chapter. Ensure that the input and output shafts turn freely, then follow Steps 19 and 20

6.18b . . . and tighten the cover bolts to the specified torque

Chapter 3
Cooling system (liquid-cooled engines)

Refer to the beginning of Chapter 1 for model identification details

Contents

Coolant hoses – removal and installation 8	Cooling system checks .... see Chapter 1
Coolant level check .... see *Daily (pre-ride) checks*	Cooling system draining, flushing and refilling ...... see Chapter 1
Coolant reservoir – removal and installation 2	General information 1
Coolant temperature gauge/warning light and sender – check and renewal 4	Radiator – removal and installation 6
	Thermostat – removal, check and installation 5
Cooling fan, motor and switch – check and renewal 3	Water pump – check, removal and installation 7

Degrees of difficulty

Easy, suitable for novice with little experience	Fairly easy, suitable for beginner with some experience	Fairly difficult, suitable for competent DIY mechanic	Difficult, suitable for experienced DIY mechanic	Very difficult, suitable for expert DIY or professional

Specifications

Thermostat
Opening temperature	69.5 to 72.5°C
Valve lift	3.5 mm at 80°C

Torque settings
Temperature gauge sender	6 to 8 Nm
Thermostat housing screws	3 to 4 Nm
Water pump mounting bolts (LEADER models)	3 to 4 Nm

1 General information

The cooling system uses a water/anti-freeze coolant to carry excess energy away from the engine in the form of heat. The cylinder is surrounded by a water jacket through which the coolant is circulated by thermo-syphonic action in conjunction with a water pump. On early models, the pump is mounted inside the crankcases and is driven by a shaft running off the oil pump. On LEADER engined models, the water pump is mounted externally on the alternator cover.

The heated coolant passes upwards to the thermostat and through to the radiator. The coolant then flows across the radiator core, where it is cooled by the passing air, to the water pump and back to the engine where the cycle is repeated.

A thermostat is fitted in the system to prevent the coolant flowing through the radiator when the engine is cold, therefore accelerating the speed at which the engine reaches normal operating temperature. A coolant temperature sender mounted in the cylinder head transmits information to the temperature gauge on the instrument panel. On Hexagon and LEADER engined models, a thermostatically-controlled cooling fan is fitted behind the radiator to aid cooling in extreme conditions. On liquid-cooled LEADER engined models, a coolant circuit from the thermostat housing supplies the heater mounted on the right-hand side of the carburettor (see Chapter 4).

⚠ **Warning: Do not remove the reservoir cap when the engine is hot. Scalding hot coolant and steam may be blown out under pressure, which could cause serious injury.**

⚠ **Warning: Do not allow anti-freeze to come in contact with your skin or painted or plastic surfaces of the scooter. Rinse off any spills immediately with plenty of water. Anti-freeze is highly toxic if ingested. Never leave anti-freeze lying around in an open container or in puddles on the floor; children and pets are attracted by its sweet smell and may drink it. Check with the local authorities about disposing of used anti-freeze. Many communities will have collection centres which will see that anti-freeze is disposed of safely.**

Caution: At all times use the specified type of anti-freeze, and always mix it with distilled water in the correct proportion. The anti-freeze contains corrosion inhibitors which are essential to avoid damage to the cooling system. A lack of these inhibitors could lead to a build-up of corrosion which would block the coolant passages, resulting in overheating and severe engine damage. Distilled water must be used rather than tap water to avoid a build-up of scale which would also block the passages.

3•2 Cooling system (liquid-cooled engines)

2.2 Detach the hoses (arrowed) and drain the reservoir

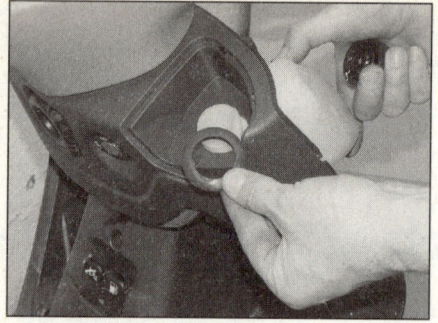

2.4a Remove the seal from the reservoir neck

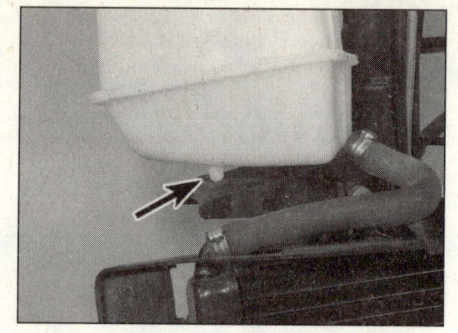

2.4b Note how the lugs locate in the grommets (arrow)

2 Coolant reservoir – removal and installation

Removal

⚠ **Warning: Ensure that the engine is cold before working on the coolant reservoir.**

1 The coolant reservoir is located at the front of the scooter and is housed within the front bodywork panels. Remove the panels for access (see Chapter 7).

2 Release the clip securing the hose to the top of the reservoir and detach the hose **(see illustration)**.

3 Place a suitable container underneath the reservoir, then release the clip securing the hose to the base of the reservoir. Detach the hose and allow the coolant to drain into the container **(see illustration 2.2)**.

4 Unscrew the reservoir mounting screw (where fitted). If not already done, unscrew the reservoir cap and remove the seal around the reservoir neck **(see illustration)**. Lift out the reservoir, noting how the lugs locate in the bracket **(see illustration)**.

Installation

5 Installation is the reverse of removal. Make sure the hoses are correctly installed and secured with their clips. On completion, refill the reservoir as described in Chapter 1.

3 Cooling fan, motor and switch – check and renewal

Cooling fan and motor
Check

1 If the engine is overheating and the cooling fan isn't coming on, first check the cooling fan circuit fuse (see Chapter 9) and then the fan switch as described in Steps 8 and 9 below.

2 If the fan does not come on (and the fan switch is good), the fault lies in either the cooling fan motor or the relevant wiring. Test all the wiring and connections as described in Chapter 9.

3 To test the cooling fan motor, remove the front bodywork panels (see Chapter 7), and disconnect the fan wiring connector **(see illustration)**. Using a 12 volt battery and two jumper wires, connect the battery positive (+ve) lead to the red/black wire terminal and the battery negative (-ve) lead to the green wire terminal on the fan motor side of the connector. Once connected the fan should operate. If it does not, and the wiring is all good, then the fan motor is faulty. Individual components are not available for the fan assembly.

Renewal

⚠ **Warning: The engine must be completely cool before carrying out this procedure.**

4 Disconnect the battery negative (-ve) lead.

5 If required, remove the radiator (see Section 6). Remove the screws securing the fan assembly to the radiator and separate them, noting how they fit **(see illustration)**. If fitted, slacken the clamp securing the fan shroud to the motor and draw the shroud off.

6 Installation is the reverse of removal.

7 Install the radiator (see Section 6). Reconnect the battery (-ve) lead.

Cooling fan switch
Check

8 If the engine is overheating and the cooling fan isn't coming on, first check the cooling fan circuit fuse (see Chapter 9). If the fuse is blown, check the fan circuit for a short to earth (see the wiring diagrams at the end of this book).

9 If the fuse is good, remove the front bodywork panels (see Chapter 7), and disconnect the wiring connectors from the fan switch. On all scooters except GT125/200 models, the switch is on the side of the

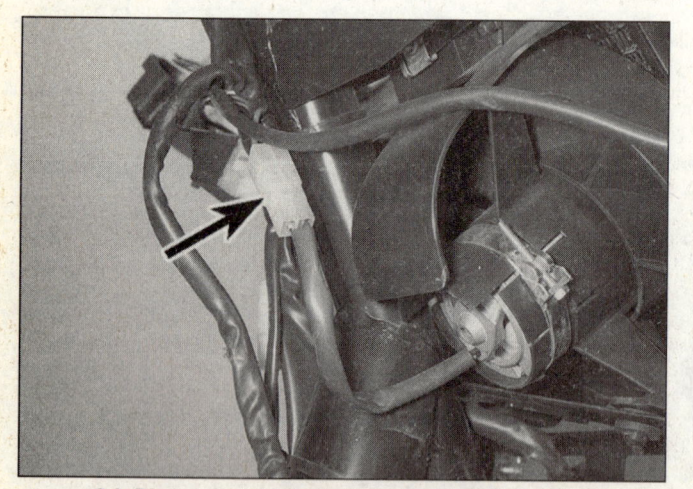

3.3 Disconnect the fan wiring connector (arrowed)

3.5 Fan assembly is secured by four screws (arrowed) – GT200 shown

Cooling system (liquid-cooled engines) 3•3

radiator **(see illustration)**. On GT125/200 models, the switch is located on the coolant union underneath the floor panel below the right-hand radiator **(see illustration)**. Using a jumper wire, connect the wiring connector terminals together. The fan should come on when the ignition is turned ON. If it does, the fan switch is confirmed faulty and must be renewed. If it does not come on, the fan should be tested (see Step 3).

10 If the fan is on the whole time, even when the engine is cold, disconnect the wiring connectors and keep them apart. The fan should stop. If it does, the fan switch is defective and must be renewed. If it keeps running, check the wiring between the switch and the fan motor for a short to earth.

Renewal

⚠️ **Warning: The engine must be completely cool before carrying out this procedure.**

11 Disconnect the battery negative (-ve) lead. Drain the cooling system (see Chapter 1).

12 Remove the front bodywork panels to access the fan switch (see Chapter 7). Disconnect the wiring connectors from the switch, then unscrew it and withdraw it from the radiator or coolant union, as applicable. Discard the seal, as a new one must be used.

13 Apply a suitable sealant to the switch threads, then install the switch using a new seal and tighten it securely. Take care not to overtighten the switch as the radiator could be damaged.

14 Reconnect the switch wiring and refill the cooling system (see Chapter 1). Reconnect the battery (-ve) lead.

4 Coolant temperature gauge/warning light and sender – check and renewal

Check

1 The circuit consists of the sender mounted on the cylinder head and the gauge assembly or coolant warning light (as applicable) mounted in the instrument panel. If the system malfunctions, check first that the battery is fully-charged and that the fuses are all good. In the case of models with a warning light check

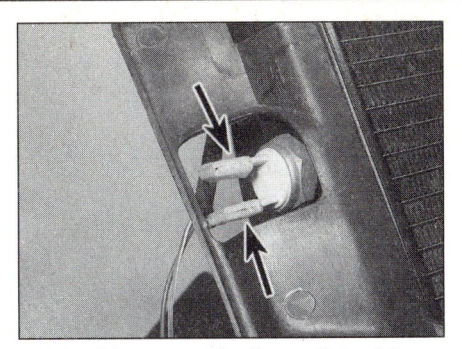

3.9a Disconnect the fan switch wiring connectors (arrowed)

that the bulb has not blown (see Chapter 9).

2 If the gauge is not working, or to test the warning light circuit, remove the access panel for the engine (see Chapter 7). Pull the rubber cover off the terminal and disconnect the wire from the sender, then turn the ignition switch ON **(see illustrations)**. The temperature gauge needle should be on the (C) on the gauge, or the bulb should be extinguished. Now earth the sender wire on the engine. The needle should swing immediately over to the (H) on the gauge or the bulb should illuminate. If the gauge or warning light operate as described above, the sender is proven defective and must be renewed.

Caution: Do not earth the wire for any longer than is necessary to take the reading, or the gauge may be damaged.

3 If the needle movement is still faulty, or if it does not move at all, the fault lies in the wiring or the gauge itself. Check all the relevant wiring and wiring connectors (see Chapter 9). If all appears to be well, the gauge is defective and must be renewed. If the bulb does not illuminate and has not blown, check the bulb wiring and wiring connectors.

Renewal

4 The temperature gauge is integral with the instrument cluster, for which individual instruments are not available. If the gauge is faulty, the entire cluster must be renewed (See Chapter 9). For warning light bulb renewal refer to Chapter 9.

⚠️ **Warning: The engine must be completely cool before carrying out this procedure.**

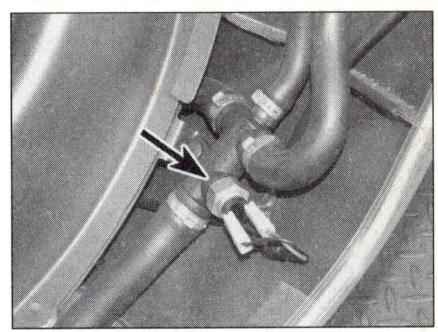

3.9b Location of the fan switch on GT125/200 models

5 To renew the sender, first drain the cooling system (see Chapter 1). Disconnect the battery negative (-ve) lead.

6 Disconnect the sender wiring connector **(see illustrations 4.2b)**. Unscrew the sender from the cylinder head.

7 Apply a smear of sealant to the threads of the new sender, then install it into the cylinder head and tighten it to the specified torque. Connect the sender wiring.

8 Refill the cooling system (see Chapter 1). Reconnect the battery negative (-ve) lead.

5 Thermostat – removal, check and installation

⚠️ **Warning: The engine must be completely cool before carrying out this procedure.**

Removal

1 The thermostat is automatic in operation and should give many years service without requiring attention. In the event of a failure, the valve will probably jam open, in which case the engine will take much longer than normal to warm-up. Conversely, if the valve jams shut, the coolant will be unable to circulate and the engine will overheat. Neither condition is acceptable, and the fault must be investigated promptly.

2 Remove the access panel to the engine (see Chapter 7) and drain the cooling system (see Chapter 1).

3 The thermostat is located in the cylinder head. Detach the hoses from the thermostat housing if required, though it is not necessary.

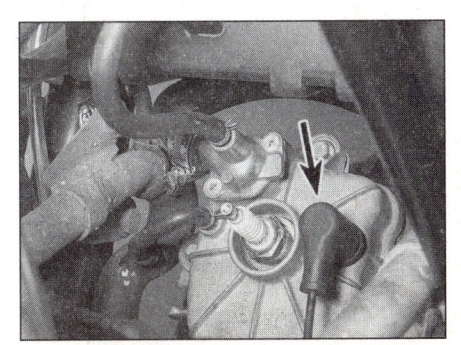

4.2a Lift off the rubber cover (arrowed) . . .

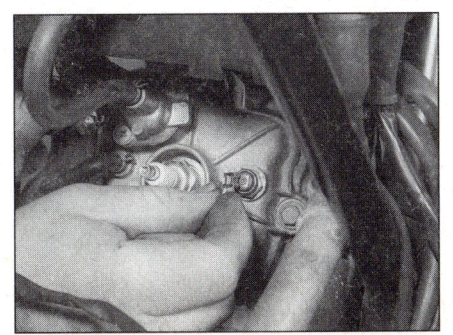

4.2b . . . and disconnect the wiring connector from the sender

4.2c Location of the sender (arrowed) on the LEADER cylinder head

3•4 Cooling system (liquid-cooled engines)

5.3a On two-stroke engines remove the screws (arrowed)

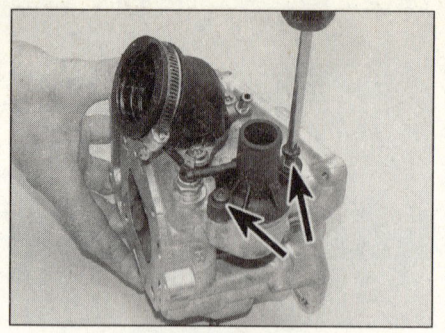

5.3b On LEADER engines remove the screws (arrowed)

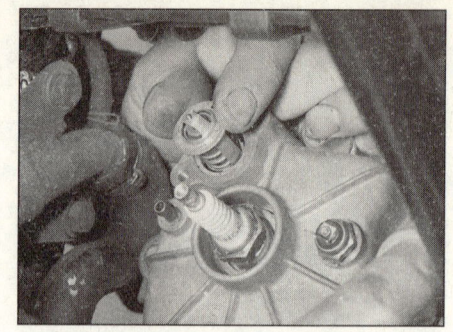

5.3c Removing the thermostat on two-stroke engines

5.3d Removing the thermostat on LEADER engines

5.5 Set-up for testing the thermostat

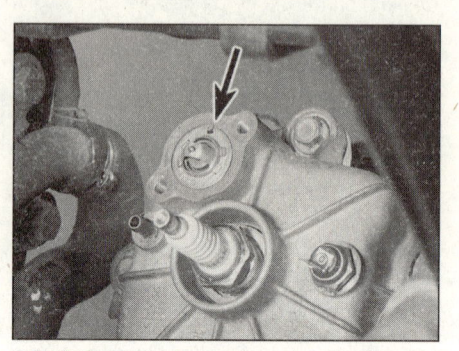

5.7 On two-stroke engines, locate the cut-out over the lug (arrowed)

Remove the two screws securing the housing and remove the housing **(see illustrations)**. Lift out the thermostat, noting how it fits **(see illustrations)**. Discard the cover O-ring, if fitted, as a new one must be used.

Check

4 Examine the thermostat visually before carrying out the test. If it remains in the open position at room temperature, it should be renewed.

5 Suspend the thermostat in a container of cold water. Place a thermometer capable of reading temperatures up to 100°C in the water so that the bulb is close to the thermostat **(see illustration)**. Heat the water, noting the temperature when the thermostat opens, and compare the result with the specifications given at the beginning of this Chapter. Also check the amount the valve opens after it has been heated at 80°C for a few minutes and compare the measurement to the specifications. If the readings obtained differ from those given, the thermostat is faulty and must be renewed.

6 In the event of the thermostat jamming closed, *as an emergency measure only*, it can be removed and the machine used without it. **Note:** *Take care when starting the engine from cold, as it will take much longer than usual to warm-up.* Ensure that a new unit is installed as soon as possible.

Installation

7 Fit the thermostat into the cylinder head. On two-stroke engines, locate the cut-out around the lug, making sure that the thermostat seats correctly **(see illustration)**.

8 If applicable, fit a new O-ring onto the housing, using a dab of grease to keep it in place if required **(see illustration)**.

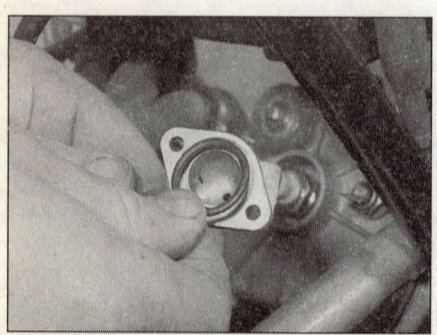

9 Fit the housing, then install the two screws and tighten them to the specified torque **(see illustrations 5.3a or 5.3b)**.

10 Refill the cooling system (see Chapter 1).

6 Radiator – removal and installation

⚠️ **Warning:** *The engine must be completely cool before carrying out this procedure.*

Removal

1 Disconnect the battery negative (-ve) lead. Remove the front bodywork panels (see Chapter 7) and drain the cooling system (see Chapter 1).

2 If applicable, disconnect the fan motor wiring connector and the wiring connectors from the fan switch in the radiator **(see illustrations 3.3 and 3.9a)**.

3 Slacken the clips securing the radiator hoses to the radiator and detach them from the radiator **(see illustration and Haynes hint)**. **Caution:** *The radiator unions are fragile. Do not use excessive force when attempting to remove the hoses.*

4 Remove the screws securing the radiator to the frame **(see illustration)**. Lift the radiator off; note that on some models, lugs on the bottom of the shroud or radiator body fit into grommets in the frame **(see illustration)**.

5 If necessary, separate the cooling fan from the radiator (see Section 3).

5.8 Fit a new O-ring into the groove in the housing

6.3 Release the clips and detach the hoses

Cooling system (liquid-cooled engines) 3•5

HAYNES HiNT

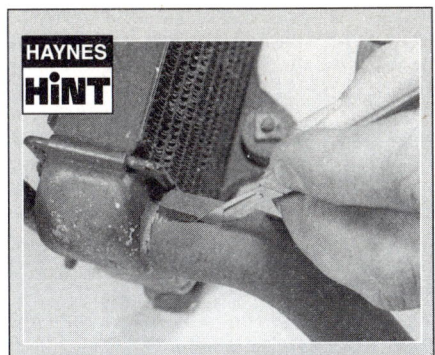

If a radiator hose is corroded in place on its union, slit it with a sharp knife and peel it off the union. A new hose will obviously be needed.

6 Check the radiator for signs of damage and clear any dirt or debris that might obstruct airflow and inhibit cooling (see Chapter 1, Section 9). If the radiator fins are badly damaged or broken the radiator must be renewed. Also check the rubber mounting grommets, and renew them if necessary.

Installation

7 Installation is the reverse of removal, noting the following.
 a) Make sure the locating lugs fit correctly into the rubber grommets.
 b) Make sure that the fan wiring is correctly connected.
 c) Ensure the coolant hoses are in good condition (see Chapter 1, Section 9), and are securely retained by their clips; fit new clips if necessary.
 d) On completion refill the cooling system as described in Chapter 1.
 e) Reconnect the battery negative (-ve) lead.

7 Water pump – check, removal and installation

Non-LEADER engines
Check

1 The water pump is located within the crankcase. The pump is driven by a shaft which is driven by the oil pump.

6.4a Remove the screw securing the assembly to the frame

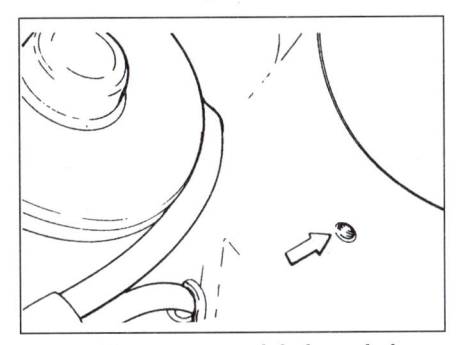

7.2 Water pump seal drainage hole (arrowed) in crankcase left-hand half

2 A seal prevents leakage of coolant from the pump housing into the crankcase. A drainage hole on the left-hand crankcase half drains any coolant should the seal fail. If the drainage hole shows signs of leakage, the pump shaft must be removed and the seal renewed **(see illustration)**.

Removal

Note: *If the crankcase halves are being separated, the water pump assembly can be removed afterwards (see Chapter 2B).*

3 Drain the coolant (see Chapter 1) and remove the alternator cover (see Chapter 2B).
4 Remove the screw or screws securing the coolant pipe bracket and pull the pipe out of its bore in the right-hand crankcase half, below the alternator **(see illustration)**. Discard the pipe O-ring as a new one must be used.
5 Remove the oil pump and its drivebelt and driven pulley (see Chapter 2B).
6 Remove the water pump driveshaft star clip

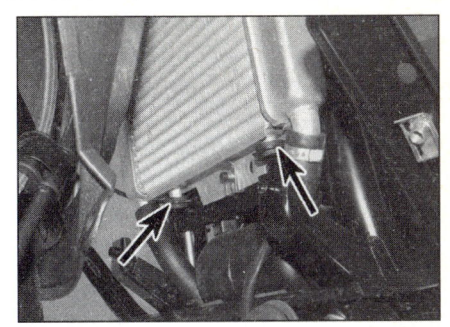

6.4b Radiator is supported in rubber grommets – X8 shown

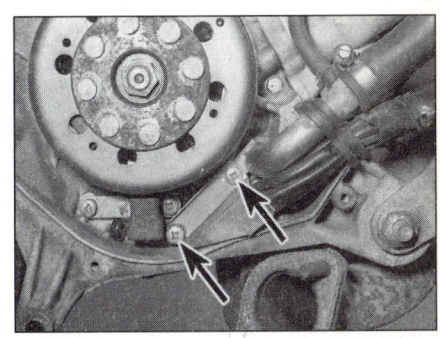

7.4 Remove the screws (arrowed) and pull the coolant pipe out of its bore

and discard it, as a new one must be used, then remove the washer from behind the star clip **(see illustration 7.9)**.
7 Locate an 8 mm socket wrench through the water pipe bore in the right-hand crankcase half and locate it on the hexagon in the centre of the pump impeller. Hold the left-hand end of the pump shaft to prevent it turning, then unscrew the impeller, noting that it has a **left-hand thread** and must therefore be unscrewed in a clockwise direction **(see illustration)**. Draw the shaft, complete with its bearings, out of the crankcase. Check the condition of the bearings on the shaft. If they do not run smoothly and freely the shaft must be renewed as the bearings are not available individually. The new shaft will be supplied with the bearings already in place **(see illustration)**.
8 Using an expanding bearing/seal puller and slide-hammer attachment, remove the water pump seal and discard it **(see illustration)**.

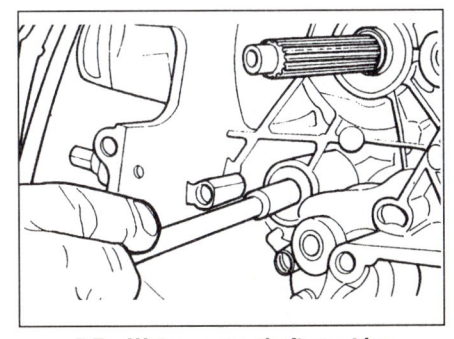

7.7a Water pump shaft must be unscrewed clockwise

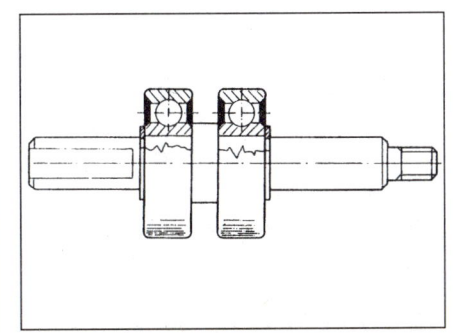

7.7b Cross-section of water pump shaft complete with bearings

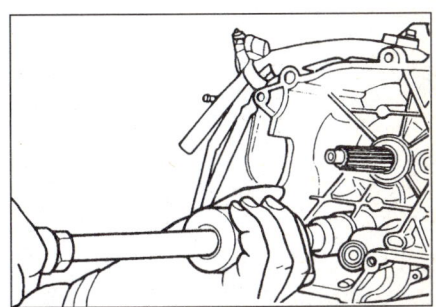

7.8 Use a slide-hammer with internally-expanding attachment to extract the water pump seal

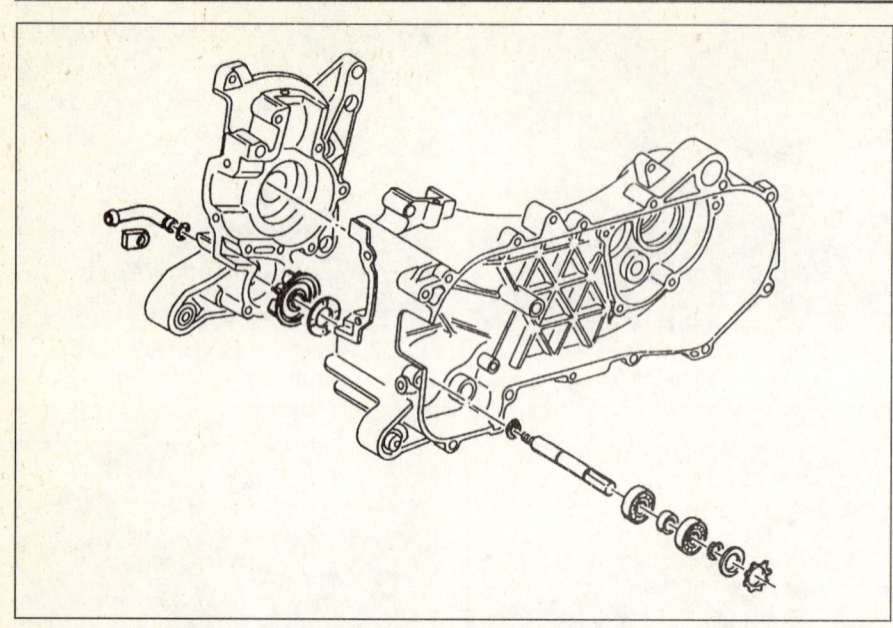

3•6 Cooling system (liquid-cooled engines)

7.9 Water pump assembly for liquid-cooled two-stroke engines

9 To remove the water pump impeller, the crankcase halves must be separated (see Chapter 2B). The impeller can then be lifted out of its housing **(see illustration)**.

Installation

10 If the crankcases have been split, install the water pump assembly before joining the crankcase halves (see Chapter 2B).

11 If the crankcases have not been disassembled, first ensure the seal housing is clean, then oil the seal and fit it into the housing, making sure it fits squarely. Use a drift which bears on the outer edge of the seal to drive it into the crankcase; ensure that the drainage hole in the crankcase remains uncovered.

12 Press the pump shaft and bearings into the crankcase. Support the impeller with the 8 mm socket as on removal and locate the impeller onto the end of the shaft. Hold the shaft to prevent it turning and thread on the impeller, not forgetting that it has a **left-hand thread** and must therefore be tightened anti-clockwise.

13 Fit the washer onto the end of the shaft, then fit a new star clip.

14 Install the oil pump and its drivebelt and gear (see Chapter 2B).

15 Fit a new O-ring onto the water pipe and fit it into its bore, then fit the bracket screw(s) **(see illustration 7.4)**.

16 Fit the alternator cover and refill the cooling system (see Chapter 1).

LEADER engines

Check

17 The water pump is located on the alternator cover **(see illustration)**. The pump is driven via dampers on the alternator rotor **(see illustration 7.29)**.

18 The pump body to alternator cover joint is sealed by an O-ring. A ceramic seal and rubber gasket in the alternator cover prevents coolant leaking down the pump impeller shaft into the cover. A hole in the bottom of the cover drains any coolant should the seal fail. If the drainage hole shows signs of leakage, the pump impeller must be removed and the seal renewed.

Removal

19 Drain the cooling system and disconnect the coolant hoses from the water pump (see Chapter 1). Undo the screws securing the pump body and lift it off; discard the O-ring, as a new one must be used **(see illustrations)**.

20 Remove the alternator cover (see Chapter 2F).

21 The impeller is a press-fit in the pump bearings **(see illustration)**. The remove the impeller, support the alternator cover upside down on the work surface with sufficient clearance below it to allow the impeller to be driven out **(see illustration)**. **Note:** *Take great care not to damage the sealing surface of the*

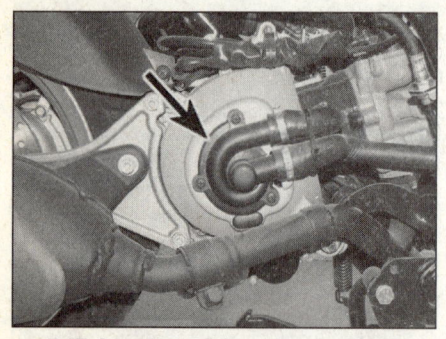

7.17 Location of the water pump on LEADER engines

7.19a Note how the O-ring locates in the pump body

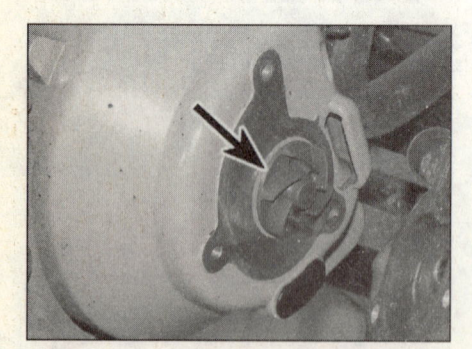

7.19b Pump impeller (arrowed) is located in the alternator cover

7.21a Location of the pump impeller shaft (arrowed)

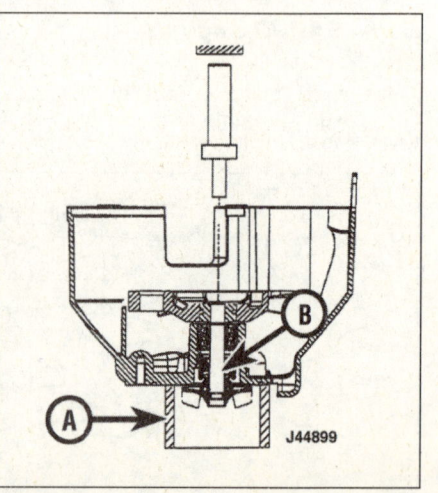

7.21b Place a suitable support (A) under the cover to drive out the impeller (B)

Cooling system (liquid-cooled engines) 3•7

alternator cover. Use a soft drift (preferably aluminium or brass) to carefully drive the impeller out.

22 Turn the cover over and carefully lever out the seal **(see illustration)**. Take care not to damage the edge of the seal housing. Lift out the rubber gasket. **Note:** *Once the seal and gasket are removed new ones must be fitted; do not re-use the old seal and gasket.*

23 Check the condition of the two bearings in the alternator cover. If they do not run smoothly they must be renewed. Note the position of the bearings; the innermost bearing is fitted flush with the inside lip of the bearing housing in the cover. Support the cover so that it is level, then use a suitable drift to drive the bearings out **(see illustration)**. If the bearings are a tight fit, heat the housing inside the cover with a hot air gun. **Note:** *Heat the cover gently to avoid damaging the paint finish.*

24 Ensure the bearing housing is clean and free from corrosion, then heat the housing again to aid fitting the new bearings. Install the bearings from the inside of the cover and ensure that the first (outermost) bearing fits against its seat before driving in the second bearing with a suitable socket or bearing driver.

25 Check the impeller for wear and damage. If the shaft is corroded, fit a new impeller.

Installation

26 Lubricate the new gasket and ceramic seal with anti-freeze and press them carefully into place with a suitably-sized socket.

27 To prevent the bearings being displaced when the impeller is fitted, support them from the inside of the cover, leaving sufficient space for the impeller shaft when it is installed. Carefully press the impeller shaft into the bearings from the outside. Ensure the impeller turns freely once fitted.

28 Fit a new O-ring into the groove in the pump body, then install the pump body and tighten the screws to the specified torque setting.

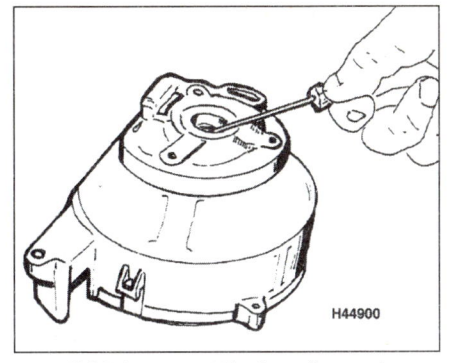

29 Align the dampers on the alternator rotor with the pump drive and install the alternator cover **(see illustration)**.

30 Refill the cooling system (see Chapter 1).

8 Coolant hoses – removal and installation

Removal

1 Before removing a hose, drain the coolant (see Chapter 1).

2 Release or slacken the hose clips, either with a screwdriver or pliers depending upon the design of the clip, then slide them back along the hose and clear of the union spigot **(see illustrations)**. **Note:** *Some clips cannot be re-used – check before removing a coolant hose and be prepared to fit new clips of the correct size.*

3 Pull the hose off its union. If a hose proves stubborn, release it by rotating it on its union before working it off. If all else fails, slit the hose with a sharp knife at each union (see *Haynes hint* in Section 6).

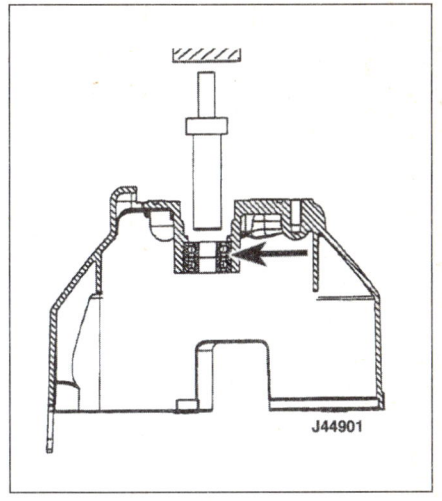

Caution: *The radiator unions are fragile. Do not use excessive force when attempting to remove the hoses.*

Installation

4 Slide the clips onto the hose and then work it on to its respective unions.

> **HAYNES HINT** *If the hose is difficult to push on its union, it can be softened by soaking it in very hot water, or alternatively a little soapy water can be used as a lubricant.*

5 Rotate the hose on its unions to settle it in position before sliding the clips into place and tightening them securely.

7.22 Lever out the impeller seal

7.23 Location of the water pump bearings (arrowed)

7.29 Align the pump drive dampers (arrowed)

8.2a Release the clip with a screwdriver ...

8.2b ... or with pliers as required

Chapter 4
Fuel and exhaust systems

Refer to the beginning of Chapter 1 for model identification details

Contents

Air filter cleaning . . . . see Chapter 1	Fuel tap and filter – check, removal and installation 2
Air filter housing – removal and installation 3	General information and precautions 1
Carburettor overhaul – general information 5	Idle fuel/air mixture adjustment – general information 4
Carburettor – (two-stroke engines) – overhaul 7	Idle speed – check . . . . see Chapter 1
Carburettor – (four-stroke engines) – overhaul 8	Oil pump and drivebelt – removal, installation and
Carburettor – removal and installation 6	bleeding . . . . see Chapter 2A
Catalytic converter 12	Reed valve (two-stroke engines) – removal, inspection
Exhaust system – removal and installation 11	and installation 9
Fuel pump – check and renewal 13	Throttle cable and oil pump – check and adjustment . . . see Chapter 1
Fuel system – check . . . . see Chapter 1	Throttle cable – removal and installation 10

Degrees of difficulty

Easy, suitable for novice with little experience	**Fairly easy,** suitable for beginner with some experience	**Fairly difficult,** suitable for competent DIY mechanic	**Difficult,** suitable for experienced DIY mechanic	**Very difficult,** suitable for expert DIY or professional

Specifications

Fuel
Fuel type and tank capacity . . . . see Chapter 1

Automatic choke
Resistance @ 20°C
    Walbro carburettor . . . . 30 to 40 ohms
    Keihin carburettor (Fly 125, LX4 125 and GT125/200 models) . . . . . . 20 ohms
    All others . . . . 30 to 40 ohms
Plunger protrusion
    Walbro carburettor
        Initial @ 20°C . . . . 12.5 to 13.0 mm
        Final (after 5 minutes constant power) . . . . 18.5 to 19.0 mm
    Keihin carburettor (Fly 125 and LX4 125 models) . . . . 10.0 mm
    All others
         Initial @ 22°C . . . . 10.9 to 11.5 mm
        Final (after 5 minutes constant power) . . . . 14.0 to 15.0 mm

Sfera 50 with Dell'Orto carburettor
Type/ID no. . . . . Dell'Orto PHVA 12
Pilot screw setting (turns out)
    With 0.8 mm thread pitch . . . . 2 to 2 1/4 turns out
    With 0.5 mm thread pitch . . . . 3 1/2 to 4 turns out
Fuel level . . . . 5 mm (not adjustable)
Idle speed . . . . see Chapter 1
Starter jet 50
Pilot jet 34
Main jet 56
Needle (clip position) . . . . SA2 (3rd notch from top)

Sfera 50 (RST model) with Dell'Orto carburettor
Type/ID no. .... Dell'Orto PHVA 12
Pilot screw setting (turns out) .... not available
Fuel level .... 5 mm (not adjustable)
Idle speed .... see Chapter 1
Starter jet 60
Pilot jet 36
Main jet 70
Needle (clip position) .... A12 (2nd notch from top)

Sfera 50 (RST model) with Weber carburettor
Type/ID no. .... Weber 12 OM
Pilot screw setting (turns out) .... not available
Fuel level .... 3.5 mm (not adjustable)
Idle speed .... see Chapter 1
Starter jet 50
Pilot jet 34
Main jet 78
Needle (clip position) .... F (3rd notch from top)

Sfera 80 with Dell'Orto carburettor
Type/ID no. .... Dell'Orto PHVA 17.5
Pilot screw setting (turns out) .... not available
Fuel level .... 5 mm (not adjustable)
Idle speed .... see Chapter 1
Starter jet 50
Pilot jet 34
Main jet 65
Needle (clip position) .... A7 (3rd notch from top)

Sfera 125 with Mikuni carburettor
Type/ID no. .... Mikuni BS24-1J
Pilot screw setting (turns out) .... not available
Float height .... 12.2 mm
Idle speed .... see Chapter 1
Starter jet 40
Pilot jet 20
Main jet 87.5
Needle (clip position) .... 4CZ6 (3rd notch from top)

Typhoon 50 with Dell'Orto carburettor
Type/ID no. .... Dell'Orto PHVA 12
Pilot screw setting (turns out) .... not available
Fuel level .... 5 mm (not adjustable)
Idle speed .... see Chapter 1
Starter jet 60
Pilot jet 36
Main jet 70
Needle (clip position) .... A12 (2nd notch from top)

Typhoon 80 with Dell'Orto carburettor
Type/ID no. .... Dell'Orto PHVA 17.5
Pilot screw setting (turns out) 4 1/2
Fuel level .... 5 mm (not adjustable)
Idle speed .... see Chapter 1
Starter jet 60
Pilot jet 34
Main jet 62
Needle (clip position) .... A7 (4th notch from top)

Typhoon 125 with Mikuni carburettor
Type/ID no. .... Mikuni VM 20-325
Pilot screw setting (turns out) 1 3/8
Fuel level .... 3.5 ± 0.5 mm
Idle speed .... see Chapter 1
Starter jet 40
Pilot jet 35
Main jet 82.5
Needle (clip position) .... 3CK01 (3rd notch from top)

Fuel and exhaust systems

Zip and early Zip RST with Dell'Orto carburettor
Type/ID no.	Dell'Orto PHVA 12 DD
Pilot screw setting (turns out)	not available
Fuel level	5 mm (not adjustable)
Idle speed	see Chapter 1
Starter jet	60
Pilot jet	38
Main jet	70 (Zip), 72 (Zip RST)
Needle (clip position)	A15 (2nd notch from top)

Later Zip RST with Dell'Orto carburettor
Type/ID no.	Dell'Orto PHVA 12 DD
Pilot screw setting (turns out)	not available
Fuel level	5 mm (not adjustable)
Idle speed	see Chapter 1
Starter jet	60
Pilot jet	35
Main jet	72
Needle (clip position)	A29 (3rd notch from top)

Zip SP with Dell'Orto carburettor
Type/ID no.	Dell'Orto PHV12 QD
Pilot screw setting (turns out)	not available
Fuel level	5 mm (not adjustable)
Idle speed	see Chapter 1
Starter jet	50
Pilot jet	34
Main jet	75
Needle (clip position)	SA2 (3rd notch from top)

Zip 50 with Dell'Orto carburettor
Type/ID no.	Dell'Orto PHVA 17.5 RD
Pilot screw setting (turns out)	1 1/2
Fuel level	5 mm (not adjustable)
Idle speed	see Chapter 1
Starter jet	50
Pilot jet	32
Main jet	56
Needle (clip position)	A22 (1st notch from top)

ET4 50, Liberty 50 4T and Zip 50 4T with Keihin carburettor
Type/ID no.	Keihin CVK 18
Pilot screw setting (turns out)	not available
Float height	not available
Idle speed	see Chapter 1
Starter jet	42
Pilot jet	35
Main jet	75
Needle (clip position)	NACA (not adjustable)

Skipper with Dell'Orto carburettor
Type/ID no.	Dell'Orto PHVB 20.5
Pilot screw setting (turns out)	2 to 2 1/4
Fuel level	5.0 ± 0.5 mm
Idle speed	see Chapter 1
Starter jet	60
Pilot jet	45
Main jet	86
Needle (clip position)	M6 (2nd notch from top)

Skipper with Mikuni carburettor
Type/ID no.	Mikuni VM 20
Pilot screw setting (turns out)	1 3/8
Fuel level	3.5 ± 0.5 mm
Idle speed	see Chapter 1
Starter jet	50
Pilot jet	35
Main jet	82.5
Needle (clip position)	3CK01 (3rd notch from top)

Skipper ST125 and Zip 125 with Walbro carburettor
Type/ID no.	Walbro WVF/6A
Pilot screw setting (turns out)	not available
Float height	see Section 8
Idle speed	see Chapter 1
Starter jet	48
Pilot jet	34
Main jet	82
Needle (clip position)	52K (2nd/3rd notch from top)

NRG MC² with Dell'Orto carburettor
Type/ID no.	Dell'Orto PHVA 12DD
Pilot screw setting (turns out)	not available
Fuel level	5 mm (not adjustable)
Idle speed	see Chapter 1
Starter jet	60
Pilot jet	38
Main jet	66
Needle (clip position)	A15 (2nd notch from top)

NRG MC³ DT and DD, NRG Power DT and DD, Fly 50 and LX2 50 with Dell'Orto carburettor
Type/ID no.	Dell'Orto PHVA 17.5RD
Pilot screw setting (turns out)	1 1/2
Fuel level	5 mm (not adjustable)
Idle speed	see Chapter 1
Starter jet	50
Pilot jet	32
Main jet	53
Needle (clip position)	A22 (1st notch from top)

Zip RST, Zip SP and NRG MC² with Weber carburettor
Type/ID no.	Weber 12 OM
Pilot screw setting (turns out)	not available
Fuel level	3.5 mm (not adjustable)
Idle speed	see Chapter 1
Starter jet	50
Pilot jet	34
Main jet	75
Needle (clip position)	S (3rd notch from top)

Hexagon with Mikuni carburettor
Type/ID no.	Mikuni VM 20-315
Pilot screw setting (turns out)	1 3/8
Fuel level	3.5 ± 0.5 mm
Idle speed	see Chapter 1
Starter jet	40
Pilot jet	35
Main jet	82.5
Needle (clip position)	3CK01 (3rd notch from top)

Super Hexagon with Walbro carburettor
Type/ID no.	Walbro WVF/7A
Pilot screw setting (turns out)	3
Float height	see Section 8
Idle speed	see Chapter 1
Starter jet	50
Pilot jet	34
Main jet	108
Needle (clip position)	51c (2nd notch from top)

Liberty 50 with Weber carburettor
Type/ID no.	Weber 12 OM
Pilot screw setting (turns out)	not available
Fuel level	3.5 mm (not adjustable)
Idle speed	see Chapter 1
Starter jet	50
Pilot jet	38 L
Main jet	63
Needle (clip position)	V (2nd notch from top)

Fuel and exhaust systems

Liberty 125 with Walbro carburettor
Type/ID no.	Walbro WVF/6B
Pilot screw setting (turns out)	not available
Float height	see Section 8
Idle speed	see Chapter 1
Starter jet	48
Pilot jet	33
Main jet	84
Needle (clip position)	52K (2nd/3rd notch from top)

ET2 with Weber carburettor
Type/ID no.	Weber 12 OM
Pilot screw setting (turns out)	2 1/2 to 3 1/2
Fuel level	3.5 mm (not adjustable)
Idle speed	see Chapter 1
Starter jet	50
Pilot jet	34
Main jet	76
Needle (clip position)	V (2nd notch from top)

Fly 50 4T and LX4 50 with Keihin carburettor
Type/ID no.	Keihin CVK 18
Pilot screw setting (turns out)	1 3/4
Float height	not available
Idle speed	see Chapter 1
Starter jet	40
Pilot jet	35
Main jet	75
Needle	NGBA

ET4 125 with Mikuni carburettor
Type/ID no.	Mikuni BS24-J
Pilot screw setting (turns out)	not available
Float height	12.2 mm
Idle speed	see Chapter 1
Starter jet	35
Pilot jet	20
Main jet	87.5
Needle (clip position)	4CZ6 (2nd notch from top)

Fly 125 and LX4 125 with Keihin carburettor
Type/ID no.	Keihin CVEK 26
Pilot screw setting (turns out)	1 3/4
Float height	not available
Idle speed	see Chapter 1
Starter jet	42
Pilot jet	35
Main jet	82
Needle	NELA

X8 125 and GT125 with Walbro carburettor
Type/ID no.	Walbro WVF/7R
Pilot screw setting (turns out)	2 7/8
Float height	see Section 8
Idle speed	see Chapter 1
Starter jet	48
Pilot jet	38
Main jet	103
Needle (clip position)	653 (2nd notch from top)

X9 125 with Walbro carburettor
Type/ID no.	Walbro WVF/7C
Pilot screw setting (turns out)	not available
Float height	see Section 8
Idle speed	see Chapter 1
Starter jet	50
Pilot jet	36
Main jet	110
Needle (clip position)	51C (2nd notch from top)

B125 with Walbro carburettor

Type/ID no.	Walbro WVF/7G
Pilot screw setting (turns out)	2 5/8
Float height	see text
Idle speed	see Chapter 1
Starter jet	50
Pilot jet	36
Main jet	108
Needle (clip position)	51c (2nd notch from top)

GT125 with Keihin carburettor

Type/ID no.	Keihin CVEK 30
Pilot screw setting (turns out)	2
Float height	not available
Idle speed	see Chapter 1
Starter jet	42
Pilot jet	38
Main jet	98
Needle	NDVA

GT200 with Keihin carburettor

Type/ID no.	Keihin CVEK 30
Pilot screw setting (turns out)	2 1/4
Float height	not available
Idle speed	see Chapter 1
Starter jet	42
Pilot jet	38
Main jet	92
Needle	NDAA

GT200 with Walbro carburettor

Type/ID no.	Walbro WVF/7P
Pilot screw setting (turns out)	2
Float height	see Section 8
Idle speed	see Chapter 1
Starter jet	45
Pilot jet	36
Main jet	95
Needle (clip position)	495 (2nd notch from top)

1 General information and precautions

The fuel system consists of the fuel tank, fuel tap with filter, carburettor, fuel hoses and control cables. Due to the position of the fuel tank, Hexagon, B125, X8 125, X9 125 and Power DT and DD models have a fuel pump. GT 125/200 models are also equipped with fuel pumps.

The fuel tap is automatic in operation and is opened by engine vacuum. The fuel filter is fitted inside the fuel tank and is part of the tap. On some models, an additional fuel filter is fitted in the fuel line.

Typhoon 80 and 125 models have two fuel tanks; the main tank is located beneath the rear bodywork and an auxiliary tank is located behind the fairing. A balance pipe links the two fuel tanks, and a vacuum-operated pump located under the footboard pumps fuel from the auxiliary tank to the main fuel tank.

For cold starting, an electrically-operated automatic choke is fitted in the carburettor. Some models also have an electrically-operated carburettor heater.

Air is drawn into the carburettors via an air filter which is housed above the transmission casing.

The exhaust system is a two-piece design.

Many of the fuel system service procedures are considered routine maintenance items and for that reason are included in Chapter 1.

Precautions

Warning: *Petrol is extremely flammable, so take extra precautions when you work on any part of the fuel system. Don't smoke or allow open flames or bare light bulbs near the work area, and don't work in a garage where a natural gas-type appliance is present. If you spill any fuel on your skin, rinse it off immediately with soap and water. When you perform any kind of work on the fuel system, wear safety glasses and have a fire extinguisher suitable for a class B type fire (flammable liquids) on hand.*

- Always perform service procedures in a well-ventilated area to prevent a build-up of fumes.
- Never work in a building containing a gas appliance with a pilot light, or any other form of naked flame. Ensure that there are no naked light bulbs or any sources of flame or sparks nearby.
- Do not smoke (or allow anyone else to smoke) while in the vicinity of petrol or of components containing it. Remember the possible presence of vapour from these sources and move well clear before smoking.
- Check all electrical equipment belonging to the house, garage or workshop where work is being undertaken (see the *Safety first!* section of this manual). Remember that certain electrical appliances such as drills, cutters, etc, create sparks in the normal course of operation and must not be used near petrol or any component containing it. Again, remember the possible presence of fumes before using electrical equipment.
- Always mop-up any spilt fuel and safely dispose of the rag used.
- Any stored fuel that is drained off during servicing work must be kept in sealed containers that are suitable for holding petrol, and clearly marked as such; the containers themselves should be kept in a safe place.
- Read the *Safety first!* section of this manual carefully before starting work.

Fuel and exhaust systems 4•7

2 Fuel tap and filter – check, removal and installation

Hexagon, B125, X8 125, X9 125 and NRG Power DT and DD models

1 These models do not have a separate fuel tap – instead the fuel pump acts as a tap, only allowing fuel to flow when the engine is turning over. Some models are fitted with a non-return valve which prevents fuel draining back into the tank when the engine is not running (see illustration). See Section 13 for fuel pump check and renewal.

2 On Hexagon, X9, X8 and B125 models, the fuel filter is fitted in the fuel line and is secured by two clips (see illustration). Remove any body panels as required by your model and trace the fuel hose from the carburettor to the filter (see Chapter 7). Note that on some machines, a filter element is also fitted to the outlet union inside the fuel tank (see illustration 2.8).

3 Check the filter for signs of sediment or a clogged element. The filter is a sealed unit – if it is dirty or clogged, fit a new one.

4 To remove the filter, loosen the clips securing the fuel hoses to each end, being prepared to catch any residual fuel, and detach the hoses. Withdraw the filter from its clamp, noting which way up it fits.

5 Install the new filter in its clamp, making sure it is the correct way up – there should be an arrow marked on the body denoting direction of fuel flow. Attach the fuel hoses and secure them with the clips. If the old clips are corroded or deformed, fit new ones (see illustration 2.2).

6 On NRG Power DT and DD models, the fuel filter is integral with the outlet union on the fuel tank – remove any body panels as required to access the tank (see Chapter 7).

7 Before removing the union, disconnect the fuel supply hose from the tank to the fuel pump at the fuel pump and insert its end in a container suitable and large enough for storing the petrol (see illustration). Allow the tank to drain.

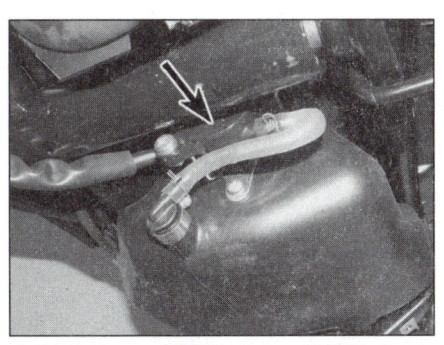

8 Slacken the clamp securing the union and

2.1 Location of non-return valve – X8 125 shown

2.2 The fuel filter (arrowed) is secured by two hose clips

2.7 Disconnect the fuel supply hose from the pump (arrowed)

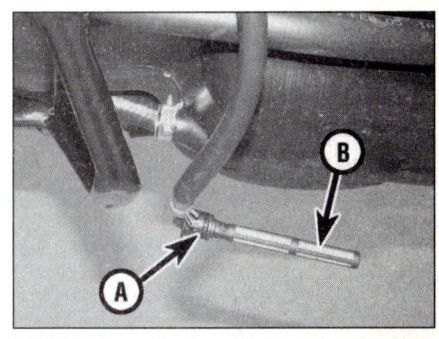

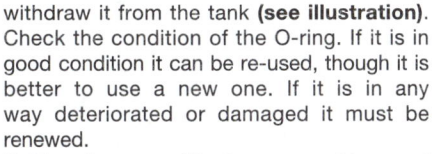

2.8 Withdraw the hose union from the tank – note the O-ring (A) and filter gauze (B)

withdraw it from the tank (see illustration). Check the condition of the O-ring. If it is in good condition it can be re-used, though it is better to use a new one. If it is in any way deteriorated or damaged it must be renewed.

9 Clean the gauze filter to remove all traces of dirt and fuel sediment. Check the gauze for holes. If any are found, a new union should be fitted as the filter is not available individually.

10 Install the union into the tank, preferably using a new O-ring, and tighten the clamp securely. Connect the fuel supply hose and secure it with the clips – if the old clips are corroded or deformed, fit new ones.

All other models – fuel tap

Check

11 The fuel tap is located on the underside of the fuel tank (see illustration 2.15). Remove any body panels as required by your model for access (see Chapter 7). The tap is automatic, operated by a vacuum created when the engine is running which opens a diaphragm inside the tap. If the tap is faulty, it must be renewed – it is a sealed unit for which no individual components are available. The most likely problem is a hole or split in the tap diaphragm.

12 To check the tap, detach the fuel hose from the carburettor and place the open end in a small container (see illustration). Detach the vacuum hose from the intake manifold or carburettor, according to model (see illustrations), and apply a vacuum to it (suck on the pipe end) – if you are not sure which hose is which on your model, trace the hoses from the tap (see illustration 2.15). Fuel should flow from the tap and into the

2.12a Detach the fuel hose from the carburettor

2.12b Detach the vacuum hose from the intake manifold . . .

2.12c . . . or from the carburettor, as applicable

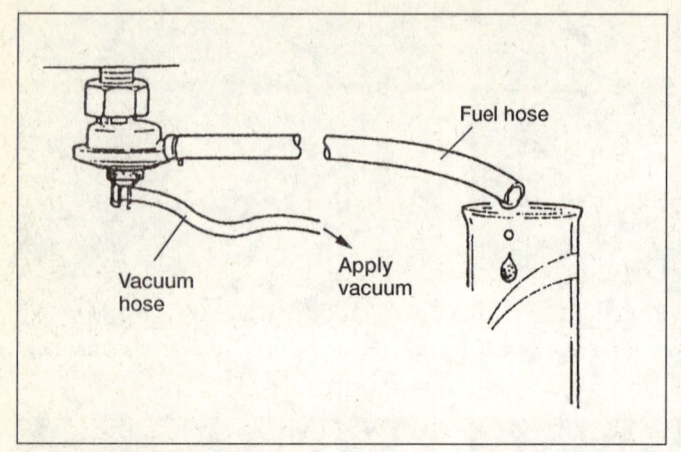

4•8 Fuel and exhaust systems

2.12d Place the fuel hose in a container and apply suction to the vacuum hose

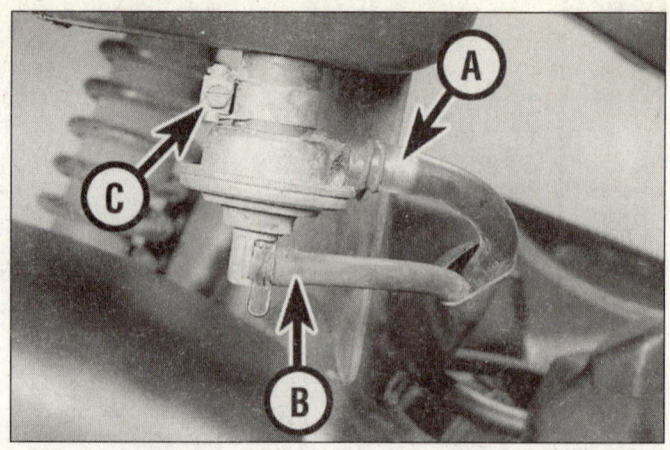

2.15 Fuel hose (A), vacuum hose (B), tap retaining clamp (C)

container – if it doesn't, the diaphragm is probably split **(see illustration)**.
13 Before renewing the tap, check that the vacuum hose is securely attached, and that there are no splits or cracks in the hose. If in doubt, attach a spare hose to the vacuum union on the tap and again apply a vacuum. If fuel still does not flow, remove the tap and fit a new one.

Removal

14 The tap should not be removed unnecessarily from the tank otherwise the O-ring or filter may be damaged.

15 Before removing the tap, connect a drain hose to the fuel hose union and insert its end in a container suitable and large enough for storing the petrol **(see illustration)**. Detach the vacuum hose from the intake manifold and apply a vacuum to it, and allow the tank to drain.
16 Slacken the clamp securing the tap and withdraw the tap assembly **(see illustration)**. Check the condition of the O-ring. If it is in good condition it can be re-used, though it is better to use a new one. If it is in any way deteriorated or damaged it must be renewed.
17 Clean the gauze filter to remove all traces of dirt and fuel sediment. Check the gauze for

holes. If any are found, a new tap should be fitted as the filter is not available individually.

Installation

18 Install the fuel tap into the tank, preferably using a new O-ring, and tighten the clamp securely.
19 Fit the fuel and vacuum hoses onto their respective unions and secure them with their clips.

GT125 and GT200 models – fuel filter

Check

20 In addition to the filter in the fuel tap (see Step 17) a filter is fitted in the fuel line between the fuel pump and the carburettor. To access the filter, first remove the right-hand side panel (see Chapter 7).
21 Release the clip securing the fuel hose to the fuel tap and disconnect the hose, being prepared to catch any residual fuel **(see illustration)**. Remove the two screws securing the fuel pump to the underside of the fuel tank and displace the pump – the fuel filter is attached to a bracket retained by the screws **(see illustration)**.
22 Check the filter for signs of sediment or a clogged element. The filter is a sealed unit – if it is dirty or clogged, fit a new one.
23 To remove the filter, loosen the clips securing the fuel hoses to each end and detach the hoses **(see illustration)**. Withdraw the filter from its clamp, noting which way up it fits.
24 Install the new filter in its clamp, making sure it is the correct way up – there should be an arrow marked on the body denoting direction of fuel flow. Attach the fuel hoses and secure them with the clips. If the old clips are corroded or deformed, fit new ones.
25 Align the filter bracket and fuel pump with the mounting on the underside of the fuel tank, then connect the hose to the tap and secure it with the clip. Install the fuel pump mounting screws and tighten them securely.

2.16 Withdraw the fuel tap and filter from the tank

2.21a Disconnect the fuel hose (arrowed) from the tap

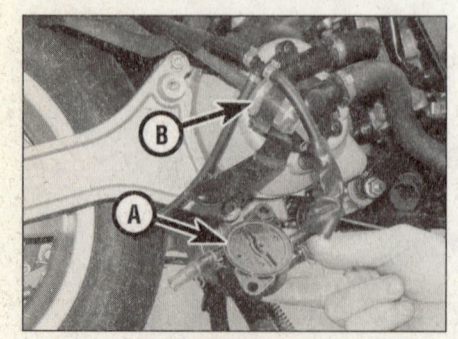

2.21b Displace the fuel pump (A) and in-line filter (B)

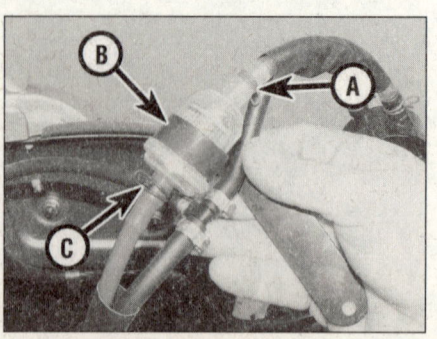

2.23 Fuel filter is secured by hose clips (A) and clamp (B)

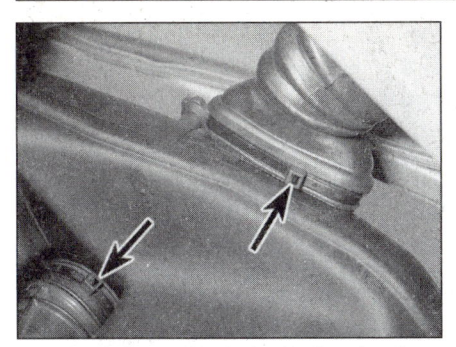

Fuel and exhaust systems 4•9

3.1a Release the ties securing the air ducts (arrowed)...

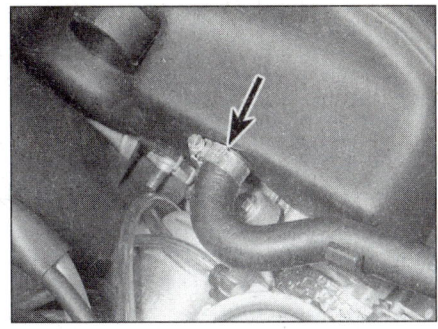

3.1b ...and the clamp securing the breather hose (arrowed), where fitted...

3 Air filter housing – removal and installation

Removal

1 Where applicable, remove the bodywork to access the filter housing, which is located above the drivebelt cover on the left-hand side of the scooter. Release the clips or cut the plastic ties securing the air inlet and outlet ducts and, where fitted, the breather hose, and detach them from the housing **(see illustrations)**. Where applicable, release the idle speed adjuster from its clip on the front of the housing.

2 Remove the bolts securing the air filter housing to the engine and manoeuvre the housing away, noting how it fits **(see illustrations)**.

Installation

3 Installation is the reverse of removal. Use new plastic cable ties to secure the air inlet and outlet ducts where the originals were cut free.

4 Idle fuel/air mixture adjustment – general information

⚠ **Warning: Adjustment of the pilot screw is made with the engine running. To prevent accidents** caused by the rear wheel contacting the ground, ensure that the scooter is on its centre stand and if necessary place a support under the scooter to prevent the rear wheel contacting the ground.

1 Idle fuel/air mixture is set using the pilot screw **(see illustration 7.1 or 8.1)**. Adjustment of the pilot screw is not normally necessary and should only be performed if the engine is running roughly, stalls continually, or if a new pilot screw has been fitted.

2 If the pilot screw is removed during a carburettor overhaul, record its current setting by turning the screw it in until it seats lightly, counting the number of turns necessary to achieve this, then unscrew it fully. On installation, turn the screw in until it seats lightly, then back it out the number of turns you've recorded. If fitting a new pilot screw, turn the screw in until it seats, then back it out the number of turns specified at the beginning of the Chapter.

3 Pilot screw adjustment must be made with the engine running and at normal working temperature. Stop the engine and screw the pilot screw in until it seats lightly, then back it out the number of turns specified at the beginning of this Chapter. Start the engine and set the idle speed to the specified amount (see Chapter 1).

4 Now try turning the pilot screw inwards by no more than a 1/4 turn, noting its effect on the idle speed, then repeat the process, this time turning the screw outwards.

5 The pilot screw should be set in the position which gives the most consistent, even idle speed without the automatic transmission engaging, and so that the engine does not stall when the twistgrip is opened. **Note:** *It will not be possible to achieve an even idle speed if the spark plug needs adjustment or if the air filter element is dirty. On four-stroke engines, ensure the valve clearances are correctly set.*

6 Once a satisfactory pilot screw setting has been achieved, further adjustments to the idle speed can be made with the idle speed adjuster screw (see Chapter 1).

7 If it is not possible to achieve a satisfactory idle speed after adjusting the pilot screw, take the scooter to a Piaggio dealer and have the fuel/air mixture adjusted with the aid of an exhaust gas analyser.

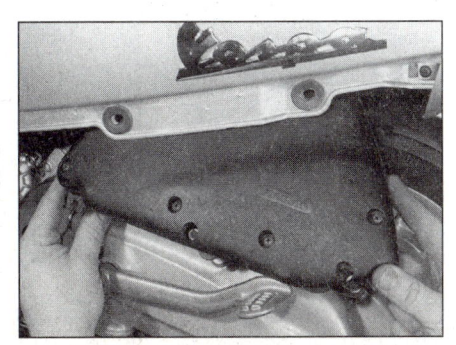

5 Carburettor overhaul – general information

1 Poor engine performance, difficult starting, stalling, flooding and backfiring are all signs that carburettor maintenance may be required.

2 Keep in mind that many so-called carburettor problems can often be traced to mechanical faults within the engine or ignition system malfunctions. Try to establish for certain that the carburettor is in need of maintenance before beginning a major overhaul.

3 Check the fuel tap and filter, the fuel and vacuum hoses, the fuel pump (where fitted), the intake manifold joint clamps, the air filter, the ignition system and the spark plug before assuming that a carburettor overhaul is required.

4 Most carburettor problems are caused by dirt particles, varnish and other deposits which build-up in and eventually block the fuel jets and air passages inside the carburettor. Also, in time, gaskets and O-rings deteriorate and cause fuel and air leaks which lead to poor performance.

5 When overhauling the carburettor, disassemble it completely and clean the parts thoroughly with a carburettor cleaning solvent. If available, blow through the fuel jets and air passages with compressed air to ensure they are clear. Once the cleaning process is complete, reassemble the carburettor using new gaskets and O-rings.

6 Before disassembling the carburettor, make sure you have the correct carburettor gasket set, some carburettor cleaner, a supply of clean rags, some means of blowing out the carburettor passages and a clean place to work.

6 Carburettor – removal and installation

⚠ **Warning:** *Refer to the precautions given in Section 1 before starting work.*

3.2a ...then unscrew the bolts (arrowed)...

3.2b ...and remove the housing

4•10 Fuel and exhaust systems

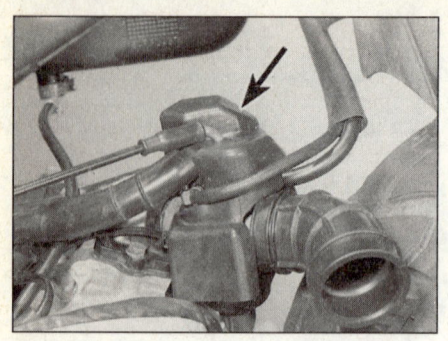

6.1 Remove the cover (arrowed), noting how it fits

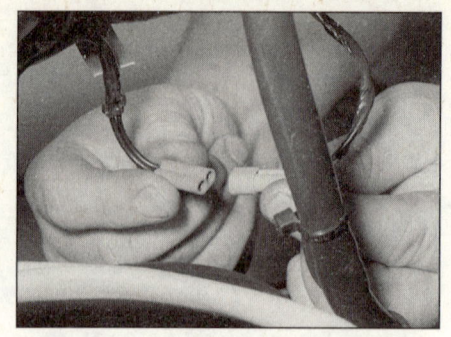

6.2a Disconnect the choke wiring at the connector

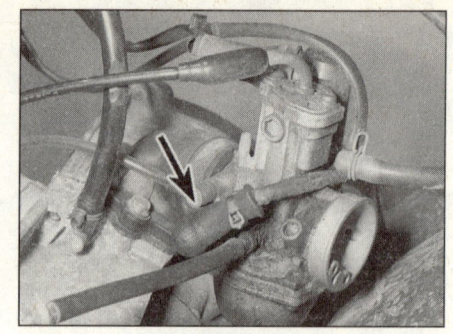

6.2b Trace the wiring from the carburettor heater (arrowed)

6.5a Release the clamp or tie (arrowed) . . .

6.5b . . . and detach the air duct from the carburettor

Removal

1 Remove the bodywork as required by your model to access the carburettor (see Chapter 7). Where fitted, remove the carburettor cover, noting how it fits **(see illustration)**.
2 Trace the wiring from the automatic choke unit and disconnect it at the connector **(see illustration)**. On Skipper, Typhoon 125, Hexagon, NRG Power DT, Fly 50, LX2 50 and air-cooled four-stroke LEADER engined models, trace the wiring from the carburettor heater and disconnect it at the connector **(see illustration)**. Free the wiring from any clips or ties. On NRG Power DD and liquid-cooled LEADER engined models, undo the bolt securing the heater union to the side of the carburettor.
3 To detach the throttle cable from the carburettor on two-stroke engines, first remove the screw securing the top cover, noting that the cover is under spring pressure, then lift the cover and withdraw the throttle slide **(see illustrations 10.5a and 10.5b)**. To detach the throttle cable on four-stroke engines, first unscrew the nut securing the outer cable in its bracket and lift the cable out of the bracket, then detach the cable nipple from the cam on the carburettor **(see illustrations 10.14a and 10.14b)**.
4 On Sfera 125 and ET4 models, release the idle speed adjuster from its clip on the front of the air filter housing and feed it through to the base of the carburettor.
5 Release the clip or cut the tie securing the air intake duct and detach it from the carburettor **(see illustrations)**.
6 Release the clips securing the fuel hose and vacuum hose, and oil hose on two-stroke engines, noting which fits where **(see illustration and 2.7a and 2.7b)**. Be prepared to catch any residual fuel in a suitable container. The fuel and oil hoses should be clamped to prevent leakage using any of the methods shown (see Section 13 **Tool Tips**). The breather and drain hoses can usually be left attached and withdrawn with the carburettor as their lower ends are not secured. Note their routing as they are withdrawn. **Note:** *The vacuum hose can be left attached to the manifold if the carburettor is being removed without it (see Step 8).*
7 Loosen the drain screw and drain all the fuel from the carburettor into a suitable container **(see illustration)**. Discard the drain screw O-ring, as a new one must be used. On installation, fit the new O-ring and tighten the drain screw securely. **Note:** *If a cleaning solvent is going to be used, fit the new O-ring after the cleaning process.*
8 Either loosen the clamp securing the

6.6 Detach the various hoses (arrowed) from the carburettor, as required

6.7 Carburettor drain screw (arrowed)

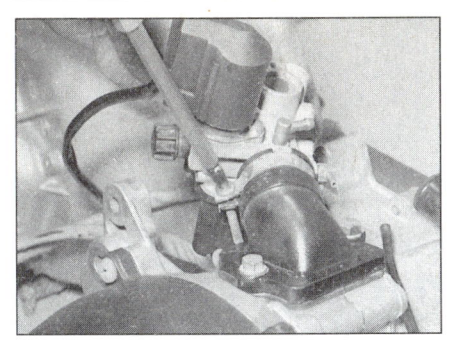

Fuel and exhaust systems 4•11

6.8a Either slacken the clamp . . .

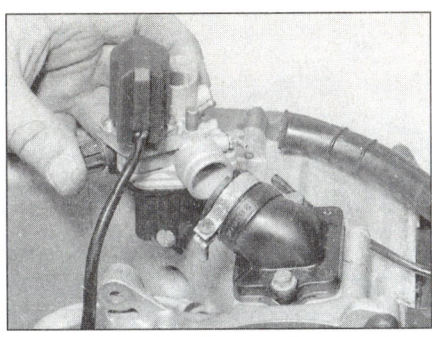

6.8b . . . and detach the carburettor from the manifold . . .

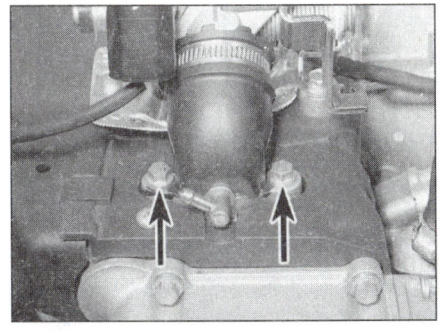

6.8c . . . or remove the manifold bolts (arrowed) . . .

6.8d . . . and remove the carburettor with it attached

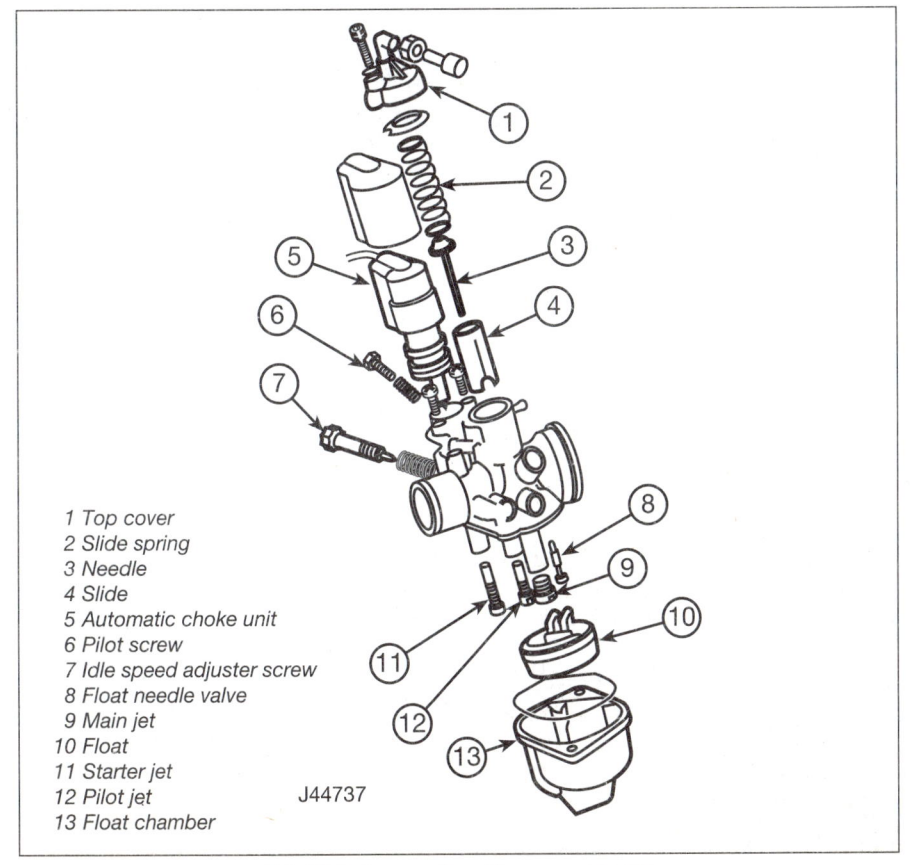

carburettor to the intake manifold on the engine and remove the carburettor, or undo the bolts securing the manifold to the engine and remove it and the carburettor together **(see illustrations)**.

Caution: Stuff clean rag into the intake after removing the carburettor to prevent anything from falling inside.

Installation

9 Installation is the reverse of removal, noting the following.
 a) *Make sure the carburettor is fully engaged with the intake manifold and the clamp is securely tightened.*
 b) *Make sure all hoses are correctly routed and secured and not trapped or kinked.*
 c) *Refer to Section 10 for installation of the throttle cable. Check the operation of the cable and adjust it as necessary (see Chapter 1).*
 d) *On liquid-cooled models, top-up the cooling system if necessary.*
 e) *Check the idle speed and adjust as necessary (see Chapter 1).*

7 Carburettor (two-stroke engines) – overhaul

Note: *Carburettor design differs for 2-stroke and 4-stroke engines. Two-stroke engines use a slide type carburettor, whereas four-stroke engines use a constant-vacuum (CV) type – ensure that you follow the correct procedure in this Section or Section 8.*

Warning: Refer to the precautions given in Section 1 before starting work.

Disassembly

1 Remove the carburettor (see Section 6). Take care when removing components to note their exact locations and any springs or O-rings that may be fitted **(see illustration)**.

2 Where fitted, remove the cover on the automatic choke unit, then remove the clamp securing the choke in the carburettor **(see illustrations)**. Withdraw the choke, noting how it fits **(see illustration)**.

3 The carburettor top cover and throttle slide assembly will have already been removed to

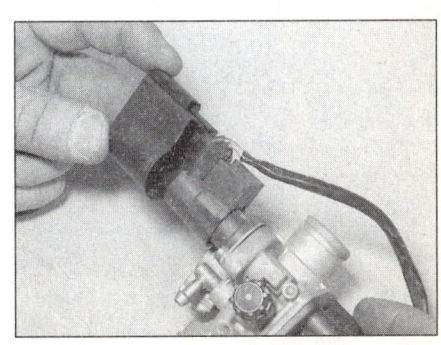

1 Top cover
2 Slide spring
3 Needle
4 Slide
5 Automatic choke unit
6 Pilot screw
7 Idle speed adjuster screw
8 Float needle valve
9 Main jet
10 Float
11 Starter jet
12 Pilot jet
13 Float chamber

7.1 Slide type carburettor components

7.2a Remove the choke cover . . .

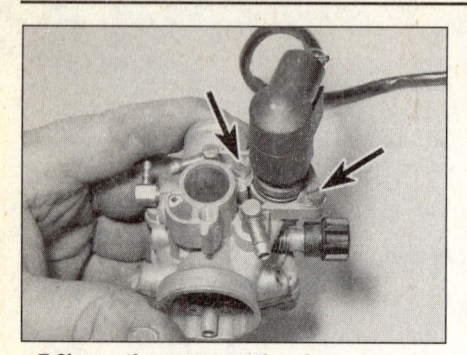

4•12 Fuel and exhaust systems

7.2b ... then remove the clamp screws (arrowed) ...

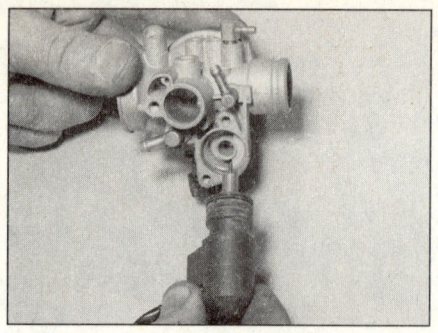

7.2c ... and withdraw the choke unit

7.3 Remove the needle from the throttle slide if required

detach the throttle cable from the carburettor. Disconnect the cable from the slide, then remove the spring seat, spring and cover from the cable (see section 10). Lift the needle out of the throttle slide **(see illustration)**.

4 Undo the screws securing the float chamber to the base of the carburettor and remove it **(see illustrations)**. Discard the gasket, as a new one must be used.

5 Using a pair of thin-nose pliers, carefully withdraw the float pin **(see illustration)**. If necessary, displace the pin using a small punch or a nail. Remove the float and unhook the float needle valve, noting how it fits onto the tab on the float.

6 Unscrew and remove the pilot jet and the starter jet, then unscrew the main jet from the base of the needle jet **(see illustration)**.

7 The needle jet is a press-fit in the carburettor body; if required, displace the jet, noting how it fits.

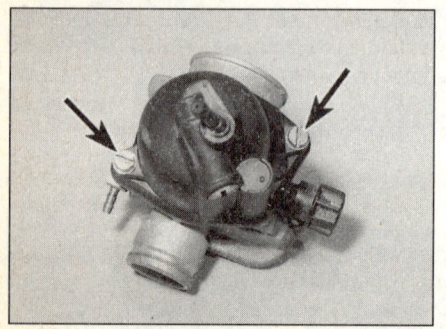

8 The pilot screw can be removed if required, but note that its setting will be disturbed (see **Haynes Hint**). Unscrew and remove the pilot screw along with its spring and O-ring, where fitted.

HAYNES HiNT *To record the pilot screw's current setting, turn the screw in until it seats lightly, counting the number of turns necessary to achieve this, then unscrew it fully. On installation, turn the screw in until it seats, then back it out the number of turns you've recorded.*

Cleaning

Caution: Use only a petroleum-based solvent for carburettor cleaning. Don't use caustic cleaners.

9 Submerge the metal components in carburettor cleaning solvent for approximately thirty minutes (or longer, if the directions recommend it).

10 After the carburettor has soaked long enough for the cleaner to loosen and dissolve most of the varnish and other deposits, use a nylon-bristled brush to remove the stubborn deposits. Rinse it again, then dry it with compressed air.

11 If available, use compressed air to blow out all the fuel jets and the air passages in the carburettor body, not forgetting the passages in the carburettor intake.

Caution: Never clean the jets or passages with a piece of wire or a drill bit, as they will be enlarged, causing the fuel and air metering rates to be upset.

Inspection

12 If removed, check the tapered portion of the pilot screw and the spring for wear or damage. Fit a new O-ring and renew the screw or spring if necessary.

13 Check the carburettor body, float chamber and top cover for cracks, distorted sealing surfaces and other damage. If any defects are found, renew the faulty component, although a new carburettor will probably be necessary (check with a Piaggio dealer on the availability of separate components).

14 Insert the throttle slide in the carburettor body and check that it moves up-and-down smoothly. Check the surface of the slide for wear. If it's worn excessively or doesn't move smoothly, renew the components as necessary.

15 Check the needle for straightness by rolling it on a flat surface such as a piece of glass. Fit a new needle if it's bent or if the tip is worn. Check the position of the clip on the needle (see Specifications at the beginning of this Chapter).

16 Inspect the tip of the float needle valve and the valve seat. If either has grooves or scratches in it, or is in any way worn, they must be renewed as a set. **Note:** *On Hexagon models with a pumped and pressurised fuel system, a worn or incorrectly-sized carburettor float needle valve seat will not be able to shut off the fuel supply sufficiently to*

7.4a Undo the screws (arrowed) ...

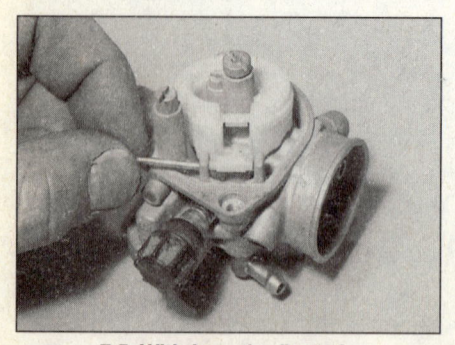

7.4b ... and lift off the chamber

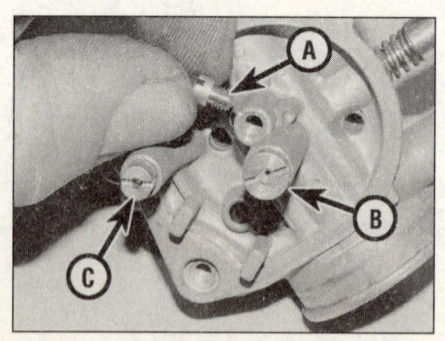

7.5 Withdraw the float pin

7.6 Pilot jet (A), main jet (B) and starter jet (C)

Fuel and exhaust systems 4•13

prevent carburettor flooding and excessive use of fuel.

17 Check the float for damage. This will usually be apparent by the presence of fuel inside the float. If the float is damaged, it must be renewed.

18 Inspect the automatic choke unit plunger and needle for signs of wear and renew the unit if necessary **(see illustration)**. The resistance of the choke unit should be checked with a multi-meter after the engine has been warmed to normal operating temperature and then allowed to cool for ten minutes. With an ambient (air) temperature of 20°C, disconnect the choke unit wiring connector and measure the resistance between the terminals on the choke unit side of the connector **(see illustration)**. If the result is not as specified at the beginning of the Chapter, renew the choke unit. To check that the plunger is not seized in the choke body, first measure the protrusion of the plunger from the body. Next, use jumper wires to connect a good 12 V battery to the choke unit terminals and measure the protrusion again after 5 minutes. If the measurements are not as specified the unit is faulty and should be renewed.

Reassembly and fuel level check

Note: *When reassembling the carburettor, be sure to use new O-rings and gaskets. Do not overtighten the carburettor jets and screws as they are easily damaged.*

19 If removed, install the pilot screw, spring and O-ring; adjust the screw to the setting as noted on removal (see Step 8).

20 If removed, install the needle jet. Where applicable, ensure the flat in the bottom of the jet aligns with the pin in the carburettor. Screw the main jet into the end of the needle jet.

21 Install the pilot jet and the starter jet **(see illustration 7.6)**.

22 Hook the float needle valve onto the float tab, then position the float assembly in the carburettor, making sure the needle valve enters its seat. Install the float pin, making sure it is secure **(see illustration 7.5)**.

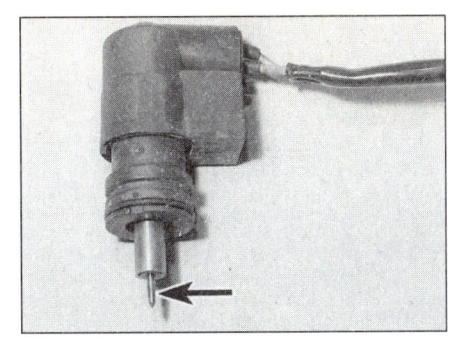

7.18a Check the automatic choke unit plunger and needle condition

23 Fit a new gasket onto the float chamber, making sure it is seated properly in its groove, then install the chamber onto the carburettor and tighten the screws securely **(see illustrations 7.4b and 7.4a)**.

24 The carburettor fuel level should be checked at this point to ensure that the float and needle valve are working correctly. Support the carburettor upright in a vice and connect a length of clear fuel hose to the drain union on the base of the float chamber. Secure the hose up against the side of the carburettor and mark it level with the float chamber joint **(see illustration)**. Carefully pour a small amount of fuel into the carburettor via the fuel hose union, then undo the drain screw in the bottom of the float chamber enough to allow fuel to flow into the clear hose. Continue pouring fuel into the carburettor until the float needle valve shuts off the supply, at which point the level in the clear hose should be the specified distance below the mark (see Specifications at the beginning of the Chapter). If the fuel level is incorrect, and the float needle valve and the valve seat are good, check the float tab for wear or damage. If the float tab is metal it can be adjusted carefully to correct the fuel height, otherwise a new float will have to be fitted.

25 Install the choke unit and secure it with

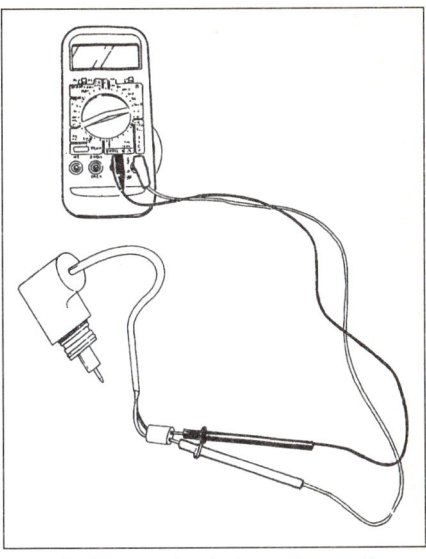

7.18b Automatic choke unit operation check

the clamp and screws **(see illustration)**. Install the choke unit cover, if fitted.

26 Install the carburettor (see Section 6). Install the jet needle in the throttle slide, then follow the procedure in Section 10 to install the throttle slide assembly onto the cable and fit the carburettor top cover.

8 Carburettor (four-stroke engines) – overhaul

Note: *Carburettor design differs for 2-stroke and 4-stroke engines. Two-stroke engines use a slide type carburettor, whereas four-stroke engines use a constant-vacuum (CV) type – ensure that you follow the correct procedure in this Section or Section 7.*

⚠ **Warning:** *Refer to the precautions given in Section 1 before proceeding.*

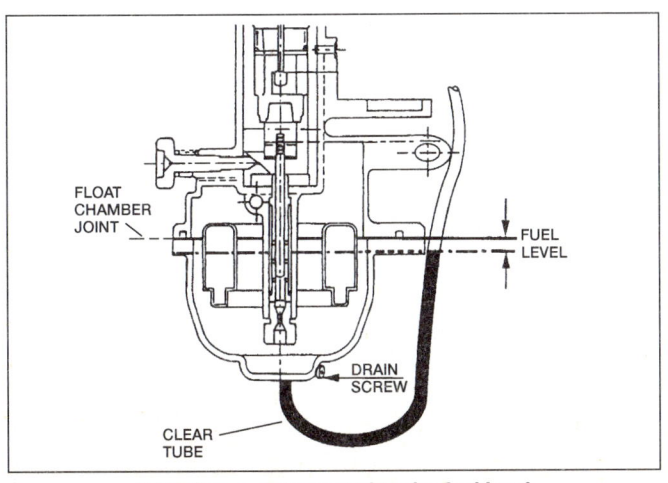

7.24 Set-up for measuring the fuel level

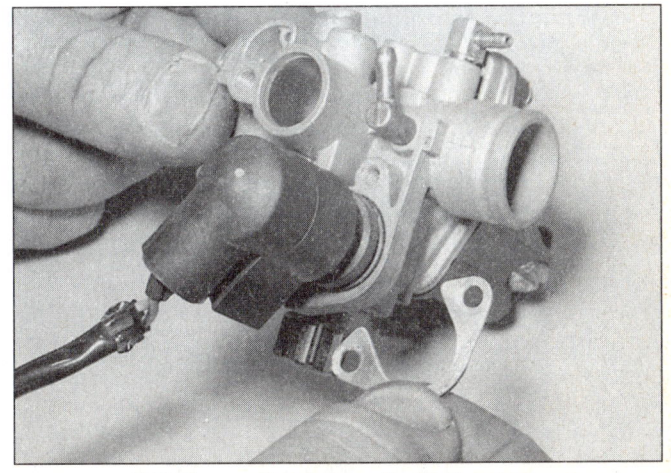

7.25 Secure the choke unit with the clamp

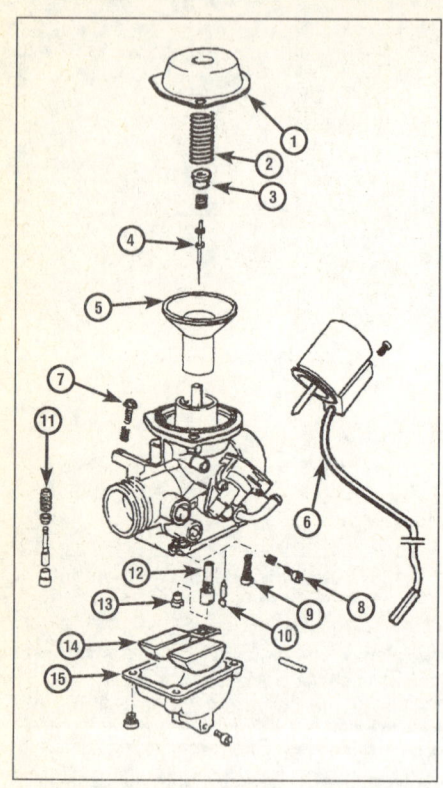

4•14 Fuel and exhaust systems

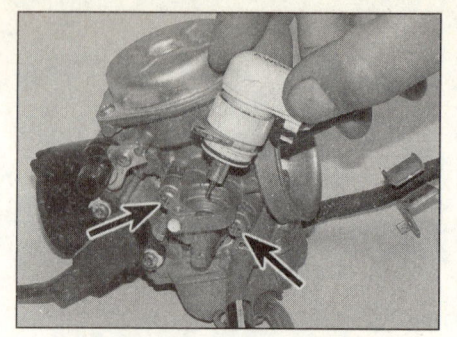

8.2 Remove the choke unit. Screws (arrowed) secure the mounting

8.3a Remove the screws and the cover...

8.3b ... then withdraw the spring ...

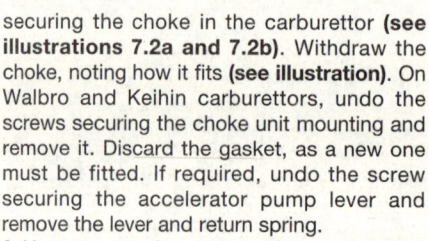

8.3c ... and the diaphragm/piston assembly

8.1 Constant vacuum (CV) type carburettor components

1 Top cover
2 Spring
3 Needle retainer
4 Needle
5 Diaphragm and piston assembly
6 Automatic choke unit
7 Idle speed adjuster screw
8 Pilot screw
9 Pilot jet
10 Float needle valve
11 Accelerator pump assembly
12 Needle jet
13 Main jet
14 Float
15 Float chamber

Disassembly

1 Remove the carburettor (see Section 6). Take care when removing components to note their exact locations and any springs or O-rings that may be fitted **(see illustration)**.
2 Where fitted, remove the cover on the automatic choke unit, then remove the clamp securing the choke in the carburettor **(see illustrations 7.2a and 7.2b)**. Withdraw the choke, noting how it fits **(see illustration)**. On Walbro and Keihin carburettors, undo the screws securing the choke unit mounting and remove it. Discard the gasket, as a new one must be fitted. If required, undo the screw securing the accelerator pump lever and remove the lever and return spring.
3 Unscrew and remove the top cover retaining screws, then lift off the cover and remove the spring from inside the piston **(see illustrations)**. Carefully peel the diaphragm away from its sealing groove in the carburettor and withdraw the diaphragm and piston assembly **(see illustration)**. Note how the tab on the diaphragm fits in the recess in the carburettor body.
Caution: Do not use a sharp instrument to displace the diaphragm as it is easily damaged.
4 On Walbro and Mikuni carburettors, unscrew the jet needle retainer, then remove the retainer, the spring and spring seat (where fitted) **(see illustration)**. On Keihin carburettors, lift out the needle retainer. Push the needle up from the bottom of the piston and withdraw it from the top **(see illustration)**.
5 Undo the screws securing the float chamber to the base of the carburettor and remove it **(see illustration)**. Discard the gasket, as a new one must be used.
6 On Mikuni and Keihin carburettors, withdraw the accelerator pump spring and plunger from the carburettor body, noting how it fits **(see illustration)**. On Walbro carburettors, unscrew the accelerator pump

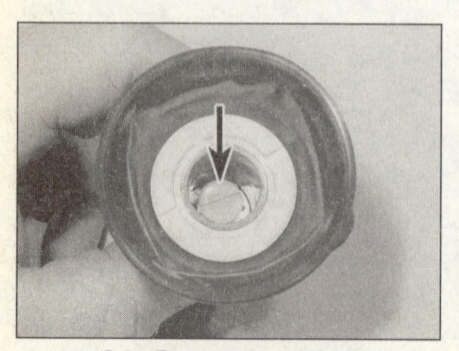

8.4a Remove the retainer (arrowed)

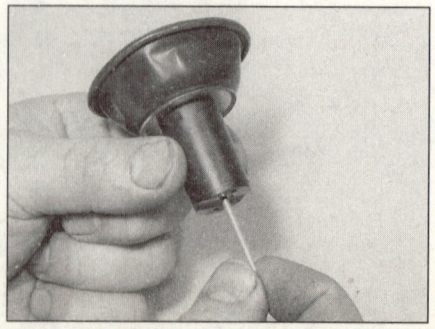

8.4b Push the needle up from the bottom

8.5 Float chamber screws (arrowed)

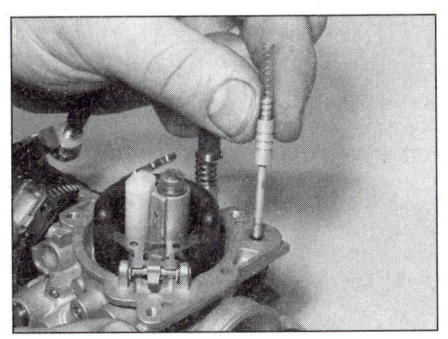

Fuel and exhaust systems 4•15

8.6a Withdraw the accelerator pump plunger . . .

8.6b . . . or unscrew the assembly (arrowed) from the float chamber

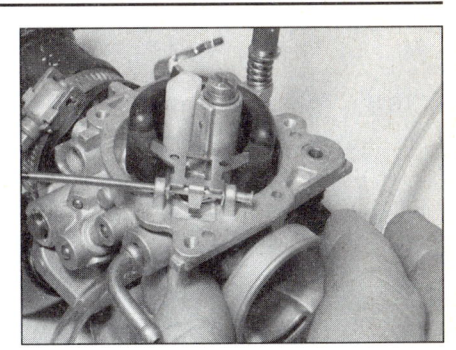

8.7a Remove the float pin

assembly from the float chamber **(see illustration)**. Discard the O-ring, as a new one must be fitted.

7 Using a pair of thin-nose pliers, carefully withdraw the float pin; if necessary, displace the pin using a small punch or a nail **(see illustration)**. Remove the float and unhook the float needle valve, noting how it fits onto the tab on the float **(see illustrations)**.

8 Undo the screw securing the float needle valve seat clamp, then withdraw the valve seat **(see illustrations)**. Discard the O-ring, as a new one should be used.

9 Remove the plastic jet cover from the starter jet **(see illustration)**. **Note:** *The starter jet is a press-fit in the carburettor body and should not be removed.* Unscrew the pilot jet and the main jet **(see illustration)**. On Walbro and Keihin carburettors, unscrew the needle jet. The fuel atomiser is retained by the needle jet; if the atomiser is loose, remove it for safekeeping.

10 The pilot screw can be removed if required, but note that its setting will be disturbed (see **Haynes Hint**). Unscrew and remove the pilot screw along with its spring and O-ring, where fitted.

Note: *Do not remove the screws securing the throttle butterfly to the throttle shaft.*

> **HAYNES HINT** *To record the pilot screw's current setting, turn the screw in until it seats lightly, counting the number of turns necessary to achieve this, then unscrew it fully. On installation, turn the screw in until it seats, then back it out the number of turns you've recorded.*

Cleaning

Caution: *Use only a petroleum-based solvent for carburettor cleaning. Don't use caustic cleaners.*

11 Follow Steps 9 to 11 in Section 7 to clean the carburettor body and internal components. Also unscrew the float chamber drain screw and clean the float chamber, paying particular attention to the fuel passage for the accelerator pump. The accelerator fuel passage is fitted with a one-way valve; blow through the fuel passage with compressed air from the bottom of the pump piston housing.

Caution: *Never clean the jets or passages with a piece of wire or a drill bit, as they will be enlarged, causing the fuel and air metering rates to be upset.*

Inspection

12 If removed, check the tapered portion of

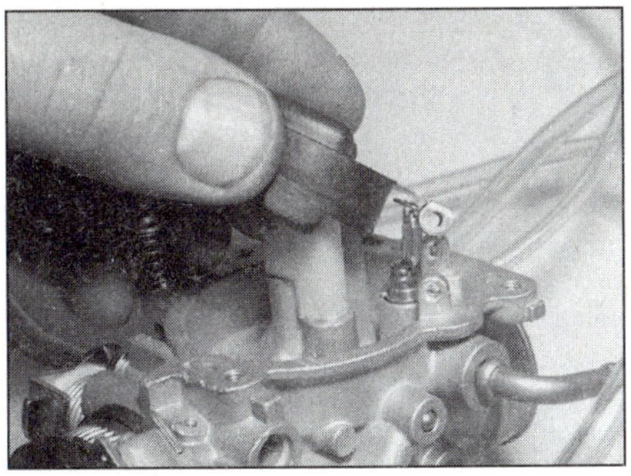

8.7b Lift out the float . . .

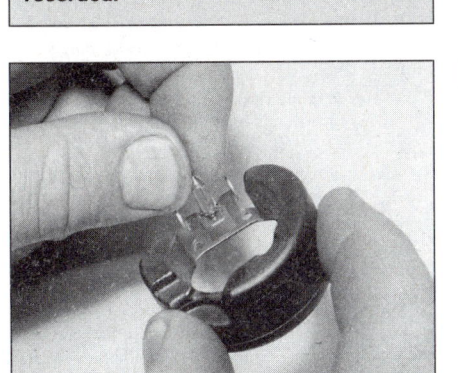

8.7c . . . and unhook the needle valve

8.8a Remove the clamp screw (arrowed) . . .

8.8b . . . and withdraw the valve seat

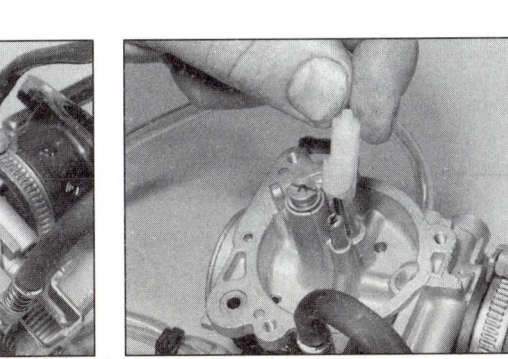

8.9a Remove the plastic jet cover

8.9b Pilot jet (A), main jet (B)

4•16 Fuel and exhaust systems

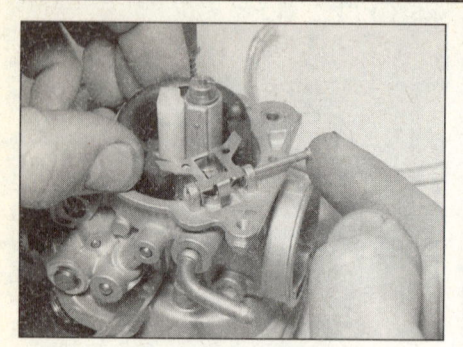

8.25 Install the float pin

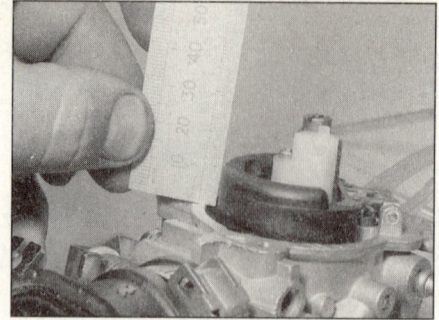

8.26a Measuring the float height

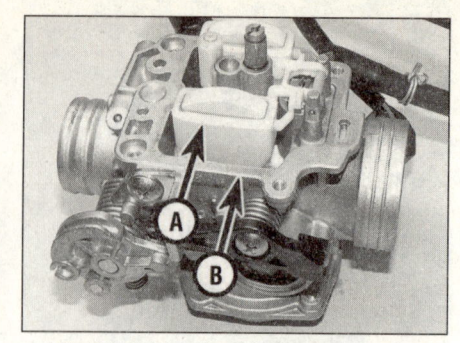

8.26b Straight-edge (A) should be parallel with gasket face (B)

the pilot screw and the spring for wear or damage. Fit a new O-ring and renew the screw or spring if necessary.

13 Check the carburettor body, float chamber and top cover for cracks, distorted sealing surfaces and other damage. If any defects are found, renew the faulty component, although renewal of the entire carburettor will probably be necessary (check with a Piaggio dealer on the availability of separate components).

14 Inspect the piston diaphragm for splits, holes and general deterioration. Holding it up to a light will help to reveal problems of this nature. Insert the piston in the carburettor body and check that the piston moves up-and-down smoothly. Check the surface of the piston for wear. If it's worn excessively or doesn't move smoothly, renew the components as necessary.

15 Check the needle for straightness by rolling it on a flat surface such as a piece of glass. Fit a new needle if it's bent or if the tip is worn.

16 Inspect the tip of the float needle valve and the valve seat. If either has grooves or scratches in it, or is in any way worn, they must be renewed as a set. **Note:** *On scooters with a pumped and pressurised fuel system, a worn or incorrectly-sized carburettor float needle valve seat will not be able to shut off the fuel supply sufficiently to prevent carburettor flooding and excessive use of fuel.*

17 Operate the throttle shaft to make sure the throttle butterfly valve opens and closes smoothly. If it doesn't, cleaning the throttle linkage may help. Otherwise, renew the carburettor.

18 Check the float for damage. This will usually be apparent by the presence of fuel inside the float. If the float is damaged, it must be renewed.

19 Follow the procedure in Section 7, Step 18, to check the automatic choke unit.

20 Inspect the accelerator pump piston and its seat in the float chamber for signs of wear. Ensure that the spring and the rubber boot are not damaged or deformed and renew them if necessary.

Reassembly and float height check

Note: *When reassembling the carburettor, be sure to use new O-rings and seals. Do not overtighten the carburettor jets and screws as they are easily damaged.*

21 If removed, install the pilot screw, spring and O-ring; adjust the screw to the setting as noted on removal (see Step 10).

22 On Walbro and Keihin carburettors, install the fuel atomiser if removed, then install the needle jet.

23 Install the main jet and the pilot jet and fit the plastic cover on the starter jet **(see illustrations 8.9b and 8.9a)**.

24 Install the float needle valve seat using a new O-ring, then fit the clamp and tighten the screw **(see illustrations 8.8a and 8.8b)**.

25 Hook the float needle valve onto the float tab, then position the float assembly in the carburettor, making sure the needle valve enters its seat **(see illustrations 8.7c and 8.7b)**. Install the pin, making sure it is secure **(see illustration)**.

26 The carburettor float height should be checked at this point. Turn the carburettor upside-down and measure the distance between the gasket face and the bottom of the float with an accurate ruler **(see illustration)**. The correct measurement for Sfera and ET4 models is given in the Specifications at the beginning of the Chapter. For all LEADER engined models, the bottom straight-edge of the float should be parallel with the gasket face **(see illustration)**. If the float height is incorrect, it can be adjusted by carefully bending the metal float tab a little at a time until the correct height is obtained.

27 On Mikuni and Keihin carburettors, install the accelerator pump spring and plunger in the carburettor body **(see illustration)**. On Walbro carburettors, fit a new O-ring to the accelerator pump assembly, then screw the assembly into the float chamber **(see illustration 8.6b)**. Fit a new gasket onto the float chamber, making sure it is seated properly in its groove, then install the chamber onto the carburettor and tighten the screws securely **(see illustration)**.

28 Check that the clip is correctly positioned on the jet needle (see Specifications at the beginning of the Chapter) then insert the jet needle into the piston **(see illustration)**. On Walbro and Mikuni carburettors, install the spring and spring seat (where fitted) and the

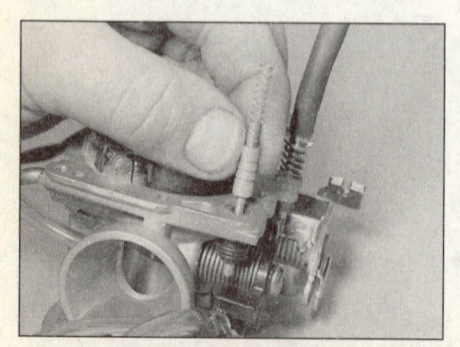

8.27a Install the plunger, making sure the spring is on its end

8.27b Ensure the float chamber gasket is correctly located

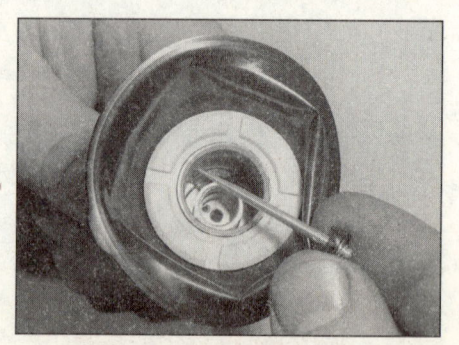

8.28a Install the jet needle . . .

Fuel and exhaust systems 4•17

jet needle retainer **(see illustrations)**. On Keihin carburettors, install the needle retainer.

29 Insert the piston assembly into the carburettor body and push it down lightly, ensuring the needle is correctly aligned with the needle jet **(see illustration 8.3c)**. Align the tab on the diaphragm with the recess in the carburettor body, then press the diaphragm outer edge into its groove, making sure it is correctly seated **(see illustration)**. Check the diaphragm is not creased, and that the piston moves smoothly up-and-down in its bore.

30 Install the spring into the piston and fit the top cover to the carburettor, making sure the spring locates over the raised section on the inside of the cover, then tighten the cover screws securely **(see illustration)**.

31 On Walbro and Keihin carburettors, install the choke unit mounting with a new gasket.

32 Install the automatic choke unit and secure it with its clamp **(see illustration 7.25)**. If fitted, install the choke unit cover.

33 If removed, install the accelerator pump lever and return spring and secure them with the screw.

34 Install the carburettor (see Section 6).

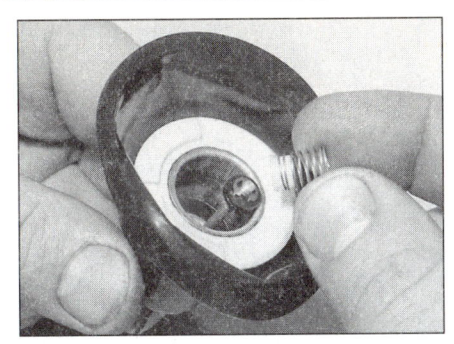

8.28b . . . the spring and spring seat . . .

8.28c . . . and the retainer

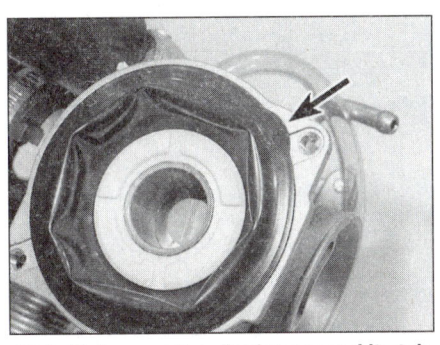

8.29 Make sure the diaphragm and its tab (arrowed) are correctly seated

8.30 Locate the cover onto the spring and fit it onto the carburettor

9 Reed valve (two-stroke engines) – removal, inspection and installation

Removal

1 Remove the carburettor along with the intake manifold (see Section 6).
2 Withdraw the reed valve from the crankcase, noting which way round it fits **(see illustration)**.

Inspection

3 Check the reed valve body closely for cracks, distortion and any other damage, particularly around the mating surfaces between the crankcase and the intake manifold – a good seal must be maintained between the components, otherwise crankcase pressure and therefore engine performance will be affected.

4 Check the reeds themselves for cracks, distortion and any other damage. Check also that there are no dirt particles trapped between the reeds and their seats. The reeds should sit flat against the valve body so that a good seal is obtained when the crankcase is under pressure **(see illustration)**. After prolonged use, the reeds tend to become bent and will not seal properly, in which case they should be renewed. A good way to check is to hold the valve up to the light – if light is visible between the reeds and the body they are not sealing properly. If the engine is difficult to start or idles erratically, this could be the problem. Check with your Piaggio dealer as to the availability of individual reeds – otherwise the complete valve must be renewed.

Installation

5 Installation is the reverse of removal. Ensure that the mating surfaces between the reed valve and crankcase, and between the reed valve and inlet manifold are clean and perfectly smooth. Check that the stopper plate retaining screws are tight; severe engine damage could result from a screw falling into the engine.

9.2 Withdraw the reed valve from the crankcase

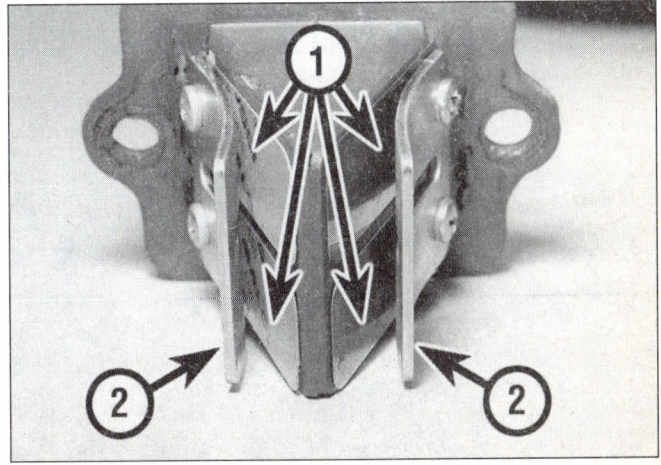

9.4 Check that the reeds (1) sit flat against the valve body when the valve is closed. Stopper plates (2)

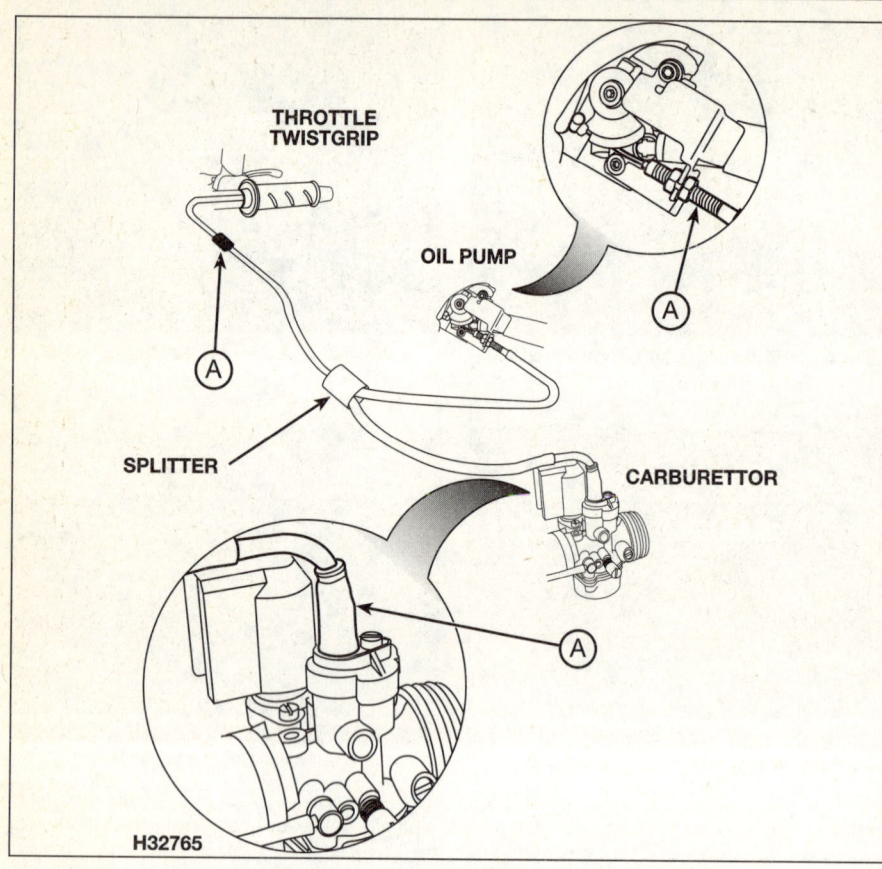

4•18 Fuel and exhaust systems

10.1 Throttle cable arrangement for two-stroke engines
Location of cable adjusters (A)

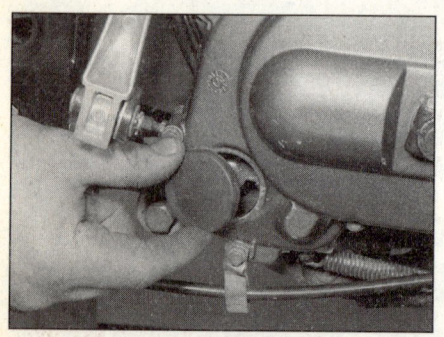

10.2 Remove the rubber plug to access the oil pump cable

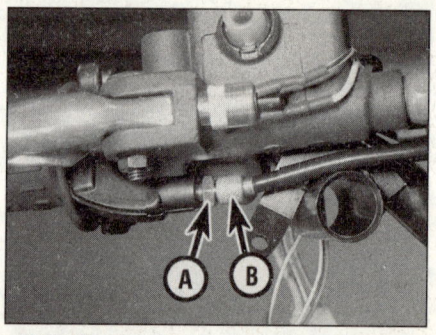

10.3a Slacken the locknut (A) and thread the adjuster (B) fully in

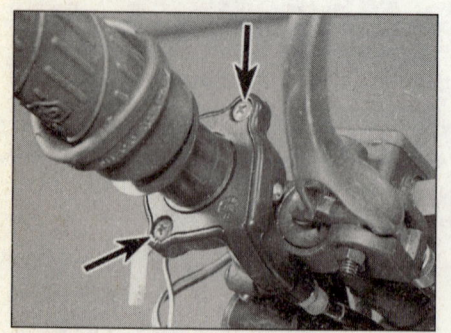

10.3b The plate is secured by two screws (arrowed)

10.3c Detach the nipple (arrowed) from the twistgrip...

10.3d ...then remove the elbow...

10 Throttle cable – removal and installation

Warning: *Refer to the precautions given in Section 1 before proceeding.*

Two-stroke engines
Removal

1 Three separate cables are fitted – the main cable from the throttle twistgrip goes into a splitter located under the floorboard, with separate cables from this going to the carburettor and oil pump **(see illustration)**. If a cable problem is diagnosed, check which cable is faulty before renewing all three. Across the range of models, two types of throttle twistgrip and two types of cable splitter are used. On some models, a motorcycle-type throttle is used, where the nipple on the end of the inner cable fits into a socket in the twistgrip. On other models, a sliding type twistgrip is used, where the end of the inner cable is secured in a slider, which locates into a diagonal track inside the twistgrip. Of the two types of splitter, one operates with the main cable pulling on a pivoted cam, while the other operates with the main cable pulling on a slider. Be sure to correctly identify which type is fitted on your model before buying new cables. Before removing a cable, make a careful note of its routing to ensure correct installation.

2 To access the cable at the throttle twistgrip, remove the handlebar front cover (see Chapter 7). To access the cable at the carburettor, remove the storage compartment and any bodywork as required according to model (see Chapter 7). To access the cable at the oil pump, remove the rubber plug in the transmission cover **(see illustration)**. To access the cable splitter, remove the floorboard (see Chapter 7).

3 On models with a motorcycle-type twistgrip, slacken the cable adjuster locknut and thread the adjuster fully into the housing **(see illustration)**. Pull back the twistgrip rubber, then remove the screws securing the cover plate and remove the plate, noting how it fits **(see illustration)**. Detach the cable nipple from its socket, then remove the cable elbow, noting how it fits **(see illustrations)**.

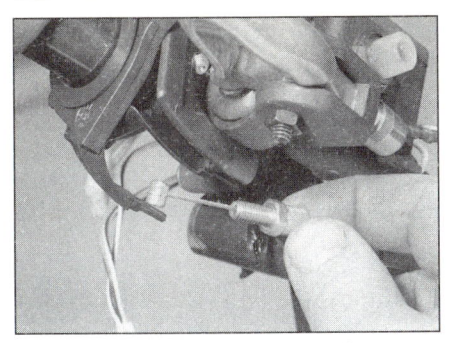

Fuel and exhaust systems 4•19

10.3e ... and unscrew the adjuster

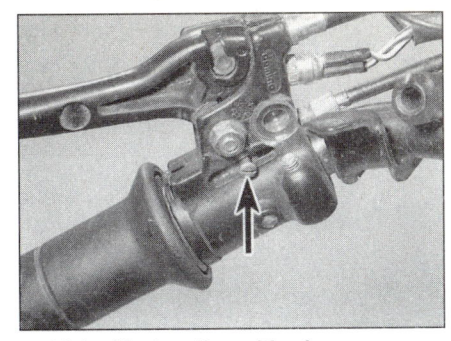

10.4a Slacken the cable clamp screw (arrowed) ...

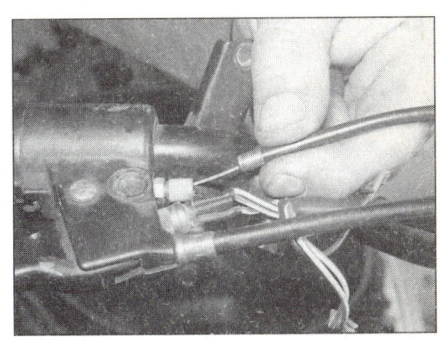

10.4b ... and draw out the cable

Now unscrew the cable adjuster from its housing and remove the cable via the slot in the housing **(see illustration)**.

4 On models with a sliding twistgrip, slacken the screw securing the end of the cable in the slider, then draw the cable out **(see illustrations)**. Make a note of the distance from the end of the cable where the screw located as an aid for correctly setting the new cable. Note that the inner cable is available separately from the outer cable. To remove the slider, remove the grub screw securing the twistgrip in the housing, then draw the twistgrip out of the housing, noting how the return spring ends locate on the housing and the twistgrip **(see illustration)**. Remove the slider, noting how it locates in the track in the twistgrip and in the housing **(see illustration)**.
5 To detach the cable from the carburettor, remove the screw securing the carburettor top cover, noting that the cover is under

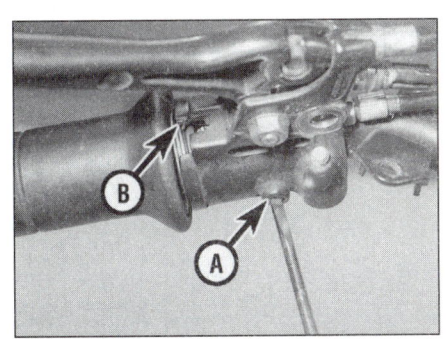

10.4c Remove the grub screw (A), noting how the return spring end (B) locates ...

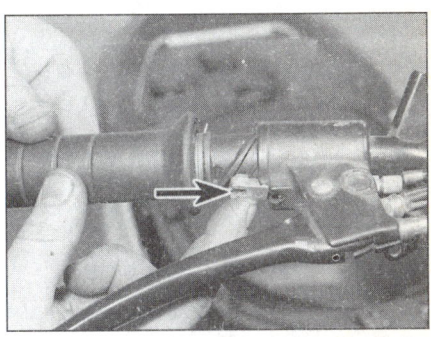

10.4d ... then draw the twistgrip out, noting how the slider (arrowed) locates in its track

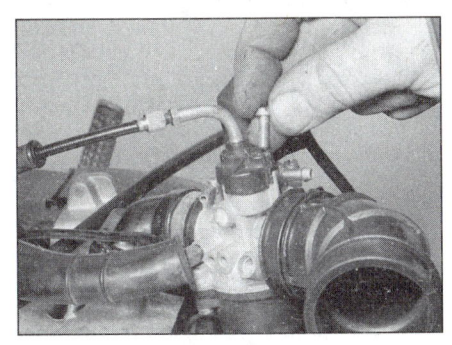

spring pressure, then lift the cover and withdraw the throttle slide **(see illustrations)**. Holding the cover, push the slide to compress the spring, thereby creating freeplay in the

cable. Free the cable nipple from its slot in the bottom of the slide and align it with the larger adjacent hole so that the slide can be drawn off the cable **(see illustration)**. Remove the

10.5a Remove the screw ...

10.5b ... and lift off the cover and throttle slide

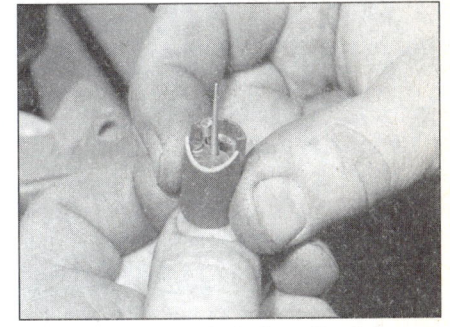

10.5c Free the nipple from its slot ...

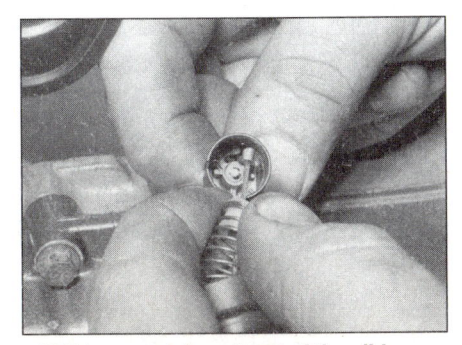

10.5d ... and draw it out of the slide ...

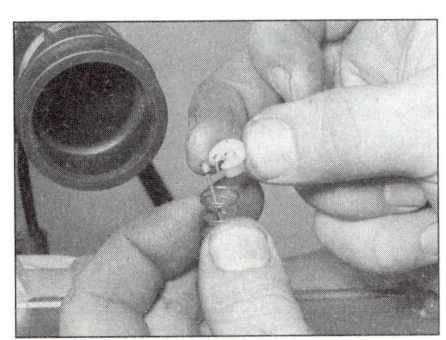

10.5e ... then remove the spring seat ...

10.5f ... and the spring ...

4•20 Fuel and exhaust systems

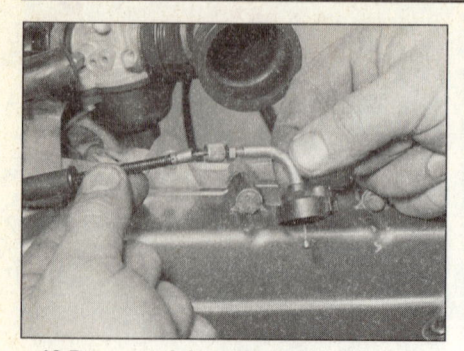

10.5g . . . and draw the cable out of the top cover

10.6a Lever up the tab securing the nipple . . .

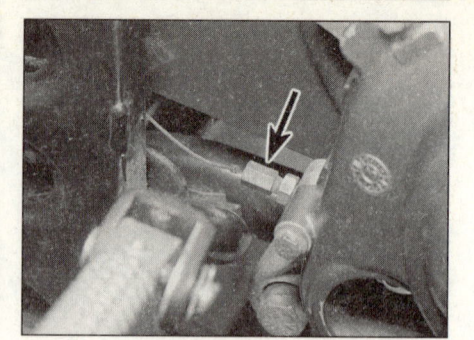

10.6b . . . and draw the cable out of the adjuster (arrowed)

10.7a Draw off the splitter cover . . .

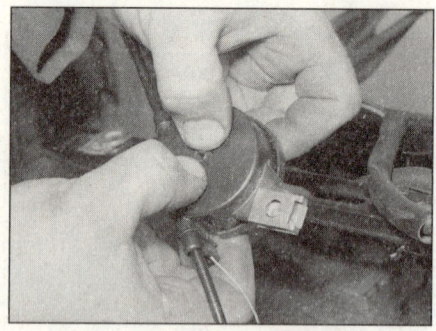

10.7b . . . then press in the tabs . . .

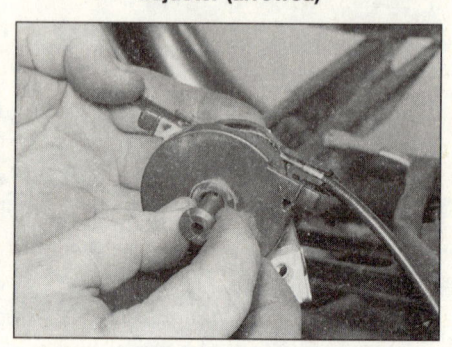

10.7c . . . withdraw the peg and remove the cover

10.7d Draw out the outer cables . . .

10.7e . . . then remove the cam and detach the cable nipples

slide and the spring seat, noting how they fit, then remove the spring and draw the cable out of the elbow on the top of the cover **(see illustrations)**.

6 To detach the cable from the oil pump, lever up the tab securing the cable nipple, then release the cable from its channel and draw it out of the front of the transmission housing **(see illustrations)**. Manually move the oil pump cam round to provide some slack in the cable if required (doing this will certainly help installation of the cable). If required, slacken the locknut on the cable adjuster, then unscrew the adjuster from the transmission housing.

7 On models with the cam type cable splitter, first detach the cable being renewed from the twistgrip, carburettor or oil pump as relevant. Remove the screw (on the underside of the bellypan) securing the splitter to its mounting. Draw the cable rubber covers off the splitter, then depress the tabs on the bottom of the peg securing the splitter cover and draw the peg out of the splitter and remove the cover **(see illustrations)**. Draw the outer cables out of their sockets, then lift the cam off its pivot and detach the cable nipples from the cam as required, noting their relative positions **(see illustrations)**.

8 On models with the slider type splitter, first detach the cables from the carburettor and the oil pump as described above. Detach the splitter holder from the frame and draw the rubber covers off the splitter **(see illustrations)**.

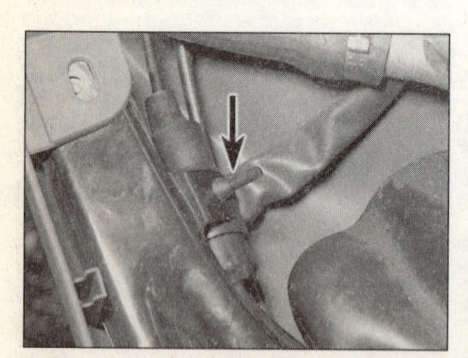

10.8a Free the splitter from its bracket (arrowed) . . .

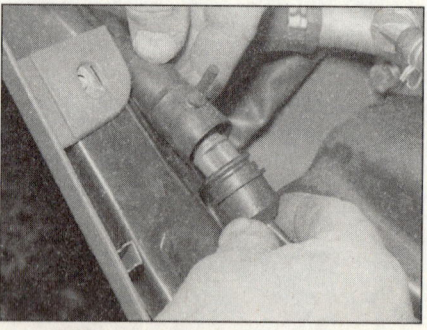

10.8b . . . and draw off the covers

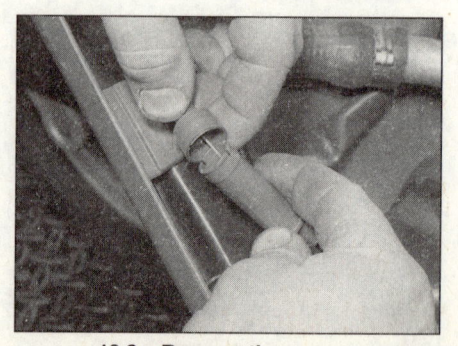

10.8c Remove the cap . . .

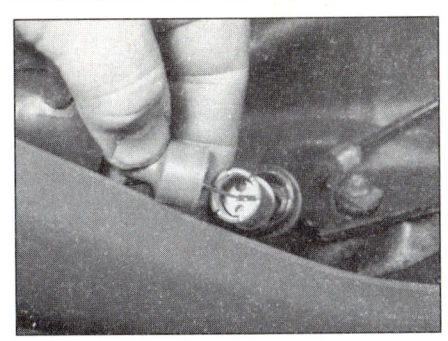

Fuel and exhaust systems 4•21

10.8d . . . and draw out the slider

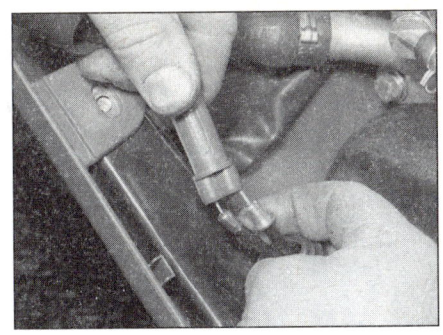

10.8e Note how the outer cables locate in the splitter

Remove the cap from the splitter and draw the slider out of the housing using the main cable from the twistgrip **(see illustrations)**. Detach the cable(s) from the splitter as required, noting their relative positions **(see illustration)**.

Installation

9 Installation is the reverse of removal, noting the following points:
  a) Lubricate the cable nipples with multi-purpose grease.
  b) Make sure the cables are correctly routed. They must not interfere with any other component and should not be kinked or bent sharply. Turn the handlebars back-and-forth to make sure the cable doesn't cause the steering to bind.
  c) Operate the throttle to check that it opens and closes smoothly and freely.
  d) Check and adjust the cable freeplay and the oil pump setting (see Chapter 1). This is very important to ensure that the engine receives the correct lubrication supply.
  e) Start the engine and check that the idle speed does not rise as the handlebars are turned. If it does, a cable is routed incorrectly. Correct the problem before riding the scooter.

Four-stroke engines

Removal

10 Two types of throttle twistgrip are used. Some models have a motorcycle-type twistgrip, where the nipple on the end of the inner cable fits into a socket in the twistgrip. Other models have a sliding type twistgrip, where the end of the inner cable is secured in a slider, which locates into a diagonal track inside the twistgrip.

11 To access the cable at the throttle twistgrip, remove the handlebar front cover. To access the cable at the carburettor, remove the storage compartment (see Chapter 7).

12 On most models with a motorcycle type twistgrip, slacken the cable adjuster locknut and thread the adjuster fully into the housing **(see illustration 10.3a)**. Pull back the twistgrip rubber, then remove the screws securing the cover plate and remove the plate, noting how it fits **(see illustration 10.3b)**. Detach the cable nipple from its socket, then remove the cable elbow, noting how it fits **(see illustrations 10.3c and 10.3d)**. Now unscrew the cable adjuster from its housing and remove the cable via the slot in the housing **(see illustration 10.3e)**. Note that on B125 models the twistgrip housing is in two halves. Slacken the throttle cable adjuster, then undo the screw securing the halves of the housing together and separate them **(see illustration)**. Detach the cable nipple from the twistgrip and pull the cable out **(see illustration)**. Note how the pin in the front half of the housing locates in the handlebar **(see illustration)**.

13 On models with a sliding twistgrip, slacken the screw securing the end of the cable in the slider, then draw the cable out **(see illustrations 10.4a and 10.4b)**. Make a note of the distance from the end of the cable where the screw located as an aid for correctly setting the new cable. Note that the inner cable is available separately from the outer cable. To remove the slider, remove the grub screw securing the twistgrip in the housing, then draw the twistgrip out of the housing, carefully noting how the return spring ends locate on the housing and the twistgrip **(see illustration 10.4c)**. Remove the slider, noting how it locates in the track in the twistgrip and in the housing **(see illustration 10.4d)**.

14 Unscrew the nut securing the outer cable in its bracket on the carburettor and lift the cable out of the bracket, then detach the cable nipple from the cam on the carburettor noting how it fits **(see illustrations)**. Withdraw the cable from the scooter noting the correct routing.

10.12a On B125 models, undo the screw to split the twistgrip housing . . .

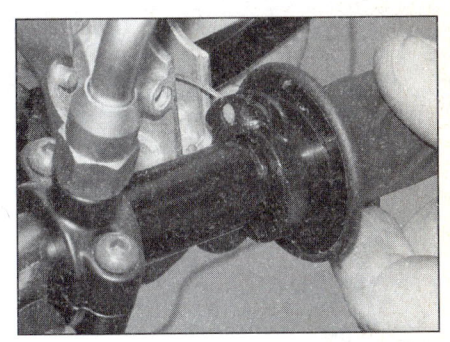

10.12b . . . then detach the cable nipple from the twistgrip . . .

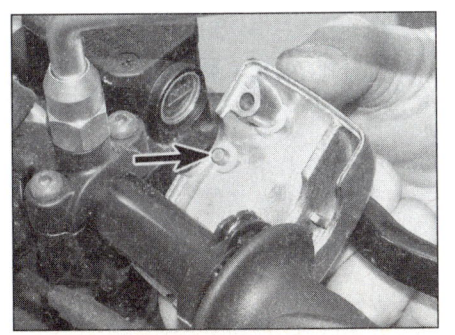

10.12c . . . noting how the pin (arrowed) locates in the handlebar

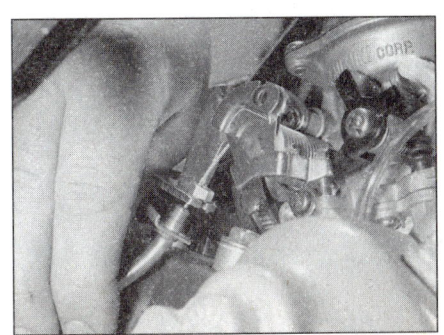

10.14a Detach the cable from the bracket . . .

10.14b . . . then detach the cable nipple from the cam

4•22 Fuel and exhaust systems

11.2a Unscrew the two nuts (arrowed) . . .

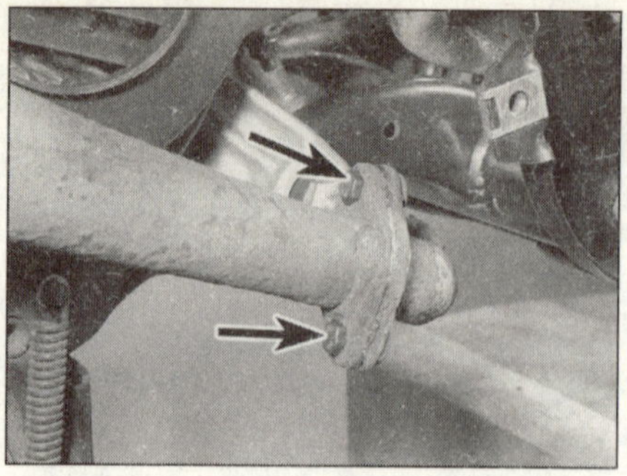

11.2b . . . and the two bolts (arrowed)

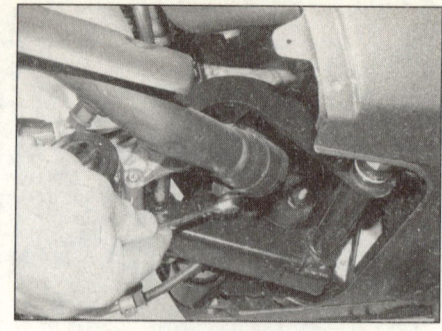

11.3a Loosen the silencer clamp

Installation

15 Installation is the reverse of removal, noting the following points:
 a) Lubricate the cable nipple(s) with multi-purpose grease.
 b) Make sure the cable is correctly routed. It must not interfere with any other component and should not be kinked or bent sharply. Turn the handlebars back-and-forth to make sure the cable doesn't cause the steering to bind.
 c) Operate the throttle to check that it opens and closes smoothly and freely.
 d) Check and adjust the cable freeplay (see Chapter 1).
 e) Start the engine and check that the idle speed does not rise as the handlebars are turned. If it does, the cable is routed incorrectly. Correct the problem before riding the scooter.

11 Exhaust system – removal and installation

Note: Some models are fitted with a one-piece exhaust system. Follow the procedure for removing the complete system.

⚠️ **Warning:** If the engine has been running the exhaust system will be very hot. Allow the system to cool before carrying out any work.

Downpipe removal

1 Remove the engine access panel and, if required by your model, the right-hand side panel (see Chapter 7).
2 Unscrew the two nuts securing the downpipe to the cylinder or cylinder head and the two bolts or clamp securing the downpipe to the silencer and remove the downpipe **(see illustrations)**. Remove the gasket from the exhaust port and from the downpipe to silencer joint. Discard them, as new ones must be used.

> **HAYNES HiNT** Exhaust system clamp bolts tend to become corroded and seized. It is advisable to spray them with penetrating oil before attempting to loosen them.

Silencer removal

Note: On all later models, the silencer incorporates a catalytic converter – handle the silencer with care to avoid damage.

3 Undo the two bolts or loosen the clamp securing the silencer to the downpipe **(see illustration)**. Support the silencer, then remove

11.3b Silencer mounting bolts – ET4

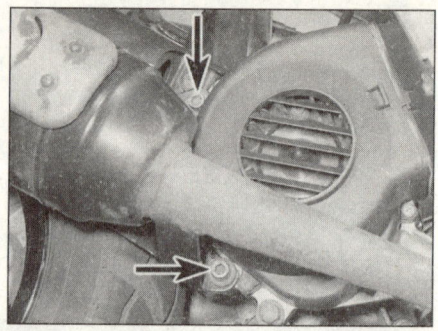

11.3c Silencer mounting bolts – Typhoon

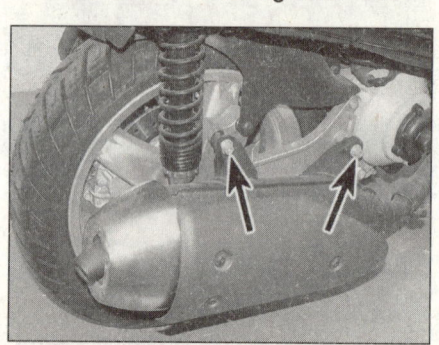

11.3d Silencer mounting bolts – X9

the bolts securing it to the engine or rear subframe and lift off **(see illustrations)**. Where fitted, note the spring washer between the silencer bracket and the engine casing **(see illustration)**. If fitted, remove the gasket from the silencer to downpipe joint **(see illustration)**. Discard it, as a new one must be used.

11.3e Remove the silencer carefully to avoid damaging the catalytic converter

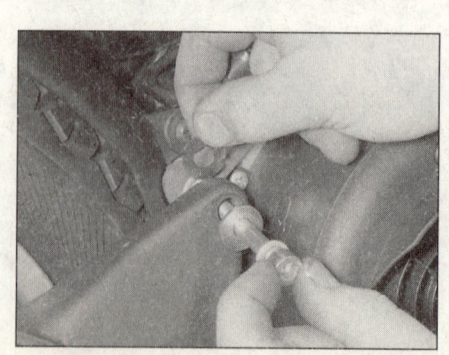

11.3f Note the location of the washers behind the silencer bracket

11.3g Remove the gasket and discard it

Fuel and exhaust systems 4•23

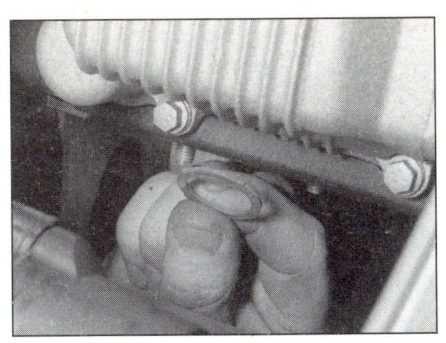

11.5 Remove the gasket from the exhaust port

Complete system removal

4 Remove the engine access panel and, if required by your model, the right-hand side panel (see Chapter 7). On two-stroke models fitted with a secondary air system (see Chapter 1, Section 21), loosen the clip securing the air hose to the extension on the exhaust downpipe and disconnect the hose.

5 Unscrew the two nuts securing the downpipe to the cylinder or cylinder head and the bolts securing the silencer to the engine and remove the exhaust system **(see illustrations 11.2a, 11.3b, 11.3c and 11.3d)**. Remove the gasket from the exhaust port. Discard it, as a new one must be used **(see illustration)**.

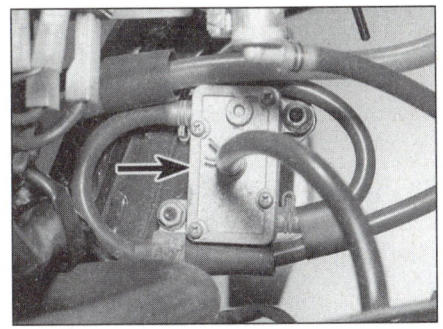

13.2a Fuel pump (arrowed) – Hexagon

Installation

6 Installation is the reverse of removal, noting the following:
a) When installing the silencer or the complete system, install the silencer-to-engine bolts first to take the weight – do not allow the other mountings to take the weight by themselves. Don't forget to fit the spring washers between the silencer bracket and the engine if applicable.
b) Leave all fasteners loose until the entire system has been installed, making alignment of the various sections easier. Tighten the silencer mountings last. Note that on some models the top silencer mounting bolt threads into a nut which sits captive, but not fixed, in a slot in the crankcase – make sure the nut is correctly positioned.
c) Use a new gasket in the exhaust port and between the downpipe and the silencer, where fitted.
d) Run the engine and check the system for leaks.

12 Catalytic converter – general information

1 To minimise the amount of engine exhaust pollutants escaping into the atmosphere, all two-stroke and four-stroke models with Hi-Per2 and Hi-Per4 engines, and later LEADER-engine models, are fitted with an exhaust system incorporating a simple, open-loop catalytic converter.

2 The catalytic converter works in conjunction with the secondary air system which promotes the burning of any excess fuel present in the exhaust gases. Ensure the secondary air system and system filters are checked at the specified service interval (see Chapter 1, Section 21).

3 The catalytic converter has no link with the fuel and ignition systems, and requires no routine maintenance. However the following points should be noted:

a) Always use unleaded fuel – the use of leaded fuel or LRP will destroy the converter.
b) Do not use any fuel or oil additives.
c) Keep the fuel and ignition systems in good order – if the fuel/air mixture is suspected of being incorrect, have it checked by a Piaggio dealer on an exhaust gas analyser.
d) When the exhaust system is removed from the scooter handle it with care to avoid damaging the catalytic converter.

13 Fuel pump – check and renewal

Warning: Refer to the precautions given in Section 1 before proceeding.

Hexagon, B125, X8 125, X9 125, GT125, GT200 and NRG Power DT and DD models

Check

1 The fuel system is pressurised. The fuel pump is operated by the alternating vacuum and pressure in the crankcase when the engine is running which opens and closes a diaphragm in the pump. On later Hexagon two-stroke models, the pump supplies fuel to a header tank which ensures a supply of fuel to the carburettor when the scooter has been standing unused. On all other models, the pump supplies fuel direct to the carburettor. The most likely cause of pump failure will be a split in the diaphragm.

2 On Hexagon models, remove the seat (see Chapter 7); the fuel pump is mounted on the frame above the engine **(see illustration)**. On B125, X8 125, X9 125 and NRG Power DT and DD models, remove the belly panel (see Chapter 7); the fuel pump is mounted on the frame alongside the fuel tank **(see illustration)**. On GT125 and GT200 models, the fuel pump is mounted on the underside of the fuel tank **(see illustration)**.

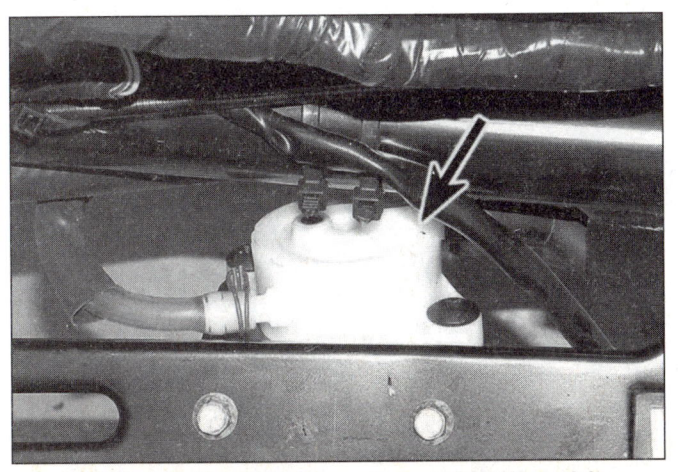

13.2b Location of fuel pump (arrowed) on X9 model

13.2c Location of the fuel pump (arrowed) on GT125 models

4•24 Fuel and exhaust systems

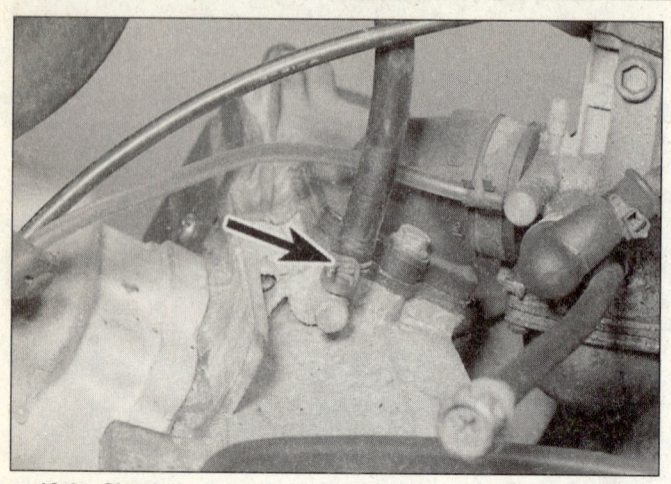

13.4a Check the vacuum hose from the crankcase (arrowed)

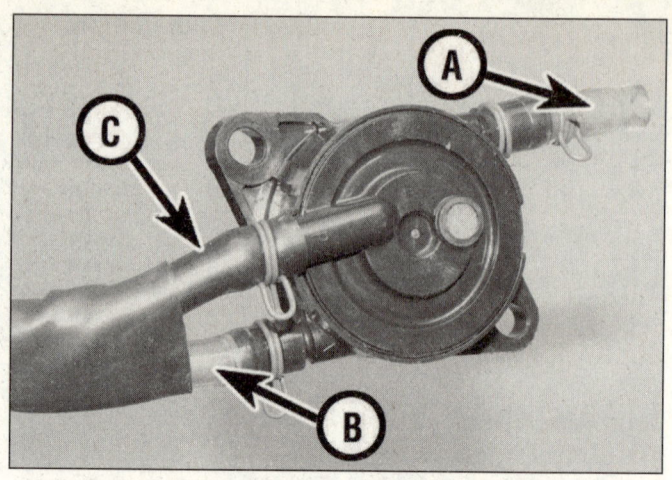

13.4b Fuel supply hose from tank (A), feed hose to carburettor (B) and vacuum hose (C)

3 To check whether the pump is operating, release the clip securing the fuel supply hose to the carburettor or header tank as applicable, and detach the hose. Place the open end in a container suitable for storing petrol. Turn the engine over on the starter motor and check whether fuel flows from the hose into the container. If fuel flows, the pump is working correctly. On later Hexagon two-stroke models, if the pump is good but fuel is not reaching the carburettor, check that the vent pipe from the header tank to the fuel tank is not blocked or kinked.

4 If no fuel flows from the pump hose, first check that this is not due to a blocked filter or fuel hose, or due to a split in the vacuum hose from the crankcase, before renewing the pump **(see illustration)**. Check all the hoses for splits, cracks and kinks, and check that they are securely connected on each end by a good clip **(see illustration)**. If all the hoses are good, renew the pump. On Hexagon two-stroke models, it is possible to disassemble the pump for cleaning or inspection – holding the diaphragm up to the light will reveal any splits or holes – but no individual components are available.

Renewal

5 Remove the bodywork as required by your model to access the fuel pump (see Chapter 7).
6 Release the clips securing the fuel and vacuum hoses and detach them from the pump, noting which fits where. Be prepared to catch any residue fuel in a suitable container. The fuel hoses should be clamped to prevent fuel leakage using any of the methods shown (see *Tool Tips*).
7 On Hexagon models, unscrew the nuts securing the pump to the frame. On all other models undo the screws securing the pump to the pump bracket **(see illustration)**. Remove the pump, noting which way up it fits.
8 Install the new pump, making sure the hoses are correctly attached and secured with the clips. If the old clips are corroded or deformed, fit new ones.

Typhoon 80 and 125 models
General

9 These models have two fuel tanks; the main fuel tank below the rear bodywork and an auxiliary fuel tank behind the fairing **(see illustrations)**. Fuel added via the filler cap in the main fuel tank is distributed evenly between both tanks via a balance pipe which

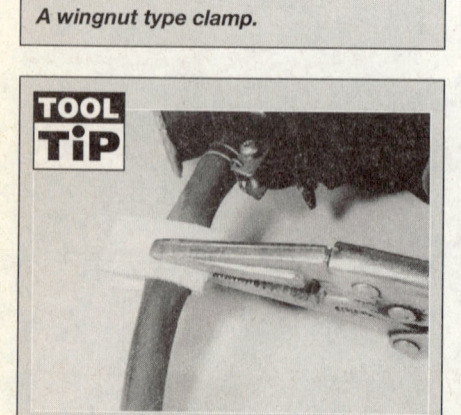

A wingnut type clamp.

Two sockets and self-locking grips.

Thick card and self-locking grips.

An automotive brake hose clamp.

13.7 Pump is secured to the bracket by two screws

Fuel and exhaust systems 4•25

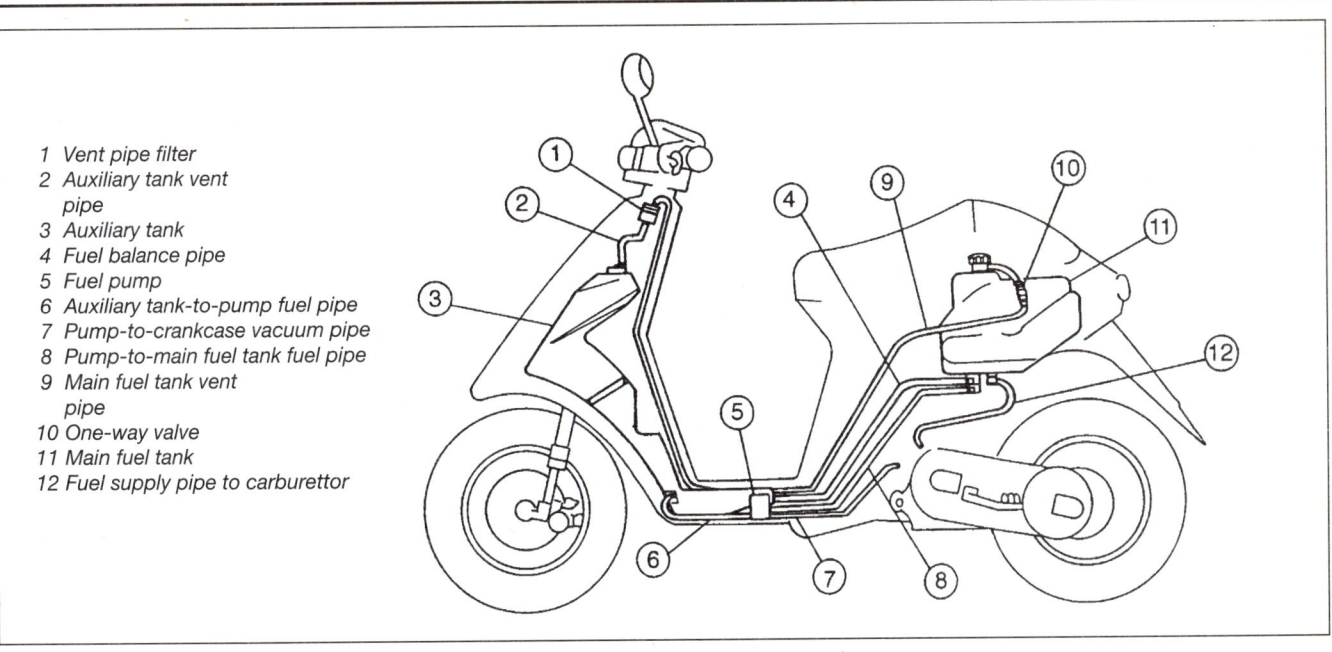

1 Vent pipe filter
2 Auxiliary tank vent pipe
3 Auxiliary tank
4 Fuel balance pipe
5 Fuel pump
6 Auxiliary tank-to-pump fuel pipe
7 Pump-to-crankcase vacuum pipe
8 Pump-to-main fuel tank fuel pipe
9 Main fuel tank vent pipe
10 One-way valve
11 Main fuel tank
12 Fuel supply pipe to carburettor

13.9a Fuel supply system components

runs under the footboard. A vent hose runs from the top of the auxiliary tank to the filler neck of the main fuel tank.

10 As the fuel level in the main fuel tank drops to show a 1/4 tank capacity on the gauge, a pump located under the footboards, pumps fuel from the auxiliary tank into the main tank until the auxiliary tank is drained. The pump is vacuum-operated via a hose from the engine.

Note: *The fuel supply to the carburettor is not pressurised. If the pump fails, it will not be possible to transfer fuel from the auxiliary tank to the main tank.*

Check

11 To check the operation of the pump, remove the filler cap from the main fuel tank. With the engine running it should be possible to see pumped fuel coming out of the supply pipe in the bottom of the tank.

12 Check for trapped or kinked pipes under the footboard. Check the auxiliary tank vent hose and the operation of the one-way valve **(see illustration 13.9b)**.

13 Check the main tank vent hose and the vent control valve. Disconnect the vent hose from the tank. There should be slight resistance when you blow through the hose from the tank end and no resistance when you blow through it from the open end.

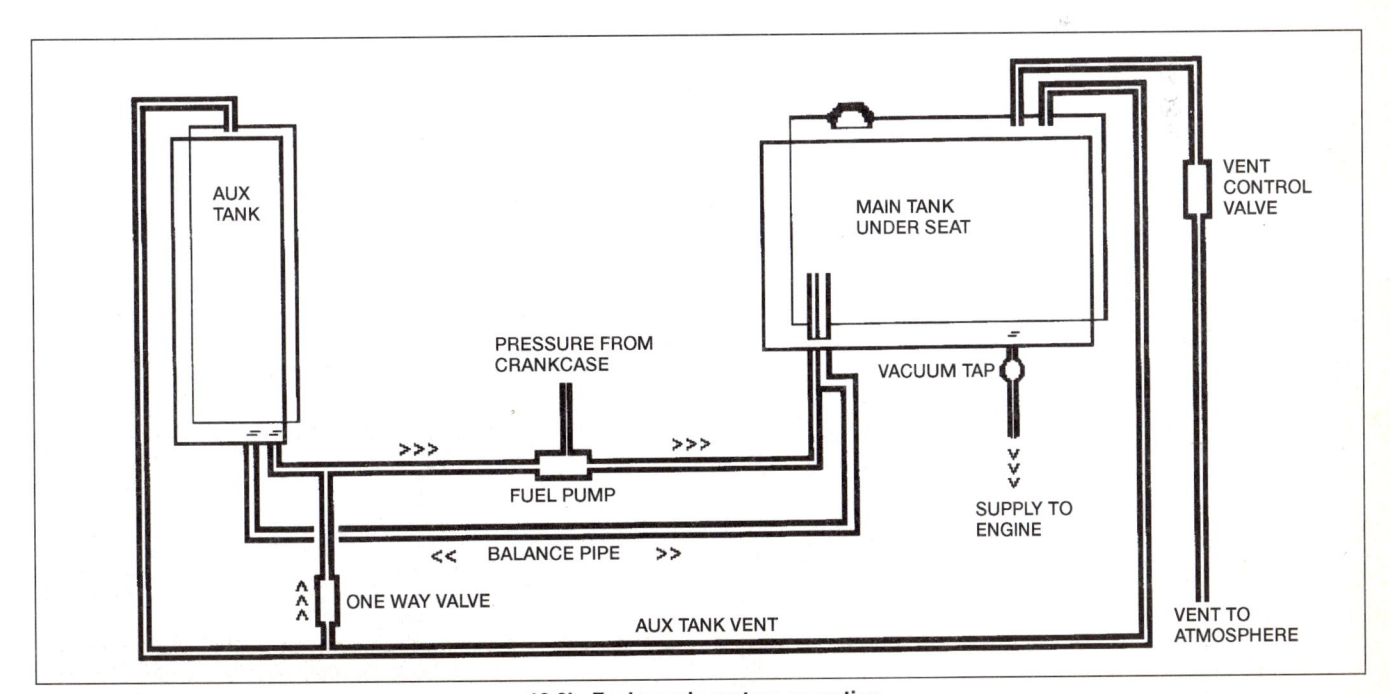

13.9b Fuel supply system operation

Chapter 5
Ignition system

Refer to the beginning of Chapter 1 for model identification details

Contents

General information 1	Source coil and pulse generator coil – check,
Ignition (main) switch – check, removal and	removal and installation 4
installation . . . . see Chapter 9	Spark plug – gap check and renewal . . . . see Chapter 1
Ignition control unit (ICU) and HT coil –	Immobiliser system (ET4) – general information,
check, removal and installation 3	programming and check 6
Ignition system – check 2	Immobiliser system (LEADER) – general information,
Ignition timing – general information and check 5	programming and check 7

Degrees of difficulty

Easy, suitable for novice with little experience	**Fairly easy,** suitable for beginner with some experience	**Fairly difficult,** suitable for competent DIY mechanic	**Difficult,** suitable for experienced DIY mechanic	**Very difficult,** suitable for expert DIY or professional

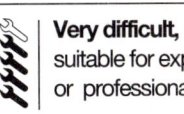

Specifications

Spark plug
Type and gap . . . . See Chapter 1
Cap resistance . . . . 5 K ohms

Ignition timing
Ignition full advance
  Sfera 50, Typhoon 50, Zip . . . . 15 to 17° BTDC @ 4000 rpm
  Sfera 50 RST, NRG MC2/MC3, NRG Power DT, ET2, Zip SP, Zip 50,
    Liberty 50, Fly 50, LX2 50 . . . . 16 to 18° BTDC @ 4000 rpm
  Sfera 80, Typhoon 80 . . . . 19 to 21° BTDC @ 4000 rpm
  LX4 50 . . . . 21° BTDC @ 4000 to 7000 rpm
  Fly 50 4T . . . . not available
  Zip 50 4T, Liberty 50 4T, ET4 50 . . . . 26° BTDC @ 5000 to 6000 rpm
  Skipper, Typhoon 125 . . . . 18 to 20° BTDC @ 4000 rpm
  Sfera 125 . . . . 31 to 33° BTDC @ 7500 rpm
  ET4 125, GT200 . . . . 31 to 33° BTDC @ 6000 rpm
  Hexagon . . . . 21 to 23° BTDC @ 6000 rpm
  Zip 125, Skipper ST . . . . 28° BTDC @ 6000 rpm
  Liberty 125 . . . . 27 to 29° BTDC @ 6000 rpm
  Fly 125, LX4 125 . . . . not available
  B125, Super Hexagon, X8 125, X9 125, GT125 . . . . 33 to 35° BTDC @ 6000 rpm

Ignition source coil
Coil resistance
  ET2 . . . . 850 to 1050 ohms
  ET4 . . . . 300 to 400 ohms
  NRG Power DT and DD, Fly 50 4T, LX4 50 . . . . 1.0 ohm
  Fly 50, LX2 50 . . . . 800 to 1100 ohms
  Sfera 125 . . . . 330 to 370 ohms
  Hexagon . . . . 122 to 132 ohms
  All LEADER-engined models . . . . 0.7 to 0.9 ohm
  All other models . . . . 930 to 1030 ohms

Ignition pulse generator coil
Coil resistance
- ET2 .... 100 to 130 ohms
- ET4, Fly 50, LX2 50 .... 90 to 140 ohms
- NRG Power DT and DD, Fly 50 4T, LX4 50 .... 170 ohms
- Sfera 125 .... 105 to 135 ohms
- Hexagon .... 102 to 112 ohms
- All LEADER-engined models .... 1.5 to 124 ohms
- All other models .... 83 to 93 ohms

Coil output voltage
- LEADER-engined models .... Less than 2 V

Ignition HT coil – 125 cc models
Primary circuit resistance .... 0.48 to 0.52 ohm
Secondary circuit resistance
- LEADER-engined models .... 2.7 to 3.3 K ohms
- All other models .... 4.6 to 5.2 K ohms

Immobiliser
Transponder aerial resistance .... 7 to 9 ohms

1 General information

All models are fitted with a fully-transistorised electronic ignition system, which because to its lack of mechanical parts is totally maintenance-free. The system comprises a source coil, rotor, pulse generator coil, ignition control unit and ignition HT coil (refer to the wiring diagrams at the end of Chapter 9 for details). On all 50 cc and 80 cc models the HT coil is integral with the ignition control unit.

The ignition trigger, which is on the alternator rotor on the right-hand end of the crankshaft, magnetically operates the pulse generator coil as the crankshaft rotates. The pulse generator coil sends a signal to the ignition control unit which then supplies the integral (50/80 cc) or separate (125/200 cc) ignition HT coil with the power necessary to produce a spark at the plug.

The ignition control unit (ICU) incorporates an electronic advance system controlled by signals generated by the ignition trigger and the pulse generator coil. There is no provision for adjusting the ignition timing on these scooters.

Depending upon the model and specification, some Piaggio scooters were fitted with an ignition immobiliser. On later models the ignition system incorporates a safety circuit which prevents the engine from being started unless one of the brake levers is pulled in and the side stand is up.

Because of their nature, the individual ignition system components can be checked but not repaired. If ignition system troubles occur, and the faulty component can be isolated, the only cure for the problem is to renew the part. Keep in mind that most electrical parts, once purchased, cannot be returned. To avoid unnecessary expense, make very sure the faulty component has been positively identified before buying a new part.

2 Ignition system – check

Warning: The energy levels in electronic systems can be very high. On no account should the ignition be switched on whilst the plug or plug cap is being held – shocks from the HT circuit can be most unpleasant. Secondly, it is vital that the engine is not turned over with the plug cap removed, and that the plug is soundly earthed when the system is checked for sparking. The ignition system components can be seriously damaged if the HT circuit becomes isolated.

1 As no means of adjustment is available, any failure of the system can be traced to failure of a system component or a simple wiring fault. Of the two possibilities, the latter is by far the most likely. In the event of failure, check the system in a logical fashion, as described below.

2 Disconnect the HT lead from the spark plug. Connect the lead to a spare spark plug and lay the plug on the engine with the thread contacting the engine. If necessary, hold the spark plug with an insulated tool.

Warning: Do not remove the spark plug from the engine to perform this check – atomised fuel being pumped out of the open spark plug hole could ignite, causing severe injury.

3 Having observed the above precautions, turn the ignition switch ON and turn the engine over on the starter motor. If the system is in good condition a regular, fat blue spark should be evident at the plug electrodes. If the spark appears thin or yellowish, or is non-existent, further investigation will be necessary. Before proceeding further, turn the ignition OFF.

4 The ignition system must be able to produce a spark which is capable of jumping a particular size gap. Piaggio do not provide a specification, but a healthy system should produce a spark capable of jumping at least 6 mm. A simple testing tool can be made to test the minimum gap across which the spark will jump (see **Tool Tip**).

5 Connect the spark plug HT lead to the protruding electrode on the test tool, and clip the tool to a good earth on the engine. Turn the ignition switch ON and turn the engine over on the starter motor. If the system is in good condition, a regular, fat blue spark should be seen to jump the gap between the nail ends. If the test results are good the entire ignition system can be considered good. If the spark appears thin or yellowish, or is non-existent, further investigation will be necessary.

6 Ignition faults can be divided into two categories, namely those where the ignition system has failed completely, and those which are due to a partial failure. The likely faults are listed on the next page, starting with the most

A simple spark gap testing tool can be made from a block of wood, a large alligator clip and two nails, one of which is fashioned so that a spark plug cap or bare HT lead end can be connected to its end. Make sure the gap between the two nail ends is the same as specified.

Ignition system 5•3

3.1 Combined ignition control unit and HT coil on Typhoon 50

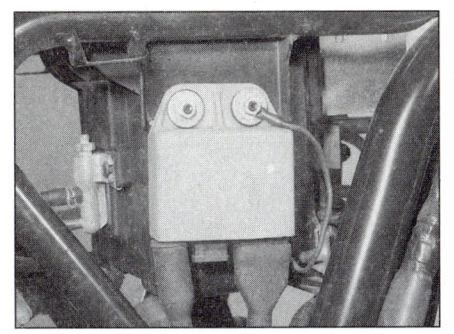

3.2a Ignition control unit on Hexagon

3.2b HT coil on Hexagon

3.2c Ignition control unit on ET4

3.2d HT coil on ET4

probable source of failure. Work through the list systematically, referring to the subsequent sections for full details of the necessary checks and tests. **Note:** *Before checking the following items ensure that the battery is fully-charged and that all fuses are in good condition.*

a) Loose, corroded or damaged wiring connections, broken or shorted wiring between any of the component parts of the ignition system (see Chapter 9).
b) Faulty HT lead or spark plug cap, faulty spark plug with dirty, worn or corroded plug electrodes, or incorrect gap between electrodes.
c) Faulty ignition (main) switch (see Chapter 9).
d) Faulty pulse generator coil or damaged trigger on rotor.
e) Faulty ignition HT coil/ignition control unit (50 and 80 cc).
f) Faulty ignition HT or control unit (125 cc).

7 If the above checks don't reveal the cause of the problem, have the ignition system tested by a Piaggio dealer.

3 Ignition control unit (ICU) and HT coil – check, removal and installation

Check – 50 and 80 cc models

1 On all 50 and 80 cc models the ICU and HT coil are integrated in one unit **(see illustration)**. Piaggio provide no test specifications for this unit. In order to determine conclusively that the unit is defective, it should be substituted with a known good one. If the fault is rectified, the original unit is faulty.

Check – 125 and 200 cc models

2 On models with 125 and 200 cc engines, the ICU and HT coil are separate **(see illustrations)**. Piaggio provide no test specifications for the ICU. In order to determine conclusively that the unit is defective, it should be substituted with a known good one. If the fault is rectified, the original unit is faulty.

3 The coil should be checked visually for cracks and other damage, then the primary and secondary coil resistance should be measured with a multi-meter. To test the HT coil, first remove the engine cover or bodywork as required according to model (see Chapter 7). Disconnect the battery negative (-ve) lead.

Non LEADER models

4 Disconnect the primary circuit electrical connector and the HT lead from the coil.

5 To check the condition of the primary windings, set the meter to the ohms x 1 scale and measure the resistance between the primary circuit terminal on the coil and the coil mounting which goes to earth **(see illustration)**. If the reading obtained is not within the range shown in the Specifications, it is likely that the coil is defective and must be renewed.

6 To check the condition of the secondary windings, set the meter to the K ohm scale, then measure the resistance between the HT lead socket on the coil and the coil mounting

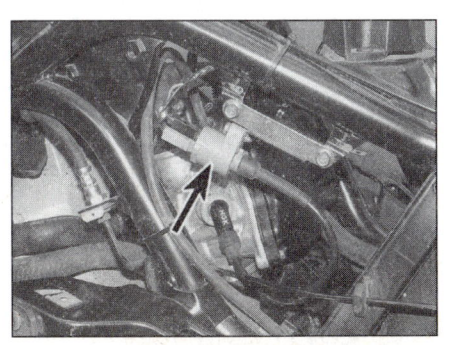

3.2e HT coil on X9

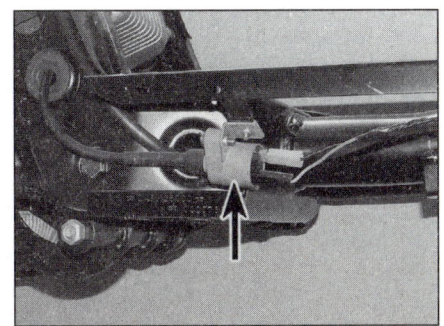

3.2f HT coil on Zip 125

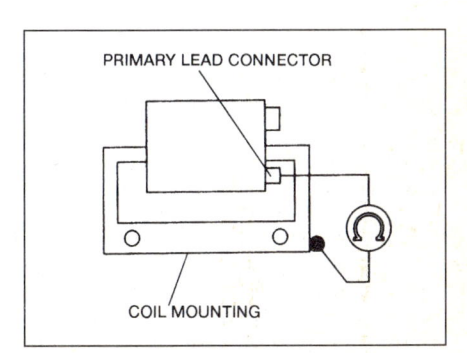

3.5 HT coil primary winding check – 125 models

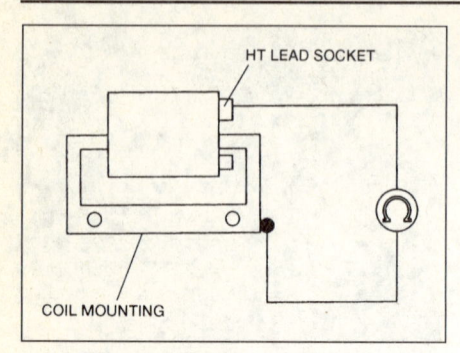

5•4 Ignition system

3.6 HT coil secondary winding check – 125 models

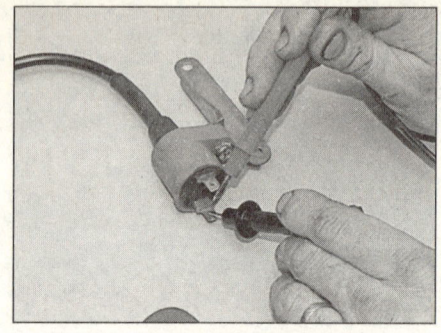

3.8 HT coil primary winding check – LEADER

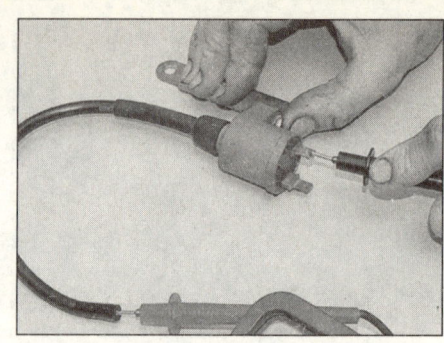

3.9 HT coil secondary winding check – LEADER, plug cap removed

which goes to earth **(see illustration)**. If the reading obtained is not within the range shown in the Specifications, it is likely that the coil is defective and must be renewed.

LEADER models

7 Disconnect the primary circuit electrical connectors from the coil, noting where they fit, and the spark plug cap from the plug.
8 To check the condition of the primary windings, set the meter to the ohms x 1 scale and measure the resistance between the primary circuit terminals on the coil **(see illustration)**. If the reading obtained is not within the range shown in the Specifications, it is likely that the coil is defective and must be renewed.
9 To check the condition of the secondary windings, set the meter to the K ohm scale, then measure the resistance between the spark plug terminal inside the cap and the black wire terminal on the coil **(see illustration)**. If the reading obtained is not within the range shown in the Specifications, unscrew the plug cap from the HT lead and check again between the black wire terminal and the core of the HT lead. If the reading is still not within the specified range, it is likely that the coil is defective and must be renewed.

Removal

10 Remove the engine cover or bodywork as required according to model (see Chapter 7). Disconnect the battery negative (-ve) lead.
11 Disconnect the electrical connectors from the unit and where applicable disconnect the HT lead from the spark plug. **Note:** *Mark the locations of all wires before disconnecting them.*
12 Unscrew the two bolts securing the unit and remove it. Note the routing of the wiring.

Installation

13 Installation is the reverse of removal. Make sure the wiring connectors and HT lead are securely connected.
Caution: If the ignition control unit has been renewed on a model fitted with an immobiliser, refer to a Piaggio dealer for details of how to programme it.

4 Source coil and pulse generator coil – check, removal and refitting

Check

1 Remove the engine cover or bodywork as required according to model (see Chapter 7) and disconnect the battery negative (-ve) lead.

Non LEADER models

2 Trace the source coil and pulse generator coil wiring from the back of the alternator housing and disconnect it at the connector on the ICU **(see illustrations)**. Using a multimeter set to the ohms x 100 scale, measure the source coil resistance by connecting the meter probes between the green and white terminals on the connector. Also measure the pulse generator coil resistance by connecting the meter probes between the red and white terminals on 50/80 cc models with integral ignition control unit and HT coil, and between red and brown on 125 cc models with separate HT coil.
3 Compare the readings obtained with those given in the Specifications at the beginning of the Chapter. If the readings obtained differ greatly from those given, particularly if the meter indicates a short circuit (no measurable resistance) or an open circuit (infinite, or very high resistance), the entire alternator stator assembly must be renewed as no individual components are available. However, first check that the fault is not due to a damaged or broken wire from the coil to the connector; pinched or broken wires can usually be repaired.

LEADER models

4 To check the source coil, first disconnect the alternator wiring multi-pin connector **(see illustration)**. Using a multi-meter set to the ohms scale, measure the coil resistance by connecting the meter probes between the yellow wire terminals on the alternator side of the connector. Compare the result with the Specifications at the beginning of the Chapter. Also check for continuity between each terminal and earth – there should be no continuity. If the results are good, reconnect the alternator connector and trace the wiring to the regulator. Disconnect the regulator wiring connector and repeat the test between the wire terminals **(see illustrations)**. If the

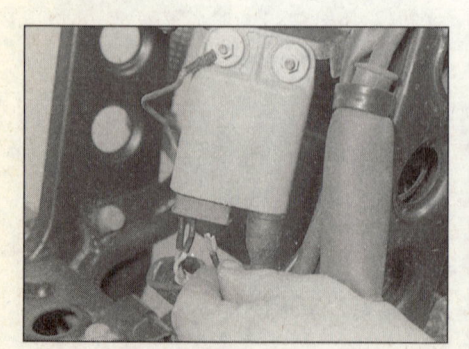

4.2a Disconnecting the pulse generator coil wiring on Typhoon 50

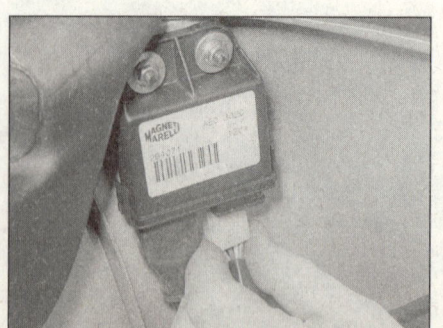

4.2b Disconnecting the pulse generator coil wiring on ET4

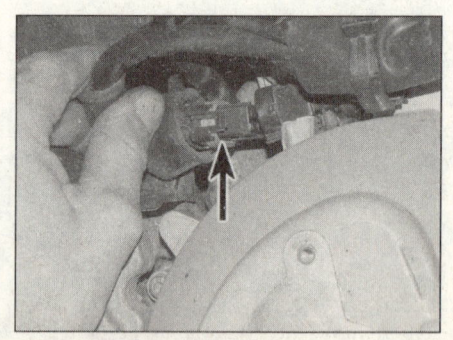

4.4a Disconnecting the alternator wiring connector (arrowed) on X9

Ignition system 5•5

4.4b Disconnect the regulator wiring connector . . .

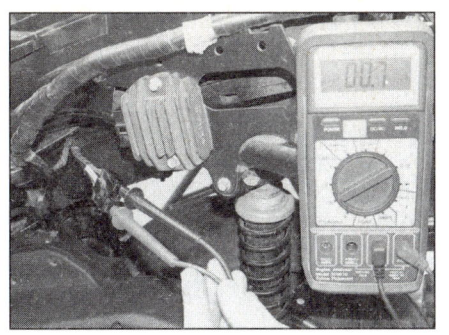

4.4c . . . and check the source coil resistance

readings differ from those given, there is a fault in the wiring between the alternator connector and the regulator connector.

5 To check the pulse generator coil resistance, connect the meter probes between the green wire terminal and earth (ground). Compare the result with the Specifications at the beginning of the Chapter. If the result is good, reconnect the alternator connector and trace the wiring to the ICU. Disconnect the ICU wiring connector and repeat the test between the green wire terminal in the connector and the black (earth/ground) wire terminal. If the reading differs from that given, there is a fault in the wiring between the alternator connector and the ICU connector. Now set the multimeter to the volts (DC) scale, connect the positive (+) meter probe to the green wire terminal and the negative (-) probe to the black wire terminal. Use the starter motor to turn the engine over and measure the pulse generator coil voltage, then compare the result to the Specifications.

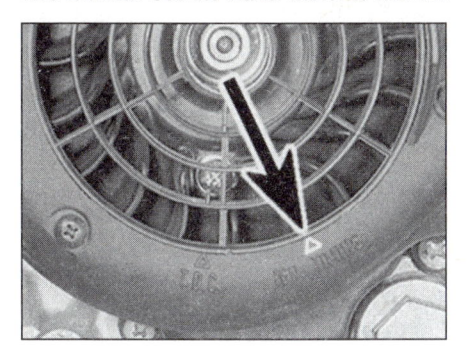

6 If any of the readings obtained differ greatly from those given, particularly if the meter indicates a short circuit (no measurable resistance) or an open circuit (infinite, or very high resistance), the entire alternator stator/pulse generator coil assembly must be renewed as no individual components are available. However, first check that the fault is not due to a damaged or broken wire from the coil to the connector; pinched or broken wires can usually be repaired.

Renewal

7 The source coil and pulse generator coil are integral with the alternator stator. Refer to the relevant Section of Chapter 2 for the removal and installation procedure.

5.4a Static timing mark at idle speed on ET4 (arrowed)

5.4b The timing mark on the rotor is an arrow (arrowed)

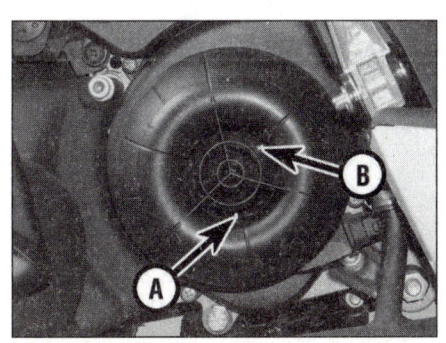

5.5 Remove the inspection cap – liquid-cooled LEADER

5.7 Static mark (A) on cover and timing mark (B) on rotor cooling fan highlighted for clarity

5 Ignition timing – general information and check

General information

1 Since no provision exists for adjusting the ignition timing and, since no component is subject to mechanical wear, there is no need for regular checks; only if investigating a fault such as a loss of power or a misfire, should the ignition timing be checked.

2 The ignition timing is checked dynamically (engine running) using a stroboscopic lamp. The inexpensive neon lamps should be adequate in theory, but in practice may produce a pulse of such low intensity that the timing mark remains indistinct. If possible, one of the more precise xenon tube lamps should be used, powered by an external source of the appropriate voltage. **Note:** *Do not use the machine's own battery as an incorrect reading may result from stray impulses within the machine's electrical system.*

Check

3 Warm the engine up to normal operating temperature then turn it OFF.

All non-LEADER engines

4 First identify the static reference mark on the alternator cover. The location of the reference mark will vary according to the machine and its age. Some scooters have two marks – one indicates the timing at idle, the other the TDC position (not relevant for ignition timing) **(see illustration)**. Some machines, especially liquid-cooled models, have an inspection hole in the cover, rather than a mark. If no reference mark is obvious, remove the cover and use the sensor on the pulse generator coil as a static guide. The timing mark is on the alternator rotor **(see illustration)** – if necessary, remove the alternator cover and the cooling fan on the right-hand side of the engine to locate the timing mark (see Chapter 2A, 2B, 2C or 2D).

LEADER engines

5 On all models, the static reference mark is on the alternator cover – on liquid-cooled models, remove the inspection cap, the reference mark is inside the hole **(see illustration)**. On air-cooled models, the timing mark is on the cooling fan; on liquid-cooled models the timing mark is on the water pump drive.

All engines

> **HAYNES HiNT** *The timing marks can be highlighted with white paint to make them more visible under the stroboscope lamp.*

6 Connect the timing light to the spark plug HT lead as described in the manufacturer's instructions.

7 Start the engine and aim the lamp at the static reference mark **(see illustration)**. With

5•6 Ignition system

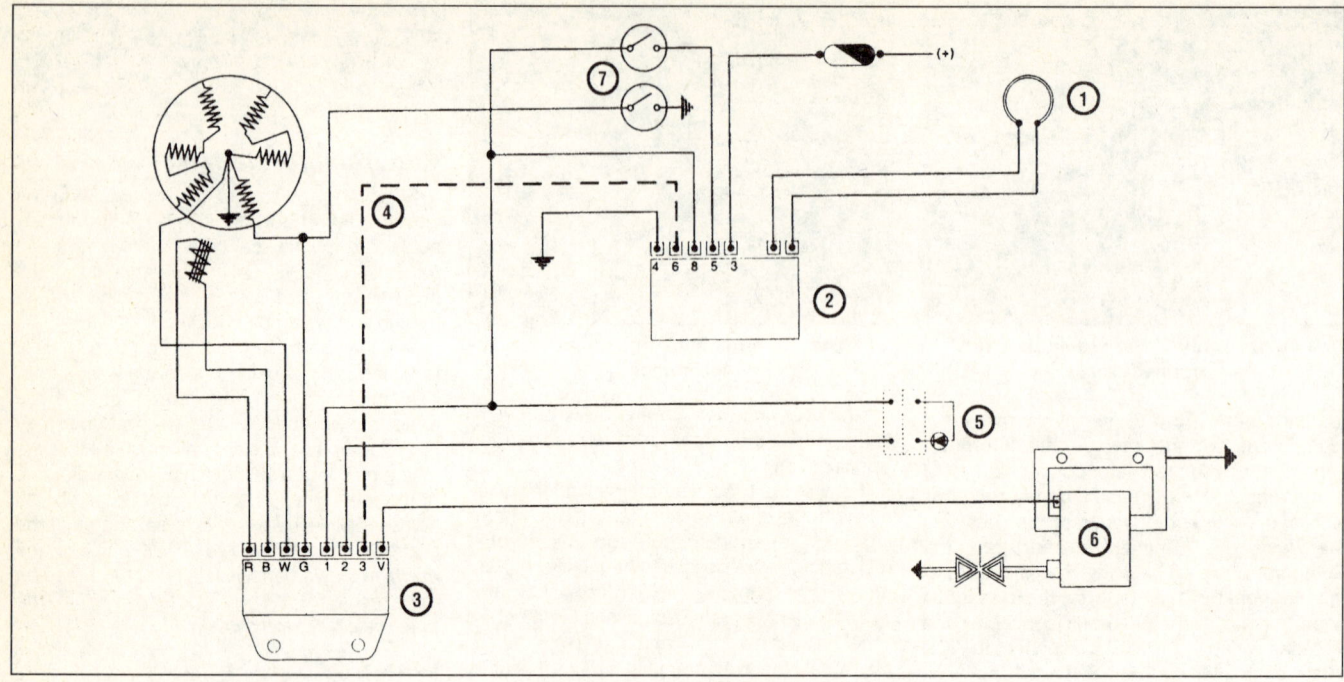

6.1 Immobiliser circuit diagram as fitted to ET4

1 Immobiliser transponder aerial
2 Decoder unit
3 Ignition control unit
4 Orange serial line cable
5 Diagnostic tester connector and diode
6 Ignition HT coil
7 Ignition (main) switch

the machine idling at the specified speed, the timing mark on the rotor should align with the idle reference mark.
8 Slowly increase the engine speed whilst observing the timing mark. The timing mark should move anti-clockwise, increasing in relation to the engine speed until it reaches the full advance reference mark (where present).
9 As already stated, there is no means of adjustment of the ignition timing on these machines. If the ignition timing is incorrect, or suspected of being incorrect, one of the ignition system components is at fault, and the system components must be tested as described in the preceding Sections of this Chapter.
10 When the check is complete, install the alternator cover or inspection cap.

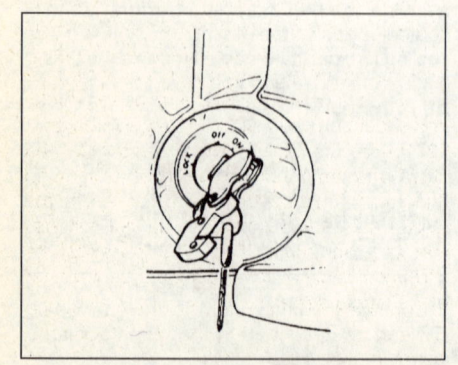

6.9 Immobiliser programming check using red-tagged key

6 Immobiliser system (ET4) – general information, programming and check

Note: *The immobiliser described in this section is fitted as standard to non-LEADER engined ET4 models. A similar version may be fitted as optional equipment on other models.*

General information

1 The ET4 model is equipped with an electronic immobiliser system **(see illustration)**. The system functions using a coded key.
2 Two keys and a code card are supplied with the vehicle from new, and the system will already have been programmed with your code. The red-tagged key is the master key and should be kept in a safe place along with the code card – if the red-tagged key is lost you will need a new immobiliser system! If required, additional blue-tagged keys can be programmed (to a maximum of seven).
3 Whenever the key is inserted, the immobiliser is disarmed (assuming the code is accepted). When the key is removed, with the ignition in either the OFF or LOCK positions, the system is automatically activated.
4 If the machine does not start when the key is inserted in the lock and the ignition is switched ON, turn the switch back to the OFF position and try again. If the machine still does not start, use the red-tagged master key. If the machine still does not start, contact your Piaggio dealer. They have a special electronic analyser which can locate the fault in the system. There are no testing specifications or procedures which can be applied at home using normal test equipment.
5 If the immobiliser decoder unit (located behind the legshield panel on ET4 models) or the ignition control unit are renewed, the system must be reprogrammed.

Programming

6 With the ignition switch in the OFF position, insert the red-tagged key. Turn the switch on for 1 to 3 seconds, then turn it OFF again. Remove the key.
7 Within 10 seconds of removing the red-tagged key, insert the blue-tagged key. Immediately turn the switch on for 1 to 3 seconds, then turn it OFF again. Remove the key. If required, repeat this procedure for any additional blue-tagged keys.
8 Within 10 seconds of removing the blue-tagged key, insert the red-tagged key again. Immediately turn the switch on for 1 to 3 seconds, then turn it OFF again. Remove the key.
Caution: *The use of the correct spark plug and suppresser cap is essential to prevent interference with the immobiliser system.*

Check

9 To check the system after programming, insert the red-tagged key and flip open the hinged section of the tag. Turn the switch ON and try to start the engine **(see illustration)**. It

Ignition system 5•7

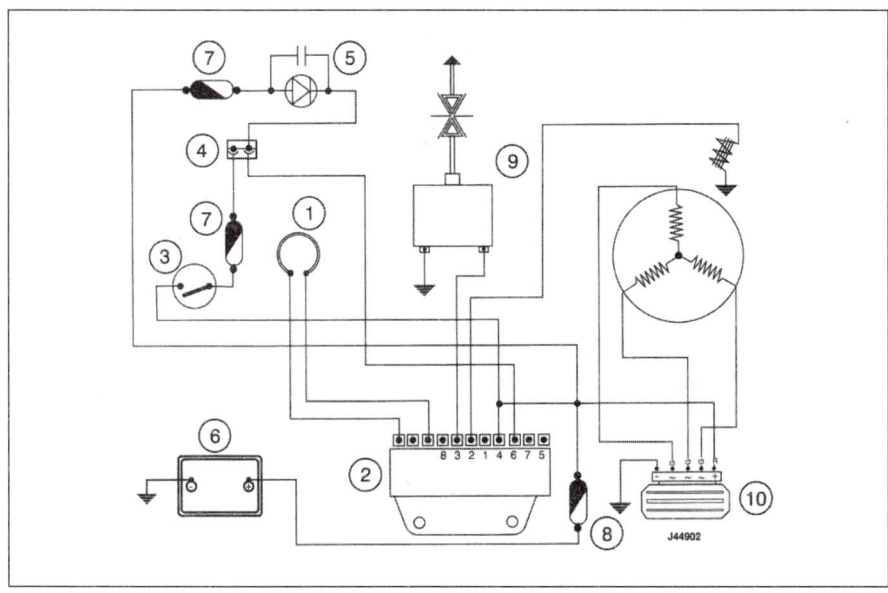

7.1 Immobiliser circuit diagram as fitted to X9

1 Immobiliser transponder aerial
2 ICU
3 Ignition (main) switch
4 Diagnostic tester connector
5 Immobiliser LED
6 Battery
7 10 A fuse
8 15 A fuse
9 Ignition HT coil
10 Regulator

should not start. Now insert a blue-tagged key and try to start the engine. It should start.

10 If the system does not perform as described, perform the programming sequence again. If the system still does not perform, contact your Piaggio dealer. They have a special electronic analyser which can locate the fault in the system. There are no testing specifications or procedures which can be applied at home using normal test equipment.

7 Immobiliser system (LEADER) – general information, programming and check

General information

1 The LEADER engined models are equipped with an electronic immobiliser system **(see illustration)**. The system functions using a coded key.

2 Two keys and a code card are supplied with the vehicle from new, and the system will already have been programmed with your code. The red or brown-tagged key is the master key and should be kept in a safe place along with the code card – if the master key is lost you will need a new immobiliser system! The blue or black-tagged keys are the service keys for everyday use – additional service keys can be programmed (to a maximum of seven).

3 Whenever the key is inserted, the immobiliser is disarmed (assuming the code is accepted). When the key is removed, with the ignition in either the OFF or LOCK positions, the system is automatically activated.

4 If the machine does not start when the service key is inserted in the lock and the ignition is switched ON, turn the switch back to the OFF position and try again. If the machine still does not start, use the master key. If the machine still does not start, contact your Piaggio dealer. They have a special electronic analyser which can locate the fault in the system. If the engine starts but will not rev above 2000 rpm (slightly more than idle speed) the immobiliser needs reprogramming (see Steps 8 to 10).

5 The immobiliser LED flashes for 48 hours and then goes out to minimise battery discharge, although the immobiliser system remains active.

6 The LED should flash once when the ignition is switched ON. If the LED stays off, use a multi-meter to check for battery voltage at the ICU. Remove the engine cover or bodywork as required according to model to access the ICU (see Chapter 7). Ensure the ignition is OFF, then disconnect the ICU wiring connector and check for battery voltage between the red/black wire terminal in the connector and earth (ground), and then between the red/black wire terminal and the black wire terminal. If there is no voltage, inspect the wiring between the ICU and the battery and check the ICU 15 amp fuse (see wiring diagrams at the end of Chapter 9).

7 Ensure that the engine kill switch on the handlebar is in the RUN position and that the side stand (where a side stand switch is fitted) is up. Turn the ignition ON and check for battery voltage between the light blue wire terminal in the ICU connector and the black wire terminal. If there is no voltage, refer to Chapter 9 and check the individual components in the starting system. If there is battery voltage, the ICU is probably faulty and should be checked by a Piaggio dealer.

Programming

8 With the ignition switch in the OFF position, insert the master key. Turn the switch on for 1 to 3 seconds, then turn it OFF again. Remove the key.

9 Within 10 seconds of removing the master key, insert the service key. Immediately turn the switch on for 1 to 3 seconds, then turn it OFF again. Remove the key. If required, repeat this procedure for any additional service keys.

10 Within 10 seconds of removing the service key, insert the master key again. Immediately turn the switch on for 1 to 3 seconds, then turn it OFF again. Remove the key. The immobiliser system is now programmed.

Caution: The use of the correct, resistor type, spark plug and suppresser cap is essential to prevent interference with the immobiliser system and possible loss of key programming.

Malfunction codes

11 The LED should flash once when the ignition is switched ON. If the LED then flashes twice and then stays on permanently to indicate an ignition fault, try using the master key to turn the ignition ON. If this works, the service key has lost its programme. If the fault persists, remove the bodywork as required according to model to access the immobiliser transponder aerial located behind the ignition switch (see Chapter 7). Trace the transponder wiring and disconnect it at the connector. Use a multi-meter set to the ohms scale to check the resistance of the aerial. If the result is not as specified, fit a new aerial. If the result is good, the ICU is probably faulty and should be checked by a Piaggio dealer.

12 If the LED flashes three times and then stays on permanently to indicate an ignition fault, try using the master key to turn the ignition ON. If this works, the service key has lost its programme. If the fault persists, the ICU is probably faulty and should be checked by a Piaggio dealer.

Notes

Chapter 6
Steering and suspension

Refer to the beginning of Chapter 1 for model identification details

Contents

Front suspension – disassembly, inspection and reassembly 5	Steering head bearings – freeplay check and adjustment .... see Chapter 1
General information 1	Steering head bearings – inspection and renewal 4
Handlebars and levers – removal and installation 2	Steering stem – removal and installation 3
Rear shock absorber – preload adjustment 7	Suspension – check .... see Chapter 1
Rear shock absorber – removal, inspection and installation 6	Swingarm – removal, inspection and installation 8

Degrees of difficulty

Easy, suitable for novice with little experience	Fairly easy, suitable for beginner with some experience	Fairly difficult, suitable for competent DIY mechanic	Difficult, suitable for experienced DIY mechanic	Very difficult, suitable for expert DIY or professional

Specifications

Front forks

Zip
  Fork oil type .... 20W fork oil
  Fork oil capacity
    Zip .... 30 cc each leg
    Zip 50, Zip 50 4T, Zip 125 .... 25 cc each leg
Liberty 50, Liberty 50 4T, Fly 50, Fly 50 4T
  Fork oil type .... 20W fork oil
  Fork oil capacity .... 30 cc each leg
Liberty 125
  Fork oil type .... 20W fork oil
  Fork oil capacity .... 90 cc each leg
X8 125
  Fork oil type .... 10W fork oil
  Fork oil capacity .... 125 cc each leg
X9 125
  Fork oil type .... 20W fork oil
  Fork oil capacity .... 90 cc each leg
B125
  Fork oil type .... 10W fork oil
  Fork oil capacity .... 102 cc each leg
Typhoon, Skipper (1998 to 2000 models), Skipper ST and all NRG models
  Grease type .... Esso Beacon ET2 or Tradal Complex 2

Torque settings

Handlebar stem bolt nut
  Hexagon 125 .... 38 Nm
  Liberty 125 .... 55 Nm
  X8 125 .... 43 to 47 Nm
  Fly 50 4T .... 50 to 55 Nm
  All other models .... 45 to 50 Nm
Handlebar stem bolt (Zip models) .... 13 to 16 Nm
Steering head bearing adjuster nut
  Initial setting for all models with ball race bearings (see text) ...... 50 to 60 Nm
  Initial setting for all models with taper roller bearings (see text) .... 20 to 25 Nm
  Final setting for all models with taper roller bearings (see text) ..... 10 to 13 Nm
Steering head bearing locknut
  Models with taper roller bearings .... 30 to 33 Nm
  Models with ball race bearings .... 40 Nm

6•2 Steering and suspension

Torque settings (continued)

Front monoshock mounting nuts
   Sfera, Hexagon, Skipper (1993 to 1997), Zip SP, ET2, ET4,
   all LX and GT models .... 20 to 30 Nm
Front monoshock mounting bolts
   Sfera, Hexagon, Skipper (1993 to 1997), Zip SP, ET2 and ET4 ..... 20 to 25 Nm
   All LX and GT models .... 20 to 27 Nm
Front monoshock upper mounting
   Super Hexagon 125 .... 30 Nm
Front monoshock lower mounting
   Super Hexagon 125 .... 27 Nm
Upside-down telescopic forks
   Upper and lower fork assembly bolts .... 8 to 10 Nm
Motorcycle-type forks
   Top bolt .... 15 to 30 Nm
   Fork leg clamp bolts
      X8 125 .... 20 to 25 Nm
      All Fly models .... 15 to 20 Nm
   Damper bolt
      All Fly models .... 15 to 20 Nm
      All other models .... 25 to 35 Nm
Rear shock absorber upper mounting
   Sfera 125 and ET4 .... 20 to 27 Nm
   B125, X9 125 .... 41 Nm
   All other models .... 20 to 25 Nm
Rear shock absorber lower mounting
   Sfera 125 and ET4 .... 20 to 27 Nm
   All other models .... 33 to 41 Nm
Swingarm pivot bolt
   Sfera 125 and ET4 .... 20 to 27 Nm
   Fly 50, Fly 50 4T, NRG Power DT and DD .... 64 to 72 Nm
   All LX models .... 44 to 52 Nm
   X9 125, B125, Fly 125, Liberty 125 (LEADER), X8 125, GT125/200 .. 64 to 72 Nm
   All other models .... 33 to 41 Nm
Swingarm to frame bolt
   Fly 125 .... 33 to 41 Nm
   X9 125, B125, X8 125, GT125/200 .... 64 to 72 Nm

1 General information

Front suspension is by conventional telescopic forks, upside-down telescopic forks, or by a single-sided trailing arm acting on a shock absorber (monoshock). The front suspension is not adjustable on any model. The model application of front suspension types is detailed in the model specifications in Chapter 1.

At the rear, single or twin oil-damped shock absorbers are mounted between the engine unit and the frame. The shock absorbers are adjustable for spring preload.

2 Handlebars and levers – removal and installation

Handlebars

Removal

1 Remove the handlebar covers (see Chapter 7). If required, the handlebars can be displaced from the steering head for access to the bearings without having to detach any cables, or remove the brake lever brackets or brake master cylinder. If this is the case, ignore the Steps which do not apply.

2 Disconnect the wiring from each brake light switch **(see illustration)**.

3 Detach the throttle cable from the twistgrip and slide the twistgrip off the end of the handlebar (see Chapter 4).

4 If either a front or rear disc brake is fitted with the hydraulic reservoir mounted on the handlebars, unscrew the master cylinder assembly clamp bolts and position the assembly clear of the handlebar, making sure no strain is placed on the hydraulic hose **(see illustration)**. Keep the hydraulic reservoir upright to prevent air entering the system.

5 On models with a cable-operated front brake, detach the cable from the lever (see Chapter 8), then remove the bolt securing the

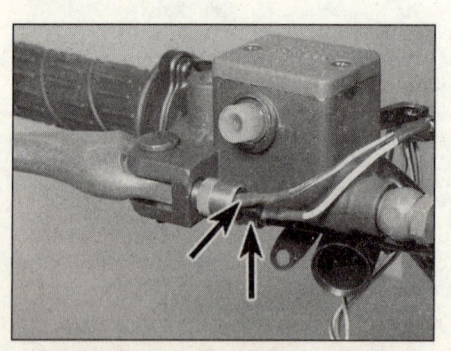

2.2 Disconnect the wiring connectors (arrowed) from each brake light switch

2.4 Disc brake master cylinder clamp bolts (arrowed)

Steering and suspension 6•3

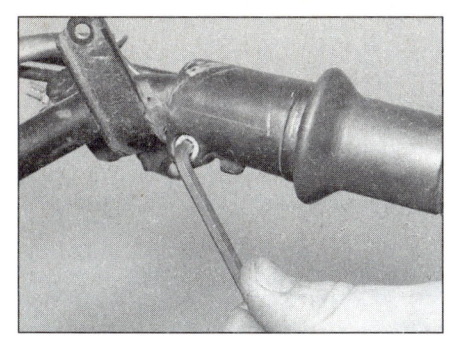

2.5 Unscrew the brake lever bracket bolt

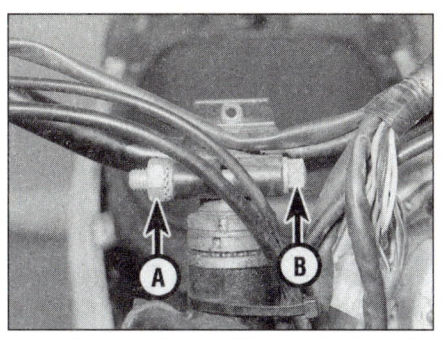

2.7a Unscrew the nut (A) and withdraw the pinch-bolt (B)

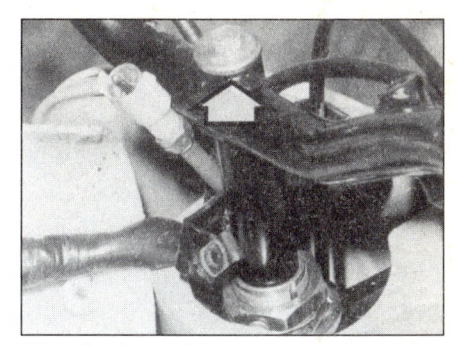

2.7b On Zip models remove the long stem bolt and washer (arrowed)

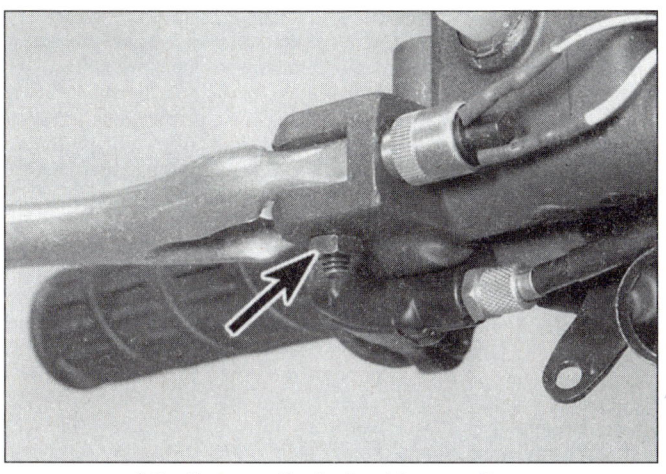

2.9a Unscrew the locknut (arrowed) . . .

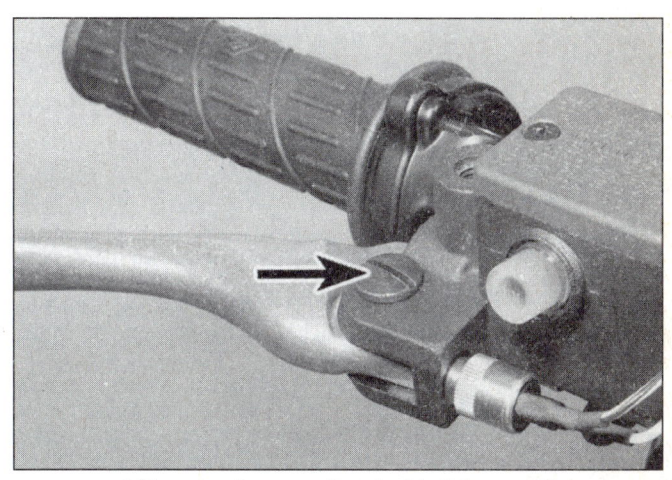

2.9b . . . and remove the pivot bolt (arrowed)

brake lever bracket and slide that off the end of the handlebar **(see illustration)**.

6 On models with a cable-operated rear brake, remove the left-hand grip (peel the grip off the bar end, or if necessary cut it off), then detach the rear brake cable from the lever (see Chapter 8). Remove the bolt securing the rear brake lever bracket and slide it off the end of the handlebar.

7 On models with the handlebars secured by a clamp and pinch-bolt, remove the nut and withdraw the bolt, then lift the handlebars off the stem **(see illustration)**. On Zip models, loosen the bolt that passes down through the handlebar stem, then strike the bolt with a soft-faced mallet to free the cone inside the steering stem **(see illustration)**. Lift off the handlebars. If the handlebar components have been left attached, position the handlebars so that no strain is placed on any of the cables, hose or wiring. If you are removing the handlebars completely, make note of how the wiring is taped to the handlebar before freeing it.

Installation

8 Installation is the reverse of removal, noting the following.
 a) *Refer to the Specifications at the beginning of the Chapter and tighten the nut on the handlebar clamp bolt and on Zip models the stem bolt, to the specified torque setting.*
 b) *Do not forget to reconnect the brake light switch wiring connectors.*
 c) *Use a suitable adhesive between the left-hand grip and the handlebar.*

Brake levers

Removal

9 Unscrew the lever pivot bolt locknut, then withdraw the pivot bolt and remove the lever **(see illustrations)**. If applicable, detach the brake cable from the lever as you remove it.

Installation

10 Installation is the reverse of removal. Apply grease to the pivot bolt shank and the contact areas between the lever and its bracket, and to the brake cable nipple (where applicable).

3 Steering stem – removal and installation

Removal

1 Remove the front wheel (see Chapter 8) and the handlebars (see Section 2). On drum brake models, detach the brake cable from the drum (see Chapter 8). On disc brake models, displace the brake caliper and secure it with a cable tie to avoid straining the hydraulic hose (see Chapter 8) – note that there is no need to disconnect the hydraulic hose. On all models, detach the speedometer cable from the wheel hub (see Chapter 9). Although not essential, it is advisable to remove the front body panel to avoid the possibility of damaging any paintwork (see Chapter 7).

2 Where fitted, lift the lower handlebar cover **(see illustration)**.

3 Unscrew and remove the bearing adjuster

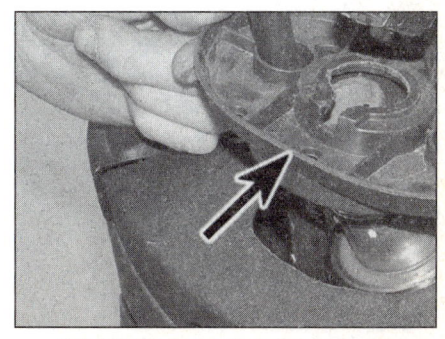

3.2 Lift the lower handlebar cover (arrowed)

6•4 Steering and suspension

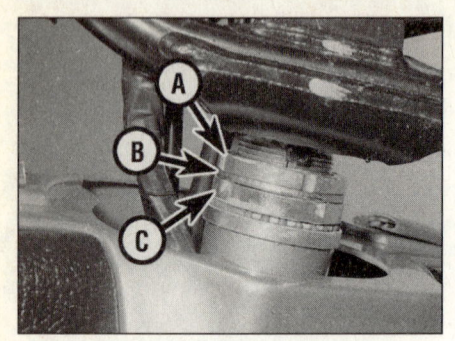

3.3a Locknut (A), washer (B), bearing adjuster nut (C)

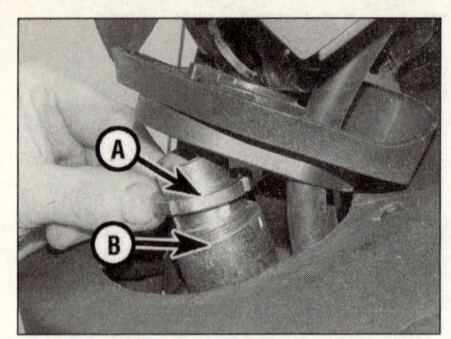

3.3b Remove the adjuster nut (A) and spacer (B)

3.4 Lower the steering stem out of the frame

locknut using either a suitable C-spanner, a peg-spanner or a drift located in one of the notches **(see illustration)**. Remove the washer, noting how it fits. Supporting the steering stem, unscrew the adjuster nut using either a C-spanner, a peg-spanner or a drift located in one of the notches. Remove the nut and the spacer where fitted **(see illustration)**.
4 Gently lower the steering stem out of the frame **(see illustration)**.
5 As applicable, remove the upper bearing balls from the top of the steering head – the lower bearing balls and inner race will be on the steering stem. **Note:** *On some later models, the upper bearing is a caged ball-bearing which is a press-fit in the steering head and the lower bearing is a taper roller bearing – see Section 4.* Remove all traces of old grease from the bearings and races and check them for wear or damage as described in Section 4. **Note:** *Do not attempt to remove the outer races from the frame or the lower bearing inner race from the steering stem unless they are to be renewed.*

Installation

6 Smear a liberal quantity of grease on the bearing outer races in the frame. Also grease both the upper and lower bearing assemblies. If removed, install the lower bearing assembly over its inner race.
7 Carefully lift the steering stem up through the frame. If removed, install the upper bearing assembly. If fitted, install the spacer, then thread the adjuster nut onto the steering stem. Tighten the adjuster nut to the initial torque setting specified at the beginning of the Chapter. On models with ball race bearings, now slacken the nut off approximately 90° and check the adjustment as described in Chapter 1 **(see illustration)**. On models with taper roller bearings, slacken the nut completely, retighten it to the final torque setting specified, then slacken it by 90°. To apply the torque setting, a service tool (Part No. 020055Y) or a suitable old socket fabricated into a peg spanner is required. If it is not possible to apply a torque wrench to the adjuster nut, tighten the nut and adjust the bearings as described in Chapter 1 after the installation procedure is complete.
Caution: Take great care not to apply excessive pressure because this will cause premature failure of the bearings.
8 When the bearings are correctly adjusted, install the washer, making sure the tab locates in the slot on the steering stem **(see illustration)**. Install the locknut and tighten it to the specified torque setting, using the same tool as above, if available.
9 Install the remaining components, then carry out a check of the steering head bearing freeplay as described in Chapter 1, and if necessary re-adjust.

4 Steering head bearings – inspection and renewal

Inspection

1 Remove the steering stem (see Section 3).
2 Remove all traces of old grease from the bearings and races and check them for wear or damage.
3 The outer races in the steering head should be polished and free from indentations. Inspect the ball or roller bearings for signs of wear, damage or discolouration, and examine the bearing retainer cage for signs of cracks or splits **(see illustration)**. Spin the bearing by hand. It should spin freely and smoothly. If there are any signs of wear on any of the above components both upper and lower bearing assemblies must be renewed as a set. Only remove the races if they need to be renewed – do not re-use them once they have been removed. **Note:** *If the upper bearing is a caged ball-bearing, turn it by hand to check for roughness and indentations in the race. The bearing is sealed and cannot be cleaned or regreased. Only remove the bearing if it is going to be renewed (see Steps 4, 5 and 6).*

Renewal

4 The outer races are an interference fit in the frame and can be tapped from position with a suitable drift **(see illustration)**. Tap firmly and evenly around each race to ensure that it is driven out squarely. It may prove advantageous to curve the end of the drift slightly to improve access.
5 Alternatively, the races can be pulled out using a slide-hammer with internal expanding extractor.
6 The new outer races can be pressed into the frame using a drawbolt arrangement (see

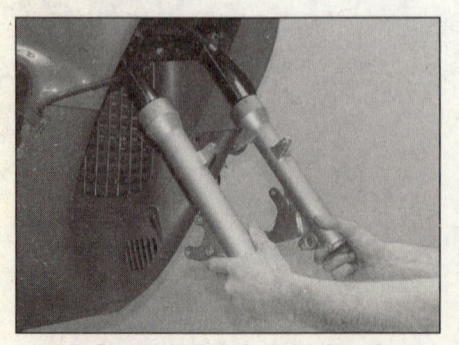

3.7 Check the bearings for freeplay

3.8 Ensure tab (arrowed) locates in the slot in the stem

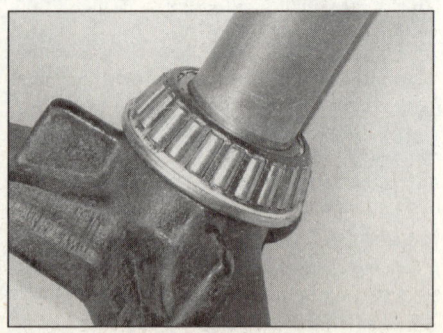

4.3 Examine the bearings and the bearing cage – roller bearing

Steering and suspension 6•5

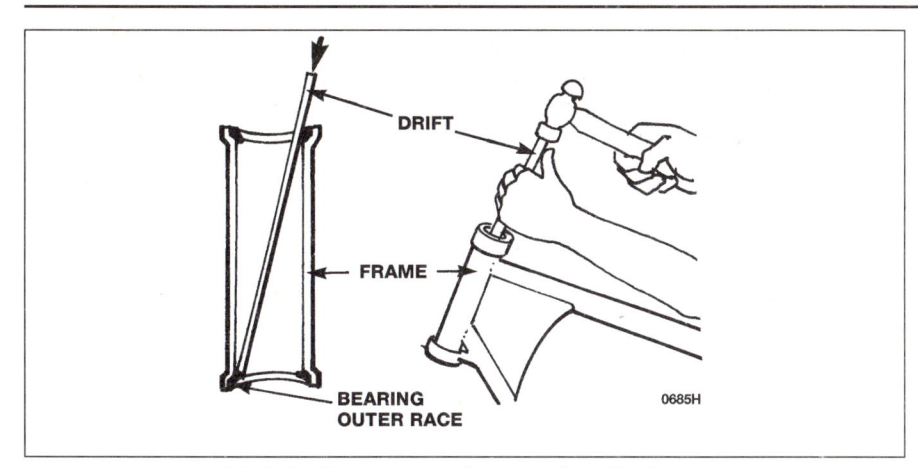

4.4 Drive the bearing outer races from the frame

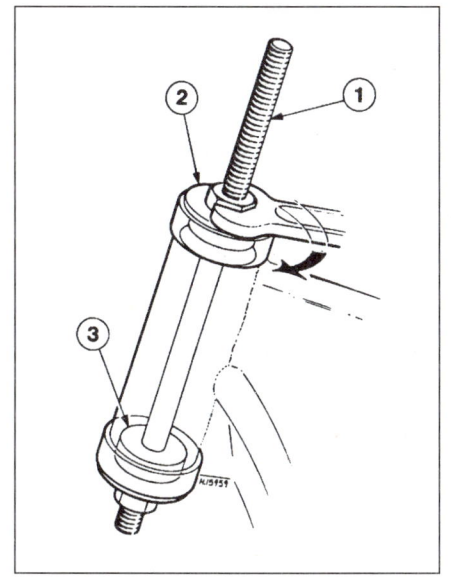

4.6 Drawbolt arrangement for fitting steering head bearing outer races
1 Long bolt or threaded bar
2 Thick washer
3 Guide for lower outer race

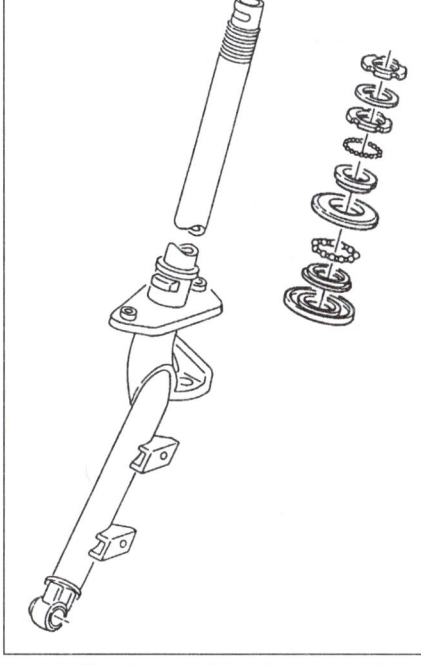

4.8 Steering head bearing assembly

illustration), or by using a large diameter tubular drift which bears only on the outer edge of the race. Ensure that the drawbolt washer or drift (as applicable) bears only on the outer edge of the race and does not contact the working surface. Alternatively, have the races installed by a Piaggio dealer equipped with the bearing race installing tools.

> **HAYNES HiNT** *Installation of new bearing outer races is made much easier if the races are left overnight in the freezer. This causes them to contract slightly making them a looser fit.*

7 To remove the lower bearing inner race from the steering stem, use two screwdrivers placed on opposite sides of the race to work it free. If the bearing is firmly in place it will be necessary to use a bearing puller, or drive a chisel between the underside of the race and the bearing seat. Take the steering stem to a Piaggio dealer if required. Check the condition of the dust seal that fits under the race and renew it if it is worn, damaged or deteriorated.
8 Fit the new lower inner race bearing onto the steering stem (see illustration). A length of tubing with an internal diameter slightly larger than the steering stem will be needed to tap the new bearing into position. Ensure that the drift bears only on the inner edge of the race and does not contact its working surface.
9 Install the steering stem (see Section 3).

5 Front suspension – disassembly, inspection and reassembly

Single-side trailing arm monoshock

Disassembly

1 Remove the front wheel (see Chapter 8). Where applicable, remove the suspension cover and the trailing link trim (see illustrations).

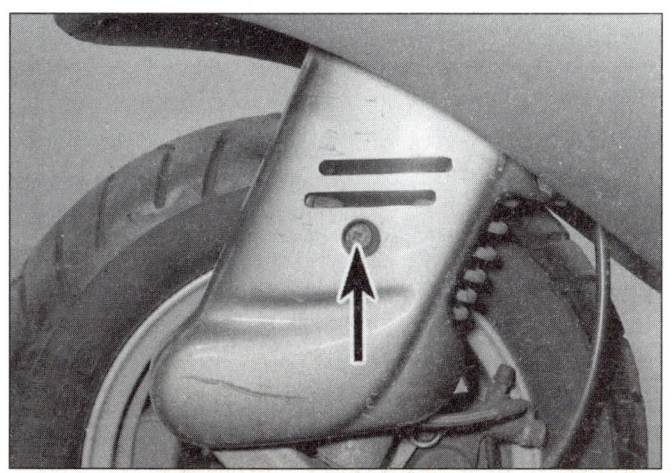

5.1a Suspension cover screw (arrowed) – Hexagon

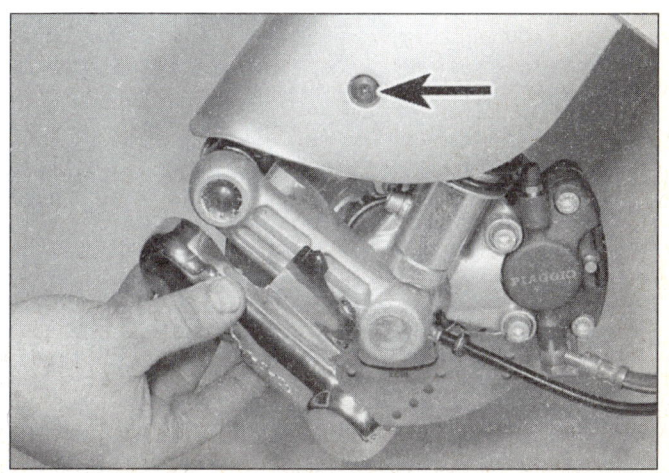

5.1b Suspension cover screw (arrowed) and trim – ET2 and ET4

6•6 Steering and suspension

5.2a Remove the two bolts (arrowed) ...

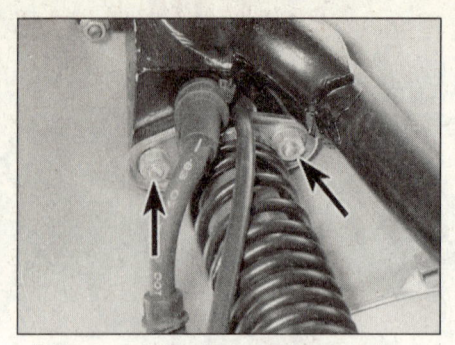

5.2b ... and the two nuts (arrowed) ...

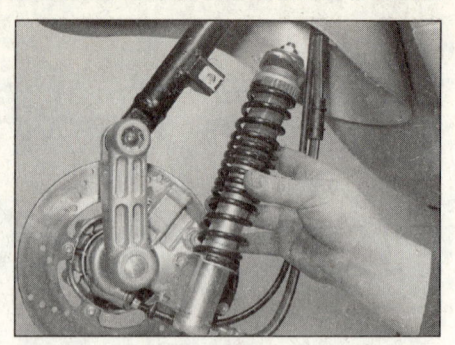

5.2c ... and remove the shock absorber

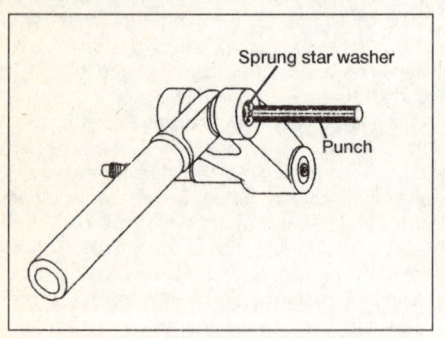

5.4 Removing the trailing link arm sprung star washers with a 20 mm diameter punch

5.6 Remove the circlip (arrowed) and draw the bracket off the trailing link arm

2 Remove the two bolts securing the bottom of the shock absorber to the bracket, noting the washers, and the two nuts securing the top to the steering stem **(see illustrations)**. Manoeuvre the shock absorber away from the scooter **(see illustration)**.

3 Before separating the trailing link arm from the steering stem, check the condition of the bearings by moving the arm laterally against the steering stem. If any play is felt between the arm and the stem, the bearings and spacer pin must be renewed. Also move the arm up and down. If any roughness is felt or the arm does not move smoothly and freely, the bearings and spacer pin must be renewed. If the bearings and pin are good, there is no need to separate the trailing link arm from the steering stem, unless required for other purposes.

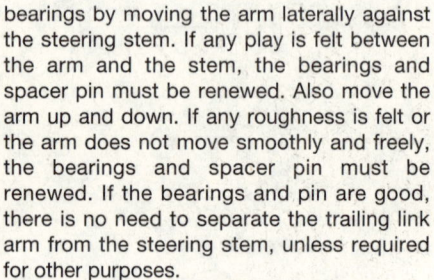

4 To remove the trailing link arm, first remove the wheel hub assembly (see Chapter 8). To separate the arm from the steering stem, remove the sprung star washer from each side of the arm. The washers can be removed either by hitting them centrally with a suitable punch or drift, which should be wide enough to cover the raised inner section of the washer **(see illustration)**, or be levering up the outer tangs of the washer with a suitable screwdriver. Discard the washers, as new ones must be used.

5 Drive or press out the bearing spacer pin from the middle of the arm and separate the arm from the stem. Remove the O-rings and dust seals.

6 Check for any play in the two needle roller bearings between the trailing link arm and the brake caliper/shock absorber mounting bracket as described in Step 3. If required, remove the circlip and slide the bracket off the trailing link arm, using a soft-faced mallet to tap the end of the wheel axle through if necessary **(see illustration)**.

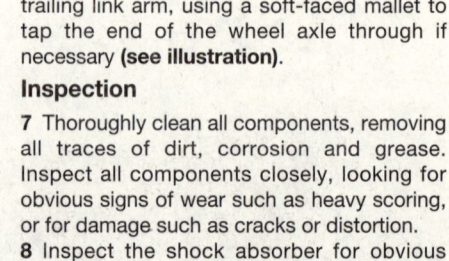

Inspection

7 Thoroughly clean all components, removing all traces of dirt, corrosion and grease. Inspect all components closely, looking for obvious signs of wear such as heavy scoring, or for damage such as cracks or distortion.

8 Inspect the shock absorber for obvious physical damage and the coil spring for looseness, cracks or signs of fatigue.

9 Inspect the damper rod for signs of bending, pitting and oil leakage.

10 Inspect the mountings at the top and bottom of the shock for wear or damage.

11 If required, the shock absorber can be disassembled and individual components renewed **(see illustration)**. Compress the

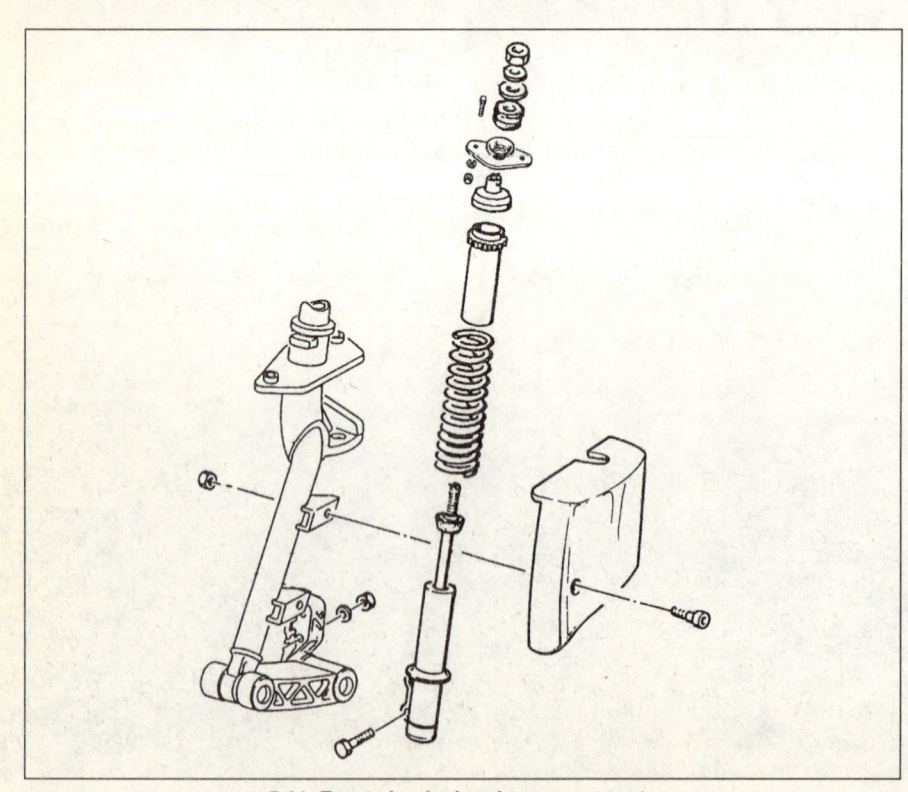

5.11 Front shock absorber components

Steering and suspension 6•7

5.23 Tighten the shock absorber mounting bolts and nuts to the specified torque

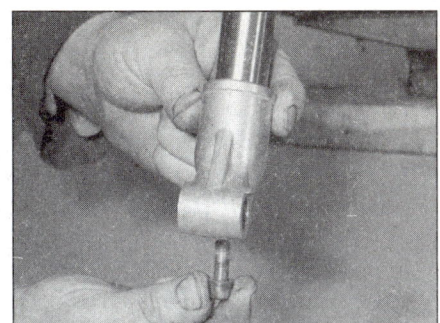

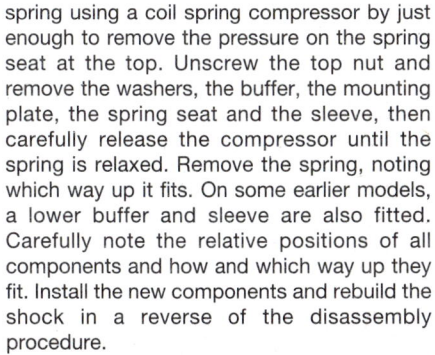

5.26a Remove the bolt and slide off the axle/brake caliper bracket

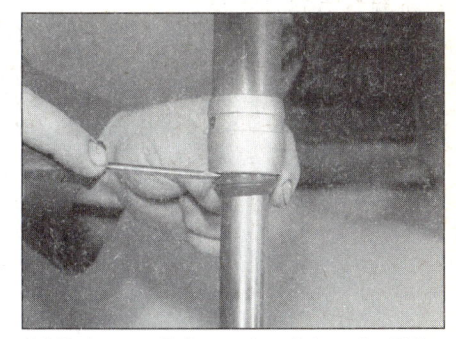

5.26b Lever off the seal and draw it off the slider

spring using a coil spring compressor by just enough to remove the pressure on the spring seat at the top. Unscrew the top nut and remove the washers, the buffer, the mounting plate, the spring seat and the sleeve, then carefully release the compressor until the spring is relaxed. Remove the spring, noting which way up it fits. On some earlier models, a lower buffer and sleeve are also fitted. Carefully note the relative positions of all components and how and which way up they fit. Install the new components and rebuild the shock in a reverse of the disassembly procedure.

12 Visually check the condition of the needle roller bearings in the trailing link arm and the brake caliper/shock absorber mounting bracket.

13 Worn bearings can be drifted out of their bores, but note that removal will destroy them; new components should be obtained before work commences. Before removing the bearings, carefully measure or mark their set depth within the bore so that the new ones can be correctly installed. The new ones should be pressed or drawn into their bores rather than driven into position. In the absence of a press, a suitable drawbolt arrangement can be made up as described below.

14 Obtain a long bolt or a length of threaded rod from a local engineering works or some other supplier. The bolt or rod should be about one inch longer than the combined width of the arm and one bearing. Also required are suitable nuts and two large and robust washers having a larger outside diameter than the bearing housing. In the case of the threaded rod, fit one nut to one end of the rod and stake it in place for convenience.

15 Fit one of the washers over the bolt or rod so that it rests against the head or staked nut, then pass the assembly through the bore. Over the projecting end place the bearing, which should be greased to ease installation, followed by the remaining washer and nut.

16 Holding the bearing to ensure that it is kept square, slowly tighten the nut so that the bearing is drawn into its bore.

17 Once it is fully home, remove the drawbolt arrangement and repeat the procedure to fit the other bearing.

18 Lubricate the needle roller bearings with molybdenum disulphide grease.

19 Fit new dust seals and O-rings.

Reassembly

20 Slide the brake caliper/shock absorber mounting bracket onto the trailing link arm and secure it with the circlip, making sure it sits properly in its groove **(see illustration 5.6)**.

21 Lubricate the bearing spacer pin with molybdenum disulphide grease. Align the trailing link arm with the steering stem and drive or press the pin through the arm and stem.

22 Fit the new sprung star washers and drive them into place using a piece of tubing that bears only on the section between the raised inner section and the raised outer tangs.

23 Install the shock absorber and tighten the nuts and bolts to the torque settings specified at the beginning of the Chapter **(see illustration)**.

24 Install the hub assembly and the front wheel (see Chapter 8) and the covers, where applicable.

Upside-down telescopic forks

Seal renewal

25 Remove the front wheel and, if applicable, displace the front brake caliper (see Chapter 8).

26 Remove the Allen bolt from the base of the fork slider and draw the axle/brake caliper bracket off the bottom **(see illustration)**. If necessary, heat the bracket with a hot air gun to aid removal. Lever the seal out of the bottom of the fork tube and remove it from the slider **(see illustration)**.

27 Clean the bottom of the slider and the inside of the axle/brake caliper bracket and remove any traces of corrosion **(see illustration)**.

28 Apply grease to the inside and outside of the new seal, then fit it over the slider and press it into position in the bottom of the tube **(see illustration)**.

29 Apply Loctite 242E or a similar locking compound to the bottom of the slider, then fit the axle/brake caliper bracket and tighten the bolt securely. Use the axle inserted through the bracket to prevent the fork slider rotating when tightening the bolt **(see illustration)**.

30 Install the front wheel (see Chapter 8). Check the operation of the front forks.

5.27 The sliders are prone to pitting and corrosion, which will ruin the seal

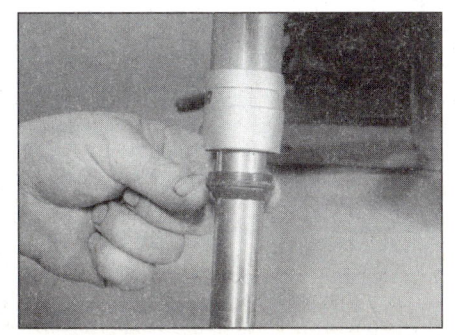

5.28 Press the new seal up into the tube

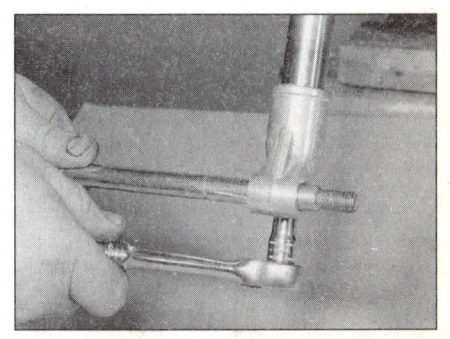

5.29 Use the axle to prevent the bracket rotating

5.32a Removing the circlip

Disassembly

Note: *The internal components of these forks are retained by a series of circlips which makes them difficult to disassemble. Also, some models have had undocumented changes to the internal components and may differ to those described. A certain amount of reader input and common sense will have to be applied if the forks are to be disassembled completely. It is advised that the procedure is carried out by a Piaggio dealer.*

Note: *Always dismantle the fork legs separately to avoid interchanging parts and thus causing an accelerated rate of wear. Store all components in separate, clearly-marked containers.*

31 Remove the front wheel and, if applicable, displace the front brake caliper (see Chapter 8). Follow the procedure in Step 26 and remove the axle/brake caliper bracket and seal.

32 Remove the circlip from inside the bottom of the fork tube using a pair of internal circlip pliers **(see illustration)**. The slider assembly is retained by a circlip that fits in a tapered groove on the inside of the fork tube; dislodge the circlip by pulling the slider down sharply. If necessary, screw a suitable bolt into the thread in the bottom of the slider, then tighten the bolt in a vice. Strike the underside of the steering stem with a heavy mallet to dislodge the circlip **(see illustration)**. **Note:** *On all NRG models, Skipper (1998 to 2000) and Skipper ST models, the left-hand fork contains an integral damper cartridge, secured by a nut on the top of the fork tube. Unscrew the nut to release the damper rod before attempting to disassemble the fork leg. If water has*

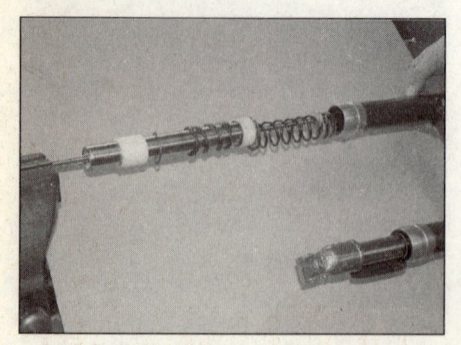

5.33 Pull the slider out of the fork tube

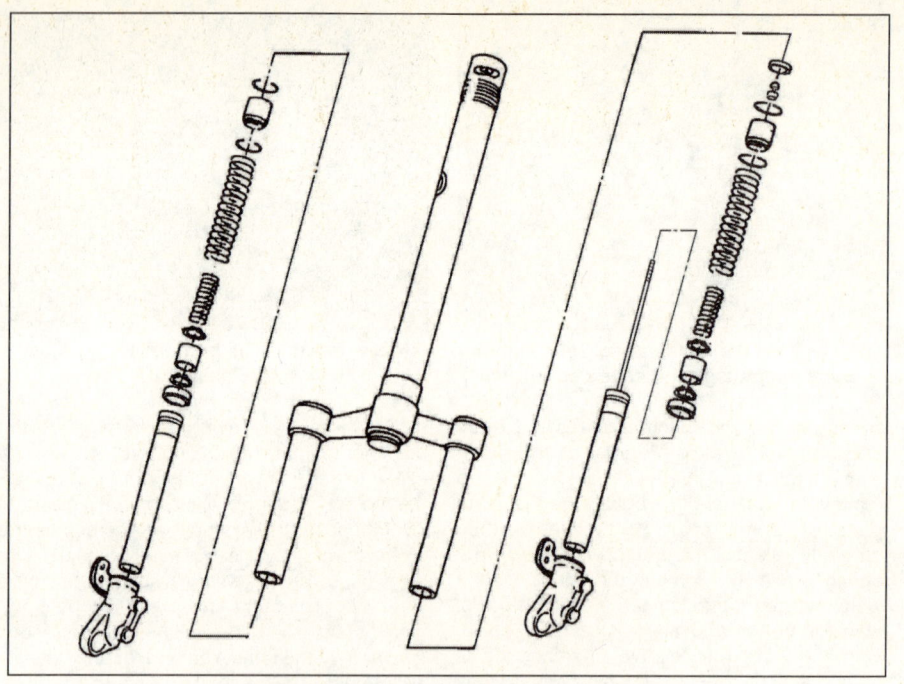

5.32b Upside-down front fork assembly

penetrated the seal, it is likely that the circlip will be very difficult to remove.

33 Pull the slider out of the fork tube, together with the lower bush, retaining circlip, rebound spring, upper bush, spring seat and compression spring. Note the order of the fork components for reassembly **(see illustration)**. Remove the upper bush lower circlip, the bush and the upper circlip from the slider. Discard the circlips if they are corroded and fit new ones on reassembly.

Inspection

34 Clean all parts in solvent and blow them dry with compressed air, if available. Check the sliders for score marks, scratches, flaking of the chrome finish and excessive or abnormal wear. Look for dents in the fork tube and fit a new steering stem assembly if any are found. Check the action of the damper, where fitted; if the rod slides freely in and out of the cartridge, or if the rod binds in the cartridge, fit a new damper. **Note:** *The damper is an integral part of the slider and cannot be removed from it.*

35 If available, check the fork sliders for runout using V-blocks and a dial gauge, or have it done by a Piaggio dealer. If the amount of runout is excessive, the sliders should be renewed.

⚠ **Warning:** *If the slider is bent, it should not be straightened; renew it.*

36 Check the springs for cracks and other damage. If they are defective, bent or sagged, renew them both. Never renew only one spring.
37 Examine the working surfaces of each bush; if worn or scuffed they must be renewed.

Reassembly

38 Install the various components in the reverse order of removal, coating them with grease as you install them. Fit the slider assembly into the tube, then, if applicable, secure the damper rod with the nut on the top of the fork tube. Use a suitable length of tubing to install the retaining circlip, the lower bush and the lower circlip squarely into the fork tube and ensure the circlips are securely located in their grooves before preceding to the next step. Use the tubing to press the seal into the bottom of the tube.

39 Install the axle/brake caliper bracket (see Step 29). If applicable, install the front brake caliper, then install the front wheel (see Chapter 8). Check the operation of the front forks.

Conventional telescopic forks

Note: *Two types of conventional telescopic fork are fitted to the scooters covered by this manual. On the first type, the tubes are an integral part of the fork yoke (Steps 40 to 51), on the second, motorcycle-type fork, the tubes are clamped in the yoke and can be removed individually for disassembly (Steps 52 to 76).*

Note: *Always dismantle the fork legs separately and store all components in separate, clearly marked containers to avoid interchanging parts. Check the availability of new parts and the type and quantity of fork oil required with a Piaggio dealer before disassembling the forks. Note that on some scooters the forks are lubricated with grease.*

Disassembly

40 Remove the front wheel (see Chapter 8).
41 Place a suitable oil drain tray below the

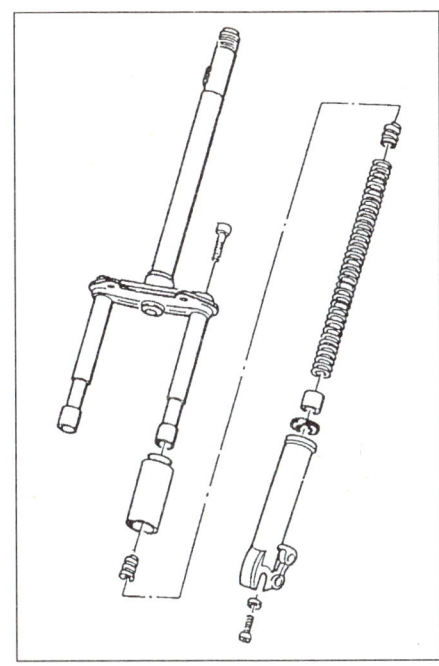

Steering and suspension 6•9

5.41 Conventional forks with integral yoke and tubes

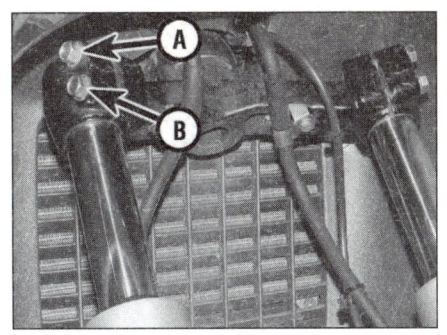

5.54 Loosen clamp bolt (A) and remove clamp bolt (B)

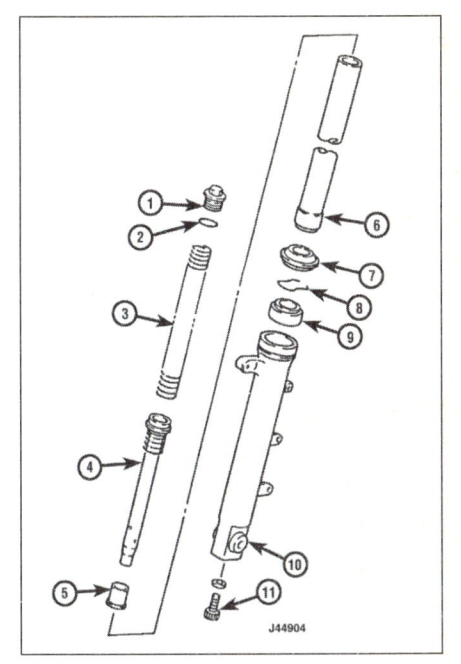

5.57 Motorcycle-type fork components

1 Top bolt
2 O-ring
3 Spring
4 Damper
5 Damper seat
6 Fork tube
7 Dust seal
8 Circlip
9 Oil seal
10 Fork slider
11 Damper bolt

fork, then unscrew the bolt in the bottom of the fork slider and allow the oil to drain, whilst holding the slider in place **(see illustration)**. When the oil has drained, draw the slider down off the tube. For oil seal renewal only, the spring can be left in place secured in the top of the fork tube. A buffer is fitted in between the bottom of the spring and the slider – remove it if required.

42 To remove the oil seal, remove the circlip from the top of the slider, then remove the oil seal, either using the Piaggio service tool (Part No. 021467/17/18Y), a commercially-available expanding puller, or by carefully levering it out using a screwdriver. Take care not to gouge the rim of the slider when doing this.

43 To remove the spring, unscrew the bolt in the top of the fork tube and draw the spring out of the tube. Hold the spring to prevent it from turning with the bolt.

Inspection

44 Clean all parts in solvent and blow them dry with compressed air, if available. Check each fork tube for score marks, scratches, flaking of the chrome finish and excessive or abnormal wear. Look for dents in the tube and renew the tube in both legs if any are found. Check the fork seal seat for nicks, gouges and scratches. If damage is evident, leaks will occur.

45 Check the spring for cracks and other damage. If it is defective, bent or sagged, renew the springs in both legs with new ones. Never renew only one spring.

Reassembly

46 Press the new oil seal squarely into its recess in the slider as far as possible, then either use the Piaggio service tool (Part No. 040971Y), or a suitable piece of tubing or a socket to tap the seal fully into place until the circlip groove is visible above the seal.

> **HAYNES HiNT** *Place the old oil seal on top of the new one to protect it when driving the seal into place.*

47 Once the seal is correctly seated, fit the circlip, making sure it is correctly located in its groove.

48 If removed, fit the buffer into the bottom of the fork slider. Check that both plugs are in the ends of the spring, then insert the spring into the slider. Install the bolt into the bottom of the slider and thread it into the plug in the base of the spring. Hold the spring to prevent it from turning with the bolt.

49 Slowly pour in the specified quantity of the specified grade of fork oil.

50 Apply some fork oil to the lips of the seal, then insert the top of the spring into the bottom of the fork tube. Lift the slider so that the bottom of the tube fits squarely through the oil seal and into the slider, and raise it until the spring contacts the top of the tube. Holding the slider in position, install the bolt and thread it into the plug in the top of the spring.

51 Install the front wheel (see Chapter 8). Check the operation of the front forks.

Motorcycle-type fork

Note: *Two types of conventional telescopic fork are fitted to the scooters covered by this manual. On the first type, the tubes are an integral part of the fork yoke (Steps 40 to 51), on the second, motorcycle-type fork, the tubes are clamped in the yoke and can be removed individually for disassembly (Steps 52 to 76).*

Note: *Always dismantle the fork legs separately and store all components in separate, clearly marked containers to avoid interchanging parts. Check the availability of new parts and the type and quantity of fork oil required with a Piaggio dealer before disassembling the forks. Note that on some scooters the forks are lubricated with grease.*

Removal

52 Remove the front wheel and displace the brake caliper (see Chapter 8).

53 Remove the front mudguard and, where fitted, the fork leg shrouds (see Chapter 7).

54 Remove each fork leg individually. Loosen the top fork leg clamp bolt and undo and remove the lower clamp bolt **(see illustration)**. Remove the fork leg by twisting it and pulling it downwards.

> **HAYNES HiNT** *If the fork legs are seized in the yoke, spray the area with penetrating oil and allow time for it to soak in before trying again.*

Installation

55 Remove all traces of corrosion from the fork tubes and the yoke. Install each fork leg individually. Slide the leg up through the yoke until the top edge of the fork tube is level with the top edge of the yoke. Ensure the location groove for the lower clamp bolt is correctly aligned. Tighten the clamp bolts securely or to the torque setting specified at the beginning of the Chapter.

56 Install the remaining components in the reverse order of removal. Check the operation of the front forks.

Disassembly

57 Remove the fork leg (see Steps 52 to 54). Always dismantle the fork legs separately to avoid interchanging parts. Store all components in separate, clearly-marked containers **(see illustration)**.

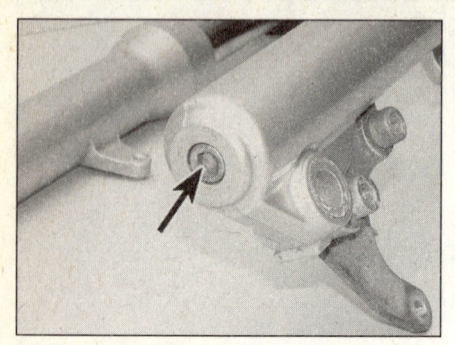

6•10 Steering and suspension

5.58 Loosen the damper bolt (arrowed)

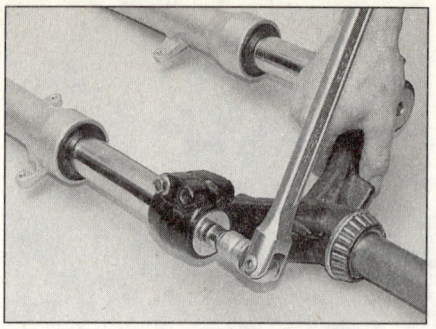

5.59 Clamp the fork tube to loosen the top bolt

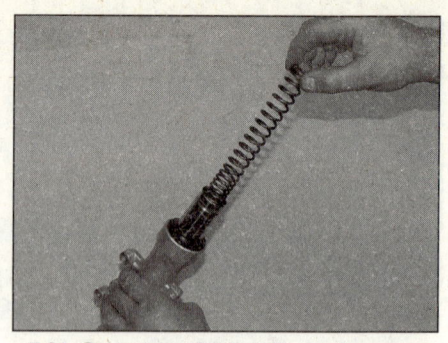

5.61 Compress the fork leg and remove the spring

58 The damper bolt should be loosened at this stage. Invert the fork leg and compress the fork tube in the slider so that the spring exerts maximum pressure on the damper head, then loosen the bolt in the base of the fork slider **(see illustration)**.

59 To remove the fork top bolt, clamp the fork tube in a vice equipped with soft jaws, taking care not to overtighten or score the tube's surface, and loosen the top bolt. **Note:** *If the steering stem has been removed, temporarily clamp the fork leg in the yoke using the lower clamp bolt only* **(see illustration)**.

60 Unscrew the top bolt and remove it. Note the O-ring fitted to the top bolt; if it is damaged, fit a new one on reassembly.

⚠ **Warning: The fork spring is pressing on the fork top bolt with considerable pressure.**

Unscrew the bolt very carefully, keeping a downward pressure on it and release it slowly as it is likely to spring clear. It is advisable to wear some form of eye and face protection when carrying out this operation.

61 Slide the fork tube down into the slider and withdraw the spring **(see illustration)**. Note which way up the spring is fitted.

62 Carefully prise out the dust seal from the top of the slider, then prise out the oil seal retaining clip **(see illustrations)**.

63 Invert the fork leg over a suitable container and pump the fork vigorously to expel as much fork oil as possible.

64 Remove the previously-loosened damper bolt and its sealing washer from the bottom of the slider. Discard the sealing washer, as a new one must be used on reassembly. If the damper bolt was not loosened before dismantling the fork, temporarily install the spring and press down on it to prevent the damper from turning.

65 Pull the fork tube out of the slider.

66 Withdraw the damper and the damper seat from inside the fork slider.

67 Carefully prise the oil seal out of the slider. Discard the oil and dust seals, as new ones must be used on reassembly.

Inspection

68 Follow the procedure in Steps 44 and 45 to clean and check the fork components. If either of the fork tubes appears bent, have them both checked by a scooter dealer or specialist engineer. If necessary, fit new fork tubes, do not have them straightened.

Reassembly

69 Insert the damper into the bottom of the fork tube and install the damper seat on the bottom of the damper **(see illustration)**.

70 Lubricate the fork tube with the specified fork oil and insert the assembly into the slider. Fit a new sealing washer to the damper bolt and apply a few drops of a suitable, non-permanent thread-locking compound, then install the bolt into the bottom of the slider and tighten it to the torque setting specified at the beginning of the Chapter. If the damper rotates inside the tube, hold it with spring pressure as on disassembly (see Step 64).

71 Push the fork tube fully into the slider, then lubricate the inside of the new oil seal with fork oil and slide it over the tube with its markings facing upwards **(see illustration)**. Press the seal into place in the slider. If necessary, use a suitable piece of tubing to tap the seal carefully into place; the tubing must be slightly larger in diameter than the fork tube and slightly smaller in diameter than the seal recess in the slider. Take care not to scratch the fork tube during this operation; if the fork tube is pushed fully into the slider any accidental scratching is confined to the area above the seal.

72 Fit the retaining clip, making sure it is correctly located in its groove. Lubricate the inside of the new dust seal then slide it down the fork tube and press it into position.

73 Slowly pour in the correct quantity of the specified grade of fork oil and carefully pump the fork to distribute the oil evenly.

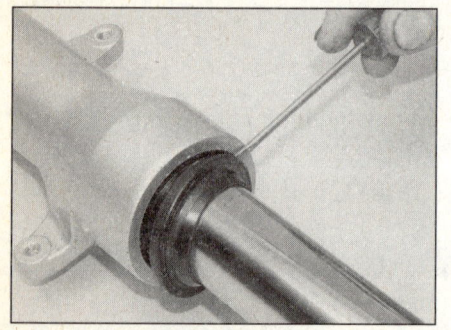

5.62a Prise out the dust seal . . .

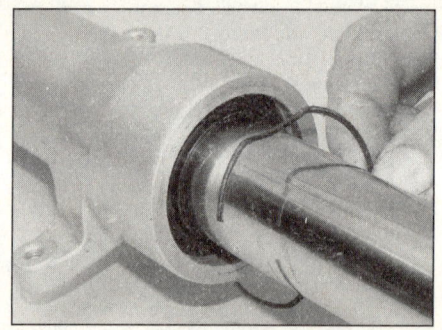

5.62b . . . then prise out the retaining clip

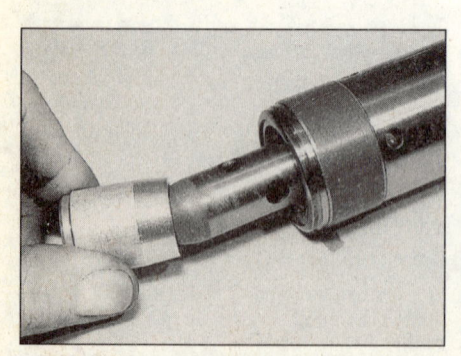

5.69 Fit the seat onto the bottom of the damper

5.71 Install the oil seal with markings facing up

Steering and suspension 6•11

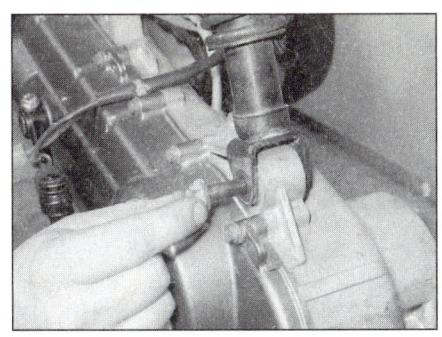

6.2a Unscrew the nut and withdraw the bolt

6.2b Right-hand lower shock absorber mounting (arrowed)

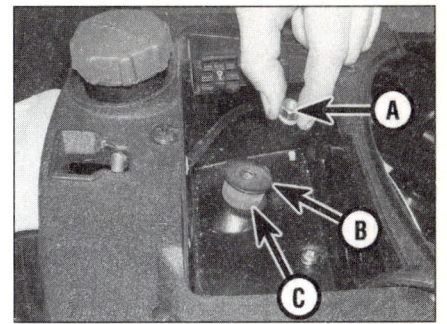

6.3a Unscrew the nut (A) and remove the washer (B) and rubber bush (C)

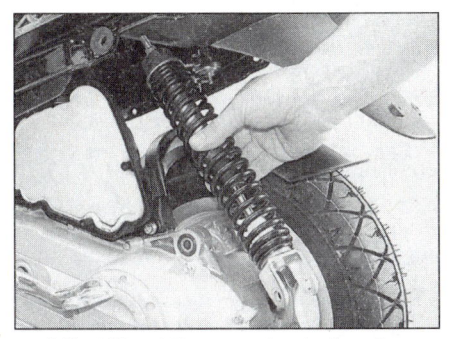

6.3b Lift out the rear shock absorber

6.4 Withdraw the bolt, noting the spacer (arrowed)

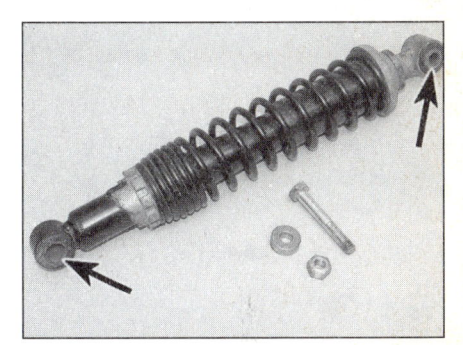

6.7 Check the mounting bolts and bushes (arrowed) for wear

74 Pull the fork tube out of the slider to its full extension and install the spring.

75 If necessary, fit a new O-ring to the fork top bolt. Keep the fork leg fully extended and press down on the spring whilst threading the top bolt into the top of the fork tube. Turn the bolt carefully to ensure it is not cross-threaded. Hold the fork leg and tighten the top bolt to the torque setting specified at the beginning of the Chapter.

⚠️ **Warning: It will be necessary to compress the spring by pressing it down with the top bolt in order to engage the threads of the top bolt with the fork tube. This is a potentially dangerous operation and should be performed with care, using an assistant if necessary. Wipe off any excess oil before starting to prevent the possibility of slipping.**

76 Install the fork leg (see Steps 55 and 56).

6 Rear shock absorber – removal, inspection and installation

Note: *Some scooters are fitted with twin rear shock absorbers; individual components are not available for these units.*

Removal

1 Support the scooter on its centre stand, then position a support under the rear wheel so that the engine does not drop when the shock absorber is removed. Check that the weight of the machine is off the rear suspension so that the shock is not compressed.

2 The lower end of the shock absorber is secured to the gearbox casing and, on twin shock models, to a stud on the right-hand subframe. Unscrew the nut and, where fitted, remove the bolt securing the bottom of the shock absorber and pull the shock away from its mounting **(see illustrations)**.

3 On single shock models, the upper end of the shock absorber is secured to the frame by a nut and washer assembly. Lift up or remove the seat and remove the battery and battery tray as required according to model to access the fixing (see Chapters 7 and 9). Position a ring spanner on the nut and hold the centre of the damper rod with a screwdriver to prevent it turning, then undo the nut. Note the location of the washers and rubber bush, then manoeuvre the shock away from the machine **(see illustrations)**.

4 On twin shock models, remove the body panels as necessary to access the upper shock mountings (see Chapter 7). Undo the upper mounting nut, then support the shock and withdraw the bolt, noting the position of any spacers **(see illustration)**.

Inspection

5 Inspect the shock absorber for obvious physical damage and the coil spring for looseness, cracks or signs of fatigue.

6 Inspect the damper rod for signs of bending, pitting and oil leaks.

7 Inspect the pivot hardware at the top and bottom of the shock for wear or damage **(see illustration)**.

8 Individual parts can be obtained for the shock absorber on certain models – check availability with a Piaggio dealer before dismantling the unit. Carefully note the relative positions of all components, and how and which way up they fit **(see illustration)**. Compress the spring using a coil spring

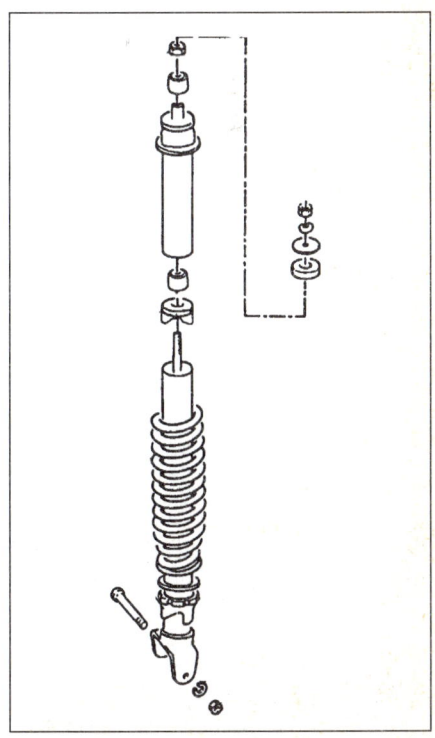

6.8 Rear shock absorber components

6•12 Steering and suspension

7.1 Adjusting the rear suspension using the tool provided

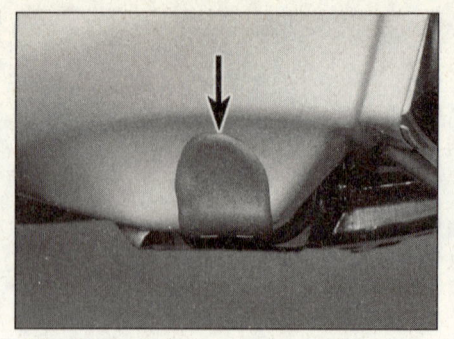

8.1a Remove the cover (arrowed) on each side . . .

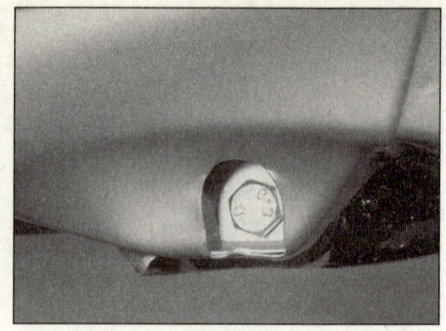

8.1b . . . to access the swingarm nut and pivot bolt

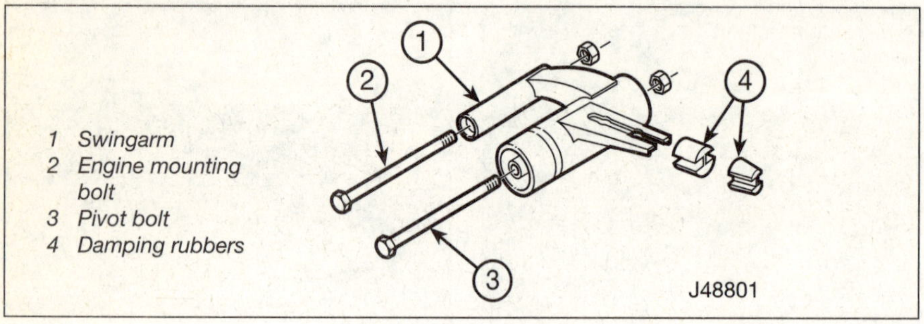

8.2a One-piece swingarm

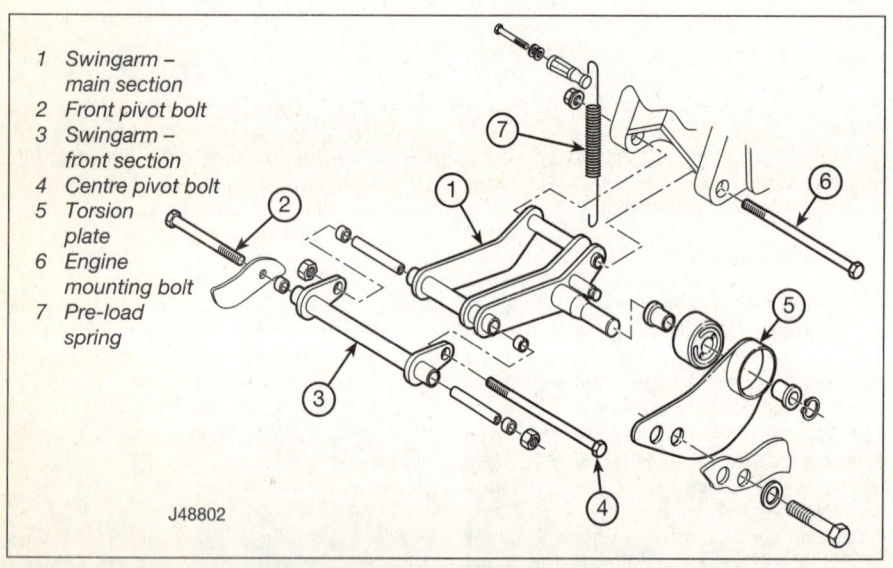

1 Swingarm
2 Engine mounting bolt
3 Pivot bolt
4 Damping rubbers

8.2b Built-up swingarm assembly

1 Swingarm – main section
2 Front pivot bolt
3 Swingarm – front section
4 Centre pivot bolt
5 Torsion plate
6 Engine mounting bolt
7 Pre-load spring

8.3a Withdraw the pivot bolt . . .

8.3b . . . and remove the swingarm

compressor by just enough to remove the pressure on the spring seat at the top. Unscrew the top nut and remove the various components according to model, noting their order, then carefully release the compressor until the spring is relaxed. Remove the spring, noting which way up it fits. Install the new components and rebuild the shock in a reverse of the disassembly procedure.

Installation

9 Installation is the reverse of removal. Tighten the shock absorber mountings to the torque settings specified at the beginning of the Chapter.

7 Rear shock absorber – preload adjustment

1 Preload adjustment is made using a suitable C-spanner (one is provided in the toolkit) to turn the spring seat on the bottom of the shock absorber **(see illustration)**. Align the setting required with the adjustment stopper.
2 To increase the preload, turn the spring seat anti-clockwise. To decrease the preload, turn the spring seat clockwise.

8 Swingarm – removal, inspection and installation

Removal

1 Remove the engine (see Chapter 2A, 2B, 2C, 2D, 2E or 2F). Where fitted, remove the cover to access the front mounting for the swingarm **(see illustrations)**.
2 Two different designs of swingarm are used. All 50 cc machines have a simple, one-piece unit; most 125 and 200 cc machines have a more complex built-up assembly with a pre-load spring **(see illustrations)**.
3 The one-piece swingarm is secured to the frame by the pivot bolt. Unscrew the nut on the end of the pivot bolt, then withdraw the bolt and remove the swingarm, noting how it fits **(see illustrations)**.
4 The built-up swingarm assembly is secured

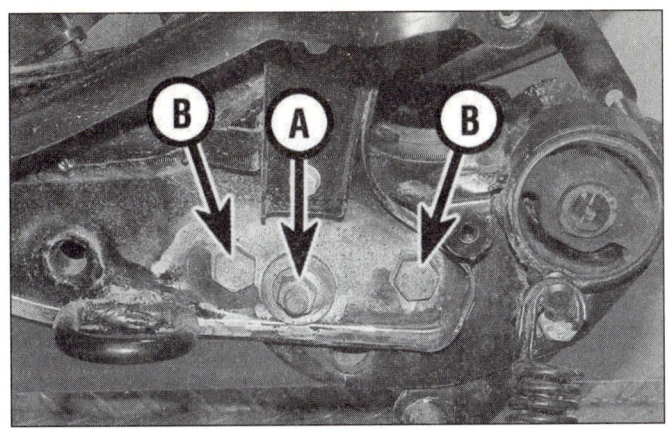

Steering and suspension 6•13

8.4a Swingarm assembly front pivot bolt (A) and torsion plate bolts (B)

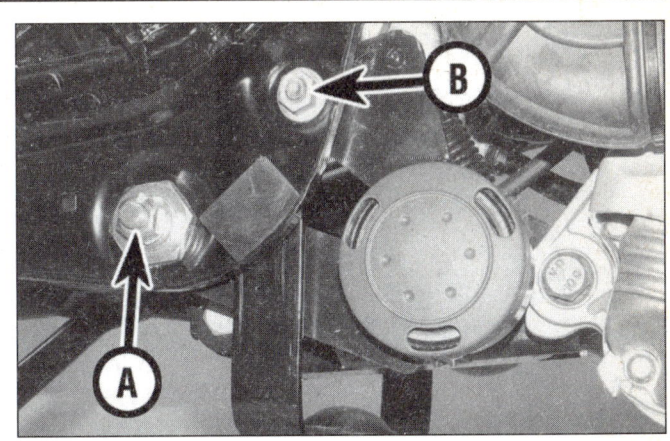

8.4b Swingarm assembly front pivot bolt (A) and torsion plate bolt (B) – X8 model

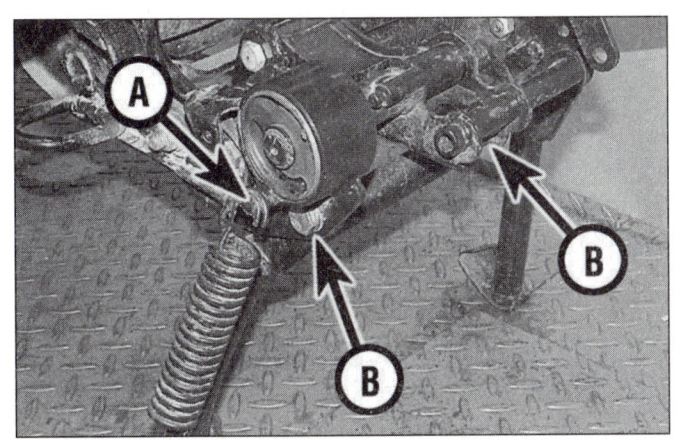

8.4c Centre stand spring location (A) and pivot bolts (B)

8.4d Remove the swingarm and its bracket as an assembly

to the frame by the front pivot bolt and torsion plate mounting bolt(s) **(see illustrations)**. On some models, the centre stand is bolted to the swingarm assembly – before removing the swingarm, support the machine on an auxiliary stand, then undo the centre stand pivot bolts and lift off the stand, noting how the stand springs locate **(see illustration)**. Unhook the swingarm pre-load spring, noting how it fits, then undo the front pivot bolt and withdraw it. Undo the torsion plate bolts and lift off the swingarm assembly **(see illustration)**.

Inspection

5 Thoroughly clean all components, removing all traces of dirt, corrosion and grease.
6 On the built-up swingarm assembly, lift off the torsion plate, then undo centre pivot bolt and withdraw it to separate the assembly. Note the location of the pivot bushes and spacers **(see illustration 8.2b)**.
7 Inspect all components closely, looking for obvious signs of wear such as heavy scoring, and cracks or distortion due to accident damage. Any damaged or worn component must be renewed. Check with a Piaggio dealer as to the availability of components.
8 Check the swingarm pivot bolt(s) and the engine mounting bolt for straightness by rolling them on a flat surface such as a piece of plate glass (first wipe off all old grease and remove any corrosion using fine emery cloth).
9 Check the various bushes and seals for cracks and deterioration **(see illustration)**. On some models, the silentbloc bushes can be renewed although they are a very tight fit and the job is best done by a Piaggio dealer or specialist engineer. On other models a new swingarm will have to be fitted.
10 Check the condition of the swingarm damping rubbers, where fitted, and renew them if necessary **(see illustration)**.

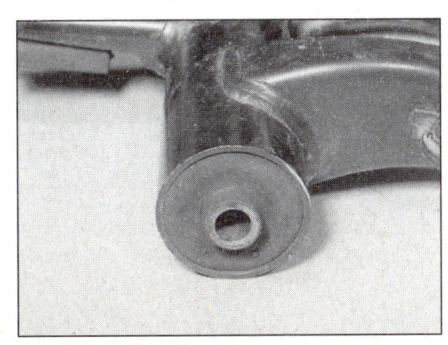

Installation

11 Installation is the reverse of removal. Smear some grease onto the pivot bolt(s) before assembly and tighten the swingarm bolts to the torque settings specified at the beginning of the Chapter. On models with a built-up swingarm assembly, install the pre-load spring.
12 Install the engine.
13 Check the operation of the rear suspension before taking the machine on the road.

8.9 Check the condition of the bushes . . .

8.10 . . . and the damping rubbers, where fitted

Chapter 7
Frame and bodywork

Refer to the beginning of Chapter 1 for model identification details

Contents

B125 body panels – removal and installation 12	Passenger footrests – removal and installation 4
Body panels removal and installation – general information 5	Rear view mirrors – removal and installation 3
ET2 and ET4 body panels – removal and installation 10	Sfera and Skipper body panels – removal and installation 7
Fly body panels – removal and installation 17	Stands – removal and installation 2
General information 1	Typhoon and NRG MC^2 and MC^3 body panels
GT body panels – removal and installation 15	– removal and installation 6
Hexagon and Super Hexagon body panels –	X8 body panels – removal and installation 19
removal and installation 9	X9 body panels – removal and installation 13
Liberty body panels – removal and installation 14	Zip 50 and Zip 125 body panels – removal and installation 11
LX body panels – removal and installation 16	Zip and Zip SP body panels – removal and installation 8
NRG Power body panels – removal and installation 18	

Degrees of difficulty

Easy, suitable for novice with little experience	Fairly easy, suitable for beginner with some experience	Fairly difficult, suitable for competent DIY mechanic	Difficult, suitable for experienced DIY mechanic	Very difficult, suitable for expert DIY or professional

1 General information

All Piaggio models are fitted with a tubular and pressed steel one-piece frame. The ET2, ET4, GT and LX models are fitted with a monocoque body, traditional to the Vespa design.

The engine and transmission assembly are linked to the frame by a swingarm at the front of the engine and by the rear shock absorber(s), making the engine an integral part of the rear suspension.

All models are fitted with a centre stand, which bolts either onto the bottom of the engine or to the frame. Some models are also fitted with a side stand which bolts to the frame.

All functional components are enclosed by body panels, including the floor panel, making removal of some or all of them a necessary part of most servicing and maintenance procedures. Be sure to follow the advice given in Section 5 before removing the panels.

2 Stands – removal and installation

Centre stand

1 Support the scooter securely using an auxiliary stand, making sure that it is not positioned directly against the body panels which could easily break.
2 On models where the stand bolts onto the frame, unhook the centre stand springs,

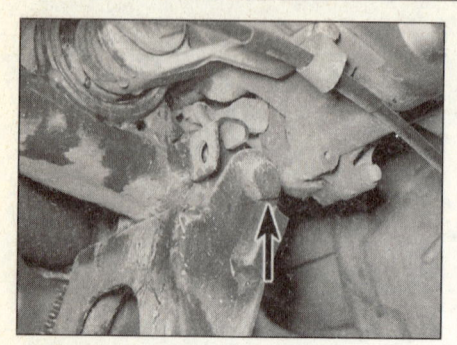

7•2 Frame and bodywork

2.2 Centre stand pivot bolt (arrowed)

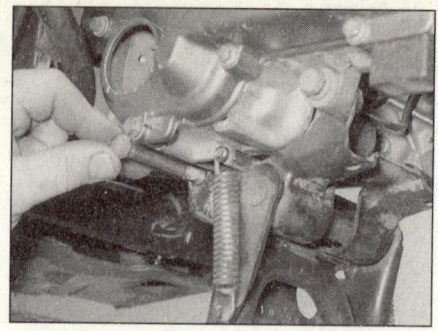

2.3a Withdraw the stand bracket bolts . . .

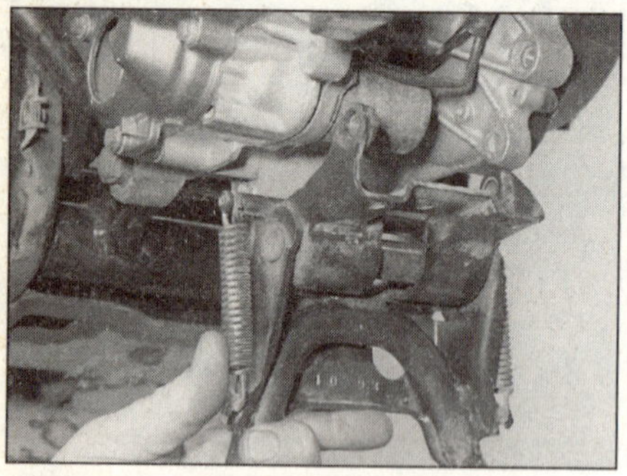

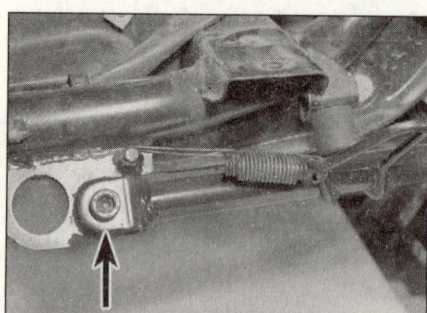

2.3b . . . and remove the stand assembly

2.7 Unhook the springs and remove the pivot bolt (arrowed)

noting where they fit. Unscrew the nut and withdraw the stand pivot bolt, then remove the stand, noting how it fits **(see illustration)**. **Note:** *On some models a left and right-hand pivot bolt is fitted.*

3 On models where the stand pivots in a bracket which bolts to the engine, unscrew the nuts and withdraw the bolts securing the bracket to the underside of the engine, then remove the stand, noting how it fits **(see illustrations)**.

4 Thoroughly clean the stand and remove all road dirt and old grease.

5 On installation apply grease to all pivot points and tighten the nuts securely. Check that the springs hold the stand securely up when not in use – an accident is almost certain to occur if the stand extends while the machine is in motion.

Side stand

6 Support the scooter using the centre stand.
7 Unhook the side stand springs, noting where they fit, then unscrew the nut and remove the pivot bolt securing the stand to the frame **(see illustration)**.

8 Thoroughly clean the stand and remove all road dirt and old grease.

9 On installation apply clean grease to the pivot bolt shank and tighten the nut securely. Reconnect the side stand springs and check that they hold the stand securely up when not in use – an accident is almost certain to occur if the stand extends while the machine is in motion.

3 Rear view mirrors – removal and installation

Removal

1 Where the mirror threads into a housing, slacken the locknut then unscrew the mirror **(see illustrations)**. Note that on some scooters, it may be necessary to remove the cover from the brake master cylinder to gain access to the locknut.

2 Where the mirror passes through a bore and is secured by a nut, unscrew the nut from the underside and remove the mirror **(see illustration)**.

3 Where the mirror is secured by mounting screws, peel back the rubber cover on the mirror bracket and undo the screws, then lift off the mirror assembly **(see illustrations)**. On X8 models, lift up the rubber cover, then push the plastic cover up and unclip it to

3.1a Slacken the nut . . .

3.1b . . . then unscrew the mirror

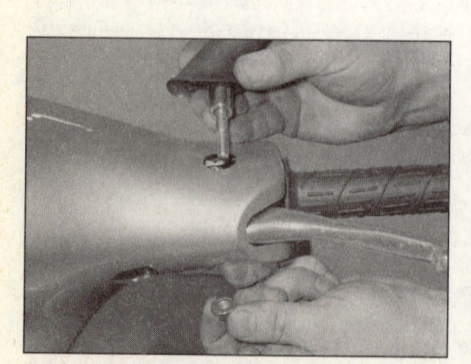

3.2 Remove the nut from the bottom of the stem and remove the mirror

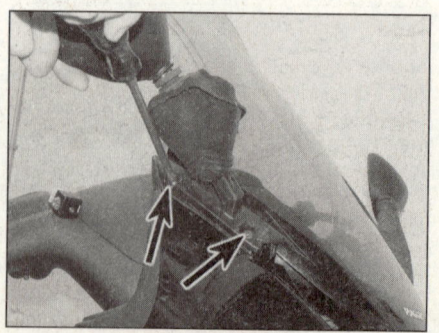

3.3a Peel back the rubber cover to access the screws (arrowed) . . .

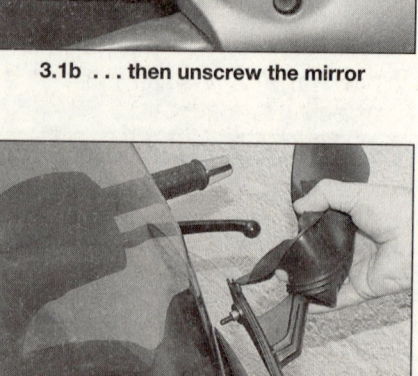

3.3b . . . then lift off the mirror assembly

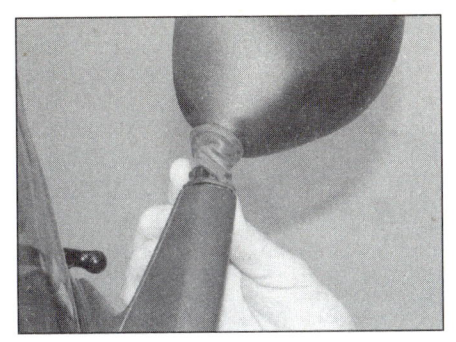

Frame and bodywork 7•3

3.3c On X8 models, push the rubber cover up ...

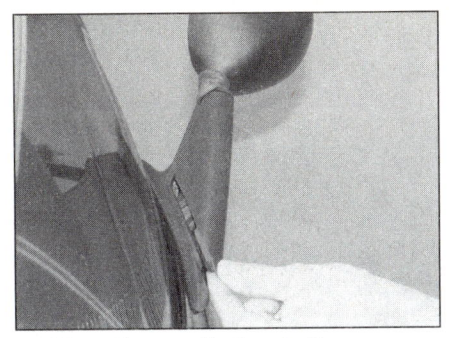

3.3d ... then unclip the plastic cover ...

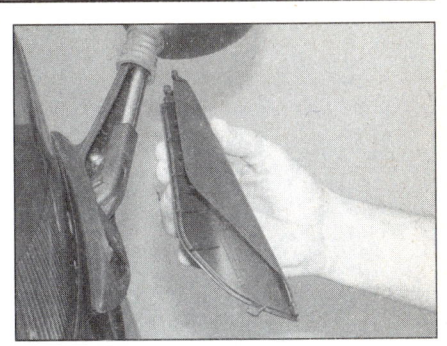

3.3e ... and lift it off

access the front mounting screws **(see illustrations)**.

4 On NRG Power models, first remove the plug in the mirror stem, then undo the bolt that secures the mirror stem to the handlebar bracket **(see illustrations)**.

Installation

5 Installation is the reverse of removal. Position the mirror as required then tighten the nut.

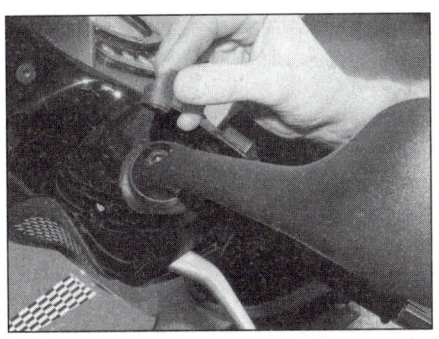

4 Passenger footrests – removal and installation

Note: *Where the procedure differs from standard refer to the specific model details given later.*

Removal

1 Remove the split pin and washer from the bottom of the footrest pivot pin, then withdraw the pivot pin and remove the footrest **(see illustration)**. Note the fitting of the detent plate, ball and spring, and take care that they do not spring out when removing the footrest.

Installation

2 Installation is the reverse of removal.

5 Body panels removal and installation – general information

When attempting to remove any body panel, first study it closely, noting any fasteners and associated fittings, to be sure of returning everything to its correct place on installation. In some cases the aid of an assistant will be required when removing panels, to help avoid the risk of damage to paintwork. Once the evident fasteners have been removed, try to withdraw the panel as described but DO NOT FORCE IT – if it will not release, check that all fasteners have been removed and try again. Where a panel engages another by means of tabs, be careful not to break the tab or its

3.4a Lift out the plug ...

mating slot or to damage the paintwork. Remember that a few moments of patience at this stage will save you a lot of money in renewing broken body panels!

When installing a body panel, first study it closely, noting any fasteners and associated fittings removed with it, to be sure of returning everything to its correct place. Check that all fasteners are in good condition, including all trim nuts or clips and damping/rubber mounts; any of these must be renewed if faulty before the panel is reassembled. Check also that all mounting brackets are straight and repair or renew them if necessary before attempting to install the panel. Where assistance was required to remove a panel, make sure your assistant is on hand to install it.

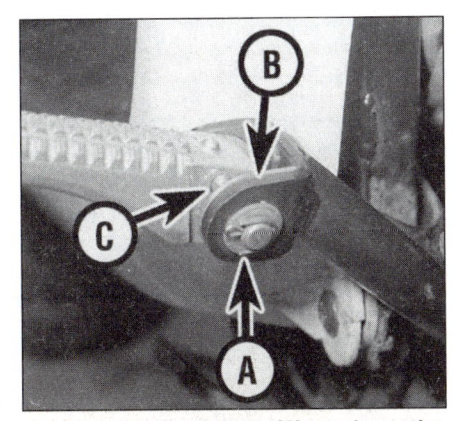

4.1 Remove the split pin (A) to release the pivot pin. Note how the detent plate (B) and ball (C) fit

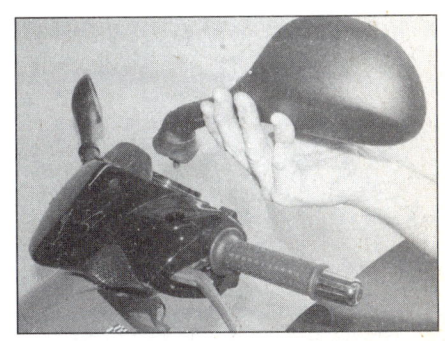

3.4b ... then unscrew the mirror

Tighten the fasteners securely, but be careful not to overtighten any of them or the panel may break (not always immediately) due to the uneven stress. Where quick-release fasteners are fitted, turn them 90° anti-clockwise to release them, and 90° clockwise to secure them.

> **HAYNES HiNT** *A small amount of lubricant (liquid soap or similar) applied to rubber mounting grommets will assist the lugs to engage without the need for undue pressure.*

In the case of damage to the body parts, it is usually necessary to remove the broken component and use a new (or used) one. There are, however, some shops that specialise in 'plastic welding', so it may be worthwhile seeking the advice of one of these specialists before consigning an expensive component to the bin. Additionally proprietary repair kits can be obtained for repair of small components.

6 Typhoon and NRG body panels – removal and installation

Seat

1 Unlock the seat using the ignition key and swing it upright.
2 Remove the screws securing the seat hinge

7•4 Frame and bodywork

6.2 Remove the two screws securing the seat hinge

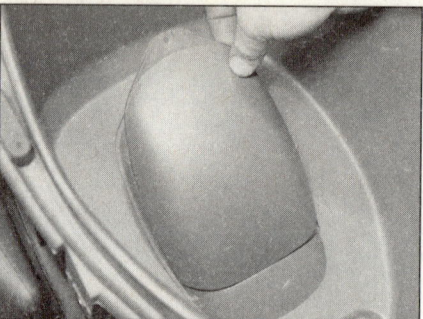

6.5 Removing the engine access panel

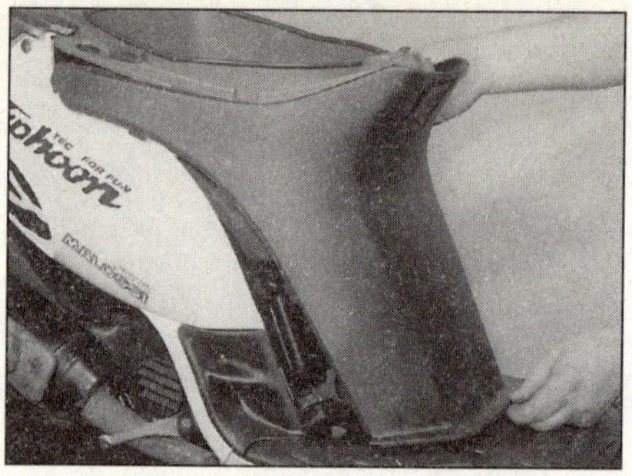

6.7 Removing the engine cover

to the storage compartment and remove the seat **(see illustration)**.
3 Installation is the reverse of removal.

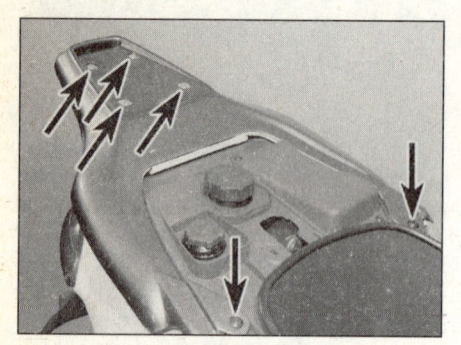

6.10a Remove the six screws (arrowed)...

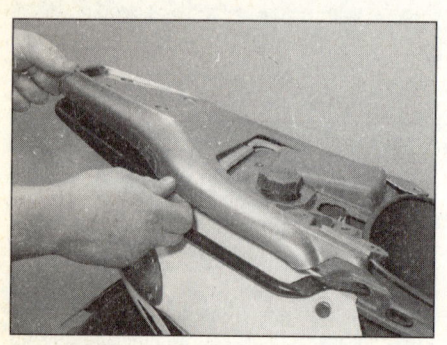

6.10b ...and remove the cover

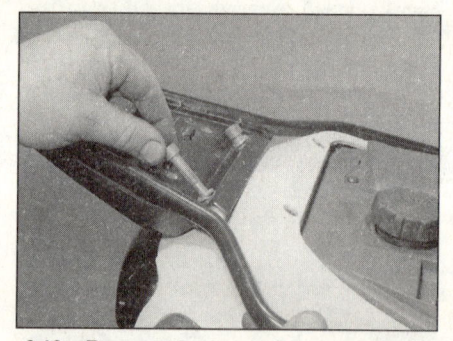

6.10c Remove the two bolts securing the rack...

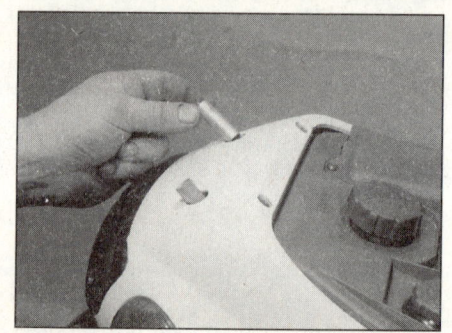

6.10d ...noting the spacers

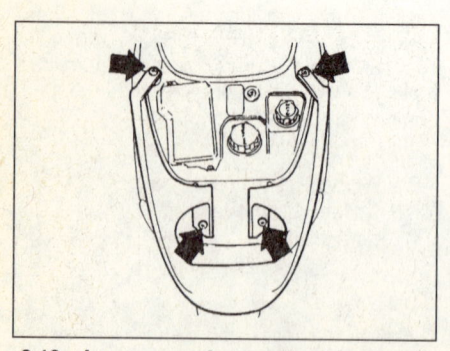

6.10e Luggage rack mountings (arrowed) on early models

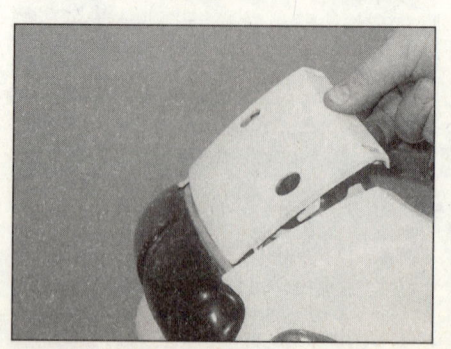

6.13 Slide the cover up to release the tabs from the side panels

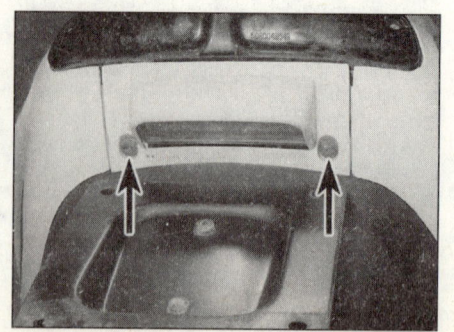

6.14 The number plate light holder is secured by two screws (arrowed)

Engine access panel

4 Unlock the seat using the ignition key and swing it upright.
5 Remove the single screw securing the access panel in the bottom of the storage compartment and remove the panel **(see illustration)**.
6 Installation is the reverse of removal.

Engine cover

7 Remove the seat. Remove the three screws securing the engine cover to the storage compartment, one at the front and one on each side along the top. Release the two pegs and the tabs which locate against related panels and remove the cover, noting how it fits **(see illustration)**.
8 Installation is the reverse of removal.

Rear carrier

9 Unlock the seat using the ignition key and swing it upright.
10 On early models, remove the six screws securing the carrier cover and remove the cover, then remove the two bolts securing the carrier and remove the carrier and the spacers **(see illustrations)**. On RST models, remove the two screws at the front and the bolts at the back, then remove the carrier **(see illustration)**.
11 Installation is the reverse of removal.

Side panels

12 Remove the engine cover and the carrier.
13 Remove the two screws securing the tail light top cover and slide the cover up, noting how its tabs locate into each side panel **(see illustration)**.
14 If both side panels are being removed, remove the two screws securing the number plate light holder and displace the holder, noting how it hooks under the tail light **(see illustration)**. If required, disconnect the wiring connectors and remove the holder. If only one

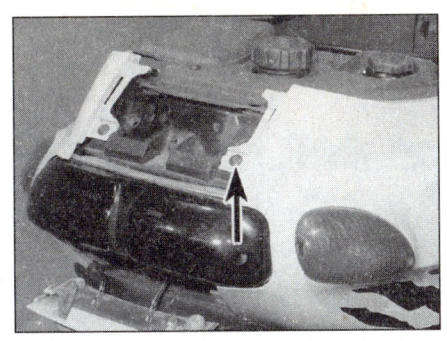

Frame and bodywork 7•5

6.15a Remove the screw at the back (arrowed) ...

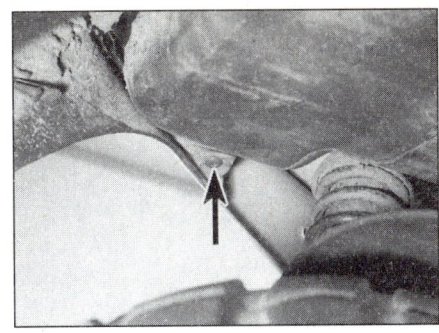

6.15b ... on the underside (arrowed) ...

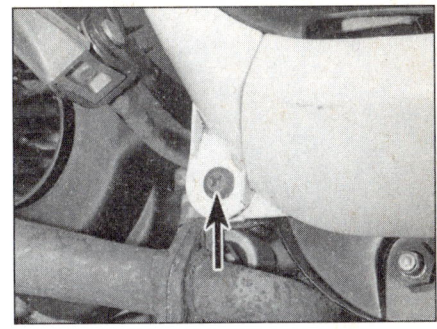

6.15c ... at the bottom (arrowed) ...

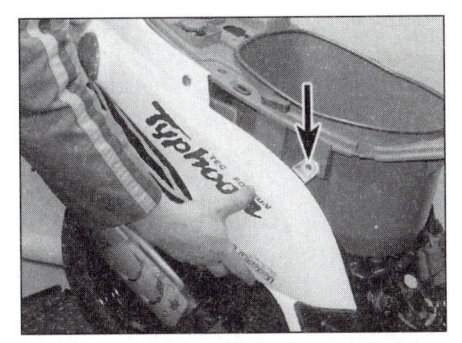

6.15d ... and the middle (arrowed), then displace the panel ...

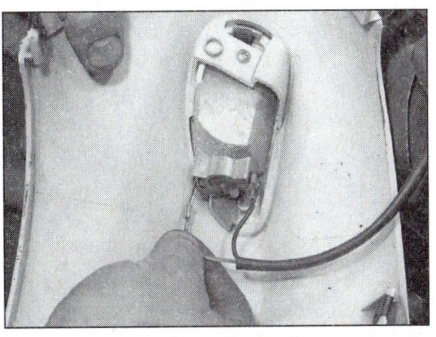

6.15e ... and disconnect the turn signal wiring connectors

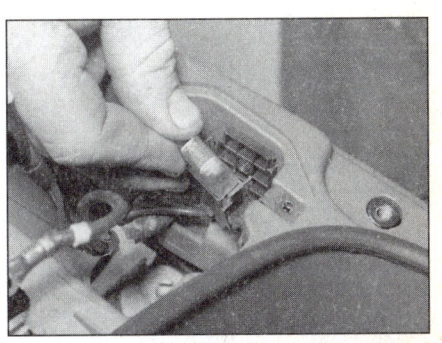

6.20 Unclip the fuse holder and feed the wiring through the hole ...

side panel is being removed, it is only necessary to remove the number plate light holder screw for the side being worked on.

15 Remove the remaining screws securing the side panel to the frame and the storage compartment and remove the panel, disconnecting the rear turn signal wiring as it becomes accessible **(see illustrations)**.

16 Installation is the reverse of removal.

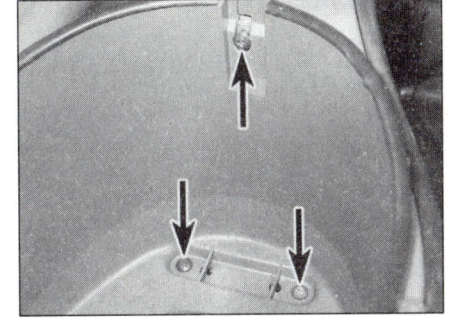

Storage compartment

17 Remove the side panels.
18 Remove the battery (see Chapter 9).
19 Remove the fuel and oil tank filler caps.
20 Unclip the fuse holder from its bracket in the battery compartment and feed it and the battery cables through the wiring hole in the side of the compartment **(see illustration)**.
21 Remove the screws securing the storage compartment to the frame and lift the compartment out, taking care not to snag the wiring as you do so **(see illustration)**. Note how the lug on the underside at the front locates into the hole in the frame **(see illustration)**. As soon as the storage compartment is free, refit the fuel and oil tank filler caps.
22 Installation is the reverse of removal.

Kick panel

23 Remove the nine screws in the kick panel, noting that two of them secure the headlight unit in the front panel **(see illustration)**. As the headlight is now loose it is advisable to tape it in place, unless the front panel is being removed, in which case remove the headlight completely (see Chapter 9).

6.21a ... then remove the three screws (arrowed) ...

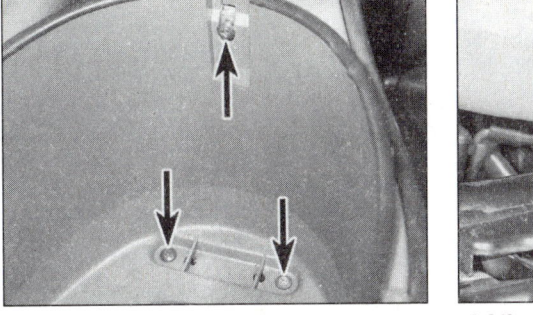

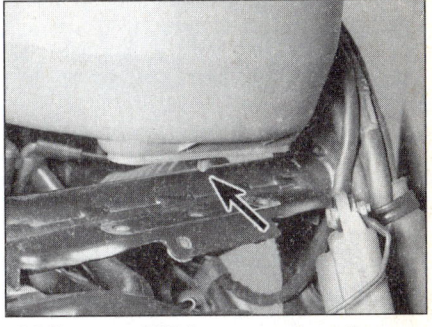

6.21b ... and lift the compartment away, noting how the lug (arrowed) locates

24 Draw the kick panel away from the front panel until the screw securing the front brake master cylinder reservoir becomes accessible. Remove the screw, then remove the reservoir cap and carefully draw the reservoir through the hole in the cover **(see illustration)**. Fit the reservoir cap and support the reservoir against the steering stem in an upright position, using a cable tie if required to prevent it tipping upside down.

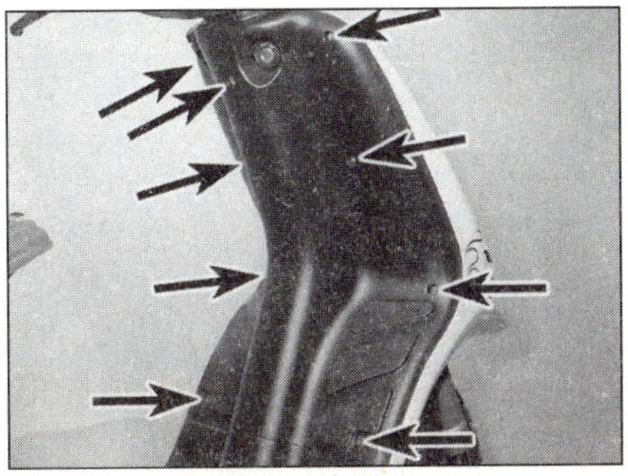

6.23 Remove the nine screws (arrowed) ...

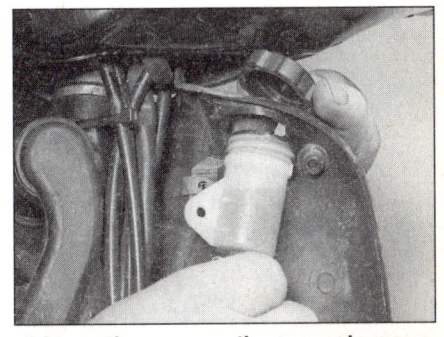

6.24 ... then remove the reservoir screw and cap

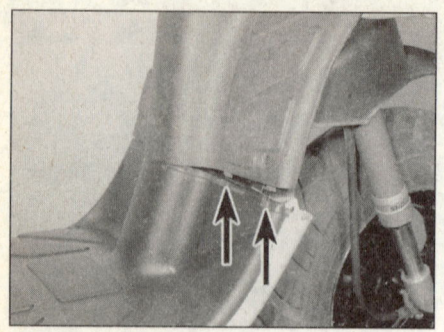

7•6 Frame and bodywork

6.25a Note how the tabs at the bottom (arrowed) . . .

6.25b . . . and the lugs in the middle (arrowed) locate

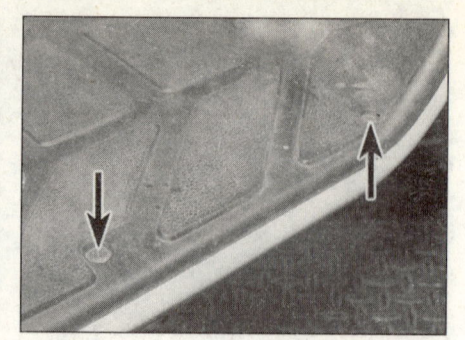

6.28a Remove the two screws (arrowed) on each side . . .

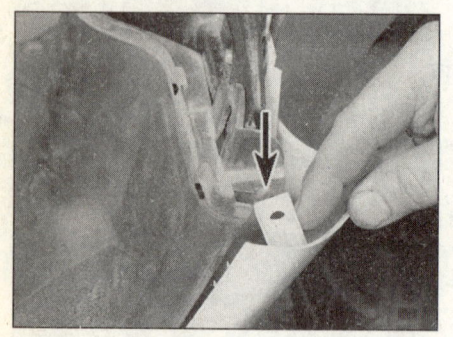

6.28b . . . then pull the belly panel away to release the lug (arrowed) . . .

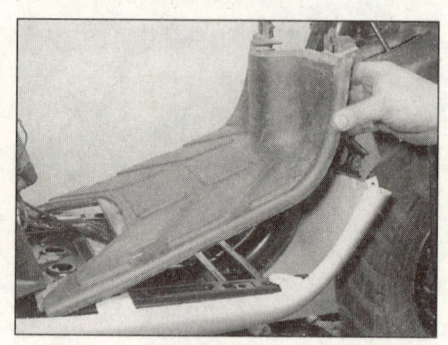

6.28c . . . and remove the floor panel

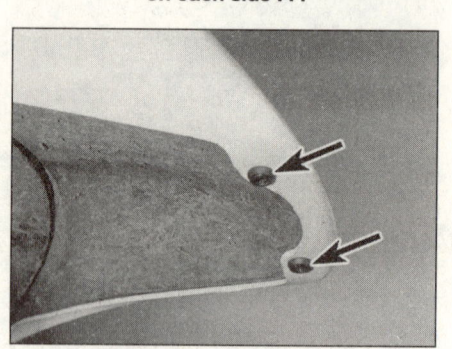

6.31 The front panel is secured to the mudguard by two screws (arrowed)

25 Remove the panel from the machine, noting how the tabs at the bottom locate into the floor panel and the lugs in the middle locate into the frame (see illustrations).
26 Installation is the reverse of removal.

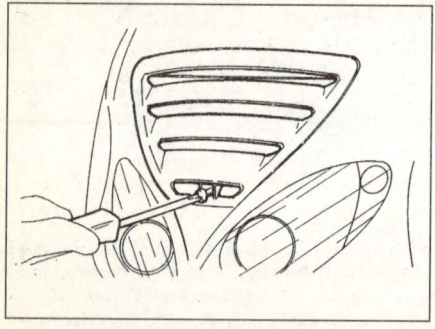

6.34 Air grille retaining screw

Floor panel

27 Remove the kick panel.
28 Remove the four screws securing the floor panel (see illustration). Pull each front corner of the belly panel away to free the lugs on the floor panel from the holes in the belly panel and lift the floor panel away, noting how it fits (see illustrations).
29 Installation is the reverse of removal.

Front panel

Typhoon

30 Remove the headlight (see Chapter 9) and the kick panel.
31 Remove the two screws securing the underside of the front panel to the mudguard and the two screws behind the front wheel securing the front panel to the frame and the belly panel (see illustration). Release the lugs on the front panel from the holes in the belly panel and remove the front panel.
32 Installation is the reverse of removal.

NRG

33 Remove the kick panel.
34 Remove the single screw securing the air grille in the front panel and remove the grille (see illustration).
35 On liquid-cooled models remove the two screws securing the air duct on the inside of the front panel and remove the duct (see illustration).
36 Remove the two screws securing the underside of the front panel and the two screws securing the front panel to the frame and the belly panel (see illustration).
37 On liquid-cooled models remove the two screws securing the inside of the radiator housing at the top (see illustration). Carefully

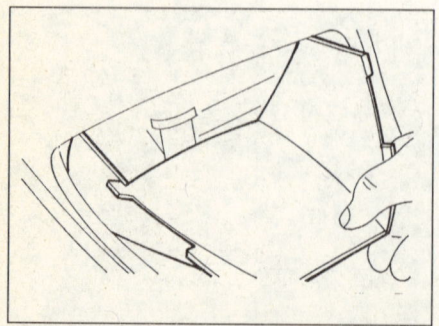

6.35 Remove the air ducts from the inside of the front panel

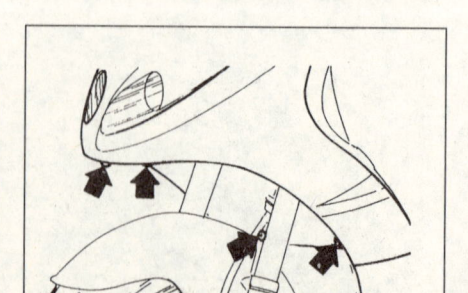

6.36 Remove the front panel retaining screws (arrowed) . . .

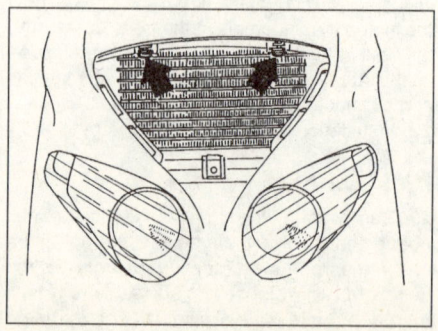

6.37a . . . plus the two in the radiator housing . . .

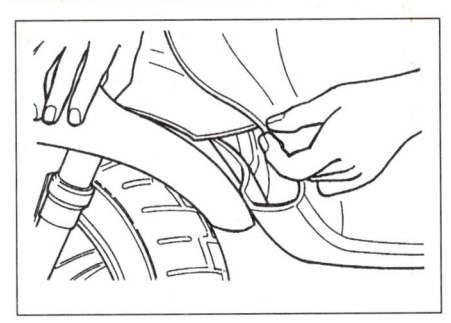

Frame and bodywork 7•7

6.37b ... and release the lower edges

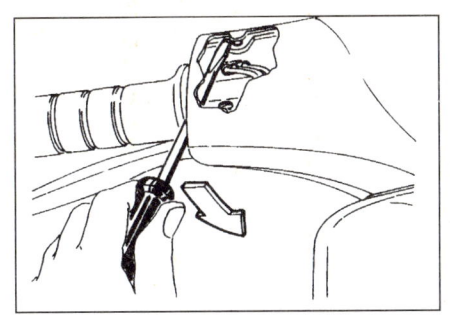

6.40 Carefully lever front cover pegs free

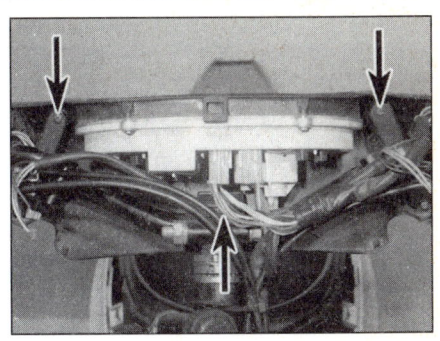

6.41 The rear cover is secured by three screws (arrowed)

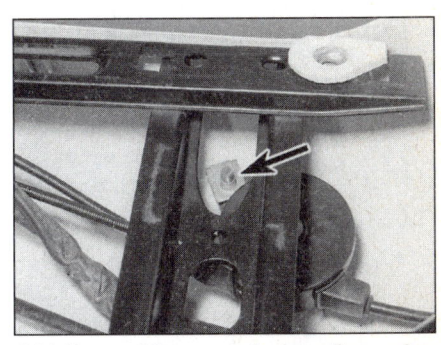

lever the front panel away at the bottom to release the tabs to remove it **(see illustration)**.
38 Installation is the reverse of removal.

Handlebar covers

39 Remove the rear view mirrors.
40 To remove the front cover, remove the screws from the rear cover **(see illustration 10.20a)**, then carefully lever up the top outer edge of the front cover to release the pegs which locate into holes in the top edge of the rear cover **(see illustration)**. These pegs are quite a tight fit and a certain amount of leverage is required, but take care not to apply excessive force as the cover could break. Once these pegs are free, manoeuvre the front cover to release its central tabs from the rear. If the cover is being completely removed rather than just displaced for access, disconnect the front turn signal wiring connectors, noting which fits where, then remove the cover.
41 To remove the rear cover, first remove the front cover. Remove the screws securing the rear cover to the brackets on the handlebars **(see illustration)**. If the cover is being completely removed rather than just displaced for access, disconnect the instrument cluster and handlebar switch wiring connectors, noting which fits where, and the speedometer cable, then remove the cover. If required, separate the instrument cluster from the cover (see Chapter 9 if necessary).
42 Installation is the reverse of removal. Make sure the wiring connectors are correctly and securely connected, and check the operation of all switches and lights.

Belly panel

43 Remove the front panel and the floor panel.

44 Remove the screw from the left-hand underside of the belly panel which secures the throttle cable splitter to the inside of the panel **(see illustration)**.
45 The belly panel is secured by screws which also secure other panels, most of which have already been removed. If the side panels have not been removed, remove the screw on each side which secures the belly panel and side panel together and to the frame **(see illustration 6.15c)**.
46 Installation is the reverse of removal.

Front mudguard (NRG)

47 Remove the two screws on each side securing the mudguard to the forks and lift the guard away, noting how it fits.
48 Installation is the reverse of removal.

Rear mudguard

49 Remove the screws securing the mudguard to the engine and remove the guard, noting how it fits.
50 Installation is the reverse of removal.

7 Sfera and Skipper body panels – removal and installation

Seat

1 Unlock the seat using the ignition key and swing it upright.
2 Remove the screws securing the seat hinge to the storage compartment and remove the seat.
3 Installation is the reverse of removal.

6.44 Remove the screw (arrowed) securing the cable splitter from the underside

Engine access panels

4 To remove the access panel in the engine cover, remove the single screw and detach the panel from the cover **(see illustration)**.
5 To remove the access panel in the storage compartment, unlock the seat using the ignition key and swing it upright. Remove the single screw securing the access panel in the bottom of the storage compartment and remove the panel.
6 Installation is the reverse of removal.

Engine cover

7 Remove the seat.
8 Remove the three screws securing the engine cover to the storage compartment **(see illustration)**. Release the two pegs and the tabs which locate against related panels and remove the cover, noting how it fits **(see illustration)**.
9 Installation is the reverse of removal.

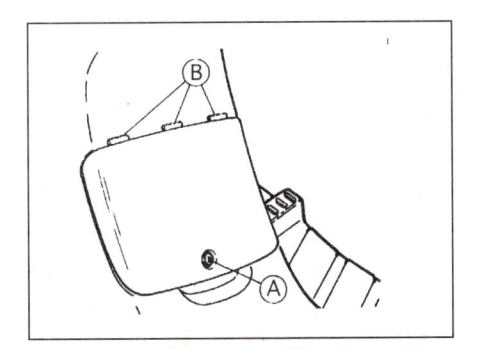

7.4 Access cover screw (A) and retaining tabs (B)

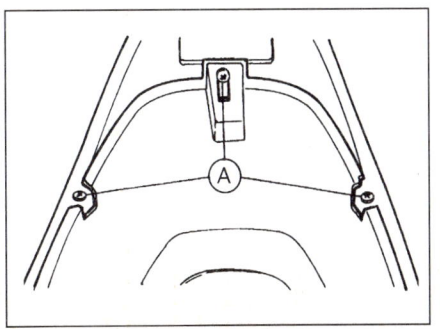

7.8a Remove the three screws (A) from the storage compartment ...

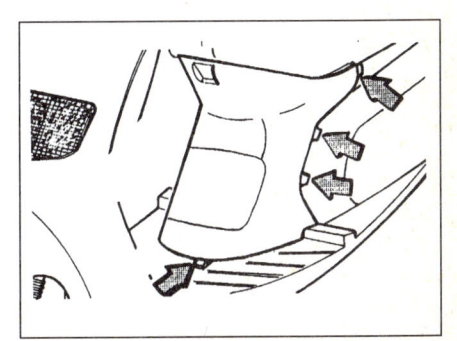

7.8b ... then release the pegs and tabs to free the engine cover

7•8 Frame and bodywork

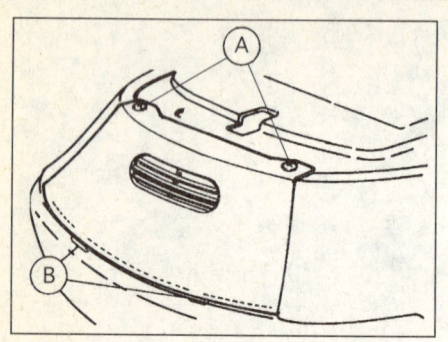

7.14 Tail light top cover screws (A) and tabs (B)

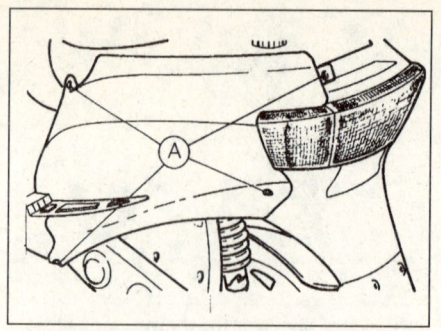

7.15 Side panel retaining screws (A)

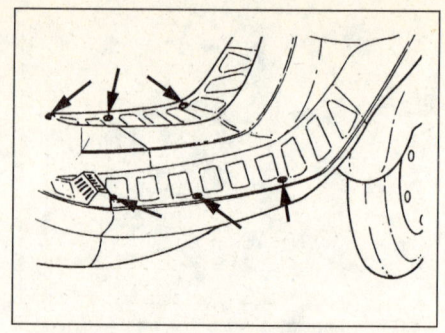

7.23 Floor panel screws (arrowed) – either 4 or 6 screws

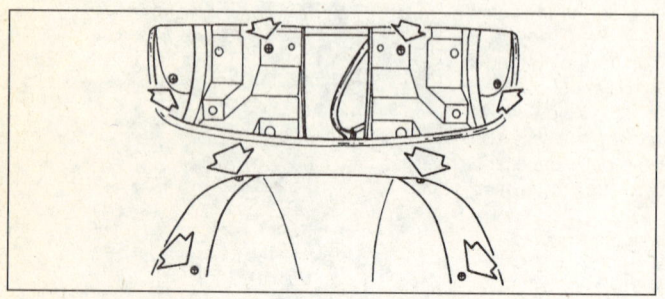

7.26a Front panel screw locations in the headlight housing and front panel lower edge . . .

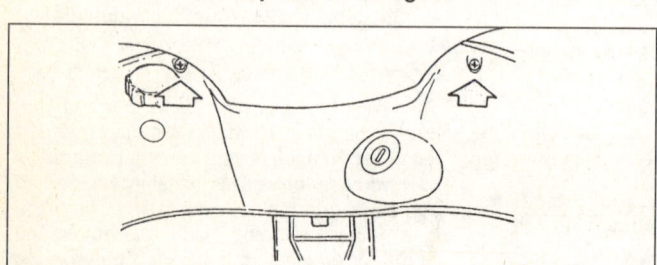

7.26b . . . and at the top of the kick panel

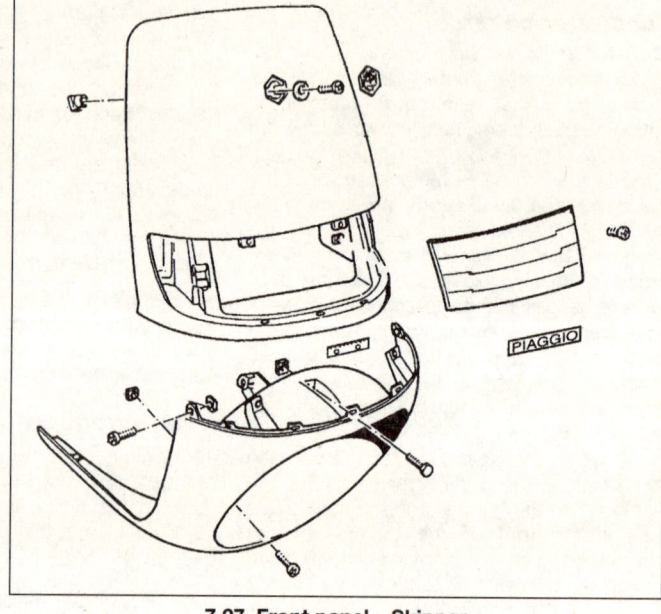

7.27 Front panel – Skipper

Rear carrier

10 Unlock the seat using the ignition key and swing it upright.
11 Remove the four bolts securing the carrier and remove it.
12 Installation is the reverse of removal.

Side panels

13 Remove the engine cover and the rear carrier.
14 Remove the two screws securing the tail light top cover and remove the cover, noting how it locates into each side panel (see illustration).
15 Remove the four screws securing the side panel to the frame and the storage compartment and remove the panel (see illustration).
16 Installation is the reverse of removal.

Storage compartment

17 Remove the side panels.
18 Remove the battery (see Chapter 9).
19 Remove the fuel and oil tank filler caps (except Sfera 125 and Skipper ST).
20 Unclip the fuse holder from its bracket in the battery compartment and feed it and the battery cables through the wiring hole in the side of the compartment.
21 Remove the screws securing the storage compartment to the frame and lift the compartment out, taking care not to snag the wiring as you do so.
22 Installation is the reverse of removal.

Floor panel

23 Remove the screws securing the floor panel (see illustration). Lift the floor panel away, noting how its tabs at the front locate into the kick panel.
24 Installation is the reverse of removal.

Front panel

25 Remove the headlight/turn signal assembly (see Chapter 9).
26 Depending on your model, the front panel is secured by a number of screws, some inside the headlight housing (see illustration), some around the base of the front panel, two on the top of the kick panel (see illustration), and one behind the badge in the front panel (early models), which must be carefully levered off using a screwdriver. Check that all fasteners for your model have been removed, then remove the front panel, noting how it fits.
27 On early models where the front panel is in two parts, to remove the lower section it is first necessary to remove the steering stem (see Chapter 6), then remove the screws securing the lower section and remove it, noting how it fits (see illustration).
28 Installation is the reverse of removal.

Kick panel

29 Remove the floor panel and the front panel.
30 Remove the screws securing the kick panel (see illustrations).
31 On disc brake models with the front brake master cylinder reservoir mounted behind the kick panel, draw the panel back to access the screw securing the reservoir. Undo the screw, then remove the reservoir cap and carefully draw the reservoir through the hole in the panel. Fit the reservoir cap and secure the reservoir against the steering stem in an upright position with a cable tie.
32 Remove the kick panel from the machine.
33 Installation is the reverse of removal.

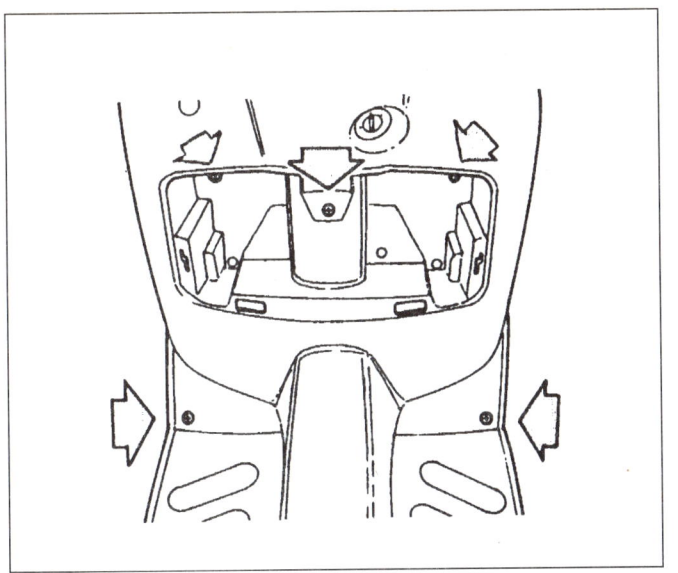

Frame and bodywork 7•9

7.30a Kick panel retaining screws (arrowed) – later model

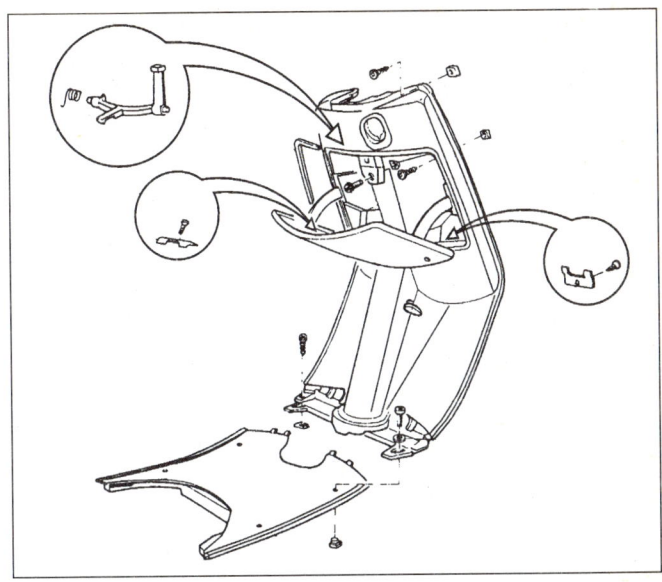

7.30b Kick panel – Skipper

Handlebar covers

34 Remove the rear view mirrors.
35 To remove the front cover, remove the screws from the rear cover **(see illustration)**, then carefully lever up the top outer edge of the front cover to release the pegs which locate into holes in the top edge of the rear cover **(see illustration 6.40)**. These pegs are quite a tight fit and a certain amount of leverage is required, but take care not to apply excessive force as the cover could break. Once these pegs are free, manoeuvre the front cover to release its central tabs from the rear. On the Skipper model, if the cover is being completely removed rather than just displaced for access, disconnect the headlight wiring connectors, noting which fits where, then remove the cover.
36 To remove the rear cover, first remove the front cover. Remove the two screws securing the rear cover to the brackets on the handlebars **(see illustration)**. If the cover is being completely removed rather than just displaced for access, disconnect the instrument cluster and handlebar switch wiring connectors, noting which fits where, and the speedometer cable, then remove the cover. If required, separate the instrument cluster from the cover (see Chapter 9 if necessary).
37 Installation is the reverse of removal.

Rear mudguard

38 Remove the screws securing the mudguard to the engine and remove the guard, noting how it fits.
39 Installation is the reverse of removal.

8 Zip and Zip SP body panels – removal and installation

Note: *For new body style see Zip 50 and Zip 125, Section 11.*

Seat

1 Unlock the seat using the ignition key and swing it upright.
2 Remove the screws securing the seat hinge to the storage compartment and remove the seat.
3 Installation is the reverse of removal.

Engine access panels

4 To remove the access panel in the engine cover, remove the single screw and detach the panel from the cover.
5 To remove the access panel in the storage compartment, unlock the seat using the ignition key and swing it upright. Remove the single screw securing the access panel in the bottom of the storage compartment and remove the panel.
6 Installation is the reverse of removal.

Floor panel

7 Remove the access panel in the engine cover.
8 Remove the four screws securing the floor panel and lift it away, noting how it fits.
9 Installation is the reverse of removal.

Side panels

10 Remove the access panel in the engine cover and the floor panel.
11 Each side panel is secured by four screws and a peg **(see illustration)**. Remove the screws, one at the front, one on the side, one at the back and one inside the access panel.

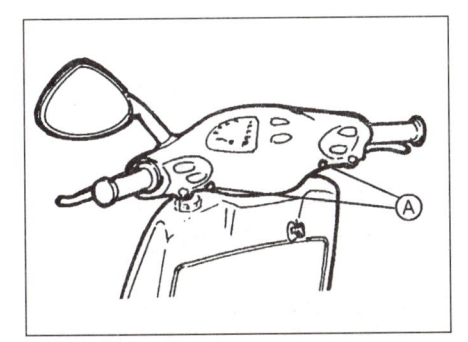

7.35 Handlebar cover screws (A)

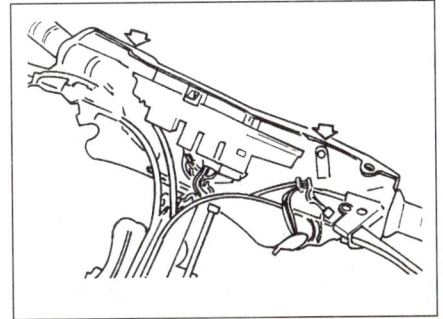

7.36 Handlebar cover rear section screws (arrowed)

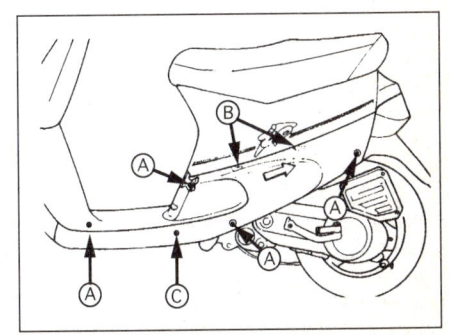

8.11 Side panel screws (A), slots (B) and peg (C)

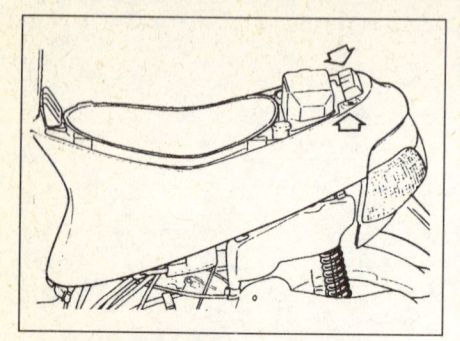

7•10 Frame and bodywork

8.17 Engine cover retaining screws (arrowed)

8.25 Front panel retaining screws on front face (top screw is under badge)

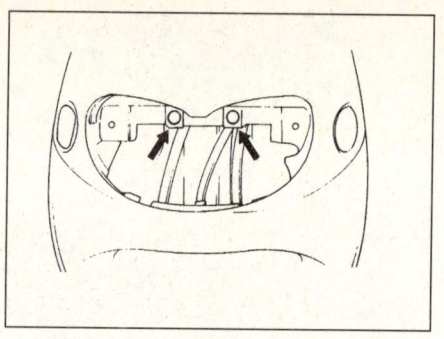

8.29 Screw locations inside headlight housing

Pull the side panel away at the front to disengage the lug from its grommet, then slide the panel backwards approximately 10 mm until the tabs on the engine cover disengage from the slots in the side panel. If removing the left-hand side panel, note that the throttle/oil pump cable splitter must first be detached.
12 Installation is the reverse of removal.

Rear carrier

13 Unlock the seat using the ignition key and swing it upright.
14 Undo the bolts and remove the carrier.
15 Installation is the reverse of removal.

Engine cover

16 Remove the seat, the carrier and the side panels.
17 Remove the screws securing the engine cover and remove the cover, noting how it fits **(see illustration)**.
18 Installation is the reverse of removal.

Storage compartment

19 Remove the engine cover.
20 Remove the battery (see Chapter 9).
21 Remove the fuel and oil tank filler caps.
22 Unclip the fuse holder from its bracket in the battery compartment and feed it and the battery cables through the wiring hole in the side of the compartment.
23 Remove the screws securing the storage compartment to the frame and lift the compartment out, taking care not to snag the wiring as you do.
24 Installation is the reverse of removal.

Front panel
Zip

25 Remove the three screws from the front of the panel, one of which is behind the badge, which must be carefully levered off using a screwdriver **(see illustration)**.
26 Push the ignition lock in to release the catch on the glove compartment and swing the door down.
27 Remove the two screws on the inside of the compartment to allow the turn signals to be withdrawn from the front panel and their wiring disconnected **(see illustration 8.33)**. Remove the two screws from the top of the kick panel then remove the front panel, noting how it fits.
28 Installation is the reverse of removal.

Zip SP

29 Remove the headlight (see Chapter 9). Remove the screws from inside the headlight housing **(see illustration)**.
30 Push the ignition lock in to release the catch on the glove compartment and swing the door down. Remove any screws on the inside of the compartment which secure the front panel.
31 Remove the two screws securing the top rim of the front panel and the two screws at the bottom front edge of the panel. Remove the front panel, noting how it fits.
32 Installation is the reverse of removal.

Kick panel

33 On Zip models, remove the screws from the kick panel **(see illustration)**; support the front turn signals to prevent them becoming dislodged from the front panel. On Zip SP models, remove the front panel as described above.
34 On all models, remove the floor panel. Remove the screw on each side which secures the front portion of each side panel to the kick panel **(see illustration 8.11, front screw A)**. Remove the kick panel.
35 Installation is the reverse of removal.

Handlebar covers

36 Remove the rear view mirrors.
37 To remove the front cover, remove the two screws from the rear cover and the single screw from the lower part of the front cover **(see illustration)**. If the cover is being completely removed rather than just displaced for access, disconnect the headlight (Zip) or front turn signal (Zip SP) wiring connectors, noting which fits where, then remove the cover.
38 To remove the rear cover, first remove the front cover. Remove the three screws securing the rear cover to the brackets on the handlebars **(see illustration)**. If the cover is being completely removed rather than just displaced for access, disconnect the instrument cluster and handlebar switch wiring connectors, noting which fits where, and the speedometer cable, then remove the cover. If required, separate the instrument cluster from the cover (see Chapter 9 if necessary).
39 Installation is the reverse of removal. Make sure the wiring connectors are correctly and securely connected, and check the operation of all switches and lights.

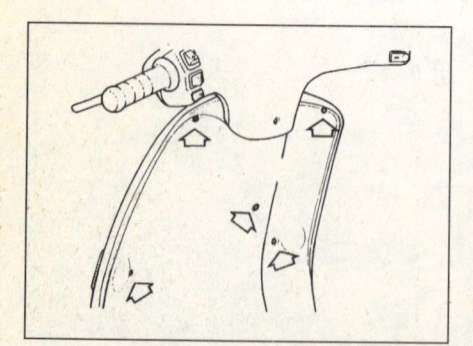

8.33 Kick panel retaining screws – Zip

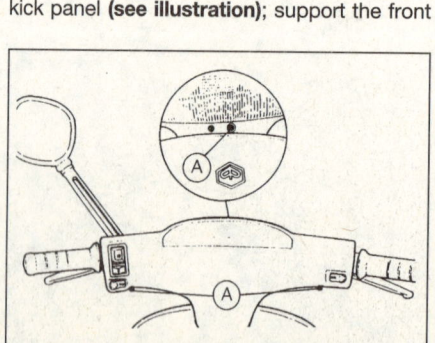

8.37 Handlebar front cover retaining screws (A)

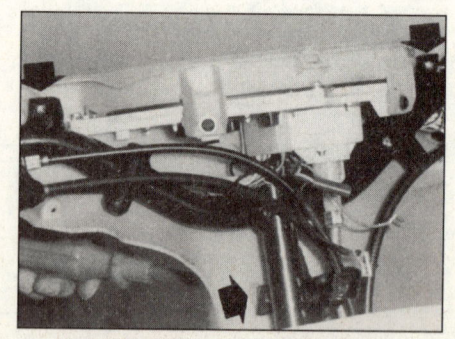

8.38 Handlebar rear cover retaining screws (arrowed)

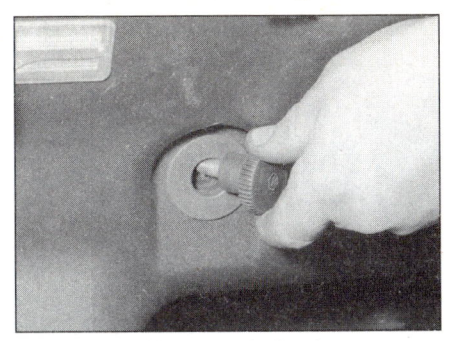

Frame and bodywork 7•11

9.2a Unscrew the knob . . .

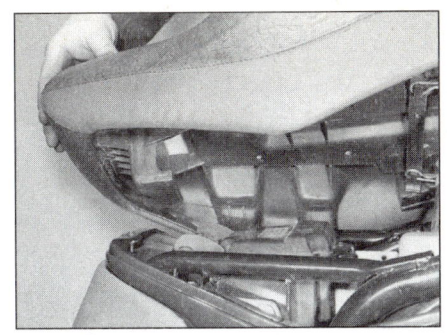

9.2b . . . and remove the seat

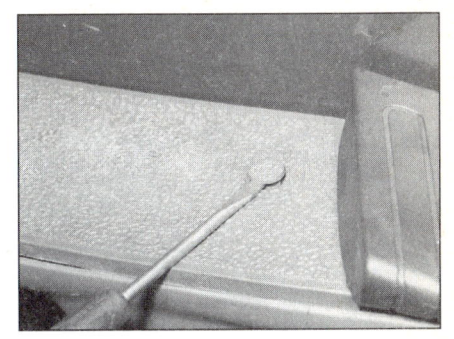

9.6a Lever up the fasteners . . .

9.6b . . . and lift the mats away

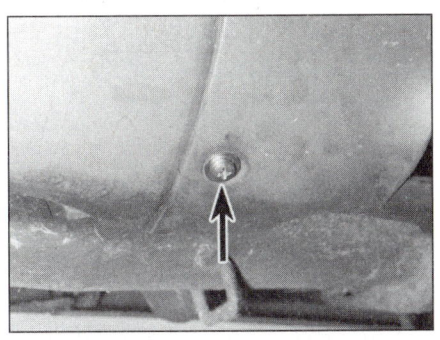

9.7a The screw securing the front is on the underside of the panel (arrow)

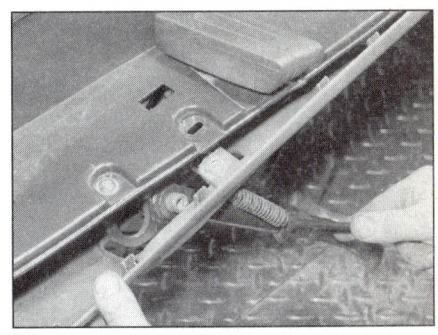

9.7b Pull the panel away at the front . . .

9.7c . . . then draw it forwards . . .

9.7d . . . to release the tabs

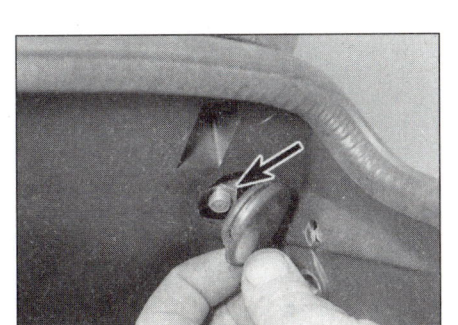

9.11a Remove the cover and unscrew the nut (arrowed) . . .

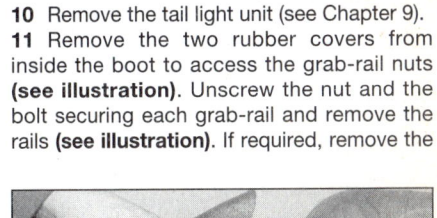

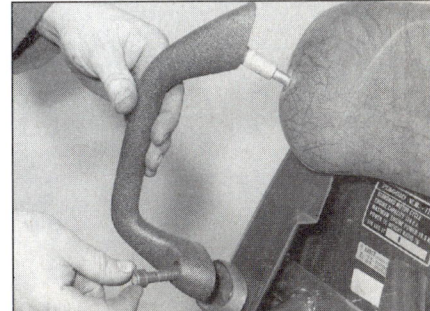

9.11b . . . and the bolt and remove the grab-rail . . .

Rear mudguard

40 Remove the screws securing the mudguard to the engine and remove the guard, noting how it fits.
41 Installation is the reverse of removal.

9 Hexagon and Super Hexagon body panels – removal and installation

Seat

1 Unlock the boot using the ignition key and swing it open.
2 Unscrew the knob inside the boot to release the seat and remove the seat **(see illustrations)**.
3 Installation is the reverse of removal.

Engine access panel

4 Remove the single screw securing the access panel below the front of the seat and remove the panel, noting how it fits.
5 Installation is the reverse of removal.

Lower trim panels

6 Remove the floor panel mats by levering up the fasteners using a screwdriver and pulling the mats up **(see illustrations)**.
7 Each lower trim panel is secured by four screws. Remove the screws, one on the underside at the front, two on the floor panel and one at the back **(see illustration)**. Pull the panel away at the front to disengage the clips from the side of the floor panel, then slide the panel forwards approximately 10 mm until the tabs disengage from the slots in the side panel **(see illustrations)**.
8 Installation is the reverse of removal.

Side panels

9 Remove the lower trim panels.
10 Remove the tail light unit (see Chapter 9).
11 Remove the two rubber covers from inside the boot to access the grab-rail nuts **(see illustration)**. Unscrew the nut and the bolt securing each grab-rail and remove the rails **(see illustration)**. If required, remove the

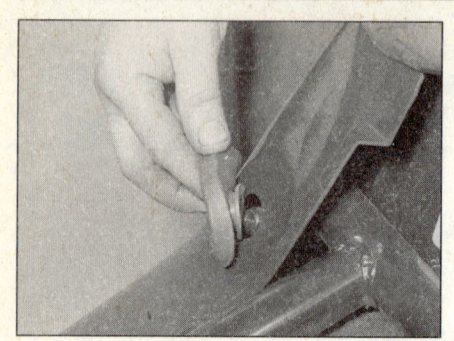

7•12 Frame and bodywork

9.11c ... and if required the rubber pad

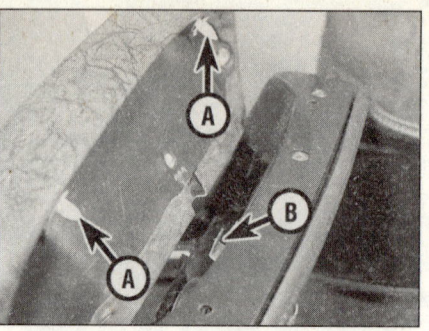

9.12a Release the pegs (A) and lift the cushion, noting the support (B)

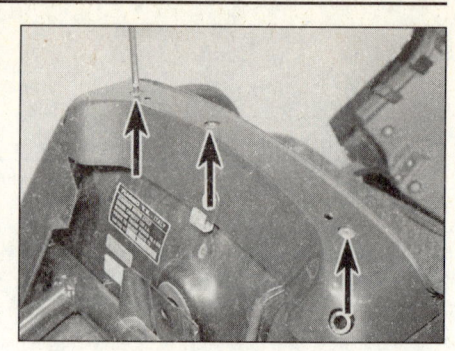

9.12b Remove the three screws (arrowed) and remove the trim

rubbers for the lower mountings (see illustration).

12 Remove the rear cushion by pulling it up to release the two pegs from the boot trim, noting how it slots onto the support, then remove the three screws securing the trim and remove it (see illustrations).

13 Remove the passenger footrest rubbers, noting which way round they fit, then unscrew the bolts securing the footrests, accessing them using a socket extension via the holes in the top (see illustrations).

14 Each side panel is secured by eight screws, three along the floor panel, two in the middle which secure the panels together, two along the top edge of the panel, and one at the rear (see illustrations). Remove all the screws, then carefully remove the panel, noting how it fits.

15 Installation is the reverse of removal.

Floor panel

16 Remove the floor panel mats by levering up the fasteners using a screwdriver and pulling the mats up (see illustrations 9.6a and 9.6b).

17 Remove the side panels as described above.

18 Open the fuel and oil filler cover lid using the ignition key and swing it upright. Remove the fuel and oil filler (where applicable) caps, then remove the drain trays and refit the caps (see illustrations).

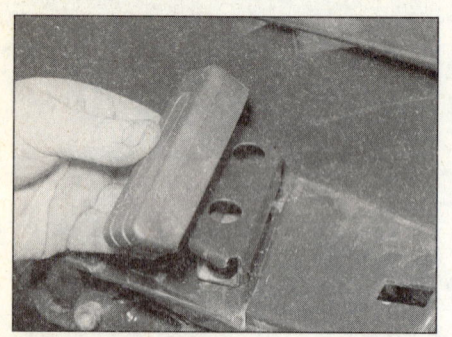

9.13a Remove the footrest rubber ...

9.13b ... to access the footrest bolts (arrowed)

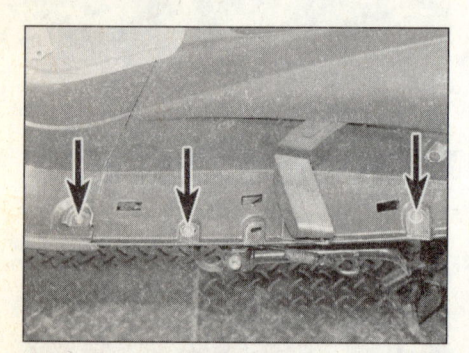

9.14a Remove the three screws (arrowed) on the floor panel ...

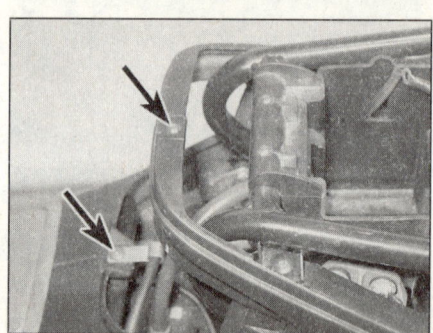

9.14b ... the two in the middle (arrowed) ...

9.14c ... the two on the top (arrowed) ...

9.14d ... and the single screw at the rear (arrowed)

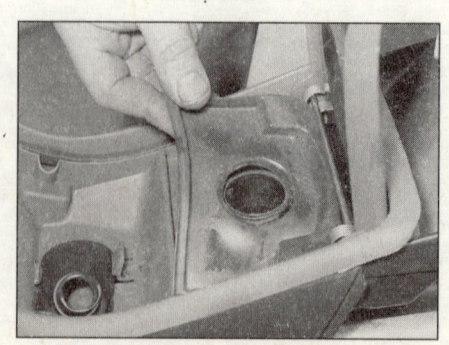

9.18a Remove the fuel ...

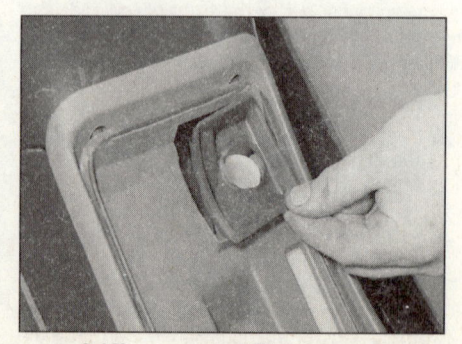

9.18b ... and oil filler trays ...

Frame and bodywork 7•13

19 Remove the six screws securing the filler cover and remove the cover **(see illustration)**.
20 Remove the four screws securing the floor panel and remove the panel, noting how it fits **(see illustration)**.
21 Installation is the reverse of removal.

Front panel

22 Remove the headlight (see Chapter 9).
23 The front panel is secured by nine screws, four inside the headlight housing, one on the underside at the front, two on the top of the kick panel and one half-way down each side of the kick panel **(see illustrations)**. Remove all the screws, then carefully draw the front panel forward and off the machine, noting how it fits.
24 Installation is the reverse of removal.

Kick panel

25 Remove the front panel.
26 Remove the screw securing the fuse holder panel, then lift the panel out of it slots and pass it through the hole in the kick panel **(see illustration)**. Disconnect the turn signal bleeper cancel switch wiring connector from the rear of the panel **(see illustration)**.
27 Remove the screw securing the coolant reservoir, then remove the reservoir cap and rubber surround. Lift the reservoir out of its mounting grommets, then draw the filler neck out of the hole in the top of the kick panel **(see illustration)**. Secure the reservoir in an upright position against the steering stem with a cable tie.
28 Remove the two screws securing the kick panel to the frame, one of which also secures a bracket holding the turn signal beeper, beeper relay and headlight relay **(see illustration)**.
29 Remove the two screws securing the bottom of the kick panel to the mudguard and remove the panel, noting how it fits **(see illustration)**.
30 Installation is the reverse of removal.

Handlebar covers and windshield

31 Remove the rear view mirrors.
32 To remove the front handlebar cover,

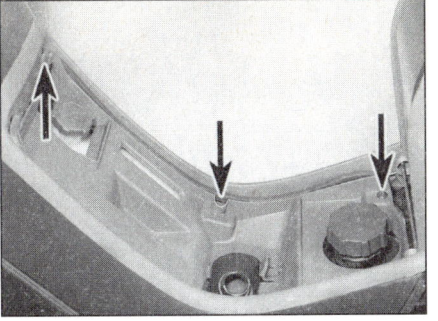

9.19 ... then remove the three screws (arrowed) on each side

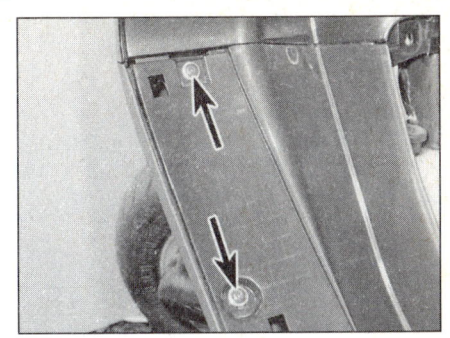

9.20 The panel is secured by two screws (arrowed) on each side

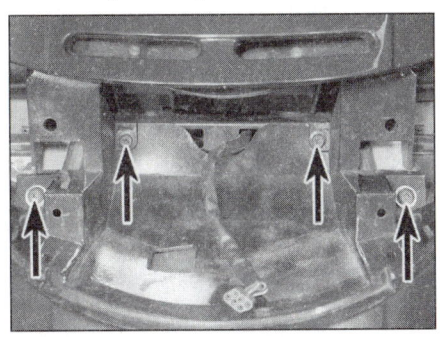

9.23a Remove the four screws (arrowed) in the headlight housing ...

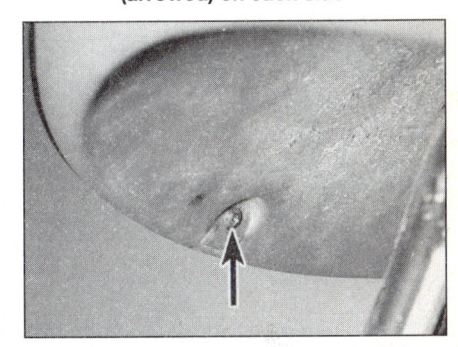

9.23b ... the screw on the underside (arrowed) ...

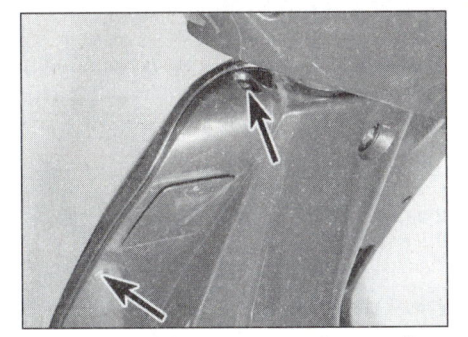

9.23c ... and the two screws (arrowed) on each side of the kick panel

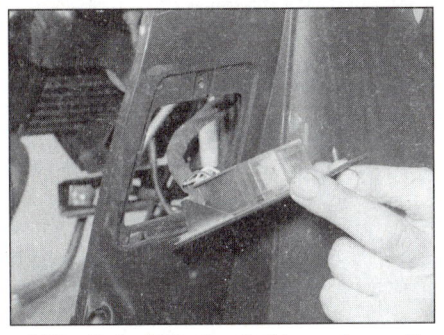

9.26a Detach the fuseholder and pass it through the hole ...

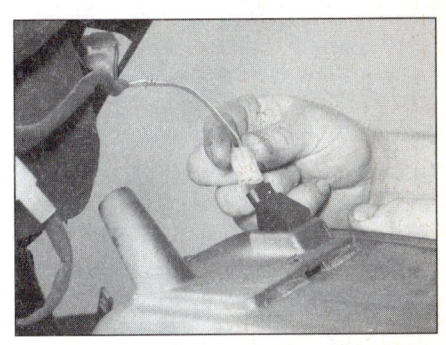

9.26b ... and disconnect the wiring from the back of the cancel switch

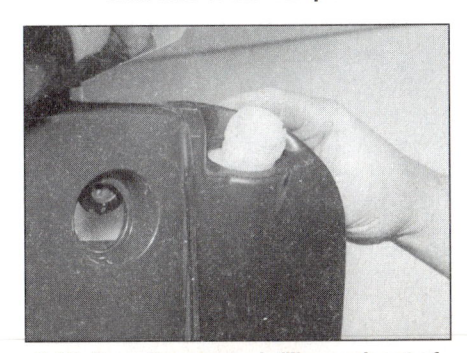

9.27 Draw the reservoir filler neck out of the panel

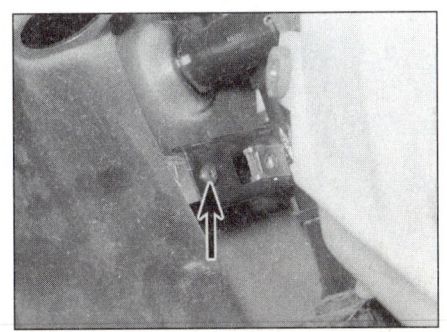

9.28 Remove the screw (arrowed) on each side of the bracket on the frame

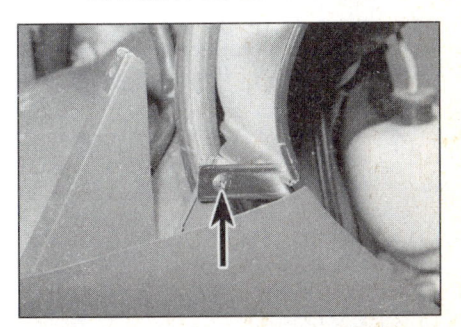

9.29 Remove the screw on each side (arrowed) securing the panel to the mudguard

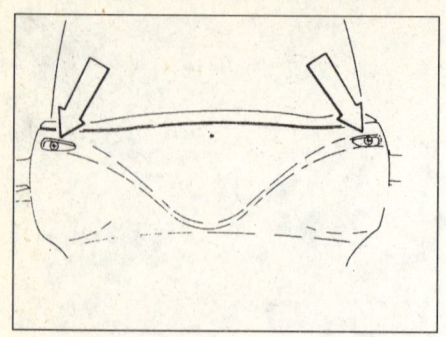

7•14 Frame and bodywork

9.32a The front cover is retained by two screws on the front face (arrowed) . . .

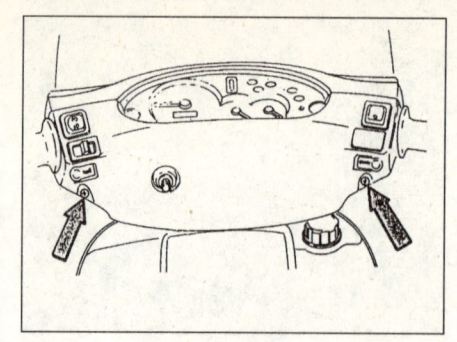

9.32b . . . and two screws (arrowed) on the rear cover

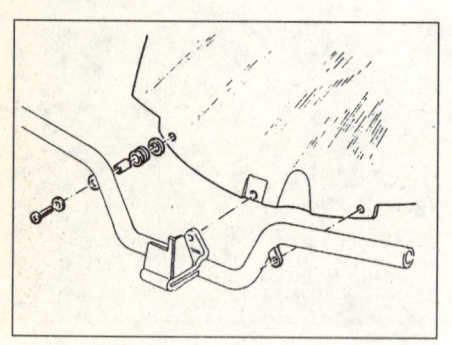

9.33a Windshield mounting arrangement

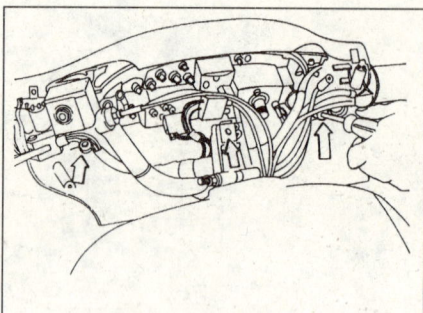

9.33b Rear cover mounting points (arrowed)

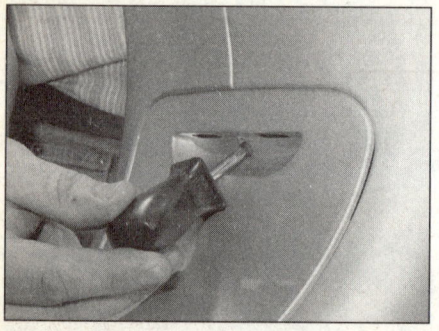

10.4a Remove the screw . . .

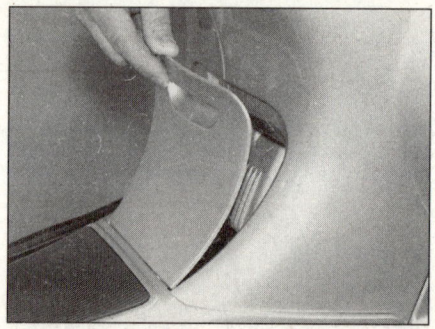

10.4b . . . to release the access panel

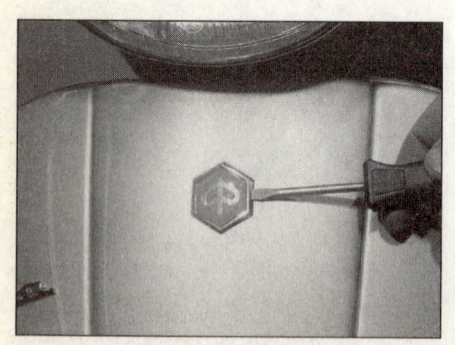

10.6a Lever off the badge . . .

10.6b . . . and remove the screw (arrowed) . . .

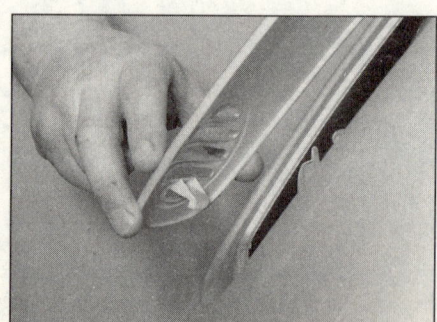

10.6c . . . to release the grille

remove the two screws at the top below the windshield and the two screws below the switches in the rear cover **(see illustrations)**.

33 To remove the rear cover, first remove the front cover. Remove the screws securing the windshield to the brackets on the handlebars **(see illustration)**. Remove the two screws from the front side of the rear cover and the single screw from the rear side **(see illustration)**. If the cover is being completely removed rather than just displaced for access, disconnect the instrument cluster and handlebar switch wiring connectors, noting which fits where, and the speedometer cable, then remove the cover. If required, separate the instrument cluster from the cover (see Chapter 9 if necessary).

34 Installation is the reverse of removal. Make sure the wiring connectors are correctly and securely connected, and check the operation of all switches and lights.

Rear mudguard

35 Remove the screws securing the mudguard to the engine and remove the guard, noting how it fits.

36 Installation is the reverse of removal.

10 ET2 and ET4 body panels – removal and installation

Seat

1 Unlock the seat using the ignition key and swing it upright.
2 Remove the screws securing the seat and remove the seat.
3 Installation is the reverse of removal.

Engine access panel

4 Remove the single screw securing the access panel below the seat and remove the panel **(see illustrations)**.
5 Installation is the reverse of removal.

Front panel grille

6 Carefully lever off the badge in the grille, then remove the screw behind it and remove the grille **(see illustrations)**.
7 Installation is the reverse of removal.

Kick panel

8 Remove the front panel grille, then remove

Frame and bodywork 7•15

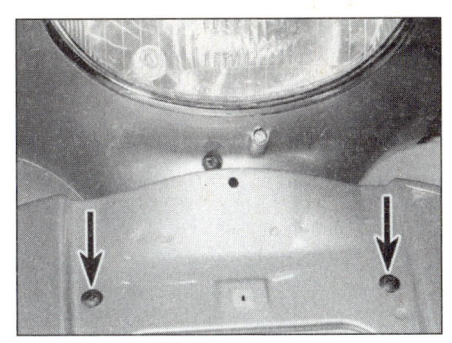

10.8 Remove the two screws (arrowed)

10.9a Open the glove compartment . . .

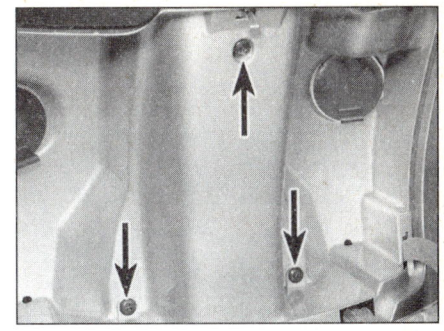

10.9b . . . then remove the screws (arrowed) . . .

the two screws located behind it **(see illustration)**.
9 Press in the ignition switch to release the glove compartment door and swing the door down **(see illustration)**. Remove the three screws inside the compartment, then remove the kick panel, noting how it fits **(see illustrations)**.
10 Installation is the reverse of removal.

Floor panel

11 Remove the kick panel.
12 Remove the floor panel mats, then remove the five screws securing the panel and remove it, noting how it engages with the side panels at the back **(see illustrations)**.
13 Installation is the reverse of removal.

Side panels

14 Lift the back of each floor panel mat and remove the screws joining the side panels to the floor panel **(see illustration)**.
15 Each side panel is secured to the main body by three pegs which locate in rubber grommets, and by tabs at the front and rear.

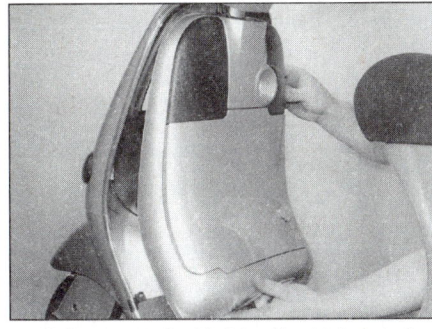

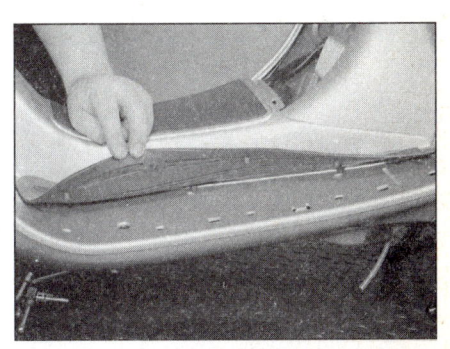

10.9c . . . and withdraw the kick panel

10.12a Pull the floor panel mats away . . .

Pull the back of each panel away to release the rear tabs, then pull the pegs out of the grommets and pull the panel back to disengage the front tab **(see illustrations)**.
16 Installation is the reverse of removal.

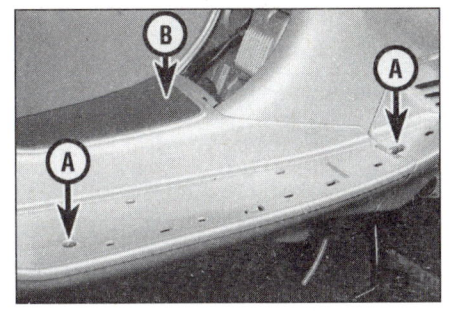

10.12b . . . then remove the two screws on each side (A) and the screw under the centre mat (B) . . .

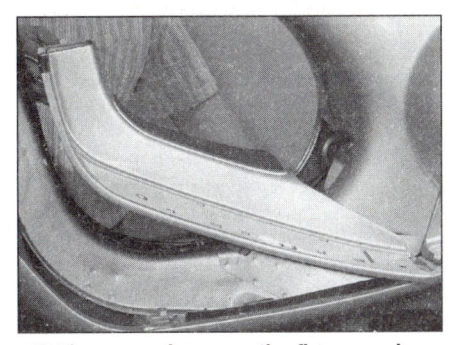

10.12c . . . and remove the floor panel . . .

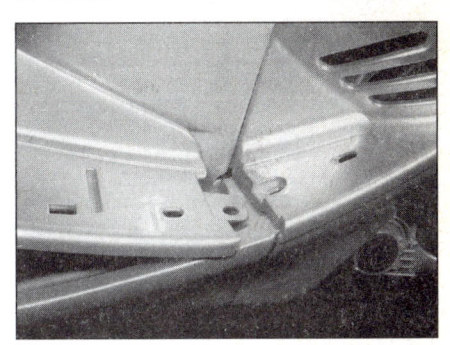

10.12d . . . noting how it engages with the side panel

10.14 Lift the back of the mat and remove the screw (arrowed)

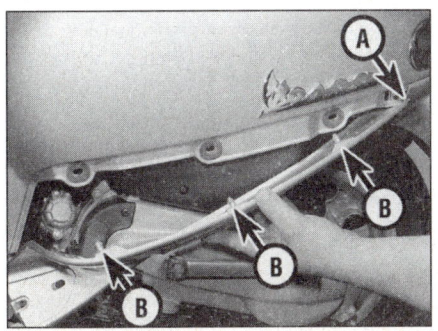

10.15a Pull out the rear of the panel to release the tab (A), then pull out the pegs (B) . . .

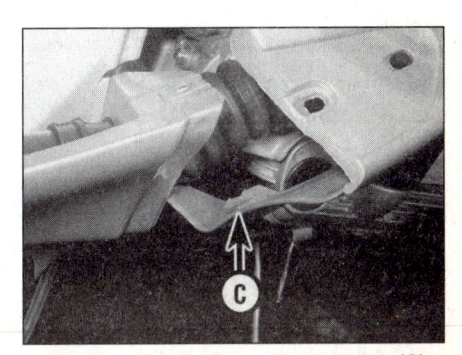

10.15b . . . and release the front tab (C)

7•16 Frame and bodywork

10.17 The storage compartment simply lifts out

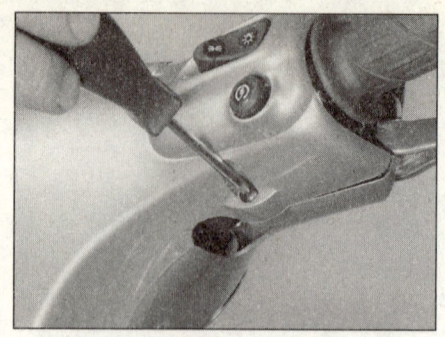

10.20a Remove the screws in the rear cover . . .

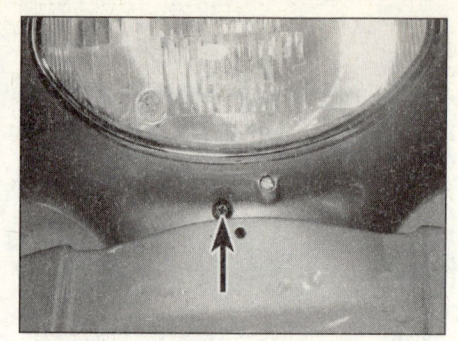

10.20b . . . and the screw below the headlight (arrowed) . . .

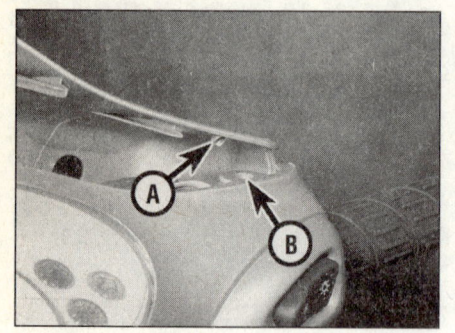

10.20c . . . then lever each end to release the tab (A) from its socket (B) . . .

10.20d . . . and pull the cover away to release the central tabs

Storage compartment

17 Unlock the seat using the ignition key and swing it upright, then lift out the storage compartment **(see illustration)**.
18 Installation is the reverse of removal.

Handlebar covers

19 Remove the rear view mirrors.
20 To remove the front cover, remove the screws from the rear cover and the screw below the headlight, then carefully lever up the top outer edge of the front cover to release the pegs which locate into holes in the top edge of the rear cover **(see illustrations)**. These pegs are quite a tight fit and a certain amount of leverage is required, but take care not to apply excessive force as the cover could break. Once these pegs are free, manoeuvre the front cover to release its central tabs from the rear **(see illustration)**. If the cover is being completely removed rather than just displaced for access, disconnect the headlight wiring connectors, noting which fits where, then remove the cover.
21 To remove the rear cover, first remove the front cover. Remove the screws securing the rear cover to the brackets on the handlebars **(see illustration)**. If the cover is being completely removed rather than just displaced for access, disconnect the instrument cluster and handlebar switch wiring connectors, noting which fits where, and the speedometer cable, then remove the cover. If required, separate the instrument cluster from the cover (see Chapter 9).
22 Installation is the reverse of removal.

Make sure the wiring connectors are correctly and securely connected, and check the operation of all switches and lights.

Rear mudguard

23 Remove the screws securing the mudguard to the engine and remove the guard, noting how it fits.
24 Installation is the reverse of removal.

11 Zip 50 and Zip 125 body panels – removal and installation

Seat

1 Unlock the seat using the ignition key and swing it upright, then remove the screws securing the seat hinge to the storage compartment and remove the seat.
2 Installation is the reverse of removal.

Engine access panels

3 To remove the access panel in the storage compartment, lift up the seat and remove it if necessary (see Step 1). Undo the four screws securing the access panel in the bottom of the storage compartment and remove the panel.
4 To remove the spark plug access panel in the engine cowling, first remove the panel in the bottom of the storage compartment. Undo the catch on the top edge of the panel and slide it out of the cowling **(see illustration)**.

10.21 The rear cover is secured by three screws (arrowed)

11.4 Removing the spark plug access panel

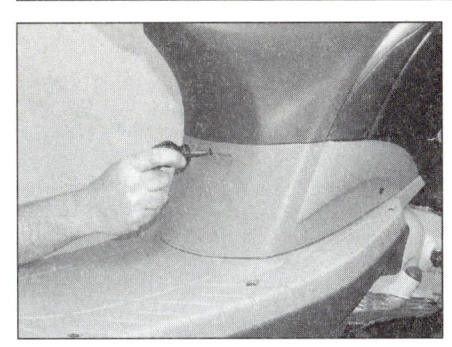

… Frame and bodywork 7•17

11.5a Remove the three fixing screws . . .

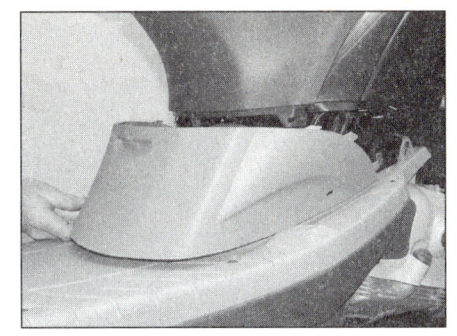

11.5b . . . and pull the panel forwards

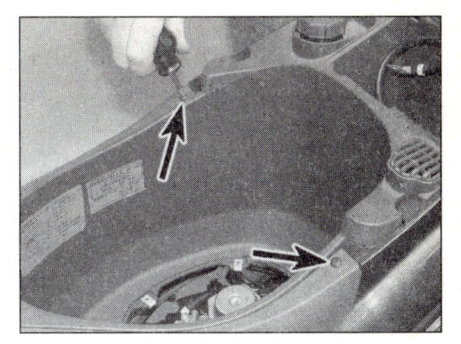

11.7a Remove the two screws (arrowed) . . .

5 To remove the front access panel, remove the three screws securing the panel, then draw the panel forwards to detach it **(see illustrations)**.
6 Installation is the reverse of removal.

Front underseat panel

7 To remove the underseat panel, first remove the front engine access panel (see Step 5). Undo the two screws securing the rear top edge of the panel, then carefully lift the panel out and disengage the tabs from the forward edge of the seat cowling **(see illustrations)**.
8 Installation is the reverse of removal, ensuring the tabs are correctly located in the seat cowling.

Tail light panel

9 Undo the four screws securing the panel, noting where they fit, then lift out the spacers for the two rear screws **(see illustrations)**.
10 Lift off the panel and disconnect the tail light wiring connector, then remove the panel **(see illustration)**.
11 Installation is the reverse of removal, ensuring the spacers are in place before installing the screws.

Seat cowling

12 To remove the seat cowling, first remove the front engine access panel, the front underseat panel and the tail light panel. Undo the screws that secure the rear mudguard to the underside of the cowling and the screws that secure the cowling to the storage compartment and the floor panel **(see illustrations)**.
13 Ease the sides of the cowling apart and withdraw it to access the turn signal wiring

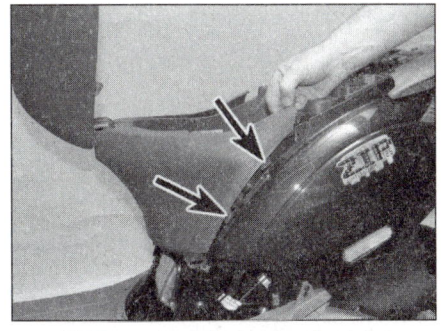

11.7b . . . and disengage the tabs (arrowed)

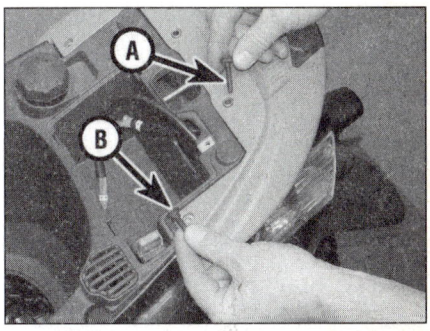

11.9a Note rear screws (A) are longer than front screws (B)

connectors, then disconnect the connectors and remove the cowling **(see illustration)**.
14 Installation is the reverse of removal, ensuring the lower rear edge of the cowling

11.9b Lift out the spacers for the rear screws

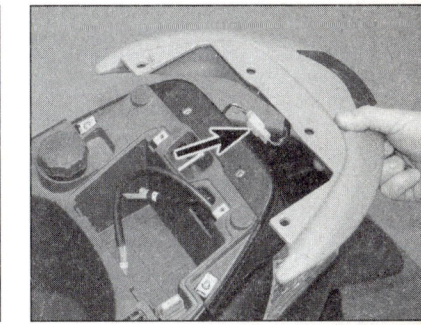

11.10 Disconnect the wiring connector (arrowed)

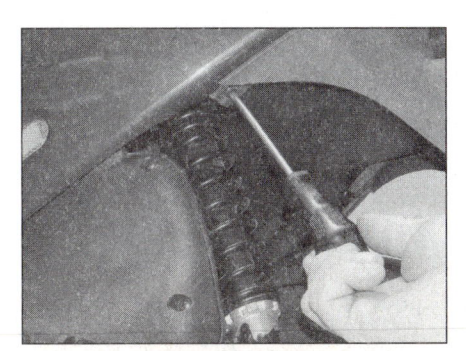

11.12a Mudguard is secured to the underside of the cowling

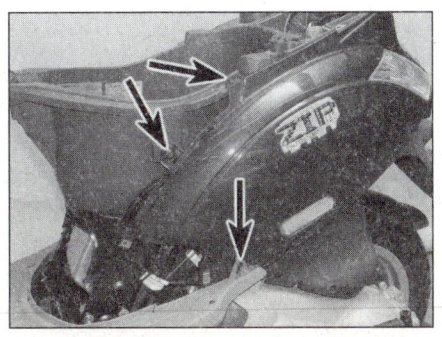

11.12b Cowling is secured to the storage compartment and floor panel

11.13 Ease the panel off and disconnect the wiring connectors

7•18 Frame and bodywork

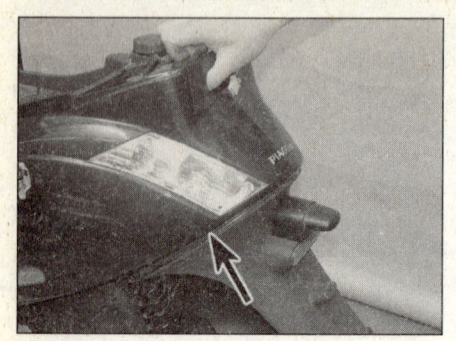

11.14 Ensure cowling locates in groove in mudguard (arrowed)

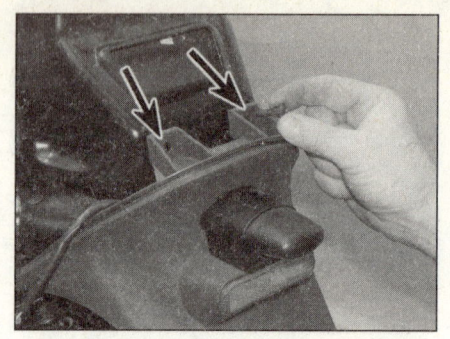

11.15 Remove the two screws (arrowed)

11.16a Hugger is secured by one screw on the right-hand side . . .

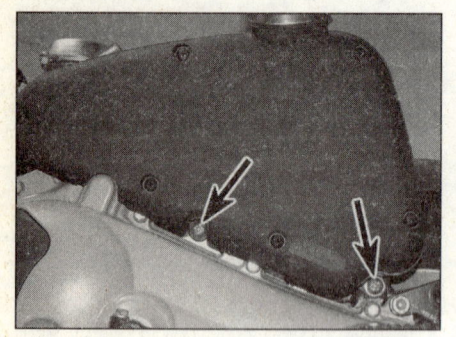

11.16b . . . and two screws on the underside of the air filter housing

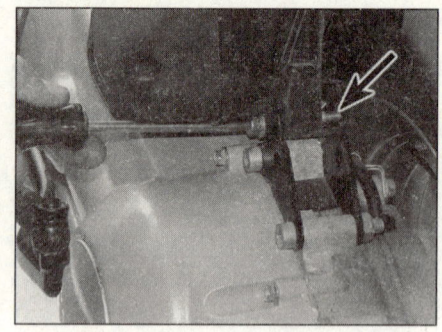

11.17 Ensure the screws locate through the air filter housing

locates correctly in the groove in the mudguard **(see illustration)**.

Rear mudguard and hugger

15 First remove the seat cowling then disconnect the wiring for the number plate light. Undo the screws securing the mudguard to the frame and remove the mudguard **(see illustration)**.
16 The hugger is secured by one screw on the right-hand side at the back of the engine unit, and two screws on the left-hand side which also secure the back of the air filter housing **(see illustrations)**. Undo the screws and remove the hugger.
17 Installation is the reverse of removal, ensuring the screws on the left-hand side are correctly located through the back of the air filter housing **(see illustration)**.

Storage compartment

18 Remove the battery and unclip the fuse holder (see Chapter 9).
19 Remove the seat cowling.
20 On four-stroke models, undo the screw that secures the air filter housing intake to the side of the storage compartment **(see illustration)**. Remove the fuel tank cap and, on two-stroke models, the oil tank cap.
21 Undo the two screws that secure the bottom of the storage compartment to the frame, then lift out the storage compartment **(see illustration)**. Refit the fuel and oil tank caps to avoid anything falling into the tanks. If required, remove the screws securing the seat hinge to the storage compartment and remove the seat.
22 Installation is the reverse of removal.

Kick panel

23 Disconnect the battery negative (-ve) terminal (see Chapter 9).
24 Undo the seven screws securing the kick panel **(see illustration)**.
25 Ease the panel back and release the tabs along its lower edge from the slots in the floor panel, then disconnect the wiring connectors for the reset button and the fuse holder **(see illustrations)**. Remove the kick panel.

11.20 Remove the air intake

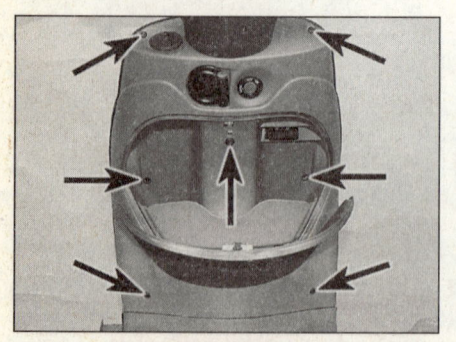

11.21 Remove the two screws (arrowed)

11.24 Remove the kick panel screws (arrowed)

11.25a Disconnect the wiring for the reset button . . .

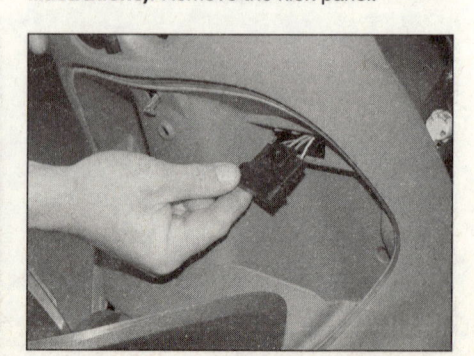

11.25b . . . and the fuse holder

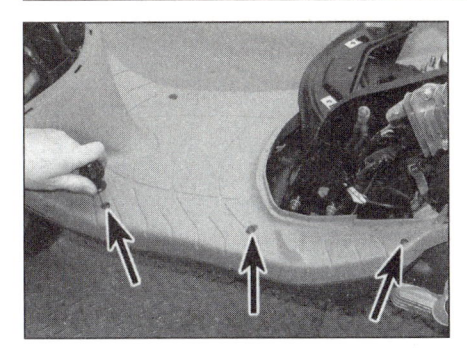

Frame and bodywork 7•19

11.28 Floor panel is secured by three screws on each side

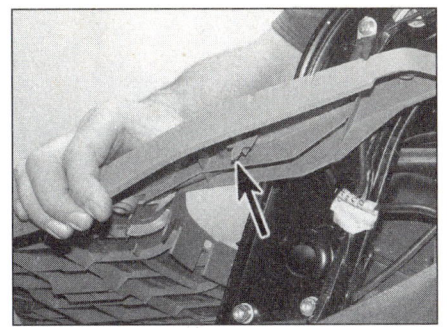

11.29 Take care to avoid damaging the tabs

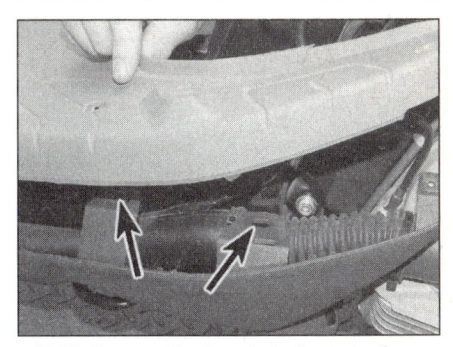

11.30 Ensure the brackets (arrowed) are properly located on the frame

26 Installation is the reverse of removal. Ensure the wiring is firmly connected and that the tabs locate correctly in the floor panel. Take care not to overtighten the screws that locate in the lugs on the back of the front panel.

Floor panel

27 Remove the front engine access panel (see Step 5) and the kick panel. **Note:** *It is possible to remove the floor panel without removing the kick panel but damage to the tabs on the lower edge of the kick panel may result.*

28 Undo the two screws securing the floor panel to the seat cowling **(see illustration 11.12b)**, then undo the six screws securing the panel to the frame **(see illustration)**.

29 Tabs on the underside of the floor panel locate in slots in the belly panel; lift the floor panel carefully to disengage the tabs, then remove it **(see illustration)**.

30 Installation is the reverse of removal. Ensure the brackets on the belly panel are correctly located on the frame supports before clipping the floor and belly panels together with the tabs **(see illustration)**.

Belly panel

31 Remove the floor panel. Undo the two screws that secure the left and right-hand lower edges of the front panel to the belly panel **(see illustration)**.

32 Undo the screws on the underside of the front mudguard that secure the mudguard to the fork yoke and displace the mudguard.

Undo the two screws that secure the front panel and the belly panel to the frame **(see illustration)**.

33 Detach the tabs on the belly panel from the lower edge of the front panel, then lift the brackets on the belly panel off the supports on the frame **(see illustration 11.30)** and drop the belly panel down and remove it.

34 Installation is the reverse of removal.

Front mudguard

35 Remove the front wheel (see Chapter 8).
36 Undo the screws on the underside of the mudguard that secure the mudguard to the fork yoke and displace the mudguard. Undo the screws that secure the clips for the front brake hose and the speedometer cable to the mudguard and remove the mudguard **(see illustration)**.
37 Installation is the reverse of removal.

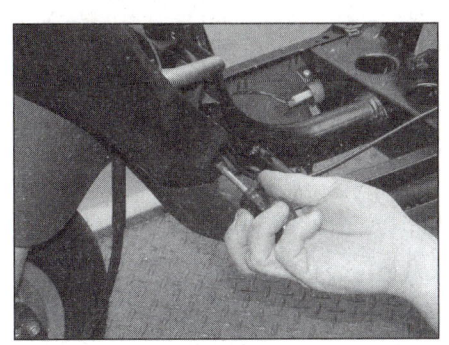

11.31 Remove the left and right-hand screws

Front panel

38 Remove the kick panel (see Steps 23 to 25).
39 Undo the screws that secure the turn signal/sidelight assemblies and displace the assemblies, then remove the turn signal bulbholders and disconnect the sidelight wiring connectors (see Chapter 9).
40 Undo the screws that secure the lower edge of the front panel to the frame **(see illustration 11.32)**.
41 Undo the screw in the centre of the front panel grille, then lower the panel over the front forks and remove it **(see illustration)**.
42 Installation is the reverse of removal.

Handlebar covers

43 To remove the rear cover, undo the three screws and unclip the cover from the front cover **(see illustration)**. Disconnect the wiring

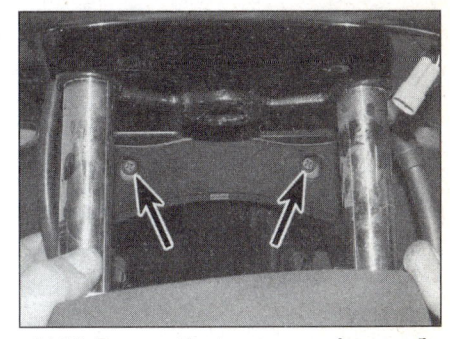

11.32 Remove the two screws (arrowed)

11.36 Displace the mudguard and release the clips (arrowed)

11.41 Remove the screw (arrowed)

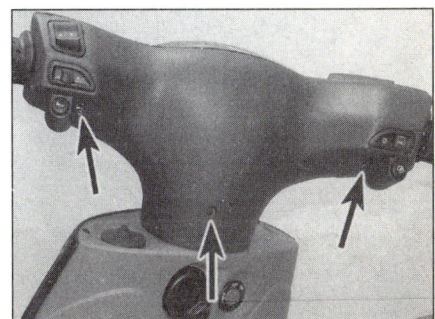

11.43 Remove the three screws (arrowed)

7•20 Frame and bodywork

12.1 Remove the seat hinge screws

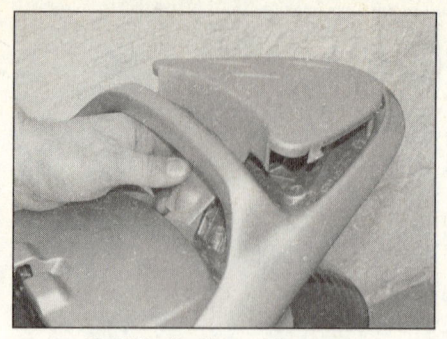

12.5 Unclip the carrier cover

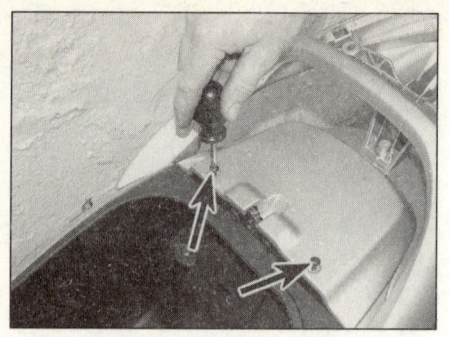

12.6a Undo the two screws (arrowed) . . .

connectors from the handlebar switches, noting where they fit, and remove the cover.
44 To remove the front cover, first remove the rear cover and the rear view mirrors, then undo the three screws securing the front cover to the handlebars and remove it.
45 Installation is the reverse of removal. Check the operation of the switches before riding the scooter.

12 B125 body panels – removal and installation

Seat
1 Unlock the seat using either the electronic seat release button or the left-hand lever in the glovebox, and swing it upright. Remove the screws securing the seat hinge to the storage compartment and remove the seat **(see illustration)**.
2 Installation is the reverse of removal.

Engine access panel
3 To remove the access panel in the storage compartment, lift up the seat and remove it if necessary (see Step 1). Undo the two screws securing the access panel in the bottom of the storage compartment and remove the panel.
4 Installation is the reverse of removal.

Rear carrier
5 Unclip the catch on the front edge of the cover, then carefully lift off the cover noting how the tabs locate in the carrier **(see illustration)**.
6 Undo the two screws securing the battery cover and lift off the cover, noting how it fits **(see illustrations)**.
7 Undo the three bolts securing the carrier and lift if off **(see illustration)**.

Floor centre panel
8 Undo the four screws securing the panel to the kick panel **(see illustration)**.
9 Remove the fuel filler cap and lift off the seal **(see illustration)**.
10 Lift up the front edge of the panel and release the tabs on the rear edge, then disconnect the cable from the lever mechanism **(see illustrations)**.
11 Installation is the reverse of removal, ensuring that the cable is correctly located on the lever mechanism before installing the fixing screws.

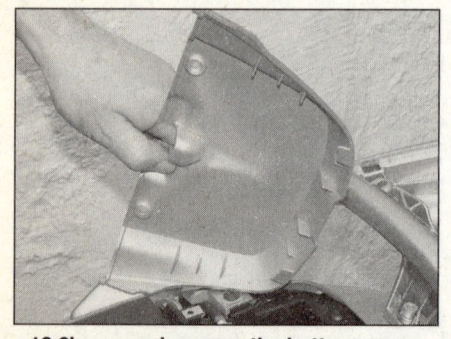

12.6b . . . and remove the battery cover, noting how it fits

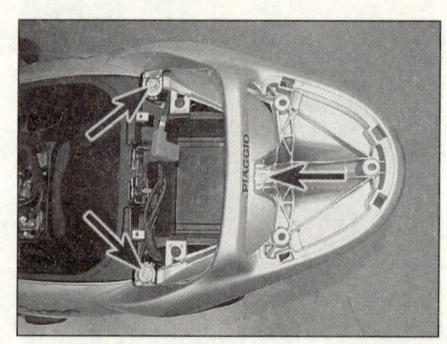

12.7 Undo the three bolts (arrowed)

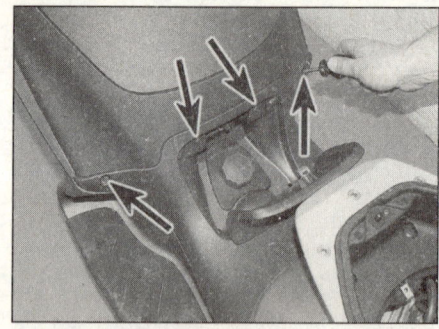

12.8 Remove the four screws (arrowed)

12.9 Lift off the fuel filler cap seal

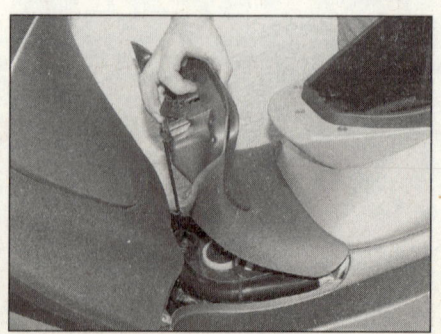

12.10a Lift up the centre panel . . .

12.10b . . . and disconnect the cover release cable

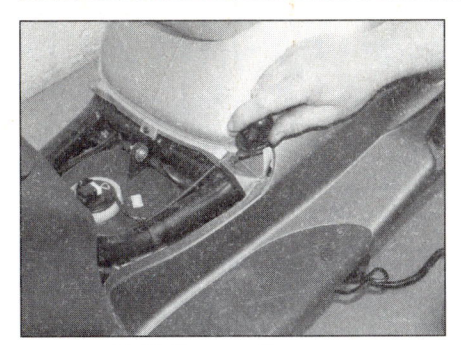

Frame and bodywork 7•21

12.12 Remove the screw

12.13a Remove the passenger footrest...

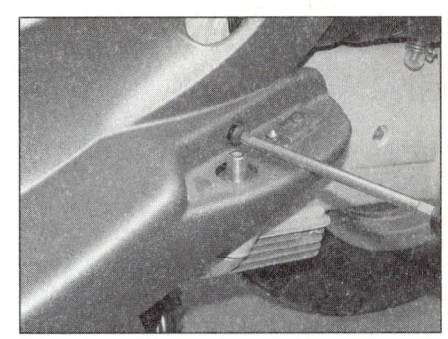

12.13b ...and the panel screw behind it

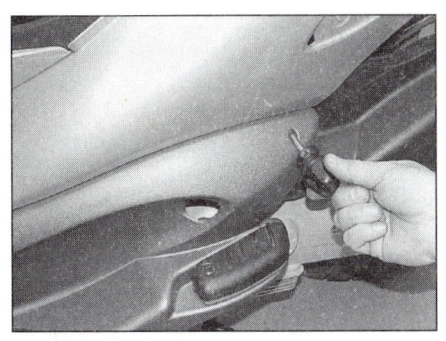

12.14a Undo the screws at the rear...

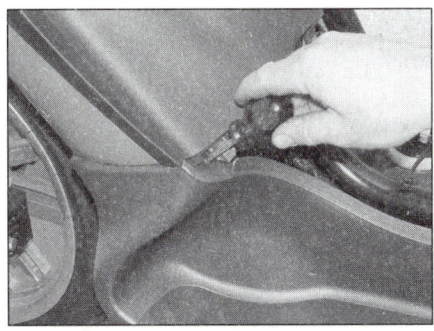

12.14b ...front inside edge...

Floor panels

Note: *The left and right-hand floor panels are separate items. The removal procedure is the same for both panels.*

12 Remove the floor centre panel and undo the floor panel fixing screw **(see illustration)**.
13 Undo the screw and remove the passenger footrest, then undo the screw securing the rear of the panel to the frame **(see illustrations)**.
14 Undo the four screws around the edge of the panel **(see illustrations)**.
15 Lever out the fasteners for the rubber mat using a small screwdriver, then fold back the mat and undo the two panel fixing screws **(see illustrations)**. Lift off the floor panel **(see illustration)**.
16 Installation is the reverse of removal. Ensure that all the panel fixing tabs are aligned with the adjacent panels before installing the screws.

Front underseat panel

17 To remove the underseat panel, first remove the seat (see Step 1). Undo the centre fixing screw and lift off the panel **(see illustration)**.
18 Installation is the reverse of removal.

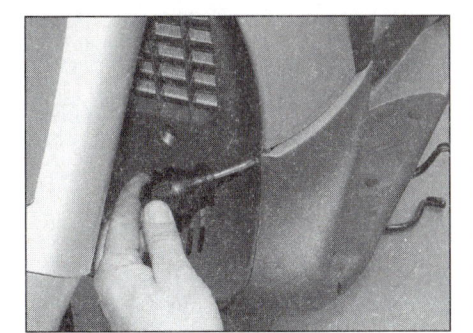

12.14c ...front outside edge...

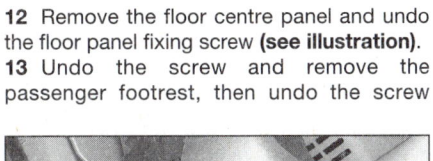

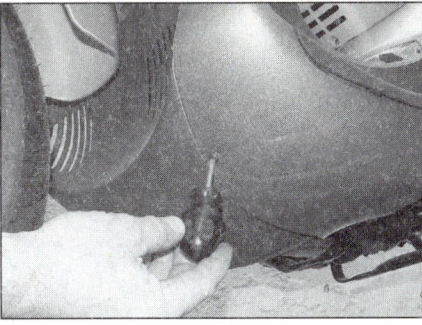

12.14d ...and front lower edge of the panel

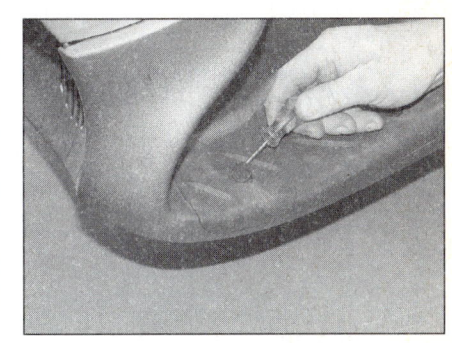

12.15a Lever out the mat fasteners

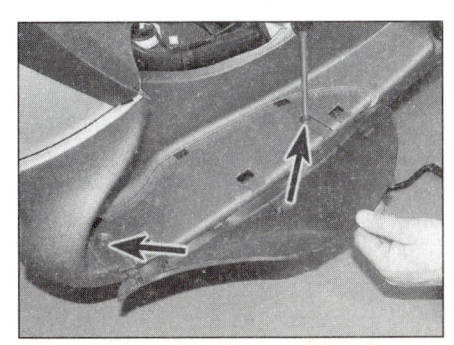

12.15b Remove the two screws (arrowed)

12.15c Lift off the floor panel

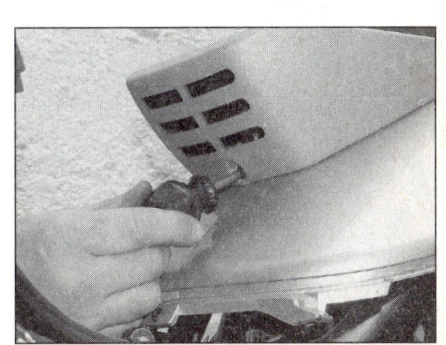

12.17 Remove the screw

7•22 Frame and bodywork

12.20a Undo the screw . . .

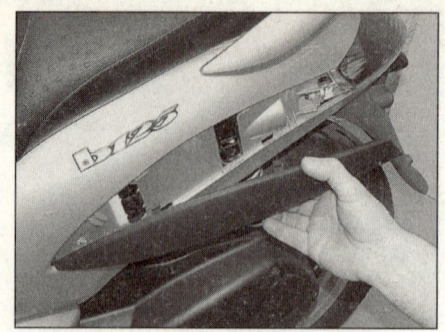

12.20b . . . then remove the trim

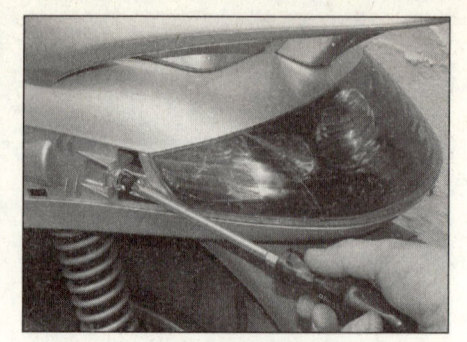

12.21a Light unit is secured by one screw on each side . . .

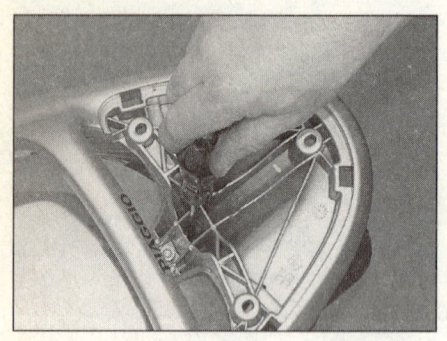

12.21b . . . and one screw in the centre top

12.22a Undo the front . . .

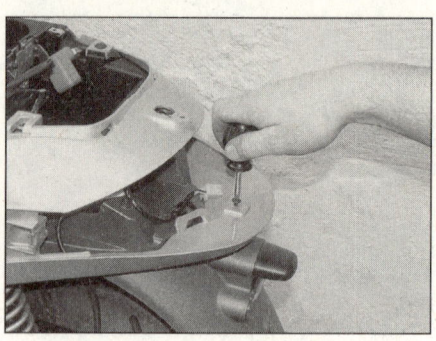

12.22b . . . and rear assembly screws

Side panels

19 To remove the side panels, first remove the rear carrier, floor centre panel, floor panels and front underseat panel.
20 Undo the screws securing the left- and right-hand side panel trims, then lift off the trims noting how they fit **(see illustrations)**.
21 Undo the screws securing the tail light/turn signal unit – note the screw in the top centre of the unit **(see illustrations)**. Withdraw the tail light and disconnect the wiring connector.

22 The side panels are joined by one screw at the front and one at the rear – undo the joining screws **(see illustrations)**.
23 Each panel is secured to the frame by two screws along the top edge – undo the screws for one panel at a time, then carefully lift off the appropriate panel, taking care not to break the overlapping tabs at the front and back of each panel **(see illustrations)**.
24 Installation is the reverse of removal, ensuring the tabs are correctly aligned before installing the fixing screws.

Rear mudguard

25 First remove the side panels.
26 The mudguard is secured by two screws on each side. Disconnect the number plate wiring connector, then undo the fixing screws and lift off the mudguard **(see illustration)**.
27 Installation is the reverse of removal.

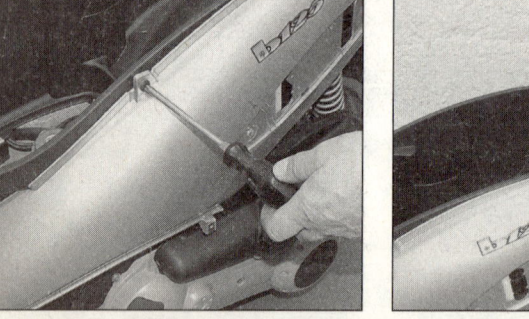

12.23a Undo the screws . . .

12.23b . . . along the top edge

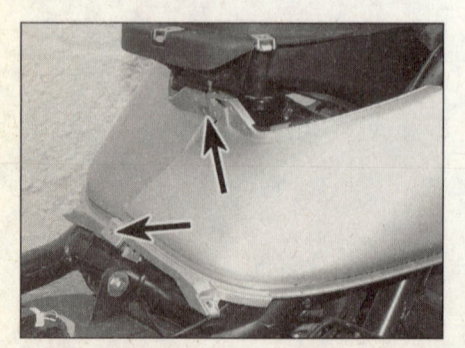

12.23c Take care not to break the tabs at the front . . .

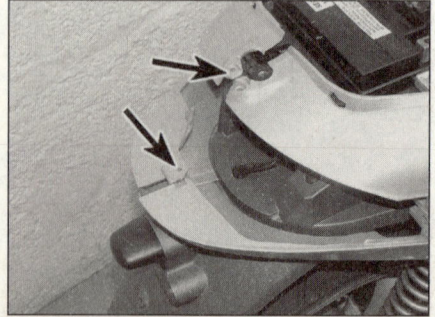

12.23d . . . and rear of the panels

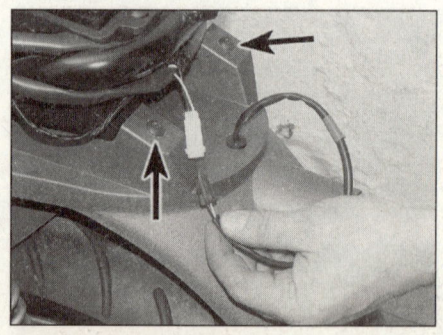

12.26 Disconnect the wiring connector and undo the screws (arrowed)

Frame and bodywork 7•23

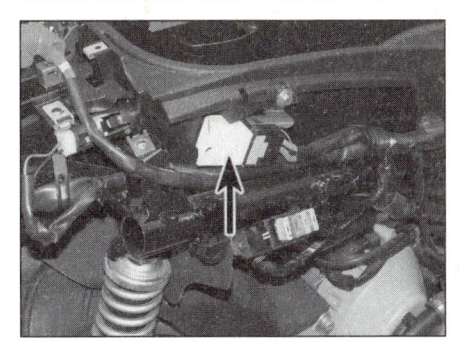

12.29 Displace the starter relay (arrowed)

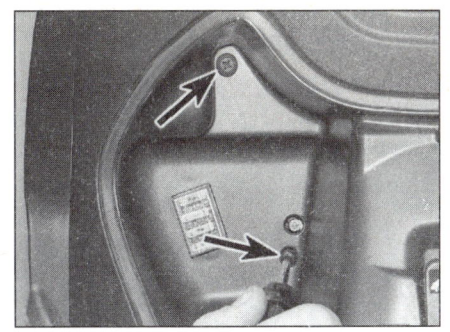

12.32a Headlight unit is secured by two screws (arrowed) on each side

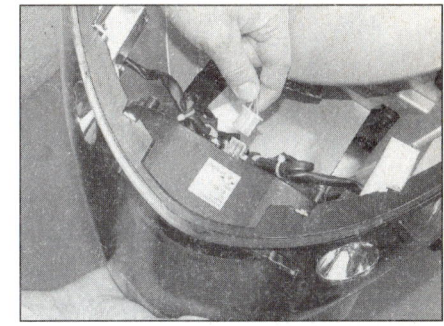

12.32b Disconnect the headlight wiring connector

Storage compartment

28 First remove the side panels.
29 Undo the bolt securing the starter relay bracket on the right-hand side of the storage compartment and displace the relay **(see illustration)**.
30 Undo the four screws securing the bottom of the storage compartment to the frame, then lift out the storage compartment.
31 Installation is the reverse of removal.

Front panel

32 Undo the four screws inside the glovebox that secure the front headlight unit, then displace the unit and disconnect the wiring connector **(see illustrations)**. **Note:** *On the right-hand side, the screw just below the uppermost screw secures the coolant reservoir and should not be undone (see Step 39).*
33 Undo the screw that secures the coolant reservoir cap cover and remove the cover, then undo the panel screw next to the filler cap **(see illustrations)**.
34 Undo the screw on the left-hand top edge of the kick panel and the two screws on the front underside of the front panel **(see illustrations)**.
35 Carefully lever off the badge on the front of the panel, then remove the screw behind it and lift off the front panel **(see illustrations)**.
36 Installation is the reverse of removal.

12.33a Remove the cover ...

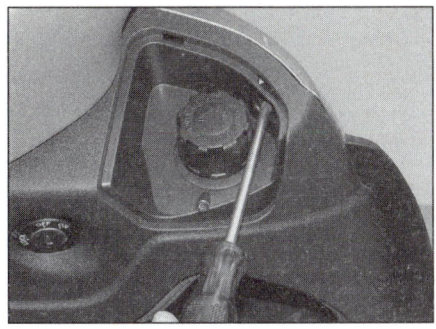

12.33b ... and undo the front panel screw

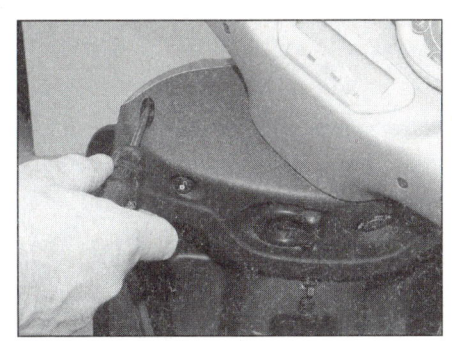

12.34a Undo the left-hand front panel screw ...

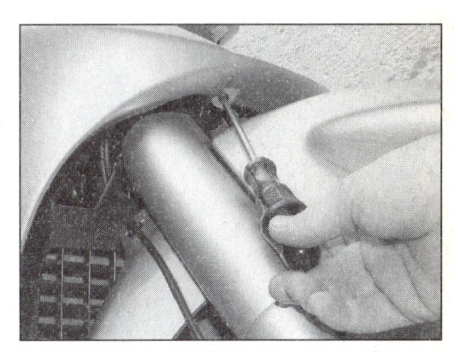

12.34b ... and two screws on the underside of the panel

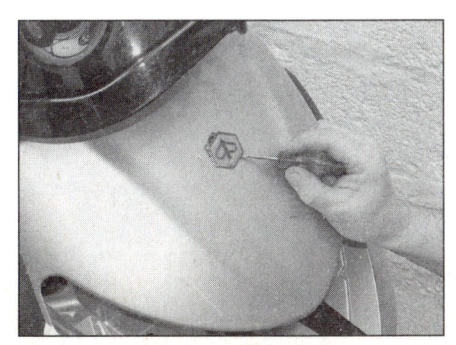

12.35a Remove the badge ...

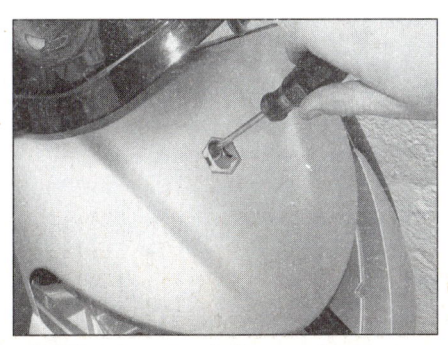

12.35b ... and undo the panel screw ...

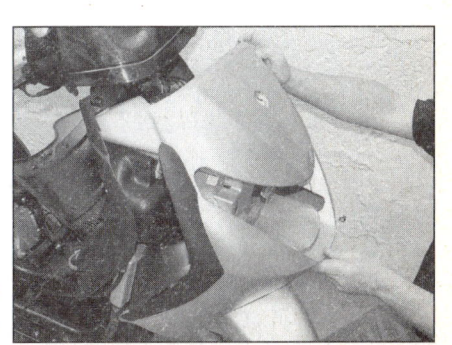

12.35c ... then lift off the front panel

7•24 Frame and bodywork

12.38a Displace the fusebox . . .

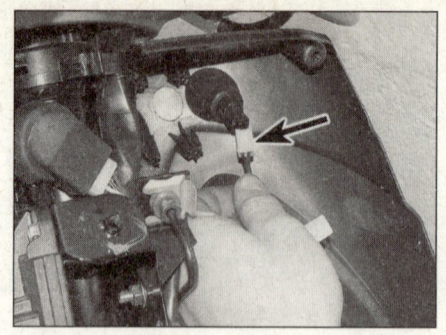

12.38b . . . and disconnect the wiring for the seat release button

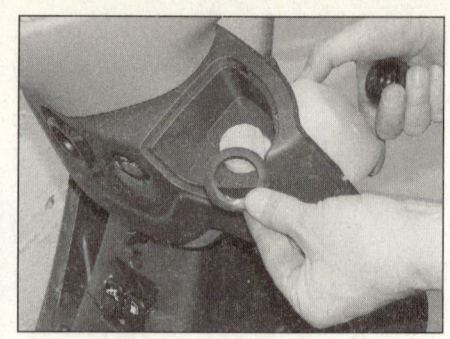

12.39a Remove the collar . . .

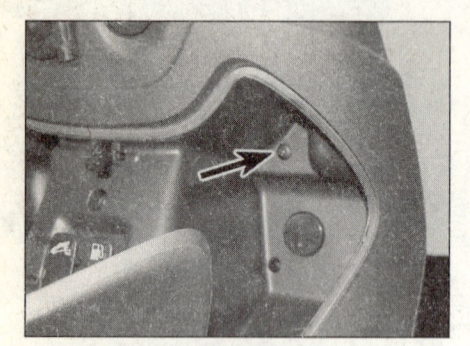

12.39b . . . then undo the fixing screw . . .

Kick panel

37 First remove the front panel.
38 Undo the screws that secure the fusebox and displace the fusebox, then disconnect the wiring for the electronic seat release button **(see illustrations)**.
39 Undo the coolant reservoir filler cap and remove the rubber collar **(see illustration)**. Support the reservoir, then undo the screw inside the glovebox that secures the coolant reservoir and displace the reservoir **(see illustrations)**. Secure the reservoir with a cable tie to avoid spillage and straining the coolant hose.
40 Undo the screw in the centre of the kick panel, pull the panel back and disconnect the cables for the seat catch and the fuel filler flap, then lift off the panel **(see illustration)**.
41 Installation is the reverse of removal, ensuring that the cables for the seat catch (left) and fuel filler flap (right) are correctly located on the lever mechanism.

Front mudguard

42 First remove the front wheel (see Chapter 8).
43 Undo the bolt that secures the front brake hose guide, then undo the screws that secure the fork leg shrouds and remove the shrouds **(see illustrations)**.
44 Unclip the speedometer cable from the front mudguard **(see illustration)**.

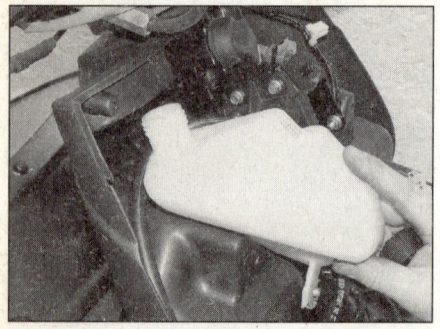

12.39c . . . and displace the reservoir

12.40a Remove the screw . . .

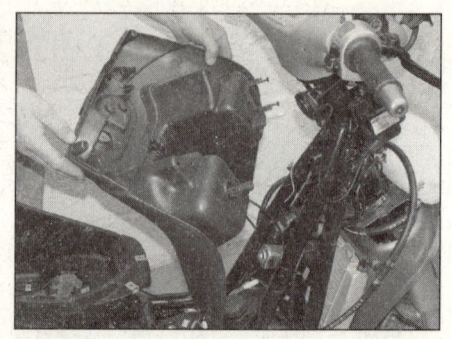

12.40b . . . then pull back the panel and disconnect the cables

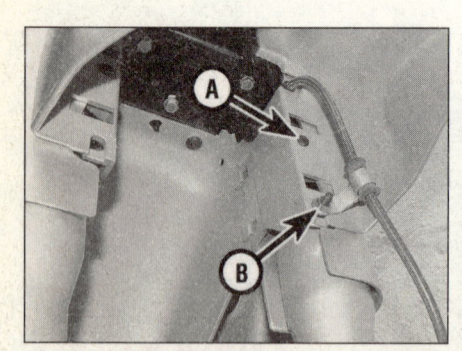

12.43a Bolt (A) secures brake hose guide, screw (B) secures shroud

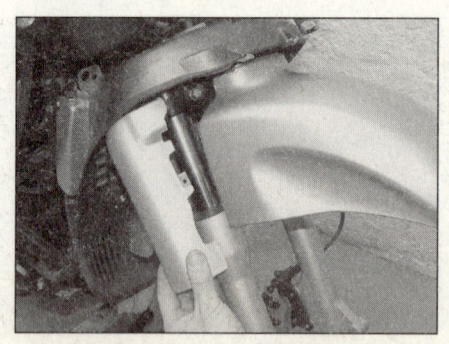

12.43b Lift off the fork shrouds

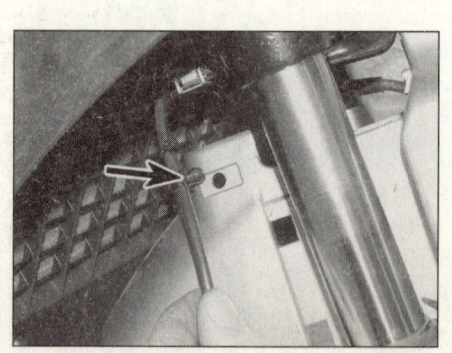

12.44 Release the speedometer cable clip (arrowed)

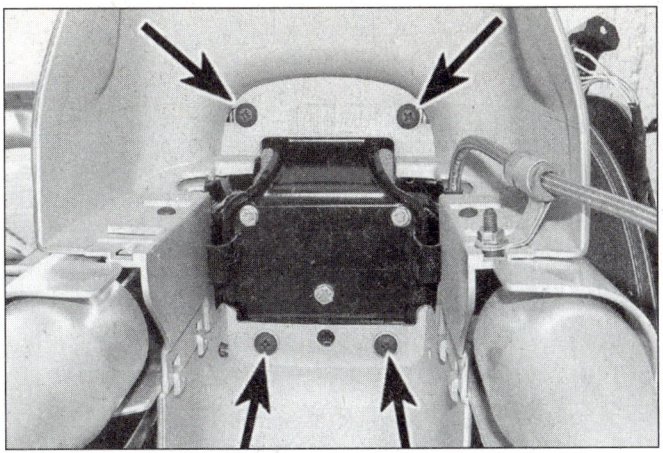

Frame and bodywork 7•25

12.45a Remove the screws (arrowed)

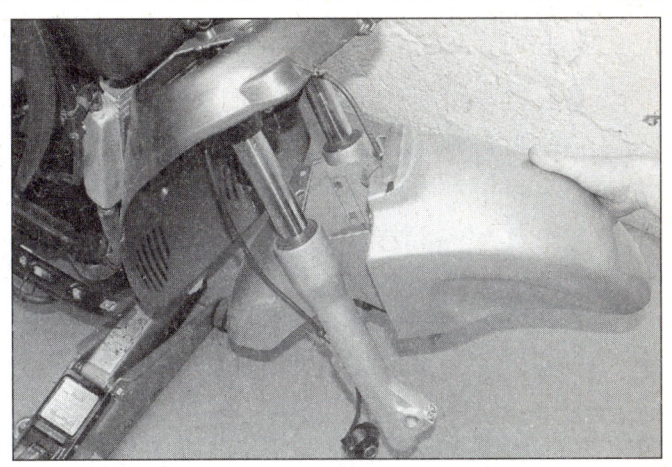

12.45b ... and lift off the mudguard

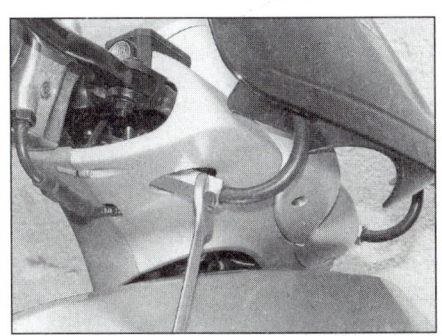

12.47a Loosen the nuts ...

45 Undo the screws that secure the mudguard to the bracket on the underside of the fork yoke and remove the mudguard **(see illustrations)**.
46 Installation is the reverse of removal.

Handlebar covers

47 Loosen the long nuts on the screen brackets and pull the brackets out of the lugs on the handlebars **(see illustrations)**.
48 Undo the two screws on the underside of the front cover, then undo the two screws on the back of the rear cover and remove the rear cover **(see illustrations)**.
49 Undo the two screws securing the front cover and the instrument cluster to the handlebars and remove the front cover **(see illustrations)**.
50 Installation is the reverse of removal, ensuring that the throttle cable is correctly routed between the two covers.

13 X9 body panels – removal and installation

Seat

1 Unlock the seat using the right-hand lever in the glovebox, and swing it upright.
2 Remove the split pin and washer from the

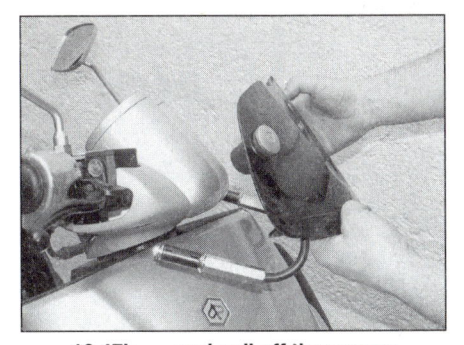

12.47b ... and pull off the screen

12.48a Undo the two screws on the lower edge ...

12.48b ... and the screws in the rear cover ...

12.48c ... then lift off the rear cover

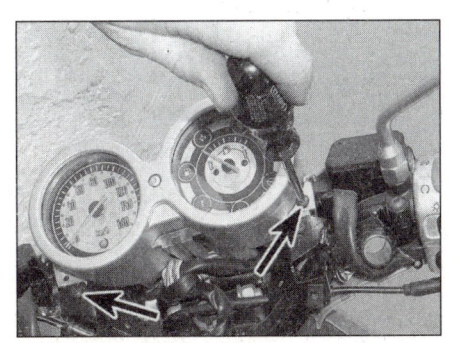

12.49a Remove the two screws ...

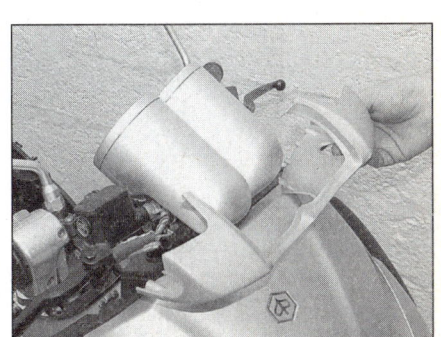

12.49b ... and lift off the front cover

7•26 Frame and bodywork

13.2a Remove the split pin and washer (arrowed)

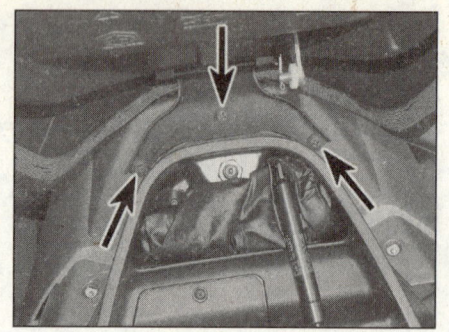

13.2b Remove the three hinge screws

13.6 Remove the two cover screws

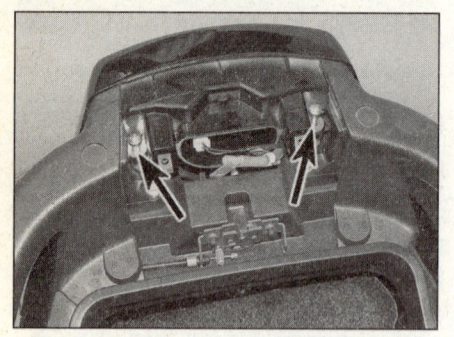

13.7a Remove the two panel screws . . .

seat support pivot pin and withdraw the pivot pin, then undo the screws securing the seat hinge to the storage compartment and remove the seat **(see illustrations)**.

3 Installation is the reverse of removal; fit a new split pin and ensure the ends are bent securely.

Engine access panel

4 To remove the access panel in the storage compartment, first lift up the seat. Undo the screw securing the panel and remove the panel.
5 Installation is the reverse of removal.

Brake light panel

6 First lift the seat and undo the two screws securing the rear cover and lift off the cover **(see illustration)**.
7 Undo the two screws securing the brake light panel, then lift the panel to release the tabs from the slots in the side panels; disconnect the brake light wiring connector **(see illustrations)**.
8 Installation is the reverse of removal.

Rear trim panel and lower side panels

9 First remove the brake light panel, then undo the four screws securing the trim panel and remove it **(see illustrations)**.
10 Undo the two screws securing each lower side panel and lift off the panels, noting how the tabs locate in the adjacent panels **(see illustrations)**.
11 Installation is the reverse of removal, ensuring the tabs are correctly located before installing the screws.

Rear mudguard

12 First remove the lower side panels. Undo

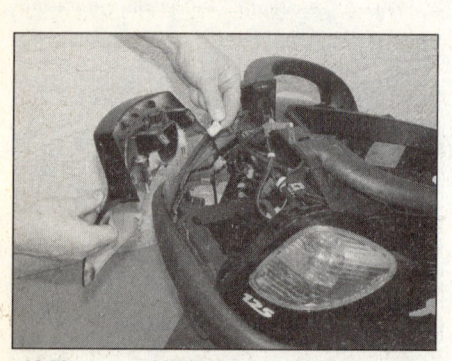

13.7b . . . and lift off the brake light panel

13.9a Remove the two screws on each side . . .

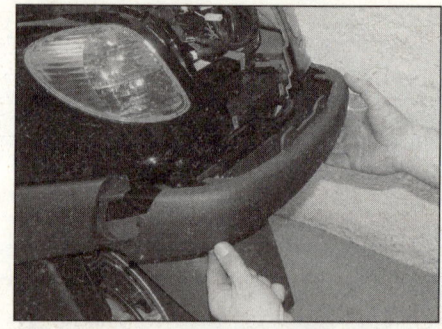

13.9b . . . then lift off the panel

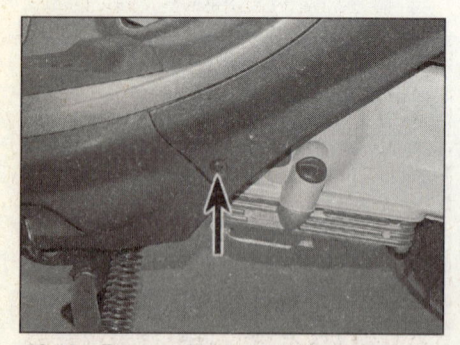

13.10a Remove the lower fixing screw . . .

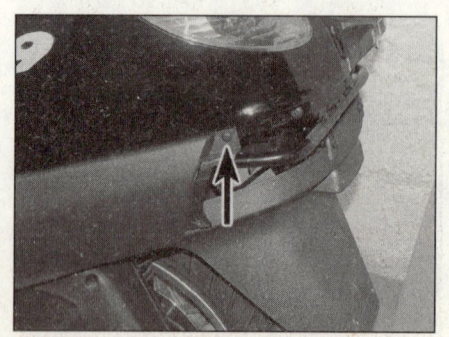

13.10b . . . then the upper fixing screw . . .

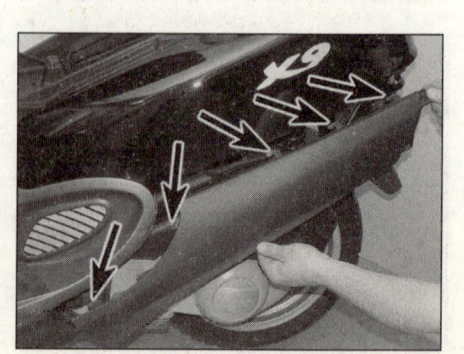

13.10c . . . then ease the panel off to release the tabs (arrowed)

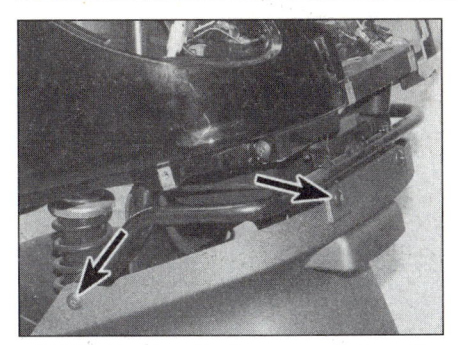

Frame and bodywork 7•27

13.12a Remove the two screws on each side

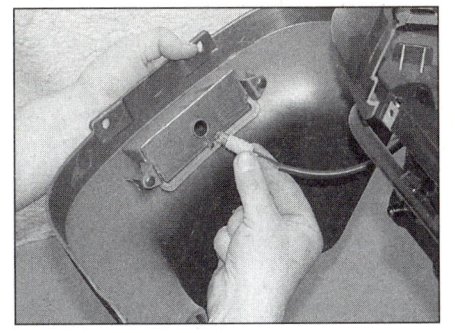

13.12b Pull out the number plate light socket

13.16a Lever out the screw cover

the screws securing the mudguard to the bracket and displace the mudguard, then pull the number plate light socket out of the light unit **(see illustrations)**.
13 Installation is the reverse of removal.

Side panels

14 To remove the side panels, first remove the rear trim panel and lower side panels.
15 Disconnect the tail light and turn signal wiring connectors.
16 Remove the grab handles. Lever out the cover for the top fixing screw, then undo the four screws that secure each handle **(see illustrations)**.
17 Each side panel is secured by three screws **(see illustrations)**. Undo the screws and lift off the panel, noting how the tabs locate in the rear edge of the floor panel.
18 Installation is the reverse of removal, ensuring the tabs are correctly located in the rear edge of the floor panels before installing the screws.

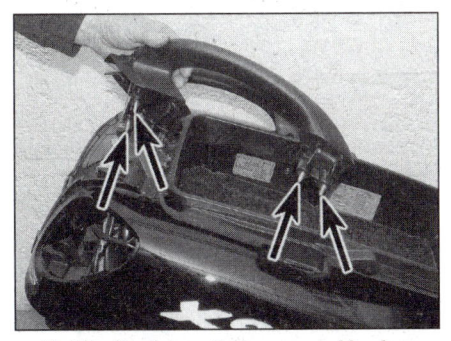

13.16b Each handle is secured by four screws

Floor panels

19 To remove the centre floor panel, first remove the seat (see Steps 1 and 2).
20 Open the fuel filler flap and undo the two screws securing the panel **(see illustration)**.

13.17a Side panel is secured by a screw on the rear lower edge . . .

Remove the filler cap and lift off the seal **(see illustration)**.
21 Lift the rear of the panel and tip it forwards to access the catch mechanism for the fuel filler flap, then disconnect the cable **(see illustrations)**. Lift off the centre panel.

13.17b . . . front lower edge . . .

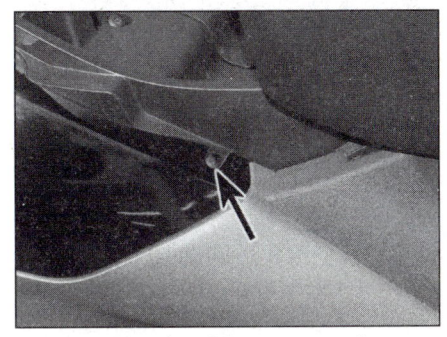

13.17c . . . and front upper edge

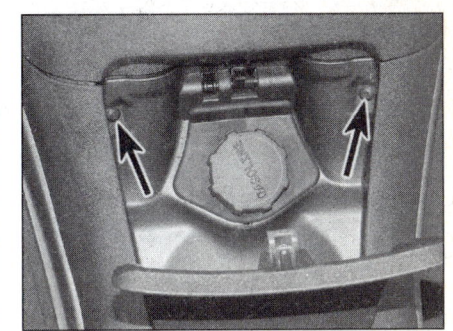

13.20a Remove the two screws

13.20b Remove the filler cap seal

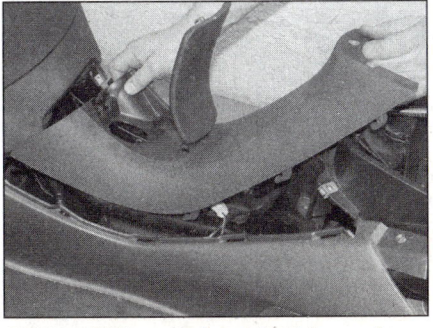

13.21a Lift the panel and tip it forwards . . .

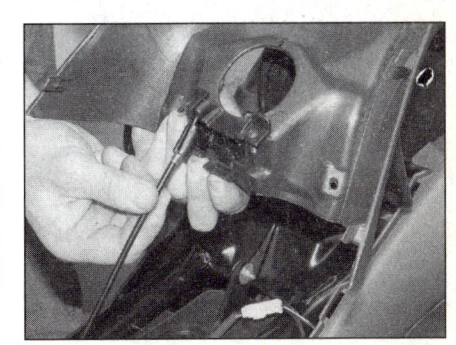

13.21b . . . to access the catch mechanism

7•28 Frame and bodywork

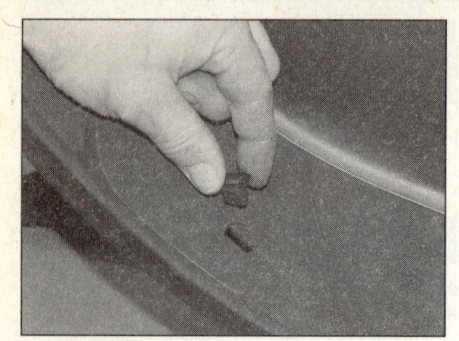

13.22a Lever out the fasteners

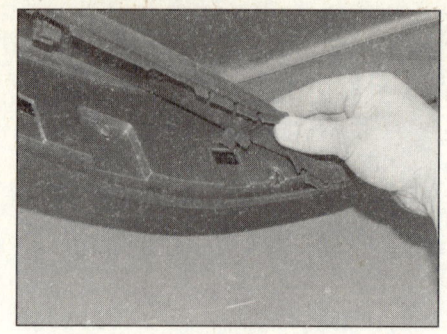

13.22b Note how the mats locate in the floor panels . . .

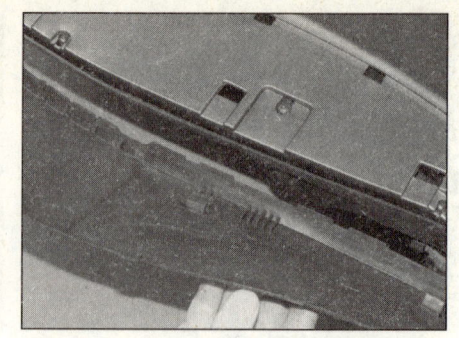

13.22c . . . and along the edge of the floor and belly panels

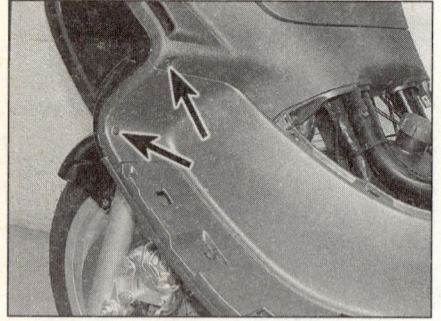

13.23a Remove the upper . . .

22 Lever out the fasteners for the rubber mats using a small screwdriver, then remove the mats noting how they locate in the floor panels and along the outside edge of the floor panels and belly panel **(see illustrations)**.
23 Undo the screws securing the floor panels to the belly panel and the lower edge of the kick panel, and the screws securing the floor panels to the frame **(see illustrations)**. **Note:** *It is not necessary to remove the passenger footrest rubbers.* Lift off the floor panels.
24 Installation is the reverse of removal. Ensure that all the panel fixing tabs are aligned with the adjacent panels before installing the screws.

Belly panel

25 To remove the belly panel first remove the floor panels.
26 Undo the four screws that secure the belly panel to the radiator grille.
27 Undo the two screws that secure the rear ends of the belly panel to the frame **(see illustration)**.
28 Carefully ease the brackets on the belly panel off the mounting points on the frame and lower the panel off **(see illustration)**.
29 Installation is the reverse of removal. Ensure that the mounting brackets are aligned with the floor panel screw holes before installing the belly panel screws.

Front panel

30 To remove the front panel, first remove the front insert panel and the headlight unit. Undo the five screws securing the insert panel; peel back the rubber covers on the rear view mirror mountings to access two of the screws **(see illustrations)**.

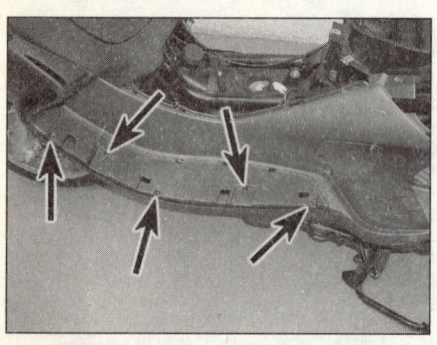

13.23b . . . and lower fixing screws

13.27 Remove the screw on each side

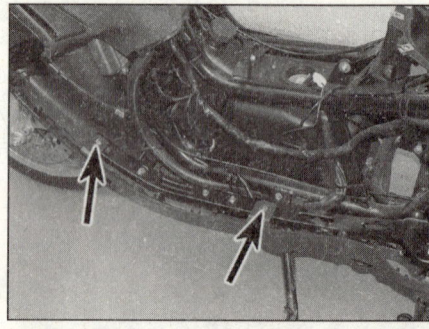

13.28 Ease the brackets off the mountings

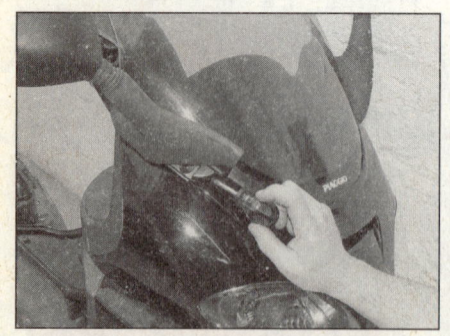

13.30a Remove the screws under the mirror mounting covers . . .

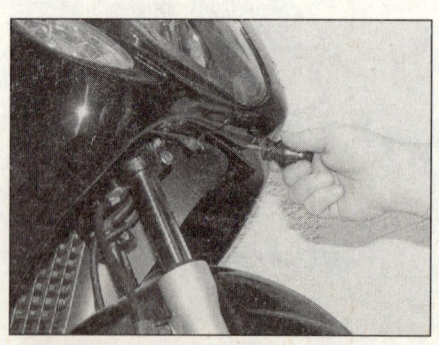

13.30b . . . on the lower front edge . . .

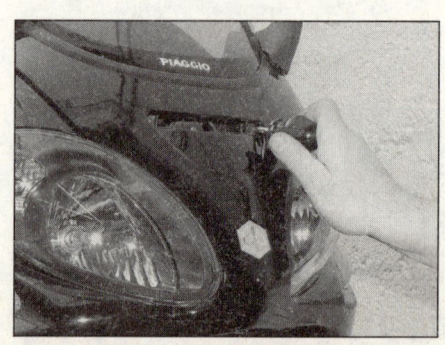

13.30c . . . and in the centre

Frame and bodywork 7•29

13.31a Remove the three screws . . .

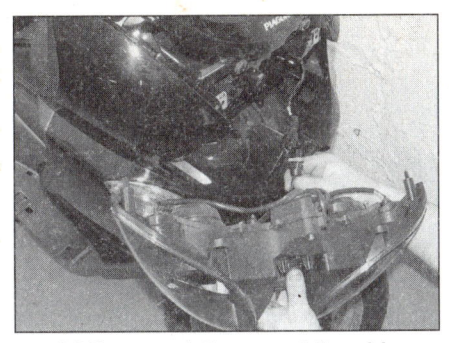

13.31b . . . and disconnect the wiring connector

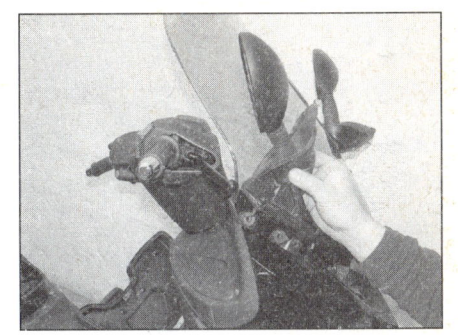

13.32 Remove the rear view mirrors

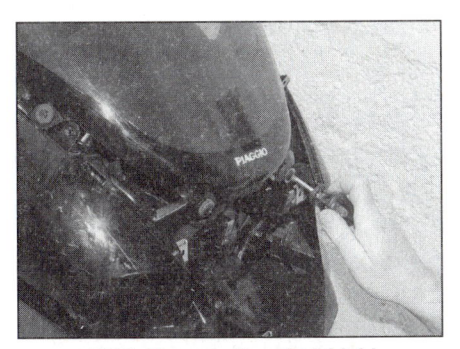

13.33 Remove the windshield

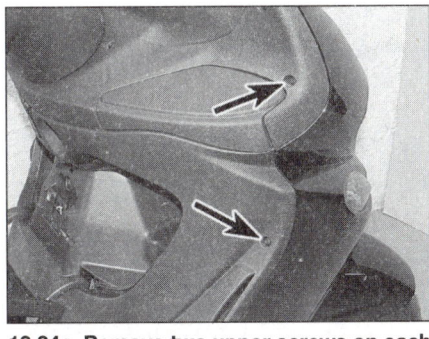

13.34a Remove two upper screws on each side . . .

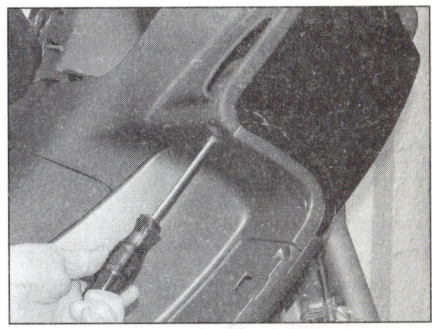

13.34b . . . and the screws on the lower edge

31 Undo the three screws securing the headlight unit and pull the unit forward, then disconnect the unit wiring connector and remove the unit **(see illustrations)**.

32 Peel back the rubber covers on the rear view mirror mountings and undo the mounting bolts, then lift off the mirrors **(see illustration)**.

33 Undo the screws securing the windshield and remove the windshield **(see illustration)**. Note the position of the washers and grommets on the windshield screws. Fit new grommets on reassembly if they are damaged or perished.

34 Undo the fixing screws in the kick panel **(see illustrations)**.

35 Undo the screw in the centre of both rear view mirror brackets **(see illustration)**.

36 Undo the two screws on the lower edge of the front panel **(see illustration)**.

37 Support the front panel, then undo the upper and lower centre mounting bolts and remove them, noting where they fit **(see illustrations)**.

38 Pull the panel forwards and release the tabs from the kick panel **(see illustration)**.

13.35 Remove the screw in the centre of the mirror bracket

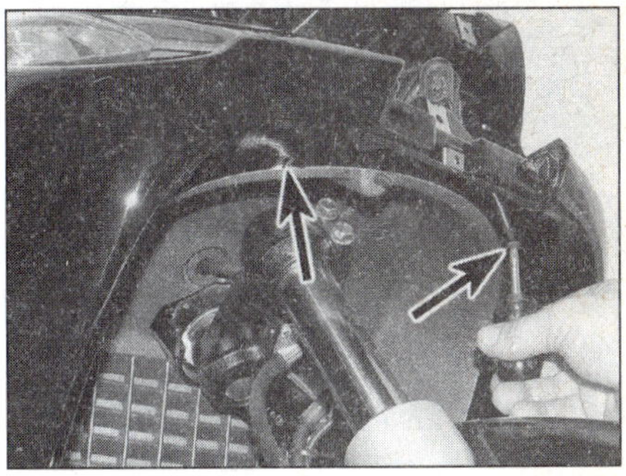

13.36 Remove the two screws on the panel lower edge

13.37a Remove the upper . . .

13.37b . . . and lower centre fixings

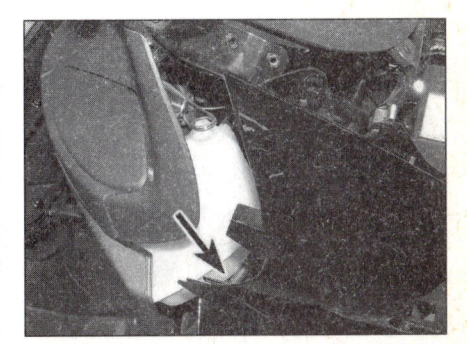

13.38a Release the panel tabs (arrowed) . . .

7•30 Frame and bodywork

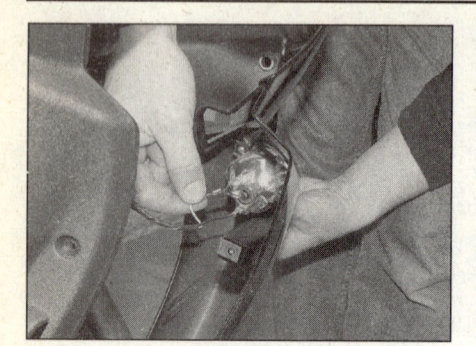

13.38b ... then disconnect the turn signal ...

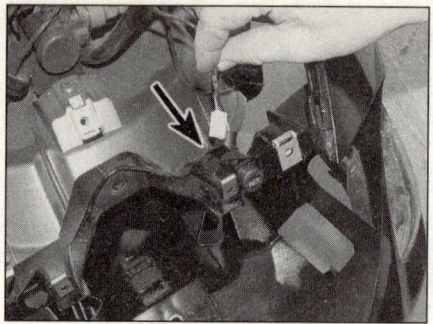

13.38c ... and reset button wiring connectors

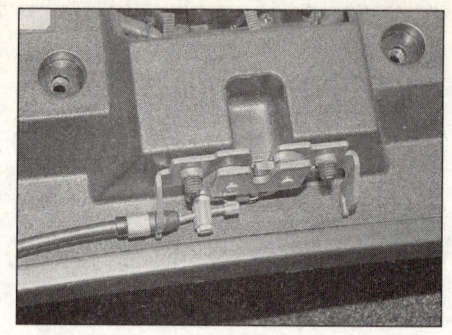

13.41 Disconnect the cable from the seat catch

13.42 Detach the fusebox from the kickpanel

Disconnect the wiring for the turn signals and the reset button, then lift the panel off **(see illustrations)**.

39 Installation is the reverse of removal. Ensure the tabs on the back edge of the panel align correctly with the kick panel.

Kick panel

40 To remove the kick panel, first remove the floor panels and the front panel.
41 Disconnect the cable from the seat catch and release it from any ties **(see illustration)**.
42 Undo the screws securing the fusebox to the kick panel **(see illustration)**.
43 Remove the coolant reservoir cap and lift off the seal **(see illustration)**.

44 Undo the four screws securing the top edge of the kick panel to the instrument panel **(see illustration)**.
45 Undo the fixing screw inside the glovebox **(see illustration)**. Lift off the kick panel, then disconnect the cable from the catch.
46 Installation is the reverse of removal.

Handlebar covers

47 Undo the screws and remove the covers for the front and rear brake hydraulic reservoirs **(see illustration)**.
48 Undo the three screws and displace the digital instrument panel **(see illustrations)**. Disconnect the wiring connectors and remove the panel.

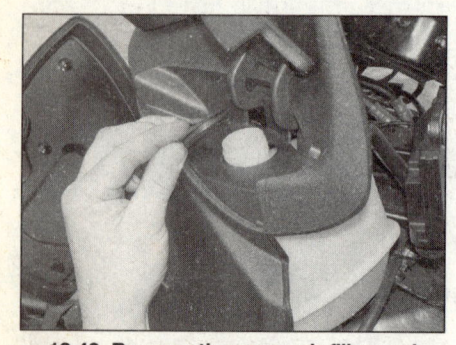

13.43 Remove the reservoir filler seal

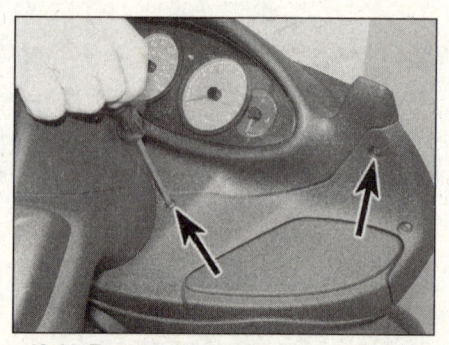

13.44 Remove two screws on each side

13.45 Remove the centre screw inside the glovebox

13.47 Remove the hydraulic reservoir covers

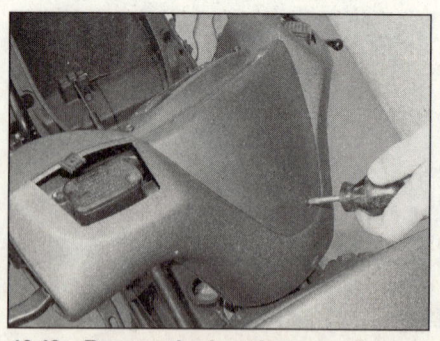

13.48a Remove the front instrument panel screw ...

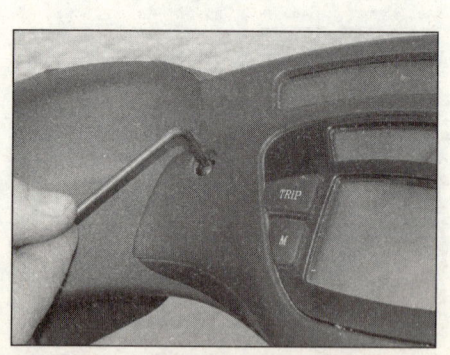

13.48b ... and the left and right-side screws

Frame and bodywork 7•31

13.49a Remove the lower fixing screw on each side . . .

13.49b . . . and lift off the front cover

49 Undo the two screws that secure the front cover, then carefully unclip the front cover from the back cover and lift it off **(see illustrations)**.
50 The back cover is secured to the handlebars with three screws **(see illustration)**. To remove the cover, undo the screws and displace the cover, then disconnect the switch wiring connectors, noting where they fit **(see illustration)**.
51 Installation is the reverse of removal. Check the operation of the instruments and switches before riding the scooter.

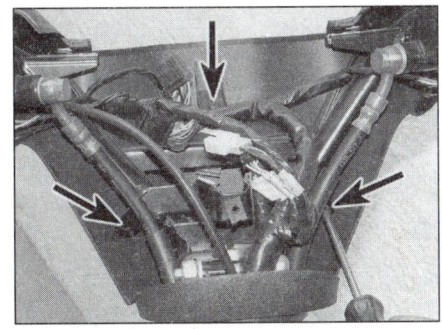

Front mudguard

52 Undo the screws securing the left and right-hand hydraulic hose clips to the mudguard, then undo the front mudguard mounting screws and lift off the mudguard **(see illustration)**.
53 Installation is the reverse of removal.

13.50a Remove the three screws

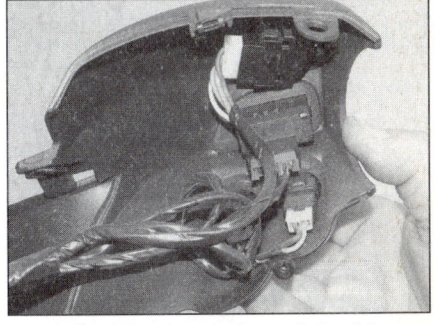

13.50b Disconnect the switch wiring connectors

6 Undo the three bolts securing the carrier and lift if off **(see illustration)**.
7 Installation is the reverse of removal. Ensure that all the tabs are correctly aligned before pressing the cover into position.

Seat cowling

8 To remove the seat cowling, first remove the seat, engine access panel and rear carrier (see above).
9 Remove the screws securing the tail light and rear turn signal assemblies, then disconnect the wiring connectors and remove the assemblies (see Chapter 9).
10 The seat cowling is secured by one screw on each side and two screws inside the

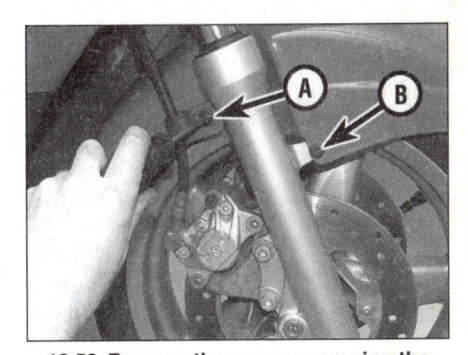

13.52 Remove the screws securing the hose clips (A) and mudguard (B)

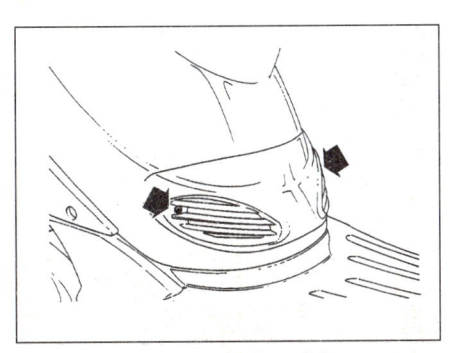

14 Liberty body panels – removal and installation

Seat

1 Unlock the seat using the ignition key and swing it upright, then remove the screws securing the seat hinge to the storage compartment and remove the seat.
2 Installation is the reverse of removal.

Engine access panel

3 To remove the front access panel, remove the two screws securing the panel, then pull the panel forwards to detach it **(see illustration)**.
4 Installation is the reverse of removal.

Rear carrier

5 Where fitted, unclip the cover, then carefully lift it off noting how the tabs locate in the carrier.

14.3 Remove the panel retaining screws (arrowed)

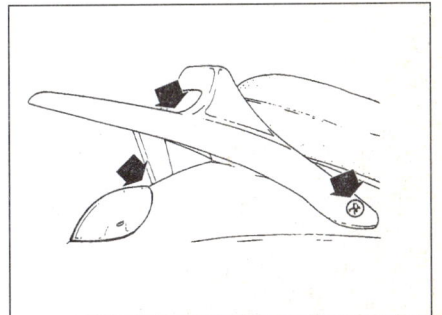

14.6 Carrier is secured by three bolts (arrowed)

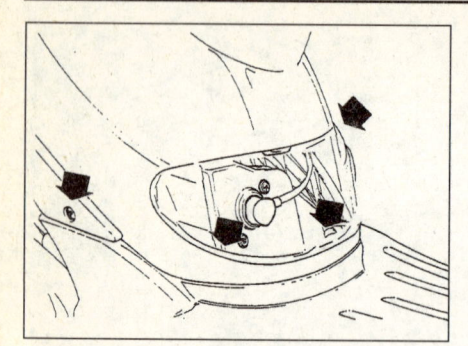

7•32 Frame and bodywork

14.10 Seat cowling is retained by four screws (arrowed)

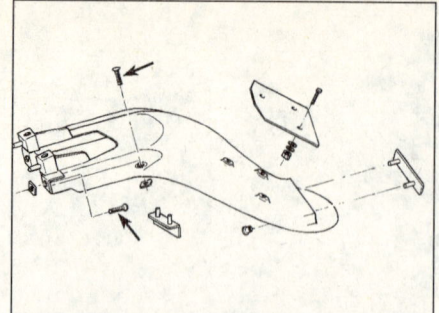

14.12 Mudguard assembly is secured by two screws (arrowed) on each side

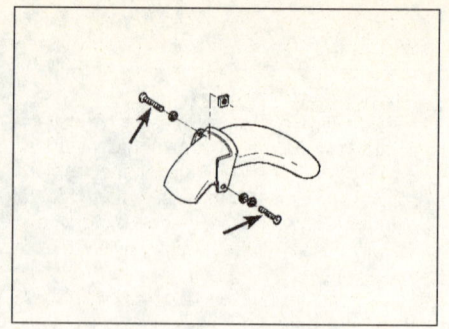

14.13 Rear hugger is secured by two screws (arrowed)

engine access aperture **(see illustration)**. Remove the screws, then carefully lift the cowling off, noting how the tabs on the lower front edge locate in the floor panel.

11 Installation is the reverse of removal. Check the operation of the tail light and turn signals before riding the scooter.

Rear mudguard and hugger

12 First remove the seat cowling then disconnect the wiring for the number plate light. Undo the screws securing the mudguard to the frame and remove the mudguard **(see illustration)**.

13 The hugger is secured by one screw on the right-hand side at the back of the engine unit, and one screw on the left-hand side which also secures the back of the air filter housing **(see illustration)**. Undo the screws and remove the hugger.

14 Installation is the reverse of removal, ensuring the screw on the left-hand side is correctly located through the back of the air filter housing.

Storage compartment

15 First remove the seat cowling.

16 Remove the battery, then undo the screw securing the starter relay bracket on the right-hand side of the storage compartment and displace the relay (see Chapter 9). Undo the screw that secures the air filter housing intake to the side of the storage compartment.

17 Remove the fuel tank cap and, on Liberty 50 models, the oil tank cap.

18 Undo the two screws securing the storage compartment to the frame, then lift out the storage compartment **(see illustration)**. Replace the fuel and oil tank caps to avoid anything falling into the tanks.

19 Installation is the reverse of removal.

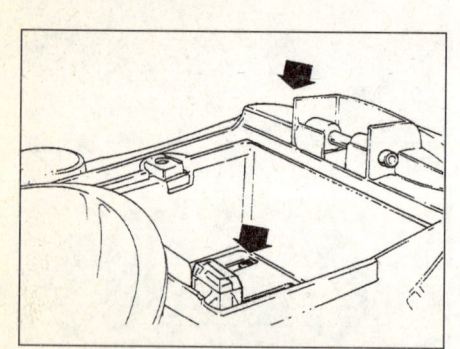

14.18 Remove the screws (arrowed) retaining the storage compartment

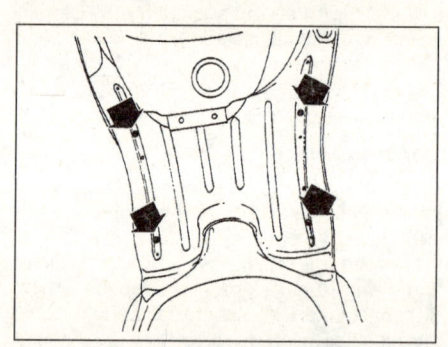

14.22 Lift the rubber strips to access the fixing screws (arrowed)

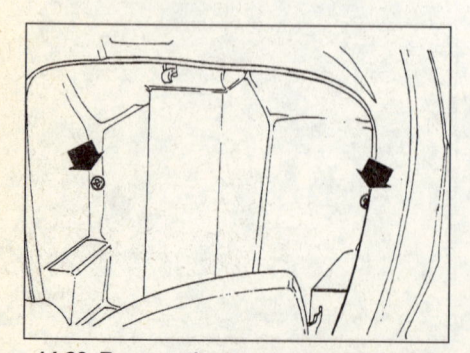

14.26 Remove the two screws (arrowed) inside the glove box

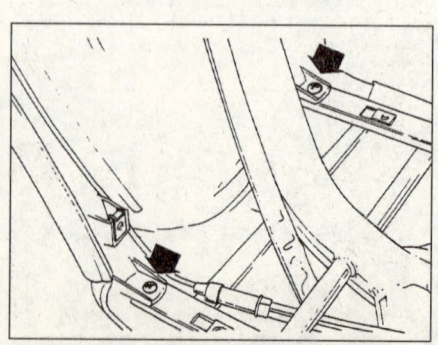

14.34 Remove the screws (arrowed) on the front edge of the belly panel

Floor panel

20 Remove the seat cowling (see Steps 8 to 10).

21 Remove the passenger footrests.

22 Lift the outer rubber strips on the floor panel and remove the four fixing screws **(see illustration)**. Lift the back edge of the panel and disengage it from the tabs on the lower edge of the kick panel, then remove the floor panel off.

23 Installation is the reverse of removal.

Kick panel

24 Remove the floor panel (see above).

25 Undo the two screws securing the bag hook and remove it.

26 Open the glove box and remove the two screws securing the kick panel **(see illustration)**.

27 Remove the two screws on the lower edge of the kick panel. Ease the panel back and remove it.

28 Installation is the reverse of removal

Front panel

Note: *The front panel cannot be removed from the machine without first removing the steering stem (see Chapter 6).*

29 Remove the kick panel (see above).

30 Carefully lever off the badge on the front centre panel, then remove the screw behind it and lift off the centre panel.

31 Remove the screws securing the front turn signal assemblies, then disconnect the wiring connectors and remove the assemblies (see Chapter 9).

32 Installation is the reverse of removal. Check the operation of the turn signals before riding the scooter.

Belly panel

33 Remove the kick panel (see Steps 24 to 27).

34 Remove the two screws securing the front edge of the panel to the frame **(see illustration)**.

35 Carefully ease the brackets on the belly panel off the mounting points on the frame and lower the panel off.

36 Installation is the reverse of removal.

Handlebar covers

37 Remove the screw underneath the headlight, then undo the two screws that

Frame and bodywork 7•33

secure the front cover to the rear cover **(see illustrations)**. Carefully unclip the front cover from the rear cover and lift it away, then disconnect the headlight wiring connector and remove the front cover.
38 The rear cover is secured to the handlebars with three screws **(see illustration)**. To remove the cover, first undo the screws and displace the cover. Disconnect the speedometer cable, instrument cluster wiring connectors and switch wiring connectors, noting where they fit (see Chapter 9).
39 Installation is the reverse of removal. Check the operation of the headlight, instruments and switches before riding the scooter.

Front mudguard

Note: *The front mudguard cannot be removed from the machine without first removing the steering stem (see Chapter 6).*
40 Undo the screws securing the mudguard to the steering stem and lift it off **(see illustration)**.

15 GT body panels – removal and installation

Seat

1 Unlock the seat, using either the electronic release button on the kick panel or the lever inside the glovebox, and swing it upright.
2 Remove the screws securing the seat hinge and remove the seat.
3 Installation is the reverse of removal.

Storage compartment – engine access

4 Unlock the seat and swing it upright, then lift out the storage compartment.
5 Installation is the reverse of removal.

Front panel grille

6 Carefully lever off the badge in the grille, then remove the screw behind it and remove the grille **(see illustrations)**.
7 Installation is the reverse of removal.

Side panels

8 Remove the screws joining the side panel to the main body panel **(see illustration)**.

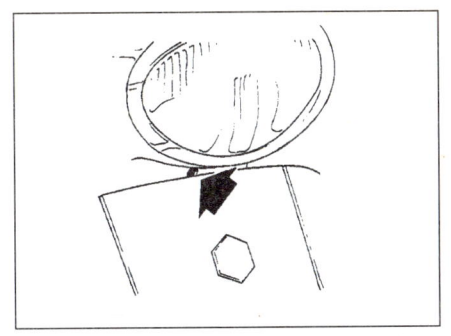

14.37a Remove the screw (arrowed) underneath the headlight . . .

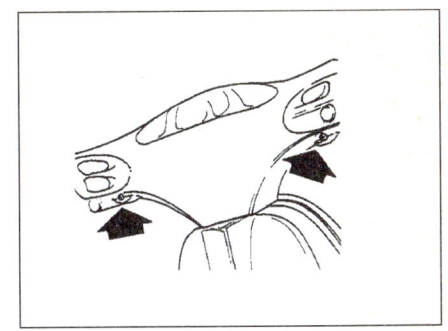

14.37b . . . then the two screws (arrowed) on the rear cover

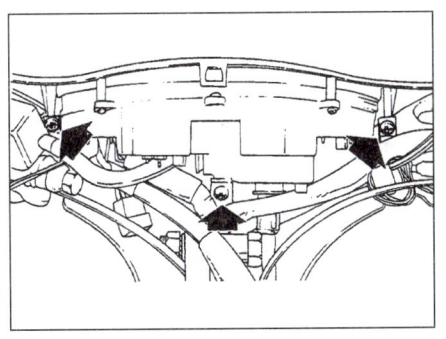

14.38 The rear cover is secured by three screws (arrowed)

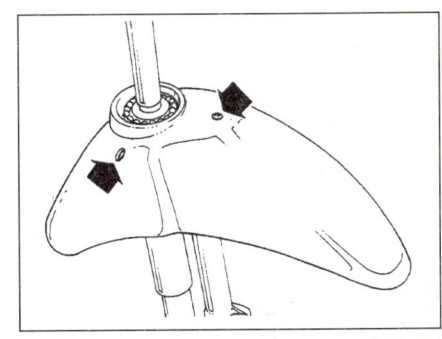

14.40 Remove the screws (arrowed) then lift off the mudguard

9 Each side panel is secured to the main body by three pegs which locate in rubber grommets, and by tabs at the front and rear. Pull the back of each panel away to release the rear tabs, then pull the pegs out of the grommets and pull the panel back to disengage the front tab **(see illustration)**.
10 If required, remove the screw securing the side trim panel and pull it off **(see illustration)**.
11 Installation is the reverse of removal.

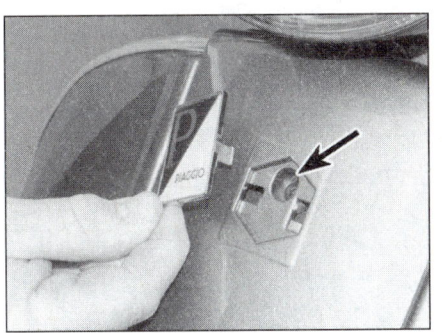

15.6a Remove the screw (arrowed) behind the badge . . .

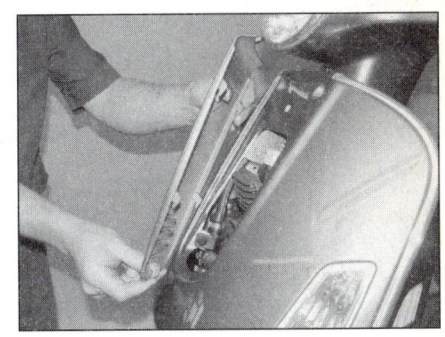

15.6b . . . and lift off the grille

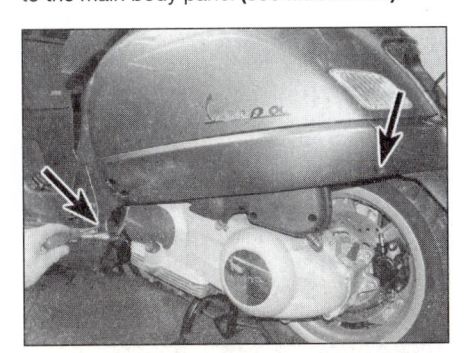

15.8 Remove the screws (arrowed)

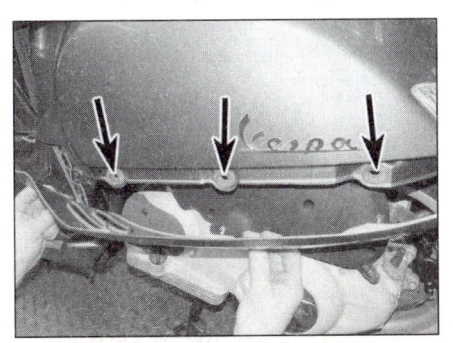

15.9 Note how the pegs locate in the grommets (arrowed)

15.10 Trim panels are secured by single screw on each side

7•34 Frame and bodywork

15.12 Remove the two screws (arrowed)

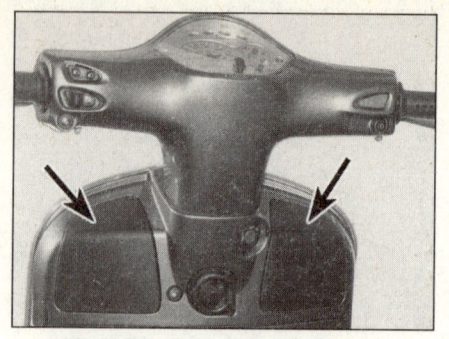

15.13 Remove the access panels (arrowed)

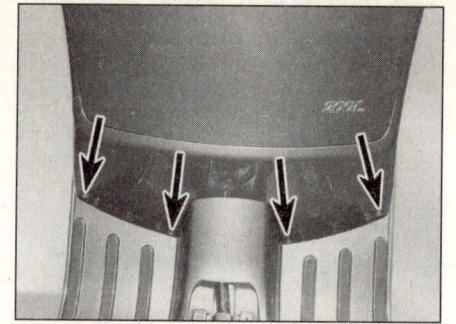

15.14a Remove the screws along the lower edge (arrowed) . . .

Kick panel

12 Disconnect the battery negative (-ve) terminal (see Chapter 9). Remove the front panel grille, then remove the two screws located behind it **(see illustration)**.
13 Remove the screws securing the left and right-hand access panels and remove the panels **(see illustration)**.
14 Remove the screws securing the lower edge of the kick panel – note that these screws are longer than the other panel screws **(see illustrations)**.
15 Press in the ignition switch to release the glovebox door and swing the door down. Remove the two screws on the top of the kick panel and the screw inside the compartment **(see illustration)**.
16 Unscrew the coolant reservoir filler cap **(see illustration)**.
17 Ease the kick panel up to disengage it from the front edge of the floor panel, then pull it back to gain access to the seat release button wiring connector – disconnect the connector and unclip the fuse holder from the back of the kick panel **(see illustrations)**.

18 Release the end of the seat opening cable from the lever inside the glovebox, then pull the cable stop out of the kickpanel **(see illustrations)**. Note how the catch for the glovebox aligns with the catch mechanism,

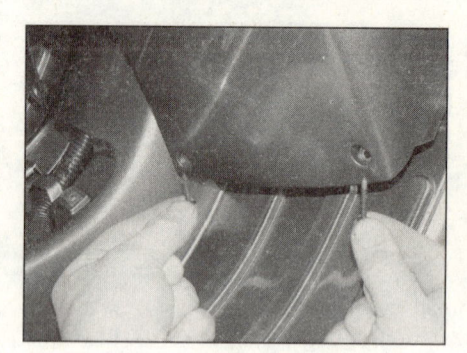

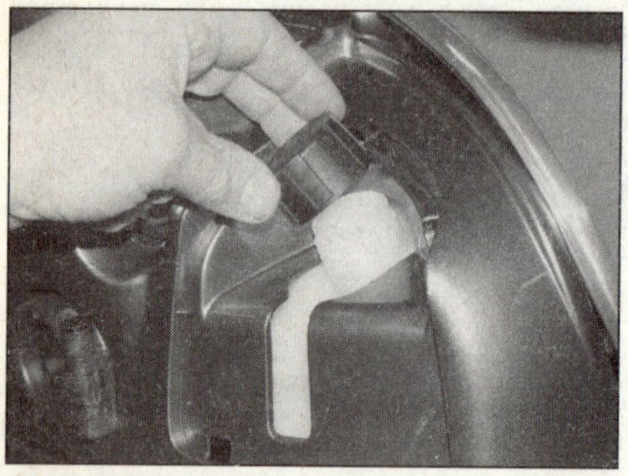

15.14b . . . noting their length

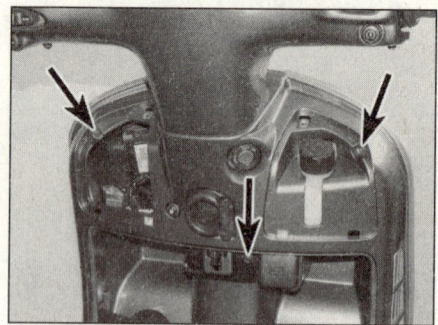

15.15 Remove the screws as described

15.16 Remove the coolant reservoir filler cap

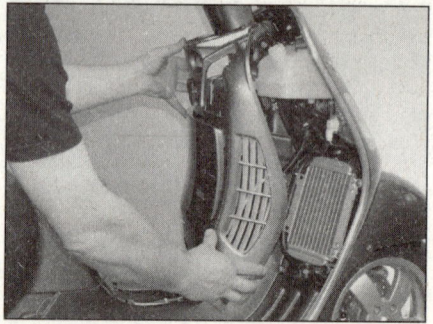

15.17a Ease the kick panel back . . .

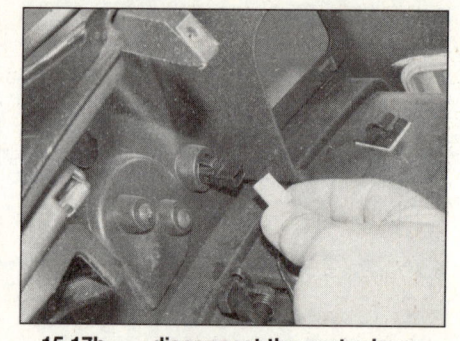

15.17b . . . disconnect the seat release wiring connector . . .

15.17c . . . and unclip the fuse holder

15.18a Release the cable end (arrowed) from the lever . . .

15.18b . . . and pull the cable stop out of the panel

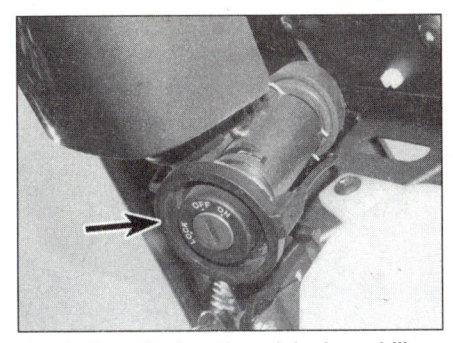

Frame and bodywork 7•35

15.19 Note the location of the immobiliser transponder aerial (arrowed)

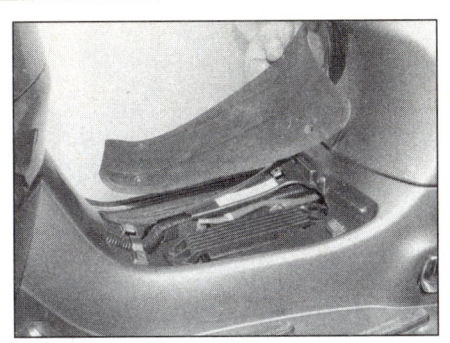

15.20 Remove the centre mat

back of the panel. Connect the seat release cable and check the operation of the seat release and glovebox door mechanisms before installing the fixing screws.

Floor panel

20 Remove the side panels and the side trim panels. Undo the four screws and remove the centre mat (see illustration).
21 Remove the kick panel.
22 Undo the screws securing the passenger footrest assemblies and remove them (see illustrations).
23 Remove the three screws securing the back edge of the floor panel (see illustration).
24 Pull the outer rubber strip from its channel in the floor panel, noting how it fits, then remove the six screws securing the panel (see illustrations).
25 Lift up the front edge of the floor panel and manoeuvre the panel off (see illustration).
26 Installation is the reverse of removal.

Handlebar covers

27 Undo the screws securing the brake master cylinder covers and remove the covers, then remove the rear view mirrors (see illustrations). Remove the front panel grille.
28 To remove the front cover, remove the screws from the underside of the rear cover and the screw below the headlight (see

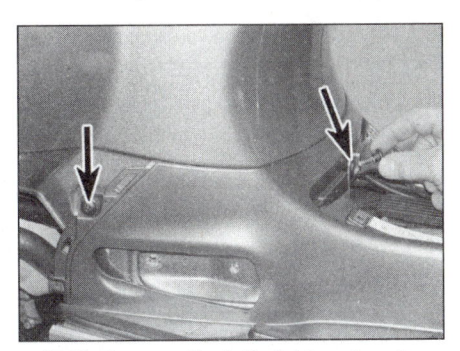

15.22a Undo the screws (arrowed) . . .

15.22b . . . and remove the passenger footrests

then lift the kick panel off. Temporarily install the coolant reservoir cap.
19 Installation is the reverse of removal. Ensure the ignition immobiliser transponder

aerial is correctly positioned on the ignition (main) switch (see illustration). Don't forget to connect the seat release button wiring connector and install the fuseholder in the

15.23 Remove the left, right and centre floor panel screws

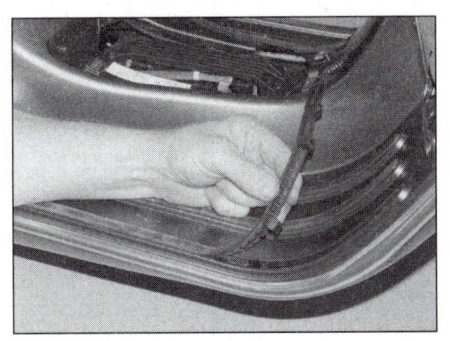

15.24a Pull up the rubber strip on each side . . .

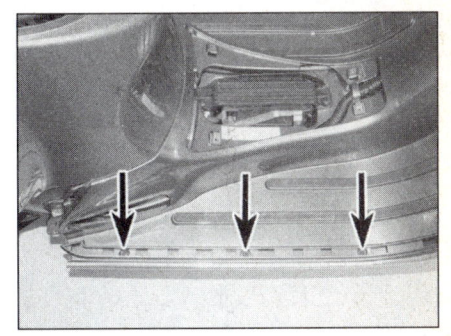

15.24b . . . and remove the screws underneath

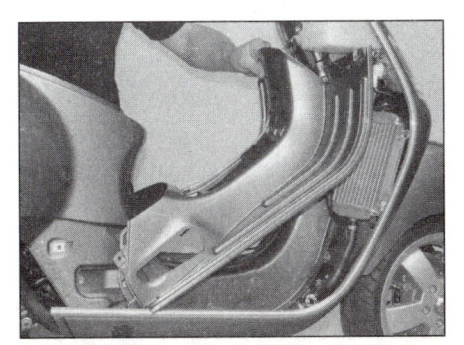

15.25 Manoeuvre the floor panel out

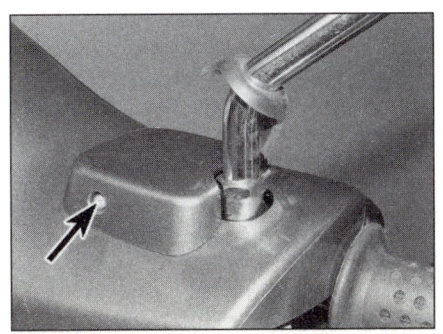

15.27a Each cover is secured by a single screw (arrowed)

15.27b Unscrew the rear view mirrors

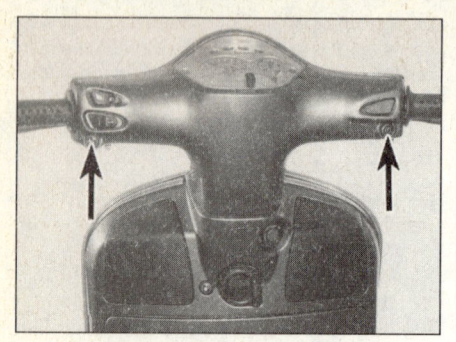

7•36 Frame and bodywork

15.28a Remove the screws on the underside of the rear cover...

15.28b ...and the screw below the headlight

15.28c Ease the pegs (arrowed) away carefully

illustrations). Carefully ease away the top edge of the front cover to release the pegs which locate into holes in the top edge of the rear cover **(see illustration)**. The cover is quite a tight fit and a certain amount of leverage is required, but take care not to apply excessive force as the cover could break. Once the cover is free, disconnect the headlight wiring connectors and remove the cover.

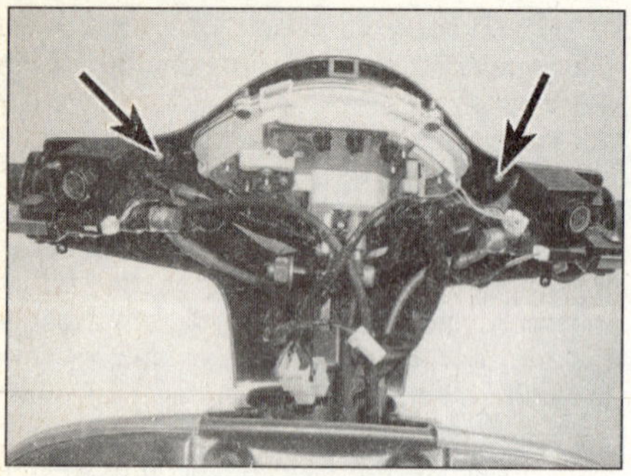

29 To remove the rear cover, first remove the front cover. Remove the screws securing the rear cover to the brackets on the handlebars **(see illustrations)**. Remove the screw securing the instrument cluster to its support bracket **(see illustration)**. If the cover is being completely removed rather than just displaced for access, disconnect the instrument cluster and handlebar switch wiring connectors, noting which fits where, and the speedometer cable, then remove the cover. If required, separate the instrument cluster from the cover (see Chapter 9).

30 Installation is the reverse of removal. Make sure the wiring connectors are correctly and securely connected, and check the operation of all switches and lights.

Rear carrier

31 Remove the storage compartment.
32 If applicable, remove the screws securing the carrier cover and remove the cover.
33 Remove the screw securing the carrier to the rear of the main body **(see illustration)**.
34 Remove the fuel filler cap and lift off the seal **(see illustration)**.
35 If a top box is fitted to the carrier, support the carrier, then undo the four bolts securing the grab handles **(see illustration 15.33)**. Remove the handles – note that the front bolts are shorter than the rear bolts – and lift off the carrier **(see illustrations)**. Temporarily install the fuel filler cap.
36 Installation is the reverse of removal.

15.29a Rear cover is secured by two screws (arrowed) at the top...

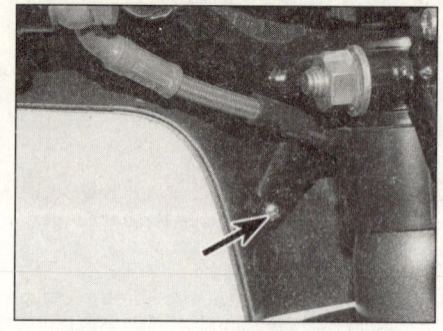

15.29b ...and one below (arrowed)

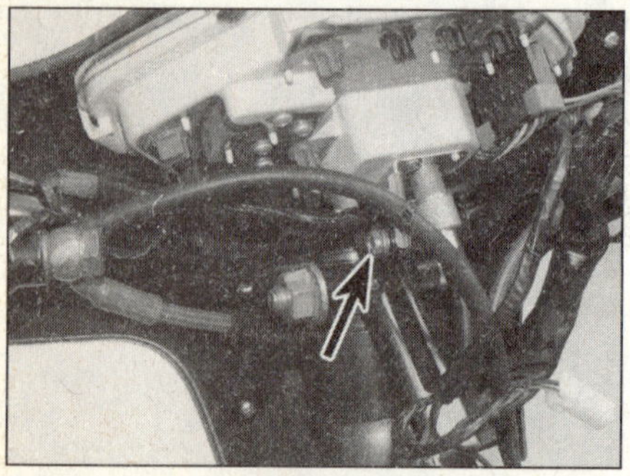

15.29c Remove the support bracket screw (arrowed)

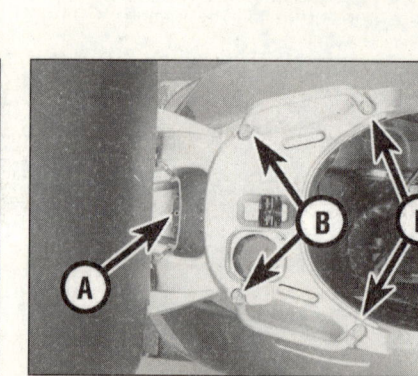

15.33 Remove the screw (A). Screws (B) secure grab handles

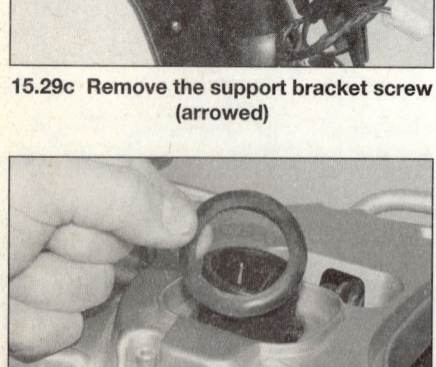

15.34 Remove the fuel filler cap seal

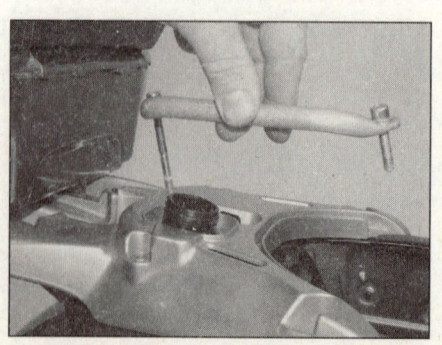

15.35a Remove the grab handles...

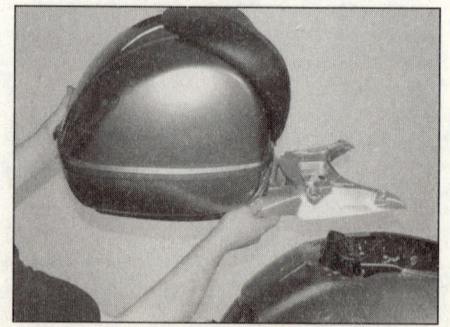

15.35b ...and lift off the carrier

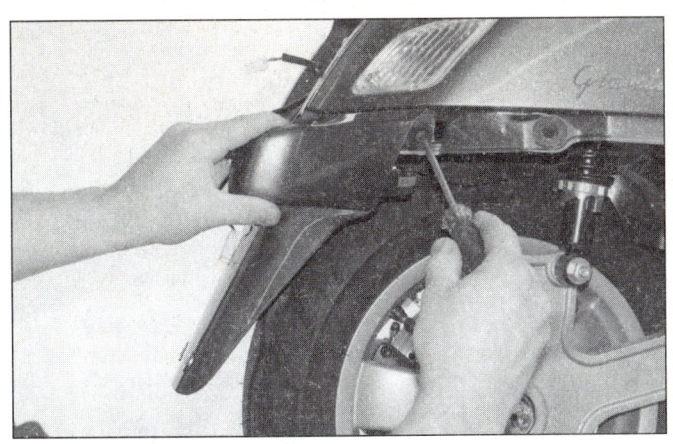

Frame and bodywork 7•37

15.39 Remove the mudguard fixing screws

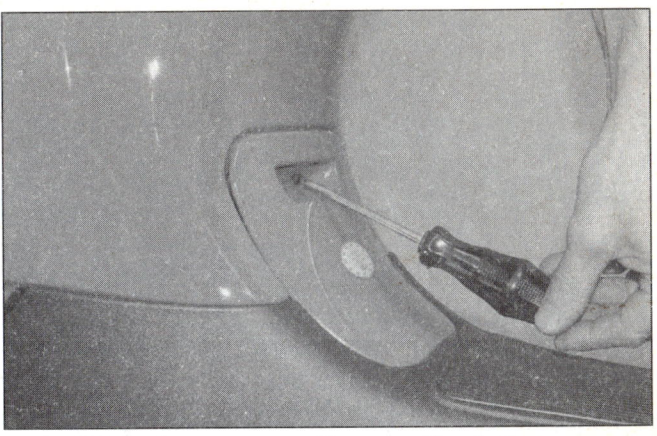

16.6 Engine access panel is secured by single screw

Rear mudguard

37 Refer to the procedure in Chapter 9, Section 9, and remove the number plate light and the tail light assembly.
38 Remove the side panels.
39 Remove the screws securing the mudguard to the main body and lift it off **(see illustration)**.
40 Installation is the reverse of removal. Check the operation of the tail light and turn signals before riding the scooter.

16 LX body panels – removal and installation

Seat

1 Unlock the seat using the ignition key and swing it upright.
2 Remove the screws securing the seat hinge and remove the seat.
3 Installation is the reverse of removal.

Storage compartment – engine access

4 Unlock the seat using the ignition key and swing it upright, then lift out the storage compartment.
5 Installation is the reverse of removal.

Engine access panel

6 Remove the single screw securing the access panel below the seat and remove the panel **(see illustration)**.
7 Installation is the reverse of removal.

Front panel grille

8 Carefully lever off the badge in the grille, then remove the screw behind it and remove the grille, noting how it fits **(see illustrations)**.
9 Installation is the reverse of removal.

Side panels

10 Remove the screws joining the side panel to the main body panel **(see illustration)**.
11 Each side panel is secured to the main body by two pegs which locate in rubber grommets, and by a tab at the rear. Pull the front of each panel away to release the pegs from the grommets, then pull the panel back to disengage the rear tab **(see illustrations)**.
12 Installation is the reverse of removal.

Kick panel

13 Remove the fairing grille, then remove the two screws located behind it **(see illustration 10.8)**.
14 Press in the ignition switch to release the glovebox door and swing the door down. Remove the three screws inside the compartment **(see illustration 10.9b)**.
15 Ease the kick panel up, then pull it away

16.8a Remove the central screw . . .

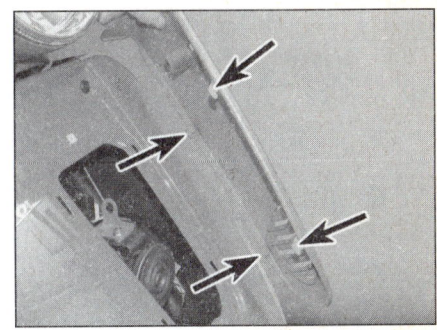

16.8b . . . and lift off the grille, noting how the tabs (arrowed) locate

16.10 Remove the screws (arrowed)

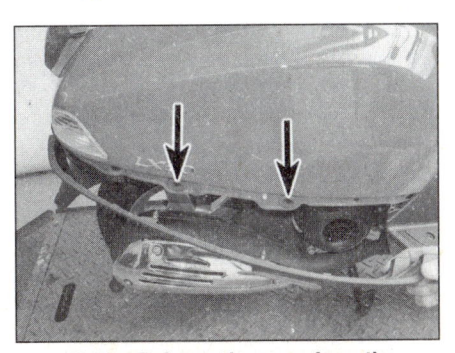

16.11a Release the pegs from the grommets (arrowed) . . .

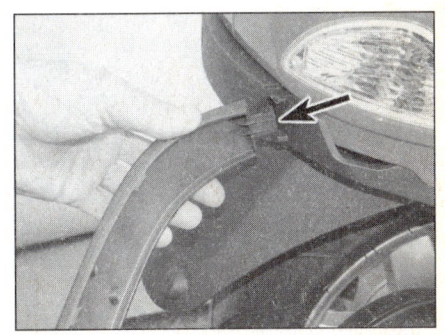

16.11b . . . and release the tab at the rear

7•38 Frame and bodywork

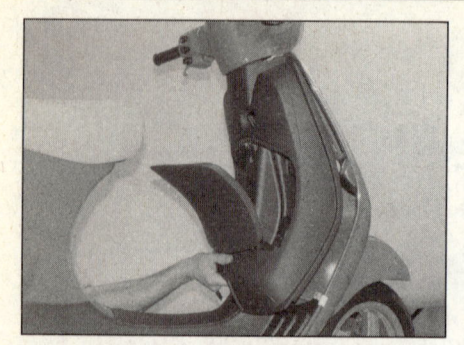

16.15a Ease the kick panel off . . .

16.15b . . . note how the catch mechanism (arrowed) aligns

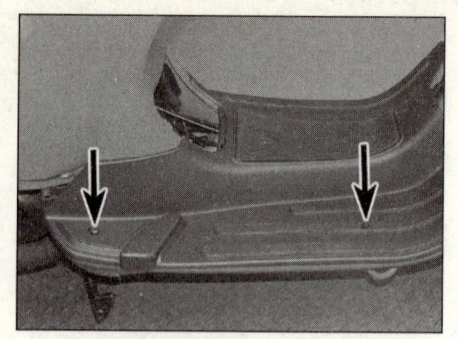

16.19 Floor panel is secured by two screws (arrowed) on each side . . .

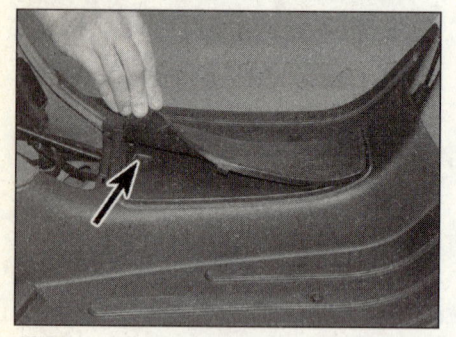

16.20 . . . and one (arrowed) under the mat

16.21 Remove the chrome trim fixing screws

from the front panel – note how the catch for the glovebox aligns with the catch mechanism around the ignition switch **(see illustrations)**.
16 Installation is the reverse of removal. Check the operation of the glovebox door release mechanism before installing the fixing screws.

Floor panel
17 Remove the kick panel.
18 Remove the engine access panel.
19 Remove the two screws on each side securing the floor panel **(see illustration)**.
20 Pull up the floor panel centre mat, then remove the screw underneath the mat **(see illustration)**.
21 Remove the screw on each side securing the lower edge of the front panel chrome trim **(see illustration)**.
22 Draw the floor panel forwards and manoeuvre it off **(see illustration)**. If required, remove the side trim panels, noting how they are secured by the rear floor panel screws **(see illustration)**.
23 Installation is the reverse of removal.

Handlebar covers
24 Remove the rear view mirrors. Remove the front panel grille.
25 To remove the front cover, remove the screws from the rear cover and the screw below the headlight, then carefully ease the edge of the front cover away to release the pegs which locate into holes in the top edge and sides of the rear cover **(see illustrations)**. These pegs

16.22a Lift the floor panel off

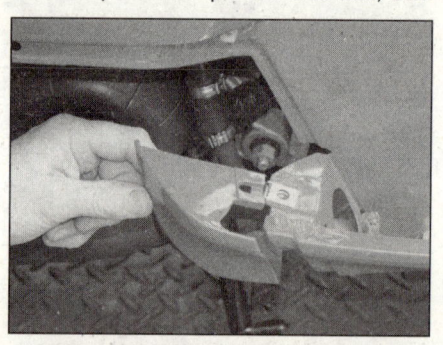

16.22b Note how the trim panels locate

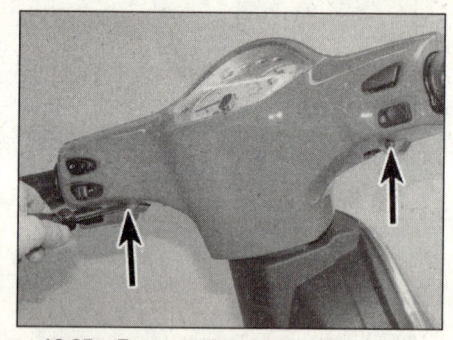

16.25a Remove the screws in the rear cover (arrowed) . . .

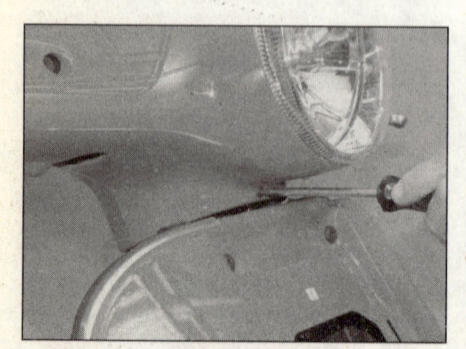

16.25b . . . and the screw below the headlight

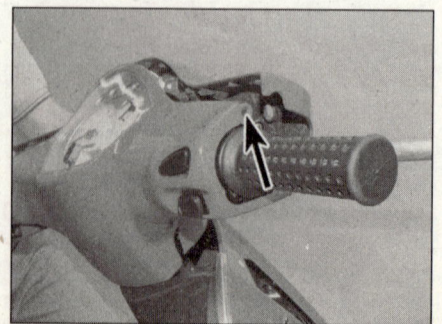

16.25c Pegs locate in both sides of the rear cover . . .

16.25d . . . and in the centre of the top edge

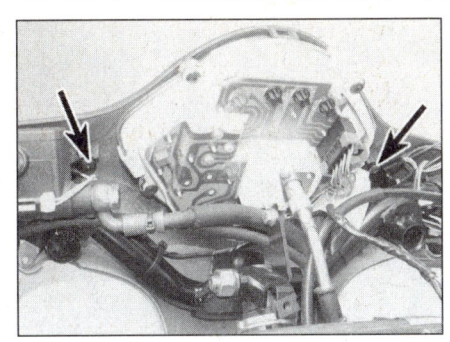

Frame and bodywork 7•39

16.26a Rear cover is secured by two screws (arrowed) at the top . . .

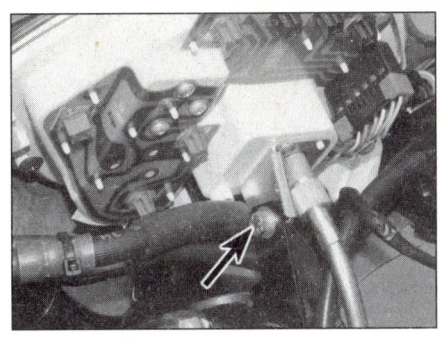

16.26b . . . and by the instrument cluster support bracket screw (arrowed)

16.29 Remove the oil filler seal

are quite a tight fit and a certain amount of leverage is required, but take care not to apply excessive force as the cover could break. Once the cover is free, disconnect the headlight wiring connectors and remove the cover.

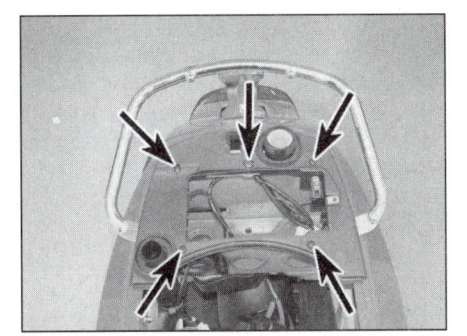

26 To remove the rear cover, first remove the front cover. Remove the screws securing the rear cover to the brackets on the handlebars **(see illustration)**. Remove the screw securing the instrument cluster to its support bracket **(see illustration)**. If the cover is being completely removed rather than just displaced for access, disconnect the instrument cluster and handlebar switch wiring connectors, noting which fits where, and the speedometer cable, then remove the cover. If required, separate the instrument cluster from the cover (see Chapter 9).
27 Installation is the reverse of removal. Make sure the wiring connectors are correctly and securely connected, and check the operation of all switches and lights.

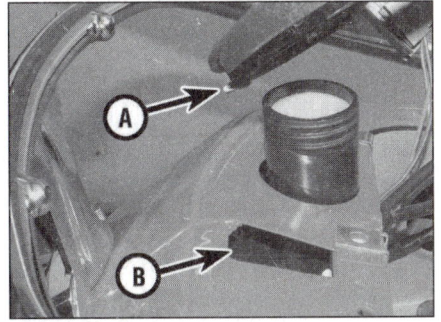

Battery panel and grab handle

28 Remove the storage compartment. Remove the battery (see Chapter 9).
29 Remove the fuel filler cap and, on two-stroke models, oil filler cap and lift off the seal **(see illustration)**.
30 Remove the screws securing the battery panel and lift it up, noting how it locates at the back, then detach the fuse holder from panel and remove the panel **(see illustrations)**. Temporarily install the fuel filler and oil filler caps.
31 Undo the screw securing the badge to the grab handle and lift it off **(see illustrations)**.
32 Remove the four bolts securing the grab handle and lift it off **(see illustration)**.
33 Installation is the reverse of removal.

Rear mudguard

34 Remove both side panels.
35 Remove the screws securing the mudguard to the main body and lift it off **(see illustration)**.
36 Installation is the reverse of removal.

16.30a Remove the battery panel screws (arrowed)

16.30b Note how tab (A) locates in slot (B)

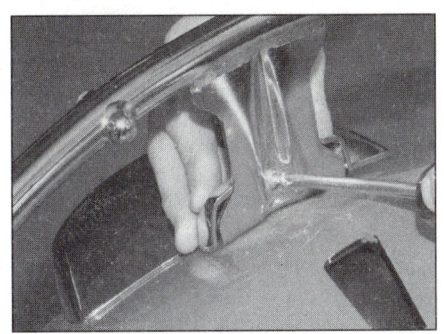

16.30c Detach the fuse holder (arrowed) from the panel

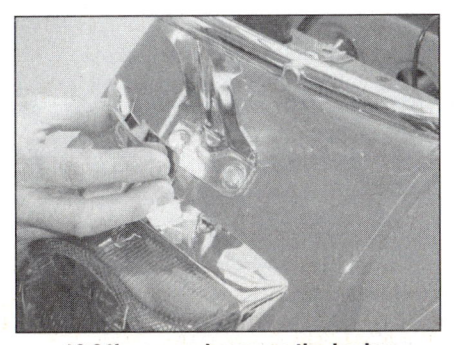

16.31a Undo the screw . . .

16.31b . . . and remove the badge

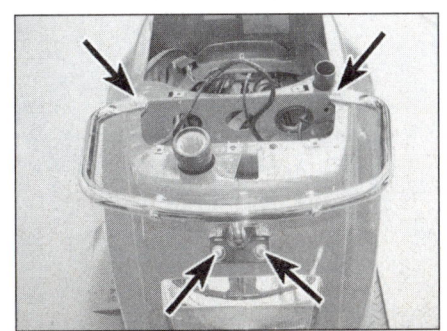

16.32 Grab handle is secured by four bolts

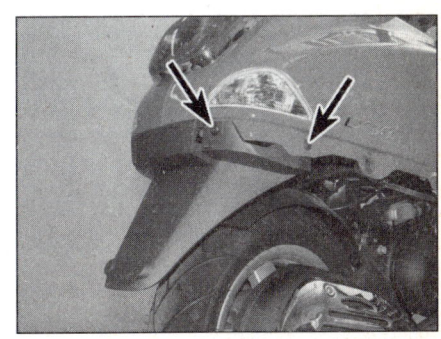

16.35 Mudguard is secured by two screws on each side

7•40 Frame and bodywork

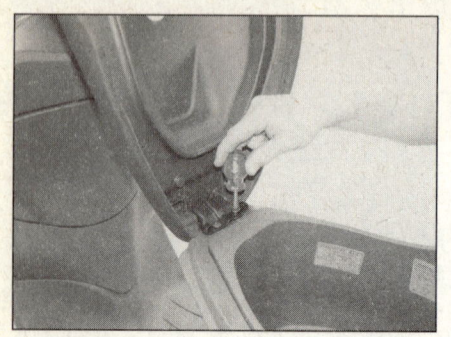

17.1 Remove the two hinge screws

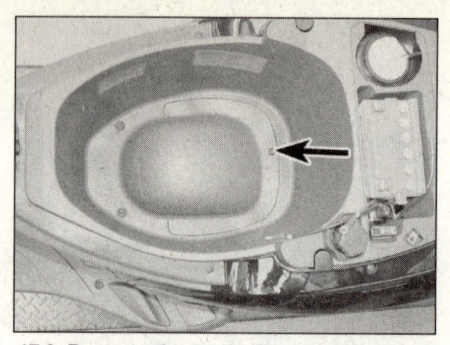

17.3 Remove the screw (arrowed) to open the access panel

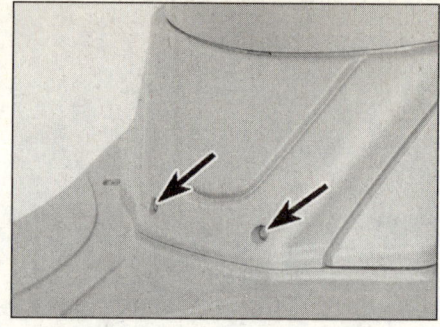

17.4a Remove the screws (arrowed) . . .

17 Fly body panels – removal and installation

Seat

1 Unlock the seat using the ignition key and swing it upright, then remove the screws securing the seat hinge to the storage compartment and remove the seat (see illustration).
2 Installation is the reverse of removal.

Engine access panels

3 To remove the access panel in the storage compartment, lift up the seat and remove it if necessary (see Step 1). Undo the screw securing the access panel in the bottom of the storage compartment and remove the panel (see illustration).
4 To remove the front access panel, remove the two screws securing the panel, then draw the panel forwards to detach it (see illustrations).
5 Installation is the reverse of removal.

Side panels

6 Remove the front engine access panel.
7 Each side panel is secured by three screws – undo the screws then ease the panel off, noting how the tabs on the top edge locate in the lower edge of the seat cowling (see illustrations).
8 Installation is the reverse of removal.

Front underseat panel

9 First remove the seat, the front engine access panel and both side panels

10 Undo the two screws securing the top edge of the panel, then lift the panel off (see illustrations).
11 Installation is the reverse of removal.

Seat cowling

12 First remove the front underseat panel.
13 Remove the four screws securing the grab handle and lift it off (see illustration).
14 Undo the screws securing the tail light unit and lift it off, then lift out the left and right-hand rear turn signal assemblies (see Chapter 9, Sections 9 and 12). If required, tag the wiring connectors to aid reassembly.
15 The left and right-hand cowlings are separate panels. Remove the rear fixing screw as appropriate, then remove the two screws on the top edge, the screw on the lower front edge and the screw on the underside of the

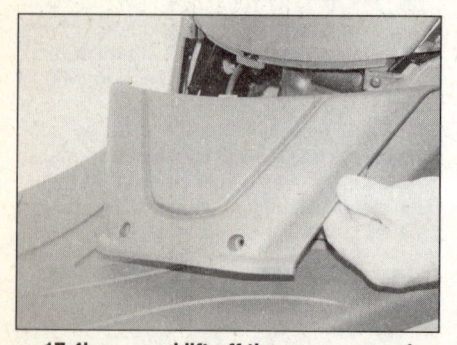

17.4b . . . and lift off the access panel

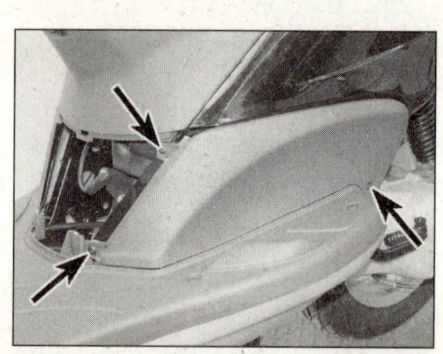

17.7a Each side panel is secured by three screws

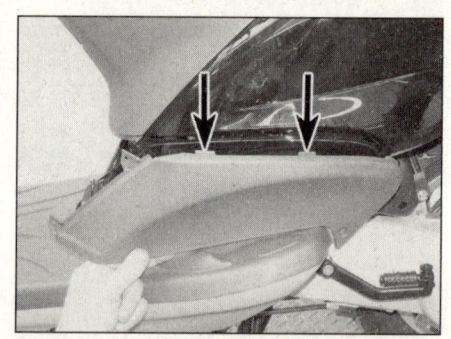

17.7b Note the tabs (arrowed) locate in the seat cowling

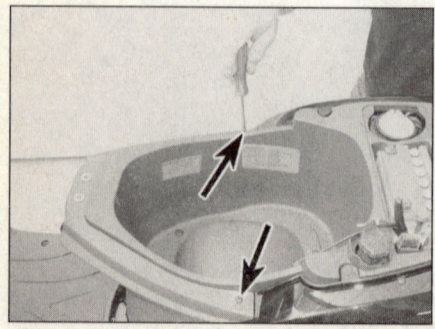

17.10a Undo the screws (arrowed) . . .

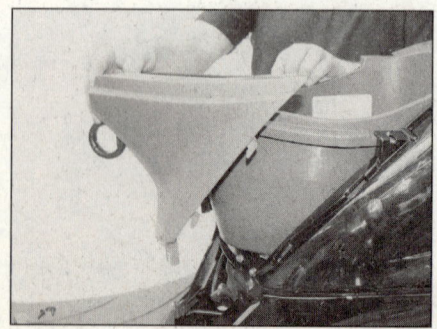

17.10b . . . and lift off the underseat panel

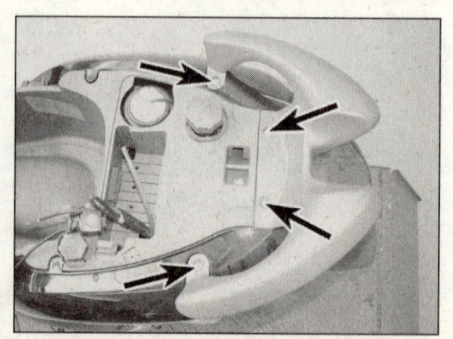

17.13 Grab handle is secured by four screws

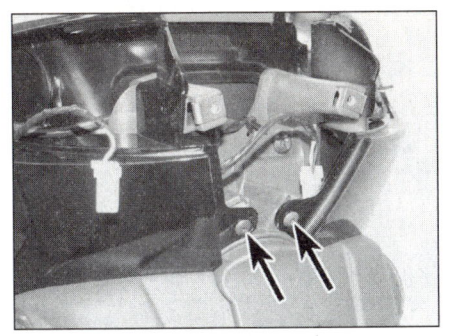

Frame and bodywork 7•41

17.15a Side cowlings are secured by screws (arrowed) at the back . . .

17.15b . . . and four screws on each side

17.18a Remove the screws (arrowed) . . .

panel **(see illustrations)**. Lift the cowling panel off.
16 Installation is the reverse of removal. Check the operation of the tail light and turn signals before riding the scooter.

Rear mudguard and hugger

17 First remove the seat cowling.
18 Undo the screws securing the mudguard to the frame and remove the mudguard **(see illustrations)**.
19 The hugger is secured by one screw on the right-hand side at the back of the engine unit, and two screws on the left-hand side which also secure the back of the air filter housing. Undo the screws and remove the hugger.
20 Installation is the reverse of removal. When refitting the hugger, ensure the screws on the left-hand side are correctly located through the back of the air filter housing.

Storage compartment

21 Remove the battery and unclip the fuse holder (see Chapter 9).
22 Remove the seat cowling.
23 Remove the fuel filler cap and, on two-stroke models, the oil filler cap.
24 Undo the two screws that secure the bottom of the storage compartment to the frame, then lift out the storage compartment **(see illustrations)**. Temporarily install the fuel filler and oil filler caps.
25 Installation is the reverse of removal.

Kick panel

26 Undo the screw securing the front access panel and remove the panel **(see illustration)**.

17.18b . . . and lift off the rear mudguard

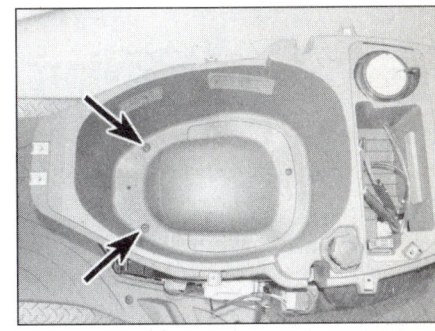

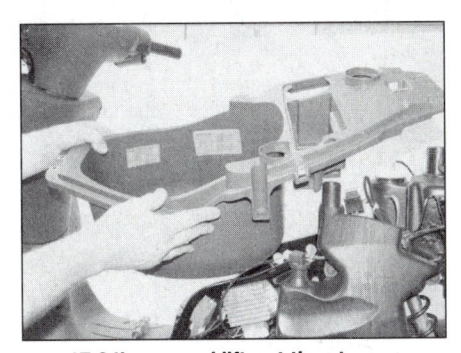

17.24b . . . and lift out the storage compartment

27 Undo the two screws inside the front access panel opening **(see illustration)**.
28 Undo the four screws securing the outer edge of the kick panel; press in the ignition switch to release the glovebox door and swing the door down, then remove the three screws inside the compartment **(see illustration)**.

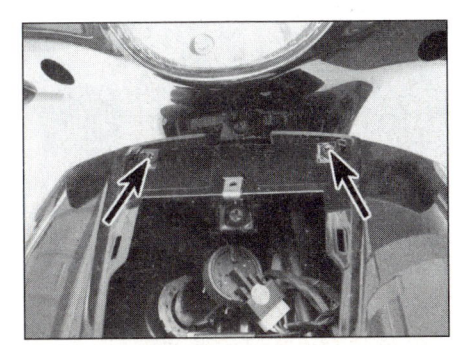

17.27 Remove the screws (arrowed) . . .

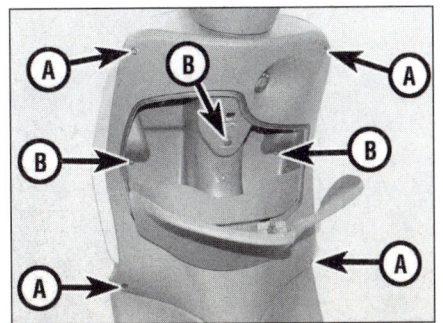

17.28 . . . then remove the outer screws (A) and the screws (B) inside the glovebox

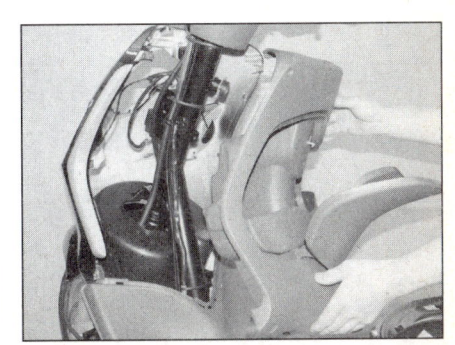

17.24a Remove the screws (arrowed) . . .

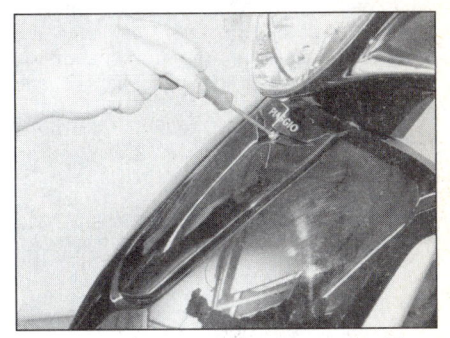

17.26 Front access panel is secured by single screw

29 Ease the panel back and release the tabs along its lower edge from the slots in the floor panel – note how the catch for the glovebox aligns with the catch mechanism around the ignition switch, then remove the kick panel **(see illustration)**.
30 Installation is the reverse of removal.

17.29 Remove the kick panel as described

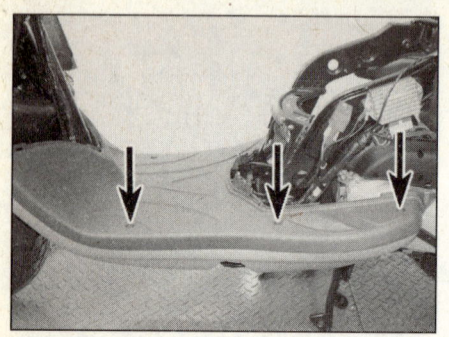

7•42 Frame and bodywork

17.32a Top of the floor panel is secured by three screws on each side . . .

17.32b . . . and two screws through the belly panel

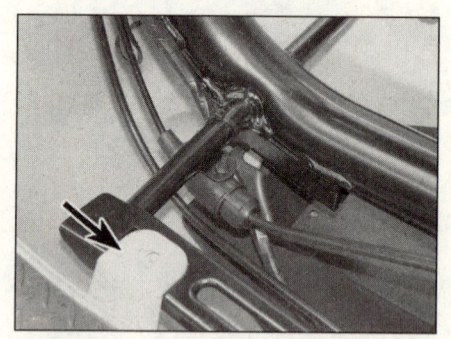

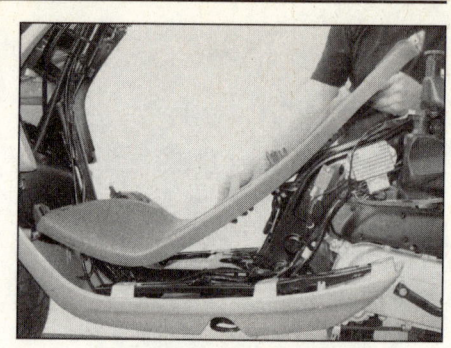

17.33 Lift the floor panel off

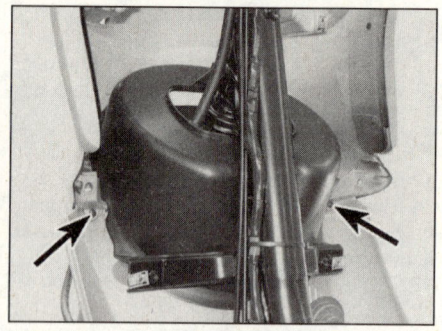

Check the operation of the glovebox door release mechanism before installing the fixing screws.

Floor panel

31 First remove both side panels and the kick panel.
32 Undo the six screws securing the top of the floor panel to the frame and the two screws at the rear of the belly panel (see illustrations).
33 Lift the floor panel and manoeuvre it off (see illustration).
34 Installation is the reverse of removal. Ensure the brackets on the belly panel are correctly located on the frame supports before installing the floor panel screws (see illustration).

Belly panel

35 Remove the floor panel.

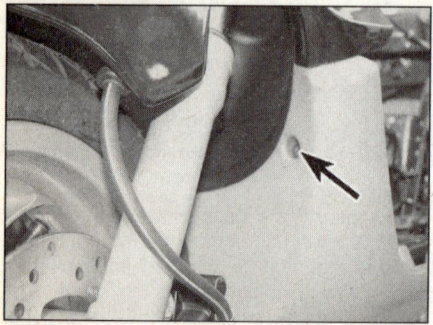

17.34 Note the location of the belly panel brackets

36 Undo the two screws that secure the left and right-hand lower edges of the front panel to the belly panel (see illustration).
37 Undo the two screws that secure the belly panel to the frame (see illustration).

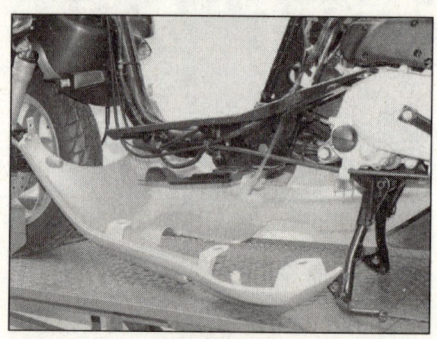

17.36 Remove the screws (arrowed) inside the panels

38 Ease the brackets on the belly panel off the supports on the frame and drop the belly panel down and remove it (see illustration).
39 Installation is the reverse of removal.

Front panel

40 Remove the floor panel.
41 Disconnect the front turn signal wiring connectors.
42 Undo the two screws that secure the left and right-hand lower edges of the front panel to the belly panel (see illustration 17.36).
43 Undo the screws that secure the lower edge of the front panel to the mudguard liner (see illustration).
44 Undo the screw in the centre of the front access panel opening, then lift the panel off (see illustrations).
45 Installation is the reverse of removal. Check the operation of the turn signals before riding the scooter.

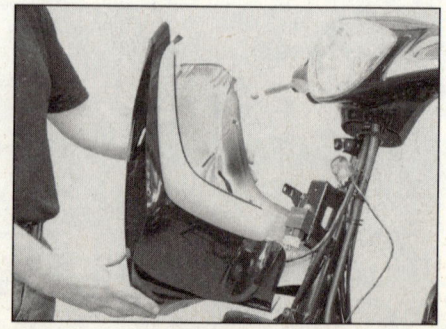

17.37 Remove the single screw (arrowed) on each side

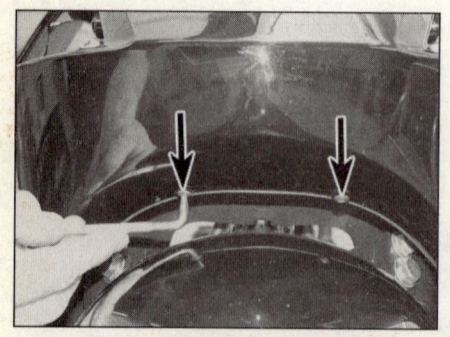

17.38 Lower the belly panel off the frame supports

17.43 Remove the screws (arrowed) on the underside of the front panel

17.44a Remove the screw (arrowed) . . .

17.44b . . . and lift off the front panel

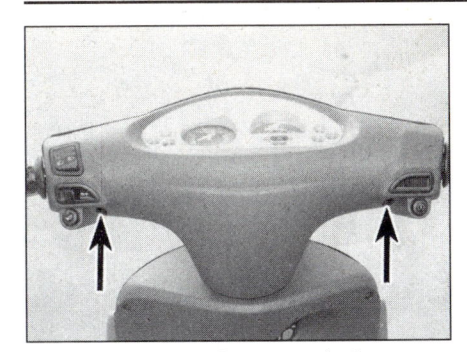

Frame and bodywork 7•43

17.47a Remove the screws in the rear cover (arrowed) . . .

17.47b . . . and the screw below the headlight . . .

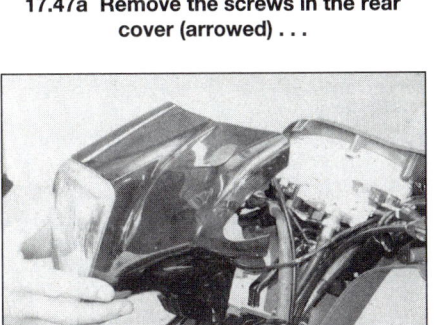

17.47c . . . then ease the cover off as described

17.48 Rear cover is secured by two screws (arrowed) on each side

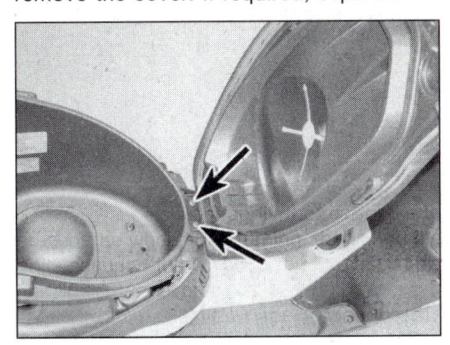

18.1 Remove the two hinge screws

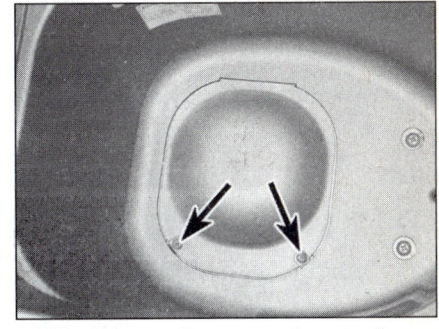

18.3a Remove the screws (arrowed) . . .

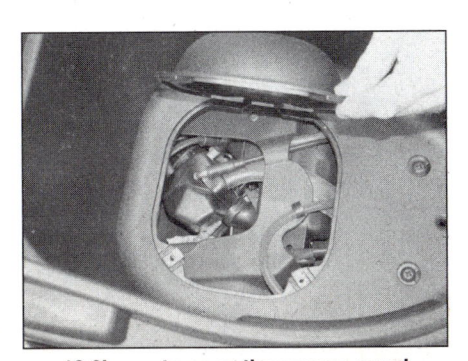

18.3b . . . to open the access panel

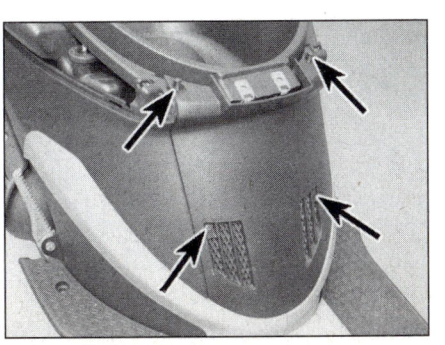

18.4a Remove the screws (arrowed) . . .

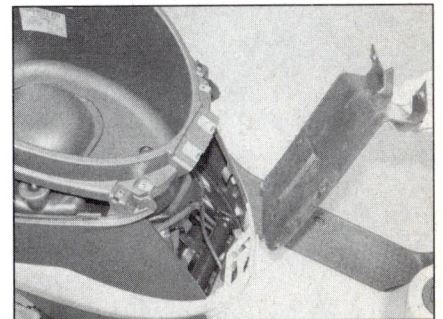

18.4b . . . and lift off the access panel

Handlebar covers

46 Remove the rear view mirrors. Remove the front access panel (see Step 26).
47 To remove the front cover, remove the screws from the rear cover and the screw below the headlight, then carefully ease the edge of the front cover away to release the pegs which locate into holes in the top edge and sides of the rear cover **(see illustrations)**. These pegs are quite a tight fit and a certain amount of leverage is required, but take care not to apply excessive force as the cover could break. Once the cover is free, disconnect the headlight wiring connectors and remove the cover.
48 To remove the rear cover, first remove the front cover. Remove the screws securing the rear cover to the brackets on the handlebars **(see illustration)**. If the cover is being completely removed rather than just displaced for access, disconnect the instrument cluster and handlebar switch wiring connectors, noting which fits where, and the speedometer cable, then remove the cover. If required, separate the instrument cluster from the cover (see Chapter 9).
49 Installation is the reverse of removal. Check the operation of the switches and the headlight before riding the scooter.

18 NRG Power body panels – removal and installation

Seat

1 Unlock the seat by pressing the ignition switch and swing it upright, then remove the screws securing the seat hinge to the storage compartment and remove the seat **(see illustration)**.
2 Installation is the reverse of removal.

Engine access panels

3 To remove the access panel in the storage compartment, lift up the seat and remove it if necessary (see Step 1). Undo the two screws securing the access panel in the bottom of the storage compartment and remove the panel **(see illustrations)**.
4 To remove the front access panel, remove the four screws securing the panel, then draw the panel forwards to detach the tabs on the bottom edge **(see illustrations)**.
5 Installation is the reverse of removal.

Upper side panels

6 Lift up the seat and remove it if necessary (see Step 1).

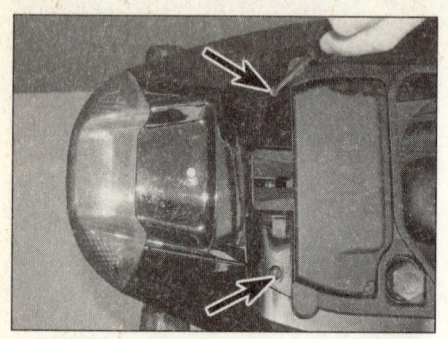

7•44 Frame and bodywork

18.7a Remove the screws (arrowed) . . .

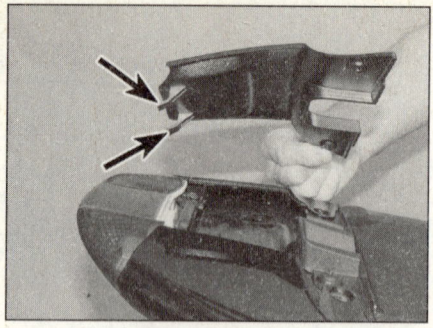

18.7b . . . and lift off the panel, noting the tabs (arrowed)

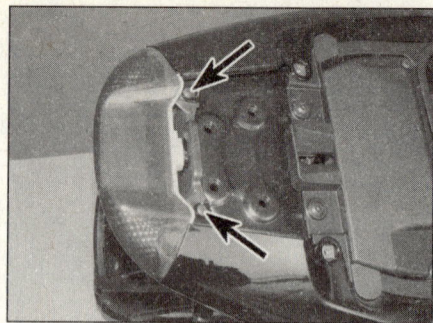

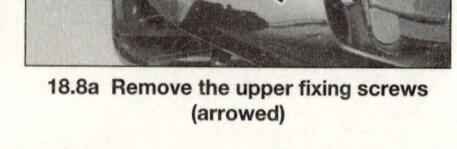

18.8a Remove the upper fixing screws (arrowed)

18.8b Remove the lower fixing screws (arrowed)

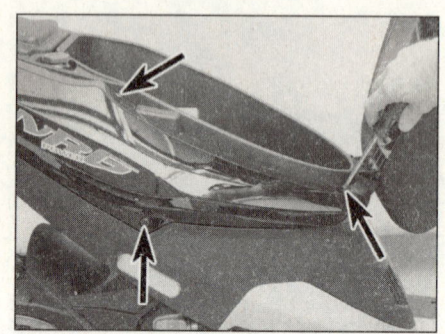

18.9 Remove the fixing screws (arrowed) on each panel

in the upper edge of the lower side panel **(see illustration)**.
10 Installation is the reverse of removal.

Lower side panels

11 Remove the upper side panels. Remove the front engine access panel.
12 Remove the screw joining the panels together at the front **(see illustration)**.
13 Remove the screws securing the number plate panel and draw it off, then disconnect the tail light and turn signal wiring connectors **(see illustration)**. If required, tag the wiring connectors to aid reassembly.
14 Each panel is secured by two screws – undo the screws then ease the panel off, noting how the tabs on the lower front edge locate in the floor panel **(see illustrations)**.
15 If required, undo the screw securing the

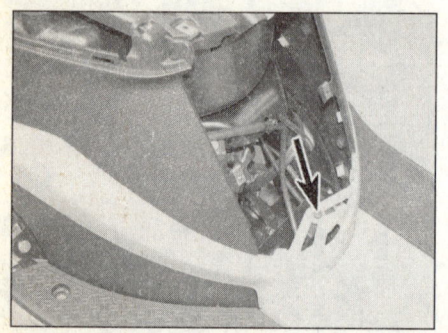

7 Undo the screws securing the rear joining panel and lift it off, noting how the tabs locate **(see illustrations)**.
8 Remove the two upper fixing screws **(see illustration)**. Remove the two screws underneath the rear light unit **(see illustration)**.
9 Each panel is secured by three screws – undo the screws then ease the panel off, noting how the tabs on the lower edge locate

18.12 Remove the screw (arrowed) joining the panels

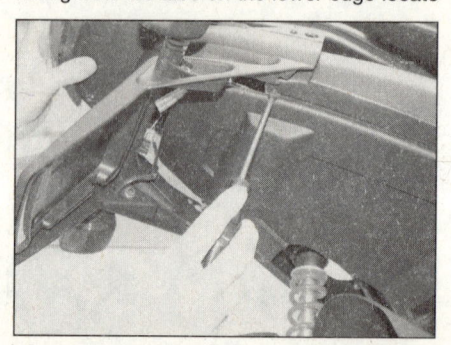

18.13a Remove the screws underneath . . .

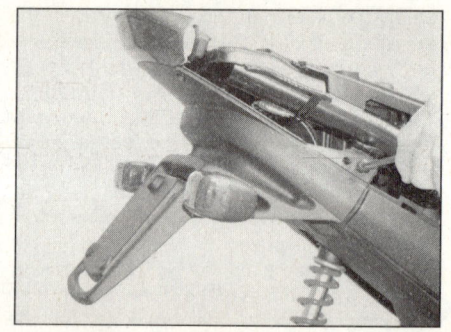

18.13b . . . and on both sides of the panel . . .

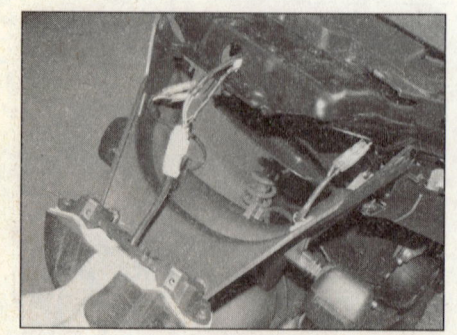

18.13c . . . then draw it off to access the wiring connectors

18.14a Remove the fixing screws (arrowed) . . .

18.14b . . . and lift the panel off, noting the tabs (arrowed)

Frame and bodywork 7•45

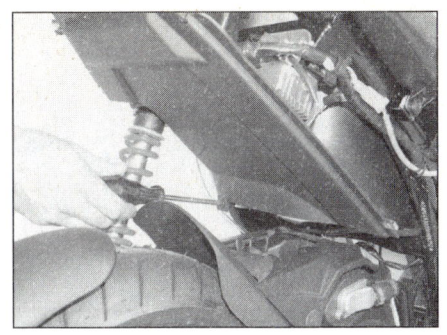

18.15 Undo the mudguard liner screw

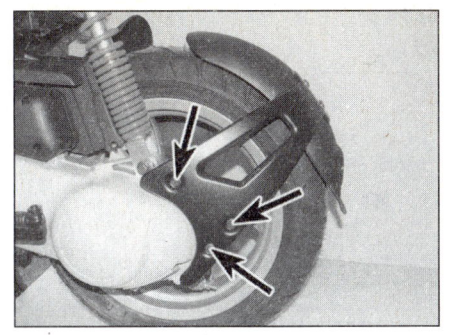

18.17 Mudguard assembly is secured by three screws

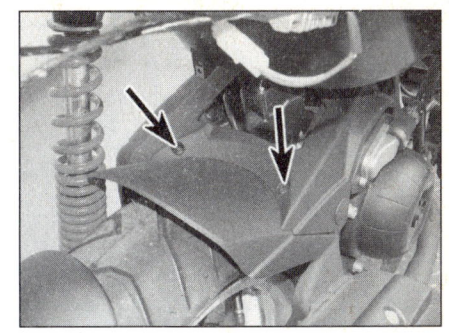

18.18 Undo the screws (arrowed)

mudguard liner and remove it **(see illustration)**.
16 Installation is the reverse of removal. Check the operation of the tail light and turn signals before riding the scooter.

Rear mudguard and hugger

17 Undo the three screws securing the mudguard assembly to the gearbox and lift it off **(see illustration)**.
18 Undo the screws securing the upper engine cover to the hugger **(see illustrations)**.
19 The hugger is secured by one screw on the right-hand side at the back of the engine unit, and two screws on the left-hand side which also secure the back of the air filter housing **(see illustrations)**. Undo the screws and remove the hugger.
20 Installation is the reverse of removal. When refitting the hugger, ensure the screws

on the left-hand side are correctly located through the back of the air filter housing.

Storage compartment

21 Remove the battery and unclip the fuse holder (see Chapter 9).
22 Remove the seat and upper side panels. Remove the front engine access panel.
23 Undo the two screws that secure the bottom of the storage compartment to the frame and the two screws that secure the rear edge of the storage compartment **(see illustrations)**.
24 Remove the oil filler cap and lift off the seal **(see illustration)**.
25 Lift out the storage compartment **(see illustration)**. Temporarily install the oil filler cap.
26 Installation is the reverse of removal.

Floor centre panel

27 First remove both lower side panels

18.19a Hugger is secured by one screw on the right-hand side . . .

28 Undo the two screws securing the back edge of the panel, then undo the three screws securing the panel around the fuel filler cap **(see illustration)**. Note that only three of the

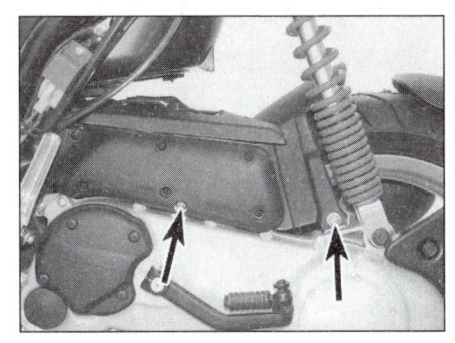

18.19b . . . and two screws on the left-hand side

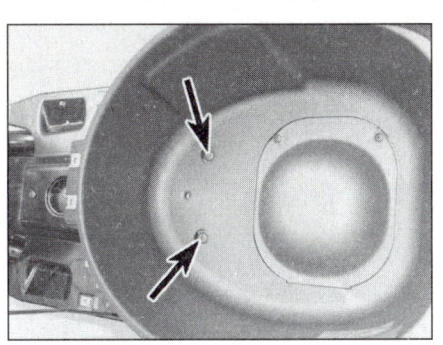

18.23a Remove the two screws in the bottom of the storage compartment . . .

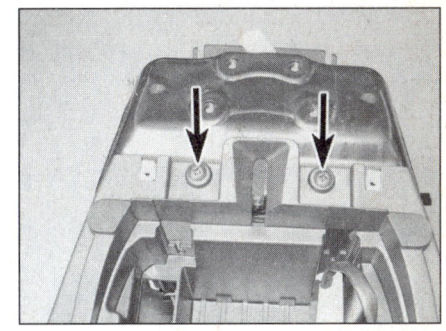

18.23b . . . and the two screws on the rear edge

18.24 Remove the oil filler cap and seal

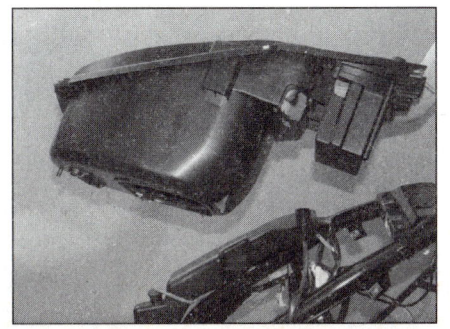

18.25 Lift out the storage compartment

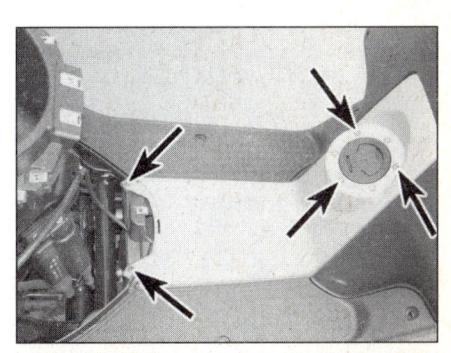

18.28 Undo the screws on the back edge of the panel and around the fuel filler cap

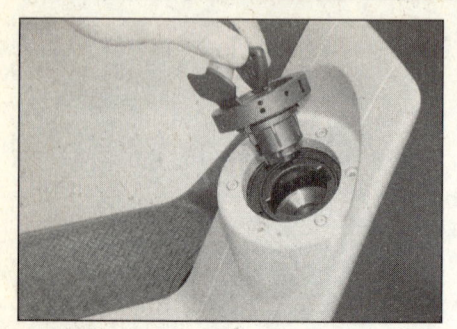

7•46 Frame and bodywork

18.29a Remove the fuel filler cap . . .

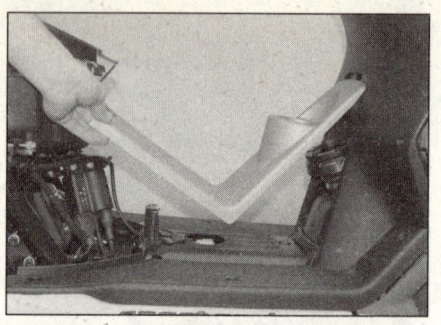

18.29b . . . and lift the floor centre panel off

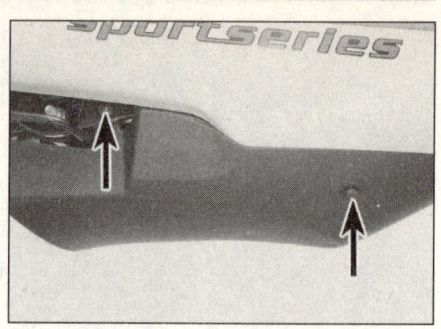

18.31a Belly panel is secured by two screws on each side . . .

six filler cap screws are real screws, the other three are part of the plastic moulding.
29 Unlock the fuel filler cap and remove it, then lift the panel off **(see illustrations)**. Temporarily install the filler cap.
30 Installation is the reverse of removal.

Belly panel
31 The belly panel is secured by two screws on each side and two screws at the front. Remove the front screws, then support the panel and remove the screws in the side and lower the panel down **(see illustrations)**.
32 Installation is the reverse of removal.

Floor panel
33 First remove the floor centre panel.
34 Disconnect the fuel level sender wiring connector **(see illustration)**.
35 Undo the six large screws securing the top of the floor panel to the frame, the two small screws in the lower edge of the kick panel and the two small screws at the rear of

the panel next to the passenger footrests **(see illustrations)**.
36 Lift the floor panel and manoeuvre it off **(see illustration)**.
37 Installation is the reverse of removal. Ensure the brackets on the floor side panels are correctly located on the frame supports before installing the floor panel screws.

Floor side panels
38 First remove the belly panel and the floor panel.
39 Undo the screw securing the floor side panel to the front panel, then lift the side panel off **(see illustrations)**.
40 Installation is the reverse of removal.

18.31b . . . and two screws at the front

18.34 Disconnect the wiring connector

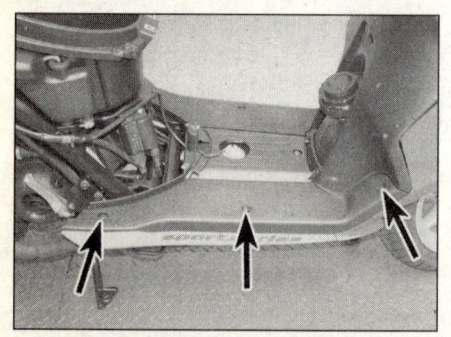

18.35a Floor panel is secured by three large screws on each side . . .

18.35b . . . two screws (arrowed) in the centre front . . .

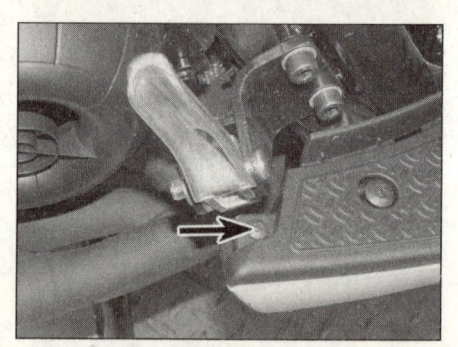

18.35c . . . and a screw (arrowed) next to each passenger footrest

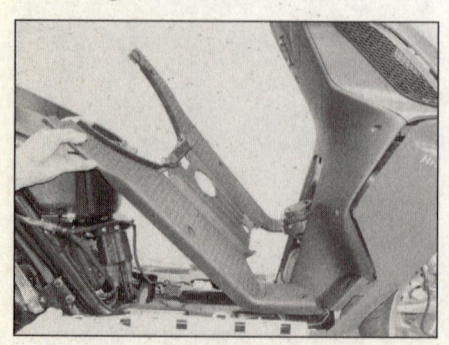

18.36 Lift off the floor panel

18.39a Remove the screw (arrowed) . . .

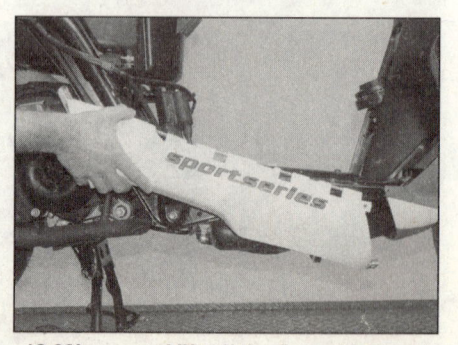

18.39b . . . and lift off the floor side panel

Frame and bodywork 7•47

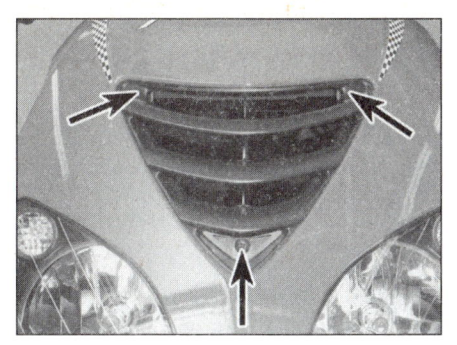

18.41 Front panel grille is secured by three screws (arrowed)

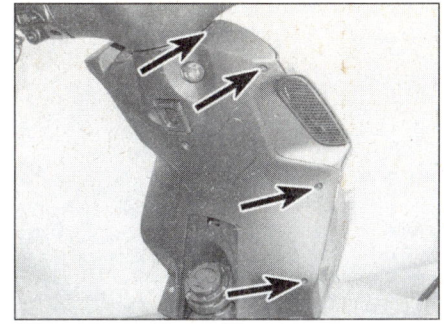

18.45 Remove the four screws (arrowed) on each side . . .

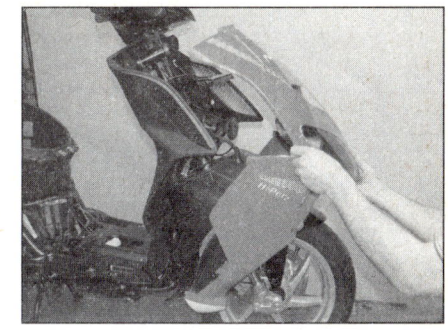

18.46 . . . then lift the panel off

Front panel

41 Undo the three screws securing the front panel grille and remove the grille **(see illustration)**. Remove the two screws located behind the grille.
42 Disconnect the headlight wiring connector and the front turn signal wiring connectors.
43 Remove the floor panel and the floor side panels.
44 Remove the four screws located behind the front forks and front wheel that secure the front panel to the mudguard liner.
45 Undo the eight screws that secure the left and right-hand edges of the front panel to the kick panel **(see illustration)**.
46 Lift the panel off **(see illustration)**.
47 Installation is the reverse of removal. Check the operation of the headlight and turn signals before riding the scooter.

Kick panel

48 Remove the front panel.
49 Undo the three screws securing the fuel filer cap **(see illustration)**.
50 Loosen the hose clip securing the fuel filler neck to the top of the fuel tank, then pull the filler neck off **(see illustrations)**. Stuff a clean rag into the fuel tank opening to prevent anything falling inside.
51 Remove the screw in the centre of the kick panel below the bag hook.
52 Remove the two screws securing the lower edges of the kick panel to the frame **(see illustration)**.
53 Ease the panel back, then lift it out from

18.49 Remove the screws (arrowed) . . .

18.50b . . . and pull the filler neck off

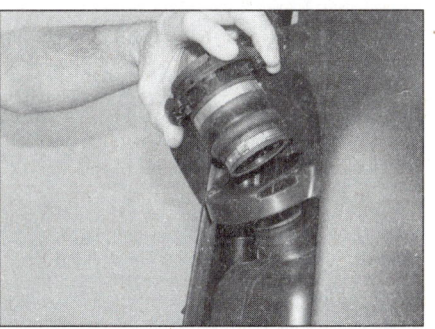

underneath the handlebar covers and lift it off **(see illustrations)**.
54 Temporarily install the fuel filler neck.
55 Installation is the reverse of removal. Ensure that the hose clip on the fuel filler neck is tightened securely **(see illustration)**.

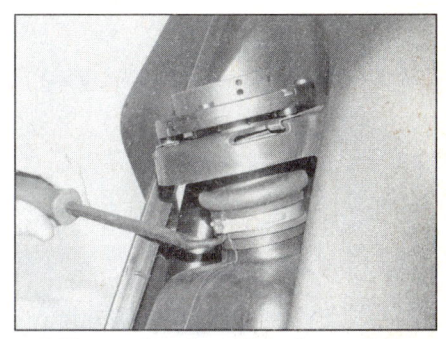

18.50a . . . then loosen the hose clip . . .

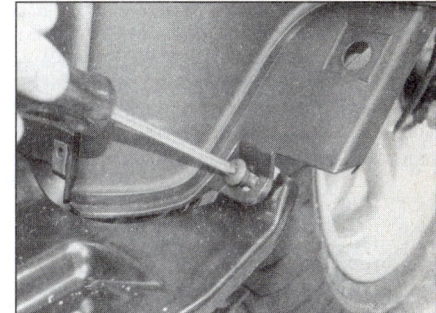

18.52 Remove the lower screws on both sides

Handlebar covers

56 Remove the rear view mirrors. Note that it is not necessary to remove the fly screen on the front handlebar cover.
57 To remove the front cover, remove the

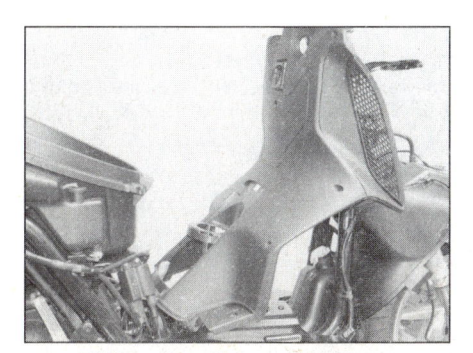

18.53a Ease the panel back . . .

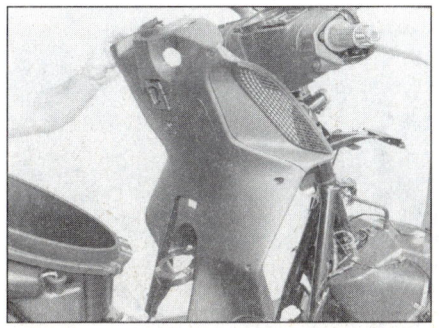

18.53b . . . and away from underneath the handlebar covers

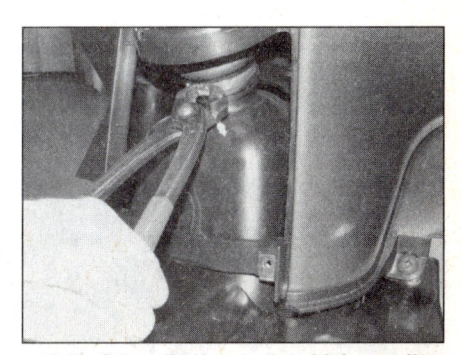

18.55 Crimp the hose clip with hose clip pliers

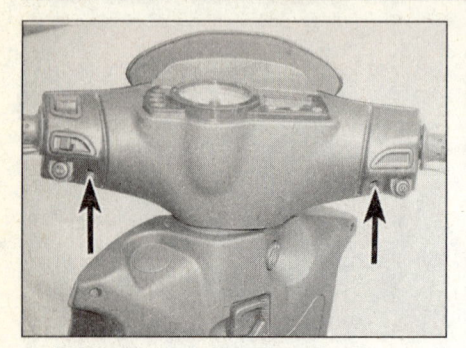

7•48 Frame and bodywork

18.57a Remove the screws in the rear cover (arrowed)

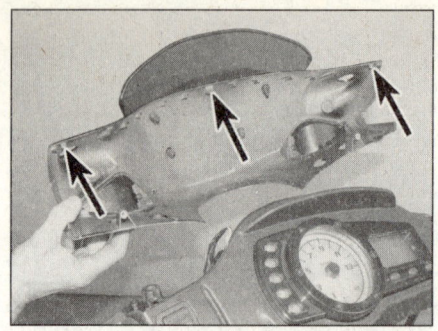

18.57b Note how the pegs on the front cover . . .

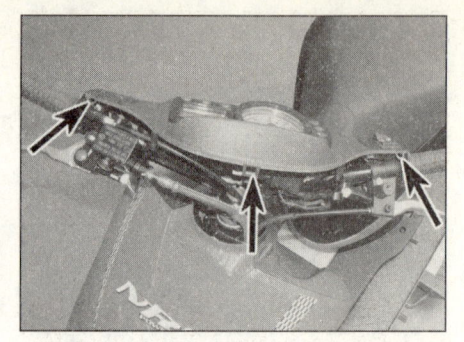

18.57c . . . locate in the holes in the rear cover

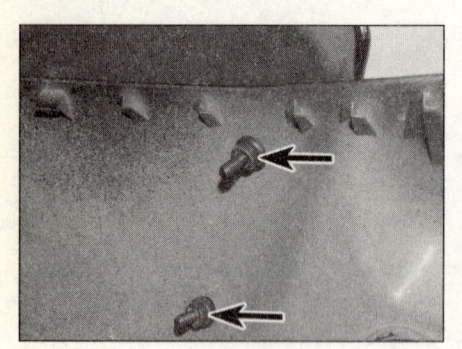

18.58 Flyscreen screws locate in wellnuts (arrowed)

18.59 Rear cover is secured by three screws (arrowed)

screws from the rear cover, then carefully ease the edge of the front cover away to release the pegs which locate into holes in the top edge of the rear cover **(see illustrations)**. These pegs are quite a tight fit and a certain amount of leverage is required, but take care not to apply excessive force as the cover could break.
58 The flyscreen is secured by four screws and wellnuts – if the screws are loosened the wellnuts can become detached from the front cover panel **(see illustration)**. If you need to remove the flyscreen, first remove the front cover as a precaution. Hold the wellnuts and tighten the screws before installing the front cover.
59 To remove the rear cover, first remove the front cover. Remove the screws securing the rear cover to the brackets on the handlebars **(see illustration)**. If the cover is being completely removed rather than just displaced for access, disconnect the instrument cluster and handlebar switch wiring connectors, noting which fits where, and the speedometer cable, then remove the cover. If required, separate the instrument cluster from the cover (see Chapter 9).
60 Installation is the reverse of removal. Check the operation of the switches before riding the scooter.

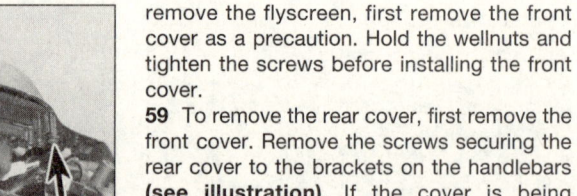

19 X8 body panels – removal and installation

Seat

1 Unlock the seat, using either the electronic release button on the left handlebar or the lever inside the fuel filler flap, and swing it upright.
2 Remove the three screws securing the seat hinge and remove the seat.
3 Installation is the reverse of removal.

Engine access panels

19.4a Engine access panel on the right-hand side

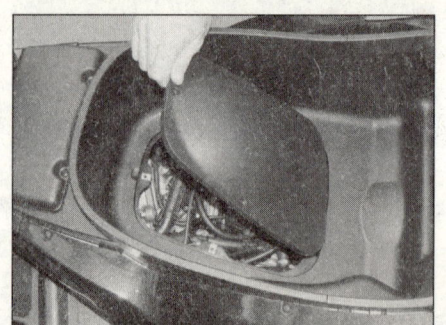

19.4b Engine access panel inside the storage compartment

4 Undo the screw securing the panel and lift it off **(see illustration)**. To remove the access panel in the storage compartment, first lift up the seat. Undo the three screws securing the panel and remove the panel **(see illustration)**.
5 Installation is the reverse of removal.

Number plate light panel

6 Undo the two screws securing the light panel, then pull the panel back to release the tabs on the top edge **(see illustrations)**. Disconnect the wiring connector.
7 Installation is the reverse of removal.

Grab handle

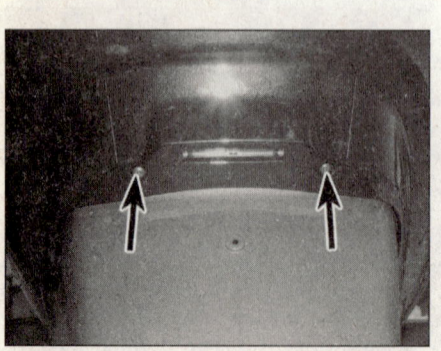

19.6a Undo the screws (arrowed) . . .

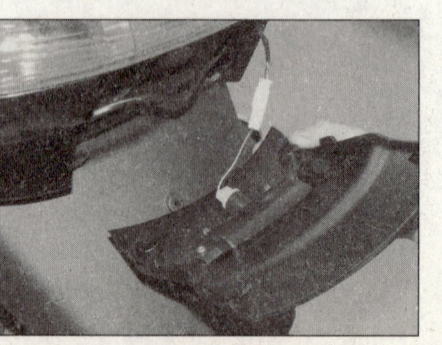

19.6b . . . and pull the panel back

8 Lift up the seat, then open the boot, using either the electronic release button on the

Frame and bodywork 7•49

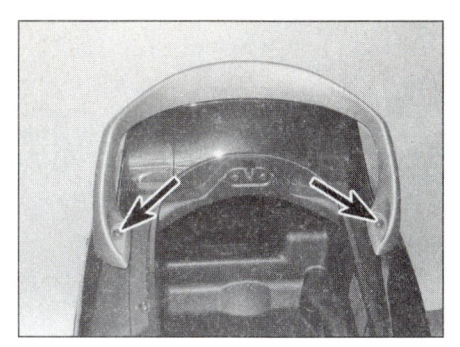

19.9a Undo the screws (arrowed) . . .

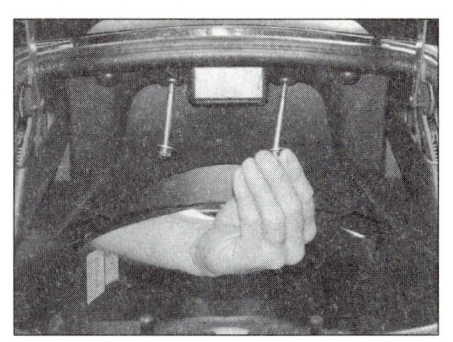

19.9b . . . and the bolts inside the boot . . .

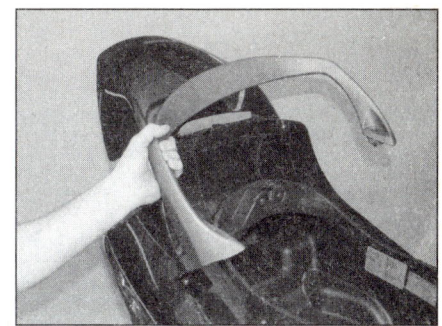

19.9c . . . and lift off the grab handle

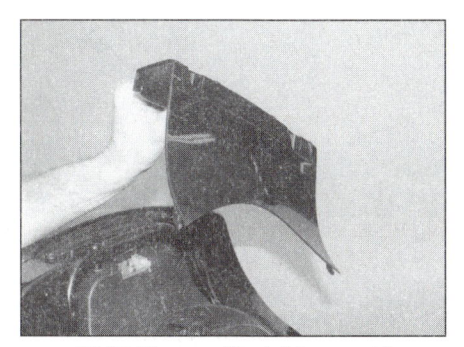

19.12 Remove the joining panel

19.13a Undo the screws (arrowed) at the rear . . .

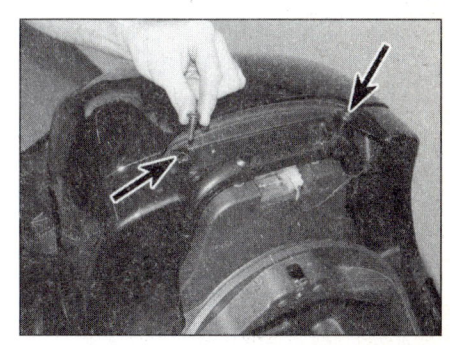

19.13b . . . and on the top edge

right handlebar or the lever inside the fuel filler flap.
9 Undo the two screws securing the handle to the sides of the scooter, then undo the two bolts inside the boot and lift the handle off. **(see illustrations)**.
10 Installation is the reverse of removal.

Side panels
11 First remove the tail light and turn signal lights (see Chapter 9). Remove the number plate light panel and the grab handle.
12 Ease the rear joining panel up and lift it off, noting how the tabs locate **(see illustration)**.

13 Undo the two shouldered screws at the rear of the side panels and the two on the rear upper edge **(see illustrations)**.
14 Undo the two screws on the edge of each side panel, inside the boot lid opening **(see illustration)**.
15 Undo the two screws on the top edge of each side panel, the screw on the back edge of the floor panel, and the screw on the lower edge of the side panel **(see illustration)**.
16 Ease the panel back, noting how the tabs on the upper front edge locate inside the rear edge of the front underseat panel, and lift it off **(see illustration)**.

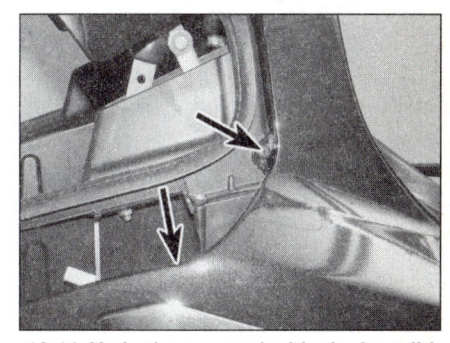

19.14 Undo the screws inside the boot lid on both sides

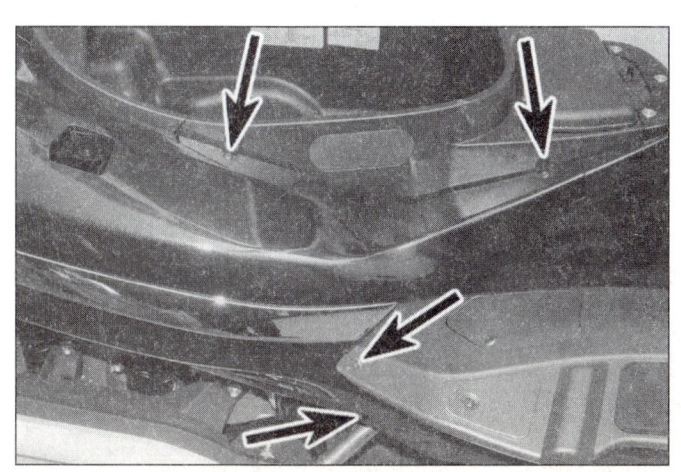

19.15 Undo the four screws on each side as described

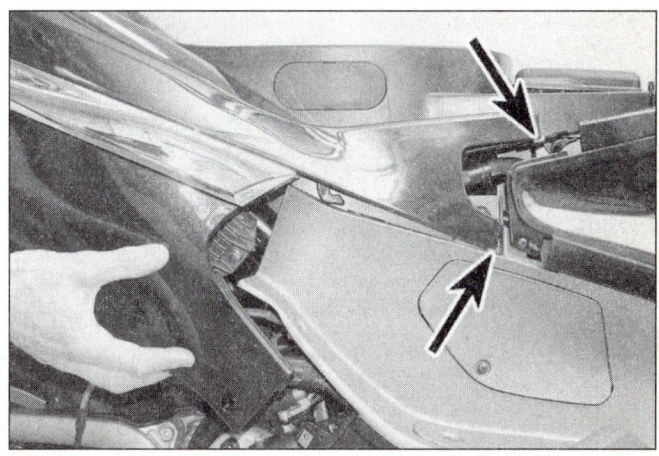

19.16 Note how the tabs (arrowed) locate

7•50 Frame and bodywork

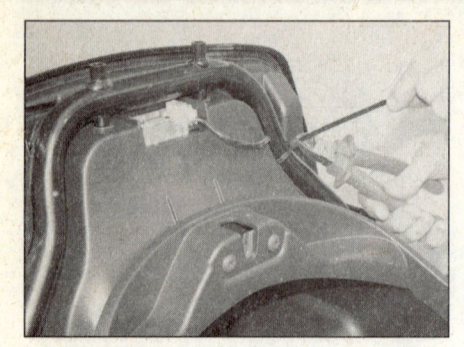

19.19a Unclip the wiring connector

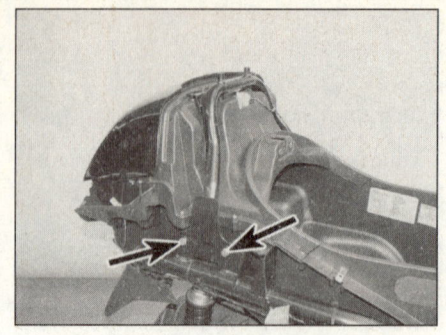

19.19b Undo the bolts on each side . . .

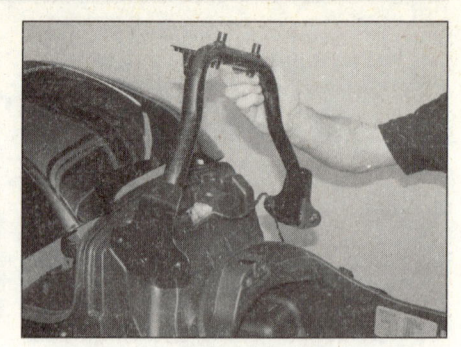

19.19c . . . and lift the bracing bar off

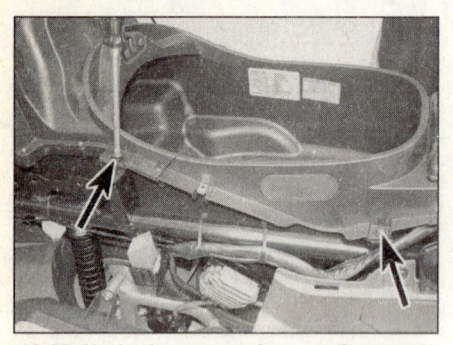

19.20 Undo the screws (arrowed) on each side

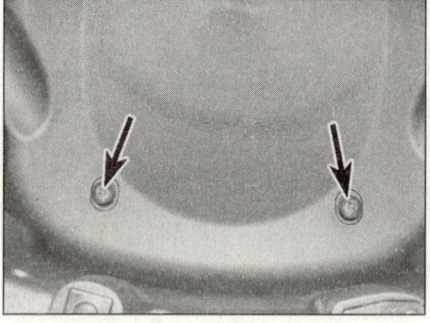

19.21 Undo the screws inside the boot

19.22 Undo the screw on each side of the mudguard

19.23 Manoeuvre the mudguard out as described

17 Installation is the reverse of removal. Check the operation of the tail light and turn signals before riding the scooter.

Rear mudguard

18 First remove the side panels.
19 Unclip the boot light wiring from the bracing bar, then undo the four bolts that secure the bar to the frame and lift it off **(see illustrations)**.
20 Undo the two screws on each side that secure the outer edge of the storage compartment to the frame **(see illustration)**.

21 Undo the two screws inside the bottom of the boot **(see illustration)**.
22 Undo the screw on each side of the mudguard **(see illustration)**.
23 Ease the rear of the boot/storage compartment up and lift the inner edge of the mudguard over the studs on the frame and draw it out **(see illustration)**.
24 Installation is the reverse of removal.

Front panel

25 First remove the mirrors (see Section 3).
26 Remove the four screws securing the front insert panel and lift it off **(see illustrations)**.

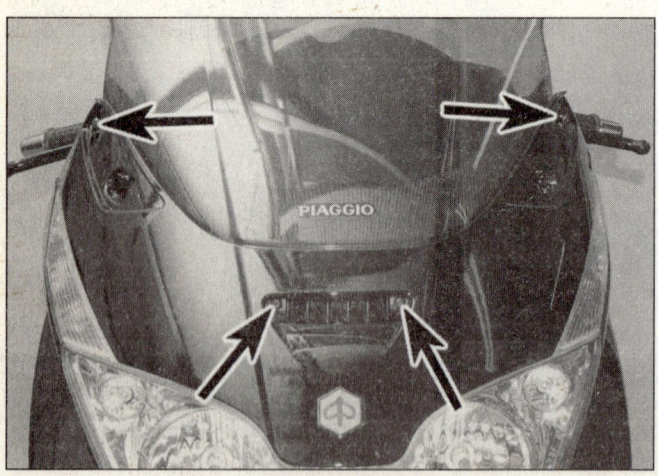

19.26a Remove the screws (arrowed) . . .

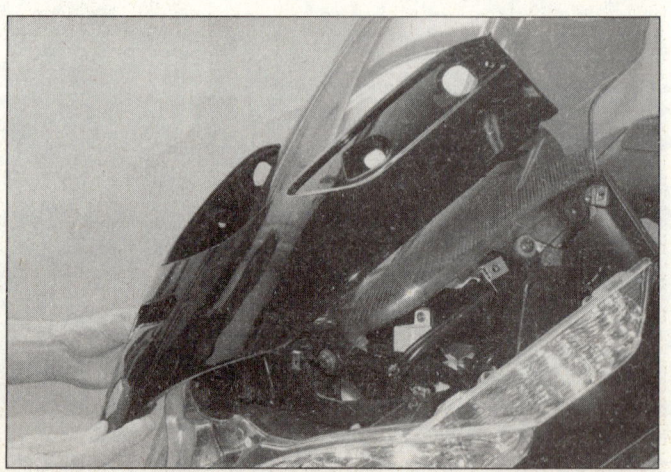

19.26b . . . and lift the insert panel off

Frame and bodywork 7•51

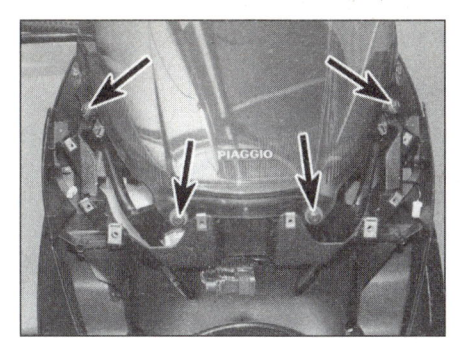

19.28a Undo the screws (arrowed) . . .

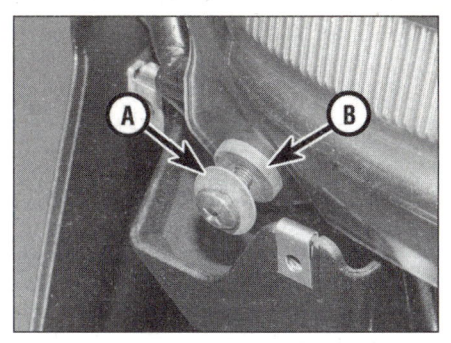

19.28b . . . note the position of the washer (A) and grommet (B) . . .

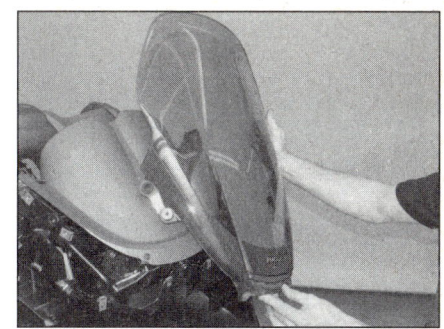

19.28c . . . then lift the windshield off

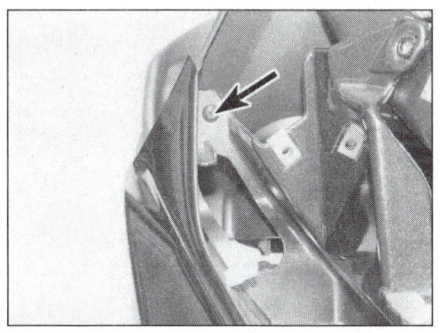

19.29 Undo the screw (arrowed) on each side

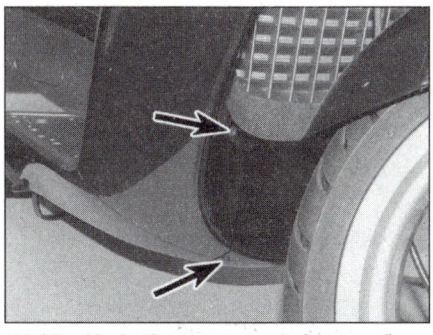

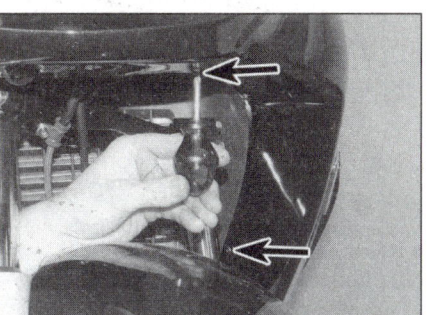

19.30a Undo the two screws (arrowed) on each side . . .

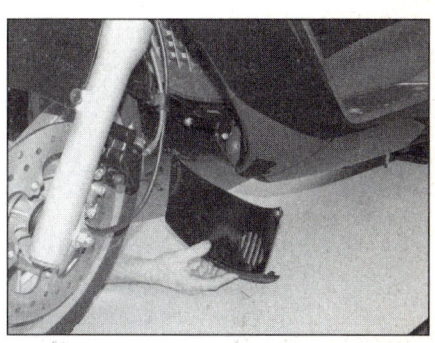

19.30b . . . and remove the insert panel

27 Follow the procedure in Chapter 9 and remove the turn signals and headlight assembly.
28 Undo the four screws securing the windshield, noting the position of the washers and grommets on the screws, then remove the windshield (see illustrations). Fit new grommets on reassembly if they are damaged or perished.
29 Undo the screw inside the top edge of the front panel on each side (see illustration).
30 Undo the two screws on each side securing the lower insert panel at the bottom of the front panel and remove the insert panel (see illustrations).
31 Undo the two screws on each side securing the front panel to the radiator cowling (see illustration).

32 Pull back the floor mat and undo the four screws on each side securing the front panel to the kick panel (see illustrations).
33 Undo the two screws on each side

19.31 Undo the two screws (arrowed) on each side

securing the front panel to the floor panel (see illustration).
34 Unclip the connector for the headlight wiring from its bracket (see illustration).

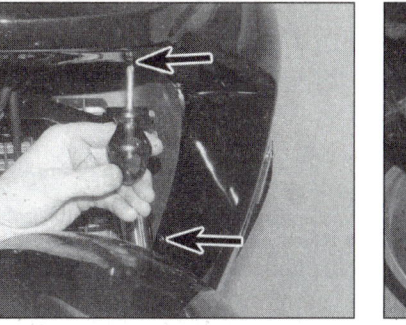

19.32a Pull back the floor mat . . .

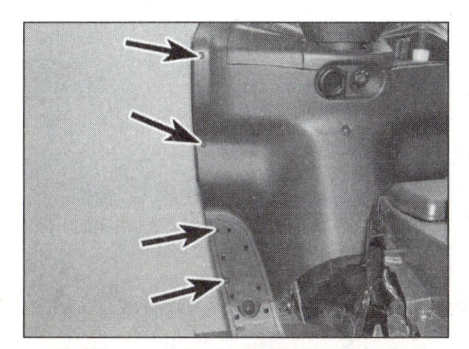

19.32b . . . then undo the four screws (arrowed) on each side

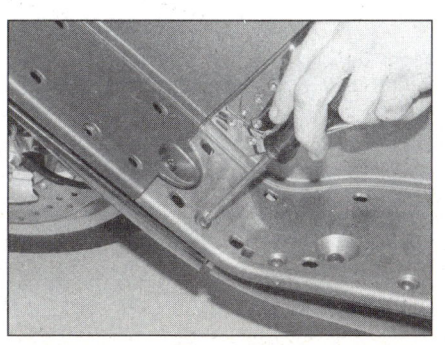

19.33 Undo the single screw on each side

19.34 Unclip the headlight wiring connector

7•52 Frame and bodywork

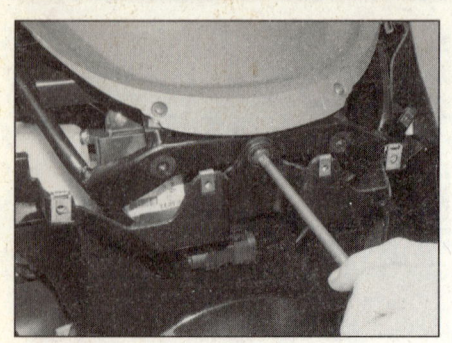

19.35a Undo the centre mounting screw

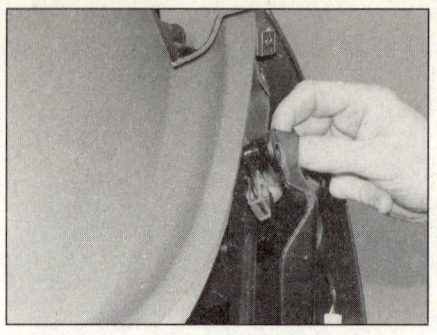

19.35b Ease the mounting lugs off the mirror brackets

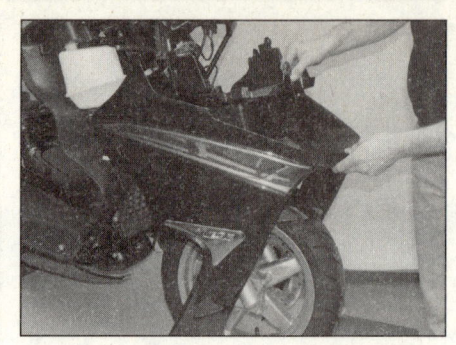

19.36 Manoeuvre the front panel off

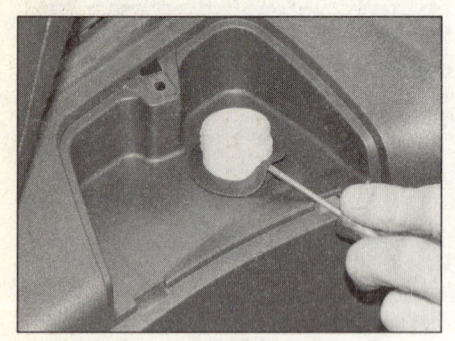

19.39a Remove the seal from the reservoir neck

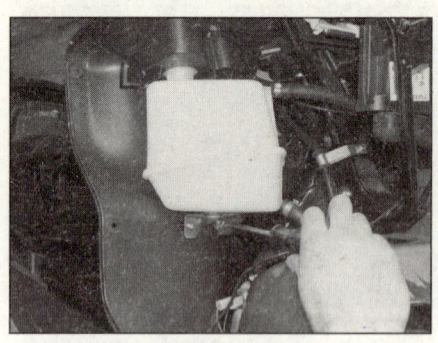

19.39b Remove the reservoir support bracket

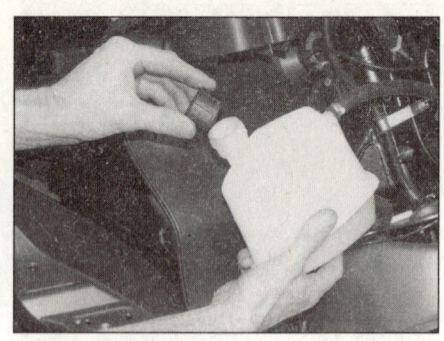

19.39c Secure the reservoir and refit the cap

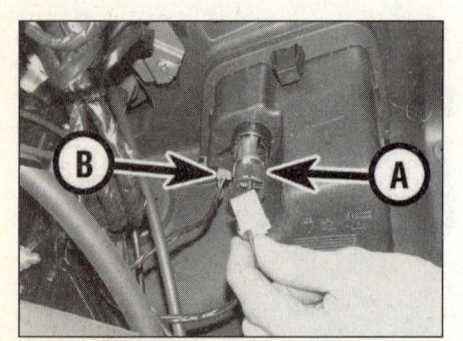

19.40 Disconnect the auxiliary socket (A) and clock reset button (B) connectors

35 Undo the centre mounting screw, then ease the lugs on the front panel off the mirror brackets **(see illustrations)**.
36 Pull the front panel forwards and lift it off **(see illustration)**.
37 Installation is the reverse of removal. Check the operation of the headlight and turn signals before riding the scooter.

Kick panel

38 First remove the seat and the front panel. Disconnect the battery negative (-ve) terminal (see Chapter 9).
39 Remove the coolant reservoir cap and prise out the seal **(see illustration)**. Undo the screws securing the reservoir bracket to the inside of the kick panel and lower the reservoir out of the kick panel; install the cap and secure the reservoir to the frame with a cable tie to avoid straining the coolant hose **(see illustrations)**.
40 Disconnect the wiring connectors for the auxiliary socket and clock reset button **(see illustration)**.
41 Undo the two screws on each side securing the top edge of the kick panel **(see illustration)**.
42 Undo the screw securing the small chrome panel on each side and remove the panel **(see illustration)**.
43 Undo the screw on each side securing the lower edge of the kick panel to the floor centre panel, then undo the shouldered screw on each side securing the kick panel to the frame **(see illustration)**.
44 Undo the screw in the centre of the kick panel **(see illustration)**.

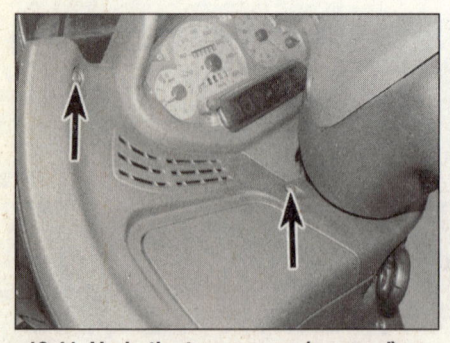

19.41 Undo the two screws (arrowed) on each side

19.42 Chrome panel is secured by single screw

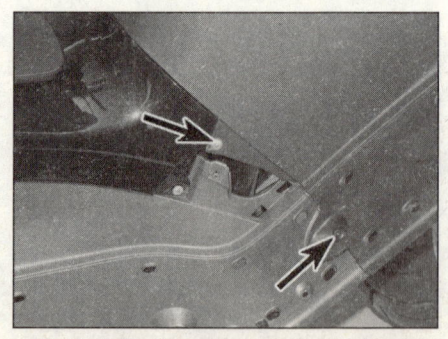

19.43 Undo the screws on each side as described

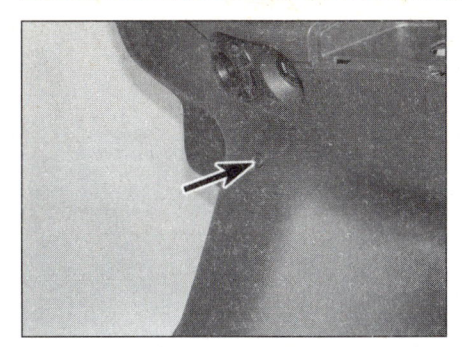

Frame and bodywork 7•53

19.44 Undo the screw in the centre of the panel

19.45a Lift the lower edge of the kick panel . . .

19.45b . . . then manoeuvre it off

19.46 Note the location of the immobiliser transponder aerial (arrowed)

19.48 Undo the two screws (arrowed) on each side

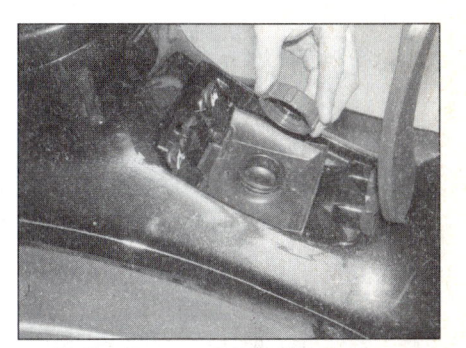

19.49a Remove the fuel filler cap . . .

45 Lift the kick panel to release the tabs on its lower edge from the floor centre panel, then manoeuvre it off **(see illustrations)**.
46 Installation is the reverse of removal. Ensure the ignition immobiliser transponder aerial is correctly positioned on the ignition (main) switch **(see illustration)**.

Floor and belly panels

47 First remove the side panels and the kick panel.
48 Undo the two screws on each side securing the floor centre panel to the floor panels **(see illustration)**.
49 Open the fuel filler flap; remove the filler cap and lift off the seal **(see illustrations)**. Ease the floor centre panel up until it is clear of the top edges of the floor panels.
50 Undo the screws securing the floor panel to the frame and lift the panel off **(see illustrations)**. Note that one half of the belly panel will come off

with the floor panel; on the left-hand side, extend the side stand and ease the belly panel off over the stand. Temporarily install the fuel filler cap.
51 Installation is the reverse of removal.

Floor centre panel

52 First remove the floor and belly panels.

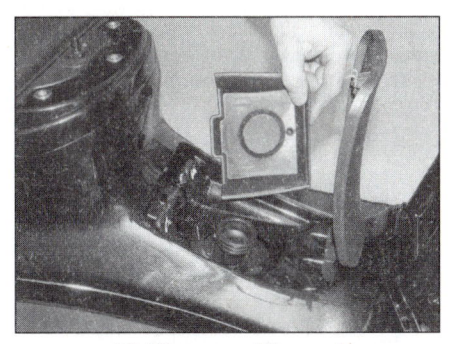

19.49b . . . and the seal

53 Identify the cables running from the levers in the floor centre panel to the seat (upper) and boot lid (lower) actuators. Disconnect the inner cable ends from the actuators and ease the outer cables out of the cable stops **(see illustration)**. Release the cables from any ties securing them to the frame **(see illustration)**.

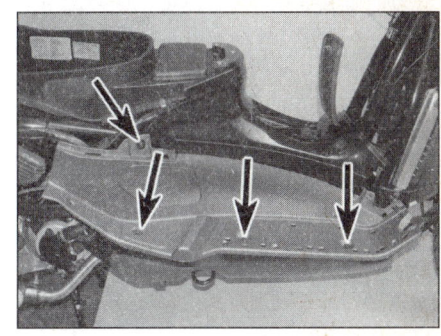

19.50a Remove the screws (arrowed) . . .

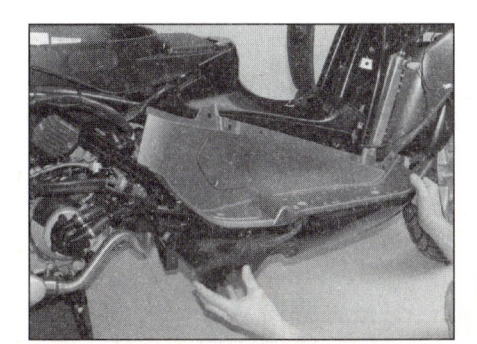

19.50b . . . and lift the panel off

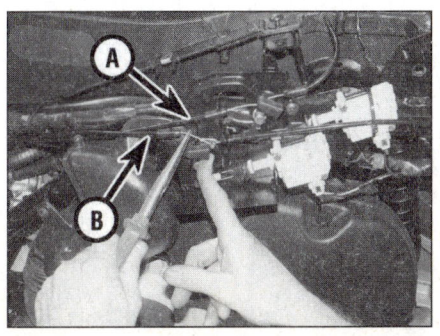

19.53a Disconnect the cables connected to the seat (A) and boot lid (B) actuators

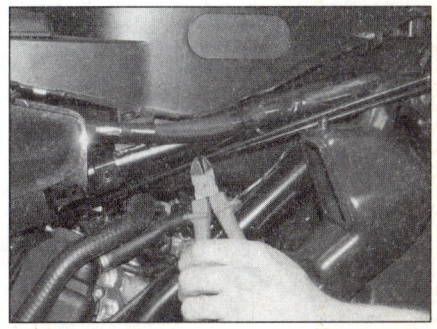

19.53b Release the cables from any ties

7•54 Frame and bodywork

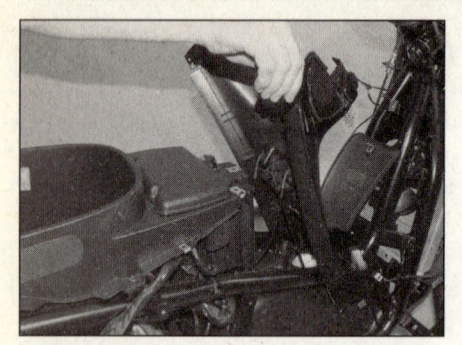

19.54a Tip the panel forwards to access the catch mechanism . . .

19.54b . . . then disconnect the fuel filler flap cable . . .

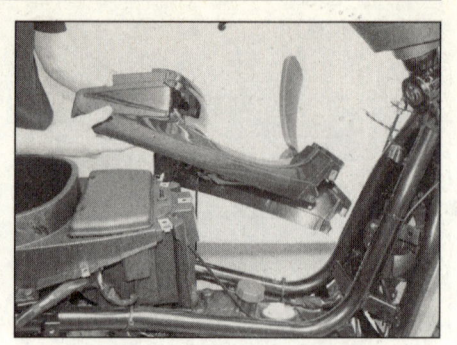

19.54c . . . and lift the panel off

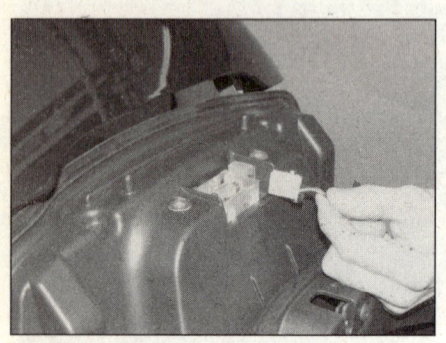

19.59a Disconnect the boot light wiring connector

19.59b Prise out the boot light unit

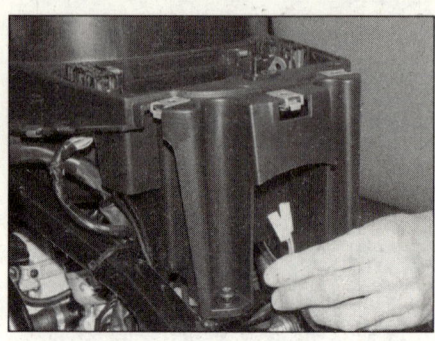

19.60a Disconnect the seat open switch . . .

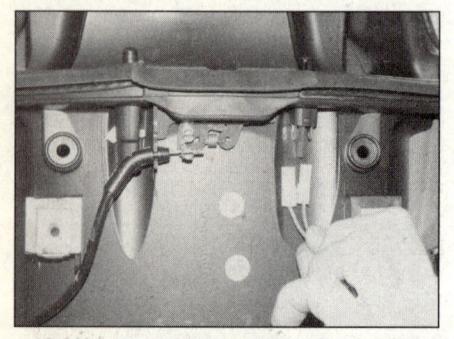

19.60b . . . and boot open switch wiring connectors

54 If not already done, remove the fuel filler cap, then lift the rear of the floor centre panel and tip it forwards to access the catch mechanism for the fuel filler flap **(see illustration)**. Disconnect the cable and lift the panel off **(see illustrations)**. Temporarily install the fuel filler cap.
55 Installation is the reverse of removal. Check the operation of the seat, boot lid and fuel filler flap release mechanisms before installing the fixing screws.

Storage compartment (boot)

56 First remove the side panels, seat and floor centre panel.
57 Remove the battery (see Chapter 9).

58 Unclip the boot light wiring from the bracing bar, then undo the four bolts that secure the bar to the frame and lift it off **(see illustrations 19.19a, 19b and 19c)**.
59 Disconnect the boot light wiring connectors **(see illustration)**. If required, displace the boot light unit **(see illustration)**.
60 Disconnect the seat open light switch and the boot lid open light switch wiring connectors **(see illustrations)**.
61 Disconnect the inner cable ends from the seat and boot lid actuators and ease the outer cables out of the cable stops **(see illustration)**
62 Undo the two screws on each side that secure the outer edge of the storage

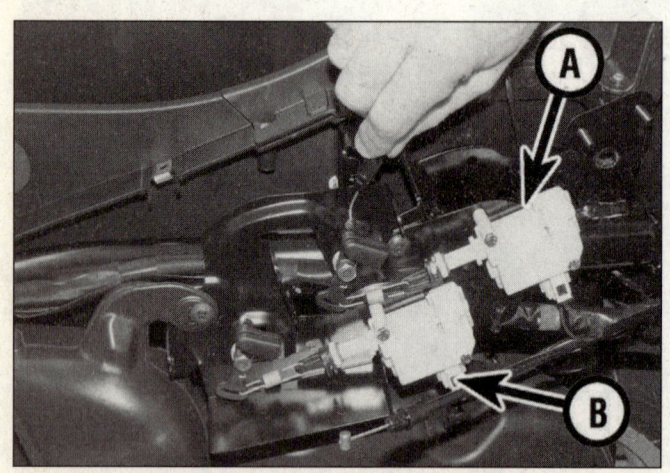

19.61 Disconnect the cables from the seat catch (A) and boot catch (B) actuators

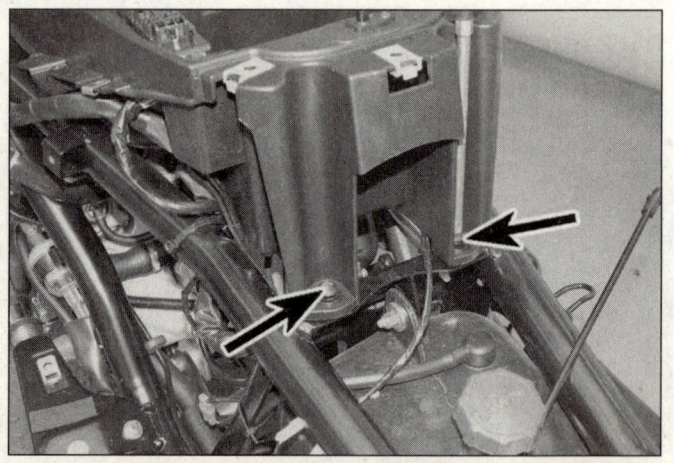

19.64 Undo the screws (arrowed) at the front of the storage compartment

Frame and bodywork 7•55

19.65a Unclip the fuse holders . . .

19.65b . . . and lift out the storage compartment

19.65c Note the location of the plain washers

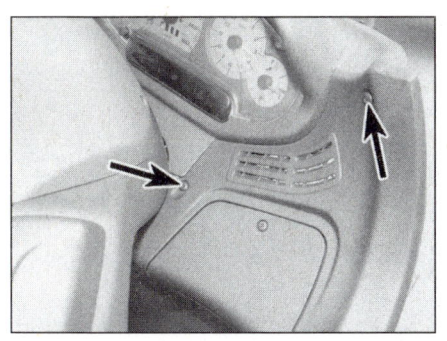

19.68 Undo the screws (arrowed) on each side

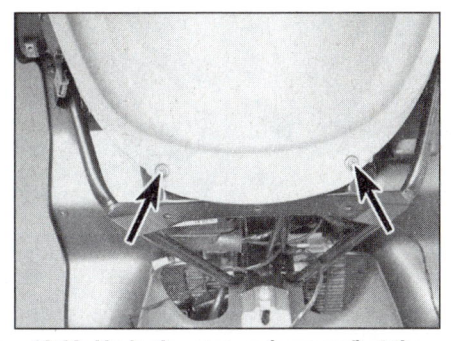

19.69 Undo the screws (arrowed) at the front

19.70a Disconnect the speedometer cable (arrowed) . . .

compartment to the frame **(see illustration 19.20)**.
63 Undo the two screws inside the bottom of the boot **(see illustration 19.21)**.
64 Undo the two screws securing the front of the storage compartment **(see illustration)**.
65 Raise the front of the storage compartment and unclip the fuse holders, then lift the storage compartment out **(see illustrations)**. Note the location of the plain washers on the front mounting lugs **(see illustration)**.
66 Installation is the reverse of removal. Check the operation of the seat and boot lid release mechanisms before installing the fixing screws.

Cockpit trim panel

67 Follow the procedure in Steps 25 to 28

and remove the turn signals, headlight assembly and windshield.
68 Undo the two screws on each side on the top edge of the kick panel **(see illustration)**.
69 Undo the two screws on the front edge of the cockpit trim panel **(see illustration)**.
70 Ease the trim panel up and disconnect the speedometer cable, then disconnect the instrument cluster wiring connectors and lift the panel off **(see illustrations)**. If required, separate the instrument cluster from the trim panel (see Chapter 9).
71 Installation is the reverse of removal. Check the operation of the instruments and warning lights.

Handlebar covers

72 Undo the screws and remove the centre cover **(see illustration)**.
73 Undo the screws and remove the covers

for the front and rear brake hydraulic reservoirs **(see illustration)**.
74 Undo the screws on the underside of the front cover, then ease the edge of the front cover away to release the pegs which locate

19.70b . . . and the instrument cluster wiring connectors

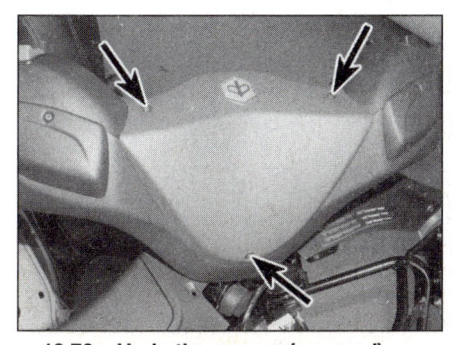

19.72a Undo the screws (arrowed) . . .

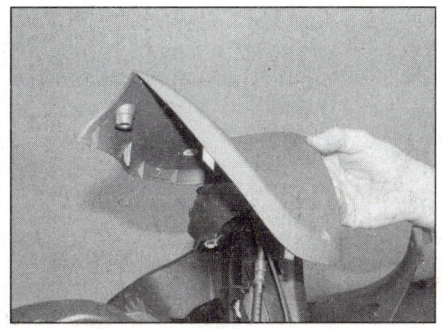

19.72b . . . and lift off the cover

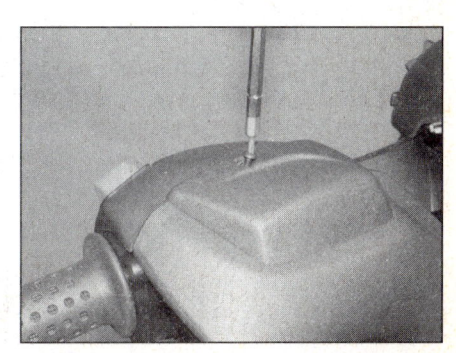

19.73 Brake reservoir covers are secured by single screw

7•56 Frame and bodywork

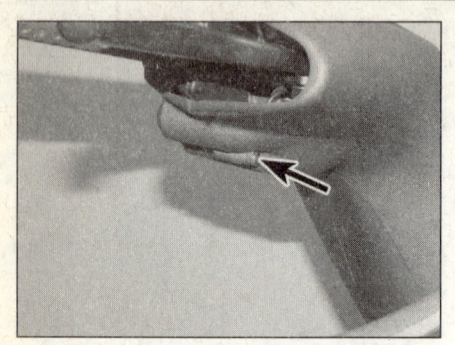

19.74a Undo the single screw on each side . . .

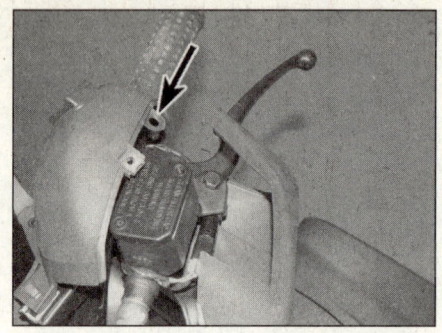

19.74b . . . then ease the pegs out of the holes (arrowed) as described . . .

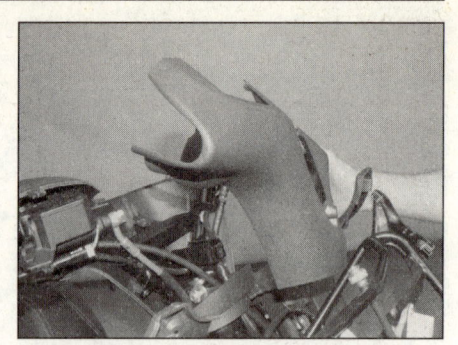

19.74c . . . and lift the cover off

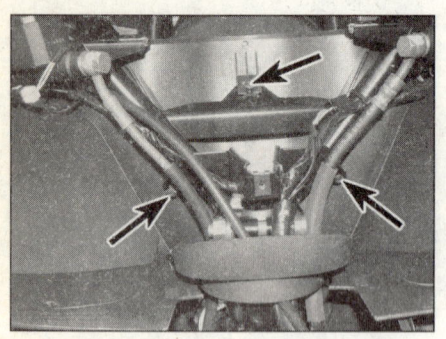

19.75a Back cover is secured by three screws (arrowed)

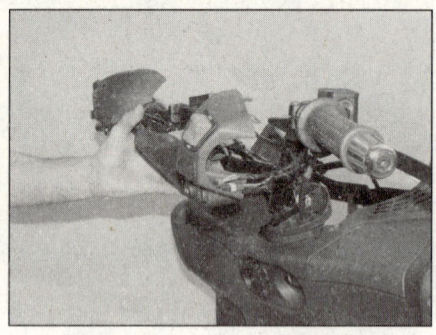

19.75b Draw the cover back and disconnect the switch wiring connectors

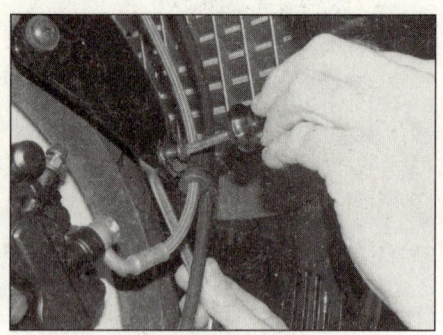

19.77 Release the brake hose and speedometer cable clip from the mudguard

into holes in the top edge of the rear cover **(see illustrations)**.

75 The back cover is secured to the handlebars with three screws **(see illustration)**. To remove the cover, undo the screws and displace the cover, then disconnect the switch wiring connectors, noting where they fit **(see illustration)**.

76 Installation is the reverse of removal. Check the operation of the switches before riding the scooter.

Front mudguard

77 Counterhold the nut and undo the screw securing the hydraulic hose and speedometer cable clip to the mudguard **(see illustration)**. Undo the four mudguard mounting screws and lift off the mudguard.

78 Installation is the reverse of removal.

Chapter 8
Brakes, wheels and tyres

Refer to the beginning of Chapter 1 for model identification details

Contents

Brake cables – renewal 10	Front wheel and hub assembly – removal and installation 13
Brake fluid level check .... see *Daily (pre-ride) checks*	General information 1
Brake light switches – check and renewal .... see Chapter 9	Rear disc brake – inspection, removal and installation 6
Brake hoses, pipes and unions – inspection and renewal 7	Rear wheel and hub assembly – removal and installation 14
Brake shoe/pad wear check .... see Chapter 1	Tyres – general information and fitting 16
Brake system bleeding (disc brake models) 8	Tyres – pressure, tread depth and condition see *Daily (pre-ride) checks*
Brake system check .... see Chapter 1	Wheels – general check .... see Chapter 1
Drum brakes (front and rear) – check and shoe renewal 9	Wheel bearings – check .... see Chapter 1
Front brake caliper – removal, overhaul and installation 3	Wheel bearings – removal, inspection and installation 15
Front brake disc – inspection, removal and installation 4	Wheels – alignment check 12
Front brake master cylinder – removal and installation 5	Wheels – inspection and repair 11
Front brake pads – removal, inspection and renewal 2	

Degrees of difficulty

Easy, suitable for novice with little experience	**Fairly easy,** suitable for beginner with some experience	**Fairly difficult,** suitable for competent DIY mechanic	**Difficult,** suitable for experienced DIY mechanic	**Very difficult,** suitable for expert DIY or professional

Specifications

Brakes (disc type)
Fluid type	DOT 4
Pad minimum thickness	1.5 mm
Disc maximum runout	0.1 mm

Brakes (drum type)
Lining minimum thickness	1.5 mm
Brake lever freeplay	10 to 15 mm

Wheels
Maximum wheel runout (front and rear)
Axial (side-to-side)	2.0 mm
Radial (out-of-round)	2.0 mm
Maximum axle runout (front and rear)	0.2 mm

Tyres
Tyre pressures and sizes	see Chapter 1

8•2 Brakes, wheels and tyres

Torque settings

Front brake pad pins	19 to 25 Nm
Brake caliper mounting bolts	20 to 25 Nm
Brake disc mounting bolts	
All LX and GT models, X8 125	5 to 6.5 Nm
All other models	8 to 10 Nm
Brake hose banjo bolts	15 to 25 Nm
Front wheel bolts (monoshock models)	20 to 25 Nm
Front hub nut (monoshock models)	
Super Hexagon 125	85 Nm
All other models	75 to 90 Nm
Front axle nut (telescopic fork models)	40 to 50 Nm
Front axle pinch-bolts	7 Nm
Rear hub nut	
Zip 125, ET4 (LEADER), B125, X9 125	125 Nm
All Fly models, all LX models, NRG Power DT and DD,	
Hexagon, Super Hexagon, Liberty 125, X8 125, all GT models	104 to 126 Nm
All other models	90 to 110 Nm
Rear wheel bolts (disc brake models)	
B125, Liberty 125	34 to 38 Nm
NRG MC3 DD and Power DD, Hexagon, Super Hexagon,	
X9 125, all GT models	20 to 25 Nm

1 General information

The front brake system varies according to model. Some are fitted with a cable-operated single leading shoe drum brake, while others have a single hydraulic disc with an opposed-piston caliper. NRG Power models have a single piston floating caliper and Fly, X8 and GT models have a two-piston floating caliper. The X9 model has twin front discs – early models were fitted with opposed piston calipers, later models with two-piston floating calipers. On some front disc brake models, the master cylinder is integral with the fluid reservoir on the right handlebar, whereas on others it is mounted on the steering stem and activated by a cable from the brake lever.

The rear brake system is either a cable-operated single leading shoe drum or a hydraulically-operated disc. The brake master cylinder is integral with the fluid reservoir on the left handlebar. On X9 models, the operation of the front left-hand and rear disc brakes is linked.

All models covered in this manual are fitted with cast alloy wheels designed for tubeless tyres only.

Caution: *Disc brake components rarely require disassembly. Do not disassemble components unless absolutely necessary. If a hydraulic brake line is loosened, the entire system must be disassembled, drained, cleaned and then properly filled and bled upon reassembly. Do not use solvents on internal brake components. Solvents will cause the seals to swell and distort. Use only clean brake fluid or denatured alcohol for cleaning. Use care when working with brake fluid as it can injure your eyes and it will damage painted surfaces and plastic parts.*

2 Front brake pads – removal, inspection and renewal

⚠️ **Warning:** *The dust created by the brake system may contain asbestos, which is harmful to your health. Never blow it out with compressed air and don't inhale any of it. An approved filtering mask should be worn when working on the brakes.*

Note: *On some models, due to a lack of clearance, it may be necessary to either displace the brake caliper or remove the front wheel to enable the pads to be removed.*

Opposed piston caliper

1 Where fitted, remove the pad cover from the caliper **(see illustration)**. Remove the E-clip from the end of the pad retaining pin, then withdraw the pin, noting how it keeps the pad spring pressed onto the pads, and remove the spring, noting which way round it fits **(see illustrations)**. If required, drive the pin out from the inside using a suitable drift and draw

2.1a Remove the cover . . .

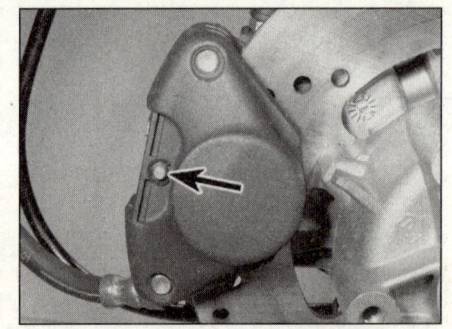

2.1b . . . then remove the E-clip

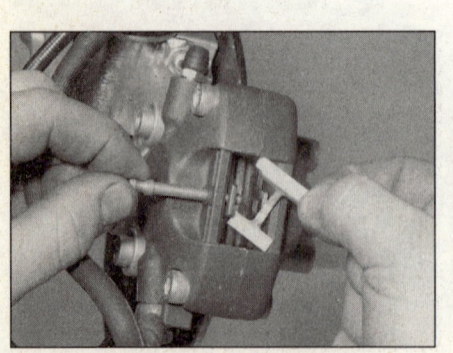

2.1c Withdrawing the pad pin and removing the spring – Piaggio type caliper

2.1d Withdrawing the pad pin and removing the spring – Brembo type caliper

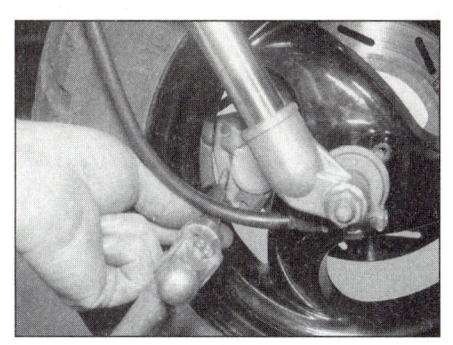

Brakes, wheels and tyres 8•3

2.1e Use a drift to drive out the pin . . .

2.1f . . . and withdraw it using a pair of pliers

2.1g Withdraw the pads from the caliper

it out using pliers **(see illustrations)**. Lift the pads out of the caliper **(see illustrations)**.

2 Inspect the surface of each pad for contamination and check that the friction material has not worn to or beyond the minimum thickness of 1.5 mm **(see illustration)**. If either pad is worn down to, or beyond, the service limit, fouled with oil or grease, or heavily scored or damaged by dirt and debris, both pads must be renewed as a set. **Note:** *It is not possible to degrease the friction material; if the pads are contaminated in any way they must be renewed.*

3 If the pads are in good condition clean them carefully, using a fine wire brush which is completely free of oil and grease to remove all traces of road dirt and corrosion. Any areas of glazing may be removed using emery cloth.

4 Check the condition of the brake disc (see Section 4).

5 Remove all traces of corrosion from the pad pin. Inspect the pin and spring for signs of wear and renew them if necessary.

6 If new pads are being fitted, push the pistons as far back into the caliper as possible using hand pressure or a piece of wood as leverage. Due to the increased friction material thickness of new pads, it may be necessary to remove the master cylinder reservoir cover and diaphragm and syphon out some fluid.

7 Smear the backs of the pads and the shank of the pad pin with copper-based grease, making sure that none gets on the front or sides of the pads **(see illustration)**.

8 Installation of the pads is the reverse of removal. Insert the pads into the caliper so

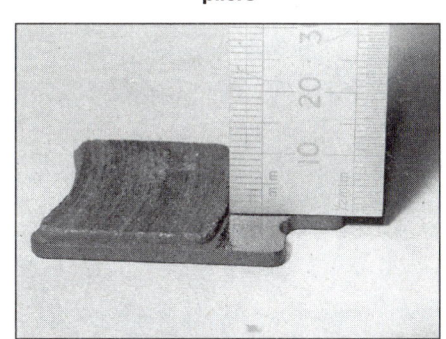

2.2 Check the amount of friction material remaining on each pad

that the friction material faces the disc, then slide the pad retaining pin through the hole in the outer pad **(see illustration)**. Fit the pad spring, making sure it locates correctly onto the pads **(see illustrations)**. Press down on the spring and slide the pin across so that it

2.7 Apply copper grease to the back of each pad . . .

locates in the groove in the middle of the spring and passes through the hole in the inner pad. Tap on the end of the pin to make sure it is fully home, then fit the retaining clip onto its end **(see illustration)**. Where fitted, install the pad cover **(see illustration)**.

2.8a . . . then install the pads

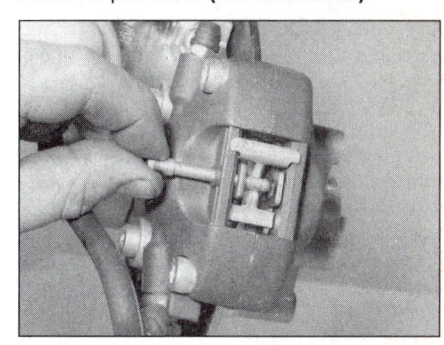

2.8b Fitting the pad pin and spring – Piaggio type caliper

2.8c Fitting the pad pin and spring – Brembo type caliper

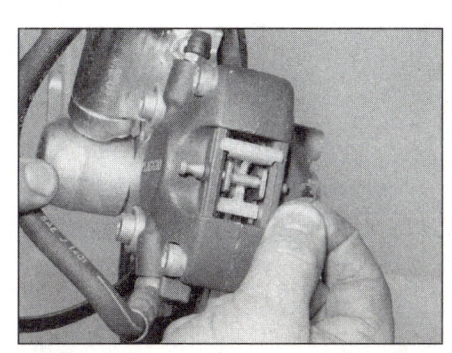

2.8d Fit the E-clip onto the end of the pin . . .

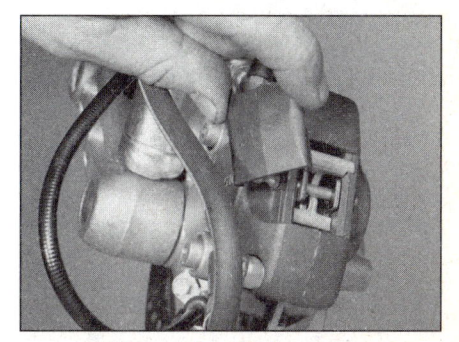

2.8e . . . then fit the cover

8•4 Brakes, wheels and tyres

2.11a Remove the caliper mounting bolts . . .

2.11b . . . and slide the caliper off the disc

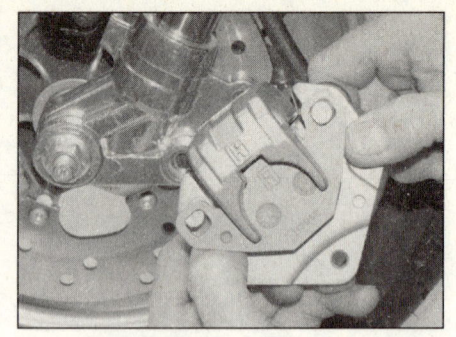

2.12a Push the piston back . . .

2.12b . . . then remove the outer brake pad . . .

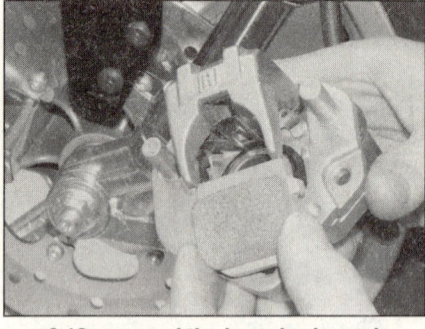

2.12c . . . and the inner brake pad

2.13a Inspect the friction material for wear and contamination

9 Top up the master cylinder reservoir if necessary (see *Daily (pre-ride) checks*), and refit the reservoir cover and diaphragm.
10 Operate the brake lever several times to bring the pads into contact with the disc. Check the operation of the brake before riding the scooter.

Single piston floating caliper

11 Undo the caliper mounting bolts and remove the bolts and washers, then slide the caliper off the disc **(see illustrations)**. Note that the lower bolt is longer than the upper bolt.
12 Push the piston as far back into the caliper as possible using hand pressure or a piece of wood as leverage, then lift the outer (larger) pad off the pad pins **(see illustrations)**. Lift the inner pad out of the caliper, noting how it fits **(see illustration)**.
13 Follow the procedure in Steps 2 to 5 to inspect and clean the pads and disc **(see illustration)**. If required, remove any corrosion from the pad pins and spring **(see illustration)**. Check that the caliper bracket slides freely in and out of the caliper – if not, pull it all the way out, clean any old grease or corrosion off the slider pins, then smear them with fresh grease **(see illustration)**. Renew the pin seals if they are damaged, then slide the bracket back into the caliper.
14 If new pads are being fitted, push the piston as far back into the caliper as possible using hand pressure or a piece of wood as leverage. Due to the increased friction material thickness of new pads, it may be necessary to remove the master cylinder reservoir cover and diaphragm and syphon out some fluid.
15 Smear the backs of the pads and the shanks of the pad pins with copper-based grease, making sure that none gets on the front or sides of the pads.

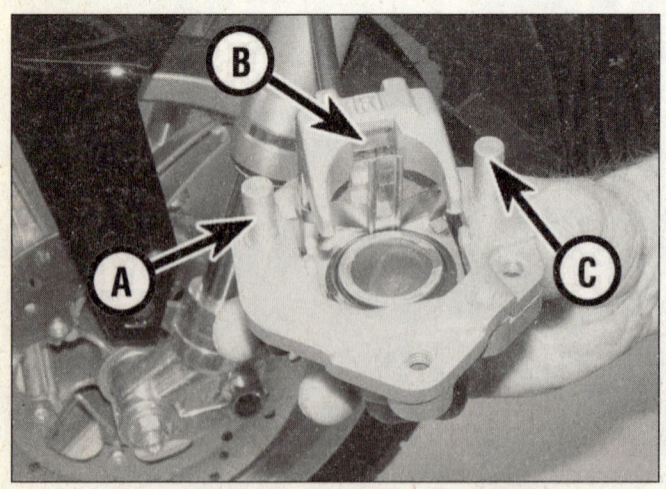

2.13b Inspect the pad pins (A) and spring (B)

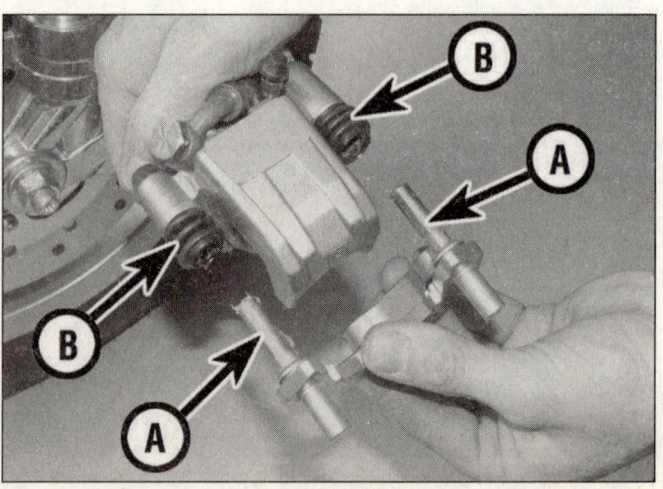

2.13c Inspect the slider pins (A) and pin seals (B)

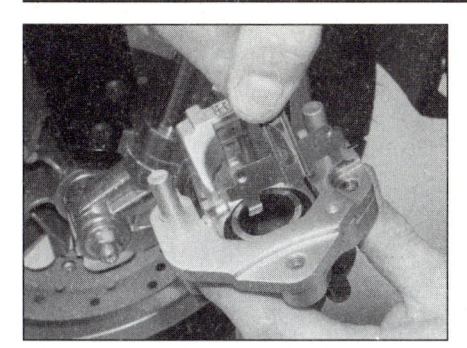

Brakes, wheels and tyres 8•5

2.16a Ensure the pad spring is correctly installed

2.16b Install the pads as described

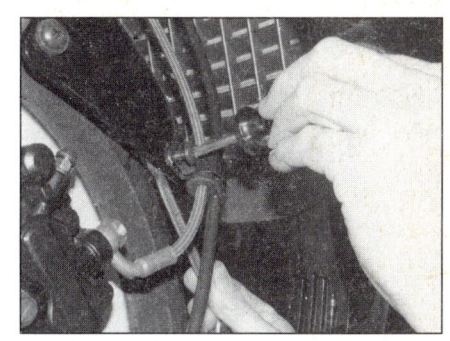

2.18a Free the brake hose from the clip

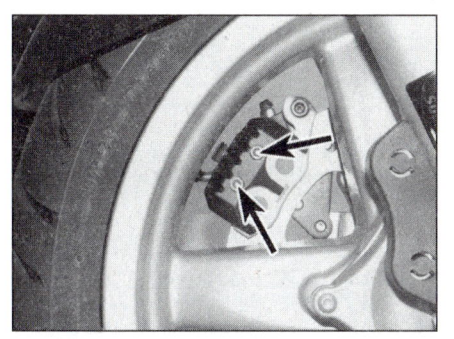

2.18b Loosen the pad retaining pins (arrowed)

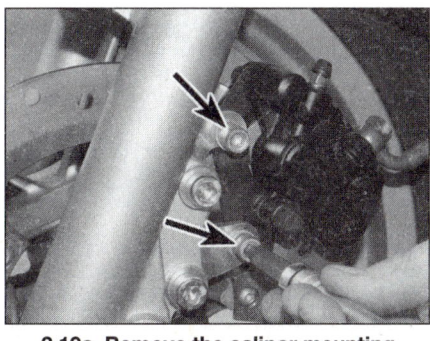

2.19a Remove the caliper mounting bolts . . .

2.19b . . . and slide the caliper off the disc

16 Ensure the pad spring is correctly fitted inside the caliper **(see illustration)**. Install the pads in the reverse order of removal so that the friction material faces the disc, then slide the caliper onto the disc **(see illustration)**.

17 Install the caliper mounting bolts and washers, noting that the longer bolt is fitted in the lower position, then tighten the bolts to the torque setting specified at the beginning of the Chapter.

Two-piston floating caliper

18 Where fitted, free the brake hose from the clip on the front mudguard **(see illustration)**. Before displacing the brake caliper, loosen the pad retaining pins from the opposite side of the front wheel **(see illustration)**.

19 Undo the caliper mounting bolts and remove the bolts and washers, then slide the caliper off the disc **(see illustrations)**.

20 Remove the pad pins and lift the outer pad out of the caliper, noting how it locates, then lift out the inner pad **(see illustrations)**. Note the location of the pad spring **(see illustration)**.

21 Follow the procedure in Steps 2 to 5 to inspect and clean the pads and disc **(see illustration)**. If required, remove any corrosion from the pad pins and spring. Check that the caliper bracket slides freely in and out of the caliper – if not, pull it all the way out, clean any

2.20a Remove the pad pins . . .

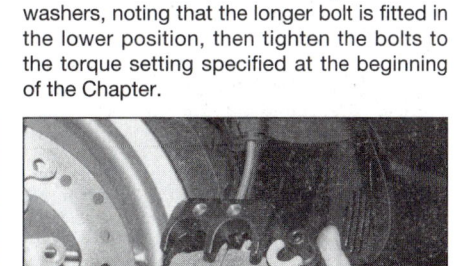

2.20b . . . then lift out the outer brake pad . . .

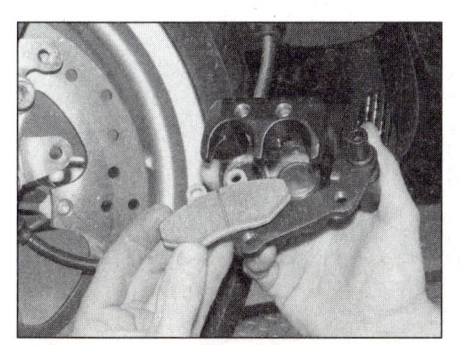

2.20c . . . and the inner brake pad

2.20d Note the location of the pad spring (arrowed)

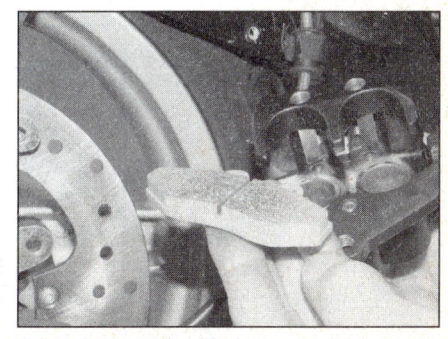

2.21a Inspect the friction material for wear and contamination

8•6 Brakes, wheels and tyres

2.21b Pull the bracket out of the caliper ...

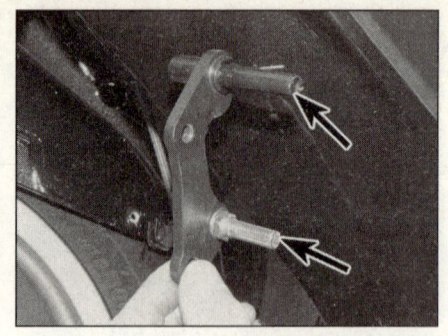

2.21c ... then clean and lubricate the slider pins (arrowed)

2.22 Push the pistons back into the caliper

old grease or corrosion off the slider pins, then smear them with fresh grease **(see illustrations)**. Renew the pin seals if they are damaged, then slide the bracket back into the caliper.

22 If new pads are being fitted, push the pistons as far back into the caliper as possible using hand pressure or a piece of wood as leverage **(see illustration)**. Due to the increased friction material thickness of new pads, it may be necessary to remove the master cylinder reservoir cover and diaphragm and syphon out some fluid.

23 Smear the backs of the pads and the shanks of the pad pins with copper-based grease, making sure that none gets on the front or sides of the pads.

24 Ensure the pad spring is correctly fitted inside the caliper **(see illustration 2.20d)**. Install the pads in the reverse order of removal so that the friction material faces the disc, then push the pads against the pad spring and insert the pad pins **(see illustration)**. Apply a suitable non-permanent thread locking compound to the threads of the pad pins, then tighten them to the torque setting specified at the beginning of the Chapter **(see illustration)**. Alternatively, tighten the pad pins once the caliper has been installed.

25 Slide the caliper onto the disc. Install the caliper mounting bolts and washers, then tighten the bolts to the torque setting specified at the beginning of the Chapter.

2.24a Install the pads as described

2.24b Apply thread locking compound to the pad pins

3 Front brake caliper – removal, overhaul and installation

⚠️ **Warning:** If a caliper indicates the need for an overhaul (usually due to leaking fluid or sticky operation), all old brake fluid should be flushed from the system. Also, the dust created by the brake system may contain asbestos, which is harmful to your health. Never blow it out with compressed air and don't inhale any of it. An approved filtering mask should be worn when working on the brakes. Do not, under any circumstances, use petroleum-based solvents to clean brake parts. Use clean brake fluid, brake cleaner or denatured alcohol only.

Note 1: There is no clear information as to the availability of caliper rebuild kits for the models covered. Before overhauling the caliper, check with a Piaggio dealer as to the availability of seals and pistons for your model. Otherwise an entire new caliper must be installed.

Note 2: On some models, due to a lack of clearance, it may be necessary to remove the front wheel to enable the caliper to be removed.

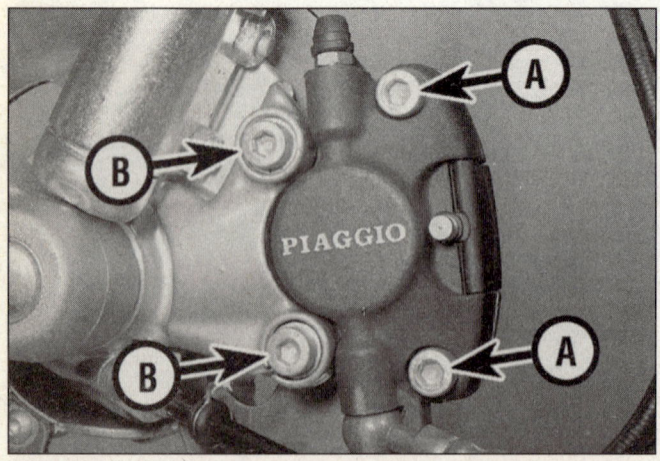

3.1a Caliper half joining bolts (A), caliper mounting bolts (B) – Piaggio type caliper

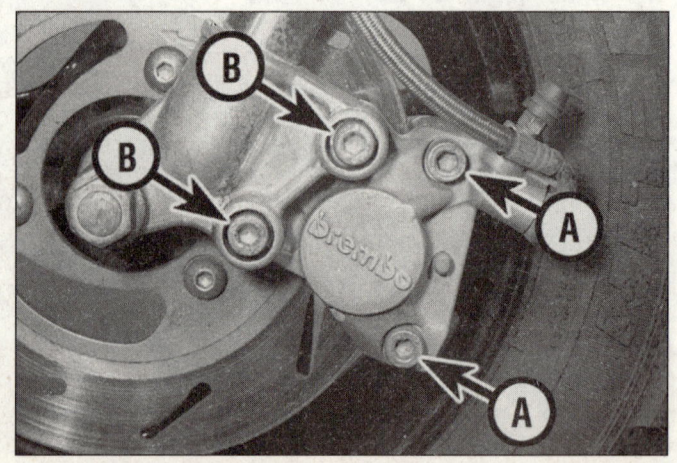

3.1b Caliper half joining bolts (A), caliper mounting bolts (B) – Brembo type caliper

Brakes, wheels and tyres 8•7

Opposed piston caliper

Removal

1 If the caliper is being overhauled (see **Note 1** overleaf), remove the brake pads (see Section 2), then slacken and lightly retighten the bolts which join the caliper halves **(see illustrations)**. If the caliper is just being removed, the pads can be left in place and the caliper half joining bolts should not be disturbed.

2 If the caliper is just being displaced and not completely removed or overhauled, do not disconnect the brake hose. If the caliper is being overhauled, note the alignment of the hose on the caliper, then remove the brake hose banjo bolt and separate the hose from the caliper **(see illustrations)**. Plug the hose end or wrap a plastic bag tightly around it to minimise fluid loss and prevent dirt entering the system. Discard the sealing washers, as new ones must be used on installation. **Note:** *If you are planning to overhaul the caliper and don't have a source of compressed air to blow out the pistons, just loosen the banjo bolt at this stage and retighten it lightly. The bike's hydraulic system can then be used to force the pistons out of the body once the pads have been removed. Disconnect the hose once the pistons have been sufficiently displaced.*

3 Unscrew the caliper mounting bolts **(see illustrations 3.1a and 3.1b)**, and slide the caliper off the disc **(see illustrations)**.

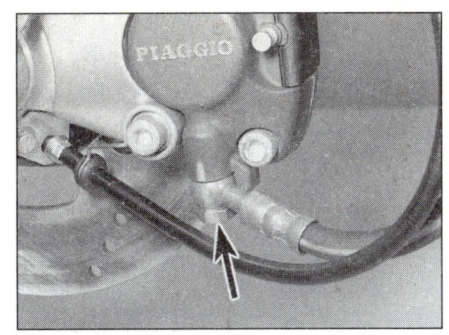

Overhaul

4 Clean the exterior of the caliper with denatured alcohol or brake system cleaner.

5 Displace the pistons as far as possible from the caliper body, either by pumping them out by operating the front brake lever, or by forcing them out using compressed air. If the compressed air method is used, place a wad of rag between the pistons and the caliper to act as a cushion, then use compressed air directed into the fluid inlet to force the pistons out of the body. Use only low pressure to ease the pistons out and make sure both pistons are displaced at the same time. If the air pressure is too high and the pistons are forced out, the caliper and/or pistons may be damaged. Unscrew the joining bolts and separate the caliper halves. Mark each piston head and caliper body with a felt marker to ensure that the pistons can be matched to their original bores on reassembly. Remove the caliper O-ring seal from either half of the caliper body and discard it, as a new one must be used.

⚠ **Warning:** *Never place your fingers in front of the pistons in an attempt to catch or protect them when applying compressed air, as serious injury could result.*

6 Using a wooden or plastic tool, remove the dust seals from the caliper bores **(see illustration)**. Discard them, as new ones must

3.2a Brake hose alignment and banjo bolt (arrowed) – Piaggio type caliper

3.2b Brake hose alignment and banjo bolt (arrowed) – Brembo type caliper

3.3a Remove the caliper mounting bolts . . .

3.3b . . . and slide the caliper off the disc

be used on installation. If a metal tool is being used, take great care not to damage the caliper bores.

7 Remove and discard the piston seals in the same way.

8 Clean the pistons and bores with denatured alcohol, clean brake fluid or brake system cleaner. If compressed air is available, use it to dry the parts thoroughly (make sure it's filtered and unlubricated).

Caution: *Do not, under any circumstances, use a petroleum-based solvent to clean brake parts.*

9 Inspect the caliper bores and pistons for signs of corrosion, nicks and burrs and loss of plating. If surface defects are present, the caliper assembly must be renewed. If the caliper is in bad shape the master cylinder should also be checked.

10 Lubricate the new piston seals with clean

3.6 Remove the dust seal with a plastic or wooden tool (a pencil works well) to avoid damage to the bore and seal groove

brake fluid and install them in their grooves in the caliper bores.

11 Lubricate the new dust seals with clean brake fluid and install them in their grooves in the caliper bores.

12 Lubricate the pistons with clean brake fluid and install them closed-end first into the caliper bores. Using your thumbs, push the pistons all the way in, making sure they enter the bore squarely.

13 Fit a new caliper seal into one half of the caliper body, then join the halves together and tighten the bolts. If required, to provide support, they can be fully tightened after the calipers have been installed.

Installation

14 Install the caliper on the brake disc making sure the pads sit squarely each side of the disc (if they weren't removed) **(see illustration)**.

3.14 Slide the caliper onto the disc . . .

8•8 Brakes, wheels and tyres

15 Install the caliper mounting bolts, and tighten them to the torque setting specified at the beginning of the Chapter (see illustration).
16 If the caliper was overhauled and the joining bolts were not fully tightened earlier, tighten them securely.
17 If removed, connect the brake hose to the caliper, using new sealing washers on each side of the fitting. Align the hose as noted on removal (see illustrations 3.2a and 3.2b). Tighten the banjo bolt to the torque setting specified at the beginning of the Chapter. Top-up the master cylinder reservoir with DOT 4 brake fluid (see *Daily (pre-ride) checks*) and bleed the hydraulic system as described in Section 8.
18 If removed, install the brake pads (see Section 2).
19 Check for leaks and thoroughly test the operation of the brake before riding the scooter.

Single piston floating caliper

Removal

20 If the caliper is just being displaced and not completely removed or overhauled, do not disconnect the brake hose. If the caliper is being overhauled, note the alignment of the hose on the caliper, then remove the brake hose banjo bolt and separate the hose from the caliper. Plug the hose end or wrap a plastic bag tightly around it to minimise fluid loss and prevent dirt entering the system. Discard the sealing washers, as new ones must be used on installation. **Note:** *If you are planning to overhaul the caliper and don't have a source of compressed air to blow out the piston, just loosen the banjo bolt at this stage and retighten it lightly. The bike's hydraulic system can then be used to force the piston out of the body once the pads have been removed. Disconnect the hose once the piston has been sufficiently displaced.*
21 If the caliper is being overhauled (see **Note 1** overleaf), remove the brake pads, pull the caliper bracket off and prise out the pad spring (see Section 2). If the caliper is just being removed, the pads and bracket can be left in place.

Overhaul

22 Clean the exterior of the caliper with denatured alcohol or brake system cleaner.
23 Displace the piston as far as possible from the caliper body, either by pumping it out by operating the front brake lever, or by forcing it out using compressed air. If the compressed air method is used, place a wad of rag between the piston and the caliper to act as a cushion, then use compressed air directed into the fluid inlet to force the piston out of the body. Use only low pressure to ease the piston out – if the air pressure is too high and the piston is forced out, the caliper and/or piston may be damaged. ⚠ **Warning:** *Never place your fingers in front of the piston in an attempt to catch or protect it*

3.15 . . . then install the bolts and tighten them to the specified torque

when applying compressed air, as serious injury could result.
24 Using a wooden or plastic tool, remove the dust seal from the caliper bore, taking care not to damage the surface of the bore (see illustration 3.6). Discard it, as new one must be used on installation.
25 Remove and discard the piston seal in the same way.
26 Clean the piston and bore with denatured alcohol, clean brake fluid or brake system cleaner. If compressed air is available, use it to dry the parts thoroughly (make sure it's filtered and unlubricated).
Caution: Do not, under any circumstances, use a petroleum-based solvent to clean brake parts.
27 Inspect the caliper bore and piston for signs of corrosion, nicks and burrs and loss of plating. If surface defects are present, the caliper assembly must be renewed. If the caliper is in bad shape the master cylinder should also be checked.
28 Lubricate the new piston seal with clean brake fluid and install it in its groove in the caliper bore.
29 Lubricate the new dust seal with clean brake fluid and install it in its groove in the caliper bore.
30 Lubricate the piston with clean brake fluid and install it closed-end first into the caliper bore. Using your thumbs, push the piston all the way in, making sure it enters the bore squarely.

Installation

31 If removed, install the pad spring, caliper bracket and brake pads (see Section 2).
32 Install the caliper on the brake disc making sure the pads sit squarely each side of the disc (see illustration 2.16b).
33 Install the caliper mounting bolts, and tighten them to the torque setting specified at the beginning of the Chapter (see Step 2.17).
34 If removed, connect the brake hose to the caliper, using new sealing washers on each side of the fitting. Align the hose as noted on removal. Tighten the banjo bolt to the torque setting specified at the beginning of the Chapter. Top-up the master cylinder reservoir with DOT 4 brake fluid (see *Daily (pre-ride) checks*) and bleed the hydraulic system as described in Section 8.

35 Check for leaks and thoroughly test the operation of the brake before riding the scooter.

Two-piston floating caliper

Removal

36 If the caliper is just being displaced and not completely removed or overhauled, do not disconnect the brake hose. If the caliper is being overhauled, note the alignment of the hose on the caliper, then remove the brake hose banjo bolt and separate the hose from the caliper (see illustration). Plug the hose end or wrap a plastic bag tightly around it to minimise fluid loss and prevent dirt entering the system. Discard the sealing washers, as new ones must be used on installation. **Note:** *If you are planning to overhaul the caliper and don't have a source of compressed air to blow out the piston, just loosen the banjo bolt at this stage and retighten it lightly. The bike's hydraulic system can then be used to force the piston out of the body once the pads have been removed. Disconnect the hose once the piston has been sufficiently displaced.*
37 If the caliper is being overhauled (see **Note 1** overleaf), remove the brake pads, pull the caliper bracket off and prise out the pad spring (see Section 2). If the caliper is just being removed, the pads can be left in place.

Overhaul

38 Clean the exterior of the caliper with denatured alcohol or brake system cleaner.
39 Displace the pistons as far as possible from the caliper body, either by pumping them out by operating the front brake lever, or by forcing them out using compressed air. If the compressed air method is used, place a wad of rag between the pistons and the caliper to act as a cushion, then use compressed air directed into the fluid inlet to force the pistons out of the body. Use only low pressure to ease the pistons out and make sure both pistons are displaced at the same time. If the air pressure is too high and the pistons are forced out, the caliper and/or pistons may be damaged. Mark each piston head and the caliper body with a felt marker to ensure that the pistons can be matched to their original bores on reassembly.

3.36 Note the alignment of the brake hose – GT model shown

Brakes, wheels and tyres 8•9

⚠️ **Warning: Never place your fingers in front of the pistons in an attempt to catch or protect them when applying compressed air, as serious injury could result.**

40 Follow the procedure in Steps 24 to 30 to remove the old seals, inspect the pistons and caliper bores, and install new seals.

Installation

41 If removed, install the pad spring, caliper bracket and brake pads (see Section 2). Don't forget to apply a suitable non-permanent thread locking compound to the threads of the pad pins before final tightening **(see illustration 2.24b)**.
42 Install the caliper on the brake disc making sure the pads sit squarely each side of the disc **(see illustration 2.24a)**.
43 Install the caliper mounting bolts, and tighten them to the torque setting specified at the beginning of the Chapter (see Step 2.25).
44 If removed, connect the brake hose to the caliper, using new sealing washers on each side of the fitting. Align the hose as noted on removal. Tighten the banjo bolt to the torque setting specified at the beginning of the Chapter. Top-up the master cylinder reservoir with DOT 4 brake fluid (see *Daily (pre-ride) checks*) and bleed the hydraulic system as described in Section 8.
45 Check for leaks and thoroughly test the operation of the brake before riding the scooter.

4 Front brake disc – inspection, removal and installation

Inspection

1 Visually inspect the surface of the disc for score marks and other damage. Light scratches are normal after use and won't affect brake operation, but deep grooves and heavy score marks will reduce braking efficiency and accelerate pad wear. If a disc is badly grooved it must be machined or renewed.
2 To check the disc runout, position the scooter upright so that the wheel is raised off the ground. Mount a dial gauge on a fork leg or the steering stem, with the plunger on the

4.2 Set up a dial gauge with the probe contacting the brake disc, then rotate the wheel to check for runout

gauge touching the surface of the disc about 13 mm (1/2 in) from the outer edge **(see illustration)**. Rotate the wheel and watch the gauge needle, comparing the reading with the limit listed in the Specifications at the beginning of the Chapter. If the runout is greater than the service limit, check the wheel bearings for play (see Chapter 1). If the bearings are worn, renew them (see Section 15) and repeat this check. If the disc runout is still excessive, it will have to be renewed, although machining by an engineer may be possible.
3 The disc must not be allowed to wear or be machined too thin. Piaggio provide no minimum thickness specification, although if the disc is obviously worn where the pads are in contact, and a substantial ridge can be felt between the rim and the contact area, it must be renewed.

Removal

4 Remove the front wheel (see Section 13). On models with monoshock front suspension, also remove the wheel hub assembly.

Caution: Do not lay the wheel down and allow it to rest on the disc – the disc could become warped. Set the wheel on wood blocks so the disc doesn't support the weight of the wheel.

5 Mark the relationship of the disc to the wheel or hub assembly, so it can be installed in the same position. Unscrew the disc retaining bolts, loosening them a little at a time in a criss-cross pattern to avoid distorting the disc, then remove the disc **(see illustration)**.

Installation

6 Install the disc, making sure the directional arrow points in the direction of normal wheel rotation **(see illustration)**. Align the previously-applied matchmarks (if you're reinstalling the original disc).
7 Apply a suitable non-permanent thread locking compound to the disc retaining bolts, then install the bolts and tighten them in a criss-cross pattern evenly and progressively. Clean off all grease from the brake disc using acetone or brake system cleaner. If a new brake disc has been installed, remove any protective coating from its working surfaces.
8 Install the wheel hub assembly (monoshock models) and the wheel (see Section 13).
9 Operate the brake lever several times to bring the pads into contact with the disc. Check the operation of the brakes carefully before riding the scooter.

5 Front brake master cylinder – removal and installation

Note 1: *Master cylinder rebuild kits are not available for the models covered. If the master cylinder is leaking fluid, or if the lever does not produce a firm feel when the brake is applied, bleeding the brakes does not help (see Section 8) and the hydraulic hoses are all in good condition, then the master cylinder must be renewed.*

Note 2: *On models with a handlebar-mounted master cylinder, the master cylinder and lever assembly can be displaced from the handlebars without any disassembly of its related components if required – follow Steps 6 and 8.*

Handlebar-mounted

Removal

1 The front brake master cylinder is mounted on the right handlebar. The master cylinder has an integral reservoir and is activated directly by pressure from the brake lever. Remove the handlebar covers for access (see Chapter 7).
2 Loosen, but do not remove, the screws holding the reservoir cover in place **(see illustration)**.

4.5 Brake disc mounting bolts

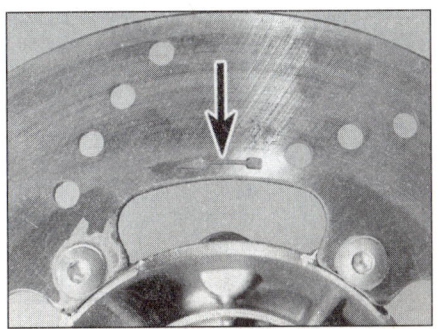

4.6 Disc directional arrow

5.2 Slacken the reservoir cover screws

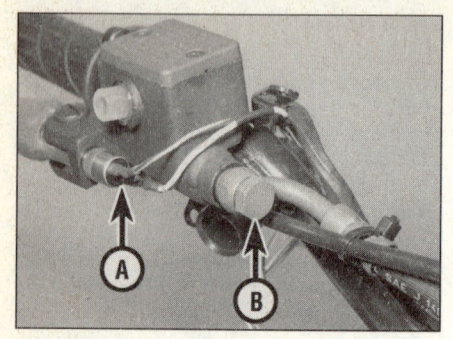

8•10 Brakes, wheels and tyres

5.4 Brake switch electrical connectors (A), brake hose banjo bolt (B)

5.6 Master cylinder clamp bolts (arrowed)

5.13 Fit the diaphragm, plate and cover onto the reservoir

3 Remove the front brake lever (see Chapter 6).
4 Disconnect the electrical connectors from the brake light switch **(see illustration)**. If required, remove the switch.
5 Unscrew the brake hose banjo bolt and separate the hose from the master cylinder, noting its alignment **(see illustration 5.4)**. Discard the two sealing washers as they must be renewed. Wrap the end of the hose in a clean rag and suspend it in an upright position or bend it down carefully and place the open end in a clean container. The objective is to prevent excessive loss of brake fluid, fluid spills and system contamination.
6 Unscrew the master cylinder clamp bolts, then lift the master cylinder and reservoir away from the handlebar **(see illustration)**.
7 Remove the reservoir cover retaining screws and lift off the cover, the diaphragm plate and the rubber diaphragm. Drain the brake fluid from the reservoir into a suitable container. Wipe any remaining fluid out of the reservoir with a clean rag.

Installation

8 Attach the master cylinder to the handlebar and fit the clamp, then tighten the bolts securely **(see illustration 5.6)**.
9 Connect the brake hose to the master cylinder, using new sealing washers on each side of the union, and aligning the hose as noted on removal **(see illustration 5.4)**. Tighten the banjo bolt to the torque setting specified at the beginning of this Chapter.
10 Install the brake lever (see Chapter 6).
11 If removed, install the brake light switch and connect the wiring connectors **(see illustration 5.4)**.
12 Fill the fluid reservoir with new DOT 4 brake fluid as described in *Daily (pre-ride) checks*. Refer to Section 8 of this Chapter and bleed the air from the system.

13 Fit the rubber diaphragm, making sure it is correctly seated, the diaphragm plate and the cover onto the master cylinder reservoir **(see illustration)**.
14 Check the operation of the front brake before riding the scooter.

Steering stem-mounted

Removal

15 Where the master cylinder is mounted on the steering stem, it is activated by a cable from the brake lever, and there is a separate reservoir mounted behind the kick panel. Remove the front panel for access (see Chapter 7).
16 Remove the E-clip on the cable pivot pin, then draw or drive out the pin and detach the cable from the master cylinder lever arm **(see illustration)**.
17 Unscrew the brake hose and separate the hose from the master cylinder **(see illustration)**. Wrap the end of the hose in a clean rag and suspend it in an upright position or bend it down carefully and place the open end in a clean container. The objective is to prevent excessive loss of brake fluid, fluid spills and system contamination.
18 If not already done when removing the front panel, remove the screw securing the reservoir, then remove the reservoir cap and drain the brake fluid from the reservoir into a suitable container. Release the clamp securing the reservoir hose to the union on the master cylinder, then detach the reservoir hose from its union **(see illustration)**. Wipe any remaining fluid out of the reservoir with a clean rag.
19 Unscrew the master cylinder bolts and remove the cylinder **(see illustration)**.

Installation

20 Install the master cylinder onto the steering stem bracket and tighten its mounting bolts securely **(see illustration 5.19)**.
21 Secure the fluid reservoir to the kick panel with its screw. Ensure that the hose is correctly routed, then connect it to the union on the master cylinder and secure it with the clamp **(see illustration 5.18)**. Check that the hose is secure and clamped at the reservoir end as well. If the clamps have weakened, use new ones.

5.16 Remove the E-clip and draw out the pin

5.17 Unscrew and detach the caliper brake hose (arrowed)

5.18 Release the clip (arrowed) and detach the reservoir brake hose

5.19 Master cylinder mounting bolts (arrowed)

Brakes, wheels and tyres 8•11

22 Connect the brake hose to the master cylinder and tighten it securely, but take care not to overtighten it **(see illustration 5.17)**.
23 Align the cable end with the lever arm, then install the pivot pin and secure it with the E-clip, using a new one if the old one was deformed on removal **(see illustration 5.16)**.
24 Fill the fluid reservoir with new DOT 4 hydraulic fluid (see *Daily (pre-ride) checks*) and bleed the system following the procedure in Section 8.
25 Install the front panel (see Chapter 7).
26 Check the operation of the brake carefully before riding the scooter.

6 Rear disc brake – inspection, removal and installation

1 The procedures for removal, inspection and renewal of the rear disc brake pads, caliper, disc and master cylinder are the same as for the front brake, with the following additions.

NRG MC³ DD and Power DD, Hexagon, Beverly, GT and X9 models

2 Remove the rear wheel (see Section 14). Remove the E-clip and pad retaining pin, noting the location of the pad spring **(see illustrations)**.
3 On some models the caliper must be displaced before the pads can be removed – a flexible brake hose will be fitted to these models. Undo the caliper mounting bolts and draw the caliper off the disc, then withdraw the pads from the caliper **(see illustrations)**. Follow the procedure in Section 2, Steps 2 to 10, for inspection and installation of the pads. **Note:** *Do not operate the brake lever while the caliper is off the disc.* Note the routing of the rear brake hose **(see illustrations)**.
4 On models fitted with a rigid brake pipe, withdraw the pads from the top of the caliper.
5 To remove the disc and hub assembly, first displace the caliper. On models fitted with a flexible brake hose, undo the caliper mounting bolts and slide the caliper off the disc, then secure the caliper to the machine with a cable tie to avoid straining the hose **(see illustration)**. On models fitted with a rigid brake pipe, note the alignment of the banjo union on the caliper, then remove the banjo bolt and separate the union from the caliper **(see illustration)**. Discard the sealing washers as new ones must be used on installation.

Undo the caliper mounting bolts and slide the caliper off the disc. **Note:** *Do not operate the brake lever while the caliper is off the disc.*
6 Draw the hub off the driveshaft, noting which way round it fits **(see illustration)**. Note

6.2a Remove the E-clip . . .

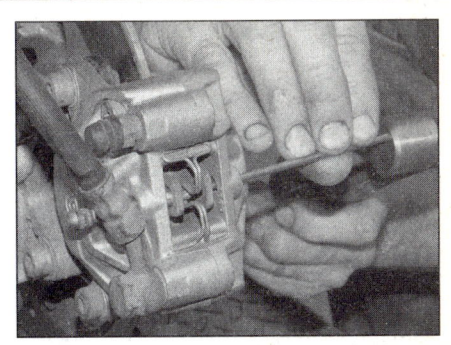

6.2b . . . then drive out the pad retaining pin

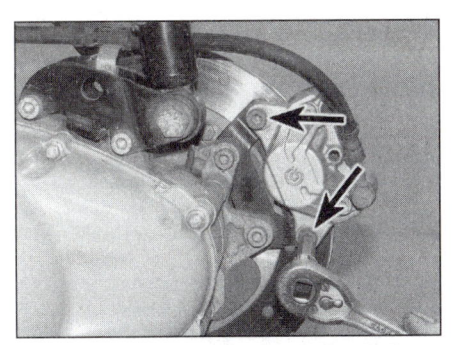

6.3a Undo the caliper mounting bolts (arrowed)

6.3b Remove the pads from the caliper

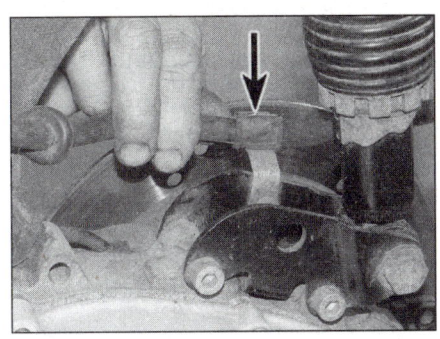

6.3c Brake hose is clipped forward of the left-hand shock . . .

6.3d . . . and forward of the rear hugger

6.5a Remove the brake caliper (arrowed)

6.5b Note the alignment of the banjo union (arrowed) with the caliper – GT model shown

6.6 Draw the hub assembly off the driveshaft

8•12 Brakes, wheels and tyres

6.8a Remove the caliper mounting bolts (arrowed) ...

6.8b ... and slide the caliper off

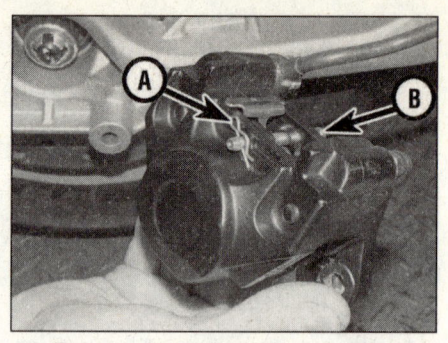

6.9 Remove the R-clip (A) then pull out the pad pin (B)

the directional arrow on the disc **(see illustration 4.6)**. Mark the relationship of the disc to the wheel so it can be installed in the same position. Unscrew the disc retaining bolts, loosening them a little at a time in a criss-cross pattern to avoid distorting the disc, then remove the disc **(see illustration 4.5)**.

X8 models

7 Remove the exhaust silencer (see Chapter 4).
8 Undo the caliper mounting bolts and slide the caliper off the disc **(see illustrations)**. **Note:** *Do not operate the brake lever while the caliper is off the disc.*
9 Remove the R-clip then pull out the pad retaining pin **(see illustration)**. Lift out the pad spring, then draw the brake pads out from the caliper. Follow the procedure in Section 2, Steps 2 to 10, for inspection and installation of the pads. On installation, apply a suitable non-permanent thread locking compound to the threads of the caliper mounting bolts.
10 To remove the disc, follow the procedure in Section 14, Steps 22 to 26, and remove the wheel. Note the directional arrow on the disc **(see illustration 4.6)**. Mark the relationship of the disc to the wheel so it can be installed in the same position. Unscrew the disc retaining bolts, loosening them a little at a time in a criss-cross pattern to avoid distorting the disc, then remove the disc **(see illustration 4.5)**.

All models

11 Follow the procedure in Section 3, Steps 4 to 13, to overhaul the brake caliper.
12 Follow the procedure in Section 4 for inspection of the disc.
13 To install the disc, position it onto the wheel or hub as applicable, making sure the directional arrow points in the direction of normal wheel rotation. Align the previously-applied matchmarks (if you're reinstalling the original disc).
14 Install the bolts and tighten them in a criss-cross pattern evenly and progressively. Clean off all grease from the brake disc using acetone or brake system cleaner. If a new brake disc has been installed, remove any protective coating from its working surfaces.

15 Install the remaining components in the reverse order of removal.
16 The rear brake master cylinder has an integral reservoir and is mounted on the left handlebar.
17 Operate the brake lever several times to bring the pads into contact with the disc. Check the operation of the brakes carefully before riding the scooter.

7 Brake hoses, pipes and unions – inspection and renewal

Inspection

Note: *On models fitted with a rear disc brake it will be necessary to remove the floor panel to inspect the rear brake pipe (see Chapter 7).*
1 Brake hose and pipe condition should be checked regularly and the hoses renewed at the specified interval (see Chapter 1).
2 Twist and flex the hose while looking for cracks, bulges and seeping fluid. Check extra carefully around the areas where the hose connects with the master cylinder and caliper, as these are common areas for hose failure. On models where the master cylinder is mounted on the steering stem (see Section 5), refer to the procedure in Chapter 7 and remove the front panel to check the hose connections. On X9 models, remove the front panel to inspect the unions on the linked brake splitter valve **(see illustration)**.
3 Inspect the union fittings connected to the

7.2 Hose unions on the X9 linked brake splitter valve

brake hose. If the fittings are rusted, scratched or cracked, renew them.

Renewal

4 Cover the surrounding area with plenty of rags and unscrew the banjo bolt or nut at each end of the hose, noting its alignment. Free the hose from any clips or guides and remove it. Discard the sealing washers as new ones must be used.
5 Position the new hose, making sure it isn't twisted or otherwise strained, and abut the tab on the hose union with the lug on the component casting, where present. Otherwise align the hose as noted on removal. Install the hose banjo bolts using new sealing washers on both sides of the unions. Tighten the banjo bolts to the torque setting specified at the beginning of this Chapter. Make sure the hoses are correctly aligned and routed clear of all moving components.
6 Keep the hydraulic reservoir topped-up with new DOT 4 brake fluid and flush the old brake fluid from the system (see *Daily (pre-ride) checks*) and bleed the air from the system (see Section 8). Check the operation of the brake carefully before riding the scooter.

8 Brake system bleeding (disc brake models)

1 Bleeding the brakes is simply the process of removing all the air bubbles from the brake fluid reservoir, master cylinder, the hose and the brake caliper. Bleeding is necessary whenever a brake system hydraulic connection is loosened, when a component or hose is renewed, or when the caliper is overhauled. Leaks in the system may also allow air to enter, but leaking brake fluid will reveal their presence and warn you of the need for repair.
2 To bleed the brake, you will need some new DOT 4 brake fluid, a length of clear vinyl or plastic tubing, a small container partially-filled with clean brake fluid, some rags and a spanner to fit the brake caliper bleed valve.
3 Cover any painted components to prevent damage in the event that brake fluid is spilled.

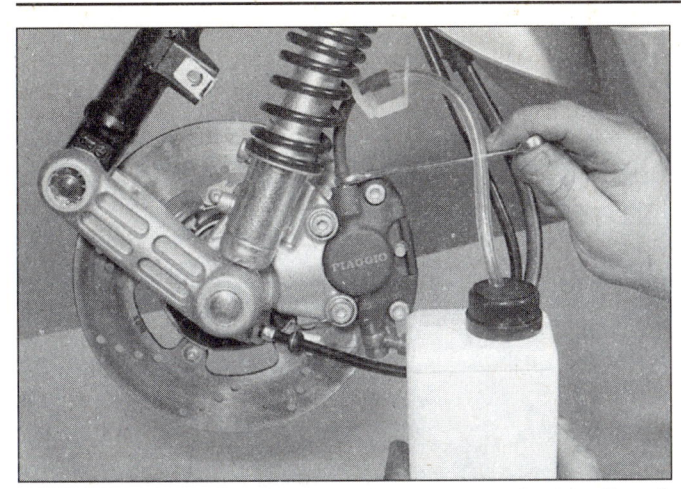

Brakes, wheels and tyres 8•13

8.6a To bleed the brakes, you need a spanner, a short section of clear tubing, and a clear container half-filled with brake fluid

8.6b Bleed valve (arrowed) on the X9 linked brake splitter valve

4 As applicable, remove the body panels for access to the fluid reservoir (see Chapter 7).

5 Remove the reservoir cap or cover, diaphragm plate and diaphragm and slowly pump the brake lever a few times, until no air bubbles can be seen floating up from the holes in the bottom of the reservoir. Doing this bleeds the air from the master cylinder end of the line. Loosely refit the reservoir cap or cover.

6 Pull the dust cap off the bleed valve. Attach one end of the clear vinyl or plastic tubing to the bleed valve and submerge the other end in the brake fluid in the container (see illustration). On X9 models, the operation of the front left-hand and rear disc brakes is linked via a splitter valve (see illustration). Bleed air from the splitter valve first, then the rear caliper and then the front caliper.

7 Remove the reservoir cap or cover and check the fluid level. Do not allow the fluid level to drop below the lower mark during the bleeding process.

8 Carefully pump the brake lever three or four times and hold it in while opening the caliper bleed valve. When the valve is opened, brake fluid will flow out of the caliper into the clear tubing and the lever will move toward the handlebar.

9 Retighten the bleed valve, then release the brake lever gradually. Repeat the process until no air bubbles are visible in the brake fluid leaving the caliper and the lever is firm when applied. On completion, disconnect the bleeding equipment, then tighten the bleed valve and fit the dust cap.

HAYNES HiNT *Old brake fluid is invariably much darker in colour than new fluid, making it easy to see when all old fluid has been expelled from the system.*

10 Install the reservoir cap or diaphragm and cover assembly, wipe up any spilled brake fluid and check the entire system for leaks.

HAYNES HiNT *If it's not possible to produce a firm feel to the lever the fluid may be aerated. Let the brake fluid in the system stabilise for a few hours and then repeat the procedure when the tiny bubbles in the system have settled out. To speed this process up, tie the brake lever to the handlebar so that the system is pressurised.*

9 Drum brakes (front and rear) – check and shoe renewal

⚠ **Warning: The dust created by the brake system may contain asbestos, which is harmful to your health. Never blow it out with compressed air and don't inhale any of it. An approved filtering mask should be worn when working on the brakes.**

Check

1 Remove the wheel (see Section 13 or 14). On Zip models (front wheel), remove the brake plate from the wheel. Remove the brake shoes (see below).

2 Check the condition of the friction material on the brake shoes (see illustration). No minimum thickness specification is given, but if the thickness of material remaining at the cam end (the thinnest point) of the shoe is 1.5 mm or less, the shoes should be renewed.

3 Inspect the surface of each shoe for contamination. If either shoe is fouled with oil or grease, or heavily scored or damaged by dirt and debris, both shoes must be renewed as a set. Note that it is not possible to degrease the friction material; if the shoes are contaminated in any way they must be renewed.

4 If the shoes are in good condition clean them carefully, using a fine wire brush which is completely free of oil and grease to remove all traces of road dirt and corrosion. If the material appears glazed, roughen up the surface using emery cloth, bearing in mind the *Warning* above.

5 Check the condition of the brake shoe springs and renew them if they appear weak or are obviously deformed or damaged.

6 Clean the brake drum surface using brake cleaner or a rag soaked in solvent. Examine the surface for scoring and excessive wear (see illustration). While light scratches are expected, any heavy scoring or cracks will impair braking and there is no satisfactory

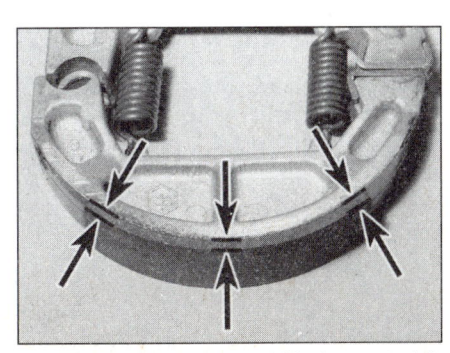

9.2 Check the amount of friction material remaining on each shoe

9.6 Check the surface of the drum for scoring and wear

8•14 Brakes, wheels and tyres

9.11a Apply some copper grease to the cam

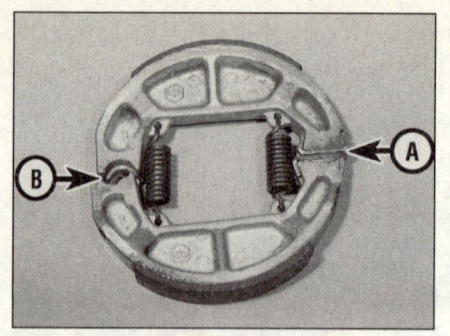

9.11b Fit the springs and locate the flat ends (A) against the cam and the rounded ends (B) against the pivot

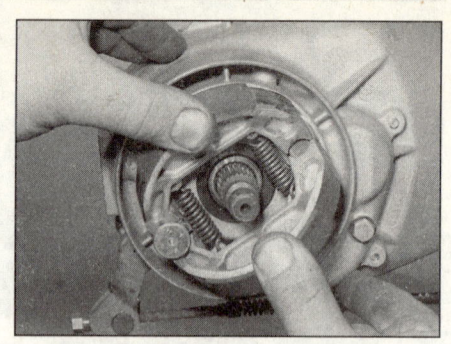

9.11c Installing the brake shoes

way of removing them; in this event the wheel should be renewed, although you could consult an engineer who might be able to skim the surface.

7 Check that the brake cam operates smoothly and to its full limits of travel by operating the lever arm. Clean off all traces of old and hardened grease from the cam. If the bearing surfaces of the cam are worn or damaged it should be renewed.

Shoe renewal

8 Remove the wheel (see Section 13 or 14). On Zip models (front wheel), remove the brake plate from the wheel.
9 Grasp the outer edge of each shoe and fold them upwards and inwards to form a V **(see illustration 9.11c)**, noting that they are under pressure from the springs, then remove them from the plate noting how they locate around the cam and the pivot. Remove the springs from the shoes.
10 Check the shoes and the drum as outlined above.
11 Apply some copper grease to the bearing surfaces on the cam, taking care not to apply too much as it could find its way onto the shoes **(see illustration)**. Install the brake shoes in a reverse of the removal procedure. Fit the springs onto the shoes and position them so that the flat end of each shoe fits on the cam and the rounded end on the pivot **(see illustration)**. Make sure the shoes sit correctly on each side of the cam and the pivot as you fold them flat onto the plate **(see illustration)**. Operate the lever arm to check that the cam and shoes work correctly.
12 Install the wheel. Check the operation of the brake before riding the scooter.

10 Brake cables – renewal

Front brake cable

Zip and Sfera with drum brake

1 Release the outer cable from its housing at the lower end.
2 Fully unscrew the adjuster nut on the lower end of the inner cable, then draw the cable out of the brake lever arm.
3 Remove the handlebar front cover (see Chapter 7).
4 Draw the outer cable out of the brake lever bracket and free the inner cable nipple from its socket in the underside of the lever **(see illustrations 10.17a and 10.17b)**.
5 Withdraw the cable, noting its routing and any guides it passes through.
6 Install the new cable in a reverse of the removal procedure. Apply some grease to the nipple on the end of the inner cable at the top, and to the roller in the brake lever arm. Check and adjust the cable freeplay (see Chapter 1).

All other models

7 Remove the fairing (see Chapter 7).
8 Remove the E-clip on the cable pivot pin, then draw or drive out the pin and detach the cable from the master cylinder lever arm **(see illustration 5.16)**.
9 Slacken the cable adjuster locknut, then thread the adjuster out of its holder **(see illustration)**.
10 Remove the handlebar front cover (see Chapter 7).
11 Draw the outer cable out of the brake lever bracket and free the inner cable nipple from its socket in the underside of the lever **(see illustrations 10.17a and 10.17b)**.
12 Withdraw the cable, noting its routing and any guides it passes through.
13 Install the new cable in a reverse of the removal procedure. Apply some grease to the ends of the inner cable. Check and adjust cable freeplay (see Chapter 1).

Rear brake cable

14 Remove the outer cable clamp bolt at the lower end of the cable and free the cable from its holder **(see illustration)**. On some models the bolt fits from the outside.
15 Fully unscrew the adjuster nut on the lower end of the cable, then draw the cable out of the brake lever arm **(see illustration)**.
16 Remove the handlebar front cover (see Chapter 7).
17 Draw the outer cable out of the brake

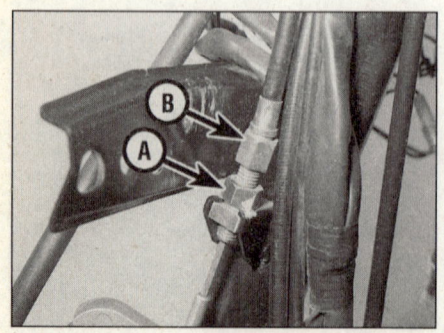

10.9 Slacken the locknut (A) and unscrew the adjuster (B)

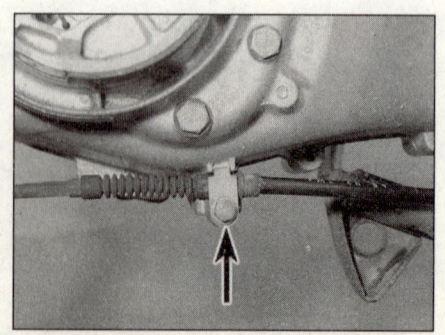

10.14 Unscrew the bolt (arrowed), remove the clamp and release the outer cable

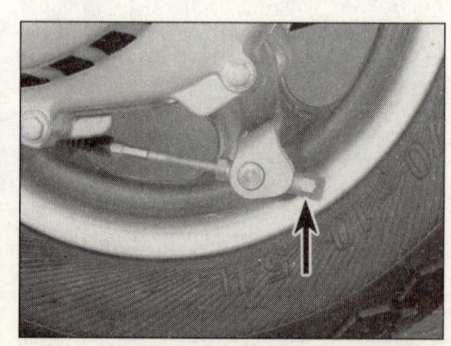

10.15 Unscrew and remove the adjuster nut (arrowed)

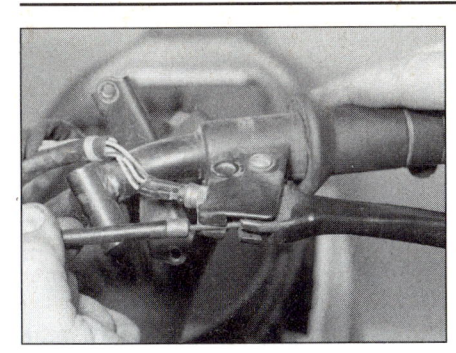

Brakes, wheels and tyres 8•15

10.17a Draw the outer cable from the bracket...

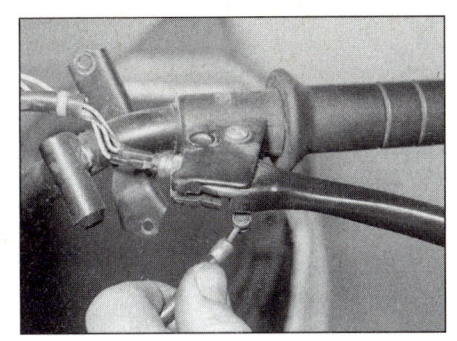

10.17b ...and release the inner cable nipple from the lever

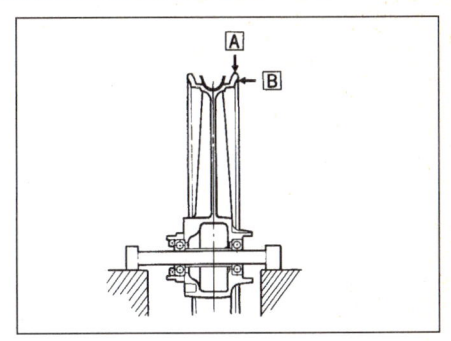

11.2 Check the wheel for radial (out-of-round) runout (A) and axial (side-to-side) runout (B)

lever bracket and free the inner cable nipple from its socket in the underside of the lever **(see illustrations)**.
18 Referring to Chapter 7, remove the legshield panel and footboard to enable access to the cable's guides and indicate correct routing. Withdraw the cable, noting its routing and any guides it passes through.
19 Install the new cable in a reverse of the removal procedure. Apply some grease to the nipple on the end of the inner cable at the top, and to the roller in the brake lever arm. Check and adjust the cable freeplay (see Chapter 1).

11 Wheels – inspection and repair

1 In order to carry out a proper inspection of the wheels, it is necessary to support the scooter upright so that the wheel being inspected is raised off the ground. Clean the wheels thoroughly to remove mud and dirt that may interfere with the inspection procedure or mask defects. Make a general check of the wheels (see Chapter 1) and tyres (see *Daily (pre-ride) checks*).
2 Attach a dial gauge to a fork leg or the steering stem (front, as applicable) or the transmission casing (rear) and position its stem against the side of the rim **(see illustration)**. Spin the wheel slowly and check the axial (side-to-side) runout of the rim. In order to accurately check radial (out of round) runout with the dial gauge, the wheel would have to be removed from the machine, and the tyre from the wheel. With the axle clamped in a vice or jig and the dial gauge positioned on the top of the rim, the wheel can be rotated to check the runout.
3 An easier, though slightly less accurate, method is to attach a stiff wire pointer to the fork leg or steering stem (front, as applicable) or the transmission casing (rear) and position the end a fraction of an inch from the wheel (where the wheel and tyre join). If the wheel is true, the distance from the pointer to the rim will be constant as the wheel is rotated. **Note:**

If wheel runout is excessive, check the wheel or hub bearings (front) or transmission driveshaft bearings (rear) very carefully before renewing the wheel.
4 The wheels should also be visually inspected for cracks, flat spots on the rim and other damage. Look very closely for dents in the area where the tyre bead contacts the rim. Dents in this area may prevent complete sealing of the tyre against the rim, which leads to deflation of the tyre over a period of time. If damage is evident, or if runout in either direction is excessive, the wheel will have to be renewed. Never attempt to repair a damaged cast alloy wheel.

12 Wheels – alignment check

1 Misalignment of the wheels can cause strange and possibly serious handling problems. Note that the wheels are unlikely to go out of alignment on this type of machine, and alignment need only be checked if the scooter has been involved in an accident or if a handling problem occurs. Poor wheel alignment will most likely be due to bent frame or suspension components, although check that the wheel bearings are not at fault. Have the frame checked by a Piaggio dealer.

2 To check the alignment you will need an assistant, a length of string or a perfectly straight piece of wood and a ruler. A plumb bob or other suitable weight will also be required.
3 In order to make a proper check of the wheels it is necessary to support the scooter in an upright position on its centre stand. Measure the width of both tyres at their widest points. Subtract the smaller measurement from the larger measurement, then divide the difference by two. The result is the amount of offset that should exist between the front and rear tyres on both sides. Note that certain models use the same diameter tyres front and back.
4 If a string is used, have your assistant hold one end of it about halfway between the floor and the rear axle, touching the rear sidewall of the tyre.
5 Run the other end of the string forward and pull it tight so that it is roughly parallel to the floor. Slowly bring the string into contact with the front sidewall of the rear tyre, then turn the front wheel until it is parallel with the string. Measure the distance from the front tyre sidewall to the string **(see illustration)**.
6 Repeat the procedure on the other side of the scooter. The distance from the front tyre sidewall to the string should be equal on both sides. Where the tyre diameters are the same front and back, the string should of course touch the front tyre sidewall directly.

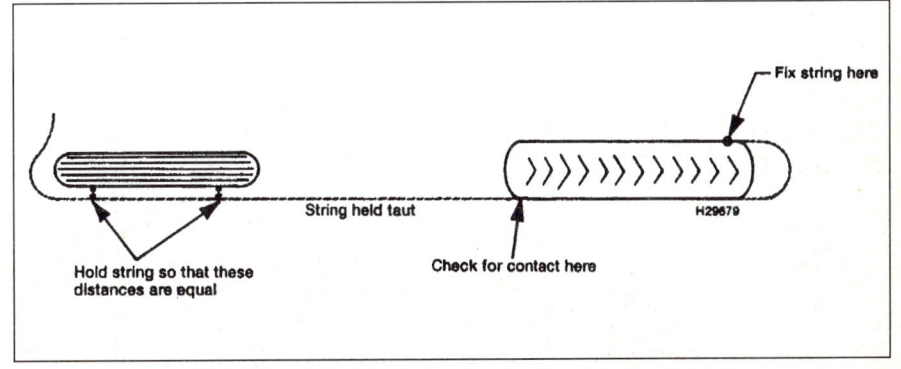

12.5 Wheel alignment check using the string method
Tyres of different widths front and rear illustrated

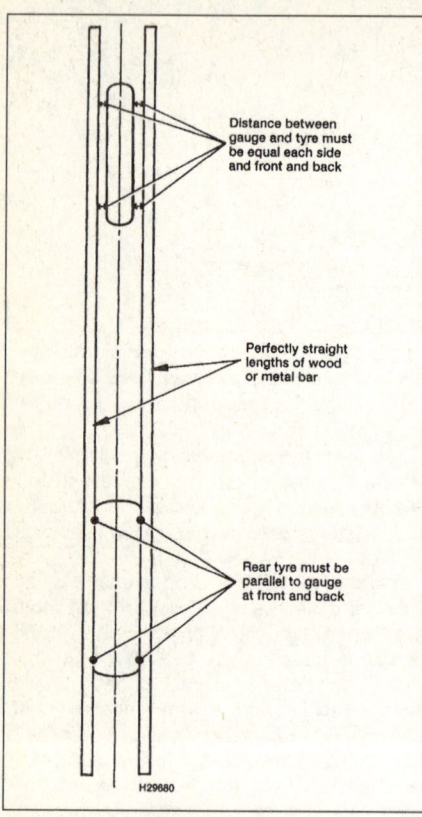

8•16 Brakes, wheels and tyres

12.7 Wheel alignment check using a straight-edge
Tyres of different widths front and rear illustrated

13.2a Unscrew the bolts (arrowed) . . .

13.2b . . . and remove the wheel

7 As was previously pointed out, a perfectly straight length of wood may be substituted for the string. The procedure is the same **(see illustration)**.

13 Front wheel and hub assembly – removal and installation

Monoshock models

Wheel removal and installation

1 Position the scooter upright so that the front wheel is off the ground; make sure it is properly supported.
2 On Sfera 50/80 models with a drum front brake, the procedure for removing the front wheel is similar to that for the rear wheel – refer to Section 14 for details. On all other models, unscrew the five bolts securing the wheel to the hub assembly and draw the wheel off the hub, noting the large washer on the inside of the wheel **(see illustrations)**.
3 Fit the washer to the inside of the wheel, then install the bolts with their washers and tighten them to the torque setting specified at the beginning of the Chapter **(see illustration)**.

Hub assembly removal

4 Remove the wheel (see above). Detach the speedometer cable from the hub and withdraw the drive gear (see Chapter 9).
5 On models with a disc brake, remove the brake caliper mounting bolts and slide the caliper off the disc (see Section 3). Support the caliper with a piece of wire or a bungee cord so that no strain is placed on its hydraulic hose. There is no need to disconnect the hose from the caliper. **Note:** *Do not operate the brake lever with the caliper removed.*
6 Remove the split pin from the hub cage nut and remove the cage nut **(see illustrations)**. Discard the split pin; a new one must be used.
7 Unscrew the hub nut **(see illustration)**.
8 Draw the hub assembly off the axle **(see illustration)**. The hub assembly is quite a tight fit – if it is difficult to remove, fit a strong washer with an external diameter the same as the recess in the wheel and with an internal diameter smaller than the diameter of the axle (so that the washer cannot slide over the axle)

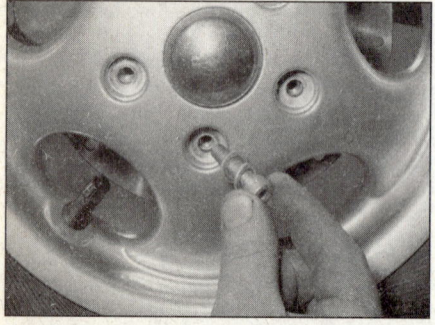

13.3 Do not omit the washers with each bolt

13.6a Remove the split pin (arrowed) . . .

13.6b . . . and the cage nut

13.7 Remove the hub nut

13.8a Draw the hub assembly off the axle

Brakes, wheels and tyres 8•17

into the wheel **(see illustration)**. Place the wheel against the axle, then install the wheel bolts and tighten them evenly and a little at a time in a criss-cross sequence until the hub is drawn off **(see illustration)**.

9 Check the condition of the bearings in the hub (see Section 15), and of the grease seal in the speedometer drive gear housing. Lever out the old seal from the drive housing and fit a new one if it is worn, damaged or deteriorated **(see illustration)**.

Hub assembly installation

10 Installation is the reverse of removal, noting the following:
 a) Apply grease to the axle, and to the bearings and speedometer drive in the hub **(see illustration)**.
 b) Tighten the hub nut to the torque setting specified at the beginning of the Chapter **(see illustration)**.
 c) Use a new split pin to secure the cage nut **(see illustration)** and bend its ends correctly **(see illustration 13.6a)**.

Telescopic fork models

Wheel removal

11 Position the scooter so that its front wheel is off the ground. Always make sure the scooter is properly supported.

12 On Zip models with a drum brake, disconnect the brake cable (see Section 10). On all other models, remove the brake caliper mounting bolts and slide the caliper off the disc (see Section 3). Support the caliper with a piece of wire or a bungee cord so that no strain is placed on its hydraulic hose. There is no need to disconnect the hose from the caliper. **Note:** *Do not operate the front brake lever with the caliper removed.*

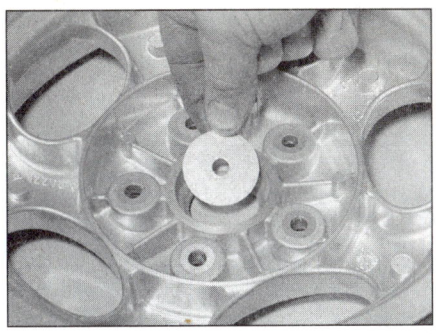

13 Pull back the rubber boot on the end of the speedometer cable, then unscrew the knurled ring and draw the cable out of the drive gear housing. **Note:** *Some later models are fitted with electronically-operated speedometers – do not try to disconnect the cable from the drive gear housing (see Chapter 9).*

14 Where fitted, loosen the axle pinch-bolts **(see illustration)**. Unscrew the axle nut, then support the wheel and withdraw the axle from the wheel **(see illustrations)**. Use a drift to knock the axle through if necessary. Remove the speedometer drive housing and thrustwasher, where fitted, noting how they fit. **Caution: *Don't lay the wheel down and allow it to rest on the disc – the disc could become warped. Set the wheel on wood blocks so the disc doesn't support the weight of the wheel.***

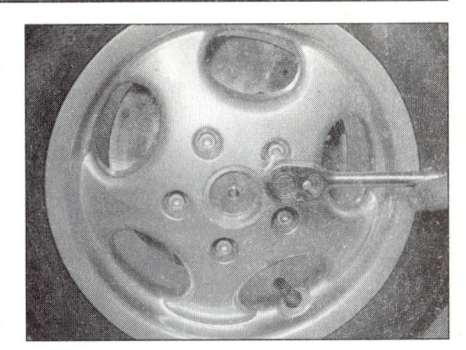

15 Check the axle for straightness by rolling it on a flat surface such as a piece of plate glass (first wipe off all old grease and remove

13.8b Fit the washer into the inside of the wheel . . .

13.8c . . . and tighten the bolts as described

13.9 Lever out the old seal using a screwdriver

13.10a Apply grease to the axle and drive housing seal

13.10b Tighten the hub nut to the specified torque

13.10c Use a new split pin to secure the cage nut

13.14a Loosen the axle pinch-bolts

13.14b Unscrew the axle nut (arrowed) . . .

13.14c . . . then withdraw the axle

8•18 Brakes, wheels and tyres

13.17a Fit the thrustwasher . . .

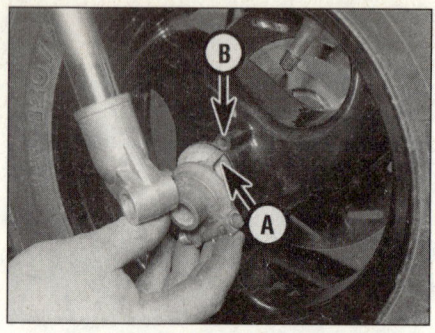

13.17b . . . and the speedometer drive, locating the tab (A) in the hole (B) . . .

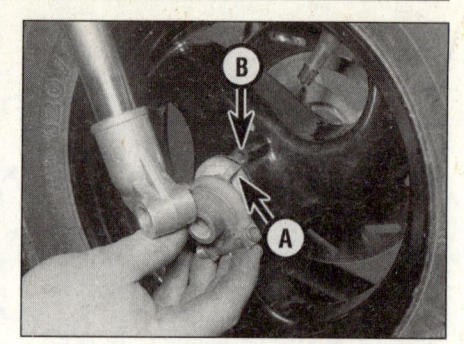

13.17c . . . or aligning the tabs (arrowed) with the drive housing

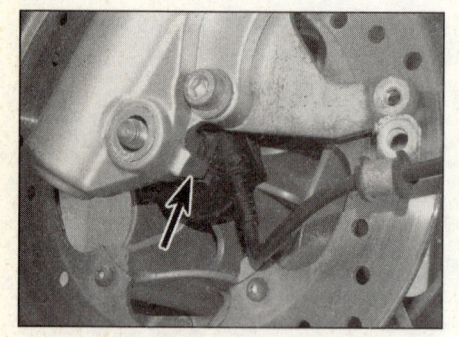

13.18 Speedometer drive housing should locate against lug (arrowed)

13.19a Fit the axle nut . . .

13.19b . . . and tighten it to the specified torque

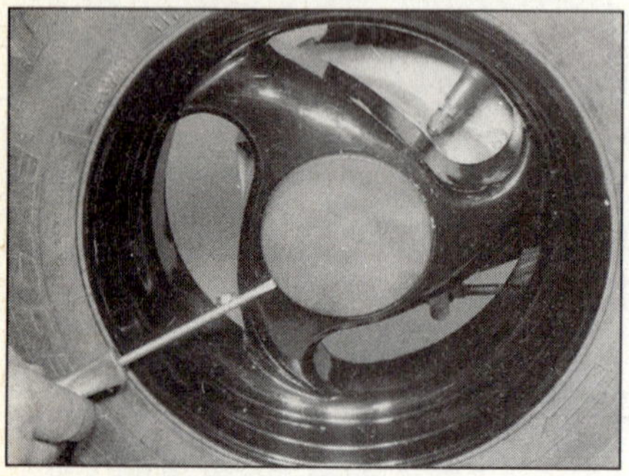

14.2a Lever off the cover . . .

14.2b . . . and remove the split pin (arrowed)

14.3a Unscrew the nut . . .

any corrosion using fine emery cloth). If the equipment is available, place the axle in V-blocks and measure the runout using a dial gauge. If the axle is bent or the runout exceeds the limit specified, renew it.

16 Check the condition of the wheel bearings (see Section 15).

Wheel installation

17 Manoeuvre the wheel into position, making sure the directional arrow is pointing in the normal direction of rotation. Apply some grease to the inside of the speedometer drive housing. If applicable, fit the thrustwasher, then install the drive housing onto the wheel, making sure the drive tab locates correctly **(see illustrations)**. Apply a thin coat of grease to the axle.

18 Lift the wheel into place between the forks, making sure the stepped section on the outside of the speedometer drive housing locates correctly against the corresponding section on the inside of the bottom of the fork **(see illustration)**. Install the axle.

19 Install the axle nut and tighten it to the torque setting specified at the beginning of the Chapter **(see illustrations)**. If applicable, tighten the axle pinch-bolts to the specified torque setting.

20 Install the brake caliper, making sure the pads sit squarely on each side of the disc (see Section 3). Tighten the caliper mounting bolts to the specified torque setting.

21 If applicable, connect the speedometer cable and tighten the knurled ring. On Zip models with a drum brake, connect the brake cable (see Section 10).

22 With the exception of Zip models, apply the front brake a few times to bring the pads back into contact with the disc. Move the scooter off its stand, apply the front brake and pump the front forks a few times to settle all components in position.

23 Check for correct operation of the front brake before riding the scooter.

14 Rear wheel and hub assembly – removal and installation

Drum brake models
Removal

1 Position the scooter on its centre stand and support it so that the rear wheel is off the ground. Remove the silencer (see Chapter 4).

2 Lever off the wheel cover using a small flat-bladed screwdriver **(see illustration)**. Remove the split pin from the end of the axle then remove the cage nut **(see illustration)**. Discard the split pin, as a new one must be used.

3 Unscrew the wheel nut, whilst applying the rear brake to prevent the wheel from turning **(see illustration)**. Remove the washer and

Brakes, wheels and tyres 8•19

14.3b ... remove the washer ...

14.3c ... and draw the wheel off the driveshaft

14.6 Tighten the nut to the specified torque

14.7 Use a new split pin (note that cage nut should be fitted first)

14.17 Remove the hugger fixing screws

14.18a Undo the lower shock fixing ...

draw the wheel off the driveshaft **(see illustrations)**.
4 Check the splines on the driveshaft and on the inside of the wheel for wear and damage and renew either or both components as required.

Installation

5 Apply some grease to the splines on the shaft and slide the wheel into position **(see illustration 14.3c)**.
6 Fit the washer and the wheel nut **(see illustrations 14.3b and 14.3a)**, then tighten the wheel nut to the torque setting specified at the beginning of the Chapter, applying the rear brake to prevent the wheel from turning **(see illustration)**.
7 Fit the cage nut and secure the nut using a new split pin, bending its ends around the cage nut **(see illustration)**.
8 Fit the wheel cover.

Disc brake models with single rear shock absorber

Removal

9 Position the scooter on its centre stand and support it so that the rear wheel is off the ground. Remove the silencer (see Chapter 4).
10 Have an assistant apply the rear brake to prevent the wheel from turning, then undo the bolts securing the wheel to the hub assembly and lift the wheel off the hub.
11 If required, follow the procedure in Section 6 to remove the rear hub assembly.
12 Check the splines on the driveshaft and on the inside of the hub for wear and damage and renew either or both components as required.

Installation

13 If removed, install the hub assembly and install the rear brake caliper (see Section 6).
14 Fit the wheel onto the hub. Have an assistant apply the rear brake and tighten the wheel bolts to the torque setting specified at the beginning of the Chapter.
15 Install the remaining components in the reverse order of removal.

Disc brake models with twin rear shock absorbers

16 Position the scooter on its centre stand and support it so that the rear wheel is off the ground. Remove the silencer (see Chapter 4).
17 Where fitted, undo the screw securing the rear hugger to the subframe **(see illustration)**.

Removal – Hexagon, Beverly, GT and X9 models

18 Undo the nut securing the lower end of the right-hand shock absorber to the subframe and displace the shock, then undo the bolts securing the subframe to the engine casing **(see illustrations)**.
19 Remove the split pin from the end of the driveshaft then remove the cage nut **(see illustration)**. Discard the split pin, as a new one must be used. Have an assistant apply the rear brake, then unscrew the hub centre

14.18b ... and the subframe mounting bolts

14.19a Remove the split pin (A) and the cage nut (B)

8•20 Brakes, wheels and tyres

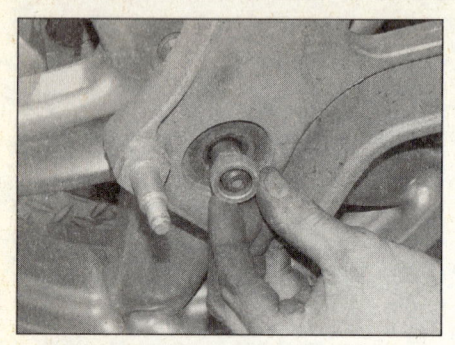

14.19b Note the position of the large washer

14.20a Remove the subframe . . .

14.20b . . . and slide the spacer off the driveshaft

14.21a Undo the bolts . . .

14.21b . . . and lift off the wheel

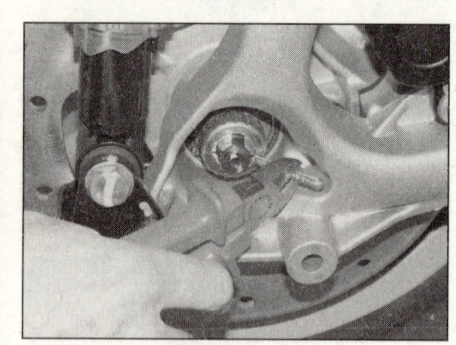

14.22a Pull out the split pin . . .

nut and remove the nut and large washer **(see illustration)**.

20 Lift off the subframe and slide the spacer off the driveshaft, noting which way round it fits **(see illustrations)**.

21 Undo the bolts securing the wheel to the hub assembly and remove the wheel **(see illustrations)**. If required, follow the procedure in Section 6 to remove the rear hub assembly.

Removal – X8 models

22 Remove the split pin from the end of the driveshaft then remove the cage nut **(see illustrations)**. Discard the split pin, as a new one must be used. Have an assistant apply the rear brake, then unscrew the hub centre nut and remove the nut and large washer **(see illustration)**.

23 Remove the brake caliper mounting bolts and displace the caliper **(see illustrations 6.8a and 8b)**. Support the caliper with a piece of wire or a bungee cord so that no strain is placed on its hydraulic hose. There is no need to disconnect the hose from the caliper. **Note:** *Do not operate the front brake lever with the caliper removed.*

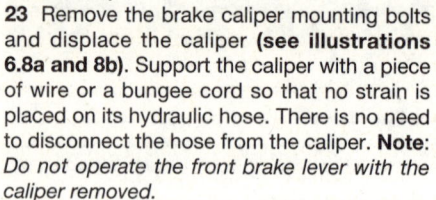

24 Undo the bolts securing the lower end of the right-hand shock absorber to the subframe and displace the shock **(see illustrations)**.

25 Undo the bolts securing the subframe to the engine casing and lift the subframe off **(see illustrations)**.

26 Slide the spacer off the driveshaft, noting

14.22b . . . then remove the cage nut

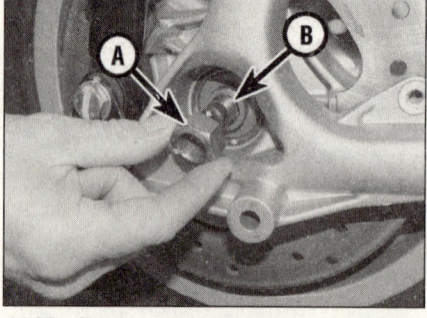

14.22c Remove the hub centre nut (A) and washer (B)

14.24a Remove the bolts (arrowed) . . .

14.24b . . . and displace the lower end of the shock

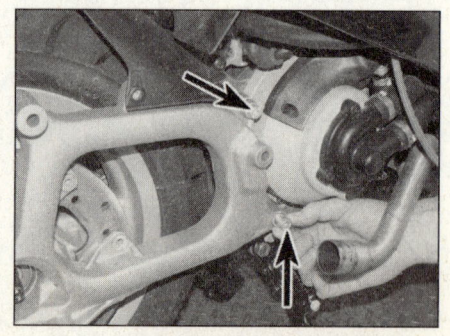

14.25a Undo the bolts (arrowed) . . .

Brakes, wheels and tyres 8•21

14.25b ... and lift the subframe off

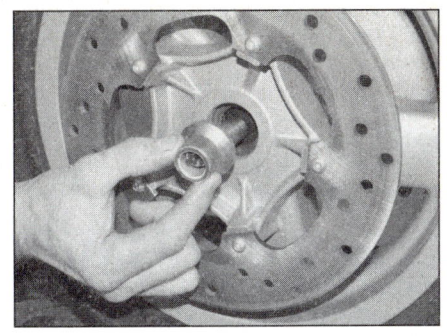

14.26 Slide the spacer off, noting how it fits

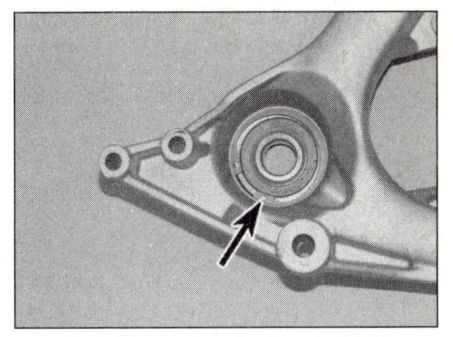

14.27 Subframe bearing is retained by a circlip (arrowed)

which way round it fits **(see illustration)**. Draw the wheel off the driveshaft. If required, follow the procedure in Section 6 to remove the brake disc.
Caution: Don't lay the wheel down and allow it to rest on the disc – the disc could become warped. Set the wheel on wood blocks so the disc doesn't support the weight of the wheel.

Check – all models

27 Check the condition of the bearing in the subframe – the bearing is sealed on both sides (see Section 15, Step 7). If there is any doubt about the condition of the bearing, renew it. Note that the bearing is retained by a circlip **(see illustration)**. Remove the circlip, then drive the bearing out from the other side. Follow the procedure in Section 15, Step 14, to install the new bearing.

28 Check the splines on the driveshaft and on the inside of the hub for wear and damage and renew either or both components as required **(see illustrations)**.

Installation – all models

29 Installation is the reverse of removal, noting the following:
 a) Tighten the wheel bolts securely.
 b) Install the spacer on the driveshaft between the wheel and the subframe.
 c) Install the large washer on the driveshaft,

14.28a Check the condition of the splines on the driveshaft ...

then the hub centre nut. Tighten the nut to the specified torque setting.
 d) Fit the cage nut and secure the nut using a new split pin, bending its ends around the cage nut.

15 Wheel bearings – removal, inspection and installation

Front wheel bearings
Monoshock (except Sfera with drum brake)

1 The bearings for the front wheel on these

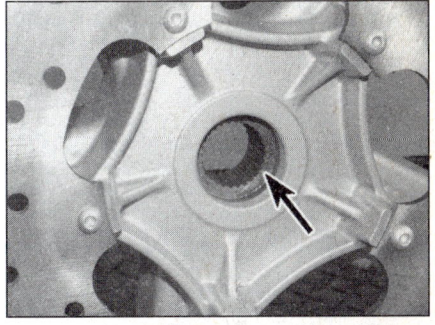

14.28b ... and the corresponding splines inside the hub

models are housed within the hub assembly. Remove the wheel and the hub assembly (see Section 13).

2 Remove the circlip retaining the caged ball-bearing using a pair of internal circlip pliers **(see illustration)**. Also remove the grease seal on the inside of the hub.

3 Set the hub assembly on blocks to allow the bearings to be driven out.

4 Using a metal rod (preferably a brass drift punch) inserted through the centre of the needle roller bearing on the inside of the hub, tap evenly around the outer race of the caged ball-bearing to drive it from the hub **(see illustration)**.

5 Lay the hub on its other side so that the

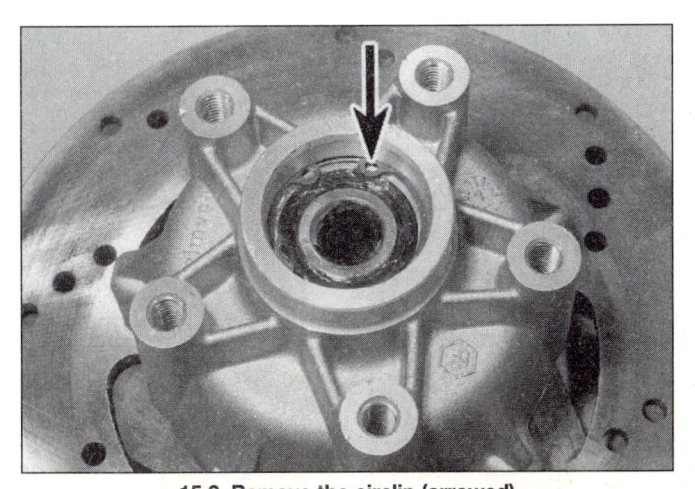

15.2 Remove the circlip (arrowed)

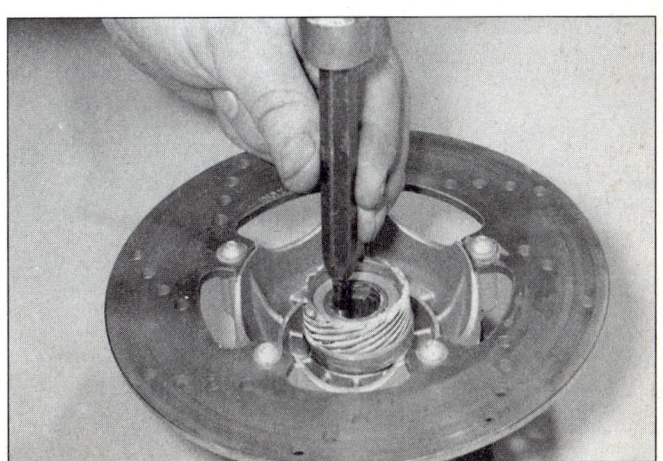

15.4 Drive the bearing out

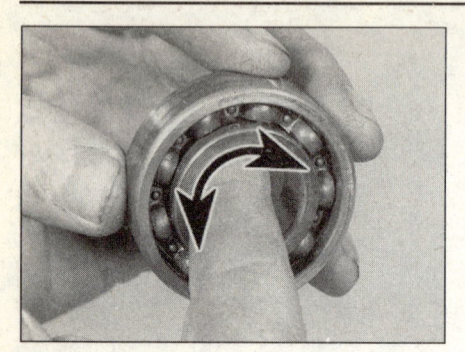

15.7 Hold the bearing outer race and listen whilst the inner race is spun

needle roller bearing faces down. Drive the bearing out of the hub using the same technique as above. Note that the needle bearing cannot be re-used after it has been driven out.

6 If the caged ball-bearing is of the unsealed type or is only sealed on one side, clean it with a high flash-point solvent (one which won't leave any residue) and blow it dry with compressed air (don't let the bearing spin as you dry it). Apply a few drops of oil to the bearing. **Note:** *If the bearing is sealed on both sides don't attempt to clean it.*

7 Hold the outer race of the bearing and rotate the inner race – if the bearing doesn't turn smoothly, has rough spots or is noisy, renew it **(see illustration)**.

8 If the bearing is good and can be re-used, wash it in solvent once again and dry it, then pack the bearing with grease.

9 Thoroughly clean the assembly, then install the bearings. Apply grease to the outside of the new needle bearing and press, rather than drive, it home until it is fully seated. In the absence of a press, a suitable drawbolt arrangement can be made up as described below.

10 Obtain a long bolt or a length of threaded rod from a local engineering works or some other supplier. The bolt or rod should be about one inch longer than the combined width of the hub and bearing. Also required are suitable nuts and two large and robust washers having a larger outside diameter than the caged ball-bearing housing. In the case of the threaded rod, fit one nut to one end of the rod and stake it in place for convenience.

11 Fit one of the washers over the bolt or rod so that it rests against the head or staked nut, then pass the assembly through the hub from the outside. Over the projecting end place the needle bearing, which should be greased to ease installation, followed by the remaining washer and nut.

12 Holding the bearing to ensure that it is kept square, slowly tighten the nut so that the bearing is drawn into its bore.

13 Once it is fully home, remove the drawbolt arrangement. Install a new oil seal into the hub.

14 Install the caged ball-bearing with the marked or sealed side facing outwards. Using the old bearing (if a new one is being fitted), a bearing driver or a socket large enough to contact the outer race of the bearing, drive it in squarely until it is completely seated. Fit the bearing retaining circlip, making sure it fits properly in its groove.

15 Install the hub assembly and the wheel (see Section 13).

Telescopic forks (and Sfera with drum brake)

Note: *Always renew the wheel bearings in pairs. Never renew the bearings individually. Avoid using a high pressure cleaner on the wheel bearing area.*

16 Remove the wheel (see Section 13).

17 Set the wheel on blocks. Do not to allow the weight of the wheel to rest on the brake disc (where applicable).

18 To remove the grease seals, which are metal and cannot, therefore, be levered out without damaging them, use either an expanding bearing puller and slide-hammer, or a suitable drift (such as a metal rod or a brass drift punch) inserted from the opposite side to the bearing being removed **(see illustrations)**. The tool used must locate on the rim of the shouldered spacer which locates behind the seal. Drawing or driving out the spacer will bring the seal with it. If the bearings are being removed, rather than just inspected, it is possible to locate the tool on the bearing inner race and to draw or drive the bearing, spacer and seal out together. If a drift is being used, and it is difficult to locate on the spacer or bearing due to the steep angle (the bearing must be face down and the drift inserted from the top), locate it on the upper rim of the central bearing spacer, which will be just below the inner race of the top bearing, and drive the central spacer, bearing, spacer and seal out together.

Caution: If driving against the central spacer, make sure you have the drift correctly located and are not trying to drive the top bearing into the wheel.

19 Lay the wheel on its other side and draw or drive the seal/spacer/bearing out of the wheel using the same technique as above.

20 If the bearings are of the unsealed type or are only sealed on one side, clean them with a high flash-point solvent (one which won't leave any residue) and blow them dry with compressed air (don't let the bearings spin as you dry them). Apply a few drops of oil to the bearing. **Note:** *If the bearing is sealed on both sides don't attempt to clean it.*

21 Hold the outer race of the bearing and rotate the inner race – if the bearing doesn't turn smoothly, has rough spots or is noisy, renew it **(see illustration 15.7)**.

22 If the bearings are in good condition and can be re-used, wash them in solvent once again and dry them, then pack the bearings with grease.

23 Thoroughly clean the hub area of the wheel. First install a bearing into its recess in one side of the hub, with the marked or sealed side facing outwards. Using the old bearing (if new ones are being fitted), a bearing driver or a socket large enough to contact the outer race of the bearing, drive it

15.18a Using a puller to remove the seals and bearings

15.18b Using a drift to remove the seals and bearings

15.23 Using a socket to drive in the bearings

15.25a Fit the shouldered spacer ...

15.25b ... then the seal

in until it is completely seated **(see illustration)**.
24 Turn the wheel over and install the bearing central spacer. Drive the other bearing into place as described above.
25 Fit the shouldered spacers onto the wheel so that the shoulder is against the bearing, then press the grease seals into the wheel, using a socket to drive them into place if required **(see illustrations)**.
26 With the exception of Zip and Sfera models, clean off all grease from the brake disc using acetone or brake system cleaner then install the wheel (see Section 13).

Rear wheel bearings

27 The rear wheel itself has no bearings. Refer to Chapter 2G for renewal of the driveshaft bearings in the gearbox. On models fitted with twin rear shock absorbers, also check the condition of the bearing in the rear subframe (see Section 14).

16 Tyres – general information and fitting

General information

1 The wheels fitted to all models are designed to take tubeless tyres only. Tyre sizes are given in the Specifications at the beginning of Chapter 1.
2 Refer to *Daily (pre-ride) checks* at the beginning of this manual for tyre maintenance.

Fitting new tyres

3 When selecting new tyres, refer to the tyre information label on the scooter and the tyre options listed in the owner's handbook. Ensure that front and rear tyre types are compatible, the correct size and correct speed rating; if necessary seek advice from a Piaggio dealer or tyre fitting specialist.
4 It is recommended that tyres are fitted by a motorcycle tyre specialist rather than attempted in the home workshop. This is particularly relevant in the case of tubeless tyres because the force required to break the seal between the wheel rim and tyre bead is substantial, and is usually beyond the capabilities of an individual working with normal tyre levers. Additionally, the specialist will be able to balance the wheels after tyre fitting.
5 Note that punctured tubeless tyres can in some cases be repaired. Piaggio recommend that such repairs are carried out only by an authorised dealer.

Notes

Chapter 9
Electrical system

Refer to the beginning of Chapter 1 for model identification details

Contents

Alternator coils – check (Typhoon 125, Hexagon, Skipper and LEADER engines) 30
Alternator – removal and installation .... see Chapter 2
Battery – charging 4
Battery – removal, installation and checks 3
Brake light switches – check and renewal 14
Brake/tail light bulb – renewal 9
Charging system – leakage and output test 29
Charging system testing – general information and precautions ... 28
Coolant temperature gauge and sender .... see Chapter 3
Diode (two-stroke engines) – check and renewal 23
Electrical system – fault finding 2
Fuel gauge and level sender, and low level warning circuit – check and renewal 18
Fuses – check and renewal 5
General information 1
Handlebar switches – check 21
Handlebar switches – removal and installation 22
Headlight aim – check and adjustment .... see Chapter 1
Headlight assembly – removal and installation 8
Headlight bulb and sidelight bulb – renewal 7
Horn – check and renewal 24
Ignition (main) switch – check, removal and installation 20
Ignition system components .... see Chapter 5
Instrument cluster bulbs and clock battery – renewal 17
Instrument cluster – check, removal and installation 15
Lighting system – check 6
Oil level warning circuit (two-stroke engines) – check 19
Regulator/rectifier – renewal 31
Side stand switch – check and renewal 32
Speedometer cable – renewal 16
Starter motor – disassembly, inspection and reassembly 27
Starter motor – removal and installation 26
Starter relay – check and renewal 25
Tail light assembly – removal and installation 10
Turn signal assemblies – removal and installation 13
Turn signal bulbs – renewal 12
Turn signal circuit – check 11

Degrees of difficulty

| **Easy**, suitable for novice with little experience | **Fairly easy**, suitable for beginner with some experience | **Fairly difficult**, suitable for competent DIY mechanic | **Difficult**, suitable for experienced DIY mechanic | **Very difficult**, suitable for expert DIY or professional |

Specifications

Battery
Capacity
  Zip 50 .... 12 V, 3.6 Ah
  Typhoon 50, Sfera 50, Zip, Zip SP, NRG (all models),
    ET2, Liberty 50, Fly 50, LX2 50 .... 12 V, 4 Ah
  Typhoon 80, Sfera 80 .... 12 V, 5 Ah
  Typhoon/Sfera 125, ET4, Hexagon, Skipper, Skipper ST,
    Liberty 50 4T, Liberty 125, ET4 50, Zip 50 4T, Zip 125,
    Fly 50 4T, Fly 125, LX4 50, LX4 125 .... 12 V, 9 Ah
  Super Hexagon 125, B125, X8, X9, GT125/200 .... 12 V, 12 Ah
Specific gravity (all models)
  Fully charged .... 1.26 to 1.28
  Uncharged 0.84
Charging rate (all models) .... 0.5 A for 6 to 8 hrs

9•2 Electrical system

Alternator
Unregulated voltage output
   Typhoon 50/80, Sfera 50/80/125, ET2, ET4 125, Zip, Zip SP, Zip 50,
      NRG (all models), Liberty 50, LX 50, Fly 50 . . . . 25 to 30 V (ac) at 3000 rpm
   ET4 50, Liberty 50 4T, Zip 50 4T, LX4 50, Fly 50 4T . . . . 25 to 35 V (ac) at 3000 rpm
   Typhoon 125, Hexagon/Super Hexagon, Skipper, Skipper ST,
      Liberty 125, Zip 125 . . . . 27 to 31 V (ac) at 2000 rpm

Charging coil resistance
   LX 50, Fly 50 . . . . 800 to 1100 ohms
   X8, LX 125, Fly 125, GT125/200 . . . . 0.7 to 0.9 ohms

Regulator/rectifier
Regulated current output
   Typhoon 50/80, Sfera 50/80/125, ET2, Zip, Zip SP, Zip 50,
      NRG (all models), Liberty 50, LX 50, Fly 50, LX4 50,
      Fly 50 4T, NRG Power DT and DD . . . . 1.5 to 2.0 A at 3000 rpm
   ET4 50, Liberty 50 4T, Zip 50 4T . . . . 4.5 A at 4000 rpm
   Skipper ST 125, Liberty 125, ET4 125, Zip 125 . . . . above 1.8 A at 3000 rpm
   Typhoon 125, Hexagon, Skipper . . . . 8.5 A at 2000 rpm
   B125, X9 . . . . 8.0 A at 3000 rpm
Regulated voltage output – X8, LX 125, Fly 125, GT125/200 . . . . 14.0 to 15.2 V at 3000 rpm

Fuses
Note: *Use the information on the fusebox lid or in the owners handbook if it differs from that given below.*

Typhoon 50/80, Sfera 50/80/125, NRG (all models),
   Zip, Zip SP, Zip 50, Liberty 50, ET2, Fly 50,
   LX2 50 (without immobiliser) . . . . 7.5 A
ET4 125, ET2 (with immobiliser) . . . . 7.5 A
Typhoon 125, Skipper, Super Hexagon, Liberty 125, Zip 125,
   ET4 50, Liberty 50 4T, Zip 50 4T, Fly 50, Fly 50 4T, LX4 50 . . . . 10 A
Fly 125, LX 125
   Main . . . . 15 A
   Others . . . . 7.5 A
B125, X9
   Main . . . . 15 A
   Others . . . . 10 A , 7.5 A , 4 A
X8, GT125/200
   Main . . . . 15 A
   Others . . . . 10 A , 7.5 A , 5 A
Skipper ST
   Main . . . . 15 A
   Others . . . . 7.5 A, 5A
Hexagon
   Main . . . . 25 A
   Others . . . . 10 A , 7.5 A , 4 A

Bulbs
Headlight (main/dipped)
   Hexagon, all Fly models, LX4 50, GT125/200 . . . . 60/55 W
   Super Hexagon, B125, X8, X9 . . . . 55/55 W
   All other models . . . . 35/35 W
Sidelight
   ET2, ET4, Super Hexagon, Liberty 125, B125, X9, all Fly models,
      LX 50, LX4 50 . . . . 5 W
   NRG Power DT and DD models . . . . 3 W
   All other models . . . . 4 W
Brake/tail light
   X8 . . . . 10/5 W
   GT125/200 . . . . 2.3 W
   NRG Power DT and DD models . . . . LED
   All other models . . . . 21/5 W
Number plate light (where fitted) . . . . 5 W
Turn signal lights
   X8 front turn signals . . . . 5 W
   All other models . . . . 10 W
Instrument and warning lights . . . . 1.2 and/or 2.0 W
Storage compartment light . . . . 5 W

Electrical system 9•3

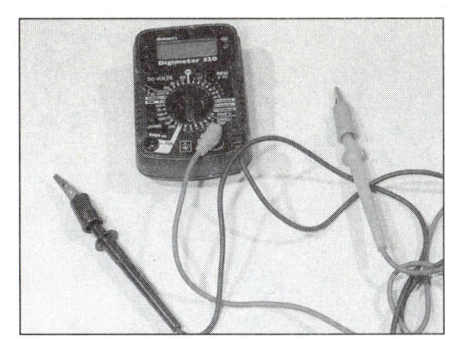

2.5 A multimeter is capable of reading ohms, amps and volts

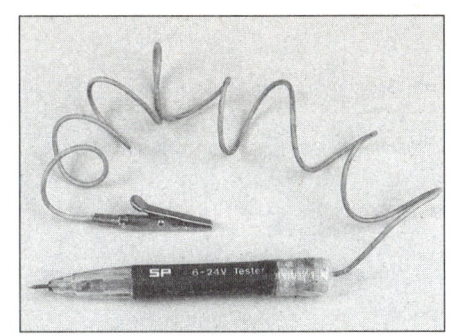

2.6a A simple test light . . .

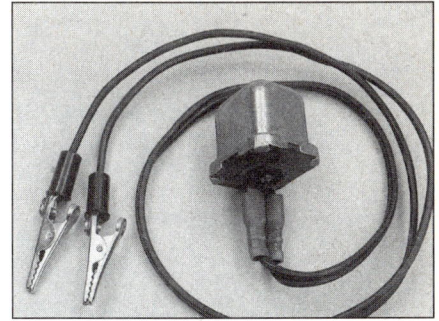

2.6b . . . or a buzzer can be used for simple voltage checks

1 General information

All models have a 12 volt electrical system charged by a three-phase alternator with a separate regulator/rectifier.

The regulator maintains the charging system output within the specified range to prevent overcharging, and the rectifier converts the AC (alternating current) output of the alternator to DC (direct current) to power the lights and other components and to charge the battery. The alternator rotor is mounted on the right-hand end of the crankshaft.

All models are fitted with an electric starter motor. The starting system includes the motor, the battery, the relay and the various wires and switches.

Note: *Keep in mind that electrical parts, once purchased, cannot be returned. To avoid unnecessary expense, make very sure the faulty component has been positively identified before buying a new part.*

2 Electrical system – fault finding

⚠ **Warning:** *To prevent the risk of short circuits, the ignition (main) switch must always be OFF and the battery negative (-ve) terminal should be disconnected before any of the bike's other electrical components are disturbed. Don't forget to reconnect the terminal securely once work is finished or if battery power is needed for circuit testing.*

Tracing faults

1 A typical electrical circuit consists of an electrical component, the switches, relays, etc, related to that component, and the wiring and terminals that connect the component to both the battery and the frame. To aid in locating a problem in any electrical circuit, refer to the wiring diagrams at the end of this Chapter.

2 Before tackling any troublesome electrical circuit, first study the wiring diagram thoroughly to get a complete picture of what makes up that individual circuit. Trouble spots, for instance, can often be narrowed down by noting if other components related to that circuit are operating properly or not. If several components or circuits fail at one time, chances are the fault lies in the fuse or earth connection.

3 Electrical problems often stem from simple causes, such as loose or corroded connections or a blown fuse. Prior to any electrical fault finding, always visually check the condition of the fuse, wires and connections in the problem circuit. Intermittent failures can be especially frustrating, since you can't always duplicate the failure when it's convenient to test. In such situations, a good practice is to clean all connections in the affected circuit, whether or not they appear to be good. All of the connections and wires should also be wiggled to check for looseness which can cause intermittent failure.

4 If testing instruments are going to be utilised, use the wiring diagram to plan where you will make the necessary connections in order to accurately pinpoint the trouble spot.

Using test equipment

5 The basic tools needed for electrical fault finding include a battery and bulb test circuit, a continuity tester, a test light, and a jumper wire. A multi-meter capable of reading volts, ohms and amps is also very useful as an alternative to the above, and is necessary for performing more extensive tests and checks **(see illustration)**.

6 Voltage checks should be performed if a circuit is not functioning properly. Connect one lead of a test light or voltmeter to either the negative battery terminal or a known good earth **(see illustrations)**. Connect the other lead to a connector in the circuit being tested, preferably nearest to the battery or fuse. If the bulb lights, voltage is reaching that point, which means the part of the circuit between that connector and the battery is problem-free. Continue checking the remainder of the circuit in the same manner. When you reach a point where no voltage is present, the problem lies between there and the last good test point. Most of the time the problem is due to a loose connection. Keep in mind that some circuits only receive voltage when the ignition is ON.

7 One method of finding short circuits is to remove the fuse and connect a test light or voltmeter in its place to the fuse terminals. There should be no load in the circuit (it should be switched off). Move the wiring harness from side-to-side while watching the test light. If the bulb lights, there is a short to earth somewhere in that area, probably where insulation has rubbed off a wire. The same test can be performed on other components in the circuit, including the switch.

8 An earth check should be done to see if a component is earthed properly. Disconnect the battery and connect one lead of a self-powered test light (continuity tester) to a known good earth **(see illustrations)**.

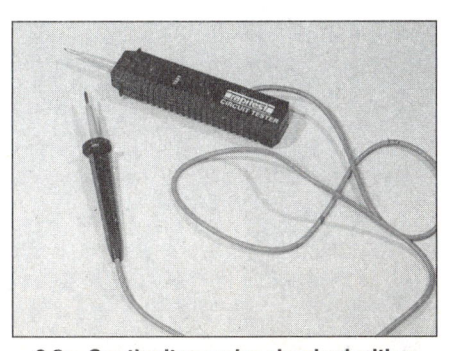

2.8a Continuity can be checked with a battery-powered tester . . .

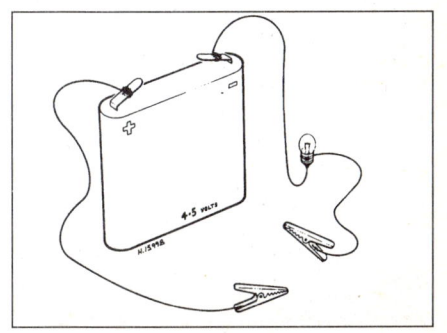

2.8b . . . or a battery and bulb circuit

9•4 Electrical system

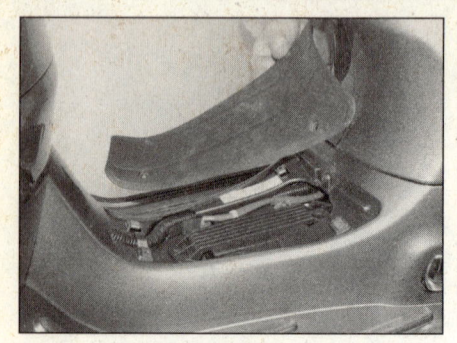

3.1a On GT models, first remove the centre mat . . .

3.1b . . . then remove the battery cover (arrowed)

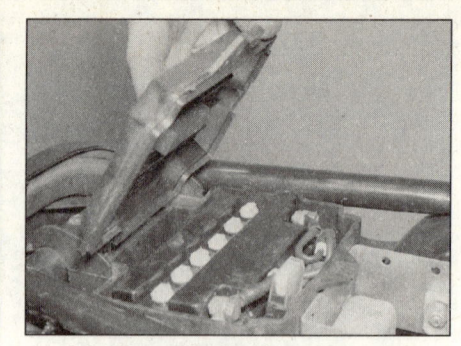

3.1c Removing the battery cover – Hexagon

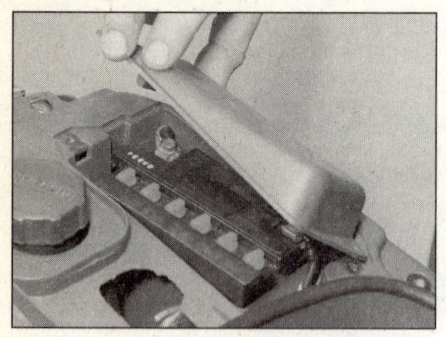

3.1d Removing the battery cover – Typhoon

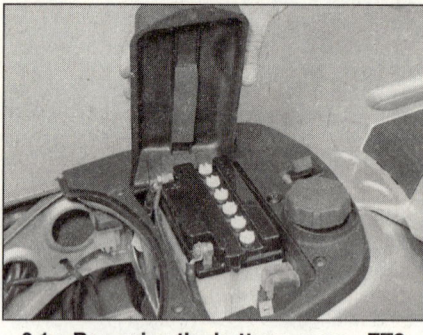

3.1e Removing the battery cover – ET2 and ET4

3.1f Removing the battery cover – X8

Connect the other lead to the wire or earth connection being tested. If the bulb lights, the earth is good. If the bulb does not light, the earth is not good.

9 A continuity check is performed to see if a circuit, section of circuit or individual component is capable of passing electricity through it. Disconnect the battery and connect one lead of a self-powered test light (continuity tester) to one end of the circuit being tested and the other lead to the other end of the circuit. If the bulb lights, there is continuity, which means the circuit is passing electricity through it properly. Switches can be checked in the same way.

3 Battery – removal, installation and checks

Caution: Be extremely careful when handling or working around the battery. The electrolyte is very caustic and an explosive gas (hydrogen) is given off when the battery is charging.

Removal and installation

1 On GT125/200 models, the battery is located between the left and right-hand floor panels – undo the four screws securing the centre mat and lift it off, then remove the screws securing the battery cover and lift the cover off the battery **(see illustrations)**. On all other models, the battery is located under the seat; on Hexagon models, remove the seat (see Chapter 7), on all other models, unlock the seat and raise it upright. Remove the screw or screws securing the battery cover and lift the cover off the battery **(see illustrations)**.

2 Unscrew the negative (-ve) terminal bolt first and disconnect the lead from the battery, then unscrew the positive (+ve) terminal bolt and disconnect the lead **(see illustration)**. Lift the battery from its holder **(see illustration)**.

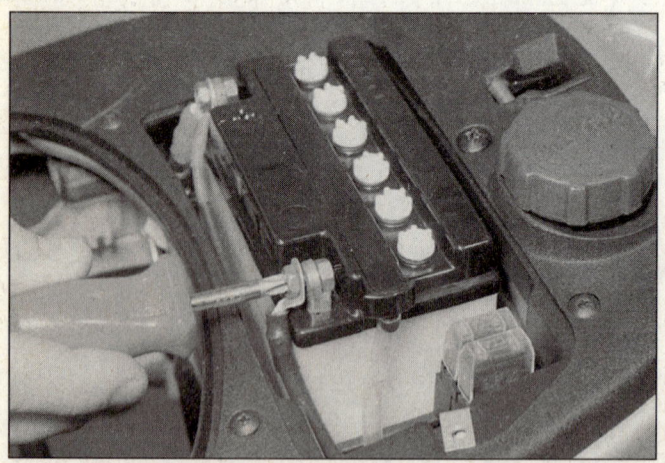

3.2a Disconnect the negative (-ve) lead first, then the positive (+ve) lead . . .

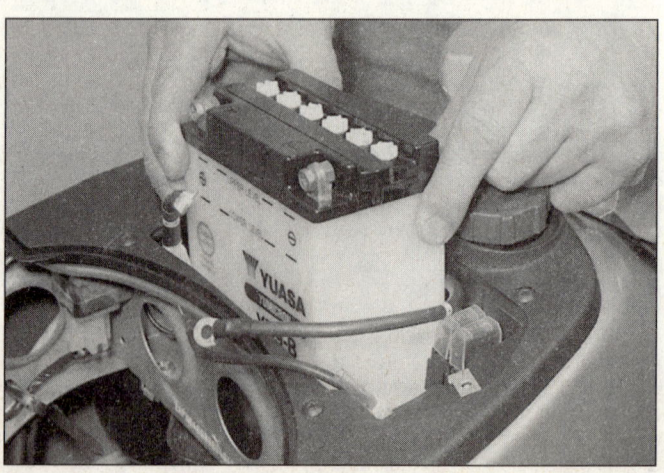

3.2b . . . and remove the battery

Electrical system 9•5

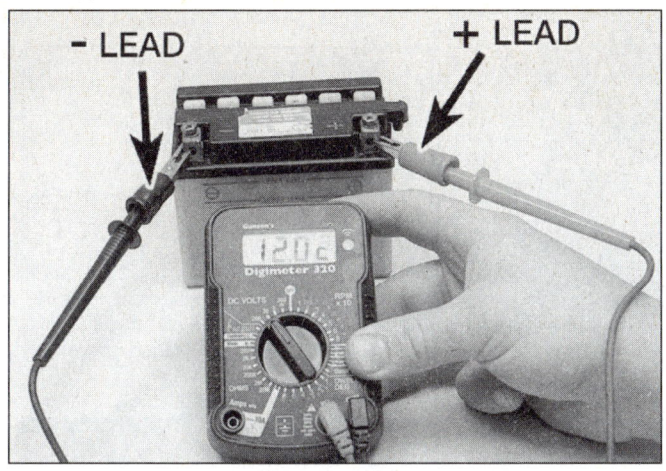

3.11 Measuring battery open-circuit voltage

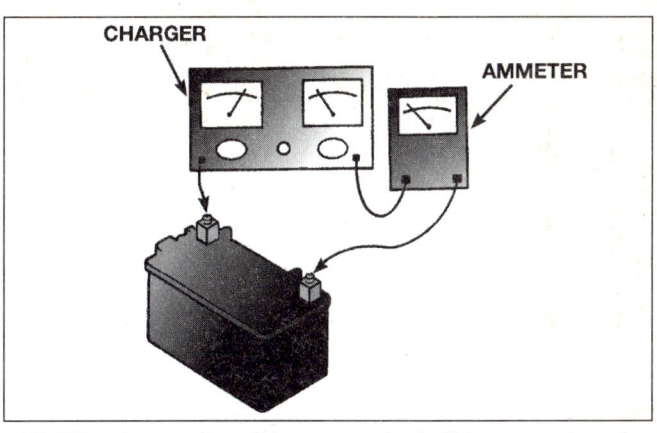

4.2 If the charger doesn't have ammeter built in, connect one in series as shown. DO NOT connect the ammeter between the battery terminals or it will be ruined

3 On installation, clean the battery terminals and lead ends with a wire brush or knife and emery paper. Reconnect the leads, connecting the positive (+ve) terminal first.
4 Fit the battery cover and install or lower the seat.

Inspection and maintenance

Conventional battery

5 The battery fitted as standard to most models is of the conventional lead-acid type, requiring regular checks of the electrolyte level (see Chapter 1) in addition to those detailed below.
6 Check the battery terminals and leads for tightness and corrosion. If corrosion is evident, unscrew the terminal bolts and disconnect the leads from the battery, disconnecting the negative (-ve) terminal first, and clean the terminals and lead ends with a wire brush or knife and emery paper. Reconnect the leads, connecting the negative (-ve) terminal last, and apply a thin coat of petroleum jelly to the connections to slow further corrosion.
7 The battery case should be kept clean to prevent current leakage, which can discharge the battery over a period of time (especially when it sits unused). Wash the outside of the case with a solution of baking soda and water. Rinse the battery thoroughly, then dry it.
8 Look for cracks in the case and renew the battery if any are found. If acid has been spilled on the battery holder or surrounding bodywork, neutralise it with a baking soda and water solution, dry it thoroughly, then touch up any damaged paint.
9 If the scooter sits unused for long periods of time, disconnect the cables from the battery terminals, negative (-ve) terminal first. Refer to Section 4 and charge the battery once every month to six weeks.
10 The condition of the battery can be assessed by measuring the specific gravity of the electrolyte. To do this an hydrometer is needed. Remove the cell caps from the battery. Insert the hydrometer nozzle into each cell in turn and squeeze the hydrometer pump to draw some electrolyte from the cell. Check the reading on the float at the level of the electrolyte and compare it to the Specifications at the beginning of the Chapter. If necessary, remove the battery and recharge it as described below in Section 4.
11 The condition of the battery can also be assessed by measuring the voltage present at the battery terminals. Connect the voltmeter positive (+ve) probe to the battery positive (+ve) terminal, and the negative (-ve) probe to the battery negative (-ve) terminal **(see illustration)**. While Piaggio provide no specifications, when fully-charged there should be more than 12.5 volts present. If the voltage falls below 12.0 volts the battery must be removed, disconnecting the negative (-ve) terminal first, and recharged as described below in Section 4. **Note:** *Before taking the measurement, wait at least 30 minutes after any charging has taken place (including running the engine).*

Maintenance-free battery

12 Several later models are fitted with an MF battery as standard. Maintenance-free batteries require little in the way of regular checks and are of sealed construction. All that is required is a check of terminal condition and the battery case as described above in Steps 6 to 9.
13 The specific gravity cannot be measured due to its sealed construction, although voltage can be checked as described in Step 11.

4 Battery – charging

Caution: Be extremely careful when handling or working around the battery. The electrolyte is very caustic and an explosive gas (hydrogen) is given off when the battery is charging.

1 Remove the battery (see Section 3). Connect the charger to the battery, making sure that the positive (+ve) lead on the charger is connected to the positive (+ve) terminal on the battery, and the negative (-ve) lead is connected to the negative (-ve) battery terminal.
2 Piaggio recommend that the battery is charged at a maximum rate of 0.5 amps for 6 to 8 hours. Exceeding this figure can cause the battery to overheat, buckling the plates and rendering it useless. Few owners will have access to an expensive current-controlled charger, so if a normal domestic charger is used check that after a possible initial peak, the charge rate falls to a safe level **(see illustration)**. If the battery becomes hot during charging **stop**. Further charging will cause damage. **Note:** *In emergencies the battery can be charged at a higher rate of around 3.0 amps for a period of 1 hour. However, this is not recommended and the low amp charge is by far the safer method of charging the battery.*
3 Note that when charging an MF battery make sure that you use a regulated battery charger. If using a constant voltage charger, ensure that the voltage does not exceed 15.2 V otherwise the battery could be ruined.
4 If the recharged battery discharges rapidly if left disconnected it is likely that an internal short caused by physical damage or sulphation has occurred. A new battery will be required. A sound item will tend to lose its charge at about 1% per day.
5 Install the battery (see Section 3).
6 If the scooter sits unused for long periods of time, charge the battery once every month to six weeks and leave it disconnected.

5 Fuses – check and renewal

1 The electrical system is protected by a fuse or fuses of different ratings (see Specifications). On models with only one fuse, and on ET2 and ET4 models, the fuse(s) is/are

9•6 Electrical system

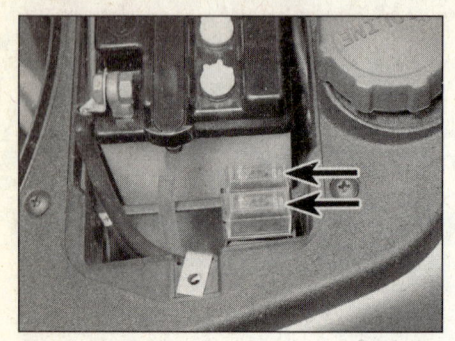

5.1a Fuseholders (arrowed) – ET2 and ET4

5.1b Fuseholder (all except main fuse) – Hexagon

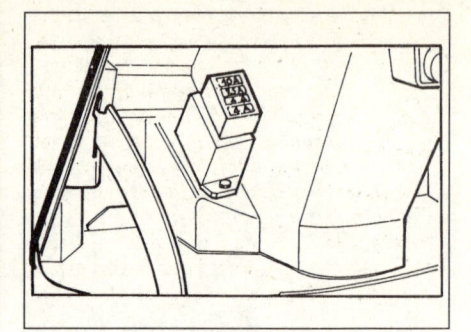

5.1c Fuseholder – Skipper

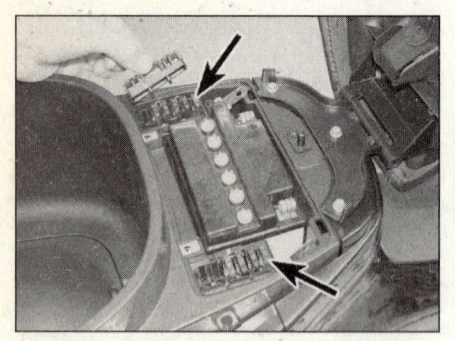

5.1d Fuseholders (arrowed) next to the battery – X8

5.1e Fuseholder – B125

5.1f Fuseholder – X9

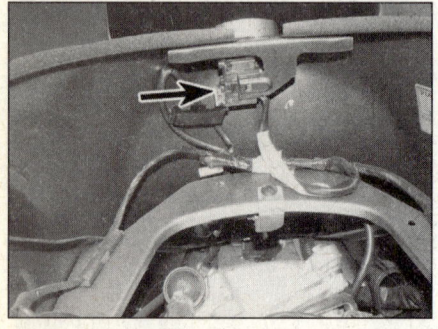

5.1g Location of main fuse (arrowed) . . .

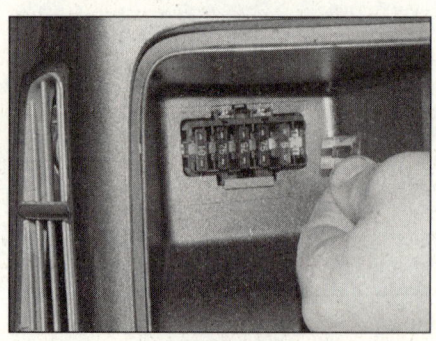

5.1h . . . and multiple fuseholder on GT models

located in a holder next to the battery (see illustration). On most other models with multiple fuses, the main fuse is located in a holder next to the battery and all other fuses are located in a holder located behind the access panel in the right-hand side of the kick panel on the Typhoon 125, behind the access panel in the left-hand side of the kick panel on the Hexagon (see illustration), or inside the glove compartment on the Skipper (see illustration). On the X8 all the fuses are located in holders next to the battery (see illustration). On the B125 the fuses are located inside the glove compartment and behind the right-hand side panel trim (see illustration). On the X9 the fuses are located inside the glove compartment and at the back of the storage compartment (see illustration). On GT models the main fuse is located inside the bodywork underneath the seat hinge – lift up the seat and lift out the storage compartment to access the fuse (see illustration); all other fuses are located inside the glove compartment (see illustration).

2 The fuses can be removed and checked visually. Remove the fuseholder cover, then pull out the fuse (see illustrations). If you can't pull it out with your fingers, use a pair of suitable pliers. A blown fuse is easily identified by a break in the element (see illustration). Each fuse is clearly marked with its rating and

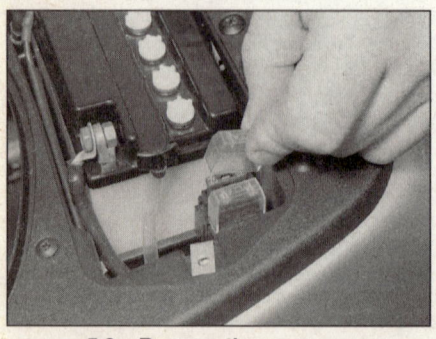

5.2a Remove the cover . . .

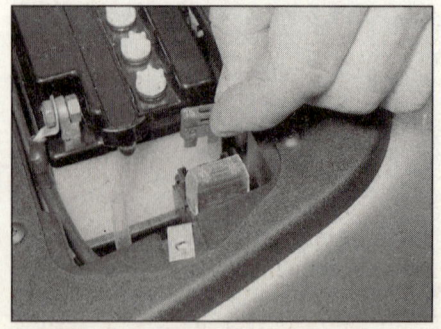

5.2b . . . and pull out the fuse

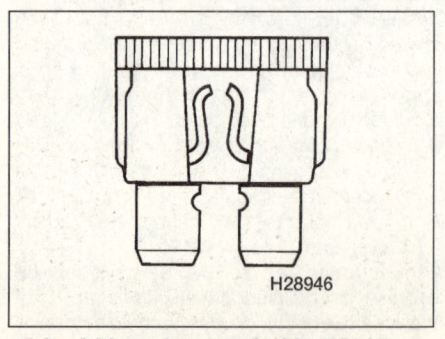

5.2c A blown fuse can be identified by a break in its element

Electrical system 9•7

must only be substituted by a fuse of the correct rating. It is advisable to carry a spare fuse of each rating on the scooter at all times.

> ⚠️ **Warning:** *Never put in a fuse of a higher rating or bridge the terminals with any other substitute, however temporary it may be. Serious damage may be done to the circuit, or a fire may start.*

3 If a fuse blows, be sure to check the wiring circuit very carefully for evidence of a short circuit. Look for bare wires and chafed, melted or burned insulation. If the fuse is renewed before the cause is located, the new fuse will blow immediately.

4 Occasionally a fuse will blow or cause an open circuit for no obvious reason. Corrosion of the fuse ends and fuseholder terminals may occur and cause poor fuse contact. If this happens, remove the corrosion with a wire brush or emery paper, then spray the fuse end and fuseholder terminals with electrical contact cleaner.

6 Lighting system – check

1 The battery provides power for operation of the headlight, tail light, brake light and instrument cluster lights. If none of the lights operate, always check battery voltage before proceeding. Low battery voltage indicates either a faulty battery or a defective charging system. Refer to Section 3 for battery checks and Sections 30 and 31 for charging system tests. Also, check the condition of the fuse(s).

Headlight

2 If the headlight fails to work, first check the fuse (see Section 5), and then the bulb (see Section 7). If they are both good, the problem lies in the wiring or one of the switches in the circuit. Refer to Section 21 for the switch testing procedures, and also the wiring diagrams at the end of this Chapter.

3 Hexagon, B125, X8, X9, and GT models are fitted with a headlight relay, located behind the front panel and mounted to the frame on a bracket **(see illustrations)**. Remove the front panel for access to the relay (see Chapter 7).

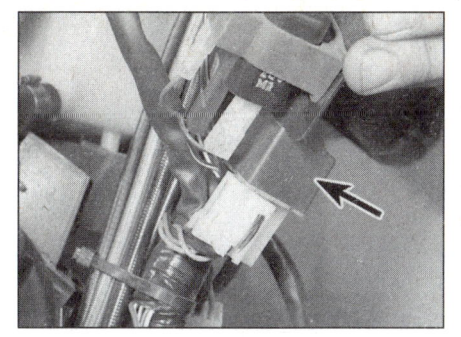

6.3a Headlight relay (arrowed) – Hexagon

6.3b Headlight relay – GT models

There are no test details for checking the relay; if it is suspected of being faulty, substitute it with another relay, although it is worth checking the power supply to and from the relay beforehand.

4 Check the power supply to the relay by checking for battery voltage at the No. 30 terminal of the relay. If no voltage is present, check the wiring between the relay and the fuse (see wiring diagrams at the end of the Chapter). If the wiring is good, check for voltage at the No. 87 terminal on the relay with the ignition and lighting switches ON. If voltage is present, the relay is functioning correctly and the fault must lie in the wiring between the relay and the dip switch, or between the dip switch and the headlight. If no voltage is shown at terminal No. 87, either the relay is faulty or there is a fault between the relay and the lighting switch or between the lighting switch and the ignition switch.

Tail light

5 If the tail light fails to work, first check the bulb and the bulb terminals (see Section 9). **Note:** *On NRG Power models, the brake/tail light consists of a number of LEDs in a sealed unit – when a single LED fails it cannot be renewed, but the failure of one LED will not affect the function of the others.* Next check the fuse (see Section 5), then check for battery voltage at the terminal on the supply side of the tail light. If voltage is present, check the earth (ground) circuit for an open or poor connection.

6 If no voltage is indicated, check the tail light wiring circuit (see wiring diagrams at the end of the Chapter).

Brake light

7 If the brake light fails to work, check the bulb and the bulb terminals first (see Section 9), then the fuse (see Section 5), then check for battery voltage at the terminal on the supply side of the brake light, with the brake lever pulled in. If voltage is present, check the earth (ground) circuit for an open or poor connection.

8 If no voltage is indicated, check the brake light switches (see Section 14), then the brake light wiring circuit (see wiring diagrams at the end of the Chapter).

Instrument and warning lights

9 See Section 17 for instrument and warning light bulb renewal.

Turn signal lights

10 See Section 11 for the turn signal circuit check.

7 Headlight bulb and sidelight bulb – renewal

Note: *If the headlight bulb is of the quartz-halogen type, do not touch the bulb glass as skin acids will shorten the bulb's service life. If the bulb is accidentally touched, it should be wiped carefully when cold with a rag soaked in methylated spirit and dried before fitting.*

> ⚠️ **Warning:** *Allow the bulb time to cool before removing it if the headlight has just been on.*

Headlight

1 On NRG models, remove the grille and, where fitted, the air duct in the front panel. On other models with the headlight mounted in the front panel, remove the headlight (see Section 8). On models with the headlight mounted on the handlebar, remove or displace the handlebar covers (see Chapter 7).

2 Where fitted, remove the rubber dust cover and disconnect the electrical connector from the bulb **(see illustration)**. Either twist the bulbholder anti-clockwise and draw it out of the headlight, or release the bulb retaining clip **(see illustration)**. Remove the bulb, noting how it fits.

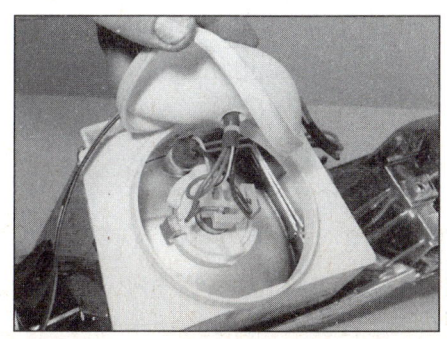

7.2a Lift the rubber cover to access the connector and bulb

7.2b Release the wire clip (arrowed)

9•8 Electrical system

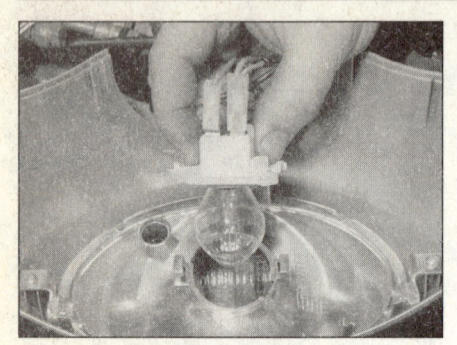

7.3a Remove the bulbholder . . .

7.3b . . . then the bulb

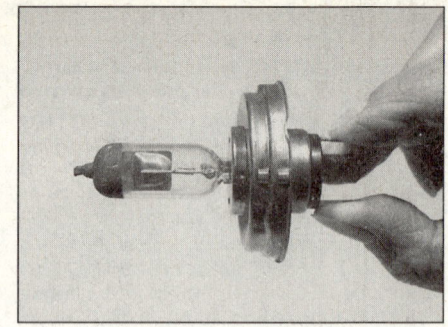

7.4 Handle quartz halogen bulbs by their wire terminals only – do not touch the glass

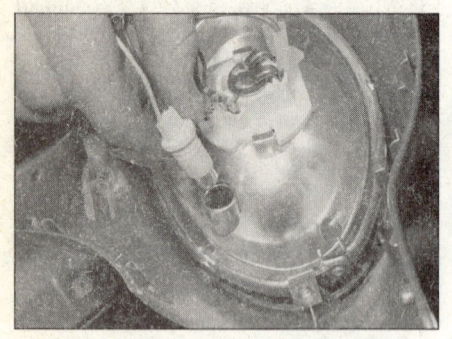

7.8a Remove the sidelight bulbholder . . .

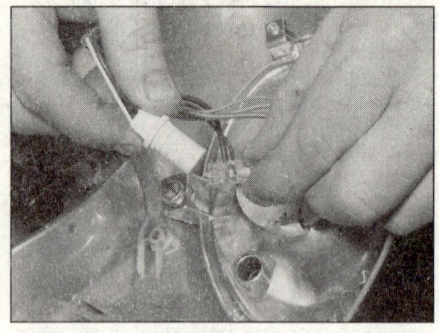

7.8b . . . and gently pull out the capless bulb

HAYNES HiNT *Always use a paper towel or dry cloth when handling new bulbs to prevent injury if the bulb should break and to increase bulb life.*

8 Headlight assembly – removal and installation

3 On all other models, twist the bulbholder anti-clockwise and draw it out of the headlight, then push the bulb in and twist it anti-clockwise to release it from the holder **(see illustrations)**.
4 Fit the new bulb and install the holder, bearing in mind the information in the **Note (see illustration)**. Make sure the pins on the bulb fit correctly in the slots in the bulbholder. The bulb types and wattage differ between the Piaggio models – refer to the Specifications at the beginning of this Chapter or note the wattage marked on the cap of the original bulb, and fit a bulb of the same type and wattage.
5 If applicable, connect the wiring connector and install the dust cover, making sure it is correctly seated **(see illustration 7.2a)**.
6 Check the operation of the headlight.

Sidelight

7 On NRG models, remove the grille and, where fitted, the air duct in the front panel. On other models with the headlight mounted in the front panel, remove the headlight (see Section 8). On models with the headlight mounted on the handlebar, remove or displace the handlebar covers (see Chapter 7).
8 Pull the bulbholder out of its socket in the headlight, then carefully pull the bulb out of the holder **(see illustrations)**. **Note:** *The type of bulb commonly used is capless and is a push-fit – if a bayonet type bulb is encountered (pins on the bulb cap), the bulb is pushed gently into its holder and turned anti-clockwise to release it.*
9 Carefully press the new bulb into the bulbholder, then install the bulbholder by pressing it in. If a rubber cover is fitted ensure it is correctly seated.
10 Check the operation of the sidelight.

Removal
Handlebar-mounted headlight

1 Remove or displace the handlebar covers (see Chapter 7). Either disconnect the headlight wiring connectors, or remove the bulbholder by twisting it anti-clockwise **(see illustration 7.3a)**. Also pull the sidelight bulbholder out of its socket **(see illustration 7.8a)**. Remove the screws securing the headlight to the front cover or to the handlebars and remove the headlight **(see illustration)**.

Front panel-mounted headlight

2 On the Typhoon the headlight is secured by the two screws in the kick panel; remove the screws and draw the headlight assembly out of the front panel **(see illustrations)**. On the Sfera and Zip SP the headlight it is secured by two screws inside the glove compartment, and on the Hexagon it is secured by a screw located behind each access panel in the kick panel. Remove the screws and draw the

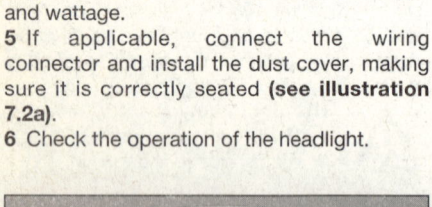

8.1 Remove the screws securing the headlight to the handlebar cover

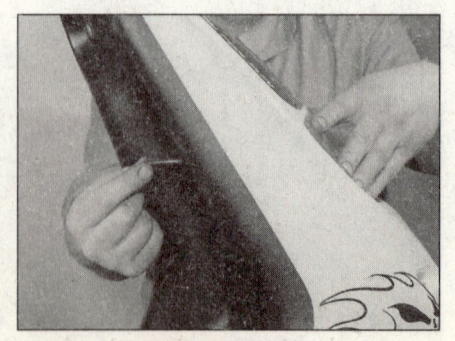

8.2a On the Typhoon, remove the screws . . .

8.2b . . . then withdraw the headlight and disconnect the wiring connectors

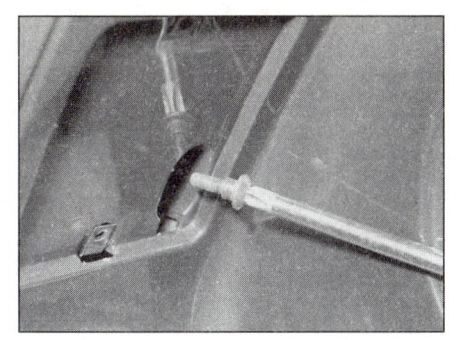

Electrical system 9•9

8.2c On the Hexagon, remove the screws...

8.2d ...withdraw the headlight assembly...

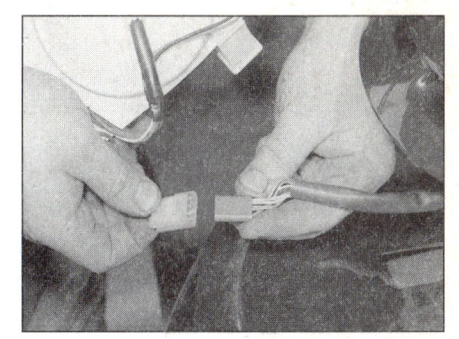

8.2e ...and disconnect the wiring connector

headlight assembly out of the front panel, then disconnect the wiring connector(s) when accessible **(see illustrations)**. On the Sfera and Hexagon, separate the turn signal units from the headlight if required. On the B125 the headlight is secured by four screws inside the glove compartment (see Chapter 7).

3 On NRG MC² and MC³ models, remove the front panel, then disconnect the wiring connectors (see Chapter 7). Either remove the screws securing each headlight to the bracket and remove the headlights separately, or remove the screws securing the bracket and remove the complete assembly. On NRG Power DT and DD models, remove the front panel, then disconnect the wiring connectors (see Chapter 7). Remove the screws securing the headlight assembly and lift it off **(see illustration)**. On X8 models, first remove the front insert panel (see Chapter 7). Undo the screws securing each turn signal assembly, then disconnect the assembly wiring connectors and lift them off **(see illustrations)**. Undo the three screws securing the headlight assembly and draw it forward, then disconnect the assembly wiring connector **(see illustrations)**. On the X9 remove the front insert panel to access the three headlight retaining screws (see Chapter 7).

Installation

4 Installation is the reverse of removal. Make sure all the wiring is correctly connected and secured. Check the operation of the headlight and sidelight. Check the headlight aim (see Chapter 1).

9 Brake/tail light bulb – renewal

Note 1: *It is a good idea to use a paper towel or dry cloth when handling new bulbs to prevent injury if the bulb should break and to increase bulb life.*

Note 2: *On NRG Power models, the brake/tail light consists of a number of LEDs in a sealed unit – when a single LED fails it cannot be renewed, but the failure of one LED will not affect the function of the others. When sufficient LEDs have failed so as to impair the safe operation of the scooter, renew the tail light assembly (see Step 10).*

1 On the B125, undo the screws securing the tail light/turn signal unit (see Chapter 7, Section

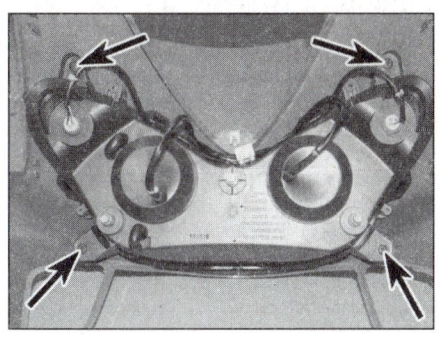

8.3a Headlight assembly is secured by four screws – NRG Power models

8.3b On X8 models, remove the screws securing each turn signal assembly...

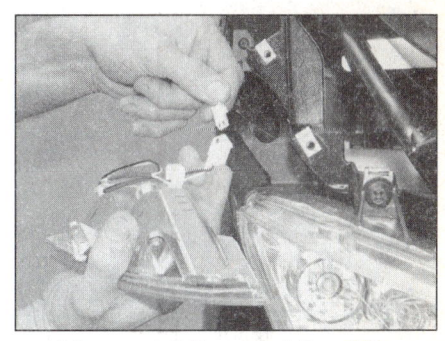

8.3c ...and disconnect the wiring connectors

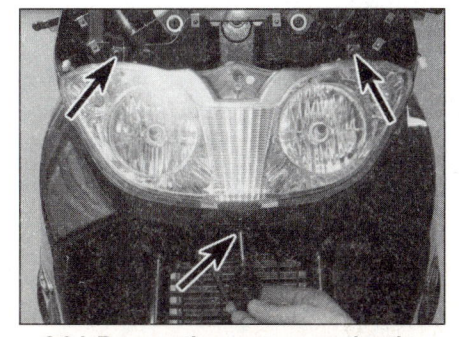

8.3d Remove the screws securing the headlight assembly...

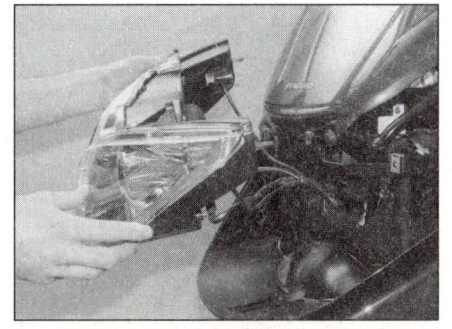

8.3e ...then draw it forward...

8.3f ...and disconnect the wiring connector

9•10 Electrical system

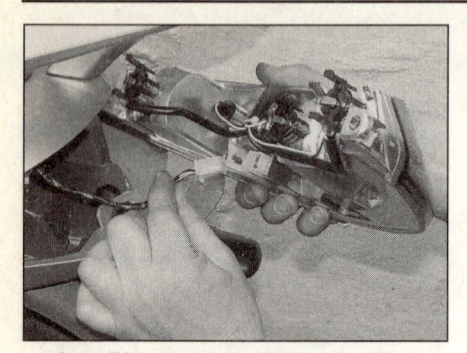

9.1a Disconnect the light unit wiring connector – B125

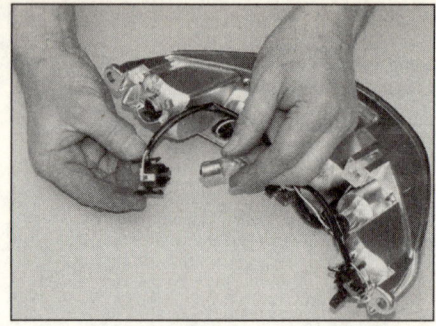

9.1b Remove the bulbholder and bulb as described

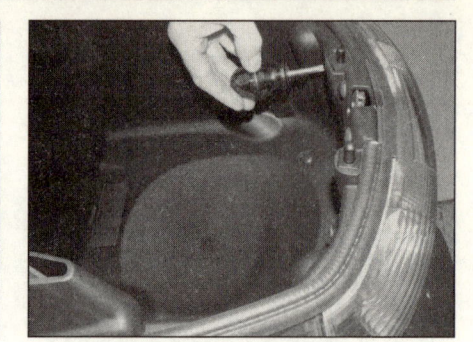

9.2a Undo the screws . . .

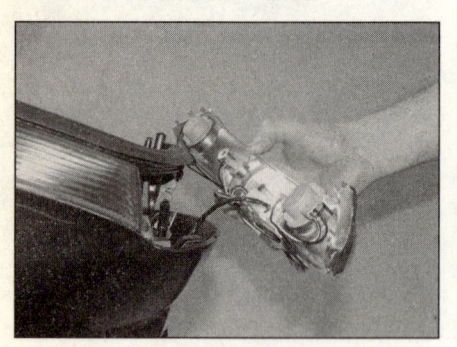

9.2b . . . and draw out the tail light assembly – X8 models

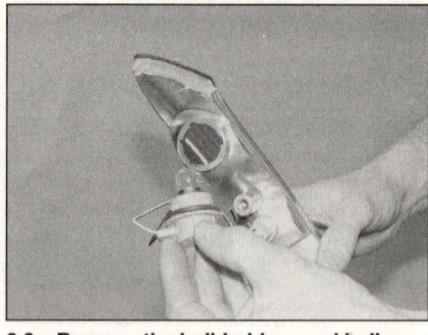

9.2c Remove the bulbholders and bulbs as described

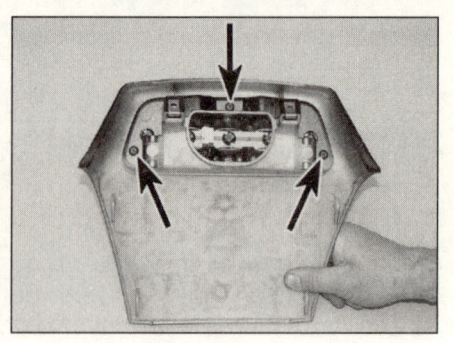

9.3a Brake light unit is secured by three screws – X9

21). Remove the unit and disconnect the wiring connector **(see illustration)**. Press the tabs on the bulbholder and pull it out of the light unit, then push the bulb into the holder and twist it anti-clockwise to remove it **(see illustration)**. Check the socket terminals for corrosion and clean them if necessary. Line up the pins of the new bulb with the slots in the socket, then push the bulb in and turn it clockwise until it locks into place. **Note:** *The pins on the bulb are offset so it can only be installed one way.*

2 On the X8, open the boot lid and undo the screws securing the tail light assembly, then draw the assembly out **(see illustrations)**.

The two centre bulbs are the tail light bulbs – pull the bulbholder out of the assembly then push the bulb into the holder and twist it anti-clockwise to remove it. The two outer bulbs are the brake light bulbs – twist the bulbholder anti-clockwise to remove it **(see illustration)**.

3 On the X9, first remove the brake light panel (see Chapter 7). To renew the brake light bulbs, undo the three screws securing the brake light unit and remove it **(see illustration)**. Twist the bulbholder and remove it from the unit, then carefully pull the bulb out of the holder **(see illustrations)**. **Note:** *The bulb used is of the capless type.* To renew the tail light bulbs, undo the screw securing the light unit and remove it, noting how the tabs locate in the side panel **(see illustrations)**. Press the tabs on the bulbholder and pull it out of the light unit, then push the bulb into the holder and twist it anti-clockwise to remove it **(see illustration)**.

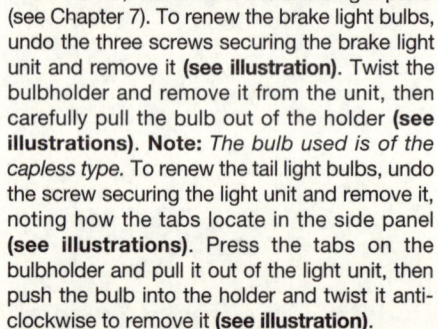

4 On GT models, first remove the screws

9.3b Twist the bulbholder to remove it . . .

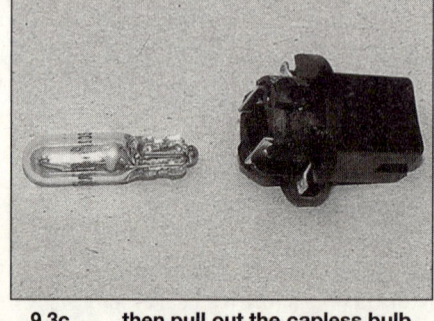

9.3c . . . then pull out the capless bulb

9.3d Undo the tail light unit screw . . .

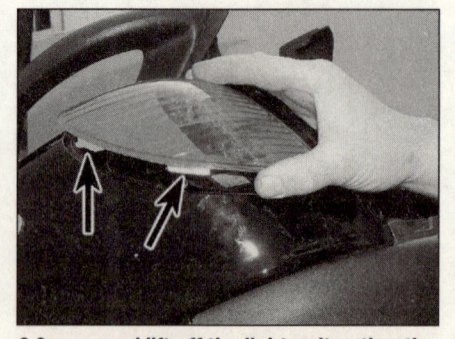

9.3e . . . and lift off the light unit noting the tabs (arrowed) – X9

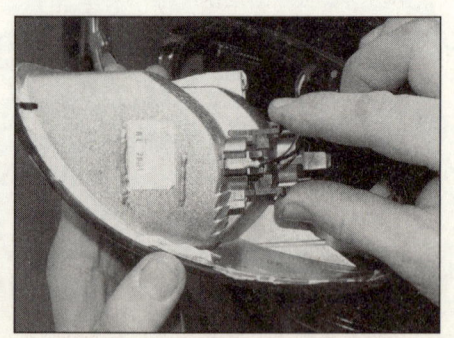

9.3f Press the tabs to release the bulbholder

Electrical system 9•11

9.4a Number plate light is secured by two screws – GT models

9.4b Bulbholder is a push fit in the unit

9.4c Remove the screws securing the tail light assembly . . .

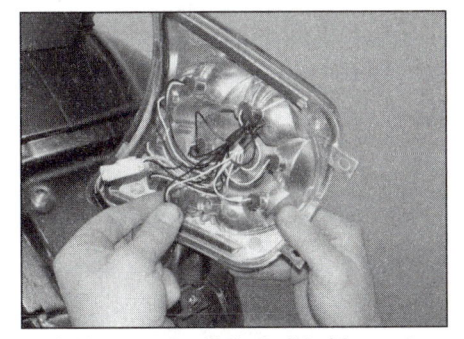

9.4d . . . and pull the bulbholders out carefully

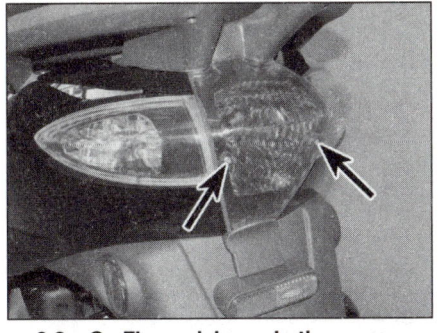

9.6a On Fly models, undo the screws (arrowed) . . .

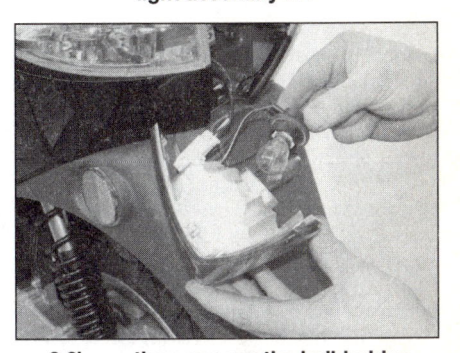

9.6b . . . then remove the bulbholder

securing the number plate light **(see illustration)**. Either pull the bulbholder out of the light unit or disconnect the wiring connector and remove the unit **(see illustration)**. Remove the screws securing the tail light assembly and lift it off – the bulbholders are a push fit in the assembly **(see illustrations)**. The bulbs used are the capless type – pull them out of the bulbholders carefully. To remove the tail light assembly from the scooter, disconnect the single assembly wiring connector.

5 On the Skipper, raise up the seat, then remove the two screws securing the cover above the tail light and slide the cover up until its tabs disengage from their slots. Remove the cover, noting how it locates. Remove the two screws securing the tail light and draw the light out of its housing. Remove the lens.

6 On Fly and LX models, remove the screws securing the tail light unit and lift it off, then twist the bulbholder anti-clockwise to remove it **(see illustrations)**. Push the bulb, into the holder and twist it anti-clockwise to remove it. Check the socket terminals for corrosion and clean them if necessary. Line up the pins of the new bulb with the slots in the socket, then push the bulb in and turn it clockwise until it locks into place. **Note:** *The pins on the bulb are offset so it can only be installed one way.*

9.6c On LX models, undo the screws (arrowed) . . .

7 On all other models, remove the screws securing the tail light lens and remove the lens, noting how it fits **(see illustrations)**. Push the bulb into the holder and twist it anti-clockwise to remove it **(see illustration)**. Check the socket terminals for corrosion and clean them if necessary. Line up the pins of

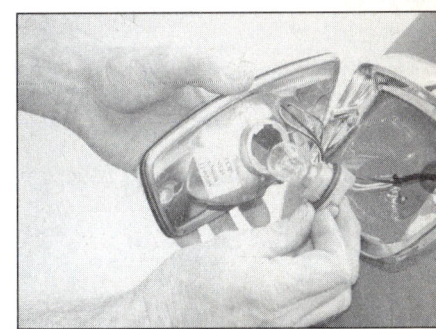

9.6d . . . then remove the bulbholder

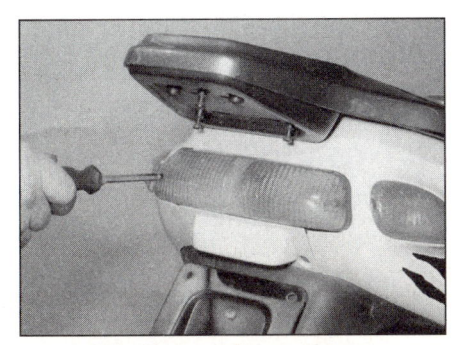

9.7a Remove the screws . . .

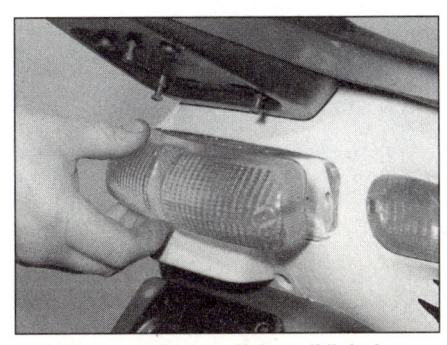

9.7b . . . and take off the tail light lens

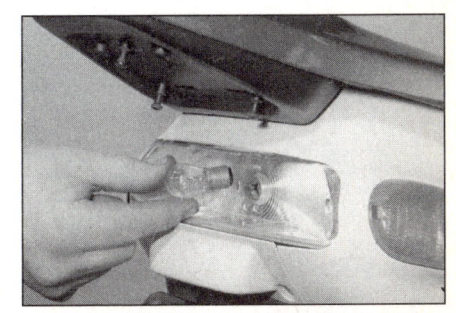

9.7c Push the bulb in and twist it anti-clockwise to remove it

9•12 Electrical system

the new bulb with the slots in the socket, then push the bulb in and turn it clockwise until it locks into place. **Note:** *The pins on the bulb are offset so it can only be installed one way.*

10 Tail light assembly – removal and installation

Removal

1 On B125, X8, X9, GT, Fly and LX models, follow the procedure in Section 9 to remove the tail light assembly. On Zip 50 and Zip 125 models, follow the procedure in Chapter 7 to remove the tail light panel. On NRG Power models, follow the procedure in Chapter 7 to remove the number plate unit, then remove the screws securing the tail light to the unit.

2 On Skipper models, raise up the seat, then remove the two screws securing the cover above the tail light and slide the cover up until its tabs disengage from their slots. Remove the cover, noting how it locates. Remove the two screws securing the tail light and draw the light out of its housing, disconnecting the wiring connector when accessible.

3 On all other models, remove the screws securing the tail light lens and remove the lens **(see illustrations 9.7a and 9.7b)**. On many models, these screws also secure the tail light bulbholder/reflector, so it can be drawn away, then removed after disconnecting the wiring. Otherwise, remove the screws securing the bulbholder/reflector and disconnect the wiring **(see illustrations)**. Where the turn signals are integral with the tail light, also remove the turn signal lenses and disconnect the wiring.

Installation

4 Installation is the reverse of removal. Check the operation of the tail light and the brake light.

11 Turn signal circuit – check

1 The battery provides power for operation of the turn signal lights, so if they do not operate, always check the battery voltage first. Low battery voltage indicates either a faulty battery

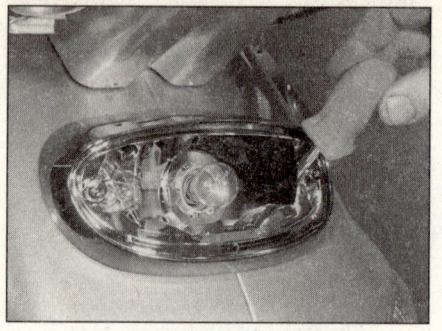

10.3a Remove the screws ...

or a defective charging system. Refer to Section 3 for battery checks and Sections 28 to 31 for charging system tests. Also, check the fuse (see Section 5) and the switch (see Section 21).

2 Most turn signal problems are the result of a burned out bulb or corroded socket. This is especially true when the turn signals function properly in one direction, but fail to flash in the other direction. Check the bulbs and the sockets (see Section 12).

3 Note that some Piaggio/Vespa models use a conventional turn signal system, where the turn signals are operated by a separate relay, whereas on others the turn signal relay is combined in the regulator/rectifier unit. Refer to the wiring diagram for your machine to establish which type is fitted and test according to the relevant procedure.

With a turn signal relay

4 If the bulbs and sockets are good, using a multi-meter set to the 0 to 20 DC volts range, check for voltage at the B terminal on the turn signal relay with the ignition ON. Battery voltage should be shown. Turn the ignition OFF when the check is complete.

5 If no power was present at the relay, check the wiring from the relay to the ignition (main) switch for continuity.

6 If power was present at the relay, using the appropriate wiring diagram at the end of this Chapter, check the wiring between the relay, turn signal switch and turn signal lights for continuity. If the wiring and switch are sound, renew the relay.

Without a turn signal relay

7 If the bulbs and sockets are good, using a

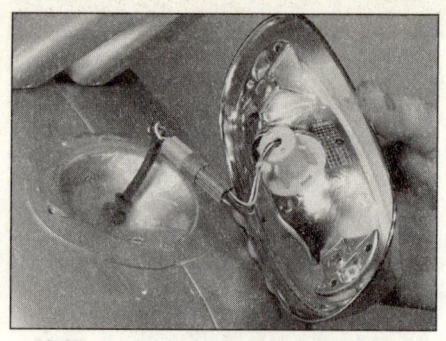

10.3b ... then remove the bulbholder/reflector unit and disconnect the wiring connector

multi-meter set to the 0 to 20 DC volts range, check for voltage at terminal No. 5 of the regulator/rectifier unit with the ignition ON. Battery voltage should be shown. Turn the ignition OFF when the check is complete.

8 If no power was present at the regulator/rectifier, check back through the wiring from the regulator/rectifier to the ignition (main) switch for continuity.

9 If power was present at terminal No. 5 of the regulator/rectifier, check for voltage at terminal No. 7 with the ignition ON. The voltage should fluctuate around 6 V, although this may vary depending on the tester used. The important factor is that the voltage is supplied in pulses. Turn the ignition OFF when the check is complete.

10 If no voltage is indicated at terminal No. 7, the regulator/rectifier should be renewed. If the voltage reading produces the expected result and the turn signals still do not work, then the fault must lie in the turn signal switch or the wiring between terminal No. 7 of the regulator/rectifier and the switch.

12 Turn signal bulbs – renewal

1 On Sfera and Hexagon models, to access the front turn signal bulbs, remove the headlight (see Section 8). To access the rear turn signal bulbs, remove the screws securing the tail light lens, then remove the tail light lens followed by the turn signal lens, noting how they fit **(see illustrations)**.

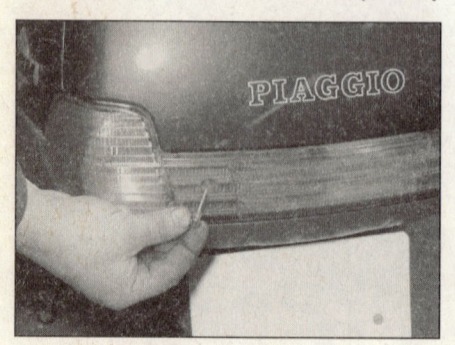

12.1a Remove the screws ...

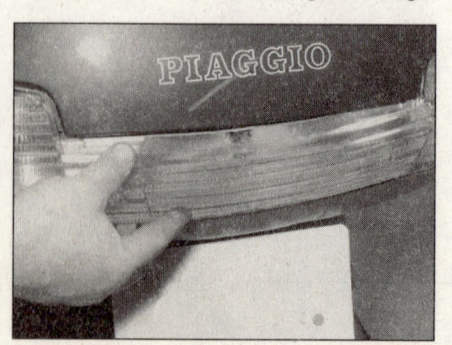

12.1b ... the tail light lens ...

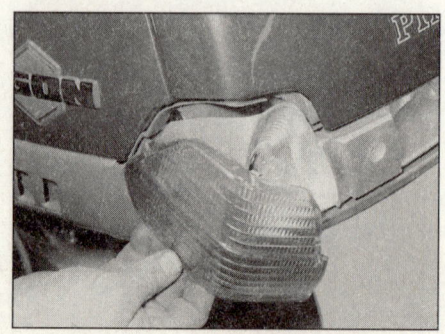

12.1c ... and then the turn signal lens

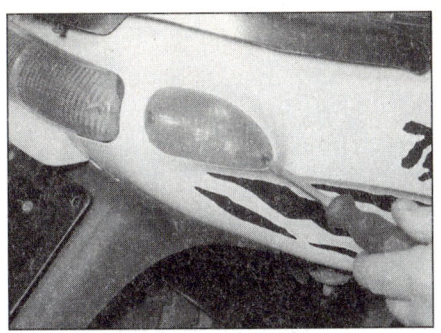

Electrical system 9•13

12.2a Remove the screw...

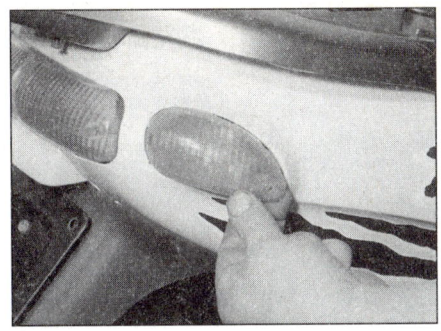

12.2b ...and detach the lens

12.3a Open the glove compartment...

12.3b ...and take off the cover

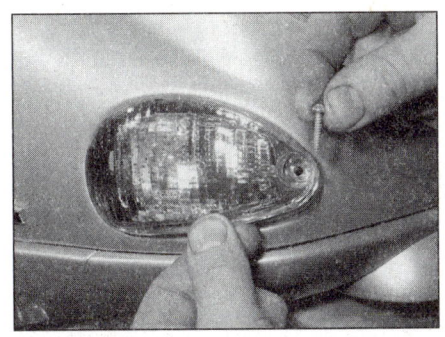

12.3c Remove the screw and detach the lens...

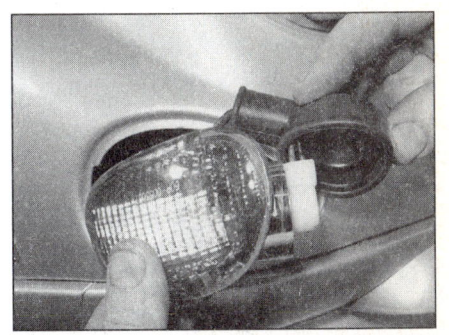

12.3d ...then pull back the cover

2 On Typhoon, Zip SP, Zip 50, Zip 125, Liberty and NRG models, remove the screw securing the turn signal lens and remove the lens **(see illustrations)**, noting that on Zip SP models at the rear it is the screws securing the tail light lens that must be removed.

3 On ET2 and ET4 models, to access the front turn signal bulbs, open the glove compartment and remove the cover from the back of the turn signal **(see illustrations)**. To access the rear turn signal bulbs, remove the screw(s) securing the lens and remove the lens, then pull back the bulb cover **(see illustrations)**.

4 On the Skipper model, to access the front turn signal bulbs, remove the two screws securing the grille in the front panel and remove the grille. Then remove the screw securing the turn signal assembly. To access the rear turn signal bulbs, carefully lever off the inner section of the lens using a small flat-bladed screwdriver inserted in the notch in its base. This provides access to the screw securing the turn signal.

5 On B125 models, to access the front turn signal bulbs, remove the headlight assembly (see Section 8). To access the rear turn signal bulbs, remove the tail light assembly (see Section 10).

6 On X8 models, to access the front turn signal bulbs, follow the procedure in Section 8 to remove the appropriate signal assembly **(see illustration 8.3a and 3b)**. Pull the bulbholder out of the assembly and pull the bulb out of the bulbholder **(see illustration)**. To access the rear turn signal bulbs, follow the procedure in Section 9 and remove the tail light unit. Undo the screw securing the signal assembly and lift it out, then pull the bulb out of the bulbholder **(see illustrations)**.

7 On X9 models, to access the front turn signal bulbs, remove the screw securing the turn signal lens and remove the lens. To access the rear turn signal bulbs, follow the procedure in Section 9 and remove the tail light unit. Press the tabs on the bulbholder and pull it out of the light unit.

8 On Fly models, to access the front turn signal bulbs, undo the screw securing the turn

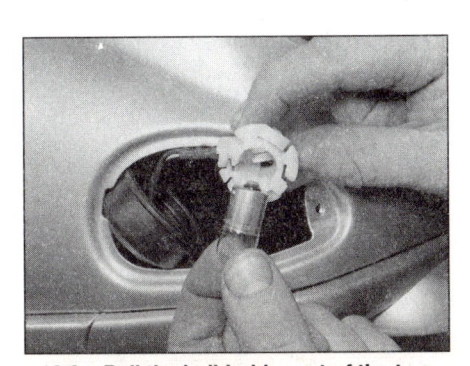

12.6a Pull the bulbholder out of the turn signal assembly – X8 models

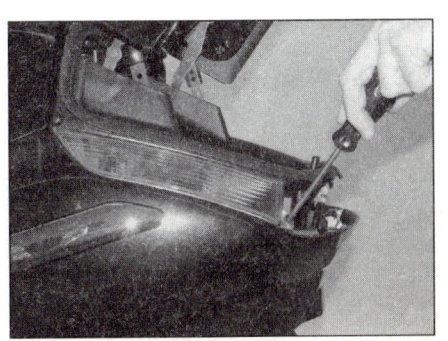

12.6b Remove the turn signal assembly...

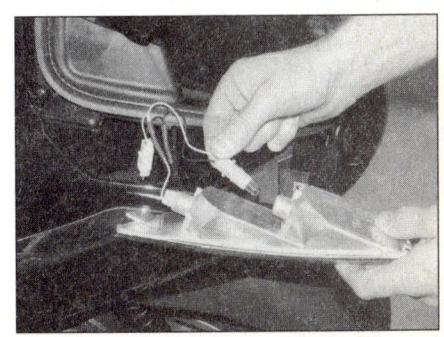

12.6c ...and pull the bulbholder out

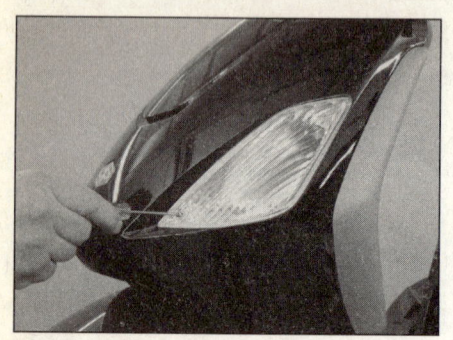

9•14 Electrical system

12.8a On Fly models, undo the screw . . .

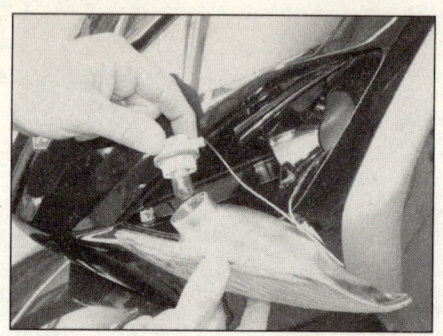

12.8b . . . and displace the signal assembly to access the bulb

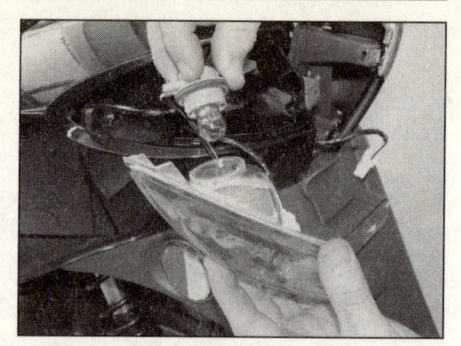

12.8c Turn the bulbholder anti-clockwise to remove it

12.9a On NRG Power models, undo the screw . . .

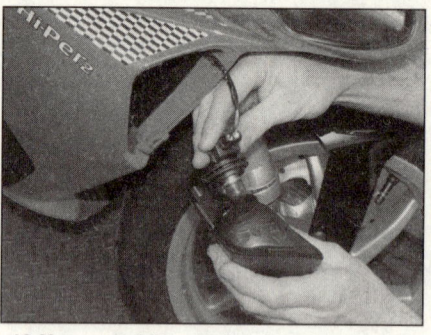

12.9b . . . and lift out the signal assembly to access the bulb

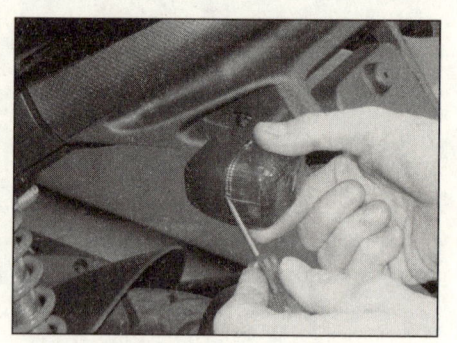

12.9c Lever the lens off carefully . . .

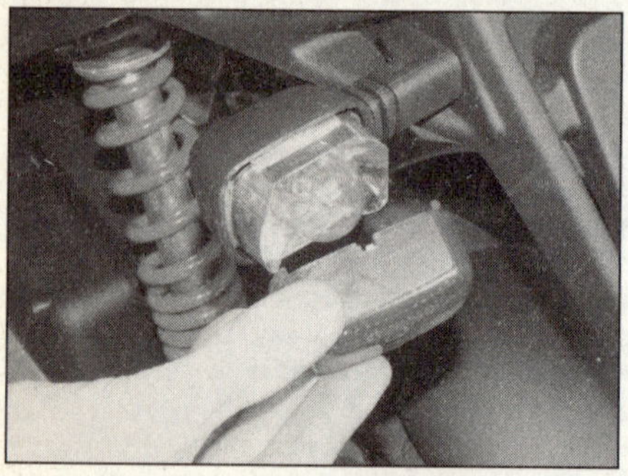

12.9d . . . noting how it fits . . .

12.9e . . . then release the tabs on the bulb cover

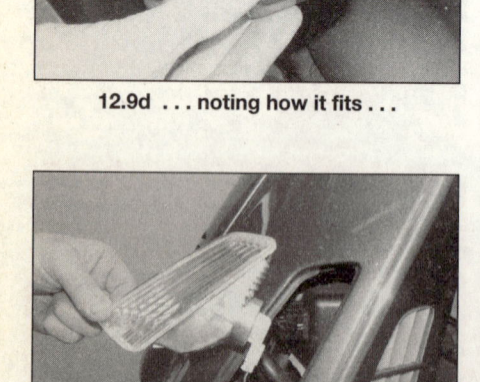

12.10a Removing the front turn signal assembly – GT models

12.10b On LX models remove the screw (arrowed) . . .

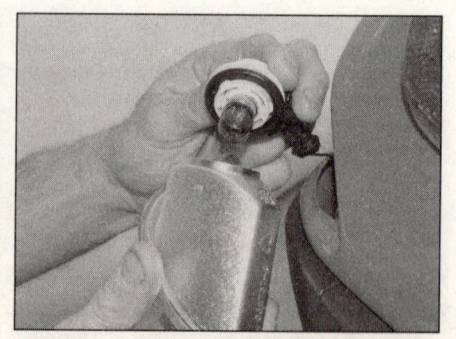

12.10c . . . then turn the bulbholder anti-clockwise to remove it

signal assembly and lift it out, then turn the bulbholder anti-clockwise and withdraw it from the assembly **(see illustrations)**. To access the rear turn signal bulbs, follow the procedure in Section 9 and remove the tail light unit, then lift out the turn signal assembly. Turn the bulbholder anti-clockwise and withdraw it from the assembly **(see illustration)**.

9 On NRG Power models, to access the front turn signal bulbs, undo the screw securing the turn signal assembly and lift it out, then turn the bulbholder anti-clockwise and withdraw it from the assembly **(see illustrations)**. To access the rear turn signal bulbs, carefully lever off the lens using a small, flat-bladed screwdriver, then ease the cover off the bulb **(see illustrations)**.

10 On GT and LX models, the front and rear turn signal assemblies are each secured by a single screw; undo the screw and lift out the assembly, then turn the bulbholder anti-clockwise and withdraw it from the assembly **(see illustrations)**.

11 Where appropriate, turn the bulbholder

Electrical system 9•15

12.11a Removing the front turn signal bulbholder – Hexagon

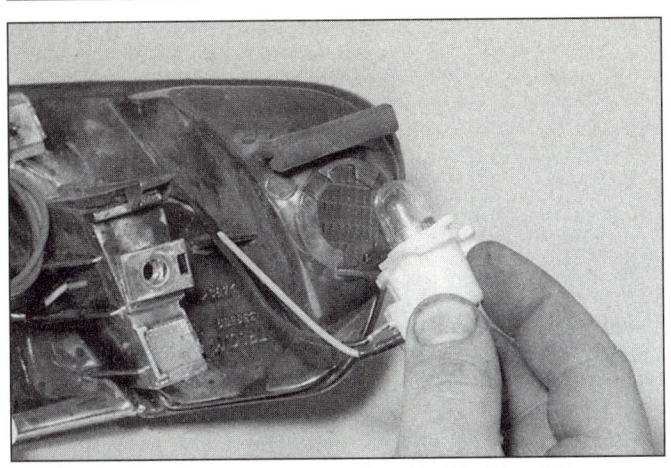

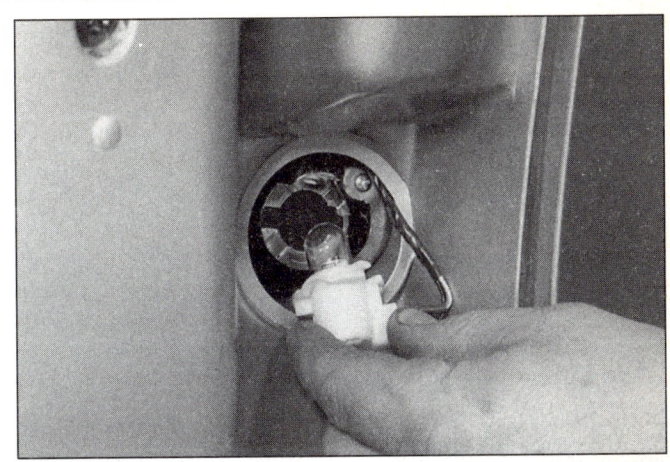

12.11b Removing the front turn signal bulbholder – ET2 and ET4

anti-clockwise and withdraw it from the lens **(see illustrations)**.

12 Push the bulb into the turn signal or bulbholder and twist it anti-clockwise to remove it **(see illustration)**. Check the socket terminals for corrosion and clean them if necessary. Line up the pins of the new bulb with the slots in the socket, then push the bulb in and turn it clockwise until it locks into place.

13 Installation is the reverse of removal.

13 Turn signal assemblies – removal and installation

Removal

1 On models where the turn signals are integral with either the headlight or tail light, refer to Section 8 or 10 as appropriate for removal of those assemblies. If applicable, separate the front turn signals from the headlight unit, noting how they fit.

2 On models with separate turn signals, follow the procedure in Section 12 for accessing the bulb, then remove the screw securing the bulbholder if necessary and/or disconnect the wiring connector. On X9 models, the front turn signals are separate units secured in the front panel. Follow the procedure in Chapter 7 to remove the panel, then undo the screw securing the unit and remove it.

Installation

3 Installation is the reverse of removal.

14 Brake light switches – check and renewal

Circuit check

Note: *On some later models, the brake switch is part of the safety circuit which prevents the engine from starting unless the side stand is up and the brake lever is pulled in. If the starter circuit is faulty, follow the procedure in Steps 2 and 3 to check the switch. If the switch is good, check the starter circuit relay (Section 25) and other components in the starter circuit as described in the relevant Sections of this Chapter. If all components are good, check the wiring between the various components (see wiring diagrams at the end of this Chapter).*

1 Before checking any electrical circuit, check the bulb (see Section 9) and fuse (see Section 5).

2 Remove the front handlebar covers (see Chapter 7) and disconnect the wiring connectors from the switch **(see illustration)**. Using a continuity tester, connect a probe to each terminal. With the brake lever at rest, there should be no continuity. Pull the brake lever in – there should now be continuity. If not, renew the switch.

3 If continuity is shown with the lever pulled in, the switch is functioning correctly and the fault must lie elsewhere in the circuit. Using a multi-meter or test light connected to a good earth, check for voltage at the brake light switch wiring connectors with the ignition ON (one of them should show battery voltage). If there's no voltage present, check the wire between the switch and the ignition switch (see the wiring diagrams at the end of this Chapter).

4 If both continuity and voltage are obtained, the switch and its power supply are proved good. Go on to check the wiring between the switch and the brake light bulb (see the wiring diagrams at the end of this Chapter).

Switch renewal

5 The switches are mounted in the brake lever brackets. Remove the handlebar covers (see Chapter 7), then disconnect the wiring connectors from the switch **(see illustration 14.2)**. Using pliers on the knurled section of the switch, unscrew it from the lever bracket.

6 Installation is the reverse of removal. The switch isn't adjustable.

15 Instrument cluster – check, removal and installation

Check

1 Special instruments are required to properly check the operation of the speedometer. If it is believed to be faulty, take the scooter to a Piaggio dealer for assessment, although check first that the drive cable is not broken. Refer to Section 18 to check the fuel gauge. Individual components are not available, so if an instrument is faulty, the entire cluster must be renewed.

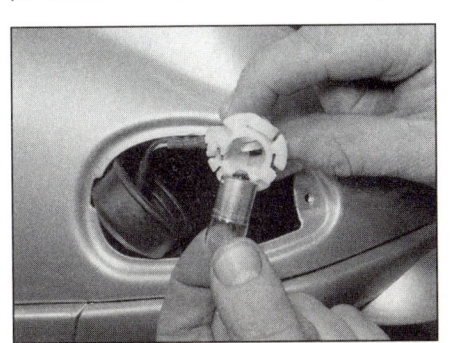

12.12 Push the bulb in and twist it anti-clockwise to release it

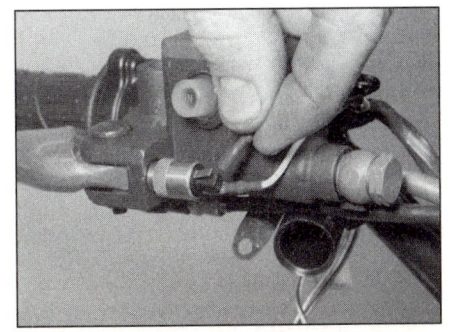

14.2 Disconnect the wiring connectors from the brake light switch

9•16 Electrical system

15.3a On B125 models, lift off the instrument cluster . . .

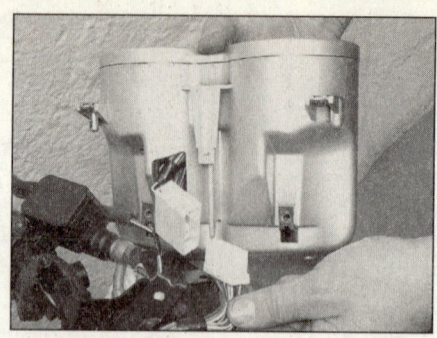

15.3b . . . and disconnect the wiring connector

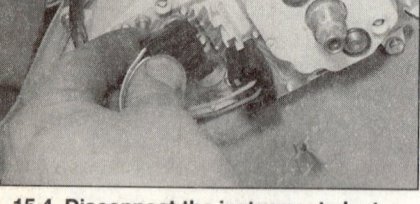

15.4 Disconnect the instrument cluster wiring connectors

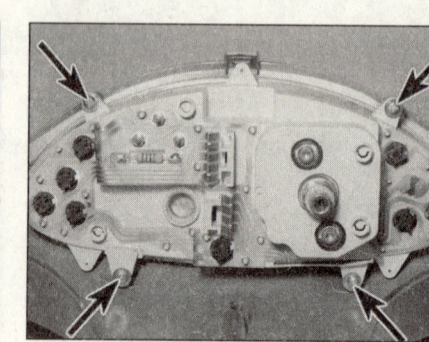

15.5 Remove the screws securing the cluster to the handlebar cover

Removal

2 Depending on the model, the instrument cluster is secured to the front or rear handlebar cover, the top of the kick panel (X9) or the cockpit trim panel (X8). Refer to the appropriate section in Chapter 7 and remove the bodywork as required by your model.

3 On B125 models, the instrument cluster is secured to the handlebars by the front cover screws. Lift off the cluster and disconnect the wiring connector **(see illustrations)**.
4 If not already done, disconnect the instrument cluster wiring connectors **(see illustration)**. Also unscrew the knurled ring or release the clip securing the speedometer cable to the back of the speedometer and detach the cable **(see illustrations 16.2a and 16.2b)**.
5 Remove the screws securing the instrument cluster to the handlebar cover or body panel and carefully lift the cluster away **(see illustration)**.

Installation

6 Installation is the reverse of removal. Make sure that the speedometer cable and wiring connectors are correctly routed and secured.

16 Speedometer cable – renewal

Note: *Some models are fitted with an electronically-operated speedometer – the 'cable' is a wire connecting the drive housing to the speedometer. Do not try to disconnect the cable from the drive gear housing.*

Removal

1 Remove the bodywork as required by your scooter to gain access to the underside of the instrument cluster (see Chapter 7).
2 Unscrew the knurled ring or release the clip securing the speedometer cable to the back of the speedometer and detach the cable **(see illustrations)**.
3 On models with monoshock front suspension, first remove the brake caliper lower mounting bolt, which also secures the cable guide, noting the washer behind it **(see illustration)**. Now fully slacken the bolt securing the cable retaining plate, then draw the cable out of the rubber grommet **(see illustrations)**. There is no need to remove the retaining plate unless necessary. If required, remove the plate, then lever out the rubber grommet and withdraw the drive gear for

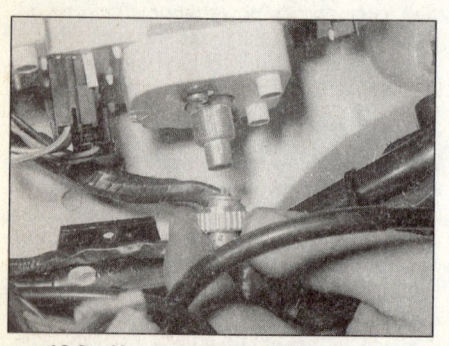

16.2a Unscrew the knurled ring . . .

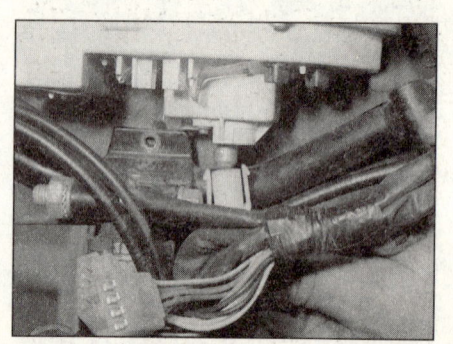

16.2b . . . or press in the clips to detach the cable

16.3a Remove the caliper lower mounting bolt . . .

16.3b . . . then slacken the retaining plate bolt . . .

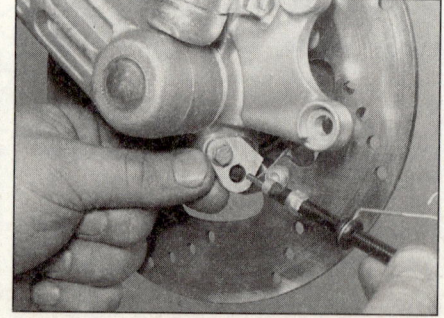

16.3c . . . and withdraw the cable

Electrical system 9•17

16.3d Remove the drive gear and regrease it

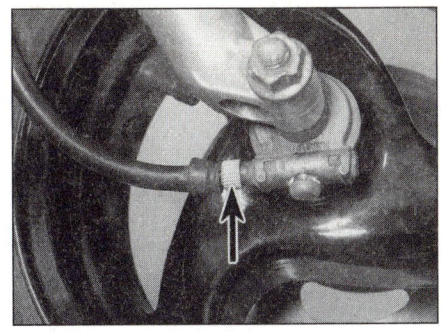

16.4a Draw back the rubber boot and unscrew the knurled ring (arrowed)

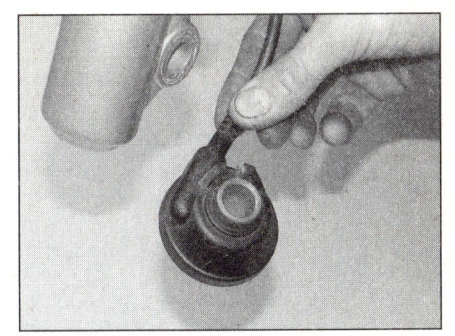

16.4b Drive gear housing for electronically-operated speedometer

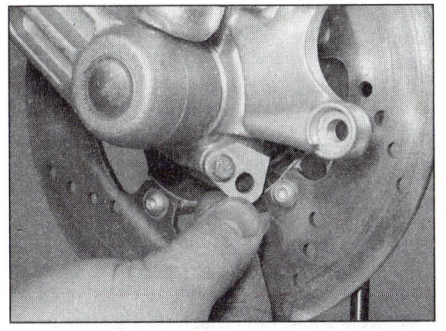

16.8a Fit the retaining plate loosely

16.8b Fit the caliper bolt washer behind the cable guide

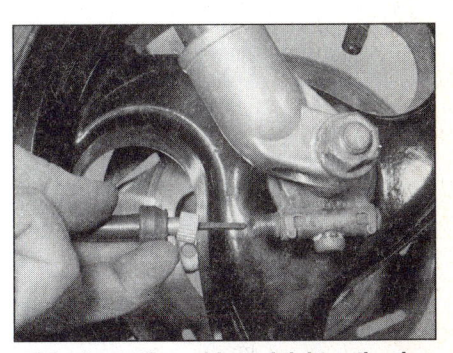

16.9a Insert the cable and tighten the ring

regreasing **(see illustration)**. Renew the grommet if it is damaged or deteriorated.

4 On models with telescopic forks, pull back the rubber boot on the bottom of the cable, then unscrew the knurled ring and draw the cable out of the housing **(see illustration)**. On models with electronically-operated speedometers do not try to disconnect the cable **(see illustration)**.

5 Withdraw the cable, releasing it from its guides, and remove it from the scooter, noting its correct routing.

Installation

6 Route the cable up through its guides to the back of the instrument cluster.

7 Connect the cable upper end to the speedometer and tighten the retaining ring or fit the clip **(see illustrations 16.2a or 16.2b)**.

8 On models with monoshock front suspension, if removed, clean and regrease the drive gear, then install the gear, its collar and the rubber grommet into the housing **(see illustration 16.3d)**. Fit the retaining plate and loosely install the bolt **(see illustration)**. Fit the cable end through the plate and fully into the rubber grommet, then tighten the plate bolt so that the plate compresses the grommet, thereby securing the cable **(see illustration 16.3c)**. Locate the cable guide in the brake caliper lower mounting, then install the caliper bolt, with its washer behind the cable guide, and tighten it to the torque setting specified at the beginning of Chapter 8 **(see illustration)**.

9 On models with telescopic forks, connect the cable lower end to the drive housing and tighten the knurled ring securely **(see illustration)**. Where fitted, remove the cap from the grease point on the underside of the drive housing and press some grease up into it, then refit the cap **(see illustrations)**.

10 Check that the cable doesn't restrict steering movement or interfere with any other components.

11 Install the bodywork as required by your scooter (see Chapter 7).

17 Instrument cluster bulbs and clock battery – renewal

1 Remove the bodywork as required by your scooter to gain access to the underside of the instrument cluster (see Chapter 7). **Note:** *Access to some bulbholders is restricted and it may be necessary to displace or remove the instrument cluster (see Section 15).*

2 Twist the bulbholder anti-clockwise and draw it out of the instrument casing, then pull the bulb out of the bulbholder **(see illustration)**. Check the wattage of the old

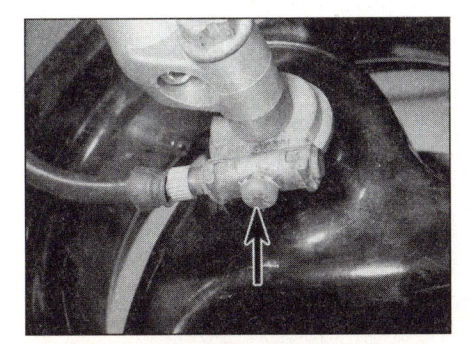

16.9b Remove the cap (arrowed) . . .

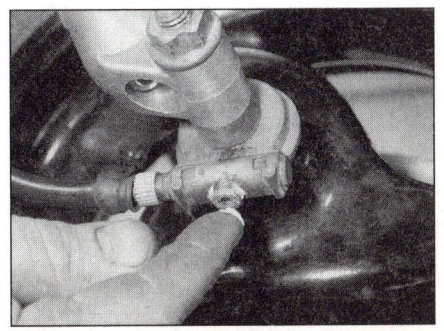

16.9c . . . and press some grease up into the housing

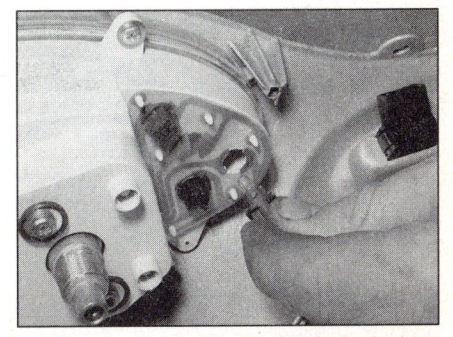

17.2 Twist the bulbholder anti-clockwise and draw it out of the casing

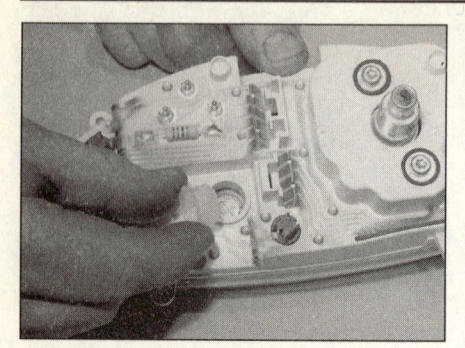

9•18 Electrical system

17.3a Remove the plug . . .

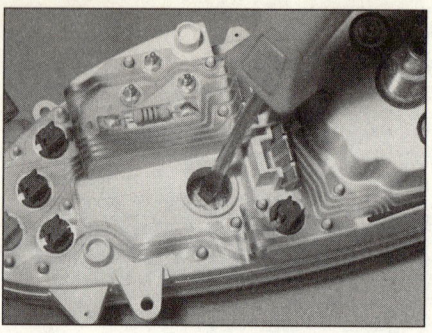

17.3b . . . and the cap to access the clock battery

18.1a Fuel level sender wiring connector (arrowed) – Hexagon

bulb and make sure that you fit a new one of the same wattage. If the socket contacts are dirty or corroded, scrape them clean and spray with electrical contact cleaner before a new bulb is installed. Carefully push the new bulb into the holder and install the handlebar cover.

3 Where a clock is fitted, the battery is secured in the back of the instrument cluster by a cap. Remove the plastic plug, then turn the cap anti-clockwise using a screwdriver and remove the cap and the battery, noting which way up it fits **(see illustrations)**. Fit the new battery, making sure it is the correct way up, then refit the cap.

18 Fuel gauge and level sender, and low level warning circuit – check and renewal

⚠️ **Warning: Petrol (gasoline) is extremely flammable, so take extra precautions when you work on any part of the fuel system. Don't smoke or allow open flames or bare light bulbs near the work area, and don't work in a garage where a natural gas-type appliance is present. If you spill any fuel on your skin, rinse it off immediately with soap and water. When you perform any kind of work on the fuel system, wear safety glasses and have a fire extinguisher suitable for a class B type fire (flammable liquids) on hand.**

Fuel gauge

Check

1 Remove the bodywork as required by your model to access the top of the fuel tank (see Chapter 7). Disconnect the wiring connector from the top of the fuel level sender **(see illustrations)**.
2 Connect a jumper wire between the white/green and black terminals on the wiring loom side of the connector. With the ignition switched ON, the fuel gauge should read FULL. If it doesn't, check the wiring between the connector and the gauge, and check for voltage at the supply terminal on the instrument cluster wiring connector. If the wiring is good and there is voltage at the terminal, then the gauge is confirmed faulty. The supply terminal of the instrument cluster wiring connector can be identified from the wiring diagrams at the end of this Chapter.

Removal and installation

3 The fuel gauge is integral with the instrument cluster, for which no individual parts are available. If the fuel gauge is faulty, the entire cluster must be renewed (see Section 15).

Fuel level sender

Check

4 If the fuel gauge is confirmed good, the fault may lie in the level sender unit in the fuel tank. Remove the bodywork as required by your model to access the top of the fuel tank (see Chapter 7).
5 Disconnect the wiring connector from the top of the sender **(see illustrations 18.1a and 18.1b)**.
6 Using an ohmmeter set to the ohms x 100 scale, connect its probes to the white/green and black terminals on the sender. Check the resistance reading with the tank empty and full. Piaggio provide no specifications, but when the tank is full, a low resistance reading should be obtained, and when the tank is empty a higher reading should be obtained. Alternatively, remove the sender from the tank (see below) and, with the meter connected as above, manually move the float up and down to emulate the different positions.
7 If the sender is good, check the wiring between the sender and the gauge (see wiring diagrams at the end of the Chapter).

Removal and installation

8 Remove the bodywork as required by your model to access the top of the fuel tank (see Chapter 7). Disconnect the wiring connector from the top of the sender **(see illustrations 18.1a and 18.1b)**, then turn the sender anti-clockwise and withdraw it from the tank, taking care not to bend the float arm **(see illustrations)**. Discard the O-ring, as a new one must be used.
9 Install the sender by reversing the removal process, using a new O-ring.

Low level warning circuit check

10 If the warning light in the instrument

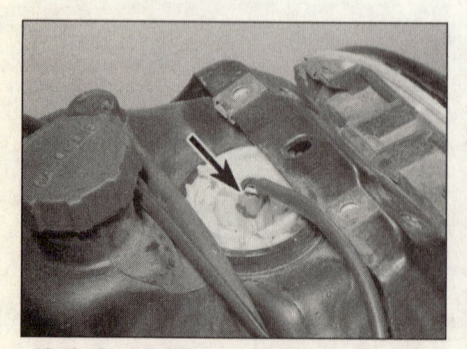

18.1b Fuel level sender wiring connector (arrowed) – Typhoon

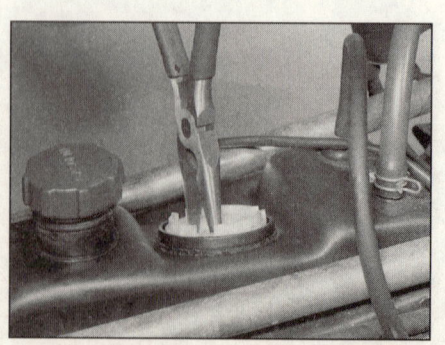

18.8a Twist the sender anti-clockwise . . .

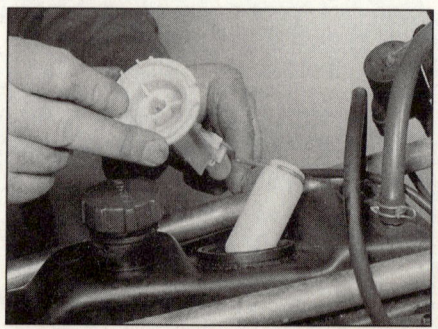

18.8b . . . and withdraw it from the tank

Electrical system 9•19

cluster fails to come on when the fuel is low, first check the bulb (see Section 17). If the bulb is good, remove the sender (see above).

11 Using a continuity tester, connect the probes between the yellow/green and black terminals on the sender. Start with the float in the full position, then slowly lower it to the empty position. There should be no continuity until the float nears the empty position, when continuity should be shown. If this is not the case, renew the sender.

12 If the sender is good, check the wiring between the sender and the instrument cluster (see wiring diagrams at the end of the Chapter).

19 Oil level warning circuit (two-stroke engines) – check

Note: *The oil level warning circuit is fitted to all models with two-stroke engines (see Model Specifications in Chapter 1).*

1 If the warning light in the instrument cluster fails to come on when the oil is low, first check the bulb (see Section 17). If the bulb is good, remove the bodywork as required by your model to access the top of the oil tank (see Chapter 7). Trace the wiring from the top of the sensor and disconnect it at the connector **(see illustration)**. Withdraw the sensor from the tank **(see illustration)**.

2 Using a continuity tester, connect the probes between the two wire terminals on the sensor side of the connector. Start with the float in the full position, then slowly lower it to the empty position. There should be no continuity until the float nears the empty position, when continuity should be shown. If this is not the case, renew the sensor.

3 If the sensor is good, check the wiring between the sensor and the instrument cluster (see wiring diagrams at the end of the Chapter).

4 The starter motor circuit incorporates a bulb check function, which illuminates the oil level warning light when the starter button is pressed. This ensures that the bulb is sound. The light should extinguish when the starter button is released, unless the oil level is low.

20 Ignition (main) switch – check, removal and installation

⚠️ **Warning: To prevent the risk of short circuits, disconnect the battery negative (-ve) lead before making any ignition (main) switch checks.**

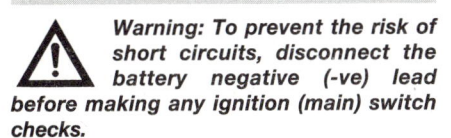

Check

1 Remove the front panel and kick panel and, on ET2 and ET4, the grille in the front panel (see Chapter 7). Trace the wiring back from

19.1a Trace the wiring back from the sensor (arrowed) and disconnect it . . .

the ignition (main) switch and disconnect it at the connector.

2 Using an ohmmeter or a continuity tester, check the continuity of the connector terminal pairs (see the wiring diagrams at the end of this Chapter). Continuity should exist between the connected terminals when the switch is in the indicated position.

3 If the switch fails any of the tests, renew it.

Removal

4 To remove the electrical section from the back of the switch, pull back the rubber cover, then lift up the spring clip and withdraw the electrical section of the switch, noting how it fits **(see illustrations)**.

5 Where an immobiliser is fitted, remove the sensor ring from around the front of the switch – it is a clip-fit **(see illustration)**. To remove the barrel of the switch, insert a small

19.1b . . . then withdraw the sensor from the tank

screwdriver into the hole in the housing behind the front of the switch. Push on the retaining tongue with the screwdriver and draw the barrel out of its housing.

Installation

6 Fit the key into the switch and turn it to the ON position. Offer the switch up to its housing, making sure the anchor tang faces down. Insert the switch about half-way into the housing, then simultaneously turn the key to the OFF position and push the switch fully in until the anchor tang is felt to locate.

7 Install the electrical section and immobiliser ring (where fitted), making sure the electrical section locates correctly and is secured by the spring clip **(see illustrations 20.4a, 20.4b, 20.4c and 20.5)**.

8 Reconnect the battery negative (-ve) lead once all electrical connections have been made to the switch.

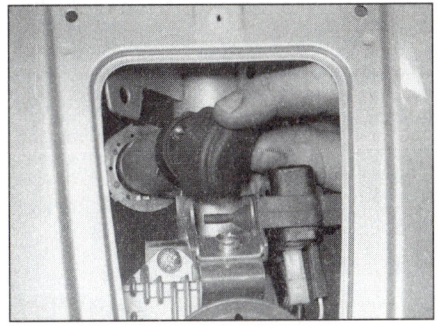

20.4a Pull off the rubber cover . . .

20.4b . . . then lift up the clip . . .

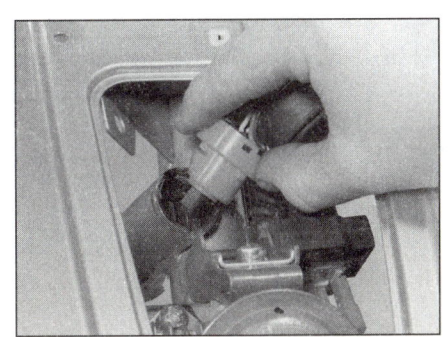

20.4c . . . and withdraw the electrical section

20.5 Where fitted, unclip the immobiliser ring

9•20 Electrical system

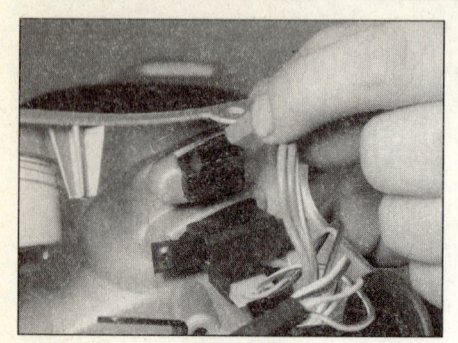

21.3 Disconnect the wiring connector from the switch

21.6a Undo the switch unit screw . . .

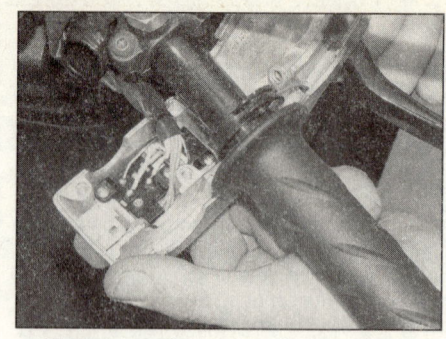

21.6b . . . and separate the two halves

21 Handlebar switches – check

Note: *B125 models are fitted with motorcycle-type handlebar switches – see Step 6.*

1 Generally speaking, the switches are reliable and trouble-free. Most troubles, when they do occur, are caused by dirty or corroded contacts, but wear and breakage is a possibility that should not be overlooked. If breakage does occur, the switch will have to be renewed.

2 The switches can be checked for continuity using an ohmmeter or a continuity test light. Always disconnect the battery negative (-ve) cable, which will prevent the possibility of a short circuit, before making the checks.

3 Remove the handlebar front cover (see Chapter 7). If required for improved access, also displace or remove the rear cover, in which the switches are housed. Disconnect the wiring connector from the switch being tested **(see illustration)**.

4 Check for continuity between the terminals of the switch harness with the switch in the various positions (i.e., switch off – no continuity, switch on – continuity) – see the wiring diagrams at the end of this Chapter and use the wire colours to identify terminals where a switch has more than two terminals.

5 If the continuity check indicates a problem exists, spray the switch contacts with electrical contact cleaner (refer to Section 22 and remove the switch if required). If they are accessible, the contacts can be scraped clean with a knife or polished with crocus cloth. If switch components are damaged or broken, it should be obvious when the switch is operated.

6 To check the switches on B125 models, first remove the rear handlebar cover and trace the wiring from the switch unit to be tested to the connector (see Chapter 7). Disconnect the wiring connector, then follow the procedure in Step 4 to check for continuity. To inspect the switch contacts, undo the screw securing the two halves and separate them, noting how they fit, then follow the procedure in Step 5 **(see illustrations)**.

22 Handlebar switches – removal and installation

Note: *B125 models are fitted with motorcycle-type handlebar switches – see Step 3.*

Removal

1 Remove the handlebar front cover (see Chapter 7). If required for improved access, also displace or remove the rear cover, in which the switches are housed.

2 Disconnect the wiring connector from the switch being removed **(see illustration 21.3)**, then remove the screws or release the clips securing the switch to the handlebar cover and remove the switch, noting how it fits **(see illustration)**.

3 On B125 models, first remove the rear handlebar cover and trace the wiring from the switch unit to the connector (see Chapter 7). Disconnect the wiring connector, then undo the screw securing the two halves of the unit and separate them **(see illustrations 21.6a and 21.6b)**. Note that to remove the front half of the right-hand switch unit the throttle cable must be disconnected from the twistgrip (see Chapter 4).

Installation

4 Installation is the reverse of removal. Make sure the wiring connectors are secure.

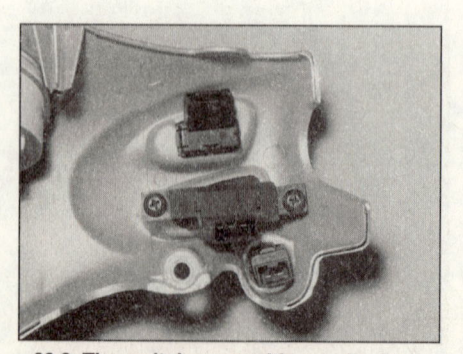

22.2 The switches are either a clip-fit or are screwed onto the cover

23 Diode (two-stroke engines) – check and renewal

Check

Note: *The following test applies to models fitted with two-stroke engines (see Model Specifications, Chapter 1). Refer to the Wiring diagrams at the end of this Chapter to confirm the location of the diode. On some models the warning light check function is controlled by the regulator/rectifier unit.*

1 The diode is part of the starter circuit which illuminates the oil level warning light, and on certain models the fuel level warning light, when the starter button is pressed. This serves as a check of the warning light bulb.

2 Locate the diode; if necessary trace the green/black wire from the starter relay to locate it. Disconnect the wires from the diode terminals.

3 Referring to the wiring diagrams at the end of this Chapter, note that the diode will only allow current to pass in the direction of the arrowhead.

4 Using an ohmmeter or continuity tester, connect the positive (+ve) probe to the green/black wire terminal of the diode and the negative (-ve) probe to the other terminal – wire colour differs according to model. The diode should show continuity. Now reverse the probes. The diode should show no continuity. If it doesn't behave as stated, renew the diode.

5 Where two diodes are shown, connect the negative probe to the other terminal to test the other diode.

6 If the diode is good, check the other components in the circuit, and check the wiring between the various components (see the wiring diagrams at the end of this Chapter).

Renewal

7 Trace the green/black wire from the starter relay to the diode, then disconnect the diode wiring connectors.

Electrical system 9•21

24.1a Location of horn on lower frame – X9

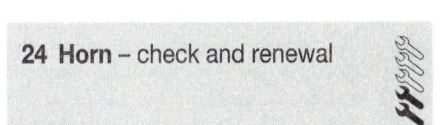

24.1b Location of horn (arrowed) behind front grille – GT models

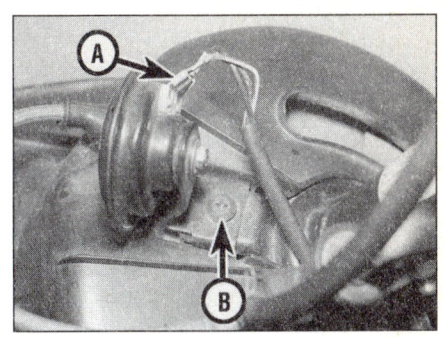

24.5 Horn wiring connectors (A) and mounting screw (B)

24 Horn – check and renewal

Check

1 The horn is mounted behind the front panel or the belly panel **(see illustrations)**. Remove the panels as necessary, or on ET2, ET4 and GT models, the front panel grille, to access the horn (see Chapter 7).
2 Unplug the wiring connectors from the horn **(see illustration 24.5)**. Using two jumper wires, apply battery voltage directly to the terminals on the horn. If the horn sounds, check the switch (see Section 21) and the wiring between the switch and the horn (see the *wiring diagrams* at the end of this Chapter).
3 If the horn doesn't sound, renew it.

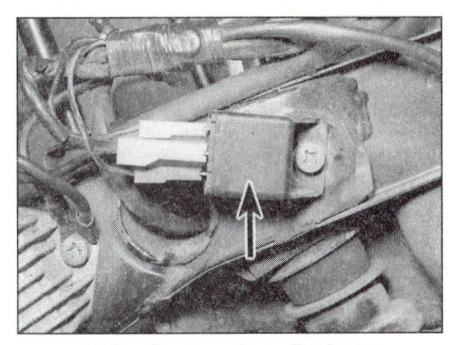

Renewal

4 Remove the panels as necessary to access the horn (see Step 1).
5 Unplug the wiring connectors from the horn, then remove the screw or bolt securing the horn and remove it **(see illustration)**.
6 Install the horn and securely tighten the screw or bolt. Connect the wiring connectors to the horn.

25 Starter relay – check and renewal

Check

1 If the starter circuit is faulty, first check the fuse (see Section 5). Also check that the battery is fully-charged (see Section 3). If the brake switches are part of the starting system, check the operation of the switches and the switch wiring (see Section 14). If a side stand switch is fitted, check the operation of the switch (see Section 32).
2 To locate the starter relay, trace the lead from the positive terminal of the battery that connects to the relay (the other one connects to the ignition switch). Alternatively, trace the lead back from the starter motor to the relay **(see illustrations)**.
3 On scooters where the wires are connected to the relay terminals with individual connectors, disconnect the battery lead (terminal No. 30) and starter motor lead (terminal No. 87) from the relay **(see illustrations 25.2a 2b)**. With the ignition switch ON, press the starter switch. The relay should be heard to click. If the relay doesn't click, switch off the ignition and test it as follows.
4 On scooters where the relay plugs into a multi-pin connector **(see illustration 25.2c)**, or as a further check of the relay, disconnect the relay wiring/connector and test it as follows on the bench.
5 Set a multi-meter to the ohms x 1 scale and connect it across the relay's battery lead and starter motor lead terminals. Using a fully-charged 12 volt battery and two insulated jumper wires, connect across the starter switch and earth (ground) terminals of the relay **(see illustration)**. At this point the relay should be heard to click and the multi-meter read 0 ohms (continuity). If this is the case the relay is proved good. If the relay does not click when battery voltage is applied and indicates no continuity (infinite resistance) across its terminals, it is faulty and must be renewed.
6 If the relay is good, check for battery voltage across the green/black (starter switch)

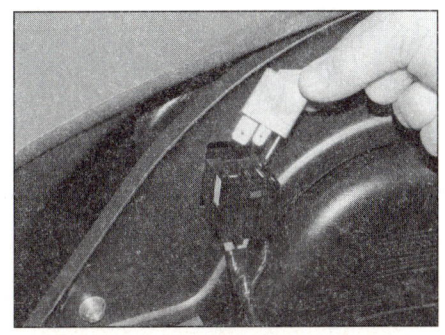

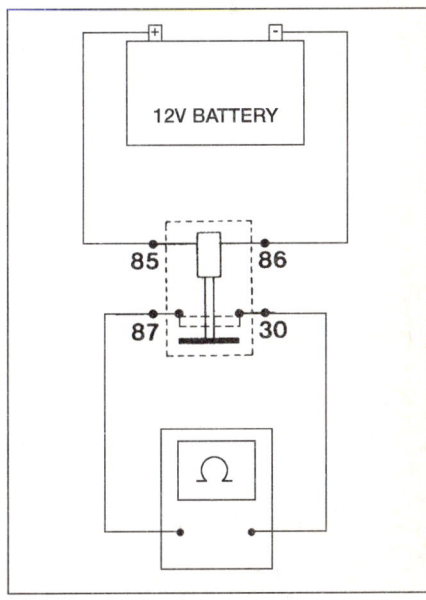

25.2a Starter relay – Typhoon

25.2b Starter relay – Hexagon

25.2c Starter relay with multi-pin connector – GT model shown

25.5 Starter relay test

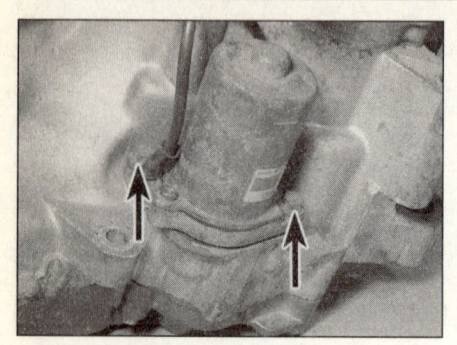

9•22 Electrical system

26.2a Remove the two bolts (arrowed), noting the earth cable . . .

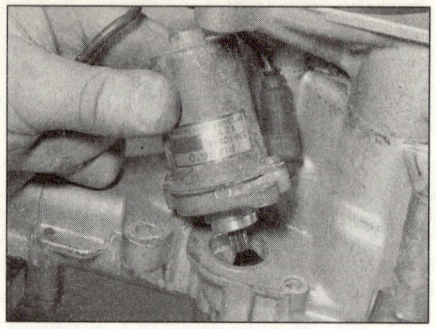

26.2b . . . then remove the starter motor . . .

26.2c . . . and detach the lead

wire and the white/black (earth) wire on the loom side of the relay connectors when the starter button is pressed. **Note:** *Wire colour codes may vary according to model – check the wiring diagrams at the end of this Chapter.* Check the other components in the starter circuit as described in the relevant sections of this Chapter. If all components are good, check the wiring between the various components (see the wiring diagrams).

Renewal

7 Disconnect the battery terminals, remembering to disconnect the negative (-ve) terminal first.
8 To locate the starter relay, trace the lead from the positive terminal of the battery that connects to the relay (the other one connects to the ignition switch). Alternatively, trace the lead back from the starter motor to the relay.
9 If applicable, make a careful note of which

wire fits on which terminal (the terminals are numbered), then disconnect the relay wiring connectors and remove the relay **(see illustrations 25.2a, 2b and 2c)**.
10 Installation is the reverse of removal. Connect the negative (-ve) lead last when reconnecting the battery.

26 Starter motor – removal and installation

Removal

Two-stroke engines

1 On two-stroke engines the starter motor is mounted underneath the engine. Disconnect the battery negative (-ve) lead.
2 Unscrew the two bolts securing the starter motor to the crankcase, noting the earth cable

secured by the upper bolt **(see illustration)**. Slide the starter motor out from the crankcase, then peel back the rubber terminal cover and remove the screw securing the starter lead to the motor **(see illustrations)**. Detach the lead and remove the starter motor.

Four-stroke engines

3 On four-stroke engines the starter motor is mounted on top of the engine, behind the carburettor. Remove the body panels as required according to model (see Chapter 7). Disconnect the battery negative (-ve) lead.
4 Peel back the rubber terminal cover, then remove the screw securing the starter lead to the motor and detach the lead **(see illustration)**.
5 Where fitted, unscrew the two bolts securing the starter motor pinion cover to the crankcase and remove the cover, noting the rubber pad on its inside **(see illustration)**. Unscrew the two bolts securing the starter motor to the crankcase, noting the earth lead and cable clip secured by them **(see illustration)**. Withdraw the bolts and remove the spacers, then lift the starter motor out of the crankcase **(see illustration)**.
6 Remove the O-ring on the end of the starter motor and discard it, as a new one must be used.

Installation

7 Installation is the reverse of removal. On four-stroke engines, fit a new O-ring on the end of the starter motor, making sure it is seated in its groove, and apply a smear of engine oil to it **(see illustration)**.

26.4 Pull back the rubber boot and remove the screw (arrowed) securing the lead

26.5a Remove the pinion cover where fitted . . .

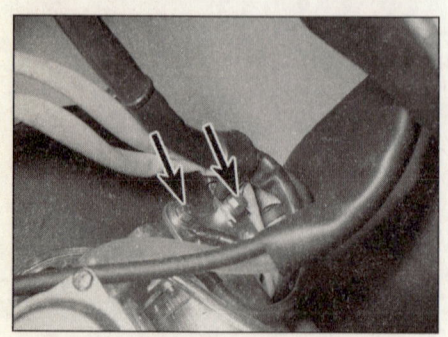

26.5b . . . then remove the two bolts (arrowed) . . .

26.5c . . . and lift the motor off the engine

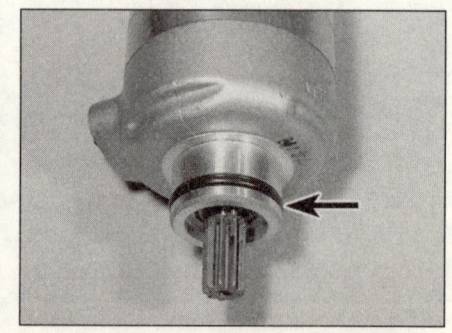

26.7 Fit a new O-ring on four-stroke models

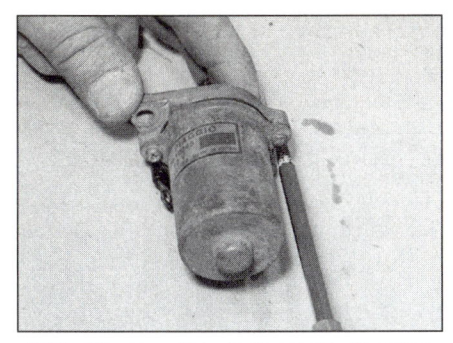

Electrical system 9•23

27.3a Remove the starter motor housing screws . . .

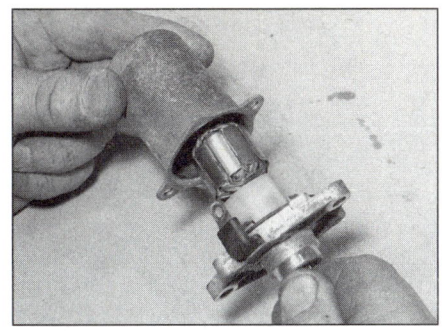

27.3b . . . and draw off the housing – Typhoon 50

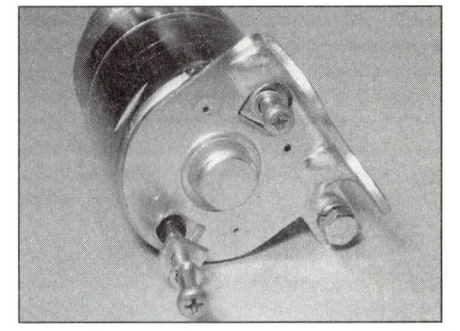

27.3c Remove the starter motor housing screws . . .

27 Starter motor – disassembly, inspection and reassembly

Disassembly

Note: *A number of different starter motors are fitted across the range of models. Before disassembling the motor, note that no individual components are available, so if the motor is faulty, a new one must be fitted. It may be worthwhile consulting an auto-electrician before buying a new motor, as sometimes, depending on the nature of the fault, they can be repaired. When disassembling the motor, carefully note the correct fitted position of each component before removing it, as the procedure given below is general and does not cover the specific components of each type of motor.*

1 Remove the starter motor (see Section 26).
2 Note the alignment mark between the main housing and the cover, or make your own if it isn't clear.
3 Remove the screws or bolts securing the cover to the main housing and draw the housing off, leaving the armature in place in the cover **(see illustrations)**. It may be necessary to grasp the end of the starter motor shaft to prevent the magnets in the housing drawing the armature away with it – note that illustration 27.3d shows a clamp fitted around the shaft to prevent this.

27.3d . . . and draw off the housing – ET4

4 Withdraw the armature from the cover, noting any shims or washers on either or both ends of the armature shaft, and noting how the brushes locate onto the commutator **(see illustration)**.
5 Slide the brushes out from their holders, noting how they locate against the brush springs **(see illustration)**.

Inspection

6 The parts of the starter motor that are most likely to wear and require attention are the brushes. Piaggio provide no specifications as to the minimum service length of the brushes, although those on the ET4 illustration measured 11 mm (new). If any of the brushes are excessively worn cracked, chipped, or otherwise damaged, they should be renewed. Check with a Piaggio dealer on the availability

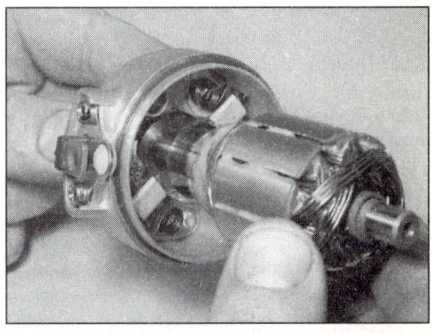

27.4 Withdraw the armature, noting how it fits

of new brushes – if none are available, a new starter motor must be fitted.
7 Inspect the commutator bars on the armature for scoring, scratches and discoloration. The commutator can be cleaned and polished with crocus cloth, but do not use sandpaper or emery paper. After cleaning, wipe away any residue with a cloth soaked in electrical system cleaner or denatured alcohol.
8 Using an ohmmeter or a continuity test light, check for continuity between the commutator bars **(see illustration)**. Continuity should exist between each bar and all of the others. Also, check for continuity between the commutator bars and the armature shaft **(see illustration)**. There should be no continuity (infinite resistance) between the commutator and the shaft. If the checks indicate otherwise, the armature is defective.

27.5 Slide the brushes out of their holders, noting how they fit

27.8a Continuity should exist between the commutator bars

27.8b There should be no continuity between the commutator bars and the armature shaft

9•24 Electrical system

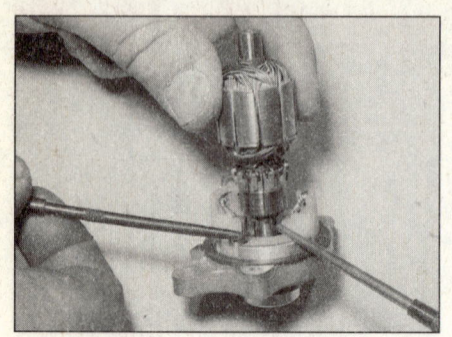

27.14a Hold the brushes back against the springs to allow the armature to be installed

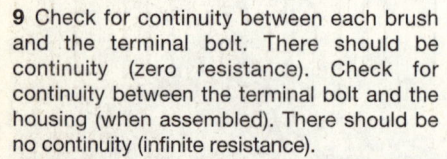

27.14b Where possible, locate the spring ends (arrowed) onto the brush holders so that there is no pressure on the brushes . . .

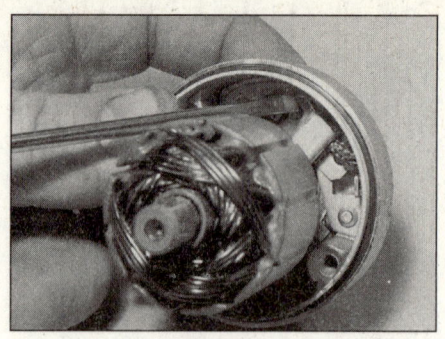

27.14c . . . then locate them back onto the brushes after the armature has been installed

9 Check for continuity between each brush and the terminal bolt. There should be continuity (zero resistance). Check for continuity between the terminal bolt and the housing (when assembled). There should be no continuity (infinite resistance).
10 Check the front end of the armature shaft for worn, cracked, chipped and broken teeth. If the shaft is damaged or worn, renew the armature (or complete starter motor).
11 Inspect the end cover for signs of cracks or wear. Inspect the magnets in the main housing and the housing itself for cracks.
12 Inspect the armature shaft bearing surfaces in the cover and main housing and the cover seal.

Reassembly

13 Reassemble the starter motor in a reverse of the disassembly procedure.
14 When fitting the armature, note that it will be necessary to hold the brushes back against the pressure of their springs. There are a number of ways of doing this, all of which can be tricky, especially without the aid of an assistant. A pair of thin-ended angled scribes, or something similar, can be used **(see illustration)**. On some models it is possible to locate the spring ends onto the top of the brush holder so that there is no pressure on the brushes, which can be slid fully back into their holders as the armature is installed **(see illustration)**. Install the armature, then place the spring ends back onto the brushes so that the brushes are then pressed onto the commutator bars **(see illustration)**. Check that each brush is securely pressed against the commutator by its spring and is free to move easily in its holder.
15 Renew the cover O-ring if it is damaged **(see illustration)**.

28 Charging system testing – general information and precautions

1 If the performance of the charging system is suspect, the system as a whole should be checked first, followed by testing of the individual components. **Note:** *Before beginning the checks, make sure the battery is fully charged and that all system connections are clean and tight.*
2 Checking the output of the charging system and the performance of the various components within the charging system requires the use of a multi-meter (with voltage, current and resistance checking facilities).
3 When making the checks, follow the procedures carefully to prevent incorrect connections or short circuits, as irreparable damage to electrical system components may result if short circuits occur.
4 If a multi-meter is not available, the job of checking the charging system should be left to a Piaggio dealer.

29 Charging system – leakage and output test

1 If the charging system of the machine is thought to be faulty, perform the following checks.

Leakage test

Caution: *Always connect an ammeter in series, never in parallel with the battery, otherwise it will be damaged. Do not turn the ignition ON or operate the starter motor when the ammeter is connected – a sudden surge in current will blow the meter's fuse.*

2 Turn the ignition switch OFF and disconnect the lead from the battery negative (-ve) terminal.
3 Set the multi-meter to the amps function and connect its negative (-ve) probe to the battery negative (-ve) terminal, and positive (+ve) probe to the disconnected negative (-ve) lead **(see illustration)**. Always set the meter to a high amps range initially and then bring it down to the mA (milli Amps) range; if there is a high current flow in the circuit it may blow the meter's fuse.

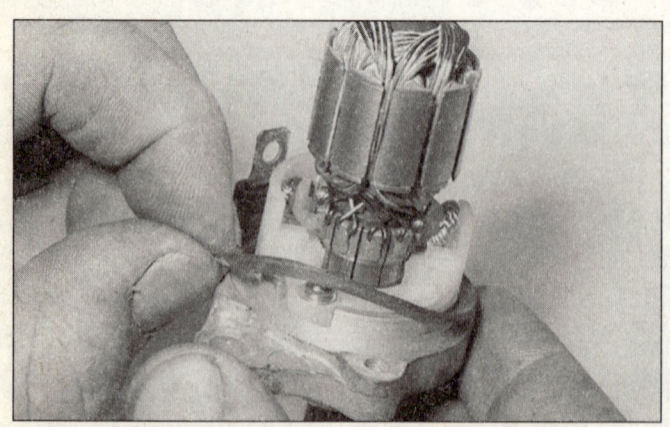

27.15 Renew the cover sealing O-ring if damaged

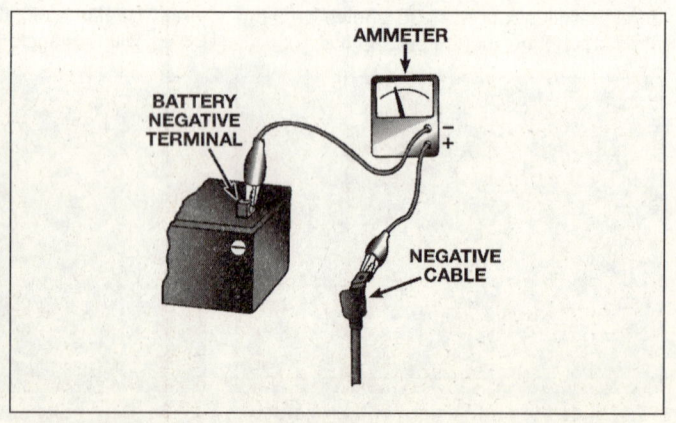

29.3 Checking the charging system leakage rate – connect the meter as shown

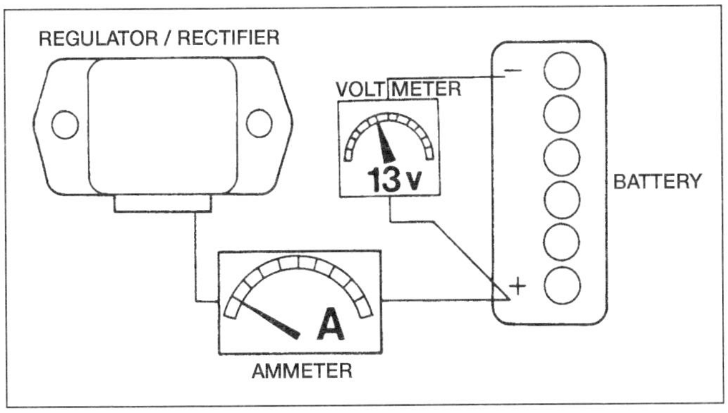

Electrical system 9•25

29.9 Checking the regulated current output

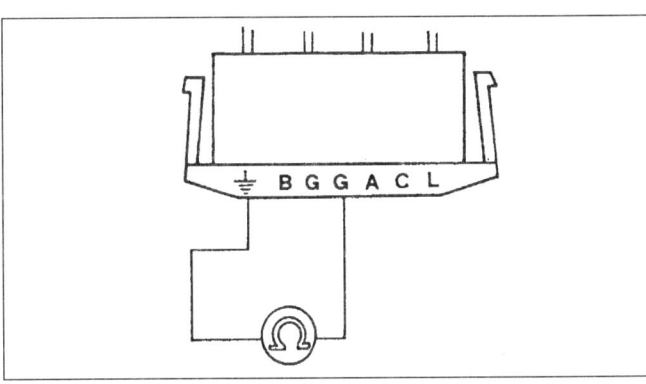

30.2 Checking the alternator coil insulation on Typhoon, Hexagon and Skipper

4 While Piaggio do not specify an amount, if the current leakage indicated exceeds 1 mA, there is probably a short circuit in the wiring. Disconnect the meter and connect the negative (-ve) lead to the battery, tightening it securely.

5 If leakage is indicated, use the wiring diagrams at the end of this book to systematically disconnect individual electrical components and repeat the test until the source is identified.

Alternator output test

6 To check the unregulated voltage output, first start the engine and warm it up to normal operating temperature. Stop the engine and turn the ignition OFF. Support the scooter on its centre stand with the rear wheel clear of the ground.

7 Disconnect the regulator wiring connector (see Section 31). Connect a voltmeter set to the 0 – 50 volts ac scale between the wire with the violet cap and earth (Sfera 50/80, Typhoon 50/80, NRG MC2, Zip and Zip SP models), or between the grey/blue terminal and earth (Sfera 125, Liberty 50, Liberty 50 4T, Zip 50, Zip 4T, ET2, ET4 50, ET4 125, LX 50, LX4 50, Fly 50, Fly 50 4T, NRG Power models), or between the yellow and black wire terminals (Typhoon 125, Zip 125, Liberty 125, B125, X9, Hexagon and Skipper models).

8 Allow the engine to idle, then slowly increase the engine speed to 2000 or 3000 rpm according to model (see Specifications) and note the reading obtained. The unregulated voltage should be as specified at the beginning of the Chapter. Turn the ignition OFF, disconnect the voltmeter and reconnect the regulator connector. If the voltage is within the specified limits, follow the procedure in Step 8 and check the regulated current output. On Typhoon 125, Hexagon and Skipper models, and all LEADER engined models (see Model Specifications, Chapter 1), also check the alternator coils (see Section 30).

9 To check the regulated current output, disconnect the battery positive (+ve) lead and connect a multi-meter set to the 0 to 20 amps DC scale (ammeter) in series between the lead and the battery positive (+ve) terminal (see illustration). Connect another multi-meter set to the 0 to 20 volts DC scale (voltmeter) across the battery terminals (meter positive (+ve) probe to battery positive terminal, and meter negative (-ve) probe to battery negative terminal). Start the engine and allow it to idle, then slowly increase the engine speed to 2000 or 3000 rpm according to model (see Specifications) and note the reading obtained. The regulated current should be as specified at the beginning of the Chapter with battery voltage at 13 V.

10 If the regulated current is outside these limits, yet the unregulated voltage output from the alternator is as specified (see Steps 7 and 8), renew the regulator (see Section 31).

30 Alternator coils – check (Typhoon 125, Hexagon, Skipper and LEADER engines)

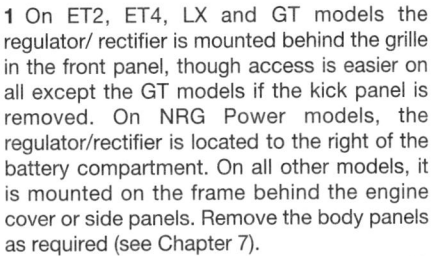

1 On ET2, ET4, LX and GT models the regulator/rectifier is mounted behind the grille in the front panel, though access is easier on all except the GT models if the kick panel is removed. On NRG Power models, the regulator/rectifier is located to the right of the battery compartment. On all other models, it is mounted on the frame behind the engine cover or side panels. Remove the body panels as required (see Chapter 7).

2 Using a multi-meter set to the ohms x 10 range, connect one probe to one of the yellow (G terminal) wires in the connector and the other probe to the black (earth) wire terminal in the connector (see illustration). If the alternator stator insulation is in good condition, no continuity (high resistance) should be indicated. Repeat the test between the other yellow wire terminal and the black wire terminal.

3 Next connect the meter probes between the two yellow wire terminals of the connector. Continuity (zero resistance) should be shown.

4 If the test results indicate that the alternator coils are open circuit or that there is a short to earth, have your findings confirmed by a Piaggio dealer or auto-electrician before fitting a new alternator stator. Check that the fault is not due to broken or shorted wiring between the alternator and regulator/rectifier connector.

31 Regulator/rectifier – renewal

1 On ET2, ET4, LX and GT models the regulator/rectifier is mounted behind the grille in the front panel, though access is easier on all except the GT models if the kick panel is removed (see illustration). On NRG Power models, the regulator/rectifier is located to the right of the battery compartment (see illustration). On all other models, it is

31.1a Regulator/rectifier location – ET2, ET4 and LX

31.1b Regulator/rectifier location – NRG Power DT

9•26 Electrical system

31.1c Regulator/rectifier location – Typhoon

31.1d Regulator/rectifier location – Hexagon

31.1e Regulator/rectifier location – B125

31.1f Regulator/rectifier location – X9

mounted on the frame behind the engine cover or side panels **(see illustrations)**. Remove the body panels as required (see Chapter 7).

2 Pull the rubber cover off the wiring connector and disconnect the connector **(see illustration)**.

3 Remove the two screws securing the regulator/rectifier and remove it, noting the earth cable secured by one of the screws on some models.

4 Install the new unit and tighten its screws securely, not forgetting the earth cable, where fitted. Connect the wiring connector.

32 Side stand switch – check and renewal

Check

1 Where fitted, the side stand switch is mounted on the top of the side stand bracket **(see illustration)**. The switch is part of the safety circuit which prevents the engine from starting unless the side stand is up and the brake lever is pulled in. Before checking the electrical circuit, check the ignition circuit fuses (see Section 5).

2 To access the wiring connector, remove the floor panel (see Chapter 7). Trace the wiring from the switch and disconnect it at the connector **(see illustration)**.

3 Check the operation of the switch using a multi-meter or continuity tester. Connect the meter probes to the terminals on the switch side of the connector. With the side stand up there should be continuity (zero resistance) between the terminals, and with the stand down there should be no continuity (infinite resistance).

4 If the switch does not perform as expected, it is defective and must be renewed.

5 If the switch is good, check the starter relay (Section 25) and other components in the starter circuit as described in the relevant Sections of this Chapter. If all components are good, check the wiring between the various components (see wiring diagrams at the end of this Chapter).

Renewal

6 The side stand switch is mounted on the top of the side stand bracket. Remove the floor panel, then trace the wiring from the switch and disconnect it at the connector **(see illustration 32.2)**. Release the wiring from any cable ties and feed it back to the switch noting the correct routing.

7 Remove the side stand and remove the switch, noting how it fits (see Chapter 7).

8 Install the new switch, then install the stand.

9 Make sure the wiring is correctly routed up to the connector and retained by all the necessary ties. Reconnect the wiring connector and check the operation of the switch, then install the floor panel.

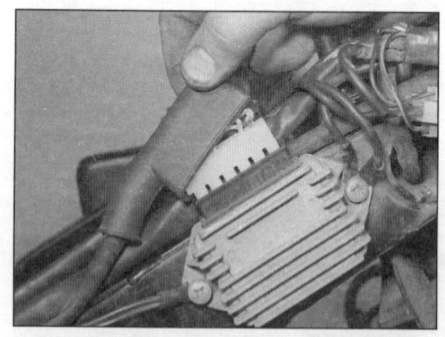

31.2 Lift the cover and disconnect the connector

32.1 Location of the side stand switch

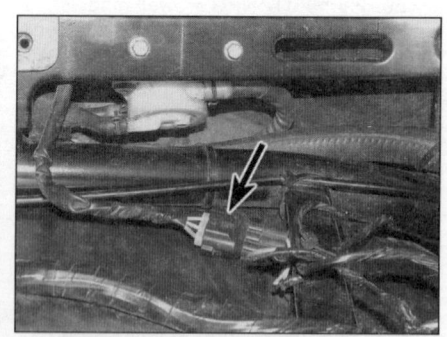

32.2 Location of the switch wiring connector (arrowed)

Wiring diagrams 9•27

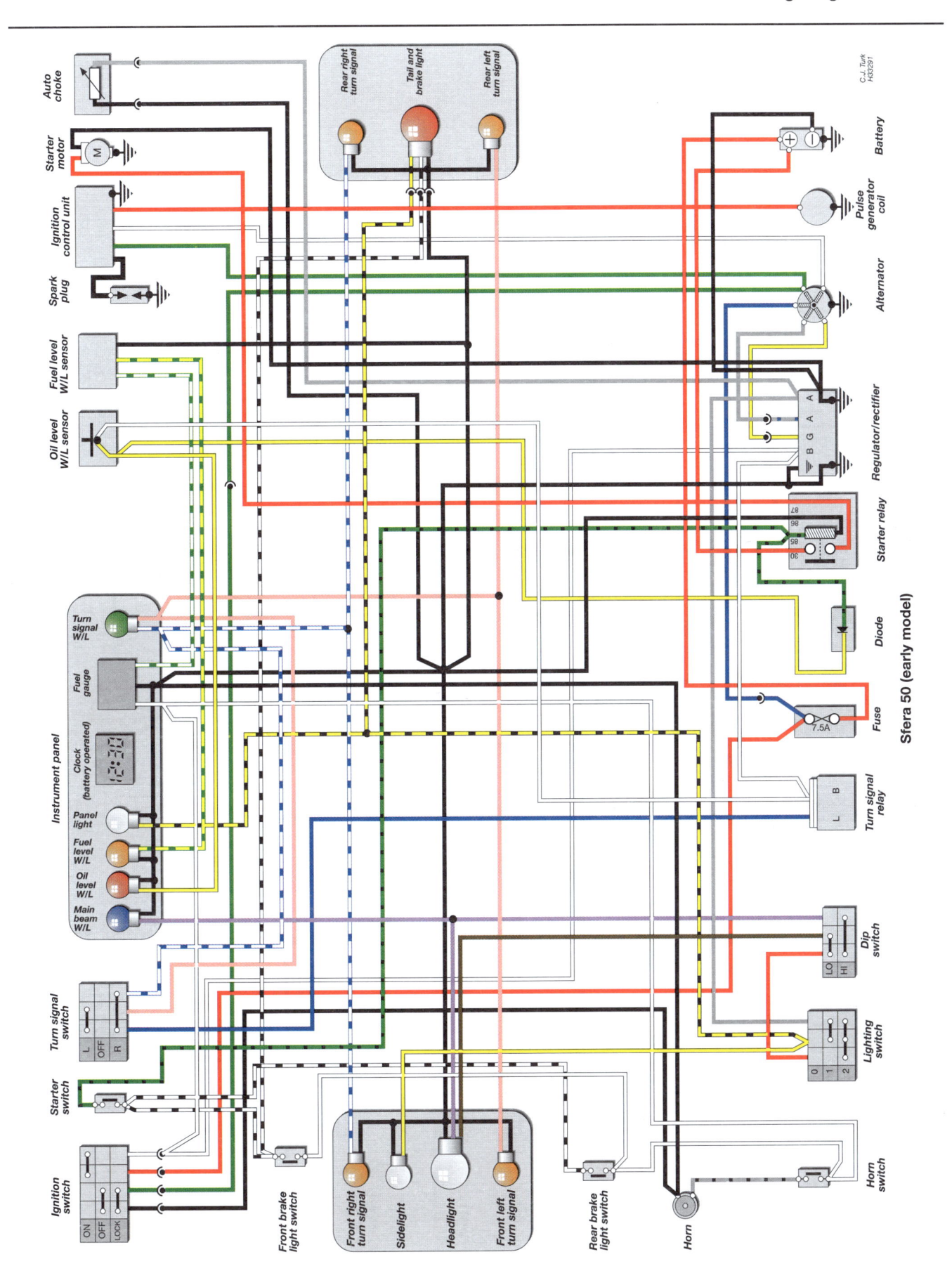

Sfera 50 (early model)

9•28 Wiring diagrams

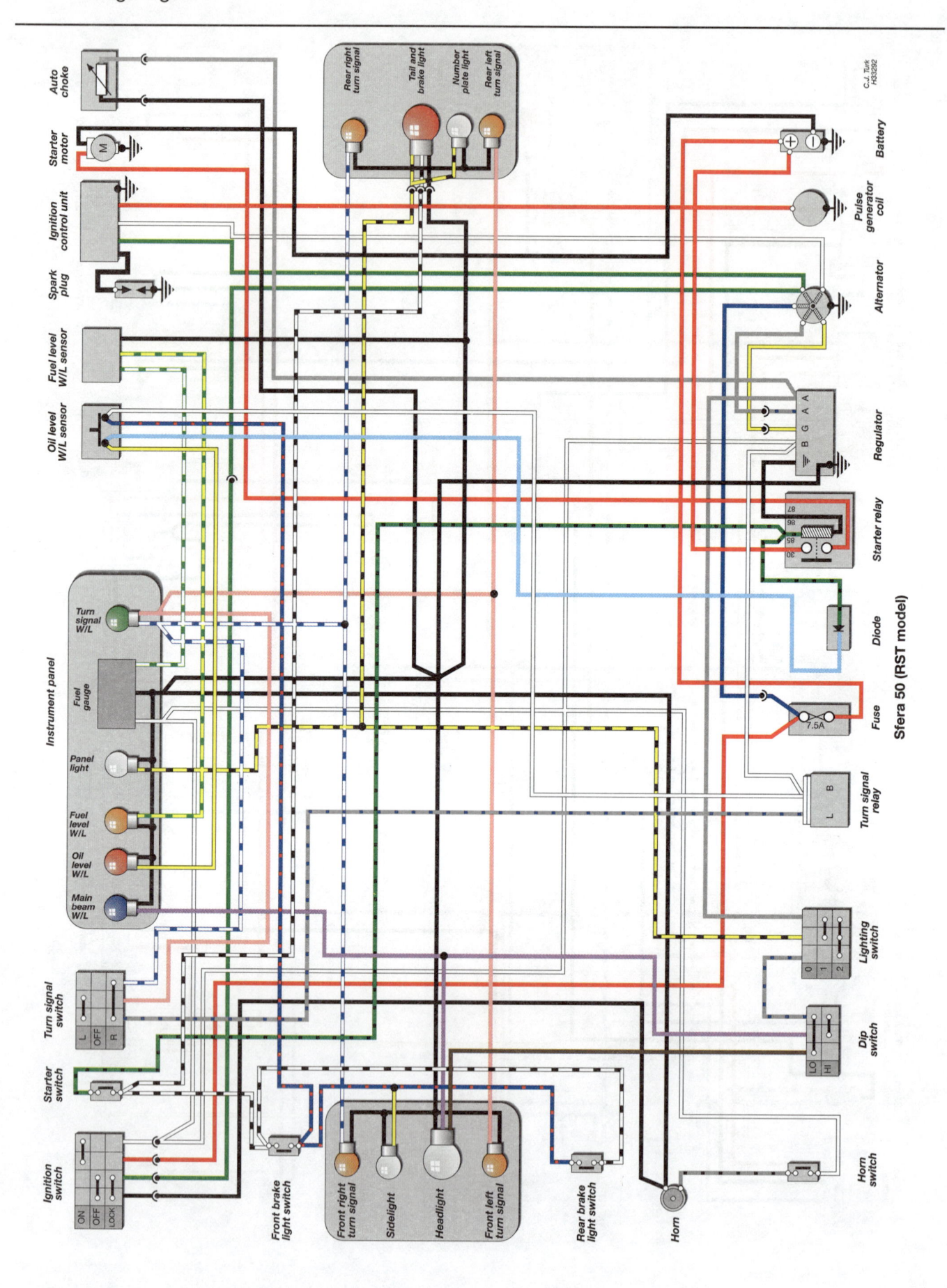

Sfera 50 (RST model)

Wiring diagrams 9•29

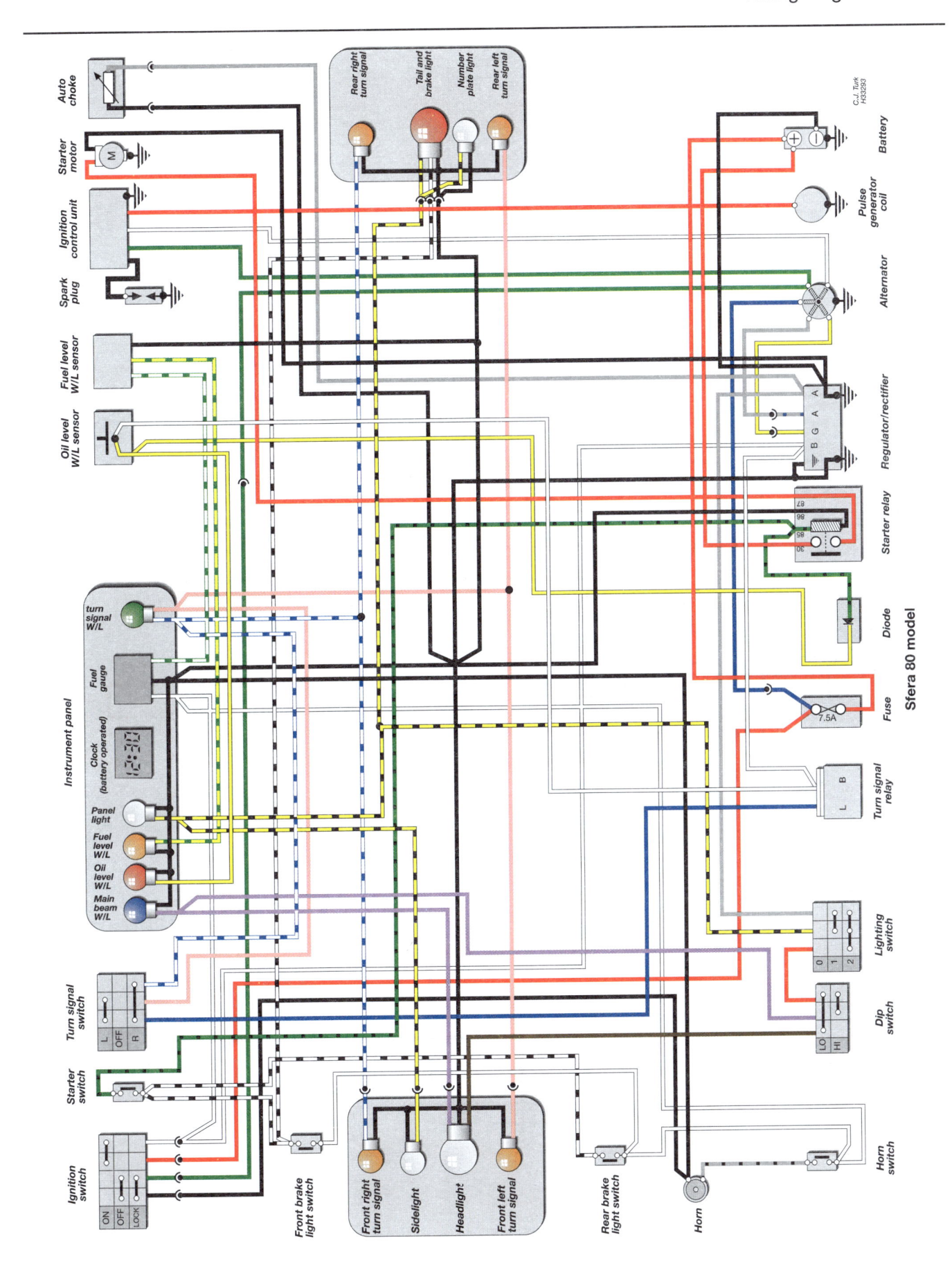

Sfera 80 model

9•30 Wiring diagrams

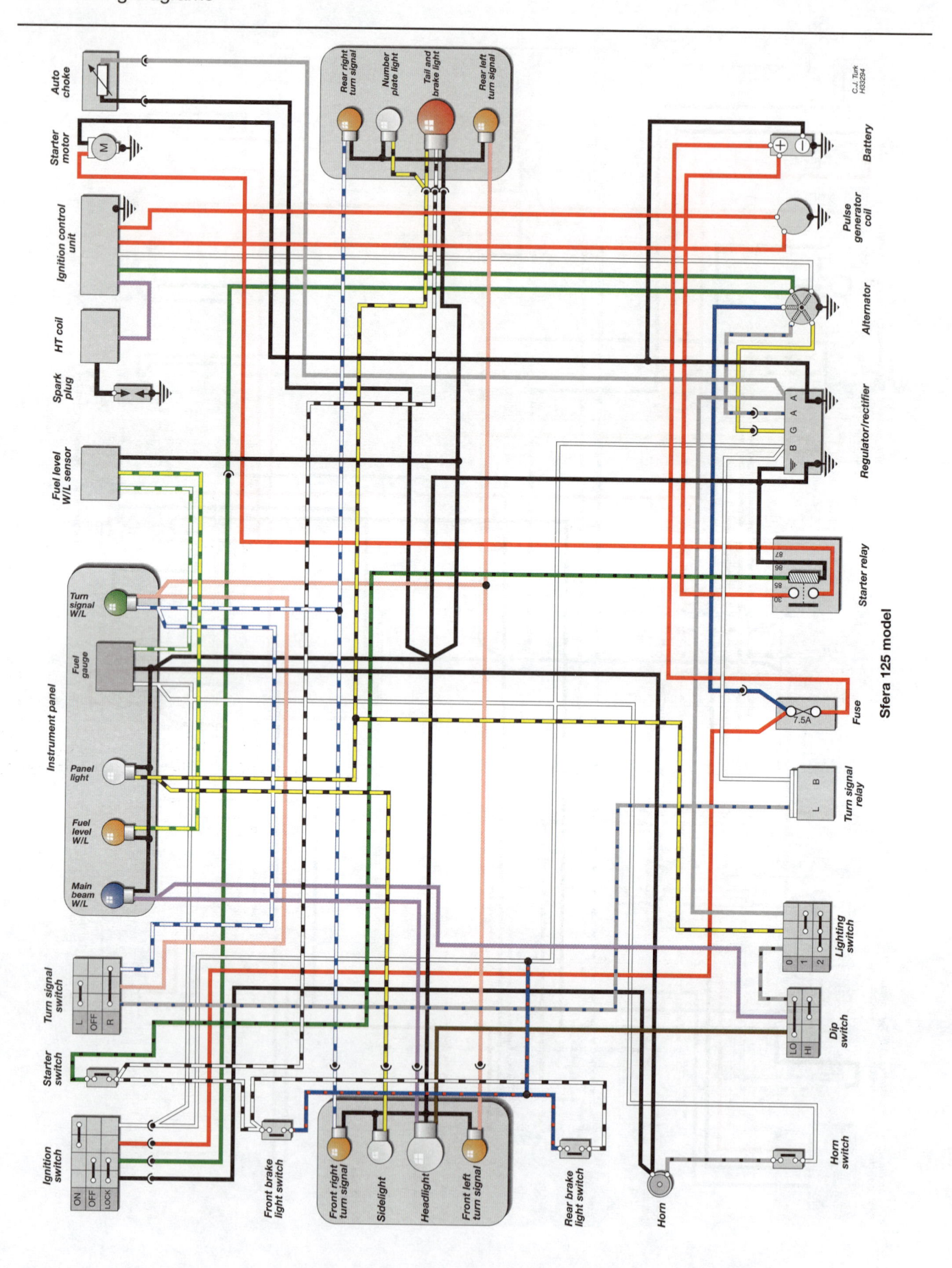

Sfera 125 model

Wiring diagrams 9•31

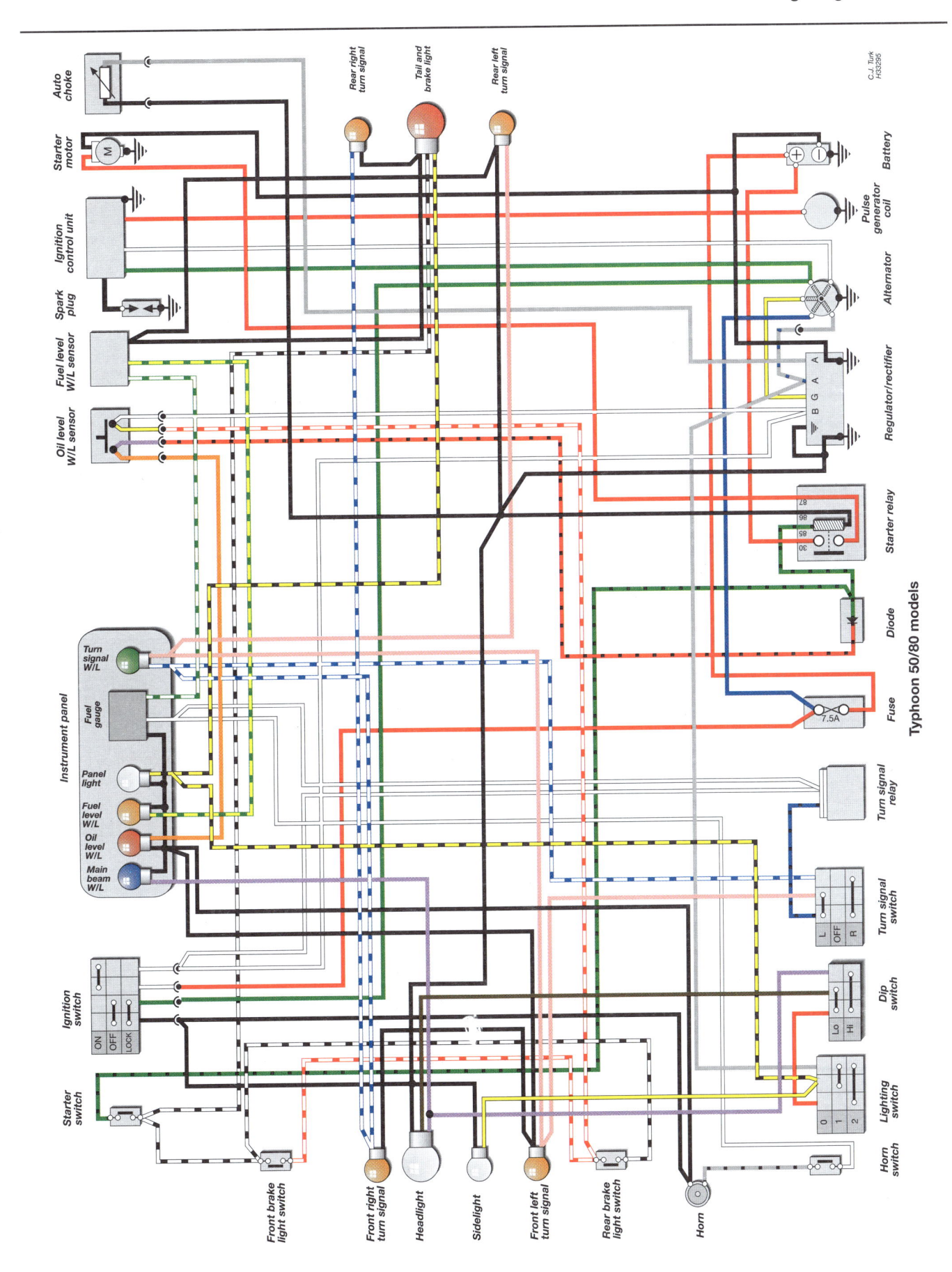

Typhoon 50/80 models

9•32 Wiring diagrams

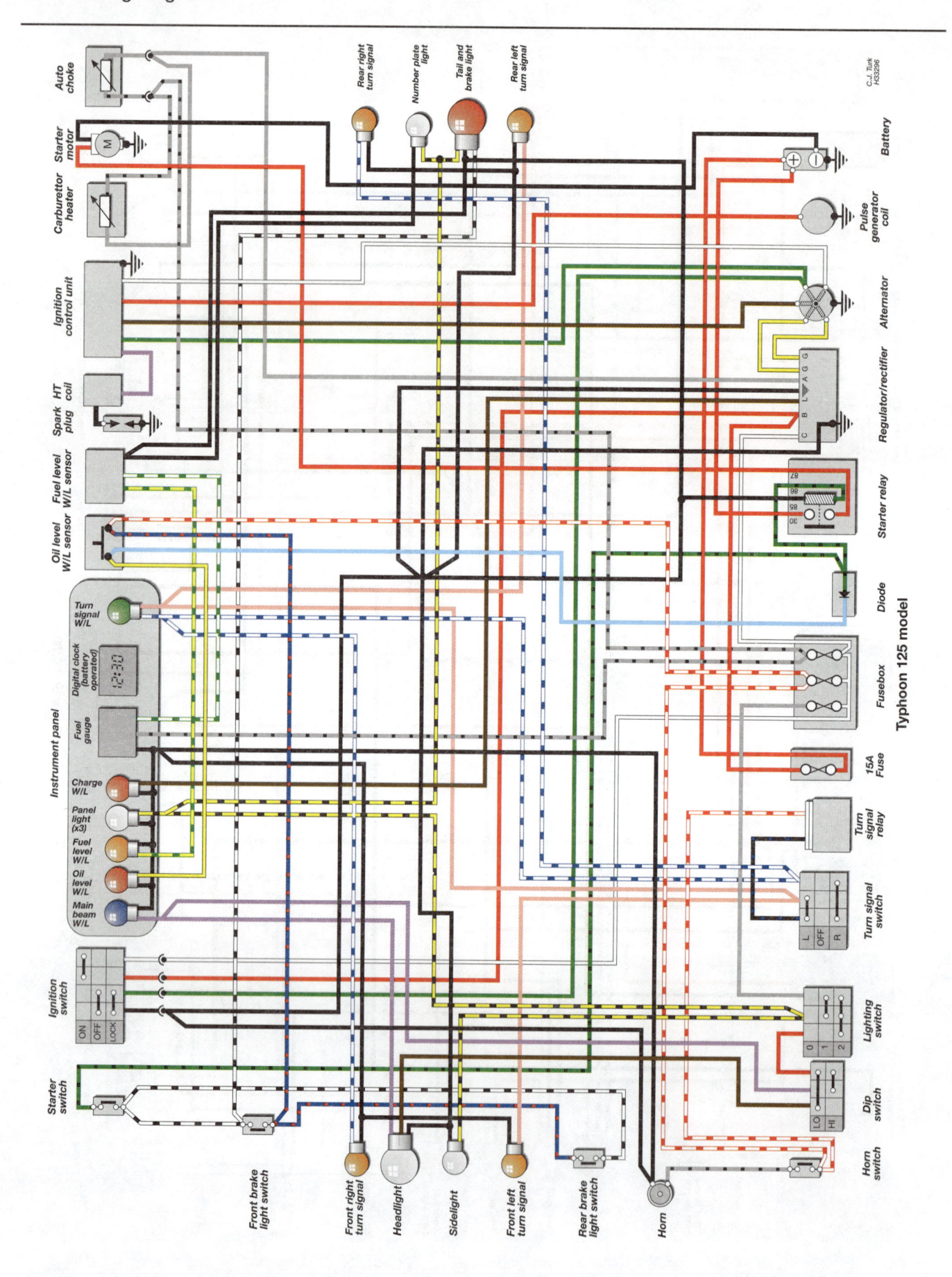

Typhoon 125 model

Wiring diagrams 9•33

Fly 50 CAT and Liberty 50 CAT models

9•34 Wiring diagrams

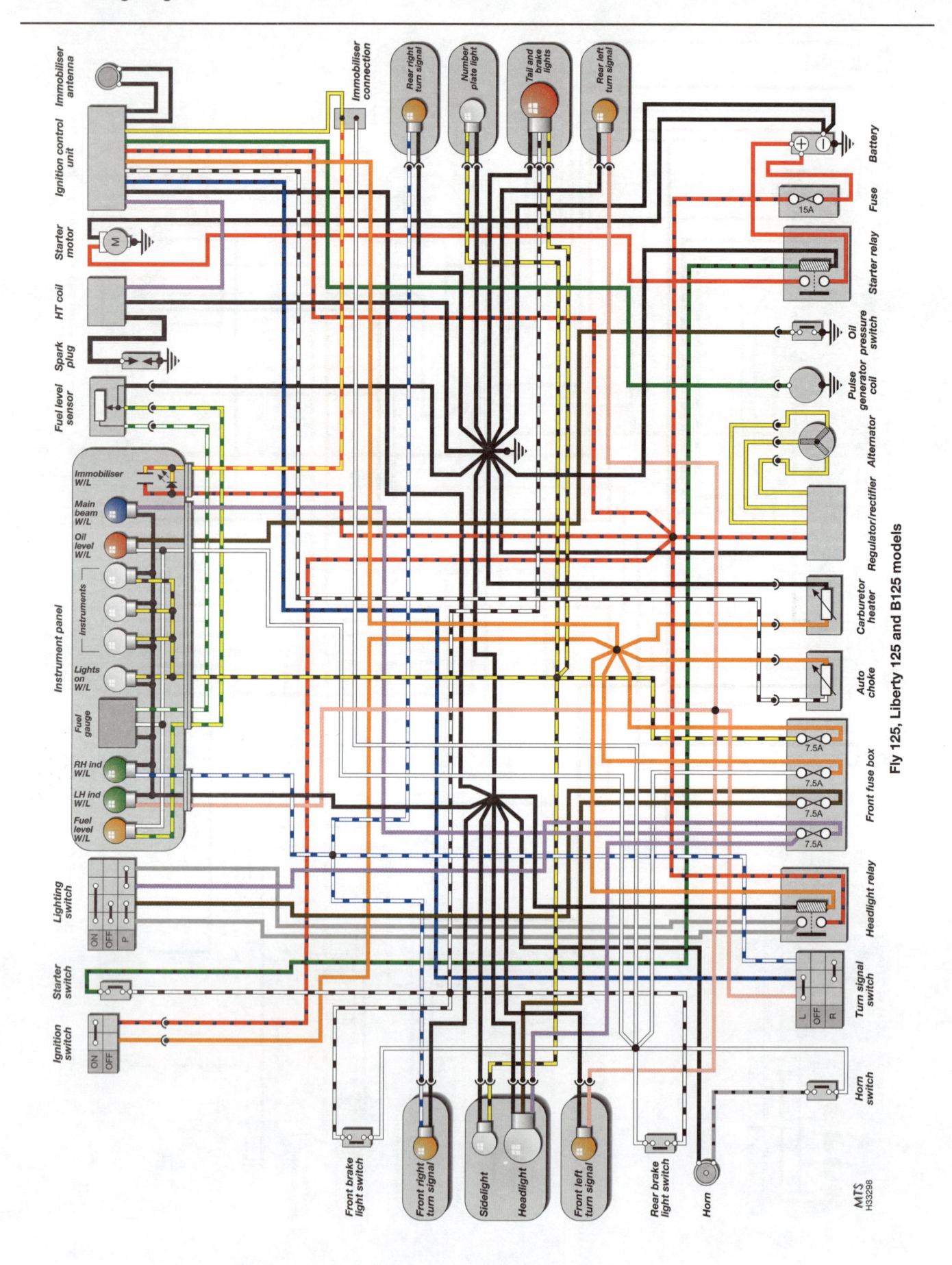

Fly 125, Liberty 125 and B125 models

Wiring diagrams 9•35

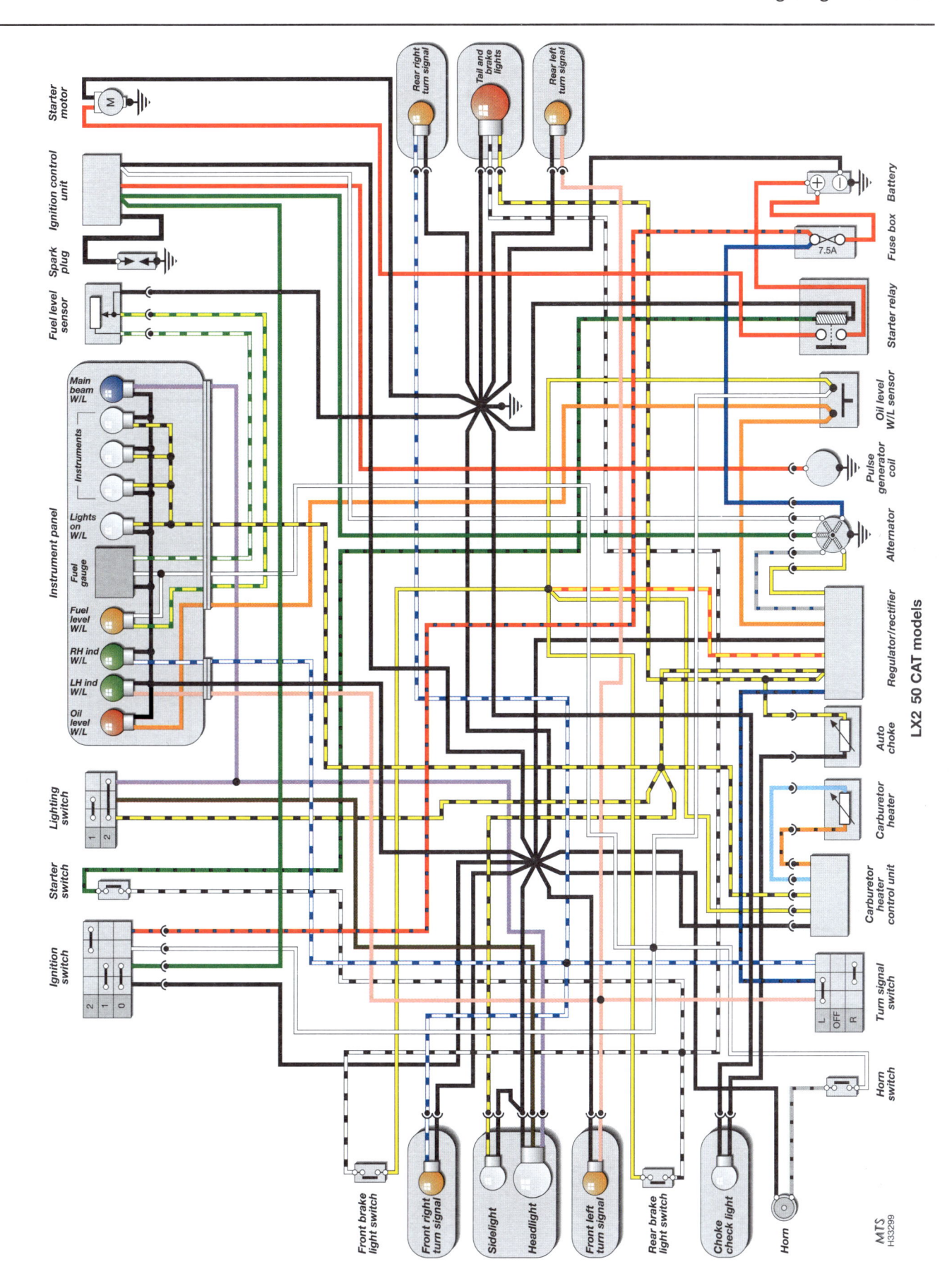

LX2 50 CAT models

9•36 Wiring diagrams

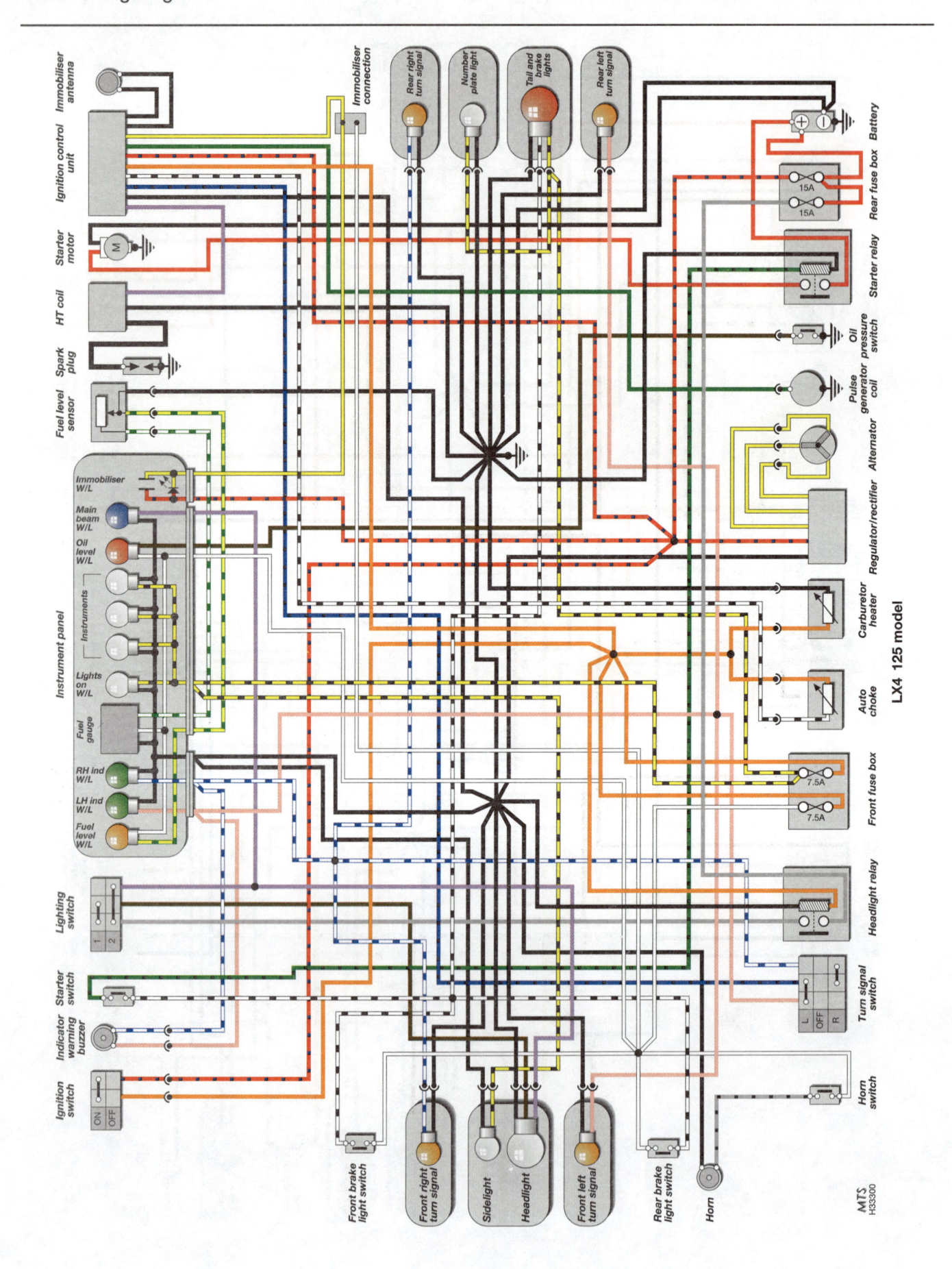

Wiring diagrams 9•37

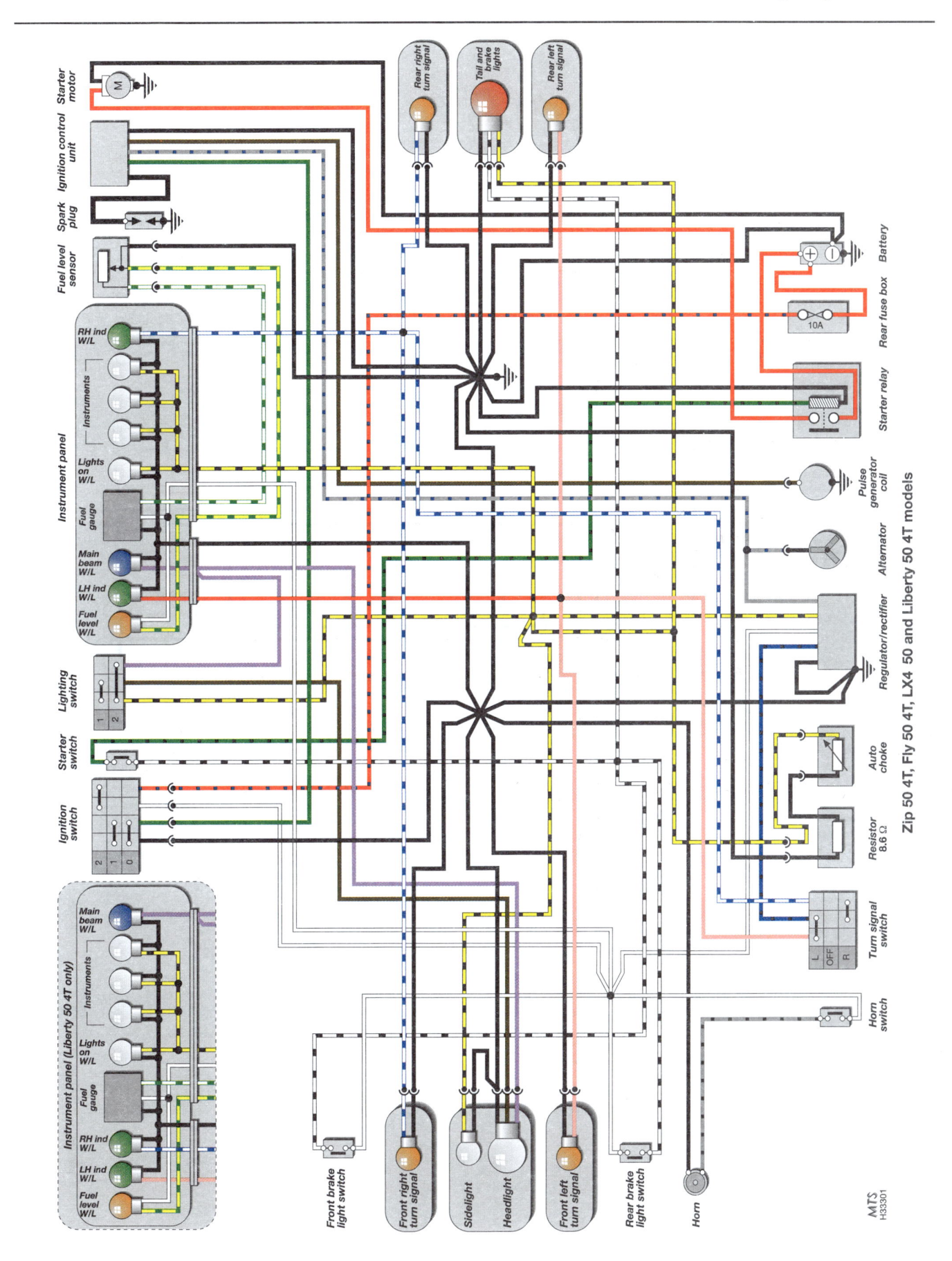

Zip 50 4T, Fly 50 4T, LX4 50 and Liberty 50 4T models

9•38 Wiring diagrams

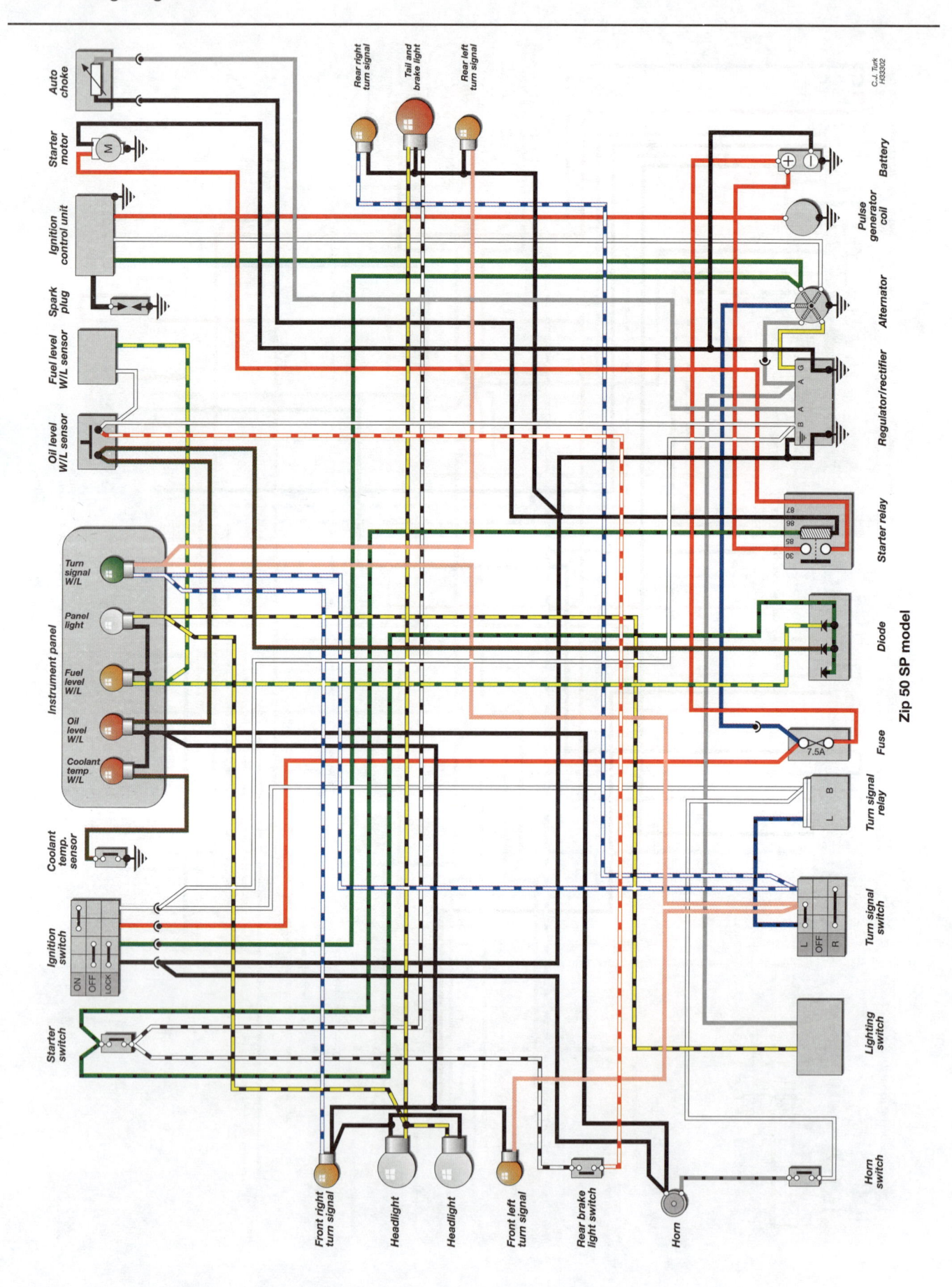

Wiring diagrams 9•39

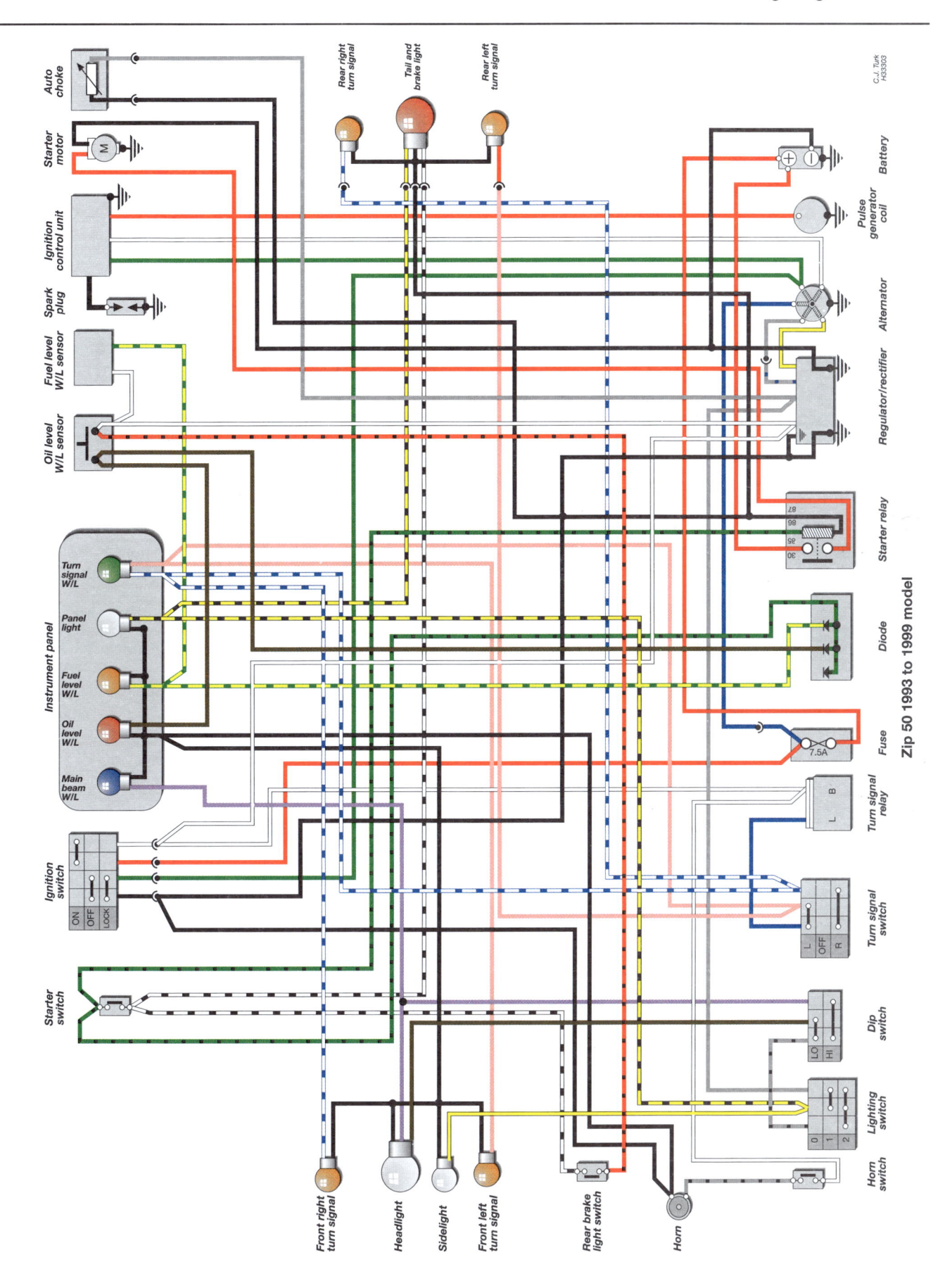

Zip 50 1993 to 1999 model

9•40 Wiring diagrams

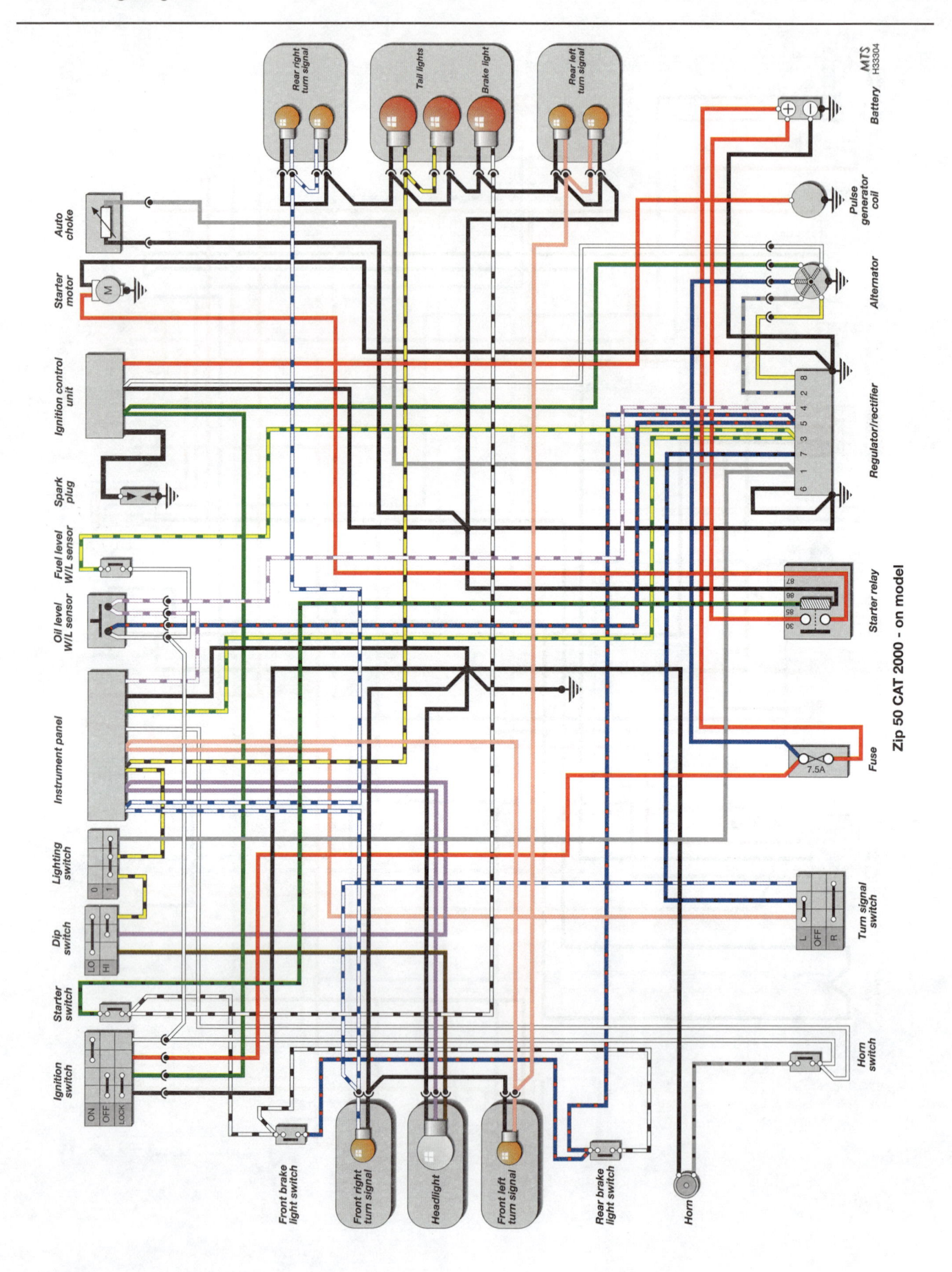

Wiring diagrams 9•41

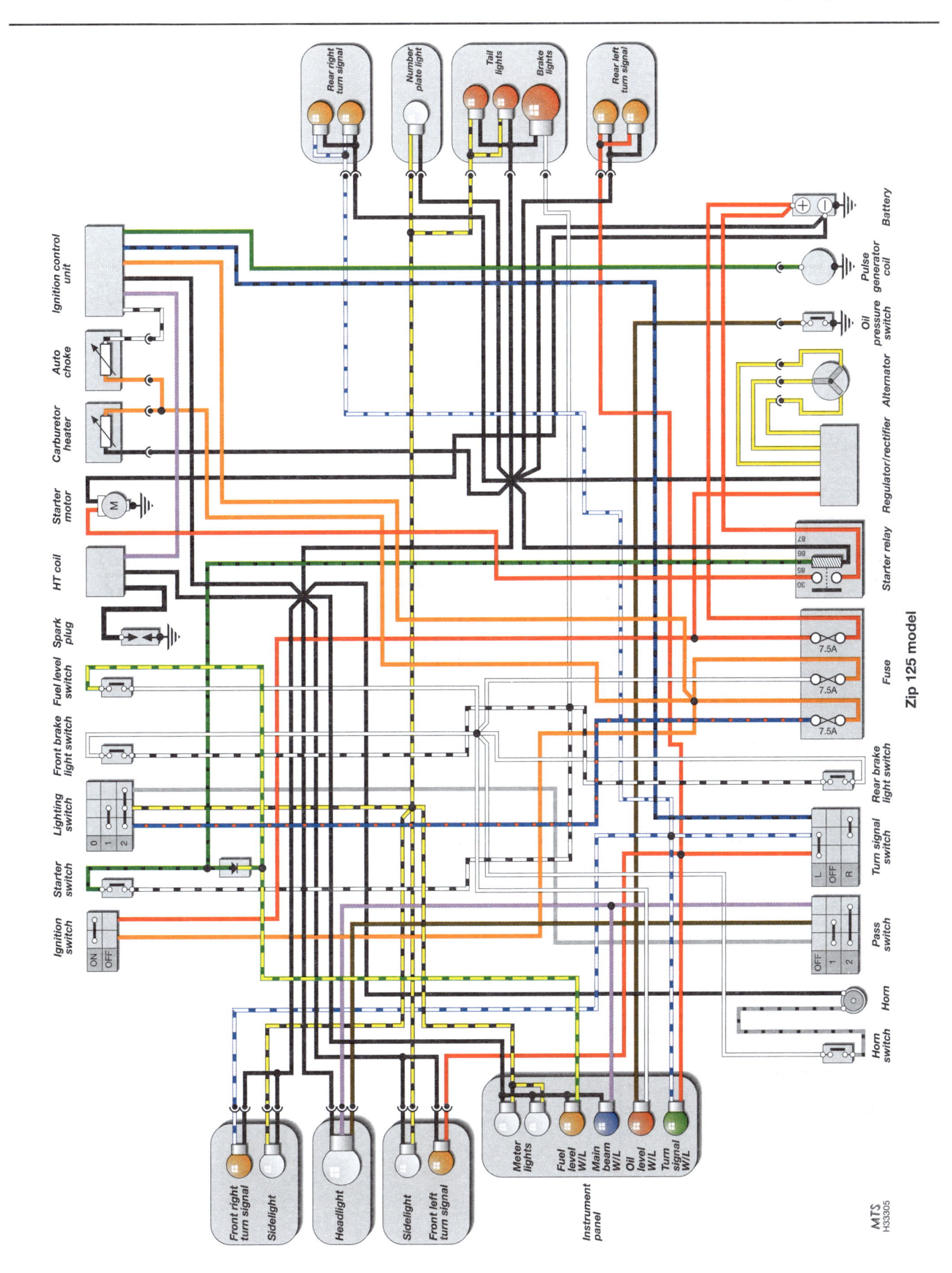

Zip 125 model

9•42 Wiring diagrams

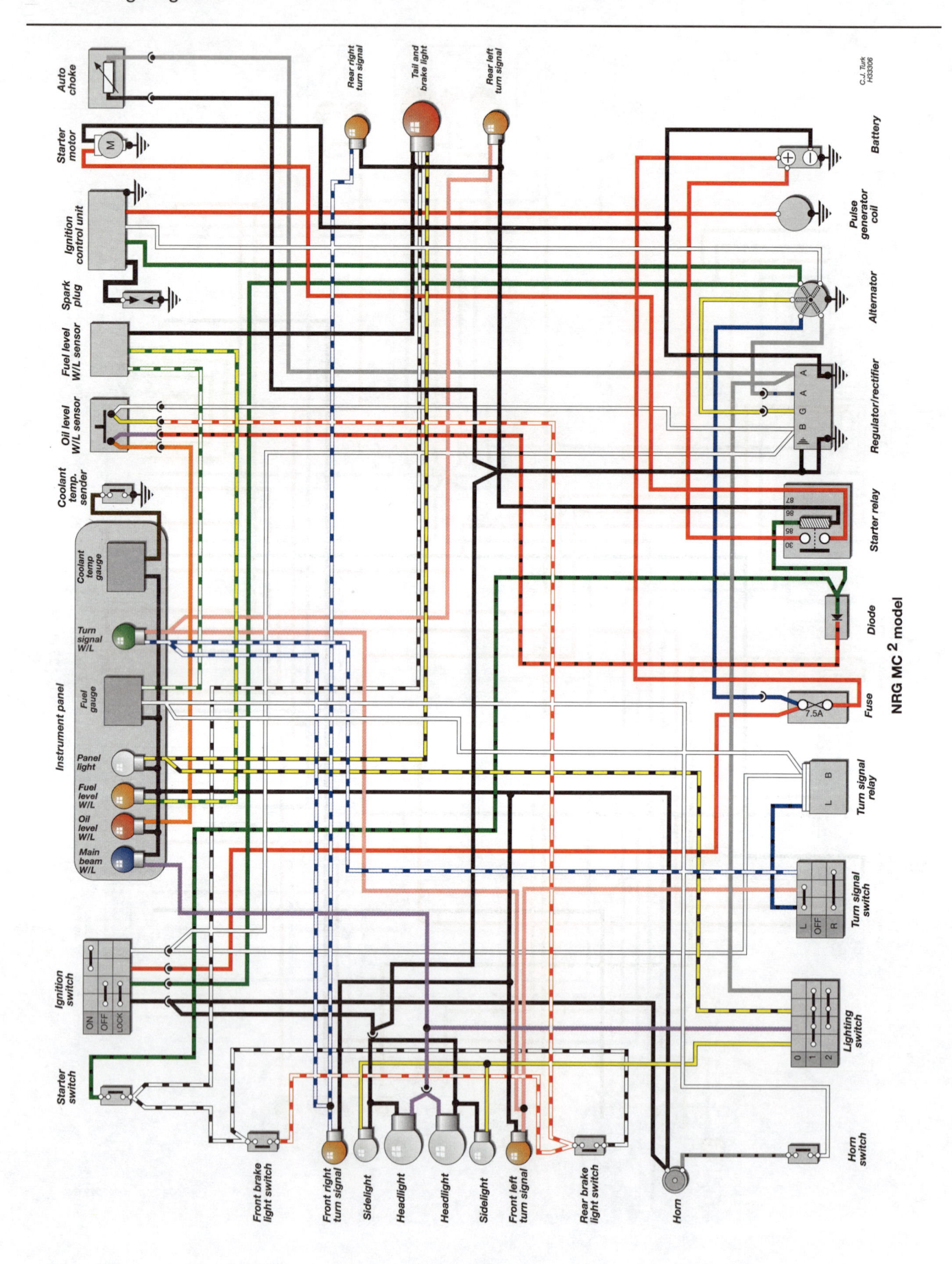

Wiring diagrams 9•43

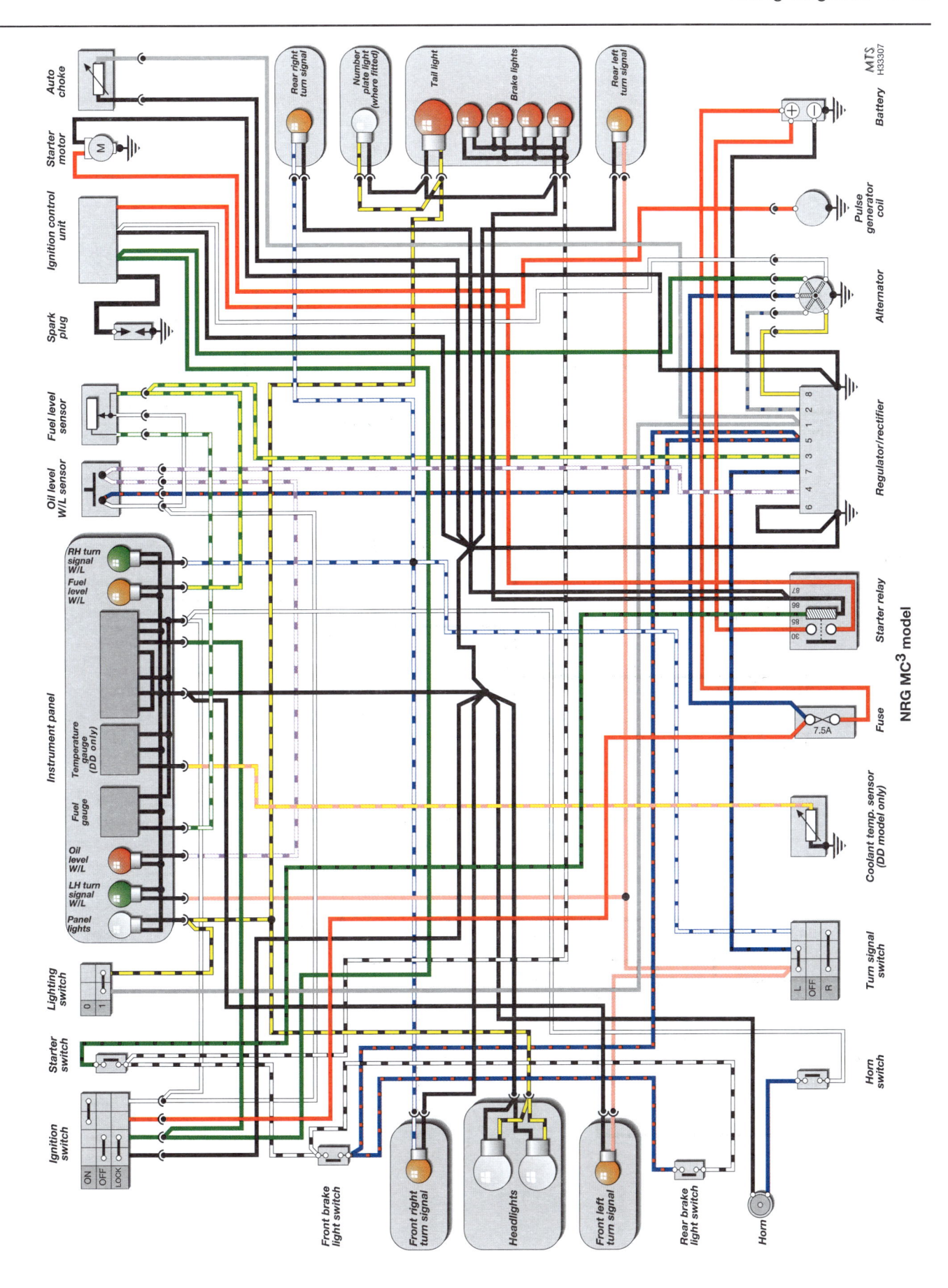

NRG MC³ model

9•44 Wiring diagrams

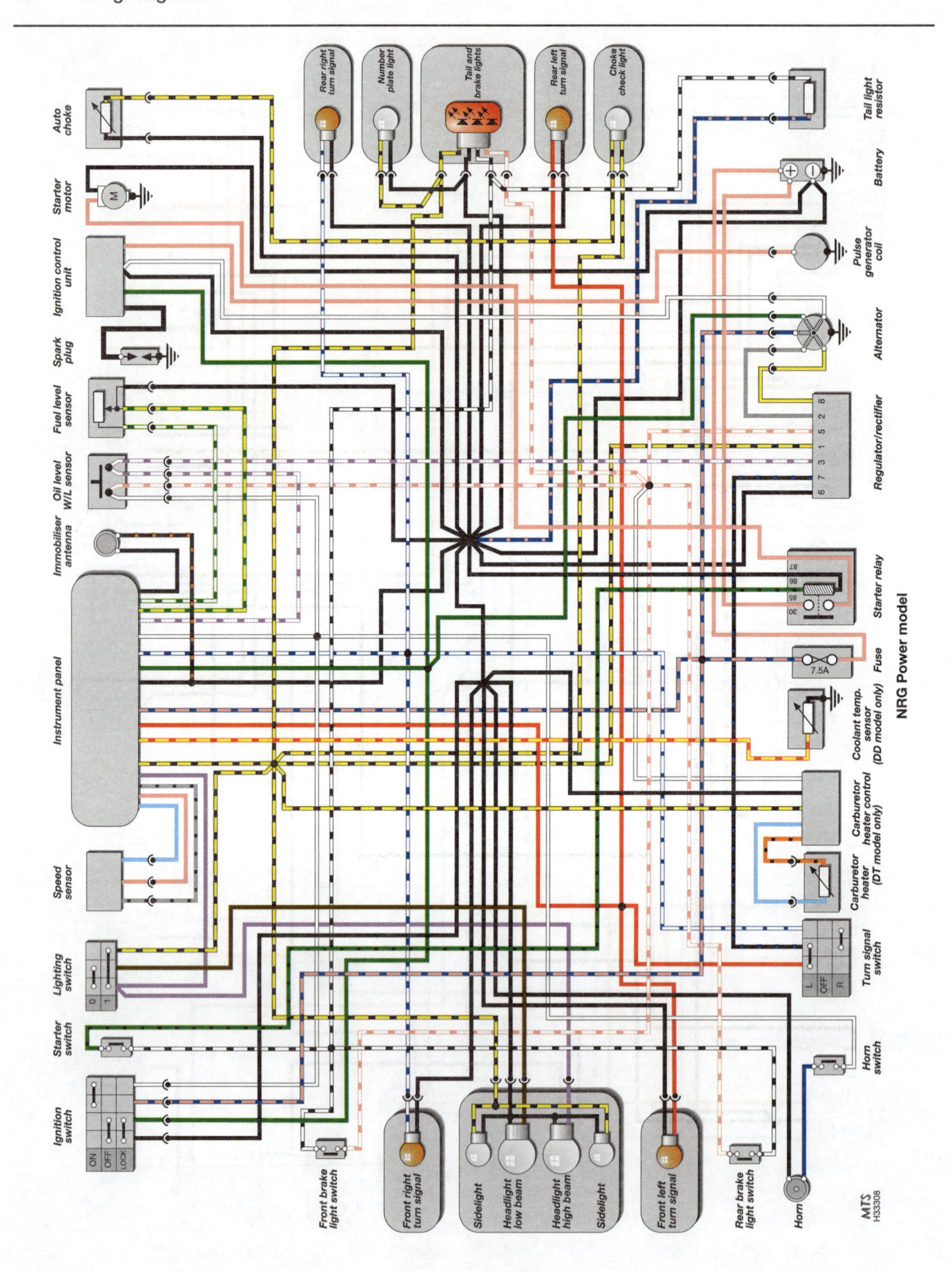

NRG Power model

Wiring diagrams 9•45

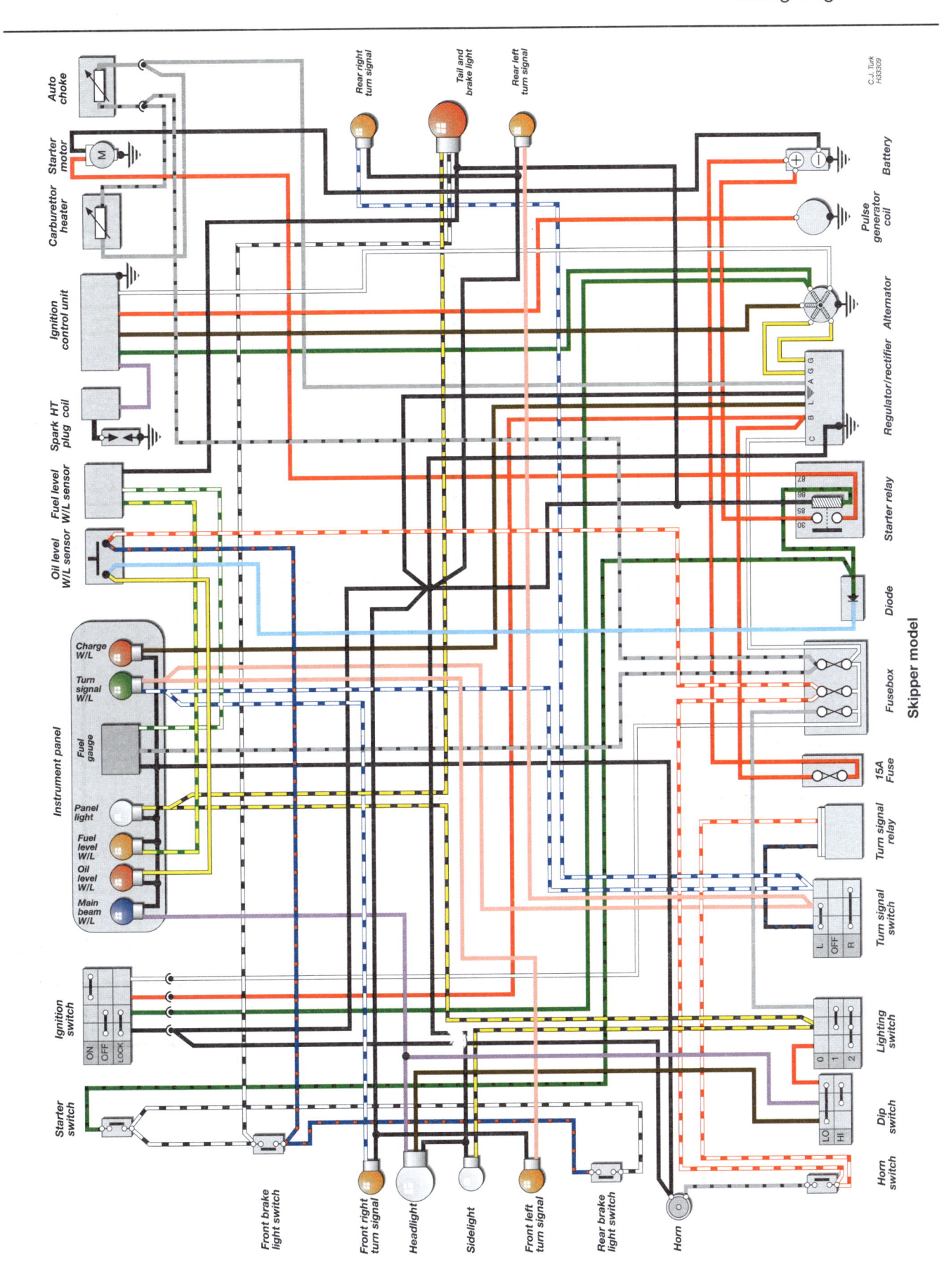

Skipper model

9•46 Wiring diagrams

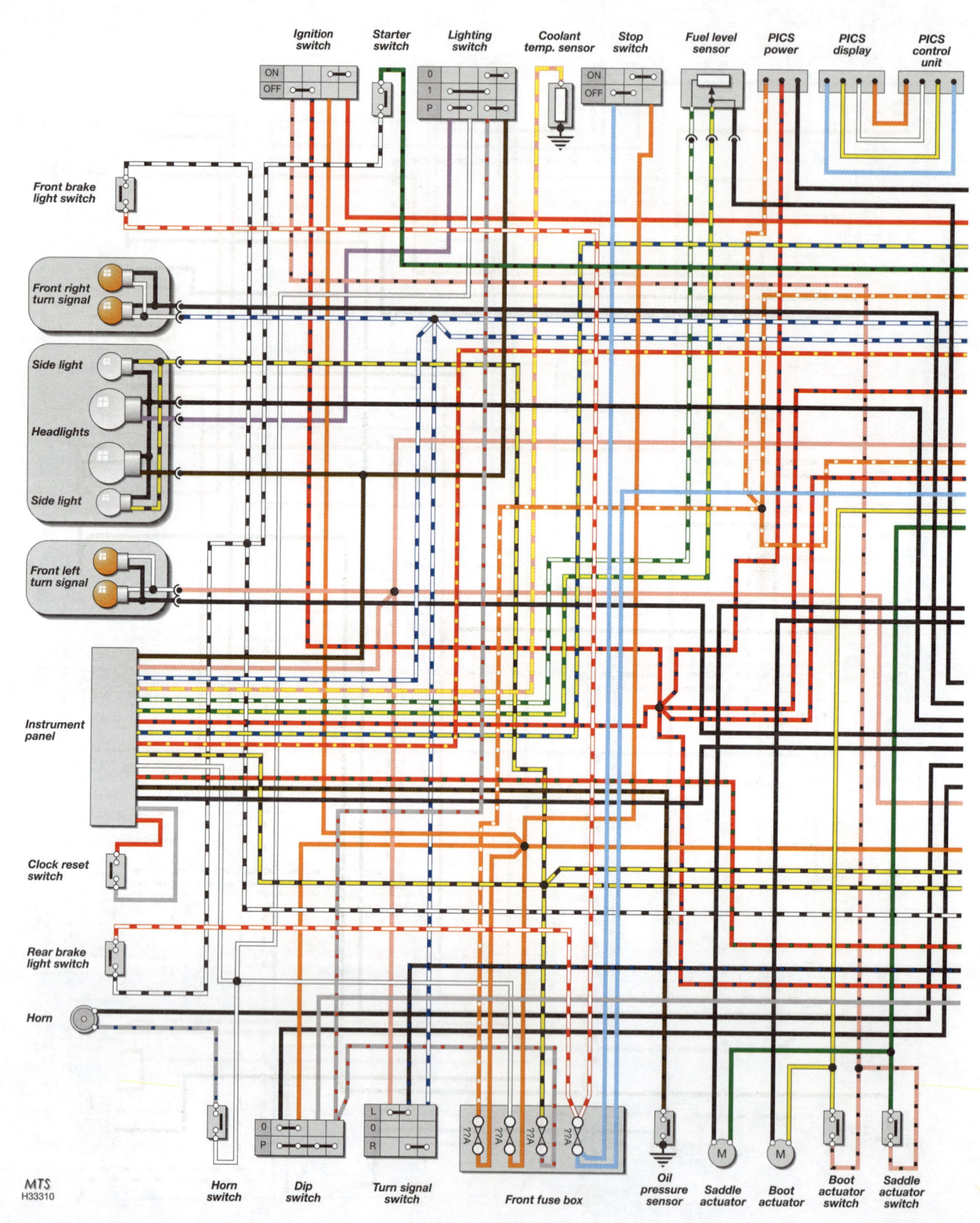

X8 125 model

Wiring diagrams 9•47

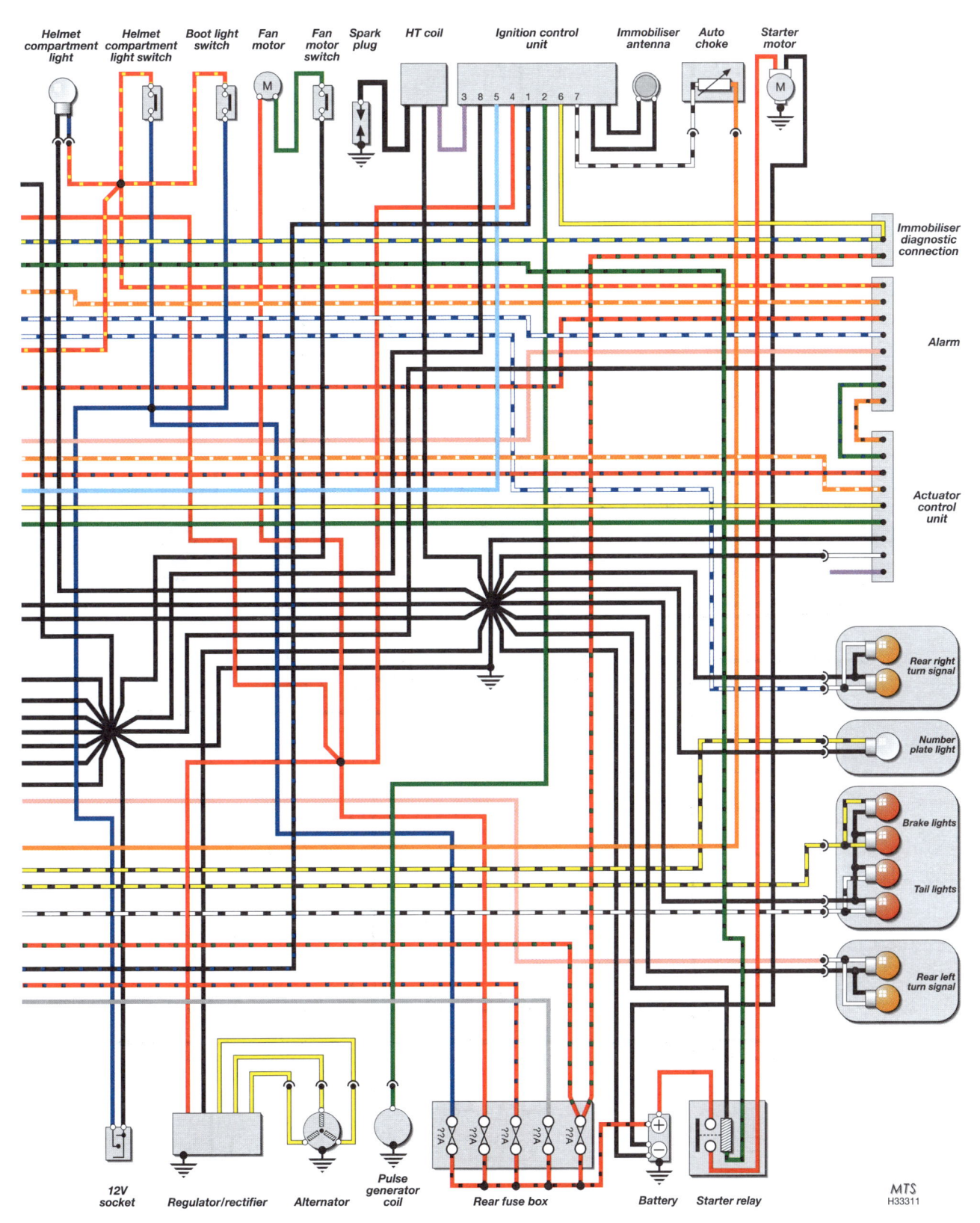

X8 125 model continued

9•48 Wiring diagrams

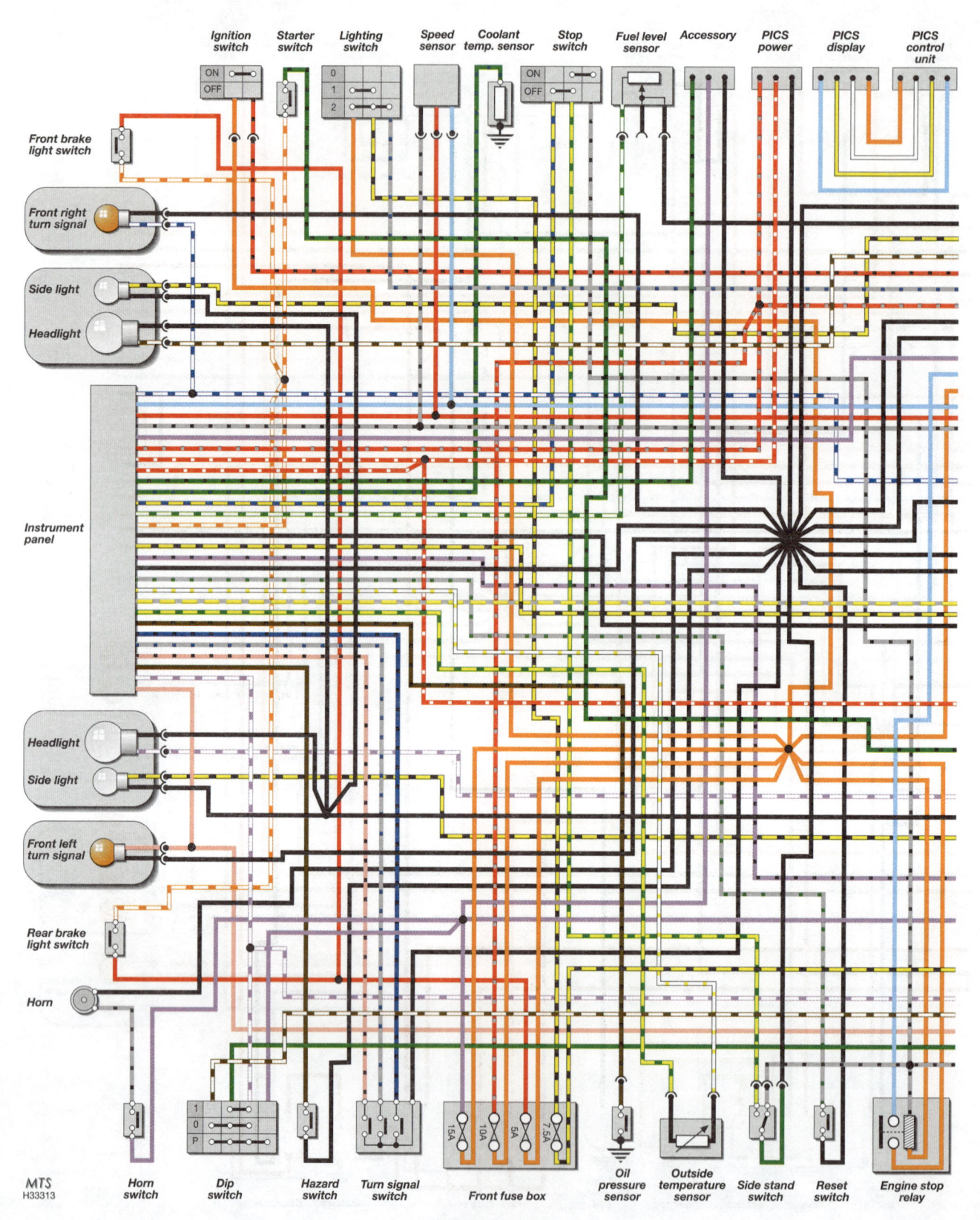

X9 125 model

Wiring diagrams 9•49

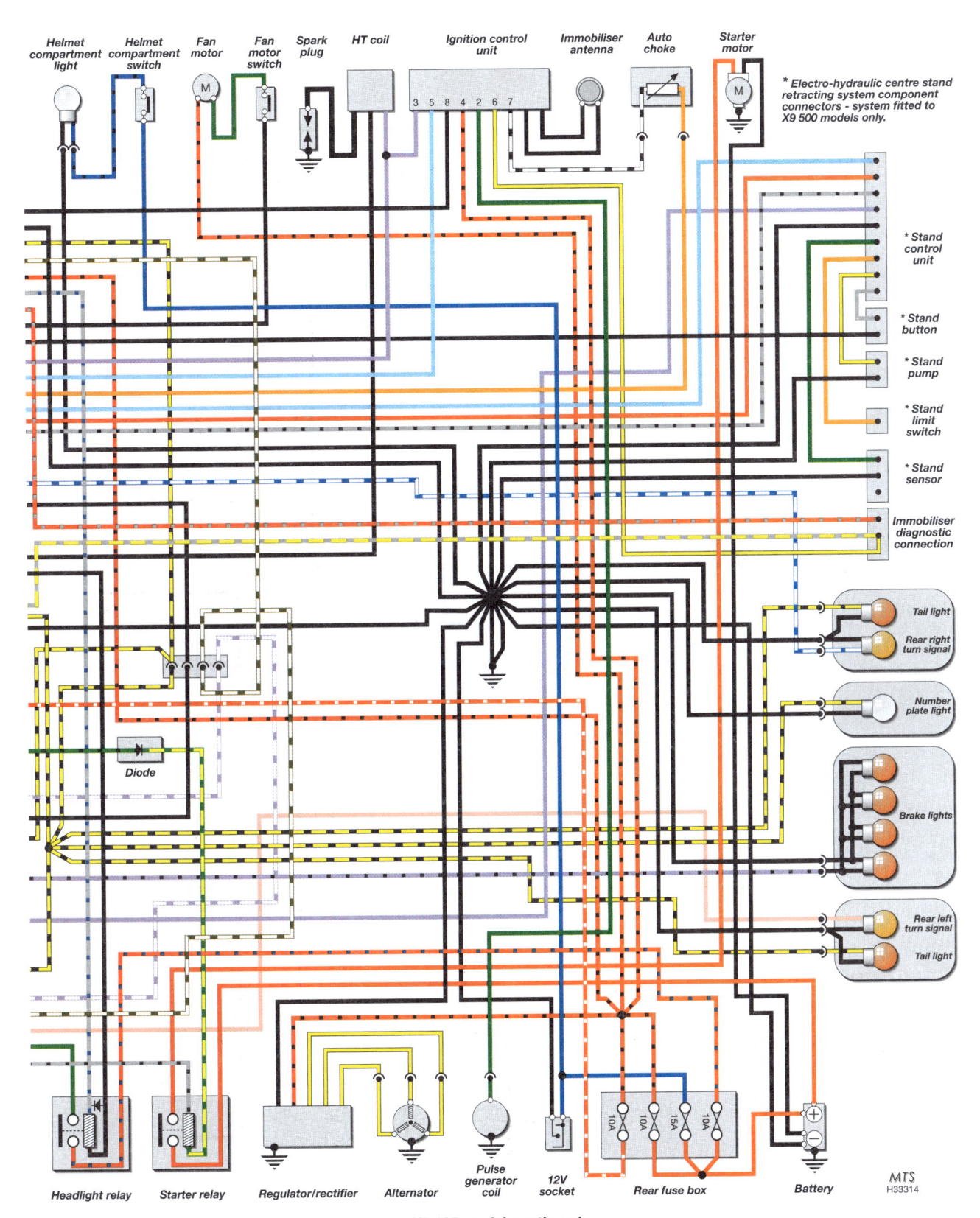

X9 125 model continued

9•50 Wiring diagrams

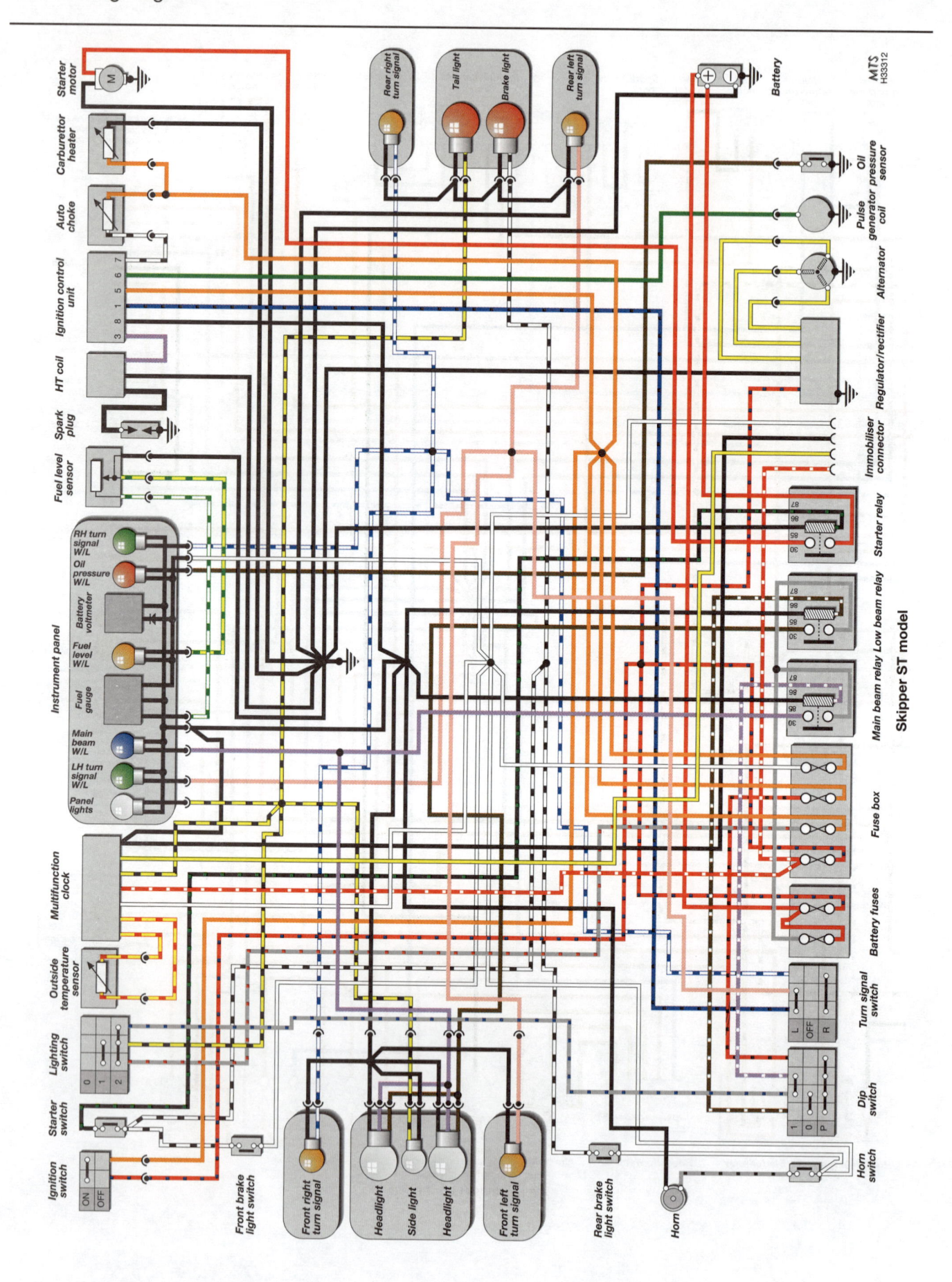

Wiring diagrams 9•51

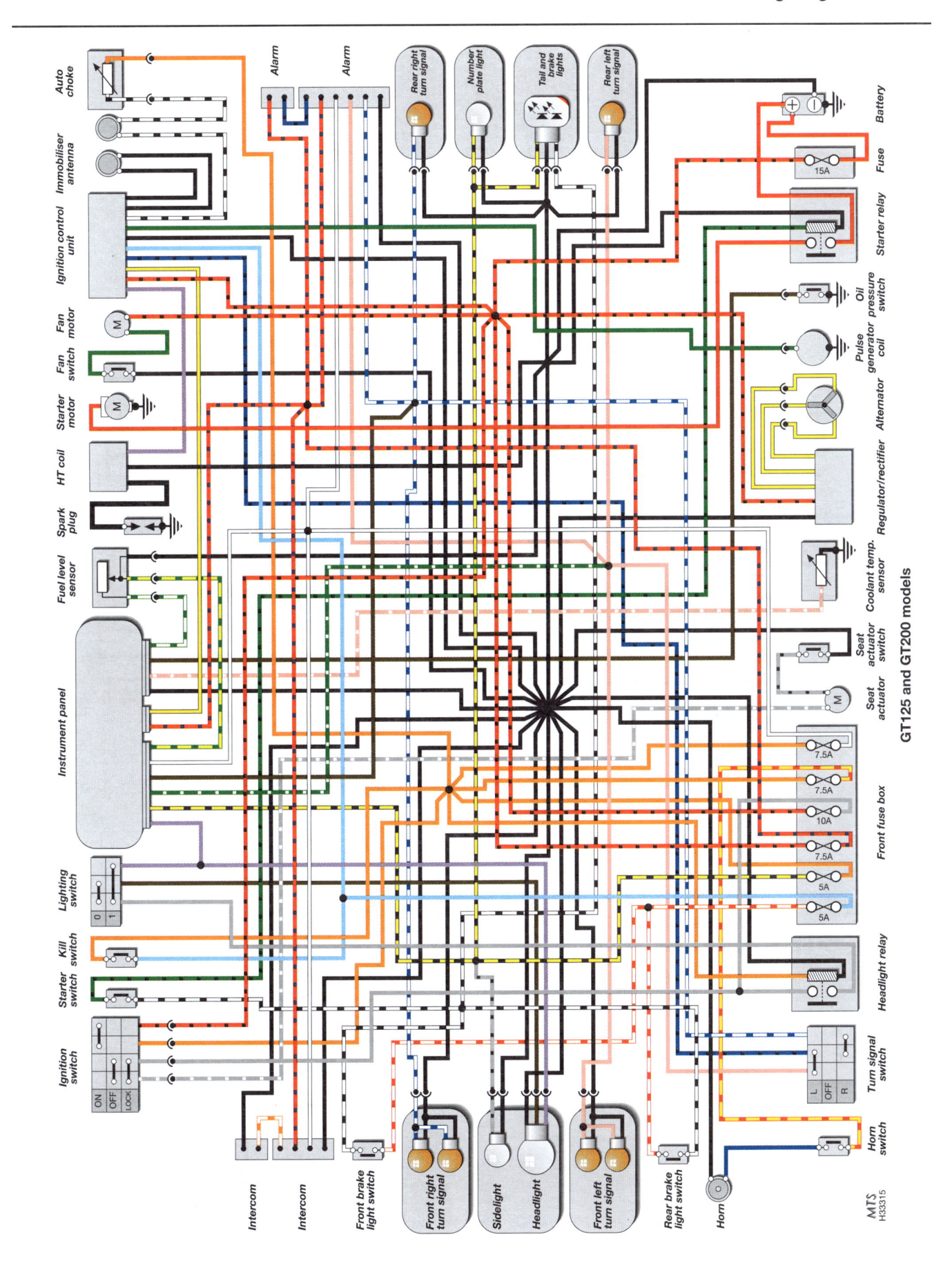

GT125 and GT200 models

9•52 Wiring diagrams

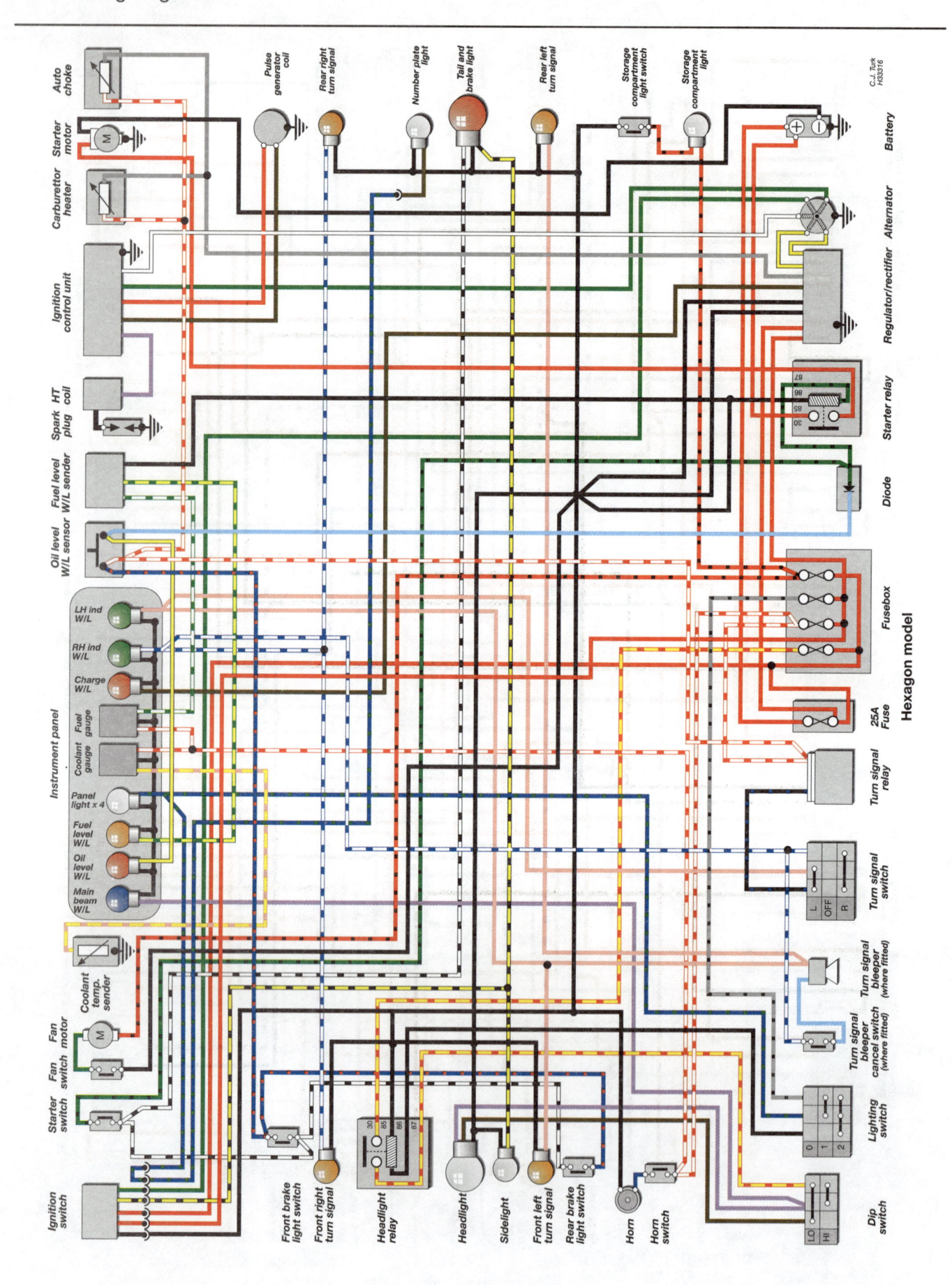

Hexagon model

Wiring diagrams 9•53

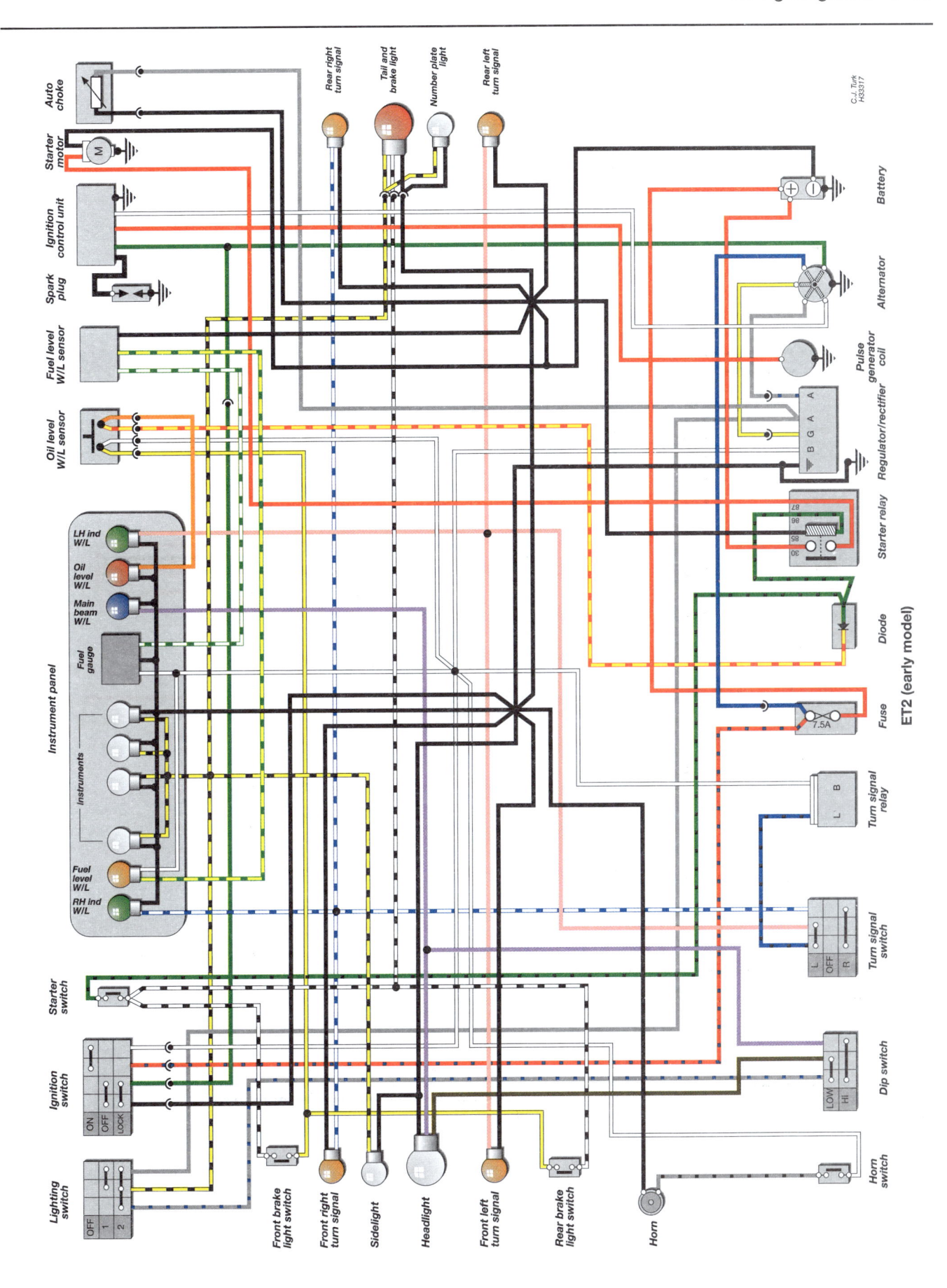

ET2 (early model)

9•54 Wiring diagrams

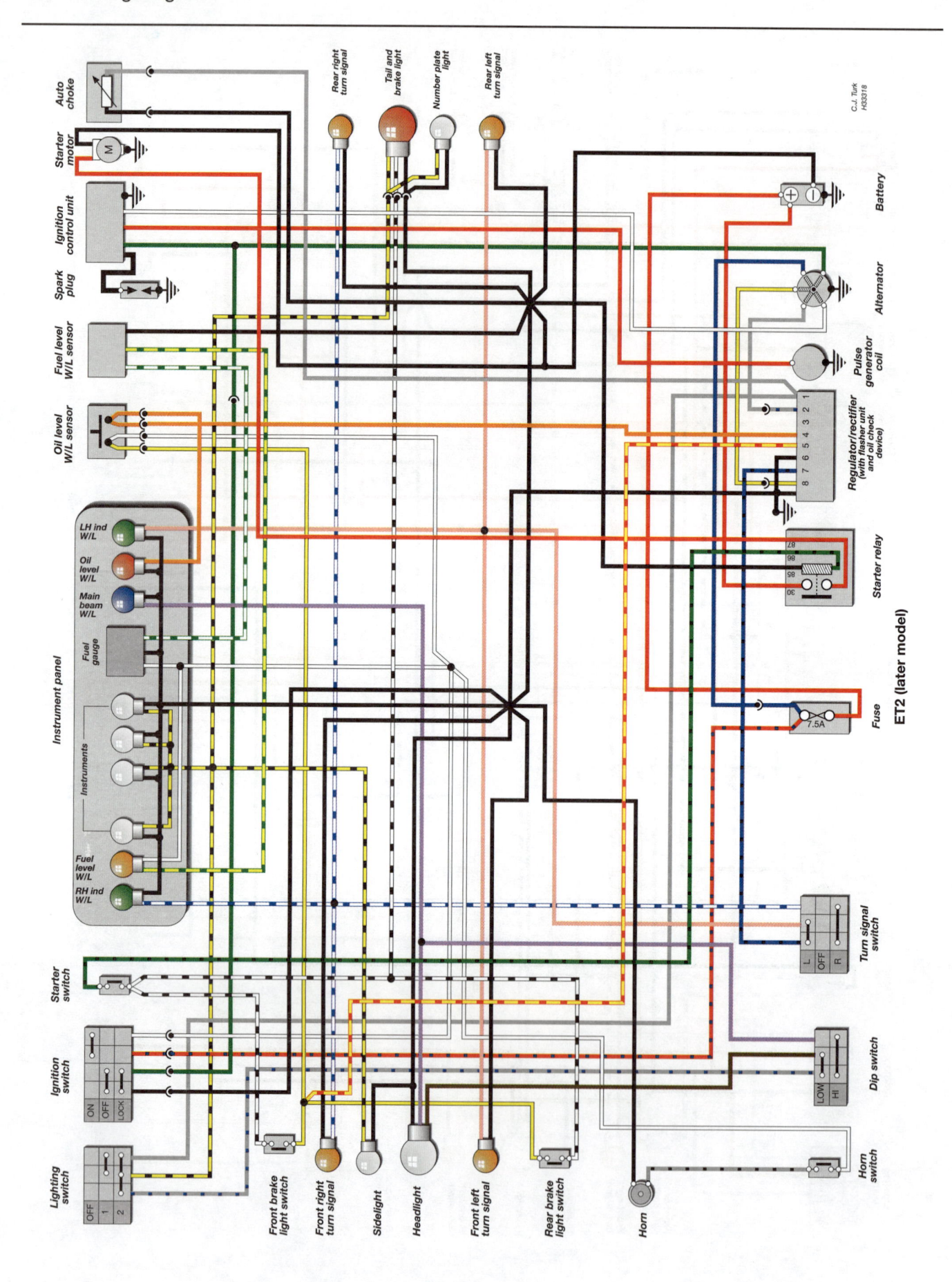

ET2 (later model)

Wiring diagrams 9•55

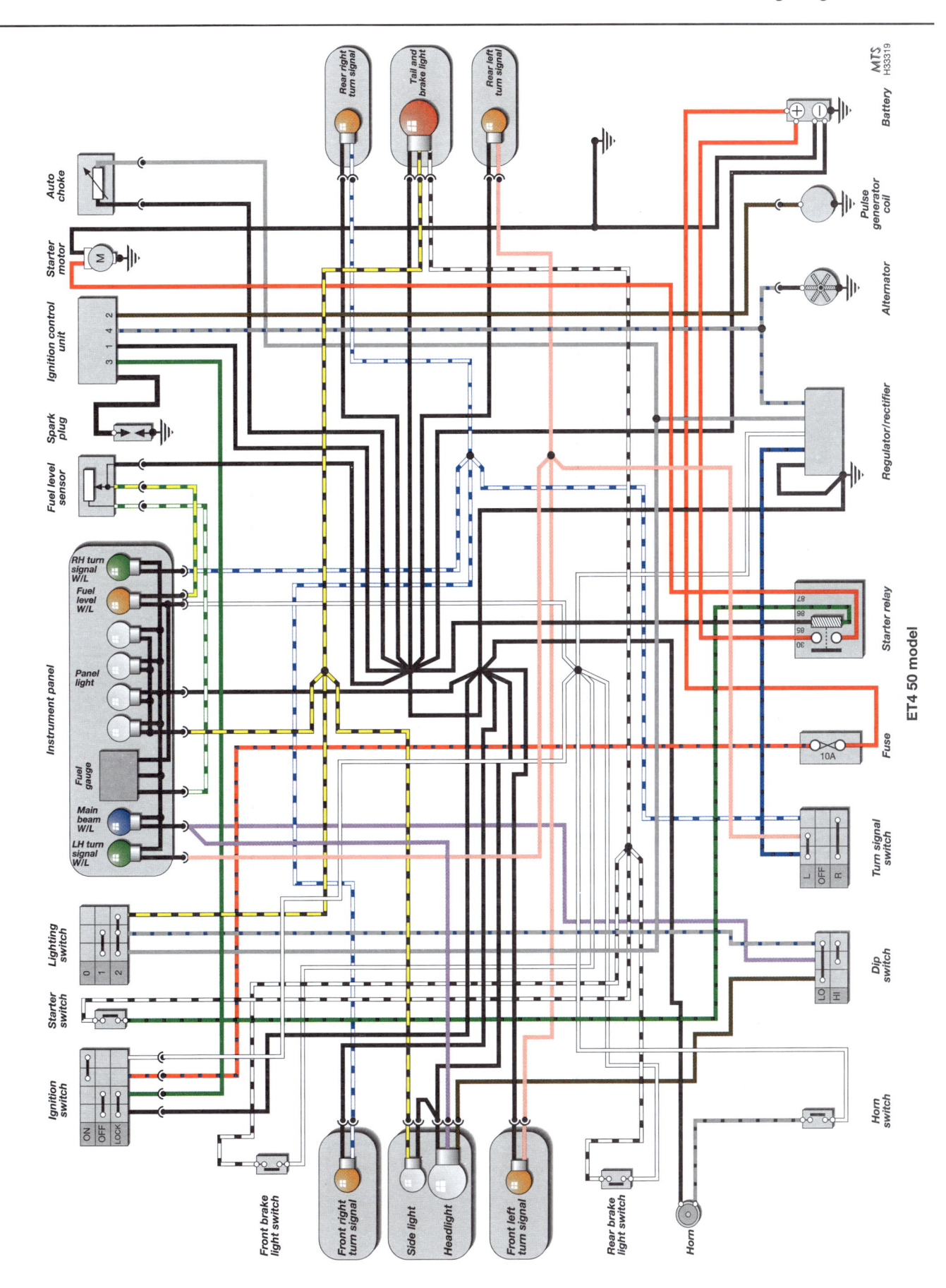

9•56 Wiring diagrams

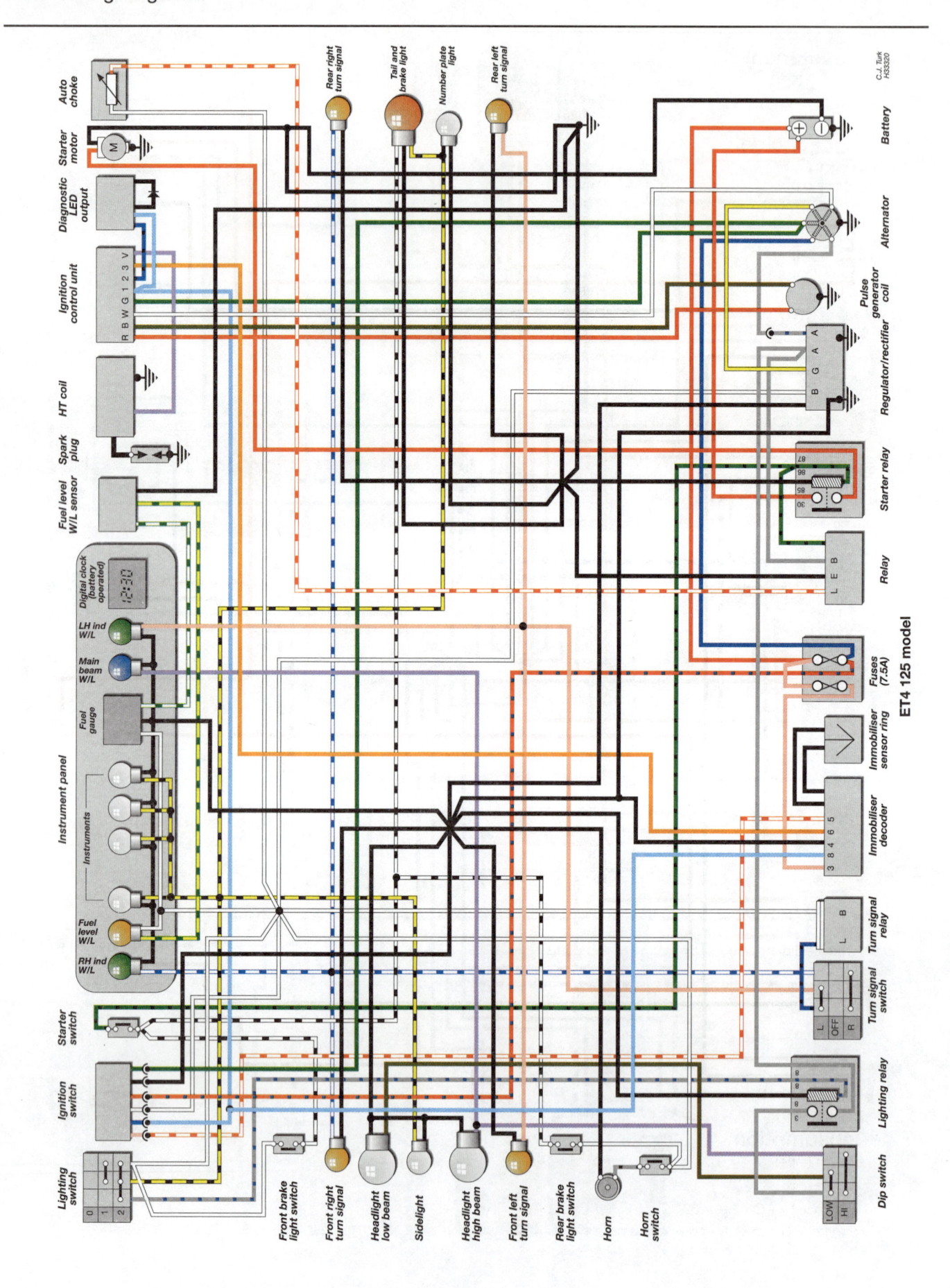

Conversion factors REF•1

Length (distance)
Inches (in)	x 25.4	= Millimetres (mm)	x 0.0394	= Inches (in)
Feet (ft)	x 0.305	= Metres (m)	x 3.281	= Feet (ft)
Miles	x 1.609	= Kilometres (km)	x 0.621	= Miles

Volume (capacity)
Cubic inches (cu in; in^3)	x 16.387	= Cubic centimetres (cc; cm^3)	x 0.061	= Cubic inches (cu in; in^3)
Imperial pints (Imp pt)	x 0.568	= Litres (l)	x 1.76	= Imperial pints (Imp pt)
Imperial quarts (Imp qt)	x 1.137	= Litres (l)	x 0.88	= Imperial quarts (Imp qt)
Imperial quarts (Imp qt)	x 1.201	= US quarts (US qt)	x 0.833	= Imperial quarts (Imp qt)
US quarts (US qt)	x 0.946	= Litres (l)	x 1.057	= US quarts (US qt)
Imperial gallons (Imp gal)	x 4.546	= Litres (l)	x 0.22	= Imperial gallons (Imp gal)
Imperial gallons (Imp gal)	x 1.201	= US gallons (US gal)	x 0.833	= Imperial gallons (Imp gal)
US gallons (US gal)	x 3.785	= Litres (l)	x 0.264	= US gallons (US gal)

Mass (weight)
Ounces (oz)	x 28.35	= Grams (g)	x 0.035	= Ounces (oz)
Pounds (lb)	x 0.454	= Kilograms (kg)	x 2.205	= Pounds (lb)

Force
Ounces-force (ozf; oz)	x 0.278	= Newtons (N)	x 3.6	= Ounces-force (ozf; oz)
Pounds-force (lbf; lb)	x 4.448	= Newtons (N)	x 0.225	= Pounds-force (lbf; lb)
Newtons (N)	x 0.1	= Kilograms-force (kgf; kg)	x 9.81	= Newtons (N)

Pressure
Pounds-force per square inch (psi; lbf/in^2; lb/in^2)	x 0.070	= Kilograms-force per square centimetre (kgf/cm^2; kg/cm^2)	x 14.223	= Pounds-force per square inch (psi; lbf/in^2; lb/in^2)
Pounds-force per square inch (psi; lbf/in^2; lb/in^2)	x 0.068	= Atmospheres (atm)	x 14.696	= Pounds-force per square inch (psi; lbf/in^2; lb/in^2)
Pounds-force per square inch (psi; lbf/in^2; lb/in^2)	x 0.069	= Bars	x 14.5	= Pounds-force per square inch (psi; lbf/in^2; lb/in^2)
Pounds-force per square inch (psi; lbf/in^2; lb/in^2)	x 6.895	= Kilopascals (kPa)	x 0.145	= Pounds-force per square inch (psi; lbf/in^2; lb/in^2)
Kilopascals (kPa)	x 0.01	= Kilograms-force per square centimetre (kgf/cm^2; kg/cm^2)	x 98.1	= Kilopascals (kPa)
Millibar (mbar)	x 100	= Pascals (Pa)	x 0.01	= Millibar (mbar)
Millibar (mbar)	x 0.0145	= Pounds-force per square inch (psi; lbf/in^2; lb/in^2)	x 68.947	= Millibar (mbar)
Millibar (mbar)	x 0.75	= Millimetres of mercury (mmHg)	x 1.333	= Millibar (mbar)
Millibar (mbar)	x 0.401	= Inches of water (inH$_2$O)	x 2.491	= Millibar (mbar)
Millimetres of mercury (mmHg)	x 0.535	= Inches of water (inH$_2$O)	x 1.868	= Millimetres of mercury (mmHg)
Inches of water (inH$_2$O)	x 0.036	= Pounds-force per square inch (psi; lbf/in^2; lb/in^2)	x 27.68	= Inches of water (inH$_2$O)

Torque (moment of force)
Pounds-force inches (lbf in; lb in)	x 1.152	= Kilograms-force centimetre (kgf cm; kg cm)	x 0.868	= Pounds-force inches (lbf in; lb in)
Pounds-force inches (lbf in; lb in)	x 0.113	= Newton metres (Nm)	x 8.85	= Pounds-force inches (lbf in; lb in)
Pounds-force inches (lbf in; lb in)	x 0.083	= Pounds-force feet (lbf ft; lb ft)	x 12	= Pounds-force inches (lbf in; lb in)
Pounds-force feet (lbf ft; lb ft)	x 0.138	= Kilograms-force metres (kgf m; kg m)	x 7.233	= Pounds-force feet (lbf ft; lb ft)
Pounds-force feet (lbf ft; lb ft)	x 1.356	= Newton metres (Nm)	x 0.738	= Pounds-force feet (lbf ft; lb ft)
Newton metres (Nm)	x 0.102	= Kilograms-force metres (kgf m; kg m)	x 9.804	= Newton metres (Nm)

Power
Horsepower (hp)	x 745.7	= Watts (W)	x 0.0013	= Horsepower (hp)

Velocity (speed)
Miles per hour (miles/hr; mph)	x 1.609	= Kilometres per hour (km/hr; kph)	x 0.621	= Miles per hour (miles/hr; mph)

Fuel consumption*
Miles per gallon (mpg)	x 0.354	= Kilometres per litre (km/l)	x 2.825	= Miles per gallon (mpg)

Temperature

Degrees Fahrenheit = (°C x 1.8) + 32   Degrees Celsius (Degrees Centigrade; °C) = (°F - 32) x 0.56

It is common practice to convert from miles per gallon (mpg) to litres/100 kilometres (l/100km), where mpg x l/100 km = 282

REF•2 Fault finding

1 Engine doesn't start or is difficult to start
- [ ] Starter motor doesn't rotate
- [ ] Starter motor rotates but engine does not turn over
- [ ] Starter works but engine won't turn over (seized)
- [ ] No fuel flow
- [ ] Engine flooded
- [ ] No spark or weak spark
- [ ] Compression low
- [ ] Stalls after starting
- [ ] Rough idle

2 Poor running at low speed
- [ ] Spark weak
- [ ] Fuel/air mixture incorrect
- [ ] Compression low
- [ ] Poor acceleration

3 Poor running or no power at high speed
- [ ] Firing incorrect
- [ ] Fuel/air mixture incorrect
- [ ] Compression low
- [ ] Knocking or pinking
- [ ] Miscellaneous causes

4 Overheating
- [ ] Engine overheats
- [ ] Firing incorrect
- [ ] Fuel/air mixture incorrect
- [ ] Compression too high
- [ ] Engine load excessive
- [ ] Lubrication inadequate
- [ ] Miscellaneous causes

5 Transmission problems
- [ ] No drive to rear wheel
- [ ] Vibration
- [ ] Poor performance
- [ ] Clutch not disengaging completely

6 Abnormal engine noise
- [ ] Knocking or pinking
- [ ] Piston slap or rattling
- [ ] Valve noise
- [ ] Other noise

7 Abnormal frame and suspension noise
- [ ] Front end noise
- [ ] Shock absorber noise
- [ ] Brake noise

8 Excessive exhaust smoke
- [ ] White smoke (four-stroke engines)
- [ ] White/blue smoke (two-stroke engines)
- [ ] Black smoke
- [ ] Brown smoke

9 Poor handling or stability
- [ ] Handlebar hard to turn
- [ ] Handlebar shakes or vibrates excessively
- [ ] Handlebar pulls to one side
- [ ] Poor shock absorbing qualities

10 Braking problems – disc brakes
- [ ] Brakes are ineffective
- [ ] Brake lever pulsates
- [ ] Brakes drag

11 Braking problems – drum brakes
- [ ] Brakes are ineffective
- [ ] Brake lever pulsates
- [ ] Brakes drag

12 Electrical problems
- [ ] Battery dead or weak
- [ ] Battery overcharged

1 Engine doesn't start or is difficult to start

Starter motor doesn't rotate
- [ ] Fuse blown. Check fuse and starter circuit (Chapter 9).
- [ ] Battery voltage low. Check and recharge battery (Chapter 9).
- [ ] Starter motor defective. Make sure the wiring to the starter is secure. Make sure the starter relay clicks when the start button is pushed. If the relay clicks, then the fault is in the wiring or motor.
- [ ] Starter relay faulty. Check it (Chapter 9).
- [ ] Starter switch on handlebar not contacting. The contacts could be wet, corroded or dirty. Disassemble and clean the switch (Chapter 9).
- [ ] Wiring open or shorted. Check all wiring connections and harnesses to make sure that they are dry, tight and not corroded. Also check for broken or frayed wires that can cause a short to earth (see wiring diagram, Chapter 9).
- [ ] Ignition (main) switch defective. Check the switch according to the procedure in Chapter 9. Replace the switch with a new one if it is defective.

Starter motor rotates but engine does not turn over
- [ ] Starter pinion assembly defective. Inspect and repair or replace (Chapter 2).
- [ ] Damaged pinion assembly or starter gears. Inspect and replace the damaged parts (Chapter 2).

Starter works but engine won't turn over (seized)
- [ ] Seized engine caused by one or more internally damaged components. Failure due to wear, abuse or lack of lubrication. On all engines damage can include piston, cylinder, connecting rod, crankshaft, bearings and additionally on four-strokes, valves, camshaft, camchain. Refer to Chapter 2 for engine disassembly.

No fuel flow
- [ ] No fuel in tank. On Typhoon 80 and 125 models (with an auxiliary fuel tank) check that the fuel hoses are not trapped and that tank vent pipe is clear.
- [ ] Fuel tap filter clogged. Remove the tap and clean it and the filter (Chapter 4). On Hexagon models, check the in-line fuel filter.
- [ ] Fuel tap vacuum hose split or detached. Check the hose.
- [ ] Fuel tap diaphragm split. Replace the tap (Chapter 4).
- [ ] Fuel line clogged. Pull the fuel line loose and carefully blow through it.
- [ ] Float needle valve or carburettor jets clogged. The carburettor should be removed and overhauled if draining the float chamber doesn't solve the problem.

Fault finding REF•3

Engine flooded
- [ ] Float height too high. Check as described in Chapter 4.
- [ ] Float needle valve worn or stuck open. A piece of dirt, rust or other debris can cause the valve to seat improperly, causing excess fuel to be admitted to the float chamber. In this case, the float chamber should be cleaned and the needle valve and seat inspected. If the needle and seat are worn, then the leaking will persist and the parts should be replaced with new ones (Chapter 4).

No spark or weak spark
- [ ] Ignition switch OFF.
- [ ] Battery voltage low. Check and recharge the battery as necessary (Chapter 9).
- [ ] Spark plug dirty, defective or worn out. Locate reason for fouled plug using spark plug condition chart at the end of this manual and follow the plug maintenance procedures (Chapter 1). Condition is especially applicable to two-stroke engines due to the oily nature of their lubrication system.
- [ ] Spark plug cap or secondary (HT) wiring faulty. Check condition. Replace either or both components if cracks or deterioration are evident (Chapter 5).
- [ ] Spark plug cap not making good contact. Make sure that the plug cap fits snugly over the plug end.
- [ ] Ignition control unit defective (125 models). Check the unit, referring to Chapter 5 for details.
- [ ] Pulse generator or source coil defective. Check the unit, referring to Chapter 5 for details.
- [ ] Ignition HT coil defective. Check the coil, referring to Chapter 5.
- [ ] Ignition switch shorted. This is usually caused by water, corrosion, damage or excessive wear. The switch can be disassembled and cleaned with electrical contact cleaner. If cleaning does not help, replace the switch (Chapter 9).
- [ ] Wiring shorted or broken. Make sure that all wiring connections are clean, dry and tight. Look for chafed and broken wires (Chapters 5 and 9).

Compression low
- [ ] Spark plug loose. Remove the plug and inspect its threads (Chapter 1).
- [ ] Cylinder head not sufficiently tightened down. If the cylinder head is suspected of being loose, then there's a chance that the gasket (4-stroke engines) or head is damaged if the problem has persisted for any length of time. The head nuts should be tightened to the proper torque in the correct sequence (Chapter 2).
- [ ] Low crankcase compression on two-stroke engines due to worn crankshaft oil seals. Condition will upset the fuel/air mixture. Renew the seals (Chapter 2A or 2B).
- [ ] Improper valve clearance (four-strokes). This means that the valve is not closing completely and compression pressure is leaking past the valve. Check and adjust the valve clearances (Chapter 1).
- [ ] Cylinder and/or piston worn. Excessive wear will cause compression pressure to leak past the rings. This is usually accompanied by worn rings as well. A top-end overhaul is necessary (Chapter 2).
- [ ] Piston rings worn, weak, broken, or sticking. Broken or sticking piston rings usually indicate a lubrication or carburation problem that causes excess carbon deposits or seizures to form on the pistons and rings. Top-end overhaul is necessary (Chapter 2).
- [ ] Piston ring-to-groove clearance excessive. This is caused by excessive wear of the piston ring lands. Piston replacement is necessary (Chapter 2).
- [ ] Cylinder head gasket damaged (4-stroke engines). If a head is allowed to become loose, or if excessive carbon build-up on the piston crown and combustion chamber causes extremely high compression, the head gasket may leak. Retorquing the head is not always sufficient to restore the seal, so gasket replacement is necessary (Chapter 2).
- [ ] Cylinder head warped. This is caused by overheating or improperly tightened head nuts. Machine shop resurfacing or head replacement is necessary (Chapter 2).
- [ ] Valve spring broken or weak (four-stroke engines). Caused by component failure or wear; the springs must be replaced (Chapter 2).
- [ ] Valve not seating properly (four-stroke engines). This is caused by a bent valve (from over-revving or improper valve adjustment), burned valve or seat (improper carburation) or an accumulation of carbon deposits on the seat (from carburation or lubrication problems). The valves must be cleaned and/or replaced and the seats serviced if possible (Chapter 2).

Stalls after starting
- [ ] Faulty automatic choke. Check connections and movement (Chapter 4).
- [ ] Ignition malfunction (Chapter 5).
- [ ] Carburettor malfunction (Chapter 4).
- [ ] Fuel contaminated. The fuel can be contaminated with either dirt or water, or can change chemically if the machine is allowed to sit for several months or more. Drain the tank and float chambers (Chapter 4).
- [ ] Inlet air leak. Check for loose carburettor-to-inlet manifold connections, loose carburettor top (Chapter 4).
- [ ] Engine idle speed incorrect. Turn idle adjusting screw until the engine idles at the specified rpm (Chapter 1).

Rough idle
- [ ] Ignition malfunction (Chapter 5).
- [ ] Idle speed incorrect (Chapter 1).
- [ ] Carburettor malfunction (Chapter 4).
- [ ] Fuel contaminated. The fuel can be contaminated with either dirt or water, or can change chemically if the machine is allowed to sit for several months or more. Drain the tank and float chambers (Chapter 4).
- [ ] Inlet air leak. Check for loose carburettor-to-inlet manifold connections, loose carburettor top (Chapter 4).
- [ ] Air filter clogged. Clean the air filter element (Chapter 1).

2 Poor running at low speeds

Spark weak
- [ ] Battery voltage low. Check and recharge battery (Chapter 9).
- [ ] Spark plug fouled, defective or worn out. Refer to Chapter 1 for spark plug maintenance.
- [ ] Spark plug cap or HT wiring defective. Refer to Chapters 1 and 5 for details on the ignition system.
- [ ] Spark plug cap not making contact.
- [ ] Incorrect spark plug. Wrong type, heat range or cap configuration. Check and install correct plug listed in Chapter 1.
- [ ] Ignition control unit defective. See Chapter 5.
- [ ] Pulse generator defective. See Chapter 5.
- [ ] Ignition HT coil defective (125 cc engines). See Chapter 5.

Fuel/air mixture incorrect
- [ ] Pilot screw out of adjustment (Chapter 4).
- [ ] Pilot jet or air passage clogged. Remove and overhaul the carburettor (Chapter 4).
- [ ] Air bleed hole clogged. Remove carburettor and blow out all passages (Chapter 4).
- [ ] Air filter clogged, poorly sealed or missing (Chapter 1).
- [ ] Air filter housing poorly sealed. Look for cracks, holes or loose screws and replace or repair defective parts.
- [ ] Fuel level too high or too low. Check the float height (Chapter 4).
- [ ] Carburettor inlet manifold loose. Check for cracks, breaks, tears or loose clamps.

REF•4 Fault finding

2 Poor running at low speeds (continued)

Compression low

- ☐ Spark plug loose. Remove the plug and inspect its threads (Chapter 1).
- ☐ Cylinder head not sufficiently tightened down. If the cylinder head is suspected of being loose, then there's a chance that the gasket (four-stroke engines) or head is damaged if the problem has persisted for any length of time. The head nuts should be tightened to the proper torque in the correct sequence (Chapter 2).
- ☐ Improper valve clearance (four-stroke engines). This means that the valve is not closing completely and compression pressure is leaking past the valve. Check and adjust the valve clearances (Chapter 1).
- ☐ Low crankcase compression on two-stroke engines due to worn crankshaft oil seals. Condition will upset the fuel/air mixture. Renew the seals (Chapter 2A or 2B).
- ☐ Cylinder and/or piston worn. Excessive wear will cause compression pressure to leak past the rings. This is usually accompanied by worn rings as well. A top-end overhaul is necessary (Chapter 2).
- ☐ Piston rings worn, weak, broken, or sticking. Broken or sticking piston rings usually indicate a lubrication or carburation problem that causes excess carbon deposits or seizures to form on the pistons and rings. Top-end overhaul is necessary (Chapter 2).
- ☐ Piston ring-to-groove clearance excessive. This is caused by excessive wear of the piston ring lands. Piston replacement is necessary (Chapter 2).
- ☐ Cylinder head gasket damaged (four-stroke engines). If a head is allowed to become loose, or if excessive carbon build-up on the piston crown and combustion chamber causes extremely high compression, the head gasket may leak. Retorquing the head is not always sufficient to restore the seal, so gasket replacement is necessary (Chapter 2).
- ☐ Cylinder head warped. This is caused by overheating or improperly tightened head nuts. Machine shop resurfacing or head replacement is necessary (Chapter 2).
- ☐ Valve spring broken or weak (four-stroke engines). Caused by component failure or wear; the springs must be replaced (Chapter 2).
- ☐ Valve not seating properly (four-stroke engines). This is caused by a bent valve (from over-revving or improper valve adjustment), burned valve or seat (improper carburation) or an accumulation of carbon deposits on the seat (from carburation or lubrication problems). The valves must be cleaned and/or replaced and the seats serviced if possible (Chapter 2).

Poor acceleration

- ☐ Carburettor leaking or dirty. Overhaul the carburettor (Chapter 4).
- ☐ Faulty automatic choke (Chapter 4).
- ☐ Timing not advancing. The pulse generator or the ignition control unit may be defective (Chapter 5). If so, they must be replaced with new ones, as they can't be repaired.
- ☐ Engine oil viscosity too high (four-stroke engines). Using a heavier oil than that recommended in Chapter 1 can damage the oil pump or lubrication system and cause drag on the engine.
- ☐ Brakes dragging. On disc brakes, usually caused by debris which has entered the brake piston seals, or from a warped disc or bent axle, or cable out of adjustment where appropriate. On drum brakes, cable out of adjustment, shoe return spring broken. Repair as necessary (Chapter 8).
- ☐ Clutch slipping, drive belt worn, or speed governor faulty (Chapter 2G).

3 Poor running or no power at high speed

Firing incorrect

- ☐ Air filter clogged. Clean filter (Chapter 1).
- ☐ Spark plug fouled, defective or worn out. See Chapter 1 for spark plug maintenance.
- ☐ Spark plug cap or HT wiring defective. See Chapters 1 and 5 for details of the ignition system.
- ☐ Spark plug cap not in good contact (Chapter 5).
- ☐ Incorrect spark plug. Wrong type, heat range or cap configuration. Check and install correct plug listed in Chapter 1.
- ☐ Ignition control unit or HT coil defective (Chapter 5).

Fuel/air mixture incorrect

- ☐ Main jet clogged. Dirt, water or other contaminants can clog the main jet. Clean the fuel tap filter, the in-line filter (Hexagon), the float chamber area, and the jets and carburettor orifices (Chapter 4).
- ☐ Main jet wrong size. The standard jetting is for sea level atmospheric pressure and oxygen content.
- ☐ Air bleed holes clogged. Remove and overhaul carburettor (Chapter 4).
- ☐ Air filter clogged, poorly sealed, or missing (Chapter 1).
- ☐ Air filter housing or duct poorly sealed. Look for cracks, holes or loose clamps or screws, and replace or repair defective parts.
- ☐ Fuel level too high or too low. Check the float height (Chapter 4).
- ☐ Carburettor inlet manifold loose. Check for cracks, breaks, tears or loose clamps.

Compression low

- ☐ Spark plug loose. Remove the plug and inspect its threads. Reinstall and tighten to the specified torque (Chapter 1).
- ☐ Cylinder head not sufficiently tightened down. If the cylinder head is suspected of being loose, then there's a chance that the gasket (four-stroke engines) or head is damaged if the problem has persisted for any length of time. The head nuts should be tightened to the proper torque in the correct sequence (Chapter 2).
- ☐ Improper valve clearance (four-stroke engines). This means that the valve is not closing completely and compression pressure is leaking past the valve. Check and adjust the valve clearances (Chapter 1).
- ☐ Low crankcase compression on two-stroke engines due to worn crankshaft oil seals. Condition will upset the fuel/air mixture. Renew the seals (Chapter 2A or 2B).
- ☐ Cylinder and/or piston worn. Excessive wear will cause compression pressure to leak past the rings. This is usually accompanied by worn rings as well. A top-end overhaul is necessary (Chapter 2).
- ☐ Piston rings worn, weak, broken, or sticking. Broken or sticking piston rings usually indicate a lubrication or carburation problem that causes excess carbon deposits or seizures to form on the pistons and rings. Top-end overhaul is necessary (Chapter 2).
- ☐ Piston ring-to-groove clearance excessive. This is caused by excessive wear of the piston ring lands. Piston replacement is necessary (Chapter 2).

Fault finding REF•5

- ☐ Cylinder head gasket damaged (four-stroke engines). If a head is allowed to become loose, or if excessive carbon build-up on the piston crown and combustion chamber causes extremely high compression, the head gasket may leak. Retorquing the head is not always sufficient to restore the seal, so gasket replacement is necessary (Chapter 2).
- ☐ Cylinder head warped. This is caused by overheating or improperly tightened head nuts. Cylinder head skimming or head replacement is necessary (Chapter 2).
- ☐ Valve spring broken or weak (four-stroke engines). Caused by component failure or wear; the springs must be replaced (Chapter 2).
- ☐ Valve not seating properly (four-stroke engines). This is caused by a bent valve (from over-revving or improper valve adjustment), burned valve or seat (improper carburation) or an accumulation of carbon deposits on the seat (from carburation or lubrication problems). The valves must be cleaned and/or replaced and the seats serviced if possible (Chapter 2).

Knocking or pinking

- ☐ Carbon build-up in combustion chamber. Use of a fuel additive that will dissolve the adhesive bonding the carbon particles to the crown and chamber is the easiest way to remove the build-up. Otherwise, the cylinder heads will have to be removed and decarbonised (Chapter 2). On two-stroke engines, the regular service interval for cylinder head decarbonisation should be adhered to.
- ☐ Incorrect or poor quality fuel. Old or improper grades of fuel can cause detonation. This causes the piston to rattle, thus the knocking or pinking sound. Drain old fuel and always use the recommended fuel grade.
- ☐ Spark plug heat range incorrect. Uncontrolled detonation indicates the plug heat range is too hot. The plug in effect becomes a glow plug, raising cylinder temperatures. Install the proper heat range plug (Chapter 1).
- ☐ Improper air/fuel mixture. This will cause the cylinders to run hot, which leads to detonation. Clogged jets or an air leak can cause this imbalance. See Chapter 4.

Miscellaneous causes

- ☐ Throttle valve doesn't open fully. Adjust the throttle grip freeplay (Chapter 1).
- ☐ Clutch slipping, drive belt worn, or speed governor faulty (Chapter 2G).
- ☐ Timing not advancing (Chapter 5).
- ☐ Engine oil viscosity too high. Using a heavier oil than the one recommended in Chapter 1 can damage the oil pump or lubrication system and cause drag on the engine.
- ☐ Brakes dragging. On disc brakes, usually caused by debris which has entered the brake piston seals, or from a warped disc or bent axle, or cable out of adjustment where appropriate. On drum brakes, cable out of adjustment, shoe return spring broken. Repair as necessary (Chapter 8).

4 Overheating

Engine overheats – liquid-cooled engines

- ☐ Coolant level low. Check and add coolant (Chapter 1).
- ☐ Leak in cooling system. Check cooling system hoses and radiator for leaks and other damage. Repair or replace parts as necessary (Chapter 3).
- ☐ Thermostat sticking open or closed. Check and replace as described in Chapter 3.
- ☐ Coolant passages clogged. Drain and flush the entire system, then refill with fresh coolant.
- ☐ Water pump defective. Remove the pump and check the components (Chapter 3).
- ☐ Clogged radiator fins. Clean them by blowing compressed air through the fins from the rear of the radiator.
- ☐ Cooling fan or fan switch fault (Hexagon) (Chapter 3).

Engine overheats – air-cooled engines

- ☐ Air cooling ducts blocked or incorrectly fitted.
- ☐ Problem with cooling fan.

Firing incorrect

- ☐ Spark plug fouled, defective or worn out. See Chapter 1 for spark plug maintenance.
- ☐ Incorrect spark plug.
- ☐ Ignition control unit defective (Chapter 5).
- ☐ Faulty ignition HT coil (125 cc engines) (Chapter 5).

Fuel/air mixture incorrect

- ☐ Main jet clogged. Dirt, water or other contaminants can clog the main jet. Clean the fuel tap filter, the in-line filter (Hexagon and certain LEADER engines), the float chamber area, and the jets and carburettor orifices (Chapter 4).
- ☐ Main jet wrong size. The standard jetting is for sea level atmospheric pressure and oxygen content.
- ☐ Air bleed holes clogged. Remove and overhaul carburettor (Chapter 4).
- ☐ Air filter clogged, poorly sealed, or missing (Chapter 1).
- ☐ Air filter housing or duct poorly sealed. Look for cracks, holes or loose clamps or screws, and replace or repair defective parts.
- ☐ Fuel level too high or too low. Check the float height (Chapter 4).
- ☐ Carburettor inlet manifold loose. Check for cracks, breaks, tears or loose clamps.

Compression too high

- ☐ Carbon build-up in combustion chamber. Use of a fuel additive that will dissolve the adhesive bonding the carbon particles to the piston crown and chamber is the easiest way to remove the build-up. Otherwise, the cylinder head will have to be removed and decarb-onised (Chapter 2). On two-stroke engines, the regular service interval for cylinder head decarbonisation should be adhered to.
- ☐ Improperly machined head surface or installation of incorrect size cylinder base gasket during engine assembly.

Engine load excessive

- ☐ Clutch slipping, drive belt worn, or speed governor faulty (Chapter 2G).
- ☐ Engine oil level too high (four-stroke engines). The addition of too much oil will cause pressurisation of the crankcase and inefficient engine operation. Check Specifications and drain to proper level (Chapter 1).
- ☐ Engine oil viscosity too high (four-stroke engines). Using a heavier oil than the one recommended in Chapter 1 can damage the oil pump or lubrication system as well as cause drag on the engine.
- ☐ Brakes dragging. On disc brakes, usually caused by debris which has entered the brake piston seals, or from a warped disc or bent axle, or cable out of adjustment where appropriate. On drum brakes, cable out of adjustment, shoe return spring broken. Repair as necessary (Chapter 8).

REF•6 Fault finding

4 Overheating (continued)

Lubrication inadequate

- [ ] Engine oil level too low (four-stroke engines). Friction caused by intermittent lack of lubrication or from oil that is overworked can cause overheating. The oil provides a definite cooling function in the engine. Check the oil level (Chapter 1).
- [ ] Oil pump out of adjustment (two-stroke engines). Adjust pump cable (Chapter 1).
- [ ] Poor quality oil or incorrect viscosity or type. Oil is rated not only according to viscosity but also according to type. Some oils are not rated high enough for use in this engine. Check the Specifications section and change to the correct oil (Chapter 1). On two-stroke engines, make sure that you use a two-stroke oil which is suitable for oil injection engines.

Miscellaneous causes

- [ ] Modification to exhaust system. Most aftermarket exhaust systems cause the engine to run leaner, which make them run hotter. When installing an accessory exhaust system, always obtain advice on rejetting the carburettor.

5 Transmission problems

No drive to rear wheel

- [ ] Drive belt broken (Chapter 2G).
- [ ] Clutch not engaging (Chapter 2G).
- [ ] Clutch or drum excessively worn (Chapter 2G).

Transmission noise or vibration

- [ ] Bearings worn. Also includes the possibility that the shafts are worn. Overhaul the transmission (Chapter 2G).
- [ ] Gears worn or chipped (Chapter 2G).
- [ ] Clutch drum worn unevenly (Chapter 2G).
- [ ] Worn bearings or bent shaft (Chapter 2G).
- [ ] Loose clutch nut or drum nut (Chapter 2G).

Poor performance

- [ ] Speed governor worn or insufficiently greased (Chapter 2G).
- [ ] Weak or broken driven pulley spring (Chapter 2G).
- [ ] Clutch or drum excessively worn (Chapter 2G).
- [ ] Grease on clutch friction material (Chapter 2G).
- [ ] Drive belt excessively worn (Chapter 2G).

Clutch not disengaging completely

- [ ] Weak or broken clutch springs (Chapter 2G).
- [ ] Engine idle speed too high (Chapter 1).

6 Abnormal engine noise

Knocking or pinking

- [ ] Carbon build-up in combustion chamber. Use of a fuel additive that will dissolve the adhesive bonding the carbon particles to the piston crown and chamber is the easiest way to remove the build-up. Otherwise, the cylinder head will have to be removed and decarbonised (Chapter 2). On two-stroke engines, always decarbonise the cylinder head and piston crown at the recommended service interval (Chapter 1).
- [ ] Incorrect or poor quality fuel. Old or improper fuel can cause detonation. This causes the pistons to rattle, thus the knocking or pinking sound. Drain the old fuel and always use the recommended grade fuel (Chapter 4).
- [ ] Spark plug heat range incorrect. Uncontrolled detonation indicates that the plug heat range is too hot. The plug in effect becomes a glow plug, raising cylinder temperatures. Install the proper heat range plug (Chapter 1).
- [ ] Improper air/fuel mixture. This will cause the cylinder to run hot and lead to detonation. Clogged jets or an air leak can cause this imbalance. See Chapter 4.

Piston slap or rattling

- [ ] Cylinder-to-piston clearance excessive. Caused by improper assembly. Inspect and overhaul top-end parts (Chapter 2).
- [ ] Connecting rod bent. Caused by over-revving, trying to start a badly flooded engine or from ingesting a foreign object into the combustion chamber. Replace the damaged parts (Chapter 2).
- [ ] Piston pin or piston pin bore worn or seized from wear or lack of lubrication. Replace damaged parts (Chapter 2).
- [ ] Piston ring(s) worn, broken or sticking. Overhaul the top-end (Chapter 2).
- [ ] Piston seizure damage. Usually from lack of lubrication or overheating. Replace the piston and where possible, rebore the cylinder, as necessary (Chapter 2). On two-stroke engines, check that the oil pump is correctly adjusted.
- [ ] Connecting rod upper or lower end clearance excessive. Caused by excessive wear or lack of lubrication. Replace worn parts.

Valve noise – four-stroke engines

- [ ] Incorrect valve clearances. Adjust the clearances by referring to Chapter 1.
- [ ] Valve spring broken or weak. Check and replace weak valve springs (Chapter 2).
- [ ] Camshaft bearings worn or damaged. Lack of lubrication at high rpm is usually the cause of damage. Insufficient oil or failure to change the oil at the recommended intervals are the chief causes. (Chapter 2).

Other noise

- [ ] Exhaust pipe leaking at cylinder head connection. Caused by improper fit of pipe or loose exhaust flange. All exhaust fasteners should be tightened evenly and carefully. Failure to do this will lead to a leak.
- [ ] Crankshaft runout excessive. Caused by a bent crankshaft (from over-revving) or damage from an upper cylinder component failure.
- [ ] Engine mounting bolts loose. Tighten all engine mount bolts (Chapter 2).
- [ ] Crankshaft bearings worn (Chapter 2).
- [ ] Camshaft drive gear assembly defective (four-stroke engines). Replace according to the procedure in Chapter 2.

Fault finding REF•7

7 Abnormal frame and suspension noise

Front end noise
☐ Steering head bearings loose or damaged. Clicks when braking. Check and adjust or replace as necessary (Chapters 1 and 6).
☐ Bolts loose. Make sure all bolts are tightened to the specified torque (Chapter 6).
☐ Fork tube bent. Good possibility if machine has been dropped. Replace tube with a new one (Chapter 6).
☐ Front axle nut loose. Tighten to the specified torque (Chapter 8).
☐ Loose or worn wheel or hub bearings. Check and replace as needed (Chapter 8).

Shock absorber noise
☐ Fluid level incorrect. Indicates a leak caused by defective seal. Shock will be covered with oil. Replace shock or seek advice on repair from a Piaggio dealer (Chapter 6).
☐ Defective shock absorber with internal damage. This is in the body of the shock and can't be remedied. The shock must be replaced with a new one (Chapter 6).
☐ Bent or damaged shock body. Replace the shock with a new one (Chapter 6).
☐ Loose or worn suspension linkage components. Check and replace as necessary (Chapter 6).

Brake noise
☐ Squeal caused by dust on brake pads or shoes. Usually found in combination with glazed pads or shoes. Clean using brake cleaning solvent (Chapter 8).
☐ Contamination of brake pads or shoes. Oil, brake fluid or dirt causing brake to chatter or squeal. Clean or replace pads or shoes (Chapter 8).
☐ Pads or shoes glazed. Caused by excessive heat from prolonged use or from contamination. Do not use sandpaper, emery cloth, carborundum cloth or any other abrasive to roughen the pad surfaces as abrasives will stay in the pad material and damage the disc or drum. A very fine flat file can be used, but pad or shoe replacement is advised (Chapter 8).
☐ Disc or drum warped. Can cause a chattering, clicking or intermittent squeal. Usually accompanied by a pulsating lever and uneven braking. Check the disc runout and the drum ovality (Chapter 8).
☐ Loose or worn wheel (front) for transmission (rear) bearings. Check and replace as needed (Chapters 8 or 2G).

8 Excessive exhaust smoke

White smoke – four-stroke engines (oil burning)
☐ Piston oil ring worn. The ring may be broken or damaged, causing oil from the crankcase to be pulled past the piston into the combustion chamber. Replace the rings with new ones (Chapter 2).
☐ Cylinder worn, cracked, or scored. Caused by overheating or oil starvation. The cylinder will have to be rebored and an oversize piston installed (Chapter 2).
☐ Valve oil seal damaged or worn. Replace oil seal with new ones (Chapter 2).
☐ Valve guide worn. Measure the valve guides and if worn seek the advice of a Piaggio dealer (Chapter 2).
☐ Engine oil level too high, which causes the oil to be forced past the rings. Drain oil to the proper level (Daily (pre-ride) checks).
☐ Head gasket broken between oil return and cylinder. Causes oil to be pulled into the combustion chamber. Replace the head gasket and check the head for warpage (Chapter 2).
☐ Abnormal crankcase pressurisation, which forces oil past the rings.

White/blue smoke – two-stroke engines (oil burning)
☐ Oil pump cable adjustment incorrect. Check throttle cable/oil pump cable adjustment (Chapter 1).
☐ Accumulated oil deposits in the exhaust system. If the scooter is used for short journeys only, the oil residue from the exhaust gases will condense in the cool silencer. Take the scooter for a long run in hot weather to burn off the accumulated oil residue.

Black smoke (over-rich mixture)
☐ Air filter clogged. Clean the element (Chapter 1).
☐ Main jet too large or loose. Compare the jet size to the Specifications (Chapter 4).
☐ Automatic choke faulty (Chapter 4).
☐ Fuel level too high. Check and adjust the float height as necessary (Chapter 4).
☐ Float needle valve held off needle seat. Clean the float chamber and fuel line and replace the needle and seat if necessary (Chapter 4).

Brown smoke (lean mixture)
☐ Main jet too small or clogged. Lean condition caused by wrong size main jet or by a restricted orifice. Clean float chambers and jets and compare jet size to Specifications (Chapter 4).
☐ Fuel flow insufficient. Float needle valve stuck closed due to chemical reaction with old fuel. Float height incorrect. Restricted fuel line. Clean line and float chamber and adjust floats if necessary.
☐ Carburettor inlet manifold clamps loose (Chapter 4).
☐ Air filter poorly sealed or not installed (Chapter 1).
☐ Ignition timing incorrect (Chapter 5).

REF•8 Fault finding

9 Poor handling or stability

Handlebar hard to turn
- [ ] Steering head bearing adjuster nut too tight. Check adjustment as described in Chapter 1.
- [ ] Bearings damaged. Roughness can be felt as the bars are turned from side-to-side. Replace bearings and races (Chapter 6).
- [ ] Races dented or worn. Denting results from wear in only one position (eg, straight ahead), from a collision or hitting a pothole or from dropping the machine. Replace races and bearings (Chapter 6).
- [ ] Steering stem lubrication inadequate. Causes are grease getting hard from age or being washed out by high pressure car washes. Disassemble steering head and repack bearings (Chapter 6).
- [ ] Steering stem bent. Caused by a collision, hitting a pothole or by dropping the machine. Replace damaged part. Don't try to straighten the steering stem (Chapter 6).
- [ ] Front tyre air pressure too low (Daily (pre-ride) checks).

Handlebar shakes or vibrates excessively
- [ ] Tyres worn (Chapter 8).
- [ ] Swingarm pivots worn. Replace worn components (Chapter 6).
- [ ] Wheel rim(s) warped or damaged. Inspect wheels for runout (Chapter 8).
- [ ] Wheel bearings worn. Worn wheel bearings (front) or transmission bearings (rear) can cause poor tracking. Worn front bearings will cause wobble (Chapter 8).
- [ ] Handlebar mountings loose (Chapter 6).
- [ ] Front suspension bolts loose. Tighten them to the specified torque (Chapter 6).
- [ ] Engine mounting bolts loose. Will cause excessive vibration with increased engine rpm (Chapter 2).

Handlebar pulls to one side
- [ ] Frame bent. Definitely suspect this if the machine has been dropped. May or may not be accompanied by cracking near the bend. Replace the frame (Chapter 6).
- [ ] Wheels out of alignment. Caused by improper location of axle spacers or from bent steering stem or frame (Chapter 6 or 8).
- [ ] Steering stem bent. Caused by impact damage or by dropping the machine. Replace the steering stem (Chapter 6).
- [ ] Fork tube bent (telescopic fork models). Disassemble the forks and replace the damaged parts (Chapter 6).

Poor shock absorbing qualities
Too hard:
a) Fork grease or oil quantity excessive (Chapter 6).
b) Fork grease or oil viscosity too high. Use the correct grade (see the Specifications in Chapter 1).
c) Suspension bent. Causes a harsh, sticking feeling (Chapter 6).
d) Fork internal damage (Chapter 6).
e) Shock internal damage (Chapter 6).
f) Tyre pressure too high (Chapter 1).

Too soft:
a) Fork grease or oil viscosity too light. Use the correct grade (see the Specifications in Chapter 1).
b) Fork or shock spring(s) weak or broken (Chapter 6).
c) Shock internal damage or leakage (Chapter 6).

10 Braking problems – disc brakes

Brakes are ineffective
- [ ] Air in brake line. Caused by inattention to master cylinder fluid level or by leakage. Locate problem and bleed brake (Chapter 8).
- [ ] Pads or disc worn (Chapters 1 and 8).
- [ ] Brake fluid leak. Locate problem and rectify (Chapter 8).
- [ ] Contaminated pads. Caused by contamination with oil, grease, brake fluid, etc. Clean or replace pads. Clean disc thoroughly with brake cleaner (Chapter 8).
- [ ] Brake fluid deteriorated. Fluid is old or contaminated. Drain system, replenish with new fluid and bleed the system (Chapter 8).
- [ ] Master cylinder internal parts worn or damaged causing fluid to bypass (Chapter 8).
- [ ] Master cylinder bore scratched by foreign material or broken spring. Repair or replace master cylinder (Chapter 8).
- [ ] Disc warped. Replace disc (Chapter 8).
- [ ] On models where the master cylinder is operated by a short cable from the handlebar lever, check that the cable is correctly adjusted and moves freely (Chapter 8).

Brake lever pulsates
- [ ] Disc warped. Replace disc (Chapter 8).
- [ ] Axle bent. Replace axle (Chapter 8).
- [ ] Brake caliper bolts loose (Chapter 8).
- [ ] Wheel warped or otherwise damaged (Chapter 8).
- [ ] Wheel or hub bearings damaged or worn (Chapter 8).

Brakes drag
- [ ] Master cylinder piston seized. Caused by wear or damage to piston or cylinder bore (Chapter 8).
- [ ] Lever balky or stuck. Check pivot and lubricate (Chapter 8).
- [ ] Brake caliper piston seized in bore. Caused by wear or ingestion of dirt past deteriorated seal (Chapter 8).
- [ ] Brake pads damaged. Pad material separated from backing plate. Usually caused by faulty manufacturing process or from contact with chemicals. Replace pads (Chapter 8).
- [ ] Pads improperly installed (Chapter 8).

Reference REF•9

11 Braking problems – drum brakes

Brakes are ineffective
☐ Cable incorrectly adjusted. Check cable (Chapter 1).
☐ Shoes or drum worn (Chapters 1 and 8).
☐ Contaminated shoes. Caused by contamination with oil, grease, brake fluid, etc. Clean or replace shoes. Clean drum thoroughly with brake cleaner (Chapter 8).
☐ Brake lever arm incorrectly positioned, or cam excessively worn (Chapter 8).

Brake lever pulsates
☐ Drum warped. Replace drum (Chapter 8).
☐ Axle bent. Replace axle (Chapter 8).
☐ Wheel warped or otherwise damaged (Chapter 8).
☐ Wheel/hub bearings (front) or transmission bearings (rear) damaged or worn (Chapter 8).

Brakes drag
☐ Cable incorrectly adjusted or requires lubrication. Check cable (Chapter 1).
☐ Shoe return springs broken (Chapter 8).
☐ Lever balky or stuck. Check pivot and lubricate (Chapter 8).
☐ Lever arm or cam binds. Caused by inadequate lubrication or damage (Chapter 8).
☐ Brake shoe damaged. Friction material separated from shoe. Usually caused by faulty manufacturing process or from contact with chemicals. Replace shoes (Chapter 8).
☐ Shoes improperly installed (Chapter 8).

12 Electrical problems

Battery dead or weak
☐ Battery faulty. Caused by sulphated plates which are shorted through sedimentation. Also, broken battery terminal making only occasional contact (Chapter 9).
☐ Battery cables making poor contact (Chapter 9).
☐ Load excessive. Caused by addition of high wattage lights or other electrical accessories.
☐ Ignition (main) switch defective. Switch either earths internally or fails to shut off system. Replace the switch (Chapter 9).
☐ Regulator/rectifier defective (Chapter 9).
☐ Alternator stator coil open or shorted (Chapter 9).
☐ Wiring faulty. Wiring either shorted to earth or connections loose in ignition, charging or lighting circuits (Chapter 9).

Battery overcharged
☐ Regulator/rectifier defective. Overcharging is noticed when battery gets excessively warm (Chapter 9).
☐ Battery defective. Replace battery with a new one (Chapter 9).
☐ Battery amperage too low, wrong type or size. Install manufacturer's specified amp-hour battery to handle charging load (Chapter 9).

Index

Note: References throughout this index are in the form - *"Chapter number"* • *"Page number"*

A

Air filter
   general information and cleaning – 1•68
   housing removal and installation – 4•9
Alternator coils – 9•25
Alternator rotor and
   stator – 2A•11, 2B•6, 2C•15, 2D•13, 2E•17, 2F•11

B

Battery
   check – 1•69
   charging – 9•5
   removal, installation and checks – 9•4
Battery panel and grab handle
   LX – 7•39
Belly panel
   Fly – 7•42
   Liberty – 7•32
   NRG Power – 7•46
   Typhoon and NRG MC – 7•7
   X8 – 7•53
   X9 – 7•28
   Zip 50 and Zip 125 – 7•19
Belt (drive) – 1•73, 2G•11
Body panels removal and refitting
   B125 – 7•20
   ET2 and ET4 – 7•14
   Fly – 7•40
   general information – 7•3
   GT – 7•33
   Hexagon and Super Hexagon – 7•11
   Liberty – 7•31
   LX – 7•37
   NRG Power – 7•43
   Sfera and Skipper – 7•7
   Typhoon and NRG MC – 7•3
   X8 – 7•48
   X9 – 7•25
   Zip and Zip SP – 7•9, 7•16

Brake
   bleeding – 8•12
   cable – 1•70, 8•14
   caliper – 8•6
   disc – 8•9, 8•11
   drum – 1•70, 1•71, 8•13
   fluid change – 1•70
   fluid level check – 0•12
   general information – 8•2
   hose, pipes and unions – 1•70, 8•12
   light switches – 9•15
   lever – 1•70, 6•3
   master cylinder – 8•9
   pads/shoes – 1•71, 8•2
   specifications – 8•1
   system check – 1•69
Brake/tail light bulbs – 9•9
Brake light panel
   X9 – 7•26
Bulbs – 9•2, 9•7, 9•9, 9•12, 9•17

C

Cables
   brake – 1•70, 8•14
   oil pump – 1•82
   speedometer – 1•81, 9•16
   throttle – 1•82, 4•18
Caliper (brake) – 8•6
Cam chain
   blades and sprockets – 2C•6, 2D•7, 2E•8, 2F•6,
   tensioner – 2C•5, 2D•6, 2E•7, 2F•6
Camshaft holder, camshaft and rockers – 2C•7, 2D•9, 2E•10, 2F•8
Carburettor
   general information – 4•9
   overhaul (four-stroke engines) – 4•13
   overhaul (two-stroke engines) – 4•11
   removal and installation – 4•9
Catalytic converter – 4•23
Charging system – 9•5
Clock battery – 9•17
Clutch and driven pulley – 1•84, 2G•8

Index REF•11

Cockpit trim panel
   X8 – 7•55
Conversion factors – REF•1
Coolant level check – 0•11
Cooling fan (air-cooled engines) – 2A•11, 2C•15, 2D•13, 2E•17
Cooling system (liquid-cooled engines)
   checks – 1•71
   coolant reservoir – 3•2
   draining flushing and refilling – 1•72
   fan – 3•2
   general information – 3•1
   hoses – 3•7
   radiator – 3•4
   specifications – 3•1
   temperature gauge/warming light and sender – 3•3
   thermostat – 3•3
Crankcase halves, crankshaft, connecting rod and bearings – 2A•14, 2B•7, 2C•18, 2D•15, 2E•20, 2F•12
Cylinder – 2A•7, 2B•6, 2C•12, 2D•12, 2E•14, 2F•10
Cylinder head
   decarbonisation – 1•73
   removal and installation – 2A•6, 2B•5, 2C•9, 2D•10, 2E•11, 2F•8,
   valves – 2C•10, 2D•12, 2E•12, 2F•9

D

Decarbonisation (2-stroke engines) – 1•73
Diode (2-stroke engines) – 9•20
Disc (brake) – 8•9, 8•11
Drive pulley and variator – 2G•5
Drivebelt – 1•73, 2G•11
Drivebelt and support roller – 2G•11
Drivebelt cover and kickstart – 2G•2

E

Electrical system – 9•1 et seq
   alternator coils – 9•25
   battery charging – 9•5
   battery removal, installation and checks – 9•4
   brake light switches – 9•15
   brake/tail light bulbs – 9•9
   charging system – 9•24
   coolant temperature gauge – 3•3
   diode – 9•20
   fault finding – 9•3
   fuel gauge and level sender – 9•18
   fuses – 9•2, 9•5
   general information – 9•3
   handlebar switches – 9•20
   headlight aim – 1•76
   headlight assembly – 9•8
   headlight bulb and sidelight bulb – 9•7
   horn – 9•21
   ignition main switch – 9•19
   instrument cluster bulbs – 9•17
   instrument cluster check – 9•15
   lighting system – 9•7
   oil level warning circuit – 9•19
   regulator/rectifier – 9•25
   side stand switch – 9•26
   specifications – 9•1
   speedometer cable – 1•81, 9•16
   starter motor – 9•22, 9•23
   starter relay – 9•21
   tail light assembly – 9•12
   turn signal assemblies – 9•15
   turn signal bulbs – 9•12
   turn signal circuit – 9•12
   wiring diagrams – 9•27 to 9•56
Engine (two-stroke) – 2A•1 et seq and 2B•1 et seq
   cooling fan – 2A•11
   crankcase halves, crankshaft and connecting rod and bearings – 2A•14, 2B•7
   cylinder – 2A•7, 2B•6
   cylinder head – 2A•6, 2B•5
   disassembly and reassembly – 2A•6, 2B•4
   fault finding – REF•2 to REF•8
   general information – 2A•5, 2B•4
   oil level check – 0•10
   oil pump – 2A•12, 2B•7
   piston – 2A•8, 2B•6
   piston rings – 2A•10, 2B•6
   removal and installation – 2A•5, 2B•4
Engine (four-stroke) – 2C•1, 2D•1, 2E•2 and 2F•1 et seq
   cam chain tensioner, blades and sprockets – 2C•5, 2C•6, 2D•6, 2D•7, 2E•7, 2E•8, 2F•6
   camshaft holder, camshaft and rockers – 2C•7, 2D•9, 2E•10, 2F•8
   cooling fan – 2C•15, 2D•13, 2E•17
   crankcase halves, crankshaft and connecting rod and bearings – 2C•18, 2D•15, 2E•20, 2F•12
   cylinder – 2C•12, 2D•12, 2E•14, 2F•10
   cylinder head and valves – 2C•10, 2D•12, 2E•12, 2F•9
   disassembly and reassembly – 2C•3, 2D•5, 2E•6, 2F•5
   fault finding – REF•2 to REF•8
   general information – 2C•3, 2D•4, 2E•4, 2F•4
   oil level check – 0•10
   oil filter change – 1•73
   oil pump – 2C•15, 2D•14, 2E•18, 2F•11
   piston – 2C•13, 2D•13, 2E•15, 2F•11
   piston rings – 2C•15, 2D•13, 2E•16, 2F•11
   removal and installation – 2C•3, 2D•4, 2E•5, 2F•4
   valve clearances – 1•83
   valve cover removal and installation – 2C•4, 2D•6, 2E•6, 2F•6
   valves/valve seats/valve guides overhaul – 2C•9, 2D•11, 2E•12, 2F•9
Engine access panel
   B125 – 7•20
   ET2 and ET4 – 7•14
   Fly – 7•40
   GT – 7•33
   Hexagon and Super Hexagon – 7•11
   Liberty – 7•31
   LX – 7•37
   NRG Power – 7•43
   Sfera and Skipper – 7•7
   Typhoon and NRG MC – 7•4
   X8 – 7•48
   X9 – 7•26
   Zip 50 and Zip 125 – 7•16
   Zip and Zip SP – 7•9
Engine cover
   Sfera and Skipper – 7•7
   Typhoon and NRG Power – 7•4
   Zip 50 and Zip SP – 7•10
Engine number – 0•8
Exhaust system – 4•22

F

Fan
   air-cooled models – 2A•11, 2C•15, 2D•13, 2E•17
   liquid-cooled models – 3•2

Index

Fault finding – REF•2 to REF•9
Filter
　air and transmission filter – 1•68, 4•9
　fuel – 4•7
　oil – 1•73
Floor panel
　B125 – 7•20
　ET2 and ET4 – 7•15
　Fly – 7•42
　GT – 7•35
　Hexagon and Super Hexagon – 7•12
　LX – 7•38
　NRG Power – 7•45, 7•46
　Sfera and Skipper – 7•8
　Typhoon and NRG MC – 7•6
　X8 – 7•53
　X9 – 7•27
　Zip 50 and Zip 125 – 7•19
　Zip and Zip SP – 7•9
Footrests – 7•3
Frame number – 0•8
Front panel
　B125 – 7•23
　ET2 and ET4 – 7•14
　Fly – 7•42
　GT – 7•33
　Hexagon and Super Hexagon – 7•13
　Liberty – 7•32
　LX – 7•37
　NRG Power – 7•47
　Sfera and Skipper – 7•8
　Typhoon and NRG MC – 7•6
　X8 – 7•50
　X9 – 7•28
　Zip 50 and Zip 125 – 7•19
　Zip and Zip SP – 7•10
Front underseat panel
　B125 – 7•21
　Fly – 7•40
　Zip 50 and Zip 125 – 7•17
Front wheel – 8•16
Fuel gauge – 9•18
Fuel pump – 4•23
Fuel system
　carburettor – 4•11, 4•13
　check – 1•74
　general information – 4•6
　specifications – 4•1
Fuel tap and filter – 4•7
Fuses – 9•2, 9•5

G

Gearbox
　general information – 2G•2
　oil level check and oil change – 1•75
　removal, inspection and installation – 2G•12
Grab handle
　X8 – 7•48

H

Headlight – 9•7, 9•8
Headlight aim – 1•76

Handlebar covers
　B125 – 7•25
　Fly – 7•43
　GT – 7•35
　Hexagon and Super Hexagon – 7•13
　Liberty – 7•32, 7•33
　LX – 7•38
　NRG Power – 7•47
　Sfera and Skipper – 7•9
　Typhoon and NRG MC – 7•7
　X8 – 7•55
　X9 – 7•30
　Zip 50 and Zip 125 – 7•19
　Zip and Zip SP – 7•10
Handlebars and levers – 6•2
Horn – 9•21
HT coils – 5•3
Hugger/mudguards
　B125 – 7•22, 7•24
　ET2 and ET4 – 7•16
　Fly – 7•41
　GT – 7•37
　Hexagon and Super Hexagon – 7•14
　Liberty – 7•32
　LX – 7•39
　NRG Power – 7•45
　Sfera and Skipper – 7•9
　Typhoon and NRG MC – 7•7
　X8 – 7•50, 7•56
　X9 – 7•26, 7•31
　Zip 50 and Zip 125 – 7•18, 7•19
　Zip and Zip SP – 7•11

I

Idle fuel/air mixture adjustment – 4•9
Idle speed check and adjustment – 1•76
Ignition
　control unit (ICU) and HT coil – 5•3
　pulse generator – 5•4
　specifications – 5•1
　system check – 5•2
　timing – 5•5
Ignition (main) switch – 9•19
Immobiliser (ET4) – 5•6
Immobiliser (LEADER) – 5•7
Initial start-up – 2A•17, 2B•7, 2C•19, 2D•16, 2E•22, 2F•12
Instruments – 9•15, 9•16, 9•17

K

Kick panel
　B125 – 7•24
　ET2 and ET4 – 7•14
　Fly – 7•41
　GT – 7•34
　Hexagon and Super Hexagon – 7•13
　Liberty – 7•32
　LX – 7•37
　NRG Power – 7•47
　Sfera and Skipper – 7•8
　Typhoon and NRG MC – 7•5
　X8 – 7•52
　X9 – 7•30
　Zip 50 and Zip 125 – 7•18
　Zip and Zip SP – 7•10
Kickstart – 2G•2

Index

L

Levers – 6•2
Lighting system – 9•7
Lower trim panel
  Hexagon and Super Hexagon – 7•11

M

Master cylinder – 8•9
Mirrors – 7•2
Model specifications – 1•2 to 1•67
Mudguards
  B125 – 7•22, 7•24
  ET2 and ET4 – 7•16
  Fly – 7•41
  GT – 7•37
  Hexagon and Super Hexagon – 7•14
  Liberty – 7•32
  LX – 7•39
  NRG Power – 7•45
  Sfera and Skipper – 7•9
  Typhoon and NRG MC – 7•7
  X8 – 7•50, 7•56
  X9 – 7•26, 7•31
  Zip 50 and Zip 125 – 7•18, 7•19
  Zip and Zip SP – 7•11

N

Nuts and bolts tightness check – 1•76
Number plate light panel
  X8 – 7•48

O

Oil cooler and pipes – 2C•4
Oil level check – 0•10
Oil pump
  2-stroke engines – 2A•12, 2B•7
  4-stroke engines – 2C•15, 2D•14, 2E•18, 2F•11

P

Pads (brake) – 1•71, 8•2
Piston – 2A•8, 2B•6, 2C•13, 2D•13, 2E•15, 2F•11
Piston rings – 2A•10, 2B•6, 2C•15, 2D•13, 2E•16, 2F•11
Pulse generator coil – 5•4
Pump
  fuel pump – 4•23
  oil pump – 2A•12, 2B•7, 2C•15, 2D•14, 2E•18, 2F•11
  water pump – 3•5

R

Radiator – 3•4
Rear carrier
  B125 – 7•20
  GT – 7•36
  Liberty – 7•31
  Sfera and Skipper – 7•8
  Typhoon and NRG MC – 7•4
  Zip and Zip SP – 7•10

Rear shock absorbers
  preload adjustment – 6•12
  removal, inspection and installation – 6•11
Rear trim panel
  X9 – 7•26
Rear view mirrors – 7•2
Rear wheel – 8•18
Regulator/rectifier – 9•25
Reed valve (two-stroke engines) – 4•17
Running-in procedure – 2A•17, 2B•7, 2C•19, 2D•16, 2E•22, 2F•12

S

Safety – 0•9
Seat
  B125 – 7•20
  ET2 and ET4 – 7•14
  Fly – 7•40
  GT – 7•33
  Hexagon and Super Hexagon – 7•11
  Liberty – 7•31
  LX – 7•37
  NRG MC – 7•3
  NRG Power – 7•43
  Sfera and Skipper – 7•7
  Typhoon – 7•3
  X8 – 7•48
  X9 – 7•25
  Zip 50 and Zip 125 – 7•17
  Zip and Zip SP – 7•9
Seat cowling
  Liberty – 7•31
  Zip 50 and Zip 125 – 7•17
Secondary air system – 1•77
Shoes (drum brake) – 1•71
Side panels
  B125 – 7•22
  ET2 and ET4 – 7•15
  Fly – 7•40
  GT – 7•33
  Hexagon and Super Hexagon – 7•11
  LX – 7•37
  NRG Power – 7•43
  Sfera and Skipper – 7•8
  Typhoon and NRG MC – 7•4
  X8 – 7•49
  X9 – 7•26, 7•27
  Zip 50 and Zip 125 – 7•16
  Zip and Zip SP – 7•9
Sidelight – 9•7
Silencer – 4•22
Source coil and pulse generator coil – 5•4
Spark plug
  gap check and adjustment – 1•79
  renewal – 1•80
Specifications – 2A•1, 2B•1, 2C•1, 2D•1, 2E•1, 2F•1, 2G•1, 3•1, 4•1, 5•1, 6•1, 8•1, 9•1
Speedometer cable – 1•81, 9•16
Speedometer head – 9•15, 9•16, 9•17
Stands – 1•81, 7•1
Starter motor – 9•22, 9•23
Starter pinion assembly – 2A•12, 2B•7, 2C•15, 2D•14, 2E•18, 2F•11
Steering
  checks – 0•13
  head bearings – 1•81, 6•4
  stem removal and installation – 6•3

Storage compartment
    B125 – 7•23
    ET2 and ET4 – 7•16
    Fly – 7•41
    GT – 7•33
    Liberty – 7•32
    LX – 7•37
    NRG Power – 7•45
    Sfera and Skipper – 7•8
    Typhoon and NRG MC – 7•5
    X8 – 7•54
    Zip 50 and Zip 125 – 7•18
    Zip 50 and Zip SP – 7•10
Suspension
    checks – 0•13, 1•82
    front suspension – 6•5
    general information – 6•2
    rear shock absorbers – 6•11, 6•12
Swingarm – 6•12

T

Tail light – 9•9, 9•12
Tail light panel
    Zip 50 and Zip 125 – 7•17
Thermostat – 3•3
Throttle cable – 1•82, 1•84, 4•18
Transmission
    clutch – 2G•8
    drivebelt – 1•73, 2G•11
    gearbox – 2G•12
    general information – 2G•2
    specifications – 2G•1
    variator – 1•84, 2G•5
Turn signals – 9•12, 9•15
Tyres
    check – 0•13
    general information and fitting – 8•23

V

Variator – 1•84, 2G•5
Valve clearances – 1•83
Valve cover removal and installation – 2C•4, 2D•6, 2E•6, 2F•6,
Valves/valve seats/valve guides
    overhaul – 2C•9, 2D•11, 2E•12, 2F•9

W

Warning lights – 9•17
Water pump – 3•5
Wheel
    alignment check – 8•15
    bearings – 1•84, 8•21
    front wheel hub and assembly – 8•16 to 8•21
    general check – 1•84
    inspection – 8•15
    rear wheel hub and assembly – 8•18
Windsheild
    Hexagon and Super Hexagon – 7•13
Wiring diagrams – 9•27 to 9•56

Preserving Our Motoring Heritage

The Model J Duesenberg Derham Tourster. Only eight of these magnificent cars were ever built – this is the only example to be found outside the United States of America

Almost every car you've ever loved, loathed or desired is gathered under one roof at the Haynes Motor Museum. Over 300 immaculately presented cars and motorbikes represent every aspect of our motoring heritage, from elegant reminders of bygone days, such as the superb Model J Duesenberg to curiosities like the bug-eyed BMW Isetta. There are also many old friends and flames. Perhaps you remember the 1959 Ford Popular that you did your courting in? The magnificent 'Red Collection' is a spectacle of classic sports cars including AC, Alfa Romeo, Austin Healey, Ferrari, Lamborghini, Maserati, MG, Riley, Porsche and Triumph.

A Perfect Day Out

Each and every vehicle at the Haynes Motor Museum has played its part in the history and culture of Motoring. Today, they make a wonderful spectacle and a great day out for all the family. Bring the kids, bring Mum and Dad, but above all bring your camera to capture those golden memories for ever. You will also find an impressive array of motoring memorabilia, a comfortable 70 seat video cinema and one of the most extensive transport book shops in Britain. The Pit Stop Cafe serves everything from a cup of tea to wholesome, home-made meals or, if you prefer, you can enjoy the large picnic area nestled in the beautiful rural surroundings of Somerset.

John Haynes O.B.E., Founder and Chairman of the museum at the wheel of a Haynes Light 12.

The 1936 490cc sohc-engined International Norton – well known for its racing success

The Museum is situated on the A359 Yeovil to Frome road at Sparkford, just off the A303 in Somerset. It is about 40 miles south of Bristol, and 25 minutes drive from the M5 intersection at Taunton.
Open 9.30am - 5.30pm (10.00am - 4.00pm Winter) 7 days a week, *except Christmas Day, Boxing Day and New Years Day*
Special rates available for schools, coach parties and outings Charitable Trust No. 292048

Haynes Motorcycle Manuals – The Complete List

Title	Book No
APRILIA RS50 (99 - 06) & RS125 (93 - 06)	4298
Aprilia RSV1000 Mille (98 - 03) ♦	4255
BMW 2-valve Twins (70 - 96) ♦	0249
BMW K100 & 75 2-valve Models (83 - 96) ♦	1373
BMW R850, 1100 & 1150 4-valve Twins (93 - 04) ♦	3466
BMW R1200 (04 - 06) ♦	4598
BSA Bantam (48 - 71)	0117
BSA Unit Singles (58 - 72)	0127
BSA Pre-unit Singles (54 - 61)	0326
BSA A7 & A10 Twins (47 - 62)	0121
BSA A50 & A65 Twins (62 - 73)	0155
DUCATI 600, 620, 750 and 900 2-valve V-Twins (91 - 05) ♦	3290
Ducati MK III & Desmo Singles (69 - 76) ◊	0445
Ducati 748, 916 & 996 4-valve V-Twins (94 - 01) ♦	3756
GILERA RUNNER, DNA, Ice & SKP/Stalker (97 - 04)	4163
HARLEY-DAVIDSON Sportsters (70 - 03) ♦	2534
Harley-Davidson Shovelhead and Evolution Big Twins (70 - 99)	2536
Harley-Davidson Twin Cam 88 (99 - 03) ♦	2478
HONDA NB, ND, NP & NS50 Melody (81 - 85) ◊	0622
Honda NE/NB50 Vision & SA50 Vision Met-in (85 - 95) ◊	1278
Honda MB, MBX, MT & MTX50 (80 - 93)	0731
Honda C50, C70 & C90 (67 - 03)	0324
Honda XR80/100R & CRF80/100F (85 - 04)	2218
Honda XL/XR 80, 100, 125, 185 & 200 2-valve Models (78 - 87)	0566
Honda H100 & H100S Singles (80 - 92) ◊	0734
Honda CB/CD125T & CM125C Twins (77 - 88) ◊	0571
Honda CBR125R (04 - 06)	4620
Honda CG125 (76 - 05) ◊	0433
Honda NS125 (86 - 93) ◊	3056
Honda MBX/MTX125 & MTX200 (83 - 93) ◊	1132
Honda CD/CM185 200T & CM250C 2-valve Twins (77 - 85)	0572
Honda XL/XR 250 & 500 (78 - 84)	0567
Honda XR250L, XR250R & XR400R (86 - 03)	2219
Honda CB250 & CB400N Super Dreams (78 - 84) ◊	0540
Honda CR Motocross Bikes (86 - 01)	2222
Honda CRF250 & CRF450 (02 - 06)	2630
Honda CBR400RR Fours (88 - 99) ◊ ♦	3552
Honda VFR400 (NC30) & RVF400 (NC35) V-Fours (89 - 98) ◊ ♦	3496
Honda CB500 (93 - 01) ◊ ♦	3753
Honda CB400 & CB550 Fours (73 - 77)	0262
Honda CX/GL500 & 650 V-Twins (78 - 86)	0442
Honda CBX550 Four (82 - 86) ◊	0940
Honda XL600R & XR600R (83 - 00)	2183
Honda XL600/650V Transalp & XRV750 Africa Twin (87 - 02) ♦	3919
Honda CBR600F1 & 1000F Fours (87 - 96) ♦	1730
Honda CBR600F2 & F3 Fours (91 - 98) ♦	2070
Honda CBR600F4 (99 - 02) ♦	3911
Honda CB600F Hornet (98 - 02) ◊ ♦	3915
Honda CBR600RR (03 - 06) ♦	4590
Honda CB650 sohc Fours (78 - 84)	0665
Honda NTV600 Revere, NTV650 and NT650V Deauville (88 - 05) ◊ ♦	3243
Honda Shadow VT600 & 750 (USA) (88 - 03)	2312
Honda CB750 sohc Four (69 - 79)	0131
Honda V45/65 Sabre & Magna (82 - 88)	0820
Honda VFR750 & 700 V-Fours (86 - 97) ♦	2101
Honda VFR800 V-Fours (97 - 01) ♦	3703
Honda VFR800 V-Tec V-Fours (02 - 05) ♦	4196
Honda CB750 & CB900 dohc Fours (78 - 84)	0535
Honda VTR1000 (FireStorm, Super Hawk) & XL1000V (Varadero) (97 - 00) ♦	3744
Honda CBR900RR FireBlade (92 - 99) ♦	2161
Honda CBR900RR FireBlade (00 - 03) ♦	4060
Honda CBR1000RR Fireblade (04 - 06) ♦	4604
Honda CBR1100XX Super Blackbird (97 - 02) ♦	3901
Honda ST1100 Pan European V-Fours (90 - 02) ♦	3384
Honda Shadow VT1100 (USA) (85 - 98)	2313

Title	Book No
Honda GL1000 Gold Wing (75 - 79)	0309
Honda GL1100 Gold Wing (79 - 81)	0669
Honda Gold Wing 1200 (USA) (84 - 87)	2199
Honda Gold Wing 1500 (USA) (88 - 00)	2225
KAWASAKI AE/AR 50 & 80 (81 - 95)	1007
Kawasaki KC, KE & KH100 (75 - 99)	1371
Kawasaki KMX125 & 200 (86 - 02) ◊	3046
Kawasaki 250, 350 & 400 Triples (72 - 79)	0134
Kawasaki 400 & 440 Twins (74 - 81)	0281
Kawasaki 400, 500 & 550 Fours (79 - 91)	0910
Kawasaki EN450 & 500 Twins (Ltd/Vulcan) (85 - 04)	2053
Kawasaki EX500 (GPZ500S) & ER500 (ER-5) (87 - 05) ♦	2052
Kawasaki ZX600 (Ninja ZX-6, ZZ-R600) Fours (90 - 00) ♦	2146
Kawasaki ZX-6R Ninja Fours (95 - 02) ♦	3541
Kawasaki ZX600 (GPZ600R, GPX600R, Ninja 600R & RX) & ZX750 (GPX750R, Ninja 750R) Fours (85 - 97) ♦	1780
Kawasaki 650 Four (76 - 78)	0373
Kawasaki Vulcan 700/750 & 800 (85 - 04) ♦	2457
Kawasaki 750 Air-cooled Fours (80 - 91)	0574
Kawasaki ZR550 & 750 Zephyr Fours (90 - 97) ♦	3382
Kawasaki ZX750 (Ninja ZX-7 & ZXR750) Fours (89 - 96) ♦	2054
Kawasaki Ninja ZX-7R & ZX-9R (94 - 04) ♦	3721
Kawasaki 900 & 1000 Fours (73 - 77)	0222
Kawasaki ZX900, 1000 & 1100 Liquid-cooled Fours (83 - 97) ♦	1681
MOTO GUZZI 750, 850 & 1000 V-Twins (74 - 78)	0339
MZ ETZ Models (81 - 95) ◊	1680
NORTON 500, 600, 650 & 750 Twins (57 - 70)	0187
Norton Commando (68 - 77)	0125
PEUGEOT Speedfight, Trekker & Vivacity Scooters (96 - 05) ◊	3920
PIAGGIO (Vespa) Scooters (91 - 06)	3492
SUZUKI GT, ZR & TS50 (77 - 90) ◊	0799
Suzuki TS50X (84 - 00) ◊	1599
Suzuki 100, 125, 185 & 250 Air-cooled Trail bikes (79 - 89)	0797
Suzuki GP100 & 125 Singles (78 - 93) ◊	0576
Suzuki GS, GN, GZ & DR125 Singles (82 - 05) ◊	0888
Suzuki 250 & 350 Twins (68 - 78)	0120
Suzuki GT250X7, GT200X5 & SB200 Twins (78 - 83) ◊	0469
Suzuki GS/GSX250, 400 & 450 Twins (79 - 85)	0736
Suzuki GS500 Twin (89 - 02) ♦	3238
Suzuki GS550 (77 - 82) & GS750 Fours (76 - 79)	0363
Suzuki GS/GSX550 4-valve Fours (83 - 88)	1133
Suzuki SV650 & SV650S (99 - 05) ♦	3912
Suzuki GSX-R600 & 750 (96 - 00) ♦	3553
Suzuki GSX-R600 (01 - 02) & GSX-R750 (00 - 02) & GSX-R1000 (01 - 02) ♦	3986
Suzuki GSX-R600/750 (04-05) & GSX-R1000 (03-06) ♦	4382
Suzuki GSF600 & 1200 Bandit Fours (95 - 04) ♦	3367
Suzuki 700, 750, 800 Intruder, Marauder, Volusia & Boulevard (85 - 06)	2618
Suzuki GS850 Fours (78 - 88)	0536
Suzuki GS1000 Four (77 - 79)	0484
Suzuki GSX-R750, GSX-R1100 (85 - 92), GSX600F, GSX750F, GSX1100F (Katana) Fours (87 - 96)	2055
Suzuki GSX600/750F & GSX750 (98 - 02) ♦	3987
Suzuki GS/GSX1000, 1100 & 1150 4-valve Fours (79 - 88)	0737
Suzuki TL1000S/R & DL1000 V-Strom (97 - 04) ♦	4083
Suzuki GSX1300R Hayabusa (99 - 04) ♦	4184
TRIUMPH Tiger Cub & Terrier (52 - 68)	0414
Triumph 350 & 500 Unit Twins (58 - 73)	0137
Triumph Pre-Unit Twins (47 - 62)	0251
Triumph 650 & 750 2-valve Unit Twins (63 - 83)	0122
Triumph Trident & BSA Rocket 3 (69 - 75)	0136
Triumph Bonneville (01 - 05) ♦	4364
Triumph Daytona, Speed Triple, Sprint & Tiger (97 - 05) ♦	3755
Triumph Triples & Fours (carburettor engines) (91 - 99) ♦	2162
VESPA P/PX125, 150 & 200 Scooters (78 - 03)	0707
Vespa Scooters (59 - 78)	0126

Title	Book No
YAMAHA DT50 & 80 Trail Bikes (78 - 95) ◊	0800
Yamaha T50 & 80 Townmate (83 - 95) ◊	1247
Yamaha YB100 Singles (73 - 91) ◊	0474
Yamaha RS/RXS100 & 125 Singles (74 - 95)	0331
Yamaha RD & DT125LC (82 - 87) ◊	0887
Yamaha TZR125 (87 - 93) & DT125R (88 - 02) ◊	1655
Yamaha TY50, 80, 125 & 175 (74 - 84) ◊	0464
Yamaha XT & SR125 (82 - 02) ◊	1021
Yamaha Trail Bikes (81 - 00)	2350
Yamaha 250 & 350 Twins (70 - 79)	0040
Yamaha XS250, 360 & 400 sohc Twins (75 - 84)	0378
Yamaha RD250 & 350LC Twins (80 - 82)	0803
Yamaha RD350 YPVS Twins (83 - 95)	1158
Yamaha RD400 Twin (75 - 79)	0333
Yamaha XT, TT & SR500 Singles (75 - 83)	0342
Yamaha XZ550 Vision V-Twins (82 - 85)	0821
Yamaha FJ, FZ, XJ & YX600 Radian (84 - 92)	2100
Yamaha XJ600S (Diversion, Seca II) & XJ600N Fours (92 - 03) ♦	2145
Yamaha YZF600R Thundercat & FZS600 Fazer (96 - 03) ♦	3702
Yamaha YZF-R6 (99 - 02) ♦	3900
Yamaha YZF-R6 (03 - 05) ♦	4601
Yamaha 650 Twins (70 - 83)	0341
Yamaha XJ650 & 750 Fours (80 - 84)	0738
Yamaha XS750 & 850 Triples (76 - 85)	0340
Yamaha TDM850, TRX850 & XTZ750 (89 - 99) ◊ ♦	3540
Yamaha YZF750R & YZF1000R Thunderace (93 - 00) ♦	3720
Yamaha FZR600, 750 & 1000 Fours (87 - 96) ♦	2056
Yamaha XV (Virago) V-Twins (81 - 03) ♦	0802
Yamaha XVS650 & 1100 Drag Star/V-Star (97 - 05) ♦	4195
Yamaha XJ900F Fours (83 - 94) ♦	3239
Yamaha XJ900S Diversion (94 - 01) ♦	3739
Yamaha YZF-R1 (98 - 03) ♦	3754
Yamaha YZF-R1 (04 - 06) ♦	4605
Yamaha FZS1000 Fazer (01 - 05) ♦	4287
Yamaha FJ1100 & 1200 Fours (84 - 96) ♦	2057
Yamaha XJR1200 & 1300 (95 - 03) ♦	3981
Yamaha V-Max (85 - 03) ♦	4072
ATVs	
HONDA ATC70, 90, 110, 185 & 200 (71 - 85)	0565
Honda Rancher, Recon & TRX250EX ATVs	2553
Honda TRX300 Shaft Drive ATVs (88 - 00)	2125
Honda TRX300EX, TRX400EX & TRX450R/ER ATVs (93 - 06)	2318
Honda Foreman 400 and 450 ATVs (95 - 02)	2465
KAWASAKI Bayou 220/250/300 & Prairie 300 ATVs (86 - 03)	2351
POLARIS ATVs (85 - 97)	2302
Polaris ATVs (98 - 06)	2508
YAMAHA YFS200 Blaster ATV (88 - 02)	2317
Yamaha YFB250 Timberwolf ATVs (92 - 00)	2217
Yamaha YFM350 & YFM400 (ER and Big Bear) ATVs (87 - 03)	2126
Yamaha Banshee and Warrior ATVs (87 - 03)	2314
Yamaha Kodiak and Grizzly ATVs (93 - 05)	2567
TECHBOOK SERIES	
ATV Basics	10450
Twist and Go (automatic transmission) Scooters Service and Repair Manual	4082
Motorcycle Basics TechBook (2nd Edition)	3515
Motorcycle Electrical TechBook (3rd Edition)	3471
Motorcycle Fuel Systems TechBook	3514
Motorcycle Maintenance TechBook	4071
Motorcycle Modifying	4272
Motorcycle Workshop Practice TechBook (2nd Edition)	3470

◊ = not available in the USA   ♦ = Superbike

The manuals on this page are available through good motorcycle dealers and accessory shops.
In case of difficulty, contact: **Haynes Publishing**
(UK) +44 1963 442030   (USA) +1 805 498 6703
(FR) +33 1 47 17 66 29   (SV) +46 18 124016
(Australia/New Zealand) +61 3 9763 8100

MCL21.9/06